Histor

"Elder" John Whipple

of

Ipswich, Massachusetts

His English Ancestors and American Descendants

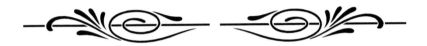

• WWW. BlaineWhipple.com

WRITTEN AND COMPILED BY BLAINE WHIPPLE

E-mail: • blaine whipple @ eschelon.com
(or) • b whipple 2 @ msn.com
Mr. Lewis Dale Whipple:
• Ldalewhip @ aol.com

From The Library Of
WILBURN M. POTTER

Mr. Weldon Whipple:
• www. whipple.org

Published by Whipple Development Corporation
in cooperation with Trafford on-demand publishing service

Victoria, British Columbia, 2003

Production by Roberta Lampert.

Printed in Victoria, Canada.

National Library of Canada Cataloguing in Publication

Whipple, Blaine
    History and genealogy of "Elder" John Whipple of Ispwich, Massachusetts and his English ancestors / Blaine Whipple.
Includes bibliographical references and index.
ISBN 1-55395-676-1
      I. Title.
CS71.W44 2003   929'.2'0973   C2003-901644-7

TRAFFORD

This book was published on-demand in cooperation with Trafford Publishing. On-demand publishing is a unique process and service of making a book available for retail sale to the public taking advantage of on-demand manufacturing and Internet marketing. On-demand publishing includes promotions, retail sales, manufacturing, order fulfilment, accounting and collecting royalties on behalf of the author.

Suite 6E, 2333 Government St., Victoria, B.C. V8T 4P4, CANADA
Phone   250-383-6864   Toll-free 1-888-232-4444 (Canada & US)
Fax   250-383-6804   E-mail sales@trafford.com
Web site www.trafford.com   TRAFFORD PUBLISHING IS A DIVISION OF TRAFFORD
                                HOLDINGS LTD.
Trafford Catalogue #03-0039   www.trafford.com/robots/03-0039.html
10   9   8   7   6   5   4   3

CONTENTS

ILLUSTRATIONS

ACKNOWLEDGMENTS

I would not have been able to prepare this book without the help of hundreds of descendants of Elder John Whipple who unselfishly shared their hard work in compiling their line of descent. Without their cooperation, the book would not be published. Not only did they provide the information, they took the time to proofread and edit their submission when it was returned to them for final approval.

I am deeply grateful to the Multnomah County librarians in Portland, Oregon who were so helpful in obtaining books through inter-library loans, in searching their stacks for little-used volumes, and in granting me access to their Rare Book Collection. This book was a long time in the making and thanks is due to the many Whipple descendants from all sections of the country who wrote, e-mailed, and called encouraging me to keep at it.

I appreciate the enthusiasm of Ralph Crandall, Executive Director of the New England Historic Genealogical Society for this book and the special interest he took in it from long distance by expediting the mailing of various documents from the society's fine library. Thanks to Weldon Whipple, Webmaster of the Whipple Website at www.whipple.org, who wrote the introduction and published a number of articles developed during the course of my research on the Whipple Website. His support helped build interest in the book.

AUTHOR'S PREFACE

Four male Whipples arrived in the new world in the 1630s. Two were named John, one Matthew, and one Paul. The two Johns and Matthew settled in the Massachusetts Bay colony; Paul on Providence Island in the West Indies. The two named John have created confusion for descendants searching for their ancestors. The search is complicated because some sources place brothers Matthew and John on the *Lyon* when it arrived in Boston in September 1632.

In fact, Matthew and John, both mature men with families, arrived in 1638 and settled in Ipswich, Essex County, Massachusetts. The other John, a teenager, was a passenger on the *Lyon* in 1632 and settled in Dorchester, Suffolk County, Massachusetts as an apprentice to Israel Stoughton. This book should help eliminate the confusion surrounding the two — the Ipswich John known as "Elder" and the Dorchester John as "Captain" — and help descendants trace their origin to the right ancestor.

Poet-author T. K. Whipple wrote in *Study Out the Land* that "All America lives at the end of the wilderness road, and our past is not a dead past, but still lives in us. Our forefathers had civilization inside themselves, the wild outside. We live in the civilization they created, but within us the wild still lingers. What they dreamed we live, and what they lived we dream."[1]

This book is divided into historical and genealogical sections. The pedigree approach to family history, the collection of names and dates, rarely captures the uniqueness or complexity of our collective past. It ignores interpreting the lives of our ancestors. The historical approach seeks to include the richness and complexity of the past. While not a trained researcher and writer of history, I have tried to portray the richness and complexity of the family from Bocking, Essex County, England prior to leaving the old home and after their arrival in Ipswich. While the ordinary life of our ancestors can never be known you will find herein the author's interpretation of some of those lives beginning with Matthew, John's father, a successful Clothier in Bocking.

The social history is from two main sources: speculation based on sociological and historical research and specific information about individuals and their associates. Insofar as possible, I have portrayed the people from available facts in the public record. However, the limited supply of family written records makes it difficult to construct what really happened. Where the individual's character is alluded to, the reader should understand that it is the author's imagination and interpretation and not necessarily the reality of their Whipple ancestors.

The American historical portion begins with Elder John and ends with his great great grandson, General William Whipple, who represented New Hampshire in the Continental Congress and signed the Declaration of Independence. To the best of my knowledge, the chapter on General Whipple is the most complete biographical sketch ever written on that great American.

Blaine Whipple
Portland, Oregon
November, 2003

---

1. T. K. Whipple, Study Out the Land, Berkeley/Los Angeles: U. of California Press, 1943. Whipple lived from 1890 to 1939. He was graduated with the Princeton class of 1912.

FOREWORD

As a Whipple growing up, I was unaware of other Whipples except for my parents and brothers and some cousins and uncles in a neighboring state. When I was a teenager my brother Bill informed me that a William Whipple had signed the Declaration of Independence. I assumed we were his descendants and imagined that other Whipples also traced their ancestry to William.

Later, documents from my great (2) grandfather's family organization confirmed that we descended from Captain John Whipple of Providence, Rhode Island. William Whipple was no where in my ancestry and no one seemed to know where Captain John came from. According to some sources, he had a brother and a father named Matthew. However, the birth dates of these two Matthews didn't seem to make sense when compared with Captain John's presumed birth date. Something had to be amiss.

Today it is well established that there were two New World immigrants named John Whipple and a third named Matthew, all with living descendants. This book is about the John frequently referred to as "Elder" John Whipple whose brother and father are named Matthew. We still lack information on Captain John's parents and whether he had siblings.

Among Elder John's descendants are Americans who have made significant contributions to our lives and culture. Following are a few of them:

- William Whipple, signer of the Declaration of Independence 90
- Susan B. Anthony, pioneer of women's rights .G 98
- Clara Barton, founder of the American Red Cross . . . . .G 120
- Calvin Coolidge, 30th President of the United States . . . . .G 216
- Robert Goddard, pioneer rocket scientist . . . . .G 212
- James Russell Lowell, diplomat, author, editor, literary critic . . . . .G 135
- Charles Pratt, founder of the Pratt Institute in Brooklyn, N. Y. . . . . . .G 83
- Brigham Young, Mormon colonizer of the American West . . . . .G 106

Blaine's book is not like any other genealogy I have read. He is not content with simply enumerating as many Whipple descendants as possible. His exploration of events that happened during the lives of Whipple forefathers in England, New England, and other sections of the United States make the book far more interesting than most genealogies.

He begins the historical section with a depiction of what life was like for the Whipple family of Bocking, England in the last half of the fifteenth and first third of the sixteenth centuries. He places the family in context of some of the major happenings of those times, the reign of Queen Elizabeth, King James and Charles, the Spanish Armada, the rise of Puritanism, the economics of the clothier's business, the important holidays during the year, quality of medical and dental care, the education of children, and many other aspects of everyday social, political, and religious customs that the family of Matthew Whipple, Sr. experienced.

The same approach is followed in his presentation of the life in early New England, beginning in 1638. He introduces us to Elder John, who along with brother Matthew and Capt. John, are the progenitors of the American line of Whipples. John gave yeoman service to his town as selectman, to his county as clerk of writs, to his colony as a long-time member of the general court (legislature), to his church as both deacon and ruling elder.

American Whipples are proud of William Whipple, the signer of Declaration of Independence who bears our surname. They will be prouder still after reading Blaine's chapter on this great American who was one of the leaders in the Continental Congress for passage of the Declaration of Independence and on the battle field at the October 1777 Battle of Saratoga, designated by most military historians the turning point of the Revolutionary War. The American victory is credited with bringing France, Spain, and Holland into the war on our side.

Blaine Whipple's book has enhanced my appreciation of my Whipple heritage, of the trials and tribulations our Whipple ancestors endured in settling the New World, and of the part they played in establishing the United States of America. I hope it does the same for you.

Weldon Whipple Webmaster,
Whipple Website
www.whipple.org.
Orem, Utah, USA

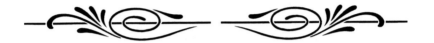

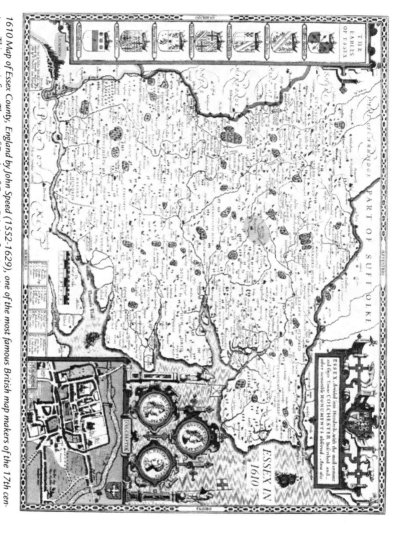

1610 Map of Essex County, England by John Speed (1552-1629), one of the most famous British map makers of the 17th century. This map is from Theatre of Empire of Great Britain, first issued in 1611 by John Sudbury and George Humble and printed by William Hall and John Beale. The engraving is by Jodocus of Amsterdam. Reproduced as John Speed's England, a colored facsimile of the first edition, Part II, edited by John Arlott. Phoenix House Limited, 1953, folio 31-32.

Bocking is a little left of center about a third of the way from the top. It was one of 72 communities in the Hundred of Hinkford.

1 THE WHIPPLES OF BOCKING, ESSEX COUNTY, ENGLAND[1]

1629: Massachusetts Bay colony founded. 1630: Francis Higginson's, "New England's Plantation," an account of living conditions in America, published. 1631: English mathematician William Oughtred proposes symbol "X" for multiplication. 1632: First coffee shop opens in London. 1635: London sets speed limit of 3 mph for hackney coaches. First inland postal service in Britain between London and Edinburgh. 1636: Roger Williams founds Providence, Rhode Island. 1637: William Prynne, Puritan parliamentarian, condemned for seditious writing, to be pilloried and mutilated. 1638: William Chillingworth wrote "The Religion of Protestants, a Safe Way to Salvation."

The children of Matthew and presumably Joan (maybe Stephens) Whipple were born and married in Bocking, Essex County, England. Following are their christening dates:

i.   Anne (Anna), 9-1-1583; married John Pepper, 1-13-1605/06.

ii.   Margaret, 3-26-1585; buried, 2-13-1607/08; married Laurence Arthur, 7-5-1603.

iii. Jane (Jana), 9-13-1587; married (1) Henry Caldam, 1613, (2) Edward Feast, 1618 or 1619.

iv.   Matthew, about 1590; died, Ipswich, Mass 9-28-1647; married (1) Anne Hawkins, 5-7-1622, (2) Rose Chute 11-13-1646 in Ipswich, Essex County, Massachusetts.

v.   Elizabeth, 4-14-1594, married Isaac Green, 9-3-1618.

vi.   John, 8-29-1596, died, Ipswich, Mass. 6-30-1669; married (1) Susanna (probably Stacy), 1620, (2) Janet Dickinson after 1662 in Ipswich.

vii. Mary (Maria) about 1599; died before 2-26-1663; married Richard Baker, 1625.

viii. Amy, 1-20-1605; married William Hoston, 10-31-1626.

Both a Jane and Johane are in Matthew's Will written in 1616. Johane is not in the parish records.

Information on the Matthew Whipple, Sr. family is sketchy but enough is known to establish the beginning. Parents of Matthew and his wife Joan have not been identified. The Margaret Whipple buried in Bocking[2] June 13, 1577 is presumed to be Matthew's mother.[3] The custom at the time was to be buried in a shroud and mourned by one's family for three to four years.

Parish records from Bocking's St. Mary's church, Matthew's Will dated 19 December 1616,[4] *Abstracts of English Records For The Ancestry of Matthew Whipple c 1560-1618,*[5] and original research of adjacent parish records in 1988 and 1990 by Debrett Ancestry Research Limited of Alresford, Hampshire, England are some of the sources for information on the family. The sources do not always agree.

No direct evidence has been found for dates of birth for Matthew and Joan but the christening record for Anne, their first child, indicates both were born in the early 1560s. Joan was buried in Bocking May 19, 1612, thought to be in her late forties or early fifties. Since he didn't remarry, it is presumed Matthew mourned her the rest of his life. If so, mirrors in the home were either covered or turned to the wall. The family coach was painted black. All rooms in the home were hung in black and he slept in a mourning bed enclosed by black draperies. Matthew was buried January 16, 1618/19, probably in his late fifties. If the family followed tradition, a pot of wine was placed on his chest so those who came to pay their last respects could do so with a toast.[6]

Matthew's Will was very particular in its details. He noted his "messauge with the yard and garden and orchards" was located on "Bradford street in Bocking." He named eldest son Matthew and son John, daughters Jane, Elizabeth, Maria, Amy, Johane, and Anne Pepper; grandchildren Hercules and Margaret Arthur and Henry and Ande Caldam, "my sister, the wife of Richard Rathbone," and Hercules Stephens. With the exception of Stephens, every beneficiary was identified as a relative.

Stephens may have been a brother to the Joan Whipple buried in 1612, making him Matthew's brother-in-law. The Bocking parish records include a Joanna Stephens christened November 15, 1562. This makes her a plausible age to be the mother of Anna christened September 1, 1583 and identified as the daughter of Matthew Whipple. The following christening dates for Matthew's other children, for Hercules Stephens' children, and for Richard Rathbone's child are in the parish records. Note how the dates track — Rathbone was married to Matthew's sister Marion.

Matthew Whipple		Hercules Stephens		Richard Rathbone	
Margaret	3-26-1585[7]				
Jana	9-3-1587	Hercules	1-20-1586		
Elizabeth	4-14-1594	Ann	3-3-1594	Gamalielus	3-17-1594[8]
John	8-29-1596	John	5-2-1596		
Amy	1-20-1605	Tabitha	4-22-1599		

Margaret married Laurence Arthur when she was 18 and died just before her 23rd birthday, probably when delivering her third child. Her children, Hercules and Margaret, would have been in their early teens when their grandfather Matthew died. Anne and Amy married at 22, Elizabeth and John at 24, ages that seem normal for that time.[9]

A reading of the history and literature of the times allows us to speculate on the early life of Matthew and Joan. Matthew's 1616 will was written in English and the probate in Latin leading us to believe he was educated.[10] While elementary age girls didn't go to school, Joan probably learned the alphabet from a hornbook and help from her grandmother.[11] School for boys began at age 7 and Matthew probably had a new satchel to carry books and papers, a sharp penknife, and some candles when he arrived for his first day of school.[12] The boys sat on hard benches, two sharing each of the slanted oak desks set in rows in a heavy-beamed, high-ceiling room. The school, always cold in wintertime, brought on an endless runny nose and fingers stiff as twigs. In summer afternoons the room was as sweaty as a chimney corner. There Matthew would have labored every day except Sunday under the unblinking gaze of the tall, thin, weary master, perched on a stool in front of the class with a supple birch rod ready for use. Behind, unseen but always felt, was the usher watching everything. It was a long, heavy-lidded day from first light until first stars.

The curriculum included mathematics, English, Greek, Hebrew and Latin. Students learned to write, in prose and verse in the slowly dying tongue of Caesar and Cicero. Their memory was enhanced by a ferule[13] laid smartly across an open palm or swollen knuckles and/or by the master's birch rod as it struck the flinching bare flesh of their backside. William Lily's *A Short Introduction of Grammar* and Nicholas Udall's *Flowers of Latin Speaking* were the Latin texts.[14] The Hebrew grammar was also by Udall. Latin was learned by heart through ceaseless exercises of recitation. The Greek text was William Camden's 1597 grammar.[15] Reading assignments included authors Aesop, Cato, Homer, Horace, Ovid, Theognis, and Virgil.[16]

His father would have taught him how to ride, to fish in the river, ponds, and creeks, to snare and catch birds, and to defend himself with an old English walking staff.

As a teenager Matthew would have joined his family and other fairgoers from the various towns in the shires of Essex, Sussex, Cambridge, Hertford, Middlesex, and Kent and from the continent at the annual Colchester fair. People went there to buy, sell, and pleasure themselves. Strange odors filled the air from the smoke of cook fires mingling with the scents of the enormous market of spices and herbs. The languages of other places and various dialects of his own tongue, the sight of strange faces with different cuts and lengths of beard and hair, the many different kinds of clothing people wore, and the taste of foreign food tingling his mouth helped him understand there was more to the world than Bocking and its close neighbor, Braintree. But even moving among the crowd and touching the soft fur worn by a Dane, the perfumed leather of a French wine dealer, or the sleek Italian silk of a Venetian there to sell the spices of the East, or to feel and heft foreign coins in his palms never led him to believe he would experience any of these things other than at the fair. It was hard to imagine life among strangers in other countries.

As he headed toward manhood, he would have listened and occasionally participated in the endless debates on religion. His fellow citizens talked freely and openly and passionately on delicate subjects such as transubstantion,[17] predestination, the true and proper nature and number of the holy sacraments; the virtues and faults and strengths and weaknesses of the *Book of Common Prayer*,[18] the best ways and means to translate the scriptures into the common tongue; the thorny questions of whether good works count with God or whether man could be justified by faith alone; whether the Pope in Rome is the anti-Christ; the place and purpose, if any, for altars and images and vestments and candles and incense, whether these were morally neutral or merely tolerable and foolish things or whether there was any place for these things in a reformed and purified service of worship; if there should be by name and title, bishops; if priests should marry; if married people may ever lawfully divorce; should private conscience or civil and public ordinances prevail.

He was probably about 16 when he made his first London trip. He had listened many times to travelers speak of the city and had undoubtedly formed an impression — probably Jerusalem and Babylon with bits and pieces of Sodom and Gomorrah. But he was probably not prepared for what he experienced. On his first visit he would have been amazed by the number of birds in the countryside and the sounds of bells tolling and ringing to each other in the towns and villages he passed through on the 45 mile journey. There were bells in every tone of voice from cockcrow day bell at first light until evening curfew and finally ending with the solemn tolling of midnight. Many towns and villages had their own language of bells — bells to announce birth, death, baptism, burial, the marriage feast, and the call to prayer and communion.

There was the barking of the chained dogs, the crying out of street vendors, the clear voices of children singing or reciting lessons together emanating from open windows. The song of the wood saw, the hammer and chisel of the stone mason, the rattle of the cart maker, and the clang of the blacksmith pounding slow clean tunes on his anvil were in every village he passed through. As he neared London, a man in the meadow was probably sharpening his scythe and it sounded like the busywork of summer bees. And the thousands of yellow butterflies reminded him of the beauty of April's daffodils.

Eventually the city appeared straight ahead of him, across fields with scattered houses, buildings, and churches, rising to fill the wide horizon. There stood the battlement wall, like a vast painted cloth, with its gates and gate houses and towers. The spires and the steeples of the churches must have seemed like a wild forest stretching from the White Tower to the Tower of London to St. Paul's church atop its hill. Weathervanes sparkled from the four corners of each. The towers and long roof of St. Peter's church at Westminster Abbey, the Old Palace, Whitehall Palace, and the great houses lining the banks of the Thames must have been beyond his imagination. This ancient city, built between and among low hills and marshy ground by a river, would have seemed newly baptized to the eyes of this sixteen-year old.

As any first time visitor would, he explored it all. He would have gone to the Smithfield market, easy to identify by its odors of hay and manure and the warm scents of cows, horses, sheep, and swine. On to St. Nicholas Shambles (next to Newgate) where the smell of the butcher and poulterer mingled. He found the market where butchers and fishmongers offered their wares where Cornhill meets Three Needle street and Lombard, and East Cheap where butchers worked close by the smoke of many cookshops and the odor of fish married the smoke of the cookshops on Thames street near Fishmonger's Row. He followed his nose around London and found the dry fatty stink of the skinners tanning their furs in an area known as the Peltry. The musty odors of all kinds of grain were on Lombard street near its intersection with Bridge street. Fresh fruits and vegetables mixing with the odors of bake house and brew house meant he was just south of St. Paul's churchyard in Carter lane. Just west of Knightrider on Thames street was the garlic market.

As he explored the wonders of this city, a new essence suddenly exploded upon him. His sense of smell would have been flooded with a paradise of spices — mace and cinnamon, almonds and anise, ginger and clove and nutmeg. The essence of all these were happily confused with black English peppermint, rosemary, wild thyme, sweet violet, chamomile, lemon scented sweet flag, sweet cicely, and sweet woodruff, as licorice as any anise seed.

And for a penny he could climb the tower of St. Paul's, see the Tower of London and the wondrous zoo there, get a guided tour of Westminster Abbey and touch the graves of kings. At the King's Head tavern he would have been introduced to oysters in bastard gravy — cooked with ale and bread crumbs and seasoned with ginger and pepper and sugar and saffron. On to the Mermaid for a salad of boiled turnips and beets and carrots followed by sturgeon cooked in claret, some chicken and fruit in a pie, and ending with a sweet pie of apples and oranges.

He must have believed it was a meal even the Queen couldn't top. If he had heard that *spiritus dulcis*, an alchemical creation composed of sack distilled twice over and flavored with spirit of roses and candy and clears nose and throat, cleans the eyes with fresh tears, tingles the toes and fingernails, and causes the stomach to leap and rejoice like a young lamb," he would have ordered a cup with his meal.[19]

Matthew and Joan were probably in their early twenties when they married. Once it was determined she should marry, Joan's parents would have searched for a suitable husband, taking care to balance social position and status as dowries were critical to a desirable match. The wedding was probably in late 1582 since Anne, their oldest, was born in September 1583. Before they had children, Matthew and Joan probably journeyed to London to watch the hangings decreed by the quarter law court sessions. Prisoners, brought in from all the prisons, were tried and those condemned to the rope were carted off by the hangman to Tyburn, the place of public execution. It was a major spectator event attended by thousands.[20]

Anne was 10 before the family purchased its home in Bocking so they probably lived with his parents for the first 11 years of their marriage. The Statute of Apprentices made labor compulsory and required seven years' apprenticeship for all trades. Since he was a clothier, Matthew probably apprenticed to his father as sons usually followed their fathers' occupations.[21]

Seventeenth century *village houses*

Sometime prior to 1593 Matthew paid £40 to Robert and Joan Ardley for a house, barn, large garden, and apple orchard on Bradford street in Bocking.[22] The Ardley's failed to perform as agreed so Matthew took them to court for specific performance and won. The court directed the Ardleys to deed the property to Matthew and his heirs forever.[23] In April 1594, Matthew was on an inquest jury at Epping to determine how 11-year-old Margaret Moyer died. In August, he was one of 11 witnesses in the court session at Brentwood. There were seven defendants, all brought to court from confinement at Colchester prison.[24] He was assessed taxes in 1599, 1600, and 1608 for lay subsidies.[25] He was bequeathed five shillings by Richard Tebold of Bocking in 1603.[26]

Bradford street, named for Great Bradfords, a farm on the Coggesall Road,[27] was one of the prettiest streets in Bocking, especially in early spring when the trees, just beginning to leaf, were not yet too thick to hide the red brown roofs and the pink stuccoed walls of the houses behind them. Houses on the street dating from the sixteenth and seventeenth centuries, several decorated with rough patterns in stucco, were still standing in 1906.[28]

Joan's child bearing extended over 22 years, from Anne born in September 1583 to Amy in January 1605. Matthew, Jr. was the first of two sons and fifth born of the nine known children. When he was born about 1590, Anne, Margaret, Jane, and Joanna were probably eagerly awaiting a brother.[29] The first four daughters were born at two year intervals. Three years separated Joanna and Matthew; four years Matthew and Elizabeth; four years Elizabeth and John; one year John and Mary; four years Mary and Amy. Infant mortality was so high in those days, one wonders if other children were born during those four year intervals.[30]

Joan's duties as wife and mother were many: cook, baker, and doctor; brew home beer and wine; make medicine; sew, spin, and embroider; look after hens and the dairy; launder; raise vegetables and flowers; make her own beauty aids. She would have joined the other women at the town mills to grind the family corn and probably baked bread in common ovens. When shopping, she had little choice between salted meat in winter and bad meat in summer. Fresh meat was in limited supply and came from shops cooking beef, mutton, veal, pork, and lamb on spits.[31]

Breakfast of cold meats, cheese, herring, salted, pickled, or dried, and oysters was served between 6 and 7 a.m. A special dinner with guests might include all or some of the following: fricassee of rabbits and chickens; a leg of mutton, boiled; three carp in a dish; a side of lamb; a dish of roasted pigeons; four lobsters; three tarts; a lamprey pie, considered rare;[32] and a dish of anchovies. Vast quantities of ale, cider, or beer would be consumed.[33] Wealthy families served French and Italian wines.

After dinner "Crambo, Hunt the Slipper, Blind Man's Bluff", and "Hot Cockles" were played. "I love my love with an apple because she is angelic" was the game played in mixed company. Family members confined indoors by weather, gout, or if female, by a state of chronic pregnancy, had lots of pastimes to alleviate boredom. "Rise Pig and Go," "One Penny Follow Me," "I Pray My Lord give Me a Curse in Your Park," and "Fire" were among the favorites. On special occasions Matthew may have hired a fiddler, a gittern[34] player, a piper, and a drummer and the home would enjoy dancing that night.

By the time of Amy's birth in 1606, the family should have been able to celebrate Christmas in grand style. The citizens of Bocking and Braintree joyously celebrated the birth of Jesus. The inns, taverns, and alehouses were wreathed with Christmas greenery and within those warm, noisy, crowded places, good beer and ale and all the best wines were served. All houses from leading citizens to the lowly rat catcher were open to hospitality. Few if any went hungry, including prisoners who received baskets of good things to eat and drink.

At night the streets were lit with lanterns and torches, minstrels played music, and young men rang church bells until it seemed the spires and steeples would tumble down in a heap like the walls of Jericho. Firewood sprinkled with the musk[35] and leaves of flowers was burned in place of the usual stinking sea coal. The firewood brought the congenial sounds of axes, the rasping hum and whining singsong of long and short saws, and the creaking of the carts of the wood bearers who looked forward to their best season of the year.

A great blast from a ram's horn announced the opening of Bocking's manor house and owner Sir Robert Barker dispensed Christmas hospitality to all. Servants served tankards of nappy ale and wonderful cakes and cream. A fiddler played country dances enjoyed by all, especially Sir. Robert who was light of foot and quick as a fox. No one was better at "Shake-a-Trot" or "Bishop of Chester's jig."

If the Whipples celebrated Christmas in grand style, they would have opened their home to employees, neighbors, and strangers. The usual torches and plain tallow candles and sputtering rushes dipped in fat were replaced with the best candles of berry and beeswax scented with herbs and perfumes. They burned night and day along with the perfumed oil in the lamps and the yule log in the hearth of the hall lighted with a brand preserved from last year's log.[36] All chambers in the house seemed to be choirs of candle flame.

Wreaths and branches of evergreen would have been hung throughout the home. They included slender, brittle branches of potted rosemary with narrow, shiny leaves;[37] bluegreen juniper with stiff, bristling, little leaves like those that sheltered and concealed the Holy Family from Herod's murderous soldiery; strong scented myrtle in honor of true and unfeigned love; glossy, fragrant leaves of bay; ivy with clusters of black berries and thin, smooth, shiny, sharp-pointed, leaves, each looking snipped and cut out of tin and then painted with rich green. And because it was Christmas, they scattered the three herbs strewn in the manager in Bethlehem in the yard, barn, and shed: wild thyme, grounsel,[38] and sweet woodruff[39] which made the oldest hay smell newly mown.

Mistletoe, its twin leaves like a pair of slender, delicate wings and berries like tiny pearls, and smooth, prickled holly brightened by round, blood-red berries were hung as "remembrance of the most precious blood of Our Lord and Savior." These evergreens remained in place until Candlemas, when for good luck they were fed to the fires and replaced through Lent until Easter Day with the deep green leaves of the box tree.

It was time for Christmas cakes and ale; to wear their most gaudy, light-colored, light-hearted costumes; to put on jewels both true and paste; time for hobby horses, for dancing with strings and ropes of little bells twisted around each leg; time for mumming and masking and disguising; time to tune instruments, make music, and sing the ancient and ageless carols. When the tables were finally cleared of the Christmas feast, Matthew and Joan would have watched the children play their games and join in late singing and dancing.

As the evening wore on, Matthew, feeling the need for fresh air, might have gone outside alone to stand in the cold, star-dazzled night, thanking God for his family and his good fortune. Full of love and charity, he would wish on a star seeking good fortune for both friend and enemy, wishing the dead from Adam and Eve to now their rest in peace, and the living, from the beggar in his hedge to the queen in her soft bed, the best life had to offer. As he made these wishes he would have wondered what the queen was thinking: was there a place in her dreams for the Bocking clothier and his family, for the plowman, the butcher, the baker, the beggar and the school master? As the last echoes of the midnight bells faded into silence, he reentered the home and joined Joan in bed.

The day after Christmas, the Whipples would have prayed and feasted in honor of the martyrdom of St. Stephen[40] and the second day rejoiced in honor of St. John the Evangelist. On the third day they prayed and fasted in honor of Childermas the day they were to think upon the blood slaughter of the Holy Innocents by king Herod.[41] If Matthew wasn't one to relinquish all the old ways for the sake of the new, he probably said a private silent prayer on December 29 for the blessed English saint, Thomas à Becket of Canterbury, for whose death an English king once bared his body and knelt to be whipped in penance.[42] It was not an easy thing for an Englishman, no matter what he professed or whatever his religious persuasion, to forget communion of English saints and martyrs.

The Whipples would have celebrated feasts and holy days in January beginning on the first with the Feast of Circumcision[43] (also the time for giving of gifts), the Feast of the Holy Name of Jesus on the second, and the Epiphany on the sixth which was the end of holidays and idleness. On that day plows were blessed and the following Monday, Plow Monday, plowing began at sunrise. There were no more holidays until Candlemas. After two weeks of eating and drinking and living like a lord, it was time to return to work, make plans to endure the rigors of Lent, and get ready to feast again at Easter. This was the time of the leanest diet of the year. But helped by the memory of the good belly cheer of Christmastime, it wasn't too difficult to be content with roast meat on two days a week.

The Whipple children would have looked forward to market day[44] because they often included entertainment such as mummers,[45] a dancing bear, a juggler who could balance a sword on his nose, and a band of gypsies (who called themselves Frenchmen) with a gaily-painted, high-wheeled horse cart who were there to perform tricks and otherwise entertain the people. One could swallow fire from a torch, another could walk on a rope tied across the square from one rooftop to another, all could tumble, leap, and somersault. As some were performing their tricks and shows, others, given half a chance, stole valuables from their unsuspecting audience. They could empty a purse as quick as the fishmonger could gut a trout.

The kids would have spent their allowance on gingerbread toys and pink pigs made from marchpane.[46] Joan would wander through the market looking at the goods, especially savoring the fine things they couldn't afford. It was fun to "window shop." Matthew probably did a lot of trading and when he couldn't trade, he would buy, using gold coins called angels and sovereigns. The angel had a likeness of the winged St. George, busily slaying the dragon with a short spear on one side and a ship and the arms of England on the other. They contained 80 grains of old gold and unlike silver did not glitter in the light. The sovereign was more than double the size of the angels and three times its weight. The queen, full-faced, crowned, seated on a throne, and holding her mystical orb, was on one side, the arms of England on the other. It was the largest coin made in the Tower mint. Five sovereigns was the equivalent of a year's wages for a skilled blacksmith in 1602.[47]

Joan's home remedies were many and peculiar. Dried, powdered hen's dung was blown in sore eyes; an ointment of white dog's turd,[48] white frankincense,[49] aloes,[50] yolk of egg, and oil of roses was used to treat hemorrhoids. A peck of roasted snails mixed with earthworms, slit and scoured in salt water, and added to various herbs, strong ale, and white wine, was the cure for jaundice and consumption. Wounds were staunched with a patch dipped in frog's spawn.[51] Fried horse dung was applied to the kid's bruises; it was used unfried and strained to soothe a severe burn or scald. A hoarhound potion quieted a bad cough. The warming pan with fresh coals helped when mother was ill. Father's aching knee or gouty toe meant a trip to the apothecary shop for a jar of leeches to suck out the bad blood.

A swollen cheek and pain darkened hollows beneath the eyes was a sure sign of a recurring toothache. If laudanum[52] and ground cloves didn't work, the tooth puller was called. Tooth pulling was pure agony. The gagging caused by the clumsy iron forceps fastened on the tortured molar magnified the grinding splintering shocks of pain as the puller sweated and jerked with one hand while forcing his patient's head back with the other. But agony was followed by the ecstacy of relief when the bloody tooth was waived in the air and the tooth puller left with payment of sixpence for his service.[53]

Anne was five when war with Spain began in 1588. Rumors that the Spanish Armada would land an army in Essex, caused great excitement and concern.[54] Essex's proximity to the Netherlands, where

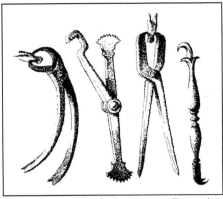

Dental Instruments *for levering an pulling teeth in England in the seventeenth century*

the Spanish army was assembled, made it the logical invasion site. Spain also felt Essex's large Catholic population would help overthrow Elizabeth and the Anglican Church.[55] The Privy Council organized, at least on paper, an impressive national levy to fund the army. Essex offered a potential of 13,062 infantry and 300 horse, and promised almost 4,000 men fully armed with musket, shot, and pike.[56] By July, before North Sea winds blew the Armada off course and aborted the invasion, the army was assembled at Fort Tilbury in Essex.[57] Its captain general, the earl of Leicester, sourly announced he was more "cook, caterer, and huntsman" than a captain general when 4,000 Essex men arrived without a barrel of beer or a loaf of bread.[58]

Elizabeth rallied her people in August at Tilbury.[59] Matthew, Sr., about 28, was probably a member of the Essex troop on parade in full war regalia on the18th when Elizabeth, in what was undoubtedly the most dramatic moment of her reign, inspected her troops.[60]

She was clad all in white velvet with a silver cuirass[61] embossed with a mythological design, and bore in her right hand a silver truncheon chased in gold. She rode bare-headed, and there was a tuft of plumes, the sheen of pearls, and the glitter of diamonds in her hair. Elizabeth carried her 55 years well.

The day was so successful she decided to repeat it the next day. This time there was a review and march past, followed by cavalry exercises which amounted to an impromptu tournament. She dined in state in the general's pavilion where all the captains of her army came to kiss her hand. Sometime during the activities of the second day, she stirred Matthew and the other soldiers with words they would always cherish:

"My loving people, we have been persuaded by some that are careful for our safety, to take heed how we commit ourselves to armed multitudes, for fear of treachery. But I assure you, I do not desire to live to distrust my faithful and loving people. Let tyrants fear. I have always so behaved myself so that, under God, I have placed my chiefest strength and safeguard in the loyal hearts and good will of my subjects; and therefore I am come amongst you as you see, at this time, not for my recreation and disport, but being resolved, in the midst and heat of the battle, to live or die amongst you all, and to lay down for my God and for my kingdom and for my people, my honor and my blood, even in the dust . . . that any Prince of Europe should dare to invade the borders of my realm; to which rather than any dishonor shall grow by me, I myself will take up arms, I myself will be your general, judge, and rewarder of every one of your virtues in the field. I know already for your forwardness you deserve rewards and crowns; and we do assure you, in the word of a prince, they shall be duly paid you."[62]

Work was important to the Whipple family and they were engaged in Bocking's chief industry — cloth making. As a clothier, Matthew produced lighter worsteds and "new draperies" out of wool and other raw materials. Clothiers contracted with carders, combers, spinners, weavers, fullers, and other craftsmen and sold the finished product at home or to an export company.[63] England's economy depended on the cloth trade and fortunately for the Whipples, business was good the first 15 years of the seventeenth century. The highest cloth export year was 1614. Beginning in 1618, traditional continental markets softened and by 1622, exports had dropped by half.[64] The depression of 1620-24 resulted in high unemployment. Exports declined further during the 1629-31 period. In 1636 and 1637, London, Norwich, Sandwich, and many other cities were hit hard by the plague.

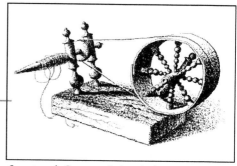
Seventeenth Century *spinning wheel*

Economic recovery, already painfully slow and uneven, was suspended for months at a time. The Whipple's final 19 years in England were extremely trying economically, and undoubtedly caused the family to wonder if its clothier business would survive.

Since the economy was dependent on cloth export, the country's woes were blamed on clothiers and their public standing reached an all-time low in the decades of the 20s and 30s. A member of parliament complained to the House of Commons that clothiers "give not the poor competent wages three pence a day and no more to divers."

A famous ballad chanted about the time Charles I was crowned (1625) recited, in rude rhymes, the grievances of the cloth workers. It was called *The Clothiers Delight.*[65] It's opening three verses:

Of all sorts of calling that in England be,
There is none that liveth so gallant as we;
Our trading maintains us as brave as a Knight,
We live at our pleasure, and take our delight;
We heapeth up riches and treasure great store,
Which we get by griping and grinding the poor.

Chorus
And this is a way for to fill up our purse,
Although we do get it with many a curse.

Through the whole kingdom, in country and town,
There is no danger of our trade going down,

So long as the Comber can work with his comb,
And also the Weaver with his lomb;
The Tucker and Spinner that spins all the year,
We will make them to earn their wages full dear.

Repeat chorus

In former ages we us'd to give,
So that our work folks like farmers did live;
But the times are altered, we will make them know
All we can to bring them all under our bow;
We will make to work hard for sixpence a day,
Though a shilling they deserve if they had their just pay

Repeat chorus

When Elizabeth died in 1603, she was the only sovereign Matthew and Joan had known. Under Elizabeth, except for the time of the Armada, they knew nothing but peace.[66] So there was great excitement in their home when James VI, King of Scots, was announced as England's new king.[67] In addition to James' coronation, other royal pomp the family may have witnessed was the investiture of Henry and Charles as Prince of Wales.[68]

After it was published in 1611, the King James version of the Bible must have become the family's favorite book. It was full of people, beasts, fishes, birds and of war, horror, love, death, and miracles. Its stories were about kings and princes; about soldiers and shepherds and beggars; about the rich and the poor, the sick and the healthy and the proud and the humble. It told of splendid feasts and bitter famine; of present joy and perennial sorrow; of the hope of heaven and the horror of hell; of sowing and reaping; of good and bad harvests. If it hadn't been for things like the desert, the Red Sea, cedar and olive trees, plants, people, and places with outlandish names, the Bible's countryside could have been England. What happened in the Bible could so easily happen and did happen to its readers.

Elizabeth's reign and the flowering of Protestantism added spice and interest to the life of the Whipple family. But what of life's contradictions? Were the children awed by the luminous quiet in St. Mary's Deanery church as they stood in the center aisle staring at the great leaded windows, tinted in jeweled greens, blues, and golds, deepened here and there by spots of translucent crimson? Or was the family already committed to the Puritan creed and considered the beautifully colored windows an idolatrous bauble left from the old days?

The Whipple children probably studied the shivery woodcuts of tortures and burnings in John Foxe's *Acts and Monuments*, the most widely circulated book in England after the Bible.[69] If the family didn't own a copy, they read it at the parish church as it was one of four chained books in all cathedrals and parish churches in the land. But how did they resolve the religious questions of that time? If papists were bad, were all Protestants good? How could that be since there were two kinds of Protestants: those who had candles and a cross like in St. Mary's and who bowed at the name of Jesus and who kept Saints' days and Christmas; and Puritans who hated all those things, who relied only on the Word of God, and who worshiped several days a week in private homes.

Everyone talked religion. It was the subject in broadsides and newsletters. An individual might not approve of a particular religious group but he would not be indifferent. Almost everyone had a religious affiliation and defended it with all the warmth and vehemence an age of religious controversy breeds in its people.[70]

Based on their membership in the Ipswich, Mass. church, it seems apparent that Matthew, Jr. and John Whipple embraced Puritanism before leaving England and probably attended a nonconformist church where the minister bravely ignored the ceremonies ordained by the bishops.[71]

Reverends Richard Rogers and his nephew John Rogers were among the leaders of the Essex Puritan movement. Richard organized congregational prayer meetings, composed treatises on the Christian life, and generally set an example for fellow converts. John, of Wetherfield, had the ability to bring trembling and sudden conversion to his hearers.

St. Mary's Deanery Church *from the west front. From a nineteenth century print. A good example of Gothic architcture.*

The Rood Screen, St. Mary's Deanery Church. *Rood comes from the old Saxon* roda, *meaning a cross. They were used to divide parts of the church, e.g. separating the chancel from the nave. Above the rood screen was the Cross of Christ. On either side of the cross were figures of St. Mary the Virgin and St. John the Evangelist.*

Details of wood-carvings and ironwork *on the south door of* St. Mary's Deanery Church

The Baptistry, St. Mary's Deanery Church

Essex produced the second highest number of emigrants from England with several Puritan preachers influencing the 244 residents who migrated to the American colonies between 1620 and 1650.[72]

Puritans believed the Bible was the complete religious authority; that the

St. Mary's Deanery Church *from the Southeast. The foundation of the Bocking church was dedicated to the Blessed Virgin Mary over 1,000 years ago in the reign of King Æthelred*

original texts of the 66 books of the old and new testaments were the only authority to be recognized;[73] that the principles of all truth and a complete guide to life were found in scripture.[74] Puritanism encompassed theology, ethics, economics, politics, ecclesiastical discipline, academics. No corrupting fancies of carnal reason were to be permitted in interpreting the Bible. In case of doubt, consider the context of the difficult passage, compare it with other parts of scripture, and fit it to the general pattern of faith as set forth in the Bible. Scripture was a matter of harmony, not strife. Puritans believed the end of the world was eminent, that the papacy was the Antichrist whose approaching final ruin would herald the great day of the second coming.[75]

Prayer was considered especially important. It was the means by which man might feel the power of God's love. It need not be audible since God was all hearing but the voice might be used in private to prevent wandering and in public to attract people.[76]

A standard Puritan day included family prayers and a survey of one's spiritual estate. Recurring sermon days took the place of the festivals of the church year. They did not object to music in church if it aided proper worship.[77] Psalm singing commonly preceded and followed the sermon but only biblical passages were sung. The minister could preach the Word in his own phrases but the hymn writer had to use those of the Holy Spirit. Art was in the same category. It could be enjoyed in moderation at home and had its place in church if it did not perpetuate superstition or obstruct the scriptural message. Outside the church, the Puritan remained generally indifferent to the fine arts.

Puritans believed that abstinence humbled the body and the mind. Want in body caused one to feel the want in his soul and turned one to God. Consequently, they fasted frequently when nothing at all, except in case of necessity, was to be eaten for 24 hours. So far as possible, sleep was to be omitted. Other than times of fast, there was no disapproval of food, clothing, or sleep. Gorgeous, even sumptuous attire, was allowed to those of exalted station as necessary means of maintaining dignity and status.

In amusements, it was the abuse, not the use that was objectionable. Dancing, undeniably a biblical activity, helped keep the body healthy and limber. Like music, it was taught to children as part of their education and special dance steps were taken to New England.

They were expected to obey superiors, love their neighbors, do works of charity, show compassion toward all men, have a calling and pursue it as zealously as the Christian life.[78] Marriage was a divine institution ordained before the Fall and open to every man. To deny clergy, as Catholic doctrine did, the right to marry was more than flesh and blood could endure without sin. Therefore, ministers were expected to marry.

Man was exalted as lord and master. Women were the "weaker vessel," made of poorer stuff and legally subject to husbands. The Bible made that clear. But rulership did not mean tyranny. The husband was to love and cherish his wife as his own flesh. She was not to be made into a drudge[79] or ordered about like a servant but was, like a judge, joined with her husband to help rule his household. While English common law permitted a husband to beat his wife with a rod no bigger than his thumb, Puritans forbade this practice.

"If he cannot reform his wife without beating, he is worth to be beaten for choosing no better; when he hath used all means that he may and yet she is like herself, he must take her for his cross and say with Jeremiah, 'This is my cross and I will bear it.' But if he strike her, he takes away his hand from her, which was the first part he gave her to join them together; and she may put up her complaint against him that he hath taken away part of her goods. Her cheeks are made for thy lips and not for thy fists."[80]

The choice of a life partner was a matter of parental decision, not individual choice. No free play or new and original traits of character were allowed to develop in Puritan children. The ruler of the household was to train the child in the Puritan way. They were to remember the fifth commandment and obey their parents. There was no such thing as too much severity. To smile or laugh at naughty words or "unhonest" deeds was unacceptable. Education was important. Children were expected to read and write, "for it may be unto them a great help in the course of this life and a treasure of much greater account than money" to read the word of God "to their comfort and instruction to salvation. He that hath learning, although it be but small, shall much better understand the preachers and take endless comfort than he that hath no learning."[81] Parents were to choose schoolmasters carefully and pay them well, just as they would a good horse trainer.

Based on the high office he held in the Ipswich, Mass. church, John may have been a more dedicated Puritan than Matthew, Jr.[82] If so, he would have committed himself to a rigid course of discipline as a youth. He would have refrained from smoking, read only the scriptures, spoke no ungodly words, and kept the Sabbath with careful piety.

As a committed Puritan, he was expected to renounce and repent of every known sin. He was to study God's requirement as set forth in the Bible, realize his shortcomings, and "rip up" his heart in genuine penitence. He was to dissect his conscience, past and present, examine even the slightest failing or secret desire, and when the depth of his transgression became apparent, it was to be contrasted with God's standard. Only then could he realize the hopelessness of his situation if no outside aid were forthcoming.

In this state of "holy desperation," convinced of his extreme sinfulness and inability to help himself, the Puritan cast himself wholly on the mercy of God. Then came peace and the assurance of salvation as the Holy Spirit convinced him that by justifying faith he was numbered among the elect.[83] _—August 28, 1621 – London_

John's marriage to Susanna in 1620 would have been arranged.[84] If they were Puritans, they were married in the briefest of ceremonies, first standing, then kneeling by the altar rail, both dressed in black, as were the handful of family who crowded behind them in the bare isles. There were no candles or flowers and no rings were exchanged.[85] Maybe they weren't married in the church since Jesus said that in heaven there was no marriage or giving in marriage so some Puritans considered a civil contract sufficient.

Matthew, Jr. would have presided at the reception since their father died the previous year. In his toast to Susanna, with pewter mug filled with sweet bride ale, he might have said: "I drink to the good health of the new Mistress Whipple. You have become my sister and I am sure with God's direction you will do credit to your new state and be a true helpmeet to your husband." Turning to his younger brother he might have said: "On this your wedding day I give you my blessing with the prayer that our gracious Lord will make the light of His countenance shine in your heart, from henceforward."

When punishing their children, John probably delivered one stroke with a hazel stick for each sin and then read to the child from Ecclesiastics:

"He that loveth his son causeth him oft to feel the rod, that he may have joy of him in the end . . . a horse not broken becometh headstrong . . . cocker [86] thy child and he shall make thee afraid . . . give him no liberty in His youth . . . wink not at his follies . . . bow down his neck while he is young, and beat him on the sides while he is a child lest he was stubborn and disobedient . . . and so bring sorrow to thine heart."[87]

Following the reading, the child was to affirm his full contrition and repentance and announce his determination never again to offend "our most loving God."[88] _Stephens⁻¹_

By Joan's death in 1612, only Anne and Margaret had married so Matthew⁻¹ had daughters Jane, 24, Elizabeth, 18, and Mary, 13, to help manage the household and raise 6 year old Amy.[89] He was a widower for his final seven years, with four grandchildren to enjoy.[90] His Will indicates he was successful and had achieved financial independence. His home with its great chamber, little chamber, lodging chamber, old parlor and loft is evidence of his success.[91] He bequeathed more than £200 to family members, some to be distributed within one month following his death, indicating he had liquid assets. Other bequeaths of silver spoons, high latten candlesticks,[92] brass pots, pewter dishes, a table, stools, three different types of chests, five beds, fine linen, bolsters, blankets, etc. confirms his station in life. Matthew, Jr. was named sole executor of the estate. The author has emphasized parts of the will in boldface, added the information in brackets, and added spaces between bequeaths to various individuals.

WILL OF MATTHEW WHIPPLE[93]

In the name of God amen **the nineteenth day of December** anno domini **one-thousand-six-hundred-sixteen** and in the fourteenth year of the reign of our Sovereign Lord James by the Grace of God King of England, France, and Ireland and the fiftieth of Scotland, defender of the faith, etc., I **Matthew Whipple the elder of Bocking in the county of Essex, Clothier**, and of the diocese of Canterbury, being at this present of good and perfect memory, thanks be given to God, and calling to my mind the uncertainty of the continuance of man's transitory life in this present world and the certainty of death when it shall please God to appoint the time, and being willing and desirous to devise and set in order such goods, chattels, and tenements as God of his mercy and goodness hath blessed me withall, do therefore make and declare this my present testament and last Will in manner and form following (renouncing and revoking all former Wills by me heretofore made), first and principally, I commend my soul to Almighty God my Creator and to Jesus Christ my only Savior and Redeemer by and through whose death merits and passion I trust assuredly to have free pardon for all my sins. And my body to the earth to be decently buried by my executors when it shall please God to take my life from me.

Item. My meaning is that my **messuage or tenement with the yard and garden and orchards**, members and appurtenances whatsoever, to the same capital messuage belonging or appertaining, **situate in Bradford street in Bocking** aforesaid, now in the occupation of me the said Matthew, from and after my decease shall remain to **Matthew Whipple, mine oldest son**, [age 26] the heirs of his body lawfully begotten, upon this condition nevertheless that he, the said Matthew my son, his heirs or assigns, shall well and truly satisfy and pay or cause to paid to **my son John Whipple**, [20] four score pounds [£80] of lawful money of England within three months next and immediately following after my decease. And also that he, the said Matthew, my son, his heirs or assigns, shall likewise satisfy and pay or cause to be paid to **my daughter Jane**, [29] thirty pounds [£30] of like lawful money of England within two months next after my death.

And likewise shall satisfy and pay or cause to be paid to **my daughter Elizabeth**, [22] thirty pounds [£30] of like money within twelve months next after my decease and likewise to **my daughter Marye**, [17] thirty pounds [£30] of like money at her age of one and twenty or at the day of her marriage which shall first happen. And likewise to **my daughter Amye** [11], thirty pounds [£30] of like money at her age of one and twenty years or at the day of her marriage, which shall first happen, upon reasonable demand made by the said Jane, Elizabeth, Mary, and Amye and provided always that if my son Matthew do refuse and do not pay to my son John Whipple the four score pounds as aforesaid and thirty pounds apiece to my four daughters aforesaid; at the several days and times limited and appointed as is afore rehearsed, then I do devise, give, and bequeath all my capital messuage or tenement aforesaid, with all and singular the premises members and appurtenances whatsoever, with the furnishings in and about all the rooms therein being, to my son John Whipple and to his heirs or assigns, forever. And that then he the said John, my son, his heirs or assigns, shall discharge and pay or cause to be paid to my afore named four daughters their portions of thirty pounds apiece of lawful money of England in manner and form as aforesaid.

Item. I give and bequeath to my daughter **Anne (Anna) Pepper** [33] six silver spoons of the better sort, two high latten candlesticks, my biggest brass pot and three pounds, six shillings and eight pence in money to be paid and delivered to her within one month next after my decease.

Item. I give to **my daughter Johane**[94] forty shillings lawful money of England to be paid to her within one month next after my decease.

Item. I give to **my daughter Jane** two silver spoons, two pewter platters of the greater sort, one pewter candlestick, one half headed bedstead, my best flock bed and flock bolster and coverlet and a pair of blankets.

Item. I give to **my daughter Elizabeth** two silver spoons, one pewter candlestick, two pewter platters of the greater sort, a half headed bedstead, next the best and flock bed and flock bolster and coverlet and pair of blankets and the little chest which was her mothers.

Item. I give to **my daughter Mary** two silver spoons, two pewter platters and a pewter salt and trundle bedstead and flock bed and flock bolster and coverlet and pair of blankets.

Item. I give to **my daughter Amye** two silver spoons, two pewter platters and pewter salt and trundle bedstead and flock bed and flock bolster and a pair of blankets.

Item. I give to my son John a joined table and frame standing in **my old parlor** with eight joined stools to it, a great joined chest standing in **my great chamber**, one silver spoon and another spoon silver, and my bed bedding and bedstead furnished whereon I do now lie standing in **my little chamber**.

Item. All my best linen I do give among to my children as the same hath been viewed, parted, and divided out to them.

Item. I give to **my sister, the wife of Richard Rathbone**, seventy shillings and to **Hercules Stephens**, ten shillings.

Item. I give to my daughter Mary one plain chest standing in my lodging chamber. And I do give to **my daughter Amye** my long chest standing in the **old parlor**.

Item. I give to **my grandchildren viz: Hercules Arthur, Margaret Arthur,**[95] **Henry Calham**, and **Ande Calham**, to each of them six shillings eight pence apiece, to be paid to them at their several ages of of one and twenty years.

Item. I give to **my son John** five curtains next **the loft**.

Item. I give to **the poor people of Bocking** twenty shillings to be distributed among them.

All the rest of my goods and chattels whatsoever (my debts being paid and my funeral discharged), I give to Matthew, my son. And **I do make and ordain the said Matthew, my son, sole executor** of this, my last will and testament. In witness whereof, I have hereunto set my hand and seal the day and year first above written.

The Will was signed by Matthew and witnessed by Thursby and Taylor.

Unfortunately, no inventory of Matthew's estate exists. Essex, unlike other

English counties, has few surviving inventories for the seventeenth century, particularly for the decades of the great migration to New England.[96]

Matthew's grandson, Hercules Arthur, acquired the manor of Fryers in Bocking June 4, 1632.[97] Located on Bradford street on the lane called Fryers, it had a court baron and several quit rents.[98] The mansion house was on the right side of the road leading from Bocking to Braintree. Hercules died without issue, leaving the manor to his half brother, John Arthur of Clapham in Surrey. John Arthur, a child of Laurence's second marriage, married Anne Corbet. Their children were John, Jr. Henry,[99] Anne, Elizabeth, and Dorothy. The Manor was bequeathed to John Arthur, Jr. who eventually sold it to John Maysent, Jr. of Bocking, a grandson of Margaret and great grandson of Matthew Whipple, Sr.[100]

John Hawkins, a respected citizen and trustee for the poor of Bocking married Mary Levitt February 21, 1603/04.[101] At the time of this marriage, he had at least two daughters by a previous wife: Eleanor, baptized March 6, 1595 and buried in 1610; and Mary, who married Matthew Wright November 8, 1610.[102] His daughters with Mary Levitt, Anne and Sarah, both married in 1622 Anne to Matthew Whipple, Jr. on May 7, and Sarah to William Coppin on September 26. His son John, Jr. lived in Braintree.[103] Hawkins died in 1619; Mary Levitt Hawkins died May 3, 1635.[104]

The Hawkins were among Braintree's notable families. Braintree was ruled by a "Select Vestry" known as the "Four and Twenty," a self perpetuating oligarchy of a few of the substantial church members. Three successive generations of Hawkins served on the Four and Twenty.[105]

John Hawkins, Jr. carried the title of Gentleman and is believed to have lived in a fine mansion in Great Square. A tablet identifying his tomb is in the north chancel wall of St. Michael the Archangel church at Braintree. He was a member of the Grocers' Company, and an alderman of the city of London in 1626.[106] At his death September 8, 1633, his estate included messuages and tenements in Tolleshunt, Bushes, Salcott, Wigborough, and Verley,[107] the messuage where the family lived in Braintree, and two little tenements adjoining the Braintree churchyard. The Braintree messuage and two tenements were left to his wife Sara, "so long as she remained a widow," and to his son Abraham. Abraham also received other lands and tenements. "Sister Whipple," brother Francis, other children, sisters, mother, aunts and a cousin were also remembered.[108]

His son Robert Hawkins, esquire, owned Lyons, a capital messuage located about a mile east south east from St. Mary's Church and about a mile south of the manor of Boones in Bocking.[109] He also owned considerable property in Braintree, passed by marriage to Sir John Dawes of Putney, knight and baronet, who married his only daughter Frances.[110]

The Will of Thomas Trotter, a London merchant, born at Braintree, suggests a possible relationship between the Whipple and Whaple families. The Trotter will refers to "my cousin Laurence Arthur's wife," and "my cousin Robert Whaples' wife."[111] Arthur was named a supervisor of the Trotter estate which included property in both Bocking and Braintree. Trotter left £50 to the poor in several parishes and named Matthew, Jr. and Arthur to oversee its distribution in Bocking, giving the same assignment to John Hawkins for Braintree.[112]

The Stone family of Great Bromley,[113] later of Boxted, both in Essex, is of interest because Mary Whipple, daughter of John and Susanna, united the two

(or) Sarah Hawkins

families by marrying Deacon Simon Stone in New England in 1655.[114] Simon, born at Boxted about 1630, moved to Massachusetts Bay with his family in 1635 where they settled at Mount Auburn in Watertown. The family can be traced to Walter atte (sic) Stone, born about 1285 and living in 1327.[115] David Stone was born in Great Bromley, Essex about 1540, the same birth year estimated for Matthew, Sr.'s mother. His son Simon, father of Deacon Simon, was christened February 6, 1586 at Great Bromley, making him a contemporary of Matthew, Jr.[116]

Early in his reign, Charles I (1625-49) caused the Articles "for the avoiding of diversities of opinions, and for the establishing of consent touching true religion" agreed to in 1562 be reprinted. As Defender of the Faith and Supreme Governor of the Church, he acted to conserve and maintain the Church in the "unity of true religion" and to eliminate "unnecessary disputations, altercations, or questions which may nourish faction both in the Church and Commonwealth."

He claimed the 1562 document contained "the true Doctrine of the Church of England agreeable to God's Word" and required "all our loving subjects to continue in the uniform profession thereof." While denying anyone the right to vary from the doctrine and discipline of the Church of England, he acknowledged "curious and unhappy differences" throughout the land. All were to submit "in the plain and full meaning thereof: and shall not put his own sense or comment to be the meaning of the Article, but shall take it in the literal and grammatical sense." Puritanism was widespread by this time and its followers were enraged. Many determined they could no longer tolerate the restrictions on their right to freedom of religion and vowed to leave the land of Charles I — it seems Matthew and John Whipple were among them.[117]

By elevating Laud to the bishopric of London in 1628 and to archbishop of Canterbury in 1633, Charles I showed further determination to enforce absolute conformity to his high church views. In 1637, three men of thoroughly respectable origin issued a series of pamphlets against the archbishop. They were William Prynne, a barrister, Henry Burton, a former court chaplain dismissed for his Puritanism, and John Bastwich, a doctor of medicine. Among their pamphlets were *News from Ipswich, For God and the King, Flagellum Pontificis,* and *The Litany of John Bastwich.* They attacked Laud in terms that ensured wide readership. The result was trial in the star chamber with a sentence of life imprisonment, a fine of £5,000 each, and loss of ears.[118] This action greatly inflamed feeling against Laud and the three were regarded as living martyrs by Puritans who dipped sponges and handkerchiefs in their blood, hardly consistent considering Puritan opinion on the relics of Catholicism.

In December of 1637, Laud's agents captured John Lilburne, the "notoriousest dispenser of scandalous books in the kingdome."[119] When Lilburne was sentenced to be whipped through the streets and set in the pillory, it reaffirmed belief that reform of the church was hopeless and that Puritan life in England was impossible. The Lilburne sentence may have helped John Whipple decide he wasn't going to be able to practice his Puritan beliefs in England.

Most people think all emigrants left for religious reasons. Not so. Of the 60,000 going to America between 1630-43, many went to better themselves.[120] Matthew Whipple was probably among this group. The several financial depressions must have diminished the family business. He may have been among Essex and Suffolk clothiers to petition the King and the two houses of parliament because London merchants were not buying their product. "Our cloths for the most part, for the space of this 18 months, remain upon our hands, our stocks lying dead therein, and we can maintain our trading no longer," the petition stated. "The cries for food by many thousands of poor, who depend on this trade, do continually press us, not without threats, and some beginnings of mutinies; so that, if some speedy relief do not intervene, we can expect no less than confusion."[121] And as a father concerned about his family's health — his first two sons and John's two sons and two daughters died in infancy — Matthew probably believed New England offered a better environment for his family. If his thoughts were on the future, he had to consider the new world and its opportunities.

This author believes a combination of religion, economics, and health caused Matthew and John Whipple to migrate and change, in mid career, their settled English vocations for a life in a pioneering agricultural community of uncertain prospects.[122] Why choose New England where the craft which had given them income and status in the old world didn't exist; where they would never again see family and old friends?

New England was not the only option. They could have moved to The Netherlands, the most economically advanced area in the whole of Europe, where every kind of craft, especially worsted weaving, was in high demand. More emigrants went to Holland than to New England because of its economic opportunities and because it welcomed nonconformists.[123] And Holland was a known entity, close to home, and moving there would be relatively easy compared to a journey across the Atlantic. That many from their area of Essex were going to New England must have also been a major influence. On the 1632 voyage of the *Lyon*, 58 were followers of rev. Thomas Hooker and were from the Braintree-Bocking area. Lionel and Rose Chute (Rose was Matthew, Jr.'s second wife) lived in Dedham, Essex before migrating in 1630. Rose's family roots were in Ardleigh, Essex. Ozias and William Goodwin left Bocking for New England in 1632. Ozias' wife, Mary Woodward was born in Braintree, her family roots were in Earl's Colone, and her marital home was Bocking. The family of the Stone brothers, Simon and Gregory, had lived in Tendring Hundred near Colchester, Essex since 1300. They went to New England in 1635. Brothers Abraham and Robert Hawkins of Braintree settled in Charleston, Mass. in 1635.[124] Simon Stacy and his wife Elizabeth Clark left Bocking for Ipswich, Mass. in 1636 as did Robert Lord of Sudbury and his wife Mary Waite of Wethersfield. Thomas Fitch and his wife Anne Stacy of Bocking settled in Hartford, Conn. about 1638 and Dr. John Dane, Jr. and his wife Eleanor Clarke were in Ipswich by 1636.[125]

The *Zealous Puritan*, a popular ballad at the time may have helped influence Puritans to pick New England:

Stay not among the wicked,
Lest that with them you perish,
But let us to New England go
And the pagan people cherish.

For company I fear not,
There goes my cousin Hannah,
And Reuben so persuades to go
My cousin Joyce, Sussannah.

With Abigail and Faith,
And Ruth no doubt comes after
And Sarah kind, will not stay behind;
My cousin Constance daughter.[126]

For whatever reason, New England was chosen. The question of pounds, shillings, and pence, of a decreasing income, and an unfavorable balance sheet, the recurring outbreaks of the plague and other killing diseases prompted many to leave. Hope for freedom to worship freely as Puritans, for economic opportunity, and for a healthier environment were undoubtedly among the motivations to leave.

Imagine the agonizing decision to sell the family home and business; to give up the known for a new life on an almost unknown continent. Imagine how Anne and Susanna felt, realizing they would never again see their sisters, brothers, aunts, and a host of cousins, nieces and nephews. No longer would their homes be surrounded by associations stretched further than their memories. They were leaving a world that was "time honored" for one that was primeval but one that eventually would become "time honored" because of their willingness to be pioneers. Difficult as it was, the decision was made in 1637 or 1638.[127]

A move of this magnitude suggests some knowledge of the destination. The next chapter examines the literature available to those contemplating a move and describes a typical ocean voyage. But first, a challenge to future Whipple historians to trace the family beyond Matthew, Sr. Records confirm that a number of Whipple families lived in Bocking and Braintree and a careful search of the records on the following may extend the line: Thomas Whyppll, living in Braintree in 1540 was elected constable in 1542, included in the Essex lay subsidies in 1546, and sold property in August 1547. The name was spelled Whipple in the final two references. Ossee, William, Robert, Pleasance, and Elizabeth Whaples were mentioned in John Pryor's Will in October 1576. Pryor was from Braintree. A Robert Whaples was mentioned in the minutes of Braintree's "Select Vestry," on March 4, 1622/23.[128] The family is also found in Brooke, Broomfield, Chelmsford, Harleston with Redenhall, Starston, Sisted, and Thorley, Essex.

Matthew's 1616 Will and parish records suggest other names to be researched, including the Laurence Arthur, Henry Caldam, Hercules Stephens, John Pepper, Edward Feast, John Wallys, Nicholas Ives, Isaac Green, Richard Baker, Henry Pye, and William Horton or Hoston families.

Because of the prominence of the Hawkins family, an effort to extend the line beyond John Hawkins should be successful. He was Anne (Hawkins) Whipple's father. A Richard Hawkins and his wife Jane were living in Ipswich in 1637.

Wife: Mary Levitt Hawkins, (ca. 1570 – 1635) -1

Thomas Whipple -3 (ca. 1475 – 1535/37)

Thomas Whipple -2 (1510 – ?)

Matthew Whipple -1 (1550 – 1618/19)

Elder John Whipple 0 (1596 – 1669)

ENDNOTES — CHAPTER 1

1. That England had its share of notable personages during the life of Matthew and Joan and their children is apparent from the following:

    1552-1599. Edmund Spenser, author of *Faerie Queen*, a treasure house of allegory, adventure, neoplatonic ideas, patriotism, and protestant morality.

    1554-1618. Sir Walter Raleigh, poet, historian, courtier, explorer, and soldier.

    1561-1626. Francis Bacon, philosopher, essayists, and statesman. In 1617, he became Lord Keeper to King James I.

    1564-1593. Christopher Marlowe, great dramatist and poet. Probably the greatest English dramatists before Shakespeare.

    1564-1616. William Shakespeare, dramatist and poet, considered the greatest playwright who ever lived. Emerged as a playwright in London in 1592, retired in 1613 to his birthplace, Stratford-on-Avon.

    1572-1637. Ben Jonson, the dominant literary figure of James I reign. The brilliance of his language earned him a reputation as one of the great playwrights in English history.

    1572-1631. John Donne, considered the greatest of the metaphysical poets and one of the most eloquent preachers of his day.

    1599-1659. John Milton, one of England's greatest poets. His *Paradise Lost* and *Paradise Regained* are considered among the greatest epic poems in the English language.

    1628-1688. John Bunyan, author of *Pilgrim's Progress*, considered one of the world's great works of literature. His prose unites the eloquence of the Bible with the vigorous realism of common speech.

2. Bocking was in the Hundred of Hinkford. Other communities in the same Hundred in 1611 were: Braintree, Alphamston, Ashden, Ashfield, Balingdon, Belchampwater, Belchamp S. Paul, Belchampotten, Bewereshamlet, Boreley, Bowrehall, Brokehall, Brunden, Brundenhall, Bruntahall, Bulmer, Bumsteedsteeple, Burbrooke, Bymhall, Clarrethall, Codham, Cusslehall, Dawardes, Dyneshall, Felsteede, Fincingfield, Foxearth, Gestlingthorpe, Goldingham, Gosfield, Heninghamsible, Hennye-little, Hennye-great, Hipford, Kirkby, Lamer, Lyston, Lystonhall, Maplesteed-great, Maplesteed-little, Maplesteed-hall, Middleton, Moynes, Old Hall, Ouington, Panfield, Pebmershe, Penlowe, Petches, Rayne-little, Ridgeswell, Roydenhall, Royeshall, Salingould, Sapines, Shalford, Stanborne, Stanborne-hall, Stebbing, Sturmer, Systeed, Thurston, Tilbury, Tilburyhall, Topefield, Twinsteed, Wethersfeld, Wickham S. Paul, Yealdhamhall, Yealdam-little. Since families generally remained in the same general area, research in these parishes, villages, and towns may find the missing link to earlier Whipple generations.

3. Some of her children probably died between 1557-59 when an epidemic caused a burial rate more than double the annual average. A Margaret Whipple's death is recorded in parish records and since Matthew's second born was named Margaret, it is likely that this Margaret is Matthew's mother.

4. The author went to England in 1963 where he viewed the parish records at Bocking's St. Mary's Church and acquired a copy of Matthew's Will from the Principal Probate Registry, Strand, London, W.C.Z. St. Mary's records are extracts from a transcript made by James J. Goodwin in 1903 and represent the earliest available register. According to the Essex county archivist, a second register is missing. The third register includes baptisms from 1655 to 1668 and marriages and burials from 1655 to 1670. Missing are baptisms from 23 March 1571 to 5 May 1583, from 28 April 1588 to 8 Oct. 1592, from 21 Oct. 1599 to 12 Oct. 1602. Marriages are missing from 24 May 1613 to 3 Sept. 1618 and from 1639 to 1655. Burials from August 1580 to September 1583 and from 1627 to 1655 are missing.

5. Mary Lovering Holman and George R. Marvin, M.A., Editors, *Abstracts of English Records Gathered Principally in Devonshire and Essex in a Search for the Ancestry of Roger Dearing c. 1624-1676 and Matthew Whipple c. 1560-1618*, 150 copies privately printed. (Boston, 1929).

6. The circumstances described were the custom for widowers who did not remarry as is the description of Matthew's mourning ritual. Mortality among wives was high and many men married three or four times.

7. She named her son Hercules.

8. All christening dates are from St. Mary's Parish records of 1561-1605 (years 1572-82 are missing). Film# 0472340, Family History Library, Salt Lake City, Utah. Filmed in 1968.

9. Couples did not marry younger than we marry now. In fact, they were older in relation to life expectancy.

10. The author had the Will and Probate translated by professors Valdis Lennicks, Ph.D. and Richard Van Fossom, Ph.D. of Cornell College in Mt. Vernon, Iowa. They were able to read all but a few words and described the Latin as, some very good, part poor.

11. A hornbook was a sheet of parchment with the alphabet, table of numbers, etc. on it. It was mounted on a small board with a handle and protected by a thin transparent plate of horn. It was used as a child's primer.

12. Schools for boys were mandatory. They had to be able to read when they enrolled.

13. Ferule: A flat stick or ruler used for punishing children.

14. Lily, born ca 1468, died 25 Feb. 1522 was one of the first teachers of Greek in England. He studied the classics in Italy and in 1512 was appointed high master of Colet's school in St. Paul's Churchyard. He wrote the national Latin grammar first published in 1513, revised in 1540, altered and reissued in 1574. Udall, born in 1505, died in 1556, was an English dramatist and Latin scholar. He was headmaster at Eton in 1534 and of Westminster School (ca 1554-56). He published his translation of the *Apothegms of Erasmus* in 1542 and translated Erasmus' paraphrase on Luke in 1542-45.

15. William Cramer was born in London 2 May 1551 and died 9 Nov. 1623. He was an English historian and antiquary noted for his study of Elizabethan times. He was headmaster at Westminster School of London (1593-97) and authored *Britannia* (first edition in 1586), a survey of the British Islands written in Latin; first translated into English in 1610.

   Theognis of Megara was one of the early Greek elegiac poets, flourishing about the middle of the sixth century B.C. Virgil, born about 1470 in Castro in Etruria, was educated at Bologna and went to England in 1501 and became bishop of Bath and Wells in 1504. He wrote *Historia Anglica* and *Liber de Prodigiis*, the latter in 1526. Etruria is an ancient country occupying what is now Tuscany and part of Umbria in Italy.

16. Aesop, supposedly born about 620 B.C., was brought to Athens as a slave while young and was eventually enfranchised by Iadom the Samian. Fables bearing his name were popular in Athens. A complete collection of the Aesopian fables, 231 in number, was published in 1810.

   Marcus Porcius Cato was born in 234 B.C. and died 149 B.C. He was a Roman statesman, general, and writer who wrote *Deagri Cultura* (also called *De re Rustica*) and *Origines*. Homer was the first and greatest poet. He probably lived in the 10th or 11th century and developed epic poetry as an art. His *Iliad* and *Odyssey* were certainly on Matthew's reading list.

   Horace lived from 65 to 8 B.C. No ancient writer has been so familiarly known and so generally appreciated in modern times. He was a moralist and a lyric poet. Among his works Matthew probably read were *Satires*, *Epodes*, and *Epistles*.

   Ovid, the last in order of time of the poets of the August, was born in 43 B.C., the year of Cicero's death. He lived in Rome and among his notable works were *Amores* (Art of Love) and the *Herodies*. He died at age 61 in 17 A.D., third year of the reign of Tiberius.

17. The doctrine, that in the Eucharist, the whole substances of the bread and of the wine are changed into the body and blood of Christ, only the incidences of bread and wine remaining.

18. The Book of Common Prayer occupies a place of great importance in the history of the English people. The Church of England has used it as the basis for religion, education, and standards of doctrine since 1559. It includes copious amounts of Holy Scripture and contributed to the formation of the modern English language. The first two prayer books, 1549 and 1552, were not generally accepted. Elizabeth's in 1559 became an integral part of English life. During the reign of Edward VI (1547-1553), Parliament passed, on 1 Jan. 1549, an Act of Uniformity to which was appended *The Book of Common Prayer*. The first copies were on sale by March 7 and was to be in use by Whit Sunday, June 9. The title page indicates it was meant to cover the services previously contained in the *Breviary* (a book containing the prayers, hymns, etc. that priests and certain other clerics of the Roman Catholic church are required to recite daily), the *Missal* (the official, liturgical book of the Roman rite containing all the prayers, rites, etc. used by a priest in celebrating the Mass throughout the year), the *Processional* (a book setting forth the ritual to be observed in church processions), and the manual; the *Pontificals* (having to do with or celebrated by a Bishop or other high-ranking prelate) remained in force for the time being. Its contents formed the use of the whole Church of England, and all diocesan uses were superseded. The preface pointed out that the only other book needed for the conduct of services was the *Bible*, though a separate *Psalter* would be a convenience. It came under immediate attack by those who

resisted liturgical reform and by those who wished to have a more thoroughly reformed order of worship. On 14 April 1552, the second Act of Uniformity, with a revised prayer book, was passed. It was to be in use from All Saints' Day, 1 Nov. It was outlawed during the reign of queen Mary (1553-1558). The 1559 Act of Uniformity included the Elizabethan prayer book and was enforced by statute, royal and local. Visitations were conducted to see to it that the law was obeyed and failure to attend prayer book worship was punishable by law. The Puritans viewed it as popish and ungodly and sought to displace it. But many of them conformed, and made use of the "corrected" prayer book attached to the Geneva Bible and felt by so doing they were obedient to the law. The Roman Catholics were torn. Some resisted, paid their fines, and attended Mass in secret. Others conformed, attended prayer book worship, perhaps with rosaries to occupy time, and then attended Mass when reasonably safe to do so. The book included all the services needed for the regular weekday and Sunday worship of the church and occasional services to meet pastoral needs, emphasizing the great events of life: birth, marriage, sickness, and death.

The Church of England only allowed male priests. According to Graham Heathcote of the Associated Press in a news story in the Portland *Oregonian* 12 Nov. 1992 (page 1 and 20) with a London dateline, the Church of England voted 11 Nov. to ordain women as priests. If parliament and queen Elizabeth endorse the decision as expected, the first woman priest would be ordained in 1994. The Anglo-Catholic wing of the church objected on the grounds ordination of women would be a bar to closer relations with Rome. Evangelicals protested that Christ was male, chose male disciples, and no warrant existed in the Bible for women priests. Canon Christopher Colvern of London responded that "The maleness of Christian ministerial priesthood may be an obstacle to some, madness to others, but I have yet to be convinced that it's not part of God's revelation for the salvation of us all." George Carey, archbishop of Canterbury, pointed out that "ordination of women to the preiesthood alters not a word in the creeds, the Scriptures, or the faith of our church." A two-thirds majority was required in each of the three houses of the church's general synod. It was approved 39-13 by the bishops, 176-74 by the clergy, and 169-82 by the laity. A switch of two votes among lay delegates would have blocked the path to priesthood for the church's 1,350 women deacons. Women bishops are not permitted, parishes may refuse to accept a woman as priests, and bishops cannot be compelled to ordain or accept women as priests in their dioceses. The synod approved severance pay for any full-time priest who felt compelled to resign.

19. Much of the description of London is from George Garrett, *The Succession*, a novel of Elizabeth and James. Doubleday & Company, Inc. (Garden City, NY. 1983).

20. Roger Hart, *English Life in Tudor Times*, Wayland Publishers, (London, 1972). 47-8.

21. The English apprentice statute was passed in 1563 and remained on the statute book for 250 years, being repealed in 1813. The working day was 12 hours in summer and daylight hours in winter. The tradition of apprentices stretches through history to ancient Babylon 4,000 years ago with terms of apprenticeship included in the *Code of Hammurabi*. Then came the industrial revolution. Manufacturing adopted an assembly-line process. Tasks were divided and subdivided and subdivided again into tiny, repetitive routines or reduced to machine watching, requiring no particular hierarchy of skills. Except for certain construction trades, apprenticeship was largely relegated to a historical footnote. In the U.S. in 1989, only 263,000 workers out of a blue-collar force of 35 million were registered apprentices. Their average age was in the mid-20s.

22. The property was known as a capital messuage. A messuage is a dwelling house with out buildings and adjacent land. A capital messuage includes the dwelling occupied by the owner plus several additional messuages. The other dwellings probably housed the married members of the family, the servants, and work force associated with the clothier business.

23. Holman and Marvin. p. 479.

24. *Ibid.* 536-7.

25. *Ibid.* 463. A lay subsidy is a tax on persons based on the payor's reputed estate in lands or goods, or customs imposed on any of the staple commodities.

26. *Ibid.* 479-63. Tebold was a yeoman whose Will was proved 12 Feb. 1603. Was there a family relationship between the families? Hopefully someone will pursue this lead.

27. May Cunnington and Stephen A. Warner, Braintree and Bocking, *A Pictorial Account of Two Essex Townships*, Arnold Fairbairns Printers. 34.

28. Bequeathed as "Bredfords" by John Peppis of Braintree in his Will of 1518.

29. This birth year has been estimated by many previous genealogists. The author feels the year is suspect since parish records show his marriage to Anne Hawkins as May 7, 1622. If born in 1590, Matthew would have been 33 when he married, an age considerably older than the norm. The

date raises questions: was he born later or did he marry earlier, losing his first wife at childbirth or to disease. Or was he his father's chief assistant in operating the clothier business and it became his obligation to run the business after his father's death which occurred three years before he married Anne Hawkins?

30. Infants had about one chance in three of surviving to age one and if surviving, faced the same odds of reaching age five.

31. Spit: A thin, pointed rod or bar on which meat is impaled for broiling or roasting over a fire.

32. A lamprey is an eel-like fish.

33. Beer was introduced into England by the Dutch in the fifteenth century.

34. Gittern: A wire-strung instrument somewhat like a guitar.

35. Musk: Any of several plants having a musky scent.

36. Brand: A stick that is burning or partially burned.

37 Rosemary leaves were placed beneath pillows or under the children's beds to drive away nightmares before they could begin.

38. Groundsel: Plants of the *composite Senecio* family usually with yellow, rayed flower heads. An annual, it is slightly acrid and was used as a domestic remedy for various aliments.

39. Woodruff: A rubiaceous herb scented like the sweet vernal and sweet clover and used to flavor the spring beverage called May drink.

40. Celebrated 26 Dec. from the end of the fourth century. St. Stephen was one of "the seven" appointed by the Apostles to "serve tables" in Jerusalem (Acts 6.5) and one of the most popular saints of the Middle Ages. He preached and performed miracles (Acts 6.8ff), thus incuring the hostility of the Jews who accused him to Sandhedrin. The Sanhedrin was the highest court and council of the ancient Jewish nation with religious and civil functions.

41. Childermas: The popular name of Holy Innocents' Day, a feast day observed in the Anglican and Roman Catholic churches on 28 Dec. to honor the children of the slaughter in and near Bethlehem, as narrated in Mat. ii 16-18. Also Childermas day.

42. The king was Henry II who ruled 1154-89. à Becket was born in London 21 Dec. 1118 and was murdered at the behest of Henry 29 Dec. 1170. He had become chancellor to Henry in 1155 and was elected archbishop in 1162. After becoming archbishop, he resigned his chancellorship and from then on there was strife between king and bishop with à Becket working to extend the authority of the pope and Henry trying to subject the church to his will.

43. The Feast of Circumcision is observed on the octave (the eighth day following a church festival, counting the festival day as the first) of Christmas day (1 Jan.), in honor of the circumcision of Christ. Also commemorates the death of St. Basil.

44. If it rained on market day the family prayed it would be in the early evening. "Rain before seven, clear by eleven," was the old saying.

45. Mummers were masked and costumed people who traveled to fairs and festivals acting out short pantomimes

46. Marchpane: A confection of ground almond, sugar, and egg white made into a paste of various shapes and colors.

47. During Elizabeth's reign (1558-1603), the country had two issues of milled coinage in gold and silver. First issue gold: Sovereign, Ryal, Angel, Half angel, Quarter angel, Pound, Half pound, Crown, and Half crown. Silver issue: Crown, Half crown, Shilling, Sixpence, Groat, Threepence, Half groat, Three halfpence, Penny, Three farthings, Halfpenny. Second issue gold: Half sovereign, Crown, and Half crown. Silver issue: Shilling, Sixpence, Groat, Threepence, Half groat, Three farthings. During the reign of James I (1602-25), there were four issues. First issue gold: Quarter angel, Sovereign, Half sovereign, Crown, and Half crown. Silver issue: Crown, Half crown, Shilling, Sixpence, Half groat, Penny, and Halfpenny. Second issue gold: Unite, Double, Britain crown, Half crown, and Thistle crown. Silver issue: Crown, Half crown, shilling, Sixpence, Half groat, Penny, and Halfpenny. Third issue gold: Rose ryal, Spur ryal, Angel, Half angel; no silver issue. Fourth issue gold: Rose ryal, Spur ryal, Angel, Laurel, Half laurel, and Quarter laurel. Silver issue: Crown, Half crown, Shilling, Half groat, Penny, Halfpenny. Copper and Billon issue: Copper farthing token, both the Harrington and Lennox type. During the reign of Charles I (1625-49), two issues. First issue gold: Angel, Unite, Double crown (half unite), and Britain crown. Silver issue: Crown, Half crown, Shilling, Sixpence, Half groat, Penny, Halfpenny. Copper and Billon issue: Copper farthing token (Richmond and Maltravers types). Second issue gold (Briot's coinage): Angel, Unite, Double crown (half unite), and Crown. Silver issue: Crown, Half crown,

Shilling, Sixpence, half groat, and Penny. The following provincial mints also struck coins for Charles I: York, Aberystwyth, Shewsbury, Oxford, Bristol, Lundy Island, Truro, Exeter, Combe Martin, Weymouth, Salisbury, Worcester, and Chester. The following towns struck siege pieces during his reign: Carlise, Colchester, Newark, Pontefract, and Scarborough. Stephen Mitchell and Brian Reeds, editors, *Coins of Great Britain and The United Kingdom*, 24th Edition. London: Seaby. Adapted with additional material from catalogues originally compiled by H.A. and P.J. Seaby.

48. It's not clear whether the dog or the turd was white.

49. White frankincense: A gum resin obtained from various Arabian and northeast African trees.

50. Aloes: A bitter, laxative drug made from the juice of certain aloe leaves. Aloe is a plant of the lily family, native to South Africa.

51. Spawn: The mass of eggs produced by the frog.

52. Laudanum: Any of various preparations containing opium.

53. Primitive as these remedies were, medicine evolved slowly and 90% of today's health care did not exist in 1950. The power of the doctor to cure and alleviate disease began its meteoric rise about 1930. Before then the doctor could do little once disease set in except relieve some of the symptoms and let nature take its course. Of the 80 milestones in the history of medicine beginning in 2700 B.C., 29 date from the last 65 years, meaning 36% of medicine's most noteworthy advances have occurred in just the last 2.2% of medicine's history.

54. Armada is a Spanish word meaning an armed force or fleet. Here, it designates the expedition of about 120 ships sent out against England in 1588 by Philip of Spain. His principal motive was to strike a decisive blow at the Protestant faith, of which England was then the bulwark.

55. The dread of a great secret Catholic conspiracy of unknown strength was in many men's minds. It was a chief source of tension in that uneasy summer of 1588. Common gossip suggested at least a third of the English were Catholics and that when Spanish armies landed it would be the signal for a widespread uprising. Under these circumstances, the privy council, unsure that English patriotism (and hatred of foreigners) was stronger than the bonds of religion, placed leading recusants (a Roman Catholic who refused to attend the services of the Church of England or to recognize its authority) in protective custody. But the open avowed Catholics were a mere handful while the crypto-Catholics and conforming Anglicans with strong Catholic leanings were more numerous. Some privy councilors and county magnates urged strong measures be taken against all persons in any way suspected. "It were hard for any man to face the enemy with a stout heart," wrote one of them, "if he thought his house [could] at any time to be burned behind his back." But it was hard for Elizabeth to believe in religion as an overriding motive except for a few crackbrained fanatics who might be annoying but not dangerous. She refused to suspect popery and treason whenever one found a sentimental attachment to old ways. Garrett Mattingly, *The Armada*. Houghton Mifflin Company. (Boston. 1959). 346.

56. Pike: A weapon used by foot soldiers, consisting of a metal spearhead on a long wooden shaft; used to pierce or kill.

57. Tilbury Fort was the country's most developed center of defense. The secondary camp in Kent was scarcely more than a potential replacement depot for the navy and the great reserve army near Westminster, intended as a bodyguard for the queen in case of invasion, existed mainly on paper.

58. Lacey Baldwin Smith, *The Horizon Book of the Elizabethan World*, American Heritage Publishing Company, Inc., (New York, 1968). 289, 344.

59. The size of the army was undoubtedly less than planned and certainly less than the 23,000 William Camden, a contemporary of the time, speaks of so confidently, but surely more than the "between five and six thousand" which is all skeptics will allow. Mattingly. 347.

60. This inspection took place ten days after the Armada had fled northward. The Whipples had three children at the time: Anne, almost 5, Margaret, 3, and Jane, 10 months. On the morning of August 18, the queen in her royal barge, departed St. James preceded by her music blowing loudly on silver trumpets and accompanied by many other barges with gentlemen pensioners of her household dressed in half armor with plumed morions (a hatlike, crested helmet without beaver or visor and with a curved brim coming to a peak in front and in back) and the full strength of the yeomen of the guard. This military show was comforting to the people of London who lined the shore to cheer as the barges swept grandly through the ebb tide. The army assembled at Tilbury lined up by regiments of foot, with coats all (or nearly all) alike, and troops of horsemen in armor with nodding plumes. The camp was gay and clean, its ditches dug and palisades emplaced, the particolored pavilions of the nobles and gentlemen bright and unfaded, the green booths where the rank and file slept not yet bedraggled and foul. At that moment, Tilbury

combined the glamour of a military spectacle with the innocent cheerfulness of a country fair. The queen informed Robert Dudley, earl of Leicester, her captain general, she had come to see the army (and to let them see her) and did not intend they look at each other across the broad shoulders of her yeomen of the guard or through the thicket of her gentlemen's plumes. She needed no guards among fellow countrymen in arms for her service. The inspection party consisted of Thomas Butler, earl of Ormonde, on foot in front carrying ceremoniously the Sword of State. Behind him walked two pages in white velvet, one with the queen's elaborate silver casque (helmet) on a white velvet cushion, the other leading her horse. Three mounted figures followed: the queen, riding between her captain general and her master of the horse, 23-year-old Robert Devereux, earl of Essex. Behind them on foot was sir John Norris, a veteran soldier who had fought with distinction with William of Orange. When this inspection party advanced into the ranks of the militia, it exploded in a roar of cheers. Mattingly. 342, 347, 348. The earl of Essex, 33 years younger than the queen, was neither adept as a military commander nor comfortable in taking orders, least of all from a woman. Openly insubordinate to the queen after bungling a military campaign in Ireland, he was banished from the court in 1599. In February 1601, Essex and a band of followers tried to stir a popular rebellion against the queen's councillors, and perhaps the queen herself. He was arrested, tried for treason, and beheaded. Elizabeth's chilly postmortem: "I warned him that he should not touch my scepter." Doug Stewart, "Elizabeth Reign On", *Smithsonian*, June 2003, 72

61. A piece of closefitting armor for protecting the breast and back.

62. Lacey Baldwin Smith. pp. 289-90. J. E. Neale, *Essays in Elizabethan History*. (London. 1958). 104-06.

63. A card is a brush with wire teeth, used in disentangling fibers of wool, flax, or cotton, laying them parallel to one another preparatory to spinning. Two brushes, one in each hand, are drawn past each other, with the fibers between them. A carder does this work thus preparing the cloth for spinning. A comber is a person who combs wool or flax. Fulling is the process of shrinking and compacting woollen fabric to felt and joining the fibers to and make the cloth stronger and firmer. Felt is an unwoven fabric of wool matted together with the aid of moisture and heat, by rolling, beating, and pressure. Thus, fullers are the workers who improve the texture of fabric by making them thicker, closer, and heavier.

64. Matthew, Sr. died in 1619 so didn't have to contend with the economic downturn. Matthew, Jr. was married in 1622 and was undoubtedly concerned about starting a family under the dire financial conditions of the time.

65. E. Lipson, *The Economic History of England*, Vol. III, A. & C Black, Ltd., (London, 1931). 250-1.

66. Matthew was approximately 43. James I was the second ruler they would know. A flood of books and poems mourned Elizabeth. A century later, the date Elizabeth was crowned, 17 Nov., was still celebrated with bonfires, and children were taught verses about a queen they never knew: "Gone is Elizabeth, /whom we have lov'd so deare. / She our kind Mistris was, / full four and forty years." Doug Stewart, 72

67. He was the first King of England named James.

68. Henry on June 5, 1610. Mathew, Jr. would have been approximately 20. Henry was the first Prince of Wales since Henry VIII in 1503. He died in 1612 and Charles, James' second and favorite son, was given the title and succeeded to the throne in 1625.

69. *Acts and Monuments* was published in 1563 and it went through five printings in the sixteenth century. Sir Francis Drake took a copy around the world with him in 1577. Those who couldn't read identified with its woodcuts, grouped both thematically, as in the sequence illustrating the conflict between papal and monarchial claims of supremacy, and illustrations of stories of martyrs. The pictures supplemented the text and made the book's central message accessible to all. Later it was known as the *Book of Martyrs*. It is available in one of the following editions: William Byron Forbush, D.D., editor, *Fox's Book of Martyrs*, Holt, Rinehart, and Winston, (New York, 1926. Renewed in 1954 and 1961). G. A. Williamson, editor, *Foxe's Book of Martyrs*, Little, Brown and Company, (Boston, Toronto, 1965).

70. The Essex Sessions Rolls include an account of a dinner conversation among the servants of Mr. Wentworth of Bocking as they were "reasoning upon" the sermon they had listened to the previous Sunday. John Harvard, apparently of the old faith, said "it was never merry in England since the scriptures were so commonly preached and talked upon among such as persons as they were." A man named King responded, saying he "hoped they should live to see no other time but when the gospel should be preached here in England." M. M. Knappen, *Tudor Puritanism*, The University of Chicago Press, (Chicago & London, 1939; First Phoenix Edition, 1965). 290-91.

71.   The Sunday morning service consisted of: a confession of sins; a prayer for pardon; a metrical psalm; a prayer for illumination; scripture reading; sermon; baptisms and publications of banns of marriage; long prayer (of intercessions and petitions) and the Lord's Prayer; the Apostles' Creed (recited by the minister); a metrical psalm; and the blessing (Aaronic or Apostolic).

Puritans established worship of the Apostolic church based on six ordinances — prayer, praise, the reading and preaching of the word, the administration of the sacraments of baptism and the Lord's Supper, catechizing, and the exercise of discipline. Authority for Apostolic worship was Acts 2:41-42: "Then they that gladly received his word were baptized; and that same day there were added to the church about three thousand souls. And they continued in the Apostles doctrine and fellowship, and breaking of bread and prayers." (From the Genevan version of the Bible, 1560). The types of prayer, supplications, intercessions, thanksgivings, were derived from I Timothy 2:1ff; invocation or adoration and confession from the example of the Lord's Prayer; praise from Ephesians 5:19, with its reference to "psalms, and hymns, and spiritual songs, singing and making melody to the Lord in your hearts."

The proclamation of the Gospel was the central feature of worship. Its importance was attested to by the entire corpus of the Scriptures, which provided a saving knowledge of God, especially II Corinthians 1:12 and Romans 10:14-15. Authority for the "Gospel Sacraments" was Matthew 28:19-20 and I Corinthians 11:23-26. Though they rejected set sermons and set forms of prayer, they accepted a set form of words for catechism from II Timothy 1:13: "Keep the true pattern of the wholesome words which ye has heard of me in faith and love which is in Christ Jesus." Matthew 18:15-18 and 18:2, I Corinthians 5:3-5, and the Third Epistle of John 10 allowed ecclesiastical censures by providing the complete procedure for admonishment, excommunication, and readmission of penitent offenders. Davies. 159, 174,273.

In their preaching, John and Nathaniel Rogers probably followed the structure of the Puritan sermon developed by Bishop John Hooper, the father of nonconformity. (See W.M.S. West, "John Hooper and the Origins of Puritanism," *Baptist Quarterly*, (October 1954-April 1955). The primary purpose of preaching was to present the claims of God on man through the criticism and comfort of the Gospel so the structure of the sermon had to be simple, memorable, and practical if it were to produce the light and heat, illumination of mind, and warming of affections required.

William Perkins, lecturer at St. Andrew's Church, Cambridge, the most eminent Puritan scholar of Elizabethan times, said the preacher's task was: (1) to read the Text distinctly out of the Canonicall Scriptures; (2) to give the sense and understanding of it being read, by the Scripture iself; (3) to collect a few and profitable points of doctrine out of the natural sense; (4) to apply (if he have the gift) thee doctrines rightly collected to the ife and manners of men in a simple and plain speech.

The goal of the Puritan sermon was to change man's mind, to improve his behavior. There was little interest in speculative thought or speculative divinity. Godliness, to know the will of God in order to follow it, was the paramount concern. Metaphors, similes, and *exempla* provided the illustrations that wer the windows of the sermon, illuminating the doctrine while sustaining interest, and provoking action. Davies 304-5.

Sermons were expected to be delivered without a manuscript, consequently Puritan preachers developed excellent memories. This allowed them to develop a firm structure, a clear progression, and the advantage of order and flexibility. By watching the congregation, they could explain further or add illustrations if they sensed incomprehension.

William Perkins (*The Workes of that Famous and Worthy Minister of Christ in the University of Cambridge*, M. William Perkins. 3 Vols. Cambridge, 1613) advised would-be ministers on voice and gesture. He advised that the voice be moderate when inculcating the doctrine but "more fervent and vehement in exhortation." His general rule for gestures was they should be grave so the body may grace the messenger of god: "It is fit therefore that the trunk or stalk of the body being erect and quiet, all the other parts, as the arm, the hand, the face and eyes, have such motions as may express and (as it were) utter the godly affections of the heart. The lifting up of the eye and the hand signifieth confidence. 2 Chron. 6. 13-14 . . . Acts, 7.55 . . . the casting down of the eyes signifieth sorrow and heaviness. Luke. 18-13." *Workes*, II, 672.

72.   Other Puritan pastors from Essex included: Thomas Weld, vicar of Terlin, later pastor at Roxbury, Mass. (1632-41); Thomas Hooker, who preached at Chelmsford until silenced by Laud, went to Holland in 1631 and to New England in 1633 where he was minister at Newtown until moving to Hartford in 1636; Thomas Shepard, pastor at Earle's Colne near Coggeshall became the minister at Newtown (later Cambridge, Mass.) in 1636; Daniel Rogers, son of Richard, was a

lecturer at Wetherfield; Nathaniel Ward, rector of Little Leighs, later pastor at Ipswich, Mass.; Stephen Marshall, vicar of Finchinfield; Samuel Wharton, vicar of Felsted; and John Beadle, rector of Little Leighs (he submitted to Laud in 1633). Martin Holbeach, a prominent Puritan, was headmaster of Felsted school where a number of prominent Puritans were educated. Michael McGiffert, Editor, *God's Plot, The Paradoxes of Puritan Piety, Being the Autobiography & Journal of Thomas Shepard*, University of Massachusetts Press, (1972). Felsted, Finchinfield, and Wetherfield were all in the Hinkford Hundred. Earle's Colne was nearby.

73. "If any man shall add unto these things, God shall add unto him the plagues that are written in this book." Rev. 22:18.

74. The scriptures provided authority for their occasional ordinances. Prophesyings were sanctioned by I Corinthians 14:1 and 31. If a day of humiliation was held for the expression of the people's penitence following a great natural, political, or military calamity, the invariable order was fasting, prayer, and sermon, as in Acts 13:1-3 and 14:23. When the sick were anointed with oil and their recovery prayed for, it was according to James 5:14-15. Even the frequency of divine services was foretold. The double burnt offering in Numbers 28:9 sanctioned two services on the Lord's Day; the necessity for the Lord's Supper to be preceded by a sermon was determined by Acts 20:27. Corinthians 16:2 and Acts 4:36 determined who should collect the offertory and at what point in the service it should be presented. Since marriage was not included in the list of pastoral duties in II Timothy 4:2ff, it did not require the services of a minister for its solemnization. A text became pretext when Matthew 11:28, "Come unto me, all ye that are weary & laden, and I will ease you," was taken as proof that the only appropriate posture at the Lord's table was sitting, as witnessing to the rest that Christ promised to his disciples. Stability of position in worship v. the mobility of the one presiding over Anglican worship who moves from prayer desk to lectern to pulpit to altar was drawn from Acts 1:15: "Peter stood up in the midst of the disciples." The denial of response in public prayers was forbidden in Leviticus. Davies. 260.

75. Puritans were careful not to name any exact time for the event.

76. The most important of the prayer books used by the Puritans was probably "John Knox's Genevan Service Book" whose correct title was *The Forme of Prayers and Ministrations of the Sacraments, etc. used in the English Congregation at Geneva: and approved by the famous and godly learned man, John Calvyn.* Imprinted at Geneva by John Crespin. MDLVI.

77. The booming and rolling of the organs were open to objection and hundreds were removed from the churches. There was no particular objection to music outside the church.

78. A calling was an occupation or job.

79. Drudge: A person who does hard, menial, or tedious work.

80. M. M. Knappen. 454-55.

81. *Ibid.* 468.

82. John was a Ruling Elder. The Will of John Abies of Bocking, proved 16 April 1647, links Rev. Rogers and John: "I give the piece of cloth at home unto Mr. Rogers, John Whipple and a jerkin cloth of it to Mr. Norton of Ipswich, NE." Rogers and Norton were Puritan preachers in Ipswich. Holman and Marvin. 468. See also Henry F. Waters, *Genealogical Gleanings in England*, Vol. I, first published in 1907; Genealogical Publishing Co, (Baltimore, 1969). 466.

83. The most important Puritan doctrine was predestination. From eternity God had predestined some to live and reprobated others to death. Man did nothing to deserve election. The will of God was the only cause. A limited and definite number were predestined to be saved.

84. This marriage is not listed in St. Mary's parish register. John was about 23 at the time of his wedding. Henry Burnett Whipple, *Matthew Whipple of Bocking, England and Descendants*, privately published (High Point, N. C., Vol. I October 1965, Vol. II, June 1969. Vol 1: 8. Permission to use material from these two volumes was granted this author by Mildred D. Whipple, widow of Henry B. Whipple. In a letter to the author dated 8 March 1986 at High Point, N.C., she wrote: "I'm sure Henry would be glad for you to use any portion of his books for your book and I therefore authorize you to include such sections as applicable."

85. Puritans believed the wedding ring was a superstition to be abolished like all the other Roman follies which tarnished God's revealed word.

86. Cocker: To coddle, pamper.

87. They had 10 children in England but six died in infancy. An eleventh, Sarah, was born in Ipswich.

88. As the monastery was the training ground of Catholic spirituality, the family was the seed plot of Puritan Christian life. The Puritan household was a little church with father, as father-in-God,

conducting weekday prayers, morning and evening, for wife, children, servants, and apprentices. After returning from Sunday worship, he rehearsed the children in their catechism, checked to see if they had memorized and understood the main points of the sermon, and read aloud from the *Bible* or some other godly books usually sermons of an approved minister of the *Book of Martyrs*.

This spirituality was mingled with the joy of psalm singing to catchy tunes and motivated by the sense that this is exactly how God's elect must live in a world of snares and traps laid by the ungodly, until rewarded by entering the everlasting community of the friends of Christ. This spirituality was aided by two powerful factors. First, religion was not associated with a sacred building as it was for Catholics and High Church Anglicans. They called their houses of worship meetinghouses, not churches. To them the word church referred exclusively to the company of God's faithful people gathered to hear the reading and exposition of the oracles of God. Thus they could conceive of the "church in the house" as the gathering of persecuted Christians of the primitive church.

Second was the new significance given family life by the reformers. God's covenant, invariably read at baptismal services, was "to you and your children." This recognition helped weld family life into an enduring solidarity in Christ. The head of the family promised at the baptism to supervise his children's Christian nature and was duty bound to teach his children the Scriptures and to make sure they understood the main points of Christian doctrine, behavior, and worship. The father's promises at baptism and his commitment in the covenant of church membership were God's marching orders and these responsibilities must be accounted for to God at the Great Day of Judgment, thus validating his duty to be a prophet and priest to his own household. Davis. 429-30

89. Jane married Henry Caldam a year after her mother's death. Johane's age is uncertain, but apparently she was older than Elizabeth. Elizabeth didn't marry until six years after her mother's death.

90. The two Arthur teenagers and the two Caldam toddlers.

91. Most cottages of that time consisted of a single room.

92. Latten is brass or brasslike alloy hammered into thin sheets.

93. Proved in the Superior Probate Court, the Prerogative Court of Canterbury in 1619. It is written in old English and Latin. The Latin introduction to the probate is reproduced on page 1 of the genealogy section.

94. Johane is not listed in the St. Marys parish records. Some people have concluded that Jane and Johane are the same person. If that is the case, why is Jane given £30 within two months after Matthew's death in an earlier section of the Will and Johane 40 shillings one month after his death? If they were the same the interpreter misread the old English the Will was written in.

95. Through Margaret Arthur, the family continued in the clothier business. She married Henry Pye and their daughter Judith married John Maysent. Judith and John's son, John, Jr. were identified, along with the Ruggles and Inglish families as being the major cloth making families in Bocking-Braintree in the 1760s. Rev. Philip Morant, *The History and Antiquities of the County of Essex*, published in two volumes between 1763 and 1768. 386-8.

96. A review of Wills of men who lived in seven Essex communities who contributed settlers to Ipswich divulged no inventories. F. G. Emmison, editor, *Wills at Chelmsford, 1400-1853*, 3 vols. II, 1620-1720. (London. 1958-1969). Passim.

97. He purchased it from Richard Windle who had inherited it 8 Dec. 1625 from his father Jonas Windle, Bocking clothier. Morant, 386. Hercules was licensed to wed Ann Broune on 27 Oct. 1632. She was identified as a spinster of White Notly. The wedding was to be solemnized in the Notly church. See Holman and Marvin. 517.

98. A court baron is a domestic court for redressing misdemeanors, etc. in the manor and for settling tenant's disputes. It consisted of the freemen or freehold tenants of the manor, presided over by the lord or his steward. Quit rent is rent paid by the freeholders and copyholders of a manor in discharge or acquittance of other services. Also called chief rent. Copyhold — a tenure of lands of a manor, according to the custom of the manor, and by copy of a court roll; or a tenure for which the tenant has nothing to show except the rolls made by the steward of the lord's court which contains entries of the admission of the original or former tenant, his surrender to the use of another, or alienation, or his death, and the claim and admission of the heir or devise. Acquittance — discharging from a debt or any other liability.

99. Killed in a duel. The duel may be connected with the role his grandfather, Miles Corbet, regicide,

played in the death of Charles I.

100. John Arthur, Jr. was the nephew of Hercules Arthur. John Maysent, Jr. was the grandson of Margaret Arthur who was the granddaughter of Matthew Whipple. John Maysent, Jr. married Judith Maysent (perhaps they were cousins), daughter of Joseph Maysent, Gentleman of Hatfield-Peverell. John and Judith had three sons who died young, and six daughters, including Susanna, born 26 March 1691, who married Rev. John Palmer of Coventry; and Judith, born 29 March 1696, and who married William Rayment, Gentleman, attorney of Braintree and later of Black Notley. John Maysent, Jr. died 7 Oct. 1723. He and his wife were buried in the Bocking churchyard in a tomb. By Will dated 8 Aug. 1723, he left the Fryers estate to his younger brother Jeremiah. The Will also provided 40 shillings per annum forever for the repairing of his tomb and vault with "the over plus to the poor of this parish." On 14 Nov. 1721, John and William Maysent were named trustees by the Will of John Mathum of Braintree to pay £20 forever to 20 poor people in Bocking." Morant. 386-8. Morant identified the Maysent, Ruggles, and Inglish families as being the major cloth making families in the 1760s.

Since John Arthur was a half brother to Hercules and Margaret Arthur, grand children of Matthew, readers may be interested in the family of John's wife, Anne, daughter of Miles Corbet, esquire, the regicide. Corbet was the second son of Sir Thomas Corbet, knight, of Sprowston, County Norfolk, and Anne, daughter of Edward Barret of Belhouse, County Essex. His brother was Sir John Corbet, Knight, and his uncle was Clement Corbet, named Chair of Law at Gresham College in 1607. A barrister, Corbet represented Great Yarmouth in Parliament in 1628 and 1640. He was on the Parliamentary side during the civil war, representing County Norfolk. He was chairman of the committee that drew up the charges against Laud and was zealous in the prosecution of the Archbishop. He became notorious as chairman of the committee of examinations whose arbitrary and inquisitorial procedure made him very unpopular. Parliament appointed him clerk of the Court of Wards in May 1644 and he was made one of the registrars of the Court of Chancery 7 March 1648. In October 1650, Parliament named him one of four commissioners to settle the affairs of Ireland, promoting him to chief Baron of the Exchequer in Ireland 13 June 1655. He remained in Ireland until the end of the Protectorate. Yarmouth elected him to Parliament in 1660 but his election was annulled 18 May causing him to flee England.

Indicted by a Grand Jury 19 Jan. 1660 for his part in the 30 Jan. 1649 execution of Charles I, Corbet's role as a regicide was so prominent he was one of only nine to suffer the hideous death given traitors. In December 1649 when plans for the king's trial were being laid, Oliver Cromwell, with his fellow soldiers (Corbet was a Colonel) who were members of Parliament, played key roles. On 6 Jan. 1649, the House of Commons declared that Commons alone constituted a true Parliament and could legislate for the nation (heretofore the King and House of Lords shared in this power) and enacted a plan for a High Court of Justice to try the King. Corbet was selected to inform the King. The King's position was that he was the ultimate authority and no one could try him. He was tried anyway and Corbet was one of the 59 Commissioners to indict, try, judge, condemn, and sign the death warrant. Corbet was in Westminster Hall when the trial began Saturday afternoon 20 January. When the King entered, the clerk read the charge of high treason and the Commissioners, "on behalf of the people of England impeach Charles Stuart as a tyrant, traitor, murderer, and implacable enemy to the Commonwealth of England."

After finding him guilty and signing the death warrant, which was to sever his head from his body, the Commissioners ordered the railing of the scaffold be hung with black so the actual execution would be screened from spectators. On execution day, while on the scaffold speaking to Bishop Juxton, the King noticed someone touching the axe, causing him to become afraid the edge would be blunted. He could not forget how his grandmother, Mary, Queen of Scots, had been hacked to death by blow after blow. "Hurt not the axe," he said, "that it may not hurt me." Spectators saw only the flash of the upraised axe before it crashed down and killed the King at its first falling. The assistant to the executioner picked up the head and held it high for all to see, then threw it down with such violence the still warm cheek was badly bruised.

At Cromwell's death, his son Richard ruled for about a year before abdicating. The monarchy was restored with Charles II, the King's oldest living son, assuming the throne 29 May 1660. The first Parliament of the new reign, overwhelmingly Royalist and vindictive, authorized the Grand Jury to decide the fate of the surviving commissioners who indicted Charles I. Fifteen had fled the country. Three, John Dixwell, Edward Whalley, and William Goffe, crossed the Atlantic and found safety in New England. Corbet, John Okey, and John Barkstead went to Holland where they were betrayed by a colleague, Sir George Downing, who had served Cromwell in high diplomatic position and became the tool of Charles II. [Downing, son of Emanuel Downing of Salem, Mass., went to England in 1645 at age 20 and eventually became a preacher in Col. Okey's regiment. He was also a nephew of Massachusetts governor John Winthrop.] All three were returned, tried, convicted, and sentenced to death. Before the execution 19 April 1662 at Tyburn, Corbet, whose wife was beside herself with grief, tried to steady her by a familiar family joke and "though tears were ready to start from [his] eyes, yet he conquered himself, and taking his wife by the hand, said, 'O, my dear wife, shall we part in a shower? God will be a husband and a father to thee and thine;' and so kissing her, turned to his son Miles, whom he took by the hand and blessed him also;" and went to his execution, "desiring a friend to stay with his wife and his son, to comfort them." In his dying speech he said, "For this for which we are to die I was no contriver of it; when the business was mentioned, I spoke against it, but being passed in Parliament I thought it my duty to obey." He said a sense of public duty, not self-interest, had motivated his public life. Corbet was hung but his body cut down immediately so he would be fully conscious while he was castrated, disemboweled, and quartered. Others killed the same way were Okey, Barkstead, John Jones, Adrian Scroope, John Carew, Thomas Scot, Gregory Clement, and Thomas Harrison. William Henry Harrison, eighth president of the U.S., descended from Harrison. Samuel Pepys was present when Corbet, Okey, and Barkstead were executed. "They all look very cheerful," he wrote, "but I hear they all die defending what they did to the King to be just." For the story of the regicides, see Hugh Ross Williamson, *The Day They Killed the King*, The MacMillan Company, (New York, 1956); C. V. Wedgwood, *A Coffin for King Charles*, The MacMillan Company, (New York, 1964); and *The Trials of Charles The First and of Some of The Regicides*, published by John Murray, (London, 1832).

101. John Hawkins was the eldest son and heir of John Hawkins of Braintree. Holman and Marvin, 518.

102. *Ibid*. 518.

103. John, Jr.'s mother's identity is unknown.

104. Holman and Marvin. 518.

105. W.F. Quin. 127. In Braintree, the court leet jury, which sought out and punished infractions, functioned in the early seventeenth century but it consisted mainly of men from the Four and Twenty. The court leet did appoint some minor manorial officers, such as ale and flesh tasters, or sealers of leather, but the town's constables were apointed by them only after selection by the Four and Twenty. The Company of Four and Twenty agreed in their April 1629 meeting that all constables, churchwardens, and overseers of the poor would henceforth be "yearly elected out of the company," and five years later the town surveyors were chosen in that fashion, "being one of the company, every year as it falls to every one by turn." These officials — churchwardens, overseers, constables, and surveyors — also served as executive officers for the governing council, the Four and Twenty, so they not only absorbed the court leet in terms of personnel but also in the services it provided. Allen. 149 He cites "Minutes of Company of Four and Twenty," D/P 264/8/3, 13 April 1629, 7 April 1634, Essex R.O. Allen discusses the Four and Twenty in more detail in pages 358-68.

106. Cunnington and Warner. 16-20. The Braintree church dates from 1199. Unfortunately, the church register only dates from 1660. The Grocers' Company was founded in 1345 from the Fraternity of St. Anthony which was under the protection of the Abbot of Bury St. Edmunds.

107. Purchased from Sir Edward Bullicke, knight, Francis and Elizabeth Steele, John and Elizabeth Hewes, John Osborne, and others.

108. His will, dated 3 Sept. 1633, was proved 18 Oct. 1633. Sister Whipple was Anne (Hawkins) Whipple, wife of Matthew, Jr. Bequeaths also went to: Eldest son John, messuages and lands in Barking and other parishes; son Robert, messuages and tenements in Old Newton, Suffolk; daughter Sara, £600 at age 18 and 21; daughter Margaret, £500 at age 18 and 21; daughter Mary, messuages, etc. in Bradwell next the sea; daughter Judith, messuages, etc. in Finchfield, Essex; brother-in-law John Kent, 100 marks for his care and pains to be taken as one of the executors; to my loving friend Mr. Collins of Braintree, 40 shillings to buy him a ring and 4 per annum during his ministry there; my mother, Mary Hawkins, widow, £16 a year, etc; my friend William Lingwood, £20; my sister Kent and my sister Edes, 30 shillings apiece to make them rings; my brother Francis Hawkins, my sister Archer, and my sister Whipple, 40 shillings apiece as remembrances from me; my cousin Tomson, my aunt Woodward and my aunt Goodaye, 10 shillings apiece; loving friends and neighbors Adrian Mott and Joseph Loomys were also mentioned. Loomys was one of the witnesses. Henry F.. Waters, Vol. I. 466-7. *Court of Wards*. Inquisition taken at Braintree April 16, 1634 after John, Jr.'s death. The jurors say that long before his death he was seized in his demesne as of fee (*inter alia*) of a capital messuage in Braintree, in his own tenure or occupation held of Robert, the Earl of Warwick a leader of the national Puritan movement, as of his manor of Braintree by fealty and rent, and of two cottages there in the occupation of Robert Woodward and Jeremie Gray; also of Drakes Croft, formerly Broom Croft, in Braintree, held of Katherine Lady

Wentworth, as of her Manor of Codham Hall in Wethersfield; also of six acres of land in the occupation of Martin Skinner, lately purchased of Isaac Skinner, son of the said Martin and Anne, his wife; also of three rods, parcel of Braintreefield with the messuage built thereon, and of other buildings belonging purchased of Richard Green and Richard Bedwell, and held of the manor of Black Notley; also of two parcels of land, called Copfield, and two parcels of land, called Crossfield, all in Bocking, and held of Roger Wentworth as of his manor of Bocking; also of two other parcels of land, called Swallow Lovells, in Bocking, now or late in the occupation of John Curtis and purchased of Henry Edes and John Edes, clerk, and of a messuage in Bocking, called Pirles or Brocks, purchased of the said John Curtis, the said Swallow Lovells and Pirles are held of Roger Wentworth, esquire, as of his manor of Bocking Hall by fealty, suit at Court and yearly rent. His will dated 3 Sept. last before this inquisition is quoted as far as concerns his lands. The said John Hawkins, the elder, also held lands in many other parts of Essex, also in the Isle of Ely, county of Cambridge, and in the county of Suffolk. John Hawkins, aged 17 on 30 Jan. last past, is his son and next heir. Holman and Marvin. 540-1. Hawkins was a man of wealth and left a relatively young family. The Robert Woodward occupying one of the cottages in Braintree was probably a cousin and son of his aunt Woodward. From this Will we learn that Anne Hawkins Whipple had a brother Francis. Sister Mary, who had married William Coppin, was not mentioned. She may have died or been widowed and remarried and could be the sister Archer, Edes, or Kent. Anne's mother, Mary Levitt Hawkins, outlived her step-son, John Hawkins, Jr. by a little more than a year, dying 3 May 1635. Daughter Sarah, who married Sir Stephen White, apparently died at an early age. In 1640, her husband established a charity of "six pounds thirteen shillings and fourpence yearly out of a farm in Black and White Notley, for the giving, upon All Saints day, unto six poor women of Braintree, of honest and good behavior, and frequenters of the Church and divine service there; to each a gown of good cloth ready made of the value of 14s and to each of the said women, four 2-penny loaves of wheaten bread upon the first Sunday of every month in the year, after Sermon in the afternoon, and to the upper Church warden, one shilling and four-pence." This charity is "to be the love and affection" which he bore to his "late wife and to the parishioners of this town, for the sake of her and her friends." Morant. 398.

109. Lyons is one of the subordinate manors owned in 1425 by John Doreward, Speaker of the House of Commons.

110. Sir John and Frances (Hawkins) Dawes had sons Robert, John, and William, and daughter Elizabeth, who married Peter Fisher, D.D. The estate went to Sir Robert, the eldest son, who, along with his brother John, died without issue, so the estate went to the youngest son, Sir William Dawes, D.D., who was born 12 Sept. 1671 at Lyons. Sir William married Frances Darcy, a sister and co-heir of Sir Robert Darcy of Great Brancksted, Baronet. Upon Sir William's death, the estate went to his son Sir Darcy Dawes, and a daughter, wife of Sir William Milner of Yorkshire, Baronet. Morant. 387 and 397.

111. Trotter's Will is in Waters, Vol. II, 1114-15. Also see Morant, 397-8 for further details on Trotter's bequeaths to Braintree residents. ". . . my cousin Laurence Arthur's wife" would be Laurence Arthur's second wife since Margaret Whipple, his first wife, had been dead for 23 years.

112. Trotter apparently had a strong sense of community. In addition to this bequeath by Will, he gave, by deed dated September 1630, an annuity of 36 shillings, 8-pence out of a house in Braintree. The money was to be "paid yearly to 30 poor people of honest life, that are men of trade, viz: weavers, combers, and fullers (he was probably a clothier), 14 days before or after St. Thomas's day." The Will was proved 12 March 1631. The Braintree bequeath was in the form of "a house, barn, and four acres of arable land, then of the yearly value of £5 10s to be disposed of, viz: 10s toward the reparation of the church, 6s 8d to the Vicar of Braintree, 5s to the Church Wardens, 5s to the Overseers of the Poor, 3s 4d to the Sexton, and the remaining 4s to 20 aged poor and impotent people of Braintree, being of honest life and conversation, by two equal payments, viz: 2s each on 18 Nov. and the like sum on 24 Feb. or within 14 days, either before or after." The tenement on the premises burnt down in 1651, reducing the charity to £4 per annum. Morant. 388, 397-8.

113. Great Bromley was apparently a hotbed of Puritanism. The churchwardens' account book reveals fines of 5s. 4d. paid "at the court for our absolution being excommunicate," £3 10s. "for making of the rail at the communion table," and 2s. 4d. "for certifying into the court for getting up the rails and bringing the rail from Colchester." Evidently the churchwardens had been excommunicated for neglecting to replace the communion rail after it had been torn down, a practice Puritans heartily encouraged. The ecclesiastical visitation to several parishes near Great Bromley in northeast Essex in 1633 demonstrated just how far apart both sides were. The detailed listing of every single departure from conformity, whether great or small, testified to the degree

to which authorities planned to carry their reform as well as to the inability of Puritan communities to accept those changes. Rev. H. H. Minchin, *The Churches of Great and Little Bromley*, Essex Archaeological Society, Transactions, N.S., VIII. (1903). 292-3. J. Gardner Bartlett, *Gregory Stone Genealogy: Ancestry and Descendants of Dea. Gregory Stone of Cambridge, Mass., 1320-1917.* (Boston. 1918). 43.

114. Simon was son of Simon Stone and Joan Clark. On page 199 of his book, Allen indicates the Stones' were a wealthy family. "The wealthy of East Anglicans was revealed in more indirect ways. Two men were indicted and appeared before court for breaking into Gregory Stone's house and stealing the sizeable sum of £86." His citation is Queen's Bench Indictments, Ancient 698. [t/ o. 23. T/A 428 Essex R.O.

115. J. Gardner Bartlett, *Simon Stone Genealogy*, 1926. 36. See also the *Utah Genealogical and Historical Magazine*, Vol. 22, (Salt Lake City, January, 1931). 14-16.

116. The wealth and status of certain emigrants from East Anglia county can be derived from the listing in English lay subsidy tax rolls. For town after town one finds the names of men who later would be prominent in town affairs in New England: men such as Matthew Whipple of Bocking-Ipswich and Simon Stone of Boxted-Watertown. The names of the men on lay subsidy lists were far fewer than the total number of emigrants from these towns in the 1620-30s, confirming, along with other evidence, that many more of the East Anglian emigrants came from lower or middle class origins.

117. Thirty nine Articles of Religion were set forth for all Englishmen to follow:

I. Of Faith in the Holy Trinity. There is but one living and true God, everlasting, without body, parts or passions; of infinite power, wisdom, and goodness; the Maker, and Preserver of all things both visible and invisible. And in unity this Godhead there be three Persons, of one substance, power, and eternity; the Father, the Son, and the Holy Ghost.

II. Of the Word of Son of God, which was made very Man. The Son, which is the Word of the Father, begotten from everlasting of the Father, the very and eternal God, and of one substance with the Father, took Man's nature in the womb of the blessed Virgin, of her substances; so that two whole and perfect natures, that is to say, the Godhead and Manhood, were joined together in one Person, never to be divided, whereof is one Christ, very God, and very Man; who truly suffered, was crucified, dead and buried, to reconcile his Father to us; and to be a sacrifice, not only for original guilt, but also for all actual sins of men.

III. Of the going down of Christ into Hell. As Christ died for us, and was buried, so also is it to be believed that he went down into Hell.

IV. Of the Resurrection of Christ. Christ did truly rise again from death, and took again his body, with flesh, bones, and all things appertaining to the perfection of Man's nature; wherewith he ascended into Heaven, and there sitteth, until he return to judge all Men at the last day.

V. Of the Holy Ghost. The Holy Ghost, proceeding from the Father and the Son, is of one substance, majesty, and glory, with the Father and the Son, very and eternal God.

VI. Of the Sufficiency of the holy Scriptures for salvation. Holy Scripture containeth all things necessary to salvation: so that whatsoever is not read therein, nor may be proved thereby, is not to be required of any man, that it should be believed as an article of the Faith, or be thought requisite or necessary to salvation. In the name of the holy Scripture we do understand those canonical Books of the Old and New Testament, of whose authority was never any doubt in the Church. Of the Names and Numbers of the Canonical Books: Genesis, Exodus, Leviticus, Numbers, Deuteronomy, Joshua, Judges, Ruth, The First Book of Samuel, The Second Book of Samuel, The First Book of Kings, The Second Book of Kings, The First Book of Chronicles, The Second Book of Chronicles, The First Book of Esdras, The Second Book of Esdras, The Book of Esther, The Book of Job, The Psalms, The Proverbs, Ecclesiastes or Preacher, Cantica, or Songs of Solomon, Four Prophets the greater, Twelve Prophets the less. And the other Books (as Hierome saith) the Church doth read for example of life and instruction of manners; but yet doth it not apply them to establish any doctrine; such are these following: The Third Book of Esdras, The Fourth Book of Esdras, The Book of Tobias, The Book of Judith, The rest of the Book of Esther, The Book of Wisdom, Jesus the Son of Sirach, Baruch the Prophet, The Song of Three Children, The Story of Susanna, Of Bel and the Dragon, The Prayer of Manasses, The First Book of Maccabees, The Second Book of Maccabees. All the Books of the New Testament, as they are commonly received, we do receive, and account them Canonical.

VII. Of the Old Testament. The Old Testament is not contrary to the New: for both in the Old and New Testament everlasting life is offered to Mankind by Christ, who is the only Mediator between God and Man, being both God and Man. Wherefore they are not to be heard, which feign that the old Fathers did look only for transitory promises. Although the Law given from God by Moses, as touching ceremonies and rites, do not bind Christian men, nor the civil precepts thereof ought of necessity to be received in any commonwealth; yet notwithstanding, no Christian man whatsoever is free from the obedience of the Commandments which are called moral.

VIII. Of the Three Creeds. The Three Creeds, Nicene Creed, Athanasius's Creed, and that which is commonly called the Apostles' Creed, ought thoroughly to be received and believed: for they may be proved by most certain warrants of holy Scripture.

IX. Of Original or Birth sin. Original Sin standeth not in the following of Adam, (as the Pelagians do vainly talk;) but it is the fault and corruption of the Nature of every man, that naturally is engendered of the offspring of Adam; whereby man is very far gone from original righteousness, and is of his own nature inclined to evil, so that the flesh lusteth always contrary to the spirit; and therefore in every person born into this world, it deserveth God's wrath and damnation. And this infection of nature doth remain, yea in them that are regenerated; whereby the list of the flesh, called in Greek, phronema sarkos, which some do expound the wisdom, some sensuality, some the affection, some the desire, of the flesh, is not subject to the Law of God. And although there is no condemnation for them that believe and are baptized, yet the Apostle doth confess, that concupiscence and lust hath of itself the nature of sin.

X. Of Free Will. The condition of Man after the fall of Adam is such, that he cannot turn and prepare himself, by his own natural strength and good works, to faith, and calling upon God: Wherefore we have no power to do good works pleasant and acceptable to God, without the grace of God by Christ preventing us, that we may have a good will, and working with us, when we have that good will.

XI. Of the Justification of Man. We are accounted righteous before God, only for the merit of our Lord and Savior Jesus Christ by Faith, and not for our own works or deservings: Wherefore, that we are justified by faith only is a most wholesome Doctrine, and very full of comfort, and more largely is expressed in the Homily of Justification.

XII. Of Good Works. Albeit that Good Works, which are the fruits of Faith, and follow after Justification, cannot put away our sins, and endure the severity of God's Judgment; yet are they pleasing and acceptable to God in Christ, and do spring out necessarily of a true and lively Faith; insomuch that by them a lively Faith may be as evidently known as a tree discerned by the fruit.

XIII. Of Works before Justification. Works done before the grace of Christ, and the Inspiration of his Spirit, are not pleasant to God, forasmuch as they spring not of faith in Jesus Christ, neither do they make men meet to receive grace, or (as the School authors say) deserve grace of congruity: yea rather, for that they are not done as God hath willed and commanded them to be done, we doubt not but they have the nature of sin.

XIV. Of Works of Supererogation. Voluntary Works besides, over and above, God's Commandments, which they call Works of Supererogation, cannot be taught without arrogancy and impiety: for by them men do declare, that they do not only render unto God as much as they are bound to do, but that they do more for his sake, than of bounden duty is required: whereas Christ saith plainly, When ye have done all that are commanded to you, say, We are unprofitable servants.

XV. Of Christ alone without Sin. Christ in the truth of our nature was made like unto us in all things, sin only except, from which he was clearly void, both in his flesh, and in his spirit. He came to be the Lamb without spot, who, by sacrifice of himself once made, should take away the sins of the world, and sin as Saint John saith, was not in him. But all we the rest, although baptized, and born again in Christ, yet offend in many things; and if we say we have no sin, we deceive ourselves, and the truth is not in us.

XVI. Of Sin after Baptism. Not every deadly sin willingly committed after Baptism is sin against the Holy Ghost, and unpardonable. Wherefore the grant of repentance is not to be denied to such as fall into sin after Baptism. After we have received the Holy Ghost, we may depart from grace given, and fall into sin and by the grace of God we may arise again, and amend our lives. And therefore they are to be condemned, which say, they can no more sin as long as they live here, or deny the place of forgiveness to such as truly repent.

XVII. Of Predestination and Election. Predestination to Life is the everlasting purpose of God, whereby (before the foundations of the world were laid) he hath constantly decreed by his counsel secret to us, to deliver from curse and damnation those whom he hath chosen in Christ out of mankind, and to bring them by Christ to everlasting salvation, as vessels made to honour.

Wherefore, they which be endued with so excellent a benefit of God be called according to God's purpose by his Spirit working in due season: they through Grace obey the calling: they be justified freely: they be made sons of God by adoption: they be made like the image of his only begotten Son Jesus Christ: they walk religiously in good works, and at length, by God's mercy, they attain to everlasting felicity. As the godly consideration of Predestination, and our Election in Christ, is full of sweet, pleasant, and unspeakable comfort to godly persons, and such as feel in themselves the working of the Spirit of Christ, mortifying the works of the flesh, and their earthly members, and drawing up their mind to high and heavenly things, as well because it doth greatly establish and confirm their faith of eternal Salvation to be enjoyed through Christ, as because it doth fervently kindle their love towards God: So, for curious and carnal persons, lacking the Spirit of Christ, to have continually before their eyes the sentence of God's Predestination, is a most dangerous downfall, whereby the Devil doth thrust them either into desperation, or into wretchlessness of most unclean living, no less perilous than desperation. Furthermore, we must receive God's promises in such wise, as they be generally set forth to us in holy Scripture: and, in our doings, that Will of God is to be followed, which we have expressly declared unto us in the Word of God.

XVIII. Of Obtaining eternal Salvation only by the Name of Christ. They also are to be had accursed that presume to say, that every man shall be saved by the Law or Sect which he professeth, so that he be diligent to frame his life according to that Law, and the light of Nature. For holy Scripture doth set out unto us only the Name of Jesus Christ, whereby men must be saved.

XIX. Of the Church. The visible Church of Christ is a congregation of faithful men, in the which the pure Word of God is preached, and the Sacraments be duly ministered according to Christ's ordinance in all those things that of necessity are requisite to the same. As the Church of Jerusalem, Alexandria, and Antioch, have erred; so also the Church of Rome hath erred, not only in their living and manner of Ceremonies, but also in matters of Faith.

XX. Of the Authority of the Church. The Church hath power to decree Rites or Ceremonies, and authority in Controversies of Faith: And yet it is not lawful for the Church to ordain any thing that is contrary to God's Word written, neither may it so expound one place of Scripture, that it be repugnant to another. Wherefore, although the Church be a witness and a keeper of holy Writ, yet, as it ought not to decree any thing against the same, so besides the same ought it not to enforce any thing to be believed for necessity of Salvation.

XXI. Of the Authority of General Councils. General Councils may not be gathered together without the commandment and will of Princes. And when they be gathered together, (forasmuch as they be an assembly of men, whereof all be not governed with the Spirit and Word of God,) they may err, and sometimes have erred, even in things pertaining unto God. Wherefore things ordained by them as necessary to salvation have neither strength nor authority, unless it may be declared that they be taken out of holy Scripture.

XXII. Of Purgatory. The Romish Doctrine concerning Purgatory, pardons, Worshiping and Adoration, as well of Images as of Reliques, and also invocation of Saints, is a fond thing vainly invented, and grounded upon no warranty of Scripture, but rather repugnant to the Word of God.

XXIII. Of Ministering in the Congregation. It is not lawful for any man to take upon him the office of public preaching, or ministering the Sacraments in the Congregation, before he be lawfully called, and sent to execute the same. And those we ought to judge lawfully called and sent, which be chosen and called to this work by men who have public authority given unto them in the Congregation, to call and send Ministers into the Lord's vineyard.

XXIV. Of speaking in the Congregation in such a Tongue as the people understandeth. It is a thing plainly repugnant to the Word of God, and the custom of the Primitive Church, to have public Prayer in the Church, or to minister the Sacraments in a tongue not understood of the people.

XXV. Of the Sacraments. Sacraments ordained of Christ be not only badges or tokens of Christian men's profession, but rather they be certain sure witnesses, and effectual signs of grace, and God's good will towards us, by the which he doth work invisibly in us, and doth not only quicken, but also strengthen and confirm our Faith in him. There are two Sacraments ordained of Christ our Lord in the Gospel, that is to say, Baptism, and the Supper of the Lord. Those five commonly called Sacraments, that is to say Confirmation, Penance, Orders, Matrimony, and extreme Unction, are not to be counted for Sacraments of the Gospel, being such as have grown partly of the corrupt following of the Apostles, partly are states of life allowed in the Scriptures; but yet have not like nature of Sacraments with Baptism, and the Lord's Supper, for that they have not any visible sign or ceremony ordained of God. The Sacraments were not ordained of Christ to be gazed upon, or to be carried about, but that we should duly use them. And in such only as worthily receive the same they have a wholesome effect or operation: but they that receive them unworthily purchase to themselves damnation, as Saint Paul saith.

XXVI. Of the Unworthiness of the Ministers, which hinders not the effect of the Sacrament. Although in the visible Church the evil be ever mingled with the good, and sometimes the evil have chief authority in the Ministration of the Word and Sacraments, yet forasmuch as they do not the same in their own name, but in Christ's, and do minister by his commission and authority, we may use their Ministry, both in hearing the Word of God, and in the receiving of the Sacraments. Neither is the effect of Christ's ordinance taken away by their wickedness, nor the grace of God's gifts diminished from such as by faith and rightly do receive the Sacraments ministered unto them; which be effectual, because of Christ's institution and promise, although they be ministered by evil men. Nevertheless, it appertaineth to the discipline of the Church, that enquiry be made of evil Ministers, and that they be accused by those that have knowledge of their offenses; and finally being found guilty, by just judgement be deposed.

XXVII. Of Baptism. Baptism is not only a sign of profession, and mark of difference, whereby Christian men are discerned from others that be not christened, but it is also a sign of Regeneration or new Birth, whereby, as by an instrument, they that receive Baptism rightly are grafted into the Church; the promises of the forgiveness of sin, and of our adoption to be the sons of God by the Holy Ghost, are visibly signed and sealed; Faith is confirmed, and Grace increased by virtue of prayer unto God. The Baptism of young Children is in any wise to be retained in the Church, as most agreeable with the institution of Christ.

XXVIII. Of the Lord's Supper. The Supper of the Lord is not only a sign of the love that Christians ought to have among themselves to another; but rather it is a Sacrament of our Redemption by Christ's death: insomuch that to such as rightly, worthily, and with faith, receive the same, the Bread which we break is a partaking of the Body of Christ; and likewise the Cup of Blessing is a partaking of the Blood of Christ. Transubstantiation (or the change of the substance of Bread and Wine) in the Supper of the Lord, cannot be proved by holy Writ; but it is repugnant to the plain words of Scripture, overthroweth the nature of a Sacrament, and hath given occasion to many superstitions. The Body of Christ is given, taken, and eaten, in the Supper, only after an heavenly and spiritual manner. And the mean whereby the Body of Christ is received and eaten in the Supper is Faith. The Sacrament of the Lord's Supper was not by Christ's ordinance reserved, carried about, lifted up, or worshipped.

XXIX. Of the Wicked which eat not the Body of Christ in the use of the Lord's Supper. The Wicked, and such as be void of a lively faith, although they do carnally and visibly press with their teeth (as Saint Augustine saith) the Sacrament of the Body and Blood of Christ, yet in no wise are they partakers of Christ: but rather, to their condemnation, do eat and drink the sign or Sacrament of so great a thing.

XXX. Of both kinds. The Cup of the Lord is not to be denied to the Lay people: for both the parts of the Lord's Sacrament, by Christ's ordinance and commandment, ought to be ministered to all Christian men alike.

XXXI. Of the one Oblation of Christ finished upon the Cross. The Offering of Christ once made is that perfect redemption, propitiation, and satisfaction, for all the sins of the whole world, both original and actual; and there is no other satisfaction for sin, but that alone. Wherefore the sacrifices of Masses, in the which it was commonly said, that the Priest did offer Christ for the quick and the dead, to have remission of pain or guilt, were blasphemous fables, and dangerous deceits.

XXXII. Of the Marriage of Priests. Bishops, Priests, and Deacons, are not commanded by God's Law, either to vow the estate of single life, or to abstain from marriage: therefore it is lawful also for them, as for all other Christian men, to marry at their own discretion, as they shall judge the same to serve better to godliness.

XXXIII. Of Excommunicate Persons, how they are to avoided. That person which by open denunciation of the Church is rightly cut off from the unity of the Church, and excommunicated, ought to be taken of the whole multitude of the faithful, as an Heathen and Publican, until he be openly reconciled by penance, and received into the church by a Judge that hath authority thereunto.

XXXIV. Of the Traditions of the Church. It is not necessary that Traditions and Ceremonies be in all places one, or utterly like; for at all times they have been divers, and may be changed according to the diversities of countries, times, and man's manners, so that nothing be ordained against God's Word. Whosoever though his private judgement, willingly and purposely, doth openly break the traditions and ceremonies of the church, which be not repugnant to the Word of God, and be ordained and approved by common authority, ought to be rebuked openly, (that others may fear to do the like,) as he that offendeth against the common order of the church, and hurteth the authority of the Magistrate, and woundeth the consciences of the weak brethren. Every particular or national church hath authority to ordain, change, and abolish, ceremonies or rites of the Church ordained only by man's authority, so that all things be done to edifying.

XXXV. Of Homilies. The second Book of Homilies, the several titles whereof we have joined under this Article, doth contain a godly and wholesome Doctrine, and necessary for these times, as doth the former Book of Homilies, which were set forth in the time of Edward the Sixth; and therefore we judge them to be read in churches by the Ministers, diligently and distinctly, that they may be understanded of the people. Of the Names of the Homilies: 1. Of the right Use of the Church. 2. Against peril of Idolatry. 3. Of the repairing and keeping clean of Churches. 4. Of good Works: first of Fasting. 5. Against Gluttony and Drunkenness. 6. Against Excess of Apparel. 7. Of Prayer. 8. Of the Place and Time of Prayer. 9. That Common Prayers and Sacraments ought to be ministered in a known tongue. 10. Of the reverend estimation of God's Word. 11. Of Alms-doing. 12. Of the Nativity of Christ. 13. Of the Passion of Christ. 14. Of the Resurrection of Christ. 15. Of the worthy receiving of the Sacraments of the Body and Blood of Christ. 16. Of the Gifts of the Holy Ghost. 17. For the Rogation days. 18. Of the state of Matrimony. 19. Of Repentance. 20. Against Idleness. 21. Against Rebellion.

XXXVI. Of Consecration of Bishops and Ministers. The Book of Consecration of Archbishops and Bishops, and Ordering of Priests and Deacons, lately set forth in the time of Edward the Sixth, and confirmed at the same time by authority of Parliament, doth contain all things necessary to such consecration and Ordering: neither hath it any thing, that of itself is superstitious and ungodly. And therefore whosoever are consecrated or ordered according to the Rites of that Book, since the second year of the forenamed King Edward unto this time, or hereafter shall be consecrated or ordered according to the same Rites; we decree all such to be rightly, orderly, and lawfully consecrated and ordered.

XXXVII. Of the Civil Magistrates. The King's Majesty hath the chief power in this Realm of England, and other his Dominions, unto whom the chief Government of all estates of this Realm, whether they be Ecclesiastical or Civil, in all causes doth appertain, and is not, nor ought to be, subject to any foreign Jurisdiction. Where we attributed to the King's Majesty the chief government, by which titles we understand the minds of some slanderous folks to be offended; we give not to our Princes the ministering either of God's Word, or of the Sacraments, the which thing the Injunctions also lately set forth by Elizabeth our Queen do most plainly testify; but that only prerogative which we see to have been given always to all godly Princes in holy Scriptures by God himself; that is, that they should rule all estates and degrees committed to their charge by God, whether they be Ecclesiastical or Temporal, and restrain with the civil sword the stubborn and evil-doers. The Bishop of Rome hath no jurisdiction in this Realm of England. The Laws of the Realm may punish Christian men with death, for heinous and grievous offenses. It is lawful for Christian men, at the commandment of the Magistrate, to wear weapons, and serve in the wars.

XXXVIII. Of Christian men's Goods, which are not common. The Riches and Goods of Christians are not common, as touching the right, title, and possession of the same, as certain Anabaptists do falsely boast. Notwithstanding, every man ought, of such things as he possesseth, liberally to give alms to the poor, according to his ability.

XXXIX. Of a Christian man's Oath. As we confess that vain and rash Swearing is forbidden Christian men by our Lord Jesus Christ, and James his Apostle, so we judge, that Christian Religion doth not prohibit, but that a man may swear when the Magistrate requireth, in a cause of faith and charity, so it be done according to the Prophet's teaching, in justice, judgement, and truth. The Ratification. This Book of Articles before rehearsed, is again approved, and allowed to be holden and executed within the Realm, by the assent and consent of our Sovereign Lady ELIZABETH, by the grace of God, of England, France, and Ireland, Queen, Defender of the Faith, &c. Which Articles were deliberately read and confirmed again by the subscription of the hands of the Archbishop and Bishops of the Upper-house, and by the subscription of the whole Clergy of the Netherhouse in their Convocation, in the Year of our Lord 1571. A Table of Kindred and Affinity wherein whosoever are related are forbidden by the Church of England to marry together. A Man may not marry his: mother, daughter, father's mother, mother's mother, son's daughter, daughter's daughter, sister, father's daughter, mother's daughter, wife's mother, wife's daughter, father's wife, son's wife, father's wife, mother's father's wife, wife's father's mother, wife's mother's, wife's son's daughter, wife's daughter's, son's wife, daughter's son's wife, father's sister, mother's sister, brother's daughter, sister's daughter. A Woman may not marry her: father, son, father's father, mother's father, son's son, daughter's son, brother, father's son, mother's son, husband's father, husband's son, mother's husband, daughter's husband, father's mothers's husband, husband's father's father, husband's mother's father, husband's son's son, husband's daughter's son, son's daughter's husband, daughter's daughter's husband, father's brother, mother's brother, brother's son, sister's son. *The Book of Common Prayer and Administration of the Sacraments and other Rites and Ceremonies of the Church According to the Use of The Church of England together with The Psalter or Psalms of David Pointed as they are to be Sung or Said in Churches; and the Form and Manner of Making, Ordaining, and Consecrating of Bishops, Priests, and Deacons.* Oxford University Press. (Oxford, New York, Toronto, Dehli, Bombay, Calcutta, Madras, Karachi, Petaling, Jaya, Singapore, Hong Kong, Tokyo, Nairobi, Dar es Salaam, Cape town, Mebourne, Auckland and associated companies in Beriut, Berlin, Idadan, Nicosia). 689-714.Allen, 199-200.

118. Prynne's ears were docked in 1634 and finally sliced off in 1637.

119. R. H. Parry, editor, *The English Civil War and After*, University of California Press, (Berkeley and Los Angeles, 1970). 34.

120. Twenty thousand went to New England; 40,000 to Virginia.

121. R. H. Parry. 9.

122. Matthew would have been about 48, John 42.

123. In a six month period in 1637, 193 left Yarmouth for Massachusetts Bay; 414 sailed from the same port to Holland.

124. It is possible that Abraham and Robert may have been related to Anne Hawkins, Matthew's first wife. Robert Hawkins was admitted to the first church in Charlestown, Mass. on 2: mo: day 17 1636 (17 April). His wife was Mary (___). Three Hawkins sons were baptized in the church: Eleazar, 10th mo: day 25 1636 (Dec.); Zachary, 8th mo: day 25 1639 (Oct.); and Joseph 2nd mo: day 3 1642 (April) *Register*, 23:279; 25:148, 150, 340.

125. Roger Thompson, *Mobility and Migration East Anglian Founders of New England, 1629-1640*. Amherst, Mass.: The University of Massachusetts Press, 1994, 130-31, 145, 147, 160, 176, 187, 193-4, 199.

126. David Hackett Fischer, *Albion's Seed*, New York: Oxford University Press, 1989. Endnote 2, page 25-26.

127. These dates are presumed. Allen. (pp. 307-8) says the Whipple brothers were granted land in Ipswich in March 1637 and July 1647. John was also granted land in November 1645 and September 1647. George A. Schofield, editor, *The Ancient Records of the Town of Ipswich 1634-1650*, Vol. 1, Chronical Motor Press. (Ipswich, 1899) says they were granted land in September 1638. 38-9. Governor Winthrop states that many ships came in 1638 bringing approximately 3,000 new settlers. The name of the ship the Whipple's sailed on is unknown. The author has no evidence that any of the Whipple sisters joined their brothers in the move. If their husbands were not interested in the new world, they would have remained in England. It is possible the family business continued, operated by an in-law or grandchild of Matthew, Sr.

128. W. F. Quin. 142. Is the Robert Whaples mentioned in the Pryor Will and the Braintree Select Vestry the same Robert Whaples mentioned in Trotter Will (page 104)?

2 | SEA VOYAGE TO NEW ENGLAND

1607: Jamestown settled by London Company. 1619: First legislature in the New World met in Jamestown. 1620: Pilgrims landed at Plymouth. 1624: New Netherlands (New York) settled by the Dutch. 1630: Settlement of Massachusetts Bay began. 1632: Young John Whipple arrived on the Lyon and settled at Dorchester, Mass. 1633: Agawam (Ipswich, Mass) settled by John Winthrop, Jr. 1634: Maryland settled by Proprietor Lord Baltimore. 1635: Connecticut Valley settled. 1636: Roger Williams founded Providence, R.I. 1637: New Haven founded. 1638: Matthew and John Whipple families settle in Ipswich. 1639: "Fundamental Orders of Connecticut," first colonial constitution adopted.

THE VIGOR OF AMERICA springs from its early English emigrants and the seed of that stock is now found in each of the 50 United States. That seed was planted in the decade 1630-40 when approximately 20,000 English, the Whipples among them, settled in New England. After 1640, the Long Parliament[1] resolved many of the grievances of the nonconformists and immigration suddenly ceased. It was almost 200 years before the English again flocked to American shores.

One does not leave the known for the unknown without some idea of the destination — especially families with children. In 1638, Matthew and Anne had five: Mary, 12; Anne, 10; Elizabeth, 9; John, 6; Matthew, 3. John and Susanna also had five: Susanna, 16; John, 13; Elizabeth, 11; William, 8; Mary, 4. If they were members of group of Puritans traveling together, the group would have planned carefully before leaving.

The emigrants to America had a number of published works to review and it is presumed the Whipples read at least some of them. Sir Humphrey Gilbert is believed to have written, in the early 1570s, the essay "Discourse of a New Passage to Cathaia," in which he proposed settlements in America. Richard Hakluyt, the noted English editor of various voyages of discovery, interviewed Newfoundland fishermen in 1578 about places suited for settlement.

By the latter part of the sixteenth century it was known in England that America was a source for fish and naval stores, that tropical products were available in the West Indies, that a northwest passage might be found to the Far East, that unoccupied regions of America might produce gold and silver. The French and the Spanish published many accounts of their work in the new world in the late 1500s. In 1600 *Hakluyt's Voyages*[2] which included over 200 narratives of voyages to the new world, was published. Samuel Purchas published accounts of 1200 more voyages in 1613/14.[3]

But the Whipples probably gained most of their information from William Wood's *New England's Prospect*[4] This slender volume was first offered for sale in 1634 by London bookseller John Bellamie at his Three Golden Lions shop in Cornhill. Wood had recently returned from four years in Massachusetts and wanted to share his excitement and knowledge of the new world. His readers were promised "A true, lively, and experimental description of that part of America, commonly called New England, the state of that country, both as it stands to our newcome English planters; and to the old native inhabitants, laying down that which may both enrich the knowledge of the mind traveling reader or benefit the future voyager."[5]

Unlike other authors, Wood focused on the land and its vegetation, on its human and animal inhabitants. His book detailed problems of frontier life: the difficulty of clearing land, the shortage of draft animals[6] and beer, the need for interpreters. Other mundane aspects of colonization were addressed. Hazards such as high mortality and widespread suffering and religious controversies were ignored. Essentially promotional, the book was written to convince others to leave home and settle in New England.

New England was known as a place where many settlers had died. Wood addressed this negative straight away. New settlers, he wrote, died of a sickness caused by a sea diet of tainted and rotten food and because they arrived in the fall with no time to build adequate shelter for protection from the cold winter. He offered advice on how to avoid these problems. The discerning reader would have questioned his contradictions as he also told settlers not to be concerned about their health: More would probably die at home than went. Many which have come with foul bodies to sea as did make their days uncomfortable on land have been so purged and clarified at sea that they have been more healthful for after times, their weak appetites being turned to good stomachs, not only desiring but likewise digesting such victuals as the sea affords.[7]

New Englanders, he argued, were not subject to the common diseases of England such as measles, greensickness,[8] headaches, stone, consumption, etc. He claimed settlers with lingering diseases were restored to their former strength and health. Noting that much of England's water was not fit to drink, he said New England water was so good many preferred it to "beer, whey, and buttermilk and those that drink it be as healthful, fresh, and lusty as they that drink beer."[9]

He described the land as forested with enough trees to build houses, mills, ships, and to provide fuel. He identified the trees — walnut, cedar, fir, pine, ash, and beach — and told how each could be used. He claimed winters weren't as raw as in England; that fishermen went to sea in January and February and got better catches than in summer; that winter crops gave better yields than spring crops because the long lasting snow kept the plants warm and provided nourishment when it melted. He agreed that summers were hotter than in England but they were tolerable because of the cooling effect of fresh winds.[10] He noted that Indian corn thrived on heat and lack of rain was not a problem for English corn (wheat) because it got adequate moisture from the nightly dew. Settlers, he said, could supplement their food supply with wild game such as: deer, available for the taking; raccoon, as good as lamb; grey squirrels, almost as big as an English rabbit; turkeys, up to 40 pounds; partridges, bigger than in England; rabbits, much like those at home; geese and ducks, in flocks of 3,000; codfish, larger than in Newfoundland; sturgeon, up to 18 feet long; halibut, up to two yards and a foot thick; bass, fine, fat, and delicate, three to four feet with a bone in the head containing a saucer full of marrow that is sweet, good, and pleasant to the palate and wholesome to the stomach; herring and alewives, so thick at spring spawning they can be had by the bucketful; shad, bigger than the English shad; mackerel up to 18 inches long; lobsters, up to 20 pounds. Mussels and clams were so plentiful, they were fed to the swine.

There was an abundance of wolves, wildcats, hawks, humbirds (sic), crows, cormorants, ravens, owls, cranes, and pigeons. Of the latter, he said there were millions, that flocks flew overhead for up to five hours, blotting out the sun.

Settlers had to cope with "evil and hurtful things," he wrote. Ravenous wolves killed the weaker cattle and rattlesnakes were dangerous to people. The latter were described as "generally a yard and a half long and as thick in the middle as the small of a man's leg." Death followed an hour after being bitten unless an antidote of snakeweed root was taken. The antidote "must be champed, the spittle swallowed, and the root applied to the sore . . . whosoever is bitten by these snakes his flesh becomes as spotted as a leper until he be perfectly cured. It is reported that if the party live that is bitten, the snake will die, and if the party die, the snake will live."[11] Wood ridiculed reports that rattlesnakes could fly and kill with their breath. He reported large numbers of troublesome flies and large populations of frogs, toads, spiders, wild bees, and "a great green fly," similar to the English horsefly, and large populations of small black flies, fleas, and wasps.

Of existing plantations,[12] he ranked Dorchester[13] the greatest in New England because of its reasonable harbor, good arable ground for hay, corn, and gardens, plentiful woods and water supply, and large supply of cattle, goats, and swine. Boston was the chief place for shipping and merchandise but not suitable for farming. Salem was recommended for its excellent farm land and water transportation. It had more canoes than in the rest of the colony combined, canoes made of "whole pine trees . . . about two foot and a half over, and 20 foot long . . . every house having a water horse or two."[14]

Ipswich, nine miles north of Salem, was a spacious place for a plantation with "great meads and marshes, plain plowing grounds, many good rivers and harbors, and no rattlesnakes." Near the sea, it was well stocked with fish, fowl, and beasts. Newbury, eight miles beyond Ipswich, was equally desirable and the two communities had enough land to accommodate "twice as many people as are yet in New England."[15]

Wood reported that the Indians were affable, courteous, loving, and of great help, teaching the English when and how to plant Indian corn, how to worm, weed, prune, dress it, and how to cull the finest seed for next year's crop. He decried the "needless fear" that had been "deeply rooted" in the English mind by previous authors about Indians. The truth, he said, is that Indians are "wise in their carriage, subtle in their dealings, true in their promise, honest in defraying of their debts . . . constant in friendship . . . much civilized since the English colonies were planted, though but little edified in religion."[16]

Earlier writers had written of "great want" in the colonies. Wood dismissed these concerns: Don't blame the new country. Any who bring provisions enough for a year and a half need not fear want.[17] I advise men that are of weak constitutions to keep at home. For all [in] New England must be workers in some kind; must have more than a boy's head and no less than a man's strength to live comfortably.[18]

The Englishman enduring hard times at home would live much better in the new world, Wood argued. He outlined what the emigrant should do to prepare for the voyage and suggested what necessities should be taken to insure a good life in the colonies.

One way passage was £5 with a children's fare as follows: Suckling children not to be reckoned; such as under four years of age, three for one fare; under eight, two for one; under 12, three for two.[19] It cost £4 a ton to ship household goods. Medical care was extra and cost 2 shillings 6 pence per person.[20]

Food and drink were included in the fare. The staples were salt beef and pork, salt fish, butter, cheese, peas, pottage,[21] water gruel,[22] biscuits, water, and "six-shilling beer." Those who could afford it were told to bring their own provisions of "conserves and good claret wine . . . salad oil . . . a comfortable thing for the stomach for such as are sea sick. Prunes are good to be stewed; sugar for many things; white biscuits, eggs, bacon, rice, poultry, and sheep to kill aboard; fine flour-baked meats will keep about a week or nine days at sea. Juice of lemons well put up is good either to prevent or cure the scurvy.[23]

Wood saw no contradiction in recommending one thing while describing another. He recommended a long coarse coat for protection against ropes and planks, noting that as the boat pitched, the passenger fell. But he wrote that the ship at sea is like a cradle rocked by a careful mother's hand. He told those concerned about sinking or being captured by pirates or enemies of England not to worry because they would be "in the careful hand of Providence."

There was no artificial light so bedtime was at sundown. Passengers provided their own bedding. Age or coarseness didn't matter but it should be clean and warm. He encouraged wearing old clothes while aboard ship. Since few products were available for sale in New England, Wood encouraged colonists to bring: great iron pots, warming pans, stewing pans, all manner of ironware, pewter and brass dishes, cups, and goblets; nails for houses, spikes for boats, ships, and fishing stages; broad and narrow hoes, broad and pitching axes, augers, piercing bits, ship saws, two-handed saws, froes,[24] both for the riving[25] of pales[26] and laths, beetle heads[27] and iron wedges; glass, well leaded and carefully packed. Fishing gear such as barbels, splitting knives, leads, hooks and lines for cod, mackerel, and sharks, seines or bass and herring nets; good poldavies[28] to make sails for boats, anchors for boats and pinnacles; seacoal, iron, lead and millstones, flints, ordnance, and whatever can be used for ballast.[29]

Noting the serious shortage of groceries and apparel in New England, he suggested bringing an adequate supply because they were "dearer in New England than in England." Grocery wares such as sugar, prunes, raisins, currants, honey, nutmeg, cloves, etc., soap, candles, lamps, etc. were in short supply. The Whipples would have easily been able to follow his recommendations on apparel. He wrote:

"Woollen cloth is a very good commodity and line better, as holland,[30] lockram,[31] flaxen,[32] hempen,[33] calico stuffs,[34] linsey-woolseys,[35] and blue calico, green sayes[36] for housewives' aprons, hats, boots, shoes, good Irish stockings, which if they be good are much more serviceable than knit ones."[37]

Since every man in the colonies had to bear arms,[38] he suggested they bring drums, English colors, halberds,[39] pikes, muskets, and bandoleers[40] with swords, shot, and powder. Bird hunters should include 6-foot guns with good powder and shot of all sort. Excess supplies would bring a good price because of shortage.

Some writers, based on Spain's claim to the country, discouraged settlement. They feared Spain would invade New England as it did St. Cristophers and St. Martins in the West Indies. Wood rejected this notion, arguing that Spanish strongholds in the West Indies were too far away, that New England plantations were too poor to plunder, and that Virginia, 400 miles closer to the Spanish settlements, had never been bothered.

Wood also had an opinion on who should colonize New England: Men of good working and contriving heads for the good of the body politic; a well-skilled husband-man for tillage and improvements of grounds; an ingenious carpenter; a cunning joiner; a handy cooper; a good brick maker; a tiler[41] and a smith; a leather dresser; a gardener; a tailor and fisherman.[42]

For those possessing these skills but lacking the resources to make the journey, Wood recommended they find an honest master and come as an indentured servant. There was more freedom and liberty for servants than in England, he wrote, and a greater opportunity to do well.[43]

After a careful review of the available literature, considering recommendations from Essex friends who had preceded them,[44] and giving serious consideration to the pros and cons of moving, the Whipples made the decision to sell their Bocking property, give up known comforts, and begin a new adventure. The cost in pounds and shillings was calculated,[45] passage arranged, goods packed[46] and carted to the port of departure, and they set sail.

The Whipples were among 3,000 sailing on 20 ships for Massachusetts Bay in the summer and fall of 1638. Winthrop called the new arrivals "people of good quality and estate, notwithstanding the council's order that none such should come without the king's license; but God so wrought, that some obtained license, and others came away without."[47]

Most colonists were landsmen who had no experience with the sea. To them, the sea was filled with marvels and dread terrors. They boarded the ship with misgivings, realizing they would experience some violent weather during their nearly 3,000 mile voyage. Almost everyone was seasick the first few days.

Even if the travelers escaped major storms they endured choppy seas, unending swells, and stiff gales[48] with heavy rain. Sometimes, storms continued for days with no headway made. One fearful Puritan described the nightmare of a storm: "the wind blew mightily, the rain fell vehemently, and the sea roared . . . and the waves powered themselves over the ship." In the pitch-black darkness the anxiety of passengers was deepened by the tenseness and fears of the crew "running here and there, loudly crying to pull at this and that rope."[49] But landsmen soon learned that storms were part of the sea and ships seldom perished because of them.

There were few amusements to relieve boredom on the long voyage. If they sailed the northern route, they were amazed by the icebergs, the many kinds of fishes, and the huge whales spouting water steams. They were thankful to escape epidemics of small pox, yellow fever, and the plague which occasionally raced through ships, leaving survivors the sad task of burying the victims at sea. The first things they saw of New England were immense forests with occasional clearings of Indian villages. Maples and oaks covered the land and pines grew down to the shore. These forests represented great wealth to the emigrant: lumber for houses, timber, pitch, and tar for ships, and towering masts for the royal navy.

It is not known what vessel the Bocking Whipples booked but the first Whipple to arrive in New England, John Whipple, a teen-aged indentured servant and no relation, sailed on the *Lyon* leaving London June 22, 1632, arriving at Boston 12 weeks later.[50] They were eight weeks from Land's End[51] and experienced five days of east wind and thick fog. John, was one of 123 passengers, including 50 children. The ship's carpenter was their only fatality, falling overboard while caulking a port.

The *Lyon* with a rampant lion on the prow, at 250 tons,[52] was one of the smaller vessels plying the New England trade. Its voyages in 1629/30/31/32 were as regular and safe as a ferry. William Pierce, its master, was noted for his skillful seamanship and his support of Puritan leaders. His first trip was in 1623 when, as master of the *Anne*, he brought 60 persons to Plymouth. In 1625, as master of the *Jacob*, he delivered a load of cattle to Plymouth.

Before leaving England, emigrants had to swear "Allegiance and Supremacy" to the king, affirm "they are no subsidy man," and buy a certificate from their parish attesting that they conformed to the orders and disciplines of the Church of England. Masters of the ships carrying the emigrants had to subscribe to the following articles:

1. That all and every person aboard their ships now bound for New England as aforesaid, that shall blaspheme or profane the Holy name of God be severely punished.

2. That they cause the prayers contained in *the Book of Common Prayer* established in the Church of England be said daily at the usual hours for morning and evening prayers and that they cause all persons aboard their ships to be present at same.

3. That they do not receive aboard or transport any person that hath not Certificate from the officers of the port where he is to embark that he hath taken both the oaths of Allegiance and Supremacy.

4. That upon their return to this Kingdom they certify to the Board the names of all such persons as they shall transport together with their proceedings in the execution of the aforesaid articles.[53]

The ships were not built for passengers, so the colonists had to adjust to the inconveniences of a freight-carrying vessel. The bow, with its high forecastle deck, was occupied by the seamen; the still higher poop deck on the stern housed the officers. The space in between, open on small vessels and fitted with a deck and a hold in large craft, was for cargo, ordnance, and the stowing of the long boats.

The more important passengers booked tiny cabins in the poop containing an upper and lower bunk no larger than coffins. Though unbelievably cramped, these cabins were luxurious compared to the rest of the passengers who slept on hammocks and pallets in the hold. Cabin passengers had a tiny square porthole and a bucket dangling on a rope for the disposal of bodily wastes. The common folk had no privacy at all and were kept under the hatches during prolonged storms. It is left to the reader's imagination how sanitary needs were met. Livestock were carried on the same ships and suffered more than the passengers as they were housed on the storm-swept decks.

Since few had been to sea before, they were unprepared for the long journey and ignorant of the inadequacy of the ships, especially during times of storms. English author Edward Johnson wrote of the giant waves hurling their goods from place to place because of improper stowage.[54]

To feed their passengers, ships carried 16 hogsheads of meat including 8,000 pounds of beef, 2,800 pounds of pork, a quantity of beef tongues, 600 pounds of salt codfish and 100 pounds of suet, presumably for cooking purposes; 20,000 biscuits, of which 15,000 were brown, 5,000 white; a barrel of flour, 30 bushel of oatmeal, 11 firkin[55] of butter, 40 bushel of dried peas, their only vegetable; and a bushel and a half of mustard seed. Deep sea fishing supplemented their larder, weather permitting.[56] The Whipples probably brought small supplies of food and cooking utensils aboard for their own use.[57]

If the voyage extended over six weeks, scurvy was an almost certainty. Their main reliance was on beer as water could not be preserved on long voyages. In addition to quenching thirst, beer was a mild antiscorbutic.[58] A ship of 350 tons would carry 42 ton of beer,[59] 14 ton of water,[60] two hogsheads of vinegar. This supply could be rationed over 12 weeks.

There were few nautical tools. Navigators measured the elevation of the sun with a cross staff [61] to determine the degrees of latitude.[62] East and west positions were expressed in terms of dead reckoning by estimating the marine leagues sailed from day to day.

As the ship passed Land's End, the Whipple families would have been on the crowded deck watching the granite cliffs and the lighthouse fade into the sky. Even the rambunctious youngsters would have been quiet, sensing it was the last time they would see England. After the second week homesickness was dulled and a daily routine established. In fair weather nine of the Whipple children probably squatted by the windlass[63] playing at "Hot Cockles," with Susanna, the oldest, as umpire.

On their initial tour of what would be their home for up to 12 weeks, Matthew and John probably began by descending through the hatch by ladder to the 'tween decks,' an area six feet high, where many of the passenger's hammocks were slung. Even though the stench was strong and the light poor, it was the preferred space since it had portholes. Down another hatch was the dark, smoky hold where a small hearth had been built of fire bricks. Here the ship's cook made a stew of salt beef and dried peas in an enormous iron pot, dinner for the common folk and the sailors. Officers and cabin passengers had a separate galley under the poop.

A number of ships probably sailed simultaneously so they could help one another in case of need. Several ministers were usually passengers on each ship. Tuesdays and Wednesdays were days of catechism. If there were a death, passengers and crew would assemble on deck, bareheaded, for burial services. After the minister read from the prayer book, the canvass-wrapped-and-weighted-bundle was dropped into the sea; the silence broken by a shrill scream from a survivor. Then the captain ordered an extra ration of beer for everyone and the ship's life continued.

Acceptable behavior for all passengers and crew was published and posted. Usually the first to break the rules were two young men who were fighting. Their punishment was to walk the deck until night with their hands bound behind them. The punishment for the man who used contemptuous speech was to be laid in bolts[64] until confessing his offense. Two sailors were flogged by the bosun[65] for fighting and two drunken passengers were disciplined in an improvised pillory. A servant who filched food and sold it to other servants had his hands tied to a bar and stood for two hours with a basket full of stones hung about his neck.

After the second day at sea, the sick were brought on deck and stood on each side of a rope stretched from the steerage to the mainmast. They swayed up and down until they were warm and soon most grew well and merry.

It was not unusual for a great storm to bring wind so strong and rain so hard it split and tore the foresail in pieces and caused the topsail to be taken in. As the storm grew, a minister led the passengers in prayer while another was above decks with the mariners, committing their souls and bodies to the Lord. The clouds were so dark by midnight that the crew lost sight of all other vessels. The wind slacked by morning but the sea was so high it tossed the ship more, causing the captain to use only the mainsail. By mid afternoon of the second day, the sea was so high the ship made little headway. By supper, the wind shifted into the west so the captain tacked and stood into the head sea, to avoid rolling the ship. No way was made as the sea beat the ship back as much as the wind put it forward. The weather was cold but most passengers had their sea legs by then and didn't get sick even though tossed about for 72 hours, 48 by the storm and 24 the next day and night when the ship drifted without a sail for want of wind and rolled continually in a high sea.

Usually about half way a women tween decks would begin to rant and prophesy. First she was a merman,[66] then a sea serpent, finally she cried out against witchcraft, claiming the Devil lurked in the sail lock. One or two like her unnerved the landsmen on every voyage.

About the seventh week, many of the ships were still battered by contrary winds and suffered fog so heavy they lost sight of the other vessels. Sudden gales and fierce rainstorms kept passengers below deck. The ship suffered the usual accidents: The flying jib[67] tore off in a heavy sea, some of the shrouds[68] on the mizzen[69] parted, and a sailor fell from the rigging[70] of the mainmast,[71] breaking a leg.

When they sighted a ship with an unfamiliar rig, they probably thought it was an enemy privateer and manned the guns. But usually it turned out to be a harmless Danish trader bound for home with cod from the Grand Banks.[72] Pods of whales, each almost as big as the ship, frolicked too close for comfort. When goats or cattle died they were quickly eaten since several casks of provisions spoiled on every voyage.

Frequently when the ship reached the Grand Banks the fog was so thick the captain hove to[73] and the sailors fished for cod. By now provisions were in scant supply. It was time to replenish. Even the captain's mess was reduced to half rations of salt beef and peas for every meal. There were several cases of scurvy and much coughing and sniffles for the weather had turned bitter and there was no way to get warm but lie in sour, verminous bedding, or to fight for a place near the cooking hearth. Knowing there were dangerous shoals to the south, the captain ordered a new mainsail be fitted. Being so close to completing a successful voyage, he would take no chances with his passengers.

Usually by the ninth week passengers were roused by the clear voice of the lookout shouting, "Land Ho!" They crowded on deck and saw land in the distance. Immediately the crew began taking periodic soundings as the ship sailed down the coast past Piscataqua[74] and other places with Indian names. The weather was now fair and sunny and the air so sweet, it came off the shore like the smell of a flower garden. They rounded Cape Ann, sailed past Salem, and the following evening sailed in Boston harbor.

The gentry stood on the poop deck, Matthew and John in their finest clothes – colorful silk doublets,[75] trimmed with gold braid, a two-inch deep ruff with Mechelen lace,[76] hat with gilt band and buckle. The Whipple women were dressed in their elegant brightly colored best. They were thinner than when they left, Anne probably had some scurvy sores around the mouth and it is likely that Susanna's plump cheeks had sagged, but none of the family looked too peaked.

It took a couple days before their ship was unloaded and a few more to arrange for permission to settle at Ipswich. Then the two families were off to begin life at one of the more remote outposts of the colony.

Let's contrast today's London to New York sea voyage with the Whipple's 1638 voyage.

The modern day Whipple would depart Southampton on a gyroscopically stabilized ship and arrive in New York five days later. Depending on the fare the family was willing to pay,[77] it could choose from cabins on at least six decks. Two pieces of checked and one carry-on bag per family member, not to exceed 70 pounds per bag, is allowed.

The stateroom is a sitting room by day, a comfortable bedroom by night. Decorated with warm pastels colors, it features ample closets, mirrors, a spotless bathroom, and air conditioning to adjust to personal comfort. Elevators take the family to the broad teak decks for golf, tennis, and jogging or a refreshing dip in the glistening pools — indoor and outdoor.

Days can be relaxing or energetic. Deck or indoor games help work up an appetite. Other options are to lie in the sun and tan, get a massage, use the sauna, walk off some calories, read, write, converse, or meet and make new friends. Evenings offer music, dancing, gala dinners, first run movies, musical revues, costume balls, and a casino.

Master chefs prepare a variety of superb cuisine from continental breakfasts in bed to full course breakfasts in the dining room, to colorful luncheon buffets, to thrilling ala carte dinners to special Gala nights. The passenger can select from main or late dining and if a special diet is required, it will be prepared. The wine connoisseur has access to a well stocked wine cellar.

Other conveniences include a telephone system with direct dial ship-to-shore satellite calling, conference capability, FAX capability, one-digit dialing to important shipboard locations, and automatic wake-up calls; a television network with up-to-the-minute news plus information on shipboard activities; a six-channel radio featuring satellite news broadcasts; a ship's doctor; a beauty salon and barber shop; laundry and pressing services; library; safe deposit boxes; a daily newspaper; computer center; and a shopping promenade.

For younger children there is a playroom complete with colorful toys, games, and child-size furniture, fully supervised by fulltime governesses; a special cinema showing cartoons and Walt Disney films; a club for kids 7 to 17 years with juke box, ping pong, air hockey, computer games, etc.

These voyages, essentially the same distance on the same ocean, are so far from reality for the two sets of time travelers, it staggers the imagination. The traveling Whipple of today should be thankful he didn't live "in the good old days."

ENDNOTES — CHAPTER 2

1. The Long Parliament convened 3 Nov. 1640 and included in its membership was Puritan leader Oliver Cromwell who opposed the policies of Charles I. The governing classes were divided into two parties: parliamentarians who distrusted the king and demanded more restrictions on his power, and royalists who were unhappy about reducing the power of the crown. This Parliament did not hesitate to act because of the King's objections and from 1640-60 controlled the course of English affairs just as Charles had the preceding 15 years. The King agreed not to dissolve Parliament without its consent and to abolish prerogative courts, the Star Chamber, and the ecclesiastical court of High Commission. All taxes from ship money to impositions, which had been levied without parliamentary consent, were declared illegal. Archbishop Laud was imprisoned and a grand remonstrance against all grievances against the crown was passed. Appointment of army officers and ministers of state without parliamentary approval was prohibited.

2. Richard Hakluyt was a preacher and sometimes student of Christ-Church in Oxford. His book was *Hayluyt's Voyages,* imprinted by George Bishop, Ralfe Newberie, and Robert Barker, (London, 1600). Reprinted by the Viking Press, Irwin R. Blackner, Editor, (New York, 1965). Reprinted by Houghton Mifflin Company, Richard David, Editor, (Boston, 1981).

3. The name of the book: *Hakluytus Postumus* or *Purchas His Pilgrimes.* Reprinted by James MacLehose and Sons, (Glasgow, 1905). 20 volumes.

4. Printed by Thomas Cotes (London 1634). Reissued in 1635 and 1639. Professor Alden T. Vaughan, editor, The University of Massachusetts Press (Amherst, 1977), published a modern and annotated version for contemporary readers.

5. See the prolix in Wood's book: *William Wood, New England's Prospect.* London: John Bellamie, Bookseller, Three Golden Lions Shop in Cornhill, 1634.

6. Leading some settlers to consider harnessing moose.

7. Vaughn. 70.

8. Greensickness: An anemic disease of young women, giving a greenish tinge to the complexion.

9. Vaughn. 37

10. Contrary to Wood's claim, settlers found it difficult to adjust, finding the extremes of heat and cold much greater than in England. But they welcomed the dry American air which they found more invigorating than the damp winds in England.

11. Vaughan. 65.

12. All new settlements in the colony were called plantations. Early settlers were called planters, not in the agricultural sense, but as persons engaged in planting a colony under the flag of England.

13. Now part of Boston.

14. Vaughan. 61.

15. Vaughan. 65.

16. Vaughan. 97.

17. He recommended a hogshead and a half of meal for everyone in the family plus malt, beef, butter, cheese, peas, good wines, vinegar, strong waters, etc. After a year and a half the first crop should be ready to harvest.

18. Vaughan. 69.

19. Charles Edward Banks, *The Winthrop Fleet of 1630,* Genealogical Publishing company, (Baltimore, 1961). 24-32.

20. Maritime law required ships carrying large numbers of passengers to have medical men on board. Known as chirugeons, they were expected to have a certificate from the "Barber-Surgeons Hall," carry a chest well furnished for both physical and surgical problems, and attend to the sick and cure the wounded. They were governed by Section 47 of the Regulations of the Guild of Barber Surgeons.

21. A kind of thick soup or stew.

22. Water gruel: Thin, easily digested broth made by cooking meal in water.

23. Vaughan. 69-70. Scurvy — a disease resulting from a deficiency of vitamin C, characterized by weakness, anemia, spongy gums, bleeding from the mucous membranes, etc.

24. Froe: A wedge-shaped cleaving tool with a handle set into the blade at right angles to

the back; used in splitting staves for casks and the like. It is driven by a mallet. Frow is the preferred spelling.

25. Riving: The act of cleaving or separating. A riving knife is a tool for splitting shingles, staves, etc.
26. Pales: A narrow, upright, pointed stake used in fences; picket.
27. Beetle heads: A heavy mallet, usually wooden.
28. Poldavies: Coarse canvas or sacking.
29. Vaughan. 71
30. Holland: Unbleached line cloth; sometimes glazed; used for clothing, window shades, etc.
31. Lockram: A kind of linen, usually of a coarse and cheap sort.
32. Flaxen: A linen thread made from the fibers of the flax stem.
33. Hempen: Tough strong fiber used for weaving into coarse fabrics.
34. Calico stuffs: Any white cotton cloth. First manufactured in India, then introduced into Europe.
35. Linsey-woolseys: Cloth made of linen and wool.
36. Sayes: A fine textured cloth used for clothing.
37. Vaughan. 71.
38. Males of 14 and up were included in the military drills held every three weeks.
39. Halberd: A combination spear and battle-ax.
40. Bandoleer: A broad belt worn over one shoulder and across the chest, with pockets for carrying ammunition, etc.
41. Tiler: A person who makes roofing tiles. The best qualities of brick earth are used for making tiles, and the process is similar to that of brick making.
42. Vaughan. 72.
43. The teen-aged John Whipple who settled in Dorchester, Mass. did extremely well after starting out as an indentured servant.
44. Ninety-two Essex county residents were in the Winthrop fleet which arrived in New England in 1630. James Kendall Hosmer, ed., *Winthrop's Journal, History of New England, 1630-1648* Vol. I, Barnes & Noble, Inc. (New York, reprinted 1959), records the following arrivals which may have included friends of the Whipples. 1630. October 30, the *Handmaid* arrived at Plymouth after 12 weeks at sea with about 60 passengers and 28 cows. She lost her masts and 10 cows. John Grant was master. (p. 53). November 2, William Pierce brought the *Lyon* into Natascot after 10 weeks at sea. His 60 passengers included Gov. Winthrop's wife Margaret and daughter Ann, age one-and-a-half. She was one of two children lost at sea.

1632. Two vessels arrived in June: The *James* with 12 passengers and 61 heifers after an eight week voyage from London. Forty of the cattle were lost. (p. 81). Mr. Thomas, master of an unnamed vessel arrived with about 60 passengers. They left London March 9. (p. 81). The *Charles* left Barnstable April 10 with about 20 passengers, 80 cows, and six mares. (p. 81).

1633. Three vessels arrived in May: The *William and Jane*, Mr. Murdock master, arrived from London after six weeks carrying 30 passengers and 10 cows. (p. 100). The *Mary and Jane*, Mr. Rose master, came from London in seven weeks with 196 passengers. Two children died. (p. 100). The *Elizabeth Bonadventure*, Mr. Graves master, arrived from Yarmouth after six weeks at sea with 95 passengers, 74 Dutch sheep, and two mares. Forty sheep were lost enroute. (p. 102). The *Griffin*, a ship of 300 ton, arrived September 4 from Downs with about 200 passengers. They lost four en route. Rev. John Cotton was aboard. (p. 105).

1634. Six ships arrived in March carrying passengers and cattle. About 100 settled at Agawam. [renamed Ipswich] (pp. 125-6). In June, 14 ships arrived at Boston, one at Salem. (p. 127). Nathaniel Ward, who became the minister at Ipswich, arrived this year. Later he wrote the *Body of Liberties* and the *Simple Cobbler of Agawam*. (p. 145). ⌐1634

1635. The *James*, a ship of 300 tons, Mr. Graves master, arrived in June from Southampton with passengers and cattle. Mr. Graves had come every year for seven years. Within the next six weeks, seven other ships came to Boston, one to Salem, and four to the mouth of the bay, all with passengers and cattle. (p. 152).

1636. Three ships-full of passengers arrived at Boston from London in mid November. One had been at sea 26 weeks, the other two ships sometime less. Their beer was consumed a month before their arrival so they were forced to "drink stinking water (and that very little) mixed with sack or vinegar." The provisions were in short supply. They encountered continual tempests. One of the ships was "overset" in the night by a sudden gust "and lay so half an hour, yet righted herself." Mr. Nathaniel Rogers, who was installed minister at Ipswich, was a passenger on one of the ships. (p.200)

45. Traveling with five children each, it would have cost at least £35 per family. If they traveled cabin class and transported more than a ton each, the cost would have been greater. Based on the retail price index and annual inflation rates and estimates of consumer prices back to 1270, £35 in 1638 would be $1,898.40 in 1989. Source: a letter to the author from the Economics Division, Bank of England, London, dated August 24, 1989. Signed by Andrew Cope.

46. Including packets of seed such as hollyhock, marigold, violets, and wall flowers. A wall flower includes any number of perennial or annual garden plants of the mustard family.

47. On hearing the reports that thousands were preparing to leave, the archbishops issued orders that no ships could sail. But upon petition of the masters suggesting the Commonwealth would suffer great damage by hindering the Newfoundland trade, they were allowed to leave. Customs didn't search for goods so emigrants took what they desired without question or control. The Lords of Council were amazed to see rich and poor, servants and others, men of all conditions, readily leaving for New England when they had to force people to go to the other plantations. Hosmer, 271-4.

48. Governor John Winthrop, who arrived in 1630 aboard the *Arbella*, described the gales as "swift, pretty, and handsome" and said they were followed by "high or raging seas." Banks, *The Winthrop Fleet of 1630*. 33.

49. Michael Kraus, *The United States to 1865*, The University of Michigan Press, (Ann Arbor, 1959). 33.

50. Arriving Sunday evening September 16. See Banks, *Planters of the Commonwealth*, 99-103.

51. Land's End: Cape in Cornwall at the southwestern most point of England.

52. Some accounts indicate 100 tons.

53. Tepper. 73-4.

54. J. Franklin Jameson, Editor, *Johnson's Wonder-Working Province*, 1628-1651, (New York, 1910).

55. Firkin: A small wooden tub.

56. Banks, *The Winthrop Fleet of 1630*. 24-32.

57. All personalized references concerning the journey are conjecture.

58. Scorbutic: of like, or having scurvy.

59. About 10,000 gallons.

60. About 3,500 gallons.

61. Cross staff: An instrument used to take the altitude of the sun or stars. It was supersed by the quadrant. Also called forestaff. It was in the form of a cross, the intersection of which was surrounded by a graduated circle, the periphery divided into four equal arcs.

62. It was the latter half of the 1700s before longitude could be determined.

63. Windlass: A simple kind of winch worked by a crank for lifting an anchor.

64. Bolts: An iron for fastening the leg; a fetter.

65. Bosun: The ship's warrant or petty officer in charge of the deck crew, the rigging, anchors, boats, etc.

66. Merman: An imaginary sea creature with the head and upper body of a man and the tail of a fish.

67. Flying jib: A triangular sail projecting ahead of the foremast.

68. Shrouds: Any of a set of ropes stretched from a ship's side to a masthead to offset lateral strain on the mast.

69. Mizzen: A fore and aft sail set on the mizzenmast. Mizzenmast — the mast closest to the stern in a ship with two or more masts.

70. Rigging: Tackle, especially the chains, ropes, etc. used for supporting and working the masts, sails, yards, etc. of a vessel.

71. The principal mast of a vessel.

72. Grand Banks: Large shoal in the North Atlantic, southeast of Newfoundland; noted fishing grounds; approximately 500 miles long.

73. Hove to: Stop forward movement by hauling in or shortening sail and heading into the wind.

74. Piscataqua: Now Portsmouth, N.H. The Isle of Shoals, off Portsmouth and exactly on the 43 degree north latitude, was a favored land site. The Islands, well off shore and charted by Capt. John

Smith, are an unmistakable land formation, and within sight of Piscataqua on a non-foggy day.

75. Doublet: A man's close-fitting jacket with or without sleeves.

76. A fine lace made in Mechelen, Belgium, with the design clearly outlined by a thread.

77. Super thrift excursion fares can be purchased for as low as $995 per person to $7,910 for four persons per cabin. Children staying in a room with two adults pay half fare, children under 2, $100. Luxury duplex apartments range from $15,335 to $29,275. Port taxes and charges are $90 per person. The rate for passage on freighters would be significantly less, the time at sea longer.

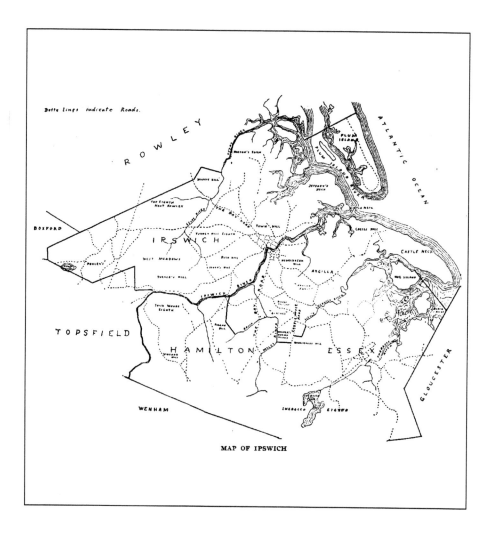

MAP OF IPSWICH

3 THE "ELDER" JOHN WHIPPLE FAMILY

John[1] Whipple (Matthew[A]) baptized 29 August 1596 in Bocking, Essex County, England; died 30 June 1669 in Ipswich, Essex County, Massachusetts. He married (1) Susanna (probably Stacey) abt 1620 at Bocking; died after 13 July 1661 in Ipswich, Massachusetts (2) the widow Janet (Jennet) Dickinson after 1662 at Ipswich. A clothier, John appears to have emigrated in 1638. He farmed and engaged in several business ventures, was an eight term delegate to the general court, Ipswich clerk of writs for several terms, deacon, and ruling elder of the Ipswich church.

∠1642   ∠1658

Children of John and Susannah Whipple, all but Sarah born in Bocking:

 i.   *Susanna, born 1 July 1622; married Lionel Worth in Ipswich.*
 ii.   *John, born 11 January 1623/24; buried 4 August 1624 in Bocking.*
 iii. *John (Captain), born 21 December 1625; died 10 August 1683 in Ipswich; married (1) Martha Reynor, (2) Elizabeth (Coggswell) Paine, both in Ipswich*
 iv.   *Elizabeth, born 1 November 1627; died 15 December 1648 without issue; married Anthony Potter in Ipswich.*
 v.   *Matthew, born 7 October 1628; died 12 October 1634 in Bocking.*
 vi.   *William, born October 1631; died 4 June 1641 in Ipswich.*
 vii. *Anne, born 2 June 1633; died 4 May 1634 in Bocking.*
 viii *Mary, born 20 February 1634; died 2 June 1720 in Watertown, Mass.; married Simon Stone in Watertown.*
 ix.   *Judith, born August 1636; died 27 June 1637 in Bocking.*
 x.   *Matthew, born 17 February 1637/38; died 30 March 1637/38 in Bocking.*
 xi.   *Sarah, born 3 November 1641 in Ipswich; died there 23 July 1681; married Joseph Goodhue in Ipswich.*

1677

The John Whipple House *(ca 1655)*, 1 South Village Green, Ipswich, Massachusetts 01938. Open 10 to 4 from early May to the middle of October. Closed Mondays and Tuesdays. Telephone 508-356-2811. The house was designated a Registered National Historic Landmark in 1966. Photo, courtesy Ipswich Historical Society.

JOHN'S FIRST MARRIAGE is not listed in St. Mary's parish register. Some genealogists have identified his wife as Sarah Hawkins, others as Susannah Stacy or Clark. It seems more plausible to this author that it was Susannah Stacy or Clark. Hawkins has been proposed by those who claim that the Whipple brothers married Hawkins sisters. Sarah and Anne Hawkins were married in Bocking in 1622: Anne to Matthew Whipple on May 7 and Sarah to William Coppin on September 26. Their brother, John Hawkins, Jr., by Will dated September 3, 1633 (proved October 18) made a bequeath to "my sister Whipple."[1] Hawkins' used names and identifying terms throughout the Will: wife Sara; children John, Robert, Sara, Margaret, Mary, Judith; mother Mary; brother Francis; sisters (by married name) Kent, Edes, Archer and Whipple; and brother-in-law John Kent. To be consistent, if he had two sisters who married Whipple men, he would have distinguished between them.

That John married Susannah Stacy is suggested by Elizabeth (Clark) Stace's (Stacy) 1670 nuncupative will[2] made in Ipswich, Mass., her daughter Ann Stacy's will in 1681/82, and a letter written by John Whipple's daughter Sarah in 1681 to her husband Joseph Goodhue.

Elizabeth Clark married Simon Stacy, Sr.[3] a clothier from Bocking November 6, 1620. Her maiden name was Clerke which may have evolved into Clark[4] The Stacy's immigrated at the same time as Matthew and John Whipple and Simon was granted "six acres of planting ground beyond the swamps next to John Whipple" in 1638.[5] Elizabeth's verbal will, proved 29 March 1670,[6] was expressed by her to her children Simon, Sarah, and Ann. In that will, She referred to her cousin John Whipple [Jr.]. Ann Stacy names her brother Simon, Jr. and sister Sarah in her will dated February 13, 1681/82 and appointed "my cuzen John Whipple [Jr.] senior executor". Whipple later presented the inventory of the estate to the court.[7] Sarah Whipple, in anticipation of death (she died a week later), wrote a letter to her husband deacon Joseph Goodhue on July 14, 1681 suggesting her husband give their 2-year-old son John to "her cuzen Simon Stacy"[8] to raise after her death.[9]

At that time, in addition to meaning the children of your aunt or uncle, cuzen was used to claim kinship or a relationship, hence the conclusion that Elder John Whipple's wife was either a sister of Simon Stacy or of his wife Elizabeth Clerke (Clark). Other Whipple-Stacy relationships are suggested by the fact that seven of the 12 persons named as heirs to Simon Stacy, Jr.'s estate sold their rights to col. Francis Wainwright of Ipswich, husband of "cuzen John Whipple's" daughter Sarah.[10] Also, Matthew, Jonathan, and James Whipple, grandsons of Matthew Whipple, were in possession of land in 1709 that had belonged to Thomas Stacy, son of Simon Stacy, Sr.[11]

John and Susanna were probably married in 1620 in Bocking and she died after 13 July 1661 in Ipswich.[12] John married Jennet (Brook) Dickinson, probably after April 1662. She was the widow of Thomas Dickinson who died in March 1662. The Dickinsons were among the early residents of Rowley, Mass. where he was a large landowner and held many positions of trust. They had six children. It appears John and Thomas had both been Clothiers. Dickinson's will dated March 8, 1661/62 bequeathed his "looms and furniture belonging thereto" to his son James.[13]

Of John and Susanna's 11 children, ten were born in Bocking and of those 10, six died at an early age ranging from one month to 10 years. Five of the six died in Bocking with William dying three years after they settled in Ipswich. Of their four sons, only Capt. John lived to marry and raise a family. Consequently, the number of descendants bearing Elder Whipple's surname is considerable less than for his brother Matthew and Capt. John Whipple of Dorchester, Mass. and Providence, R. I.

Elder John was the first of the Whipples to play a major role in the development of New England. The Whipples contributed to all aspects of early American life on the local and national level, serving in government, church, education, and the military. When a job was to be done or a controversial issue to be tackled, the Whipples were usually in the vanguard. It is a remarkable family that through subsequent generations continues to serve community, church, and state. *Emigrated 1638; settled Ipswich, MA 1639.*

The first reference in Ipswich records to the Whipples was September 1, 1638[14] when the seven selectmen granted Matthew "six acres of planting ground near the river" and John "six acres of planting ground next his brother on this side the swamp." They were jointly granted "two hundred acres" plus "meadow not to exceed forty five acres . . .to begin at Mr. Woodmansee's farm running toward Mr. Hubbard's farm." The acreage was to be "divided as they shall agree."[15]

Though not university trained his judicious nature and religious bent led John into a leadership role, holding significant power over the lives of his townsmen.[16] He was called on to lay out the land of new settlers, arrange for the exchange of land between citizens and the town, determine boundaries of lots granted by the town, construct fences, oversee the building of the cart bridge, etc.[17] He eventually played a major role in the religious life of the community, becoming a deacon in 1642 and a ruling elder in 1658. He associated with the Winthrops, Dudleys, Saltonstalls, Bradstreets, Denisons, Paines, Dodges, Lummuses, Wards, Symonds, Nortons, Hubbards — all leaders in Massachusetts church, political, and social life.

His first town assignment was keeping a herd of 86 young cattle from April 20, 1639 until the end of harvest. He was paid £15: 12d a head at the outset, 12d a head after midsummer, and 18d a head at the end of the term. He had help every other Sabbath[18] and had to pay for corn damaged because of his neglect.

Other assignments came quickly. On January 11, 1640/41, he and Matthew were named to the committee for "furthering trade amongst us." The committee was to arrange for the "putting up the buoys, beacons, and providing of salt, cotton, sewing of hemp seed, flax seed, and card wyer canes."[19] He received a second assignment the same day: to serve on the committee to advance fishing.[20]

On February 10, 1640/41, he was elected selectman[21] for a term of six months. He first served on the grand jury in 1641 and repeated that assignment on several occasions. He served several terms as a grand juror[22] and on June 14, 1642 was appointed clerk of writs for the Ipswich quarterly sessions court.[23]

As clerk of writs, he was especially busy just prior to the first, fourth, seventh, and ninth months of the year. The Ipswich court met the last Tuesday of the first and seventh months; the Salem court met the last Tuesday of the fourth and ninth months. One of the more interesting writs was issued September 4, 1653 to Edmon (Edmond) Marshall charged with defaming the wives of William Vincen (Vinset) and William Evans. Marshall called the women witches.[24] The most common writs were attachments of house and grounds, orchards, goods, cows, ground and garden, and disputes over accounts.

John was made a freeman May 13, 1640 and was immediately elected to the first of his eight terms as deputy to the general court by the freemen of Ipswich[25] Thomas Dudley was elected governor that year, defeating the incumbent, John Winthrop.[26] Richard Bellingham was elected deputy governor and Israel Stoughton of Dorchester an assistant. The Whipple-Stoughton conversation upon first meeting would have been interesting as Stoughton certainly would have inquired about a possible relationship with young John Whipple[27] who was indentured to Stoughton in 1632.

Deputies, while sharing fundamental beliefs with the magistrates, disagreed with them about the relationship between the citizen and government. Deputies supported an active political role for freemen and opposed divine magisterial power. They rejected the idea that their or God's happiness required government leaders to possess arbitrary power and insisted on a greater voice in defining the character of the common good.[28] This background should help us understand the dynamics of the general court when John arrived. His first session was the seventh session that magistrates had to compromise with deputies to pass legislation and run the commonwealth.

The court convened annually in Boston for four short periods requiring deputies to be away from work and family during both the planting and harvesting season. During this time, Susanna had to adjust to life in a rough frontier village. Lonely nights with young children must have been particularly hard because of the ever present threat of wolves and Indians. Anxiety for John's safety and fears for her own illness and exhaustion must have filled her mind and she must have pined for the graciousness and comfort of Old England. When John was home, she would have joined him in receiving and entertaining his guests.

During his eight terms, John had to take a position on many difficult issues with the three most controversial being formation of an interim governing committee,[29] the magisterial veto,[30] and the codification of Massachusetts law.[31] Each was a round in an ongoing fight.

The colony began registering land ownership as early as 1634 and in John's first term, the general court passed legislation that gave priority to recorded grants. Under this law, individuals who failed to record their purchases could lose their land to any later purchaser if the second purchaser recorded his deed first and did not know of the earlier sale. Soon thereafter the law was amended requiring the grantor's signature be witnessed and acknowledged by a government official or notary public.[32] These Massachusetts precedents became colonial law except in the southern colonies.[33]

Mundane assignments were also a part of legislative service and John got his share. In May 1640, he was on the committee to value horses, mares, cows, goats, and hogs in Ipswich; in June 1641, the committee to view where Rowley "may have their addition without prejudice to Cochituate, and to determine the bounds between them;" in December 1641, the committee to value the house and grounds William Whitred gave to Mr. William Tynge; in June 1642, the committee to levy and apportion a rate of £800 on the towns of the colony for the central government.[34]

John's first legislative session opened with controversy when the deputies chose rev. Nathaniel Ward of Ipswich to preach the election sermon. Outgoing governor Winthrop and the magistrates objected since Ward was no longer a practicing pastor. The deputies prevailed. On Ward's urging, a bill was introduced to prohibit magistrates from reviewing cases in advance of public hearings. Deputies supported the proposal, magistrates opposed.

John Humphrey, an original member of the Company of the Massachusetts Bay in New England, was the source of another controversy. He lost his barn, hay, and corn in a fire that winter, petitioned the court for help, and was awarded £250. Outraged by this special treatment, the public caused deputies to introduce a bill "to deny future benevolence." The magistrates opposed, arguing "the court should not deprive itself of its honor and blemish itself," that passing the bill would weaken the court's reputation "for wisdom and faithfulness." The bodies compromised by prohibiting future similar grants until the colony's debts were paid and the treasury replenished, "except upon foreign occasions, etc."[35]

The 1640 session adopted punishment for unmarried fornication. The debate centered around master and servant with the court deciding to follow the law of God by requiring a guilty master to marry the maid or pay a sum of money to her father. Servants were to be whipped for abusing the master in his house.[36]

Richard Bellingham was elected governor in May 1641, John's second term. The governor's November marriage caused an uproar as the bride had previously "contracted" to marry a friend of Bellingham who lived in the governor's home. The governor claimed his bride was not "absolutely" promised and that "the strength of his affection" justified his action. The couple did not publish their intentions and the governor violated general practice by conducting the marriage ceremony, thereby ending his promising political career. Winthrop was elected governor in 1642.[37]

John's second session (1641) was probably the most important of his eight terms. After three years of review by the freemen in all towns, Nathaniel Ward's *Body of Liberties* was adopted as the law of the commonwealth. The new laws extended dower rights of women and abolished pure primogeniture,[38] concepts that were radically different from English law. It included strict rules against battering wives or servants, rules unheard of elsewhere. Laws protecting "Brute Creatures" were the first extensive animal protection laws ever. There was no reference to crown, the charter, or to English authority. With the exception of the section on "Capital Laws," which listed crimes punishable by death taken from the Old Testament, it was a totally new initiative in law making. John and his fellow deputies were both visionary and radical: visionary in guaranteeing human dignity and radical for going beyond English precedence. All Americans are in their debt for this bold action.

A great thunder and lightning storm began as the court was sitting June 22 1642. Lightning struck the upper sail of the windmill by the ferry, shattering it into many pieces, setting the mill on fire, and knocking the miller unconscious. The hair on one side of his head and beard was singed and one of his shoes torn off. It was the next day before he regained his senses, giving the lawmakers cause for concern that God might be trying to tell them something.[39]

A memorable constitutional change — the bicameral legislature — evolved from this session. The catalyst was Capt. Robert Keayne, an unpopular, well-to-do, highly connected merchant from Boston. After the elders cleared Keayne of extorting a pig from Goody Sherman, a poor Boston widow, she appealed to the inferior court. Keayne won again and was awarded £3 costs and £20 damages. A witnesses later admitted he lied to the inferior court so the general court agreed to hear the case. John and his fellow legislators spent the best part of seven days examining witnesses and debating the case but failed to reach the required majority decision by both deputies and magistrates.[40]

Based on Keayne's reputation — previously censored by both the court and his church — the public sided with Sherman. When she lost in the legislature, many freemen spoke "unreverently of the court, especially the magistrates" feeling their "negative voice had hindered the course of justice and that magistrates must be put out so the power of the negative voice might be taken away."[41] Two years of political maneuvering followed before the legislators agreed to divide the general court into two separate houses, each possessing veto power over decisions of the other.[42]

Apparently the clerk of writs job was so demanding John didn't return to the general court until May 1646 when he and Mr. William Hubbard were elected to represent Ipswich.[43] Winthrop was governor that year, Dudley deputy governor. This was John's first bicameral session and he undoubtedly welcomed the opportunity to debate issues free from the magistrate's intimidating presence. Deputies now recognized their importance in Bay politics and valued themselves as more than freemen whose only official responsibility was carrying town grievances to the general court; they had developed a pride in their independent role within the legislature.[44]

Religion[45] and a need for a body of laws to protect all citizens dominated the session. Some elders (church leaders) asked the court to authorize a synod[46] to be held at the end of summer. The magistrates agreed but the deputies believed civil authorities should not require churches to send messengers to it. Deputies argued that Christ had not given them that power or authorized a synod to agree on a uniform practice and compel all churches to conform. The magistrates insisted they had power to compel advice in ecclesiastical matters, either of doctrine or discipline; that they were bound by God to maintain the churches in purity and truth; that the synod would only offer counsel from the word of God with the court at liberty to authorize or ignore its actions. The debate resulted in an amended bill allowing a synod which could recommend but not command the churches to send representatives.[47]

The Grand Remonstrance was a major issue in the 1646 session. John and his colleagues debated the merits of a petition by Robert Child and six other non-freemen claiming the colony's government was arbitrary and failed to follow the laws of England as required by the charter. They denied the government's right to require church attendance, to levy taxes to support Puritan ministers, and to restrict freeman-ship, which included the right to vote and hold office, to church members. They sought a body of laws to replace the incomplete *Body of Liberties*, demanded all members of the Church of England be admitted to communion, and threatened to appeal to parliament if their demands were rejected. Granting their demands they said would result in "piety quickened, discontents allayed, business improved, taxes lightened."[48]

Because the Remonstrance was presented near the end of the session, formal consideration was postponed to the autumn session. In the interim, Remonstrance backers generated widespread support, especially among the younger generation, causing Ipswich magistrate Samuel Symonds to seek Winthrop's support to offset the proponents. Ministers denounced the petitioners as sons of Levi,[49] sons of Belial,[50] and subverters of church and state. Robert Child, leader of the petitioners, was labeled a Jesuit because he had once visited Rome.

When the court reconvened, governor Winthrop and deputy governor Dudley were ready. To the charge of unjust taxes they asked how the government could be more penurious, noting that some magistrates served without salary, that no money was spent on feasting, pensions, public gratuities, and the like. Regarding the rights of Englishmen, they denied there ever was a right to vote. On the issue of church membership, they said if the petitioners are as sober and godly as they claim, they should not 'boggle at the covenants of these churches' but should join and become freemen. They suggested those who espoused religious toleration as a practical policy move to Rhode Island.

The general court adopted a "Declaration of 1646" attacking the Remonstrance and claiming the colonial government was consistent with the charter and the laws of England. Magistrates Saltonstall, Bradstreet, and Bellingham dissented. The remonstrants[51] were fined and summoned before the court and informed they had transgressed the Apostle's rule "that ye study to be quiet and to do your own business (Thess.[52] IV, II)" and likened to Korah, Dathan, and Abiram,[53] who "gathered themselves together against Moses and against Aaron. . ." To offset concerns in England, the court[54] sent Mr. Edward Winslow to London with two sets of instructions: one general in nature to be published, and one secret to be used only if specific questions were asked.[55]

What was John's position on the Remonstrance? Did he debate the proper relation of a dependency to the mother state as a deacon advocating the conservative views of the church or did he share the more progressive views of his friend and confidant, magistrate Saltonstall? His great great grandson, General William Whipple, New Hampshire signer of the Declaration of Independence, would have recognized the answers to the objections as ideas which eventually led to the American revolution.

Supporters of the Remonstrance made an effort to elect a new governor and magistrates in 1647 but Winthrop won with an overwhelming margin.[56] The mind of the commonwealth was clearly for the existing order.

It was May 1650 before John again represented Ipswich in the general court. He served four consecutive terms before abandoning legislative service to concentrate on his religious duties. Mr. William Bartholomew was Ipswich's other deputy. Maj. Daniel Denison was his fellow deputy in 1651 and 1652, serving as speaker in 1652. John probably received major assignments and leadership roles that session. Joining John as Ipswich delegates in 1653 were Mr. George Gittens and Mr. Samuel Winsley.[57]

The court preserved class distinctions in 1650 by excluding whipping as a punishment for those titled Master and Mistress.[58] In 1651 it prohibited women from wearing gold, silver, or bone lace that cost more than 2s per yard, or silk hoods or scarfs unless their husbands were worth £200.[59] The penalty was 10s for each offense. Among those later charged with violating this law was Martha, the wife of Capt. John Whipple.[60]

While playing a major role in the development of the Bay colony in the 1640s and 1650s, John was a farmer and businessman, served as clerk of writs, as feoffee[61] of the grammar school, as witness and executor of wills, as feoffe in trust to the unfortunate.[62] Richard Saltonstall gave him power of attorney to act as his business agent when he returned to England in 1647.[63] By 1661, John had a 15-year-old servant, Cornelius Kent, to help in his many endeavors.[64]

In 1647, the year Matthew died, John formed a partnership with Robert and William Payne, John Whittingham, Jonathan Wade, and William Bartholomew to conduct a trade at Ipswich. The partnership expired January 24, 1652[65] and on September 28, as clerk of writs, John had to serve former partners, Robert and William Payne, who were being sued by another former partner, Jonathan Wade.

John also had his day in court. He sued Samuel Archer for illegally taking his horse, he and Edward Browne sued the town of Ipswich in January 1642, and he and his business partners sued Mr. Robert Knight in September 1647. The court ordered Knight to pay a bill of exchange for £220 13s. A Capt. Brigham sued John and William Paine; Payne countersued Brigham in January 1649. The issue was over a fishing voyage.[66]

He steadily increased his land holdings, adding to his acreage at various times. The town granted him eight acres March 25, 1643; four acres of meadow on the southeast side of the Mill river near his farm in 1644 or 1645, six acres of meadow on the other side of the Mill river February 7, 1647/48. He exchanged a parcel of upland by his meadow for a similar acreage elsewhere December 11, 1649.[67] By the time of his death in 1669, his farm contained about 360 acres and he had a house and approximately 100 acres in town.

John was also a leader in education.[68] Ipswich may have had a grammar school as early as 1636,[69] probably not a free school as there is no record of public support until 1643 when the town voted to raise £112 annually to run the school. Lionel Chute was school master until his death in 1644. Chute's widow, Rose, became John's sister-in-law in November 1646 when she married widower Matthew Whipple. There is no record of another school until January 11, 1650, when the Town granted "all that Neck beyond Chebacco river and the rest of the groups (up to Gloucester) line adjoining to it to benefit the school."[70] To provide income for the school, the land was leased "forever" to John Cogswell, Jr., his heirs, and assigns, for £5 in pork and beef, £5 in corn, and £4 in butter and cheese "at the current price" annually. Robert and William Payne, major Daniel Denison, and William Bartholomew were named feoffees.[71] On January 26, 1650/51, John was named one of five additional feoffees.[72]

The feoffees were to build, maintain, administer, and enlarge the school as needed; select the master; determine tuition; regulate all matters concerning the master and scholars; and "consider the best way to make provision for teaching to write and cast accounts." They hired Ezekiel Cheever as master[73] and he and his second wife Ellen Lathrop moved into a house on two acres donated by Robert Payne. Cheever's daughter and three sons were born there. Ipswich's grammar school, with its emphasis on reading, writing, and arithmetic, became famous for preparing students for entrance to Harvard.[74] Cheever's Latin grammar, The Accidence, the first elementary book for learners, was used for more than a century in New England schools.[75] John Whipple and Ezekiel Cheever became fast friends and jointly served in a variety of civic activities.[76]

John's religious service began when he was elected deacon sometime prior to October 1642.[77] He and Robert Payne were elected ruling elders in 1658 when Mr.

Hubbard was elected to serve as teacher with Mr. Norton. The ordination was November 17.[78]

The Cambridge Platform defined church officers as extraordinary or ordinary. Apostles, prophets, and evangelists were extraordinary. Elders and deacons were ordinary and fasted before ordination which was by the imposition of hands and prayer.

The Whipple of today may find interesting the qualifications and job description of deacons and elders. To be elected,[79] both deacons and elders had to demonstrate they were "tried and proved, honest, and of good report." Scripture determined qualifications. "Elders must be blameless, sober, apt to teach, and imbued with such other qualifications as are laid down in 1 *Timothy*: 3 and 2; *Titus*: 1, 6 to 9." Qualifications for deacons were outlined in *Acts*: 6, 3; 1 *Timothy*: 3, 8 to 11. Failure to live up to the qualifications resulted in removal by a vote of the congregation.

Deacons, sometimes called "Helps," were responsible for the temporal, not the spiritual, needs of the church. They were to have "the mystery of the faith in a pure conscience, endued with the Holy Ghost," to be "grave, not double tongued, not given too much to wine, not given to filthy lucre." They received offerings and gifts, kept the treasury, and served the Tables of the church: "the Lord's Table, the table of the ministers, and of such as are in necessity, to whom they are to distribute in simplicity." When contributions waned, they spurred greater giving. Contributions were collected on the Sabbath, not the Lecture day.[80]

They were to keep dogs out of the meeting house on Sabbath or Lecture days between noon and 3:00, keep the meeting house water tight, and approve construction of a gallery for use by "young men and youth". When the town voted to repair the meeting house on January 4, 1646/47, the deacons were responsible for overseeing the £20 repair.[81] The following year they were authorized to hire a man to keep the meeting house clean and to ring the bell and to determine a fair payment for the work.[82]

John's legislative service probably served him well in the Ipswich-Boston controversy over Mr. Norton in 1655. Before a teacher could be hired by a new church, permission was required from the existing church. A Boston church wanted to hire Norton but on February 23, 1655, Ipswich refused permission. Boston continued to press for the move so the general court ordered representatives of 12 churches to meet in council in Ipswich the second Tuesday of June 1655 and deliberate to a decision. Boston prevailed and Norton began duties there in 1656.

Elders joined pastors and teachers in acts of spiritual rule but did not participate in teaching and preaching.[83] They were expected to have attained "wisdom and judgment endued with the Spirit of God, able to discern between cause and cause, between plea and plea, and accordingly to prevent and redress evils, always vigilant and intending to see the statutes, ordinances, and laws of God kept in the church, and that not only by the people in obedience, but to see the officers do their duties." They "must be of life likewise unreprovable, governing their own families orderly . . . of manners sober, gentle, modest, loving, temperate."[84]

Ruling meant they were to call the church together upon any weighty occasion. Members were obliged to attend, could not leave until dismissed, could not speak until recognized by the elders, could be silenced in mid sentence, and could not contradict the judgment or sentence of elders without "sufficient and weighty cause." These rules were supposed to insure order and avoid disturbance and confusion.

Prospective members were subjected to a searching private examination by the elders, both as to "their knowledge in the principles of religion, of their experience in the ways of grace, and of their godly conversation amongst men." To qualify, applicants had to relate an instance of "the transforming operation of God in their lives." The examination determined their repentance from sin and faith in Jesus Christ. They had to "profess and hold in such sort, as may satisfy rational charity that the things are there indeed."[85] The weakest measure of faith was to be accepted "because weak Christians, if sincere, have the substance of that faith, repentance, and holiness which is required in church members and such have most need of the ordinances for their confirmation and growth in grace."[86]

Candidates for church membership were announced in church. Those "unfit to join" were to be reported to the elders. Approved candidates, if no one objected, were presented on the Sabbath, usually after evening exercises. All members were to be present. The candidate testified to the work of grace on his soul, professed faith, and stated his view of the constitution of the church and its officers, members, and their respective duties. A question-answer format was used for those who needed help. A show of hands confirmed acceptance and the ceremony concluded with the elders reading the covenant and the candidate promising to perform, with divine help, his obligations. Church membership meant access to the sacrament of the Lord's Supper, baptism for their children, and qualified males to be freemen of the commonwealth.[87]

Children of members were entitled to church privileges except the Lord's Supper. For this, they had to profess personal regeneration. So solemn was the privilege of baptism, non-regenerate members could not claim it for their children without acknowledging the truths of the Gospel and promising fidelity and submission to church discipline.[88]

It seems likely that John was a participant in the Boston Synod of 1662 which gave standing to these moral but non-regenerate members by establishing the Half-Way Covenant. This covenant provided a half way house between the world and full Christian discipleship. Candidates were required to display knowledge of religious truth, to publicly profess to guide their lives by gospel principles, and to commit to raise their children in the fear of God. A personal sense of "a change of heart" was not required. The Synod adopted seven propositions delegates believed conformed to Scripture as to "Who are the subjects of baptism?"[89]

The synod denied baptism to children of those not in covenant. It determined that "owning the covenant" was a solemn personal acceptance of a formal declaration of intention to do the best to lead a Christian life by association in worship and discipline with the recognized people of God.

The Anabaptism controversy became an issue in the last year of John's life. Anabaptists denied the validity of infant baptism and only baptized adults. They also advocated other religious and social reforms. The controversy began in March 1668 when Thomas Gould of Middlesex county refused to worship with the established church and, along with William Turner and John Farnham, Sr., established a Baptist church. The elders opposed the new church believing it would result in "a free school of seduction, wherein false teachers may have open liberty to seduce the people into ways of error, which may not be suffered." If Baptists were tolerated, "where shall we stop," they asked? They answered their own question, saying "Familists,[90] Socinians,[91] Quakers,[92] Papists"[93] would creep in "under the mask of Anabaptism."

After hearing the elders testify that God had given many warnings that "Anabaptism . . .hath proved an incendiary and vexation to church and state" and to allow the Baptists to flourish would open a "door for all sorts of abominations, to the disturbance not only of our ecclesiastical enjoyments, but also contempt of our civil order, and the authorities here established," the general court forbade the Baptists to hold meetings and ordered Gould, Turner, and Farnham out of its jurisdiction before July 20, 1668.[94]

The keeping of a journal seems to have been an important part of Puritan piety. John's Puritan credentials are unquestioned so the reader might assume he kept such a journal. If only such a legacy survived to modern times. The author has tried to imagine some of its contents in this recap of John's life. But the surface is only scratched. The fullness of his life as husband, father, legislator, farmer, businessman, grand juror, clerk of writs, deacon, elder, and observer of strange phenomenons staggers the imagination.

What, for example, did he write in his journal about the first comet to appear in the heavens of New England? It blazed forth from Orion[95] December 9-22, 1652. Another appeared from February 3 to March 28, 1661. Those who saw it shuddered at the tail of fire and believed famine, plague, or disaster would follow. They were told it was the beginning of the burning of the world. Church membership increased as a consequence and ordinances and services were more carefully observed as members prepared their souls for the great change that might come immediately and without further warning. Another "great and dreadful" comet streaked across the skies November 9, 1664, continuing, night after night, all winter. Its size and extreme brilliancy created great alarm. People believed it was "sent by God to awake the secure world," that it caused the plague in England the next summer, the war with the Dutch, and the burning of London the second year following.[96] The people turned to their elder and long-time community leader for answers and reassurance but John was probably as frightened as they. It is easy to imagine the people turning to him and equally difficult to imagine how he responded.

While no self-revealing journal survives, a letter written July 14, 1681 by his youngest daughter, Sarah Whipple Goodhue (wife of deacon Joseph Goodhue), reveals much of the characteristics and qualities of the family. Written under a strangely realized premonition her death would occur at the birth of her twins — her ninth and tenth children — the letter presents a fascinating picture of early Puritan life.[97]

It is the letter of a woman who would be rare in any age or era and reflects a deeply religious nature. It is filled with the spirit of self sacrifice, of courage, of fearlessness of death. It is full of love of parents, husband, children, affection for friends and neighbors, adoration of God. It reflects mental poise, moral purity, refinement of thought, and a cultural background. It paints a picture of the ideals of Puritanism and Puritan life.

Sherman L. Whipple, noted Massachusetts attorney and descendant of Matthew, said at the rededication of the Whipple House in Ipswich in September

1929, that Sarah's letter "not only exalts Puritanism to its proper place, but does honor to the parents to whom God sent this child as a priceless blessing."[98]

It is apparent that John Whipple was a man of strength, character, and good works. Few in Ipswich matched his labors on behalf of the public good. But he also had major personal losses to overcome. He lost his 10-year-old son William June 4, 1641, three years after settling in Ipswich. His brother Matthew died September 28, 1647, leaving him with responsibility for the joint family farm and business operations and probably as guardian of nephews John 15, Matthew 12, and Joseph 7. Susanna, his wife of 41 years died after July 13, 1661.[99]

As he neared the end of his life he probably thought about England and his home town of Bocking. His daughter Sarah and nephew Joseph, the only children not born in England, would have asked him about the land they would never see. John probably responded that when you lived to be as old as he, memory is a deceiver. His age showed in his sagging muscles, now turned to fat, joints needled with aches and pains, faded eyesight and diminished hearing. Eating was no longer enjoyable as there was little difference between sweet odors and foul, most food was tasteless, and his guts were often in windy rebellion, and fasting or purging didn't help.

But as is often the case with the elderly, the memories of youth probably returned. If so, he probably remembered the best of times, recalling childhood baths in a wooden tub with steamy water scented with powdered herbs and oils of flowers; Shrove-tide pancakes served with meat of a boiled hen;[100] black pudding when a pig was killed in the fall; a fat goose for Michaelmas;[101] cream and the tarts of fresh-picked berries on May Day; venison and frumenty — the red wheat perfectly boiled in cream and then cooked with sugar and eggs and saffron and cinnamon — on Twelfth Night;[102] fresh pears in August for Bartholomew tide;[103] new cider in the fall. But his best memory might have been of the black iron pot simmering on the hearth, a steam of rich odors rising from it; so thick you could float a pewter spoon on it.

His memory of the English weather would have been mostly in shades of gray — cold mists rising up ghostlike from gray earth and gray water. The remembrance of springtime may have included trees in their flower, leaves as delicate as if beaten into shape and brightness by goldsmiths, a sky filled with bird songs, meadows and pastures carpeted with red clover and loud with bees, and full of butterflies. He would have remembered orchards, gardens, grass and fields; the swollen Blackwater river surging over its banks; and the wasteland yellow and green with clusters of dandelions and buttercups, ragwort,[104] bright torches of delicate, ivy-leaved, yellow toad-flax,[105] golden bells of cowslip,[106] and yellow-white-eyed daisies.

Remembrances of the preparations for Midsummer Eve[107] probably flooded his memory. This was the time when five, fat, yellow fingers of St. James' wort and the blue feathery flowers of larkspur[108] were set over the doorway, crescents[109] held lights at doorways and gateways, bonfires prepared and tubs filled with water in case of fire, and fresh birch boughs gathered for decorations. It was a night of dancing, singing, eating, and drinking. Except for the old and sick and the very young, there was no sleeping on Midsummer Eve. It was a time of vigil, much like All Hallow's Eve,[110] to prevent your soul from escaping from your sleeping body. If unwatched, the soul of those supposed to die in the year to come left to inspect its final resting place. Only by staying awake in the company of others could you prevent the soul from leaving. Sometimes they waited by the churchyard to watch for lost souls flying by.

High summer would have been remembered as the last, long, soft days of August when harvest had begun with reaping and binding and stacking. He would have recalled fields of growing grain with the blue of the cornflower,[111] the purple patches of corn cockles,[112] and the scarlet poppies which danced in the breeze like a college of drunken cardinals. The family garden rich with red and white roses, iris, violets, pansy, the gilly-flower's[113] awash in butterflies; vegetables and various berries, melon, pumpkin, and squash in abundance would have come to mind as would the orchard with its apples, cherries, peaches, pears, walnuts, hazelnuts, and chestnuts.

Fall brought memories of the fair and a sky blue and gold with light changes casting long shadows; sunsets like coals of dying fire; a moon, huge and fat, a ruddy face among the glitter of crowded stars. The weeks of September before Michaelmas was harvest time; the reapers would sweep across the fields, stooping and kneeling with their sickles. The corn was cut and stacked, left to dry, then carted home to the barns; straw and stover[114] gathered. Nights belonged to the owls, days to crows and gulls gleaning the fields. The winter firewood was cut and stored close at hand. The year's last fruits were brought in and carefully stored. And then the rains began with its patter on the roof and gurgling down the spouts. That was when they sat by the fire with new cider, hazelnuts, and roasted chestnuts and darkened their teeth and tongues with the sticky sweetness of new-picked blackberries.

He would have told them of the grand parents they never met, of the life of a clothier, of queen Elizabeth and king James, of the old Whipple homestead on Bradford street in Bocking. John was glad Sarah and Joseph had bothered to ask. The memories were good.

John Whipple died June 30, 1669, two months shy of his 74th birthday. He made out his Will May 10 with his good friends rev. William Hubbard and Robert Day present to witness his mark. Physical weakness apparently caused him to sign with a mark. We know he could write as his signature is preserved in many documents. His Will was filed but not recorded. The Will and inventory — his estate was large for that period, totaling £444 1s — were presented in court at Ipswich September 28. Both can be found in Appendix 1 along with information on the John Whipple House built circa 1655. He had a farm of 360 acres, houses, and land "in ye Towne," with a hundred acres, plate valued at £6, books at £2, 8s., as well as the usual and some unusual household and farm gear.[115]

Bequeaths were give to this three daughters Susannah Worth of Newbury, "my eldest daughter," Mary Stone, and Sarah Goodhue and to son-in-law Anthony Potter. Jennett, his "beloved wife" was left ten pounds plus the fourteen pounds and the annuity of six pounds a year engaged unto her in the Articles of Agreement before our marriage. The fourteen which is to paid (both for time and manner of pay) according to said Agreement, viz: one third part in wheat, malt, and Indian corn, in equal proportions, the other two thirds in neat cattle under seven years old. Mr. William Hubbard and Mr. John Rogers, both ministers in Ipswich, were appointed overseers with "power to determine any difference that may arise betwixt my executor, and any of the legatees, aforesaid, about the payments aforesaid." Son John Whipple was named sole executor and given all the rest of the estate, both houses, lands, cattle, debts from whomsoever due, and to his heirs forever.

Less than half of his life — 31 years — were spent in Massachusetts Bay. But what a productive and meaningful 31 years. The people of Ipswich and the commonwealth were the beneficiaries of his time among them.

ENDNOTES — CHAPTER 3

1. His Will, dated 3 Sept. 1633, was proved 18 Oct. 1633. He left his "sister Whipple 40 shillings as remembrance from me."

2.. A nuncupative will is an oral declaration of a person made before witnesses during a last illness, where a written will would not be possible. Such oral wills are rarely upheld today because of the opportunity for fraud and because of the detailed requirements for their validity. Today they are most often used by persons in military service and are generally restricted to personalty and cannot transfer real property.

3. Also spelled Stace.

4. "Stacy, Simon, of Bocking, co. Essex, clothier, and Elizabeth Clerke, of Theydon Garnon, said county, spinster, daughter of Stephen Clerke, of same, yeoman — at Theydon Mount, co. Essex, 6 Nov. 1620." Joseph Foster, editor, *London Marriage Licenses, 1521-1869*. Bernard Quaritch. (London. 1887). p. 1273.

5. George A. Schofield, editor and publisher, *The Ancient Town of Ipswich, 1634-1650*, Vol. 1, Chronicle Motor Press, Ipswich, 1899. There is no page numbering in this publication. However, the author has numbered the pages and this reference is on pages 38-9.

6. *Essex County, Probate Files*, No. 26069.

7   *Essex County, Probate Files*, No. 26052. Ann died in Ipswich 21 Feb. 1681. *Ipswich Vital Records*, Deaths, 682. Simon Stace, Jr. and John Whipple, Jr. were appointed on 27 April 1678 to take the inventory of the estate of Edward Chapman of Ipswich (*Essex County Probate Files*, Docket 5018) and on 30 May 1680 to take the inventory of the estate of Renold Foster, Sr. of Ipswich (*Ipswich Deeds*, vol. 4:402-4). On 29 March 1659, Elder John Whipple and Thomas Stace were appointed overseers for the two children of William Adams, Jr. of Ipswich (*Ipswich Quarterly Court Records*, vol. 1:74 and vol. 5:56). William Adams' wife was Elizabeth Stacy. Their children were Simon, John, and William Adams.

8. This would be Capt. Simon (Symon) Stace, Jr. and his wife Sarah Wallis. They had no children. Both died in Ipswich; Simon on 27 October 1699 and Sarah on 21 Nov. 1711. Simon's Will mentions cornett John Whipple. *Essex Co., Mass., Probate*, 307: 105.

9. This is the third reference in 13 years to a relationship between the Whipples and the Stacys In all instances the word "cuzen" is used. Alternative spelling is "cosen". Kenneth W. Kilpatrick, *The Loving Cosens: Herbert Pelham, Sir Arthur Hesilrige, and Gov. Edward Winslow*. The NEHGS *Register* defines the term as follows: In the 17th century, when a man {A} called another man {B} 'cosen', {A} meant one of two things: either he was an uncle to {B}, or he and {B} were cousins in the modern sense, whether directly or by marriage — in other words, either {A} and {B}, or their wives (or one of the two men, and the other's wife), shared an ancestor in common. (As people of that era took very seriously the notion that, sacrament of marriage rendered a couple of one flesh— and therefore of one blood, as well — men who were cousins only by marriage, via their wives, nevertheless considered themselves every bit as genuinely related, and in exactly the same sense, as though they themselves shared the common ancestry.) In footnote 3 and 6 of the *Register* article, page 80, Prof. David H. Kelley writes "Cousin as a term of *address*, may in special circumstances, be extended to quite remote relatives — through association, common interest, courtesy in a special situation etc. — but 'cousin' as a term of *reference* is normally much more sharply limited— seldom applied to third cousins (except where the [sur]name is the same) and very rarely indeed to more remote relatives."

10. *Essex County Probate Records*, Vol. 310: 435; Essex County Deeds, Vols. 14, 26, 28; 16: 4-6.

11. *Essex County Deeds*, Vol. 21, 88.

12. Joseph B. Felt in *History of Ipswich, Essex, and Hamilton, Mass.*, first published in Cambridge, Mass. in 1834 calls her Sarah and gives her date of death as 14 June 1658 (p. 159.), Abraham Hammatt, *The Hammatt Papers, Early Inhabitants of Ipswich, Massachusetts, 1633-1700*, Genealogical Publishing Co., Inc. (Baltimore. 1980. Originally published in seven parts, Ipswich, 1880-1889), (p.405) repeats both statements. Neither offer proof. This author poses the date "after 13 July 1661" which is the date Elder John Whipple signed the Marriage Contract between the Whipple and Goodhue families arranging the marriage of Sarah Whipple and Joseph Goodhue. In the contract John Whipple states, "I do promise and engage that at ye decease of my wife Susanna and Myself that I give unto my daughter Sarah . . ." (See Appendix 1 for the Marriage Contract.

13. Many Rowley men were clothiers or cloth-workers and were noted throughout the colony for this skill. A small woolen and fulling was built there in 1643. The Dickinson's daughter Sarah

married Jeremiah Jewett, son of Joseph Jewett, one of the founders of Rowley. Amos Everett Jewett and Emily Mabel Adams Jewett, *Rowley Massachusetts Mr. Ezechi Rogers Plantation 1639-1850.* Rowley, MA: *The Jewett Family of America,* Newcomb & Gauss Co., Printer, Salem, Mass. 1946, 117, 119, 147, 150, 211-12, 304-5.

14. Other writers have placed them there earlier. The year 1636 is frequently mentioned. The author has not been able to find any documentation showing them in Massachusetts earlier than September 1638.

15. At this same meeting, three six acre lots were reserved for three of Rev. Rogers' friends. The sites adjoined Rogers' 20 acre site near Heartbreak Hill. Simon Stace was granted six acres of planting ground "beyond the swamps next to John Whipple. Schofield. 38-9.

16. It is necessary to understand John was a businessman in England and that his experiences were quite different from many of the fellow townspeople. His habits differed from those who were farmers, laborers, and craftsmen in East Anglica. Each type of man had a distinct framework of reference, as well as a distinct realm of experience which generated tensions in the early years. As representatives of different areas arrived in New England, they were forced to adjust to each other's habits as they attempted to modify the basic English institutions and customs.

17. Schofield. 91, 93, 106, 113.

18. *Ibid.* 69

19. Card weyer cane: A brush with wire teeth used in disentangling fibers of wool, flax, or cotton and laying them parallel to one another preparatory to spinning.

20. Other members of the trade committee were Mr. Bradstreet, Mr. Robert Payne, Capt. Denison, Mr. Tuttle, and Mr. Saltonstall. Bradstreet, Mr. Hubbard, Mr Symonds, and Payne joined him on the fishing committee.

21. The other selectmen were Mr. Hubbard, Capt. Denison, Goodman Giddings, Mark Symonds, John Perkins, Sr., and Mr. William Payne. They were elected on condition they "give no lands, nor meddle with dividing or stinting of the commons." Schofield. 71-4, 78, 83, 85. Duties included land distribution, appointment of town officers, economic regulations and taxes, church affairs, farming, resolving personal quarrels in the community, relations with neighboring towns, relations with Indians, and relations with the government of the commonwealth.

22. Grand Jurors oath: You swear by the living God, that you will diligently inquire and faithfully present to this court whatsoever you know to be a breach of any law established in this jurisdiction according to the mind of God; and whatsoever criminal offenses you apprehend fit to be here presented, unless some necessary and religious tie of conscience truly grounded upon the word of God bind you to secrecy. And whatsoever shall be legally committed by this court to your judgment, you will return a true and just verdict therein according to the evidence given you, and the laws established amongst us: So help you God, &c. William H. Whitmore, Record Commissioner, *The Colonial Laws of Massachusetts,* reprinted from the editions of 1672, with the supplements through 1686, 2 vols. Boston: Rockwell and Churchill, City Printers, 1980, 2:167.

23. Replacing Mr. Giles Firman, Ipswich physician. Nathaniel B. Shurtleff, ed. *Records of Massachusetts 1628-1641.* Boston: 1853, 1:14. He was still serving as clerk in 1654. A writ is the document used to file causes for action. His duties: record births, deaths, and marriages, keep track of the town's brand marks, grant summons and attachments in civil actions, record horses shipped off, and keep a tollbook of all cattle sold. He was to provide the above information yearly to the clerk of the county court. Whitmore, 2: 173-4.

24. *The Essex Antiquarian,* Vol. 10, No. 1, January 1906. 84. This monthly magazine, whose first issue was January 1897, was devoted to the biography, genealogy, history, and antiquities of Essex County, Massachusetts. It terminated publication with Vol. 13, No. 4 when the editor wrote he was "worn out" after 13 years of researching original records about the county. In his "Notice of Discontinuance," he pointed out that 95% of its contents were researched and written by the editor and that he lacked the strength to continue "this labor of love." During its existence, it published genealogies of all families from Abbe to Brown; all gravestone inscriptions dated prior to 1800 in Amesbury, Andover, Beverly, Boxford, Brandford, Danvers, Essex, Georgetown, Gloucester, Groveland, Hamilton, Haverhill, and Ipswich; all wills proved in the county prior to June 1666; the record of the Essex county revolutionary soldiers and sailors alphabetically to Brown; abstracts of the old Norfolk records to 1675; Salem and Ipswich quarterly court records and files to 1659; and abstracts of all records in the first 10 volumes of the Suffolk county registry of deeds relating to Essex county persons and property, where parties resided or property was located in Essex county, for the period prior to 1678.

25. The governor, deputy governor, and assistants were also elected annually. John also served in 1641, 42, 46, 50, 51, 52, and 53. The terms deputy and representative are used interchangeably as are assistant and magistrate. The general court is known as the state legislature today. Prior to 1634, the general court (hereafter usually referred to as court) only included magistrates. Their arbitrary use of power caused the freemen to insist on being represented in that body and in May 1634, towns elected their first deputies. The court exercised the chief civil power of the commonwealth. Its power was as follows: . . . only hath power to raise money and taxes upon the whole country, and dispose of lands, viz. to give and confirm properties, appertaining to and immediately derived from the country; and may act in all affairs of this Commonwealth according to such power, both in matters of counsel, making of laws, and matters of judicature, by impeaching and sentencing any person or persons, according to law, and by receiving and hearing any complaints orderly presented against any person or courts; and it is agreed that this Court will not proceed to judgment in any cause, civil or criminal, before the deputies have taken this oath following:

    I do swear by the most great and dreadful name of the everliving God, that in all cases wherein I am to deliver my vote or sentence against any criminal offense, or between parties in any civil case; I will deal uprightly and justly, according to my judgment and conscience; and I will according to my skill and ability, assist in all other public affairs of this Court, faithfully and truly, according to the duty of my place, when I shall be present to attend the service. Whitmore, 2:34.

    No person could acquire ruling authority except at the polls. Freemen, either in person or by proxy, "were required by the patent, without any summons, to elect and send their deputies to the general court with full power to consult and determine such matters, as concern the welfare of this Commonwealth; from which general court no magistrate or deputy shall depart or be discharged, without the consent of the major part both of magistrates and deputies, during the first four days of the first session, under the penalty of one-hundred pounds, nor afterwards under such penalty as the Court shall impose . . ." Whitmore, 2:35.

    The magistrates' obligation to the towns or to the freemen who elected them was never clearly defined. What was magisterial authority? Governor Winthrop's position was their "authority came from God, in the way of an ordinance, such as hath the image of God eminently stamped upon it." He felt magistrates were free to govern the commonwealth as they alone saw fit. Ruling was reserved for a small and select group. Only the governor, deputy governor, and assistants were full-fledged magistrates. Winthrop believed John's duties as deputy were incidental responsibilities, detracting from his regular calling; that the Lord had not granted special ruling skills to such lesser officials. In short, deputies were not real magistrates. T.H. Breen, *The Character of the Good Ruler*, W. W. Norton and Company, Inc. (New York. 1974). xii, 59, 60.

    No one campaigned for office. To do so would cause dissension and demonstrate that the people who had covenanted with God were no longer united. However, freemen kept informed of their deputies' behavior, especially in time of crisis, and frequently instructed them how to handle specific legislation. And they checked to see if their instructions were followed, thus deputies could not ignore them.

    When John first joined the general court, the pay was 2s 6d a day for deputies; 3s 6d for magistrates. Towns, not the central government, paid them. The 1646 session enacted a law stating "that no more than a member and his horse shall be maintained." This suggests some representatives may have had family members fed and lodged at public expense.

26. It would be interesting to know who John supported. Dudley won in a close election, supported by those who were concerned that Winthrop had been in office too long and that the office would become hereditary if a change weren't made. As a fellow Ipswich resident, he undoubtedly supported Dudley.

27. Young John would have been in the colony eight years by 1640.

28. Breen. 69-70.

29. The issue was powers held by magistrates between sessions. Magistrates assumed both executive and judicial functions. They also heard cases of both original and appellate jurisdiction, raising serious questions about conflict of interest, since they were ruling on the fairness of decisions they had made earlier as judges in the lower courts. Deputies opposed this unrestricted interim power as it allowed the magistrates to indulge their arbitrary desires as soon as the representatives left the capital. Breen. 75-7.

30. Magisterial veto is also known as the negative voice

31. Massachusetts law was codified in Ward's *Body of Liberties* which deputies felt was ill-defined and

open to interpretation by individual judges. They wanted the colony's laws printed in alphabetical order so every man could see for himself the limits of magisterial authority. The magistrates resisted, believing codification a threat to their fundamental prerogatives. The deputies won this battle and in 1648, the court adopted *The Laws and Liberties of Massachusetts*. Breen. 81-2.

32. See *The Laws and Liberties of Massachusetts*, 13-14.

33. Virginia set a southern precedent by passing a law in 1639 protecting the original grantee if the grantor later conveyed to someone else even if the deed wasn't recorded. George R. Ryskamp, "Common-Law Concepts for the Genealogist: Real-Property Transactions," *National Genealogical Society Quarterly*, Vol. 84, No. 3, 177-8.

34. Shurtleff. 1:295, 319, 346, 2:13.

35. James Kendall Hosmer. ed., *Winthrop's Journal, History of New England, 1630-1648*. Two volumes. New York: Barnes & Noble, Inc., 1959, II:12, 38. Humphrey's wife Susan was a sister of the Earl of Lincoln. He was to be deputy-governor to Winthrop in 1630 but didn't arrive until June 1634. He settled in Lynn and was made an assistant. Life in the Bay was too arduous for his family so he sought and received appointment as governor of Providence in the West Indies. He made a major effort to recruit Bay folk to join him but the Spanish captured Providence before they left.

36. Hosmer II:43-4.

37. Hosmer, II:43-4, 58.

38. Primogeniture in law was the exclusive right of the eldest son to inherit his father's estate.

39. Hosmer. II:63.

40. The law required a majority of both magistrates and deputies to pass a bill. Two magistrates, Bellingham and Saltonstall, and 15 deputies voted for Sherman; seven magistrates and eight deputies for Keayne; seven deputies were undecided.

41. A minority of the court magistrates could veto bills supported by a majority of deputies. The first attack on the negative voice occurred in 1634. It was smoothed over with no action taken. In this instance, although losing, the representatives made it clear they were in a fight to the finish to eliminate the negative veto.

42. Hosmer. II:64-6.

43. The session lasted three weeks before adjourning to 7 Oct. Mr. Norris of Salem preached the election sermon. Deputy Endicott, who was serjeant (sic) general, and Mr. Pelham were elected commissioners for the United Colonies. Heretofore, magistrates and deputies chose the commissioners but freemen now considered them general officers subject to general election.

44. Breen. 83-4.

45. Two laws against Anabaptists and other heretics were extended this session.

46. Synod: A meeting of representatives of the churches. The Congregationalism of the 17th century required officers of civil government be consulted in all affairs concerning churches.

47. Hosmer. *Winthrop's Journal*, I:274. The congregations at Salem, Hingham, and Concord disputed the general court's authority and did not send representative to the meeting which began 1 Sept. Thirty to 40 of Boston's members opposed and on 3 Sept., at the regular church lecture, rev. John Norton of Ipswich, later to be teacher at the Boston church, preached to the Boston church. His text was of Moses and Aaron meeting on the Mount and kissing each other. He said the work of the synod would be consultative and declarative, not co-active; he documented the power of civil magistrates to call such assemblies; stressed the duty of churches to yield obedience; and emphasized the great offence and scandal refusing to attend would give. On Sunday 6 Sept., a majority of Boston's members voted to attend.

The Synod adjourned in Mid September, reassembled at Cambridge 8 June 1647 and concluded at Cambridge 15 Aug. 1648 by adopting a *Platform of Church Discipline*, primarily the work of Richard Mather of Dorchester and the rev. John Cotton of Boston. It established a standard by which New England churches might be regulated and innovation resisted and was presented in a manner that was not offensive to the Puritan party in England, whether Presbyterian or Independent, or to parliament.

It became known as the Cambridge Platform and represented the clearest reflection of Congregationalism by the first generation on American soil. It followed nearly 20 years of practical experience and resulted in the non recognition of the democratic element in politics while urging the right of civil magistrates to interfere in matters of doctrine and practice. It upheld Congregationalism as a polity of exclusive divine warrant. Williston Walker. *The Creeds and Platforms of Congregationalism.* The Pilgrim Press. (Boston. 1960. First published in 1893), 173, 182, 184, 185.

48.   Samuel Eliot Morrison, *Builders of the Bay Colony.* (Boston: Houghton Mifflin Company, 1930), 250-1.

49.   The treachery of Levi and Simeon towards a community which had received the rite of connubium with Israel is represented as a crime, which imperiled the position of the Hebrews and was fatal to the future of the tribes directly involved. Connubium: 1) lawful marriage 2) the right to intermarry.

50.   Belial: A Hebrew word often used as a proper name, but really an abstract term meaning worthless or wickedness.

51.   Child, who Winthrop styled "a stranger, a leader to the rest, and who carried himself proudly, etc., in the court," was fined £50; Mr. John Smith, being also a stranger, £40; Mr. Thomas Fowle, Mr. Thomas Burton, Mr. David Yale, and Mr. John Dane, £30 each; and Mr. Samuel Maverick, "because he had not as yet appealed," £10. It is believed that all petitioners except Maverick left the Bay Colony. Hosmer. *Winthrop's Journal,*. II:304-5.

52.   Thessalonians. Books of the new testament, the epistles from Apostle Paul to the Christians of Thessalonica.

53.   Reubenites who led a revolt against Moses in the interval between the return of the spies and the final march toward Canaan. In NU: 15-17, the revolt of Dathan and Abiram is confused with another revolt, that of Korah. It is impossible to interpret the narrative as it stands.

54.   The session began 4 Nov., and that night a northeaster struck, blowing off roofs, breaking anchors, and driving ships from their moorage.

55.   The secret instructions:

Objection 1. Why we make not our process in the king's name? You shall answer: 1) That we should thereby waive the power of our government granted to us, for we claim not as by commission, but by a free donation of absolute government. 2) For avoiding appeals, etc.

Objection 2. That our government is arbitrary. Answer: We have four or five hundred express laws, as near the laws of England as may be; and yearly we make more, and where we have no law, we judge by the word of God, as near as we can.

Objection 3. About enlarging our limits, etc. Answer: Such Indians as are willing to come under our government, we know no reason to refuse. Some Indians we have subdued by just war, as the Pequids. Some English also, having purchased lands of the Indians, have submitted to our government.

Objection 4. About our subjection to England. Answer: 1) We are to pay the one-fifth part of ore of gold and silver. 2) In being faithful and firm to the state of England, endeavoring to walk with God in upholding his truth, etc., and praying for it. 3) In framing our government according to our patent, so near as we may.

Objection 5. About exercising admiral jurisdiction. Answer: 1) We are not restrained by our charter. 2) We have power given us to rule, punish, pardon, etc., in all cases, ergo in maritime. 3) We have power granted us to defend ourselves and offend our enemies, as well by sea as by land, ergo we must needs have power to judge of such cases. 4) Without this, neither our own people nor strangers could have justice from us in such cases.

Objection 6. About our independency upon that state. Answer. Our dependency is in these points: 1) We have received our government and other privileges by our charter. 2) We owe allegiance and fidelity to that state. 3) In erecting a government here accordingly and subjecting thereto, we therein yield subjection to that state. 4) In rendering the one-fifth part of ore, etc. 5) We depend upon that state for protection and immunities as freeborn Englishmen.

Objection 7. Seeing we hold of East Greenwich, etc., why every freeholder of forty shillings per annum have not votes in elections, etc., as in England. Answer: Our charter gives that liberty expressly to the freemen only.

Objection 8. By your charter, such as we transport are to live under his majesty's allegiance. Answer: So they all do, and so intended, so far as we know.

Objection 9. About a general governor. Answer: 1) Our charter gives us absolute power of government. 2) On the terms above specified, we conceive the patent hath no such thing in it, neither expressed, nor implied. 3) We had not transported ourselves and families upon such terms. 4) Other plantations have been undertaken at the charge of others in England, and the planters have their dependence upon the companies there, and those planters go and come chiefly for matter of profit; but we came to abide here, and to plant the gospel, and people the country, and herein God hath marvelously blessed us. Hosmer. Winthrop's Journal, II: 314-15.

56. John did not stand for election in 1647, probably because of Matthew's (presumed) illness made additional demands on him to oversee their farming operation. Matthew died in September.

57. Shurtlett, 3:183, 220, 259, 297.

58. The ordinary respectable people were known as goodman and good wife, or goody.

59. Legislation was passed in 1639 against "women's sleeves more than half an ell (measure of length equal to 45 inches) wide in the widest places, immoderate great breeches, broad shoulder bands and rayles, silk roses, double ruffs and cuffs, etc." Short, cropped hair, in obedience to Paul's injunction, was the ideal of the sterner Puritans but from the beginning the more frivolous wore long hair. Rev. Ezekiel Rogers of Rowley was so bitter in his detestation of long hair he disinherited his nephew because he persisted in wearing his long. On 10 May 1649, governor Endicott and deputy governor Dudley and seven assistants declared: "Forasmuch as the wearing of long hair after the manner of ruffians and barbarous Indians has begun to invade New England, contrary to the rule of God's work, which says it is a shame for a man to wear long hair, etc., we, the magistrates, who have subscribed to this paper, (for the showing of our innocency in this behalf) do declare and manifest our dislike and detestation against the wearing of such long hair, as against a thing uncivil and unmanly whereby men do deform themselves, and offend sober and modest men, and do corrupt good manners. We do, therefore, earnestly entreat all the elders of this jurisdiction (as often as they shall see cause to manifest their zeal against it in their public administration) to take care that the members of their respective churches be not defiled therewith; that so such as shall prove obstinate and will not reform themselves, may have God and man to witness against them.

In 1651, the general court declared its "utter detestation and dislike that men or women of mean condition, educations, and callings should take upon them the garb of gentlemen by wearing of gold and silver lace, or buttons, or points at their knees, to walk in great boots, or women of the same rank to wear silk or tiffany hoods or scarfs, which though allowable to persons of greater estate or more liberal education, yet cannot but judge intolerable in person of such like condition." (John Lilburne published a book in 1637 setting forth 39 articles of religion for Englishmen to follow. Item 35, sub 6 includes a prohibition "against excess of apparel."

60. Her husband was able to show he was worth £200 so the charge was dismissed. Perzel, 10. However at the Ipswich quarterly court in 1653, included among the 11 women presented as being in violation was Sarah Kent, wife of Lt. John Whipple. Lt. John was the son of Matthew. The women were charged with wearing silk hoods. Lt. John was able to prove his worth exceeded £200. The Essex Antiquarian, Vol. 10, No. 2, April 1906, 85, 88. See also Hammatt, 268.

Only two of the 11 women were fined. One woman presented a letter from her husband admitting he was not worth £200 but he listed four good reasons his wife should wear a silk scarf and hood: 1) she was brought up to it. 2) I am bound by conscience and love to maintain my wife's honor and that good education she was brought up in but neither conscience nor love doth yet teach me to maintain her worse than I found her. 3) when she doth wear a scarf it is not because she would be in the fashion or that she would be as fine as other, but 4) for the necessity and preserving of health, and this appears to me thus because she ordinarily wears a scarf but two seasons, the first is in winter when it is very cold, the other season is when it is very wet weather. More, I conceive if she did wear her scarf for pride she would be as proud in summer as she is in winter and in dry weather as in wet. Morison, 162-3.

61. Feoffee: Similar to a school board member.

62. On 1 July 1652, John and Lt. Samuel Appleton were named feoffees in trust to prosecute John Langton "for evil usage" of a little child of his wife. The child was ordered to live with his grandparents, the William Varneys. The Essex Antiquarian, Vol. 7. No. 3, July 1903. 130.

63. See Ipswich Deeds 2:6. Saltonstall gave authority to John and others "to act and deal in and about all my estate and every part and parcel thereof in Ipswich.

64. Register, 6:345.

65. The Essex Antiquarian, Vol. 11, No. 2, 1907, 84-5.

66. Ibid. All citations are in Vol. 8. No. 4, October 1904, 169; No. 1, January 1904, 5, 11; No. 3, July 1904, 109.

67. Schofield, 97, 109, 122, 128.

68. The inventory of his estate included several books valued at £2 8s., indicating his personal household contained some of the literature of the time.

69. According to Abraham Hammatt, Esq., "Ipswich Grammar School," *Register*, 6: 64-5. Thomas Franklin Waters says the first grammar school was established in 1642. See *Ipswich In The Massachusetts Bay Colony*, Part I. The Ipswich Historical Society. 1905. Schofield says the town authorized a free school in November 1643 and limited the number of students "not to exceed seven." 93, 99.

70. The grant was made after Robert Payne committed to give land and a building for a school provided "certain discreet and faithful persons would manage it as feoffes" and provided the town would "devote, set apart, and give any land or other annuity" for its yearly maintenance. Payne was one of the richest of Ipswich's earliest settlers. He was deputy to the general court in 1647, '48, '49, county treasurer from 1665 to 1683, and elected ruling elder at the same time as John Whipple. He died in 1684, age 82. *Register*. 6:1852. p. 65.

71. *Register*,. 6:64.

72. Hammatt gives the year as 1650, Waters as 1652. The other four were Mr. William Hubbard, Mr. Jonathan Norton, Mr. Nathaniel Rogers, and Mr. Samuel Symonds. Hammatt described the feoffees as "remarkable men who lived in an age distinguished for other remarkable men." He speculated that some "may have had their Latin whipped into them by John Milton; some may have heard William Shakespeare 'warble his native wood notes;' and some, undoubtedly, had been exposed to Francis Bacon." He opined they realized educated citizens who knew their rights would be ready to defend them; that a portion of the people must be highly instructed so they could be the guides and teachers of others. *Register*, 6:65-7.

73. Ezekiel Cheever was born in London about 1615, educated at Emanuel, former teacher at New Haven where he was considered a brilliant success.

74. According to Cotton Mather, "When scholars had so far profited at the grammar schools that they could read any classical author into English, and readily make and speak true Latin, and write in verse as well as prose; and perfectly decline the paradigms of nouns and verbs in the Greek tongue, they were judged capable of admission in Harvard College."

75. At least 20 editions of Cheever *The Accidence* were published.

76. The will of rev. Nathaniel Rogers was proved 26 Sept. 1655 by the oaths of Deacon John Whipple and Mr. Ezekiel Cheever. *Register*, 5:139.

77. On 19 Nov. 1642 the town ordered payment "to our Deacon Jo: Whipple 15s. 6d according to money or in money being due to him as appeareth upon the account of the said Jo: Whipple delivered the 31st of the 8th mo. 1642." Thomas Franklin Waters. *The John Whipple House in Ipswich, Mass. and the People Who Have Owned and Lived In It*. Publications of the Ipswich Historical Society. XX. 1915, 8. On 3 Nov. 1655, the general court ordered Deacon John Whipple, Mr. Samuel Hall of Salisbury, and Ensign Thomas Howlet a committee to determine the boundary between Newbury and Rowley. They reached agreement and made their report to the general court 17 March 1655/56. Amos Jewett and Emily Jewett, Rowley, Massachusetts *Mr. Ezech Rogers Plantation 1639-1850*. Published by the Jewett Family of America, Newcomb & Gauss Co., Printer, Salem, Mass., 1946, 15.

78. *Ibid*.

79. Church members willingly submitted to the officers they elected.

80. Walker, 213, 214, 221.

81. £140 to pay the ministers was voted at the same election.

82. Schofield, 88, 93, 98, 113, 117.

83. Elders' duties:

1) To open and shut the doors of God's House by the admission of members approved by the church; by ordination of officers chosen by the church; and by excommunication of notorious and obstinate offenders renounced by the church; and by resorting of penitents, forgiven by the church.

2) To call the church together when there is occasion, and seasonably to dismiss them again.

3) To prepare matters in private, that in public they may be carried to end with less trouble, and more speedy dispatch.

4) To moderate the carriage of all matters in the church assembled. As, to propound matters to the church, to order the season of speech and silence; and to pronounce sentence according to the mind of Christ, with the consent of the church.

5) To be guides and leaders to the church, in all matters whatsoever, pertaining to church administrations and actions.

6) To see that none in the church live inordinately out of rank and place; with a calling, or idly in their calling.

7) To prevent and heal such offenses in life, or in doctrine as might corrupt the church.

8) To feed the flock of God with a word of admonition.

9) And as they shall be sent for, to visit and to pray over their sick brethren.

10) And at other times as opportunity shall serve unto. Walker, 212.

84. *Ibid*, 36.

85. Most first generation Puritans were unable to show sufficient evidence of faith and experience to be admitted.

86. Walker, 222.

87. Joseph B. Felt, *The Ecclesiastical History of New England*, Congregational Library Association and the Congregational Board of Publication. Vol. I. (Boston. 1855). 429-31.

88. Adult children, baptized and educated in the faith, well grounded in the knowledge of Christian truth, students of the Bible, and interested listeners in the sanctuary, who wanted to raise their families in the same way, and who were moral and earnest in their lives but could not claim the experience their parents called "a change of heart," were not full members. They were unregenerate members, entitled to transmit membership and baptism to their offspring, but their non-regenerate character denied them communion.

89. John may have played a major role in the deliberations of this synod. The Ipswich church began deliberating the concept of the Half-Way Covenant as early as 1653 when rev. Nathaniel Rogers endorsed the concept. It was not until 1656 under Rev. Thomas Cobbet that the church took a position. It was probably the first church in New England to adopt the rule of the Half-Way Covenant. They agreed as follows:

We look at children of members in full communion, which were about [i.e. not more than] 14 years old when their father and mother joined the church, or have been born since, to be members in and with their parents.

We look upon it as the elder's duty to call upon such children, being adults, and are of understanding, and not scandalous, to take the covenant solemnly before our assembly. We judge that the children of such adult persons that are of understanding, and not scandalous, and shall take the covenant, shall be baptized.

That notwithstanding the baptizing the children of such, yet we judge that these adult persons are not to come to the Lord's Supper, nor to act in church votes, unless they satisfy the reasonable charity of the elders or church, that they have a work of faith and repentance in them. Walker, 256.

The synod of 1662 deliberated to seven propositions delegates believed conformed to Scripture as to "Who are the subjects of baptism?" 1) They that according to Scripture, are members of the visible church, are the subjects of baptism. 2) The members of the visible church according to Scripture, are confederate visible believers, in particular churches, and their infant-seed, i.e. children in minority, whose parents, one or both, are in covenant. 3) The infant-seed of confederate visible believers, are members of the same church with their parents, and when grown up, are personally under the watch, discipline, and government of that church. 4) These adult persons, are not therefore to be admitted to full communion, merely because they are and continue members, without such further qualifications, as the Word of God requireth thereunto. 5) Church members who were admitted in minority, understanding the doctrine of faith, and publicly professing their assent thereto; not scandalous in life, and solemnly owning the Covenant before the church, wherein they give up themselves and their children to the Lord, and subject themselves to the government of Christ in the church, their children are to be baptized. 6) Such church members, who either by death, or some other extraordinary Providence, have been inevitably hindered from public acting as aforesaid, yet have give the church cause, in judgment of charity, to look at them as so qualified, and such as had they been called thereunto, would have so acted, their children are to be baptized. 7) The members of orthodox churches, being sound in the Faith, and no scandalous in life, and presenting due testimony thereof; these occasionally coming from one church to another, may have their children baptized in the church whither they come, by virtue of communion of churches: but if they removed their habitation, they ought orderly to covenant and subject themselves to the government of Christ in the church where they settle their abode, and so their children to be baptized. It being the church's duty to receive such unto communion, so far as they are regularly fit for the same. Walker.

90. Familists: A sect that propagated a vague philanthropism of pantheistic hue and Antinomian

tendencies. Philanthropic — implies interest in the general human welfare. Pantheism — the doctrine that God is not a personality, but that all laws, forces, manifestations, etc. of the self-existing universe are God. Antinomian — a beliver in the doctrine that faith alone, not obedience to the moral law, is necessary for salvation. Familists eventually joined the Quakers.

91. Socinians: A sect that denied the essential divinity of Christ; rejected the natural immortality of man. Toward the end of the 16th century, it moderated into Unitarianism as practiced by the upper classes.

92. Quakers: A sect founded by George Fox in England in 1650 and known as the Society of Friends. Friends have no formal creed, rites, liturgy, or priesthood, and reject violence in human relations, including war.

93. Papist: 1) a person who believes in papal supremacy. 2) a Roman Catholic. In the 1600s, a hostile term.

94. Felt. *Ecclesiastical History of New England*,.II:423-27.

95. Orion: An equatorial constellation near Taurus, containing the bright stars Rigel and Betelgeuse.

96. "Early Comets," *Essex Antiquarian.*,Vol. 2, No. 5, May 1898.

97. The letter is reproduced in Chapter 3

98. Sherman L. Whipple, Esq., and Thomas Franklin Waters, *Puritan Homes*, Publications of the Ipswich Historical Society XXVII. Newcomb & Gauss Co., Printers. (Salem. 1929), 13.

99. Felt, *History of Ipswich*, etc., 159.

100. Shrove is a time of confession; specifically the period between the evening of the Saturday before Quinquagesima Sunday and the morning of Ash Wednesday, as being the period when people were shriven in preparation for Lent. Shriven is a past participle of shrive. Shrive is to go to your confessor in the week immediately before Lent and confess your deeds and the confessor prescribes penance for sin. In Essex and Suffolk, at Shrove-tide or upon Shrove Tuesday, after the confession, it was usual for the farmer to permit his ploughman to go to the barn blindfolded and "thresh the fat hen," saying, "if you can kill her then give it to thy men and go you and dine on fritters and pancakes."

101. Michaelmas: A festival celebrated by the Roman, Anglican, and other churches on 29 Sept. in honor of the archangel Michael. It is also one of the four quarter days in England when tenants pay their quarter's rent. They bring foul at Midsummer, fish at lent, a capon at Christmas, a goose at Michaelmas. An archangel is an angel of high rank.

102. Twelfth Night: The end of the festival of the Epiphany.

103. St. Bartholomew tide: The season near St. Bartholomew's day (August 24).

104. Ragwort: An erect herb, 2 to 4 feet high, with bright yellow heads; also called St. Jameswort.

105. Yellow-toad flax: A popular name of the European plant linaria vulgaris; extended as a generic name to other species of linaria, as Ivy-leaved Toad-flax.

106. Cowslip: A wild plant in pastures and grassy banks, blossoming in the spring, with drooping umbels of fragrant yellow flowers.

107. Summer was considered to begin in May. Midsummer Eve, or the eve of the Feast of St. John Baptist, was celebrated June 24. It was the custom to kindle fires (called St. John's fires) upon hills in celebration of the summer solstice. Various superstitious practices and wild festivities were observed on this occasion.

108. Larkspur: A plant with a spur-shaped calyx. The calyx is is the outer whorl of protective leaves, or sepals of a flower, usually green. A whorl is a circular growth of leaves, petals, etc. about the same point on a stem. A sepal is any of the usually green, leaflike parts of the calyx.

109. Crescent: A device shaped like the moon during its first quarter.

110. All Hallow's Eve: The evening of 31 Oct., the eve of the vigil of All Hallows or All Saints' day (1 Nov.); known today as Halloween. All Hallow's Eve was an occasion of popular superstitions and observances in many Christian countries. Fairies, witches, and imps of all kinds were supposed to be especially active that night.

111. Cornflowers: the name given to various plants commonly found growing amongst corn.

112. Corn cockles: A plant with handsome reddish-purple flowers succeeded by capsules of numerous black seeds, which grows in cornfields, especially among wheat.

113. Gilly-flower: Plants whose flowers are scented like a clove.

114. Stover: Cured stalks of grain, without the ears, used as fodder for animals.

115. Essex Co., Probate, printed 2: 166.

4 CAPTAIN JOHN WHIPPLE FAMILY

John² Whipple (John¹, Matthew^) baptized 25 December 1625 in Bocking, Essex County, England; died 10 August 1683 in Ipswich, Essex County, Massachusetts. He married (1) Martha Reyner about 1653 at Ipswich. She died 24 February 1679 in Ipswich (2) Mrs. Elizabeth (Cogswell) Paine 28 June 1680 at Ipswich. John emigrated to Massachusetts Bay colony in 1638 with his parents when he was almost 13 years old. He was an entrepreneur and started a number of business in Ipswich. He was an officer in King Philip's War, served as selectman, Essex county treasurer, and Ipswich's representative to the general court for four years between 1674-1683. He left an estate of £3,000. John and Elizabeth had no children.

Children of John and Martha Whipple, all born in Ipswich:

    i. *John (Major), born 15 July 1657; died 12 June 1722 in Ipswich; married Kathrin Layton 6 June 1681.*

    ii. *Matthew (Major), born in 1658; died 28 January 1739 in Ipswich; married (1) about 1684 Jemima Lane (2) Johanna Appleton about 1688 (3) Mrs. Martha (Denison) Thing 11 June 1697. He and Johanna were the grandparents of Gen. William Whipple who signed the Declaration of Independence for New Hampshire.*

    iii. *Susanna, born in 1661; died 4 August 1713 in Billerica, Mass; married Major John Lane 2 January 1681.*

    iv. *Joseph, born 6 March 1664; died in August 1665 in Ipswich.*

    v. *Joseph, born 8 June 1666; died 11 May 1699 in Ipswich; married Mary Symonds 10 December 1697.*

    vi. *Sarah, born 2 September 1671; died 16 March 1709 in Ipswich; married Col. Francis Wainwright 12 March 1686. no children.*

IT IS HARD TO IMAGINE John Whipple, Jr. acquiring an estate of £3,000 and matching his accomplishments had he remained in Bocking, England. Granted, he was building on a foundation laid by his father, but he had to be a man of energy and drive to accomplish so much. A man in similar circumstances in Bocking would have spent as much labor and cost for an acre or two of land. John saw opportunity in the new land and took advantage of it.

The primeval qualities of New England were strikingly different from what John and his parents left in old England. No longer were they surrounded by associations that went back beyond memory. Nothing in their new home was "time-honored" and this proved to be a benefit to John because he was able to see opportunities and was willing to open the door when they knocked.

The general court passed a new law October 14, 1651, two years after John and Martha were married. This law encouraged people to be moderate in the "use of those blessings which, beyond our expectations, the Lord hath been pleased to afford unto us in this wilderness." The court declared its "utter detestation and dislike that men or women of meane condition, education, and calling" who wore the "garb of gentlemen" including "gold or silver lace, or buttons, or points at their knees," and who walked "in greater boots," and women who wore "silk or tiffany hoods or scarfs."

The law prohibited any person "or any of their relations depending on them" whose visible estates, real and personal, did not exceed "the true and indifferent value of £200" from wearing gold or silver lace, or gold or silver buttons, or any bone lace above two shillings per yard, or silk hoods or scarfs. The penalty per offense was set at 10 shillings.

Initially the complaints came fast and furious including one against Martha Whipple who was presented in the Ipswich court September 27, 1653 for wearing a silk hood.[1] The charge was dropped when John proved he was worth £200. Eventually the law was ignored because it exempted members of the court, making it a very unpopular law.[2] Not only was John, but her father, Humphrey Reyner who lived in Rowley, Massachusetts, was also a man of considerable means. He died in 1660 and left an estate appraised at £865. Both Martha and John were remembered in his Will where he referred to John as "my son John Whipple, Jun'r."[3]

One of John's first ventures was to open an "ordinary" (tavern) in 1662 when he was 36 years old. Ipswich's license required him to sell "at least a quart at a time and none to be drunk in house." He was not to sell by retail "to any but men of good family or good repute" and he was not to be open for business after sunset. His license also required him "to be ready to give account of what liquor he sells by retail, the quantity, time, and to whom."[4] The annual fee for liquor licenses in Ipswich was £2. By 1670 there were so many complaints of "persons spending their time and estate by drinking and tippling in taverns and alehouses," the general court ordered selectmen to "post the name of immoderate drinkers in each establishment."[5]

In 1673 he built a fulling mill at the lower and smaller falls near Ezekiel Woodward's house. The purpose of the mill was to "make finishing homespun cloth." Ipswich had a number of "clothiers" in its early population and John was undoubtedly planning on providing them cloth for their businesses. He would have had some knowledge of the business since his uncle Matthew, father John, and grandfather Matthew were clothiers in Bocking. His right to build was conditioned on not diminishing water from Mr. Saltonstall's grist mill and another fulling mill already begun at the upper falls. He was given one year to build the mill and was prohibited from cutting trees on the common for building materials.[6] John also eventually acquired a saw mill.[7]

When Plumb Island was divided among the commoners of Ipswich he received one-and-a-half shares. In 1664 at age 39 he was elected selectman. On April 29, 1668 he was made a freeman and was elected cornet of troop that same year. He came into full communion with the church February 22, 1673 and in 1674 was elected to the first of four terms (between 1674-83) to the Massachusetts general court.[8] He was on the list of commoners recorded in February 1678. He was county treasurer at his death.

In 1666 king Charles II (1660-85) challenged the right of the colonists under the original charter because the oath of allegiance and administration of justice was not done in his name. He also demanded that Church of England services be allowed, that "all good and honest people be admitted to the Lord's Supper," and "all of wisdom and integrity" to be allowed to vote. Not wanting the franchise extended or to recognize the English Church, the general court resisted the king. However, on September 14, John was one of 73 Ipswich residents to sign a petition pledging loyalty to the king. His cousin Joseph signed the same pledge.[9] This petition incurred the wrath of the general court and on September 17 petition leaders from each town were summoned to attend the general court in October and answer for the petition.[10]

In January 1680 the general court sent the residents of Ipswich a copy of capt. John Mason's claim that the grant to his father in 1622 included "the land lying between the little river which flows into the ocean at Naumkeag (Salem) and the Merrimac." The Massachusetts Bay Co. grant of 1628 extended from the Atlantic to the western ocean and from a line three miles south of the Charles river, land already granted to Mason. Mason's actions were of vital concern to Ipswich which was within the Mason grant. A copy of the Mason claim was delivered to major general Daniel Denison and the magistrates of Essex county with instructions that all terretenants (land tenants) affected by the claim be convened as soon as possible. The convention was held in Ipswich the second Wednesday of February and resulted in a petition to the general court stating they had owned their lands for 50 years, had no knowledge of Mason's claim, its bounds or limits, and they, not Mason, defended the land against the Indians in the late war at a cost of 12 dead and hundreds of pounds.[11] They concluded that any trial of the claim should be in the Massachusetts courts, not in England. The general court forwarded their concerns to Sir Lionel Jenkins, one of the king's secretaries of state.

A year later, a petition claiming rightful title to the lands based on the grant of the general court under the Bay colony charter and purchase from the natives, was addressed to the king. It was signed by representatives from Gloucester, Ipswich, Newbury, Rowley, and other nearby towns. John Whipple, Jr. was one of 15 from Ipswich to sign.[12] It was a time of high drama in Ipswich. If the Mason claim prevailed, title to their lands, houses, barns, and fences would be worthless. On March 17, the court ordered Mr. Jonathan Wade and Mr. Daniel Epps to convene the residents to determine if they agreed with the sentiments of the petition and if so, their concerns would be forwarded to England. The sentiments were endorsed with little opposition.

Mason modified his claim in 1682, asking for the common and unimproved lands only and demanded admittance to the courts to prosecute his rights. The general court told him there was no more common land, that every acre was occupied and improved. It ordered William Stoughton, esq., Peter Bulkley, esq., John Hall, esq., "together with such other magistrates in Essex county as are unconcerned in Mr. Mason's case, to convene the county court there for the trial of those cases." Records of this court have never been found so no positive knowledge exists if the case was tried. If not, it is probable no one was disturbed in the possession of his lands.

MILITARY SERVICE

John was elected cornet of the Ipswich troop in either 1663 or 1668.[13] His service in King Philip's War began at the Battle of Mount Hope in 1675 as a lieutenant in Nicholas Paige's troop. He was a captain of a troop under major Thomas Savage in a failed campaign in March 1676.[14]

By 1765 the English colonists had pushed their settlements to the edge of the frontier, forcing many Indian tribes into ghetto-like settlements that provoked the Indians to take a stand against the advancing invader. From then on, the English lived in constant fear of the lurking enemy.[15] Their military skill and bravery didn't work against the tactics of a foe who appeared where least expected, striking those least prepared, killing them in ambush or while working in their fields, torching homes and barns, and vanishing before effective resistance could be organized.[16]

This Indian warfare was matched by the ruthlessness of the English settlers. When surprised in their winter quarters, their wigwams were set afire, their food destroyed, and the old people and infants left among the flames.

On February 8, 1676 the commissioners of the United Colonies voted to raise an army of 600 for a campaign against the Indians in the west. The Massachusetts quota was 100 foot soldiers and 72 troopers. Major Savage, captain of the foot company, was named commander of all Massachusetts troops February 25. Lieutenant Benjamin Gillam and capt. William Turner commanded the two foot companies and capt. John Whipple commanded the troopers. John Curtice and six friendly Indians served as guides.[17]

On either the second or third of March the Massachusetts' forces joined the Connecticut force at Brookfield, Massachusetts commanded by major Treat. Major general Daniel Denison of Ipswich was commander-in-chief of the combined force and set up his command headquarters at Marlboro.[18] Denison ordered the combined forces to attack the Indians at Wenimesset (now New Braintree, Mass.) but the Indians left before the troops arrived.[19] Whipple's troopers followed the Indians as far as Paquayag (Athol, Mass.) before they escaped towards Northfield. Indian attacks on Westfield and Northampton were repulsed.

Savage wrote the united council on March 28 informing it the Connecticut forces had withdrawn and that the Indians were assembling a large force near Deerfield and Northfield. On April 1 the council authorized Savage to station 150 of his troops at towns needing help and to return home with the others. On their return home they were to engage the enemy if possible but not to pursue small bands of them. The march home began about April 7 with four companies commanded by Whipple, Gillam, lieut. Edward Drinker, and capt. Mosely. When they reached Brookfield a discussion was held to consider new orders from the council ordering them to attack the Indians at Wachuset.

Whipple, Mosley, Gillam, and Drinker voted not to march to Wachuset because of insufficient supplies and sickness among the troops.[20] Chaplain Samuel Nowell voted to march. The council directed gen. Denison on April 10 to inspect the army, discharge those unfit for service, and "dispose of the rest as he shall judge best."[21]

The council, responding to a letter from maj. Savage of March 28 at Hadley, included a comment in its response of April 1 about the "rebuke of God upon capt. Whipple and the poor people of Springfield [as a] matter of great shame and humbling to us." According to Savage's letter, he had word from Springfield that eight Indians assaulted 16 or 18 men besides women and children "as they were going to a meeting from a place called Long Meadow, and killed a man and a maid, wounded two men, and carried away captive two women and two children." Savage said he sent 16 men to pursue the Indians, who when they saw the English closing in, killed the two children, struck the women in the head with hatchets, left them for dead, and fled. The troopers brought the four captives back, the two women still alive, one of whom recovered. This disaster resulted in a popular rhyme of the day: "Seven Indians, and one with-out a gun, caused capt. Nixon and forty men to run."[22]

capt. Whipple?

John lived for eight years following King Philips' War running his various business enterprises and serving as executor of wills for many prominent members of the community and as an appraiser of their estates. The Ipswich probate records are full of references to his participation in these activities.

John died of an unknown sickness August 10, 1683. His Will, written eight days before his death, included language that he was "not like (sic) to escape this sickness." Elizabeth, his "beloved wife, was to enjoy one half of my dwelling house so long as she shall see cause to live therein." His daughters Sarah, 12, and Susanna, 22, wife of maj. John Lane, were each to receive £150. Susanna had already received about £70 and was to receive the balance within three years after his death. If she was willing, Sarah was to be brought up by her step-mother with her maintenance to come from the estate. She was to receive the £150 at "the time of her marriage or when she comes to one and twenty years of age."

He made specific bequests to sons John, Matthew, and Joseph. However, he provided that if his two eldest sons were not happy with their bequests, his real and personal property was to be equally divided by indifferent appraisers into five parts with John, the eldest, to receive two-fifths, Matthew and Joseph one-fifth each, and the last fifth used to pay debts and other legacies. John and Matthew were named executors with Joseph to join them when he came of age. The Will was witnessed by rev. William Hubbard, Samuel Phillips, and Daniel Epps.[23] See Appendix 1 for the full Will.

ENDNOTES — CHAPTER 4

1. *Essex County Register of Deeds* 22:192.

2. *Essex Antiquarian* 10, No. 2, April 1906.

3. The Will was dated 10 Sept. 1660 and provided for his wife Mary with reversion to his daughters Whipple and Hobson. John Sr., and Jr. were apparently in business at that time and had borrowed money from Reynor. The will referred to £300 due him "from John Whipple and John Whipple, jr." Hammatt, 276.

4. Waters, *Ipswich in the Massachusetts Bay Colony.* Part II, House and Lands.

5. *Essex Antiquarian*, Vol. 11, No. 3, March 1898.

6. Waters, *Ipswich Mills and Factories*, 104.

7. Reference to a saw mill is included in his Will dated 2 Aug. 1683. Ipswich Probate Records, 304;10

8. Hammatt, 405.

9. In addition to the 73 Ipswich residents, there were 39 signers from Newbury, 35 from Salem, and 26 from Boston. Waters, Part I, Historical.

10. Capt. John Appleton of Ipswich, Capt. William Gerrish of Newbury, Mr. Edmund Batter of Salem, and Capt. Thomas Savage, Mr. Thomas Brattle, Mr. Habakkuk Glover, and Mr. Thomas Dean of Boston. These leaders were identified as principal persons, some in public trusts, all, save one, freemen of the Colony and member of churches.

11. After meeting with Mason, Ipswich selectman Thomas Lovell recommended the Mason claim be recognized. Instead, the town replaced him as selectman with Capt. John Appleton.

12. The petition was presented to the general court February 16, 1681. Other Ipswich men signing: John and Samuel Appleton, Thomas Burnam, Thomas Cobbet, Sr., Daniel Epps, William Goodhue, William Hubbard, Thomas Knowlton, Moses Pengrey, Sr., John Perkins, John and Samuel Rogers, Symon Stace, and Jonathan Wade, Sr.

13. Cornet — an officer of the lowest rank who carried his troop's flag. George Madison Boge, *Soldiers in King Philip's War*. Baltimore: Genealogical Publishing Co., Inc., 1967, 86. (Originally published in Boston in 1906) gives the date as 1663. Felt in his *History of Ipswich*, etc. gives the date as 1668, 142.

14. Whipple received £14 14 shillings, 3 pence for his service. The following served under him: John Dodge, Marke Hascall, Wm. Smith, Richard Child, Thomas Leaver, Samuel Smith, Daniel Wycome (quartermaster), Joseph Cask, John Rayment, Thadeus Berry, Moses Cleveland, John Sawin, John Stone, Samuel Stearnes, John Wait, Samuel Cooper, James Tenney, Samuel Ladd, Christopher Palmer, Samuel Chapman, Joseph Taylor, James Hobbs, Timothy Bread, Wm. Dellow, Henry Kenny, James Lowden, Joseph Eaton, Thomas Brintnall, Thomas Hodgman, Edward Neland, Samuel Giddings, Thomas Andrews, Ephraim Fellows, and John Brown. Boge, 282-83.

15. Ipswich residents killed in 1675 included: Edward Coburn (in August) and Thomas Scott (September) at Squakeheage; Thomas Manning, Jacob Wainwright, Caleb Kimball, Samuel Whittredge, and others in September at Muddy Brook under capt. Lathrop; Benjamin Tappan (September); Freegrace Norton and John Petts (maybe Pettis) at Hatfield in October. Felt, 147

16. Examples of Indian warfare are documented in a letter from maj. Richard Waldron at Dover under date 25 Sept. 1675 to gen. Daniel Denison of Ipswich: "On Saturday and Sabbath day last at Scarborough, they killed an old man and woman and burnt their house, and at Mr. Foxwell's two young men were killed, being at the barn about the cattle. The people were alerted by a friendly Indian and fled to maj. Pendleton and maj. Phillips' home. The Indians rifled and burnt several house on the north side of the Saco river and then a party of 36 crossed the river in English canoes, which they then cut holes in and set adrift, and burned maj. Phillips' sawmill and corn mill, trying to draw the major out to defend his property. Phillips had 15 families (about 50 people) in his home. The Indians tried to fire the house with birch, pitchwood, turpentine, and powder but were driven off. They continued firing at the house all night, leaving Sabbath day morning about 9 o'clock. Waldron said he left garrisons at Sawco, Scarborough, and Falmouth so people could gather their corn, but many people had to forsake their plantations and leave their corn and cattle to the enemy." *Register*, 23:324-27.

17. Readers interested in more information are referred to the archives of Massachusetts and Connecticut.

18. General Denison's granddaughter Martha Denison married maj. Matthew Whipple, son of Capt. John Whipple, Jr.

19. Several descendants of Elder John Whipple's brother Matthew were among the early settlers of New Braintree in the mid 1700s.

20 They only had one day's provisions for a six day march. Waters, Part I, Historical.

21. *Massachusetts Archives*, 30:169; 67:201-02, 209, 215; 68:189, 191, 203, 235. Boge, 85-101; *Register*, 37:285, 362-75.

22. Boge construes the council's letter as holding Whipple responsible for the disaster. He said he knew nothing of capt. Nixon. 282-83. Rev. William Hubbard does not refer to this incident in his history of the war. The people of Ipswich appear not to have considered it rebuke by God on Whipple as an individual but as a rebuke on the people in Springfield at that time.

23. *Ipswich Probate Records*, 304:10.

5 SARAH WHIPPLE AND DEACON JOSEPH GOODHUE

Sarah² Whipple (John¹, Matthew^) born 3 November 1641 in Ipswich, Essex County, Massachusetts; died there 23 July 1681. She married Deacon Joseph Goodhue at Ipswich 13 July 1661. He died at Ipswich 2 September 1697. He married (2) Mrs. Rachel Todd at Ipswich 15 October 1684. She died in 1691 in Ipswich; (3) Mrs. Mercy Clark at Ipswich 4 July 1692. When pregnant with her last children, twins, Sarah had a premonition she would die in childbirth and wrote a Valedictory and Monitory Writing for her husband, children, and siblings. Joseph became a freeman in 1774, a deacon, and an Ipswich representative to the general court.

Children of Sarah Whipple and Joseph Goodhue, all born in Ipswich

    i.   *Mary, born about 1664; married Bonus Norton in Ipswich.*

   ii. *William, born about 1666; died 10 July 1722 in Ipswich; married Mary Lowden*

  iii. *Sarah, born about 1668; married John Kimball in Ipswich.*

  iv. *Joseph, born about 1668; died in 1768 at age 100; married Sarah Smith.*

   v. *Marjory (Margery), born about 1670; died after 1704 in Ipswich; married Thomas Knowlton.*

  vi. *John, born about 1674; married Sarah Sherwin in Ipswich.*

 vii. *Susanna, born about 1676; married Moses Kimball in Ipswich.*

viii. *Twin Baby, born 20 July 1681 and died in infancy.*

  ix. *Hannah, born 20 July 1681; married Joseph Edwards.*

Children of Joseph Goodhue and Mrs. Rachel Todd, born in Ipswich

    i.   *Ebenezer, born 25 July 1685.*

   ii. *Benjamin, born 25 January 1691*

Children of Joseph Goodhue and Mrs. Mercy Clark, born in Ipswich

    i.   *Samuel, born 6 April 1696; married Abigail Barlett.*

SARAH WAS THE only child born to Elder John and Susannah in Massachusetts, making her the first generation American of this branch of the Whipple family tree. She was exposed to the many facets of her father's life in politics, as a merchant, school leader, member of the general court, deacon, and ruling elder of the church. Unlike most girls of that time, she learned to read and write. She was a devoted member of the church.

When Sarah married Joseph, their parents, as was the custom at that time, entered into a formal wedding contract. Tradition required Joseph's father, William, a deacon in the church, to wait upon the bride's father so we can presume the terms of the settlement were agreed to and the formal instrument drawn in the Whipple home.

Deacon Goodhue agreed to give Joseph, his oldest son, the house he and his wife Margery lived in after both had died. The gift was to include the orchard and all buildings on the land and included 22 acres of salt marsh and six acres of upland at Milebrook. The agreement noted that the house and land had been purchased with funds sent from England by Joseph's maternal grandfather (__?__) Watson with instructions the property was to go to his grandson Joseph after the parents' death. John Whipple agreed to pay Joseph £40 "forthwith upon his marriage to my daughter Sarah" and to give Sarah "an equal share of my household goods with her two sisters at my and my wife Susanna's decease."

The agreement was reconfirmed July 13, 1666 when John provided that Sarah was to receive an additional £30 within six months after his and Susanna's deaths. It seems apparent that Sarah never lived in the Goodhue house since her father-in-law outlived her by 19 years, dying in 1700. (See Appendix 1 for a copy of the wedding contract.)

In July 1681, pregnant with twins and the mother of three sons and four daughters born in her first 20 years of marriage, Sarah had a strong premonition she would die in childbirth and wrote a letter to her husband found after her death. She wrote of her profoundly religious life "her joy in the Lord and her delight in sermons and all religious exercises" and of her tender affection for her husband and children.

The letter, address to her "dear and loving husband" included specific messages to her children, siblings, and in-laws. The twins were born July 20, six days after the date of the letter. She died three days later. One twin died, the other was named Hannah.

She wrote because she thought the Lord was going to make "a sudden change in thy family" and she wanted to share her thoughts but didn't want to talk about the premonition because she didn't want Joseph to worry about her.

She said she believed that the Lord had "fit me for himself" and that she would die "either at my travail, or soon after it." I am very willing to enjoy thy company and my children longer [but] if it be the will of the Lord that I must not, I hope I can say cheerfully the will of the Lord be done."

She was concerned about leaving him with so many children— the oldest 17 and the youngest 5— and suggested he ease his burden by placing some of them with relatives. If delivered of a living child, she wanted Joseph's father and stepmother to have it "if they please." She suggested her son John, about 7, be raised by her cozen Simon Stacy. Daughter Susanna, "a hearty girl," should go to her cozen Catherine Whipple because they would be helpful to each other.

She expressed "hearty and humble thanks' to the senior Goodhues for their "father and motherly love towards me and mine" and hoped they would be "a father and mother to the motherless." She told her brothers and sisters not to be discouraged by her death and to consider "to what end" God lent them any time on earth.

The message to her children was "to let the Lord Jesus Christ be precious in your sight." They were to read God's word and to pray for "hearts and wisdom to improve [their] great and many privileges, to improve [their] youthful days unto God's service . . . [to] give good attention unto sermons preached in public, and to sermons repeated in private." She reminded them they were in the bond of the covenant and to own and renew it as they grew up so they could "enjoy the Lord Jesus Christ in all his Ordinances."

She wrote that Joseph had been "loving, kind [and] tender-hearted" to her and to them and labored for their "temporal and spiritual good." She reminded them that at the end of a day's work, he took them "into his wearied arms [and they] could behold as in a glass, his tender care and love," that he had prayed "with ardent desires and tears to God" on their behalf. She told them to continue to honor him so he would continue to plead for their welfare. She instructed them to "live godly, walk soberly, modestly, and innocently; [to] be diligent and not hasty to follow new fashions and the pride of life, [or to let] pride betray the good of your immortal souls."

Sarah described herself as "weakly natured and referred to all her burdens." She thanked Joseph for his sympathy and for cheerfully helping her bear them. "There never was a man more truly kind to a woman," she wrote. She praised the Lord for "ordering their life together." She thanked Joseph for repeating the "precious sermons and prayers and tears for me and with me" when she was necessarily absent from public worship. She called him the "dearest" of her bosom friends.

In a beautiful expression of love, she concludes:

O dear heart, if I must leave thee and thine here behind,
Of my natural affection here is my heart and hand.
Be courageous, and on the living God bear up thy heart
in so great a breach as this.

Sarah's "Valedictory and Monitory Writing" is a classic in the annals of the olden times and is preserved as one of Ipswich's most precious original documents. It reveals the depths of spiritual experience that underlay the severe legalism of the old Puritan religion. The literary style, moreover, is chaste and beautiful and suggests a cultured and luminous atmosphere in her early home.

SARAH GOODHUE'S LETTER[1]
The Copy of a Valedictory and Monitory Writing[2] Left by Sarah Goodhue

Dear and loving Husband, if it should please the Lord to make a sudden change in thy family, the which I know not how soon it may be, and I am fearful of it:

Therefore in a few words I would declare something of my mind, lest I should afterwards have no opportunity: I cannot but sympathize and pity thy condition, seeing that thou hast a great family of children, and some of them small, and if it should please the Lord to add to thy number one more or two, be not discouraged, although it should please the Lord to deprive thee of thy weak help which is so near and dear unto thee. Trust in the living God, who will be an help to the helpless, and a father to the motherless: My desire is, that if thou art so contented, to dispose of two or three of my children: If it please the Lord that I should be delivered of a living child, son or daughter, my desire is, that my father and mother should have it, if they please, I freely bequeath and give it to them.[3] And also my desire is, that my cousin Symond Stacy should have John if he please, I freely bequeath and give him to him for his own if thou art willing. And also my desire is, that my cousin Catharine Whipple should have Susanna, which is an hearty girl, and will quickly be helpful to her, and she may be helpful to the child, to bring her up: These or either of these I durst trust their care under God, for the faithful discharge of that which may be for my children's good and comfort, and I hope to thy satisfaction: Therefore if they be willing to take them, and to deal well with them, answer my desire I pray thee, thou hast been willing to answer my request formerly, and I hope now thou wilt, this being the last as far as I know.

Honored and most loving father and mother, I cannot tell how to express your fatherly and motherly love towards me and mine: It hath been so great, and in several kinds; for the which in a poor requital, I give you hearty and humble thanks, yet trusting in God that he will enable you to be a father and mother to the motherless: Be not troubled for the loss of an unworthy daughter; but rejoice in the free grace of God, that there is hope of rejoicing together hereafter in the place of everlasting joy and blessedness.

Brothers and Sisters all, hearken and hear the voice of the Lord, that by his sudden providence doth call aloud on you, to prepare yourselves for that swift and sudden messenger of death: that no one of you may be found without a wedding garment; a part and portion of Jesus Christ: the assurance of the love of God, which will enable you to leave this world, and all your relations, though never so near and dear, for the everlasting enjoyment of the great and glorious God, if you do fear him in truth.

The private society, to which while here, I did belong; of God by his Providence come amongst you, and begin by death to break you; be not discouraged, but be strong in repenting, faith and prayers with the lively repeatal of God's counsels declared unto you by his faithful messengers: O pray each for another and with one another; that so in these threatening times of storms and troubles, you may be found more precious than gold tried in the fire. Think not a few hours time in your approaches to God misspent; but consider seriously with yourselves, to what end God lent to you any time at all: This surely I can through grace now say; that of the time that there I spent, through the blessing of God, I have no cause to repent, no not in the least.

O my children all, which in pains and care have cost me dear; unto you I call to come and take what portion your dying mother will bestow upon you: many times by experience it hath been found, that the dying words of parents have left a living impression upon the hearts of Children: O my children, be sure to set the fear of God before your eyes; consider what you are by nature, miserable sinners, utterly lost and undone; and that there is no way and means whereby you can come out of this miserable estate; but by the Mediation of the Lord Jesus Christ: He died a reproachful death, that every poor humble and true repenting sinner by faith on God through him, might have everlasting life: O my Children the best counsel that a poor dying Mother can give you is, to get a part and portion in the Lord Jesus Christ, that will hold, when all these things will fail; O let the Lord Jesus Christ be precious in your sight.

O children, neighbors, and friends, I hope I can by experience truly say; that Christ is the best, most precious, most durable portion, that all or any of you can set your hearts delight upon; I forever desire to bless and praise the Lord, that he hath opened mine eyes to see the emptiness of these things, and mine own; and to behold the fullness and riches of grace that is in the Lord Jesus Christ: To that and my children, I do not only counsel you, but in the fear of the Lord I charge you all, to read God's word, and pray unto the Lord that he would be pleased to give you hearts and wisdom to improve the great and many privileges that the Lord is at present pleased to afford unto you, improve your youthful days unto God's service, your health and strength whilst it lasteth, for you know not how soon your health may be turned into sickness, your strength into weakness, and your lives into death; as death cuts the tree of your life down, so it will lie; as death leaveth you, so judgment will find you out: Therefore be persuaded to agree with your adversity quickly, whilst you are in the way of these precious opportunities: be sure to improve the lively dispensations of the gospel; give good attention unto sermons preached in public, and to sermons repeated in private. Endeavor to learn to write your father's hand, that you may read over those precious sermons, that he hath taken pains to write and keep from the mouths of God's lively messengers, and in them are lively messages: I can through the blessings of God along with them, say, that they have been lively unto me: and if you improve them aright, why not to all of you? God upbraideth none of the seed of Jacob, that seek his Face in truth: My children be encouraged in this work, you are in the bond of the covenant, although you may be breakers of covenant, yet God is a merciful keeper of covenant. Endeavor as you grow up, to own and renew your covenant, and rest not if God give you life, but so labor to improve all the advantages that God is pleased to afford you, that you may be fit to enjoy the Lord Jesus Christ in all his Ordinances. What hath the Lord Jesus Christ given himself for you? If you will lay hold upon him by true faith and repentance; And what will you be backward to accept of his gracious and free offers, and not keep in remembrance his death and sufferings, and to strengthen your weak faith; I thank the Lord, in some measure, I have found that ordinance, a life-making ordinance unto my soul.

Oh the smiles and loving embraces of the Lord Jesus Christ, that they miss of, that hold off, and will not be in such near relation unto their Head and Savior. The Lord grant that Christ may be your Portions all.

My children, one or two words I have to say to you more, in the first place, be sure to carry well to your father, obey him, love him, follow his instructions and example, be ruled by him, take his advice, and have a care of grieving him:

For I must testify the truth unto you, and I may call some of you to testify against yourselves; that your Father hath been loving, kind, tender-hearted towards you all; and laborious for you all, both for your temporal and spiritual good:—You that are grown up, cannot but see how careful your father is when he cometh home from his work, to take the young ones up into his wearied arms, by his loving carriage and care towards those, you may behold as in a glass, his tender care and love to you every one as you grow up: I can safely say, that his love was so to you all, that I cannot say which is the child that he doth love best but further I may testify unto you, that this is not all your father hath been doing for you, and that some of you may bear me witness that hath given you many instructions, which hath been to the end your souls might enjoy happiness, he hath reproved you often for your evils, laying before you the ill event that would happen unto you, if you did not work in God's ways, and give your minds to do his will, to keep holy his Sabbath to attend unto reading God's Word, hearing it preached with a desire to profit by it, and declaring unto you this way that he had experienced to get good by it; that was to pray unto the Lord for his blessing with it and upon it, that it might soak into the heart and find entertainment there and that you should meditate upon it, and he you might find the sweetness of God's word.

Furthermore, my children, be encouraged in this work, your father hath put up many prayers with ardent desires and tears to God on behalf of you all: which if you walk with God, I hope you will find gracious answers and showers of blessings from those bottled tears for you. O carry it well to your father, that he may yet be encouraged to be doing and pleading for your welfare: Consider that the scripture holdeth forth many blessings to such children that obey their parents in the Lord, but there are curses threatened to the disobedient.

My children, in your life and conversation, live godly, walk soberly, modestly, and innocently: be diligent, and be not hasty to follow new fashions, and the pride of life, that now too much abounds. Let not pride betray the good of your immortal souls.

And if it please the Lord that you live to match yourselves, and to make your choice: Be sure you choose such as first do seek the kingdom of Heaven.

My first, as they name is Joseph, labor so in knowledge to increase. As to be freed from the guilt of thy sins, and enjoy eternal Peace.

Mary, labor so to be arrayed with the hidden man of the heart, that with Mary thou mayest find, thou has chosen the better part.

William, thou hadst that name for the grandfather's sake. Labor so to tread in his steps, as over sin conquest thou mayest make.

Sarah, Sarah's daughter thou shall be, if thou continuest in doing well. Labor in holiness among the daughters to walk, as that thou mayest excel.

So my children all, if I must be gone, I with tears bid you all Farewell. The Lord bless you all.

Now dear Husband, I can do no less than turn unto thee. And if I could, I would naturally mourn with thee. And in a poor requital of all they kindness, if I could, I would speak some things of comfort to thee, whilst thou dost mourn for me.

A tender-hearted, affectionate, and entire loving husband thou hast been to me several ways. If I should but speak of what I have found as to these outward things; I being but weakly natured: In all my burdens thou hast willingly with me sympathized, and cheerfully thou hast helped me bear them: which although I was but weak natured; and so the more enabled to go through those troubles in my way: Yet thou hast by thy cheerful love to me, helped me forward in a cheerful frame of spirit. But when I come to speak or consider in thy place, thy great pains and care for the good of my soul.

This twenty years of thy love to me in this kind, hath so enstamped it upon my mind, that I do think that there never was man more truly kind to a woman: I desire for ever to bless and praise the Lord, that in mercy to my soul, he by his providence ordered that I should live with thee in such a relation, therefore dear husband be comforted in this, (although God by his providence break that relation between us, that he gave being to at first) that in the place thou hast been a man of knowledge to discharge to God and my soul, that scripture commanded duty, which by the effects in me wrought, through the grace of God, thou mayest behold with comfort our prayers not hindered; but a gracious answer from the Lord, which is of great price and reward. Although my being gone be thy loss, yet I trust in and thro' Jesus Christ, it will be my gain.

Was it not to this end that the Lord was pleased to enable thee and give thee in heart to take (as an instrument) so much pains for his glory and my external good, and that it might be thy comfort: As all thy reading of scriptures and writing of sermons, and repeating of them over to me, that although I was necessarily often absent from the public worship of God, yet by thy pains and care to the good of my soul, it was brought home unto me: And blessed be the Lord who hath set home by the operation of his spirit, so many repeatals of precious sermons and prayers and tears for me and with me, for my eternal good: And now let it be thy comfort under all, go on and persevere in believing in God, and praying fervently unto God: Let not thy affectionate heart become hard, and thy tears dried away: And certainly the Lord will render a double portion of blessing upon thee and thine.

If thou couldest ask me a reason why I thus declare myself? I cannot answer no other but this; that I have had of late a strong persuasion upon my mind, that by sudden death I should be surprised, either at my travail, or soon after it, the Lord fit me for himself: although I could be very willing to enjoy they company, and my children longer, yet if it be the will of the Lord that I must not, I hope I can say cheerfully, thy will of the Lord be done, this hath been often my desire and thy prayer.

Further, if thou could'st ask me why I did not discover some of these particulars of my mind to thee before, my answer is because I knew that thou wert tender-hearted towards me, and therefore I would not create thee needless trouble.

O dear husband of all my dearest bosom friends, if by sudden death I must part from thee, let not thy trouble and cares that are on thee make thee to turn aside from the right way.

O dear heart, if I must leave thee and thine here behind, of my natural affections here is my heart and hand.

Be courageous, and on the living God bear up thy heart in so great a breach as this.

/S/ Sarah Goodhue

Dear Husband, if by sudden death I am taken away from thee, there is infolded among thy papers something that I have to say to thee and others. July 14, 1681.

ENDNOTES, CHAPTER 5

1. Thomas Franklin Waters, *Ipswich in the Massachusetts Bay Colony*. Part I. Historical. The Ipswich Historical Society. (Ipswich, MA. 1905). Appendix F.

2. A Valedictory and Monitory Writing, left by Sarah Whipple Goodhue. Cambridge, Mass., 1861. Reprinted by Samuel Hall, Salem, 1770. Reprinted by request of Jenks & Shirley, Cambridge, 1805. Reprinted by Metcalf & Co. For David Pulsifer of Boston, 1850. See also Waters, *Ipswich in the Massachusetts Bay Colony*, Appendix F, 519-25.

3. The father had to be William Goodhue because her own father died 30 June 1669. Deacon Goodhue died in 1700. Who was the mother? Deacon Goodhue's first wife, Margory, died 28 Aug. 1668; his second wife, Mrs. Mary Web, died 7 Sept. 1680; he married his third wife, Mrs. Bethia Grafton 26 July 1682. Sarah's letter is dated 14 July 1681 when William Goodhue was without a wife.

6 GENERAL WILLIAM WHIPPLE, NEW HAMPSHIRE SIGNER OF THE DECLARATION OF INDEPENDENCE

William⁵ Whipple (Capt. William⁴, Maj. Matthew³,Capt.John², John¹ ,Matthew^) born 14 January 1730/31 in Kittery, Maine; died 28 November 1785 in Portsmouth, New Hampshire. He married his cousin Katharine Moffatt at Portsmouth about 1769. She died at Portsmouth 22 November 1821. His early career was at sea where he was capt. of his own ship at age 21. He left the sea and entered the mercantile business in Portsmouth with his two younger brothers Robert and Joseph. He was active in Portsmouth public affairs, represented the city in the colonial legislature, and served three terms — from 29 February 1776 to 25 September 1779 — in the continental congress. While in the Congress he commanded a New Hampshire militia brigade in the Revolutionary War. After leaving Congress he was New Hampshire's first federal tax collector and judge and president of the court to try the first case heard under the Articles of Confederation. He again represented Portsmouth in the legislature and served as justice of the state's superior court of judicature.

Children of William and Katharine Whipple born and died in Portsmouth.
  i. *William, baptized 24 May 1772; died 11 April 1773.*

The following statements were made by general Whipple at various times during his public career: *[Thomas Paine's]* Common Sense *has made that illustrious stranger [independence] that was so much feared a friend of the southern colonies, and I hope the northern colonies will soon open their arms to receive him. It's my opinion that the salvation of America depends on him. (Philadelphia, 3-24-1776). The prospect of laying a foundation of liberty and happiness for posterity and securing an asylum for all who wish to enjoy those blessings is an object in my opinion sufficient to raise the mind above every misfortune. (Baltimore, 2-7-1777). We have nothing to fear but ourselves. (Philadelphia, 7-27-1777). Peace is desirable, but in my opinion a secondary object. War with all its horrors is preferable to an inglorious peace. I hope we never consent to a peace [that leaves our] posterity greater evils than we have suffered. (Philadelphia, 2-18-1779). The more difficulty we are in at obtaining the jewel the higher value we shall set on it, consequently shall be more careful to preserve. (Philadelphia, 8-24-1779).*

Many individuals who share the Whipple surname presume their family descends from general Whipple. His Continental Congress and revolutionary war activity make him an historic personage and one whom most Whipples would like to share kinship. However, as is noted above, he only had one child and that child died in infancy. So while we who bear the Whipple surname would like to claim him as an ancestor, we cannot.

AMERICANS FEEL THEIR Declaration of Independence is one of the great events of history. Along with the Magna Carta, the Mayflower Compact, and Abraham Lincoln's Emancipation Proclamation, it is a high point of the progress of civilization and a prophecy of what would follow. It was written by men who knew how to voice their grievances so that the whole world should hear. They knew their rights, guaranteed by the crown in their charters, and simply claimed them. The destiny of what was then the mightiest empire on earth and of what became the mightiest nation in the world was the result.

The Declaration of Independence transformed the colonies into sovereign, free, and independent states. It transformed the sentiment of nationality into the fact of nationality, announced to the world the fact of the United States of America and the justification of the fact, and changed allegiance of the individual from the monarchy to the new political unit of the United States.

General William Whipple *(1730-1785).*   Katharine (Moffatt) Whipple *(1734-1821).*
Both Photos courtesy of the National Society of the Colonial Dames of America In the State of New Hampshire, Portsmouth, N.H.

History helps us appreciate the courage, faith, and confidence of the patriots who dared sign that radical document. The colonies had few resources in 1776 and little experience of working jointly in a common cause. The country had limited transportation facilities and limited ability to quickly communicate between colonies. There were hostile native Americans on the frontier and many loyalists among the merchant class. To vote for independence meant branding yourself a traitor and rebel. It meant a price on your head, shameless death, or fleeing the country if the colonies lost the war against the largest navy and strongest army in the world. In the face of these odds, delegates from 12 colonies voted July 2, 1776 (New York abstained but voted its approval in convention July 9) for independence. Americans more than two centuries later cannot begin to comprehend the fears and pressures those patriots had to overcome before casting that fateful vote.

Of the 56 signers, eight were merchants, six physicians, five farmers, 25 lawyers. Most were tutored in the art of local politics and many had served in colonial legislatures. A majority had taken an active part in agitations against British policy and nearly all had natural talents for political management. William Whipple of Portsmouth, New Hampshire was one of the 56 to sign. He fought for his country with ideas in the congress and on the battlefield with indomitable will. His service on key congressional committees was constant, steady, and preserving. He was among the hardest working members of a congress that lacked a bureaucracy to carry out its directives. He joined Sam and John Adams and John Hancock of Massachusetts, Thomas Jefferson and Richard Henry Lee of Virginia and Stephen Hopkins of Rhode Island in opposing John Dickinson, Robert Morris, and James Wilson of Pennsylvania, James Duane and John Jay of New York, and brothers Edward and John Rutledge of South Carolina who were willing at first to give in to British threats and power. His was the New Hampshire voice most often raised in congressional debates, and it was a voice listened to, especially on marine, foreign affairs, and public administration issues. He chaired the foreign affairs committee when France pressured the congress in early 1779 to decide on issues critical to a peace conference with England. Whipple's committee decided that negotiations could only begin after Great Britain acknowledged "the absolute and unlimited liberty, sovereignty and independence" of the United States in matters of government and commerce. His incomparable letters, are witness of his ever alert, courageous, and encouraging spirit. While signers from Massachusetts, Pennsylvania, and Virginia are saluted in the history books, none worked harder or contributed more to the founding of the United States than did Whipple. His reward was not fame; it was helping to create the greatest democracy ever known.

When Whipple first arrived in Philadelphia, John Adams wrote "William Whipple, esq. [is] another excellent member in principle and disposition, as well as understanding."[1] While John Adams and Jefferson were writing state papers, Whipple applied his sound judgment and business experience to find ways to supply the navy with ships, armaments, and crews and the army with shoes and food and powder and cannon balls. He gave everything to the cause, dying just before his dream of a strong central government was realized. New Hampshire historian Richard Francis Upton, in evaluating the various delegates representing the state, placed him first and labeled him "one of the most popular and respected members of congress."[2]

Whipple was 46 when he voted to declare independence from England. Many who bear the Whipple name today proudly claim him as a direct ancestor — the author's grandfather included — but it is a false claim. The author and the Signer are fourth cousins six times removed, our common ancestor being Matthew Whipple (ca 1560-1619) of Bocking, Essex Co., England. William and Katharine (Moffatt) Whipple had one living child, a son, William, baptized at the Old North Church in Portsmouth May 24, 1772. He died 11 months later on April 29, 1773.[3] Thus this line of male Whipples ended with William's generation as brothers Robert and Joseph had no children. William is buried in a tomb near the center of Portsmouth's North Cemetery. Son William, sister Mary Traill, and mother-in-law-aunt, Katharine (Cutt) Moffatt, are in adjacent graves.[4] His epitaph: "Here are deposited the remains Of the Honorable William Whipple who departed this Life on the 28th day of November, 1785, in the 55th year of his Age. He was often elected and thrice attended the Continental Congress as Delegate for the State of New Hampshire, particularly in that memorable year in which America declared itself independent of Great Britain. He was also at the Time of his decease a Judge of the Supreme Court of Judicature. In Him a firm & ardent Patriotism was united with universal benevolence and every social Virtue."

Biographers have emphasized Whipple's lack of participation in public affairs prior to the revolution. It is obvious they failed to do their research. His participation in public life began in 1760, 16 years before he signed the Declaration of Independence. In the 1770s when problems with England escalated, his Portsmouth neighbors consistently elected him to committees to deal with these problems and to the legislature where he immediately became a leader. In 1775 he was on the provincial committee of correspondence and chairman pro tem of the committee of safety, the executive body running the province. In 1776 he was selected one of 12 councilors to run the colony.

He served in the continental congress from February 29, 1776 to September 25, 1779. Between sessions, as brigadier general of the New Hampshire militia,[5] he was one of the negotiators of gen. John Burgoyne's surrender at Saratoga in October 1777 and he commanded a militia brigade in the 1778 Rhode Island campaign. After leaving congress, he represented Portsmouth in the state legislature and was judge of the superior court. He declined federal appointment as commissioner of admiralty in 1780 but served the federal government as New Hampshire receiver of the United States and as presiding judge of the federal court hearing the 1782 dispute between Pennsylvania and Connecticut. He was ahead of his time in medical science, advocating inoculation for small pox[6] and authorized an autopsy on his body.

During his public life Whipple was associated with great men engaged in great pursuits and was their peer in greatness. His courage and fidelity made possible our comfort and prosperity. Good sense, knowledge of men and tact in dealing with them, fondness for work, steadfastness of purpose, putting the public good ahead of personal interests, breadth of view, patience, capacity for friendship, generous estimate of opponents, unquestioned integrity, unwavering loyalty, and serving the new nation with unremitting diligence are what he left us. America is indebted to this strong and noble man.

FAMILY HERITAGE AND HOME

How did Whipple, a sea captain-merchant, come to be in this unique group of patriots, all but eight born in America?[7] He grew up proud to be an Englishman. He had lived through two French wars and had grown to manhood with the burning conviction that British rights, British freedom, the British form of government, must be cherished at all costs. Why did he become a leader in the cause of revolution?

He was born January 14, 1730/31 in his grandparents, Robert and Dorcas (Hammond) Cutt's, old garrison house in Kittery, the first town in Maine (organized October 20, 1647). His parents, capt. William Whipple[8] and Mary Cutt[9] had five children: Mary, William, Hannah, Robert, and Joseph.[10] William was almost six when his grandfather Cutt died and left to "my well beloved daughter Mary Whipple" my land, dwelling house and all other buildings situated at Crooked Lane in Kittery.[11] After his father-in-law died, William, who owned and sailed ships to the West Indies and Coast of Africa, held the Cutt estate in right of his wife and thereafter was a farmer and maltster.[12]

Major Matthew Whipple (1658-1739), who represented Ipswich in the Massachusetts general court (1718, 19, 29) and was a justice of the sessions court, was William, Jr.'s grandfather. His great grandfather was capt. John Whipple, born in Bocking, Essex co., England in 1626, died in Ipswich in 1683, capt of troop during King Philip's War, a member of the general court, left an estate of £3,000; his second great grandfather was John Whipple (1598-1669), born in Bocking, died in Ipswich where he received a large grant of land in 1638 and owned the famous John Whipple House, a freeman in 1640, served eight terms in the general court, and was ruling elder of the Ipswich church; his third great grandfather was Matthew Whipple (circa 1560-1619), clothier of Bocking.

His great grandfather Robert Cutt settled in the Portsmouth area prior to 1646 and established the Kittery shipyard. His great grand uncle John Cutt was New Hampshire's first president[13] and his second great grandfather Richard Cutt was a member of parliament from Essex in the 1650s. William Jr.'s blood lines were notable and in serving the public, he was following family tradition. Titles were important in those years and in his early Portsmouth years William was known and addressed as captain Whipple. In the continental congress he was addressed as colonel, later general, Whipple.

His birth place, built about 1660, is on the east bank of the Piscataqua river a few rods from the water and about a mile from the river's mouth. Its cove (called Whipple's cove), ran halfway round it making it suitable for a garrison house. Neighbors sought refuge there in times of danger because its view up and down the harbor made it impossible to approach unseen.[14] The garrison part of the house was hewed hemlock timbers squared and dovetailed at the corners. The large doors of heavy timbers hung on wooden hinges. The upper story projected over the lower eight to ten inches, double this on some sides, making it possible to pour boiling water on the attackers and/or put out fires they started. Originally about 34 feet square, it was enlarged several times, including an addition around 1830 and today is known as the old Whipple mansion and is a private residence.[15] The Daughters of the American Revolution placed a bronze plaque on the front of the house in 1913 identifying it as the birthplace of William Whipple.

During William's youth, the window sills would have contained plants, fennel, chives, and parsley. Skillets, scoured and ready, each in its accustomed place, were hung on the kitchen hearth. He undoubtedly took the warm hearth, the warm bed, and the plentiful food laid before him for granted. The outside life must have fascinated him as he roamed his grandfather's holdings from the wide sloping meadow to the river, to the eastern boundary, to the shipyards nearby.

It is supposed he began school about age 6. Then the typical New England school was a one-room log house with fireplace, worn benches, and battered desks. No blackboard, map, or picture hung on the wall. The room was divided into sections, the smallest boys in front, the big boys behind. While one section recited, the others learned by rote whatever was placed before them, from spelling to Lily's *Latin Grammar*. Time was kept by a mark on the eastern window sill. The room was always too hot or too cold and by noon, when the hearth fire was high, the odor from boys' woolen garments made the place smell. School laws required large biweekly doses of Westminster catechism, backbone of the Congregational faith, which taught the world had been created in the year 4047 B.C., that it took six days to do it, and God rested on the seventh day. The shorter catechism with its extra proportions of hell-fire, eternal punishment, and torment was used. No earthly or heavenly rewards were offered — only the severe justice of the Old Testament. God was made sterner and more cruel than any living judge so children would learn how slight a chance even the most pure had of escaping eternal damnation. They were taught what they were to think when they reached the age of discretion.

School began at 8. The teacher, at his high desk overlooking the room, began by reading from the Bible. Drawing the *Catechism* from his desk at the prescribed

Birthplace of Gen. Wm. Whipple, *in Kittery, Maine on the east bank of the Piscataqua River. Built about 1660. It is known as the old Whipple mansion and is a private residence. A bronze plaque identifying it as the birthplace of William was placed near the front entry by the DAR in 1913. Photo, courtesy of the Thayer Cumings Library and Archives, Strawbery Banke, Portsmouth, N.H.*

periods, he asked in a voice hollow with boredom, "What is the chief end of man?" Monotonous voices answered in sing-song, "To glorify God and enjoy Him forever." "And what," the teacher continued, "is the misery of that estate whereinto man fell?" "All mankind, by their fall, lost communion with God, are under His wrath and curse, and so made liable to all the miseries of this life, to death itself, and to the pains of hell forever." It would not have occurred to William to question the catechism as to sacredness, beauty, or usefulness. He was probably able to recite the opening words by heart by age four.

He learned the alphabet from the *New England Primer*.[16] It started with Adam: "In Adam's fall, We sinned all" . . . How miserable Adam looked in the drawing, standing naked by the tree, with the serpent coiled evilly, lording it over poor shivering Eve! All the way down the alphabet death and hellfire loomed — G, as runs the Glass, Man's life doth pass. I, The idle fool is whipt at School. T fixed it irrevocably: "Time cuts down all, Both great and small." Here, Time with his hour glass marched, winged and dreadful. Beside the letter X a coffin lay open, a man's head stuck out: "Xerxes must die, and so must you and I". Next a fearful skeleton held an arrow over a child's head: Y was Youth forward slips, Death soonest nips." The picture of John Rogers, the dissenting martyr burned at the stake while his wife with nine small children and one at her breast watched, must have fascinated William. The flames flew and darted. The executioner looked wicked in helmet and armor; the children's tears fell on their pinafores and poured to the ground.

In addition to catechism, he would have studied reading, writing, arithmetic, and navigation — courses to prepare him for a life at sea. The Whipple children were also tutored by Robert Elliot Gerrish, a Harvard graduate and cousin of their mother.[17] Historian John Sanderson said Whipple "displayed throughout his whole life the marks of early attention and good elementary education. On leaving school he embarked immediately on board a merchant vessel, the constant and customary mode of commencing a commercial life at that period."[18] He was 14 when he went to sea as a cabin boy in one of his father's ships. Both France and Spain were at war with Great Britain and her American colonies at the time. His parents must have been fearful he would be captured and impressed into a foreign navy when they read of Piscataqua vessels being chased by the French fleet off Cape Sable as they returned home from Newfoundland. He was 16 when the French sent a fleet to destroy British shipping and to land forces in Canada. New Hampshire was in a state of panic until word arrived the fleet had been dispersed by a storm.[19]

SEA CAPTAIN AND TRADER

When his father died August 7, 1751, William was only 21 and already commanded his own vessel. His seafaring career took him to Europe, the West Indies, and Africa and was excellent training for his later government career. It opened his mind to new ideas, provided opportunity to observe other cultures, brought him into contact with many types of people, and exposed him to England's attitude toward America. The period 1750-56 was profitable for those in shipping. Portsmouth letterbooks and accounts show extensive exports to Europe which was closer to Portsmouth by a day or two than Boston and New York.[20] The larger ships and brigs carried fish, beef and pork, lumber, livestock (especially horses for the cane mills), masts, and "moses-boats" (lighters, used for loading sugar and other products) to the West Indies. They returned via Spain or England with hardware, cloth, salt, iron, and a multitude of other things generally described as "sundry European goods." However, privateers made it a dangerous business and may have contributed to Whipple decision to retire from the sea. The September 30, 1757 New Hampshire Gazette[21] reported 10 Piscataqua vessels captured by French privateers between August 1756 and July 1757 and taken to Guadeloupe, West Indies, an immensely wealthy sugar island owned by France. Wyseman Claggett, notary public, reported French and Spanish privateers working the West Indies captured nine Piscataqua merchantmen in both 1759 and 1760, 19 in 1761, and seven in 1762.[22] Most were Portsmouth and Kittery ships with a few from Exeter, Dover, and Berwick.[23]

At around age 30, he began a new career as a Portsmouth merchant with brothers Robert, 23, and Joseph, 22 on Spring Hill's Bow street. Fish was one of the products they sold. Robert, a bachelor, died a year-and-a-half later. Joseph's business education was learned in the counting house of Nathaniel Carter of Newburyport. He became a large landowner on the frontier, served in the state legislature, was a colonel in the militia during the revolution, and was collector of the port of Portsmouth by state appointment and after the federal constitution was adopted, by appointment of presidents George Washington and Thomas Jefferson. He held that office until a few months before his death January 30, 1816.[24] After Robert's death, the firm, was known as William and Joseph Whipple, Merchants. A merchant imported and exported and sold at wholesale.[25]

William's knowledge of the shipping business and his excellent contacts benefitted the new enterprise and it flourished from the beginning. Joseph's marriage into the prominent Billings family of Boston was helpful in developing intercoastal trade, the standing of their brothers-in-law, Robert Traill[26] and Dr. Joshua Brackett,[27] in Portsmouth's mercantile and professional life; their relationship to the Cutts, to their uncle Joseph Whipple of Hampton Falls, one of the most prominent ministers in the colony,[28] and to Jotham Odiorne, their uncle-in-law, owner of a large number of fishing vessels and a member of his majesty's council, opened many doors for the young entrepreneurs. William joined the St. John's Masonic Lodge January 1, 1752, an association which undoubtedly benefitted their business.[29] Timing was also important. The 12 years between the French & Indian War,[30] and the revolution was a time of rapid expansion of Piscataqua ports. Between 1764 and 1772, the Portsmouth custom house reported an average of 103 ship arrivals and 155 departures annually.[31]

He was an alert merchant as his letter of October 8, 1766 shows. He wrote Joseph that a load of fish was to be delivered to their warehouse and cautioned Joseph "to keep a good look out" as other fish were on board and "some of their crew are very great rascals." He referred to dealing with (name unclear) saying it would be "very imprudent to suffer any more trifling" from him and for Joseph to take the most direct method to get security" from the man.[32]

COURTSHIP AND MARRIAGE

Sometime in the 1760s, William became engaged to his cousin Mehitable, daughter of Mehitable Cutt and Jotham Odiorne. She informed him on the wedding day of her decision to postpone the ceremony. Despite his pleas, she was adamant so he left, never to call again.[33] Several years later, he married his cousin Katharine (Kitty) Moffatt (1734-1821), an heiress, belle, and acknowledged beauty who became one of the leaders of Portsmouth's society. She survived her husband by 41 years. Their wedding was not made public until it became apparent she was with child. In a January 25, 1771 letter to Katharine's sister-in-law Sarah Moffatt, then living at St. Eustatius, West Indies, capt. John Parker, one of William's closest friends, revealed the facts of the marriage. He said William and Kitty were married privately with only the minister, Dr. Brackett, and Parker present. It would have remained a secret, he wrote, as they did not live together until after the marriage was made public when "she was with child." At that point, enemies of both made sure it was the number one topic of conversation at the "Tea Tables" of Portsmouth. "When I told there was no room for their scandal, my veracity was questioned. Among the most violent was Mrs. Knight (Mrs. Wm. Knight was Kitty's sister, Mehitable) who was the last person that suspected or heard of the matter . . . (Kitty) has the misfortune to miscarry about four weeks ago & even this scandal has been very freely dealt about."[34]

Katharine's parents, Katharine Cutt and John Moffatt, were one of Portsmouth's wealthiest couples. Moffatt, born in Dunster, Somerset County, England about 1691, came to America as commander of a "mast" ship which carried masts from Piscataqua to England for use by the royal navy. They were married August 20, 1723[35] and moved from Kittery to Portsmouth in 1735. Beginning in 1741, he served four terms as selectman and served in the house of representatives in 1746. No record exists of public life thereafter. On January 30, 1746, he joined others in purchasing title to capt. John Mason's claim to New

Hampshire and became one of colony's largest landholders. Throughout the decade of the 1740s he kept a fleet of seven to eleven vessels in action and was the fourth largest trader by volume in the Piscataqua area in 1752. He was among the top six taxpayers in the colony in 1770. Not active in the events leading to the Revolution, he was blind and deaf for several years before his death. He owned land in 64 towns when he died and it took Katharine Whipple several years to settle his estate, most of which went to his grandson Robert Cutts Moffatt.[36] Their son Samuel (1738-80), a 1758 Harvard graduate, married Sarah Catherine Mason January 30, 1764. She was a direct descendant of John Mason whose claim to the New Hampshire area dates to 1623. Samuel went into the slave trading business with his wife's brother-in-law Peter Livius[37] and George Meserve, a future Stamp Act collector. Financial reverses in the slave trade forced Samuel to flee Portsmouth to avoid debtors prison. Whipple helped his cousin and future brother-in-law by taking him to St. Eustatius in the West Indies in the brig *Diana* prior to November 1767 where Samuel began a new commercial life assisted by a Philip Lewis, a merchant friend of Whipple.[38] Moffatt's wife and children Elizabeth and John Cutt did not accompany them as Sarah was pregnant at the time. They joined him after the birth of his second daughter, Mary, known as Polly.

Whipple's good deed came back to haunt him. Livius, who was known as "the Czar" and "Peter the Great," was successful in obtaining a judgment against Samuel in the amount of 1,663 sterling. Since he was out of the country, the judgment could not be served. Determined to get his money, Livius went to the province law books and found an old statute which decreed that a master or commander of a ship carrying any inhabitant out of the province without giving bond to the province secretary is subject to a fine and required to pay all damages arising thereby. Livius used this law to attach Whipple's brig *Diana* and its cargo upon its return from the West Indies. The brig was anchored subject to final settlement which meant Whipple could not use it in his business.

Samuel's debt to Meserve was also large and he monitored Livius' action closely, and was ready to attach Whipple's property if Livius was successful. It was a significant loss ending William and Joseph's business dealings because Livius and Meserve could continue to attach any new business by claiming the value of the original attachment did not nearly equal the amount of their claims. The Whipple brothers offered to give Livius bail in return for sufficient security to refund any damages they might recover if they beat him in court. Livius refused the offer.

The court awarded Livius a judgment of £2,000 and Whipple moved for an "arrest of judgment" but the court ruled in favor of Livius. John Moffatt, William, and capt. John Parker appealed the ruling to the governor and council. Whipple and Livius entered into a "Rule of Court" which referred all matters to the inferior court without a jury. That court ruled in favor of Whipple but Livius appealed to the superior court and said he would carry it to king in council if he lost at that level. The author has not been able to review the superior court ruling so does not know the final outcome.

John Moffatt was in his late 70s when business went sour for Samuel. He tried to help his son as much as possible sending him ships and goods to establish a business and encouraged him to remember that he is "a being made for eternity . . . and not neglect your duty towards God . . . always live in a prepared state . . .

as you would choose to die in." He said while he was relatively healthy he had expected Samuel to have assisted with the business in his old age because he became "disordered," causing his business "to stagnate."[39]

THE MOFFATT MANSION

John Moffatt began building a large house on Fore Street in 1760. Completed in 1763, it became the residence of Samuel and Sarah.[40] After Samuel fled to the West Indies, John paid his debts by auctioning the house's contents, which had been pledged for collateral. He had friends bid on his behalf and repurchased the contents from them. He, Katharine, and Samuel's wife, Sarah and their three children, Elizabeth, John Cutt, and the baby, Mary Tufton "Polly" Moffatt,[41] were living in the house by the time Whipple returned to Portsmouth.[42] After their marriage was publicly announced William moved in and he and Katharine became host and hostess of the great mansion. Sarah, Elizabeth, and John eventually joined Samuel Moffatt in the West Indies and Polly remained to be raised by the Whipples. They treated her as if she were their daughter. Polly eloped with Nathaniel Haven, a Portsmouth physician, in April 1786, five months after William died. She was 18.

The house was on a bank overlooking the river with a two-story coach house beside the service yard. There were a few mansions close by including Samuel Cutts' and Thomas Wallingford's. Governor John Cutt's house was a short distance away. The customs house and post office were nearby.[43] The narrow lane below was later widened and a private wharf with warehouses and sail loft was at water's edge. To the west were gardens and orchards, presumed to have been laid out when the

Moffatt-Ladd House, 154 Market Street, Portsmouth, N.H. Home of Gen. William and Katharine (Moffatt) Whipple their entire married life. Open to the public from mid-June to mid-Ocotber and by appointment. Photo courtesy of the National Society of the Colonial Dames of America in the State of New Hampshire, Portsmouth, N.H.

house was built. Two plantings survive from the eighteenth century: the English damask rose planted by Sarah Moffatt in 1768 and the enormous horse chestnut tree planted by Whipple in the fall of 1776 with chestnuts he brought to Portsmouth from Philadelphia after signing the Declaration of Independence.

Larger (50' by 40') than any other in the Piscataqua, the house is wood frame, clapboarded with quoined corners, and has a roof topped by a Captain's or Widow's Walk surrounded by a handsome railing with urn finials. It was built by highly skilled carpenters and artisans at a cost of £14,000.[44] Its most dramatic features are the great hall — nearly a quarter of the ground floor, unique in a house north of Boston — and the rich architectural detail.[45] The corner staircase with intermediate landing is the central focus. Three windows in the parlor at the back of the hall look out on the upward slope of the terraced garden with its grass steps, fruit trees, bee hives, and multitudes of flowers, providing an unexpected contrast to the wharf which fronts the busy Piscataqua river. The front parlor opens from the hall at the left of the front door and looks out on the street. Fred Myron Colby, author of "The Moffatt-Whipple Mansion" article in The *Granite Monthly New Hampshire Magazine*, speculated it is the room where the Whipples did most of their entertaining.[46] The left hall probably served as Whipple's office and library. Shelves containing a variety of bound volumes lined two sides. The house had multiple sleeping chambers — some believe as many as nine. The Whipples' chamber was on the east side of the second floor where it catches the morning sun and has a view of the harbor with Kittery in the distance.

The 1768 auction inventory shows the Whipples lived in high style. The hall was furnished with a large table, 12 French easy chairs of mahogany were in the long chamber, six leather bottom and six Windsor "cherry tree" chairs, some of which may have been in the upper hall. The drawing room had a cherry table, card table, two teaboards and eight walnut chairs. A set of penciled English cups and saucers were in the closet. The front parlor had a cherry table, card table and stand, and eight chairs of mahogany with hair bottoms. There were plates and cups and saucers in blue and white and in "burnt china" with two large bowls; a china tea tray, six patty pans, green ivory knives and forks, wine and syllabub[47] glasses and a brown urn. The kitchen had four iron kettles, a tin kitchen, brass, iron, and bell metal skillets, small and large brass kettles, two coffee pots, a copper tea kettle, and two dozen pewter plates. The Green

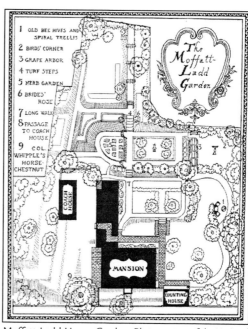

Moffatt-Ladd House Garden. *Photo courtesy of the National Society of the Colonial Dames of America in the State of New Hampshire, Portsmouth, N.H.*

Chamber upstairs had a mahogany dressing glass as well as other mahogany pieces, a painted cedar bedstead, bed and window curtain and chair covers in green check. The windows and fluted walnut bedstead in the Yellow Chamber were curtained in yellow damask, which also covered six chairs and an easy chair. A silk quilt, three window cushions, and a gilt mirror completed the effect. These rooms had "Persia carpets" and rugs were scattered throughout the third story.

In 1814 the house was transferred to John Moffatt's last heir, his grandson Robert Cutts Moffatt. Nathaniel and Polly (Moffatt) Haven purchased it from Robert's estate in 1819 for $14,000, the value established by the court in 1813, and gave it to their daughter Maria (Mrs. Alexander Ladd), John Moffatt's great granddaughter. The Ladds moved in in September 1819. Alexander H. Ladd acquired it in 1861. Except for a few boarders, only Moffatts, Whipples, and Ladds lived in the house from the time it was built until acquired by The National Society of The Colonial Dames of America in the State of New Hampshire in 1913.[48]

One of Portsmouth's most elegant historic mansions, it is known as the Moffatt-Ladd House and is located at 154 Market Street. The house, coach house, counting house, gardens, and open vista to the Piscataqua river have changed very little since it was built. In 1814, the Havens installed a side door near the foot of the stairs to provide access to the garden and counting house, hung imported Vues d'Italie scenic wallpaper, replaced door molding, installed a mantel, and added an arched niche for the sideboard in the dining room. Alexander H. Ladd added a vertical row of windows lighting the service spaces behind the kitchen chimney, modernized the original southwest corner kitchen with a cast iron stove, and changed paint colors and wallpapers throughout. The Dames discovered the fireplace and decorative ends of the original kitchen shelves in the 1960s and restored the space as the original kitchen.[49] A number of the furnishings have been there since the 1700s. Generous descendants

Kitchen, Moffatt-Ladd House. *Photo courtesy of the National Society of the Colonial Dames of America In the State of New Hampshire, Portsmouth, N.H.*

Dining Room, Moffatt-Ladd House, *with Gen. Whipple's sword on the table.. Photo courtesy of the National Society of the Colonial Dames of America In the State of New Hampshire, Portsmouth, N.H.*

Central Stairway, Moffatt-Ladd House. *Photo courtesy of the National Society of the Colonial Dames of America In the State of New Hampshire, Portsmouth, N.H.*

of the Moffatt and Ladd families have contributed to the collection. Inventories in 1768 and 1786 have helped authenticate furnishings and uses of specific rooms. The Yellow chamber on the second floor is one of the best-documented American rooms of the 18th century.

Portraits of more than a dozen family members by Gilbert Stuart, John Greenwood, Joseph Blackburn, Ulysses Dow Tenner, and Albert Gallanting Hot hang throughout the mansion. The formal

Yellow Bedroom, Moffatt-Ladd House. *Photo courtesy of the National Society of the Colonial Dames of America In the State of New Hampshire, Portsmouth, N.H.*

portrait of William Whipple in civilian dress was painted by U.D. Tenney from a likeness from John Trumbull's painting of the signing of the Declaration of Independence.[50] The portrait of Katharine Moffatt Whipple was acquired by the

New Hampshire Colonial Dames in May 1992 from Skinner's Auction Gallery in Bolton, Massachusetts.[51]

In addition to the original pieces, today's furniture includes purchases by the Society as well as gifts and loans. The parlor features a set of ornately carved Chinese Chippendale furniture said to have been imported from England by John Wentworth, New Hampshire's last royal governor and purchased in 1794 by Nathaniel A. and Polly Haven and given to their daughter, Maria (Haven) Ladd. Fine examples of New England furniture fill the rooms. A Flemish scroll chair, believed to have been "brought from Ireland in 1680" and a walnut lowboy of the same period are in the yellow chamber as are two Flemish scroll chairs with cane back supposed to have belonged to Sir William Pepperrell, a native of Kittery Point, who led the Americans troops in the 1745 battle which captured the French stronghold at Louisbourg. Pepperrell was made a baronet and became a revered figure in New England. Under the angle of the stairs stands a large gate leg table said to be the one the provincial council used at the call of gov. Benning Wentworth in the council chamber at his house at Little Harbour. The Society continues to research and add period pieces to the house in an effort to make it a museum of interest, beauty, and authenticity.[52] In 2001, the Friends of the Moffatt-Ladd House, following a successful fund raising event, added a large set of mahogany seating furniture in the fashionable Chinese Chippendale style to the house. Made around 1760 in London, it was originally owned by New Hampshire's last royal governor John Wentworth[53] The house is open to the public from mid June to mid October and by appointment.

PORTSMOUTH CIVIC ACTIVITIES, 1760 – 1775

After becoming merchants, the Whipple brothers became active in town activities and were soon elected to positions of trust. William's first election was November 24, 1760 as a petit juror. Joseph's first election was August 20, 1764, also as a petit juror.[54] As members of Portsmouth's marine society, they petitioned the state assembly on June 14, 1765 to build a lighthouse near the mouth of the Piscataqua to prevent the loss of more vessels.[55] In 1766 they were among petitioners asking the legislature to prevent hogs going at large in town.[56] On April 2, 1767 William was elected to a committee to spend £50 to pave the street leading to the market house. He was moderator of the town meeting December 6, 1768, and town agent along with Samuel Cutts[57] March 25, 1769. As agents, they had authority to commence any action, suit, or process in law on behalf of the town and/or its inhabitants and to answer and defend any suit, action, or process against the town or its inhabitants.

William and Joseph signed the petition July 12, 1769 asking the town to determine if merchants should continue the importation or sale of British goods. William, Samuel Cutts, John Sherburne, Woodbury Langdon, and Jacob Sheafe (John Penhallow and Daniel Rindge refused to serve) were named a committee to decide what to do about the Revenue Acts and the non importation of British goods. The committee reported July 24 (Langdon presented a separate report) but the town meeting adjourned without taking action. Later that year Portsmouth merchants and traders stopped importing and on April 10, 1770 William and Joseph were among those seeking a public meeting to protest several Boston merchants led by James McMasters transferring their import business to Portsmouth. The town voted April 11 to "stigmatize" McMasters, to rescind licenses of tavern keepers who accommodated such persons, and to identify importers "who go contrary to the united sentiments of the patriotic sentiments of our sister colonies as . . . enemies to America." William Whipple, John Parker, Woodbury Langdon, Sam Cutts, and Peter Pearse were named "a committee of inspection to see who imports goods contrary to the foregoing resolves" and to inform McMasters of "the mind of the town."

In the decade of the 1770s William greatly increased his public service activities.[58] He was elected a petit juror January 15, 1770, city auditor and fire warden March 26, and to a committee to apply to the general court for a valuation act March 30. Community health was also a concern and on June 30, 1772 William circulated a petition to allow inoculation for small pox. Only 15 other freeholders, including Joseph, signed. On March 25, 1773, he was elected the city's agent and to a committee to spend £100 to pave the streets and highways of the town. On March 16, 1774, William was named to a committee to instruct Portsmouth's legislative delegation on matters related to the split with England. He signed a petition June 28 asking for a determination of what to do about tea imported by Edmund Parry. The petition noted the general anxiety caused by tea landed subject to a duty imposed by parliament without consent. It referred to dependency on sister colonies for necessary supplies which would be denied if the town allowed the tea to be sold and consumed. To preserve the peace and welfare of the town and province and to prevent the tea from being destroyed by violent means, the petitioners recommended it be sent out of the port. On June 29, Joseph Whipple, Samuel Dolling, Joseph Bass, and George Tanner were named a committee to inform Parry that if the tea was not out of the harbor within four hours, the town would not be responsible for what happened to it.[59] William was named to a standing committee to inspect incoming cargo which met with Parry July 27. Parry apparently continued to import and the town instructed William on September 9 to remove and protect 30 chests of tea if Parry agreed not import any more until repeal of the Tea Act. Parry agreed at a public meeting September 10 to refuse the cargo.

William signed a petition September 15, 1774 urging his townsmen to aid the poor of Boston who were suffering greatly by closure of the port.[60] Four days later the town agreed and named him to the committee to receive donations. It collected £200 in three weeks. On November 29, William and 12 other petitioners objected to laws enacted by "a parliament in which they had no representation" and asked the town to endorse the Continental Association, a declaration of American rights, adopted by the continental congress in Philadelphia. While rejecting independence, it was an ultimatum to test allegiance to the American cause. The choice was to be for or against the Non Importation Act — either buy or don't buy British goods. It established committees of safety and inspection.[61] Whipple condemned profiteers at the town meeting, arguing, "he who increased in wealth in such times as the present, must be an enemy to his country, be his pretensions what they may."[62] The town voted unanimously to support and to "punctually and religiously execute [the Continental Association] as far as in them lies"[63] and warned traders not to raise prices. On December 8 the brothers were elected to a committee of inspection or safety "to observe that the conduct of all persons . . . adhere to the most peaceable and successful method for the removal of the distress these colonies are laboring under and the restoration of their violated rights . . ."[64]

On March 4, 1775, Portsmouth elected William agent and auditor. He was elected to two committees April 20: the 10-man committee to equip every man in Portsmouth with "one flintlock in good order, bayonet, and every other requirement to defend himself " and the five-man committee to monitor "every commerce" that may effect the interest and safety of the town. The latter committee was responsible for "regulating secret instructions in military exercises" and to coordinate the military for any emergency called by the committee of twenty-five."[65] A month later he was elected to a five-man committee to "adopt and pursue measures . . . to preserve and restore the rights of this and other colonies" and to empower "their deputation [at Philadelphia] to act on behalf of themselves."[66] He ended the year by accepting election to a five-man committee to ask the general court meeting in Exeter to do something about inflation and loss of trade."

PRE-REVOLUTION ACTIVITIES

To understand what motivated William Whipple to the cause of independence, it is necessary to know the New Hampshire of his time. When John Wentworth became royal governor in 1767, the population was 52,000. Portsmouth, the colony's commercial center, capital, and home of most royal officials, had a population of 4,500 and dominated the social and political life of the province. The rest of the colony was divided into two distinct parts: (1) the agricultural Merrimack Valley and contiguous territory; its leading towns were Londonderry with 2,389 population and Concord with 752; (2) the frontier settled by pioneers from Connecticut who lived by farming and lumbering. These settlers were far from the arm of the law and the king's name inspired little emotion.[67]

Two years after the Whipple brothers started their business, England imposed Writs of Assistance to enforce Trade and Navigation Acts. The Navigation Acts confined colonial trade to the motherland at a time colonial merchants were calling for less restrictions so they could develop their own enterprises and trade freely with the world outside Great Britain. The Writs allowed custom officers to make searches without warrant. Merchants also resisted the 1764 Sugar and Currency Acts, the 1765 Stamp Act, and the 1767 Townshend Act. The Sugar Act taxed imports coming from places other than Great Britain; the Currency Act prohibited them from issuing paper money; the Stamp Act imposed a tax on newspapers, advertisements, almanacs, legal documents, bills of lading, notes, and bonds and affected the most articulate people in the colonies — merchants, lawyers, publishers. The Townshend Act taxed tea, glass, paper, painters' colors, etc. The American economy had grown too big to be handled in outworn mercantilist relationships — a doctrine that the economic interests of a nation as a whole are of primary importance and should be strengthened by protecting home industries by tariffs, increased foreign trade, monopolies, and a balance of exports over imports.

During debate on the Currency Act, chancellor of the exchequer Charles Townshend asked testily whether "these American children, planted by our care, nourished up by our indulgence . . . and protected by our arms" would be so ungrateful as not to contribute their small share to imperial revenues?" Colonel Isaac Barrè's, who had fought at gen. James Wolfe's side at Quebec, defended the colonists, calling them Sons of Liberty. "They planted by your care! No your oppression planted them in America," he threw back at Townshend. "They fled from your tyranny to a then uncultivated, inhospitable country, where they exposed themselves to almost all the hardships to which human nature is liable. They nourished up by your indulgence! They grew by your neglect of them . . . They protected by your arms! They have nobly taken up arms in your defense; have exerted a valor amidst their constant and laborious industry, for the defense of a country whose frontier was drenched in blood, while its interior parts yielded all its little savings to your emolument." Americans long remembered Barrè's speech.

These acts disrupted Portsmouth's commerce and caused severe financial problems. Imports fell as much as 80%. The New Hampshire assembly sent the king a petition June 1, 1768 stating it was inappropriate to levy taxes on them since they had no representation in parliament. They reminded the king the province had willingly supported the government with revenues voted by itself and with indirect contributions in port duties collected in England, pointing out the latter was extremely large because of England's monopoly of American trade. The Boston Massacre, the catalyst that caused the petition to be sent, prompted gov. Wentworth to write the earl of Hillsborough that "the people will not be persuaded but that the commissioners of the customs and the revenue acts are exerted to absorb the property, and destroy the lives of the people."[68] Americans who had been proclaiming "No Representation, No Taxation" now began to cry, "No Representation, No Legislation."

On May 28, 1773 the New Hampshire assembly received a circular letter from the Virginia house of burgess recommending a standing committee of correspondence and inquiry be established. It committed its first overt act of rebellion by naming a seven-member committee the same day.[69] Similar committees were appointed in the other colonies and a confidential interchange of opinions developed. The New Hampshire committee was replaced in May 1774 with a committee of inspection and later by a committee of ways and means. All these committees were revolutionary in character and functioned alike. Other towns to establish committees of correspondence or inspection in 1774 were Exeter, Barrington, Hampton, Newcastle, Haverhill, Rochester, and Dover.[70]

Parliament passed Lord North's Tea Act in May 1773 giving the English East India company a monopoly on the sale of tea to the colonies, freezing regular merchants out of a profitable business. Colonial merchants reminded Americans that the East India company had drained Asia of its wealth and now "cast their eyes on America . . . to exercise their talents of rapine, oppression, and cruelty. The monopoly of tea, is . . . but a small part of the plan they have formed to strip us of our property." The Act was labeled an "attack upon the liberties of America" designed "to subvert our constitution, render our assemblies useless, and the government arbitrary." At the December 16 Portsmouth town meeting, the night of Boston's infamous tea party, the town resolved, "That it is the natural right of men born and inheriting estates in any part of the British dominions, to have the power of disposing of their own property, either by themselves or by their representatives." Before the meeting ended, it was agreed no tea could be landed at Portsmouth and a committee of correspondence was organized.[71]

A series of measures passed in 1774 widened the rift between Great Britain and America. Boston harbor was closed which meant the destruction of the town as it lived by and from the sea. Elements of government were removed from popular control,[72] royal officials were allowed to be tried in England to avoid judgment by a local jury, colonists were required to house British troops, and Quebec's boundaries were extended to the Ohio river thwarting the western land claims of Massachusetts, Connecticut, and Virginia.

General Thomas Gage, the new military governor, arrived in Boston May 17 to inaugurate the regime of what was dubbed the "five intolerable acts." Reactions in Portsmouth were ominous. Its committee of correspondence wrote the Boston committee May 19 that closing the port was "of the most extraordinary nature and fatal tendency." On May 27 the assembly appointed a new provincial committee of correspondence despite gov. Wentworth's lobbying efforts against it. After a fiery debate the motion carried by a majority of two and was upheld by a single vote when reconsidered the next day. Wentworth adjourned the assembly, keeping it under short adjournment, hoping to overturn the vote. After learning letters urging election of a general American congress had arrived, he dissolved the assembly June 8 which had no constitutional existence except during sessions of the assembly.

The assembly met in an extralegal (outside of legal control or authority) session July 6 in Portsmouth to consider Virginia's invitation to participate in a continental congress. The governor ordered them to disperse as they were meeting illegally in government property. They adjourned to a nearby tavern and voted to hold a provincial congress at Exeter July 21. Eighty-five delegates attended and elected John Sullivan and Nathaniel Folsom to the continental congress to be held in Philadelphia in September, instructing them to assist delegates from other colonies "to devise, consult, and adopt such measures as may have the most likely tendency to extricate the colonies from their present difficulties, to secure and perpetuate their rights, liberties, and privileges, and to restore that peace, harmony, and mutual confidence, which once happily subsisted between the parent country and her colonies."[73]

There were two governments, royal and revolutionary, in New Hampshire from the middle of 1774 to the fall of 1775.[74] Initially illegal and unconstitutional, the revolutionary government soon commanded obedience and became the real government until power was passed to the independent state government. By adopting the temporary constitution drawn up in 1775 (which lasted until a permanent constitution was adopted June 2, 1784), New Hampshire became an independent colony seven months before the Declaration of Independence was signed. The first constitution was never ratified but was accepted by the people.

The provincial committee of correspondence ordered non-importation and non-consumption agreements to begin December 1, 1774 with a non-exportation agreement to be effective September 10, 1775 unless the oppressive English acts had been repealed. Domestic manufacturing and strict economy were encouraged. Merchants who raised prices to take advantage of the temporary scarcity were to be boycotted. A warrant was sent to all towns December 2 urging appointment of local committees to enforce the measures.[75]

Two critical actions were taken March 30, 1775. First, parliament passed the New England Restraining Act which required New Hampshire, Massachusetts, Connecticut, and Rhode Island to trade only with Great Britain, Ireland, and the West Indies and forbade fisheries on the Grand Banks. The intent was to starve the New Englanders into obedience and submission.[76] Second, the king began signing commissions for generals and admirals to lead this new war. He dispatched a fleet to the colonies and ordered forces be increased to 20,000 in Boston. Vice admiral Keppel refused to go. He would fight a European army, he said, but not an American one. Lord Effingham resigned his commission when he discovered his regiment was intended for America. The king personally called on sir Jeffrey Amherst and offered him a peerage. Amherst refused saying he could not serve against the Americans, "to whom he had been so much obliged." The old Highland Watch, now stationed in Ireland, refused to "go and fight against their brethren, who last war fought and conquered by their side." William Pitt withdrew his son from the army rather than see him fight the Americans. Sir William Howe, youngest of the three military brothers, reluctantly agreed to take over Gage's command at Boston. The first thing Howe would see on landing at Boston was the monument to his brother George Augustus viscount Howe who had died fighting side by side with the Americans against the French at Ticonderoga.

Late in May 1775 capt. Andrew Barkley of the frigate *Scarborough* with 100 marines established a blockade of Portsmouth harbor. His orders were to "take every provision vessel" and convoy it to Boston for use by gen. Gage's troops. Believing a deserter from his crew was given sanctuary by the people of Portsmouth, Barkley took a crew member from a Portsmouth fishing vessel hostage causing the town to end its informal agreement with Barkley not to starve each other. When Barkley detained two Portsmouth bound vessels laden with corn, pork, flour, and other provisions, William Whipple was one of the memorialists to ask gov. Wentworth to liberate the vessels and cargoes. The signers predicted violence if lawful commerce wasn't allowed to continue. The Portsmouth committee of correspondence wrote the Newburyport committee asking it to intercept the *Canceaux*, a small ship of six or eight guns, escorting the seized vessels to Boston. Portsmouth was unable to prevent the sailing as the harbor was blocked by a 20-gun English warship and it had no vessel to retaliate.[77] By August 23, lack of food caused Barkley to sail to Boston. Governor Wentworth and family were compelled to sail with them. A mob demolished Fort William and Mary after they left.

To prevent the humiliation of the assembly meeting without his presence, Wentworth sailed to Gosport, Isle of Shoals, September 25 and sent a proclamation to Portsmouth proroguing the assembly until April 24, 1776. It was the last act of the royal government in New Hampshire. William Whipple wrote Langdon October 12, 1775 that no one paid any attention to Wentworth. "The sons of despotism dare not open their mouths except when they get together to lament their loss of power and what passes between them is of but little consequence to the public."[78]

With exception of gunpowder (Britain prohibited export of powder and arms to America), the colony was in a reasonable state of defense by October. Gun batteries had been placed at strategic points overlooking Portsmouth harbor and a boom was being built to lay across the river from Henderson's Point to Bass

Rock. Paul Revere galloped into Portsmouth December 13 with the erroneous information that Gage was sending two regiments to strengthen the fort known as the Castle. The Portsmouth committee of ways and means made immediate plans to remove the fort's munitions and armaments. The next day about 400 men from Portsmouth, Rye, and Newcastle overpowered the fort's five man garrison, seized 100 barrels of powder, and sent it up river by gundalow to Durham where it was hidden under the pulpit in the meeting house. On the night of the 15th, John Sullivan of Durham, later a member of the continental congress and a major general in the continental army, with about 40 men, seized 16 pieces of cannon, 60 muskets, and other military stores.[79] These raids marked the beginning of the rebellion in New Hampshire. Though powerless, gov. Wentworth stripped maj. John Langdon, maj. John Sullivan, and col. Nathaniel Folsom of their militia commissions and col. Josiah Bartlett of both his militia and justice of the peace commissions.[80]

Independence was hard for many Americans to accept. As late as the winter of 1775/76 the provinces of Pennsylvania, New York, New Jersey, and Maryland instructed their delegates not to vote for independence. But the king made their decision easier by proclaiming the colonies in a state of rebellion when he rejected the continental congress' Olive Branch petition authored by Pennsylvania's John Dickinson. This petition professed the attachment of the American people to the king, expressed hope for the restoration of harmony, and implored him to prevent further hostile actions against the colonies until a reconciliation could be worked out.

New Hampshire's John Sullivan and Massachusetts' John Adams led the debate against the petition. On the day he was to receive the petition, the king issued a proclamation declaring "open and avowed rebellion existed in the colonies." In a later speech to parliament, he was among the first to raise the specter of independence when he said, "the rebellious war now levied is become more general, and is manifestly carried on for the purpose of establishing an independent empire."[81] In December, parliament proclaimed the colonies an independent enemy rather than rebellious subjects by passing an act forbidding all trade and intercourse, authorizing forfeiture of captured ships and property as enemy property, and declaring the colonies out of the king's protection.

SERVICE TO THE COLONY
Convinced that England was not going to change its policies, William Whipple disposed of his business interests in 1775 and devoted the rest of his life to public service and the cause of American independence. His January 12 election to the provisional congress and May 15 election to Portsmouth's committee of safety[82] led to a remarkable third career in public service. He was one of 144 members at the second provincial congress[83] in Exeter January 25 which elected John Sullivan and John Landgon representatives to the May 10 continental congress. His leadership was immediately recognized as he was named to the provincial committee of correspondence[84] and to the committee empowered to call a provincial convention of deputies.[85]

The provincial congress, in a January 25 message, said that since the royal government had not functioned for 10 months, the people were deprived of "advantages which flow to society from legislative assemblies" and that parliament was passing measures to enslave them. "Shall we," they asked, "knowing the value of freedom, and nursed in the arms of liberty, make a base and ignominious surrender of our rights, thereby consigning all succeeding generations to a condition of wretchedness, from which, perhaps, all human efforts will be insufficient to extricate them? Duty to ourselves, and regard for country, should induce us to defend our liberties, and to transmit the fair inheritance unimpaired to posterity." The message included 12 recommendations for the people to live by.[86]

Though not legally authorized as a government, the provisional congress regulated the everyday conduct of the towns and taxed them to defray expenses of delegates to the continental congress. News of the April 19 battles at Lexington and Concord reached New Hampshire the 20th and most southern towns dispatched their troops to Boston and vicinity and the committee of correspondence called an emergency session of the provincial congress for April 21. Because of the short notice, only 68 delegates from 34 towns attended. Whipple and Joshua Brackett, his brother-in-law, represented Portsmouth. Colonel Nathaniel Folsom was appointed to command the scattered New Hampshire forces already at Boston. Each town was asked to accumulate military stores and to organize its own company of minute men. Whipple was named to two committees: one to answer a letter from the Massachusetts congress and one to procure fire arms and ammunition.[87]

On May 17 the fourth provincial congress met at Exeter and assumed authority for governing the colony. It established a provincial post office at Portsmouth, authorized three regiments of 2,000 men to serve six months, and voted a tax of £3,000 to support these forces. Whipple was on the post office committee and the committee to prepare the plan for raising, supplying, and paying the troops. He also served on the ways and means committee which seized £1,516 from royal treasurer George Jeffrey.

A committee of safety to function as an executive body was authorized May 20. In addition to Whipple, its members were Meschech Weare, chairman from 1776 to 1784,[88] Dr. Matthew Thornton, Dr. Josiah Bartlett, Nathaniel Folsom, Dr. Ebenezer Thompson, Phillips White, Pierce Long, Samuel Cutts, George Gains, Israel More, Jonathan Moulton, Wyseman Claggett, John Dudley, Timothy Walker, Jr., Nicholas and John Taylor Gilman, Dr. Nathaniel Peabody, and John McClary. These men were New Hampshire's real revolutionary government — the political power behind the scenes.[89] Notable exceptions among the revolutionary party who never served on the committee were John Langdon, John Sullivan, and Samuel Livermore. Royal authority was gone by June 28. The courts didn't function and the king's sheriffs were powerless. The committee of safety filled an obvious gap in government — a responsible executive and a compact administrative body to execute general policy efficiently with power to act secretly and speedily in emergencies. It interpreted its power broadly and never shrank from assuming doubtful jurisdiction — its powers and duties were practically dictatorial. It gave itself "general authority" between legislative sessions to consider "all matters in which the welfare of the province shall be concerned, except the appointment of field officers." It executed legislative policy; coordinated the state's military; regulated trade; was the tribunal for the defection and trial of crimes of dishonesty in government, counterfeiting, and loyalism; represented the colony in dealing with continental authorities and supervised disbursement of colonial funds. It issued £10,000 on the credit of the revolutionary government and voted to emit an additional £10,000 for other pressing needs.[90] It seized provincial records and transferred them to the provincial secretary Ebenezer Thompson at Exeter. It directed each town to appoint a committee of safety, retaining authority to command them to enforce its edicts and enforce law and order. Because of the prestige of its members, the committee's power was generally unchallenged.

As chairman of the committee of safety, Whipple wrote capt. Timothy Bedel July 7 to proceed with his company to Northumberland or Lancaster and erect a garrison suitable for defense against small arms. He was to gather intelligence, gain and keep the friendship of the Indians, examine anyone suspected of going to Canada to oppose the cause of America, and assist, to the extent possible, any individuals attacked.

The next day he wrote two letters — one to delegate Langdon, the other to the continental congress. He notified Langdon that congress never gave the colony direction and asked for a resolve legitimizing the colony's paper money. He pointed out how difficult it was for so small a colony "without any money" to raise and support troops requested by congress and noted the colony's lack of gun powder. His letter to the congress informed it that New Hampshire was wholly governed by "this congress and the committees of the respective towns," that there was great unanimity for the cause of freedom, that opponents did not dare attempt to obstruct the new government, and that the Restraining Bill was being strictly enforced on the coast by armed vessels. He said the colony had resolved to raise 2,000 men, had stationed 28 companies of 66 men each in the vicinity of Boston under the command of Nathaniel Folsom, and had posted two companies to guard the sea coast and three companies to guard the Canadian frontier. He reminded congress the colony's frontier was only two days march from French and Indian settlements and said he saw little prospect of overcoming a shortage of gun powder as the coast was patrolled by English men-of-war and cutters.[91]

On August 23, as both the nominal and actual government, the provincial congress reorganized the militia into 12 regiments under command of Folsom who was made a major general. On that date Whipple was elected to the committee that drew up instructions for delegates to the continental congress, set the salary for local representatives at six shillings a day, and organized men from 16 to 50 into regiments and companies. He was appointed colonel of the first regiment of militia August 24. His staff included Joshua Wentworth as lieut. col., Benjamin Barker first major, and Ephraim Pickering second major.[92]

After the ship *Prince George* sailed into Portsmouth harbor October 2 and was captured, gen. George Washington ordered its cargo of 1,892 barrels of flour brought to Cambridge. Whipple wrote Washington October 11 that 100 soldiers were stationed in Portsmouth, 200 more worked on the port's batteries, and they had been out of flour for weeks. To promote the common cause he said the committee ordered 100 barrels be taken for the use of the soldiers and asked permission to buy an additional 500 barrels as "the town of Portsmouth is in great want of bread."

He wrote delegates Bartlett and Langdon October 12 that since the cargo was captured by New Hampshire forces, it should be awarded the colony.[93] Bartlett and Langdon wrote him back October 26 that congress had taken no action on the flour ship, that because of a shortage of powder "no cannon [should] be fired unless drove to the last extremity," and that capt. Mowatt was expected to sail to Portsmouth with three armed transports to burn the town. "For God's sake, be you ready," they warned.[94]

That the colony was preparing for war is evident from Whipple's letter of November 12 informing Langdon they had fortified Portsmouth harbor with "three 32-pounders, one 24, one 18, six 6s, four 4s with all necessary implements on Peirces Island and one 24, six 4s & 6s on Seavy, and a battery of six guns on Kittery Point." About 250 men were stationed on New Castle and they sank the flour ship in Crooked Lane, placed a boom across the river from Henderson Point to Pierce's Island, moored four vessels above the boom which could be set afire if necessary, and gathered 20 pair of fire rafts to burn if needed.[95] He reported the burning of Falmouth, Maine by the British and said Portsmouth, expecting to be the next target, had taken appropriate defensive action by asking for assistance from towns throughout the state. The response was so great Whipple said they wished the enemy would attack so Portsmouth could avenge Falmouth. "The cruelties of the enemy have so effectually united us," he concluded "that everyone seems determined to risk all in support of his liberties and privileges. If the enemy comes we should give them a warm reception."[96] A thousand men were enlisted but they only had 17 pounds of powder.[97]

He wrote capt. Bedel November 18 from Exeter congratulating him and his troops on their part in the victory at St. Johns. The troops had been ordered to join maj. gen. Philip Schuyler's army so the committee considered them continental troops and made no provisions for their pay. However, realizing they were suffering in the severe climate and needed assistance, the committee sent "£300 L.M." (lawful money) with the caution no more would be forthcoming. He told Bedel he had written to generals Schuyler and Richard Montgomery about pay and supplies and hoped they would "safely return with the laurels of victory and be well regarded for your services and sufferings by your countrymen."[98] On December 2 he authorized capt. Joshua Martin to enlist 61 able bodied men to serve in the continental army under Washington until January 15, 1776. He ordered the company to join maj. gen. John Sullivan's brigade on Winter Hill by December 10 and said they would be paid at the continental rate beginning the day they march. Pay would include the time going to and from their destination and would be paid immediately upon dismissal. Those supplying their own provisions on the march would be reimbursed in cash.[99]

Whipple also worked to broaden the right to vote and serve in the legislature. Beginning in 1728, New Hampshire required voters to own real property worth at least £50. To qualify for election a representative had to own at least £300, thus limiting both voters and candidates. When the Revolution began, legislators were elected by the towns, by voters the selectmen deemed qualified. He was on the committee that recommended that all taxpayers be allowed to vote, that the property qualification to hold office be reduced to £200, that towns be allocated representatives for every 100 freemen, and towns with less than 100 could combine until reaching that number.[100]

From the second through the fifth provincial congresses, he was the only Portsmouth representative to serve the entire time. After the fourth congress adjourned, he shared with Langdon his hope that "God grant the next may be composed of better men than the last. A certain puppy (a member from Portsmo) who you know never acted on a just principle (notwithstanding his insignificancy) has given much trouble & taken up much time to little purpose." He also said it was his wish that America could possess Canada "or at least [keep] it out of the possession of our enemies."[101]

On October 18, New Hampshire's delegates sought advice from the continental congress on how the colony should administer justice and regulate civil police. John Adams of Massachusetts, eager for all colonies to establish their own governments, "embraced with joy the opportunity of haranguing on the subject at large and of urging congress to resolve on a general recommendation to all the states to call conventions and institute regular governments." On November 3, the continental congress suggested the colony hold a convention and let the people determine what form of government would "most effectually secure peace and good order in the province." Meeting in Exeter from December 21 to January 5, 1776, the provisional congress voted to form a civil government and "assume the name, power, and authority of a house of representatives or assembly for the colony of New Hampshire" and to choose 12 persons — five from Rockingham county, two from Strafford county, two from Hillsborough county, two from Cheshire county, and one from Grafton county — to be a distinct and separate branch of the legislature known as the Council, the president of which was to be the colony's chief executive officer.[102]

Portsmouth conservatives, concerned "the action would disaffect our friends in Great Britain as savoring of independency," wrote circular letters to other towns expressing fears about forming a government. Nine towns joined Portsmouth in petitioning the provincial congress to "reconsider" its action and to continue "to do business as the late congress had done."[103] After several days of deliberation, the provincial congress voted 2 to 1 to ratify the earlier action.

The new government was formed January 5, 1776. Twelve councilors by rank were named the next day. Meschech Weare was first, Matthew Thornton, second, Whipple, third, Josiah Bartlett, fourth, Nathaniel Folson, fifth, Thomas Westbrook Waldron, sixth, Ebenezer Thompson seventh, Wyseman Clagett eighth, Jonathan Blanchard ninth, Samuel Ashley, tenth, Benjamin Giles, eleventh, and John Hurd, twelfth. Bartlett, Langdon, and Whipple were elected delegates to the continental congress January 23 for a term of one year "any one in the absence of the others to have full power to represent the colony." Only two were to attend at one time. One hundred pounds was appropriated for Whipple's expenses on the 27th.

Accepting election to the continental congress carried negative political consequences in Portsmouth. The anonymous letter in the January 9 *New Hampshire Gazette* might have fazed a weaker man than Whipple. The letter writer said independence meant ruin and destruction and asked how the colonies, with 1,000 miles of seacoast and no ships of war, could defend themselves against "310 battle ships, completely manned and fitted?" He wondered how a country of three million who might raise an army of 30,000 could expect to win against a nation of 15 million with an army of 150,000. He said the colonies were "without arms, without ammunition, without trade, contending with a nation that enjoys the whole in the fullest latitude."

A Portsmouth town meeting adopted a petition January 18 criticizing the new government and 12 legislators protested saying "so small & inconsiderable a colony" should not take the lead "in a matter of so great importance, and that their constituents only expected "judicial & executive wheels [be set] in motion, not a new form of government" that appears independent from the mother country.[104] That there was concern about the petition of the 10 towns is evidenced by the letter sent to Whipple and Bartlett in Philadelphia February 10, 1776. The legislature wanted the continental congress to reaffirm its original recommendation to form a state government.[105]

In March congress asked New Hampshire's committee of safety to determine how its citizens felt about revolution. On April 12 the committee circulated the association test throughout the state to be signed or rejected by all white males over 21, lunatics and idiots excepted. The test asked subscribers to "solemnly engage, and promise, that we will, to the utmost of our power, at the risk of our lives and fortunes, with arms, oppose the hostile proceedings of the British fleets and armies against the United American Colonies."[106] Sentiment was fairly equally divided on the seacoast among the commercial class, including merchants, shipbuilders, and financial entrepreneurs. It was overwhelmingly revolutionary in the interior.[107] Whipple's willingness to be a leader in the cause of revolution becomes more meaningful considering many of his associates, including his brother-in-law Robert Traill, supported Great Britain. Traill fled the country and was proscribed in November 1778.[108] When the British peace commissioners arrived in the colonies in mid 1788, they brought a letter from Traill for Whipple.[109]

ENTERS THE CONTINENTAL CONGRESS

From 1774 to the autumn of 1788, New Hampshire sent 18 delegates to congress. Whipple, its fifth delegate, was elected four times: January 23, 1776, December 24, 1776, August 19, 1778, and November 3, 1779. He declined to accept the last election. He attended various sessions between February 29, 1776 and September 24, 1779 and served the state longer than any other delegate. His colleagues were Josiah Bartlett, 1776, Matthew Thornton, 1776, '77, George Frost, 1777, '78, '79, Nathaniel Peabody, 1779, and Woodbury Langdon, 1779. Of the five, he was closest to Bartlett and they became close friends and allies. He wrote Bartlett January 13, 1777 that Thornton was well and that they were agreeable, but "inter nos (between ourselves), New Hampshire is oftener divided than she used to be."

Noting Thornton's impending departure in May 1777 would require him to attend Thornton's committees as well as his own, which included the all-important secret committee,[110] he wondered why Timothy Walker, Jr. and George King, elected in March, declined to serve. "Do gentlemen still think it hazardous to appear in a character that will render them obnoxious to the British tyrant and his infernal tools? Or are they afraid their private interest will suffer? The day is not far off when some of those gentlemen who are so loath to step forth will be making interest for a seat in congress." He said those "now laboring" in congress will be remembered for serving when the country most needed them."[111] He wrote Weare in November 1777 that even those "who compose public bodies" pay more attention to their private business at the expense of public business "notwithstanding their own and their country's salvation is at stake. My desire is to animate everyone . . . in the glorious cause."[112]

When Peabody and Langdon were elected in 1779, Whipple predicted they would have difficulties working together, which he believed to be a disadvantage to the state and disagreeable to the delegates. After Peabody arrived he wrote Bartlett, "I find I am not mistaken in my conjecture respecting him and his intended colleague. Cannot something be done to prevent the evils that may be the consequence of a division of sentiment?"[113] Of the continental congress' 55 delegates, usually 35 to 40 attended. Delegates came and went, depending on conditions in their home colonies. Frequently they went home to attend to local public business they considered more important than national affairs. At times some colonies were not represented at all and others only by one member.

Most congressional history is culled from journals, diaries, notes of debates, official letters written by delegates collectively or individually to their home governments, and private letters to friends. Fortunately, Whipple and Bartlett were prolific letter writers and a large body of their letters, and those of Meshech Weare survive.[114] An example of Whipple's proclivity for letter writing is his February 7, 1777 letter to Bartlett: "Please to give best respects to Dr. Thompson. I am half a letter in debt to him, but fear I shall not be able to pay him by this conveyance, but shall very soon as I love to be punctual in paying debts, especially of this sort. I wish he and some other of my friends would increase my obligations in this way. While I am on this subject I must beg leave to remind you that I have not heard so often from you as I could wish, but flatter myself when you recollect how anxious you used to be to know how affairs were going on at home, that you will not be unmindful of me."[115]

Whipple's journey to Philadelphia by horseback with bulging saddlebags was slow, dreary, and toilsome. Extremely bad road conditions made the trip more difficult. He took lodgings with John Adams on Second street. Mrs. Sara Yard was their landlady. Philadelphia, largest city on the continent, had a population of about 20,000, a majority were Quakers who dressed plainly and lived simply. A miasma, believed to cause malaria, arose at sundown so most people hurried home to avoid the night air.[116] While it had fine houses of brick and stone most were wooden. It had a dozen churches, about 300 shops, a few manufactories, a theatre, where the play began at 6 p.m., and John Dunlap's daily newspaper, *The Pennsylvania Packet*. It lacked bridges but the "horseboat" ferries, where horses walking in a circle turning a capstan made the water wheels move, ran constantly. Whipple found these ingenious. Its citizens were more conservative than those in Portsmouth, Boston, and the South but were patriotic and supported the cause of independence. The non Quaker wealthy families lived in elegant style and entertained delegates at dinners and balls.

Bartlett was there for Whipple's first two weeks of service and was of great help in introducing him to members and the ways of congress. He served alone from March 18 to May 18 when Bartlett returned. Langdon never attended this term.[117] The 1776 congress sat longer and considered more important issues than its predecessor. It was not an easy year. The war was more costly, the army had to be renewed and maintained, continental bills of credit were depreciating, and the people's enthusiasm diminished. Since the militia was undependable, a regular army with specific enlistments and pay and better selection of officers was debated as were inducements such as enlistment bounties and land grants. Articles of war modeled after England's were adopted; disposition of lands to the westward became an issue.

Sending Silas Deane to France and other commissioners to Europe to solicit recognition, trade, and aid was the beginning of diplomatic relations with foreign powers. Life and death measures such as the Declaration of Independence, the first draft of the Articles of Confederation, the plan of treaties with foreign powers were dealt with. Any one of these, when measured by results or consequences, would distinguish the 1776 session. This was William Whipple's new world. Fortunately, he was equal to the job and thrived on the national scene.

Whipple wrote Bartlett March 24 that he needed help in representing the colony and for Bartlett to hurry to Philadelphia as the "grand question [independence] would be debated soon."[118] Four days later he wrote Bartlett the "devils from the other side of the water" are expected soon.[119] On April 5 he issued another plea to Bartlett to return and expressed frustration about not hearing from the state assembly: "I have given over all thought of hearing from anybody concerned in the legislature of New Hampshire." He had been in Philadelphia two months and had "not received a single line tho' the genl. court has been setting almost a month." He said the main business of congress was "the privateering business and regulation of trade."[120]

He wrote Langdon April 2 about the impending arrival of the British commissioners and said he hoped "you or Bartlett will be here to receive their low mightiness. Some here are for shutting them up at the moment they land. However, I hope they will be treated with civility and sent back with a flea in the ear, for I cannot possibly think they are commissioned for any good." He wondered if his Portsmouth neighbors "can yet reconcile themselves to that illustrious stranger [independence] that was so much feared. *Common Sense* has made all the southern colonies his friend, and I hope the northern colonies will soon open their arms to receive him. It's my opinion that the salvation of America depends on him."

On April 11 he asked Langdon for a report on how the British left Boston and whether "the statue of the Royal Brute in Bowling Green will soon be demolished." He reported that parliament's act declaring all American rebels caused South Carolina to seize a ship loaded with sugar bound for London. The ship and cargo were sold, the money deposited in the state treasury, and the colony was asking for congressional approval of the act. Whipple said the action was "justified" and noted South Carolina had formed a government and North Carolina and Virginia would soon follow. He wondered how lord Dunmore's declaration of war published in Virginia would impact the Olive Branch petition being considered by congress.

He wrote Weare April 12 that the colony should inform congress of its activity in the war effort, point out the disadvantages of printing colonial bills, and ask for about two-thirds of the sum required to implement its war plans. In May he informed the state it was to raise a battalion of 728 men to be stationed at Portsmouth under command of a continental officer[121] and urged it to begin manufacturing arms which were in short supply throughout the nation. He wrote Weare he expected Britain to exert the "utmost efforts for our destruction," and hoped "the Supreme governor of the Universe [would] protect, and defend us, guide our councils and prosper our arms."[122]

Whipple was an early supporter of the Articles of Confederation but initially doubted congress would ever agree on the many differences that "give great offense to some."[123] He wrote Langdon in May that "a Confederation, permanent and lasting . . . is not far off," and would lead to recognition by Europe and ". . . fill our ports with ships from all parts of the world."[124] Negotiations took place in July and August causing Whipple to postpone his return to New Hampshire to hear the debates so he could answer questions from the state assembly on his return. He had a copy with him when he arrived in Portsmouth August 31.

En route home he dined with Ezra Stiles who recorded in his diary that "col. Whipple showed me the Articles of Confederation . . . not passed but printed" for every member to consider. "He might show it but suffer no copies."[125] Most delegates agreed with Whipple about the need to confederate, but issues of taxation, commerce, boundaries of the western lands, representation for large and small states, etc. had to be resolved and provoked heated debate until August 20 when the Articles were set aside and not considered again until April 8, 1777, when as time permitted, they were debated until mid November. They were adopted November 15 and sent to the states for ratification. Legislatures had to give their delegates "competent power" to sign. New Hampshire delegates signed in July 1778.[126]

Congress made many momentous decisions in early May. Talk of independence was being replaced by preparations for war. On the 9th it authorized issuance of five million dollars in paper money.[127] On the 15th, John Adam's resolution advising the colonies to suppress crown authority and to assume power under the authority of the people passed. General Washington was summoned to Philadelphia the 16th to plan for the coming campaign and conferred with the entire congress the 24th and 25th. A committee, including Whipple, was appointed to plan the military operations.[128] Bartlett arrived the evening of May 17, "much fatigued." New Hampshire finally had two delegates to share the heavy work load.

In early June Whipple wrote Langdon a vote on independence was approaching and he believed it would pass. The change in Philadelphia is as great "since my arrival, as there was in New Hampshire between the time that the powder was taken from the fort (William and Mary) and the battle of Bunker Hill." John Hancock, president of the continental congress, asked the state to raise troops for continental service, calling the cause of freedom "a most glorious one and I trust every New Hampshire man is determined to see it gloriously ended, or to perish in the ruins of it." He said the salvation of America depended on all colonies working in common.[129] A letter, with a congressional resolution asking the state to supply 750 troops for an incursion into Canada, from Whipple and Bartlett arrived the same day. They said it was imperative to support the request noting a successful campaign "will place us out of the reach of their malice." The legislature responded July 3 by voting to recruit 1,500 men of which 115 were to be raised by Whipple's regiment, 111 by Bartlett's, and 66 by Thornton's.

SIGNS THE DECLARATION OF INDEPENDENCE

By the time Whipple reached Philadelphia February 28, only seven delegates had spoken for independence: George Wythe, Virginia; Christopher Gadsen, South Carolina; Thomas McKean, Delaware; Benjamin Franklin, Pennsylvania, Samuel Ward, Rhode Island; Silas Deane, Connecticut; Samuel Adams, Massachusetts. But after Thomas Paine's 47-page pamphlet, *Common Sense*, issued in January with over 100,000 copies reaching even the outermost parts of the colonies, generated overwhelming mass sentiment for independence, others including Whipple, Roger Sherman, Connecticut; John Adams, Massachusetts; Richard Henry Lee, Virginia joined in the call. As late as April, a majority did not exist for independence. Yet, three months later, congress voted unanimously to separate from the mother country.

Paine argued the futility of reconciliation and presented the practical benefits of independence in terms of simple common sense. "We have it in our power to begin the world over again. The birth day of a new world is at hand, and a race of men, perhaps as numerous as all Europe contains, are to receive their portion of freedom." He said independence carried a significance beyond political boundaries. "'Tis not the affair of a city, a country, a province, or a kingdom but of a continent. It is not a concern of the day but of all posterity to the end of time. All plans and proposals prior to the nineteenth of April (battle of Lexington) are like the almanacs of last year. Time hath found us! Ye that dare oppose not only the tyranny but the tyrant, stand forth!" He demolished kings everywhere, past, present, and future, and using the Old Testament proved that monarchy, far from being blessed, was cursed by scripture. Trace any royal line to its origin, said *Common Sense* contemptuously, and the first king would be seen as "nothing better than the principal ruffian of some restless gang, whose savage manners obtained him the title of chief among plunderers." Paine asked and answered the question: Where is the king of America? ". . . he reigns above, and doth not make havoc of mankind like the royal brute of Britain." These were powerful arguments for pious Americans. His manifesto ended with seven words in large black print: THE FREE AND INDEPENDENT STATES OF AMERICA.

North Carolina was the first colony to speak for independence in unmistakable tones. On April 12 its provincial congress gave its continental delegates power to declare independence and form foreign alliances. After Virginia and North Carolina instructed their delegates to offer a resolution for independence,[130] Whipple and Bartlett wrote Weare May 28 asking for "the sentiments of our colony on the important subject of a total separation from Great Britain. Let our own opinions be what they may, we think ourselves in duty bound to act agreeable to the sentiments of our constituents." When no answer had been received by June 11, they asked again because debate on the issue would begin July 1, "by which time it is expected . . . delegates . . . not already instructed will receive ample power."[131]

Virginia's R. H. Lee introduced the resolution for independence Friday June 7: "That these United Colonies are, and of right ought to be, free and independent States, that they are absolved from all allegiance to the British crown, and that all political connection between them and the state of Great Britain is, and ought to be, totally dissolved. That it is expedient forthwith to take the most effectual measures for forming foreign alliances. That a plan of confederation be prepared and transmitted to the respective colonies for their consideration and approbation." John Adams seconded. On June 10 opponents won postponement of the vote after agreeing a Declaration should be drafted and ready for the July 1 debate. Thomas Jefferson, John Adams, Benjamin Franklin, Roger Sherman, and Robert R. Livingston were named to the drafting committee June 11. On the 12th, a member from each colony was named to a committee to prepare a form of Confederation, and John Dickinson, John Adams, Benjamin Harrison, and Robert

Morris were named to a committee to develop a plan of treaties to be proposed to foreign powers. Independence meant war so a majority was unacceptable; unanimity was required. Congress convened as a committee of the whole about noon July 1. President Hancock vacated the chair so the debate and vote were unofficial. This "trial balloon" was a traditional and highly useful device to get the sense of a legislative body before official and irretrievable action was taken. Dickinson led the opposition, arguing more time was needed to reach a reconciliation and to prepare for a contest with such a powerful foe. Opponents believed a yes vote would cause the colonial union to dissolve while Whipple, Bartlett, and others believed a no vote would result in dissolution. Lee was in Virginia so John Adams carried the resolution. No notes on his speech survive, yet for the remainder of his life, it was referred to in terms of wonder and praise. "He came out with a power of thought and expression that moved us from our seats," Jefferson said years afterward. The vote was 9-4 for independence.

Bartlett and Whipple are believed to have cast the first and second votes for the declaration as the normal order of voting began with the northern colony.[132] New York refused to vote "for want of instructions from home." Pennsylvania and South Carolina voted nay. Delaware's two deputies were divided. Congress adjourned until 9 a.m. when the final vote would be taken "in full congress assembled." The large majority was a powerful inducement to the four dissenters and on July 2, twelve states voted for independence. Henry Wisner promised New York would not stand alone; it voted approval in a convention July 9.

The draft committee had given the job of writing the Declaration to Jefferson and congress spent most of July 2, 3, and 4 reviewing the draft sentence by sentence making 86 changes and eliminating 480 words. It stopped short of Paine's proposals as it only referred to the "present" king of Great Britain and would not have precluded a monarchial form of government for the United States or for any of its constituent parts. But it put into words, even more effectively than Paine did, "that all men are created equal;" that Americans were entitled to "a separate and equal station" among the nations of the earth. The words, in the form of a sacred creed, have an elemental eloquence that has been moving men ever since.

Historians agree that most of the changes were improvements, but Jefferson writhed at what he later termed the "depredations" of his work.[133] But he said years later that the Declaration's "authority rests . . . on the harmonizing sentiments of the day." Congress eliminated everything that tended to divide — references to slavery and Scotch mercenaries — and added language to strengthen the union — the reference to God so the devout could feel the revolution was being carried out under divine guidance.

Editing the Declaration did more than improve it; it led to a unity among delegates who only three weeks earlier had been at loggerheads over the question of independence. Now, with little difficulty, they agreed on a set of fundamental political beliefs. America celebrates the Fourth of July when the Declaration was adopted by congress rather than July 2 when Lee's resolution for independence was passed. However, delegates considered the Declaration a mere application of the July 2 unanimous decision which made independence a fact.

There was no question about New England. On May 14 Rhode Island informed congress its delegates should support independence.[134] Connecticut's legislature instructed its delegates on June 14 "to assent" to all elements of Lee's Resolution. New Hampshire took similar action the 18th "solemnly pledging our faith and honor that we will, on our parts, support the measure with our lives and fortunes."[135] Whipple could now vote his conviction on what he felt was the most important act of his life. On June 24 he wrote, "the middle colonies are getting in a good way. Next Monday, being the first of July, the grand question is to be debated, and I believe determined unanimously. May God unite our hearts in all things that tend to the wellbeing of the rising empire."[136] After the declaration was adopted, he wrote, "This declaration has had a glorious effect. It has made these colonies all alive."[137] On July 9 Whipple and Bartlett sent Weare a copy saying they "were so happy to agree in sentiment with our constituents, it gave us the greater pleasure . . . to vote for the enclosed declaration."[138]

Members felt the amended copy was not suitable for formal signature so on July 19 congress ordered it engrossed on parchment as "The Unanimous Declaration of the Thirteen United States of America." Most members signed August 2 and that evening feasted on sea food from a captured enemy ship destined for lord North's table in London.[139] Although celebrated as champions of liberty, approximately one-fourth of the signers didn't vote for the declaration. Only three of Pennsylvania's nine signers voted for it; three who were present didn't sign; five were not members when it was adopted. Oliver Wolcott, Connecticut; Philip Livingston and Lewis Morris, New York; R. H. Lee and George Wythe, Virginia; William Hooper, North Carolina; Samuel Chase and Charles Carroll, Maryland; and possibly others were absent on July 2. Livingston of the drafting committee, believing its adoption inexpedient, left congress when New York adopted it and never signed.[140] Matthew Thornton, New Hampshire's third signer, was not a member when it passed. He attended congress from November 4 to May 2, 1777 and signed it sometime in November.[141]

The Declaration was first proclaimed before a great crowd at noon Monday July 8, in Philadelphia's state house yard. Colonel Nixon of the Philadelphia Associators read it from atop a round scaffold about 20 feet high. Troops saluted, the people gave three great huzzahs. Whipple, Bartlett, and 47 other members of congress standing just below the platform cheered, then went back to work.

Post riders carried it to every corner of the now 13 sovereign and independent states. Townspeople gathered and cheered as the Declaration was read. Spontaneous celebrations of gunfire, bells, bonfires, pomp, and parades broke out. The lion and the unicorn would no longer prance in these American states. The king's coat-of-arms were ripped from courthouse doors. His portrait was turned to the wall. The halfpenny with its royal face was reduced to a farthing. A hundred King streets were renamed State street; Queen street became Congress Way. Meshech Weare, in a letter to president Hancock July 16, voiced the fervent desire "That He who puteth down potentates and setteth up states may guard and protect the United States of America."[142]

Abraham Clark of New Jersey expressed the opinion of many members that the Declaration was an act of treason and if the colonies failed to achieve independence, those who signed stood a good chance to suffer the penalty of traitors. Consequently, congress decided not to release the names until January 18, 1777 when it ordered an authenticated copy with names printed and sent to each state. President Hancock's January 31 letter said: "As there is not a more

The Declaration of Independence, 4 July 1776 by John Trumbull (1756-1843) Yale University ARt Gallery, New Haven, Connecticut. Trumbull Collection.

Key to signers: 1. George Wythe, VA; 2. William Whipple, NH; 3. Josiah Bartlett, NH.; 4. Thomas Lynch, SC; 5. Benjamin Harrison, VA; 6. Richard Henry Lee, VA; 7. Samuel Adams, MA.; 8. Stephen Hopkins, R I; 9. William Paca, MD; 10. Samuel Chase, MD. 11. Richard Stockton, NJ; 12. Lewis Morris, NY; 13; William Floyd, NY; 14. Arthur Middleton, SC; 15. Thomas Heyward, Jr., SC; 16. Charles Carroll of "Carrollton", MD; 17. Robert Morris, PA.; 18. Thomas Willing, PA; 19. Benjamin Rush, PA; 20. Elbridge Gerry, MA; 21. Robert Treat Paine, MA; 22. William Hooper, NC; 23. John Dickinson, PA; 24. William Ellery, RI; 25. George Clymer, PA; 26. Joseph Hewes, NC; 27. George Walton, GA; 28. James Wilson, PA; 29. Abraham Clark, NJ; 30. Francis Hopkinson, NJ; 31. John Adams, MA; 32. Roger Sherman, CT; 33. Robert R. Livingston, NY; 34. Thomas Jefferson, VA; 35. Benjamin Franklin, PA; 36. Thomas Nelson, Jr., VA; 37. Francis Lewis, NY; 38. John Witherspoon, NJ; 39. Samuel Huntington, CT; 40. William Williams, CT. 41. Oliver Wolcott, CT; 42. Charles Thomson, PA; 43. John Hancock, President, MA; 44. George Read, D   E   ; 45. George Clinton, NY; 46. Edward Rutledge, SC; 47. Thomas McKean, DE; 48. Philip Livingston, NY.

distinguished event in the history of America than the declaration of her independence — nor any, that in all probability, will so much excite the attention of future ages — it is highly proper, that the memory of that transaction, together with the causes that gave rise to it, should be preserved in the most careful manner that can be devised . . . that it may henceforth form a part of the archives of your state and remain a lasting testimony of your approbation of that necessary and important measure."[143]

Pennsylvania's Benjamin Rush wrote John Adams July 20, 1811 asking if he remembered "the day on which the vote (for independence) was taken? Do you recollect the pensive and awful silence which pervaded the house when we were called up, one after another, to the table of the president of congress to subscribe what was believed by many at that time to be our death warrants? The silence and the gloom of the morning were interrupted, I well recollect, only for a moment by col. Harrison of Virginia, who said to Mr. [Elbridge] Gerry at the table: I shall have a great advantage over you, Mr. Gerry, when we are hung for what we are now doing. From the size and weight of my body I shall die in a few minutes, but from the lightness of your body you will dance in the air an hour or two before you are dead." This speech procured a transient smile, but it was soon succeeded by the solemnity with which the whole business was concluded."[144] While two signers became president and others were heroes of American history, most sank to relative obscurity. Even those who signed with doubt probably agreed with the death bed message Pennsylvania's John Morton left for his family: "Tell them that they shall live to see the hour when they shall acknowledge it to be the most glorious service I ever rendered my country." John and Sam Adams and Jefferson, like Whipple, felt it was the most important act of their lives.

After declaring independence, there was no middle ground, no place for the lukewarm and hesitant in congress. Members were renewed, animated, enthusiastic, and buoyant with hopes of a speedy victory. However, the next year and a half saw failure and defeat on the battlefield and in organization and administration of the congress. Twice congress had to flee Philadelphia to avoid capture by the British. But despite all setbacks, it continued doggedly at its task and finally found success.

CONGRESSIONAL COMMITTEES

Whipple quickly became one of the work horses of congress. His colleagues recognized both his people skills and his broad knowledge of marine and foreign affairs, money and taxation, and commerce and military affairs. He was named to the most important committees, chaired the naval, foreign affairs, and tax committees, and was a ranking member on military and quartermaster committees. He served on scores of sub committees, chairing many of them. Committees met mornings before the general session and almost every night, even during general sessions. He wrote Langdon June 10, 1776 they were in session as late as 7 p.m.

His first appointment was March 4, 1776 to the committee of claims. One of the busiest committees in congress, it reviewed and approved payment of claims ranging from military obligations to supplies and clerical work for congress. Two weeks later he was named to the important marine committee which was to develop and oversee the navy. He became its most influential member. Whipple believed the navy to be the safest and cheapest defense of a nation. He noted it required men of some education to manage. "Illiterate men . . . may make brave and popular . . . army [officers], but they can neither navigate or fight a ship of war [so] a navy . . . will always command the best resources of our country in talents and character. It will become the depot of supernumerary sons of all the wealthy families in the U.S. It is less destructive to human life by diseases than an army, and far less so to morals. There are no taverns nor brothels in ships of war."[145] In October 1776 he was on the sub committee with R.H. Lee and Robert Morris that recommended rank and pay for naval officers.[146] In 1777, he supported establishment of a navy board in Boston and advocated a "powerful navy." He wrote Bartlett in April it was time to pay attention to protection from future invasions by building the navy.

Pierre Landais, a French navy captain, had convinced congress in 1778 to build 74-gun warships. Whipple redesigned them into frigates with thirty-two 32-pounders on the gun deck and fourteen 12-pounders on the quarter deck and forecastle. He said Landais' plan would provide more "genteel" accommodations for officers but his design would have great advantage in fighting and predicted that if built, the two-deckers would never go to sea. One 74-gun ship was eventually built. Whipple wrote Bartlett August 22 that he had conferred with Landais who offered "nothing of sufficient weight to alter my sentiments. On the contrary, since talking to him I am more confirmed in my opinion. Those Frenchmen who are not perfectly acquainted with our language have a very convenient way of getting over difficulties. When they cannot answer your objections, they do not understand you. However, experience will bring us right in time, I hope."[147] Whipple's plan was approved with amendments.[148]

Despite reluctance by fellow delegates, Whipple continued to press for funding a strong navy. Following victories by the *Warren*, *Ranger*, and *Queen of France* in April 1779, he won approval of a $500,000 appropriation for the navy's eastern department.[149] The navy received good news in July 1779 when Rhode Island's Abraham Whipple, no relation, commanded a squadron of three frigates that accomplished one of the great naval feats of the war. During a thick peasoup fog off Newfoundland the squadron sailed into a Jamaica fleet of some 60 merchantmen bound for England with rich cargoes of cotton, sugar, woods, and other tropical products and captured 11 prizes.

In March 1776, Whipple joined the qualifications committee, which recommended appointment to offices other than military. He joined the cannon committee[150] in April and the secret committee in November. The cannon committee awarded contracts for armament for the army and navy and the secret committee, one of congress' most important, was responsible for providing arms and ammunition to the army. This assignment resulted in close working relationships with generals George Washington, Horatio Gates, Charles Lee, Thomas Mifflin, John Sullivan, Philip Shuyler, and commissary general Joseph Trumbull.[151] He spent Christmas 1778 at the home of the president of Pennsylvania Joseph Reed. Other guests were George and Martha Washington, the president of congress [either John Laurens or John Jay], Don Juan de Miralles of the Spanish navy, Samuel Holten, Massachusetts member of the marine committee, and col. Lawrence, Washington's military aid.[152]

That congress recognized his military insight is evidenced by his appointment to many special committees dealing with military matters. In March 1776, he, Richard Henry (hereafter R.H.) Lee, Virginia, and Edward Rutledge, South Carolina, were the committee to work with gen. Charles Lee on "the best methods of defending New York."[153] The committee's report, in Whipple's handwriting with a few words inserted by gen. Lee, was extensive. It determined the security of Long Island was a greater priority than New York and that 8,000 troops could defend both. It called for confiscation of all Tory weapons. Congress accepted its recommendations and ordered 8,000 men to defend New York.[154] He, John Adams, Benjamin Harrison, Virginia, Joseph Hewes, North Carolina, and Robert Morris, Pennsylvania, were on the committee to plan "for fortifying the coast" in 1776. The committee was to determine construction methods and costs to fortify at least one port to protect cruisers and receive their prizes.[155]

Washington's request in May 1776 for arms was referred to Whipple, Sam Adams, George Wythe, Virginia, Caesar Rodney, Delaware, and R. H. Lee.[156] This committee was conferring with Washington as late as June 2. They were also in conference with the chiefs of the Six [Indian] Nations who had come to Philadelphia at the request of congress. Later that month he was appointed to the committee to investigate problems in the commissary department run by commissary general Joseph Trumbell.[157] This was followed by appointment to the committee to work with Washington, maj. gen. Horatio Gates, and brig. gen. Thomas Mifflin to develop "a plan of military operations for the ensuing campaign."[158] On June 24 he was named chairman of the committee "to inquire into the cause of the miscarriages in Canada. Based on the committee's report, congress ordered court martials for several officers.[159] The committee concluded that short enlistments resulted in "disorderly and disobedient" soldiers; lack of money resulted in shortage of supplies and ammunition; and an outbreak of small pox disabled many soldiers.[160] Congress addressed the enlistment problem by offering new enlistees £20 bounty and 100 acres of land and a complete suit of clothes annually. Those providing their own clothes were to be paid £20.[161] In October 1776, he, Sam Adams, and John Hart, New Jersey, were on a special committee to acquire salt for the army.[162] His concern about clothing for the army prompted him to ask Bartlett in November 1776 if he visited any army units en route home. "If so, you must be sensible of the lack of clothing [and] . . . use your influence to draw the attention of the executive power of our state to that subject."[163] He wrote Weare on the same subject November 18 and encouraged the state to work on the problem.[164] He expressed concern for the common soldier February 22, 1777 because congress was only providing a "scanty supply" of clothing. He believed each state should make up the difference and also called for great care in the appointment of regimental surgeons. On Christmas eve 1776 he and Thomas Heyward, South Carolina, joined the committee dealing with the affairs of the northern army. He was on the fiveman committee to confer with gen. Gates "upon the general affairs of state" in March 1777.[165]

In November 1778, along with Nathaniel Scudder, New Jersey, and Gouverneur Morris, New York, he was on the committee to take "proper steps" about issues recently raised by gen. Washington. Five days later they were authorized to regulate and superintend the commissary and quartermaster departments. The commissary quartermaster committee functioned for somewhat more than a year as a self-directing body and was constantly seeking provisions for the army and to control prices.

Letters sent to governors and legislatures November 11, 1778 asked for a census of food production so it could determine how surpluses could be diverted to the war effort. The census information was to be kept secret to prevent "devoted adherents of lucre" from profiting at public expense. The committee warned legislatures about "engrossers (speculators) and their evil practices which threaten the poorer people of the states" and requested local laws to fix prices and to impose heavy taxation on speculators. Legislatures were also asked to prohibit the manufacture of malt spirits, to seize distilled liquor "at a low price," sell it, and use the proceeds "for the comfort of sick and wounded soldiers."[166]

In April 1776, he was on the committee to examine and determine the value of the several species of gold and silver coin in circulation and the proportion they ought to bear to Spanish milled dollars." This committee cautioned that "enemies of American liberty" might try to "impair" the credit of continental currency by raising the nominal value of gold and silver and warned the people to be on guard against this. Its final recommendation was that bills of credit emitted by congress be equal in value to gold and silver and whoever charged or accepted more in continental currency for "land, houses, goods, wares, or merchandise than for gold or silver "ought to be deemed an enemy to the liberties of these colonies and treated accordingly" upon conviction.[167]

The day after Christmas 1776 he was named chairman of a government operations committee. Since legislative activity left little time for executive responsibility, this committee was to develop a plan to employ non delegates to conduct the executive business of congress.[168] On November 12, 1778 he was named to the commerce committee whose assignment was to recommend by the 16th proposals on how to conduct commercial affairs.[169]

Among his special commitee assignments in 1779 were those to prepare a plan to conduct the country's marine business, to plan for the needs of the board of war and ordnance, to consult with Washington, and to investigate a road project from the Penobscot river to the St. John's river, a public works project that could employ up to 1,500 men and spend up to $15,000 in his state.[170]

A sound money advocate, Whipple expressed concern about inflation and the excessive printing of paper money in a May 3, 1777 letter to Langdon. He was hoping for a foreign loan and would reluctantly support printing more money if a loan were not forthcoming because "the war must be supported."[171] He wrote Bartlett runaway inflation made "living here beyond all bounds. Everything has risen more than double since you left" and that inflation took "four months' pay of a private" to buy a bushel of wheat and a colonel's pay would not buy oats for his horse.[172]

He was chair of the January 1779 tax committee that apportioned $15,000,000 to be collected from the states. He told Langdon he was able to get New Hampshire's share lowered to $500,000 which was less than the original assessment, to give the state flexibility. He hoped the state would collect more.[173] He wrote Bartlett that taxation was the only cure for inflation and that every state should tax "as high as possible while money is plenty." He advocated quarterly collection because "most men would cheerfully pay £25 per quarter [rather] than £100 in an annual payment." He called the May 21 vote to raise $45,000,000 more in taxes "a bold political stroke" even though it added $1,500,000 to New

Hampshire obligation. He wished the whole sum "could be drawn from those speculating miscreants . . . sucking the blood of their country." He wrote Landgon that he hoped "there is still patriotism enough left to make one bold effort to save the country from impending ruin,"[174] that if people who "indulge in every luxury" would buy government bonds, inflation could be controlled, and that "speculators do more mischief than . . . any set of villains since the creation." He wished the country would rise up against them.[175] He supported price controls in a letter to Weare November 24 saying speculators were having a fatal impact on the war effort.

He told Bartlett in May 1779 that congress would soon adopt a plan to support the nation's currency and "dispel the glooms" of America's friends overseas.[176] Approximately $140,000,000 in paper money was circulating and he deplored printing more, supporting instead the proposal to redeem $41,500,000. He realized redemption would produce "convulsion in the country" but believed it would "eventually have salutary effects." Since existing bills were easy to copy, he wanted to replace them with new emissions more difficult to counterfeit.[177]

He assumed a major role in the country's foreign affairs as chair of the committee to "consider the foreign affairs of the United States and the conduct of the late and present commissioners in Europe" in 1778/79. In this capacity he had many dealings with France's minister plenipotentiary Conrad-Alexandre Gérard.[178]

NEW HAMPSHIRE'S CONTINENTAL AGENT

John Langdon served in the continental congress in 1775 and was elected to serve with Whipple and Bartlett in 1776 but never attended. Instead, he sought appointment as New Hampshire's continental agent. Whipple was successful in getting the nomination through committee but a majority of the delegates opposed a member holding a lucrative office created by congress. Not only was the job lucrative, it was powerful. Agents were responsible for construction of all naval vessels, contracted for the rigging and outfitting of naval and privately owned ships desiring continental naval commissions, received continental monies from the navy board to pay for services and goods, imported and exported supplies for the continental government, and assembled naval stores. When prizes were brought to port they prosecuted the libel in the maritime court, sold the seized ship and cargo, and distributed the prize money — one-third to the captor-crew, two-thirds to the continental government. They had advance information about demand for naval and military stores and were able to speculate accordingly.[179]

Whipple informed Langdon the marine committee was forwarding nominations for continental agents to congress April 21, 1776 and he expected to advise him of his appointment in his next letter. He said John Hancock would be in Boston for a few days the end of the month and encouraged Langdon to go there to speak to the president directly about "your ships." "Your ships" refers to the _Raleigh, Ranger,_ and _America,_ built on the Piscataqua under Langdon's supervision. The 696 ton _Raleigh_ was the first ship built by the continental navy. The keel was laid March 21, 1776 and it was launched 60 days later but it took another 14 months before it was armed and put to sea. Her first cruise began August 12, 1777 when she sailed to France to secure military stores.[180] He notified Langdon June 5 that agents had been appointed for all states from Massachusetts to North Carolina except Langdon because he was still a delegate and that acting agent, Joshua Wentworth appointed by Washington in 1775, would get the job if Langdon didn't resign. Langdon wrote Bartlett that he wanted the appointment, was relying on Whipple to get it for him, and had written "brother Whipple fully" on his desire and had resigned his seat "so there shall be no bar to my being chosen. Langdon was appointed June 25. He wrote Whipple July 6 thanking him "for his constant endeavor."

Whipple selected Thomas Thompson of Portsmouth as the *Raleigh*'s first captain and tried to get congress to name the ship *New Hampshire* but agreed to *Raleigh* in deference to Virginia, who "is entitled to compliments from New England" for its early leadership role in organizing the colonies to oppose British policies.[181]

Langdon reported to Whipple July 1 the *Raleigh* was finished "with every rope, completely rove, with men ready to join the crew." He had hired 30 to 40 crew members but had no guns, balls, powder, or provisions for the commissary. Several letters disclose how difficult it was to arm the *Raleigh*. Whipple informed Langdon that Philadelphia furnaces had met with many accidents so guns had to come from Providence "or some other furnace eastward."

Realizing how bad the Rhode Island situation was, Whipple alerted Langdon to the problem and tried to motivate him to write more often: "I have been about two months & six days from Portsmouth & have received one short letter from my professed friend, J. Langdon, esqr. Do you know that Gentn? If so, please present my regards & tell him I am ready to execute any of his commands, and do not expect he will take the trouble to write unless it immediately concerns himself. As all mankind was created mainly for his own benefit, why should one man concern himself about the advantage or disadvantage that may arise to another? The word friendship is often used but there is no substantial meaning to it in this refined age. It's quite an old fashioned word; nothing is now meant by it but that I will readily gratify the person I call my friend provided I can thereby obtain any real advantage to myself. I know you think with me this is the modern use of the word friendship, but your general conduct convinces me that your sentiments are not so far modernized as not to be actuated by the true principles of friendship, & to convince you that I am actuated by the same principles I enclose copies of the letters from Providence mentioned in my last. I don't mean by sending these letters to excite resentment, but to give you power when an opportunity offers, to vindicate yourself. Whenever the person for whom I profess a friendship is treated in a manner that appears to me injurious to his character, I esteem it an indispensable duty to vindicate him. Is that all? No I must do more. I must let him know by whom & in what manner he has been traduced in order that he may know who are his enemies, & in what manner to guard against them, this ever has been and ever shall be my conduct towards the person for whom I profess a friendship."[182]

Providence ship builder Nicholas Brown wrote Langdon August 30 the furnace hearth had given away and it would be at least 55 days before they could cast his guns and either col.Whipple or Langdon must appear in person to buy existing guns. Langdon reported to Whipple September 14 he had just returned from his third trip to Providence and that the ships' committee, chaired by Rhode Island's gov. Cooke, agreed to let him have guns if he would sign a contract to replace them at £100 per ton. He noted the price increased with each visit. The

June price was £70 per ton, raised shortly thereafter to £80, then £90. Rather than do without the guns, he agreed to the unreasonable price but then the Browns would not accept his order as agent but required his private guarantee in case congress concluded the price was too high. Even though congress had already paid for them, he agreed to pay $2,000 up front for the new guns but ultimately gave up when he realized there was "a secret determination not to let me have the guns at any rate." He noted the Browns had cast cannon for private ships and concluded that jealousy that New Hampshire's ship was four months ahead of Rhode Island's was part of the problem.[183] In the end, *Raleigh*'s ordnance was a hodgepodge of local donations, purchase, and imported French guns.[184]

THE NEW HAMPSHIRE GRANTS

On January 15, 1777, towns west of the Connecticut river organized themselves as the independent state of New Connecticut (the name was changed to Vermont in June) and petitioned the continental congress for recognition. Sixteen New Hampshire towns petitioned Vermont to join and were accepted by the Vermont assembly June 11, 1778. New York also had an interest in the area. The disputed territory was known as the New Hampshire Grants and became a continuing issue in the congress.

Whipple's first reference to the dispute was April 7, 1777 when he wrote Bartlett New York would give "an infinity of trouble" and a deputation of Green Mountain boys were in town to lobby their position before congress. On November 30, 1778 he reported to Weare that col. Ethan Allen was in Philadelphia to present the Green Mountain assembly's position on the Grants.

An early member of the Green Mountain boys was Benjamin Whipple of Bennington, Vt. One wonders if Allen, seeking common ground with delegate Whipple, told him of his Vermont Whipple colleague. Benjamin and William were fourth cousins, their common ancestor being Matthew of Bocking, England. In December, Whipple recommended to Weare that the state claim the territory, employ "an able lawyer" to master the subject and represent the state's interest rather than relying on the knowledge of the sitting delegates because western New Hampshire would be "in a perpetual broil" until jurisdiction was settled. While he didn't think there was much support to join New York, he believed towns on the eastern side of the river would join Vermont if it were accepted as a separate state.[186]

Bartlett wrote him in February 1779 that "our disaffected towns seem determined . . . to put the state to all the trouble in their power."[187] Whipple informed state leaders that New York was against forming a new state and again urged claiming the area and appointing a special representative to press the claim. The assembly agreed and directed Ebenezer Thompson to represent it at a congressional committee meeting in the Grants. During the assembly debate to accept his recommendations, Vermont was referred to as an independent state which irritated Whipple who believed such a designation was detrimental to New Hampshire's position. When Thompson failed to meet with the congressional committee, he predicted disagreeable consequences for New Hampshire.

He wrote Bartlett in August how important it was to support the claim to prevent annexation to New York. The issue, still unresolved when he left congress the end of September 1779, prompted him to write his successor, Nathaniel Peabody, that James Duane of New York would be his principal opponent. He hoped Peabody would continue in congress until the issue was settled. James Lovell of Massachusetts wrote Whipple August 30, 1782 that he would not support New Hampshire's Samuel Livermore's bargain with New York delegates to divide the country. John Taylor Gilman wrote Weare January 16, 1783 for instructions on how to vote if congress required New Hampshire and New York to settle the matter between themselves. He said gen. Whipple had been in Philadelphia for several days and they had "freely" conversed on the subject and that Whipple would report on their conversations when he returned home.[188]

CONGRESS FLEES TO BALTIMORE

Whipple informed Weare on November 18, 1776 that general Howe with 10,000 men was marching toward Philadelphia and he expected the Americans to give Howe "a good account." When a rumor spread that congress would flee, Washington was instructed (Dec. 11) to contradict the "scandalous report" and tell the country congress would not leave "until the last necessity shall direct it."[189] The next day congress adjourned to Baltimore.[190] The president and the board of war were among the first to leave so Whipple, Sam Adams, Elbridge Gerry, and William Ellery wrote Washington December 12 that 10,000 troops in Rhode Island were without a general officer and recommended either major general Nathaniel Green or Horatio Gates, with "a suitable number of brigadiers," be given command with orders to repel the progress of the enemy.[191]

In a December 22 letter to his wife postmarked Baltimore, he said he arrived there the 17th and was "lucky enough to get good accommodations." Regarding the advance on Philadelphia, he said British brutality had generated a "spirit worthy of free men" which will result in the enemy's retreat. He predicted 1777 would be good to the American cause and said he had no doubt about ultimate success. His major concern was "friends of America might lose their spirits . . . when there will be the most need of keeping them up." He assured her his anxiety "to hear from you increases with the distance that I am from you. I hope the fear of your letters falling into the enemy's hand will not discourage your writing."[192]

Before leaving Philadelphia, congress passed an extraordinary resolution giving Washington full power to run the war. These powers were extended for six months December 27 and expressed in precise terms: "full, ample, and complete powers" to raise and officer 16 battalions, along with most of the powers that would be exercised under martial law including arresting and confining "persons who refuse to take the continental currency." Whipple believed granting the power "was absolutely necessary for the salvation of America." Benjamin Rush agreed, saying "general Washington must be invested with dictatorial powers for a few months, or we are undone." Sam Adams pronounced it necessary "for a limited time."[193]

The only good news congress received in December was Washington's brilliant stroke at Trenton, New Jersey the night before Christmas. Whipple wrote Bartlett the last day of 1776 that the success at Trenton will put new life into the "Pennsylvanians and add to our strength from Jersey" and if the army were increased to 110 battalions, America's enemies will be vanquished. He expected "the tyrant" to "summon earth and hell" to execute "his infernal plans" and reported that congress had instructed its agents to assure all the European courts it was determined to support independence and that "affairs in France wore a very favorable aspect."[194]

Baltimore, while only a village, was expensive and dirty. Rain turned its streets to mud and its well water tasted of salt. Whipple complained about the lack of exercise calling the place "so intolerable muddy there is no such thing as walking, and I have no time to ride." Living costs were at least 100 percent higher than Philadelphia. His colleague Matthew Thornton found himself abed and in the care of two physicians he called "Dr. Cash" and "Dr. Surly." Sam Adams noted that congress did more important business in three weeks than it did in Philadelphia in six months. Rush was less charitable. "We live here," he wrote "in a convent, we converse only with one another. We are precluded from all opportunities of feeling the pulse of the public upon our measures."[195]

But congress preferred misery to the possibility of capture and voted to continue in Baltimore — even though only half the delegates were there — until Philadelphia seemed safe from invasion.[196] The air was so much purer than Philadelphia's the "weak nerves" of congress would be strengthened, some members opined.[197] And so they sat through the gloomy winter, much of the time no more than a rump congress, not quite despairing, yet weighted with eternal uncertainties. Whipple informed Weare February 3 that congress appropriated $100,000.00 for New Hampshire's war effort and wrote Bartlett the 7th there was "more unanimity in congress than ever. The little southern jealousies have almost subsided and the Dickinson politics are banished."

Congress adjourned February 27 and reconvened in Philadelphia March 12. Once again Whipple and John Adams shared quarters. They lived in what Adams described as "a pleasant part of the town, Walnut street, between Second and third streets at the house of Mr. Duncan, a gentleman from Boston who had a wife and three children. General [Oliver] Wolcott of Connecticut and col. Whipple of Portsmouth are in the same house. Mr. [Sam] Adams has removed to Mrs. Cheesman's in fourth Street near the corner of Market street where he has a curious group of company consisting of characters as opposite as North and South. [Pennsylvania's Jared] Ingersol, the Stamp man and Judge of Admiralty; [Connecticut's Roger] Sherman, an old Puritan, as honest as an Angel, and as staunch as a blood hound, firm as a rock in the cause of American independence as Mount Atlas, and [New Hampshire's] col. Thornton, as droll and funny as Tristram Shandy.[198] Between the fun of Thornton, the gravity of Sherman, and the formal Toryism of Ingersol, Adams will have a curious life of it. The landlady too, will add to the entertainment. Mr. Hancock has taken an house in Chestnut Street near the corner of Fourth Street near the State House.[199]

MILITARY SERVICE BETWEEN CONGRESSIONAL SESSIONS

Whipple left Philadelphia for New Hampshire June 18, 1777 the day after congress authorized a national flag with 13 stripes, alternately red and white, to represent the states; and 13 stars, white in a blue field, to represent the union. The *Ranger*, launched in Portsmouth and commanded by John Paul Jones, was the first warship to fly it. When he arrived home the legislature elected him justice of the inferior court of common pleas for Rockingham county and appointed him brigadier general of the militia replacing Nathaniel Folson who was leaving to serve in congress. After American troops were defeated at Ticonderoga, the legislature and the state committee of safety met jointly July 17 to devise a plan to protect the state. It divided the state's militia into two brigades, naming Whipple commander of the first and John Stark the second, both with the rank of brigadier general. They were accountable to the general court when in session, otherwise to the committee of safety.[200] Apparently the jail at Exeter contained important prisoners, who "were to be protected and kept secure," as Whipple was directed September 18 to place a "round-the-clock guard of 16 men with a proper officer" there for three months.[201] His general orders were to protect the seacoast but when maj. gen. Horatio Gates called for assistance, Whipple marched to the Saratoga battlefield.

Stark was the key commander at the August 16, 1777 Battle of Bennington. His untrained troops, armed with all kinds of ancient weapons, overwhelmed two bodies of trained professional soldiers. They captured four brass field pieces, 12 drums, 250 sabers, four ammunition wagons, and several hundred muskets and rifles. Their losses were 30 killed and 40 wounded compared to 207 Germans and Tories killed and 700 captured, including 30 officers. A veteran at the battle described Stark's army as wearing loose coats and waistcoats of huge dimensions, with colors as various as the barks of oaks, sumac, and other trees of our hills and swamps, homespun shirts of flax, and large round-top and broad-brimmed hats. Their arms were as various as their costumes. An old soldier carried a heavy Queen's army gun used at the conquest of Canada 20 years previously, while at his side walked a stripling boy with a Spanish fusee not half its weight or caliber which his grandfather may have taken at the Havana; some had old French pieces that dated to the battle of Louisbourg. A few had bayonets. Some of the officer's swords were made by blacksmiths from farming utensils. They looked serviceable, but heavy and uncouth. Instead of the cartridge box, a large powder horn was slung under the arm.[202] Pitted against these rustic warriors were about 650 troops led by lt. col. Friedreich Baum, a German who could not speak English.

BATTLE OF SARATOGA, TURNING POINT OF THE WAR *1777*

Whipple played a major role at the Battle of Saratoga, rated by historians as among the most decisive in history as it changed the course of the revolution by bringing France into the war on America's side.[203] Lieutenant general John (Gentleman Johnny) Burgoyne commanded the invading army from Canada.[204] Tall and handsome, with large brilliant eyes and a strong, jutting jaw, he had been a cavalry officer noted for his dash and daring on European battlefields. Major general Horatio Gates, 50, a former professional soldier in the British army, stooped, ruddy-cheeked, and cautious, commanded the American forces.[205]

Whipple's brigade was mustered Sept. 21 and its full quota of 1,070 men and officers was filled the 28th.[206] It consisted of parts of nine militia regiments and sundry other companies, and served from September 22 to October 26. He and his troops were assigned to serve under brig. general John Fellows at Batten Kill October 10.[207] Whipple, his brigade major George Gaines, and his man servant Prince, served until November 12 as they escorted Burgoyne to Boston. The march from Portsmouth to Saratoga was 216 miles. It was 290 miles home by way of Boston.[208]

Whipple and Gates were well acquainted through Whipple's service on congressional committees dealing with the army.[209] He was with Gates October 14 when Burgoyne's adjutant arrived with a flag seeking a cessation of the fighting. Gates named Whipple and col. James Wilkinson to negotiate surrender terms. Lieutenant colonel Nicholas Sutherland and capt. James Henry Craig were

Burgoyne's representatives. After agreeing to terms, Burgoyne claimed they were preliminary and asked they be more precisely defined before a conclusive treaty could be executed. Gates agreed and the negotiators met October 15 in a tent between the advance guards of the two armies and worked out Articles of Capitulation by 8 p.m.[210] About 11 p.m. Burgoyne notified the American negotiators by letter he would accept the terms and deliver a signed copy in the morning if the word "capitulation" were changed to "convention." Gates agreed. That night Burgoyne received erroneous information that some of Gates' militia had left and that British gen. Henry Clinton had reached Albany with reinforcements. Encouraged by this news, Burgoyne decided to break the convention.

He informed Gates by letter the morning of the 16th that he had "reliable" information that parts of Gates' army had left and unless convinced he was outnumbered by at least 4 to 1, would not sign. Gates gave his "word of honor" that his army did outnumber Burgoyne 4 to 1, reminded him what it meant to break his word of honor, and gave him an hour to respond or he would "adopt the most stringent measures."

After two hours passed, col. Sutherland told col. Wilkinson, who was waiting for Bugoyne's answer, that the British "officers had got the devil in their heads and could not agree." Wilkinson had Burgoyne's letter pledging to sign if capitulation was changed to convention and read it to Sutherland and pointed out how the Americans would use "it as a testimony of the good faith of a British commander." Sutherland asked to borrow it and pledged his "honor [to] return it in 15 minutes." Wilkinson gambled and gave it to Sutherland who returned to Burgoyne's headquarters. Gates, losing patience, instructed Wilkinson to break off the treaty if not immediately ratified. Wilkinson asked for an additional half hour and punctual to his promise, Sutherland returned with the signed convention making Burgoyne's army prisoners of the United States.[211] Gates' first act after winning one of history's great military victories was to send quantities of meat across Fishkill creek to feed his starving enemies.[212]

The surrender on the 17th was a colorful spectacle. Burgoyne, accompanied by his adjutants and aides, crossed the Fishkill and rode through the meadow to the American camp. British troops paraded at 10 a.m. and then marched out, as British lieut. Digby wrote, "with drums beating and the honors of war, but the drums seemed to have lost their inspiring sound, and though we beat the `Grenadier's March,' which not long before was so animating, yet then it seemed by its last effort, as it was almost ashamed to be heard on such an occasion." The troops stacked their arms in a meadow by the river, then marched through the American camp, between two lines drawn up in order. After the last of the defeated army marched past Gates' hut, a new American flag made from military coats was run up a pole. In view of both armies, Burgoyne surrendered his ivory-handled sword to Gates who took it with a courteous nod and instantly handed it back.[213]

By Gates' command, the conquering Americans were silent; not a word or taunt was uttered. A Brunswicker,[214] in some amazement, wrote this description of their conquerors: "Not one of them was properly uniformed, but each man had on the clothes in which he goes to the field, to church, or to the tavern. But they stood like soldiers, erect, with a military bearing that was subject to little criticism. Not one fellow made a motion as if to speak to his neighbor; furthermore, nature had formed all the fellows who stood in rank and file, so slender, so handsome, so sinewy, that it was a pleasure to look at them and we were all surprised at the sight of such finely built people. And their size! The officers wore very few uniforms and those they did wear were of their own invention.[215]

The two commanders, Burgoyne wearing his richest scarlet uniform and Gates in a plain blue coat, entered Gates' hut for the surrender ceremony. Four plates and two glasses sat on a plank table held up by empty barrels. The opposing generals offered toasts in rum and water — Burgoyne to George Washington, Gates to the British king. Quips and joking soon began among the other officers, and within minutes the entire party was laughing hilariously with exhaustion and relief. One British artillery major turned to an American captain and noted how they seemed the best of friends when only a fortnight ago they had been enemies trying to kill each other. It was, the major reflected, an odd old world.[216]

Brigadier general John Glover of the continental army was put in charge of removing the British army to Cambridge and Whipple was to deliver Burgoyne and his staff to Boston. The first night, Glover's militia halted a mile in the rear of the British and spent the whole night with their weapons in their hands. It took the British army more than three hours of brisk marching to pass a spot.[217] Whipple and Gates dined with Burgoyne and his staff in Albany on the 20th and Burgoyne agreed to leave the next day. However it took much longer to prepare his dispatches and he kept asking to delay the departure. They left Albany at 7 a.m. the 27th. The Berkshire's fall colors were brilliant but Burgoyne hardly noticed because of the stormy weather. Whipple's horse gave out on November 5 at Marlboro and he "hired" a replacement from a tavern keeper with instructions his was to be sent to Boston. He delivered Burgoyne to Boston on the 8th and dined with maj. gen. William Heath before leaving for Portsmouth.[218]

Whipple wrote Weare from Albany October 21 that "nothing could have been more seasonable than our success over Burgoyne" because a British army of 3 or 4,000 men were enroute to reinforce Burgoyne "but fortunately for us they are too late, and if the weather does not prevent general Gates getting his heavy artillery down, I am in great hopes . . . the plunderers from York, will soon be in the same situation with Mr. Burgoyne."[219]

Rhode Island delegate William Ellery wrote Whipple from South Kingstown October 30: "I most heartily congratulate you on your signal success at the Northward. You may say with the invincible Caesar *veni, vidi, vici* for scarcely had you arrived at the Northern Headquarters, scarcely had you seen the army of the enemy before it surrendered. Methinks I see you escorting in triumph towards Boston John Burgoyne Esq. Lieutenant General of His Majesty's armies in America, Colonel of the Queen's regiment of Light Dragoons, Governor of Fort William in North Britain, one of the representatives of the Commons of Great Britain, and late commandeering an army and fleet employed on an expedition from Canada & at the head of troops in the full powers of health, discipline and valor. Oh Lucifer, how art thou fallen! How hath the northern menacing meteor after the most portentous glare evaporated into smoke, vanished into nothing. I suppose now you have entered the military list we shall not see you in congress. Flushed with your success you will now prefer the field to the cabinet. In whatever walk you choose to tread I wish you happiness and renown."[220]

Saratoga was a monumental victory. It caused British troops to retreat to

The Surrender of General Burgoyne at Saratogy, NY *by John Trumbull (1756-1843) Copyright Yale University Art Gallery, New Haven, CT.*

Key to Surrender of Genreal Burgoyne by John Trubull: *10. Major General Phillips, British; 11. Lt. General John Burgoyne, British; 14. Maj. General Horatio Gates; 25.* **Brigadier General William Whipple, NH.**

Canada, ending a threat of a two-pronged drive that might split the colonies. Two lieutenant generals, two major generals, three brigadiers, the staffs and aides of all of them, 299 other officers of all ranks, including a dozen members of parliament, lords, and Scottish knights, and 3,379 British and 2,412 German soldiers became prisoners of war; 1,429 British and Germans were killed and wounded; 27 cannon of various calibers, 5,000 stand of small arms, and large quantities of ammunition and military equipment of all kind were seized. Doors to France and Spain were opened.

CAMPAIGN TO RETAKE RHODE ISLAND

? 1778

New Hampshire's maj. gen. John Sullivan was named commander of the campaign to retake Rhode Island in the spring of 1788. The enemy army of more than 6,000 troops was protected by a naval force of seven ships of war and two galleys. Sullivan's command, including two brigades under maj. gen. Marquis Lafayette, eventually numbered nearly 10,000. He began a siege of Newport Island's harbor August 9. General Whipple commanded a brigade of about 1,200 New Hampshire volunteers in this campaign. He served from August 3 to September 5. Unfortunately most of Sullivan's troops were recruits without discipline or knowledge of war and supplies were limited. When the French fleet under admiral count d'Estaing, which had agreed to join in the operation failed to take part despite appeals by Lafayette, American troops became disheartened and deserted in large numbers.

Sullivan wrote to gen. Washington August 23 enclosing a letter he received from D'Estaing August 21 announcing his departure for Boston and the impossibility of leaving troops to aid Sullivan because of losses sustained at sea during an "exceedingly severe storm." John Laurens, speaker of the congress, wrote Washington on the 23rd saying it was his opinion that the comte's decision to go to Boston was motivated by "the Cabal of Marine Officers who wish his destruction because he joined their Corps from land service." Laurens thought that the solemn protest of the American officers might give the comte "a justification" to act in contradiction of his officers and cause him to stay in Rhode Island. Whipple was one of 10 officers to sign the letter to the comte.[221]

Without the French troops, Sullivan retreated to the north end of the island the night of the 28th and an engagement ensued the 29th. News that the British were to be reinforced (gen. Henry Clinton arrived with 4,000 troops the next day) caused Sullivan to retreat to the mainland the evening of the 30th. Whipple and gen. Ezekiel Cornell of Rhode Island executed the withdrawal without loss or incident and Sullivan's general order of the 31st commended them for their good work.

While Whipple and his staff[222] were at breakfast in the American quarters August 29, a cannon ball tore through the building and shattered maj. John Samuel Sherburne's leg. It had to be amputated and thereafter he was called "Corkleg Sherburne." After returning to Portsmouth, Whipple wrote Bartlett the expedition failed because desertion was widespread in all units. While volunteers were recruited for an uncertain time, each had fixed an expiration date in his own mind and "when that time arrives it is as impossible to keep them even half an hour as it is to alter the course of the sun. Scarce a man was left of those I was sent to command by the day of the action." He described losses as minimal despite intense action on the 29th and said the remaining troops acquitted themselves well. In his opinion, circumstances justified the retreat.[223] Congress voted its thanks go Sullivan and his army as did the legislatures of Rhode Island and New Hampshire.[224]

DEALING WITH FRANCE AND BRITAIN

In February 1777, Whipple sent Weare a copy of a speech by "the British tyrant," saying it pleased him that the king thinks the "contest arduous. I fancy the wretch begins to see his danger." He said private letters from Spain foretold a general war in Europe and he believed France, Spain, and Prussia were "mediating some grand plan. I believe we may as well cede Hanover to Prussia and give Great Britain to France. What think you of this scheme?"[225]

When news of lt. gen. John Burgoyne's surrender at Saratoga reached Paris December 5, 1777 "the buzz of drawing rooms and coffee houses swelled into a unanimous cry for war."[226] King Louis XVI recognized the independence of the United States the next day. On February 6, 1788 France signed two treaties with the United States — one of alliance and one of amity and commerce. The latter was to maintain the "liberty, sovereignty, and independence absolute and unlimited of the United States." Foreign minister Vergennes was unsuccessful in getting Spain, worried her colonies might be encouraged to follow America's example, to join the alliance. Spain did, however, enter the war in June 1779 as an ally of France and promised not to make peace with Britain without French consent and agreed France could not make peace until American independence was secured. France sent 6,000 soldiers under the comte de Rochembeau, a fleet of 17 vessels under the comte d'Estaing, and later another of 28 vessels under admiral deGrasse to assist America. Even with this help, fighting continued for more than three years before Cornwallis surrendered his army of more than 7,000 men at Yorktown October 17, 1781. Interestingly, Burgoyne surrendered on October 17, four years earlier.[227]

After the February 1778 signing of the Franco-American alliance and before hostilities began between France and Britain in June, parliament passed two bills to end the war. The first offered to repeal the Coercive Acts of 1774 and to provide freedom from parliamentary taxation. The second established a commission to negotiate peace with America and authorized congress as a permanent body subject to parliament. The British peace commission and the French treaties arrived in America about the same time. Congress treated the British proposals with contempt and immediately ratified the Franco-American treaties. England now had to fight on several fronts and keep troops and ships at home to protect against possible invasion.[228]

Bartlett wrote Whipple June 20, 1778 that "every member of congress was firm and steady" in rejecting the overtures of the British peace commissioners then in Philadelphia. Only peace that included absolute independence, was acceptable, he said. Whipple responded that firmness with the British commissioners "must do [congress] eternal honor. No transaction of congress ever gave more general satisfaction in this quarter," he concluded.[229] He sent Weare a copy of the treaty of alliance between France and America in November.[230]

French insistence in January 1779 that congress enter into peace negotiations with England and the ongoing hearings about French commissioners Silas Deane and Charles Lee occupied a great deal of Whipple's time as chairman of the foreign affairs committee. Major ideological disputes developed from the Deane-Lee hearings which led to formation of the Federalist and anti Federalist political parties. Congressional historian Edmund C. Burnett said the controversy generated such personal antagonisms that supporters of each became irreconcilable.[231] Managing these hearings and working with the factions required great tact by Whipple, who favored Lee. The French minister plenipotentiary Conrad-Alexandre Gérard aggravated the conflict by suggesting Deane's opponents were anti-French.

Whipple's partisanship surfaced when he reported in an August 3 letter to R.H. Lee at Chantilly, Virginia that Charles Lee's statement, when read in congress, produced, "Envy, malice, and every vindictive passion that disappointed malevolence could inspire, on various countenances around the room. Fiddle head (Meriwether Smith, Virginia) shook, swivel eye (James Duane, New York) nestled and turned pale, the chair (John Jay, New York) changed color at every sentence, some others forced a sneer, endeavoring to conceal their chagrin and confusion. This, you may well suppose, afforded me no small degree of enjoyment."[232] Congress never reached a clearcut decision on the hearings. However, its refusal to approve Deane's account so embittered him he returned to Europe in 1780 and accepted a bribe to propagandize on behalf of Britain.[233]

Congress hosted Gérard at the City Tavern February 6 in honor of the first anniversary of the Franco-American alliance. He told Whipple's committee on the 15th it had to decide on issues critical to a peace conference. Whipple surveyed his committee and the consensus was that negotiations could only begin after Great Britain acknowledged "the absolute and unlimited liberty, sovereignty and independence" of the United States in matters of government and commerce.[234] Six nonnegotiable positions and six bargaining positions were also identified.

The non-negotiable issues: minimum boundary requirements, evacuation of American soil, American fishing rights in the waters off Newfoundland, navigation of the Mississippi river to the southern boundary of the U.S., free trade with a port or ports below that boundary, and cession of Nova Scotia. Four were settled easily. Fisheries and Mississippi navigation were seen as sectional issues and split the committee. New Englanders considered fishing privileges as hereditary rights; southerners insisted American progress depended on navigation of the Mississippi. Neither saw the other's viewpoint and sometimes representatives of states north of Maryland voted one way, those to the south the opposite.[235] The debate evolved into the whole subject of American foreign relations and continued for weeks.[236] The committee also had to agree on war objectives, as France and Spain were secretly doing, and elect a commissioner to negotiate peace once Britain accepted American independence.[237] Chairman Whipple had to mediate the conflicting interests.

Rumors of peace were rampant the spring of 1779. In a February letter to Bartlett, Whipple anticipated, based on all the negotiations going on in Europe, that America would receive British peace proposals in the spring. But he didn't expect them to include independence. His bottom line for an acceptable peace was independence, Britain "quitting all pretensions to Canada and Nova Scotia,"[238] and divide Florida with Spain. The latter was predicated on Spanish support of colonial currency. He wrote Weare in March that peace rumors are "idle" and that New Hampshire should vigorously recruit for the army so the country could prosecute the war "with utmost vigor."[239]

He authored the July 19, 1779 letter sent by the marine committee to Benjamin Franklin in France directing him "to destroy some of the most distinguished cities in Great Britain and the West Indies" in retaliation for Britain burning Portsmouth and Suffolk, Virginia, Fairfield, Norwalk, and Bedford, Connecticut, and some villages in New York. The committee believed "destruction of a single village would instantly convince our enemy of the danger to which they are exposed and the necessity [to] desist from the[ir] destructive mode in carrying on the war." A Resolution of congress called the British action contrary to the way the United States carried on the war and was "for the sole and direct purpose of self preservation, absolutely and indispensably necessary, [to stop] the cruel and unprecedented manner in which our enemies are daily carrying on the war."[240]

CONFERRING WITH THE BRITISH; TORIES AND LOYALISTS; PRIVATEERING

Whipple was a man of strong views with the courage to express them. There was never any doubt about his position on independence and he was among the first to advocate a federal government and was steadfast in his support of the Articles of Confederation. He held and enunciated equally strong positions on conferring with the British prior to declaring independence, on how to handle Tory-Loyalists, and in opposition to privateers.

Bartlett wrote Whipple September 3, 1776 that New Hampshire's maj. gen. John Sullivan, captured in a battle on Long Island in late August now paroled,[241] arrived at his lodgings with a message for congress from lord Howe. Howe could not acknowledge congress but wanted to confer with members as private gentlemen to resolve the conflict without war upon terms advantageous to both sides. Whipple responded that congress should not acknowledge Howe, predicting it would "cause divisions among us," give the enemy a "capital advantage," and "lessen" congress in the eyes of the public.[242]

While congress would not send members privately it agreed to send Benjamin Franklin, John Adams, and Edward Rutledge as a committee to Staten Island to confer with Howe. Howe assured them the offensive acts of parliament would be revised and instructions to governors reconsidered if the colonies would reaffirm their allegiance but that he lacked authority to negotiate with them. The committee told Howe that parliament's declaration of war provoked the Declaration of Independence, that congress did not have the power to return the states to their former dependent state, and returned to Philadelphia.[243] After maj. gen. Charles Lee was captured by the British in the New York campaign in December 1776, he wrote congress requesting two or three delegates come to New York to confer with Howe about peace terms. Whipple fervently believed that meeting with Howe would send the wrong message to potential European allies and wrote Bartlett of his total opposition to any discussion with the British commanding general. He believed Howe would offer pardon to congress if America submitted and he was unalterably opposed to any submission.[244]

Whipple was outraged by Tory-loyalists and their activities.[245] He had "no confidence in men who opposed the principles of republicanism" and who were "not heartily attached" to independence. He said his "most fervent wish" was that Heaven "guard my country against the influence of such false patriots." His willingness to suppress them negated one of the great revolutionary ideals he was fighting for, political liberty. He asked Langdon May 3, 1776, "Why . . . is it possible those pests to society should govern the town meetings in the metropolis of New Hampshire?"[246] He suggested to Bartlett that New York Tories sent to New Hampshire should be sent to lord Howe "and let him make the most of them."[247] He called them "miscreants" in a 1777 letter to Bartlett and said they "should be treated with the severity their crimes deserve." He didn't want them jailed, he wanted them run out of the country saying the cause of freedom justified "the most severe and decisive measures."[248] Three letters to Bartlett in 1779 register his disgust: On May 28 he wrote loyalists who fled the country should not be called "refugees" or "absentees." Since they either fled from justice or deserted the cause of their country, they should be called "fugitives" and every state should pass legislation to control their abandoned estates. In July he wrote it was "high time they were all hung or banished." In August he said the war would have ended long ago if there were no concealed loyalists. "However, I comfort myself with hopes that the present evils tend to future good; the more difficulty we are in at obtaining the jewel the higher value we shall set on it, consequently shall be more careful to preserve it."[249]

His intense feelings against George III were expressed in a letter to Ebenezer Thompson July 19.[250] He wondered how anyone in America could even have a "distant desire" of being under the government of "such an execrable villain . . .as that infernal barbarian who we once called king." He wrote that future generations would not believe that "such miscreants (loyalists) are permitted to remain among us. I should be happy to hear that the authority of New Hampshire were taking effectual measures to rid that state of all such miscreants. These people are justly chargeable with the greatest part of the miseries of this cruel war and still they are suffered to remain quietly among us, doing all the mischief in their power."[251]

In November 1775 congress encouraged the states to enact privateering laws and an estimated 2,000 privateers manned by 30,000 sailors were in action by war's end. By contrast, at its peak, the continental navy had 21 vessels manned by about 3,000 men and naval vessels lay idle for lack of armament because privateers outbid the government. Up to 100 privateers operated out of Portsmouth, including, much to his chagrin, Whipple's closest associates: George Gains, Jacob Sheafe, Jr., Joshua Brackett, his brother-in-law, and John Langdon. Langdon owned at least seven privateers and became rich from the war. Brackett was judge of Portsmouth's admiralty court. It was a rare issue of the *Gazette* which did not include a notice from him of a libel filed on behalf of a Portsmouth privateer.[252] Navy pay ranged from $60 monthly for a captain to $8 for an ordinary seaman. The commander of the Portsmouth privateer *General Sullivan* received £36,793 and the ordinary seaman about £2500 in 1780 as shares of a single prize. Merchants preferred privateering to foreign trade as there was less risk and the profits were enormous.[253]

Whipple called privateering "the most baneful [business] to society of any that ever a civilized people were engaged in." Saying they were "little better than freebooters," he predicted they would eventually disgrace the American flag.[254] He agreed that privateers "distressed our enemies" but believed funding the navy would accomplish the same results on better terms for the country. "I heartily wish to see the American navy respectable but do not expect it until privateering is discouraged."[255] Officers are "courted to go a privateering" and leave for the great pay. "The navy will soon be officered by tinkers, shoemakers, and horse-jockeys and no gentlemen worth employing will accept a commission."

He suggested if Bartlett spent three months in Portsmouth he would see that privateers "lose every idea of right and wrong," and their "insatiable avarice" cause them to seize "without the least compunction property of our friends as well as of our enemies." He said pay received by seamen on privateers was so great some New Hampshire towns could only recruit soldiers to serve in the 1778 Rhode Island campaign by paying $400 bounty, in addition to what the state paid. He also noted its impact on farmers who had to compete with shipbuilders for labor. Five privateers, then being outfitted in Portsmouth, expected to employ 400 men.[256]

Britain also authorized privateers. R.H. Lee's wrote Whipple in 1782 from Chantilly, Virginia that "We continue to be infested with privateers that much injure our bay and river vessels, and pester our shores extremely with night robberies and day surprises. Their crews are made up of refugees, Negroes, and such as fly from civil justice, who under the sanction of British commissions are warring upon women and children, stealing clothes and Negroes, and committing every outrage that chance can furnish them with an opportunity of perpetrating. Thus the worst passions of human nature are let loose to thrive under the patronage of George the Third, defender of the faith truly!"[257]

WHIPPLE, EVER HOPEFUL; BARTLETT, FREQUENTLY DOUBTFUL

Whipple's crowning virtue was hopefulness, something badly needed in the dark and discouraging days of 1777. By contrast, Bartlett was often the victim of doubt, despair, and gloom. The value of Whipple's persistent and contagious hopefulness was always there to inspire Bartlett during his down periods. Whipple wrote him in February 1777 "I am sorry you want any thing to keep up your spirits. I should think the glorious cause in which we are engaged is sufficient for that purpose. The prospect of laying a foundation of liberty and happiness for posterity and securing an asylum for all who wish to enjoy those blessings is an object in my opinion sufficient to raise the mind above every misfortune." In late May he told Bartlett not to be despondent because "a few scattering clouds pass between us and the sun. Proper exertion will soon dispel them." Instead of gloomy reflections, "look forward to the glorious prize with a determination to obtain it, and all those difficulties that a gloomy mind would deem insupportable will be mere mushrooms." He said new difficulties will replace old, "but patience and vigorous perseverance will surmount them all."[258]

By 1779, Bartlett, despairing of victory, began advocating peace. In a strong letter written February 18, Whipple, then chair of the foreign affairs committee, attempted to strengthen Bartlett's resolve saying the country could and would eventually win. "Peace . . . is desirable but . . . a secondary object. War with all its horrors is preferable to an inglorious peace. I hope we never consent to a peace [that leaves our] posterity greater evils than we have suffered. I [believe] there is virtue enough in the army to undergo the fatigues of one more campaign. By the last accounts from Europe, American affairs have a much better aspect there than here. [I cannot share] the particulars but . . . I shall er'er long have it in my power to . . . dispel those gloomy forebodings that . . . pervade your mind. I [expect we will] have a very respectable army in the field . . . [and do] not doubt we shall, under smiles of Heaven and assisted by our allies, humble to the dust the proudest nation in the world, have peace on our own terms, and make America the seat of happiness."[259]

He reinforced this belief March 7 when he wrote Bartlett he "heartily concurred" with his desire for peace but peace required "strenuous exertions for war." The country "ought to be united in council, formidable in the field," and "feel the importance of sovereignty."[260] He said if the United States were fully sensible of its importance among the powers of the earth it would depend on its own strength and "banish every idea of servility, which now like the tares[261] among the wheat, prevents the growth of that virtuous republican pride so essential to the happiness of America."[262] He informed Bartlett in March 1779 that peace reports were "Tory tale calculated to put people off their guard and slacken their exertions in the ensuing campaign," that Spain had offered an alliance, warships, and money on liberal terms, and that congress asked South Carolina to raise a regiment of blacks. He hoped the black regiment would be successful and "lay a foundation for the emancipation of those poor wretches and . . . be the means of dispersing the blessings of freedom to all the human race in America."[263]

While grateful for European assistance and wanting it to continue, he became concerned about foreign alliances which might "be destructive to true Republicanism." He dismissed rumors that America's allies would abandon us because England had nothing to offer France, Spain had been so abused by Britain in their last war that "we need not apprehend an apostasy there," and English insults to Holland were assurances that country would not turn back. He told Bartlett that almost every country in Europe thinks favorably of our cause so he should not be despondent. "We have nothing to fear but ourselves and such fear would be immediately dissipated if we had vigor enough to get rid of our internal enemies."[264]

When Bartlett continued to doubt America's ability to win the war Whipple told him not to allow idle reports to intimidate him. Reports that France was seeking peace with England under mediation of Spain were without foundation, he said in a July 27 letter. Accounts from Paris show the American cause popular in Europe and other alliances are being explored. There was every reason to believe Spanish assistance would continue. "Our cause is more just than Jacob's posterity," he wrote. "Miracles in favor of that people followed their own exertions and were essential for their security, so let us exert ourselves as we ought and no doubt Heaven will smile on our endeavors and crown them with success."

COMMENTS OF COLLEAGUES

Dr. Benjamin Rush, a Pennsylvania signer, described New Hampshire's signers as follows. Whipple: "Liberal in his principles and manners and a genuine friend to liberty and independence." Bartlett: "Of excellent character and warmly attached to the liberties of his country." Thornton: "He was ignorant of the world but believed to be a sincere patriot and an honest man."[265]

Bartlett wrote Whipple in September 1777 how important it was for him to accept reelection because peace negotiations were to begin and Whipple's abilities were needed. "I hope . . . you will have as great a hand in making peace and confirming our independence as you had in carrying on the war and declaring our total separation from Britain."[266] In July 1778 Bartlett wrote Whipple that because marine affairs were so important to the country, he hoped the state would have the wisdom "to appoint you to relieve me in the fall and that you will . . . forgo your own private interest for the public good." If he wouldn't accept another term, Bartlett urged him to join the navy board at Boston and use his talents to get it running efficiently.[267] Bartlett wrote him in July 1779 that the legislature was "extremely desirous you should tarry as long as possible and have ordered me to signify the same to you. They are sensible of the fatigues and hardships that you must necessarily be under by so long a stay there, but think you tarring at this time will be an essential service to this state and perhaps to the continent."[268]

Samuel Holten of Massachusetts described Whipple in November 1778 as "a man of sense and great experience in marine affairs" and hoped he would resume chairmanship of the marine committee.[269] Virginia's Richard Henry Lee in 1779 labeled Whipple and Sam Adams "wise and virtuous friends of America, who, loving their country, esteem and honor its able and virtuous citizens."[270] Further evidence of Lee's esteem is obvious in his letter of July 17, 1782 from Chantilly: "Judging of your heart by my own, I cannot suppose that either of us will conceive ourselves neglected by an interrupted correspondence in the present state of things. It must certainly be some other cause than neglect which can produce such an effect between two persons whose friendship is founded on virtue tried in severest times. For my part, I must cease to live before I cease to love those proud patriots with whom I toiled in the vineyard of American liberty. We have indeed, as you observe, suffered our part of the calamities of war, and I wish it may furnish us with the best kind of improvement which is learnt in the school of adversity."[271] Massachusetts' James Lovell described himself as "your real friend" and hoped Whipple would "return speedily" as "resolute, honest members were needed."

Whipple regretted South Carolina's Henry Laurens resignation in 1778 as president of congress. "I have so high an opinion of Mr. Laurens that I must confess I exceedingly regretted his leaving the chair." That Laurens held Whipple in similar regard was apparent in Laurens' letter to him three days after Whipple left congress in September 1779: "God bless you my dear general. I wish you every happiness and assure you with great sincerity of the love and esteem of your obedient and most humble servant."[272]

Displayed in Thomas Jefferson's home in Monticello, Virginia is a set of moose antlers that may have been a gift from Whipple to his former colleague and future president. Jefferson began collecting animal specimens in the 1780s and Whipple was one of the first people he turned to for help. The then-popular theory of the respected French naturalist Georges Louis Leclerc (1707-88) that New World animal species were inferior to Old World species, prompted Jefferson to seek Whipple's help. Knowing moose were native to New Hampshire, he posed a series of questions about the animal in January 12, 1784 letter to Whipple.[273]

Whipple sought advice from "local experts" and sent his answer March 15 along with some moose hair. He told Jefferson he would send him a complete skeleton. If he couldn't get a skeleton he would send a pair of horns and some of the animal's principal bones. Jefferson thanked Whipple in an April 27 letter postmarked Annapolis and asked him to send the horns and bones to Richmond along with answers to questions about differences between the caribou, the renne, the black moose, the grey moose, and the elk.

Jefferson's final letter, postmarked Paris January 7, 1786, a little over a month after Whipple's death, asked Whipple to send him the skin, skeleton, and horns of the moose, caribou, and elk. If all three weren't available, his preference was the moose. He requested the bones of the legs, hoofs, and head including horns be left in the skin, "so that by sewing up the incision made along the belly and neck, and stuffing the animal, we should have its true form and size." He said it would be an "acquisition here more precious than you could conceive."[274]

POST CONGRESSIONAL SERVICE

Congress created a five-member board of admiralty in October 1779 to shape and run the navy. The board consisted of two delegates and three non delegates. The non delegate salary was set at $14,000 and delegates were to receive no pay other than their congressional salary; a permanent secretary was paid $10,000. Whipple, Thomas Waring of South Carolina, and Francis Lewis of New York, were elected non delegates members. Peabody wrote Bartlett November 30 asking him to "earnestly" influence Whipple to accept the appointment. "It is a matter of the highest importance . . . that the board consist of members whose knowledge is equal to the important trust that will be reposed in them." Woodbury Langdon encouraged his acceptance. James Lovell wrote Henry Laurens December 17 predicting he would decline. Lovell was right.[275]

Whipple wrote Peabody from Portsmouth December 27 congratulating congress for taking measures to reform the naval department. He said the commission could find better qualified men than he. "I do not suppose any man who has lived a month in Philadelphia can think the [salary] is equal to the necessary expenses a man in that character must be at. This however is by no means the greatest objection I have, but time will not permit me at present to state all my objections as I am just setting out for Exeter where the assembly is now set." He officially declined in a letter to Peabody February 7, 1780. After a fortnight of consideration, he said he found "the balance so greatly against it, I was obliged on the principle of self-preservation to decline" despite having "nothing more at heart than our navy."[276]

Philadelphia had become the most expensive place in America. Living was especially hard on civil servants with fixed incomes. In early 1780 some delegates paid $1,200 and more a month for a room. John Sullivan wrote Weare January 21, 1781 he had to live by borrowing. "I have used every economy in my power and can truly say that I never lived so sparingly in my life yet I am ashamed of the nominal expense. That you may form some judgment I will give you the price of wood which is by far the cheapest article I know. It cost $630 per chord. I am convinced that three hard dollars would in 1775 purchase more than a thousand continental dollars will now do."[277]

He accepted appointment to one of the country's most difficult and unpopular jobs in May 1782 when superintendent of finance Robert Morris, his longtime friend and former colleague from Pennsylvania, convinced him to become New Hampshire's federal tax collector. His duties were to receive and transmit taxes and to expedite their collection. Times were hard and collecting federal taxes was almost impossible. Six months after the first installment was due the federal government had to send money to New Hampshire to finish a ship under construction at Portsmouth.[278] He tried to resign in August 1783. Morris refused the resignation saying "if others would have served you would have declined originally. Your original motives must continue until our affairs mend. Persist, I pray you, and be persuaded that the consciousness of having made them will be the best reward. If this is not the case I have mistaken your character."[279] It was January 1784 before his first payment, $3,000, was made to the federal treasury. He resigned July 22, 1784 and retired the following month.

In 1782, Whipple, Welcome Arnold of Rhode Island, Cyrus Griffin of Virginia, and David Brearley and William C. Houston of New Jersey were the judges deciding the Pennsylvania-Connecticut dispute over the Wyoming Valley claimed by both states. Boundaries, jurisdiction, and other matters disputed by states came under Article IX of the Articles of Confederation and this was the first case ever tried.[280] Whipple was elected president of the court.

The controversy evolved from a purchase of Indian land in 1754 by Connecticut land speculators organized as the Susquehannah company. The purchase extended into Pennsylvania but the Susquehannah Co. contended Connecticut's sea-to-sea charter included the land west of the Delaware river. Political pressure from Susquehannah's land speculators in May 1771 caused Connecticut to vigorously pursue its claim. When arbitration failed, Pennsylvania sought legal remedy with England. The case, before the privy council when the revolution broke out, was postponed until the war ended.

The Susquehannah company settled families in the Wyoming valley near Wilkes-Barre on both sides of the river and about 3,000 people lived there when the Revolution began. Their contempt for Pennsylvania law produced frictions at a time unity was essential to the revolutionary cause. Congress urged the status quo feeling the national cause should override colonial boundary disputes but Pennsylvania tried to invoke Article IX in 1779. Because the war was not over and because the Articles had not been ratified by all states, the request was denied. Pennsylvania then quit supplying troops at Wyoming believing Connecticut soldiers garrisoned there, even though in continental service, supported Connecticut's continued possession. Upon ratification of the Confederation by all states, Pennsylvania invoked Article IX.

The trial began the second week of November and proceeded in three stages: 1) introductory statements in which each side explained why the court should decide for it 2) citations of records and works of history; and 3) closing arguments. Pennsylvania's arguments included its charter boundaries, its purchases of land from the Indians, its acquisition of territorial rights from the proprietors, and its settlement in the disputed area before Connecticut made its claim. Connecticut argued its charter rights, its exercise of jurisdiction over the disputed lands since 1774, and the deed obtained from the Indians in 1754. The deed had grave defects — erasures, no consideration, and no purchase authorization from the Connecticut government — which violated colonial law. Final arguments were heard December 24 and the decision rendered December 30. It was notable for its brevity and for not publishing its reasons for deciding in favor of Pennsylvania. The judges had agreed in advance to announce a unanimous decision and never to divulge the reasoning.[281] The trial established precedence for sovereign states to settle disputes using federal authority so Whipple played another important role in the evolution of the federal government.

SLAVE TRADE AND SLAVE OWNER

Almost every author who has written about Whipple states, without documentation, he was briefly engaged in the slave trade. This author has been unable to find any confirming evidence.[282] Slavery was never widely prevalent in New Hampshire and on May 10, 1732 the assembly told the governor it had never laid an "impost on Negroes . . ." and so few were brought in "it would not be worth the public notice to make an act concerning them."

There was anti-slavery sentiment in the colony before the revolution. In a sermon at Dover in July 1774, Dr. Jeremy Belknap said it was astonishing that a few people contending for liberty "are not willing to allow liberty to others." He noted there were thousands of men, women, and children in bondage and slavery in the colonies because "their skin is darker than our own. Such is the inconsistency of our conduct."[283] When Whipple followed the sea, Massachusetts was the leading New England slave trading colony followed by Rhode Island,[284] Connecticut, and New Hampshire in that order. Most New England slavers got their cargoes on the Gold Coast or Windward Coast of Africa and sold them in the West Indies or some southern colony.[285] Their ships were sloops, schooners, topsail schooners, and brigantines, easy to handle with small crews. These are the types of ships Whipple sailed. Each ship kept a journal to record winds and currents and to log the ship's position. All ships and lands sighted and the general condition of the crew and ship were recorded by the master and first and second mates and given to the owner at the end of the voyage.[286] If Whipple's logs and journals, are ever found they will confirm whether he had any participation in the slave trade.

Dr. Robert M. Dishman, emeritus professor of history and former head of the history department at the University of New Hampshire, has been able to document one voyage by Whipple to and from Barbados and Tortola between May and November 1756. He was master of John Moffatt's brigantine *Elizabeth*. Dishman examined Whipple's log book at the Portsmouth Athenaeum and it shows no slaves on that voyage unless three men given passage were slaves.[287] The record is clear that John and Samuel Moffatt, Whipple's fatherin law and brother-in- law, were extensively involved in the African trade at a date later than 1756. [288]

Another popular story with variations is that Whipple dramatically freed his slave, Prince, just prior to the battle of Saratoga. Nathaniel Adams, in *Annals of Portsmouth*, writes, "He had with him at the capture of Burgoyne a valuable Negro servant imported from Africa named Prince. On his way to the army he said to his servant, `Should we be called into action, I hope you will behave yourself like a man of courage, and fight bravely for your country.' Prince replied, `Sir, I have no inducement to fight, but if I had my liberty, I would endeavor to defend it to the last drop of blood.' The general then said to him, `Prince, you shall have your freedom; from this time on you are your own man.'"

Variations of the story are reported by historians Charles Brewster and John Sanderson and in a 1975 *Ebony* magazine article.[289] But the record contradicts the story. Prince was one of 20 Negro or mulatto slaves to petition the legislature November 12, 1779 — two years after Saratoga — to set them free.[290] It was a thoughtful and carefully worded petition but the lower house of the legislature, of which Whipple was a member, determined June 9, 1780 that the time was not "ripe" to determine the matter and postponed it "to a more convenient opportunity.[291] Prince was allowed one of the rights of a freeman February 22,

1781 and legally manumitted by Whipple February 26, 1784.[292]

The stories about Prince Whipple and his brother (maybe cousin) Cuffee (sometimes spelled Cuff) make interesting reading but are not documented. Both are portrayed as being owned by William although it was Joseph Whipple who manumitted Cuffee July 14, 1784.[293] Portsmouth historian Charles Brewster says they were about 10 years old and sons of an African prince sent over for an education but retained in slavery when brought here before 1766.[294] Dishman doubts the claim and says it can't be supported by assuming the name was representative of status. He says the name was commonly given to slaves.[295]

New Hampshire author Valerie Cunningham says Prince and Cuffee "were young children when they arrived in Portsmouth with some other slaves from Guinea about 1760. She believes service as Whipple's body servant educated Prince to the point of understanding what was possible for blacks in Portsmouth and earned him respect and a leadership role among local slaves.[296] Four other sources, referring only to Prince, state he was born in Amabou, Africa and was purchased by Whipple in Baltimore after being illegally seized by the captain of the ship that brought him there.[297]

Four sources have Prince serving with general Washington, including being one of the oarsmen to row Washington and his party across the Delaware Christmas night of 1776 and winning the battle of Trenton, New Jersey.[298] Cuffee saw no military service but Prince served with Whipple in both the Saratoga and Rhode Island campaigns where Whipple commanded state militia brigades, not continental troops. The author has found no confirming evidence Prince was with Washington at Long Island or Trenton. He died in November 1797 and is buried in Portsmouth's North Cemetery. His headstone reads "Prince Whipple, Cont'l Troops, Rev. War."[299]

Whipple planned to erect a house on the Moffatt estate for use of Prince and Cuffee and their families but died before doing so. His widow Katharine allowed the two men to place a small two-story house on the west end of her garden on High street with the privilege to use the property during their lives and the lives of their wives.[300] Prince's wife, Dinah, was born a slave in New Castle, New Hampshire to the rev. Steven Chase family. They freed her when she reached 21 and she moved to Portsmouth where she joined the North church and was a member until her death at 86.[301] Cuffee, who died ca 1820, married Rebecca Daverson.[302] Dinah was the last of the Whipple blacks to live in the house. When it became "much dilapidated and scarcely tenable and dangerous to the neighborhood on account of fire," she was given a "life lease of a small house in Pleasant street and a small annuity."[303]

Historian Brewster described Prince as "a large, well-proportioned and fine looking man of gentlemanly manners and deportment. He was the Caleb Quotem of the old fashioned semimonthly assemblies, and at all large weddings and dinners, balls, and evening parties. Nothing could go right with out Prince and his death was much regretted by both the white and colored inhabitants of the town.[304]" He described Cuffee as being "prominent among the dark gentry."[305] The author has limited information on either family. Dr. Dishman believes both raised a large family with descendants still in the Portsmouth area.[306]

Known children of Prince and Dinah with their baptism dates are Jeremiah, December 30, 1781, Esther, December 19, 1784, Robert, April 27, 1788, a second

Jeremiah, December 6, 1789. Cuffee and Rebecca's son Daniel was baptized September 7, 1778 and daughter Mary, October 4, 1789. The christenings took place at the North church.[307] The Ladies Charitable African Society operated a school out of their home and Dinah and Rebecca taught black children of the town.[308]

STATE LEGISLATIVE SERVICE

After returning to Portsmouth, Whipple was continuously elected to represent Portsmouth in the New Hampshire legislature until 1784. He was on the committee to devise "a proper seal" for the state in March 1780, speaker pro tem in April 1781 and March 1782, and served jointly with brother Joseph in the 1782 and '83 sessions.[309] He was a prominent participant when Portsmouth proclaimed the provisional articles of peace between the U.S. and Great Britain April 28, 1783. The festivities began at 6 a.m. with salutes of 13 guns fired at the fort, Liberty bridge, and Church Hill. Religious services began at 10 in the north meeting house before a crowded audience. The proclamation was read to a large crowd at noon from the balcony of the state house. An elegant dinner was served in the assembly room followed by a splendid ball. Fireworks concluded the celebration.[310]

HIS DEATH

Whipple was appointed justice of the New Hampshire superior court of judicature January 20, 1783 and served until his death. Josiah Bartlett was a fellow justice.[311] When riding the circuits, Whipple suffered extreme chest pains, which historian John Sanderson said were "so violent . . . he proceeded with great difficulty." The problem became so acute he had to return home in the fall of 1785 before completing his circuit. Unable to lie in bed, he slept sitting in a chair in his chamber and died November 28.[312] His obituary referred to "unequaled sufferings" endured "with a firmness correspondent to the greatness of his mind" and said he faced death "in full confidence that He who made him knew best how to dispose of him."[313]

Postmortem examinations were rare but Whipple, believing medical science would benefit from knowledge of his affliction, authorized one.[314] He was probably influenced by his brother-in-law Dr. Brackett. The autopsy by Portsmouth physician-surgeon Hall Jackson (1739-97) was performed November 29 and showed an ossification in his heart — only a small aperture the size of a knitting needle was open for blood circulation. Considering how small a proportion of blood circulated through the lungs, Jackson found it "a matter of wonder and astonishment that life could be so far prolonged." Jackson believed if he had survived a short time longer, the auricle would have been completely ruptured with instantaneous death the consequence.[315]

Jackson's report was sent to William Plumer (1759-1850), a future governor and U.S. Senator. The autopsy was analyzed in 1976 by Dr. J. Worth Estes who described it as a "remarkable clinicopathologic correlation consistent with today's concept of cardiac physiology, although we are still unable to attach a modern diagnostic label to the case." He said the lesion might be so rare it didn't fit any of today's diagnostic categories and remains a challenge. The medical literature of the time is almost completely devoid of studies which might be relevant to Whipple's disease.[316]

Whipple's father-in-law died January 22, 1786, leaving his widow Katharine two estates to settle which led to two legal battles. Katharine and Joseph Whipple were executors of William's estate. They disagreed over its distribution and took their dispute to court. Portsmouth's Strawbery Banke library contains much information on the dispute but the author has not had time to review the papers.

Despite being deaf and blind, John Moffatt signed a codicil to his will a week before his death naming Katharine and Joshua Brackett executors of his estate. He left the house to his grandson Robert Cutts Moffatt, Samuel's son, giving Katharine occupancy privileges for 16 years until 1802. A seaman, Robert was living in either Baltimore or New York City in 1802 and didn't claim the house. When he finally claimed his inheritance, Katharine was unwilling to move and Robert either didn't want to dislodge her or didn't know how to proceed. Nathaniel Haven, Jr., Robert's nephew and son of his sister Mary Tufton "Polly" Moffatt, was a member of the Portsmouth law firm of Jeremiah Mason and Daniel Webster. This firm represented Moffatt, taking the case to the state supreme court where Webster's argument prevailed.[317] After the court ordered Katharine, then 82, to give Robert his inheritance, she moved to her farm at the Plain on the south outskirts of Portsmouth in December 1813. The large gambrel-roofed dwelling still stands.[318]

Katharine died at home November 22, 1821, age 90. The funeral was held November 25 at the house of the late gov. John Langdon and she was buried in the Langdon tomb at the North Cemetery. Her heirs were the children of her long-dead sister Elizabeth (Mrs. John Sherburne), whose daughter Elizabeth Sherburne was the wife of governor John Langdon.[319] She left nothing to the children of Polly (Moffatt) Haven and Robert Cutts Moffatt, who had been instrumental in forcing her to leave her long-time home in December. 1813.

Katharine Whipple's farm home *in Portsmouth, N.H. She moved here after being forced out of the Moffatt-Ladd House by the courts in a dispute with nephew Robert Cutts Moffatt. Photo by Blaine Whipple.*

WILLIAM WHIPPLE MEMORIALS

Portsmouth honored Whipple in 1890 by naming a new elementary school on State street after him. It opened in September of that year and was closed in June 1969 when Little Harbour school replaced it and two other older elementary schools. From September 1969 to June 1976 it served as an annex to the junior high school and was then sold and developed into a condominium complex.[320] The campaign to name the Whipple School began with a letter to the editor of the Portsmouth *Daily Evening Times* on May 13, 1890. The letter lamented the fact that Portsmouth's "signer of the immortal Declaration of American Independence had been long forgotten by the people of this city" and that no marble statue or public monument exists to record "one of the chiefest among our glories." It said naming the new school after Whipple would be an honor for the town and its people, and would offer children during the coming century "a daily lesson of love of country." The letter concluded with "Let us give no unmeaning name to this building, but place in the daily thought of our city [William Whipple], so deeply imbued with patriotism and every virtue." On May 16 Storer Post, No. 1, Grand Army of the Republic unanimously voted to ask the school board to name the school in honor of Whipple and on June 3 its representatives asked the board to "rescue from ignominious forgetfulness the name of an illustrious son of Portsmouth." Acknowledging the board could choose from among many good citizens, they pointed out all nominees owed their citizenship "To the Declaration of Independence," which Portsmouth's "priceless jewel," William Whipple, helped create. It was named the William Whipple School at the September 4 meeting. The largest school in the city at the time with two stories and basement, it had large play yards and was centrally located for its attendance area.[321]

On November 20, 1891, in ceremonies at the Music Hall, Storer Post presented the city an oil portrait of Whipple painted by Ulysses Dow Tenney.[322] Joseph Foster, U.S. navy paymaster and featured speaker, said Whipple was "Portsmouth's most illustrious citizen." While presented to the city, the portrait was placed in the senior class room at the Whipple School.[323] The Sons of the American Revolution of the State of New Hampshire placed a bronze tablet at the main entrance to the school October 24, 1910 to commemorate Whipple and his patriotic deeds. The ceremony took place at noon in front of the building before six hundred students from the High School and Whipple School, teachers, and many citizens. Rev. Alfred Langdon Elwyn, a direct descendant of Elizabeth (Sherburne) and gov. John Langdon, was among the speakers.[324] Today, the portrait, in a handsome gold frame, is in the Portsmouth Athenaeum.

Amesbury honors its signer, Josiah Bartlett, with a bronze statute erected on the town square in 1888. The state honors Matthew Thornton, a signer who did not vote for independence or participate in the deliberations leading to independence, with a 13-foot monument of Concord granite erected in 1892 in the Merrimack cemetery. Since the sale of the Whipple School, his only memorials are a "liberty tree" planted in 1976 and marker at Prescott Park and an historical marker at the North Cemetery in Portsmouth.[325]

Whipple was such an eminent person it is surprising that New Hampshire and Portsmouth have done so little to perpetuate his memory. Thirty-seven of the 50 states and the thousands of cities and towns who are not blessed with a signer of the Declaration of Independence would love to be able to claim a signer and would proudly share such a distinction with the rest of the country. Rather than forget Whipple, whose remarkable life contributed so much to the founding of the nation, it seems state and local governmental entities should erect a monument of some consequence to call attention to the accomplishments of Portsmouth's most eminent citizen. Some organization in New Hampshire should begin a campaign to rectify this oversight.

ENDNOTES — CHAPTER 6

1. Charles Francis Adams, *The Works of John Adams*, Vol. III. 25.

2. Richard Francis Upton, *Revolutionary New Hampshire*, (Port Washington, N.Y./London). First published in 1936. Reissued in 1970 by Kennikat Press. 84. New Hampshire's 18 delegates to the continental congress from 1774-89 were: Josiah Bartlett, 1775-6, 1778-9; Jonathan Blanchard, 1783-4; Nathaniel Folsom, 1775, 1777-80; Abiel Foster, 1783-5; George Frost, 1777-9; John Taylor Gilman, 1782-3; Nicholas Gilman, 1786-8; John Landgon,1775 and 1786-7; Woodbury Landgon, 1779-80; Samuel Livermore, 1780-3 and 1785-6; Pierce Long, 1784-6; Nathaniel Peabody, 1779-80; John Sullivan, 1774-5 and 1780-1; Matthew Thornton, 1776-8; John Wentworth, Jr., 1778-9; William Whipple, 1776-9; Philip White, 1782-3; Paine Wingage, 1787-8. During Whipple's service the congress met in Philadelphia from May 10 1775 to December 12, 1776; Baltimore from December 20 1776 to March 4, 1777; Philadelphia from March 4 to September 18, 1777; Philadelphia from July 2, 1778 to June 21, 1783. Presidents of the congress during Whipple's service: John Hancock of Mass. elected May 24, 1775; Henry Laurens of S.C. elected November 1, 1777; John Jay of N.Y. elected December 10, 1778. Charles Thomson of Pa. was elected clerk September 5, 1774 and served every session thereafter.

   The Political Register and Congressional Directory of the United States of America, compiled by Benjamin Perley Poore, Clerk of the Printing Records, U.S. Senate. Houghton, Osgood and Company. (Boston, 1878). 1-2. Thomas Whipple, Jr. represented New Hampshire in the federal House of Representatives in the 17th, 18th, 19th, and 20th congresses, serving from December 3, 1821 to March 3, 1823. He was a medical doctor from Wentworth, N.H. and died there January 23, 1835. He was born in Berkshire Co., Mass. in 1788.

3. Author Joseph Foster claims William and Katharine "had seven children, all of whom died in infancy." He provides no authority for this information. Joseph Foster, *"Lest We Forget." The Soldiers' Memorial*. Portsmouth, N.H. 1893 — 1923. Tercentenary Edition, with indexed record of the graves we decorate. Storer Post, No. 1, Department of New Hampshire, Grand Army of the Republic. (Portsmouth, N.H.). 23. The line was extended, however, through his sister Mary Whipple Traill.

4. Buried nearby are his sister Hannah Brackett (and her husband Joshua), his brother, Col. Joseph Whipple and his wife Hannah Billings, and his father-in-law, John Moffatt. William's wife Katharine is buried in gov. John Landgon's family tomb on the southern edge of the cemetery.

5. In September 1776, the New Hampshire council and assembly voted to raise 1,000 men out of the militia of several regiments. A colonel at the time, Whipple's quota was 74. In March 1777 the state authorized three continental regiments. Whipple was to raise 1,561 men as follows: 873 from Portsmouth, 85 from Newcastle, 161 from Rye, 96 from Newington, 200 from Strathan, and 146 from Greenland. They were to be part of three battalions of 2,064 privates. Isaac W. Hammond, editor, *Rolls of the Soldiers in the Revolutionary War, 1775 to May 1777*. Vol. I. Published by the authority of the Legislature. Parsons B. Cogswell, State Printer. (Concord, 1885).

6. Smallpox killed hundreds in Portsmouth. Whenever an epidemic hit, a terrifying little ribbon was placed above the door of the victim to announce the disease within. Preachers thundered the ancient arguments from their pulpits: "If God sent disease to scourge His people, what He desired was not inoculation but repentance!"

7. Of the eight, three were from Ireland, two each from England and Scotland, one from Wales.

8. William Whipple was born in Ipswich, Mass. 28, Feb. 1695, died in Kittery, Maine 7 Aug. 1751. He is buried in Kittery Point cemetery. Tombstone inscriptions: "In Memory of Capt. William Whipple Who Departed this Life August 7th, 1751, In the 56th Year of his Age." See Appendix B for his will.

9. Mary Cutt (in later years spelled Cutts), born in Kittery about 1699, died 28 Feb. 1783, married William Whipple 16 May 1722. She was daughter of Robert Cutt, II, born in 1666, died 24 Sept. 1735, Will probated 21 Oct. 1735, and Dorcas Hammond, died 17, Nov. 1757. They were married 18 April 1698. Dorcas was a daughter of Major Joseph Hammond of England whose father, an adherent of Cromwell, left England on the death of the Protector and settled in Kittery in 1658. Robert and Dorcas had four daughters: 1) Mary who married William Whipple; 2) Katherine, born 30 Sept. 1700, married John Moffatt, a Kittery merchant, (later moved to Portsmouth). Moffatt's daughter Katharine married William Whipple, Jr.; 3) Mehitable, born 18 Aug. 1703, married Jotham Odiorne, who lived in Newcastle in his youth. He died in 1761. 4) Elizabeth born 20 March 1710, married rev. Joseph Whipple (see endnote 27) of Hampton Falls, half brother of

William Whipple, Sr. Thus rev. Whipple was both uncle to William, Jr. and an uncle by marriage to Katharine; Elizabeth was an aunt to both. William, Jr.'s aunt Katharine Cutt was his mother-in-law.

The first Cutts in North America were brothers John, Robert, and Richard, supposedly born in Wales. They settled in the vicinity of Portsmouth prior to 1646. See *The New England Historical and Genealogical Register*, 49:131-2, (hereafter *Register*) for a copy of Richard's will proved 11 July 1682. When New Hampshire was separated from Massachusetts in 1697, John Cutt was named its first president. He and his second wife, Mary Hoel, had six children including Richard and Robert, II. A manuscript attributed to Joseph Whipple (*Register*, 5:246) contends Mary Hoel was the second wife of Robert, not John. "Robert settled at St. Christopher's where he married, afterwards in Barbados his second wife, Mary Hoel whom he brought with him to New England. [Their son Robert Cutt, in his Will made 18 Sept. 1734, names my uncle John Hoels formerly of Kittery deceased.] Robert's father, Richard Cutt, was a member of Parliament the year he died. [Richard Cutts was returned from Essex, for Cromwell's second parliament, in 1654, but not 1656]. After Robert Cutt I died, his widow Mary married Francis Champernon, nephew of Sir Ferdinando Gorges, the Founder of Maine. His "beloved wife Mary Champernon" was sole executrix of his Will which named my son-in-law Robert Cutts, Mary Cutts, Sarah Cutts, son-in-law [Hon] Richard Cutts, and Cutts Island in Kittery. *York Register of Deeds*, Vol. 5, fol. 55.

For information on the Cutt family, see Cecil Hampden Cutts Howard, *Genealogy of the Cutts Family in America*. Joel Munsell's Sons, Publishers. (Albany, NY, 1892); Fanny C. Heffenger, *Anecdotes and Reminiscences of the Traill, Spence, Cutt, and Whipple Families*, privately published in 1933; Nathaniel Adams, *Annals of Portsmouth*. C. Norris, Printer. (Exeter, NH, 1825). 69-70. Charles W. Brewster, *Rambles About Portsmouth*. (Portsmouth, 1859). 150-51. Chester B. Jordan, "Col. Joseph B. Whipple," *Proceedings of the New Hampshire Historical Society*, Vol. II, June 1888 to June 1895, published by the Society. (Concord, 1895). 293-94. Hereafter referred to as *Proceedings*.

Joseph Whipple said Dorcas Hammond was daughter of Major Joseph Hammond who came to America from England in Anno ____. He was of Monmoth's party and died in Wells, Province of Maine, about Anno 1700, age 102. Dorcas Hammond's mother was Katharine Frost, dau. of Nicholas Frost, who came from the west of England, and was of the Chevalier's, or King's, party in opposition to the Duke of Monmouth. A letter (*Register* 8:312) postmarked Kittery 24 March 1732 from Joseph Hammond stated his grandfather was Wm. Hammond, of Wells, county of York. He died in 1702, age 105. He left two sons, Jonathan and Joseph, my father. Joseph the son died in 1709 in his 63rd year. His son, Joseph, author of the letter to the *Register*, was 56 in 1732 and had three daughters and sons Joseph, George, John, and Jonathan. Robert and Dorcas Cutt are buried in Kittery Point Cemetery. Inscriptions: "Here lyes buried the body of Mr. Robert Cutt who dec'd Sep ye 24, 1753 in the 69th year of his age." "Here is interred the Body of Mrs Dorcas Cutt Relict of Mr. Robert Cutt who departed this Life Nov. 17th, 1757, in the 83d year of her Age."

Mary Cutt Whipple is buried in Portsmouth's North Cemetery near her son William. Inscription: "Here lies interred the Remains of Mrs. Mary Whipple, Relict of Capt. William Whipple late of Kittery deceased. She departed this life the 24th day of February, 1783, aged 84 years. Her religion was without ostentation And her Charity unlimited."

10. Mary the oldest (13 Jan. 1728-3 Oct. 1791) married Robert Traill (see endnote 26). Hannah married Joshua Brackett (see endnote 27). Robert, born 6 April 1736, died 4 May 1761, is buried in Kittery Point Cemetery. "Here lies interred ye Remains of Mr Robert Cutt Whipple who Departed this Life May ye 4th A.D. 1761, Aged 25 Years." Joseph, born 14 Feb. 1737, died 30 Jan. 1816, married Hannah Billings of Boston (see endnote 24). Throat distemper spread through the Portsmouth-Kittery area in 1736 causing 99 deaths, 81 under the age of 10, in 14 months. The Whipples were fortunate as many families were left childless. Nathaniel Adams, 164-65.

11. Robert Cutt's Will, dated 18 Sept. 1734, identified him as a Kittery shipwright. In addition to Mary, it mentions wife Dorcas Cutt and Katharine Moffatt, Mehitable Odiorne, and Elizabeth Whipple, and appoints Dorcas executrix. Dorcas' Will, dated 26 May 1749 (probated 3 Aug. 1758), bequeaths "to my beloved daughter Mary Whipple, her heirs and assigns, all my household goods and furniture, money, notes and bonds, and all my moveable or personal estate of what nature or kind or quality soever." It mentions Katharine Moffatt, Mehitable Oidorne, and Elizabeth Whipple and appoints "my son William Whipple, executor. *Maine Wills*, 360-4, 837-9.

12. Married women in this era were, in the eyes of the law, feme coverts; all their real and personal property became their husband's at the time of their marriage. Only a feme sole — a widow or unmarried woman — could buy, sell, devise, and bequeath.

13. Commission of John Cutt, 1680. The Commission constituting a President & Council for ye Province of New Hampshire in New-England. Charles ye Second, &c, to all to whom these

presents shall come Greetings. Whereas Our Colony of ye Massachusetts also Mattachusetts bay in New England in America, have taken upon themselves to exercise a Government & Jurisdiction, over ye inhabitants & Planters in ye Towns of Portsmouth, Hampton, Dover, Excester, & all other ye Towns & lands in ye Providence, lying & extending from three miles northward of Merrimack river, or any part thereof to ye Province of Maine, not having any legal right or authority so to do: Which said Jurisdiction & all further exercise thereof, We have thought fit by the advice of Our Privy Council to inhibit & restrain for the future; And do hereby inhibit and restrain ye same. And whereas ye Government of yt part of the said Providence of New Hampshire, so limited & bounded as aforesaid hath not yet been granted unto any person or persons whatsoever but ye same still remains & is under Our immediate care d& protection; To the end therefore, yt Our living Subjects, ye Planters and Inhabitants within ye limits aforesaid, may be protected and Defended in their respective rights, liberties & properties, & yt due & impartial Justice may be duly administered in all cases civil & criminal; & yt all possible care may be taken for ye quiet & orderly Government of ye same: Now know ye that We by & with ye advice of Our Privy Council, have thought fit to erect & constitute, & by these presents for us or hrs & Successors do erect, constitute, & appoint a President & Council , to take care of ye said Tract of land called The Province of New Hampshire, & of the Planters & Inhabitants thereof; & to Order, rule, & Govern ye same according to such methods & regulations, as are herein after specified & declared. And for ye better execution of Our Royal pleasure in this behalf, We do hereby nominate & appoint Our trusty & well beloved Subject John Cutt of Portsmouth Esqr to be ye first President of ye said Council, & to continue in ye said Office for the space of one whole year next ensuing ye date of these presents & so long after until We, Our heirs or successors, shall nominate & appoint some other person to succeed him in ye same. [The commission continues for several more pages announcing the appointment of council members, oaths of office, replacement of officers, ruling authority, etc.] Whereof we have Caused these our letters to be made pattens witness our self at wesminister the 18th of September In the one and thirtieth years of our Reign. Peripsom Regem Barker.

The Federal and State Constitutions Colonial Charters, and Other Organic Laws of the States, Territories, and Colonies Now or Heretofore Forming the United States of America Compiled and edited under the Act of Congress of June 30, 1906 by Francis Newton Thorpe. Washington, D.C: Government Printing Office, 1909. The Avalon Project at the Yale Law School. William C. Fray and Lisa A. Spar, Co-Directors. Http://www.yale.edu/ lawweb/avalon/states/nh08.htm.

14. *Proceedings*, II:293-4.

15. Owners Everett and Audrey Yates keep the house in immaculate condition.

16. Either the Westminster Assembly's *Shorter Catechism* or John Cotton's *Spiritual Milk for Babes* was included in all eighteenth century editions of *The New England Primer*. Some editions included both. William's first Primer would have been the 1727 version with its woodcut of George II, elegantly dressed and wearing a curly wig but no crown. Its full title: *New England Primer. Enlarged. For the more easy attaining the true reading of English.* To which is added the *Assembly of Divines Catechism.* Printed by S. Kneeland & T. Green. Sold by the Bookfellers. (Boston, 1727). The 1737 edition included a part of the "Duty of Children towards their Parents." It also contained the first printing, author unknown, of the lines: Now I lay me down to sleep, I pray the Lord my soul to keep, If I should die before I wake, I pray the Lord my soul to take. This verse was contained in almost every subsequent edition. Paul Leicester Ford, editor, *New England Primer. Classics in Education*, No. 13. Dodd, Meade and Company. (New York, 1962).

17. Gerrish taught from 1741 to 1755. Moses Atwood Safford, "General William Whipple," *Collections and Proceedings of the Maine Historical Society*, second series, vol. vi. Published by the Society. (Portland, 1895). 340-1.

18. John Sanderson, *Biography of the Signers of the Declaration of Independence*, Vol. 5. R. W. Pomeroy. (Philadelphia. 1823).

19. Nathaniel Adams, 183. William G. Saltonstall, *Ports of Piscataqua*, Russell & Russell. (New York, 1941). 30.

20. Saltonstall, 4, 5.

21. Founded by Daniel Fowle 7 Oct. 1756. Thomas Furber founded *The New Hampshire Mercury and Weekly Advertiser* in late 1764 with financial support from zealous Whigs who found the *Gazette* too timid in the cause of liberty and too much under the influence of the officers of the government. Nathaniel Adams, 210.

22. "Notary and Tabellion Public, by Authority of Parliament, of Portsmouth." Claggett's Manuscript in the Massachusetts Historical Society.

23. Saltonstall, 37-39.

24. Joseph married Hannah Billings 9 Oct. 1763. She died 30 Jan. 1811. William and Joseph worshiped at the old North Church; William occupied the first pew, Joseph's pew was adjacent to John Langdon. Joseph left family, friends, social life, civilization, and a good business in 1773 to penetrate the colony's frontier, founded the town of Jefferson in the wilderness, and set in motion numberless wheels of varied industries. See genealogy section for Joseph's biography.

25. Importers were usually men of large property, so the term merchant implied wealth and merit. The average annual income of the established merchant was well over 500 sterling; shopkeepers, traders who sold in a shop, earned less than half that. Although they had large incomes, their expenses were proportionate. Much of their profit had to be put back into business and their stock might run into thousands of pounds. It cost £80 to outfit and supply a ship; wages and other charges during the voyage exceeded £200, and cargo cost from £700 to £1,000. Frequently a large share of the merchant's assets consisted of debts, often thousands of pounds, which were of doubtful value. Jackson Turner Maine, *The Social Structure of Revolutionary America*, Princeton University Press. (Princeton, NJ, 1965). 88, 135-36. William had two subscriptions to *Prince's New England Chronology* after he became a merchant. *Register*, 6:199. The author has been unable to discover anything about this publication.

26. Traill, comptroller of the port of Portsmouth, became a loyalist, joined royal governor John Wentworth on Long Island in 1777, and was proscribed in November 1778. See *Laws of New Hampshire*, 4:177-80 for these details. He became collector of the Island of Bermuda. The Traills had three children, Robert, William, and Mary. Robert and William settled in Europe. Mary married Keith Spence, esq., a merchant from Scotland who settled in Portsmouth. Their son, Robert T. Spence, became a captain in the U.S. Navy. Keith and Mary (Traill) Spence were the parents of Harriet who married rev. Charles Lowell. Their son, James Russell Lowell (see genealogy section), born 22 February 1819 in Cambridge, Mass. is the noted American poet, critic, editor, and minister to London 1877-85. See his collected works (12 vols., 1890-92); biographies by M.B. Duberman (1966) and H.E. Scudder (2 vols., 1901). Thus William Whipple was the great grand uncle of James Russell Lowell who died in 1891. The Huntington Library of San Marino, Calif. holds the Spence-Lowell collection of original autograph manuscripts. It includes 321 pieces, 1740-1958. Subject matter: trade and privateering in the West Indies (1790-1800); the US Navy and the Tripolitan War (1802- 05); description of travel in Malaga, Gibraltar, Malta, Tunis, Algiers, Sicily, Italy, New England, and New Orleans; Whipple and Lowell families; early history of Portsmouth, N.H. Also includes 98 autograph letters collected by Mary Traill Spence (Lowell) Putnam, sister of James Russell Lowell, and written by various prominent American and European figures of the 19th century. Strongest for 1797-1810. Physical description: chiefly letters, with a few manuscripts and documents.

27. Born in Greenland, N.H. 5 May 1733, Brackett was the son of capt. John and Elizabeth (Pickering) Brackett. His father, a lawyer and farmer, was an intimate of gov. Benning Wentworth. Joshua went from the public school to the Stratham parsonage of Henry Rust who prepared him for Harvard where he studied for the ministry. After a short period of preaching, he studied medicine with Dr. Clement Jackson of Portsmouth and began his own practice in Portsmouth about 1759. He married Hannah Whipple of Kittery 14 March 1760. See the genealogical section for further biographical information on Hannah and Joshua.

28. Reverend Joseph Whipple, capt. William Whipple's half-brother, was born 31 July 1701 in that part of Ipswich, Mass. now known as the town of Hamilton to Matthew Whipple and his third wife Martha (Denison) Thing. He was graduated from Harvard's class of 1720 but remained in residence until September 1721 as a scholar of the house. He taught school at Chelmsford for three years before going to Hampton Falls where he was called to preach after a month's trial in October 1726. He was ordained by neighboring ministers 4 Jan. 1726-27 and married Elizabeth Cutt of Kittery 23 Oct. 1727. See genealogy section for a biography on rev. Joseph Whipple.

29. Dickinson Foss, *Three Centuries of Freemasonry in New Hampshire*, The New Hampshire Publishing Co. (Somersworth, N.H., 1972). 119. E. Van Krugel, MPS 320, *The New Age Magazine*. April, 1970. 47.

30. The war began in July 1754 when a youthful George Washington was sent to stop the French incursions in the Ohio country. He was badly beaten. French forces finally capitulated at Montreal on 8 Sept. 1760. The final treaty, signed in 1763, gave almost total supremacy in North America to the British.

31. The 1766 diary of Portsmouth merchant William Barrell mentions ships owned by Samuel Cutt and John Moffatt sailing directly for London. One of Cutt's ships, the *Non Pareil*, advertised transatlantic passage to Bristol. Saltonstal, 47-49. Opportunities to do business with Boston were

greatly improved 20 April 1761 when John Stavers started a stage, supposedly the first ever run in America, from Portsmouth to Boston. It left Portsmouth Monday morning and was back by Friday. The carriage was a curricle, sufficiently wide to carry three passengers. It was drawn by two horses. It stopped at Ipswich and Charlestown. Fare was 13 shillings and sixpence sterling. Nathaniel Adams, 204-05.

32. He referred to employees Coleman who he was sending home and Frank (__?__) who would return with him. Original letter in the John Carter Brown Library, Providence, R.I.

33. Brewster reports (p. 151) that Mehitable eventually married William E. Treadwell. Brewster's account and Joseph Foster's account in his article on William Whipple in *The Granite Monthly*, XLIII, No 7, New Series, 6, No 7, July 1, 1911, 218 [hereafter Foster II] of the failed engagement was embellished by Dorothy Mansfield Vaughn of Portsmouth in 1964. Vaughn says the wedding was to be in 1763 after Joseph had married. She had Mehitable's father giving his blessing and greeting the groom on the wedding day when the man had died in 1761. Vaughn does not cite sources for the 1763 date or for her enhanced treatment of the failed engagement. A letter from the author to Ms. Vaughn seeking sources was unanswered. Dorothy Mansfield Vaughn, *This Was a Man,,* a biography of General William Whipple, read by the author at a meeting of The National Society of The Colonial Dames in the State of New Hampshire 26 Feb. 1964. 500 copies printed by the Stinehour Press. (Lunenburg, Vt., 1964). Second edition of 300 printed with permission by CGC. (Rye, N.H., 1986). 6-7.

34. John Parker Letter. The whereabouts of the original of this letter is unknown. The author has a copy of the copy in possession of the Moffatt-Ladd House in Portsmouth. Portsmouth Athenaeum, Moffatt-Ladd House Collection, The National Society of Colonial Dames of America in the State of New Hampshire. (Portsmouth, N.H).

35. "Births, Marriages, and Deaths in Portsmouth," N.H. *Register*, 24:14.

36. Nathaniel Adams, p. 182. Fred Myron Colby, "The Moffatt-Whipple Mansion." *The Granite Monthly New Hampshire Magazine*, Vol. III. Republican Press Association. (Concord, N.H., 1890). 219. An old "wastebook" [Mead Papers, Kittery Point] kept by John Moffatt in 1744-45 provides a picture of a Portsmouth ship chandlery during King George's war. Moffatt dealt extensively in rum, rope, nails, rigging, lumber, spars, sugar, cider, anchors, duck and paints, not only in Portsmouth and Kittery, but in up-river Piscataqua towns. He did considerable outfitting for the snow *Nancy*, had a large interest in the ships *Neptune* and *Delight*; repaired the sloop *Unity*; and provided many masts and spars for local builders and export to England. Among merchants, shipwrights, and outfitters he dealt with extensively were John Shackford, Tobias Langdon, Mark Wentworth, James Ferguson, Nathaniel Meserve, Henry and William Sherburne, Samuel Newmarch, Charles Hoight, John Pridham, and Joseph Dam. These were all prominent builders, painters, riggers, sail and rope-makers, and merchants. Saltonstall, 30-31.

37. Sara Catherine's sister Anna Elizabeth married Peter Livius, a famous tory who fled to England after the Revolutionary war broke out. Fred Myron Colby, "The Moffatt-Whipple Mansion." *The Granite Monthly New Hampshire Magazine*. Vol III. Republican Press Association. (Concord, NH, 1890) 219-20. Livius became governor of Nova Scotia and later superior court judge in Quebec.

38. He died at Demerara, now Surinam. "An old-time chronicler remarked with disapproval that Samuel Moffatt's `college education and fashionable life, as might be supposed, had not qualified him for strict and prudent application to business.' He was heavily in debt, and in danger from that strange judicial system which made recovery impossible by locking up the debtor." Everett S. Stackpole. *Old Kittery and Her Families*. Press of Lewiston Journal Company. (Lewiston, Maine, 1903). 6.

39. Nine letters written to Samuel Moffatt in St. Ecstatics dated 4 June 1768 through 30 July 1770. Three of the letters were authored by John Moffatt and six by Capt. John Parker, a close friend of the Moffatts These letters were given to the Moffatt-Ladd House and Garden, a National Historic Landmark owned and operated by The National Society of The Colonial Dames of America in the State of New Hampshire, by John Landgon Ward.

40. Sarah wrote her father in January 1764 saying she was "now at housekeeping. . .Our house is chiefly furnished and in a very genteel manner for so large a one and young beginners." Richard M. Candee, Ph.D, "An Old Town by the Sea," *Urban Landscape and Vernacular Architecture Forum 1660-1990.* (Portsmouth, NH, 1992.) 25. Through Samuel Moffatt's marriage to Sarah Mason, the house is connected with the very beginning of the state's history.

41. Katharine wrote her brother in Surinam 19 Nov. 1769, "your dear little babes are very well. Polly was sick about three weeks ago. We all thought she would die but is got very well now. Mother lays as we all think on her death bed. She has laid twelve days helpless as a babe the greatest part

of the time insensible." Copy of letter in possession of Moffatt-Ladd House, Portsmouth, N.H.

42. Parker's letter disclosed that Mehitable and William Knight were living in John Moffatt's "old mansion house" on Buck street which John and Katharine probably moved out of after Mrs. Moffatt died 1 Dec. 1769. John Parker Letter, Portsmouth Athenaeum, Moffatt-Ladd House Collection.

43. Colby, 220.

44. Candee, 25.

45. First floor windows are surmounted by segmental pediments, second floor windows have elaborate swan-pediments, each terminating in a pair of conventionalized Tudor roses; third floor windows meet the cornice. The stairs are "exceptionally handsome, the box-paneled ends supported by richly carved brackets, and each carrying in succession a turned, a twisted, and a fluted baluster, topped by a rail well proportioned and graceful." The underside of the second halflight, which shows effectively from the entrance, is "an enriched panel with an oval centre circled by the same carving as that of the door architraves, this surrounded by elaborate moldings embracing a conventionalized Tudor rose in each corner." Philip Dana Orcutt, *The Moffatt-Ladd House, Its Garden and Its Period*. The Society of the Colonial Dames of America in the State of New Hampshire. (Portsmouth, N.H). Dr. James L. Garvin, New Hampshire's architectural historian, says the house was raised by Michael Whidden III and sheathed, shingled, and fully finished by his crew of nine apprentices and two journeymen, Richard Mills did the turnings of the stairs, and Ebenezer Dearing was responsible for the "lavish carving" that provides much of "the spectacular quality of the house's interior." He said Dearing was responsible for the sumptuous moldings and carved capitals, modillions, stair brackets, two chimney pieces, and 18 Roses." Candee, 25-26.

46. Colby, 222.

47. Syllabub: A desert or beverage made of sweetened milk or cream mixed with wine or cider and beaten to a froth.

48. The Society of Colonial Dames of America in the State of New Hampshire founded in 1892 entered into a long-term lease on the house in 1911 and later received a deed to it. The Society began restoration in 1912 following the recommendations of Luke V. Lockewood, an antique scholar. The 1768 room-by-room inventory of Samuel Moffatt's bankruptcy inspired the second round of restoration in the 1960s and is responsible for much of the museum's subsequent activity.

49. In November 1862 a Portsmouth newspaper reported repairs and improvements "in which all the rich outlines of a superb mansion of eighty years ago have been carefully preserved." Candee. 26-27.

50. The portrait is 44" by 36". Trumbull's original miniature is in the Trumbull Collection at Yale University and the Tenney portrait was lent by The Society of Colonial Dames of America in the State of New Hampshire to the United States Constitution Sesquicentennial Commission for its "Exhibition of Portraits of the Signers and Deputies to the Convention of 1787 and Signers of the Declaration of Independence In Commemoration of the 150th Anniversary of the Formation of the Constitution of the United States." The exhibition was at the Corcoran Gallery of Art in Washington, D.C. 27 Nov. 1937 to Feb. 1, 1938.

51. It came from the estate of a Mr. Macomber of Nashua, New Hampshire and is identified as Katharine Whipple but there is no confirming evidence the person is actually Katharine. Letters to the author from Nancy Douthat Goss, Museum House Chairman, Moffatt-Ladd House. 8 July 1992 and 13 July-24 Aug.1993.

52. Mrs. A. T. Dudley and William P. Dudley, *The Moffatt-Ladd House*. The National Society of Colonial Dames in the State of New Hampshire. (Portsmouth, N.H). 2-16. Jane C. Giffen, "The Moffatt-Ladd House" *The Connoisseur*, October and November, 1970. Reprinted in booklet form by the National Society of the Colonial Dames of America in the State of New Hampshire.

53. The furniture was purchased from Colonial Williamsburg, Va. who had acquired it in the early 1930s and displayed it in the restored governor's residence in the restored colonial Virginia capitol. Brock Jobe, author of *Portsmouth Furniture — Masterworks from the New Hampshire Seacoast* describes it as "extraordinary [and] the most important suite of eighteenth-century English furniture with an American provenance." Friends of the Moffatt-Ladd House, 154 Market Street, Portsmouth, N.H. 0380. (603) 430-7968; moffatt-ladd@juno.com email.

54. *Portsmouth Town Records*, Vol. 1, Part 1, 1695-1779. Works Projects Administration, Official Project No 65-1-13-2098.

55. A 78 foot wooden lighthouse built on the eastern point of Newcastle was lighted 8 June 1771.

Twenty years later Joseph Whipple, as collector of the port, ceded it to the United States. Saltonstall, 49-50.

56. *NHSP*, 269-72.

57. Cutts was heavily involved in shipping. On 22 June 1761 his brigantine *Mercury* cleared Portsmouth for the West Indies and was taken by a French privateer before arriving at its destination. William Barrell, a Portsmouth merchant, kept a diary and entries for 1766 mention Cutts and John Moffatt's ships. Cutts' ship *Non Pareil* offered trans-atlantic passage to Bristol, England. Saltonstall, 38, 47, 49.

58. Details of the various activities are found in *Portsmouth Town Records*, 2: part 1.

59. *Portsmouth, N.H. Town Records*, Vol. 2, part 1. Edmund Parry is identified as Edward Parry in *Provincial Papers*, VII, 408, 413, 415.

60. The petition is in *NHPP*. The author misplaced the volume and page number.

61. Nathaniel Bouton, editor, *Provisional Papers. Documents and Records Relating to the Province of New-Hampshire, from 1764 to 1776; Including the Whole Administration of Gov. John Wentworth; the Events Immediately Preceding the Revolutionary War; the Losses at the Battle of Bunker Hill, and the Record of all Proceedings till the end of our Provincial History*. Vol VII. Published by the authority of the legislature of New-Hampshire. Orrin C. Moore, State Printer. (Nashua, 1873). The author misplaced the volume and page number.

62. Saltonstall, 92.

63. Nathaniel Adams, 246-47.

64. *Portsmouth Town Records*. 2: Part 1.

65. *Portsmouth Town Records*. 2: Part 1.

66. *Portsmouth Town Records*. 2: Part 1.

67. Jackson Turner Maine, 38, 42.

68. *NHPP.*, 180, 187, 188, 248. A copy of the petition is in *NHPP*, VII, 248.

69. *NHPP*, VII, 331-32.

70. Upton, 302.

71. Nathaniel Adams, 239-42. Dover, Barrington, Exeter, Hampton, Haverhill, and Newcastle passed similar "tea resolves."

72. The Massachusetts Government Act, passed May 13, provided that councilors were to be chosen in England. Sheriffs and judges were to be directly responsible to the governor. Jurors were to be summoned by the sheriff, not selected by town meetings. And the town meeting, that "nest of sedition," was put under the governor's supervision.

73. Dr. Josiah Bartlett of Kingston and John Pickering, esq. of Portsmouth were initially elected to the continental congress. Pickering refused to serve and Bartlett, having recently lost his house to fire, was compelled to decline. Maj. Sullivan and col. Folsom were the second choices. *NHPP*, VII, 407. New Hampshire delegates were the first to stand and be acknowledged. On October 18, after three weeks of debate, the continental congress voted for the "Continental Association," the first instrument of their union. It contained 14 sections and 2,000 words. The address to the People of Great Britain, a daring novelty, caused much argument in congress. Heretofore, when nations wished to communicate, they addressed the monarch, not "the people."

74. New Hampshire received its first governor in its own right in 1741 in the person of Benning Wentworth, and the legislature was given increased authority. This form of government continued until changes brought about by the revolution. The last royal governor, John Wentworth II, held office from 1767 to 1775. *Federal Writers' Project of the Works Projects Administration for the State of N.H. New Hampshire A Guide to the Granite State*. Francis P. Murphy Governor, Houghton Mifflin Company. (Boston, 1938). 37-40.

75. *NHPP*, VII, 419. The first continental congress asked all colonies to adopt these measures. W. C. Ford, editor, *Journals of the Continental Congress*, Vol. I. Washington Government Printing Office. 75-80. [Hereafter Journals].

76. It was later extended to all colonies represented at the 1774 continental congress except New York and North Carolina.

77. William James Morgan, editor, *Naval Documents of the American Revolution*. Vol. 5. (Washington, 1970). 555-6. Hereafter Naval Documents.

78. Foster, II, 27.

79. Saltonstall, 89-90.

80. Upton, 24.

81. Frank Donovan, *Mr. Jefferson's Declaration*. Dodd, Mead & Company. (New York, 1968). 16-7.

82. *NHPP*, VII, 467.

83. The first provisional congress met 21 July 1774.

84. Other members: John Wentworth, Meshech Weare, Nathaniel Folson, Josiah Bartlett, Christopher Toppan, Ebenezer Thompson, Samuel Cutts, and John Pickering.

85. *NHPP*, VII, 442.

86. Measures "best calculated to restore to you that peace and harmony so ardently wished for by every good and honest American:"

    1st. That you discountenance and discourage all trespasses and injuries against individuals and their property, and all disorders of every kind: and that you cultivate and maintain peace and harmony among yourselves.

    2nd. That you yield due obedience to the magistrates within this government, and carefully endeavor to support the laws thereof.

    3rd. That you strictly adhere to the Association of the late continental congress, and deal with the violators of it in the manner therein recommended.

    4th. That you endeavor particularly to enforce the laws of the province against hawkers, peddlers, and petty chapmen.

    5th. That you abstain from the use of East India tea, whenever, or by whatever means it has or may be imported.

    6th. That you encourage and support your several committees of correspondence and inspection, in discharging the very important trust you have placed in them.

    7th. That in case any inhabitant of these colonies should be seized, in order to be transported to Great Britain, or other parts beyond the seas, to be sent for offenses supposed to be committed in America, you conduct yourself agreeable to the advice of the late continental congress.

    8th. That in your several stations you promote and encourage the manufactures of this country, and endeavor, both by precept and example, to induce all under you, and with whom you are connected, to practice economy and industry, and to shun all kinds of extravagances.

    9th. That the officers of the several regiments strictly comply with the laws of this province for regulating the militia; and as the militia upon this continent, if properly disciplined, would be able to do great service in its defence, should it ever be invaded by his majesty's enemies, that you acquaint yourselves with the manual exercise, particularly that recommended and enjoined by the captain general, the motions being natural, easy, and best calculated to qualify persons for real action; and also to improve themselves in those evolutions which are necessary for infantry in time of engagement.

    10th. That, as your enemies are using every art to impoverish and distress you, in order to induce submission to their arbitrary mandates, you carefully shun those measures which may have a tendency to distress your brethren and fellow-suffers, and avoid all unnecessary lawsuits, and endeavor to settle disputes between you in the most amicable and least expensive manner. That all debtors exert themselves in discharging their just debts, and all creditors exercise such lenity as their circumstances will admit of.

    11th. That as the inhabitants of the town of Boston, in the province of the Massachusetts Bay, are now laboring under a load of ministerial vengeance, laid upon them to enforce obedience to certain arbitrary and unconstitutional acts, which, if once submitted to, must involve all America in slavery and ruin; conscious that all these colonies are largely indebted to the virtue and fortitude of those patriotic assertors of freedom, we heartily recommend a continuation of your contributions, for the relief of that oppressed people; and that you keep yourselves in constant readiness to support them in their just opposition, whenever necessity may require.

    Lastly. We earnestly entreat you, at this time of tribulation and distress, when your enemies are urging you to despair, when every scene around is full of blood and horror, that in imitation of your pious forefathers with contrition of spirit and penitence of heart, you implore the Divine Being who alone is able to deliver you from your present unhappy and distressing situation, to espouse your righteous cause, secure your liberties, and fix them on a firm and lasting basis; and we fervently beseech Him to restore to you and your American brethren, that peace and tranquility so ardently desired, and earnestly sought for, by every true friend to liberty and mankind. *NHPP*, VII, 443-4.

87. *NHPP*, VII, 461.

88. Weare (1713-86) was a farmer and jurist. He had served in the general court since 1745. During the revolution he was the state's leader as chairman of the committee of safety and of the executive council and chief justice of the superior court under the constitution.

89. Of these, Whipple, Thornton, Bartlett, Folsom, White, Peabody, and John Taylor Gilman served in the continental congress.

90. Bills of credit were to be backed by the credit of the colony, payable at different periods from future taxes and were to bear six percent interest. Foster II, 25-6.

91. *NHPP*, VII, 670-71 and 570-61.

92. Capt. Stephen Evans was appointed colonel of the second regiment, col. Jonathan Moulton, colonel of the third, and col. Nicholas Gilman colonel of the fourth. Col. Josiah Bartlett was appointed colonel of a regiment previously commanded by col. Jonathan Greeley. *NHPP*, VII, 577.

93. Frank C. Mevers, Editor, *The Papers of Josiah Bartlett*, New Hampshire Historical Society. University Press of New England. (Hanover, N.H., 1979). 25, 29.

94. *Naval Documents*. 2:397-8, 613.

95. *Naval Documents*, 2:996-7.

96. *Naval Documents*, 2:996-7.

97. The state assembly authorized eight companies of 100 men each enlisted for two months, "exclusive of 200 montrosses before ordered." *Naval Documents*, 2:996-7.

98. *NHPP*, VII, 572-3. *Naval Documents*, 2:1064.

99. *NHSP*. Author has lost volume and page number.

100. *NHPP*, Vol. VII, 655.

101. *Naval Documents*, 2:1089.

102. NHSP, Vol. VIII, 15. Constitution of New Hampshire — 1776 (1). IN CONGRESS AT EXETER, January 5, 1776. VOTED, That this Congress take up CIVIL GOVERNMENT for this colony in manner and form following, viz. We, the members of the Congress of New Hampshire, chosen and appointed by the free suffrages of the people of said colony, and authorized and empowered by them to meet together, and use such means and pursue such measures as should judge best for the public good; and in particular to establish some form of government, provided that measure should be recommended by the Continental Congress: And a recommendation to that purpose having been transmitted to us from the said Congress: Have taken into our serious consideration the unhappy circumstances, into which this colony is involved by means of many grievous and oppressive acts of the British Parliament, depriving us of our natural and constitutional rights and privileges; to enforce obedience to which acts a powerful fleet and army have been sent to this country by the ministry of Great Britain, who have exercised a wanton and cruel abuse of their power, in destroying the lives and properties of the colonists in many places with fire and sword, taking the ships and lading from many of the honest and industrious inhabitants of this colony employed in commerce, agreeable to the laws and customs a long time used here.

The sudden and abrupt departure of his Excellency John Wentworth, Esq., our late Governor, and several of the Council, leaving us destitute of legislation, and no executive courts being open to punish criminal offenders; whereby the lives and properties of the honest people of this colony are liable to the machinations and evil designs of wicked men.

Therefore, for the preservation of peace and good order, and for the security of the lives and properties of the inhabitants of this colony, we conceive ourselves reduced to the necessity of establishing A FORM OF GOVERNMENT to continue during the present unhappy and unnatural contest with Great Britain; PROTESTING and DECLARING that we never sought to throw off our dependence upon Great Britain, but felt ourselves happy under her protection, while we could enjoy our constitutional rights and privileges. And that we shall rejoice if such a reconciliation between us and our parent State can be effected as shall be approved by the CONTINENTAL CONGRESS, in whose prudence and wisdom we confide. Accordingly pursuant to the trust reposed in us. WE DO resolve, that this Congress assume the name, power, and authority of a House of Representatives or Assembly for the Colony of New Hampshire And that said House then proceed to choose twelve persons, being reputable freeholders and inhabitants within this colony, in the following manner, viz. Five in the county of Rockingham, two in the county of Stratford, two in the county of Hillsborough, two in the county of Cheshire, and one in the county of Grafton, to be a distinct and separate branch of the Legislature by the name of a COUNCIL for this colony, to continue as such until the third Wednesday in December next; and seven of whom to be a quorum to do business. That such Council appoint their President, and in his absence that the senior counselor preside; that a Secretary be appointed by both branches, who may be a counselor, or otherwise, as they shall choose. That no act or resolve shall be valid and put into execution unless agreed to, and passed by both branches of the legislature. That all public officers for the said colony, and each county, for the current year, be appointed by the Council and assembly, except the several clerks of the Executive Courts, who shall be appointed by the Justices of the respective Courts. That all bills, resolves, or votes for raising levying, and collecting money originate in the House of Representatives. That at any session of the Council and Assembly neither branch shall adjourn from any longer time that from Sunday till Monday without consent of the other. And it is further resolved, That if the present unhappy dispute with Great Britain should continue longer than this present year, and the Continental Congress give no instruction or direction to the contrary, the Council be chosen by the people of each respective county in such manner as the Council and House of Representatives shall order. The general and field officers of the militia, on any vacancy, be appointed by the two houses, and all inferior officers be chosen by the respective companies. That all officers of the Army be appointed by the two houses, except they should direct otherwise in case of any emergency. That all civil officers for the colony and for each county be appointed, and the time of their continuance in office be determined by the two houses, except clerks of courts, and county treasurers, and recorders of deeds. That a treasurer, and a recorder of deeds for each county be annually chosen by the people of each county respectively; the votes for such officers to be returned to the respective courts of General Sessions of the Peace in the county, there to be ascertained as the Council and Assembly shall hereafter direct. That precepts in the name of the Council and Council, signed by the President of the Council, and Speaker of the House of Representatives to be returned by the third Wednesday in December then next ensuing, in such manner as the Council and Assembly shall hereafter prescribe. (1) Verified by "Acts and Laws of the State of New Hampshire in America, by order of The general Assembly. To which is prefixed, The Resolution of the American Congress for Establishing a Form of Government in New Hampshire and the Resolve of the Provincial Congress, for taking up Government in Form. With the Declaration of Independence. America; Printed at Exeter in the State of New Hampshire, MDCCLXXX. Francis Newton Thorpe, William C. Fray, and Lisa A. Spar.

103. *NHSP*, VIII:1-3, 12, 14-15, 65-67.

104. *NHSP*, VIII, 14, 33.

105. *NHSP*, VIII:1-3, 12, 14-15, 65-67.

106. *NHSP*, VIII:204-96.

107. Out of 155 towns and a population of 82,000, returns have been preserved from 77 towns including more than 50,000 men. Upton, 50-51. The Proscription Act of 1778 listed the names, occupations, and locations of 76 prominent loyalists who were banished from the state. Metcalf, *Laws of New Hampshire*, IV:171 ff.

108. Brighton, *They Came to Fish*, 2:83; NHSP, 8:659; Laws of New Hampshire, 4:177-80.

109. Mevers, 187.

110. The other members were Robert Morris, R.H. Lee, and Philip Livingston. *Washington's Correspondence*, 143.

111. Edmund C. Burnett, editor, *Letters of Members of the Continental Congress*. Vol. 2. Published by the Carnegie Institution of Washington. (Washington, 1921). *Richard Smith Diary*, Letter No. 462, 342-3. Hereafter, this reference will be *Letters* and will cite the volume, Letter No., and page.

112. Foster II, 28.

113. Mevers, 259.

114. Most letters of New Hampshire delegates in the state archives have been printed in the New Hampshire State Papers. Some unprinted letters are in the Farmer's Collection. A large selection of Josiah Bartlett's correspondence is at Dartmouth College. The Portsmouth Athenaeum owns a collection of Whipple's papers. The principal body of Weare's papers are in the Massachusetts Historical Society, others are in the New Hampshire Historical Society.

115. *The Papers of Josiah Bartlett*. Microfilm, 7 rolls. New Hampshire State Historical Society. (Concord, N.H., 1976).

116. There were a great number of mill ponds around the city. Miasma is a vapor that rose from the ponds. Joseph West Moore, *The American Congress*. Harper & Brothers Publishers. (New York, 1895). 21.

117. Langdon was elected 25 Jan. 1775 and attended 10 May to 2 Aug.; 16 Sept. to 12 Nov.; 23 Dec. to 2 Jan. 1776. He was reelected 23 Jan. 1776. Bartlett was elected 23 Aug. 1775 and attended 16 Sept. to 17 March 1776.

118. *Letters*, 1:Letter 575, 407.

119. *Naval Documents*. 4:551.

120. *Letters*, 1:Letter 590, 415. Privateers were warships owned by individuals and sanctioned by congress.

121. Eleven battalions were to be raised for the eastern department under two general officers. *Letters*, 1:Letter 646, 452-53.

122. *NHSP*, Vol. VIII, 121, 125.

123. *Letters*, 2:47-48.

124. *Letters*, 1:Letter 653, May 17, 1776 with a P.S. dated May 18, 455. 1:Letter No. 655, May 18, 456.

125. Recorded in Ezra Stiles diary. Letter2: Letter 198, fn., 47.

126. *Letters*, 2:Letter 47, 29-30. Moore, 72.

127. Another $5 million was issued two months later and an additional $5 million November 2. By then inflation and depreciation were creating new problems.

128. Burnett, 162-63. The committee conferred with Washington, maj. Gen. Horatio Gates, and brig. Gen. Thomas Mifflin on the Canadian situation. Other members were Benj. Harrison, Richard Henry Lee, John Adams, James Wilson, Robert R. Livingston, Roger Sherman, Stephen Hopkins, William Livingston, George Read, Matthew Tilghman, Joseph Hewes, Arthur Middleton, and Lyman Hall. The committee issued reports on 29, 30, 31 May and 1 June. Eight battalions from Mass., Conn., N.H., and N.Y. were ordered raised for the Canada campaign. Washington was authorised to employ Indians in Canada; 13,800 milita from Mass., Conn. N.Y., and N.J. were authorized to re-enforce N.Y.; Pa., Md., and Del. were to furnish 10,000 more for a flying camp, to serve until 1 December. Various other measurers were adopted (see the *Journals of the Continental Congress*. Washington was excused on 3 June and was back in N.Y. on 6 June. *The George Washington Papers at the Library of Congress*, 1741-1799. Vol. 5, Philadelphia, May 28, 1776. [Hereafter Washington Papers.]

129. Chandler E. Potter, *The Military History of the State of New Hampshire 1623-1861*. Genealogical Publishing Co. Inc. (Baltimore, 1972).

130. Burnett, 154-55.

131. *Letters*, 1:Letter 670, 466-67; Letter 687, 483. Burnett, 171.

132. The roll call: New Hampshire, Massachusetts, Rhode Island, Connecticut, New York, New Jersey, Pennsylvania, Delaware, Maryland, Virginia, North Carolina, South Carolina, Georgia. It is presumed Bartlett voted first because his attendance at the second congress in 1775 made him senior to Whipple. When later votes were recorded in the *Journal*, the senior delegate was always listed first.

133. Donovan, 43.

134. Burnett, 166.

135. Burnett. p. 180.

136. Burnett, 180.

137. Catherine Drinker Bowen, *John Adams and the American Revolution*. Little, Brown and Company. (Boston, 1950). 603.

138. *Letters*, 2:Letter 9, 5. See Force, *American Archives*, 4th series, VI:1029-30 for New Hampshire's instructions.

139. Lynn Montross *The Reluctant Rebels The Story of the Continental Congress 1774-1789*. Harper & Brothers Publishers. (New York, 1950). 201.

140. Donovan, 49.

141. Except for Hancock, who signed as president of the congress, delegates signed in groups, by colonies. Names on the engrossed copy from left to right begin with Georgia and continues from south to north. Signers by state: Josiah Bartlett, William Whipple, Matthew Thornton, New Hampshire; Samuel Adams, John Adams, Robert Treat Paine, Elbridge Gerry, Massachusetts; Stephen Hopkins, William Ellery, Rhode Island; Roger Sherman, Samuel Huntington, William Williams, Oliver Wolcott, Connecticut; Robert Morris, Benjamin Rush, Benjamin Franklin, John Morton, George Clymer, James Smith, George Taylor, James Wilson, George Ross, Pennsylvania; William Floyd, Philip Livingston, Frances Lewis, Lewis Morris, New York; Richard Stockton,

Jonathan Witherspoon, Francis Hopkinson, John Hart, Abraham Clark, New Jersey; Caesar Rodney, George Reed, Delaware; Samuel Chase, William Paca, Thomas Stone, Charles Carroll; Maryland; Butler Gwinnett, Lyman Hall, George Walton, Georgia; William Hopper, Joseph Hewes, John Penn, North Carolina; Edward Rutledge, Thomas Heyward, Jr., Thomas Lynch, Jr., Arthur Middleton, South Carolina; George Wythe, Richard Henry Lee, Thomas Jefferson, Benjamin Harrison, Thomas Nelson, Jr., Francis Lightfoot Lee, Carter Braxton, Virginia.

142. Burnett, 189.

143. Burnett, 197.

144. John A. Schutz and Douglas Adair, editors, *The Spur of Fame*. The Huntington Library. (San Marino, CA, 1966). 183.

145. Schutz and Adair, 250.

146. *Journals*, 6:914.

147. Meters, 192. *Josiah Bartlett Correspondence*. Microfilm, roll 2.

148. *Letters*, 3:314.

149. *Letters*, 4:Letter 97, 72; Letter 228, 178-79.

150. *Journals*, 4:182, 214, 272.

151. *Journals*, 6:1063-38.

152. *Letters*, 3:Letter 696, 55.

153. *Letters*, 1:Letter 546, 385.

154. *Journals*, 4:196, 201-04.

155. *Calendar of the Correspondence of George Washington with the Continental Congress*. Library of Congress, Government Printing Office. (Washington, 1906). 43. Hereafter Washington's Correspondence.

156. Washington's Correspondence, 47. According to the Journals, 4:337, this committee was named 8 May.

157. Other members were Elbridge Gerry, Mass. and Francis Lightfoot Lee, Va. *Journals*, 4:384.

158. *Journals*, 4:391.

159. *Journals*, 4:474.

160. *Journals*, 5:617-20. On 19 July the committee's report on "officers as may have been accessary thereto" was read and tabled. *Journals*, 5:592.

161. Potter, 186, 338, 377.

162. *Journals*, 6:950.

163. Mevers, 132.

164. Foster II, 28.

165. *Journals*, 7:175; 8:465.

166. *Letters*, 3:Letter 609, 480; Letter 620, 489-90; Letter 621, 490-91; Letter 622, 491-92.

167. Other members: James Duane, N.Y., George Wythe, Va., J. Adams, Roger Sherman, Conn., Joseph Hewes, N.C., and Thomas Johnson, Md. The report was submitted May 22 and recommended a redemption rate for continental bills of credit. It took into account the different standards in different colonies and established rates for coin then circulating in the various colonies. The report was tabled. *Journals*. 4:294, 381-83. It submitted a new report in September stating redemption of bills of credit issued by congress should be at the rate of Spanish milled dollars (otherwise called the Pillar piece of eight), now becoming the common measure of other coins, or its equivalent in gold and silver. Since the value of coins was estimated by different rules and proportions in the various states, an injustice could occur unless a common measure was established. Consequently, the committee recommended a precise weight and fineness assigned to the Spanish milled dollar to be applied to other coins and bullion to estimate their comparative value. It prepared a chart listing the value of a continental dollar as follows. Silver coins: Spanish milled dollar, the old Ecu of France, of 60 sol Tournois, or French Crown, English Crown, English Shilling, English sixpence. Gold Coins: The old Spanish Double Doubloon, the old Spanish Pistole, the Johannes of Portugal, the half Johannes, the double Moeda of Portugal, the Modea of Portugal, the old Louis d'or of France, the new Louis d'or of France, the English Guinea of William III, the English half Guinea of William III, the Hungary Ducat; the Ducat of Holland, of the bishop of Bamberg, of Brandenberg, of Sweden, of Denmark, of Poland, of Transylvania; the double Ducat of the Duke of Hanover, and the Chequins of Venice. Circulating coins not stated in this table should be assayed and inserted in the table together with their value in dollars. *Journals*, 5:724-48.

168. James Wilson, Elbridge Gerry, Mass., Thomas Nelson, Va., and Robert Morris, Pa., were the other members. Journals, 6:1042.

169. *Journals*, 12:1102, 1114-15, 1123. Letters, 3:fn, 489-90.

170. *Journals*, 13:472; 14:708, 739, 852. Letters, 4:Letter 70, 54-55; Letter 219, 173.

171. *Letters*, 2:Letter 477, 355.

172. Moore, 69.

173. *Letters*, 4:Letter 7, 5-6; Letter 47, 38; Letter 79, 59-60.

174. *Letters*, 4:Letter 228, 178-79; Letter 299, 233.

175. *Letters*, 4:Letter 126, 91-92.

176. *Letters*, 4:Letter 242, 260; Letter 362, 279-80.

177. *Journals*, 13:79. Letters, 4:Letter 82, 82-83.

178. *Journals*, 13:93-94; 148-49; 543; 988. Letters, 4:Letter 25, 35; Letter 46, 37; Letter 47, 38.

179. Upton, 113.

180. Saltonstall. 96-98. *Naval Documents*, 160.

181. *Letters*, 1:Letter 691; 479.

182. Foster II, 29.

183. *Naval Documents*, 6:360, 815-16, 1415-16, 1463-64.

184. Fowler, 214.

185. Upton, 188-98.

186. *Letters*, 3:Letter 644, 513; Letter 660, 522; Letter 673, 534-35.

187. Mevers, 245, 251.

188. *Letters*, 4:Letter 403, 310; Letter 453, 351-52; Letter 633, 508-09; Letters 6, Letter 605, 462. Upton, 195.

189. Burnett, 232.

190. Many members, concerned for their safety, returned home. Many at home remained there rather than return to the congress. Burnett, 234.

191. *Letters*, 2:Letter 243, 175.

192. *William Whipple Papers*, Manuscript Box 50 at the Portland Athenaeum, Portsmouth, NH. [Hereafter *William Whipple Papers*.]

193. Burnett, 232-33.

194. Mevers, 142.

195. Burnett. p. 233.

196. Amory, 174-75. 182-83.

197. Burnett, 232.

198. Laurence Sterne, *Life and Opinions of Tristram Shandy, Gentleman*. The Modern Library of the World's Best Books, Random House, Inc. (1950). The first two volumes were published in London in 1759. Seven other volumes appeared at intervals until 1767. Sterne, born in Ireland in 1713, was an ordained minister, educated at Jesus College, Cambridge. He held the vicarages of Sutton and Stillington, was prebend of the cathedral and Comissary of the Peculiar Court of Pickering and Pocklington in York. He died in 1768. He dedicated the book to William Pitt (1708-1778) member of parliament who favored the colonial cause in the American Revolution. Sterne's dedication said he lived "in a constant endeavor to fence against the infirmities of ill health, and other evils of life, by mirth; being firmly persuaded that every time a man smiles, — but much more so, when he laughs, it adds something to this Fragment of Life."

199. Letter to Abigail Adams March 16, 1777. L.H. Butterfield, Marc Friedlander, and Mary Jo Kline, editors, *The Book of Abigail and John*. Harvard University Press. (Cambridge and London, 1975). 170-71.

200. Regiments assigned to Whipple: his own, Evans, Moulton, Gilman, Bartlett, Thornton, Webster, Badger, and McClary. Assigned to Stark: Nichols, Ashley, Moore, Stickeny, Hale, Bellow, Hobart, Morey, and Chase. Upton, 635. Also Hammond, II, May 1777 to 1789. (1886).

201. *NHSP*, VIII, 697, 701.

202. Fred J. Cook, *Dawn Over Saratoga*. Doubleday & Company, Inc. (Garden City, NY, 1973). 97, 105.

203. Sir Edward Creasy singled out the Battle of Saratoga as the decisive battle of the revolution. The

British considered that the whole head and animus of the rebellion lay in New England and they formed a grand design to crush it with one all-powerful blow. They sent a large fleet carrying soldiers and munitions up the Hudson to form a line on the south, then massed large bodies of troops in Canada to march down from the north. It was expected that these two forces would meet and crush or capture every rebel between them. Had the plan succeeded the British would have possessed all the territory between New York City and the Lakes, and between the coast and Canada; including all New England and there would have been no force left sufficient to resist them. Sir Edward Creasy, M.A., *The Fifteen Decisive Battles of the World from Marathon to Waterloo.* London, 1872, 775-6.

204. The British war strategy was for gen. Burgoyne to lead an army south from Canada to Albany, N.Y. A smaller expedition under col. Barry St. Leger would converge on Albany from the west. By occupying Albany and controlling the Hudson river, the British intended to cut off New England from the other colonies and force an end to the American rebellion. Burgoyne left Montreal in June with about 7,000 British and Hessian troops and a number of Native American allies. He took fort Ticonderoga on lake Champlain in July without a struggle and fought a skirmish with an American force near Hubbardton, Vt. on 16 Aug. 1777. Two thousand inexperienced New Hampshire and Vermont militiamen defeated a detachment of Burgoyne's troops at Bennington, Vt. After a 3-week delay at fort Miller (now Schuylerville, N.Y. to obtain provisions, Burgoyne moved his army across the Hudson. He began to march south towards Albany on 13 Sept. but found his way blocked by some 7,000 American under maj. Gen. Horatio Gates, who had taken up an entrenched position at Bemis Heights, a densely wooded plateau a few miles south of Saratoga. The British attacked on the 19th and a furious but indecisive battle was fought at Freeman's Farm, known as the First Battle of Saratoga. Gates withdrew to Bemis Heights and Burgoyne made a camp a mile north. Meanwhile St. Leger had turned back at fort Stanwix in the Mohawk Valley and though commanding fewer than 5,000 men, Burgoyne refused to retreat. His army moved against the American position on 7 Oct leading to the Battle of Bemis Heights (the second Battle of Saratoga). Gates' well-disciplined forces drove the British back to their camp with heavy losses. Burgoyne withdrew to Saratoga, where surrounded by the American army (now numbering nearly 20,000), he surrendered on 17 October. The 2,800-acre Saratoga National Historical park is located in Stillwater, N.Y. some 30 miles north of Albany. The Hudson river and its bluffs are major features of the park and it includes the Schuyler House and the 155 ft. Saratoga Monument in Victory. Most of the American and British fortified lines where the two battles of Saratoga were fought are protected and Saratoga may be the only significant battlefield where so much of the land associated with the fighting is well protected. The typical viewer should plan on spending at least two to three hours. The first hour should be spent at the Visitor Center to view the 20-minute orientation film and browsing through the Museum and obtaining Park information. The remaining time can be spent traveling the 9.2 mile Tour Road which has 10 stops as you follow the two battles through time. Wayside audio programs are available at each stop. Self guided audiotapes are available for a slight fee at the Visitor Center

205. The congress asked Washington to name a general to command the northern army but he asked to be excused as that department had always been considered separate. On 2 Aug. 1777, New England delegates in congress suggested gen. Gates. James Lovell of Mass. wrote to Whipple 4 August that New York was pushing for Washington to succeed gen. Schuyler and opposing Gates. However, when it was proposed to the committee, they voted 11 to 1 for Gates and Washington was directed on 4 Aug. to order Gates to take command of the northern department. Burnett, vol. A, 437.

206. Howard Parker Moore, *A Life of General John Stark of New Hampshire.* Spaulding-Moss Company. (Boston, 1949). 381.

207. The route of his march and the account of his activities are in the *William Whipple Papers.* The roll of officers of Whipple's brigade: Whipple, brigadier-general; George Gains, brigade major; Prince, negro servant to Whipple; Stephen Evans, colonel; Thomas Bartlett, lieutenant colonel; Joseph Prescott, major; Thomas Peabody; surgeon; Jonathan Wentworth, adjutant; Robert Swainson, quartermaster; John Gage, sergeant major; John Philpot, quartermaster sergeant. Chandler E. Potter, *The Military History of the State of New Hampshire 1623-1861.* Genealogical Publishing Col, Inc. (Baltimore, 1972). 325.

208. Potter. 282, 433. Other signers to serve on the battlefield at various times were Benjamin Rush, Pa., Lewis Morris, N.Y., Caesar Rodney, Del., Thomas Heyward, Jr., Arthur Middleton, and Edward Rutledge, S.C.

209. Whipple was on the committee in the summer of 1776 to work with Washington, Gates, and brig.

gen. Thomas Mifflin to develop "a plan of military operations for the ensuring campaign" and on the 5-man committee to confer with Gates "upon the general affairs of state" in March 1777.

210. A copy of the surrender document dated 16 Oct. with Burgoyne's signature is in the *William Whipple Papers*.

211. Lt. James M. Hadden, *Hadden' Journal & Orderly Book*, Books for Libraries Press. (Freeport, N.H., 1884). Reprinted 1970. 558-62.

212. A. J. Langguth, *Patriots, The Men Who Started the American Revolution*. Simon and Schuster. (New York, 1988). 455-57.

213. Langguth, 455-57.

214. A soldier from the German dutchy of Brunswick.

215. Cook, 176.

216. Langguth, 455-57.

217. W. L. Stone, *Visits to the Saratoga Battlegrounds*. First published in 1895. Reissued by the Kennikat Press. Taylor Publishing Co. (Dallas, 1970). 296-97, 388-89.

218. *William Whipple Papers*.

219. Stone, 707.

220. *Rhode Island History*. Vol. 13, No. 1. The Rhode Island Historical Society. (Providence, January 1954). 11-12.

221. Other officers signing the letter were Sullivan, Greene, brig. gen. John Glover, maj. (Gen.?) John Hancock of the Massachusetts militia, and the following brigadier generals of militia: Ezekiel Cornell, R.I., John Tyler, Conn., Solomon Lovell, Mass., Jonathan Titcomb, Mass. *Washington Papers*. Vol. 12, Head Quarters, White Plains, 24 and 25 Aug. 1778.

222. Nathaniel Peabody, adjutant general, John Samuel Sherburne, brigade major, Nathaniel Garfield, brigade quartermaster, and Prince, his man servant.

223. Amory, 67-73, 336-37; Atwood, 351, 580; Sanderson, 88-91.

224. Rufus Griswold, *Washington and the Generals of the American Revolution*. Henry T. Coats and Co. (Philadelphia, 1885). 211-12.

225. *Letters*, 2:Letter 342, 238. Also, *Josiah Bartlett Correspondence*.

226. Cook, 183.

227. Edmund S. Morgan, *The Birth of the Republic 1763-89* Revised Edition. The University of Chicago Press. (Chicago and London). 83-86.

228. Jonathan R. Dull, *A Diplomatic History of the American Revolution*. Yale University Press. (New Haven and London, 1985). 99-100.

229. Mevers, 187, 195.

230. *Letters*, 3:Letter 638, 507.

231. *Letters*, 4:Preface.

232. *Letters*, 4:Letter 488, 386.

233. Dull, 51, 55-56, 61-64, 83-84, 116.

234. *Journals*, 13:239-44.

235. Montross, 267-68.

236. *Journals*, 13:455-57.

237. Dull, 116.

238. *Letters*, 4:Letter 325, 251. Letters, 4:Letter 453, 351-52.

239. *Letters*, 4:Letter 79, 59-60; Letter 163, 121-22.

240. *Letters*, 4:Letter 426, 328-30.

241. The promise of a prisoner of war that, in exchange for full or partial freedom, he will abide by certain conditions.

242. *Josiah Bartlett Correspondence*. New Hampshire State Historical Society. (Concord, NH).

243. Thomas C. Amory. *The Military Services and Public Life of Major-General Sullivan of the American Revolutionary Army*. First published 1868. Reissued by Kennikat Press. (Port Washington, NY, 1968). 29-32.

244. *Letters*, 2:Letter 428, 319.

245. See Upton, 119-25, for a recitation of New Hampshire laws dealing with them.

246. Foster, 25.

247. *Josiah Bartlett Correspondence.*

248. Upton, 119.

249. *Letters*, 4:Letter 442; Letter 489, 386-87.

250. Thompson was among the revolutionary leaders of New Hampshire. He served with Whipple as one of the 12 councilors elected in January 1776 to run the colony and served with him on the colony's committee of safety in 1775. Thompson was also the colony's provisional secretary in 1775.

251. *Letters*, 4:Letter 428, 330-31.

252. A typical verdict from the Rockingham Co. Records Office: "You are hereby required to sell at public venue (after giving reasonable notice of the time and place of sale) the Brigantine *Edinburgh*, her cargo, and appurtenances which were deemed and adjudged lawful prize by the Maritime Court held at Portsmouth on the 9th day of July current . . .the proceeds of the sale (after deducting your own legal fees) you are to distribute and pay as follows, to wit, the sum of sixteen pounds thirteen shillings in gold or sliver money for the costs and charges of Trial & Condemnation and the residue of the said proceeds you are to distribute and pay to the Agents for the use of the Captors and other concerned as the law directs. Hereof fail not and make return of this precept and your doings herein. Given under my hand and seal of the said Maritime Court. Joshua Bracket." Saltonstall, 105-112.

253. Upton, 109-14.

254. Mevers, 119.

255. *Josiah Bartlett Correspondence.*

256. *Historical Magazine*. iv.:74-75.

257. Letter offered for sale by Robert E. Batchelder, 1 West Butler Avenue, Ambler, Pa. 19002.

258. Mevers, 165.

259. *Letters*, 4:Letter 99, 73-74.

260. *Letters*, 4:Letter 125, 91.

261. Tares: A noxious weed.

262. Mevers, 251, 256.

263. *Letters*, 4:Letter 79, 59-60; Letter 163, 121-22.

264. *Letters*, 4:Letter 442, 344.

265. George W. Corner, Editor, *The Autobiography of Benjamin Rush*. Princeton University Press. (Princeton, N.J., 1948).

266. Mevers, 187, 195.

267. *Letters*, 2:Letter 238, 242. Also *Josiah Bartlett Correspondence.*

268. Mevers, 265.

269. I, 4:Letter 426.

270. *Letters*. 4:Letter 593, 481-82.

271. Letter offered for sale by Robert E. Batchelder, 1 West Butler Avenue, Ambler, Pa. 19002.

272. *Letters*, 3:Letter 672, 534-35. Letters, 4:Letter 560, 453.

273. "Are the caribou and the black moose the same animal? Has it a solid or cloven hoof? Do their feet make a loud rattling as they run? Do they sweat when run hard or only drip at the tongue?"

274. General John Sullivan sent a moose to Jefferson's specifications, along with horns from caribou, elk, deer, spiked horned buck, and roebuck, to Paris in September 1787. Jefferson presented them to Leclerce with a letter stating these species did not exist in Europe, helping to disprove Leclerce's theory of the degeneracy of American animals and the notion that the moose was the same as a Lapland deer. Leclerce promised to set things straight in his next volume but died first. Julian P. Boyd, Editor, *The Papers of Thomas Jefferson*. 7:21-24, 28-30, 317-20; 9:161-62; Susan R. Stein, *The World of Thomas Jefferson of Monticello*. Harry N. Abrams, Inc. with the Thomas Jefferson Memorial Foundation, Inc. (New York, 1993), 394; Langdon Collection, Strawbery Banke Museum, Portsmouth, N.H.

275. *Letters*, 4:Letter 649, 519; Letter 672, 531; Letter 685, 538-39; Letter 694, 545-46.

276. Sanderson, 83.

277. Fowler, 81-82; Letters, 5:541.

278. Sanderson, 92.

279. Sanderson, 92-93.

280. Whipple had been elected to New Hampshire's superior court earlier that year, Arnold's legal experience was limited to service as a justice of the peace and several years in the legislature, Griffin had been a judge of the court of appeals and capture since 1780, Houston had been admitted to the bar in 1781, serving as clerk of the supreme court of New Jersey, and Brearley had been justice of the New Jersey supreme court since 1780. Robert J. Taylor, "Trial at Trenton," *William and Mary Quarterly*, Vol. XXVI, 3d series, No. 4. October 1969. 527-28.

281. Taylor, 543.

282. Moffatt-Whipple documents are in the N.H. Historical Society's manuscript collection Concord: Box I, Folder 3: Whipple family papers (1651-1779). Robert Cutt's Will, 1738 deed from Ruth Morgaridge to Wm. Whipple, 1745 deed from Thomas and Dorcas Cutt to Wm.Whipple, seven maps showing boundaries of land relating to the Cutt estate. Three of the maps are to fragile to photocopy. The bulk of the material in Folder 4 consisted of receipts written on pieces of paper about 2x3 inches. In general, this material is too fragile for photo-copying. Most items in Folder 5 relate to Joseph Whipple. Box II, Ledger (1755-1758) and Day Book or Journal (1735-1739 of William Whipple, Sr. The Day Book or Journal is in very poor condition and the library will not permit photocopying of any of its contents. The first five pages in the Account Book are not numbered. The following legend appears on the second of these five pages: "An account of the cost of the ship that Mr. Jona. Dain is building for me. The dimensions follow. 52 feet keel, 19 feet beam, 9 feet hold, and 4 feet between decks." (Commas inserted by the transcriber). On the fifth of these unnumbered pages is the total cost in pounds, shillings, and pence as 2296 15 6.5.

There is no breakdown between cost to build the ship and cost to outfit. There is a four page itemized list with cost of labor, materials, stores, furniture, etc. but none are categorized. 4 Dec. 1739: An account of the cost of the *Sasegotha* (?) built by Mr. Jona. Dain. 2467 15 49. Included is a lengthy detailed list of all items involved. Ledger (1755-1758). This volume is too fragile for photocopying. The Ledger's description states it includes the log of the snow *Exeter*, Benjamin Russell, Master, which returned from Antigua in 1756 with a cargo of 61 slaves. However, the ledger's only reference to the *Exeter* is on a dog-eared page. The name of the master was apparently on the part of the page now missing. The reference is an accounting of the stores put aboard for its outward voyage to Guinea which began 13 November 1755. The ledger is indexed with entries beginning with R and S missing. No entries show slaves as cargo.

283. *NHPP*, IV: 67. Upton, 214-15. [Worthington, New Hampshire Churches and the American Revolution]. 65. In 1777 there were 626 slaves in New Hampshire of which 533 were in the two seacoast counties of Strafford and Rockingham. Green and Harrington, *American Population Before the Federal Census of 1790*, 72-73 and *NHPP*, VII: 724-79.].

284. Esek Hopkins of Providence, first commander of the continental navy, commanded a slaver for the Brown brothers. In the fall of 1765, as master of the brig *Sally*, he lost part of his rum cargo by leakage, most of his crew by fever, and was obliged to sell the surviving slaves for a low price. Daniel P. Mannix in collaboration with Malcolm Cowley, *Black Cargoes, A History of the Atlantic Slave Trade 1518-1865*. The Viking Press. (New York, 1962). 8-9, 112, 158.

285. John Hope Franklin, *From Slavery to Freedom*. Third edition, fourth printing. Alfred A. Knopf. (New York, 1947). 103.

286. William Burney, Maritime Dictionary. T. Cadell. (London, 1830). xvi.

287. Letter to the author from Dr. Robert B. Dishman, Durham, N.H., dated April 9, 1994. Dr. Dishman is writing a book to be titled *Masters, Servants, and Slaves on the Northeastern Frontier*. Some shipowners sent a cargo of pine lumber and salt fish to the West Indies. About a fourth of the catch of the Grand Banks fishing fleet consisted of "Jamaica fish," not good enough for the Yankees. Fed to the West Indian slaves, they were almost their only protein. The ship would return with hogsheads of molasses and might carry half a dozen slaves as part of its deck cargo. Most of the small Negro population of the Northern colonies was brought from the West Indies in this casual fashion instead of being imported directly from Africa. Mannix and Cowley, 158.

288. "John Moffatt's ship, the *Exeter* returned from Africa in 1756 with 61 slaves: 20 men, 15 women, 7 "man boys," 2 "woman girls," 10 boys, and 7 girls. The ship's carpenter, John Winkley, had contracted with Moffatt to receive in exchange for his labor on the trip free passage and his choice of "a prime slave" at the price paid "on the coast of Guinea." Valerie Cunningham, "The First Blacks of Portsmouth," *Historical New Hampshire*. Vol. 44, No. 4. New Hampshire Historical Society. (Concord, N.H., 1989). 188. Cunningham's source is John Moffatt's Ledger, 1755-1758,

90, New Hampshire Historical Society.

289. Nathaniel Adams, 283. Brewster, 152-53. Sanderson, 87. Benjamin Quarles, "A Group Portrait, Black America at the time of the American Revolution," *Ebony*. August 1975. 44.

290. *NHSP*, XVIII: 705-08.

291. "State of New Hampshire. To the Honorable, the Council, and House of Representatives of said state, now sitting at Exeter in and for said state: The petition of the subscribers, natives of Africa, now forcibly detained in slavery in said state most humbly sheweth, That the God of nature gave them life and freedom, upon the terms of the most perfect equality with other men; That freedom is an inherent right of the human species, not to be surrendered, but by consent, for the sake of social life; That private or public tyranny and slavery are alike detestable to minds conscious of the equal dignity of human nature; That in power and authority of individuals, derived solely from a principle of coercion, against the will of individuals, and to dispose of their persons and properties, consists the completest idea of private and political slavery; that all men being amenable to the Deity for the ill-improvement of the blessings of His Providence, they hold themselves in duty bound strenuously to exert every faculty of their minds to obtain that blessing of freedom, which they are justly entitled to from that donation of the beneficent Creator; That through ignorance and brutish violence of their native countrymen, and by the sinister designs of others (who ought to have taught them better), and by the avarice of both, they, while but children, and incapable of self-defence, whose infancy might have prompted protection, were seized, imprisoned, and transported from their native country, where (through ignorance and in-Christianity prevailed) they were born free, to a country, where (though knowledge, Christianity, and freedom are their boast) they are compelled and their posterity to drag on their lives in miserable servitude: Thus, often is the parent's cheek wet for the loss of a child, torn by the cruel hand of violence from her aching bosom; Thus, often and in vain is the infant's sigh for the nurturing care of its bereaved parent, and this do the ties of nature and blood become victims to cherish the vanity and luxury of a fellow mortal. Can this be right? Forbid it gracious heaven. Permit again your humble slaves to lay before this honorable assembly some of these grievances which they daily experience and feel. Though fortune hath dealt out our portion with rugged hand, yet hath she smiled in the disposal of our persons to those who claim us as their property; of them we do not complain, but from what authority they assume the power to dispose of our lives, freedom, and property, we would wish to know. Is it from the sacred volume of Christianity? There we believe it is not to be found; but here hath the cruel hand of slavery made us incompetent judges, hence knowledge is hid from our minds. is it from the volumes of the laws? Of these also slaves cannot be judges, but those we are told are founded on reason and justice; it cannot be found there. Is it from the volumes of nature? No, here we can read with others, of this knowledge, slavery cannot wholly deprive us; here we know that we ought to be free agents; here we feel the dignity of human nature; here we feel the passions and desires of men, though checked by the rod of slavery; here we feel a just equality; here we know that the God of nature made us free. Is their authority assumed from custom? If so let that custom be abolished, which is not founded in nature, reason, nor religion. Should the humanity and benevolence of this honorable assembly restore us to that state of liberty of which we have been so long deprived, we conceive that those who are present masters will not be sufferers by our liberation, as we have most of us spent our whole strength and the prime of our lives in their service; and as freedom inspires a noble confidence and gives the mind an emulation to view in the noblest efforts of enterprise, and as justice and humanity are the result of your deliberations, we fondly hope that the eye of pity and the heart of justice may commiserate our situation, and put us upon the equality of freemen, and give us an opportunity of evincing to the world our love of freedom by exerting ourselves in her cause, in opposing the efforts of tyranny and oppression over the country in which we ourselves have been so long injuriously enslaved.

Therefore, Your humble slaves most devoutly pray for the sake of injured liberty, for the sake of justice, humanity, and the rights of mankind, for the honor of religion and by all that is dear, that your honors would graciously interpose in our behalf, and enact such laws and regulations, as you in your wisdom think proper, whereby we may regain our liberty and be ranked in the class of free agents, and that the name of slave may not more be heard in a land gloriously contending for the sweets of freedom. And your humble slaves as in duty bound will ever pray. Signed: Nero Brewster, Pharaoh Rogers, Romeo Rindge, Seneca Hall, Cato Newmarch, Peter Warner, Caesar Gerrish, Pharaoh Shores, Zebulon Gardner, Winsor Moffatt, Quam Sherburne, Garrett Cotton, Samuel Wentworth, Kittridge Tuckerman, Will Clarkson, Peter Frost, Jack Odiorne, **Prince Whipple**, Cipio Hubbard. John Langdon was speaker of the house when the petition was presented to that body April 25, 1780. The house and council agreed to hear the petition the next session provided the petitioners gave notice by publication in the *New Hampshire Gazette*. The house took the following action June 9: "Agreeable to order of the day the petition of Nero Brewster and others, Negro slaves, praying to be set free from slavery, being read, considered, and argued by counsel for petitioners before this house, it appears to this house that at this time the house is not ripe for a determination in this matter; therefore, ordered that the further consideration and determination of the matter be postponed to a more convenient opportunity." Isaac W. Hammond, "Slavery in New Hampshire in the Olden time," *The Granite Monthly, A New Hampshire Magazine, Devoted to History, Biography, Literature, and State Progress*. Vol. 4. Evans & Sleeper, Printers. (Concord, N.H., 1881).109-110. Hammond said he found no further reference to the petition.

292. *Portsmouth Town Records*. Vol. III. New Hampshire State Library. (Concord, NH). 95.

293. *Portsmouth Town Records*, III:101B.

294. Brewster, 152.

295. Letter to the author, 9 April 1994.

296. North Church funeral records indicates Prince was born in 1750, Cuffee in 1753, and that Cuffee was a native of Guinea. Cunningham, fn 70, 198.

297. Sidney and Emma N. Kaplan, *Black Presence in the American Revolution* (Revised). 50. Harry A. Polski and James William Williams, compilers and editors, *Negro Almanac*. (4th Edition). John Wiley & Sons. (New York, 1938). Quarles, 44. "Heroes of The American Revolution Prince Whipple," *Boston Roxbury City News*, May 21, 1964, 4. The newspaper quotes pioneer Negro historian William Nell, writing in 1855, as its source.

298. Ploski and Williams. Quarles, 44. Franklin, 132-35. *Boston Roxbury City News*, May 21, 1964, 4.

299. Brewster, 153.

300. Brewster, 155-56.

301. *North Church Records*, 1-A, 148.

302. Cunningham, 199.

303. *Portsmouth Journal of Literature & Politics*. Feb.14, 1846. 2.

304. The author has been unable to find a definition for the sobriquet, Caleb Quotem.

305. Brewster, 86.

306. Dishman letter of 9 April 1994.

307. Charles W. Tibbetts, editor and publisher, *The New Hampshire Genealogical Record*. Vol. 7., January-April 1910. (Dover, N.H., 1910). 13, 15, 74, 75. Tibbetts' source was records from the North Church. He states Prince was baptized 19 Dec. 1784 and Cuffe on 7 Sept. 1788. 15, 75.

308. "The mere existence of The Ladies Charitable African Society implies the presence of knowledgeable leaders who were committed to improving the conditions of blacks as slavery was ending. The name is a conscious identification with similarly named groups formed in other northern black communities during the period. The name of this organization is suggestive, because these women were clearly engaging in an ethic of giving — similar to white charitable societies — while simultaneously practicing the centuries-old tradition of communal responsibility known in African cultures. The social work performed by these women, black and white, was of vital importance to the well-being of the community." Cunningham, 199. Cunningham cites James Oliver Horton and Lois E. Horton, *Black Bostonians: Family Life and Community Struggle in the Antebellum North*, (New York, 1979), 55-66. She comments that "people like the black Whipples of Portsmouth would have had knowledge of activities in Boston and consulted with the leaders and community activists there." fn. 76, 199.

309. *NHSP*, XIII, 289-91. *William Whipple Papers*.

310. Adams, 276-78.

311. *State Papers*. Vol. 3. 980.

312. Sanderson, 95-97.

313. On Monday the 28th ultimo, died, universally lamented, the Hon. General WILLIAM WHIPPLE, a Judge of the Superior-Court of this State. In him concentrated every principle that exalts the dignity of man. His disinterested patriotism and public services are now known to all; and when newspaper encomiums are lost in oblivion, the pen of the historian shall preserve the remembrance of his virtues in the breast of succeeding generations. During a long course of unequalled sufferings, he endured his lot with a firmness correspondent to the greatness of his mind. He viewed his approaching dissolution with a heroic fortitude, in full confidence, that he

who made him, best knew how to dispose of him. In his extremist agonies, his mind was still revolving schemes for the happiness of mankind, and those sentiments of benevolence which distinguished him while living, were the last that died in him. He was generous and humane, and "the elements so mixed in him, that nature might rise up and say, "THIS WAS A MAN." *New Hampshire Gazette*, December 9, 1785. 3.

314. Kenneth Iserson writes in his almanac *Death to Dust* that physicians have performed autopsies for more than 2,000 years but were rarely done except for legal purposes. The Roman physician Antistius performed one of the earliest forensic examinations on record on Julius Caesar in 44 B. C. He documented 23 wounds including a final stab to the heart. The Catholic church, in 1410 ordered an autopsy on Pope Alexander V to determine if his successor had poisoned him. No evidence of poison was found. Even in the 19th century, long after church strictures had loosened, people in the West rarely allowed doctors to autopsy their family members for medical purposes. Today, in the U.S., doctors seek so few autopsies that *The Journal of the American Medical Association* twice in recent years declared "war on the non-autopsy." During much of the 20th century, doctors diligently obtained autopsies in the majority of all deaths. Recent statistics indicate autopsies are done in less than 10 percent of deaths and many hospitals do none. This is a dramatic turnabout. Atul Gawande, "Final Cut," *The New Yorker*, 19 March 2001, 94-99.

315. *Plummer Letters*. Vol. I. New Hampshire State Library. (Concord, NH).

316. J. Worth Estes, M.D., *Bulletin, New York Academy of Medicine*. Vol. 52, No. 5, June 1976. 620-25.

317. Katharine was represented by Thomas Elwyn in her cases against Joseph Whipple and Robert Moffatt. Elwyn was the husband of her grand niece Elizabeth Langdon, daughter of gov. John Langdon. The author is indebted to Nancy Douthat Goss of North Andover, Mass. for the research regarding the house dispute. Mrs. Goss has served as Museum House Chairman of the Moffatt-Ladd House in Portsmouth. Her sources were briefs, arguments, notes, financial records, etc. at the New Hampshire Historical Society, Concord, N.H.

318. Southwest of downtown Portsmouth, its address is 248 Peverly Hill Road. The home dates to 1740.

319. *Portsmouth Journal*, November 24, 1821.

320. Letter dated April 14, 1989 to the author from Timothy F. Monahan, Portsmouth superintendent of schools.

321. Its architecture was modern. The Cabot street school, closed when the Whipple school opened, was shortly thereafter reopened as an auxiliary of the Whipple school to serve kindergarten and some first and second grade students. C. S. Gurney, *Portsmouth Historic and Picturesque*. Peter E. Randall, Publisher. (Hampton, N.H., 1981). 155.

322. Dated 1891, Tenney noted Whipple's likeness was from John Trumbell's painting of the signers of the Declaration of Independence.

323. The Presentation of the Portraits of General William Whipple, Signer of the Declaration of Independence, and of David Glasgow Farragut, Admiral, United States Navy November 20th, 1891, by Storer Post No. 1, Grand Army of the Republic, Department of New Hampshire, to the City of Portsmouth, N.H., for the Whipple and Farragut Schools. (Portsmouth, N.H., 1891).

324. Sons of the Revolution of the State of New Hampshire, *Whipple Tablet Presentation*. The Rumford Press. (Concord, N.H., 1910).

325. On October 10, 1976 the Rockingham County Bicentennial Committee replaced the original epitaph on Whipple's grave and dedicated the liberty tree and marker while the state Historical Commission placed the marker at the Maplewood Avenue location. In 1776 the state liquor commission issued a commemorative booklet compiled by Leon W. Anderson, legislative historian, accompanied by a commemorative decanter of liquor which featured the likenesses of the three signers.

APPENDIX 1
VARIOUS WILLS AND WHIPPLE HOUSE INFORMATION

LAST WILL AND TESTAMENT OF JOHN WHIPPLE, SR. OF IPSWICH
(Filed, not recorded)[1]

In the name of God, Amen. I John Whipple Senior of Ipswich in New England being in this present time of perfect understanding and memory though weak in body, committing my soul into the hands of Almighty God, and my body to decent burial, in hope of resurrection unto eternal life by the merit and power of Jesus Christ, my most merciful Savior and Redeemer, do thus dispose of the temporal estate which God hath graciously given me.

Imprimis. I give unto Susanna Worth of Newberry my eldest daughter thirty pounds and a silver beer bowl and a silver wine cup.

Item. I give unto my daughter Mary Stone twenty pounds and one silver wine cup, and a silver dram cup.

Item. I give unto my daughter Sarah Goodhue twenty pounds. And all the rest of my household goods my will is that they be equally divided betwixt my three daughters aforesaid. But for their other legacies my will is that they should be paid them within two years after my decease: and if it should so fall out that any of my daughters above said should be taken away by death before this time of payment be come, my will is the respective legacies be paid to their heirs when they come to age. Likewise I give unto Anthony Potter, my son-in-law, sometime, forty shillings.

Moreover I give unto Jennett my beloved wife ten pounds which my will is that it should be paid her besides the fourteen pounds and the annuity of six pounds a year engaged unto her in the Articles of Agreement before our marriage. Concerning the four-score pound, which is to be returned back to her after my decease, my will is that it should be paid (both for time and manner of pay) according to said Agreement, viz: one third part in wheat, malt, and Indian corn, in equal proportions, the other two thirds in neat cattle under seven years old. Further, my will is that no debt should be charged upon my said wife as touching any of her daughters, until it be first proved to arise from the account of Mercy, Sarah, or Mary.

I do appoint my loving friends, Mr. William Hubbard and Mr. John Rogers of Ipswich, the overseers of this my last will and testament, and I do hereby give them power to determine any difference that may arise betwixt my executor, and any of the legatees, aforesaid, about the payments aforesaid. lastly I ordain and appoint my son John Whipple the sole executor of this my last will and testament. To whom I give all the rest of my estate, both houses, lands, cattle, debts from whomsoever due, and to his heirs forever.

In confirmation whereof I have hereunto set my hand and seal this 10th day of May 1669. In the presence of William Hubbard, Robert Day. The mark of // Edward Lummus. The mark of John Whipple.

His daughter Elizabeth was not mentioned, although her husband, Anthony Potter, was, suggesting she was not living. Her name appears in a deed given by Mr. Potter 22 Dec. 1644.[2] His "loving friends" appointed to be overseers were both ministers of the church. Mr. Rogers was subsequently president of Harvard College.

INVENTORY OF ELDER JOHN WHIPPLE'S ESTATE

John died June 30 and the will was presented in court at Ipswich September 28 along with the inventory of his estate. The inventory was attested to on the oath of his son Cornet John Whipple "to be a full & true inventory of the estate of his father, deceased, to the best of his knowledge, and if more appears afterwards is should be added."

It. The farm containing about 360 acres		150	0
It. The houses and lands in town containing about 100 acres		250	0
It. In apparel		9	0
It. In linen		6	0
It. A feather bed with appurtenances		7	0
It. In plate		6	0
It. In pewter		4	0
It. In brass	3	10	0
It. In chairs, cushions, & other small things	1	7	0
It. A still		7	0
It. Two flock beds 1		10	0
It. One musket, one pair of mustard querns [3]		15	0
It. Andirons, firepan, & tongs		14	0
It. Two mortars, two spits		10	0
It. In books	2	8	0
Total	444	1	0

LAST WILL AND TESTAMENT OF CAPT. JOHN WHIPPLE
Son of John Whipple (In slightly abridged form)[4]

I, John Whipple, Sen. of Ipswich, having not settled my estate before, in case of death do thus order the estate which God hath graciously given me. Imprimis my will is yet **Elizabeth, my beloved wife**, shall enjoy one half of my dwelling house so long as she shall see cause to live therein, and if my executors shall provide her ye going of a cow or two with ye use of an horse for her occasions during yet time: And my will further is yet my executors shall pay or cause to be paid unto her fifteen pounds by ye year, besides what is already mentioned during ye time of her natural life.

Item, my will is yet **my daughter Susan Lane** shall have ye portion which she hath already received (which I judge to be about seventy pounds) made up an hundred and fifty pounds in like specie as before. I will also that my said daughter shall have ye remainder of her portion paid her within three years after my decease.

My will likewise is, that my youngest daughter Sarah Whipple shall be brought up with her mother (if she be willing thereunto) and my executors to allow her with maintenance as necessary thereunto, and to have likewise an hundred and fifty pounds for her portion at the time of her marriage, or when she comes to one and twenty years of age.

Concerning **my three sons**, it was my intent yet if my estate were divided into five parts, yet my eldest son should enjoy two fifths parts thereof, ye other three to be left for ye other three viz. **Matthew, Joseph, and Sarah**. But apprehending that I am not like to escape this sickness, I thus dispose concerning the same, viz. I will that **my son John** and **my son Matthew** shall be executors of this my last will and testament for ye present and yet **my son Joseph** shall be joined as an executor with them two, as soon as ever he comes to be of age. And then my will is that if my son John enjoys all ye lands, houses, buildings, and appurtenances, and privileges thereunto belong where he now lives together with ye lands in ye hands of Arthur Abbot to be added thereunto: And that my son Matthew enjoys ye lands, houses where he now lives, the appurtenances ye privileges with ye saw mill and ye land in ye tenure of Fennell Ross, yet then my son Joseph when he comes of age shall enjoy ye houses, buildings, malting office, with ye other lands, pasture, arable and meadow where I now live as his right of inheritance and portion, to him and his heirs forever, provided yet my John do help him to order and manage ye same till he himself comes of age. And also my will is that then he pay an hundred pounds out of his estate to his sister Sarah, and ye rest of her and her sister Susan's portion to be paid out of ye debts and other chattels which are found belonging to my estate.

But if my two elder sons be not satisfied with this and that my son Matthew enjoys ye lands, houses where he now lives, the appurtenances ye privileges with ye saw mill and ye land in ye tenure of Fennell Ross.

Then my son Joseph when he comes of age shall enjoy ye houses, buildings, malting office, with ye other lands, pasture, arable and meadow where I now live as his right of inheritance and portion, to him and his heirs forever, provided yet my son John do help him to order and manage ye same till he himself comes of age.

And also my will is that then he pay an hundred pounds out of his estate to his sister Sarah, and ye rest of her and her sister Susan's portion are to be paid out of ye debts and other chattels which are found belonging to my estate.

But if my two elder sons be not satisfied with this distribution of my real estate, my will is yet my whole estate (with what is in my son John's and Matthew's hand already of houses and lands) both real and personal be equally divided by indifferent appraisers into five parts, and if then my eldest son shall have two fifths thereof, my son Matthew another fifth, and if Joseph shall another fifth and yet ye last fifth shall be improved to pay debts and other legacies and yet what ever land falls to any of my three sons shall be to them and their heirs forever.

In witness whereof I have set my hand and seal this second of August 1683.
John Whipple

My will also is yet if my two sons, John and Matthew, choose to enjoy ye farms yet then Joseph shall also have yet ten acres of marsh by Quilters and Matthew as much of my marsh in ye hundreds to them and their heirs forever excepting ye March in ye Island which may be sold to pay debts. **John Whipple**

Signed, sealed, and delivered in presence of us. William Hubbard, Samuel Phillips, Daniel Epps.[5]

LAST WILL AND TESTAMENT OF CAPT. WILLIAM WHIPPLE FATHER OF GENERAL WILLIAM WHIPPLE

"In the name of God amen. I William Whipple of Kittery in the county of York in the Province of the Massa: Bay, Mariner, being sick & weak but of sound disposing mind and memory, and considering the uncertainty of life, and not knowing but that the time of my departure out of this life is near, do make this my last Will & Testament. And after humbly committing my soul to God the Father of Spirits, hoping for his pardoning mercy through the merits & mediation of Jesus Christ and my body to a decent internment according to the discretion of my executor hereinafter named, believing in the resurrection & hoping for eternal life. My worldly estate I give & devise in the following manner & form, that is to say, Impr.

My will is that all my just debts & funeral charges be paid by my executor in convenient time after my decease, and that he dispose of any of my personal estate for that purpose as soon after my decease as he can with conveniency. And if it is necessary for that end to sell any of my real estate I hereby give him full power to do it in such way & manner as he shall judge best only excepting the land I purchased of the Moggerages.

Item. Whereas by the providence of God my wife Mary Whipple is so indisposed in mind as to be incapable of business, I give her one third part of my personal estate but to remain in ye hands of my executor to be applied to her use as he shall judge proper and if it should please God to restore her to her former capacity then to be delivered to her.

Item. I give & bequeath to my daughter Mary Traill twenty shillings lawful money. She having already received her portion of my estate.

Item. My will is that my executor take the care of my children that are now at home that he take proper care of their education according to his discretion, and to put the boys to some suitable business & employment and I do hereby give him full power to bind them out by indentures of apprenticeship for that purpose if he shall see cause. I also give my executor full power & authority to sell any of my real estate (excepting as aforesaid) if he shall apprehend he can apply the money to be raised thereby more to the advantage of my children than by keeping the same for them. And that he defray the charge of their maintenance & education out of any part of my estate still excepting as aforesaid.

Item. All the residue & remainder of my estate I give, devise, and bequeath to & among my four children: William, Robert Cutt, Joseph, & Hannah equally divided (saving & excepting that I give my silver hilted sword & my watch to my son William over & above his equal share) to hold to them respectively & their respective heirs, executors, & administrators forever.

Lastly, I do hereby constitute & appoint my brother Joseph Whipple sole executor of this my last Will & Testament and revoke all other wills by me heretofore made. In witness whereof I have hereunto set my hand & seal the 21st day of June, 1751." Wm. Whipple (Seal).

Signed, sealed, & declared by the said Wm. Whipple to be his last Will & Testament in presence of us witnesses who subscribed in his presence. Ebenezer Fernald, Ebenez Fernald jun, Joanthan Fernald. Probated Sept. 3, 1751. Inventory returned Sept. 26, 1751 at £712:6:7 by Thomas Cutt, Ebenezer Fernald, and John Godsoe, appraisers.[6]

WILL OF KATHARINE WHIPPLE

Be it remembered that I Katharine Whipple of Portsmouth in the County of Rockingham and State of New Hampshire, tho' of advanced age, of sound and perfect mind and memory, do make, ordain, and publish this my last Will and Testament in manner and form following, that is to say:

First. My Will is and I direct that my funeral expenses and debts that I may owe at my decease, be paid in proper and convenient time by my Executor.

Item. I give and bequeath to Mrs. Elizabeth Elwyn, the wife of Thomas Elwyn,

Esq. of said Portsmouth all the household furniture belonging to me which shall be, at the time of my decease, in the house I now occupy, except my Plate, which I herein otherwise dispose of.

Item. I give and bequeath to my nephew the Honorable John Samuel Sherburne, Esq. of said Portsmouth my Silver Tankard, Coffee Pot, Bowl, and all the Silver and Plate which I may own, at the time of my decease. I also give and bequeath to my said nephew all my shares and stock in the New Hampshire Union Bank or elsewhere. I also give, devise, and bequeath to my said nephew John Samuel Sherburne, his heirs and assigns forever, all my lands in the town of Alton and elsewhere, and all the rest, residue, & remainder of my estate, real, personal, or mixed, of every nature or description, not herein otherwise disposed of, to him, his heirs, and assigns forever.

Lastly, I make, ordain, constitute, and appoint my said nephew the Honorable John Sam l Sherburne, Esquire, to be Executor of this my last Will and Testament, hereby revoking all other or former Wills and Testaments by me, at any time made and declaring and confirming this and this only to be my last Will and Testament.

In witness whereof I have hereunto set my hand and seal this thirty-first day of October in the year of our Lord one-thousand-eight-hundred-and-fifteen.

/s/ Katharine Whipple
Signed, sealed, published & declared by the said
Testatiex the said Katharine Whipple,
to be her last Will & Testament in presence
of us, who at her request and her presence
(& in that of each other) have herewith
subscribed our names as witnesses to the same.

/s/ Dan l Humphre   /s/ Wm. Holman   /s/ John Sparhawk

INVENTORY OF GENERAL WILLIAM WHIPPLE'S ESTATE[7]

General Whipple did not leave a will but his estate was inventoried for probate purposes.

1 small Mahogany table 36/. 1 washstand 3/	1.19
1 carpet 20/. 3 doz. Wineglasses 12/	1.12
3 doz. tumblers 12/. 7 decanters 16/ Cruets 2/	1.10
6 glass salvers 10/. 6 China dishes 10/	1.
2 China cans 4/. 3 2 doz. Yellow plates 7/	.11
4 China mugs 8/. 3 China cups	.12
4 yellow butter boats 1/4. 4 d⁰ bowles 3/	. 4.4
2 shagreen cases Ivory handle knives & forks	1.4
1 case with 8 bottles	.6
1 desk and bookcase 80/ 2 Mahogany tables 72/	7.12
1 Mahogany stand 24/. 1 Jappan'd waiter 3/	1.7
1 rail'd stand 24/. 6 leather bottom chairs	2.8
1 Mahogany bureau 60/. 1 toilet 5/	3.5
1 dressing glass 15/. 2 yds carpeting 4/. Toilet 2/	. 1.1
1 looking glass 30/. 1 dressing glass 12/. Old easy chair 12/	2.14
1 Mahogany bedstead, 1 bed, furniture check, curtains, rods & rails compleat	12

1 camp bedstead & curtains 30/. 1 old table 6/	1.16
1 pr. Handirons 10/. 2 trammels 4/6. 1 spit 3/ 1 jack 20/	1.17.6
2 spinning wheels 12/. 4 iron d hhds 12/. 5 hhds cyder 100/	6.4
2 bbs rum qv z 60 galls 150/. 15 gs Mada wine 105/	12.15
12 galls brandy 36/ 1 cow 60/ 4.16	
1 sulkey & harness /12. 1 double sleigh 40/	14.
1 pair trucks with a cart body	4.
2 crowbars 15/. 2 iron shovels 6/	1.1
Wearing apparel of the deceas^d	26.
1 musket 36/. 1 pr pistols 45/	4.1
1 hair trunk 15/. 1 portmanteau trunk 15/	1.10
32 oz s silver plate @ 6/8. Cash in silver & gold /42	52.13.4
Loan Office Certificates by scale as specie £2122.1.7	
valued now at 3/6 in the pound 371	7.3 2.
Interest Certificate £177.9.4 valued at D^o	31.1.3
Massachusetts Note £70.7.4 valued at D^o	12.6.3
One half of the store on Spring Hill	120.
1 Right or prop rs share of land in township of Trecothick 6	
10 Rights of D^o in Bretton Woods @ /6	60.
1 pr silver plated candlesticks 30/. 2 pictures 4/	1.14
1 railed tea table 48/. 1 sett China 24/	3.12
1 Mahogany table 20/. 2 pictures 3/	1.3
1 tea board & 8 cups & saucers	.4
I large & 1 small carpet	1.6
1 pier & 1 chimney glass 110/. 6 pictures 18/	6.8
1 bed common bedstead & furnr chk curtains	7.10
1 looking glass 40/. 1 small D^o 24/.	3.4
1 small bedr bedstead & coverlid	7.10
Fire dog shovel & tongs	.12
1 bed, bedstead & furn chk curtains	9.
4 old pictures 4/. 8 brass candlesticks 8/	. 12
18 pr sheets /10. 12 pr blankets 90/. 2 old quilts 10/	15.
3 skillets 10/. 2 brass kettles 24/	1.14
1 pr flat irons 6/. 1 toaster 1/6. 1 dripping pan 2/	.96
9 leather bottom chairs 36/. 1 large looking glass /9	10.16
1 large floor carpet 90/. 1 small D^o 48/. 1 bedside D^o 15/	7.13
1 Windsor chair 4/. 12 arm'd chairs with backs and	
bottoms cover'd @ 12/	7.16
	928.9.6

Portsmouth November 15th 1786
John Evans
William. Gardner

State of New Hampshire   Rockingham Co. Portsmouth Nov. 18, 1788

Mrs Catherine Whipple and Joseph Whipple, Esquire, as Administrators of the Estate of William Whipple, Esq., deceased, personally appearing and made solemn oath that the foregoing inventory contains the whole of said deceased Estate that hath come to their hands or knowledge and if any more of his Estate should come to their hands or knowledge they will exhibit an additional inventory thereof in to the office of the Registry of Probate of said wills for said county.

Sworn to before me Geo. Gaines, Justice of the Peace.

MARRIAGE CONTRACT between JOHN WHIPPLE & WILLIAM GOODHUE

Elder JOHN WHIPPLE & *Deacon* WILLIAM GOODHUE

Sarah Whipple, youngest child of elder John Whipple, married Joseph Goodhue, son of deacon William Goodhue, July 13, 1661. In accordance with the custom of the time, the elder and the deacon made a formal agreement regarding the marriage whereby Joseph was assured the possession of the house and land of his father. The document is of unique value as a specimen of the ancient marriage contracts. Courtesy required the deacon to wait upon the father of the bride which suggests terms of the settlement were discussed and the formal instrument drawn in the home of elder Whipple.

Articles agreed upon between John Whipple, Sen. of Ipswich in New England of ye one party and William Goodhue, deacon of ye church of Ipswich on ye other party in consideration of a marriage between Joseph Goodhue and Sarah Whipple, their children, in manner and form following viz. that I William Goodhue do promise and covenant that I will settle my eldest son Joseph Goodhue upon my farm according to our Agreement already made and signed upon his marriage with Sarah Whipple which is now to be consummated also I John Whipple above named have covenanted and engaged to pay or cause to be paid unto Joseph Goodhue, forthwith upon his marriage to my daughter Sarah forty pounds in good and merchantable pay also I John Whipple do engage that my daughter Sarah shall have an equal share of my household goods with her two sisters at my decease and my wife Susanna.

Also I ye above William Goodhue and Margery Goodhue my wife do engage and covenant that our eldest son Joseph Goodhue now to be married to Sarah Whipple shall have and possess ye house that I now live in with all ye orchards, and buildings upon ye land belonging to it that I bought of Mr. Giles Firman as it is bounded on ye other side at my decease and his own mothers Margery Goodhue's decease this house and land being paid for by his grandfather in England with that proviso that his grandchild Joseph Goodhue and his should enjoy it after ye death of his father and mother as an absolute and perfect inheritance for ever with parcel of salt marsh of about 22 acres bought of Mr. Thomas Firman with ten pounds of ye twenty-five pounds in silver that our father Watson sent over to me to purchase meadow and upland to lay to ye house and land above his grand child Joseph Goodhue to inherit after our death and his heirs for ever with six acres of upland at Milebrooke of that land that I had in exchange of Mr. John Appleton for land in ye Pequot lots all this housing and lands above we give grant and confirm with our son Joseph and his heirs for ever after our decease and if that he have children by his wife Sarah[8] but if he have not children or a child by her then after our son Joseph's death and Sarah his wife without children it shall be to ye rest of our children that shall outlive them. Furthermore I yet above John Whipple upon deacon Goodhue and his wife owning and confirming the house and lands above with their son Joseph Goodhue after their death I do promise and engage that at ye decease of my wife

Susanna and myself that I give unto my daughter Sarah, Joseph Goodhue's wife now to be confirmed thirty pounds in good currant merchantable pay at ye merchantable price to be paid by my heirs or executors within six months after my decease and my wife Susanna's unto Joseph Goodhue or his heirs besides ye forty pounds first agreed upon and ye share of household goods above mentioned. These several articles above agreed upon between elder John Whipple of Ipswich in ye county of Essex in New England and deacon William Goodhue of ye same town and county and his wife Margery Goodhue upon the marriage of Joseph Goodhue and Sarah Whipple, our children, we do here witness and confirm our agreements each to ye other by signing and sealing hereof ye thirteenth day of July in ye year of our Lord Sixteen hundred and Sixty One.

John Whipple, Sen. and a seal.
William Goodhue, Sen. And a seal
Marjery M. Goodhue and a seal. Her mark.

Witnesses were John Rogers, Robert Lord, and Samuel Younglieff, Sen.

THE JOHN WHIPPLE HOUSE OF IPSWICH, MASSACHUSETTS

Built in the mid 1600s, the historic John Whipple House in Ipswich, Massachusetts is a remarkable example of how a house evolved in the seventeenth century. The additions and remodeling over its first 90 years reflects the change in workmanship and architectural detail as the area developed and how six generations of owners grew away from their English origins. From its location on the northeast corner of the Village Green where the militia trained for King Philip's War 100 years before the American Revolution, the house has watched many men play their part in American history.

Elder John Whipple was the first of the family to occupy the house. His son Capt. John more than doubled its size in 1670, a year after his father's death. John the third added a leanto at the rear and expanded the second story after 1700. It was owned and lived in by family members until 1833 when it was sold to Caleb K. Moore. The Ipswich Historical Society purchased it in 1898 and restored and showcased it as an example of how America's earliest colonists lived. It was moved to its present location at 1 South Village Green in 1927. Thousands of tourists from all over the world visit it annually and marvel at its authenticity and durability.

The house was originally known as the Saltonstall house.[9] That it was the Whipple house was proved by rev. Thomas Franklin Waters, first president of the Ipswich Historical Society, who exhaustively researched Whipple deed and probate records.[10] Because it was common for deeds to describe property boundaries by including names of adjacent land owners, Waters researched ownership of adjacent land and of Saltonstall land before reaching his conclusion.

Brothers Matthew and John Whipple were granted land in Ipswich in September 1638 and John acquired the house and two-and-a-half acres of land from John Jolly, Samuel Appleton, John Cogswell, Robert Muzzey, and Humphrey Bradstreet approximately four years later. These five men had acquired it from John Fawne who moved from Ipswich to Haverhill in 1641.[11] The record of the transfer from Fawn to the five men has never been found but he retained an interest which he quit-claimed to Whipple 20 October 1650. The quit-claim deed specifically includes a house and two-and-half acres and names the sellers.

That Whipple acquired the Fawne property by at least 1642 is established by town records which ordered that he "should cause the fence to be made between the house late capt. Denison's and the said John Whipple, namely on the side next capt. Denison's." Town records of the original division of lands show that Daniel Denison received two acres near the mill, that John Fawne's houselot was to its southwest and bound by Mr. Samuel Appleton's. Relating the original land division to Denison and Appleton with Fawn's quit-claim deed of the two-and-a-half acres in 1650, Waters proved the house to be the Whipple homestead, not Saltonstall's.

The first three Whipple owners were named John. Elder John left it to his son capt. John by will dated 10 May 1669. Captain John gave it to sons John, Matthew, Joseph, and daughter Sarah by will dated 2 August 1683. He provided that his wife Elizabeth could live in one half for as long as she desired.[12] In the final division of the estate recorded 31 October 1684, son John, 26, received "the mansion house his father died in with the barn, outhouses, kiln, orchards, & homestead with commonage & privileges in and upon two acres & a half of land, be it more or less, called the homestead in Ipswich town."

The third John, known as major Whipple, bequeathed the home and property to his daughter Mary and her heirs by Will dated 30 August 1721.[13] Major John served as selectman, justice of the court of general sessions, and as county treasurer. Mary, wife of Benjamin Crocker, died at age 51 on 24 October 1734.[14] Crocker was Ipswich's school teacher from 1745 to 1753 and again in 1759 and 1760. He was a chaplain during the French and Indian War, serving in the summer of 1745. A 1713 graduate of Harvard, he represented Ipswich in the general court and was frequently called on to preach in Ipswich pulpits. On his death 9 April 1767, Benjamin left the home to John Crocker, son of Mary and Benjamin. A deacon of the South Church, John had two wives and 11 children.[15] After his death 21 April 1806, the property was divided for the first time. John, son of John's first wife Mehitable Burley of Londonderry, received the homestead with Elizabeth, daughter of second wife Elizabeth Lakeman, given the right to live in "the great chamber in the west end . . .so long as she shall remain single and unmarried."[16] Son Joseph (second wife) received the malt house and an acre of ground. Although the deed was never recorded, John apparently sold the homestead to Joseph as the inventory of his estate in 1813 includes the house, barn, malt house, and other buildings.

Joseph's half sister Lydia[17] and her second husband, col. Joseph Hodgkins (she was his third wife), purchased five-sixth of the dwelling plus the land 16 May 1813 for $750.00. Apparently Elizabeth was still single and living in the portion bequeathed to her.[18] Hodgkins, born in 1743 was a representative to the general court from 1810-16 and a lieutenant in the Ipswich company at the Battle of Bunker Hill. He also served in the battles of Long Island, Harlem Heights, White Plains, Princeton, and Saratoga. He was 86 at his death 25 Sept. 1829. Lydia continued to live in the home until her death 21 June 1833. Four months later (31 October) Nathaniel Wade and other heirs of Col. Hodgkins[19] sold the house, including an acre and 11 rods, to Caleb K. Moore of Canterbury, N. H. for $501.00. For the first time since 1642, the owner of the property didn't carry the Whipple bloodline. The remaining 11 rods was sold to James Estes for $300.00 on 11 August 1841.[20] After two centuries and six generations — three of Whipples and three of Crockers — the family could no longer claim any part of this ancient and venerable home site.

The original house was 26 feet 10 inches long and 17 feet 8 inches wide at ground level. The chimney filled one end. There were two great rooms. In the seventeenth century, the hall was where meals were cooked and eaten, spinning and weaving done, and the family gathered in the evening to enjoy the heat and light of the enormous fireplace. It was so spacious it accommodated friends and strangers who stopped to visit. That capt. John Whipple, one of Ipswich's wealthiest men, enlarged — probably doubled the original size — his father's home is suggested by rafters in the attic. Further evidence is the £330 value placed on it when the estate was inventoried in 1684. Comparing the home with those of other men of prominence confirms it ranked as one of the finest. Daniel Denison was commander of the colony's militia and a man of comparative wealth. In 1682 his home was valued at £160, less than half Whipple's value. Deputy governor Samuel Symonds' home was in the center of town and sited on two acres. It was valued at £150 in 1678.[21] Based on these comparisons, Waters concluded the Whipple house was the grandest dwelling in the immediate area of Essex county.

Major John Whipple's 1721 will and estate inventory provides the first identity of the home's rooms: parlor, parlor chamber, hall, kitchen and kitchen chamber, bedroom below, one above, and a lean-to. The kitchen and kitchen chamber were undoubtedly a part of the original. The parlor and parlor chamber were probably added by capt. John. By the time of maj. John's death, the kitchen was separate. The major added the lean-to, an eight foot wide room running the length of the house,[22] and second floor bedroom under the sloping roof. With six daughters living at home in 1700, there was a need for bedrooms. These additions changed the home's appearance to its look of today.

Beginning with capt. John, slaves were a part of the family. The first was an Indian lad named Lawrence, captured during King Philip's War. John's estate, inventoried 10 Sept. 1683, included Lawrence with a value of £4. Major John's Will mentioned a male and female slave. Benjamin Crocker owned Tom and Flora who were married in September 1726. They are the last known slaves to be part of the family. There were either freed or died between the time of their marriage and Crocker's death 30 years later as neither are mentioned in his Will or inventory.

The Ipswich Historical Society, founded 14 April 1890 to preserve the historic features of the town, first considered purchasing the Whipple House at its annual meeting in December 1897. Despite the decayed and dilapidated exterior, it was considered a good example of the town's early architecture and the interior, though mutilated by various reconstructions, was well preserved. Members believed it would make an ideal permanent home of the Society when repaired and restored. The Bond family who acquired it from Moore for $400.00 agreed to sell and the Society acquired it 12 May 1898 for $1,650.[23] The price included the house, lot, and a right-of-way in the narrow passageway separating it from the house on the corner.

Society members carefully researched early seventeenth century houses before restoration began in May 1898. Craftsmen quickly discovered they had a gem. Original sheathing and clay plaster with traces of the early color were uncovered.

The original fireplace was exposed and the wells for the ancient casement windows found. Splendid oak beams laid bare and an ancient door post, and old batten doors with huge, unshapely hinges were found. Cracks created by years of hard weather were filled. Decay was removed from portions of ornamental beams and new wood inserted. The base of the chimney was repaired and rebuilt at the top. Some of the brick that filled the space between studs from sill to plate were removed but most were left in place, making the house more fire proof. Second floor joists were in perfect condition. New sills were placed under the house, new floors laid, a large part of the lower story restudded, new clapboard installed, and the roof virtually rebuilt. Diamondpane windows, low and broad, replaced the perpendicular narrow ones and dark stain restored the exterior to its original look.

Restoration costs approximated $1,000.00[24] and the result was an outstanding reproduction of the home environment of primitive New England.[25] The west room was wainscoted with handsome paneling from the 1728 Rogers Manse. A painted panel over the mantle was a panoramic view of the town from the river showing old-fashioned shipping activity and Jeffries Neck in the background. White plaster was applied directly to the floor boards of the second story to create the ceiling of the first floor and the woodwork was painted white.

In opening remarks at the dedication ceremony 19 October 1898, president Waters said the Society did its best "to restore the house to its ancient style" and that the craftsmen "adhered slavishly to the original."[26] He noted the original builders selected the beams of "grand old oaks and stately pines" from local forests and called the home "a link that binds us to the remote past and to a solemn and earnest manner of living, quite in contrast with much in modern life." Wall panels were left open and glassed over so visitors could see early construction techniques. Waters wondered if the brick and clay filled space between studs was "to protect against Indian assaults or to keep out the biting cold of winter."[27]

As selectman, deacon, feoffee of the grammar school, deputy to the general court, clerk of writs, deacon, and church elder, John Whipple would have entertained the leaders of town, county, and colony in his home. Waters speculated they included Richard Saltonstall, a member of the colony's governing council from 1637-49 and 1664; Ezekiel Cheever, the most eminent teacher of the day; John Winthrop, Jr., founder of Ipswich and later governor of Connecticut; governor John Dudley; Ann Bradstreet, New England's first woman poet; and General Denison. Waters said church leaders — including John Norton who left the Ipswich church in 1655 to become the famous pastor of the Old South Church in Boston; William Hubbard, pastor and historian of the Indian wars; Thomas Cobbett, longtime Ipswich pastor; the famous Rogers family of ministers, Ezekiel, Nathaniel, and John; and all the other old time ministers — would have been regular callers at the home because "the Whipples and the Crockers were a godly race." He said that maj. Samuel Appleton, hero of King Philip's War, played in the house as a boy and that col. Hodgkins, who gained fame as a Revolutionary War soldier, died in the parlor. "Many notables," he concluded, "warmed themselves before the great fireplace and made themselves comfortable under its welcome roof."[28]

In the dedicatory address, rev. John C. Kimball of Hartford, Connecticut said the house "enables us to live more richly in past time, [it] stretches our existence from 70 and 80 years to over 200 years, [it puts] us in touch with our ancestors and opens a door . . .to the customs of our country's youth." He said the Whipple house is important "in the same way the ruins are to Rome, Nazareth to Palestine, Bunker Hill and Gettysburg to America" and is as much an ornament of the town as its venerable hills and river and ocean shore and as much an educational institution as its schools and library.

He asked the audience to imagine capt. John Whipple's hurrying to lead his troopers on a swift ride to Andover to repel and Indian assault; John Appleton and Thomas French "talking in this very room" of their imprisonment and trial for advocating resistance and demanding representation before they would submit to taxation; colonels Hodgkins and Wade and maj. Burnham sitting in the great room smoking and sipping their steaming cups and chatting of Bunker Hill, of Burgoyne and Cornwallis, of Washington and Lafayette.

He made the low vaulted rooms relive their past by painting a word picture of the whir of spinning wheels, the beat of the churn, the roar of great winter fires, the hissing of meats on the long spits, the voices of children at play or demurely reciting the catechism, the goodwife's chat with neighboring gossips, the loud laughter of the slaves, the tale of love, the solemn declaration of the last Will and Testament, the weeping of mourners. "The life of the ancient time," he concluded, "is revived in the Whipple house; it helps the history of other days become a living reality . . .and is a living, speaking witness to the naturalness, the simplicity, the sturdiness, the refinement, the devotion of the old Puritan home life."[29]

An extraordinary number of antiquities were given or loaned to be displayed at the opening. The lower west room was furnished with period pieces including a fine oak chest, ancient piano, antique chairs, china cabinet with rare and choice pieces, pictures, pamphlets, manuscripts, rare books, and two great bronze candelabra.[30] The andirons are cast iron figures of Hessians in grenadier caps. The iron fireback is dated 1693. The Society's library was housed there. The east room was furnished as a kitchen and featured the fireplace with 1696 andirons and ancient cooking utensils. Pewter platters and ancient fire arms adorned the walls, spinning wheels, cheese press, and butter churn were in place with a 'fine old hundred-legged table in the center.'[31] The room also featured a great winnowing fan, foot stoves, candlemould, candle sticks, needlework, samplers, lamps, pewter porringers, tinderboxes, trivets, lanthorns, trammels, and tin kitchens with spits.[32] The west chamber was arranged as a bedroom with chests, cradle, light stand, and canopy bed made up with ancient bedding. A collection of water color paintings of Ipswich's old houses added to its attraction.[33]

W. H. Downes, a student of colonial homes, called the Whipple house the "best surviving example in New England of the earliest seventeenth century colonial architecture.[34] While finer and grander specimens of later periods exist in Essex county, he said none were more "perfectly preserved and authentic." He said the beams, posts, sills, girders, joists, rafters, etc. in the west section showed "astonishing durability" for American larch or tamarack, a soft wood. The main beams in the east section added by capt. John are oak and the posts and girders are carved "with some attempt at elegance of finish." When the lean-to was added, roof rafters on the rear were supplemented by a new set, which, at one point carried the roof almost to the ground. Downes believed the original profile was very angular and high shouldered in proportion to is ground area. He said the interior had two points of architectural merit: remarkable massiveness of construction and fine, dignified proportions. "The two main rooms on the ground floor are in fact superb for the simplicity, size, and solidity. The beautiful brown tone of the old oak posts, girders, and joints gives the key of color."[35]

Miss Alice A. Gray gave up a 23-year career with the Boston Fine Art Museum to become first custodian of the home, serving without pay. She brought a beautiful collection of furniture and had great success in inducing owners to contribute antiques and money to the Society. A "disreputable-looking old tenement house" occupied the lot between the house and railroad track. Miss Gray solicited a donation of $1,800.00 from a Boston matron which allowed the Society to acquire the property 26 July 1899, demolish the building, and plant an old-fashioned garden on the site.[36] A box-bordered walk was installed that led past the well and handsome sundial of stone to the caretakers's door.

The rear portion of the house was converted into living quarters with modern conveniences for Miss Gray and her assistant Miss Julia Gutberlett. The suite included a row of little chambers with slant ceilings under the roof of the second floor. Waters said Miss Gray's "delicate taste, rare knowledge of antiques and personal antique collection were the principal factors in the attractive interior arrangement and furnishings of the house." He reported 1,681 visitors in 1900 (admittance fee 25¢) allowing the Society to retire its debt. He hoped 1901 would be as successful so Miss Gray and Miss Gutberlett, "a cherry and winsome housekeeper and chaperon of visitors during Miss Gray's absence," could be paid and a heating system installed in the curator's apartment.[37]

The house was moved to its present location in December 1927. Richard Crane wanted to build and give the town a Memorial Building. When the town rejected his offer he gave the land to the Historical Society which deemed it a much better location for its 300-year-old house than its site near the Sylvania parking area off Topsfield Road. Once the money was raised the Society hired the B. F. Goodwin Co. of Marblehead to move the house. The chimney was dismantled and each brick numbered to insure it would be replaced exactly as built. Large timbers were slid underneath and the building blocked. A large truck with winch slowly pulled it to its new location. The moved began 15 December and reached Market Square by the end of the first day. Electric and telephone crews preceded and followed to take down and replace the wires. Rollers were replaced as needed and the jacks adjusted when necessary. The historic Choate Bridge was the only major obstacle to the move. Built of stone about 1764, Ipswich residents were concerned about damage to it. However, the house was jacked up until it was higher than the bridge and guided over with no problem.[38]

The house was rededicated in September 1929 with the main address delivered by Sherman L. Whipple, prominent Boston lawyer, Democratic politician, and Society member. Descended from Elder John's brother Matthew, the modern-day Whipple said it thrilled him to walk in the rooms where his ancestors visited their kin for more than a century and where his kinsfolk walked in their daily vocations for more than two centuries. He paid homage to rev. Waters for the exhaustive research to document the house's lineage saying "no building in America has ever been more thoroughly investigated or its history written with such care and accuracy." He described elder John Whipple as "a Puritan of the Puritans, typifying their virtues and their failures."

A seventeenth century garden was created at the house in 1948 by landscape artist Arthur A. Shurcliff. Its clam shell walks and formal beds replicate what might have been Susanna Whipple's garden in 1642. Members of the Ipswich Garden Club led by Mrs. A. W. Smith researched chronicles, diaries, letters, inventories, and herbal recipes to make certain the garden would be authentic. The plants grown today are the ones most commonly grown in the seventeenth century and include burdock, comfrey, elecamapane, agrimony, lavender, thyme, parsley, and gallicas and damask roses. It elicits praise from visitors throughout the world.

The Ipswich Historical Society encourages individuals interested in the preservation of ancient American homes to join. Annual membership fee in 2003: $25.00 individual; $40.00 family/dual; $75.00 business; $60.00 sustaining; $135.00 patron; $200.00 benefactor. The Society's address is 54 South Main Street, Ipswich, MA 01938. Email: ihs@cove.com; telephone (978)356-2322.

WHIPPLE HOUSE CHAIN OF TITLE

In tracing the property's line of title, rev. Franklin Waters, first president of the Ipswich Historical Society, began with the Society's purchase from James W. Bond. The property was left to James by his father Abraham who purchased it 7 Oct. 1841 from Caleb K. Moore (*Essex Co. Deeds*, 327:157). Moore purchased the house with an acre and 11 rods from Mr. Nathaniel Wade and other, heirs of the estate of col. Joseph Hodgkins 31 Oct. 1833 (*Essex Co. Deeds*, 271:164). On 11 August 1841, the heirs sold the balance of the property, an acre and 11 rods, to James Estes. It was described in the deed as "this piece of land extended down Winter street, to the barn and land of Joseph Farley, now occupied by the buildings of the Ipswich Mill, followed the line of the Farley land to the river, extended along the river bank to the Samuel Wade property, and followed this line to Moore's boundary line." The Hodgkins property thus extended from the main road to Topsfield to the river, and measured two acres and 22 rods. (*Essex Co. Deeds*, 326-215). Col. Hodgkins and his third wife, the widow Lydia Crocker Treadwell, purchased five-sixths of the estate from the heirs of Joseph Crocker 16 May 1813 for $750.00. John Crocker received the property from his father deacon John Crocker. (*Essex Co. Probate Records*, 374:9:10). John Crocker disposed of the property to his brother Joseph (Waters was unable to find the records of this transaction). The return of the administrator of Joseph Crocker's estate dated March 1814 includes: "five-sixths of dwelling house and land sold to Joseph Hodgkins, esq., $750.00." Deacon John Crocker received the estate by inheritance from his father Benjamin Crocker. (Probate Records, 343:481). Mary Crocker, first wife of Benjamin, received the property from her father major John Whipple. (*Essex Co. Probate Records*, 313:555).

Because successive generations of Whipples were named John — capt. John, maj. John, cornet John, elder John, John, Sr., etc. Waters sought "every clue, however slight," to determine the property pedigree. That is why, in tracing the generations, he gives credence to rev. John Rogers receipt for his son's legacy "that it was in accordance with the Will of "Major John Whipple." Captain John Whipple's Will left the property to his son Joseph. (*Essex Co. Probate Records*, 304:10). However, in the final division recorded 31 Oct. 1684, John received "the mansion house his father deceased in with barn, outhouses, kiln, orchards and homestead with commonage and privilege in and upon two acres and a half of land, be it more or less, called ye homestead in Ipswich Town." (*Book 305*: folio 135). Captain John received the property by will dated 10 May 1669 from his father Elder John. The inventory of this estate was delivered in court at Ipswich 28 September 1669. Attested to by Robert Lord, clerk.

Elder John's estate included a 360 acre farm valued at £150 and "house and lands in ye town" of about 100 acres valued at £250. Waters says the two acre home lot and homestead were included in the town property. He said it didn't seem possible that capt. Whipple's mansion, which showed a great increase in value in the 14-year period 1669-83, remained the same as when owned by elder John. Indications are it was enlarged substantially and "this supposition harmonizes perfectly with the fact, apparent to every observer, that the eastern half of the present edifice was added to the western portion, and the elaborate and costly style of the newer work presupposes such ample wealth as capt. Whipple possessed. Evidently a considerable change in the chimney of the old house was involved, and in our house, it is evident that the chimney stack was enlarged when this new portion was added. The western half of our house was probably therefore elder Whipple's home, and as the fashion of houses was in those days, it was a very good and comfortable house, much larger and better than many which were built in that period."

Elder John acquired the property from John Fawne, by a recorded deed which reads as follows: Md, that I, John Fawne, gent. do by these presents, allow, certife & confirme, unto Mr. John Whipple his heirs and assigns forever, a certaine bargaine & sale of an house & house lot in Ipswich containing by estimation two acres & a half, more or less, formerly sold unto the said John Whipple by John Jolly, Samuel Appleton, John Cogswell, Robert Muzzey, & Humphrey Broadstreete & do hereby release all my right and title thereunto, as witness my hand & seal, this 10th day of October, 1650. /s/ John Fawne. [*Old Ipswich Books* (1:89)]

The original deed is not to be found, and this quit claim deed only perfects the title to the property, which was purchased by Whipple from six well-known citizens acting in some collective capacity, not yet discoverable. But it is of great value in proving Fawne's original ownership. Elder John Whipple was living on this spot in 1642, for in that year the town ordered that John Whipple "should cause the fence to be made between the house late capt. Denison's and the said John Whipple, namely on the side next capt. Denison's." But Fawne's occupancy of this location had ceased in 1638, inasmuch as in our Town Record, it was recorded in 1638, that eight acres had been "granted to Samuel Appleton above the mill, the town river on the southeast, the house lot formerly John Fawne's northeast, and the highway leading into the Common, northwest." Whipple may have been living there at that early period. It is not beyond the bounds of possibility that this western end of the old mansion may have been erected by Mr. Fawne prior to this early date.

By a singular coincidence, deputy governor Symonds gave instructions to Mr. Winthrop in 1637 for the kind of a house he wished built: "I think to make it a girt house will make it more chargeable than need; however, the side bearers for the second story being to be loaden with corn, etc. must not be pinned on, but rather either set into the studs or borne up with false studs & so tenanted in at the ends." The studs in this part of the Whipple house extend from the sill to the plate, and the side-bearers or supports for the floor joists are oak planks, some six inches wide, and two inches thick, let into the studs and fastened with oak pins, after the fashion of the modern "balloon-framed." This similarity in construction, coupled with the fact that the farm house was to be a substantial two story building with garret, 30 or 35 foot long, 16 or 18 foot broad, encourages the belief that this part of our house was one of the earliest houses, of the better sort, built by the first settlers.

These ancient grants afford us the first links in the chain of collateral evidence which confirms our identification of the property. Town records show that Mr. Fawne had a houselot adjoining to Mr. Appleton, six acres near the mill. Daniel Denison had a house lot, next Mr. Fawne's "to come to the skirt of the hill next the swamp." Denison's lot is again described as "near the mill, containing about two acres which he hath paled in and built an house upon it, having Mr. Fawne's house lot on the south west." Denison's property included the tract bounded by Market, Winter, and Union streets. The Appleton lot was on both sides of the Topsfield road, beyond the present railway crossing. Fawne's land lay between them. As he conveyed only two and a half acres to Whipple, the balance of his original grant had been sold apparently to Mr. Appleton as he always appears as the abutter on the western side. The grant to Denison originally included a lot that bounded the Whipple land on the southeast, i.e. toward the river. This was owned afterwards by John Burnham and Anthony Potter. A portion of this original Denison grant was owned by Jeremiah Belcher. On the occasion of his marriage with Mary Lockwood, Belcher conveyed to Mr. Robert Paine, Richard Brown of Newbury, and Robert Lord of Ipswich, "in behalf of the said Mary etc." his now dwelling house with out-houses, orchards, yards, gardens & all other the appurtenances and privileges thereunto belonging, which house is situate, lying & being in Ipswich aforesaid, near the mill on the north side the river, having the said river toward the southeast, and the land of John Whipple toward the northwest." [30:7:1652 (*Ipswich Deeds*, 1:239)]. Twelve years later, Jeremiah Belcher mortgaged his farm and town property to capt. Geo. Corwin. The dwelling and land about it are described as follows: "On the west side of the Mill river, having the river on the east side thereof, the land of elder Whipple on the west, and on the north, the town and mill & bordering southward upon the land of elder Whipple." (*Essex Deeds*, 2:92). On 8 April, 1672, Anthony Potter sold Samuel Belcher (son of Jeremiah) a small piece of land, "joining to the house lot of Jeremiah Belcher and bounded therewith and with the river on the south and southwest side, and with the house lot of John Whipple on the northwest and with the highway on the northeast, all which piece of land I had of John Burnham." (*Ipswich Deeds*, 3:223).

On 20 April 1672, the rev. Samuel Belcher, pastor on the Isle of Shoals, sold to Edward Lumase, on behalf of Richard Saltonstall, esq. "a parcel of ground near unto the mill, for to set a house upon for the miller, that shall keep the mills from time to time, to live and dwell in while he or they shall keep the said mills, containing about six rods of land bounded by a fence of pales toward the west, the barn of Jeremiah Belcher toward the south, down to a rock near the end of the said barn toward the east, & common land or highway, where gravel hath been digged toward the north." (*Ipswich Deeds*, 3:329). This is the only deed which contains the name of Saltonstall. Before remarking on it, let me add two others. Mary Belcher, the widow of Jeremiah, set over to her son Samuel, who then resided in Ipswich, "all that house lot given & made over to me by way of jointure on marriage, — bounded by ye grist mill in Ipswich easterly, Mr. John Appleton's land southerly, Mr. John Whipple's land northerly, the other part bounded by the way to said land or lot, and partly by land granted to major Denison, now possessed and built on by Samuel Belcher. Novem. 11:1672." (*Essex Deeds*, 49:61). On 25 September 1713, Mr. Samuel Belcher sold this property to capt. John Whipple "one half acre of land be ye same more or less with ye house, barn, and orchard standing thereupon — bounded northeasterly by a highway leading to ye mill, southeasterly by Ipswich river, southwesterly by land of col. John Appleton, northwesterly by land of ye above said capt. John Whipple." (*Essex Deeds*, 29:61). Comparing these deeds it will be seen at once that the bit of land sold to Mr. Saltonstall for the miller's house, was only a part of Samuel Belcher's land, and that the whole Belcher property was bounded then, as it had been for many years, by the Whipple estate. Apart from that, a six rod lot is rather small for a mansion like this, though it were then only half its present length. The old Jeremiah Belcher lot reappears in the "Brackenbury lot" which William Brackenbury, of North Carolina, planter, then in Ipswich, sold to Nath. Farley about 3/4 acre, which is bounded by John Crocker, the river, and other land of Farley's. On 30 April 1771 when the heirs of Joseph Crocker sold to col. Hodgkins, the lot was bounded by land of Enoch Parson and Joseph Farley, the river, etc. (*Essex Deeds*, 129:112).

Not a link of any importance is lacking. The direct pedigree of the land is through Fawne, the Whipples, and the Crockers to colonel Hodgkins. The abutting estates are always bounded by these owners. Mr. Saltonstall never owned an inch of land on this site. The estate always includes two or two and a half acres. I dwell on this only in the interest of exact historic truth. We cannot call our house by the name of Saltonstall. If any name is given it, that of Whipple has first claim.[39]

The ownership of the house was described in essentially the same terms as above in *The Essex Antiquarian*, Vol. 6, No. 7, July 1900.

ENDNOTES, APPENDIX 1

1. *The John Whipple House in Ipswich, Massachusetts & the People Who Have Owned & Lived In It.* Ipswich Historical Society., 1915, 17, 18. [Hereafter *The John Whipple House.*]

2. *Ipswich Deeds* 2:220

3. Quern: Primitive hand mill, especially for grinding grain.

4. Waters. Publication No. XX. 1915, 9-10

5. *Probate Records* 304:10, 22-23

6. William M. Sargent, ed. *Maine Wills*, 1640-1760. Brown Thurston & Company. (Portland, 1887) Probate Office, 8, 137, 656-58.

7. *Exeter Probate*, Vol. 29:221, #5167-1786

8. William Goodhue's property must have been left to his grandchildren. Sarah and Joseph had nine children. Joseph died 2 Sept. 1697 and William died in 1700. The marriage contract provided Joseph was to receive his father's property after his father's death. In turn, he was to leave it to his children by Sarah. Therefore, the property had to go to Joseph and Sarah's heirs.

9. Richard Saltonstall arrived in Ipswich in 1635 and was given permission to build the town's first grist mill. The son of Sir Richard Saltonstall, he was heavily involved in the commerce of the community. Joseph B. Felt, *History of Ipswich, Essex, and Hamilton, Mass.* Cambridge, Mass.: 1834; reprinted by the Clamshell Press, Ipswich, 1966, 13, 95.

10. Waters was pastor of Ipswich's South church. He was president of the Society from 1890 until his death in 1919. See Whipple House chain of title for the results of Waters' research.

11. "Rev. John Ward, Mr. John Fawne, and Hugh Sheratt moved to Haverhill in 1641." Felt, 72.

12. *Essex County Probate Records*, 304:10.

13. *Essex County Probate Records*, 313:458. John, his wife Katharine and daughters Katharine and Sarah are buried in Ipswich's Ancient Burial Ground.

14. Benjamin Crocker married twice after Mary's death. His second wife was the widow Experience Coolidge whom he married 17 May 1736. She died 4 Nov. 1759. His third wife was Elizabeth Williams of Weston whom he married 9 Sept. 1760 in Weston. *Essex Antiquarian*, "The John Whipple House," Vol. 6, No. 1. Salem, Mass.: January 1902, 33. Benjamin, Mary, and Experience are buried in Ipswich's Ancient Burial Ground. 11.

15 John Crocker married Mehitable Burley 3 Dec. 1747. She died 9 July 1766 in her 39th year. They had seven daughters, Mary, Mehitable, Hannah, Lydia, Martha, Sarah, and Eliza; and two sons, John and Aaron. His second wife was Elizabeth (Perkins) Lakeman. Their intentions were published 28 Nov. 1767. They had a son Joseph born 22 Oct. 1770 and a daughter Elizabeth, born 4 Dec. 1772. *The John Whipple House*, 34-35

16. The deed to Elizabeth reserved the chamber with "the privilege of going in and out at the front door, and a right to use the entry way and stairs in common, and a right to bake in the oven in the northeasterly room, to go to and from the well, and a privilege in the cellar to put and keep so much cider, vegetables, and other necessaries sufficient for her own use, also liberty to pass and repass to and from the yard at the southwest end of said house, and to keep therein wood for her own use, said reservation to continue so long as she shall remain single and unmarried, as expressed in the last Will and Testament of said John Crocker, deceased." *Essex Co. Probate Records*, 374:9, 10

17. Lydia Whipple Crocker was born 7 Nov. 1754. She married Elisha Treadwell 21 June 1780. He died 19 Dec. 1792. She married Col. Hodgkins 18 Dec. 1804. *The John Whipple House*, 38.

18. *Ibid.*, 38-39.

19. Hodgkins died 25 Sept. 1929, age 86. He had three wives: Joanna Weber, Sarah Perkins, and Lydia Crocker, daughter of deacon John Crocker and widow of Elisha Treadwell. Only one of Hodgkin's 16 children survived him. He held several town offices and was a state representative from 1810 to 1816. He was a lieutenant in the Ipswich Co. at the Battle of Bunker Hill, in the battles of Long Island, Harlem Heights, White Plains, Princeton, and at Sartoga at the capture of gen. Burgoyne's army. He succeeded col. Wade in the command of the Middle Essex Regiment. Felt, 190. Nathaniel Wade married Hodgkin's daughter Hannah, born to his second wife Sarah Perkins.

20. *The John Whipple House*, 40.

21. *Ibid.*, 23-27. Capt. John Whipple's estate was valued at £3,314, Denison at £2,105, Symonds at £2,534.

22. *Ibid*, 32. Narrow lean-to's with fireplaces were common in that era and may have served as laundry rooms or for other rough work.

23. *Essex Co. Deeds*, 1549:6.

24. Sylvester Baxter and W. H. Downes, *The Hotel Cluny of a New England Village and An Old Ipswich House with The History of the House and Proceedings at the Annual Meeting Dec. 3, 1900*. Salem, Mass.: Publications of the Ipswich Historical Society, No. X, The Salem Press Co., 1901, 6.

25. Dimensions of the building when renovated: 50' long by 36' wide. The ground floor of the great east room is 24' by 17 2' and 7' high. The fireplace is 7' 3" wide, 2' 9" deep. The oak girders are 14 by 14 inches. The windows, diamond-panes, hung on hinges, are 5' 3" wide and 2' 6" high with three sashes each. The east chamber is the same size but the fireplace is 6' 2" wide and 2' 2" deep. *The John Whipple House*, 13. [Hereafter, Baxter and Downes]

26. *Order of the Exercises at the Dedication of the Ancient House Now Occupied by the Society*. Ipswich, Mass.: Publication of the Ipswich Historical Society, No. VI., The Independent Press, 1899, 8-9. [Hereafter *Dedication*.]

27. *Dedication*, 8.

28. *Dedication*, 9.

29. *Dedication*, 12-16.

30. Among the items displayed by the Religious Society of Ipswich: *Breeches Bible* (1615); named for Gen. 3:7 "They sewed fig leaves together and made themselves breeches."; *Indwelling Sin* (London) by John Owen, 1616- 83; *Call to the Uncoverted* (London, 1658) by Richard Baxter; *Sound Believer* (London) by Thomas Shepard; *Angelagraphia* (Boston, 1696) by Increase Mather; *Safety of Appearing in ye Righteousness of Christ* (Boston, 1729) by Salam Stoddard; *Fair Warning by Woodward*; *Dying Shots*, about conversion by Crawford; *Predestination* by Cooper; *The Revelation* by Langdon; *Parable of the Ten Virgins* by Coleman; *Direction for Conversion* by Webb; *Glory of the Gospel* by Joseph Bellamy; *The Resurrection* by Ditton; *Regeneration* by Phil Doddridge; *Sinners in the Hands of an Angry God* (Salem, 1786); and *Original Sin* by Jonathan Edwards; *The Loving Invitation of Christ to the Aged, Middle-Aged, Youth, and Children from the Mouth of Elizabeth Osborn Only Three Years and Nine Months Old* (Newburyport, Mass., 1811) by her sister Jane Osborn; an autograph letter from John Winthrop, Jr. (1634); an inventory of household goods in Winthrop's Ipswich home; several petitions, deeds, wills, and other colonial and revolutionary documents. *The John Whipple House*, 14-15

31. *Dedication*, 7.

32. *The John Whipple House*, 16.

33. Loaned by artist Walker Paris of Washington, D. C. *Dedication*, 7.

34. Homes dating to the mid 1600s are rare because of the limited longevity of wood and because most early homes were temporary and abandoned or neglected after more comfortable dwellings were made possible when sawmills, forges, and roads were built. While founded in 1633, Ipswich didn't have a sawmill until 1649. Downes noted the great posts, girders, and other surviving timbers of the frame contained no axe or adze marks leading him to believe they were hand sawed.

35. *The John Whipple House*, 12-14.

36. *Essex Co. Deeds*, 1584:266. The balance of the land with the old barn was purchased 17 Nov. 1902. *Essex Co. Deeds*, 1691:470.

37. *The History of the House*, 40-43.

38. Harold D. Bowen, "Tales of Olde Ipswich." Newspaper article on file in the Ipswich public library. Name and date of newspaper missing.

39. Baxter and Downes, 18-37.

APPENDIX 2
THE WHIPPLE FLAG AND
THE WHIPPLE MUSEUM OF THE HISTORY OF SCIENCE

Most of us from the various American Whipple lineages recognize the Betsy Ross flag of 13 stars, the 48- star flag, if we were born before January 1959 (Alaska and Hawaii were admitted to the Union as the 49th and 50th states on January 3 and August 21, 1959), and the current flag of half a hundred stars. But how many Whipples know about the 48-star Whipple Flag named after its designer, Wayne Whipple?

The American flag evolved over many years and did not spring into existence when Betsy Ross finished her work in Philadelphia in May 1776. The first flag to have been raised on the North American continent was probably flown by Eric the Red or his son Leif when they raised the Viking sea rovers' banner (a black raven on a white field) in 1000 A.D. The first flag linked to the future Stars and Stripes was probably the red ensign with small white upper canton, the ancient symbol of England (the Cross of St. George) raised by the English settlers of Jamestown and Plymouth.

The stern Puritans of New England, objecting to the Cross of St. George, deleted it and flew a flag with a plain white canton[1] on the red field.[2] How prophetic! A field ready to receive white strokes with the empty canton waiting for a bright cluster of American stars.[3] The molet[4] was accepted as a star, emblems of the states joined together in solemn union.

The first documented appearance of the stripes was in mid 1775 on the regimental flag of a Philadelphia troop. The first recorded mention of a star used on an American ensign (flag) was in the *Massachusetts Spy* of May 10, 1774: "A ray of bright glory now beams from afar; The American ensign now sparkles a star; Which shall shortly flame wide through the skies."[5]

Whipple Peace Flag. *Designed by Wayne Whipple in 1912, it was selected from among 500 entries as best representing American history. Approved by president William Howard Taft, it was widely publicized and produced. Whipple called his flag the "Peace Flag" in tribute to the global peace movement in the years preceding World War 1.*

The two devices, stars and stripes, form the national flag. On June 14, 1777, the Continental Congress passed its Flag Resolution which described the flag only in general terms: "Resolved that the flag of the United States be 13 stripes alternate red and white, that the Union be 13 stars white in a blue field representing a new constellation." The *Ranger*, launched in Portsmouth, New Hampshire, commanded by John Paul Jones, was the first warship to fly it. There was no indication of shape, size, or arrangement. "What became the American flag went through several evolutions from this time forward.

From the beginning, license was taken with the number of stripes. In 1795, a "Second Flag" of 15 stars and 15 stripes was decreed by Congress in honor of Kentucky and Vermont joining the Union. Theoretically, from then on one star and one stripe were to be added for each new state. However, nine and 13 stripes continued in symbolic use simultaneously with a number corresponding to the number of states in the Union. Eventually it was found to be easier, cheaper, and more practical to keep the flag up to date by only adding stars.

Modern usage refers to the stars and stripes. But officially the stripes were named ahead of the stars in the original Flag Resolution of 1777, the second of 1795, and the final Act to Establish the Flag in 1818. Revolutionary soldiers fought under "rebellious stripes" and in some of the earlier flags, the canton of stars was so small it suggests reluctance to include them at all.

Verbally and visually the stripes prevailed for years. In 1814 Francis Scott Key hailed the "broad stripes and bright stars." In 1829 the song *Our Flag* told us to "Behold the glorious stripes and stars." In 1856 composer Edward J. Allen wrote we should "unfurl . . . the gleaming stripes and stars" and in 1861 Harrison Millard wrote of ". . . our stripes and stars, lov'd and honored by all" in his popular *Flag of the Free*.

Early U. S. Naval ensigns were dominated by two patterns: 1) staggered which placed the stars in overlapping square or rectangular units of five and 2) the plainer fashion of placing the stars in three parallel rows. The "Great Star" or "Great Luminary" pattern emerged in 1818. It was used for the first national flag of 20 stars flown over the Capitol on April 13. The 20 stars were grouped to form one large star. Ships in New York harbor on July 4, 1857 flew a variety of flags. Most had the stars arranged in five horizontal rows of six stars each (30 in all); but 31 was then the proper number. Some had one large star formed of 31 smaller stars; others had them in a diamond or a circle; another had 31 stars in the form of an anchor; another had the anchor embellished with a circle of small stars. Other flags have used the rattlesnake and the eagle, sometimes together. The many different eagle flags and "standards of the eagle" were created during the Civil War.

A contest to design the classical style of American heraldry was held in the first decade of the twentieth century. The flag designed by Wayne Whipple, well known as the author of popular works on American history, was chosen in 1912 from among 500 entries.[6] Whipple's flag was approved by president William Howard Taft, widely publicized throughout the nation, and produced. The *Whipple Flag* epitomized American history. Its 48 stars are arranged in a central six-pointed "Great Star" to symbolize the 13 original states similar to both the "Great Seal" and "Great Star" patterns of many early flags. The ring of stars around the "Great Star" represents the states admitted to the Union up to the time of the

First centennial Exposition of 1876 (25). An outer ring – with space for future additions – symbolizes the states admitted since the Centennial (10). For some unknown reason, this flag fell into disuse and the last of the "Great Star" flags disappeared.

Whipple called his flag the "Peace Flag" in tribute to the global peace movement in the years preceding World War I. In late August 1913, the "Peace Flag" name was used at a meeting of nations at The Hague, Netherlands. Unfortunately no universal Peace Flag could be decided upon. But the nations agreed that each would have as a Peace Flag its own flag surrounded by a white border. For a time thereafter, the U.S. Peace Flag was the stars and stripes within the prescribed white frame.

Originality in American flag design ended early in the twentieth century. In 1923 and 1924, patriotic associations formulated a flag etiquette which came to known as the Flag Code. It became federal law in 1942.

WHIPPLE MUSEUM OF THE HISTORY OF SCIENCE[7]

The Whipple Museum of the History of Science is at the University of Cambridge in England. It was established in 1944 when Mr. Robert Stewart Whipple presented his collection of early scientific instruments and antiquarian books to the University. The museum is housed in the historic First Cambridge Free School erected in 1618 and extensively remodeled during the 19th century. The site was acquired by the University late in the century and expanded in 1894 to provide scientific laboratories. The site underwent major internal reconstruction and restoration in the mid 1970s and reopened as the Whipple Museum in 1976. The main gallery of the Museum is housed in a large hall with Elizabethan hammerbeam roof trusses. The Whipple Library is in an adjacent room allowing visitors to combine essential sources for research in the history of science.

The Museum is preeminent in and internationally renowned for its collection of scientific instruments and models, dating from the Middle Ages to the present. Microscopes and telescopes, sundials, early slide rules, pocket electronic calculators, teaching and demonstration apparatus, as well as laboratory equipment are included in the collection. Among the specific items are: the first circular logarithmic slide rule, c. 1640,[8] a grand orrery, c. 1750,[9] an astronomical screen c. 1757,[10] a set of mathematical instruments, 1717,[11] a precision balance, 1790,[12] electro- static generator, c. 1785,[13] Azimuth compass, 1711,[14] and many others.

A part of the University's Department of History and Philosophy of Science, the Museum plays a central role in the teaching and research of the Department. Because the collection represent diverse but inter-related scientific and cultural activities a wide range of people use the Museum to study the history of science in its material and cultural contexts, including school children and enthusiasts, historians, philosophers, and practicing scientists.

Robert Whipple's donation in 1944 included one thousand scientific instruments and a similar number of rare books collected during his life-long connection with the world of scientific instruments. His father, George Mathews Whipple, was a scientist and later superintendent of the Royal Observatory at Kew where Robert started his working life as an assistant.[15] He was assistant manager at the well-known instrument maker L. P. Casella and a personal assistant to Horace

Darwin (youngest son of Charles Darwin), the founder of the Cambridge Scientific Instrument Company. He rose to become managing director of the firm and later its chairman.

He was also involved in various learned societies and institutions as a Founder-Fellow of the Institute of Physics; a Fellow of the Physical Society, serving as vice president and honorary treasurer; and president of the British Optical Instrument Manufacturers' Association.

Whipple's enthusiasm for the history of science led him to negotiate with a Committee on History of Science Lectures and the Cambridge Philosophical Society to donate his collection to the University to form the basis for a Museum within the University. The desire for the development of the history of science as a subject of study and research was emphasized as shown by the memorandum submitted to the University:

> " . . . it is important that the museum should be much more than a well arranged depositary of historic scientific apparatus. It should be designed and maintained as a valuable teaching instrument and a cultural accessory to modern research."

An exhibition was held in the East Room of the Old Schools in November 1944 to commemorate the official presentation of Whipple's collection. At the center of the Museum's library are Whipple's collection of rare books including publications on scientific instruments ranging from medieval instruments for astronomical observations to early twentieth-century industrial technology as well as the more 'canonical' books such as Sir Isaac Newton's (1642-1727) *Philosophiae Naturalis Principia Mathematica, 1687 (Mathematical Principles of Natural Philosophy)* and Christiaan Huygens' (1629-95) *Horologium oscillatorium, 1673*. From these auspicious beginnings the rare book collection has grown substantially. And as planned, the Museum and Library plays an active role in the teaching of history and philosophy in science.

Whipple started to collect antique scientific instruments and rare books of science in the 1910s. In addition to the main donation in 1944 he continued to present rare books until his death in 1953 and over the next 40 years the history of science as an academic discipline in Cambridge was built around his collection which was enlarged through Whipple's bequest, generous loans from colleges, transfer of material from the scientific departments of the University, and by gifts. It continues to grow today with new acquisitions being displayed in the main gallery.

The most distinctive feature of Whipple's collecting was the integration of scientific instruments and of books illustrating their construction and use. His interests led him to appreciate and collect both the more canonical[16] 'landmarks' of science and the works of less well known scientific practitioners. Three major fields are particularly well represented:

1. Renaissance books of astronomy and practical mathematics, including surveying and navigation.
2. Seventeenth-and-eighteenth century books on the new philosophical and optical instruments.
3. Books on nineteenth and early twentieth-century instruments.

Some books have extremely interesting provenance (origin). Included are Ben Jonson's and Monatesquieu's copies of William Gilbert's *De Magnete (On the Magnet), 1600*; Borelli's copy of Gilbert's *De Mundo nostro sublunari*; Newton's copies of Robert Boyle's (1627-91) *Tracts consisting of observations about the saltness of the sea* and of John Wallis' (1616-1703) *Opera mathematica*, Robert Hooke's (1635-1703) copy of Pierre de Fermat's (1601-65) *Varia opera mathematics*, John Flamsteed's (1646-1719) copy of Wing's *Astronomia Britannica*. Among the more recent book's in Whipple's collection are Augustus De Morgan's copy of Guericke's *Experimenta nova* and several books from Pierre Duhem's (1861-1916) library. These names, in addition to those of less-known owners, who appear in more than one book, confirm the potential of the Whipple collection as a source for documenting the history of the collecting and dissemination of science books.

In addition to the Whipple collection, the Library holds more than 3,000 volumes. Included are books on instruments and science which were acquired thank's to Whipple's special bequest, the collection of medical books bought with the Wellcome Fund, the Phrenology Collection (about 300 volumes), the Sleeman and Steward Collection of books of chemistry and physics, the collection presented by George Parker Bidder (1806-78) (books of biological sciences from the nineteenth-century onward), and some of the books originally presented to the Cavendish Laboratory by James Clerk Maxwell (1831-79). Three incunabales[17] have been added: Firmicus Maternus' *De Nativitatibus*, (Venetiae, 1499). Sacro Bosco's *Sphaera Mundi*, (Venetiae, 1482) and Solinus' *Polyhistor, sive De mirabilibus mundi*, (Venetiae, 1498).

The collection is now being fully catalogued using the information Whipple recorded in a notebook and a card catalogue. The research has led students to the intersection of the history of science and the history of the book.

Printed catalogues documenting some of Whipple's books are D. Bertoloni Meli and J.A. Bennett, *Sphaera Mundi. Astronomy Books in the Whipple Museum 1478-1600*, Cambridge, 1994; S. A. Johnston, F. H. Willmoth, and J. A. Bennett, *The Grounde of Artes Mathematical Books of 16th-century England*, Cambridge, 1985; and S. Butler, R.H. Nuttal, O. Brown, *The Social History of the Microscope*, Cambridge, 1986.[18]

ENDNOTES, WHIPPLE FLAG

1. Canton – the four square divisions placed one at each corner of a shield or escutcheon and always less than a quarter of the total service.
2. Field – the surface of a flag which functions as a background for its devices.
3. Example: The field of the canton in the Stars and Stripes is blue and bears white stars; the balance of the field consists of horizontal red and white stripes.
4. Molet – rowel of a knight's spur .
5. This was shortly after the Boston Massacre.
6. Among Whipple's books were *The Story-Life of Lincoln*, *The Story of the White House and Its Home Life*, *The Minute Man*, and *The Story of Plymouth Rock*.

WHIPPLE MUSEUM NOTES

7. D. J. Bryden, compiler, *Selected Exhibits in the Whipple Museum of the History of Science*, Eastbourne, England: Whipple Museum of the History of Science, printed by Sumfield & Day Ltd., 1978.

8. John Napier's(1550-1617) invention of logarithms (and the decimal point), published in 1614, was acclaimed throughout Europe for providing a new and immensely powerful computational tool. Edmund Gunter (1581-1626) suggested that Napier's 'artificial numbers' could be used by sailors in an instrument to form and set out logarithmically divided lines of certain trigonometrical functions on the limb of a cross-staff. William Oughtred (1574-1660) improved Gunter's ideas and invented the first circular and linear logarithmic slide rule. The present form of the slide rule was designed in 1850 by a French army officer, Amedee Manneheim. Bryden, 2.

9. An orrery is a mechanical model of the solar system. Orreries were used to teach the basic astronomy of the solar system. Bryden, 2- 3.

10. The astronomical screen came from the Royal Palace of the Yi Dynasty, Seoul, Korea and is a folding screen with eight panels. Apparently conceived as an historical record, it contrasted the then most recent mapping of the stars with the earliest recorded data held in the Korean state archives. Bryden, 4-5.

11. A set of 24 mathematical instruments made by Domenico Lusuergh, who worked in Rome, designed for the practical needs of an architect, draftsman, gunner, and surveyor and includes a set of paper-covered multiplying rods designed by John Napier and a surveying-quadrant which incorporates a vernier made to the design published by Piere Venier in 1631. Bryden, 6-7.

12. Nicolas Fortin (1750-1831) made a balance in 1788 commissioned by the French chemist Antoine Lavoisier which became the model of subsequent French manufacture of precision balances over the next 30 years. Fortin's instruments of this design performed routine weighings of up to one kilogram to an accuracy of one milligram. Bryden, 8.

13. Edward Nairne (1726-1806) patented his "Insulated Medical Electrical Machine" in 1783. The design insulated both the primary and the secondary conductors and permitted the production of positive and negative electricity. He sold these instruments to people who wished to practice medical electricity. He claimed that "the very many cures performed by electricity in the hands even of persons entirely unskilled in medicine" included nervous disorders, epileptic and hysterical cases, purulent discharges of ulcers, inflammations of the eyes, sciatica, gout, and palsy. Bryden, 9.

14. Azimuth means the distance in angular degrees in a clockwise direction from the north point or, in the Southern Hemisphere, south point; arc of the horizon measured clockwise from such a point to a vertical circle passing from the zenith through the center of a star. An azimuth compass is not an ordinary ship's steering-compass but an instrument used to ascertain the magnetic variations. That the compass needle did not indicate true north, but pointed away to what was later called magnetic north, became apparent to European sailors by the late 14th century. One hundred years later long distance navigators discovered that this magnetic variation changed markedly with their geographical location, and in the 17th century it was found that at any one place the variation changed slowly over the years. It was essential to be able to measure the magnetic variation for accurate navigation. The azimuth compass was designed to take the bearing of the sun at sunrise or sunset. The observed reading was compared with printed tables of solar amplitude and the magnetic variation determined. Readers wanting to obtain a table of the altitude and azimuth of the Sun or Moon during a specific day, at a time interval that they specify, can go to the Web Page http://aa..usno.navy.mil/data/docs/AltAZ.html and do so.

15. Robert was the oldest of five children, all boys. He was born in 1871 and died in 1953.

16. Canonical - (1) of, according to, or ordered by church canon which is a body of laws of a church. (2) authoritative; accepted. (3) belonging to the canon of the Bible.

17. Incunables - early printed books, especially printed before 1500.

18. Silvia De Renzi, UNIVERSITY OF CAMBRIDGE, Whipple Library, http://www.hps.cam.ac.uk/library/speccoll.html, 1-6.

WHIPPLE COAT OF ARMS

Arms once granted to someone with the Whipple surname do not subsequently belong to everyone with that surname. They may be inherited by the oldest male heir of the one first granted the arms. Younger sons can apply for arms that are similar to but different from the heir's arms. Who, if anyone, is entitled to use the Whipple Coat of Arms? The arms are documented in *Burke's General Armory* for a family from County Norfolk, England. Burke says the arms are authentic for the family who spelled its name both Whipple and whipley. He gives no other data. The Whipple arms shown here were drawn by an heraldic artist associated with Halberts of Bath, Ohio. Supposedly, Halberts' rendering came from ancient heraldic archives.

GENEALOGY PREFACE

THE GENEALOGICAL SECTION includes 6,910 individuals, 1,570 surnames, and 2,544 marriages. The period covered is from about 1560 in England to October 2001 in the United States and includes 15 generations. The format follows the modified Register style where all children receive an Arabic number in birth order beginning with the next number after the last number used in the previous generation. Children whose line continue have a plus (+) in front of their number. Names of main persons are printed in bold upper/lower case letters. All notes appear at the end of the genealogy.

Readers are advised that this is not a professional genealogical project. It is a compilation with hundreds of sources, many of which have not been verified by other sources. The families included herein have been identified by hundreds of family historians who claim descent from the earliest known Whipple ancestor from Bocking. Some lineages are explored more extensively than others. Some cited sources, some did not.

I used endnotes to cite the sources. They are as diverse as vital statistics, town and county histories, cemetery and church records, Bible, probate and guardianship records, deed records, personal knowledge of the provider of information, etc. Documentation is from both primary and secondary sources. The author does not know how accurately the compilers copied the sources or how correctly they appraised the information and does not vouch for the lineages herein. When a reader finds information without primary citations it should be validated with other sources of independent origins. Any single record contains the possibility of error. Corroboration and verification of sources is essential to prove any lineage.

No ancestral line is ever truly complete and all conclusions are open to critical evaluation because further evidence or evaluation may upset that conclusion. Genealogy is cumulative because people may return to a family and, often in the light of new evidence that was not previously available, add to our understanding of it.

Beginning with the 10th generation, there is an anomaly with the numbering system. Normally the individual with a plus (+) in front of their name appears in the next generation in numbered sequence. However, the numbering system becomes non-sequential beginning in the 10th generation. Apparently the genealogy software had to make numbering ajustments when generating the sequence of children born to the multiple wives of a Mormon husband. In making this adjustment, the numbering system of all children is consistent throughout the entire genealogy. Examples of the non-sequential of the of plus (+) individuals: No. 1688 is followed by 1742, 1744, and 1689. No. 7111 is followed by 1762, 1746, and 1716. Readers need to be aware of this anomaly as they track their lineage from the 10th generation.

When the genealogy was printed for the first time it took 104 pages to print the 4,523 endnotes. Many of these endnotes were "Ibid." In order to reduce the number of pages, all consecutive Ibids are combined with the original endnote citation. For example, note 3225 is followed by 42 Ibids. These 43 notes are consolidated into one, identified as Endnote 3225 through 3267 in the endnote section. However, all 4,523 endnotes are numbered consecutively (not combined) in the body of the text. Thus the reader can check, without difficulty, the appropriate citation in the endnote section.

This is the first of three volumes expected to be published on the Whipple Families of America. The second volume, on Matthew Whipple of Ipswich, will be authored by me. It is in the final stages of preparation and is expected to be published in 2004. It will include approximately 20,000 individuals, 4,500 surnames, and 8,700 marriages. The historical section will feature a biographical chapter on one family for each generation beginning with Matthew (1560-1618).

Work on the third volume, on Captain John Whipple, is expected to begin this year. The compiler-author will be Charles M. Whipple, Jr., Ph.D, Ed,D, Litt.D, emeritus professor of psychology and philosophy at the University of Central Oklahoma and former senior minister of Mayflower Congregational Church and past associate minister of Plymouth Congregational Church, both in Oklahoma City. Dr. Whipple is a descendant of Captain John and author of *Sons and Daughters of Jesse*, authorized by the Jabez Whipple Family Association and published by the Southwestern Press in Oklahoma City in 1976. Descendants of Captain John Whipple who would like to be included in the book are asked to mail their information to Dr. Whipple at 327 Sundance Lane, Edmond, OK 73034. He can also be reached at charles@whipple.net.

The author welcomes reader additions and corrections. This genealogy includes approximately 3,000 individuals whose lines are not carried forward. Thus, thousands of descendants of Elder John Whipple are not represented. A second volume will be considered if a sufficient number of submissions, along with source citations, are received. Mail additions and corrections to Blaine Whipple, 326 S.W. Sundown Way, Portland, OR 97229-6575.

The software program used to generate this genealogy is Ultimate Family Tree, copyright ©1999, The Learning Co., Inc. Ultimate Family Tree is a trademark of Learning Company Properties, Inc.

Blaine Whipple
Portland, Oregon
November, 2003

20. **Maj. Matthew[4] Whipple** (Capt. John[3], Elder John[2], Matthew[1])[53] was born in Ipswich in 1658 and died there 28 January 1739 at 80 years of age. He had a malt house and an oat mill and did a large volume of business. He held several town offices, was justice of the sessions court, and representative in 1718, 1719, 1729. He had a slave Pluto who was born in Africa, lived to age 107, and was eventually freed by Matthew. Pluto was living in Hamilton at the time of death. Matthew's Will was probated in Essex Co., 5 February 1739. He left an estate of £3,500 and bequeathed his house and lands to his two oldest sons, Matthew and John.

He married three times. (1) **Jemima Lane** in Billerica, Mass. abt 1684. Jemima,[54] daughter of Job **Lane** and Hannah Reyner, was born in Malden, Middlesex Co., Mass. 19 August 1666. (2) **Johanna Appleton** in Ipswich abt 1688. Johanna,[55] daughter of Samuel **Appleton** and Mary Oliver, died abt 1698 in Ipswich. The Appleton line has been traced to John Appleton of Waldingfield, Magna, Suffolk, England. John died in 1414. Johanna's father, Samuel, was born in Little Walddingfield, Essex Co., England in 1625 and died in Ipswich 15 May 1696. (3) **Mrs. Martha (Denison) Thing** in Ipswich 11 June 1697. Henry B. Whipple's genealogy states that Matthew's third wife was Martha Ringe (Rindge), daughter of John Ringe and granddaughter of maj. gen. Daniel Denison.[56] Charles H. Preston in *Putnams' Monthly Historical Magazine* (II:14) identifies her as Martha, widow of Jonathan Thing of Exeter, daughter of John Denison, and granddaughter of maj. gen. Daniel Denison. Henry Whipple's genealogy does not include Matthew's marriage to Jemima, daughter of Job Lane; Preston's account does. Since Job Lane's Will dated 19 May 1688 mentions daughter Jemima and son Matthew Whipple, this author is inclined to Preston's account. Martha,[57] daughter of John **Denison** and Martha Symonds, was born about 1668 and died 12 September 1728 in Ipswich at 60 years of age.

Both Matthew and his sister Susanna married into the Job Lane family. Jemima's older brother John married Matthew's sister Susanna. John and Jemima and Matthew were mentioned in Job Lane's Will.

Maj. Matthew **Whipple** and Jemima **Lane** had the following child:

68   i.   Dea. Matthew[5] **Whipple**[58] was born in Ipswich 20 October 1685 and died there 24 January 1766 at 80 years of age. He married Martha **Cogswell** in Ipswich. The date of intent to marry was 23 September 1710. Martha[59] was born in 1690 and died 7 August 1774 at 84 years of age.

       Matthew's Will mentions wife Martha, real estate "which was my father, Major Whipple's" and left property to the three sons of his brother Capt. John Whipple: Deacon Nathaniel, Capt. John, and William Whipple. A release of all claim to estate of "uncle Dea. Matthew" was signed by Capt. John Whipple and wife Dorothy (Moulton). Matthew also inherited one-fourth of the Winthrop farm in Billerica purchased by his grandfather Job Lane in 1664.

Maj. Matthew **Whipple** and Johanna **Appleton** had the following children, all born in Ipswich:

+   69   ii.   Capt. John **Whipple** was born 22 July 1689.

    70   iii.   Joanna (Johanna) **Whipple**[60] was born 22 July 1692 and died 31 August 1692 in Ipswich at less than one year of age.

    71   iv.   Appleton **Whipple**[61] was born 19 October 1693.

+   72   v.   Capt. William **Whipple** was born 28 February 1696.

Maj. Matthew **Whipple** and Mrs. Martha (Denison) **Thing** had the following children, all born in Ipswich:

73   vi.   Rev. Joseph **Whipple**[62] was born 31 July 1701 and died 17 February 1757 in Hampton Falls, N.H. at 55 years of age. He married Elizabeth **Cutt** in Kittery, Maine 23 October 1727. Elizabeth,[63] daughter of Robert **Cutt** II and Dorcas Hammond, was born in Kittery abt 1708. She married (2) Rev. John **Lowell** in Newbury, Mass. 26 September 1757 and died 22 September 1805 in Portsmouth, Rockingham Co., N.H. at 97 years, the age stated on her tombstone.

Joseph was graduated with the Harvard class of 1720 (the first Whipple Harvard graduate) and after the death on 16 August 1726 of rev. Theopilus Cotton, first minister at Hampton Falls, he was called to preach there. He was ordained 4 January 1726/27 and served the town for the next 30 years. His initial salary was £120 a year plus the use of the parsonage. The salary was raised periodically to keep pace with inflation. Joseph owned a slave (a bill of sale for the slave Pompey is in his interleaved Almanac for 1733) and was distinguished enough to dine in state with gov. Belcher (interleaved Almanac 27 April 1737). When the New Hampshire assembly sat in Hampton, it rented Joseph's home to hold its sessions. He was an active and efficient parson and was frequently called to ecclesiastical councils. The parsonage was destroyed by fire 18 February 1749 and the parish built a new one 40' long, 32' wide, two stories high with a single chimney with three flues, each as large as a bedroom. It was painted inside and out and cost £1,807 16 shillings 2 pence (Old Tenor). The home was torn down in 1837 and a new home built on the lot.

Joseph continued to keep the church diary began by rev. Cotton and these two diaries contain nearly all that is known of the church history previous to 1756. A magnifying glass is required to decipher his tiny writing. During his ministry, 79 new members accepted the church covenant, 236 were admitted to full communion, 91 were dismissed to other churches, and he performed 1,136 baptisms, 605 funerals, and 389 marriages. He baptized his wife 14 April 1728 and she was admitted to full communion in June. He officiated at both marriages of Mechech Weare (20 July 1738 to Elizabeth Shaw and 11 Dec. 1746 to Mrs. Mehitable Wainwright). Weare was leader of Revolutionary New Hampshire from 1776-84.

Several church members became Quakers which greatly agitated Joseph. He also opposed the preaching of George Whitefield, the most famous of the evangelist ministers during the Great Awakening. Whipple warned, by letter, Boston ministers of the evils that would result if they permitted Whitefield to preach in their pulpits. Some of his parishioners opposed having deacons read and turn the Psalms. This practice of deaconing the Psalms originated because there was a scarcity of Psalm books. After deacons read two lines, the congregation would sing those words with no regard to harmony and rhythm. Choirs eventually replaced the deacons but they didn't yield without a struggle.

In July 1754 John Adams traveled from Boston to Newington, N.H. a village on the south side of the Piscataqua river just above Portsmouth. It was probably the future president's first long trip away from home. His companion was a cousin, rev. Ebenezer Adams. The purpose of their trip was to visit Ebenezer's father John, Newington's minister. They visited the Whipple home enroute. In a letter of January 1822 to David Sewell of York, Maine John Adams' only surviving Harvard classmate, Adams recalled the visit to the Whipples as follows: ". . . we visited parsons Whipple whose lady persecuted me as much as she did afterward to father F. (Harvard tutor Henry Flynt). The lady had a fine figure and a fair face. At dinner I was very bashful and silent. After dinner parson W. invited us into another [room]where he took a pipe himself and offered us pipes. I was an old smoker and readily took one. The (word torn away] lady very soon came into the room, lifted up her hands, and cried out in a masculine voice, I am astonished to see that pretty little boy with a pipe in his mouth smoking that nasty poisoned tobacco. I can't bear the sight. I was as bashful and timorous as a girl, but I resented so much being called a little boy at 15 or 16 years of age and as stout as her husband, that I determined not to be frightened out of my pipe so I continued to puff away."[64]

Whipple was an active and efficient pastor. The record shows frequent cases of discipline and suspension from the church "by those who had fallen into sin." But his kindness and admonition prompted them to confess their sins and in almost every case, they were restored to church fellowship. He became ill in the fall of 1756 and died 17 February 1757.

The New Hampshire Gazette of 25 February wrote he "was a grave and solid preacher, a faithful and useful minister, and a good Christian; pleasant and agreeable in social life, a great lover and promoter of peace, order, and good will among men. A generous patron of ministers, an example of every amiable virtue, especially meekness, prudence, fidelity, charity, and hospitality. Few in his station were more extensively known, and perhaps not any more universally belov'd."

The church authorized £400 (Old Tenor, about £40 sterling) for his funeral and burial and named a committee, including col. Mechech Weare, to plan the event. Rev. John Lowell of Newbury preached the funeral sermon on the Sabbath following Whipple's death. Whipple's successor, rev. Josiah Bayley, was ordained 19 Oct. 1757. Rev. Thomas Barnard of Salem, Mass. who preached Bayley's ordination sermon, referred to Whipple as "Your last most worthy pastor . . . friend of mankind . . . is in the Providence of the Lord which he so cultivated and of which he was such a shining example."

Reverend Whipple was buried in the old cemetery in a grave adjacent to rev. Cotton. Their graves are about 20´ in front of the monument on Mechech Wear's grave. Whipple's tombstone is 34" high and 30" wide and is inscribed: "Here lies the body of Rev. Mr. Joseph Whipple who having wisely and faithfully discharged the pastoral office in Second Church in Hampton. Deceased Feby 17th in the 56th year of his age and 31st of his ministry highly esteemed and beloved in life and in death much lamented." The author visited the grave in October 1998. The tombstone still stands but is difficult to read. The cemetery is just south of State Highway 88W off Route 1 and just east of the I-95 overpass.

On 15 March 1757 the town voted to allow Mrs. Whipple, "who was much beloved by the people," use of half of the parsonage, barn, and garden, the fruit of 30 apple trees, the pasturing of a cow at the upper parsonage, the improvements of the whole lower parsonage for pasturing a horse and cutting hay for a horse and one cow, and the full produce of an acre of rye sown at the upper parsonage for one year. The Whipples had no children. About eight months after her husband's death, rev. Lowell married her and took her away. After the wedding, the people, remembering the text of his funeral sermon: "I will not leave you comfortless but will come unto you," said he was "preaching to the widow and not to us" and they did not "desire such miserable comfort." She survived her second husband.

    74   vii.   Martha **Whipple**[65] was born 7 January 1704 and died 30 January 1704 in Ipswich at less than one year of age.

    75   viii. Nathaniel **Whipple**[66] was born 2 July 1711.

+   76   ix.   Martha **Whipple** was born 2 July 1711.

21. Susanna[4] **Whipple** (Capt. John[3], Elder John[2], Matthew[1])[67] was born in Ipswich in 1661 and died 4 August 1713 in Billerica, Mass. at 52 years of age. She married **Maj. John Lane** in Salem, Essex Co., Mass. 2 January 1681. The *Register* 10: 356, and *Lane Genealogies* report a marriage date of 20 March 1680. *Ipswich Vital Records*, 2:454 gives the date as 20 December 1683. *The Compendium of American Genealogy*, 3, says their marriage occurred in 1681. Susannah, their first child, was born 24 January 1682, thus it appears *Ipswich Vital Records* is wrong. They were half second cousins, their common ancestor being (?) Reyner.

John,[68] son of Job **Lane** and Hannah Reyner, was born in Malden, Mass. in October 1661 and died 17 January 1715 in Billerica at 53 years of age. The death date may have been 7 instead of 17 January.[69] He was captain of a troop in August 1695 that was ordered to be ready to march against the Indians "at a minute's warning . . . with three days provisions." He was captain of a troop in November 1702 when he was ordered to speak with "Wotanummun and the Penocook men, and assure them of friendship with the Governour (of the Massachusetts Bay colony) and all the English." His rank was major when he commanded a troop in July 1706 of which his brother-in-law Matthew **Whipple** was a member. When John's father died 23 Aug. 1697, he left an estate of £2,036 11 shillings. John was executor of his Will and "as the only male heir of his body" was the heir of his lands in England. In a letter dated 23 March 1697/98 mailed to England from Woburn, New England and addressed to "Loving Kinsman," John asked for an accounting of what was due him in rents and requested the kinsman to continue to manage the property. He said he understood that at least £10 was now due and asked that it be paid in "Alamode 20 ells, Kentish 4 pieces, good fine Holland 6 ells, of new fashion stuffs 5 pieces, two of which I would have of a solid colour, very good and fine for my mother's and wife's own wear; a large Bible of a very good and large print in quarto; a piece of coarse Holland, a piece of good Devonshire carsey, for my own wear, 2 pieces of other carseys fit for service, and half a dozen yards of good broadcloth, if there be so much due." He ended his letter noting, "I have through God's goodness (besides 2 that I buried) 6 children, Susanna, Mary, Job, John, Martha, James."

Susanna **Whipple** and Maj. John **Lane** had the following children, all born in Billerica:

+   77   i. Susannah[5] **Lane** was born 24 January 1682/83.
+   78   ii. Mary **Lane** was born 15 May 1686.
     79   iii. Jemima **Lane**[70] was born 27 June 1688 and died 10 July 1688 in Billerica at less than one month of age.
+   80   iv. Job **Lane** was born 22 June 1689.
+   81   v. John **Lane** was born 20 October 1691.
     82   vi. Martha **Lane**[71] was born 1 October 1694 and died 18 January 1735/36 at 40 years of age. She married James **Minot** in Billerica 14 November 1716. James[72] was born abt 1695 and died 6 February 1759 at 63 years of age. He was from Concord, Mass.
+   83   vii. James **Lane** was born 12 August 1696.
     84   viii. Joseph **Lane**[73] was born 18 February 1698 and died before 1715.

23. **Joseph**[4] **Whipple** (Capt. John[3], Elder John[2], Matthew[1])[74] was born in Ipswich 8 June 1666 and died there 11 May 1699 at 32 years of age. He married **Mary Symonds** in Ipswich 10 December 1697. Mary,[75] daughter of William **Symonds**, died 20 January 1703 in Ipswich. Joseph's Will, dated 9 May 1699, identifies him as a yeoman and mentions wife Mary and daughter Mary. Administration of the estate of Mary (Symonds) **Whipple** was granted to her brothers-in-law, Matthew and Cyprian Whipple on 26 June 1703.

Joseph **Whipple** and Mary **Symonds** had the following child:
+   85   i. Mary[5] **Whipple** was born 15 February 1699.

24. **Sarah**[4] **Whipple** (Capt. John[3], Elder John[2], Matthew[1])[76] was born in Ipswich

2 September 1671 and died there 16 March 1709 at 37 years of age. She married Col. Francis Wainwright in Ipswich 12 March 1686. Francis,[77] son of Francis Wainwright and Phillis (_) (maybe Epes), was born in Ipswich 25 August 1664 and died there 2 August 1711 at 46 years of age. He was laid to rest in a tomb of his own making and Sarah Whipple, who proceeded him in death, was taken from her tomb and laid with him. Sarah is identified as the youngest daughter in her father's (Capt. John Whipple) Will.

Francis was graduated from Harvard in 1686. He joined the artillery company in 1709; was colonel of the first regiment; town clerk for several years; representative to the general court in 1699 and 1700; feoffee of the grammar school; justice of the general sessions court; and commissioner and collector of excise for Essex County.[78] When HMS *Deptford* sailed from Boston as part of the expedition against Port Royal in Canada on 13 May 1707, Francis, a colonel, was a member of the expedition. John Whipple, probably a brother-in-law, served under him The expedition was unsuccessful.

Francis was engaged to marry (2) Mrs. Elizabeth (Betty) Hirst on 31 July 1711 but was stricken on the 29th, wrote his Will on 2 August and died the next day. The following bequests were provided in his Will: To ye church of Ipswich, ye sum of £5 to be laid in a piece of plate for ye Lord's table. To Mrs. Elizabeth Hirst of Salem, with whom I had contracted for marriage, for ye love I bare to her, ye sum of £100. To my kinswoman Mrs. Mary Whipple, who hath been kind to me in health and sickness, ye sum of £10. To ye rev. Mr. John Rogers, minister, ye sum of £5. To ye rev. Mr. Jabez Fitch, ye sum of £10. To my loving and good friend Daniel Rogers, schoolmaster, £5. I will and desire my mother Epes may have a mourning suite given by my executor at my funeral. As he had already given £250 to his daughter Sarah when she married Stephen Minot of Boston, he gave the same sum to his daughters Elizabeth and Lucy. His "loving brother (in-law) Capt. John Whipple," and his son-in-law Stephen Minot were appointed executors.

The carefully preserved accounts of the administrator, Stephen Minot, reveal the extraordinary pomp and parade of that funeral. Funeral rings, scarfs, and gloves were provided for the mourners. The following orders were given to the foremost tradesmen and artificers of Boston:

Ebenezer Wentworth received orders for 2 super fine hats at 40/ each, 2 common hats at 18/ each, 9 doz. gloves and a mourning gown delivered to Mr. Minot, the whole order amounting to £15-7-6.

Ezekiel Lewis provided 6 doz. mens white and colored gloves @ 30/, 4 doz. women's white and colored gloves @ 30/, and 9 mourning fans at 4/; total cost £16-16.

Benjamin Walker's bill "for gloves of the finer quality for the inner circle of mourners; 6 yds. 3/8 fine black broadcloth; 12 yds. mourning crape @ 4/; 1 doz. men's satin topt gloves, 1 doz women's satin topt gloves; 6 pr. women's looyned Shammy"; totaled £26-1-7

Peter Cutler's account was for 1 ps. cloth rash, 7 1/2 yds; fine muslin @ 12/; 3 hats @ 08/; 3 pr. black shammy gloves 8/; 1 pr. black hose; total cost £16-13-0.

Oliver Noyes furnished 6 1/2 yds black queen's cloath @ 40/; 7 yds black queen's cloath; 7 1/2 yds. black queen's cloath; sundry silk laces and ferrett, 11/12 at a total cost of £42-11-12.

Merchant Andrew Faneuil supplied 35 1/4 ells of Jute-string @ 10/6 totaling £18-109-1.

The items of Col. Thomas Savage's bill of £85-9-2 indicate a cart blanche order for his finest goods: 200 yds. fine bro. cloath at 27/; 24 yds fine durange; 2 doz. best new fash coat buttons; 5 doz breast ditto; 5 yds white fustian; black cloth to Walker's boy; 14 yds besty Lute string @ 9/8; 38 yds black Sallopeen @5/6; 2 1/8 yd. shallon @ 4/; 13 yds finest shallop @ 4/; 6 yds 1/2 galix @ 2/; 3 doz. coat buttons; 5 pr. superfine hose @ 14; 12 yds. catgut gauze 3/4; 18 yds black cloath; 1 pr. boys gloves for Wm. Alden; 3 yds. broad Love ribbind; 2 yds. broad cadez; 4 yds. broad Italian crape; 1/2 yd. durance @ 3/; 35 yds. allamode @ 5/3; 25 yds. black & white silk cape.

The tailors and dressmakers of Boston had to fashion all this broad cloth and durance or durrange, a stout cloth made in imitation of buff leather, the fustian and the worsted fabric called shallon into men's garmets, and the lute-string and crape and ribbons into mourning garb for the daughters and bride-elect.

Dame Bridget Pead presented an account of £1-10 for ye funeral, making 3 suits of mourning. George Shore's bill for "making a black suit of cloathes, coat, cloning, breaches puffs, and buckram was £1-18-9. Peter Barber charged £1-19-0 for making a black cloath coat and west coat and breeches with leather pockets for capt. John Whipple.

Most melancholy of all was the bill rendered by John Cotts: "Sundrys for your wedding clothes" which were displayed in the bride-chamber. This bill was dated 23 July and included making a coat jacket and breaches of cloath looped with gold and wrought in vellome, 14 yds. durance, 5 1/2 yds. white dustian, pockets, 3 doz. & 1 coat buttons, 4 doz. and 1 breast buttons, 3/4 oz. of gold thread, 7/8 yd. gold lace, wodding, making a coat of black cloath, making 2 jackets & breaches of hold loopt, 11 1/2 yds. holland @ 5/, 5 1/2 yds. linen, 6 doz buttons, thread, etc.

Thomas Selby provided "a light colored Compigne Perrewig" at a cost of £6-10-00.

The order for gold rings was divided among three craftsmen: Edward Winslow provided "18 gold rings, 1 oz. 13 dwt. 12 qr. making and waste at 2/6 per ring to the half making 12 more damage." Total bill: £13-5-0. John Coney's bill for 12 gold rings and the "fashioning" was £9-14-6, and Shubel Dummer charged £8-7-6 for a similar number.

These mourning rings, usually enamelled in black or black and white, and decorated, sometimes with a death's head or a framed lock of hair, upon which the initials of the deceased were engraved or "fashioned" were given at funerals to near relatives and persons of note in the community.

Henry Sharpe furnished ye Hatchments & Escutcheons for funeral as follows: 1 Hatchment of Arms, ye freem and cloth, 26 Escutcheons and 10 yds of buckram. His charge was £10-19-0.

Escutcheons were sometimes attached to the livery of the horses or perhaps to the pall. These 25 escutcheons all found conspicuous place. John Roberts, the Boston undertaker, furnished the "paule" at an expense of 12 shillings and charged £3 and 13 shillings for his service and expense.

Presumably the account for the pall was for rental only, as it was usually of heavy purple or black broadcloth and was often owned by the Town. The pall bearers held it by the corners or sides, and the actual carrying of the body was often performed by young and vigorous men.

The custom of prayers at funerals was gaining ground in the beginning of the 18th century and Mr. Rogers and Mr. Fitch, the ministers, may have had a funeral service. Then the stately procession formed and the spacious High street was filled with a curious crowd of town folk and from all the country round to see the imposing array of pall bearers, with the hat bands and scarfs of crape, the principal mourners, Mrs. Hirst, in her new gowns of woe, the afflicted family, and the long line of relatives and friends, and not least, John Roberts, master of ceremonies, bringing the last touch of Boston display. At the grave judge Samuel Sewall or one of the ministers may have pronounced a brief eulogy.

The place of burial is marked with a flat stone, with the simple inscription: "Here lies entombed the body of Colonel Francis Wainwright, Esq., who died August 2, 1711, Aetatis 47. And his virtuous consort, Mrs. Sarah Wainwright, who died March ye 16, 1709. Aetatis 38. With three of their young sons, John, Francis, and Benjamin, who died in their infancy."

The total funeral charges amounted to £415-18-4. The real estate was inventoried at £1914, personal property at £4132-5-1. Included in the personal property was the Negro Maxey, valued at £40.

Sarah **Whipple** and Col. Francis **Wainwright** had the following children, all born in Ipswich:

86	i.	Elizabeth[5] **Wainwright**[79].
87	ii.	John **Wainwright**[80] died young.
88	iii.	John **Wainwright**[81] was born 7 January 1690.
89	iv.	Sarah **Wainwright**[82] was born 26 January 1692 and married Stephen Minott in Ipswich. The date of intent to marry was 16 September 1710.
90	v.	Francis **Wainwright**[83] was born 2 April 1697 and died 20 November 1698 in Ipswich at one year of age.
91	vi.	Benjamin **Wainwright**[84] was born 26 September 1698 and died 15 October 1698 in Ipswich at less than one year of age.
92	vii.	Lucy **Wainwright** was born 30 April 1704.[85]

25. **Deacon Simon[4] Stone** (Mary[3] **Whipple**, Elder John[2], Matthew[1])[86] was born in Watertown, Mass. 8 September 1656 and died 20 December 1741 in Groton, Mass. at 85 years of age. He married **Sarah Farnsworth** abt 1683. Sarah[87] was the daughter of Matthew **Farnsworth** and Mary **Farr**.

Simon served in King Philip's War in a garrison at Groton in January 1675/76; was in Capt. Joseph's Sill's company against the Indians in June 1676; and served in the defense of Exeter, N.H. when it was attacked by Indians 4 July 1690. He was severely wounded in this latter battle. Rev. Cotton Mather wrote that Simon was shot in nine places and that the Indians attempted to cut off his head with a hatchet. When the English returned to bury the dead, a soldier heard him gasp and revived him with strong water and he eventually recovered. Mather used his recovery as an example "that nothing may be despaired of . . ."

He was living in Groton as early as 1680 where he was a farmer. He and his brother John were a part of the Groton Garrison that defended against Indian attacks. He held several town offices, was a deacon, and represented the area in the general court. He died as 29 December 1741.[88]

Deacon Simon **Stone** and Sarah **Farnsworth** had the following children, all born in Groton:

+	93	i.	Sarah[5] **Stone** was born abt 1684.
+	94	ii.	Simon **Stone** was born 1 August 1686.
+	95	iii.	Abigail **Stone** was born in 1691.
+	96	iv.	Mary **Stone** was born about 1692.
+	97	v.	Susanna **Stone** was born 23 October 1694.
	98	vi.	Isaac **Stone**[89] was born 4 May 1697 and died 30 September 1723 in Groton at 26 years of age.
	99	vii.	Hannah **Stone**[90] was born in 1699 and died 27 September 1723 in Groton at 24 years of age.
	100	viii.	Joseph **Stone**[91] was born 8 March 1701/02 and died 10 September 1777 at 75 years of age. He married Mary **Prescott** 9 May 1728.
	101	ix.	Benjamin **Stone**[92] was born 12 August 1706 and died 23 September 1758 in Groton at 52 years of age. He married Emme **Parker** 13 May 1736.
	102	x.	Lydia **Stone**[93] was born in 1708 and died 30 September 1723 in Groton at 15 years of age.

26. **John**[4] **Stone** (Mary[3] **Whipple**, Elder John[2], Matthew[1])[94] was born in Watertown, Mass. 23 July 1658 and died there in 1735 at 76 years of age. He served in King Philip's War in 1676 and was settled in Groton by 1691. A farmer, he was active in town and church affairs. He married **Mrs. Sarah (Nutting) Farnsworth** in Watertown after 1678. Sarah (Nutting) Farnsworth[95] married (1) **Matthias Farnsworth** Jr. of Groton.

John **Stone** had the following child:

| | 103 | i. | Capt. Jonas[5] **Stone**[96] who married **Ann Stone** in Watertown 14 November 1745. Ann,[97] daughter of Ens. Jonathan **Stone** and Hepzibah **Coolidge**, was born in Watertown 9 August 1722 and died 16 June 1794 in Newton, Middlesex Co., Mass. at 71 years of age. Jonas and Ann were cousins. They had eight childen. |

John **Stone** and Mrs. Sarah (Nutting) **Farnsworth** had the following children, born in Groton:

| | 104 | ii. | John Stone[98] was born 23 September 1699 and married Elizabeth **Farwell** in Groton 26 December 1722. Elizabeth,[99] daughter of Joseph **Farwell** and Hannah (__), was born in Groton. |
| + | 105 | iii. | James **Stone** was born 23 January 1701. |

27. **Dea. Matthew**[4] **Stone** (Mary[3] **Whipple**, Elder John[2], Matthew[1])[100] was born in Watertown, Mass. 16 February 1659/60 and died there 12 August 1743 at 84 years of age. He married twice. (1) **Rachael Pond** in Dedham, Mass. in July 1681. (2) **Mary Plympton** in Massachusetts in 1696. Mary[101] was the daughter of Thomas **Plympton** and Abigail **Noyes**, and was born in Massachusetts.

Matthew served in King Philip's War at age 16 in Capt. Daniel Henchman's company in 1675. Following the war, he left Watertown for Sudbury where he was a deacon and represented the town in the general court from 1710 through 1713. He also lived in Lancaster, Mass. His Will, proved 9 Aug. 1743, directed that his house lot and buildings and "intervale land belonging thereto," 48 acres of woodland, and all his intervale and meadows in Lancaster and all his personal estate and debts due be divided into four equal parts and divided among his four children: Joseph Stone, Adams Stone, Mary George, and Rachel Cobb, "part and part alike." All his remaining lands and utensils of husbandry were to be divided between his sons Joseph and Adams and their heirs and assigns. Adams was appointed sole executor.[102]

Dea. Matthew **Stone** and Mary **Plympton** had the following children, all born in Massachusetts:

106	i.	Joseph[5] **Stone**[103] lived in Sudbury and Lancaster, Mass.
107	ii.	Mary Stone[104] married (__) George.
108	iii.	Rachel **Stone**[105] married Thomas **Cobb** 1 June 1710. He was from Barnstable, Mass.
+ 109	iv.	Adams **Stone**.

29. **Ebenezer**[4] **Stone** (Mary[3] **Whipple**, Elder John[2], Matthew[1])[106] was born in Watertown, Mass. 27 February 1662/63 and died 4 October 1754 in Newton, Mass. at 92 years of age. He married three times. (1) **Margaret Towbridge** in Newton 18 March 1686. Margaret,[107] daughter of James **Trowbridge** and Margaret **Atherton**, was born in Newton 30 April 1666 and died there 4 May 1710 at 44 years of age. Her grandfather was gen. Humphrey Atherton. (2) **Abigail Wilson** in Salem, Mass. 12 June 1711. Abigail[108] died in 1720. (3) **Mrs. Sarah (Nevinson) (Stearns) Livermore** in Newton 8 April 1724.[109]

Ebenezer settled in Cambridge Village (Newton) and became a leading and influential citizen. He was a selectman for 10 years, representative to the general court from 1720 through 1724 and 1728 and 1729 and a member of gov. Jonathan Belcher's council from 1730 through 1733. He left an estate of £3,502 divided among sons Ebenezer, John, Simon, James, children of deceased son Samuel, and daughters Margart Hammond, Mindwell Woodward, and Experience Ward, and grandsons Ebenezer and Nehemiah Stone[110]

Ebenezer **Stone** and Margaret **Towbridge** had the following children, all born in Cambridge Village:

+ 110	i.	Ebenezer[5] **Stone** was born 21 December 1686.
111	ii.	Margaret Stone[111] was born 1 August 1688 and died in 1776 at 87 years of age. She married Nathaniel **Hammond**.
+ 112	iii.	Samuel **Stone** was born 1 July 1690.
113	iv.	John Stone[112] was born 18 September 1692 and died in 1765 at 72 years of age. He married Lydia **Hyde**.
114	v.	Nathaniel Stone[113] was born 6 September 1694 and died in 1713 at 18 years of age.
+ 115	vi.	Mindwell **Stone** was born 26 June 1696.
116	vii.	David Stone[114] was born 15 May 1698 and died unmarried in 1725 at 27 years of age.
117	viii.	Mary Stone[115] was born 19 April 1700 and died 10 October 1732 at 32 years of age. She married dea. Ephraim **Ward**.
118	ix.	Simon Stone[116] was born 14 September 1702 and died in 1760 at 57 years of age. He married Priscilla **Dyke** in 1732.
119	x.	James Stone[117] was born 8 June 1704 and died 28 July 1742 in Holliston, Middlesex Co., Mass. at 38 years of age. He married Elizabeth Smith, daughter of rev. John **Swift**. Elizabeth[118] was born in Framingham, Mass. James was graduated from Harvard College class of 1724 and was the first pastor of the church in Holliston, Mass. He was ordained 20 Nov. 1728, serving until his death 14 years later.
120	xi.	Experience Stone[119] was born in 1707 and died in 1798 at 91 years of age. She married Joseph **Ward** in 1733.

30. **Mary**[4] **Stone** (Mary[3] **Whipple**, Elder John[2], Matthew[1])[120] was born in Watertown, Mass. 6 January 1665 and died 20 April 1735 in Dedham, Mass. at 70 years of age. She married **Deacon Comfort Starr** in Dedham 4 November 1683. Comfort,[121] son of John **Starr** and Martha **Bunker**, was born in Boston, Mass. 4 February 1661 and died 9 June 1729 in Dedham at 68 years of age.

Comfort descends from Thomas Starr, born abt. 1565 in England. His grandfather, Dr. Comfort Starr, was baptized 6 July 1589 at Canbrook, Kent Co. England and died 2 January 1660 in Suffolk Co., Mass. Dr. Starr moved to New England with wife Elizabeth Mitchell and children Thomas, baptized 31 December 1615, Mary, baptized 16 April 1620, and John, baptized 15 October 1626, all in county Kent. Dr. Starr bought William Penytree's homestead at Newtown (Cambridge), Mass. in 1635. Some family researchers give the marriage date as 14 Sept. 1683.

Mary **Stone** and Deacon Comfort **Starr** had the following children:

	121	i.	Mary[5] **Starr**[122] was born in Watertown 23 November 1685 and married William **Eaton** 27 April 1704.
+	122	ii.	Lydia Abiah **Starr** was born 18 February 1687.
	123	iii.	Hannah **Starr**[123] was born in Watertown 13 January 1690 and married Dr. John **Sabin** 3 November 1730. She was his second wife.
	124	iv.	Sarah **Starr**[124] was born 13 February 1692 and died 17 October 1722 at 30 years of age. She married Samuel **Morse** 8 February 1716.
	125	v.	Josiah **Starr**[125] was born 4 September 1693 and died 26 November 1693 at less than one year of age.
+	126	vi.	Susanna **Starr** was born 24 November 1694.
+	127	vii.	Comfort **Starr** was born 9 August 1696.
	128	viii.	Judith **Starr**[126] was born in Dedham, Mass. 2 September 1698 and married John **Morse** in Dedham 11 April 1728.
	129	ix.	Martha **Starr**[127] was born in Dedham 5 October 1700 and died there 13 December 1700 at less than two months of age.
	130	x.	Ruth **Starr**[128] was born in Dedham 5 October 1700 and died 20 September 1737 at 36 years of age.
	131	xi.	Elizabeth **Starr**[129] was born in Dedham 2 October 1702 and married Jonathan **Hyde** in Boston, Mass. 27 August 1724.
	132	xii.	Jonathan **Starr**[130] was born in Dedham 8 December 1704. He married an unnamed person there 22 February 1738.
	133	xiii.	Martha **Starr**[131] was born in Dedham 27 April 1708 and married an unnamed person in Boston, Mass. 5 January 1736.

31. **Rev. Nathaniel**[4] **Stone** (Mary[3] **Whipple**, Elder John[2], Matthew[1])[132] was born in Watertown, Mass. in April 1667 and died 8 February 1755 in Harwich, Mass. at 87 years and 10 months. He married **Reliance Hinckley** 15 December 1698. Reliance,[133] daughter of gov. Thomas **Hinckley** and Mary **Smith**, was born in Barnstable, Barnstable Co., Mass. 15 December 1675 and died 24 May 1759 in Harwich at 83 years of age. Reliance's father Thomas was the last governor of Plymouth Colony. She was the 17th and youngest child of the governor.

Following his graduation with the Harvard College class of 1690, Nathaniel was schoolmaster in Watertown and ordained 16 Ocober. (maybe November) 1700 as Harwich's first minister. His ordination occurred on the same day the town was organized. He had started preaching there 6 March 1697/98 before the church was formally organized and spent his entire church career there. The church and his residence were in that part of town that is now Brewster. His fame was colony wide.

Several of his sermons were printed and deposited with the Boston library: "The Way to Attain Glory by Inheritance," preached in Boston in 1718; The election sermon 25 May 1720, "Rulers are a Terror not to Good but Evil Workers," preached to gov. Samuel Shute, his majesty's council, and the representatives to the general court; "Concio ad Magistra," preached before the judges of the superior court at Barnstable 24 April 1728; "Sermon on the Absolute Freedom of Grace," in 1731; "Questions and advice to the rev. Mr. Whitefield as to his Methods," preached at Harwich 7 January 1744/45.[134]

Rev. Nathaniel **Stone** and Reliance **Hinckley** had the following children, all born in Harwich:

	134	i. Lincoln⁵ Stone[135] died 19 April 1760.
+	135	ii. **Mary Stone was born 16 September 1699.**
	136	iii. Kezia Stone[136] was born 8 April 1701 and died 2 November 1763 at 62 years of age. She married Isaac **Lincoln** 10 April 1729.
	137	iv. Reliance Stone[137] was born 26 April 1703 and died 26 March 1735 at 31 years of age. She married Joseph **Paddock**.
	138	v. Heman Stone[138] was born 4 September 1705 and died 26 April 1779 at 73 years of age. He married Temperance **Sturgis**.
+	139	vi. Rev. Nathan **Stone** was born 18 February 1708.
	140	vii. Thankful Stone[139] was born 2 March 1709 and married Seth **Bangs** 11 June 1756. She was his second wife. The marriage date may have been 4 January 1756.
	141	viii. Eunice Stone[140] was born 23 June 1711 and died 5 February 1816 in Hardwick, Worcester Co., Mass. at 104 years of age. She married David **Bangs** in Harwich 23 September 1731. She was the mother of 15 children. The family lived in Harwich until 1768 when they moved to Hardwick. She attended church on her 100th birthday and listened to a sermon that reviewed her century of life.
	142	ix. Nathaniel Stone[141] was born 29 November 1713 and died 7 January 1777 at 63 years of age. He married Mary **Bourne**.
	143	x. Achsah Stone[142] was born 1 September 1715. The birth date may have been 5 September. She married Elijah **Hersey**.
	144	xi. Hannah Stone[143] was born 30 June 1718 and died 30 July 1718 in Harwich at one month of age.
	145	xii. Hannah Stone[144] was born 26 March 1720 and died 7 June 1720 in Harwich at less than three months of age.
	146	xiii. Huldah Stone[145] was born 6 July 1722 and died 24 January 1726/27 in Harwich at 4 years of age.

32. Elizabeth⁴ Stone (Mary³ **Whipple**, Elder John², Matthew¹)[146] was born in Watertown, Mass. 9 October 1670 and married Dea. Isaac **Stearns III** abt 1696. Isaac,[147] son of Isaac **Stearns** Jr. and Sarah **Beers**, was born in Lexington, Mass. 20 May 1665 and died abt 1741.

Elizabeth **Stone** and Isaac **Stearns III** had the following children:

+	147	i. Elizabeth Mary⁵ Stearns.
+	148	ii. Rev. Ebenezer Stearns.
+	149	iii. Jonathan Stearns was born 20 November 1701.
+	150	iv. Hannah Stearns was born 26 January 1704.

34. **Susanna[4] Stone** (Mary[3] **Whipple**, Elder John[2], Matthew[1])[148] was born in Watertown, Mass. 4 November 1675 and died 4 February 1754 in Framingham, Middlesex Co., Mass. at 78 years of age. She married **Edward Goddard** in Massachusetts 17 June 1697. Edward,[149] son of William **Goddard** and Elizabeth **Miles**, was born in Watertown 24 March 1675 and died 9 February 1754 in Framingham at 78 years of age. Both Edward and Susannah and their sons Benjamin and David died in the "Great Sickness" in 1754.

Edward was the schoolmaster in Watertown until about 1707 when he moved to Boston to teach. The family moved to Framingham 25 March 1714 where he taught grammar school for several years. His parents, William and Elizabeth, were born in England where William was a citizen and grocer in London. They had six children born in London, three of whom died young. William arrived in New England in 1665 and his wife and three surviving sons in 1666. They settled in Watertown where he was admitted freeman in December 1677. The town engaged him to "teach such children as should be sent to him to learn the rules of the Latin tongue."

The sons born in London were William, Joseph, and Robert. Children born in Watertown were Thomas, 8 June 1667; Benjamin, 17 August 1668; Elizabeth, 22 July 1670; Josiah, about 1672; and Edward. The Goddard line has been traced to John Goddard of Poulton, near Marlborough, Wilts. John lived from the reign of Richard II to Henry VI (1386-1434).

Susanna **Stone** and Edward **Goddard** had the following children:

+   151   i.   Edward[5] **Goddard Jr.** was born 4 May 1698.
     152   ii.   Susanna **Goddard**[150] was born in Watertown 25 February 1700 and married twice. (1) John **Drury**. (2) Joseph **Haven**.
     153   iii.   Simon **Goddard**[151] was born in Watertown 18 February 1702 and died 3 November 1758 in Shewsbury, Mass. at 56 years of age. He married Susannah **Cloyes** 2 November 1727.
+   154   iv.   Benjamin **Goddard** was born 15 August 1704.
     155   v.   Rev. David **Goddard**[152] was born in Watertown 26 September 1706 and died 19 January 1754 in Leicester, Worcester Co., Mass. at 47 years of age. He married Mercy **Stone** 19 August 1736. They were cousins. He was a Harvard College graduate class of 1731. Mercy,[153] daughter of David **Stone** and Mary **Rice**, was born in Watertown, 2 February 1713.
     156   vi.   Mary **Goddard**[154] was born in Boston, Mass. 4 June 1711 and died there 5 August 1711 at less than one year of age.
     157   vii.   Ebenezer **Goddard**[155] was born in Boston 18 November 1712 and died young.
+   158   viii.   Ebenezer **Goddard** was born 14 February 1714.
     159   ix.   William **Goddard**[156] was born in Framingham 10 December 1720 and died there seven days later.
     160   x.   Hepsibah **Goddard**[157] was born in Framingham and christened 8 May 1723.

35. **Ens. Jonathan[4] Stone** (Mary[3] **Whipple**, Elder John[2], Matthew[1])[158] was born in Watertown, Mass. 26 December 1677 and died 7 January 1754 at 76 years of age. He married three times. (1) **Ruth Eddy** in Watertown 15 November 1699. Ruth,[159] daughter of Samuel **Eddy** and Sarah **Mead**, was born in Watertown 3 November 1681 and died there 13 October 1702 at 20 years of age. Her death date is also given as 7 October 1702. (2) **Mary (__)**[160] 24 June 1720. (3) **Hepzibah Coolidge** in

Watertown 15 November 1720. Hepzibah,[161] daughter of Nathaniel **Coolidge** and Mary **Bright**, was born in Watertown 27 February 1680/81 and died 25 March 1763 at 82 years of age.

Ens. Jonathan **Stone** and Ruth **Eddy** had the following child:
+ 161   i.   Jonathan[5] **Stone**.

Ens. Jonathan **Stone**, and Hepzibah **Coolidge** had the following children, all born in Watertown:

     162   ii.   Hepzibah **Stone**[162] was born 9 August 1722 and died 14 April 1723 in Watertown at less than one year of age.

     163   iii.   Ann **Stone**[163] was born 9 August 1722 and died 16 June 1794 in Newton, Mass. at 71 years of age. She married capt. Jonas **Stone** in Watertown 14 November 1745. Jonas and Ann were cousins and had eight childen. Jonas[164] was the son of John **Stone** (1692-1765) and grandson of Ebenezer **Stone** (1662-1754)

+ 164   iv.   Moses **Stone** was born 16 December 1723.

36. **David**[4] **Stone** (Mary[3] **Whipple**, Elder John[2], Matthew[1])[165] was born in Watertown, Mass. 19 October 1692 and died there 7 October 1750 at 57 years of age. He went blind at age 24 and was sightless for the remaining 56 years of his life. Nevertheless he was able to work and care for his family. The family remained in Watertown. He married **Mary Rice** in Watertown 12 December 1710.

David **Stone** and Mary **Rice** had the following children, all born in Watertown:

     165   i.   Mercy[5] **Stone**[166] was born 2 February 1713 and married rev. David **Goddard** 19 August 1736. They were cousins. David,[167] son of Edward **Goddard** and Susanna **Stone**, was born in Watertown 26 September 1706 and died 19 January 1754 in Leicester, Worcester Co., Mass. at 47 years of age. He was a Harvard College graduate class of 1731.

     166   ii.   Mary **Stone**[168] was born 9 December 1715.

   ‾167   iii.   Ruth **Stone**[169] married Dea. Nathaniel **Stone**. They were second cousins. He was the son of Ebenezer (1686-1784) and grandson of Ebenezer **Stone** (1662-1754). The latter Ebenezer was an older brother to her father David.

37. **Mary**[4] **Goodhue** (Sarah[3] **Whipple**, Elder John[2], Matthew[1])[170] was born in Ipswich, Mass. abt 1664 and married **Bonus Norton** in Ipswich. Bonus,[171] son of William **Norton** and Lucy **Downing**, was born in Massachusetts abt 1657 and died 30 April 1718 in Hampton, N.H. at 60 years of age. Hampton is now Seabrook. Bonus' gravestone at the Seabrook cemetery is inscribed: "Here lyes ye body of Mr. Bonus Norton. Died Apriel 30, 1718 Aged 61 years."[172] William Norton of Ipswich, "in consideration of the parental care, love and affection which he beareth to his beloved son Bonus Norton of ye same towne . . . who has entered into a marriage estate . . . gives to said son land in Ipswich. Witnesses were Marjery Whipple and Marjery Goodhue 14 April 1694.[173] Bonus took the oath of fidelity in 1678, was living in Ipswich by 1691, and in Highham by 29 Septermber 1712 where his brother John was minister. He was the sole executor of his father's estate (dated 28 April and proved 15 May 1694) and was bequeathed the "whole estate . . . except legacies and to maintain testator's beloved wife . . ."

Bonus and his daughter Sarah received bequeaths from Mrs. Anne Bradstreet, widow and second wife of gov. Simon Bradstreet. Anne's Will dated 29 September 1712 was proved 24 April 1713. Bonus was referred to as "cousin."

Anne Bradstreet's maiden name was Downing. She was the sister of Bonus' mother, Lucy Downing. Lucy and Anne's parents were Emanuel Downing and Lucy Winthrop, the latter the sister of gov. John Winthrop. Gov. Bradstreet's first wife was Anne, daughter of gov. Dudley. At the time of her marriage to gov. Bradstreet, Anne Downing was the widow of capt. Joseph Gardiner.[174] Bonus' uncle was the famed rev. John Norton, one-time minister at Ipswich and successor to rev. John Cotton as minister of the First Church of Boston in 1655.

Mary **Goodhue** and Bonus **Norton** had the following children:

168	i.	Lucy[5] **Norton**[175] was born in Ipswich.
169	ii.	Mary **Norton**[176] was born in Ipswich and married Daniel **Moody** Jr. abt 24 June 1709.
170	iii.	William **Norton**[177] was born in Ipswich 9 May 1691.
171	iv.	Sarah **Norton**[178] was born in Hingham, Mass. and married Thomas **Waite** Jr. 26 November 1713.
172	v.	Joseph **Norton**[179] was born in Ipswich 17 November 1695.
+ 173	vi.	John **Norton**.
174	vii.	Samuel **Norton**[180] was born in Ipswich 12 September 1699.
+ 175	viii.	Elizabeth **Norton** was born 31 March 1703.
+ 176	ix.	Anna **Norton** was born 20 March 1707.

38. William[4] Goodhue Sr. (Sarah[3] **Whipple**, Elder John[2], Matthew[1])[181] was born in Ipswich, Mass. abt 1666 and died there 10 July 1722 at 56 years of age. He is buried in Section D Stone 103 in the Old North Churchyard. His grave is marked with a foot stone. He married **Mary Lowden** in Ipswich abt 1686. Mary[182] died 4 September 1729 in Ipswich at 63 years of age.

William **Goodhue** Sr. and Mary **Lowden** had the following children, all born in Ipswich:

177	i.	William[5] **Goodhue**[183] was born 17 September 1687 and married Abigail **Adams**.
178	ii.	Mary **Goodhue**[184] was born 3 August 1690 and died 10 April 1694 in Ipswich at 3 years of age.
179	iii.	John **Goodhue**[185] was born 28 August 1693 and died 10 April 1694 in Ipswich at less than one year of age.
+ 180	iv.	Sarah **Goodhue** was born 24 May 1695.
181	v.	Elizabeth **Goodhue**[186] was born 7 February 1697.
182	vi.	Hannah **Goodhue**[187] was born 27 March 1699.
183	vii.	Joseph **Goodhue**[188] was born in 1701 and married Dorothy **Haskell**. Dorothy,[189] daughter of Joseph **Haskell** and Mary **Graves**, was born in 1694 and died in 1724 at 30 years of age.
184	viii.	David **Goodhue**[190] was born 26 April 1703 and died 1 September 1713 in Ipswich at 10 years of age.
+ 185	ix.	Jonathan **Goodhue** was born 28 April 1705.
186	x.	Benjamin **Goodhue**[191] was born 11 July 1707.

39. Sarah[4] Goodhue (Sarah[3] **Whipple**, Elder John[2], Matthew[1])[192] was born in Ipswich abt 1668 and married **John Kimball** there 2 December 1692. John,[193] son of John **Kimball** and Mary **Bradstreet**, was born in Ipswich 16 May 1668 and died 6 May 1761 in Preston, New London Co. Conn. at 92 years of age. Sisters Sarah and Susanna Goodhue married brothers John and Moses Kimball.

Sarah **Goodhue** and John **Kimball** had the following children:

+ 187   i. John[5] **Kimball** was born in 1693.
   188   ii. Joseph **Kimball**[194] was born in 1693 and died in 1694 at one year of age.
   189   iii. Mary **Kimball**[195] was born in 1698 and married (__) **Lawrence**.
+ 190   iv. David **Kimball** was born in 1700.
   191   v. Nathan **Kimball**[196] was born in 1702.
+ 192   vi. Isaac **Kimball** was born 19 April 1705.
+ 193   vii. Jacob **Kimball** was born 12 October 1706.
+ 194   viii. Abigail **Kimball** was born 11 October 1709.

40. **Joseph**[4] **Goodhue** (Sarah[3] **Whipple**, Elder John2, Matthew[1])[197] was born in Ipswich in 1668 and died in 1768 at 100 years of age. He married **Sarah Smith**.

Joseph **Goodhue** and Sarah **Smith** had the following child:

+ 195   i. George[5] **Goodhue** was born in 1709.

41. **Marjory (Margery)**[4] **Goodhue** (Sarah[3] **Whipple**, Elder John[2], Matthew[1])[198] was born in Ipswich abt 1670 and died there after 1704. She married **Thomas Knowlton** in Watertown, Mass. 2 December 1692. Thomas,[199] son of John **Knowlton** and Deborah (__), was born in Ipswich 16 May 1662 and married (2) **Mary Coy** in Beverly, Mass. 6 June 1706. Thomas died 4 February 1749 at 86 years of age.

Marjory (Margery) **Goodhue** and Thomas **Knowlton** had the following children:

+ 196   i. Robert[5] **Knowlton** was born 7 September 1693.
+ 197   ii. Margery **Knowlton** was born 26 March 1695.
+ 198   iii. Joseph **Knowlton** was born 3 September 1697.

42. **John**[4] **Goodhue** (Sarah[3] **Whipple**, Elder John[2], Matthew[1])[200] was born in Ipswich abt 1674 and married **Sarah Sherwin** there.

John **Goodhue** and Sarah **Sherwin** had the following children:

   199   i. Sarah[5] **Goodhue**[201] was born in 1713.
   200   ii. Hannah **Goodhue**[202] was born in 1715.
   201   iii. John **Goodhue**[203] was born in 1718 and died young.
   202   iv. Elisabeth **Goodhue**[204] was born in 1719.
+ 203   v. John **Goodhue** was born in January 1721.

43. **Susanna**[4] **Goodhue** (Sarah[3] **Whipple**, Elder John[2], Matthew[1])[205] was born in Ipswich abt 1676 and married **Moses Kimball** there 28 March 1696. Moses,[206] son of John **Kimball** and Mary **Bradstreet**, was born in Ipswich in September 1672 and died there 23 January 1750 at 77 years of age. Moses was a tailor who also dealt in real estate. The Salem records are full of transactions involving him. On 28 March 1696, his father gave him, in consideration of his marriage to Susanna Goodhue, the right to pasture three cows and a house, orchard, and one acre of land on the road to Topsfield. His son Moses Jr. was granted administration of his estate 7 May 1750.

Susanna **Goodhue** and Moses **Kimball** had the following children, all born in Ipswich:

204	i.	Sarah[5] **Kimball**[207] was christened 26 February 1713 and married John **Leatherland** in Ipswich 8 January 1733.
+ 205	ii.	Aaron **Kimball**.
+ 206	iii.	Moses **Kimball** Jr. was born 6 January 1697.
207	iv.	Ebenezer **Kimball**[208] was born 20 March 1699 and died in Ipswich 3 December 1721 at 22 years of age.
208	v.	Susanna **Kimball**[209] was born 10 June 1701 and married William **Sutton** in Ipswich. The date of intent to marry was 8 Jan. 1725.
209	vi.	Ezekiel **Kimball**[210] was born in 1705 and drowned 30 December 1730 in Ipswich at 25 years of age.
210	vii.	Katherine **Kimball**[211] was born 30 August 1706 and married John **Pindar** in Ipswich 17 August 1729.[212]
211	viii.	Mary **Kimball**[213] married Daniel **Smith** in Ipswich 11 November 1729.
212	ix.	John **Kimball**[214] married Jane **Beady** and died 6 November 1766 at 56 years of age.
213	x.	Joseph **Kimball**[215] was born 11 September 1715 and died 30 December 1730 in Ipswich at 15 years of age.

FIFTH GENERATION

47. Moses[5] **Pillsbury** (Susanna[4] **Worth**, Susannah[3] **Whipple**, Elder John[2], Matthew[1]) was born in Newbury, Mass. 4 July 1672 and died 24 March 1738 at 65 years of age. He married **Abigail Rolfe** in Newbury 5 February 1697. Abigail, daughter of Ezra **Rolfe** and Abigail **Bond**, was born in Haverhill, Mass. 17 September 1677.[216]

Moses **Pillsbury** and Abigail **Rolfe** had the following children:

+ 214	i.	Moses[6] **Pillsbury** was born 16 January 1699.
+ 215	ii.	Abigail W. **Pillsbury** was born 9 August 1700.
216	iii.	Daniel **Pillsbury**[217] was born 22 August 1707 and married Mercy **Watson**.
217	iv.	Ezra **Pillsbury**[218] was born 6 April 1708 and died in 1797 at 89 years of age.
+ 218	v.	Susanna **Pillsbury** was born 12 June 1709.
219	vi.	Mary **Pillsbury**[219] was born 27 July 1711 and married three times. (1) John **Hills** in April 1728. (2) Enoch **Hale** after 1729. (3) David Emery after 1730.
220	vii.	Edmund **Pillsbury**[220] was born 6 April 1714 and died in 1738 at 24 years of age.
221	viii.	William **Pillsbury**[221] was born 15 December 1716 and died in 1788 at 71 years of age. He married Mary **Poor**.
222	ix.	Amos **Pillsbury**[222] was born in 1721 and died in 1766 at 45 years of age. He married Anna **Chase**.

51. Caleb[5] **Pillsbury** (Susanna[4] **Worth**, Susannah[3] **Whipple**, Elder John[2], Matthew[1])[223] was born in Newbury, Mass. 27 July 1681 and died between 24 November 1758 and 25 June 1759 in Amesbury, Mass. He was a cordwainer and married **Sarah Morse** in Newbury 11 February 1702/03. Sarah,[224] daughter of Benjamin **Morse** and Ruth **Sawyer**, was born in Newbury 19 June 1680.

Caleb **Pillsbury** and Sarah **Morse** had the following children, all born in

Newbury:

223   i. Benjamin[6] **Pillsbury**[225] was christened 9 April 1705 and married Sarah **Kelley** 15 January 1735.

224   ii. Susannah **Pillsbury**[226] married David **Walker** 27 September 1733.

225   iii. Esther **Pillsbury**[227] was christened 26 December 1714 and married Daniel Parker 14 October 1743.

226   iv. Hannah **Pillsbury**[228] was christened 26 December 1714 and was living in 1758.

227   v. Ellinor **Pillsbury**[229] was christened in October 1720.

229   vii. Judith **Pillsbury**[230] was born abt 1714 and married William **Harvey** 16 January 1745/46.

+ 230   viii. Caleb **Pillsbury** Jr. was born 26 January 1717.

54. Lt. Samuel[5] **Bucknam** (Judith (Jude)[4] **Worth**, Susannah[3] **Whipple**, Elder John[2], Matthew[1])[231] was born in Malden, Mass. in 1674 and died 3 July 1751 at age 77. He married **Deborah Millen** in Malden 22 September 1697. Deborah[232] died in 1751.

Lt. Samuel **Bucknam** and Deborah **Millen** had the following children:

231   i. Phebe[6] **Bucknam**[233].

232   ii. Abigail **Bucknam**[234].

233   iii. Lydia **Bucknam**[235].

234   iv. Mehitable **Bucknam**[236].

235   v. William **Bucknam**[237].

236   vi. John **Bucknam**[238].

237   vii. William **Bucknam**[239].

238   viii. Benjamin **Bucknam**.

239   ix. Debra **Bucknam**[240].

240   x. Samuel **Bucknam**[241] was born in Malden in 1699.

55. Judith[5] **Bucknam** (Judith (Jude)[4] **Worth**, Susannah[3] **Whipple**, Elder John[2], Matthew[1])[242] was born in Malden, Mass. 6 July 1676 and died there 1 December 1767 at 91 years of age. She married twice. (1) **Zachary Hill**[243] in Malden in 1700. He died before 1725. (2) **Thomas Blanchard** 21 February 1725.

Judith **Bucknam** and Zachary **Hill** had the following children:

+ 241   i. Abiah[6] **Hill**.

242   ii. Judith **Hill**[244] was born in Charlestown, Mass. 19 September 1700 and married Jabez **Wait**.

243   iii. Eunice **Hill**[245] was born in Malden 11 February 1706 and married Joseph **Porter**.

61. Martha[5] **Whipple** (Maj. John[4], Capt. John[3], Elder John[2], Matthew[1])[246] was born in Ipswich 1 April 1682 and married **Rev. Richard Brown** there 22 April 1703. Richard,[247] son of Richard **Brown** and Mary **Jaques**, was born in Newbury, Mass. 12 September 1675 and died 20 October 1732 in Reading, Mass. at 57 years of age. (Reading is now known as Wakefield.) He was graduated from Harvard in 1697, ordained in Reading 23 June 1712, and was pastor of the first church in Reading at the time of death.

Martha **Whipple** and Rev. Richard **Brown** had the following children:

244   i. Martha[6] **Brown**[248] was born in Newbury 19 February 1704 and died in

1784 in Newburyport, Mass. at 80 years of age. She married rev. Samuel **Wigglesworth** in Ipswich 12 March 1730. Samuel was the son of rev. Michael **Wigglesworth** and Martha **Mudge**.

245	ii.	John **Brown**[249] was born in Newbury 2 March 1706.
+ 246	iii.	William **Brown** was born 24 January 1707.
247	iv.	Mary **Brown**[250] was born in Newbury 31 December 1709 and married Benjamin **Crocker**.
+ 248	v.	Katherine **Brown** was born 15 August 1712.
249	vi.	Richard **Brown**[251] was born in Reading, Mass. 20 December 1716 and died there 2 January 1717 at less than one year of age.
250	vii.	Sarah **Brown**[252] was born in Reading 4 September 1718.
251	viii.	Elizabeth **Brown**[253] was born in Reading 9 October 1720.

62. Mary[5] **Whipple** (Maj. John[4], Capt. John[3], Elder John[2], Matthew[1])[254] was born in Ipswich 20 October 1684 and died there 25 October 1734 at 50 years of age. Mary inherited her father's house which had been her grandfather's and is known today as the John Whipple House (built abt 1655, see Appendix 1 for description of house, Whipple owners, and chain of title.). They lived in the house after she married **Benjamin Crocker** in Ipswich. The date of intent to marry was 12 December 1719. She is buried in Section C Stone 38 in the Old North Churchyard. Her grave is marked with a foot stone.

Benjamin was born abt 1692.[255] and died 9 April 1767 in Ipswich at 74 years of age. He is buried in Section C Stone 44 in the Old North Churchyard. His grave is marked with a foot stone. He married (2) **Elizabeth Williams** in Ipswich. (3) **Mrs. Experience Coolidge** in Ipswich. He was graduated from Harvard College, Class of 1713 and accepted three different appointments to teach in the Ipswich grammar school. (1) from 4 June 1717 to November 1719. (2) in 1746/47. (3) in 1759/60. He served as feoffee for the school from 1749 until 1776.[256] He was also a frequent preacher in Ipswich pulpits and a representative to the general court. He was chaplain of the second company of the fifth Massachusetts regiment in the summer of 1745 during the French and Indian War. The regiment participated in the capture of the fortress of Louisbourg in Cape Brenton, Canada by English and Colonial forces.[257]

Mary **Whipple** and Benjamin **Crocker** had the following children:

+ 252	i.	Dea. John[6] **Crocker**.
253	ii.	Mary **Crocker**[258] married Joseph **Gunnison** 10 September 1738. She was christened in Ipswich, 6 November 1720.

66. Susanna[5] **Whipple** (Maj. John[4], Capt. John[3], Elder John[2], Matthew[1])[259] was born in Ipswich 3 April 1696 and died 22 October 1779 in Kittery, Maine at 83 years of age. She married **Rev. John Rogers** in Ipswich. Their date of intent to marry was 6 September 1718. John,[260] son of rev. John **Rogers** and Martha **Whittingham**, was born in Ipswich abt 1692 and died there in 1773 at 81 years of age of palsy. He was graduated from Harvard College in 1711 and was the first settled minister at Eliot, Maine.

Susanna **Whipple** and Rev. John **Rogers** had the following children:

+ 254	i.	Rev. John[6] **Rogers** was born 7 August 1719.
255	ii.	Capt. Timothy **Rogers**[261] was born in Kittery 8 September 1721 and died 22 June 1766 in Gloucester, Mass. at 44 years of age. He married

twice. (1) Lucy (__)[262] who was born abt 1726 and died 21 April 1759 at 32 years of age. (2) Mrs Esther (____) **Goldthwaite**[263] in Gloucester 4 July 1765. Timothy was a merchant at Gloucester.

256   iii.   William **Rogers**[264] was born in October 1723 and died 5 June 1747 at 23 years of age.

257   iv.   Katherine **Rogers**[265] was born in Eliot 2 December 1725 and died 17 March 1750 at 24 years of age. She married William **Leighton**, Jr.

258   v.   Nathaniel **Rogers**[266] was born in Eliot 27 April 1728 and died there 10 August 1728 at less than four months of age. The day may have been 7 August.

259   vi.   Nathaniel **Rogers**[267] was born in Eliot 2 August 1729 and died 25 March 1803 at 73 years of age. He was a farmer in Kittery. His marriage banns with Abigail **Hammond** were published 30 April 1756. Abigail died in December 1809 in her 74th year.

260   vii.   Martha **Rogers**[268] was born in Eliot 25 October 1734 an died 9 Nov. 1788 at 54 years of age. She married John **Hill** of Kittery.

+ 261   viii.   Daniel **Rogers** Esq. was born 25 October 1734.

262   ix.   Mary **Rogers**[269] was born in Kittery 4 June 1739 and died in June 1819 at 80 years of age. Her marriage banns with Thomas **Hammond** were published in Eliot 20 March 1756.

69. **Capt. John**[5] **Whipple** (Maj. Matthew[4], Capt. John[3], Elder John[2], Matthew[1])[270] was born in Ipswich 22 July 1689 and died there 9 February 1781 at 91 years of age. His Will was probated in Essex Co. 6 March 1781. He was a farmer in Kittery, Maine. He married **Hannah Whipple** in Ipswich 7 June 1714. Hannah,[271] daughter of Capt. John **Whipple** and Hannah (__), was born in Ipswich 30 June 1692 and died there 24 January 1758 at 65 years of age.

John and Hannah Whipple were third cousins. Hannah's descent is from Matthew Whipple of Ipswich: Matthew[1,] Lt. John [2], and John[3]. John and Hannah's children and succeeding generations claim double descent from Matthew Whipple (abt 1560-1619), Clothier, of Bocking, England.

Capt. John **Whipple** and Hannah **Whipple** had the following children, all born in Ipswich:

+ 263   i.   Capt. John[6] **Whipple** was born 25 June 1717.
+ 264   ii.   Dea. Nathaniel **Whipple** was born 7 October 1721.
265   iii.   William **Whipple**[272] was born 15 December 1727 and died in Ipswich 29 June 1784 at 56 years of age.

72. **Capt. William**[5] **Whipple** (Maj. Matthew[4], Capt. John[3], Elder John[2], Matthew[1])[273] was born in Ipswich, Mass. 28 February 1696 and died 7 August 1751 in Kittery, Maine at 55 years of age. He is buried at Kittery Point Cemetery. Inscription on his gravestone: "Capt William Whipple, died Aug 7th 1751." He married **Mary Cutt** in Kittery 14 May 1722. William and his half-brother rev. Joseph Whipple (see p. G 10) married sisters, Mary and Elizabeth Cutt.

Mary,[274] daughter of Robert **Cutt** II and Dorcas **Hammond**, was born in Kittery abt 1699 and died 28 February 1783 in Portsmouth, N.H. at 83 years of age. She is buried in Portsmouth's North Cemetery in a grave near the tomb of her son, gen. William Whipple. Her parents are buried in Kittery Point Cemetery. The inscription on her father's gravestone: "Robert Cutt died Sept ye 24th 1735 aged 62 years;" her mother's gravestone: "Dorcas Cutt wife of Robert Cutt died Nov

17th 1757 in the 83rd year of her age."

William's Will written in Kittery 21 June 1751 mentioned wife Mary, daughter Mary Traill, sons William, Robert, and Joseph. He named his half-brother Joseph Whipple of Hampton Falls, N.H. as sole executor. The Will was probated 3 September 1751.

Capt. William **Whipple** and Mary **Cutt** had the following children, all born in Kittery:

+ 266   i.   Mary[6] **Whipple** was born 13 January 1728.
+ 267   ii.   Gen. William **Whipple** was born 14 January 1730/31.
   268   iii.   Hannah **Whipple**[275] was born 15 February 1735 and died in May 1805 in Portsmouth at 70 years of age and is buried in the Old North Cemetery. She married Dr. Joshua **Brackett** in Kittery. The intent to marry was recorded 3 March 1760. Rev. Benjamin Stevens performed the ceremony. Joshua, son of Capt. John **Brackett** and Elizabeth **Pickering**, was born in Greenland, N.H. 5 May 1733 and died 17 July 1802 in Portsmouth at 69 years of age.

Hannah had a great interest in natural philosophy and botany and her garden included choice and rare shrubs, plants and fruits which were a help to her husband's practice.[276] The following advertisement appeared in the 23 May 1760 *New Hampshire Gazette*: "Dr. Thomson's famous Sovereign Spirit of Venice Treacle, Chymucally prepared by Dr. Joshua Brackett of Portsmouth, (Purchased of the Heirs of Mr. Clifton) and no other Person, and sold by him, which certainly cures the colick, Spring and Autumnal Fevers; is of excellent Use in surfeits, Small Pox, and Measles, and to such as go abroad early; and of particular Use to those who are at Sea; and a very great Preservative against all contagious Distempers, &c." In later years his advertisements show a stock swelled by importations such as "Lockyer's and Anderson's Pills, James's Powders, Stoughton Elexir, Jesuits Drops, Turlington's Balsam, smelling Bottels, Nipple Pipes and Shells, Court Plaster, Teeth Powder, &c. Sweet Oil, by the Flask, Linseed Oil, Currants, Almonds, Raisins and Spices of all sorts, Coffee, best Hyson and Bohea-Tea, Salt Petre, Indigo, Glue, Varnish, Brimstone, Allum, &c &c." Timothy Alden in *A Collection of American Epitaphs*, I. (New York, 1814) praised his practice as follows: "He was extremely attentive to his patients, and spared no pains to investigate the cause and nature of their maladies, and to afford relief. While a happy general success attended his professional ministrations, his tenderness and sympathy with the sons and daughters of disease and distress, were striking traits in his character.

"In his professional labors, he was peculiarly kind to the poor, and never made a charge, where he had reason to think the payment would occasion the smallest embarrassment." He was a strong advocate of smallpox inoculation and joined in establishing a hospital for that purpose, even continuing the practice after the province council forbade inoculation. He had to give bond of £100 not to continue. When he defiantly inoculated his wife he had great difficulty in getting the council to permit her to return from the pesthouse. He served in the provincial congress and the Committee of Safety in 1775 and became judge of the New Hampshire admiralty court 4 July 1776. He encouraged the war effort by supplying medicines to the army, maintaining an inoculation hospital, encouraging privateers, and urging a state navy. He also rounded up votes in the general assembly to have the state finance Jeremy Belknap's history of New Hampshire. His reputation spread and he was elected an honorary member of the Massachusetts Medical Society and was a founder of the New Hampshire Medical Society in 1791, serving as both its librarian and president. Failing health compelled him to resign the presidency in 1799. He died 17 July 1802 and by Will left a bequest to endow a professorship of Natural History at Harvard. The money was to be paid at the death of his widow. Hannah, however, did not wait and authorized the payment adding an additional sum of her own. They left no children. When she died in May 1805 she was almost as widely mourned as he. He had kept a "Register of events" which disappeared about the middle of the nineteenth century.[277]

269   iv.   Robert Cutt **Whipple**[278] was born 6 April 1736 and died unmarried 4 May 1761 in Portsmouth at 25 years of age. He is buried at Kittery Point Cemetery. Inscription on his gravestone: "Robert Cutt Whipple died May 4th 1735 aged 25."

270   v.   Col. Joseph **Whipple**[279] was born 14 February 1737/38 and died 30 January 1816 in Portsmouth at 77 years of age. He married Hannah **Billings** in Kittery. The date of intent to marry was 9 October 1762. Joseph and Hannah are buried near his older brother William in the Old North Cemetery. Hannah,[280] daughter of John **Billings** and Sarah **Endicott**, was born in Boston, Mass. 16 November 1735 and died 30 January 1811 in Portsmouth at 75 years of age. Her earliest antecedents in New England go back to Roger Billings (son of Roger Billings) born at Taunton, England about 1618 and died at Dorchester, Mass 15 Nov. 1683. Her father was a tailor in Boston. Hannah and her sister Mary received "undivided property of Tyngs Alley and Cornhill, Boston" from his estate. Mary later assigned her interest to Hannah, and Joseph sold it to Daniel Bigelow of Boston. The deed was signed 2 January 1784 by Joseph, Hannah, and others.

Joseph's business education was learned in the counting house of Nathaniel Carter of Newburyport. He joined his older brothers William and Robert and opened a mercantile business in Portsmouth about 1759. This was a time of rapid expansion of Piscataqua ports with an average of 103 ship arrivals and 155 departures annually and the firm flourished.

Joseph left family, friends, social life, civilization, and a good business in 1773 to settle on the colony's frontier where he became a successful farmer and established a variety of industries. He was the first white man to make a home in the locality of Dartmouth where he built a log cabin on the Siwooganock river with views of three mountains — Washington, Jefferson, and Adams. He eventually replaced the cabin with a 2-story mansion and sold 50-acre farms to his laborers whom he regarded as part of his family for leaving the comforts of life near the seaboard. He accepted payment for the 50-acre parcels in the form of crops from their newly cleared fields.

The Dartmouth area was granted to 70 persons in June 1772 and between 17 February 1774 and 11 February 1775, Joseph purchased 57 of those rights and owned the entire town site by 9 November 1796. He also acquired land in Bretton Woods, Bethlehem, Conway, Colebrook, Columbia, Strafford, and other towns and eventually owned thousands of acres — 25,000 acres in Jefferson alone. He built a grist and a saw mill near his home and other mills near Riverton. In December 1796 he petitioned the legislature to form a town which he named Jefferson after Thomas Jefferson. Its first town meeting was in March 1798 with 20 voters and taxpayers.

He led the movement for schools and roads in the area and represented Coos county and parts of Grafton and Carroll counties in the legislature serving in 1776, '77, '78, '82, '83, '85, where he voted against imprisonment for debt, to give prisoners better care, supported education and roads, and worked to bring new industry to Portsmouth. He was justice of the peace and of the quorum for Grafton county in 1779 and 1784 and became colonel of the 25th regiment of militia in 1784.

Dr. Jeremy Belknap, New Hampshire historian, with a party of eight including rev. Manassah Cutler of Ipswich, Mass. and rev. Daniel Little of Kennebunk, Mass. set out from Whipple's home 24 July 1784 for an ascent of Mt. Washington. Only Whipple, Belknap, and Little outlasted the bad weather and reached the summit where they engraved the initials N.H. on the highest rock and left a lead plate on which they had engraved their names. Many of the descriptions of the White Mountains in Belknap's history are believed to have come from this trip.

Joseph maintained his Portsmouth residence and was appointed impost officer at Portsmouth 4 March 1786, serving until 1789. That year president George Washington named him collector of the port where he remained until replaced by president John Adams for actively supporting Jefferson for president. He was renamed to the post 5 April 1801 following Jefferson's election. His job as collector was to collect duties on all goods imported by land or water, search for concealed goods, seize illegally imported goods, and prevent every kind of fraud attempted on the revenue. In describing his job he said he "had to contend with the adverse humor of every anti-revenue, anti-patriotic, and selfish person in the state who imported goods."[281]

Col. Joseph Whipple *(1737-1816) of Portsmouth, N.H. by Charles St. Mémin, a popular artist famous for his profile bust of some of America's best-known personalities. Joseph was a younger brother and business partner of Gen. William Whipple who signed the Declaration of Independence on behalf of New Hampshire. Gift of Lila Maria (Mrs. H.P. Garnett of York Harbor, Maine, to the National Society of the Colonial Dames of America in the State of New Hampshire for the Portsmouth Moffatt-Ladd House collecton.*

Col. Joseph Whipple's *home in Portsmouth, N.H. Built about 1760 it is one of the finest in the Piscataqua area. It was moved to 599 Middle Street in 1969 and is rented as a multiplex.*

Levi W. Dodge, writing in the *Granite Monthy* (date unknown) described Whipple as "a man of large wealth and influence living in a baronial style who employed many on his extensive holdings and kept a dozen horses for his own use and pleasure." His Dartmouth house was a large, square structure, with wings, two stories high, built to resist Indians or other foes. Its high windows were heavily shuttered and barred and there were loop-holes for rifles in the upper story. Dodge wrote the upper rooms contained valuable property such as family plate, silks, and broadcloth and a wealth of Spanish coin, "for the colonel was once a merchant . . . and his trade with the Indies had brought him great riches." The cellar was stocked with choice burgundies, maderias, and good West India rum.

The New Hampshire adjutant-general's report (305) for 1868 describes how Whipple came near falling a victim of British designs and Indian cunning in August 1781 when a party of Indians directed by the British attacked settlements in the area. Rev. B.G. Wiley reported his capture and escape in detail.[282]

His Portsmouth house, built about 1760, was one of the finest in the Piscataqua area. It and the Moffatt-Ladd house where his brother William lived, are the sole colonial examples in the area to devote nearly a quarter of the floor plan to the stair hall. He acquired it in 1766 and owned it until his death. Joseph's house was altered several times over the years and in 1969 was moved to 599 Middle Street where today it is rented as a multiplex.[283]

While collector of the port of Portsmouth in 1796, Joseph received a letter from president George Washington via secretary of treasury Oliver Wolcott asking him to locate and return Martha Washington's run-away slave attendant, Ona Maria Judge who was believed to be in Portsmouth.

Ona had been one of Martha's attendants since age 10 and was a particular favorite of the first lady. Among her skills was sewing and Martha considered her "a perfect mistress of her needle." Her escape occurred when the Washington family was packing to leave Philadelphia for Mount Vernon. After completing her personal packing she had it delivered to some black friends in Philadelphia and left Washington's house when the family was eating dinner. She retrieved her packed belongings and boarded the sloop *Nancy* which was sailing that night for Portsmouth, arriving about 1 June. She was later seen on the streets of Portsmouth by Elizabeth Langdon[284] who would have recognized her from being "in the chamber of Miss Curtis . . . when Mrs. Washington call[ed] on girls there."

The president's letter, dated 1 September 1796, included Ona's name and description and speculated that some "Seducer (for she is simple and unoffensive herself)" had enticed her to leave. He expressed the hope that she could be returned "without a fuss." He said he was sorry to put Joseph to the trouble "on such a trifling occasion, but the ingratitude of the girl, who was brought up and treated more like a child than a servant, ought not to escape with impunity if it can be avoided."

Joseph wrote Wolcott 10 September that he had confirmed that Ona was in Portsmouth and in a second letter dated 10 November, that he had personally interviewed Ona and concluded she had not been "decoyed away" but " a thirst for complete freedom which she was informed would take place on her arrival here had been her only motive for absconding."

Joseph expressed "much satisfaction" that Ona proclaimed great affection and reverence for the Washingtons and that she would willing return and serve them with "fidelity" during the rest of their lives if she could be freed upon their death but would rather suffer death than return to slavery and maybe eventually sold or given to someone else. Joseph said he believed her proposal "would be pleasing to the president and his lady" and made arrangements for her to sail to Philadelphia that evening. Contrary winds delayed the sailing and the next day some of Ona's friends talked her out of returning.

Joseph's letter also reported that many slaves from the southern states came to Massachusetts, fewer to New Hampshire, considering those states as an asylum because opinion there favored universal freedom and made it difficult to get slaves back to their masters. He said if it were necessary to return Ona involuntarily the legal way to proceed would be for an officer of the president's household to request the attorney of the United States in New Hampshire to have her returned according to methods authorized by the Constitution.

President Washington responded to Joseph's letter of 4 October on 28 November refusing Ona's terms for returning voluntarily. He argued that however disposed he might be to a gradual abolition, "or even an entire emancipation," it would neither "be politic or just to reward unfaithfulness with a premature preference; and thereby discontent before the minds of all her fellow-servants who by their steady attachments are far more deserving than herself of favor." The president said if Ona would return "without using compulsory means" she would be forgiven by her Mistress. If not, he asked Joseph to place her on board a vessel bound for Alexandria or the Federal City (Washington, D.C.) with instructions she was to be delivered to his manager at Mt. Vernon or to his secretary Tobias Lear at Alexandria. If Ona had "adherents" or "well disposed citizens" who might become upset if she were returned unwillingly and thereby "excite a mob or riot" he would forego her services altogether." The president ignored Joseph's suggestion that Ona's return be negotiated through the courts as if she had the rights of a United States citizen.

Joseph sent his last letter to president Washington 22 Dec. 1796. He reported that Ona was living with "a Free-Negro" and was "published for marriage, agreeable to our laws, to a Mulatto." He told the president that he wished "for the good of society" that some means could be adopted to abolish slavery on a gradual basis. While there was then no vessel bound for Alexandria he said when one became available, he would execute the president's request and send Ona to Alexandria if it could be done "without disagreeable consequences as I may think repugnant to your wishes."

Joseph never did place Ona on a ship bound for Alexandria making one wonder how eager he was to accommodate the president. The vital records of Greenland, N.H. include this notation by Thomas Philbrook, town clerk, dated 18 January 1797: "This may certify that Mr. John Staines and Miss Oney Judge was published in this town." Their marriage was performed by Dr. Samuel Haven in Portsmouth and announced in the 14 January *Gazette*. The Washingtons are reported to have subsequently attempted to induce Ona to return to them without success. The Stainesses settled in Portsmouth and had two daughters: Eliza, born in 1797, and Nancy, probably in 1802.[285]

Joseph prepared a genealogy on his Cutt family ancestors. See endnote 9 in Chapter 6 on General William Whipple for information from Joseph's manuscript which also includes information on his Hoels ancestors and Francis Champernon, nephew of Sir Ferdinando Gorges, founder of Maine, who married into the Cutt family. Joseph lived his last five years as a widower.

76. **Martha**[5] **Whipple** (Maj. Matthew[4], Capt. John[3], Elder John[2], Matthew[1])[286] was born in Ipswich, Mass. 2 July 1711 and married **Ebenezer Hartshorn** in Concord, Mass. before 1736. Ebenezer[287] was born in Charlestown, Mass. 29 July 1712/13 and died 5 January 1772 in Concord at 58 years of age.

Martha **Whipple** and Ebenezer **Hartshorn** had the following children, all born in Concord:

271	i.	John Denison[6] **Hartshorn**[288] was born 3 July 1736.
272	ii.	Martha **Hartshorn**[289] was born 30 May 1738 and died 12 October 1811 in Concord at 73 years of age.
273	iii.	Ebenezer **Hartshorn**[290] was born 16 April 1741[291] and married Eunice **Hapgood** in Shrewsbury, Worcester Co., Mass. 20 April 1767.
274	iv.	Elizabeth **Hartshorn**[292] was born 16 May 1745 and married John **Remington** in Concord 9 November 1769.

77. **Susannah**[5] **Lane** (Susanna[4] **Whipple**, Capt. John[3], Elder John[2], Matthew[1])[293] was born in Billerica, Mass. 24 January 1682/83 and died there 2 September 1746 at 63 years of age. She married **Nathaniel Page Jr.** in Billerica 6 November 1701. Nathaniel,[294] son of Nathaniel **Page** and Joanna (__), was born abt 1679. He married (2) **Mary Grimes** in Billerica 23 June 1748.

Susannah **Lane** and Nathaniel **Page** Jr. had the following children, all born in Billerica:

+ 275	i.	Nathaniel[6] **Page** was born 4 September 1702.
276	ii.	John **Page**[295] was born 11 October 1704.
277	iii.	Christopher **Page**[296] was born 16 July 1707 and died 11 November 1786 in Billerica at 79 years of age. He married Susanna **Weber** in Billerica 2 February 1742/43. Susanna[297] was born about 1710 and died 20 July 1792 in Billerica at 82 years of age.
278	iv.	Susanna **Page**[298] was born 29 April 1711 and married Samuel Bridge of Lexington, Mass.
279	v.	Joanna **Page**[299] was born 29 October 1714 and married Josiah **Fassett**,[300] son of Josiah **Fassett**. He was born in Billerica 11 July 1714.

78. **Mary**[5] **Lane** (Susanna[4] **Whipple**, Capt. John[3], Elder John[2], Matthew[1])[301] was born in Billerica, Mass. 15 May 1686 and died 27 March 1783 in Bedford, Mass. at 96 years of age. She married **John Whitmore** in Billerica before 1707. John[302] was born in Medford, Mass. 27 August 1683 and died 26 March 1753 at 69 years of age.

Mary **Lane** and John **Whitmore** had the following children:

280	i.	Mary[6] **Whitmore**[303] was born 17 July 1707.
281	ii.	Susanna **Whitmore**[304] was born 25 November 1708.
282	iii.	John **Whitmore**[305] was born 15 April 1711 and died 5 October 1748 at 37 years of age. He married Martha **Lane**.
+ 283	iv.	Francis **Whitmore** was born 4 October 1714.
284	v.	Martha **Whitmore**[306] was born 22 April 1716.
285	vi.	William H. **Whitmore**[307] was born 19 December 1725 and died 10 March 1760 at 34 years of age. He married Mary **Brooks** 1 October 1747.

80. **Job**[5] **Lane** (Susanna[4] **Whipple**, Capt. John[3], Elder John[2], Matthew[1])[308] was born in Billerica, Mass. 22 June 1689 and died 9 August 1762 in Bedford, Mass. at 73 years of age. Job was a deacon, a lieutenant of troops, and acted as Indian scout for Billerica where he held many town offices. He married **Martha Ruggles** in Roxbury, Mass. 17 December 1713. Martha[309] was born in Bedford 1 February 1691 and died 14 September 1740 in Billerica at 49 years of age.

Job **Lane** and Martha **Ruggles** had the following children:

286	i.	Martha[6] **Lane**[310] was born in Billerica 22 June 1716 and married (_) **Adams**.
287	ii.	Job **Lane**[311] was born in Billerica 27 September 1718.
+ 288	iii.	John **Lane** was born 2 October 1720.
+ 289	iv.	Timothy **Lane** was born 10 July 1722.
+ 290	v.	Mary **Lane** was born 24 February 1724/25.
291	vi.	Whipple **Lane**[312] was born in Billerica 15 September 1727 and died there 4 October 1728 at one year of age.
292	vii.	Benjamin **Lane**[313] was born in Billerica 29 August 1729.
293	viii.	Lucy **Lane**[314] was born in Billerica 3 May 1732 and married (_) **Stearns** in Billerica.
294	ix.	Hannah **Lane**[315] was born in Bedford, Mass. 22 September 1733 and died there 27 December 1733 at less three months of age.
295	x.	Sarah **Lane**[316] was born in Bedford 22 September 1733 and died there 7 October 1733 at less than one month of age.
296	xi.	Anna **Lane**[317] was born in Bedford in 1735 and died there 8 September 1735 at less than one year of age.

81. **John**[5] **Lane** (Susanna[4] **Whipple**, Capt. John[3], Elder John[2], Matthew[1])[318] was born in Billerica, Mass. 20 October 1691and married twice. (1) **Katherine Whiting** in Billerica 31 December 1714. Katherine,[319] daughter of Samuel **Whiting**, was born in Billerica in 1691 and died there 1 April 1731 at 39 years of age. (2) **Hannah Abbott** in Billerica.

John **Lane** and Katherine **Whiting** had the following children, all born in Billerica :

297	i.	Elizabeth[6] **Lane**[320] was born 14 October 1716.
298	ii.	Katharine **Lane**[321] was born 27 June 1717.
299	iii.	Susanna **Lane**[322] was born 8 April 1720.
+ 300	iv.	John **Lane** was born 1 July 1722.

| 301 | v. | Matthew **Lane**[323] was born 10 July 1724. |
| 302 | vi. | Samuel **Lane**[324] was born 15 April 1727 and died 1 April 1734 in Billerica at 6 years of age. |

John **Lane** and Hannah **Abbott** had the following children:

303	vii.	Hannah **Lane**[325] was born 19 May 1734 and died 2 June 1741 in Billerica at 7 years of age.
304	viii.	Samuel **Lane**[326] was born 21 October 1737.
305	ix.	Matthew **Lane**[327] was born 5 August 1741.

83. James⁵ Lane (Susanna⁴ **Whipple**, Capt. John³, Elder John², Matthew¹)[328] was born in Billerica 12 August 1696 and died there 11 April 1783 at 86 years of age. His Will was proved 14 May 1783. He married twice. (1) **Martha Minot** in Billerica 30 April 1719. The date may have been 19 January. Martha,[329] daughter of Dr. James **Minot** and Rebecca **Wheeler**, was born in Concord, Mass. 30 April 1699 and died 3 July 1762 in Billerica at 63 years of age. (2) **Charity Wellington**[330] in Billerica. She died 16 December 1764 in Billerica.

James **Lane** and Martha **Minot** had the following children, all born in Billerica:

	306	i.	Martha⁶ **Lane**[331] was born 17 March 1721/22.
+	307	ii.	Rebecca **Lane** was born 29 October 1723.
	308	iii.	James **Lane**[332] was born 8 March 1725/26 and died 24 January 1799 in Bedford, Mass. at 72 years of age.
	309	iv.	Marcy **Lane**[333] was born 24 December 1730 and died 4 March 1736/37 in Billerica at 6 years of age.
	310	v.	David **Lane**[334] was born 17 March 1733/34 and died 29 December 1756 in Billerica at 22 years of age.
	311	vi.	Love **Lane**[335] was born 13 August 1735.
	312	vii.	Susanna **Lane**[336] was born 18 July 1735 and died 24 February 1749/50 in Billerica at 13 years of age.
+	313	viii.	Samuel **Lane** was born 11 July 1737.

85. Mary⁵ Whipple (Joseph⁴, Capt. John³, Elder John², Matthew¹)[337] was born in Ipswich 15 February 1699 and died in March 1790 in Cambridge, Mass. at 91 years of age. She married twice. (1) **Maj. Symonds Epes** in Ipswich in 1715. The intent to marry was published 26 March 1715. Mary was much younger than Symonds. It is possible they went to Portsmouth, N.H. to get married. Symonds[338] was born abt 1662 and died 30 August 1741 in Ipswich at 79 years of age. (2) **Rev. Edward Holyoke** after 1741. He was president of Harvard College.

Mary **Whipple** and Maj. Symonds **Epes** had the following children:

| 314 | i. | Samuel⁶ **Epes**[339]. |
| 315 | ii. | Elizabeth **Epes**[340]. |

93. Sarah⁵ Stone (Deacon Simon⁴, Mary³ **Whipple**, Elder John², Matthew¹)[341] was born in Groton, Mass. abt 1684 and married **Stephen Farr**[342] there 28 September 1708. He was from Stowe, Mass. and was the son of Stephen **Farr** and Mary **Taylor**.

Sarah **Stone** and Stephen **Farr** had the following children, all born in Stow:

316	i.	Jemina⁶ **Farr**[343] was born 29 November 1713.
317	ii.	Joseph **Farr**[344] was born 11 April 1718.
318	iii.	Susanna **Farr**[345] was born 6 September 1724.

319   iv. Sarah **Farr**[346] was born 19 January 1734/35.

94. Simon[5] **Stone** (Deacon Simon[4], Mary[3] **Whipple**, Elder John[2], Matthew[1])[347] was born in Groton, Mass. 1 August 1686 and married twice. (1) **Elizabeth Lawrence** who married (2) **Micah Stone**. (2) **Sarah Farnsworth** in 1712.

Simon **Stone** and Elizabeth **Lawrence** had the following child:
+   320   i. Micah[6] **Stone**.

Simon **Stone** and Sarah **Farnsworth** had the following child:
+   321   ii. Amos **Stone** was born 9 September 1729.

95. Abigail[5] **Stone** (Deacon Simon[4], Mary[3] **Whipple**, Elder John[2], Matthew[1])[348] was born in Groton, Mass. in 1691 and died 29 September 1757 in Massachusetts at 66 years of age. She married **Nathaniel Holden** in Massachusetts 11 December 1718. Nathaniel[349] was born in Massachusetts abt 1691 and died 15 May 1740 in Groton at 48 years of age.

Abigail **Stone** and Nathaniel **Holden** had the following child:
+   322   i. Capt. Asa[6] **Holden** was born 23 August 1732.

96. Mary[5] **Stone** (Deacon Simon[4], Mary[3] **Whipple**, Elder John[2], Matthew[1])[350] was born in Groton, Mass. about 1692 and died 17 October 1766 in Stowe, Mass. at 74 years of age. She married **Abraham Whitney**. Abraham[351] was born 29 May 1692 and died 15 September 1778 in Stowe at 86 years of age.

Mary **Stone** and Abraham **Whitney** had the following child:
+   323   i. Mary[6] **Whitney** was born 28 October 1729.

97. Susanna[5] **Stone** (Deacon Simon[4], Mary[3] **Whipple**, Elder John[2], Matthew[1])[352] was born in Groton, Mass. 23 October 1694 and died 26 July 1774 at 79 years of age. She married **Jacob Chamberlain** in 1718/19. Jacob,[353] the son of Jacob **Chamerlain** and Experience **French**, was born 19 February 1691/92 and died 28 July 1771 at 79 years of age. He was from Newton, Mass.

Susanna **Stone** and Jacob **Chamberlain** had the following child:
+   324   i. Josiah[6] **Chamberlain** was born 13 November 1721.

105. James[5] **Stone** (John[4], Mary[3] **Whipple**, Elder John[2], Matthew[1])[354] was born in Groton, Mass. 23 January 1701 and died 27 February 1783 at 82 years of age. He married **Mary Farwell** in Groton 28 December 1726. Mary,[355] daughter of Joseph **Farwell** and Hannah (_), was born in Groton. James and John Stone married sisters Mary and Elizabeth Farwell of Groton.

James **Stone** and Mary **Farwell** had the following child:
+   325   i. Lt. James[6] **Stone** was born in 1727.

109. Adams[5] **Stone** (Dea. Matthew[4], Mary[3] **Whipple**, Elder John[2], Matthew[1])[356] was born in Massachusetts and married **Sarah Wight** 22 May 1717. They lived in Sudbury, Mass. where he was a deacon

Adams **Stone** and Sarah **Wight** had the following children, all born in Sudbury:
326   i. Benjamin[6] **Stone**[357] was born 20 February 1718/19 and married Beulah **Fiske**. Beulah[358] was the daughter of Jonathan **Fiske**.

+ 327   ii.   Bathsheba **Stone** was born 1 December 1721.
  328   iii. Elizabeth **Stone**[359] was born 2 April 1723 and married Nathaniel **Rice** 23 February 1741.
  329   iv.   Isaac **Stone**[360] was born 18 February 1736/37 and died 2 April 1798 in Massachusetts at 62 years of age. He married Sarah **Moulton** in Massachusett, about 1757.

110. Ebenezer[5] **Stone** (Ebenezer[4], Mary[3] **Whipple**, Elder John[2], Matthew[1])[361] was born in Cambridge Village, Mass. 21 December 1686 and died 1 February 1784 at 97 years of age. He married **Sarah Bond** 28 January 1712/13. Sarah,[362] daughter of John **Bond** and Hannah **Coolidge**, was born in Watertown, Mass. 25 August 1688 and died there 11 May 1754 at 65 years of age.

Ebenezer **Stone** and Sarah **Bond** had the following children:
+ 330   i.   Hannah[6] **Stone**.
+ 331   ii.   Margaret **Stone** was born 14 October 1728.

112. Samuel[5] **Stone** (Ebenezer[4], Mary[3] **Whipple**, Elder John[2], Matthew[1])[363] was born in Newton, Mass. 1 July 1690 and died 30 August 1726 at 36 years of age. He married **Hannah Searle** 21 May 1716. Hannah[364] was born in Roxbury, Mass. 9 April 1696 and died 4 November 1724 at 28 years of age.

Samuel **Stone** and Hannah **Searle** had the following child:
+ 332   i.   Mary[6] **Stone** was born 23 January 1718/19.

115. Mindwell[5] **Stone** (Ebenezer[4], Mary[3] **Whipple**, Elder John[2], Matthew[1])[365] was born in Cambridge Village, Mass. 26 June 1696 and died in 1744 at 48 years of age. She married **Ebenezer Woodward**. Ebenezer, son of John **Woodward** and Sarah **Bancraft**, was born in 1690 and died in 1770 at 80 years of age. The family lived in Newton, Mass.

Mindwell **Stone** and Ebenezer **Woodward** had the following children, all born in Newton:
  333   i.   Mindwell[6] **Woodward**[366] was born 26 February 1716/17.
  334   ii.   Eleanor **Woodward**[367] was born 20 June 1720.
  335   iii. Rev. Samuel **Woodward**[368] was born 1 February 1726/27 and died 5 October 1782 in Weston, Mass. at 55 years of age. He was graduated with the Harvard class of 1748 and was ordained minister of the church in Weston 25 Sept. 1751 where he served until his death.
  336   iv.   John **Woodward**[369] was born 4 February 1726/27.
+ 337   v.   Mary **Woodward** was born 28 February 1732/33.

122. Lydia Abiah[5] **Starr** (Mary[4] **Stone**, Mary[3] **Whipple**, Elder John[2], Matthew[1])[370] was born in Watertown, Mass. 18 February 1687/88 and died 4 March 1751 in Thompson, Windham Co. Conn. at 64 years of age. She married **Jonathan Eaton** in Dedham, Mass. 30 November 1705. Jonathan,[371] son of John **Eaton** and Alice (_), was born in Dedham 3 September 1681 and died 25 June 1748 in Thompson at 66 years of age. There is a conflict about Lydia's marriage and death locations. Some researchers give the place of marriage as Woodstock, Windham Co., Conn. and the place of death at Killingly, Windham Co., Conn.

Lydia Abiah **Starr** and Jonathan **Eaton** had the following children, all born in

Killlingly:

338   i.   Lydia[6] **Eaton**[372] was born 5 November 1707 and married twice. (1) Philemon **Chandler**. (2) Edward **Goodale**.

339   ii.   Keziah **Eaton**[373] was born 24 May 1710 and married Deliverance **Cleveland**.

340   iii.   Alice **Eaton**[374] was born 28 November 1712 and married Joseph **Leavens**.

341   iv.   Susanna **Eaton**[375] was born in April 1715 and married Thomas **Grou**.

342   v.   Jerusha **Eaton**[376] was born 16 April 1717 and married John **Bucklin**.

+ 343   vi.   Hannah **Eaton** was born 17 August 1719.

344   vii.   Jonathan **Eaton**[377] was born 10 November 1721 and died in 1775 in Adams, Berkshire Co., Mass. at 53 years of age. He married Sarah **Johnson** in 1747.

+ 345   viii.   John **Eaton** was born 18 May 1724.

346   ix.   Penelope **Eaton**[378] was born 21 March 1729.

347   x.   Comfort **Eaton**[379] was born 25 September 1730 and married Mehitable **Whitmore** in 1771.

348   xi.   Marston **Eaton**[380] was born 21 October 1731 and died 3 May 1776 in Belchertown, Mass. at 44 years of age. He married Elizabeth **Lyon** in 1762.

126. Susanna[5] **Starr** (Mary[4] **Stone**, Mary[3] **Whipple**, Elder John[2], Matthew[1])[381] was born in Dedham, Mass. 24 November 1694 and died 10 April 1731 in Promfet, Conn. at 36 years of age. She married **Samuel Dana** in Massachusetts 6 January 1719. Samuel[382] was born in Cambridge, Mass. 7 September 1694 and died 22 August 1770 at 75 years of age.

Susanna **Starr** and Samuel **Dana** had the following children:

+ 349   i.   Abigail[6] **Dana** was born 23 July 1722.

+ 350   ii.   Penelope **Dana** was born in 1731.

127. Comfort[5] **Starr** (Mary[4] **Stone**, Mary[3] **Whipple**, Elder John[2], Matthew[1])[383] was born in Dedham, Mass. 9 August 1696 and died 13 February 1775 in Thompson, Windham Co., Conn. at 78 years of age. Comfort purchased 1000 acres in Killingly, Conn., later selling part and reserving a homestead on what is known as Brandy Hill (now in the city of Thompson). He was a signer of the church covenant and prominent in church and town affairs.

He married twice. (1) **Elizabeth Perley** in Killingly about 1726. Elizabeth,[384] daughter of Isaac **Perley** and Frances (__), was born in Boxford, Mass. 10 October 1705 and died 4 March 1741 in Thompson at 35 years of age. (2) **Mrs. Sarah Knapp** in Killingly November in 1763.

Comfort **Starr** and Elizabeth **Perley** had the following children, all born in Thompson:

351   i.   Frances[6] **Starr**[385] was born 22 October 1726 and died 3 December 1737 in Thompson at 11 years of age.

352   ii.   Sarah (Sally) **Starr**[386] was born before 1 September 1728 and married Jesse **Woodward**.

+ 353   iii.   Capt. Comfort **Starr** was born 10 August 1731.

354   iv.   Isaac **Starr**[387] was born 24 June 1733 and died 22 July 1733 in Thompson at less than one month of age.

355   v.   Elizabeth **Starr**[388] was born 13 September 1734 and married Joseph **Prince** 4 February 1779.

356   vi. Isaac **Starr**[389] was born 25 October 1736 and died in October 1741 in Thompson at five years of age.

357   vii. Josiah **Starr**[390] was christened 3 August 1740.

+ 358   viii. Ebenezer **Starr** was born 24 February 1741.

135. Mary[5] **Stone** (Rev. Nathaniel[4], Mary[3] **Whipple**, Elder John[2], Matthew[1])[391] was born in Harwich, Mass. 16 September 1699 and died 22 December 1778 at 79 years of age. She married **Barnabas Freeman**.

Mary **Stone** and Barnabas **Freeman** had the following children:

359   i. Nathaniel[6] **Freeman**[392] died 22 November 1743 at less than one year of age.

360   ii. Mary **Freeman**[393] was born 18 August 1744.

139. Rev. Nathan[5] **Stone** (Rev. Nathaniel[4], Mary[3] **Whipple**, Elder John[2], Matthew[1])[394] was born in Harwich, Mass. 18 February 1708 and died 31 May 1781 in Southborough, Worcestor Co., Mass. at 73 years of age. Nathan kept a Family Register running back to his ancestral line on both sides; the paternal to Simon Stone-Joana Clark and the maternal to Thomas Hinckley-Mary Smith, the last governor of Plymouth.[395] He was graduated from Harvard College class of 1726 and was ordained minister of Southborough 21 October 1730 where he served for 51 years until his death. His son Nathan and grandson Nathaniel also were graduated from Harvard and became ministers.

He married twice. (1) **Judith Fox** 21 October 1734. Judith,[396] daughter of rev. John **Fox**, was born 10 August 1712 and died in February 1748/49 at 36 years of age. The Fox family lived in Woburn, Mass. Judith's mother, no name supplied, died 5 February 1764. (2) **Mary** Thatcher[397] in Attleborough, Mass. 16 May 1751. Mary's mother, name not provided, died 1 October 1771.

Rev. Nathan **Stone** and Judith **Fox** had the following child:

+ 361   i. Rev. Nathan[6] **Stone** was born 30 September 1737.

147. Elizabeth Mary[5] **Stearns** (Elizabeth[4] **Stone**, Mary[3] **Whipple**, Elder John[2], Matthew[1])[398] was born in Massachusetts, probably in Lexington or Cambridge. She married **Edward Estey** about 1718. Edward,[399] son of Joseph **Estey** and Jane **Stewart**, was born in Topsfield, Mass. 16 July 1693 and died 6 November 1789 at 96 years of age.

Elizabeth Mary **Stearns** and Edward **Estey** had the following children, all born in Massachusetts:

362   i. Elizabeth[6] **Estey**[400] died 26 June 1738 in Massachusetts.

363   ii. Mary **Estey**[401] was born 11 September 1719 and died in Massachussettes 9 February 1738 at 18 years of age.

364   iii. Isaac **Estey** was born 24 November 1720 and died 6 February 1738 in Massachusetts at 17 years of age.

365   iv. Jabez **Estey**[402] was born 14 November 1726 and died 2 October 1745 in Massachusetts at 18 years of age.

366   v. Martha **Estey**[403] was born 23 November 1728 and died 20 January 1738 in Massachusetts at 9 years of age.

367   vi. Stewart **Estey** was born 18 June 1730 and died about 1769.[404]

368   vii. Edward **Estey**[405] was born in Massachusetts 14 April 1732.

369   viii. Mercy **Estey**[406] was born in Massachusetts 10 May 1736.

+ 370 ix. Solomon **Estey** was born 31 December 1737.

148. Rev. Ebenezer[5] Stearns (Elizabeth[4] **Stone**, Mary[3] **Whipple**, Elder John[2], Matthew[1])[407] birth date unknown, married **Thankful Clapp**.

Rev. Ebenezer **Stearns** and Thankful **Clapp** had the following child:
+ 371 i. Eliphet[6] **Stearns**.

149. Jonathan[5] Stearns (Elizabeth[4] **Stone**, Mary[3] **Whipple**, Elder John[2], Matthew[1])[408] was born in Cambridge, Mass. 20 November 1701 and married **Experience Lincoln** in Dorchester, Mass. 26 May 1726. Experience[409] was the daughter of Samuel **Lincoln** and (__) **Briggs**.

Jonathan **Stearns** and Experience **Lincoln** had the following child:
+ 372 i. Mary[6] **Stearns**.

150. Hannah[5] Stearns (Elizabeth[4] **Stone**, Mary[3] **Whipple**, Elder John[2], Matthew[1])[410] was born in Lexington, Mass. 26 January 1704 and died 10 June 1788 at 84 years of age. She married **Ezekiel Upham** 17 November 1726. Ezekiel,[411] son of John **Upham** and Abigail (__), was born in Malden, Mass. in 1700 and died 21 April 1783 in Sturbridge, Mass. at 82 years of age.

Hannah **Stearns** and Ezekiel **Upham** had the following child:
+ 373 i. Asa[6] **Upham** was born 18 May 1736.

151. Edward[5] Goddard Jr. (Susanna[4] **Stone**, Mary[3] **Whipple**, Elder John[2], Matthew[1])[412] was born in Watertown, Mass. 4 May 1698 and died 13 October 1777 in Shrewsbury, Worcester Co., Mass. at 79 years of age. He married **Hepzibah Hapgood**. Hepzibah,[413] daughter of Thomas **Hapgood**, was born in Marlborough, Mass. 27 June 1704 and died 19 July 1763 in Shrewsbury at 59 years of age.

Edward **Goddard** Jr. and Hepzibah **Hapgood** had the following children, all born in Shrewsbury:

> 374 i. Hepzibah[6] **Goddard**[414] was born 11 February 1723 and died 7 October 1781 at 58 years of age.
> + 375 ii. Nathan **Goddard** was born 18 January 1725.
> 376 iii. Elizabeth **Goddard**[415] was born 4 September 1726 and married Daniel **Fiske** in Shrewsbury 2 November 1743.
> + 377 iv. Robert **Goddard** was born 13 August 1728.
> + 378 v. David **Goddard** was born 26 September 1730.
> 379 vi. Hezekiah **Goddard**[416] was born 13 August 1732.
> + 380 vii. Lt. Daniel **Goddard** was born 17 February 1734.
> 381 viii. Ebenezer **Goddard**[417] was born 25 November 1735 and died 9 December 1735 in Shrewsbury at less than one month of age.
> 382 ix. Ebenezer **Goddard**[418] was born 28 December 1736 and died 29 September 1738 in Shewsbury at almost two year of age.
> 383 x. Rhoda **Goddard**[419] was born 25 February 1740.
> 384 xi. Meriam **Goddard**[420] was born 30 April 1742 and died 8 November 1755 in Shrewsbury at 13 years of age.
> + 385 xii. Edward **Goddard** was born 12 March 1745.

154. Benjamin[5] Goddard (Susanna[4] **Stone**, Mary[3] **Whipple**, Elder John[2], Matthew[1])[421] was born in Watertown, Mass. 15 August 1704 and died 28 January

1754 in Shewsbury, Mass. at 49 years of age. He married **Grace Fisk** in Watertown 25 September 1733. Grace,[422] daughter of Dea. Nathan **Fiske** and Sarah **Coolidge**, was born in Watertown 9 May 1714 and died 28 October 1803 at 89 years of age.

Benjamin **Goddard** and Grace **Fisk** had the following children:

386	i.	Grace[6] Goddard[423] was born 1 January 1735 and married Jasper **Stone** 17 April 1755.
387	ii.	Benjamin Goddard[424] was born 19 February 1737 and died 23 September 1740 at 3 years of age.
388	iii.	Sarah Goddard[425] was born 6 January 1739 and married Joseph **Nichols** 20 November 1761.
389	iv.	Benjamin Goddard[426] was born 29 March 1742.
390	v.	Susanna Goddard[427] was born 4 August 1744.
+ 391	vi.	Nathan Goddard was born 4 August 1746.
392	vii.	Lydia Goddard[428] was born 2 August 1748 and died 26 February 1826 at 77 years of age.
393	viii.	Hannah Goddard[429] was born 10 October 1750.
394	ix.	Submit Goddard[430] was born 7 August 1754 and married James **Puffer** 14 February 1792.

158. Ebenezer[5] Goddard (Susanna[4] **Stone**, Mary[3] **Whipple**, Elder John[2], Matthew[1])[431] was born in Boston, Mass. 14 February 1714 and died 18 November 1762 in Athol, Worcester Co., Mass. at 48 years of age. He married **Sybil Brigham** 27 January 1736. Sybil,[432] daughter of Capt. Samuel **Brigham** and Abigail **Moore**, was born in Marlborough, Mass. 15 October 1718 and died 27 September 1807 at 88 years of age. Sybil's given name have been spelled Sibil, Sybella, or Sybilla.

The Brigham line has been traced back to Thomas Brigham, born about 1475 at Holme Upon Sapulding Moore, Yorkshire, England. The first Brigham to come to New England was Lt. Thomas Brigham, born about 1603 at Holme Upon Spaulding Moore. He arrived on the *Susan and Ellen* 18 April 1635 and settled at Watertown near the Cambridge line.

Ebenezer **Goddard** and Sybil **Brigham** had the following children, all but the youngest born in Framingham:

395	i.	Abigail[6] Goddard[433] was born 11 September 1737 and died 11 August 1759 at 21 years of age. She married (__) **White**.
396	ii.	Martha Goddard[434] was born 18 March 1739 and died 15 October 1771 at 32 years of age. She married Benoni **Hemenway**.
397	iii.	Sybil Goddard[435] was born 14 January 1741 and married Joseph **Woodward**.
+ 398	iv.	Susanna Goddard was born 25 September 1742.
399	v.	Mary Goddard[436] was born 3 August 1744 and died 1 June 1773 at 28 years of age. She married Rufus **Taylor**.
400	vi.	Sophia Goddard[437] was born 3 October 1746 and married Abner **Morton**.
401	vii.	Betty Goddard[438] was born 26 January 1748 and married Nehemiah **Howe**.
402	viii.	Easter Goddard[439] was born 15 June 1751 and died 10 March 1778 at 26 years of age. She married Samuel **Morton**.
403	ix.	Ebenezer Goddard[440] was born 9 August 1753 and died 30 March 1815 at 61 years of age. He married Hannah **Death**.
404	x.	Benjamin Goddard[441] was born 2 September 1755 and died 6

November 1771 at 16 years of age.

405   xi.   Edward **Goddard**[442] was born 16 April 1759 and married Anna **Death**.
406   xii.   Samuel **Goddard**[443] was born 16 April 1759 and married Kenzie **Pond**.
407   xiii. Abigail **Goddard**[444] was born in Athol, Mass. 16 May 1761 and married John **Tidd**.

161. **Jonathan**[5] **Stone** (Jonathan[4], Mary[3] **Whipple**, Elder John[2], Matthew[1])[445] birthdate unknown, died 27 October 1725 in Watertown, Mass. He married **Hannah Jennison** in Watertown 25 February 1725. The marriage year is also given as 1724. Hannah,[446] daughter of Samuel **Jennison** and Mary **Stearns**, was born in Watertown 17 July 1702 and died 4 December 1777 in Worcester, Worcester Co., Mass. at 75 years of age. She married (2) **John Goddard** in Watertown 4 September 1729. John Goddard was christened in Watertown 4 October 1702.

Jonathan **Stone** and Hannah **Jennison** had the following child:
+   408   i.   Jonathan[6] **Stone** was born 17 November 1725.

164. **Moses**[5] **Stone** (Jonathan[4], Mary[3] **Whipple**, Elder John[2], Matthew[1])[447] was born in Watertown, Mass. 16 December 1723 and died there 2 December 1796 at 72 years of age. Moses was a soldier in the Revolution. He married **Hannah Tainter** in Watertown 25 November 1746. Hannah was the daughter of capt. John **Tainter**. They had four children but only two are identified here.

Moses **Stone** and Hannah **Tainter** had the following children:
+   409   i.   William[6] **Stone** was born 6 October 1750.
+   410   ii.   Jonathan **Stone** was born in 1753.

173. **John**[5] **Norton** (Mary[4] **Goodhue**, Sarah[3] **Whipple**, Elder John[2], Matthew[1])[448] was born in Hingham, Mass. and married **Rebecca Wilson** 11 July 1717. Rebecca,[449] daughter of Joseph **Wilson** and Hannah **Endle, was born 16 February 1696.**

John **Norton** and Rebecca **Wilson** had the following children:
     411   i.   John[6] **Norton**[450].
+   412   ii.   Joanna **Norton** was born between 1720-24.

175. **Elizabeth**[5] **Norton** (Mary[4] **Goodhue**, Sarah[3] **Whipple**, Elder John[2], Matthew[1])[451] was born in Ipswich 31 March 1703 and died in 1759 in New Hampshire at 56 years of age. She married twice. (1) (__) **Jenness**. (2) **Benjamin Swett**[452]. Benjamin was born in New Hampshire in 1710 and died there in 1762 at 52 years of age.

Elizabeth **Norton** and Benjamin **Swett** had the following child:
+   413   i.   Moses[6] **Swett** was born in 1738.

176. **Anna**[5] **Norton** (Mary[4] **Goodhue**, Sarah[3] **Whipple**, Elder John[2], Matthew[1])[453] was born in Ipswich 20 March 1707 and married **Jonathan Towle** 10 February 1728. Jonathan,[454] son of Joseph **Towle** and Sarah **Dalton**, was born in Hampton, N.H. 5 April 1703 and died 23 April 1791 at 88 years of age.

Anna **Norton** and Jonathan **Towle** had the following children:
     414   i.   Jonathan[6] **Towle**[455] was born in Hampton, N.H. 4 July 1729 and died in Epsom, N.H. He married Elizabeth **Jenness**,[456] daughter of John

Jenness and Elizabeth **Seavey**.

415	ii.	Levi **Towle**[457] was born in Hampton 22 September 1731 and married Ruth **Marden** 11 October 1753.
416	iii.	Joseph **Towle**[458] was born 21 March 1733/34 and married Sarah **Wallis**.
417	iv.	Samuel **Towle**[459] was born 5 November 1735 and married twice. (1) Rachel **Elkins** 21 August 1760. (2) Esther **Johnson** 18 October 1762.
418	v.	James **Towle**[460] was born 28 October 1737.
419	vi.	Anna **Towle**[461] was born 28 March 1741 and married Joseph **Philbrick** 2 December 1760.
420	vii.	Nathan **Towle**[462] was born 29 May 1745.

180. Sarah[5] Goodhue (William[4], Sarah[3] **Whipple**, Elder John[2], Matthew[1])[463] was born in Ipswich 24 May 1695 and died there 2 January 1764 (a presumed death date) at 68 years of age. She married **Thomas Treadwell** in Ipswich. Their marriage banns were published 18 March 1715. Thomas,[464] son of Nathaniel **Treadwell**, was born in Ipswich 8 April 1686 and died there 17 February 1743 at 56 years of age.

Sarah **Goodhue** and Thomas **Treadwell** had the following children, all born in Ipswich:

	421	i.	Mary[6] **Treadwell**[465] was christened 19 June 1726.
	422	ii.	Mary **Treadwell**[466] was christened 21 December 1727 and died after 21 April 1769 in Ipswich,
+	423	iii.	Joseph **Treadwell** was born 3 February 1716/17.
+	424	iv.	Sarah **Treadwell** was born in 1720.
+	425	v.	Elizabeth **Treadwell** was born abt March 1722.
+	426	vi.	Thomas **Treadwell** was born 6 August 1732.

185. Jonathan[5] Goodhue (William[4], Sarah[3] **Whipple**, Elder John[2], Matthew[1])[467] was born in Ipswich 28 April 1705 and died abt 1744 in Chester, N.H. He married **Elizabeth Powell** in Exeter, Rockingham Co., N.H. 28 April 1728. Elizabeth,[468] daughter of William **Powell** and Esther **Garland**, was born abt 1708.

Jonathan **Goodhue** and Elizabeth **Powell** had the following children, born in Chester:

| + | 427 | i. | Elizabeth[6] **Goodhue** was born 16 March 1729/30. |
| | 428 | ii. | Mary **Goodhue**[469] was born 2 May 1730 and died 13 October 1809 at 79 years of age. She married Moses **Richardson**. |

187. John[5] Kimball (Sarah[4] **Goodhue**, Sarah[3] **Whipple**, Elder John[2], Matthew[1])[470] was born in 1693 and died in 1749 at 56 years of age. He married Patience **Larribee**[471] who died in 1747.

John **Kimball** and Patience **Larribee** had the following child:

| | 429 | i. | John[6] **Kimball**[472] was born in 1732. |

190. David[5] Kimball (Sarah[4] **Goodhue**, Sarah[3] **Whipple**, Elder John[2], Matthew[1])[473] was born in 1700 and died in 1776 at 76 years of age. He married Sarah **Pride**[474] who died in 1769.

David **Kimball** and Sarah **Pride** had the following children:

| | 430 | i. | Mary[6] **Kimball**[475] was born in 1727. |

431   ii. Eunice **Kimball**[476] was born in 1729.
432   iii. Nathan **Kimball**[477] was born in 1732.
433   iv. David **Kimball**[478] was born in 1734.
434   v.   Jonathan **Kimball**[479] was born in 1738.
435   vi. Sarah **Kimball**[480] was born in 1738.

192. **Isaac**[5] **Kimball** (Sarah[4] **Goodhue**, Sarah[3] **Whipple**, Elder John[2], Matthew[1])[481] was born in Ipswich 19 April 1705 and died 24 August 1749 in Preston, New London Co., Conn. at 44 years of age. He married **Prudence Parke**[482] in Preston 13 May 1729. She was born in Preston 14 October 1706.

Isaac **Kimball** and Prudence **Parke** had the following child:
+ 436   i.   John[6] **Kimball** was born 12 December 1731.

193. **Jacob**[5] **Kimball** (Sarah[4] **Goodhue**, Sarah[3] **Whipple**, Elder John[2], Matthew[1])[483] was born in Ipswich 12 October 1706 and died 4 May 1788 in Preston, New London Co., Conn. at 81 years of age. He married **Mary Parke** 24 February 1730. Mary,[484] daughter of Thomas **Parke** and Hannah **Witter**, was born 6 June 1715.

Jacob **Kimball** and Mary **Parke** had the following child:
+ 437   i.   Jacob[6] **Kimball** Jr. was born 1 December 1735.

194. **Abigail**[5] **Kimball** (Sarah[4] **Goodhue**, Sarah[3] **Whipple**, Elder John[2], Matthew[1])[485] was born in Watertown, Conn. 11 October 1709 and married **John Kilham** 3 February 1730. John[486] was born in Wenham, Mass. 7 September 1698 and died in September 1753 in Preston, New London Co., Conn. at 55 years of age.

Abigail **Kimball** and John **Kilham** had the following child:
+ 438   i   Hepsibah[6] **Kilham**.

195. **George**[5] **Goodhue** (Joseph[4], Sarah[3] **Whipple**, Elder John[2], Matthew[1])[487] was born in 1709, died in Newbury, Mass., and married **Elizabeth Sleeper**.

George **Goodhue** and Elizabeth **Sleeper** had the following child:
+ 439   i.   Samuel[6] **Goodhue** was born in 1751.

196. **Robert**[5] **Knowlton** (Marjory (Margery)[4] **Goodhue**, Sarah[3] **Whipple**, Elder John[2], Matthew[1])[488] was born in Ipswich 7 September 1693 and died 29 December 1774 in Ashford, Conn. at 81 years of age. He married **Hannah Robinson** 21 November 1717. Hannah[489] was born in Ipswich.

Robert **Knowlton** and Hannah **Robinson** had the following child:
+ 440   i.   Daniel[6] **Knowlton** was born 19 May 1726.

197. **Margery**[5] **Knowlton** (Marjory (Margery)[4] **Goodhue**, Sarah[3] **Whipple**, Elder John[2], Matthew[1])[490] was born in Ipswich 26 March 1695 and died after 1725. She married **Jabez Dodge** 25 November 1718. Jabez[491] was born in Ipswich 22 March 1686 and died October 1774 at 88 years of age.

Margery **Knowlton** and Jabez **Dodge** had the following child:
+ 441   i.   Deborah[6] **Dodge** was born 26 August 1725.

198. Joseph[5] Knowlton (Marjory (Margery)[4] **Goodhue**, Sarah[3] **Whipple**, Elder John[2], Matthew[1])[492] was born in Ipswich 3 September 1697 and died there abt 1756. He married twice. (1) **Abigail Poland** in Ipswich 8 January 1720. Abigail,[493] daughter of Samuel **Poland** and Elizabeth **Perkins**, was christened in Wenham, Mass. 24 April 1698 and died 3 July 1748 in Ipswich. (2) **Mrs. Hannah Ward** in Ipswich after July 1748.

Joseph **Knowlton** and Abigail **Poland** had the following child:
+ 442   i.   Joseph[6] **Knowlton** was born 18 October 1726.

203. John[5] Goodhue (John[4], Sarah[3] **Whipple**, Elder John[2], Matthew[1])[494] was born in Ipswich in January 1721 and died there 15 January 1815 at 94 years of age. He married **Elizabeth Lampson** in Ipswich in 1743.

John **Goodhue** and Elizabeth **Lampson** had the following child:
+ 443   i.   Ebenezer[6] **Goodhue** was born in 1754.

205. Aaron[5] Kimball (Susanna[4] **Goodhue**, Sarah[3] **Whipple**, Elder John[2], Matthew[1])[495] was christened in Ipswich 7 October 1718 and died there in May 1787. He married **Sarah Rindge** in Ipswich. The date of intent to marry was 6 November 1742.

Aaron **Kimball** and Sarah **Rindge** had the following children:
444   i.   Mary[6] **Kimball**[496] was born in 1743.
445   ii.   Susanna **Kimball**[497] was born in 1747.
446   iii.   Sarah **Kimball**[498] was born in 1748.
447   iv.   Moses **Kimball**[499] was born in 1751.

206. Moses[5] Kimball Jr. (Susanna[4] **Goodhue**, Sarah[3] **Whipple**, Elder John[2], Matthew[1])[500] was born in Ipswich 6 January 1697 and died there 29 July 1793 at 96 years of age. Moses, a carpenter and mover of buildings, was a tall man standing over 6 feet. He made Ipswich's first ox wagon and first gondola and helped build the stone bridge. Active in town affairs, he filled many offices. He downed in the Ipswich river while removing logs. He married twice. (1) **Mary Kimball** in Ipswich. The date of intent to marry was 21 May 1729. (2) **Mrs. Mary Brown** in Ipswich. The date of intent to marry was 10 September 1734.

Moses **Kimball** Jr. and Mary **Kimball** had the following children:
448   i.   Joseph[6] **Kimball**[501] was born in 1730.
449   ii.   Ebenezer **Kimball**[502] was born in 1732 and died in 1736 at 4 years of age.
450   iii.   Mary **Kimball**[503] was born in 1735 and died in 1736 at one year of age.
451   iv.   Ebenezer **Kimball**[504] was born in 1737.

SIXTH GENERATION

214. Moses[6] Pillsbury (Moses[5], Susanna[4] **Worth**, Susannah[3] **Whipple**, Elder John[2], Matthew[1]) was born in Newbury, Mass. 16 January 1699 and died in April 1787 in Boxford, Mass. at 88 years of age. He married **Mary Parker** 6 August 1728.

Moses **Pillsbury** and Mary **Parker** had the following children:

452		i.	Susannah[7] **Pillsbury**[505] was born in 1730.
+	453	ii.	Rev. Edmund **Pillsbury** was born 12 March 1738.
+	454	iii.	Parker **Pillsbury** was born in 1742.

215. Abigail W.[6] Pillsbury (Moses[5], Susanna[4] **Worth**, Susannah[3] **Whipple**, Elder John[2], Matthew[1]) was born 9 August 1700 and died before April 1765. She married **Thomas Hale** in Newbury, Mass. 12 January 1726. Thomas, son of Henry **Hale** and Sarah **Kelley**, was born 15 November 1696 and died before April 1765.

Abigail W. **Pillsbury** and Thomas **Hale** had the following children:

455		i.	Abraham[7] **Hale**.
+	456	ii.	Sarah **Hale** was born 14 August 1731.
+	457	iii.	Joseph **Hale** was born 14 October 1735.
	458	iv.	Martha **Hale** was born in 1736 and died 11 April 1809 in Northwood, Rockingham Co., N.H. at 72 years of age. She has a memorial stone in the Northwood Cemetery. She married Edmund **Pillsbury** in Haverhill, Mass. 22 October 1761.

218. Susanna[6] Pillsbury (Moses[5], Susanna[4] **Worth**, Susannah[3] **Whipple**, Elder John[2], Matthew[1]) was born in Newbury, Mass. 12 June 1709 and died there 22 December 1788 at 79 years of age. She married **Dr. James Brickett** in Newbury 7 August 1729.

Susanna **Pillsbury** and Dr. James **Brickett** had the following child:

| + | 459 | i. | Bernard[7] **Brickett** was born 25 July 1751. |

230. Caleb[6] Pillsbury Jr. (Caleb[5], Susanna[4] **Worth**, Susannah[3] **Whipple**, Elder John[2], Matthew[1])[506] was born in Newbury, Mass. 26 January 1717 and died 7 February 1778 in Amesbury, Mass. at 61 years of age. He married twice. (1) **Sarah Kimball** in Amesbury 8 July 1742. Sarah,[507] daughter of Joseph **Kimball** and Bethia **Shepard**, was born 4 August 1722. (2) **Mehitable (Buswell) Smith** in Amesbury. Mehitable[508] was the daughter of William **Buswell**.

Caleb **Pillsbury** Jr. and Sarah **Kimball** had the following children, all born in Amesbury:

460		i.	Joshua[7] **Pillsbury**[509] was born 30 March 1743 and died 21 February 1825 in Canaan, N.H. at 81 years of age. He married Elizabeth **Sawyer** in October 1770.
461		ii.	Susannah **Pillsbury**[510] was born 30 March 1745 and died abt 1788 in Methuen, Mass. She married Miles **Flint** 18 February 1768.
462		iii.	Sarah **Pillsbury**[511] was born 4 June 1747 and married twice. (1) Samuel **Morrell**. (2) Benjamin **Brown**.
463		iv.	Moses **Pillsbury**[512] was born 19 June 1750 and died 28 January 1840 in Bridgewater, N.H. at 89 years of age. He married Anna **Hoyt** 19 October 1775.
+ 464		v.	Caleb **Pillsbury** III was born 27 March 1752.
465		vi.	Elizabeth **Pillsbury**[513] was born 3 August 1754 and died in 1835 at 80 years of age. She married Samuel **Webster** in 1777.
466		vii.	Micajah **Pillsbury**[514] was born 4 May 1761 and died in 1801 in Sutton, N.H. at 40 years of age. He married Sarah **Sargent**. The date of intent to marry was 15 March 1781.

Caleb **Pillsbury Jr.** and Mehitable (Buswell) **Smith** had the following child, born in Amesbury:

467   viii.   Isaac **Pillsbury**[515] was born 19 October 1762 and died 4 May 1814 in Hallowell, Maine at 51 years of age. He married Mary **Smith** abt 1787.

241. Abiah[6] **Hill** (Judith[5] **Bucknam**, Judith (Jude)[4] **Worth**, Susannah[3] **Whipple**, Elder John[2], Matthew[1])[516] birth date unknown, died after 1770 in Massachusetts. She married **Benjamin Mooar** in Andover, Essex Co., Mass. 16 September 1740. Benjamin[517] was born in Andover 18 February 1715/16 and was buried there 8 November 1777.

Abiah **Hill** and Benjamin **Mooar** had the following children, all born in Andover:

+ 468   i.   Abiah[7] **Mooar** was born 9 November 1741.
+ 469   ii.   Benjamin **Mooar** Jr. was born 28 October 1743.
   470   iii. Joseph **Mooar**[518] was born 13 February 1745/46 and died 5 December 1747 in Andover at 2 years of age.
+ 471   iv.   Lois **Mooar** was born 10 November 1747.
   472   vi.   Mehitabel **Mooar**[519] was born 1 November 1749 and died in 1820 at 70 years of age. She married twice. (1) Emery **Chase** in Andover 25 July 1768. Emery was born in 1747 and died in 1788 at 41 years of age. (2) Aaron **Blanchard** in Andover 21 September 1789.
   473   vi.   Anne **Mooar**[520] was born 11 August 1753 and married Joel **Marshall** in Andover 30 April 1772.
   474   vii. Mary **Mooar**[521] was born 11 October 1755 and married Samuel **Stevens** 28 April 1778.

246. William[6] **Brown** (Martha[5] **Whipple**, Maj. John[4], Capt. John[3], Elder John[2], Matthew[1])[522] was born in Newbury, Mass. 24 January 1707/08 and died there 31 December 1786 at 79 years of age. He married **Ann Poor** in Newbury 23 June 1730. Ann,[523] daughter of Jonathan **Poor** and Rebecca **Hale**, was born in Newbury 25 October 1708 and died there 26 July 1792 at 83 years of age.

William **Brown** and Ann **Poor** had the following child:

+ 475   i.   Samuel[7] **Brown** was born 23 December 1752.

248. Katherine[6] **Brown** (Martha[5] **Whipple**, Maj. John[4], Capt. John[3], Elder John[2], Matthew[1])[524] was born in Reading, Mass. 15 August 1712 and died in May 1787 in Newbury at 74 years of age. She married **Col. Joseph Gerrish** in Reading 16 February 1731/32. Joseph,[525] son of Col. Joseph **Gerrish** and Mary **Little**, was born in Newbury 10 September 1708 and died there 26 May 1776 at 67 years of age.

Katherine **Brown** and Col. Joseph **Gerrish** had the following children, all born in Newbury:

   476   i.   Jane[7] **Gerrish**[526] died 31 December 1756 in Newbury.
   477   ii.   Katherine **Gerrish**[527] was born 17 November 1732.
   478   iii. Mary **Gerrish**[528] was born 1 January 1735/36.
   479   iv.   Jacob **Gerrish**[529] was born 9 February 1738/39.
   480   v.   Martha **Gerrish**[530] was born 8 October 1741 and died 1 January 1801 at 59 years of age.
   481   vi.   Stephen **Gerrish**[531] was born 20 March 1744.
+ 482   vii. Sarah **Gerrish** was born in 1752.

252. Dea. John⁶ Crocker (Mary⁵ **Whipple**, Maj. John⁴, Capt. John³, Elder John², Matthew¹)⁵³² was christened in Ipswich 21 September 1723, died there 21 April 1806, and is buried in Section B Stone 1 in the Old North Churchyard. His grave is marked with a foot stone. He married twice. (1) **Mehitable Burley** in Ipswich 3 December 1747. Mehitable⁵³³ was born abt 1727 and died 9 July 1766 in Ipswich at 39 years of age. (2) **Elizabeth Lakeman** in Ipswich. The date of intent to marry was 28 November 1767. Elizabeth⁵³⁴ was born abt 1730 and died 12 January 1803 in Ipswich at 72 years of age and is buried in Section C Stone 21 in the Old North Churchyard. Her grave is marked with a foot stone.

Dea. John **Crocker** and Mehitable **Burley** had the following children, all born in Ipswich:

+   483   i.   Mary⁷ **Crocker** was born 4 November 1748.
    484   ii. Mehitable **Crocker**⁵³⁵ was born 17 February 1750 and died 20 May 1804 in Ipswich at 54 years of age. She married Thomas **Appleton** in Ipswich 26 November 1768. Thomas⁵³⁶ was born abt 1746 and died 21 May 1810 in Ipswich at 63 years of age.
+   485   iii. Hannah **Crocker** was born 29 December 1752.
+   486   iv. Lydia **Crocker** was born 7 November 1754.
    487   v.   Martha **Crocker**⁵³⁷ was christened 19 March 1758.
    488   vi. John **Crocker**⁵³⁸ was born 13 March 1760 and married an unnamed person in Ipswich 25 May 1786.
    489   vii. Sarah **Crocker**⁵³⁹ was born 11 July 1762.
    490   viii. Aaron **Crocker**⁵⁴⁰ was christened 14 August 1763.
    491   ix. Eliza **Crocker**⁵⁴¹ was born 16 December 1764.

Dea. John **Crocker** and Elizabeth **Lakeman** had the following children, born in Ipswich:

    492   x.   Joseph **Crocker**⁵⁴² was born 22 October 1770.
    493   xi. Elizabeth **Crocker**⁵⁴³ was born 4 December 1772 and died 17 March 1817 in Ipswich at 44 years of age. She died unmarried and is buried in the Old North Churchyard, Section B Stone 4. The grave was marked with a foot stone.

254. Rev. John⁶ Rogers (Susanna⁵ **Whipple**, Maj. John⁴, Capt. John³, Elder John², Matthew¹)⁵⁴⁴ was born in Kittery, Maine 7 August 1719 and died 4 October 1782 in Gloucester, Mass. at 63 years of age. He was graduated from Harvard in 1739 where he was also a librarian. He was pastor of the church in the Town Parish of Gloucester which was organized 27 October 1743. His father preached the sermon at his ordination and his uncle rev. Nathaniel Rogers of Ipswich also participated in the services.

He married three times. (1) **Susannah Allen** in Gloucester in 1744. The date of intent to marry was 16 October 1744. Susannah⁵⁴⁵ was born abt 1723 and died 20 April 1746 in Gloucester at 22 years of age. (2) **Mary Ellery** in Gloucester 28 January 1748. Mary⁵⁴⁶ was born in Gloucester abt 1723 and died there 5 February 1766 at 42 years of age. (3) **Mrs. Abigail (__) Woodward** in Gloucester 2 April 1770. Abigail⁵⁴⁷ was born abt 1739 and died 12 March 1819 in Gloucester at 79 years of age.

Rev. John **Rogers** and Susannah **Allen** had the following child born in Gloucester:

    494   i.   Susannah⁷ **Rogers**⁵⁴⁸ was born 19 April 1746 and died 5 May 1746 in

Gloucester at 17 days of age.

Rev. John **Rogers** and Mary **Ellery** had the following child born in Gloucester:

+   495   ii. John **Rogers** was born in 1748.

261. Daniel[6] Rogers Esq. (Susanna[5] **Whipple**, Maj. John[4], Capt. John[3], Elder John[2], Matthew[1])[549] was born in Kittery, Maine 25 October 1734 and died suddenly of a paralytic stroke 5 January 1800 in Gloucester, Mass. at 65 years of age. He was a merchant in Gloucester and married twice. (1) **Mrs. Elizabeth** Gorham. The date of intent to marry was 6 November 1759. Elizabeth,[550] daughter of Col. John **Gorham**, died 4 March 1769 in Gloucester four days after the birth of her sixth child. The child is not named in the Gloucester vital records so probably died at birth or soon thereafter. (2) **Mrs.Rachel Ellery**. The date of intent to marry was 20 March 1777. Rachel[551] was born abt 1749 and died 20 November 1833 in Gloucester at 84 years of age.

Daniel **Rogers** Esq. and Mrs. Elizabeth **Gorham** had the following children all born in Gloucester:

  496   i. Lucy[7] **Rogers**[552] was born 26 August 1760.
  497   ii. John Gorham **Rogers**[553] was born 16 April 1762.
  498   iii. Eliza **Rogers**[554] was born 7 July 1764.
  499   iv. Charles **Rogers**[555] was born 15 October 1765 and died of dropsy 15 January 1809 in Gloucester at 43 years of age.
  500   v. Daniel **Rogers**[556] was born 22 July 1767 and died in December 1768 in Gloucester at one year of age.
  501   vi. Child **Rogers**[557] was born 28 February 1769.

Daniel **Rogers** Esq. and Mrs.Rachel **Ellery** had the following children, all born in Gloucester:

  502   vii. Rachel **Rogers**[558] was born 18 January 1772 and died 1 October 1773 in Gloucester at one year of age.
  503   viii. Esther **Rogers**[559] was born 9 November 1773.
  504   ix. Susanna **Rogers**[560] was born 22 February 1775.
  505   x. Daniel **Rogers**[561] was born 18 March 1778.
  506   xi. Timothy **Rogers**[562] was born 22 June 1779.
  507   xii. Mary **Rogers**[563] was born 28 September 1780.
  508   xiii. Samuel **Rogers**[564] was born 28 December 1781.
  509   xiv. Shubael Gorham **Rogers**[565] was born 17 April 1783.
  510   xv. William **Rogers**[566] was born 16 November 1784.
  511   xvi George **Rogers**[567] was born 18 April 1786 and drowned 4 July 1792 in Gloucester at 6 years of age.
  512   xvii. Judith **Rogers**[568] was born 17 November 1787.
  513   xviii. Rachel **Rogers**[569] was born 13 July 1789.
  514   xix. Fanny **Rogers**[570] was born. 6 May 1792.

263. Capt. John[6] Whipple (Capt. John[5], Maj. Matthew[4], Capt. John[3], Elder John[2], Matthew[1])[571] was born in Ipswich 25 June 1717 and died there 27 December 1794 at 77 years of age. He married **Dorothy Moulton** in Ipswich 18 August 1737. Dorothy[572] was born 9 March 1717 and died in September 1776 in Ipswich at 59 years of age.

Capt. John **Whipple** and Dorothy **Moulton** had the following children born in Ipswich:

515   i. Jemima[7] **Whipple**[573] was born 23 August 1740. She may be the Jemima Whipple who married Nathaniel Abot of Beverly, Mass. in Ipswich on 18 December 1768.[574]

+ 516   ii. John **Whipple** was born abt 1748.

264. Dea. Nathaniel[6] **Whipple** (Capt. John[5], Maj. Matthew[4], Capt. John[3], Elder John[2], Matthew[1])[575] was born in Ipswich, Mass. 7 October 1721 and died 19 December 1809 at 88 years of age. Nathaniel's name is on the list of Hamlet men who served in the Revolutionary War, thus qualifying his descendants for all patriotic societies based on that war.[576]

He married **Mary Appleton** in Ipswich. The date of intent to marry was 10 November 1744. Mary,[577] daughter of Lt. Oliver **Appleton** and Sarah **Perkins**, was born in Ipswich in 1724 and died there 2 March 1810 at 85 years of age. Nathaniel and Mary were first cousins, once removed. Mary's father was a brother to Johanna Appleton, wife of Maj. Matthew Whipple.

Her father, Oliver Appleton, was a hemophiliac (bleeder). Hemophilia is an hereditary bleeding tendency that occurs only in males and is transmitted by females. Dr. Victor A. McKusick, professor of medicine at the Johns Hopkins Hospital in Baltimore, conducted a study on hemophiliacs born in New England before 1900.

Dea. Nathaniel **Whipple** and Mary **Appleton** had the following children, all born in Ipswich:

517   i. Elizabeth[7] **Whipple**[578].

518   ii. Mary **Whipple**[579] was born 29 October 1745 and died 29 November 1838 at 93 years of age.

519   iii. Hannah **Whipple**[580] was born 17 April 1747 and died 30 October 1821 at 74 years of age.

520   iv. John **Whipple**[581] was born 28 December 1748 and died 22 January 1806 at 57 years of age. He married Jane Jewett **Rowley** in Ipswich. The date of intent to marry was 20 December 1781. Jane was from Rowley.

521   v. Sarah **Whipple**[582] was born 30 January 1751 and died 20 February 1836 at 85 years of age. She married Joseph **Poland**.

522   vi. Lucy **Whipple**[583] was born 30 October 1753 and died in 1834 at 80 years of age. She married Benjamin **Peck** in Ipswich 2 March 1779.

+ 523   vii. Martha **Whipple** was born 12 November 1755.

524   viii. Nathaniel **Whipple**[584] was born abt 1759 and died of convulsive fits 2 November 1771 in Ipswich at 12 years of age. .

266. Mary[6] **Whipple** (Capt. William[5], Maj. Matthew[4], Capt. John[3], Elder John[2], Matthew[1])[585] was born in Kittery, Maine 13 January 1728/29, died 3 October 1791 at 63 years of age, and is buried in Portsmouth's North Cemetery. She married **Robert Traill** in Kittery in a ceremony performed by rev. John Newmarch. He was born in the Orkney Island. The intent to marry was recorded 16 July 1748. Robert was a Portsmouth merchant before becoming comptroller of the Port of Portsmouth, joined the Loyalist cause during the Revolution, and fled with gov. John Wentworth to Long Island in 1777. He was proscribed by the colonial government in November 1778 and later he became collector of the Island of Bermuda.[586] His brother-in-law, gen. William Whipple, played a prominent role is removing the Loyalists from the new nation.

Mary **Whipple** and Robert **Traill** had the following children:

    525   i. Robert[7] **Traill**. He settled in Europe.
    526   ii. William **Traill**. He settled in Europe.
+ 527   iii. Mary **Traill** was born abt 1755.

267. Gen. William[6] Whipple (Capt. William[5], Maj. Matthew[4], Capt. John[3], Elder John[2], Matthew[1])[587] was born in Kittery, Maine 14 January 1730/31 and died 28 November 1785 in Portsmouth, N.H. at 55 years of age. He married **Katharine Moffatt** in Portsmouth abt 1769. Katharine, daughter of John **Moffatt** and Katherine **Cutt**, was born in Kittery, died 22 November 1821 in Portsmouth, and is buried in the tomb of gov. John Langdon on the southern edge of Portsmouth's North Cemetery. Her husband is in a separate tomb in the same cemetery. Their marriage is revealed in a letter written by John Parker owned by the Porthsmouth, N.H. Athenaeum and on loan to the Moffatt-Ladd house in Portsmouth. William and Katharine were first cousins; their mothers were sisters. She was William's widow for 36 years. See chapter 6 for a full account of Katharine Moffatt and William, great great grandson of John and Susanna Whipple.

William's tomb in the North Cemetery in Portsmouth, N. H. is engraved as follows:

> Here are deposited thie remains
> Of the Honorable William Whipple who departed this life
> on the 28th day of November, 1785.
> He was often elected
> and thrice attended
> the Continental Congress
> as Delegate for the state of New Hampshire
> particularly in that memorable
> year in which America declared itself independent of Great Britain.
> He was also at the time of his decease a Judge of the Supreme Court
> of Judicature
> In Him
> a firm and ardent Patriotism
> was united with
> universal benevolence
> and every Social Virtue.

Gen. William **Whipple** and Katherine **Moffatt** had the following child:

    528   i. William[7] **Whipple** was born in Portsmouth and christened 24 May 1772 at the Old North Church. He died in Portsmouth 11 April 1773 at less than one year of age and is buried near his father's tomb in the North Cemetery.

275. Nathaniel[6] Page (Susannah[5] **Lane**, Susanna[4] **Whipple**, Capt. John[3], Elder John[2], Matthew[1])[588] was born in Billerica, Mass. 4 September 1702 and died there 6 April 1779 at 76 years of age. He married **Hannah (__)**[589] in Billerica. and she died there 7 September 1763.

Nathaniel **Page** and Hannah (__) had the following children:

    529   i. Thomas[7] **Page**[590] was born in Billerica, Mass. 5 May 1733.

+   530   ii. Hannah **Page** was born 15 May 1736.

283. Francis[6] **Whitmore** (Mary[5] **Lane**, Susanna[4] **Whipple**, Capt. John[3], Elder John[2], Matthew[1])[591] was born 4 October 1714 and died 7 April 1794 at 79 years of age. He married **Mary Hall**[592] 1 January 1739. She was born in 1712 and died 20 October 1791 at 79 years of age.

Francis **Whitmore** and Mary **Hall** had the following child:
+   531   I. John[7] **Whitmore** was born 3 November 1781.

288. John[6] **Lane** (Job[5], Susanna[4] **Whipple**, Capt. John[3], Elder John[2], Matthew[1])[593] was born in Billerica, Mass. 2 October 1720 and died 7 December 1789 in Bedford, Mass. at 69 years of age. He married **Mrs. Sarah (Abbott) Hildreth** as his second wife. No information provided on his first wife.

John **Lane** and Mrs. Sarah (Abbott) **Hildreth** had the following child:
+   532   i. Jonathan[7] **Lane** was born in 1763.

289. Timothy[6] **Lane** (Job[5], Susanna[4] **Whipple**, Capt. John[3], Elder John[2], Matthew[1])[594] was born in Bedford, Mass. 10 July 1722 and died there 3 December 1793 at 71 years of age. He married **Lydia Davis** in Bedford 7 March 1750/51. Lydia[595] was born in Bedford 25 July 1730 and died of bilious fever there 4 August 1801 at 71 years of age.

Timothy **Lane** and Lydia **Davis** had the following children, all born in Bedford:

   533   i. Lucy[7] **Lane**[596] was born 7 November 1751.
   534   ii. Elizabeth **Lane**[597] was born 7 May 1753.
   535   iii. Stephen **Lane**[598] was born 20 August 1755.
+   536   iv. Anna **Lane** was born 30 March 1758.
   537   v. Lydia **Lane**[599] was born 16 December 1760 and died in Bedford 23 October 1765 at 4 years of age.
   538   vi. Rhoda **Lane**[600] was born 17 May 1763.
   539   vii. Pattie **Lane**[601] was born 8 November 1765.
   540   viii. Nathan **Lane**[602] was born 11 February 1768.
   541   ix. Lydia **Lane**[603] was born 16 January 1772.

290. Mary[6] **Lane** (Job[5], Susanna[4] **Whipple**, Capt. John[3], Elder John[2], Matthew[1])[604] was born in Billerica, Mass. 24 February 1724/25 and died there 24 October 1772 at 47 years of age. She married **Jonathan Hill** in Billerica 13 January 1746/47. Jonathan,[605] son of Joseph **Hill** and Susanna **Baldwin**, was born in Billerica 28 April 1718 and died there 7 April 1796 at 77 years of age. He married (2) **Sarah Stevens** in Billerica 24 May 1774. She was the widow of Samuel Whiting.

Mary **Lane** and Jonathan **Hill** had the following children, all born in Billerica:
+   542   i. Ralph[7] **Hill** was born 20 September 1747.
   543   ii. Mary **Hill**[606] was born 21 October 1748 and married Oliver **Pollard** in Billerica 19 June 1777. Oliver was from Bedford, Mass.
   544   iii. Martha **Hill**[607] was born 4 March 1749/50 and died 13 April 1750/51 in Billerica at one year of age.
   545   iv. Susanna **Hill**[608] was born 22 January 1750/51 and died 18 November 1817 in Billerica at 66 years of age.
   546   v. Benjamin **Hill**[609] was born 30 June 1752 and died 10 April 1796 in

Billerica at 43 years of age.
+ 547   vi.   Job **Hill** was born 29 May 1754.
  548   vii. Lucy **Hill**[610] was born 14 January 1756 and married Isaac **Taylor** in Billerica in October 1814. Isaac was from Dunstable, Mass.
  549   viii. Josiah **Hill**[611] was born 10 December 1757.
  550   ix.   Elizabeth **Hill**[612] was born 13 October 1759 and died 20 May 1830 in Billerica at 70 years of age.
  551   x.   Isabel **Hill**[613] was born 3 December 1761 and married Benjamin **Lane** in Billerica 26 May 1785. Benjamin was from Ashburnham, Mass.
+ 552   xi.   Jonathan **Hill** was born 28 September 1763.
  553   xii. Jane **Hill**[614] was born 17 December 1764 and died 14 September 1775 in Billerica at 10 years of age.
+ 554   xiii. Asubah **Hill** was born 1 March 1768.
+ 555   xiv. Anna **Hill** was born 11 June 1776.

300. **John**[6] **Lane** (John[5], Susanna[4] **Whipple**, Capt. John[3], Elder John[2], Matthew[1])[615] was born in Billerica, Mass. 1 July 1722 and died in 1797 at 75 years of age. He married **Martha Flagg**.

John **Lane** and Martha **Flagg** had the following child:
  556   i.   Gershom Flagg[7] **Lane** was born in 1753.

307. **Rebecca**[6] **Lane** (James[5], Susanna[4] **Whipple**, Capt. John[3], Elder John[2], Matthew[1])[616] was born in Billerica 29 October 1723 and died there 24 May 1814 at 90 years of age.   She married **Benjamin Hutchinson Jr** in Bedford, Mass. 31 July 1750. Benjamin[617] was christened in Salem Village, Mass. 30 September 1772 and died in 1813 in Bedford.

Rebecca **Lane** and Benjamin **Hutchinson** Jr had the following child:
+ 557   i.   Betsey[7] **Hutchinson** was born 20 January 1760.

313. **Samuel**[6] **Lane** (James[5], Susanna[4] **Whipple**, Capt. John[3], Elder John[2], Matthew[1])[618] was born in Billerica 11 July 1737 and died 26 June 1802 at 64 years of age. He participated in the Battle at Concord, Mass. 19 April 1775 and married **Ruth Davis** 2 October 1760. Ruth,[619] daughter of Stephen **Davis** and Elizabeth **Brown**, was born 5 December 1739 and died 21 October 1772 at 32 years of age. She was from Bedford, Mass.

Samuel **Lane** and Ruth **Davis** had the following child:
+ 558   i.   Ebenezer[7] **Lane** was born 14 May 1771.

320. **Micah**[6] **Stone** (Simon[5], Deacon Simon[4], Mary[3] **Whipple**, Elder John[2], Matthew[1])[620] birth date unknown married **Elizabeth Lawrence**. She married (2) **Simon Stone**.

Micah **Stone** and Elizabeth **Lawrence** had the following child:
+ 559   i.   Simon[7] **Stone**.

321. **Amos**[6] **Stone** (Simon[5], Deacon Simon[4], Mary[3] **Whipple**, Elder John[2], Matthew[1])[621] was born in Harvard, Middlesex Co. Mass. 9 September 1729 and died 16 September 1804 at 75 years of age. He married **Edna Hale**,[622] daughter of Ambrose **Hale** and Hannah **Symonds**.

Amos **Stone** and Edna **Hale** had the following children, probably all born in Harvard:

560   i.   Charles[7] **Stone**[623] was christened 6 May 1764.

561   ii. Huldah **Stone**[624] was christened 29 June 1766 and married Zebulon **Keene** in Greenwich Hampshire Co. Mass. 16 January 1788.

562   iii. Cyrus **Stone**[625] was christened 30 April 1769 and died abt 1833 in Hanover, Indiana.

563   iv. Hannah **Stone**[626] was born 5 February 1755 and died 26 October 1756 in Harvard at one year of age.

564   v. Ambrose **Stone**[627] was born in 1757 and died in 1850 in Goshen, Mass. at 93 years of age. He married Katherine **Partridge**. Ambrose served as a private under General Ward at Ticonderoga during the Revolutionary War (1776) and was placed on the pension role in 1833 for service in the Massachusetts Continental Line.

+ 565   vi. Capt. Amos **Stone** was born 28 September 1759.

566   vii. Hannah **Stone**[628] was born 26 February 1762.

567 viii. Oliver **Stone**[629] was christened 7 April 1771 and died 20 August 1774 at 3 years of age.

568   ix. Manasseh **Stone**[630] was christened 23 May 1773 and died abt 1804 in Castleon, N.Y.

322. Capt. Asa[6] **Holden** (Abigail[5] **Stone**, Deacon Simon[4], Mary[3] **Whipple**, Elder John[2], Matthew[1])[631] was born in Groton, Mass. 23 August 1732 and died 23 June 1813 in Shirley, Mass. at 80 years of age. He was a farmer and tanner and married **Dorothy Wait** in Groton 6 December 1757. Dorothy,[632] daughter of Phineas **Wait** and Mary **Hubbard**, was born in Groton 9 September 1734 and died 5 July 1807 in Shirley at 72 years of age.

Capt. Asa **Holden** and Dorothy **Wait** had the following child:

+ 569   i.   Phineas[7] **Holden** was born 14 July 1760.

323. Mary[6] **Whitney** (Mary[5] **Stone**, Deacon Simon[4], Mary[3] **Whipple**, Elder John[2], Matthew[1])[633] was born in Stowe, Mass. 28 October 1729 and died 18 May 1797 in Marlborough, Mass. at 67 years of age. She married **Silas Jewell**[634] who was born 4 May 1726 and died 20 May 1803 in Marlborough at 77 years of age.

Mary **Whitney** and Silas **Jewell** had the following child:

+ 570   i.   Mary[7] **Jewell** was born 22 August 1757.

324. Josiah[6] **Chamberlain** (Susanna[5] **Stone**, Deacon Simon[4], Mary[3] **Whipple**, Elder John[2], Matthew[1])[635] was born in Newton, Mass. 13 November 1721 and married **Hepsibah Cressy** in Groton, Mass. 10 June 1752. Hepsibah,[636] daughter of Jonathan **Cressy** and Eleanor **Barter**, was born 18 July 1730.

Josiah **Chamberlain** and Hepsibah **Cressy** had the following children:

571   i.   Thomas[7] **Chamberlain**[637] was born 26 March 1753.

572   ii. Jonathan **Chamberlain**[638] was born in February 1754 and died 5 November 1754 at less than one year of age.

325. Lt. James[6] **Stone** (James[5], John[4], Mary[3] **Whipple**, Elder John[2], Matthew[1])[639] was born in Groton, Mass. In 1727 and died in 1788 at 61 years of age. He lived at Groton and Harvard, Mass. was a tanner and an officer in the 1755 expedition against Crown Point. He married twice: (1) Deborah **Nutting** and (2) an unnamed second wife.

Lt. James **Stone** and Deborah **Nutting** had the following child:

+ 573   i. David[7] **Stone** was born in 1761.

327. **Bathsheba**[6] **Stone** (Adams[5], Dea. Matthew[4], Mary[3] **Whipple**, Elder John[2], Matthew[1])[640] was born in Sudbury, Mass. 1 December 1721 and married **Col. Ezekiel Howe** in Massachusetts 19 January 1744. Ezekiel[641] died in 1796 at 76 years of age. Col. Howe was the proprietor of the Red Horse Tavern (Wayside Inn) in Sudbury from 1746 until his death. Their son Adam was proprietor until 1830 and Adam's son Lyman until 1861.

Bathsheba **Stone** and Col. Ezekiel **Howe** had the following child:

+ 574   I. Adam[7] **Howe**.

330. **Hannah**[6] **Stone** (Ebenezer[5], Ebenezer[4], Mary[3] **Whipple**, Elder John[2], Matthew[1])[642]. was christened 15 November 1726 and died 26 February 1757. She married **Robert Goddard**, her second cousin, in Petersham, Worcester Co., Mass. 8 January 1751/52. Their common ancestors were Mary Whipple and Deacon Simon Stone. Robert,[643] son of Edward **Goddard** Jr. and Hepzibah **Hapgood**, was born in Petersham 13 August 1728 and died there 9 June 1807 at 78 years of age[644] He married (2) **Elizabeth Goddard** in Petersham 15 January 1760. Robert was deputy sheriff of Petersham in 1774/75 (see 377).

Robert **Goddard** and Hannah **Stone** had the following children born in Petersham:

+ 575   i. Hannah[7] **Goddard** was born 22 January 1753.
  576   ii. Sarah **Goddard**[645] was born 26 March 1755 and married Isaac Hastings.

331. **Margaret**[6] **Stone** (Ebenezer[5], Ebenezer[4], Mary[3] **Whipple**, Elder John[2], Matthew[1])[646] was born in Watertown, Mass. 14 October 1728 and married **David Goddard**. David,[647] son of Edward **Goddard** Jr. and Hepzibah **Hapgood**, was born in Shrewsbury, Mass. 26 September 1730. (See No. 378.)

David **Goddard** and Margaret **Stone** had the following children:

  577   i. Moses[7] **Goddard**[648] was born 25 July 1754.
  578   ii. Jonathan **Goddard**[649] was born 23 December 1755.
  579   iii. Hezekiah **Goddard**[650] was born 10 November 1757.
+ 580   iv. Lucy **Goddard** was born 19 June 1760.
  581   v. Catherine **Goddard**[651] was born 21 November 1762.
  582   vi. Lydia **Goddard**[652] was born 2 December 1764.
  583   vii. John **Goddard**[653] was born 20 April 1768.

332. **Mary**[6] **Stone** (Samuel[5], Ebenezer[4], Mary[3] **Whipple**, Elder John[2], Matthew[1])[654] was born 23 January 1718 and died 27 March 1776 in Newton, Mass. at 58 years of age. She married **Daniel Woodward Jr.** 16 May 1739. Daniel[655] was born in Newton 14 September 1714 and died there 30 March 1774 at 59 years of age.

Mary **Stone** and Daniel **Woodward**, Jr. had the following child:

+ 584   i. Lois[7] **Woodward**, was born 6 October 1740.

337. Mary[6] **Woodward** (Mindwell[5] **Stone**, Ebenezer[4], Mary[3] **Whipple**, Elder John[2], Matthew[1])[656] was born in Newton, Mass. 28 February 1732/33. She married **Jonathan Richardson**[657]

Mary **Woodward** and Jonathan **Richardson** had the following children:

	585	i.	Mary[7] **Richardson**[658] was born 23 September 1752.
	586	ii.	Jonathan **Richardson**[659] was born 30 December 1753.
+	587	iii.	Susanna **Richardson** was born 12 December 1755.
	588	iv.	Abigail **Richardson**[660] was born 29 October 1757.
	589	v.	Nehemiah **Richardson**[661] was born 28 June 1759.
	590	vi.	John **Richardson**[662] was born 22 April 1761.
	591	vii.	Mehitabel **Richardson**[663] was born 10 August 1764.
	592	viii.	Hannah **Richardson**[664] was born 4 February 1766.
	593	ix.	Lois **Richardson**[665] was born 16 September 1767.
	594	x.	Jonathan **Richardson**[666] was born 19 September 1768.

343. **Hannah**[6] **Eaton** (Lydia Abiah[5] **Starr**, Mary[4] **Stone**, Mary[3] **Whipple**, Elder John[2], Matthew[1])[667] was born in Killingly, Conn. 17 August 1719 and died 16 February 1757 in Stafford, Conn. at 37 years of age. She married **Seth Johnson** in Killingly 13 October 1743. Seth,[668] son of Nathaniel **Johnson** and Mehitable **Guile**, was born in Haverhill, Mass. 12 July 1720 and died abt 1804 in Floyd, N.Y. (Floyd is the presumed place of death.) He married (2) **Mary Edson** 20 April 1758. Seth and Mary had six children.

Hannah **Eaton** and Seth **Johnson** had the following children:

	595	i.	Abner[7] **Johnson**[669] was born in Killingly, 15 July 1744 and died 29 March 1751 in Stafford, Conn. at 6 years of age.
	596	ii.	Mehitable **Johnson**[670] was born in Stafford 17 July 1746 and died there 29 March 1751 at 4 years of age.
	597	iii.	Jonathan **Johnson**[671] was born in Stafford 18 September 1748 and married Hannah **Orcutt** [672] there.
	598	iv.	Hannah **Johnson**[673] was born in Stafford, 23 September 1750.
	599	v.	Mabel **Johnson**[674] was born in Stafford 9 November 1752.
+	600	vi.	Abner **Johnson** was born 15 April 1755.
	601	vii.	Lydia **Johnson**[675] was born in Stafford 7 February 1757 and died there 18 May 1776 at 19 years of age.

345. **John**[6] **Eaton** (Lydia Abiah[5] **Starr**, Mary[4] **Stone**, Mary[3] **Whipple**, Elder John[2], Matthew[1])[676] was born in Killingly, Conn. 18 May 1724 and died 19 September 1788 in East Hoosick, Berkshire Co., Mass. at 64 years of age. East Hoosick is now Adams, Mass. He married **Hannah Johnson** in Stafford Springs, Tolland Co., Conn. in 1751.

John **Eaton** and Hannah **Johnson** had the following children:

	602	I.	Rufus[7] **Eaton**.
+	603	ii.	John **Eaton** was born 14 February 1761.

349. **Abigail**[6] **Dana** (Susanna[5] **Starr**, Mary[4] **Stone**, Mary[3] **Whipple**, Elder John[2], Matthew[1])[677] was born in Promfet, Conn. 23 July 1722 and died 2 April 1808 in Newbury, Vt. at 85 years of age. She married **Joseph Grow** 4 February 1742. Joseph,[678] son of Thomas **Grow** and Rebecca **Holt**, was born in Andover, Mass. 16 October 1717 and died 21 April 1808 at 90 years of age.

Abigail **Dana** and Joseph **Grow** had the following child:

+   604   i. Joseph[7] **Grow** was born 13 March 1748.

350. Penelope[6] **Dana** (Susanna[5] **Starr**, Mary[4] **Stone**, Mary[3] **Whipple**, Elder John[2], Matthew[1])[679] was born in 1731 and married **Ephraim** Patch[680] who was born in 1723.

Penelope **Dana** and Ephraim **Patch** had the following child:

+   605   i. Thomas[7] **Patch** was born in 1753.

353. Capt. Comfort[6] **Starr** (Comfort[5], Mary[4] **Stone**, Mary[3] **Whipple**, Elder John[2], Matthew[1])[681] was born in Thompson, Conn. 10 August 1731 and died 30 November 1812 in Guilford, Vt. at 81 years of age. He was buried in Carpenter Cemetery. His military title was earned during service in the Revolutionary War when he was a captain in the militia. He paid £330 for land in Guilford in April 1777 and moved his family there in 1780. He is considered the progenitor of the Vermont line of Starrs.

He married **Judith Cooper** in Thompson 22 December 1754. Judith,[682] daughter of Timothy **Cooper** and Sarah **Guile**, was born in Killingly, Conn. 14 February 1736 and died 15 September 1815 in Guilford at 79 years of age. She is buried in Carpenter Cemetery.

Capt. Comfort **Starr** and Judith **Cooper** had the following children:

    606   i. Perley[7] **Starr**[683] was born in Thompson, 14 October 1755 and died abt 1817 in Beach Ridge, Niagara Co., N.Y. He was a farmer, operated a saw and a grist mill, and served in his father's military company in 1780 during the Revolutionary War.

+   607   ii. Sarah **Starr** was born 28 November 1760.

+   608   iii. Abigail **Starr** was born 24 November 1763.

+   609   iv. Comfort **Starr** was born 30 May 1766.

    610   v. Judith **Starr**[684] was born in Thompson 27 November 1768 and died 27 November 1815 at 47 years of age.

    611   vi. Mary **Starr**[685] was born in Thompson 27 May 1771 and died 26 February 1860 in Newfane, Windham Co., Vt. at 88 years of age. She married James **Franklin**.

    612   vii. Timothy **Starr**[686] was born in Thompson 22 December 1773 and married twice. (1) Anna K. **Chase**[687] in April 1796. (2) Demaris **Nichols** in March 1805.

+   613   viii. Martha **Starr** was born 28 May 1776.

    614   ix. Ephraim **Starr**[688] was born in Guilford 11 May 1780 and died 29 December 1862 in Illinois at 82 years of age. He married twice. (1) Hannah **Gore**. (2) (_) **Eggleston**. He was a soldier in the War of 1812.

358. Ebenezer[6] **Starr** (Comfort[5], Mary[4] **Stone**, Mary[3] **Whipple**, Elder John[2], Matthew[1])[689] was born in Thompson, Conn. 24 February 174 and died there 13 October 1804 at 63 years of age. A Quaker, he was a farmer and tavern keeper. He married twice. (1) **Sarah Porter**[690] in Connecticut 21 December 1767. (2) **Mary Stevens** in Connecticut 18 February 1773. Mary[691] was the daughter of Robert **Stevens**.

Ebenezer **Starr** and Mary **Stevens** had the following child:

+   615   i. Ebenezer[7] **Starr Jr.** was born abt 1780.

361. **Rev. Nathan**[6] **Stone** (Rev. Nathan[5], Rev. Nathaniel[4], Mary[3] **Whipple**, Elder John[2], Matthew[1])[692] was born in Southborough, Worcestor Co., Mass. 30 September 1737 and died 26 April 1804 in Dennis, Mass. at 66 years of age. He was graduated from Harvard College class of 1762 and was ordained at East Yarmouth, Mass. (now Dennis) in 1764. His father preached the sermon at his ordination. He was minister there for 40 years until his death.[693] He married **Mary** Cushing,[694] daughter of rev. Job **Cushing**.

Rev. Nathan **Stone** and Mary **Cushing** had the following child:

616   i. Rev. Nathaniel[7] **Stone**[695] was born in Dennis and was graduated from Harvard College Class of 1795 and ordained at Windham, Maine 31 Oct. 1798 where he served for six years before moving to Provincetown where he was minister for nearly 20 years. These four generations of Stone ministers, beginning with Nathaniel (1667-1755), and continuing through Nathan (1707-1781), Nathaniel (1737-1804?), and Nathaniel, served over 170 years in the ministry.

370. **Solomon**[6] **Estey** (Elizabeth Mary[5] **Stearns**, Elizabeth[4] **Stone**, Mary[3] **Whipple**, Elder John[2], Matthew[1])[696] was born 31 December 1737 and married **Phebe Dean** in Taunton, Mass. 17 May 1770. Phebe,[697] daughter of Silas **Dean** and Joanna **Whitcomb**, was born in Hardwick, Worcester Co., Mass. 14 July 1748.

Solomon **Estey** and Phebe **Dean** had the following children:

617   i. Mercy[7] **Estey**[698].
+ 618   ii. John Dean **Estey** was born about 1775.

371. **Eliphet**[6] **Stearns** (Rev. Ebenezer[5], Elizabeth[4] **Stone**, Mary[3] **Whipple**, Elder John[2], Matthew[1])[699] birth date unknown married **Hannah Clark**.

Eliphet **Stearns** and Hannah **Clark** had the following child:
+ 619   i. Phineas[7] **Stearns**.

372. **Mary**[6] **Stearns** (Jonathan[5], Elizabeth[4] **Stone**, Mary[3] **Whipple**, Elder John[2], Matthew[1])[700] birth date unknown married **Lt. Joseph Wilbor**[701] 19 January 1753. Joseph was born in 1733 and died 15 November 1803 at 70 years of age.

Mary **Stearns** and Lt. Joseph **Wilbor** had the following child:
+ 620   i. Hannah[7] **Wilbor** was born 1755.

373. **Asa**[6] **Upham** (Hannah[5] **Stearns**, Elizabeth[4] **Stone**, Mary[3] **Whipple**, Elder John[2], Matthew[1])[702] was born in Sturbridge, Mass. 18 May 1736 and died 13 September 1826 in Weathersfield, Vt. at 90 years of age. He married **Lydia Pierce** 10 December 1761. Lydia,[703] daughter of Joseph **Pierce** IV and Lydia **Walker**, was born in Weston, Mass. and died 11 December 1822 in Weathersfield.

Asa **Upham** and Lydia **Pierce** had the following child:
+ 621   i. Joseph Pierce[7] **Upham** was born 12 February 1764.

375. **Nathan**[6] **Goddard** (Edward[5], Susanna[4] **Stone**, Mary[3] **Whipple**, Elder John[2], Matthew[1])[704] was born in Shrewsbury, Mass. 18 January 1725 and died 2 February 1806 at 81 years of age. He married **Dorothy Stevens** who was born in Petersham, Mass. abt 1719. Dorothy[705] died 30 March 1808 at 88 years of age.

Nathan **Goddard** and Dorothy **Stevens** had the following children:
- 622   i. Hepzibah[7] **Goddard**[706] was born in Shrewsbury and married Jonathan **Woodward** 19 June 1770.
- 623   ii. Dolly Goddard[707].
- 624   iii. Nathan **Goddard** Jr.[708] was born in 1748 and died 8 December 1816 at 68 years of age. He married Thankful **Woodward**.
- + 625   iv. Ebenezer **Goddard** was born 19 September 1753.
- + 626   v. Asa **Goddard** was born in August 1755.

377. Robert[6] **Goddard** (Edward[5], Susanna[4] **Stone**, Mary[3] **Whipple**, Elder John[2], Matthew[1])[709] was born in Petersham, Mass. 13 August 1728[710] and died there 9 June 1807 at 78 years of age. Robert was deputy sheriff of Petersham in 1774/75. He married twice. (1) **Hannah Stone** in Petersham 8 January 1751/52. Robert and Hannah were second cousins with Mary Whipple and Deacon Simon Stone being their common ancestors. Hannah,[711] daughter of Ebenezer **Stone** and Sarah **Bond**, was christened 15 November 1726 and died 26 February 1757. (2) **Elizabeth Goddard** in Petersham, 15 January 1760. Elizabeth,[712] daughter of Benjamin Samuel **Goddard** and Mary **Kidder**, was born in Grafton, Worcester Co., Mass. 1 November 1733 and died 14 April 1820 in Rutland, Vt. at 86 years of age (see 330).

Robert **Goddard** and Hannah **Stone** had the following children:
- + 575   i. Hannah[7] **Goddard** was born 22 January 1753.
- 576   ii. Sarah Goddard[713] was born in Petersham 26 March 1755 and married Isaac **Hastings**.

Robert **Goddard** and Elizabeth **Goddard** had the following children, all born in Petersham:
- 627   iii. Hulda Goddard[714] was born 12 January 1761 and died in 1821 at 60 years of age.
- 628   iv. Rhoda Goddard[715] was born 11 February 1762 and died 29 November 1844 in Chester, Vt. at 82 years of age. She married Solomon **Wilson** 28 February 1804.
- 629   v. Joel Goddard[716] was born 8 April 1763 and married twice. (1) Anna **Goddard** 23 February 1786. (2) Hannah **Grosvenor** 31 August 1825.
- 630   vi. Nathaniel Goddard[717] was born 20 October 1764.
- 631   vii. Stephan Goddard[718] was born 6 October 1766 and died there 28 November 1768 at 2 years of age.
- 632   viii. John Goddard[719] was born 18 February 1768 and died 21 December 1768 in Peterham at less than one year of age.
- 633   ix. Stephan Goddard[720] was born 21 April 1769 and married Rachel Rhoda **Woodward** 9 November 1807.
- 634   x. John Goddard[721] was born 14 November 1770 and died in 1800 at 29 years of age. He married Delia **Kady** 11 September 1798.
- 635   xi. Levi Goddard[722] was born 25 July 1772 and married Mary **Goddard** 16 May 1799.
- 636   xii. Ashbel Goddard[723] was born 23 August 1774 and died 23 April 1776 in Petersham at less than two years of age.
- + 637   xiii. Nahum **Goddard** was born 14 February 1776.
- 638   xiv. Robert Goddard[724] was born 20 June 1778 and married Eunice **Bennett** 23 January 1805.

378. David[6] **Goddard** (Edward[5], Susanna[4] **Stone**, Mary[3] **Whipple**, Elder John[2],

Matthew[1])[725] was born in Shrewsbury, Mass. 26 September 1730 and married **Margaret Stone**. Margaret,[726] daughter of Ebenezer **Stone** and Sarah **Bond**, was born in Watertown, Mass. 14 October 1728 (See No. 331.)

David **Goddard** and Margaret **Stone** had the following children:

     577   i. Moses[7] **Goddard**[727] was born 25 July 1754.
     578   ii. Jonathan **Goddard**[728] was born 23 December 1755.
     579   iii. Hezekiah **Goddard**[729] was born 10 November 1757.
+   580   iv. Lucy **Goddard** was born 19 June 1760.
     581   v. Catherine **Goddard**[730] was born 21 November 1762.
     582   vi. Lydia **Goddard**[731] was born 2 December 1764.
     583   vii. John **Goddard**[732] was born 20 April 1768.

380. **Lt. Daniel[6] Goddard** (Edward[5], Susanna[4] **Stone**, Mary[3] **Whipple**, Elder John[2], Matthew[1])[733] was born in Shewsbury, Mass. 17 February 1734 and died there 20 September 1807 at 73 years of age. He married **Mary Willard** in Grafton, Mass. 17 November 1756. Mary[734] was born abt 1730 and died 13 January 1796 in Shrewsbury at 65 years of age. Her death record stated she was in her 66th year.

Lt. Daniel **Goddard** and Mary **Willard** had the following children, all born in Shrewsbury:

     639   i. Miriam[7] **Goddard**[735] was born 8 September 1757 and died 8 December 1792 in Shrewsbury at 35 years of age.
     640   ii. Daniel **Goddard**[736] was born 15 January 1759 and died 29 January 1759 at less than one year of age.
     641   iii. Martha **Goddard**[737] was born 4 March 1760.
     642   iv. Hepzibah **Goddard**[738] was born 2 February 1764 and died 16 May 1764 at less than one year of age.
+   643   v. Daniel **Goddard** was born 23 August 1765.
     644   vi. Calvin **Goddard**[739] was born 17 July 1768.
     645   vii. Martha **Goddard**[740] was born 1 September 1770 and died 14 September 1770 in Shrewsbury at less than one month of age.

385. **Edward[6] Goddard** (Edward[5], Susanna[4] **Stone**, Mary[3] **Whipple**, Elder John[2], Matthew[1])[741] was born in Shrewsbury, Mass. 12 March 1745 and died there 20 May 1782 at 37 years of age. He married **Margaret How**[742] in Shrewsbury 23 May 1771 and she died there 27 October 1781.

Edward **Goddard** and Margaret **How** had the following children, all born in Shrewsbury:

     646   i. Patty[7] **Goddard**[743] was born 13 June 1772.
     647   ii. Molly **Goddard**[744] was born 17 March 1776.
     648   iii. Sally **Goddard**[745] was born 20 January 1778 and died 10 April 1778 in Shrewsbury at less than three months of age.

391. **Nathan[6] Goddard** (Benjamin[5], Susanna[4] **Stone**, Mary[3] **Whipple**, Elder John[2], Matthew[1])[746] was born 4 August 1746 and died 24 July 1795 in Framingham, Mass. at 48 years of age. He married **Martha Nichols** 15 December 1772. Martha, daughter of Joseph **Nichols** and Martha **Howe**, was born in Framingham 31 October 1746.

Nathan **Goddard** and Martha **Nichols** had the following children born in Framingham:

649	i.	Nichols[7] married Charity **White**.
650	ii.	Grace **Goddard**[747] married Ephraim **Drurg**.
+ 651	iii.	Capt. Nathan **Goddard**.

398. Susanna[6] **Goddard** (Ebenezer[5], Susanna[4] **Stone**, Mary[3] **Whipple**, Elder John[2], Matthew[1])[748] was born in Framingham, Mass. 25 September 1742 and died 5 January 1837 in Hopkinton, Middlesex Co., Mass. at 94 years of age. She married **Phineas Howe** in Hopkinton 23 April 1761. Phineas,[749] son of Peter **Howe** and Thankful **Howe**, was born in Hopkinton 22 October 1735 and died there 19 September 1807 at 71 years of age.

Susanna **Goddard** and Phineas **Howe** had the following children, born in Hopkinton:

+ 652	i.	Rhoda[7] **Howe** was born 8 July 1762.
653	ii.	Susannah **Howe**[750] was born 19 February 1764 and married Phineas **Brigham**.
+ 654	iii.	Abigail (Nabby) **Howe** was born 3 May 1766.
655	iv.	Patty **Howe**[751] was born 28 February 1768 and married Elisha **Morse**.
656	v.	Ann **Howe**[752] was born 25 May 1770 and married Jereboam **Parker**.
657	vi.	Phineas **Howe**[753] was born 21 February 1773 and died unmarried.
658	vii.	Betsey **Howe**[754] was born 3 May 1774 and married John **Haven**.
659	viii.	Nehemiah **Howe**[755] was born 21 December 1776 and married Ruthy **Eames**.
660	ix.	Samuel **Howe**[756] was born 21 July 178 and married Jerusa **Cody**.
661	x.	Peter **Howe**[757] was born 11 October 1783.
662	xi.	Ruth **Howe**[758] was born 31 March 1785.

408. Jonathan[6] **Stone** (Jonathan[5], Jonathan[4], Mary[3] **Whipple**, Elder John[2], Matthew[1])[759] was born in Watertown, Mass. 17 November 1725 and died 21 December 1806 in Ward (now Auburn), Mass. He married three times. (1) **Ruth Livermore** in Watertown 21 May 1747. Ruth,[760] daughter of Oliver **Livermore** and Ruth (__) **Bowman**, was born in Watertown 23 May 1727 and died 2 September 1764 in Worcester, Mass. at 37 years of age. (2) **Mrs. Mary (Clark) Gates** in Worcester, 29 October 1765. (3) **Martha Baird** after August 1773.

Jonathan **Stone** and Ruth **Livermore** had the following children:

+ 663	i.	Ruth[7] **Stone** was born 3 August 1748.
+ 664	ii.	Lt. Jonathan **Stone** was born 8 December 1750.
+ 665	iii.	Daniel **Stone** was born 25 October 1752.
666	iv.	Rhoda **Stone**[761] was born 3 August 1754 and died 25 September 1801 at 47 years of age. She married twice. (1) Phineas **Flagg** 25 May 1777. (2) John **Sawyer** 7 November 1798.
667	v.	Joseph **Stone**[762] was born 20 March 1758 and died 2 February 1837 at 78 years of age. He married Hannah (Nichols) **Boyden**. They had no children.
668	vi.	Nathaniel **Stone**[763] was born 2 June 1761 and died 1 March 1843 at 81 years of age. He married Elizabeth **Brown**.
669	vii.	Mary **Stone**[764] was born 18 February 1763 and died 10 December 1825 at 62 years of age. She married Francis **Stevens** abt 1784.

Jonathan **Stone** and Mrs. Mary (Clark) **Gates**, had the following children:

670	viii.	Sarah **Stone**[765] was born 24 March 1768 and died 16 May 1816 at 48 years of age. She married Jonah **Cutting** 31 December 1787.

671   ix. Moses **Stone**[766] was born 28 March 1771 and died 8 January 1814 at 42 years of age. He married Pamela **Gilbert** 26 February 1795.

409. William[6] **Stone** (Moses[5], Jonathan[4], Mary[3] **Whipple**, Elder John[2], Matthew[1])[767] was born in Watertown, Mass. 6 October 1750 and died there in May 1808 at 57 years of age. He married **Hannah Barnard** in Waltham, Mass. 29 December 1774. Hannah,[768] daughter of Jonathan **Barnard** and Hannah **Stowell**, was born in Watertown 17 May 1754 and died there 3 November 1834 at 80 years of age.

William **Stone** and Hannah **Barnard** had the following children:

+ 672   i. Hannah[7] **Stone** was born 28 February 1778.

673   ii. William **Stone**[769] was born in Woodstock, Windham Co., Conn. 28 September 1781.

+ 674   iii. Susanna **Stone** was born in October 1783.

+ 675   iv. Abigail **Stone** was born in October 1783.

676   v. Leonard **Stone**[770] was born in Watertown, Mass. 16 February 1785.

677   vi. Richard **Stone**[771] was born in Watertown 12 October 1787 and died 25 April 1830 in Baltimore, Md., at 42 years of age.

678   vii. Hepzibah **Stone**[772] was born in Watertown 21 March 1789 and married Jesse **Bird**.

679   viii. Joseph **Stone**[773] was born 1 November 1790.

680   ix. Betsey **Stone**[774] was born in 1792.

+ 681   x. Elizabeth **Stone** was born 11 June 1795.

+ 682   xi. Seth **Stone** was born 2 January 1797.

683   xii. Eveline **Stone**[775] was born in Watertown 12 June 1799 and died 9 July 1861 in Belmont, Middlesex Co., Mass. at 62 years of age.

684   xiii. Caroline **Stone**[776] was born in Watertown 12 June 1799 and married George M. **Robbins**.

685   xiv. Mary **Stone**[777] was born in Woodstock and married Seth **Bird**.

686   xv. Anna **Stone**[778] was born in Watertown 2 February 1802 and married Constantine V. **Swan** 16 December 1821.

410. Jonathan[6] **Stone** (Moses[5], Jonathan[4], Mary[3] **Whipple**, Elder John[2], Matthew[1])[779] was born in Watertown, Mass. in 1753 and died in 1825 at 72 years of age. He married **Sarah Watson**. He was a soldier in the Revolution. The family lived in that part of Watertown now Belmont.

Jonathan **Stone** and Sarah **Watson** had the following child:

+ 687   i. Charles[7] **Stone** was born in 1789.

412. Joanna[6] **Norton** (John[5], Mary[4] **Goodhue**, Sarah[3] **Whipple**, Elder John[2], Matthew[1])[780] was born in Kittery, Maine bet 1720-24 and died bef 25 January 1781 in Berwick, York Co., Maine at approximately 60 years of age. She married **Joseph Billings** in 1742. Joseph[781] was the son of Joseph **Billings** and Hannah **Wilson**. He married (2) **Sarah Cox** aft 25 January 1781. Joseph died before 4 November 1797 in Berwick. His Will is dated 1 January 1794 and was probated 4 November 1797.

Joanna **Norton** and Joseph **Billings** had the following children:

688   i. Daniel[7] **Billings**[782] was christened in Kittery 5 July 1747 and married twice. (1) Hannah **Billings** in Kittery 30 December 1770. (2) Jane **Cox** in Kittery 9 December 1790.

+ 689   ii. John **Billings** was born 6 March 1743.

690   iii. Sarah **Billings**[783] was born in Berwick and died bef 1 January 1797. She married John **Norton**.

691   iv. Rebecca **Billings**[784] was born in Berwick and married Thomas **Morgrage** in Kittery 7 December 1773.

692   v. Susanna **Billings**[785] was born in Berwick,[786] christened in Kittery 24 September 1749, and died there bef 1800.

693   vi. Joanna Billings[787] was born in Berwick and died unmarried abt 2 May 1798 at approximately 47 years of age.

694   vii. Joseph **Billings**[788] was born in Berwick, christened in Kittery 2 June 1751, and died there between 1820-30. He married twice. (1) Mercy **Fernald** in Kittery 3 January 1782. (2) Margery **Pickernell** in Kittery 8 February 1816.

413. Moses[6] **Swett** (Elizabeth[5] **Norton**, Mary[4] **Goodhue**, Sarah[3] **Whipple**, Elder John[2], Matthew[1])[789] was born in New Hampshire in 1738 and died there in 1790 at 52 years of age. He married **Eunice** Rogers.[790]

Moses **Swett** and Eunice **Rogers** had the following child:

+ 695   i. Daniel[7] **Swett** was born 23 April 1763.

423. Joseph[6] **Treadwell** (Sarah[5] **Goodhue**, William[4], Sarah[3] **Whipple**, Elder John[2], Matthew[1])[791] was born in Ipswich, Mass. 3 February 1716/17 and died abt 1763 in Nova Scotia, Canada. He was in the militia at the time of his death and died at Menas Bay on the Bay of Chagnecto. He married **Sarah Hammond** in Ipswich. The date of intent to marry was 10 January 1746. Sarah,[792] daughter of David **Hammond** and Mary **Platts**, was born in Rowley, Mass. and christened there 15 February 1727/28. She married (2) **Walter Davis** in Newburyport, Mass. 25 December 1769. Walter was a yeoman who lived in Ipswich and Dracut, Mass.

Joseph **Treadwell** and Sarah **Hammond** had the following children:

696   i. Mary[7] **Treadwell**[793] was born in Rowley, christened there 5 March 1748, and married George **Tryal** in Newburyport, Mass. 30 December 1760.

+ 697   ii. Sarah **Treadwell**.

+ 698   iii. Joseph **Treadwell**.

699   iv. Elizabeth **Treadwell**[794] was born and christened in Ipswich 5 March 1748. It is believed she died young.

424. Sarah[6] **Treadwell** (Sarah[5] **Goodhue**, William[4], Sarah[3] **Whipple**, Elder John[2], Matthew[1])[795] was born in Ipswich, Mass. christened there 18 September 1720, and died there after 1769. She married **Samuel Adams Jr.** in Ipswich. The date of intent to marry was 17 August 1738. Samuel,[796] son of Samuel **Adams** and Mary **Burley**, was born in Ipswich 19 January 1710 and died there 26 August 1757 at 47 years of age.

Sarah **Treadwell** and Samuel **Adams** Jr. had the following children born in Ipswich:

700   i. Sarah[7] **Adams**.[797].

701   ii. Samuel **Adams**.[798]

425. Elizabeth[6] **Treadwell** (Sarah[5] **Goodhue**, William[4], Sarah[3] **Whipple**, Elder John[2], Matthew[1])[799] was born in Ipswich, Mass., christened there 1 April 1722, and died there (death place is presumed) 23 July 1778 at 56 years of age. She married **Aaron Caldwell** in Ipswich in 1750. The date of intent to marry was 3

June 1750. Aaron,[800] son of John **Caldwell** and Elizabeth **Lull**, was born 18 April 1721 and died before 21 September 1765 in Ipswich at approximately 44 years of age. He was a widower at the time of his marriage to Elizabeth.

Elizabeth **Treadwell** and Aaron **Caldwell** had the following children born in Ipswich:

702	i.	Elizabeth[7] **Caldwell**.[801]
703	ii.	Moses **Caldwell**.[802]
704	iii.	Stephen **Caldwell**.[803]
705	iv.	Mary **Caldwell**.[804]

426. Thomas[6] **Treadwell** (Sarah[5] **Goodhue**, William[4], Sarah[3] **Whipple**, Elder John[2], Matthew[1])[805] was born in Ipswich, Mass. 6 August 1732 and died in 1766 at 33 years of age. He was a sea captain. He married **Esther Hovey** in Ipswich 19 February 1752. Esther,[806] daughter of Nathaniel **Hovey** and Hannah **Fossee**, was born in Ipswich, christened there 23 February 1728, and died there 5 October 1808 at 80 years of age.

Thomas **Treadwell** and Esther **Hovey** had the following children, born in Ipswich:

+	706	i.	Nathaniel[7] **Treadwell** was born 20 December 1752.
	707	ii	Hannah **Treadwell**[807] was christened 12 May 1754. She may have married Stephen Wyatt, Jr. of Newburyport, Mass. 27 March 1777.
	708	iii.	Esther **Treadwell**[808] was christened 14 November 1756. She may have married Robert Newman at Ipswich 22 May 1778.

427. Elizabeth[6] **Goodhue** (Jonathan[5], William[4], Sarah[3] **Whipple**, Elder John[2], Matthew[1])[809] was born in Chester, N.H. 16 March 1729 and married **Joseph Basford** 8 January 1746. Joseph,[810] son of James **Basford** and Mary **Davis**, was born in Chester abt 1721 and died there 12 February 1791 at 69 years of age.

Elizabeth **Goodhue** and Joseph **Basford** had the following children born in Long Meadows, N.H.:

+	709	i.	Jonathan[7] **Basford** was born 1 March 1748.
	710	ii.	Joseph **Basford** Jr.[811] was born 24 August 1750.
	711	iii.	Jacob **Basford**[812] was born 5 August 1754.
	712	iv.	Benjamin **Basford**[813] was born 25 April 1756.
	713	v.	Elizabeth **Basford**[814] was born 1 October 1760.
	714	vi.	James **Basford**[815] was born in 27 September 1762.
	715	vii.	Aaron **Basford**[816] was born 17 July 1764.

436. John[6] **Kimball** (Isaac[5], Sarah[4] **Goodhue**, Sarah[3] **Whipple**, Elder John[2], Matthew[1])[817] was born in Preston, New London Co., Conn. 12 December 1731 and died in Antioch, Gibson Co., Ind. He married **Ruhumah Sanders** in Preston 21 September 1752. Ruhumah[818] was born in Lyme, Conn. 8 July 1731 and died in Antioch.

John **Kimball** and Ruhumah **Sanders** had the following children:

+	716	i.	Isaac[7] **Kimball**.
	717	ii.	Samuel **Kimball**[819] was born in 1752.
	718	iii.	Thankful **Kimball**[820] was born in 1754.
	719	iv.	Azuba **Kimball**[821] was born in 1757.
+	720	v.	Jesse **Kimball** was born 19 March 1760.

721   vi. Silvah **Kimball**[822] was born in 1763.

437. Jacob[6] **Kimball** Jr. (Jacob[5], Sarah[4] **Goodhue**, Sarah[3] **Whipple**, Elder John[2], Matthew[1])[823] was born in Preston, Conn. 1 December 1735 and died 18 May 1826 at 90 years of age. He married **Esther Phillips** in Plainfield, Conn. 16 January 1754.

Jacob **Kimball** Jr. and Esther **Phillips** had the following child:
+   722   i. Jacob[7] **Kimball** was born in 1767.

438. Hepsibah[6] **Kilham** (Abigail[5] **Kimball**, Sarah[4] **Goodhue**, Sarah[3] **Whipple**, Elder John[2], Matthew[1])[824] was born in Preston, Conn. and died 13 February 1776 in Plainfield, Conn. She married **Nehemiah Stevens** 24 January 1766. Nehemiah[825] was born 31 August 1731and died 13 February 1776 at 44 years of age.

Hepsibah **Kilham** and Nehemiah **Stevens** had the following child:
+   723   i. Roswell[7] **Stevens** was born 17 February 1772.

439. Samuel[6] **Goodhue** (George[5], Joseph[4], Sarah[3] **Whipple**, Elder John[2], Matthew[1])[826] was born in Newburyport, Mass. in 1751 and married **Martha Mitchell** there.

Samuel **Goodhue** and Martha **Mitchell** had the following child:
+   724   i. Samuel[7] **Goodhue** was born in 1778.

440. Daniel[6] **Knowlton** (Robert[5], Marjory (Margery)[4] **Goodhue**, Sarah[3] **Whipple**, Elder John[2], Matthew[1])[827] was born in Ashford, Conn. 19 May 1726 and died abt 1795. He married **Zerviah Watkins** in Ashford 7 November 1745. Zerviah[828] was born 28 April 1728 and died abt 1760.

Daniel **Knowlton** and Zerviah **Watkins** had the following child:
+   725   i. Eleanor[7] **Knowlton** was born in 1752.

441. Deborah[6] **Dodge** (Margery[5] **Knowlton**, Marjory (Margery)[4] **Goodhue**, Sarah[3] **Whipple**, Elder John[2], Matthew[1])[829] was born in Manchester, Mass. 26 August 1725 and died in July 1810 at 84 years of age. She married **Solomon Rand** 15 September 1741. Solomon[830] was born 13 March 1723 and died in July 1801 at 78 years of age.

Deborah **Dodge** and Solomon **Rand** had the following child:
+   726   i. Solomon[7] **Rand** was born 5 March 1750.

442. Joseph[6] **Knowlton** (Joseph[5], Marjory (Margery)[4] **Goodhue**, Sarah[3] **Whipple**, Elder John[2], Matthew[1])[831] was born 18 October 1726 and died 22 August 1816 in Auburn, Mass. at 89 years of age. He married **Mary Knowlton** 21 September 1749. Mary,[832] daughter of Ezekial **Knowlton** and Susannah **Morgan**, was born 16 March 1731 and died 21 August 1796 in Auburn at 65 years of age. They had 10 children but information is only available for one.

Joseph **Knowlton** and Mary **Knowlton** had the following child:
+   727   i. Nathan[7] **Knowlton** was born 15 May 1760.

443. Ebenezer[6] **Goodhue** (John[5], John[4], Sarah[3] **Whipple**, Elder John[2], Matthew[1])[833] was born in Ipswich, Mass. in 1754 and died in 1853 at 99 years of age. He married **Sarah Potter** 4 November 1777.

Ebenezer **Goodhue** and Sarah **Potter** had the following child:

+ 728   i. Ebenezer[7] **Goodhue** was born 30 September 1782.

SEVENTH GENERATION

453. Rev. Edmund[7]**Pillsbury** (Moses[6], Moses[5], Susanna[4] **Worth**, Susunnah[3] Whipple, Elder John[2], Matthew[1]) was born in Tewksbury, Mass. 12 March 1738 and died 17 August 1816 at Northwood, Rockingham Co., N.H. at 78 years of age. He began his church work as a Baptist and later became a Univeralist minister. He married three times. (1) **Sarah Hale** in Newbury, Mass. 22 November 1759 (see No 456). Sarah, daughter of Thomas **Hale** and Abigail W. **Pillsbury**, was born 14 August 1731 and died 28 May 1761 at 29 years of age. (2) **Martha Hale** in Plaistow, Rockingham Co., N.H. 22 October 1761. Martha and Sarah were sisters. (3) **Hepzieth Twombly** in Barrington, N.H. in 1809.

Rev. Edmund **Pillsbury** and Sarah **Hale** had the following child:

729   i. John[8] **Pillsbury** born in 1760 and died in 1761 at one year of age.

Rev. Edmund **Pillsbury** and Martha **Hale** had the following children:

+ 730   i. John Hale **Pillsbury** was born 27 September 1762.
731   ii. Enoch **Pillsbury** was born in 1763 and died in 1796 at 33 years of age. He married Abigail **Batchelder**.
732   iii. Thomas **Pillsbury** was born in 1765 and died in 1840 at 75 years of age. He married Betsey **Jones**.
733   iv. Sarah **Pillsbury** was born in 1768 and died in 1826 at 58 years of age. She married Benjamin **Hoitt**.
734   v. James **Pillsbury** was born in 1770 and married Rhoda **Smart**.
735   vi. Martha **Pillsbury** was born in 1771 and died in 1806 at 35 years of age, She married James **Batchelder**.

454. Parker[7] **Pillsbury** (Moses[6], Moses[5], Susanna[4] **Worth**, Susannah[3] **Whipple**, Elder John[2], Matthew[1])[834] was born in 1742 and married **Sarah Dickinson** as his second wife.

Parker **Pillsbury** and **Sarah Dickinson** had the following child:

+ 736   i. Oliver[8] **Pillsbury** was born in 1783.

456. Sarah Hale (Abigail W.[6] **Pillsbury**, Moses[5], Susanna[4] **Worth**, Susannah[3] Whipple, Elder John[2,] Matthew[1]) was born 14 August 1731 and died 28 May 1761 at 29 years of age. She married **Rev. Edmund Pillsbury** (see No. 453) in Newbury, Mass. 22 November 1759. Edmund, son of Moses **Pillsbury** and Mary **Parker**, was born in Tewksbury, Mass. 12 March 1738.

Rev. Edmund **Pillsbury** and Sarah **Hale** had the following child:

729   i. John[8] **Pillsbury** born in 1760 and died in 1761 at one year of age.

457. Joseph[7] **Hale** (Abigail W.[6] **Pillsbury**, Moses[5,] Susanna[4] **Worth**, Susannah[3] Whipple, Elder John[2], Matthew[1])[835] was born in Dunstable, N.H. 14 October 1735 and married **Hannah Lovewell** there 31 May 1761. Hannah, daughter of Zachus **Lovewell** and Esther **Hassel**, was born 17 February 1747.

Joseph **Hale** and Hannah **Lovewell** had the following children:

737	i.	Hannah[8] **Hale** was born in Dunstable, N.H. 30 July 1761.
738	ii.	Betty **Hale** was born in Dunstable 24 October 1763 and married Lemuel **Blood** 2 May 1782.
739	iii.	Cate **Hale** was born in Dunstable 2 August 1767.
740	iv.	Esther **Hale** was born 1 August 1769.
741	v.	Joseph **Hale** Jr was born in Dunstable 6 October 1771 and married Hannah **Lund** 30 March 1797.
+ 743	vi.	Zacheus **Hale** was born 2 February 1775.
744	vii.	Noah **Hale** was born 18 March 1777.
745	viii.	Mary **Hale** was born 9 February 1778
746	ix.	Eleazer **Hale** was born 27 November 1778.
747	x.	Jonas **Hale** was born 16 February 1781.
748	xi.	James **Hale** was born 21 June 1783.
749	xii.	Benjamin **Hale** was born 13 December 1785.
750	xiii.	John **Hale** was born 9 February 1788.
751	xiv.	Leonard **Hale** was born 27 March 1790.

459. Bernard[7] **Brickett** (Susanna[6] **Pillsbury**, Moses[5], Susanna[4] **Worth**, Susannah[3] **Whipple**, Elder John[2], Matthew[1]) was born in Haverhill, Mass. 25 July 1751 and died there 7 February 1829 at 77 years of age. He married **Deborah Towne** in Topsfield, Mass. 3 December 1772. Deborah was born in Topsfield 10 November 1754.

Bernard **Brickett** and Deborah **Towne** had the following child:
| + 752 | i. | Bernard[8] **Brickett** Jr. was born 17 July 1778. |

464. Caleb[7] **Pillsbury III** (Caleb[6], Caleb[5], Susanna[4] **Worth**, Susannah[3] **Whipple**, Elder John[2], Matthew[1])[836] was born in Amesbury, Mass. 27 March 1752 and died 17 September 1832 in Danville, Caledonia Co., Vt. at 80 years of age. He married **Judith Sargent** abt. 1772. Judith,[837] daughter of Benjamin **Sargent** and Ruth **Moulton**, was born in Amesbury 21 May 1757 and died 6 May 1834 in Danville at 76 years of age.

Caleb **Pillsbury** III and Judith **Sargent** had the following children:
753	i.	Nathan[8] **Pillsbury**[838] was born in Amesbury 22 December 1773 and died 19 January 1853 in Danville at 79 years of age. He married Sally **Robbins**.
754	ii.	Ruth **Pillsbury**[839] was born in Amesbury 24 March 1776 and died 18 March 1859 in Loudon, N.H. at 82 years of age. She married David **Batchelder**.
755	iii.	Sally Kimball **Pillsbury**[840] was born in Amesbury 3 November 1778.
+ 756	iv.	Judith **Pillsbury** was born 23 November 1780.
757	v.	Elizabeth **Pillsbury**[841] was born in Amesbury 15 January 1783 and married (__) **Morse**. Morse's given name is believed to be either Daniel or Moses.
758	vi.	Mary **Pillsbury**[842] was born in Amesbury 6 February 1785 and married Isaac **Robbins**.
759	vii.	Caleb **Pillsbury** IV[843] was born in Loudon 17 December 1786 and died 17 March 1874 at 87 years of age. He married Nancy **Nelson** 14 July 1808.
760	viii.	Benjamin Lewis **Pillsbury**[844] was born in Loudon 6 September 1789 and died 15 December 1823 at 34 years of age.
761	ix.	Martha **Pillsbury**[845] was born in Loudon 22 November 1791 and died

6 November 1854 at 62 years of age. She married John **Morrill**.

762   x.   Eunice B. **Pillsbury**[846] was born in Loudon 9 January 1794 and married James **Kelsey** 10 November 1810.

763   xi.   Lydia B. **Pillsbury**[847] was born in Loudon 10 October 1795 and married William **Chamberlain**.

764   xii.   Nancy **Pillsbury**[848] was born in Loudon 5 July 1797 and married Ebenezer **Hill** 21 March 1819.

765   xiii.   Ploomy **Pillsbury**[849] was born in Loudon 30 March 1800 and married Judkins **Randall**.

468. Abiah[7] **Mooar** (Abiah[6] **Hill**, Judith[5] **Bucknam**, Judith (Jude)[4] **Worth**, Susannah[3] **Whipple**, Elder John[2], Matthew[1])[850] was born in Andover, Mass. 9 November 1741 and died there 7 October 1828 at 86 years of age. She married **Joseph Burt** in Andover 23 March 1758. Joseph was born in Springfield, Mass. 21 February 1725 and died 29 December 1810 in Andover at 85 years of age and Both are buried in the West Parish Burying Ground.

Abiah **Mooar** and Joseph **Burt** had the following children born in Andover:

766   i.   Susanna[8] **Burt** was born 25 June 1758.

767   ii.   Abiah **Burt**[851] was born 13 December 1759 and married Francis **Dane** in Andover 1 May 1781.

768   iii.   Elizabeth **Burt**[852] was born 18 September 1761 and married Samuel **Clark** in Andover 16 July 1787.

+   769   iv.   Lois **Burt** was born 16 June 1763.

770   v.   Joseph **Burt** Jr.[853] was born 5 July 1765 and died 17 October 1812 at 47 years of age. He married Mary **Carlton** in Andover 4 May 1786. She died in 1825.

771   vi.   John **Burt**[854] was born 6 May 1770.

772   vii.   Jedidiah **Burt**[855] was christened 23 June 1771 and died 24 December 1831 at 60 years of age. He married Sarah **Manning** 7 February 1792. Sarah died in 1828.

773   viii.   Sarah **Burt**[856] was christened 4 December 1774 and died in 1797.

774   ix.   Fanny Mooar **Burt**[857] was born 17 October 1779 and died in November 1779 at less than one year of age.

775   x.   Hannah **Burt**[858] was born 28 October 1781 and was buried 6 June 1791 in Andover .

776   xi.   Lucy **Burt**[859] was christened 5 June 1785 and married Peter Osgood **Dane** 10 May 1805.

469. Benjamin[7] **Mooar Jr.** (Abiah[6] **Hill**, Judith[5] **Bucknam**, Judith (Jude)[4] **Worth**, Susannah[3] **Whipple**, Elder John[2], Matthew[1])[860] was born in Andover, Mass. 28 October 1743 and married **Hannah Phelps** there 29 September 1767.

Benjamin **Mooar** Jr. and Hannah **Phelps** had the following children:

777   i.   Timothy[8] **Mooar**[861].

778   ii.   Prissy **Mooar**[862].

779   iii.   Lois **Mooar**[863].

780   iv.   Joseph **Mooar**[864].

781   v.   John **Mooar**[865].

782   vi.   Hannah **Mooar**[866].

783   vii.   Benjamin **Mooar**[867].

471. **Lois**[7] **Mooar** (Abiah[6] **Hill**, Judith[5] **Bucknam**, Judith (Jude)[4] **Worth**, Susannah[3] **Whipple**, Elder John[2], Matthew[1])[868] was born in Andover, Mass. 10 November 1747 and died 29 December 1828 at 81 years of age. She married **Jonathan Stanley** in Andover 17 May 1773.

Lois **Mooar** and Jonathan **Stanley** had the following children:

784	i.	Jonathan[8] **Stanley**.
785	ii.	John **Stanley**.
786	iii.	Benjamin **Stanley**.
787	iv.	Nathaniel **Stanley**.
788	v.	Sarah **Stanley**.
789	vi.	Abiah **Stanley**.
790	vii.	Keziah **Stanley**.
791	viii.	Abner **Stanley**.

475. **Samuel**[7] **Brown** (William[6], Martha[5] **Whipple**, Maj. John[4], Capt. John[3], Elder John[2], Matthew[1])[869] was born in Newbury, Mass. 23 December 1752 and died there 24 August 1815 at 62 years of age. He married **Hannah Stone** in Newburyport, Mass. 18 November 1782. Hannah[870] daughter of John **Stone** and Sarah **Miller**, was born in Newbury 20 September 1762 and died 9 December 1801 at 39 years of age.

Samuel **Brown** and Hannah **Stone** had the following child:

+	792	i.	Hannah Stone[8] **Brown** was born 30 October 1801.

482. **Sarah**[7] **Gerrish** (Katherine[6] **Brown**, Martha[5] **Whipple**, Maj. John[4], Capt. John[3], Elder John[2], Matthew[1])[871] was born in Newbury, Mass. in 1752 and died there 12 March 1840 at 87 years of age. She married **Nathaniel Pearson**. Nathaniel,[872] son of David **Pearson** and Jane **Noyes**, was born in Newbury 6 March 1746/47.

Sarah **Gerrish** and Nathaniel **Pearson** had the following children born in Newbury:

	793	i.	Enoch[8] **Pearson**[873] was born in November 1775.
+	794	ii.	Nathaniel **Pearson** was born 25 June 1783.
	795	iii.	Gilpah **Pearson**[874] was born 13 September 1786.

483. **Mary**[7] **Crocker** (Dea. John[6], Mary[5] **Whipple**, Maj. John[4], Capt. John[3], Elder John[2], Matthew[1])[875] was born in Ipswich, Mass. 4 November 1748 and died 22 December 1771 in Ipswich at 23 years of age. She married **William Wade** in Ipswich 11 March 1769.

Mary **Crocker** and William **Wade** had the following children born in Ipswich:

796	i.	Thomas[8] **Wade**[876].
797	ii.	Samuel **Wade**[877].

485. **Hannah**[7] **Crocker** (Dea. John[6], Mary[5] **Whipple**, Maj. John[4], Capt. John[3], Elder John[2], Matthew[1])[878] was born in Ipswich, 29 December 1752. She married **Edward Waldron**.

Hannah **Crocker** and Edward **Waldron** had the following children:

798	i.	Mary[8] **Waldron**[879].
799	ii.	Abigail **Waldron**[880].

486. **Lydia**[7] **Crocker** (Dea. John[6], Mary[5] **Whipple**, Maj. John[4], Capt. John[3], Elder John[2], Matthew[1])[881] was born in Ipswich, Mass. 7 November 1754 and died there 21 June 1833 at 78 years of age. She married twice. (1) **Elisha Treadwell**[882] in Ipswich 21 June 1780. He died 19 December 1792 in Ipswich. (2) **Col. Joseph Hodgkins** in Ipswich 18 December 1804. Joseph[883] was born abt 1743 and died 25 September 1829 in Ipswich at 86 years of age. He was an officer in the Revolutionary War.

Lydia **Crocker** and Elisha **Treadwell** had the following children born in Ipswich:

800	i.	William[8] **Treadwell**[884] was born 9 February 1781.
801	ii.	Mary **Treadwell**[885] was born 11 February 1783 and died 25 June 1804 in Ipswich at 21 years of age.
802	iii.	John **Treadwell**[886] was born 14 March 1785.
803	iv.	Lydia **Treadwell**[887] was born 14 September 1787.
804	v.	Ephraim **Treadwell**[888] was born 24 September 1789.
805	vi.	Charles **Treadwell**[889] was born 26 July 1791.

495. **John**[7] **Rogers** (Rev. John[6], Susanna[5] **Whipple**, Maj. John[4], Capt. John[3], Elder John[2], Matthew[1])[890] was born in 1748 and died in 1827 at 79 years of age. He married **Sarah Smith**. John earned an A.B. in 1767and an A.M. in 1770, both from Harvard College.

John **Rogers** and Sarah **Smith** had the following child:

+ 806	i.	George[8] **Rogers** was born 17 June 1792.

516. **John**[7] **Whipple** (Capt. John[6], Capt. John[5], Maj. Matthew[4], Capt. John[3], Elder John[2], Matthew[1])[891] was born in Ipswich, Mass. abt 1748 and died in 1806 in Boylston, Worcester Co., Mass. at 58 years of age. He married **Anna Tilton** in Ipswich 15 May 1775. Anna, daughter of Joseph **Tilton** and Abigail **Brown**, was born in Ipswich 31 July 1756 and died 23 May 1844 in Boylston at 87 years of age.

John **Whipple** and Anna **Tilton** had the following children born in Ipswich:

+ 807	i.	John[8] **Whipple** was born 22 March 1776.
808	ii.	Irene **Whipple**[892] was christened 27 November 1785 and married Charles **Timson** in Ipswich 1 January 1808.
809	iii.	Sally **Whipple**[893] was christened 4 May 1878 and married Jonas **Goodenow** in Ipswich 14 July 1810.
810	iv.	Joseph **Whipple**[894] was christened 6 November 1791 and married Rebecka **Jerry**[895] 4 July 1819. Rebecka was from Shrewsbury, Mass.

523. **Martha**[7] **Whipple** (Dea. Nathaniel[6], Capt. John[5], Maj. Matthew[4], Capt. John[3], Elder John[2], Matthew[1])[896] was born in Ipswich, Mass. 12 November 1755 and died there 23 November 1849 at 94 years of age. She married **Jonathan Whipple** in Ipswich 15 November 1777. He was born in Ipswich and died there 8 September 1816 at 61 years of age. He[897] was the son of Capt. Stephen **Whipple** and Anna **Woodbury** and served in the military in New England in 1777 and was listed as the head of a family on the 1790 federal census of Ipswich. Martha and Jonathan were fifth cousins with Martha descending from Elder John Whipple and Jonathan from Matthew Whipple, the original Whipple brothers to settle in Ipswich in 1638. Thus all succeeding generations claim double descent from Matthew Whipple, Sr., Clothier of Bocking, England.

Martha **Whipple** and Jonathan **Whipple** had the following children born in Ipswich:

+ 811   i. Stephen[8] **Whipple**.
   812   ii. Elizabeth Whipple was christened 16 April 1786.[898]
   813   iii. Hannah **Whipple**[899] was christened 19 October 1788 and married Isaac **Dodge**.
   814   iv. Lucinda **Whipple**[900] was christened 18 September 1791 and married William **Brown** after 1800.
   815   v. Jonathan **Whipple**[901] was christened 23 March 1794. and married Mary **Cloutman**.
   816   vi. Nathaniel **Whipple**[902] was born 18 April 1779 and married Mary **Woodbury** in Ipswich.
   817   vii. Martha **Whipple**[903] was born 24 August 1783 and married Robert **Woodbury**.
   818   viii. Oliver **Whipple**[904] was born 15 December 1796 and married Polly **Woodbury**.
   819   ix. John **Whipple**[905] was born 3 October 1800 and married Mary **Hitchings**.

527. **Mary**[7] **Traill** (Mary[6] **Whipple**, Capt. William[5], Maj. Matthew[4], Capt. John[3], Elder John[2], Matthew[1])[906] was born in New Hampshire abt 1755 and died 10 January 1824 at 68 years of age. She is buried in Portsmouth's Old North Cemetery. Mary married **Keith Spence** in Portsmouth, N.H. He was a merchant from Scotland who settled in Portsmouth.

Mary **Traill** and Keith **Spence** had the following children:
   820   i. Robert T.[8] Spence was appointed midshipman in the U.S. Navy 13 May 1800 and distinguished himself in the attack on Tripoli 7 Aug. 1804. He was a captain in the U.S. Navy at the time of his death 26 Sept. 1826.
+ 821   ii. Harriett **Spence**.

530. **Hannah**[7] **Page** (Nathaniel[6], Susannah[5] **Lane**, Susanna[4] **Whipple**, Capt. John[3], Elder John[2], Matthew[1])[907] was born in Billerica, Mass. 15 May 1736 and died there 2 April 1793 at 56 years of age. She married **Jonas French** in Billerica 5 January 1758. Jonas[908] son of William **French** and Joanna **Hill**, was born in Billerica 18 March 1731/32 and died there 9 February 1801 at 68 years of age.

Hannah **Page** and Jonas **French** had the following children born in Billerica:
   822   i. Jonas[8] **French**[909] was born 18 September 1758 and died 4 October 1775 in Billerica at 17 years of age.
+ 823   ii. Nathaniel **French** was born 11 April 1760.
+ 824   iii. Reuben **French** was born 18 October 1761.
   825   iv. William **French**[910] was born 29 April 1765 and married Rebecca **Marshall** in Billerica 20 January 1791. Rebecca,[911] daughter of Isaac **Marshall** and Abigail **Brown**, was born in Billerica 2 March 1767.
   826   v. Hannah **French**[912] was born 23 January 1768 and married Jonathan **Heald** in Billerica 2 April 1789. Jonathan was from Carlisle, Mass.
   827   vi Ziba **French**[913] was born 9 June 1773.
   828   vii. Susanna **French**[914] was born 25 October 1775 and married Joseph **Jaquith**.

531. **John**[7] **Whitmore** (Francis[6], Mary[5] **Lane**, Susanna[4] **Whipple**, Capt. John[3],

Elder John[2], Matthew[1])[915] was born 3 November 1781 and married **Huldah Crooker** 3 November 1781. Huldah was from Bath, Maine.

John **Whitmore** and Huldah **Crooker** had the following child:
+ 829   i. William Dickman[8] **Whitmore** was born 3 November 1781.

532. **Jonathan**[7] **Lane** (John[6], Job[5], Susanna[4] **Whipple**, Capt. John[3], Elder John[2], Matthew[1])[916] was born in 1763 and died in 1808 at 45 years of age. He married **Hannah Lane**. They resided in Bedford, Mass.

Jonathan **Lane** and Hannah **Lane** had the following child:
+ 830   i. Jonathan[8] **Lane** was born in 1788.

536. **Anna**[7] **Lane** (Timothy[6], Job[5], Susanna[4] **Whipple**, Capt. John[3], Elder John[2], Matthew[1])[917] was born in Bedford, Mass. 30 March 1758 and died 20 July 1844 in Windsor, Vt. at 86 years of age. She married **Ebenezer Gould Jr.**[918] in Chelmsford, Mass. 20 May 1779. He was born in Chelmsford 27 February 1755 and died 1 April 1813 in Hartland, Vt. at 58 years of age.

Anna **Lane** and Ebenezer **Gould** Jr. had the following children:
+ 831   i. Anna[8] **Gould** was born 5 March 1780.
   832   ii. Ebenezer **Gould**[919] was born in Rindge, N.H. in July 1781 and was christened there 21 October 1781.
   833   iii. John **Gould**[920] was born in 1783.
   834   iv. Rachel **Gould**[921] was born in 1785.
   835   v. Patty **Gould**[922] was born in 1787.
   836   vi. Betsey **Gould**[923] was born in 1789.

542. **Ralph**[7] **Hill** (Mary[6] **Lane**, Job[5], Susanna[4] **Whipple**, Capt. John[3], Elder John[2], Matthew[1])[924] was born in Billerica, Mass. 20 September 1747 and died 10 April 1831 in Ashby, Mass. at 83 years of age. He married **Mary Jones** 9 April 1777. Mary was from Concord, Mass.

Ralph **Hill** and Mary **Jones** had the following children:
   837   i. Job[8] **Hill**[925] was born 7 July 1780.
   838   ii. Polly **Hill**[926] was born 5 September 1782 and married (__) **Fiske**. They lived in Barton, Vt. in 1883.
+ 839   iii. Brewster **Hill** was born 16 September 1784.
   840   iv. Elijah **Hill**[927] was born 15 July 1787 and married Cynthia **Lake**.
   841   v. Betsey **Hill**[928] was born 12 January 1790 and died in 1800 at 10 years of age.
   842   vi. Phebe **Hill**[929] was born 13 August 1792 and married Stephen **Wright**. Stephen was from Hanover, N.H.
   843   vii. Nancy **Hill**[930] was born 18 May 1795 and married Peter **Sloan**.
   844   viii. Emma **Hill**[931] was born 24 April 1798 and married Stephen **Taylor**. Stephen was from Montpelier, Vt. The family lived in Barton Vt. in 1883.
   845   ix. Abigail **Hill**[932] was born 14 February 1800 and married David **Poor**. David was from Montpelier, Vt.

547. **Job**[7] **Hill** (Mary[6] **Lane**, Job[5], Susanna[4] **Whipple**, Capt. John[3], Elder John[2], Matthew[1])[933] was born in Billerica, Mass. 29 May 1754 and died there 5 February 1824 at 69 years of age. He married **Susanna Blanchard** in Billerica 19 January

1790. Susanna,[934] daughter of Simon **Blanchard** and Rebecca **Sheldon**, was born in Billerica 2 April 1763.

Job **Hill** and Susanna **Blanchard** had the following children born in Billerica:

846   i.   Asenath[8] **Hill**[935] was born 3 June 1790.

847   ii. Job **Hill**[936] was born 5 December 1791 and married an unnamed person in Billerica 18 July 1814.

848   iii. Daniel **Hill**[937] was born 17 May 1797.

849   iv. Susanna **Hill**[938] was christened 24 August 1800 and died 23 September 1801 in Billerica at one year of age.

850   v. David **Hill**[939] was christened 24 August 1800.

851   vi. Susanna Lane **Hill**[940] was born 7 March 1803.

+ 852   vii. Jonathan **Hill** was born 24 November 1804.

853   viii. Lucretia **Hill**[941] was born 3 March 1807 and married Sewall **Stearns** in Billerica 23 June 1836. Sewall,[942] son of Timothy **Stearns** and Sarah **Lane**, was born in Billerica 21 September 1796.

552. **Jonathan**[7] **Hill** (Mary[6] **Lane**, Job[5], Susanna[4] **Whipple**, Capt. John[3], Elder John[2], Matthew[1])[943] was born in Billerica, Mass. 28 September 1763 and died there 29 January 1815 at 51 years of age. He married **Mary Proctor**[944] in Billerica 13 December 1798. She died there 1 February 1848.

Jonathan **Hill** and Mary **Proctor** had the following children born in Billerica:

854   i.   Mary[8] **Hill**[945] was born 11 June 1801 and married Samuel **Butler** in Billerica 23 November 1824. Samuel was from Leominster, Mass.

855   ii. Anna **Hill**[946] was born 15 October 1802 and married John **Simonds** in Billerica 2 June 1825.

856   iii. Jonathan **Hill**[947] was born 24 November 1804.

857   iv. Rufus **Hill**[948].

554. **Asubah**[7] **Hill** (Mary[6] **Lane**, Job[5], Susanna[4] **Whipple**, Capt. John[3], Elder John[2], Matthew[1])[949] was born in Billerica, Mass. 1 March 1768 and died bef. November 1804. She married **Josiah Snow** in Billerica 14 May 1797. Josiah[950] son of Richard **Snow** and Lydia (__), was born 25 April 1781 and died 30 September 1811 in Grafton, Vt. at 30 years of age. He married (2) **Betsey Parker** 11 November 1804.

Asubah **Hill** and Josiah **Snow** had the following children:

858   i.   Charles[8] **Snow**[951].

859   ii. Lucy Hill **Snow**[952].

860   iii. Harvey **Snow**[953].

861   iv. Alexander Hill **Snow**[954].

555. **Anna**[7] **Hill** (Mary[6] **Lane**, Job[5], Susanna[4] **Whipple**, Capt. John[3], Elder John[2], Matthew[1])[955] was born in Billerica, Mass. 11 June 1776 and died there 22 October 1807 at 31 years of age. She married **Abner Stearns** in Billerica 1 May 1796. Abner,[956] son of Edward **Stearns** and Lucy **Wyman**, was born in Billerica 9 July 1766 and died 11 December 1838 at 72 years of age. He married (2) **Anna Russell** 30 June 1808, the widow of John Estabrooks. Abner and Ann had the following children: Mary Ann, Edward H., George S., Albert T., and Henry A.

Anna **Hill** and Abner **Stearns** had the following child:

862   i.   Abner[8] **Stearns**[957] was born in Billerica 1 April 1797 and was a machinist in Winchester, N.H.

556. **Gershom Flagg^7 Lane** (John^6, John^5, Susanna^4 **Whipple**, Capt. John^3, Elder John^2, Matthew^1)[958] was born in 1753 and died in 1838 at 85 years of age. He married **Lydia Thomas**.

Gershom Flagg **Lane** and Lydia **Thomas** had the following child:
+ 863   I. Martha^8 **Lane** was born in 1788.

557. **Betsey^7 Hutchinson** (Rebecca^6 **Lane**, James^5, Susanna^4 **Whipple**, Capt. John^3, Elder John^2, Matthew^1)[959] was born in Bedford, Mass. 20 January 1760 and died 29 January 1817 in Chelmsford, Mass. at 57 years of age. She married **Samuel Parkhurst**[960] in Bedford 12 January 1788. He was born in Chelmsford 4 November 1758 and died there 15 January 1849 at 90 years of age.

Betsey **Hutchinson** and Samuel **Parkhurst** had the following child:
+ 864   i. Rev. John^8 **Parkhurst** was born 17 January 1789.

558. **Ebenezer^7 Lane** (Samuel^6, James^5, Susanna^4 **Whipple**, Capt. John^3, Elder John^2, Matthew^1)[961] was born in Bedford, Mass. 14 May 1771 and died 14 February 1846 in New York, N.Y. at 74 years of age. He is buried in Arlington, Mass. He married twice. (1) **Hannah Cunningham** in Boston 21 May 1797. Hannah,[962] daughter of James **Cunningham** and Mary **Mackintire**, was born in Balltown, Maine 19 August 1771 and died 21 November 1812 in Arlington, Middlesex Co., Mass. at 41 years of age. (2) **Mrs. Sally Weston**[963] 30 August 1815 who was born 19 March 1770 and died 28 October 1842 at 72 years of age. The family lived in Boston and West Cambridge (now Arlington).

Ebenezer **Lane** and Hannah **Cunningham** had the following child:
+ 865   i. Washington Jefferson Poor^8 **Lane** was born 16 February 1807.

559. **Simon^7 Stone** (Micah^6, Simon^5, Deacon Simon^4, Mary^3 **Whipple**, Elder John^2, Matthew^1)[964] birth date unknown married **Lydia Rice**.

Simon **Stone** and Lydia **Rice** had the following children born in West Boylston, Worcester Co., Mass:
    866   i. Nabby Sawyer^8 **Stone**[965] was born 2 November 1807.
+ 867   ii. Charlotte Woods **Stone** was born 20 August 1809.
    868   iii. Lydia **Stone**[966] was born 13 June 1811.
    869   iv. Simon **Stone**[967] was born 20 August 1813 and died 18 September 1814 in West Boylston at 1 year of age.
    870   v. Cornelia **Stone**[968] was born 30 June 1815.
    871   vi. Simon Edward **Stone** was born 27 May 1818 and died the day of birth.[969]
    872   vii. Silas Beaman **Stone**[970] was born 27 September 1822.
    873   viii. Phebe **Stone**[971] was born 13 August 1826.

565. **Capt. Amos^7 Stone** (Amos^6, Simon^5, Deacon Simon^4, Mary^3 **Whipple**, Elder John^2, Matthew^1)[972] was born in Harvard, Worcester Co., Mass. 28 September 1759 and died 17 March 1842 in Urbana, Steuben Co., N.Y. at 82 years of age. He married twice. (1) (_) **Ives** in Pennsylvania in 1788. (2) **Elizabeth Holiday**[973] in Holliday, Penn. 13 January 1790. Elizabeth was born in Pennsylvania abt 1770.

Amos enlisted in the Revolutionary War from Greenwich, Mass. and served at Ticonderoga in 1775; enlisted in 1776 for a year and served around Boston during the British evacuation; re-enlisted in May 1777 and served for 2 1/2 months as part of the reinforcement of the Northern Army; re-enlisted in September 1777 and served at the Battle of Saratoga and was present at the surrender of general John Burgoyne's army on 17 October. [It would be interesting to know if capt. Stone realized that brig. gen. William Whipple, who commanded New Hampshire troops in the battle and was a member of the team that negotiated Burgoyne's surrender, was his third cousin once removed – Elder John and Susannah Whipple being their common ancestors. Capt. Stone re-enlisted in May 1778 for eight months and served at the Battle of Momouth; re-enlisted for a five month term in April 1779 and was present on duty and witness to the hanging of maj. Andre on 2 October 1780 (the British officer Benedict Arnold dealt with for the betrayal of West Point); was discharged at West Point about January 1781. On 3 August 1833, at age 74 and a resident of Steuben Co., N.Y. he was placed on the U.S. pension roll at $80 per year. On 22 February 1804, he was commissioned as captain in the Steuben Co. militia.[974]

Capt. Amos **Stone** and Elizabeth **Holiday** had the following children:

874	i.	Amos[8] **Stone**[975].
875	ii.	Elizabeth **Stone**[976] married (__) **Bailey**.
876	iii.	Eunice **Stone**[977] married (__) **Lamb**.
877	iv.	Lucinda **Stone**[978] married (__) **Gregory**.
878	v.	George M. **Stone**[979] married Polly (__).
879	vi.	Adna **Stone**[980] married (__) **Youmans**.
+ 880	vii.	Lavinia **Stone** was born 6 November 1793.
881	viii.	Isabel **Stone**[981] was born abt 1800 and died 13 July 1801 at about one year of age.
882	ix.	Huldah **Stone**[982] was born abt 1802 and died 12 July 1806 at about four years of age.
883	x.	Sabrina **Stone**[983] was born 29 August 1808 and died 26 February 1885 in Waverly, N.Y. at 76 years of age. She married David **Bailey** 28 September 1826.

569. **Phineas**[7] **Holden** (Capt. Asa[6], Abigail[5] **Stone**, Deacon Simon[4], Mary[3] **Whipple**, Elder John[2], Matthew[1])[984] was born in Shirley, Mass. 14 July 1760 and died there 25 November 1814 at 54 years of age. He married **Miriam Longley** in Shirley 25 November 1814. The marriage may have occurred 25 November 1790. Miriam,[985] daughter of Jonas **Longley** and Esther **Patterson**, was born in Shirley 24 April 1767 and died there 13 July 1811 at 44 years of age.

Phineas **Holden** and Miriam **Longley** had the following child:
+ 884   i.   Alma Ellery[8] **Holden** was born 26 January 1792.

570. **Mary**[7] **Jewell** (Mary[6] **Whitney**, Mary[5] **Stone**, Deacon Simon[4], Mary[3] **Whipple**, Elder John[2], Matthew[1])[986] was born in Marlborough, Middlesex Co., Mass. 22 August 1757. She married **Abner Dunton**.

Mary **Jewell** and Abner **Dunton** had the following child:
+ 885   i.   Susanna[8] **Dunton** was born 6 March 1777.

573. **David**[7] **Stone** (Lt. James[6], James[5], John[4], Mary[3] **Whipple**, Elder John[2], Matthew[1])[987] was born in 1761 and died in 1851 in Waterford, Maine at 90 years of age. He was from Harvard, Mass. a soldier in the Revolution, and settled in

Waterford in 1799. He married **Lucy Sampson Thomas** [988] who was from Sweden and died in 1857 at 72 years of age.

David **Stone** and Lucy Sampson **Thomas** had the following child:
+   886   i.   Reedsburg[8] **Stone**.

574. Adam[7] **Howe** (Bathsheba[6] **Stone**, Adams[5], Dea. Matthew[4], Mary[3] **Whipple**, Elder John[2], Matthew[1])[989] was born in Sudbury, Mass. and had the following child:
        887   i.   Lyman[8] **Howe**[990] was born in Sudbury, Mass.

575. Hannah[7] **Goddard** (Robert[6], Edward[5], Susanna[4] **Stone**, Mary[3] **Whipple**, Elder John[2], Matthew[1])[991] was born in Petersham, Mass. 22 January 1753 and died in 1812 at 59 years of age. She married **Sylvanus Ward**[992] 22 November 1775. Sylvanus was born in Marlborough, Mass. 8 May 1753 and died 15 March 1834 at 80 years of age.

Hannah **Goddard** and Sylvanus **Ward** had the following child:
+   888   i.   Betsey[8] **Ward** was born 26 June 1778.

580. Lucy[7] **Goddard** (David[6], Edward[5], Susanna[4] **Stone**, Mary[3] **Whipple**, Elder John[2], Matthew[1])[993] was born 19 June 1760 and died in 1800 at 40 years of age. She married **Asa Goddard** 2 November 1779. Asa,[994] son of Nathan **Goddard** and Dorothy **Stevens**, was born in Orange, Franklin Co. Mass. in August 1755 and died 3 June 1828 at 72 years of age. Asa and Lucy are first cousins. [See No. 626.]

Asa **Goddard** and Lucy **Goddard** had the following child:
+   889   i.   David[8] **Goddard** was born in 1786.

584. Lois[7] **Woodward**, (Mary[6] **Stone**, Samuel[5], Ebenezer[4], Mary[3] **Whipple**, Elder John[2], Matthew[1])[995] was born in Newton, Mass. 6 October 1740 and died there 24 September 1811 at 70 years of age. She married **Samuel Jackson**[996] 4 November 1763. Samuel was born in Newton 16 April 1737 and died in July 1801 in Jay, Maine at 64 years of age.

Lois **Woodward**, and Samuel **Jackson** had the following child
+   890   i.   Lois[8] **Jackson** was born 17 August 1765.

587. Susanna[7] **Richardson** (Mary[6] **Woodward**, Mindwell[5] **Stone**, Ebenezer[4], Mary[3] **Whipple**, Elder John[2], Matthew[1])[997] was born in Newton, Mass. 12 December 1755 and married **Daniel Read**.

Susanna **Richardson** and Daniel **Read** had the following child:
+   891   i.   Lucy[8] **Read** was born 2 December 1793.

600. Abner[7] **Johnson** (Hannah[6] **Eaton**, Lydia Abiah[5] **Starr**, Mary[4] **Stone**, Mary[3] **Whipple**, Elder John[2], Matthew[1])[998] was born in Stafford, Conn. 15 April 1755 and died there 8 April 1794 at 38 years of age. He married **Lydia Avery** in Stafford 22 June 1780. Lydia,[999] daughter of John **Avery** and Mehitable **Buell**, was born in Goshen, Conn. 28 December 1757 and died 8 March 1810 in Hampton, Conn. at 52 years of age. She married **Nathan Jennings** in Connecticut 23 October 1801.

Abner **Johnson** and Lydia **Avery** had the following children born in Stafford, Conn.:

+ 892   i.   Lydia[8] **Johnson** was born 27 December 1780.
+ 893   ii.   John **Johnson** was born 24 April 1783.
+ 894   iii.   Laura **Johnson** was born 23 February 1785.
    895   iv.   Elizabeth **Johnson**[1000] was born 25 February 1787 and married James Corbin.
    896   v.   Mabel **Johnson**[1001] was born 21 May 1789.
    897   vi.   Abner **Johnson**[1002] was born 10 May 1791 (birth year is presumed).
    898   vii.   Welthy **Johnson**[1003] was born 16 March 1793 (birth year is presumed).

603. John[7] Eaton (John[6], Lydia Abiah[5] **Starr**, Mary[4] **Stone**, Mary[3] **Whipple**, Elder John[2], Matthew[1])[1004] was born in Killingly, Conn. 14 February 1761 and died 11 December 1835 in Little Falls, Herkimer Co., N.Y. at 74 years of age. He married **Mehitable Richardson** in East Hoosick, Berkshire Co., Mass. 6 November 1782.

John **Eaton** and Mehitable **Richardson** had the following child:
+ 899   i.   Arrunah[8] **Eaton** was born 4 February 1784.

604. Joseph[7] Grow (Abigail[6] **Dana**, Susanna[5] **Starr**, Mary[4] **Stone**, Mary[3] **Whipple**, Elder John[2], Matthew[1])[1005] was born in Promfet, Conn. 13 March 1748 and died 19 March 1813 in Hartland, Vt. at 65 years of age. He married **Tirzah Sanger**[1006] in Promfet 13 December 1770. Tirzah was born in Woodstock, Conn. 19 December 1748 and died 1 October 1824 in Hartland at 75 years of age.

Joseph **Grow** and Tirzah **Sanger** had the following child:
+ 900   i.   Samuel Porter[8] **Grow** was born 23 March 1773.

605. Thomas[7] Patch (Penelope[6] **Dana**, Susanna[5] **Starr**, Mary[4] **Stone**, Mary[3] **Whipple**, Elder John[2], Matthew[1])[1007] was born in 1753 and married **Desire Cowing**[1008] who was born in 1754.

Thomas **Patch** and Desire **Cowing** had the following child:
+ 901   i.   Luther[8] **Patch** was born in 1798.

607. Sarah[7] Starr (Capt. Comfort[6], Comfort[5], Mary[4] **Stone**, Mary[3] **Whipple**, Elder John[2], Matthew[1])[1009] was born in Thompson, Conn. 28 November 1760 and died 20 August 1805 in Guilford, Vt. at 44 years of age. She is buried in Franklin Cemetery. She married **Jabez Franklin**.

Sarah **Starr** and Jabez **Franklin** had the following child:
+ 902   i.   Luther[8] **Franklin**.

608. Abigail[7] Starr (Capt. Comfort[6], Comfort[5], Mary[4] **Stone**, Mary[3] **Whipple**, Elder John[2], Matthew[1])[1010] was born in Westborough, Worcester Co., Mass. 24 November 1763 and died in 1840 in Newark, Vt. at 76 years of age. She married **James Ball** in 1780. James,[1011] son of James **Ball** and Dinah **Fay**, died in 1840 in Newark. He served in the Revolutionary War and moved his family to Newark in 1797 where he served as selectman in 1809. He and Abigail were members of the Baptist church.

Abigail **Starr** and James **Ball** had the following children:

+ 903   i. James Bradley[8] **Ball** was born 28 July 1781.

904   ii. Peres **Ball**[1012] was born in Guilford, Vt. 15 September 1783 and died there in 1785 at one year of age.

905   iii. Perley **Ball**[1013] was born in Marlboro, Vt. 20 April 1786 and died 30 September 1884 at 98 years of age. He married Phebe **Smith**.

906   iv. Sally **Ball**[1014] was born in Marlboro 16 December 1792 and died 7 August 1845 in Newark at 52 years of age. She is buried in the Packer Mountain Cemetery and her grave is plainly marked. She married Philemon **Hartwell** in Newark.

907   v. Hannah **Ball**[1015] was born in Marlboro 19 December 1793 and died in December 1812 in Newark at 18 years of age. She is buried in the Packer Mountain Cemetery and her grave is plainly marked.

908   vi. Arad **Ball**[1016] was born in Guilford 16 December 1797 and died 17 August 1885 at 87 years of age. He married Sylvania **Beckwith**. Arad and Sylvania had six children; names not provided.

909   vii. Arnold **Ball**[1017] was born in Newark 13 July 1799 and died there 18 October 1821 at 22 years of age. Arnold is buried in the Packer Mountain Cemetery and his grave is plainly marked.

+ 910   viii. Lucius **Ball** was born 14 May 1803.

911   ix. Louisa **Ball**[1018] was born in Newark 17 September 1806 and married Benjamin **Wooster** there.

609. Comfort[7] **Starr** (Capt. Comfort[6], Comfort[5], Mary[4] **Stone**, Mary[3] **Whipple**, Elder John[2], Matthew[1])[1019] was born in Thompson, Conn. 30 May 1766 and died abt 1800 in Colchester, Chittenden Co. Vt. He married **Hannah Thurber** in Windham Co., Vt. abt 1785. Hannah,[1020] daughter of David **Thurber** and Mary **Bullock**, was born in Guilford, Vt. abt 1758 and died 7 July 1844 in Milton, Chittenden Co Vt. at 86 years of age. She married (2) **Rev. Richard Lee** after 1800.

Comfort **Starr** and Hannah **Thurber** had the following children:

912   i. Olive[8] **Starr**[1021] was born in Guilford 4 December 1786 and died 6 June 1840 in Colchester at 53 years of age. She married Eber **Coon** in Vermont 12 August 1801.

913   ii. Comfort **Starr**[1022] was born in Guilford abt 1787 and died abt 1846 in Mount Tabor, Vt. He married twice. (1) Olive **Reed**. (2) Elizo **Warner**.

914   iii. Parley **Starr**[1023] was born in Guilford 9 May 1789 and died 29 January 1853 in Milton at 63 years of age. He married Jemima **Coon**.

915   iv. Eliza **Starr**[1024] was born abt 1790 and died 26 October 1826 in Milton at 36 years of age. She married Elias **Coon**.

916   v. Mary **Starr**[1025] was born abt 1794 and died 25 January 1861 at 66 years of age. She married Henry **Austin**.

+ 917   vi. Lovel **Starr** was born 26 April 1797.

613. Martha[7] **Starr** (Capt. Comfort[6], Comfort[5], Mary[4] **Stone**, Mary[3] **Whipple**, Elder John[2], Matthew[1])[1026] was born in Thompson, Conn. 28 May 1776 and died 9 October 1839 in West Halifax, Windham Co., Vt. at 63 years of age. She married **Asahel Ballou** in Thompson 3 December 1795.

Martha **Starr** and Asahel **Ballou** had the following child:

918   i. Hosea[8] **Ballou**.[1027] He was a Univeralist minister and first president of Tufts College.

615. Ebenezer⁷ Starr Jr. (Ebenezer⁶, Comfort⁵, Mary⁴ **Stone**, Mary³ **Whipple**, Elder John², Matthew¹)[1028] was born in Thompson, Conn. abt 1780 and died 17 September 1873 in Douglas, Mass. at 93 years of age. He married **Anna Stevens Rose** 18 October 1803. Anna,[1029] daughter of Asa **Rose**, was born in Jewett City, Conn. 17 August 1783 and died 2 October 1869 at 86 years of age.

Ebenezer **Starr** Jr. and Anna Stevens **Rose** had the following child:

+ 919   i. Elsie Elizabeth⁸ **Starr** was born 26 March 1807.

618. John Dean⁷ Estey (Solomon⁶, Elizabeth Mary⁵ **Stearns**, Elizabeth⁴ **Stone**, Mary³ **Whipple**, Elder John², Matthew¹)[1030] was born about 1775. He married **Jenitha (__)** before 1800.

John Dean **Estey** and Jenitha (__) had the following children born in Kingston, Addison Co., Vt.:

+ 920   i. John Dean⁸ **Estey** Jr. was born 11 June 1800.
   921   ii. Elijab B. **Estey**[1031] was born 26 August 1802 and married Margaret **Ripley**.
   922   iii. Hiram **Estey**[1032] was born about 1808 and died about 1888. He married Sarah A. **McKillips**.

619. Phineas⁷ Stearns (Eliphet⁶, Rev. Ebenezer⁵, Elizabeth⁴ **Stone**, Mary³ **Whipple**, Elder John², Matthew¹)[1033] birth date unknown. He married **Mary Cooper**.

Phineas **Stearns** and Mary **Cooper** had the following child:

+ 923   i. Harrison⁸ **Stearns**.

620. Hannah⁷ Wilbor (Mary⁶ **Stearns**, Jonathan⁵, Elizabeth⁴ **Stone**, Mary³ **Whipple**, Elder John², Matthew¹)[1034] was born in 1755 and died 24 February 1833 at 77 years of age. She married **James Smith** in Taunton, Mass. 28 July 1774. James,[1035] son of George **Smith** and Lydia **Reed**, was born in 1750 and died 5 April 1825 at 74 years of age.

Hannah **Wilbor** and James **Smith** had the following child:

+ 924   i. George⁸ **Smith** was born 2 October 1778.

621. Joseph Pierce⁷ Upham (Asa⁶, Hannah⁵ **Stearns**, Elizabeth⁴ **Stone**, Mary³ **Whipple**, Elder John², Matthew¹)[1036] was born in Sturbridge, Mass. 12 February 1764 and died 7 October 1857 in Granville, N.Y. at 93 years of age. He married **Hulda Rosabella Smith**. Hulda,[1037] daughter of (__) **Smith** and Rosabella **Denslow**, was born in 1768 and died 16 May 1828 in Pawlet, Vt. at 59 years of age. They were living in Pawlet by 1810.

Joseph Pierce **Upham** and Hulda Rosabella **Smith** had the following child:

+ 925   i. Lucinda Chipman⁸ **Upham** was born 3 March 1792.

625. Ebenezer⁷ Goddard (Nathan⁶, Edward⁵, Susanna⁴ **Stone**, Mary³ **Whipple**, Elder John², Matthew¹)[1038] was born 19 September 1753. He married **Anna Woodward**. Anna,[1039] daughter of Jonathan **Woodward** and Mary **Brown**, was born 9 June 1753 and died 19 February 1820 at 66 years of age.

Ebenezer **Goddard** and Anna **Woodward** had the following children:

926   i. Anna[8] Goddard[1040] was born 22 August 177 and married Asbel **Ward**.
927   ii. Ebenezer **Goddard** Jr.[1041] was born in 1779 and married Sally **Wood** 8 January 1801.
+   928   iii. Enoch Elbert **Goddard** was born 26 March 1783.

626. **Asa**[7] **Goddard** (Nathan[6], Edward[5], Susanna[4] **Stone**, Mary[3] **Whipple**, Elder John[2], Matthew[1])[1042] was born in Orange, Franklin Co., Mass. in August 1755 and died 3 June 1828 at 72 years of age. He married **Lucy Goddard** 2 November 1779. Lucy,[1043] daughter of David **Goddard** and Margaret **Stone**, was born 19 June 1760 and died in 1800 at 40 years of age. Asa and Lucy are first cousins. [See No. 580.]

Asa **Goddard** and Lucy **Goddard** had the following child:
+   889   i. David[8] **Goddard** was born in 1786.

637. **Nahum**[7] **Goddard** (Robert[6], Edward[5], Susanna[4] **Stone**, Mary[3] **Whipple**, Elder John[2], Matthew[1])[1044] was born in Petersham, Mass. 14 February 1776 and died 3 August 1852 in Rochester, Windsor Co., Vt. at 76 years of age. He married **Sarah Richardson** in Petersham 1 February 1801. Sarah was born abt 1771 and died 26 June 1846 in Rochester at 74 years of age.

Nahum **Goddard** and Sarah **Richardson** had the following children:
+   929   i. Robert[8] **Goddard** was born 3 June 1803.
    930   ii. Lorinda **Goddard**[1045] was christened in Rutland, Vt. 5 July 1812 and died unmarried 10 March 1872 in Monona, Iowa at 66 years of age.

643. **Daniel**[7] **Goddard** (Lt. Daniel[6], Edward[5], Susanna[4] **Stone**, Mary[3] **Whipple**, Elder John[2], Matthew[1])[1046] was born in Shrewsbury, Mass. 23 August 1765 married **Mary Puffer** in Sudbury, Mass. 18 February 1790. Mary was from Sudbury. Her given name is listed as Mercy in the marriage record and May in birth records of her children and in her death record.

Daniel **Goddard** and Mary **Puffer** had the following children born in Shrewsbury:
    931   i. James Puffer[8] **Goddard**[1047] was born 2 February 1791.
    932   ii. Mary Willard **Goddard**[1048] was born 26 March 1792.
    933   iii. Hariot Miriam **Goddard**[1049] was born 23 August 1794.

651. **Capt. Nathan**[7] **Goddard** (Nathan[6], Benjamin[5], Susanna[4] **Stone**, Mary[3] **Whipple**, Elder John[2], Matthew[1])[1050] was born in Framingham, Mass. and died there 4 July 1822. He married twice. (1) **Prudence Hemeway** in Framingham before 1805. (2) **Polly Bacon**[1051] 6 January 1814. Polly was born in Framingham 17 August 1781 and died there 9 April 1812.

Capt. Nathan **Goddard** and Prudence **Hemeway** had the following children born in Framingham:
    934   i. Charles[8] **Goddard**[1052] was born 12 January 1805.
    935   ii. Grace **Goddard**[1053] was born 28 November 1805.
+   936   iii. George **Goddard** was born 31 August 1808.
    937   iv. Ann **Goddard**[1054] was born 31 August 1810.

Capt. Nathan **Goddard** and Polly **Bacon** had the following children born in Framingham:
    938   v. Nathan **Goddard**[1055] was born 1 October 1814.

939   vi.   Prudence **Goddard**[1056] was born 11 October 1815.

940   vii.   Patty **Goddard**[1057] was born 22 May 1817.

941   viii.   Hitty **Goddard**[1058] was born 11 January 1819.

942   ix.   Mary **Goddard**[1059] was born 30 January 1820.

652. Rhoda[7] **Howe** (Susanna[6] **Goddard**, Ebenezer[5], Susanna[4] **Stone**, Mary[3] **Whipple**, Elder John[2], Matthew[1])[1060] was born in Hopkinton, Middlesex Co., Mass. 8 July 1762 and died 14 February 1838 at 75 years of age. She married **Joseph Richards**.

Rhoda **Howe** and Joseph **Richards** had the following children:

943   i.   Rhoda[8] **Richards**[1061] was born in Framingham, Mass. 8 August 1784 and died 17 January 1879 in Salt Lake City, Utah at 94 years of age. She married Brigham **Young** in Nauvoo, Hancock Co., Ill. 31 January 1846 as his 23rd wife. Brigham,[1062] son of John **Young** and Abigail (Nabby) **Howe**, was born in Whitingham, Windham, Co., Vt. 1 June 1801 and died 29 August 1877 at Salt Lake City, Utah.

944   ii.   Hepzibah **Richards** was born in Hopkinton, Middlesex Co., Mass. 28 July 1795 and died 30 September in Far West, Caldwell Co., Mo. at 43 years of age.

654. Abigail (Nabby)[7] **Howe** (Susanna[6] **Goddard**, Ebenezer[5], Susanna[4] **Stone**, Mary[3] **Whipple**, Elder John[2], Matthew[1])[1063] was born in Hopkinton, Mass. 3 May 1766 and died 11 June 1815 in Genoa, Cayuga Co., N.Y. at 49 years of age. She had blue eyes and yellowish-brown hair and was musically inclined as were her her sisters. They sang old English madigrals at social affairs. She was an invalid for several years and died of consumption.[1064] She married **John Young** 31 October 1786.[1065] John,[1066] son of Joseph **Young** and Elizabeth **Hayden**, was born in Hopkinton 7 March 1763 and died 12 October 1839 in Quincy, Ill. at 76 years of age. John's grandparents were William Young and Susannah Cotton. William was from Boston and Susannah from Portsmouth, N.H. They were married 27 May 1722. Susannah's parents were John Cotton and Sarah Hearle. He married (2) **Hannah Dennis** in 1817. Hannah was from Tyrone, Steuben, Co., N.Y.

Abigail (Nabby) **Howe** and John **Young** had the following children:

945   i.   Nancy[8] **Young**[1067] was born in Hopkinton 6 August 1786 and died in Salt Lake City 22 September 1860 at 74 years of age. She married Daniel **Kent**.

946   ii.   Fanny **Young**[1068] was born in Hopkinton 8 November 1787 and died 11 June 1859 at 71 years of age. She married twice. (1) Robert **Carr**. (2) Roswell **Murray**.

947   iii.   Rhoda **Young**[1069] was born 10 September 1789 and died 18 January 1840 at 50 years of age. She married John Portinus **Green**.

948   iv.   John **Young**[1070] was born in Hopkinton 22 May 1791 and died 27 April 1870 at 78 years of age. He married Theodocia **Kimball**. He had other wives.

949   v.   Nabby **Young**[1071] was born in Hopkinton 22 April 1793 and died in 1807 in Smyrna, N.Y. at 14 years of age.

950   vi.   Susannah **Young**[1072] was born in Hopkinton 17 June 1795 and died 5 May 1852 at 56 years of age. She married twice. (1) James **Little**. (2) William **Stilson**.

+ 951   vii.   Joseph **Young** was born 7 April 1797.

+ 952   viii. Phineas Howe **Young** was born 16 February 1799.
+ 953   ix. Brigham **Young** was born 1 June 1801.
     954   x. Louisa **Young**[1073] was born in Smyrna, N.Y. 26 September 1804 and died in July 1833 at 28 years of age. She married Joel **Sanford**.
+ 955   xi. Lorenzo Dow **Young** was born 19 October 1807.

663. Ruth[7] **Stone** (Jonathan[6], Jonathan[5], Jonathan[4], Mary[3] **Whipple**, Elder John[2], Matthew[1])[1074] was born in Watertown, Mass. 3 August 1748 and died 24 August 1817 in Worcester, Mass. at 69 years of age. She married **Nathaniel Harrington** in Worcester 2 July 1776.

Ruth **Stone** and Nathaniel **Harrington** had the following children:
     956   i. Francis[8] **Harrington**[1075] was born 15 May 1777.
     957   ii. Jonathan **Harrington**[1076] was born 31 October 1779.
     958   iii. Sarah **Harrington**[1077] was born 14 August 1786.

664. Lt. Jonathan[7] **Stone** (Jonathan[6], Jonathan[5], Jonathan[4], Mary[3] **Whipple**, Elder John[2], Matthew[1])[1078] was born in Watertown, Mass. 8 December 1750 and died 24 November 1809 in Auburn, Mass. at 58 years of age. He married twice. (1) **Mary Harrington** in Worcester 13 February 1777. (2) **Sarah (Sally) Hall** in Ward, Mass. 23 June 1792. Sarah,[1079] daughter of Jonathan **Hall** and Mary **Stow**, was born 31 December 1763 and died 16 September 1853 in Auburn at 89 years of age.

Lt. Jonathan **Stone** and Sarah (Sally) **Hall** had the following children:
+ 959   i. Col. Jonathan[8] **Stone** was born 4 April 1793.
     960   ii. Mary (Polly) Harrington **Stone**[1080] was born 22 June 1795 and married (__) **Smith**.
     961   iii. Oliver **Stone**[1081] was born 4 March 1798.
     962   iv. Elijah **Stone**[1082] was born 22 April 1802 and died 22 June 1872 at 70 years of age.

665. Daniel[7] **Stone** (Jonathan[6], Jonathan[5], Jonathan[4], Mary[3] **Whipple**, Elder John[2], Matthew[1])[1083] was born in Worcester, Mass. 25 October 1752 and died 22 January 1792 in Charleston, Mass. at 39 years of age. He married **Abigail Jones** in Worcester 5 November 1777.

Daniel **Stone** and Abigail **Jones** had the following children:
     963   i. Amasa[8] **Stone**[1084] was born 3 February 1779.
     964   ii. Mary (or Polly) **Stone**[1085] was born 25 October 1780.
     965   iii. Abigail **Stone**[1086] was born 6 March 1783.
     966   iv. Daniel **Stone**[1087] was born 30 October 1785.
     967   v. Jonathan **Stone**[1088] was born 11 February 1790.

672. Hannah[7] **Stone** (William[6], Moses[5], Jonathan[4], Mary[3] **Whipple**, Elder John[2], Matthew[1])[1089] was born in Woodstock, Conn. 28 February 1778 and died 20 November 1841 in Watertown, Mass. at 63 years of age. She married **Daniel Bond** in Watertown 1 January 1796. Daniel[1090] was born in Watertown 10 September 1761 and died there 13 September 1842 at 75 years of age.

Hannah **Stone** and Daniel **Bond** had the following children born in Watertown:
     968   i. Hannah[8] **Bond**[1091] was born 23 September 1796.
     969   ii. Sarah **Bond**[1092] was born 3 September 1798.

970   iii.   Mary S. **Bond**[1093] was born 29 December 1800.
971   iv.   Catherine **Bond**[1094] was born 16 May 1803.
972   v.   Eliza Ann **Bond**[1095] was born 2 January 1805.
973   vi.   Jane **Bond**[1096] was born 27 January 1807.
974   vii.   William **Bond**[1097] was born 17 August 1809 and died 20 December 1815 in Watertown at 6 years of age.
975   viii. Edward **Bond**[1098] was born 11 July 1811.
976   ix.   George **Bond**[1099] was born 7 September 1813.
977   x.   Daniel **Bond**[1100] was born 6 November 1815.
978   xi.   Adeline **Bond**[1101] was born 19 April 1819.
979   xii.   William **Bond**[1102] was born 18 April 1822.

674. Susanna[7] **Stone** (William[6], Moses[5], Jonathan[4], Mary[3] **Whipple**, Elder John[2], Matthew[1])[1103] was born in Watertown,, Mass. 4 October 1783 and died 8 January 1875 in Brookline, Norfolk Co., Mass. at 91 years of age. She married **Jabez Fisher** in Boston, Mass. 7 November 1816. Jabez,[1104] son of Jabin **Fisher** and Mary **Tucker**, was born in Stoughton, Norfolk Co., Mass. 28 November 1791 and died 10 August 1889 in Washington, Sullivan Co., N.H. at 97 years of age.

Susanna **Stone** and Jabez **Fisher** had the following children born in Boston:
980   i   James Tucker[8] **Fisher**[1105] was born 12 August 1817.
981   ii.   Susan Stone **Fisher**[1106] was born 8 January 1820.
982   iii.   Harriet Louisa **Fisher**[1107] was born 23 April 1822.
983   iv.   Jabez George **Fisher**[1108] was born 5 September 1823 and died 10 January 1826 in Boston at 2 years of age.
984   v.   Eveline **Fisher**[1109] was born 17 September 1824 and died 21 March 1878 at 53 years of age.
985   vi.   Anna Maria Bird **Fisher**[1110] was born 22 December 1825.
986   vii.   George Jabez **Fisher**[1111] was born 21 February 1828.
987   viii. Mary Davenport **Fisher**[1112] was born 10 June 1830 and died in April 1831 in Boston at less than one year of age.
988   ix.   Davenport **Fisher**[1113] was born 28 March 1832.
989   x.   Charles Lowell **Fisher**[1114] was born 23 October 1836 and died in November 1843 at 7 years of age.

675. Abigail[7] **Stone** (William[6], Moses[5], Jonathan[4], Mary[3] **Whipple**, Elder John[2], Matthew[1])[1115] was born in Watertown, Mass. 12 October 1783 and died 6 January 1857 at 73 years of age. She married **Thomas Richardson** in Watertown 11 April 1805. Thomas,[1116] son of Richard **Richardson** and Mehitable **Smith**, was born in Arlington, Middlesex Co., Mass. 15 September 1780 and died 7 September 1822 in Watertown at 41 years of age.

Abigail **Stone** and Thomas **Richardson** had the following children:
990   i.   Richard[8] **Richardson**[1117] was born in 1805.
991   ii.   Thomas **Richardson**[1118] was born 13 June 1807.
992   iii.   Henry **Richardson**[1119] was born in 1809.
993   iv.   James **Richardson**[1120] was born in 1812.
994   v.   Susan Stone **Richardson**[1121] was born in 1814.
995   vi.   Hannah Stone **Richardson**[1122] was born in 1817.
996   vii.   Abigail **Richardson**[1123] was born in 1822.

681. Elizabeth[7] **Stone** (William[6], Moses[5], Jonathan[4], Mary[3] **Whipple**, Elder

John[2], Matthew[1])[1124] was born in Watertown, Mass. 11 June 1795 and married **Asa Pratt** in Boston, Mass. 19 August 1819. Asa was born in Malden, Mass. 1 March 1794 and died 8 November 1878 in Watertown at 84 years of age.[1125]

Elizabeth **Stone** and Asa **Pratt** had the following children born in Watertown:
997   i. Charles[8] **Pratt**[1126] was born 2 October 1830 and died 4 May 1891 in New York, N.Y. at 60 years of age. He married twice. (1) Lydia Ann **Richardson** in 1854. Lydia was born in Belmont, Mass. and died in 1861 in New York State.[1127] (2) Mary Helen **Richardson** in 1863. She was born in Belmont and was Lydia Ann's sister.[1128]

Charles Pratt and Lydia had a son, Charles Millard and a daughter, Lydia. Charles and Mary had sons George D., Herbert L., John T., and Frederic B. and a daughter.

Charles, a great (4) grandson of John and Susanna Whipple, was one of 11 children born to a Massachusetts cabinet maker. He joined the work force while still a child to help support the family. Because of his mother's poor health, he also helped care for his 10 siblings. From this humble beginning, he rose to be a successful businessman and philanthropist. At the time of his death he was considered to be the wealthiest man in Brooklyn, N. Y. with an estate valued at between $15 and $20 million.

At age 10 he worked on a nearby farm while attending elementary school. At 13 he was working in a Boston grocery store and at 14 was a machine apprentice in Newton, Mass. earning $1.00 a week. A strong desire for more education motivated him to save as much money as possible and with these savings he enrolled at Wesleyan Academy in Wilbraham, Mass. where he studied for three years.

In 1849 at 18, he joined a Boston company specializing in paints and whale products and two years later moved to New York City, taking a job with the paints and oil firm of Schenck and Downing. In 1854 he, along with two partners, formed Raynolds, Devoe & Pratt, a paint and oil business. He also married his first wife, Lydia in 1854 and they had two children before she died in 1861. In 1863 he married Lydia's sister Mary and they had six children.

After the discovery of oil in Pennsylvania in 1859, Pratt went into oil refining and in 1867 he left his paints and oils firm to organize Charles Pratt & Company with Henry H. Rogers. The company bought crude oil and refined it at Greenpoint, New York. The firm introduced and manufactured several new oil by products, including "Pratt's Astral Oil," an illuminating oil that became a standard household product in the United States and Europe. It was a high grade kerosene that originated the remark that "the holy lamps of Tibet are primed with 'Astral Oil.'" He built one of the first company housing complexes for workers in the U.S. at Greenpoint and he named it "the Astral."

Pratt developed the business into the most successful such company in Brooklyn. His success caught the eye of John D. Rockefeller, Sr. and in 1874 the company was acquired by Standard Oil Co. Pratt changed its name to Pratt & Rogers to maintain a degree of managerial autonomy while benefitting from Standard Oil's extensive organizational structure and its near monopoly in the field. Despite his initial reluctance to sell to Standard Oil, Pratt became a high ranking director, one of nine trustees in the parent company, and one of the most powerful men in the country.

Toward the end of his life, he turned his attention to educational philanthropy. He had always regretted his own limited education and dreamed of founding an institution where pupils could learn trades through the skillful use of their hands. This dream was realized in 1887 when the Pratt Institute opened its doors in Brooklyn endowed with two million dollars. In addition to the main campus, today it also operates a campus at 144 West 14th in New York City.

Before founding the Institute, Pratt studied technical schools in Europe which led to the Institute's offering training for artisans, designers, and architects. Enrollment grew from 12 to more than 5,000 today. He also founded the Pratt Institute Free Library, the first free public library in New York City.

He was a trustee of Adelphi Academy in Brooklyn from 1867 to 1891 and president of its board of trustees for 12 years. He contributed $160,000 to the school in 1886 for the construction of a 1,000 student dormitory. Amherst College and the University of Rochester also received considerable grants from him. He also funded the building of Emmanuel Baptist church in Brooklyn and established the Asa Pratt fund for a free reading room in Watertown, Mass. in memory of his father. Highlights of the Pratt Institute include:

1877.	Art classes opened for enrollment.
1888.	Programs in liberal arts and sciences began.
1890.	Library School opens and has the distinction of being the oldest continuous school of Library Science in the country.
1910.	School of Science and Technology created.
1936.	Industrial Design Department created.
1938.	Foundation Year initiated; first baccalaureate degrees awarded.
1946.	Interior Design Department established.
1954.	School of Architecture separated from Art School.
1964.	Cooperative Education Program initiated in School of Engineering; first of its kind in the New York metropolitan area.

Four years after the opening of Pratt Institute, Charles died leaving the job of guiding the Institute through its early years to his sons, Charles Millard, George D., Herbert L., John T., and Frederic B. as the board of trustees[1129]. The energy, foresight, money, and spirit Charles Pratt gave to his dream remains today. Careers and goals like those of its founder are encouraged. Inscribed on the seal of the Institute is the motto: Be True To Your Work And Your Work Will Be True To You.

Pratt died at his office at 20 Broadway in New York City. Following an executive committee meeting of the Standard Oil Co., he fainted about 3 p.m. Doctors were unable to revive him and his wife, son Charles, and brother Henry were called to the office. He died in his wife's arms at 6:52 p.m.. The Pratt Institute was closed and the Standard Oil Co. conducted no business until after his funeral. He was also a director of the Long Island Railroad at the time of death.

The Pratts lived in a mansion at 232 Clinton Ave. in Brooklyn, had an extensive country place at Shelter Island, and several thousand acres on Long Island. He invested in improved real estate and was a heavy stock holder in local bank and trust companies. The Charles Pratt & Company was founded after his death and served as a central administrative office providing professional financial services for his descendants and selected other private clients.

998   ii.   Henry A. **Pratt**[1130] was born in Watertown, Mass.

682. Seth[7] **Stone** (William[6], Moses[5], Jonathan[4], Mary[3] **Whipple**, Elder John[2], Matthew[1])[1131] was born in Watertown, Mass. 2 January 1797.

Seth **Stone** had the following children:

999   i.   Melvin[8] **Stone**[1132].
1000   ii.   Charles H. **Stone**[1133].

687. Charles[7] **Stone** (Jonathan[6], Moses[5], Jonathan[4], Mary[3] **Whipple**, Elder John[2], Matthew[1])[1134] was born in 1789 and died in 1862 at 73 years of age. He married **Sarah Hobart Spear**. The family lived in Watertown and Belmont, Mass. A deacon, he was also a prosperous market gardener

Charles **Stone** and Sarah Hobart **Spear** had the following child:

+ 1001   i.   Charles Hobart[8] **Stone** was born 25 May 1827.

689. John[7] **Billings** (Joanna[6] **Norton**, John[5], Mary[4] **Goodhue**, Sarah[3] **Whipple**,

Elder John[2], Matthew[1])[1135] was born in Berwick, York, Co., Maine 6 March 1743 and died there 14 March 1834 at 91 years of age. He married an unnamed person in Berwick before 21 December 1770.

John **Billings** had the following child:
+ 1002   i.   Joel[8] **Billings** was born 21 December 1770.

695. Daniel[7] Swett (Moses[6], Elizabeth[5] Norton, Mary[4] **Goodhue**, Sarah[3] **Whipple**, Elder John[2], Matthew[1])1136 was born in Gilmanton, N.H. 23 April 1763 and died in 1837 in New Hampshire at 74 years of age. He married Jane **McNeil**[1137] who was born in 1765 and died in 1829 at 64 years of age.

Daniel **Swett** and Jane **McNeil** had the following child:
+ 1003   i.   Benjamin[8] **Swett** was born 5 December 1805.

697. Sarah[7] Treadwell (Joseph[6], Sarah[5] **Goodhue**, William[4], Sarah[3] **Whipple**, Elder John[2], Matthew[1])[1138] was born in Rowley, Mass. and christened 7 July 1751. She died 25 February 1837 in Millbury, Mass. She married **David Stone** in Oxford, Worcester Co., Mass. 25 July 1776. David was born in Waltham, Middlesex Co., Mass. 6 December and died 9 December 1827 in Oxford at 77 years of age.[1139] He changed his surname from Gale to Stone.

Sarah **Treadwell** and David **Stone** had the following children born in Oxford:
1004   i.   Capt. David[8] **Stone**[1140] was born 6 April 1776 and died 29 August 1828 in Oxford at 52 years of age. He married Betsy **Hall** in Oxford 16 January 1808. Betsey was from Sutton, Mass.
1005   ii.   Joseph **Stone**[1141] was born 24 August 1780 and married Martha **Learned** in Oxford 18 April 1813.
+ 1006   iii.   Sarah (Sally) **Stone** was born 13 November 1783.
1007   iv.   Anna **Stone**[1142] was born 27 October 1787 and married Amos **Eddy** in Oxford. The date of intent to marry was in October 1813. Amos was from Millbury, Mass.
1008   v.   Jeremiah **Stone**[1143] was born 21 March 1791 and married Luella **Hawse** in Oxford 12 October 1834.

698. Joseph[7] Treadwell (Joseph[6], Sarah[5] **Goodhue**, William[4], Sarah[3] **Whipple**, Elder John[2], Matthew[1])[1144] was born in Ipswich, Mass. and was christened 5 March 1748. He was a mariner and died before 1785. He married **Susanna (__)** before 26 May 1769.

Joseph **Treadwell** and Susanna (__) had the following children:
+ 1009   i.   Joseph[8] **Treadwell** was born 12 August 1771.
1010   ii.   Benjamin **Treadwell**[1145] was born in Newburyport, Mass. 19 January 1774.

706. Nathaniel[7] Treadwell (Thomas[6], Sarah[5] **Goodhue**, William[4], Sarah[3] **Whipple**, Elder John[2], Matthew[1])[1146] was born in Ipswich, Mass. 20 December 1752 and died there 10 November 1835 at 82 years of age. He was a sea captain and his vessel the *Lucy* was captured by the French and became part of the "Spoilation Claims." He married twice. (1) **Elizabeth Stone** in Ipswich 4 May 1775. Elizabeth was born 2 November 1755 and died 25 December 1808 in Ipswich at 53 years of age.[1147] (2) **Mrs. Elizabeth (McNeal) Fuller** in Ipswich 19 March 1810 who died 26

September 1828 in Ipswich at 68 years of age.

Nathaniel **Treadwell** and Elizabeth **Stone** had the following children:

+ 1011   i. Nathaniel[8] **Treadwell** was born 13 May 1776.
+ 1012   ii. Thomas **Treadwell** was born 1 October 1779.
+ 1013   iii. Samuel **Treadwell** was born in 1781.
+ 1014   iv. Elizabeth **Treadwell** was born 18 November 1783.
+ 1015   v. John **Treadwell** was born 27 February 1786.
   1016   vi. Mehitable **Treadwell**[1148] was born in Ipswich and died there 19 January 1789 at one year of age.
+ 1017   vii. William **Treadwell** was born 10 March 1791.
+ 1018   viii. Hannah **Treadwell** was born 1 September 1793.
   1019   ix. Robert **Treadwell**[1149] was born in Ipswich 2 August 1795 and died in 1819 at 23 years of age. It is believed he was killed in Europe. His intent to marry Elizabeth Creasey of Newburyport, Mass. was published in Newburyport 7 November 1819. There is no evidence the marriage took place suggesting he was killed before the ceremony could be performed.

709. Jonathan[7] Basford (Elizabeth[6] **Goodhue**, Jonathan[5], William[4], Sarah[3] **Whipple**, Elder John[2], Matthew[1])[1150] was born in Chester, N.H. 1 March 1748 and died 31 January 1818 in Canterbury, N.H. at 69 years of age. He married **Rachel Ladd**[1151]

Jonathan **Basford** and Rachel **Ladd** had the following child:

+ 1020   i. Sarah[8] **Basford** was born 6 April 1772.

716. Isaac[7] Kimball (John[6], Isaac[5], Sarah[4] **Goodhue**, Sarah[3] **Whipple**, Elder John[2], Matthew[1]) birth date unknown, married **Sarah Warner**.

Isaac **Kimball** and Sarah **Warner** had the following child:

+ 1021   i. Jesse W.[8] **Kimball**.

720. Jesse[7] Kimball (John[6], Isaac[5], Sarah[4] **Goodhue**, Sarah[3] **Whipple**, Elder John[2], Matthew[1])[1152] was born in Preston, New London Co., Conn. 19 March 1760 and died 18 November 1857 in Antioch, Gibson Co., Ind. at 97 years of age. He married **Elizabeth Roelofson**. Elizabeth was born in 1773 and died 4 December 1843 in Antioch at 70 years of age.

Jesse **Kimball** and Elizabeth **Roelofson** had the following children:

+ 1022   i. Mary[8] **Kimball** was born in 1794.
+ 1023   ii. Sarah **Kimball** was born in 1796.
+ 1024   iii. Elisha **Kimball** was born in 1798.
   1025   iv. Amy **Kimball**[1153] was born in 1799 and died in 1820 at 21 years of age.
   1026   v. Margaret **Kimball**[1154] was born in 1800 and died in 1820 at 20 years of age.
+ 1027   vi. Easter **Kimball** was born 15 October 1802.
+ 1028   vii. Isaac **Kimball** was born in 1804.
   1029   viii. Enoch **Kimball**[1155] was born in 1806 and married Sarah **Boyle**.
+ 1030   ix. Cynthia **Kimball** was born in 1809.
   1031   x. Mahalah **Kimball**[1156] was born in 1812 and married Andrew **Baird**.

722. Jacob[7] Kimball (Jacob[6], Jacob[5], Sarah[4] **Goodhue**, Sarah[3] **Whipple**, Elder John[2], Matthew[1])[1157] was born in 1767 and died 5 October 1834 at 67 years of age. He married **Anna Ansley**. Anna,[1158] daughter of John **Ansley** and Eunice (_), was born in 1777 and died 15 April 1841 at 63 years of age. Jacob and Anna are buried at Paupack, Penn.

Jacob **Kimball** and Anna **Ansley** had the following child:
    1032   i.   Walter[8] **Kimble** was born 9 June 1808.

723. Roswell[7] Stevens (Hepsibah[6] **Kilham**, Abigail[5] **Kimball**, Sarah[4] **Goodhue**, Sarah[3] **Whipple**, Elder John[2], Matthew[1])[1159] was born in Plainfield, Conn. 17 February 1772 and died in July 1847 in Council Bluffs, Iowa at 75 years of age. He married **Sybell Spencer**.[1160] Sybell was born in Washington, Berkshire Co., Mass. 4 April 1778 and died 18 November 1862 in Holden, Utah at 84 years of age.

Roswell **Stevens** and Sybell **Spencer** had the following children:
    1033   i.   Roswell[8] **Stevens** Jr.[1161] was born in Mt. Pleasant, Great Upper Canada 17 November 1808 and died 14 May 1880 in Bluff, San Juan Co., Utah at 71 years of age. He married Valley Mariah **Doyle** in 1827. Valley,[1162] daughter of John **Doyle** and Polly (_), was born in Mt. Pleasant, Canada 29 June 1809 and died 11 August 1879 in Montpelier, Bear Lake Co., Idaho at 70 years of age.
  + 1034   ii. Julia Ann **Stevens** was born 17 February 1830.
  + 1035   iii. William **Stevens** was born 14 February 1832.

724. Samuel[7] Goodhue (Samuel[6], George[5], Joseph[4], Sarah[3] **Whipple**, Elder John[2], Matthew[1])[1163] was born in Newburyport, Mass. in 1778 and died there in 1841 at 63 years of age. He married **Elizabeth Slade Blunt** in Newburyport.

Samuel **Goodhue** and Elizabeth Slade **Blunt** had the following child:
  + 1036   i.   Samuel[8] **Goodhue** was born in 1805.

725. Eleanor[7] Knowlton (Daniel[6], Robert[5], Marjory (Margery)[4] **Goodhue**, Sarah[3] **Whipple**, Elder John[2], Matthew[1])[1164] was born in Ashford, Conn. in 1752 and married **Natham Upham** abt 1774. Natham[1165] was born 25 July 1752 and died 4 June 1818 in Colchester Co., N.S. at 65 years of age.

Eleanor **Knowlton** and Natham **Upham** had the following child:
  + 1037   i.   Elizabeth[8] **Upham** was born 8 March 1786.

726. Solomon[7] Rand (Deborah[6] **Dodge**, Margery[5] **Knowlton**, Marjory (Margery)[4] **Goodhue**, Sarah[3] **Whipple**, Elder John[2], Matthew[1])[1166] was born 5 March 1750 and died 27 April 1827 in Rindge, N.H. at 77 years of age. He married **Sarah Adams** 22 June 1774. Sarah[1167] was born 30 April 1754 and died 18 February 1815 in Rindge at 60 years of age.

Solomon **Rand** and Sarah **Adams** had the following child:
  + 1038   I.   Polly[8] **Rand** was born 14 March 1790.

727. Nathan[7] Knowlton (Joseph[6], Joseph[5], Marjory (Margery)[4] **Goodhue**, Sarah[33] **Whipple**, Elder John[2], Matthew[1])[1168] was born 15 May 1760 and died 24 May 1856 in Auburn, Mass. at 96 years of age. He married twice. (1) **Abigail Maynard** 6 January 1782. Abigail, daughter of Benjamin **Maynard** and Abigail

Rice, was born 7 June 1762 and died 21 December 1790 at 28 years of age.[1169] (2) **Olive Pomeroy** in 1791. Olive was born in Warwick, Mass. 16 August 1763 and died 3 January 1843 in Auburn at 79 years of age.[1170]

Nathan **Knowlton** and Abigail **Maynard** had the following children:

1039   i. Benjamin[8] **Knowlton**[1171] was born 3 August 1782 and died 23 August 1865 in Jamaica, Vt. at 83 years of age. He married Olive **Stone** in Ward, Mass. 22 January 1807. Olive, daughter of Israel **Stone** and Tryphena **Boyden**, was born in Ward, 19 January 1781 and died 13 December 1865 in Jamaica at 84 years of age.[1172] Olive is a direct descendant of the early Massachusetts Bay settler Gregory Stone. The descent is Gregory[1], John[2], Nathaniel[3], Hezekiah[4], and Israel[5]. Their children were Tryphema, Mary, Abigail, Israel, Candace, Marcia, and Benjamin L.

1040   ii. Sally **Knowlton**[1173] was born 16 July 1783 and died 10 April 1871 at 87 years of age. She married twice. (1) David **Gleason** after 1800. She and David had a child named Freeman Gleason. (2) Aaron **Sibley** before 1870.

1041   iii. Nathan **Knowlton**[1174] was born 23 January 1785 and died 12 March 1848 at 63 years of age. He married Sally **Gates** after 1805.

1042   iv. Maynard **Knowlton**[1175] was born 20 October 1787 and married Susannah **Gates**.[1176]

+ 1043   v. Abigail **Knowlton** was born 13 March 1790.

1044   vi. Lucretia **Knowlton**[1177] was born 3 March 1792.

1045   vii. Joanna **Knowlton**[1178] was born 23 July 1793 and died 18 August 1857 in Bennington, Vt. at 64 years of age. She married David **Rockwood** in 1815.

1046   viii. Pomeroy **Knowlton**[1179] was born 1 August 1794 and died 1 June 1874 at 79 years of age. He married Marcia **Palmer**. They had a daughter.

1047   ix. Lucinda **Knowlton**[1180] was born 3 February 1796 and died at an early age.

1048   x. Olive **Knowlton**[1181] was born 1 February 1797 and married C. **Fay** and died 3 March 1886 probably in Lawrence, Mass at 89 years of age. They had six children; names and vitals not provided.

1049   xi. Arad **Knowlton**[1182] was born 29 December 1798 and married Sophia **Wilkinson** in October 1825.

1050   xii. Mary **Knowlton**[1183] was born 16 February 1800 and died 13 September 1866 at 66 years of age. She married Luther **Waters**.

1051   xiii. Lucy **Knowlton**[1184] was born 10 December 1801 and married N.S. **Clark**.

1052   xiv. Asabel **Knowlton**[1185] was born 22 February 1803 and married Sophronia C. **Cummings** 19 January 1832.

728. Ebenezer[7] Goodhue (Ebenezer[6], John[5], John[4], Sarah[3] **Whipple**, Elder John[2], Matthew[1])[1186] was born in Massachusetts 30 September 1782 and died 10 September 1869 at 86 years of age. He married **Mehitable Knight**. She was from Antrim, N.H.

Ebenezer **Goodhue** and Mehitable **Knight** had the following child:

+ 1053   i. Benjamin[8] **Goodhue** was born 17 July 1818.

EIGHTH GENERATION

730. John Hale[8] Pillsbury (Rev. Edmund[7], Moses[6], Moses[5], Susanna[4] **Worth**, Susannah[33] **Whipple**, Elder John[2], Matthew[1])[1187] was born in Newbury, Mass. 27 September 1762 and died 14 March 1857 in S. Hampton, Rockingham Co., N.H. at 94 years of age. He married **Eliz Rowell** 27 March 1787.

John Hale **Pillsbury** and Eliz **Rowell** had the following children:

1054	i.	James[9] **Pillsbury**[1188].
1055	ii.	George **Pillsbury**[1189].
1056	iii.	Lois **Pillsbury**[1190] was born in 1787 and died in 1839 at 52 years of age. She married Samuel **Currier**.
1057	iv.	James **Pillsbury** was born in 1789 and died in 1824 at 35 years of age. He married Sally **Lane**.
1058	v.	John **Pillsbury**[1191] was born in 1790 and died in 1843 at 53 years of age.
+ 1059	vi.	Jacob **Pillsbury** was born 25 September 1791.
+ 1060	vii.	Edmund **Pillsbury** was born in 1793.
1061	viii.	Enoch **Pillsbury**[1192] was born in 1795 and died in 1851 at 56 years of age.
1062	ix.	Eliz **Pillsbury**[1193] was born in 1796 and died in 1882 at 86 years of age. She married George **Currier**.
1063	x.	William **Pillsbury**[1194] was born in 1800 and died in 1802 at 2 years of age.
1064	xi.	William **Pillsbury**[1195] was born in 1802 and died in 1839 at 37 years of age.
1065	xii.	George Washington **Pillsbury**[1196] was born in 1804 and married Betsy Fitts **Dow** 2 February 1832.

736. Oliver[8] Pillsbury (Parker[7], Moses[6], Moses[5], Susanna[4] **Worth**, Susannah[3] **Whipple**, Elder John[2], Matthew[1]) was born in 1783 and died in 1857 at 74 years of age. He married **Anna Smith**.

Oliver **Pillsbury** and Anna **Smith** had the following child:

+ 1066	i.	Josiah Webster[9] **Pillsbury** was born 20 March 1811.

743. Zacheus[8] Hale (Joseph[7], Abigail W.[6] **Pillsbury**, Moses[5], Susanna[4] **Worth**, Susannah[3] **Whipple**, Elder John[2], Matthew[1])[1197] was born in Dunstable, N.H. 2 February 1775 and married **Mary (Polly) Chase** in Hudson, N.H. 5 October 1797. Mary, daughter of Joshua **Chase** and Mary **Hadley**, was born in Hudson 2 May 1774.

Zacheus **Hale** and Mary (Polly) **Chase** had the following children:

1067	i.	Hannah[9] **Hale** was born 11 August 1799.
+ 1068	ii.	Zacheus **Hale** was born 27 March 1802.
1069	iii.	Robert **Hale** was born 1 April 1804.
1070	iv.	Frederic **Hale** was born in Dunstable, N.H. 15 August 1806.
1071	v.	Robert **Hale** was born 19 March 1809.
1072	vi.	Abel Goodrich **Hale** was born 29 September 1811.

752. Bernard[8] Brickett Jr. (Bernard[7], Susanna[6] **Pillsbury**, Moses[5], Susanna[4] **Worth**, Susannah[3] **Whipple**, Elder John[2], Matthew[1]) was born in Haverhill, Mass. 17 July 1778 and died there 15 April 1836 at 57 years of age. He married **Hannah Bryant** in Haverhill 8 April 1806. Hannah was born in 1786 and died 16 September 1818 in Haverhill at 32 years of age.

Bernard **Brickett** Jr. and Hannah **Bryant** had the following child:
+ 1073   i.   Deborah Towne[9] **Brickett** was born 14 July 1807.

756. Judith[8] **Pillsbury** (Caleb[7], Caleb[6], Caleb[5], Susanna[4] **Worth**, Susannah[3] **Whipple**, Elder John[2], Matthew[1])[1198] was born in Amesbury, Mass. 23 November 1780 and died 5 May 1848 in Wheelock, Caledonia Co., Vt. at 67 years of age. She is buried in Pope Cemetery, Danville Caledonia Co. Vt. She married twice. (1) **Joseph Hoyt** in Danville. Joseph was born in Danville in 1776 and died there 19 August 1843 at 67 years of age. He is buried in Pope Cemetery.[1199] (2) **Ward Bradley** as his second wife in Danville 12 March 1845. Ward was born in Haverhill, Mass. 16 February 177 and died 5 July 1865 in Sheffield, Caledonia Co., Vt. at 93 years of age. He is buried in Wheelock Hollow Cemetery, Wheelock, Vt. He married (1) **Hannah Nutting**.[1200]

Judith **Pillsbury** and Joseph **Hoyt** had the following children:
1074   i.   Nancy[9] **Hoyt**[1201] died unmarried 29 April 1838.
1075   ii   Sargent **Hoyt**[1202] married Mary Trew **Page** in Danville 12 June 1827.
+ 1076   iii.   Dr. Hiram Pillsbury **Hoyt** was born abt 1806.
1077   iv.   Luther **Hoyt**[1203] was born abt 1808 and died 5 June 1866 at 57 years of age. He is buried in Pope Cemetery, Danville. He married Betsey **Hill** 26 November 1845.
1078   v.   Mary Ann **Hoyt**[1204] was born in 1817 and died unmarried 19 May 1865 at 47 years of age. She is buried in Pope Cemetery, Danville.

766. Susanna[8] **Burt** (Abiah[7] **Mooar**, Abiah[6] **Hill**, Judith[5] **Bucknam**, Judith (Jude)[4] **Worth**, Susannah[3] **Whipple**, Elder John[2], Matthew[1])[1205] was born in Andover, Mass. 25 June 1758 and died in 1853 in Amherst, Mass. at 95 years of age. She married **William Dane Jr.** in Andover 31 October 1780.

Susanna **Burt** and William **Dane** Jr. had the following child:
1079   i.   Mary Baldwin[9] **Dane**[1206] was born after 1780.

769. Lois[8] **Burt** (Abiah[7] **Mooar**, Abiah[6] **Hill**, Judith[5] **Bucknam**, Judith (Jude)[4] **Worth**, Susannah[3] **Whipple**, Elder John[2], Matthew[1])[1207] was born in Andover, Mass. 16 June 1763 and died 19 September 1814 in Henderson, Jefferson Co., N.Y. at 51 years of age. She was buried in September 1814 in Henderson's Carpenter's Cemetery. She married **Thomas Blanchard** in Andover 12 March 1782. Thomas,[1208] son of Aaron **Blanchard** and Nelle **Holt**, was born in Andover 11 November 1762 and died 1 February 1837 in Henderson at 74 years of age. He was buried in Henderson's Carpenter's Cemetery. Thomas, a private in the Revolutionary War, was a farmer and blacksmith.

Lois **Burt** and Thomas **Blanchard** had the following children:
1080   i.   Lois[9] **Blanchard**[1209] was born 2 September 1783 and died before October 1874 in Andover.
1081   ii.   Lois **Blanchard**[1210] was born 24 October 1784.
+ 1082   iii.   Thomas **Blanchard** Jr. was born 1 October 1786.
1083   iv.   Molly **Blanchard**[1211] was born in Andover 16 December 1788 and died there 7 December 1789 at less than one year of age.
1084   v.   Priscy **Blanchard**[1212] was born in Andover 16 December 1788 and died there 1 January 1789 at less than one year of age.
1085   vi.   Betty **Blanchard**[1213] was born in Danville, Vt. and christened there 14

February 1790. She married Jason **Wilkins** there 10 May 1813.[1214]
+ 1086   vii. John Burt **Blanchard** was born in 1792.
  1087   viii. Priscilla **Blanchard**[1215] was born in Danville 10 September 1796.
+ 1088   ix. Salma **Blanchard** was born 24 September 1798.
+ 1089   x. Lucy **Blanchard** was born 13 May 1801.
+ 1090   xi. Aaron **Blanchard** was born 5 March 1804.
+ 1091   xii. Sophia **Blanchard** was born 24 April 1809.

792. Hannah Stone[8] Brown (Samuel[7], William[6], Martha[5] **Whipple**, Maj. John[4], Capt. John[3], Elder John[2], Matthew[1])[1216] was born in Newburyport, Mass. 30 October 1801 and died 7 June 1869 in Boston, Mass. at 67 years of age. She was buried in Roxbury, Mass. in Forest Hills Cemetery. She married **Robert Breck Williams** in Newburyport, 18 October 1821. Robert,[1217] son of Joseph **Williams** and Mrs. Abigail (Gallishan) **Wells**, was born in Newburyport 25 May 1792 and died 5 April 1872 in Boston at 79 years of age.

Hannah Stone **Brown** and Robert Breck **Williams** had the following child:
+ 1092   i. William Brown[9] **Williams** was born 10 November 1835.

794. Nathaniel[8] Pearson (Sarah[7] **Gerrish**, Katherine[6] **Brown**, Martha[5] **Whipple**, Maj. John[4], Capt. John[3], Elder John[2], Matthew[1])[1218] was born in Newbury, Mass. 25 June 1783 and died 2 May 1851 in Georgetown, Mass. at 67 years of age. He married **Rebekah Rogers** in Newbury 18 January 1805. Rebekah,[1219] daughter of Gideon **Rogers** and Hannah **Flood**, was born in Newbury 7 October 1787 and died there 13 May 1868 at 80 years of age. Nathaniel and Rebekah are buried in Byfield, Mass. in the Congregational Church Cemetery.

Nathaniel **Pearson** and Rebekah **Rogers** had the following children:
  1093   i. Luther[9] **Pearson**[1220] was born 29 August 1805 and married Phebe **Ordway**. Phebe,[1221] daughter of Thomas **Ordway** and Lydia **Hanson**, was born in Newbury 4 August 1808
  1094   ii. William Noyes **Pearson**[1222] was born 12 March 1807 and married Elizabeth **Perkins**.
  1095   iii. Daniel **Pearson**[1223] was born 15 April 1810 and married Anna Mary **Ordway**. Anna,[1224] daughter of Thomas **Ordway** and Lydia **Hanson**, was born in Newbury 19 December 1815.
  1096   iv. Joseph Gerrish **Pearson**[1225] was born 20 August 1816 and married Phebe **Nichols**.
  1097   v. Angier Morrill **Pearson**[1226] was born 8 June 1819.
  1098   vi. Eliza Farnham **Pearson**[1227] was born 25 December 1821.
+ 1099   vii. Susan Poor **Pearson** was born 15 July 1824.

806. George[8] Rogers (John[7], Rev. John[6], Suanna[5] **Whipple**, Maj. John[4], Capt. John[3], Elder John[2], Matthew[1])[1228] was born in Gloucester, Mass. 17 June 1792 and died 31 July 1864 at 72 years of age. He married **Sarah Caroline (Hovey) Doane**. Sarah,[1229] daughter of Solomon **Hovey** and Sarah **Johnson**, was born in Charlestown, Mass. 19 June 1809 and died 25 August 1898 in Brookline, Norfolk Co., Mass. at 89 years of age.

George **Rogers** and Sarah Caroline (Hovey) **Doane** had the following child:
+ 1100   i. Grace Adams[9] **Rogers** was born 22 February 1856.

807. **John**[8] **Whipple** (John[7], Capt. John[6], Capt. John[55], Maj. Matthew[4], Capt. John[3], Elder John[2], Matthew[1])[1230] was born in Ipswich, Mass. 22 March 1776 and died 22 July 1858 in Sommerville, Suffolk Co., Mass. at 82 years of age. He married **Eunice Holbrook** in Sherborn, Mass. 3 December 1805. Eunice,[1231] daughter of Micah **Holbrook** and Lydia **Kendall**, was born in Sherborn 3 May 1781 and died 14 October 1858 in Boylston, Worcester Co., Mass. at 77 years of age. Eunice was the fifth generation from Thomas Holbrook of England who settled at Dorchester, Mass and was one of the founders of Sherborn.

John **Whipple** and Eunice **Holbrook** had the following children born in Boylston:

1101	i.	Orland[9] Whipple[1232] was born 3 November 1806 and died 20 September 1850 in Stockton, San Joaquin Co., Calif. at 43 years of age.
1102	ii.	Adeline Whipple[1233] was born 10 August 1808 and died 22 November 1840 at 32 years of age. She married William **Green** 31 May 1836.
+ 1103	iii.	William Ward Whipple was born 25 August 1811.
+ 1104	iv.	John Whipple was born 26 August 1811.
1105	v.	Louisa Whipple[1234] was born 6 September 1817 and died 5 September 1847 at 29 years of age.
1106	vi.	Lyman Whipple[1235] was born 6 September 1817 and died 7 March 1891 in Shrewsbury, Mass. at 73 years of age. He married Sarah Louise **Clement**.

811. **Stephen**[8] **Whipple** (Martha[7], Dea. Nathaniel[6], Capt. John[5], Maj. Matthew[4], Capt. John[3], Elder John[2], Matthew[1])[1236] was christened in Ipswich, Mass. 11 March 1781 and died after 1850 in Cleveland, Ohio. He married **Eunice P. Smith** in Danvers, Mass. 31 January 1810. Eunice,[1237] daughter of Ephraim **Smith** and Eunice (_), was born in Danvers 5 August 1782 and died after 1840 in Cleveland. Stephen was listed as the head of a family on the 1840 Census in Cuyahoga Co., Ohio where the family was living in the first ward. Stephen is listed as a resident of a boarding house in the 1850 census. Eunice, not listed, was probably dead.

Stephen **Whipple** and Eunice P. **Smith** had the following children born in Danvers:

1107	i.	Stephen S.[9] Whipple[1238] was born 18 November 1810.
1108	ii.	Ephraim Smith Whipple[1239] was born 2 June 1812.
1109	iii.	Elvira Whipple[1240] was born 9 September 1814.
1110	iv.	Phebe Smith Whipple[1241] was born 4 September 1817 and died 7 December 1817 in Danvers at less than one year of age.
+ 1111	v.	Phebe Smith Whipple was born 31 August 1818.

821. **Harriett**[8] **Spence** (Mary[7] Traill, Mary[6] Whipple, Capt. William[5], Maj. Matthew[4], Capt. John[3], Elder John[1], Matthew[1]) birth date unknown, married **Rev. Charles Lowell**. Rev. Lowell was awarded an A.B. degree in 1800 and an A.M. degree in 1803, both from Harvard College. He was the fourth minister of the West Church in Boston, serving until his death in 1861. A "Lowell Genealogy" traces the family descent from Percival Lowle said to have been born in England in 1571 and known to have died at Newbury, Mass. 8 January 1664.[1242]

Harriett **Spence** and Rev. Charles **Lowell** had the following children:

1112	i.	Mary Traill Spence[9] Lowell. She married S. R. **Putnam**.

1113   ii. Charles **Lowell**.

1114   iii. Robert Traill Spence **Lowell**[1243] was born in Boston, Mass. 18 October 1816 and died 12 September 1891 in Schenectady, N.Y. at 74 years of age. He married Mary Ann **Duane** in Duanesburg Schenectady Co., N.Y. 28 October 1845. Their sons, gen. Charles Russell Lowell and lieut. James Jackson Lowell, were killed during the Civil War.

Robert, great (5) grandson of John and Susanna Whipple, was a man of genuine, though minor, literary originality, a poet and a novelist who entered Harvard at age 13 (1829) to study medicine. He was graduated in 1833 after taking the full medical course. Instead of practicing medicine, he went into a mercantile business with his brother Charles for a number of years and became active in military affairs as captain of a militia company in Boston.

In 1839 he decided to become an Episcopal minister and entered Union College, passed his theological examinations in 1840, and was ordained a deacon at Bermuda in December 1842. He was ordained as a minister in March 1843 and appointed domestic chaplain to the Bishop and inspector of schools in the colony Later that year he requested a transfer to a missionary post at Bay Roberts, Newfoundland where he became the representative of the English Society for the Propagation of the Gospel.

He lived through a famine winter in Newfoundland during which time he served as chairman of the relief committee of a large district. His medical training was of great help at the time and he was commended by the colonial secretary for his work. The experience broke his health and he returned to the United States in 1847 where after a long rest, he began a mission in Newark, N.J. and reestablished and rebuilt a neglected church.

From 1859 to 1869, he was rector of Christ Church at Duanesburg, N.Y. his wife's home town. She was the great granddaughter of Judge Duane, first mayor of New York City and founder of Duanesburg. Robert became headmaster of St. Mark's School in Southborough, Mass. in 1869 where he remained until 1873 when he was appointed Professor of Latin and Literature at Union College where he remained until his retirement six years later. He lived out his retirement years in Schenectady.

His published works include two novels, two volumes of poems, and a collection of short stories. His first novel, *The Story of the New Priest in Conception Bay* published in 1858, reflect memories of his Newfoundland days. The first edition sold out almost immediately. In its review of December 1858, the *Atlantic Monthly* wrote: "No candid critic can read it without pronouncing it to be a remarkable work and the production of an original mind."

His second novel, *Antony Brade: A Story of a School* (1874) is about a mysterious schoolboy hero who the townsfolk believe is a Russian prince incognito. Two years after his first novel, he published a volume of verse, *Fresh Hearts That Failed Three Thousand Years Ago.* He published *The Poems of Robert Lowell* in 1864 which included the poems of the earlier volume plus 30 more. Some of these poems appeared in magazines of the time. His last poem, *Burgoyne's Last March*, commemorated the hundredth anniversary of the battle of Bemis Heights September 19, 1777. It was published in pamphlet form.

His short story, "A Raft That No Man Made," was first printed in the *Atlantic Monthly* of March 1862, later reprinted in a series entitled "Little Classics." This story came from his experiences in Newfoundland. While at Union College, he published in 1878 three short stories under the title *A Story or Two from an Old Dutch Town.* The first two, "The Man in the Picture" and "Mr. Schermerhorn's Marriage and Widowhood," are about Schenectady in the early nineteenth century. The third, "Master Vorhagen's Wife," goes back to the days of "the second George" when the Dutch aspects of the town were still prominent and slavery was a common institution in the northern colonies.

He had a gift for poems of occasion, the nostalgic verses of class reunions, or the patriotic celebrations of heroic events. His ballad "The Relief of Lucknow," first published in the *Atlantic Monthly*, was admired by Ralph Waldo Emerson who often recited it on the public platform. Bancroft, the Secretary of the Navy, quoted "The Men of the Cumberland" in his official report of the loss of the *Cumberland* in its engagement with the Confederate iron ship *Virginia* 9 March 1862. Another of his civil war poems, "The Massachusetts Line," written at Duanesburg in May 1861 to the tune of "Yankee Doodle," was reprinted by the hundred thousand and used as a campaign song in General Benjamin Franklin Butler's successful run for the governorship of Massachusetts. His younger brother James died 12 August 1891, a month before his death. James had been ill for several months but Robert's health was such that he could not visit his brother at the end or attend the funeral.

+ 1115   iv. James Russell **Lowell** was born 22 February 1819.

823. Nathaniel[8] **French** (Hannah[7] **Page**, Nathaniel[6], Susannah[5] **Lane**, Susanna[4] **Whipple**, Capt. John[3], Elder John[2], Matthew[1])[1244] was born in Billerica, Mass. 11 April 1760 and married **Susanna Brown** there 11 September 1783. Susanna was from Concord, Mass.

Nathaniel **French** and Susanna **Brown** had the following child:
1116   i. Jonas[9] **French**[1245] was born in Billerica 7 June 1787.

824. Reuben[8] **French** (Hannah[7] **Page**, Nathaniel[6], Susannah[5] **Lane**, Susanna[4] **Whipple**, Capt. John[3], Elder John[2], Matthew[1])[1246] was born in Billerica, Mass. 18 October 1761 and married **Abigail Farmer** there 12 March 1789.

Reuben **French** and Abigail **Farmer** had the following children born in Billerica:
1117   i. Nabby[9] **French**[1247] was born 21 August 1790 and married an unnamed person.
+ 1118   ii. Reuben **French** was born 26 February 1792.
1119   iii. Charles **French**[1248] was born 13 October 1793.
1120   iv. Ziba **French**[1249] was born 3 January 1796.
1121   v. George **French**[1250] was born 8 September 1797.
1122   vi. Zoa **French**[1251] was born 15 April 1801.
1123   vii. Page **French**[1252] was born 30 April 1805 and died 14 October 1819 in Billerica at 14 years of age.

829. William Dickman[8] **Whitmore** (John[7], Francis[6], Mary[5] **Lane**, Susanna[4] **Whipple**, Capt. John[3], Elder John[2], Matthew[1])[1253] was born 3 November 1781 and married **Rhoda Woodward** 20 January 1805.

William Dickman **Whitmore** and Rhoda **Woodward** had the following children:
1124   i. Huldah[9] **Whitmore**[1254] married William G. **Barrows**. He was from Brunswick, Maine.
1125   ii. Charles **Whitmore**[1255] was born 19 December 1805 and died 24 March 1807 at one year of age.
+ 1126   iii. Charles O. **Whitmore** was born 2 November 1807.
1127   iv. Martha **Whitmore**[1256] was born 9 May 1810.

830. Jonathan[8] **Lane** (Jonathan[7], John[6], Job[5], Susanna **Whipple**, Capt. John[3], Elder John[2], Matthew[1])[1257] was born in 1788 and died in 1860 at 72 years of age. He married **Ruhamah Page**. The family moved to Boston in 1824.

Jonathan **Lane** and Ruhamah **Page** had the following child:
1128   i. Jonathan Abbot[9] **Lane** was born in 1822.

831. Anna[8] Gould (Anna[7] **Lane**, Timothy[6], Job[5], Susanna[4] **Whipple**, Capt. John[3], Elder John[2], Matthew[1])[1258] was born in Rindge, N.H. 5 March 1780, christened 13 August 1780, and died 19 December 1860 in Roxbury, Vt. at 80 years of age. She married **Darius Hatch** in Roxbury 10 April 1804. Darius was born in Hartland, Vt. 19 July 1779 and died 17 January 1861 in Roxbury at 81 years of age.[1259]

Anna **Gould** and Darius **Hatch** had the following children:

+ 1129	i.	Paschal[9] **Hatch** was born 17 October 1807.
1130	ii.	Allen **Hatch**[1260] was born in Hartland in 1810.
1131	iii.	Franklin **Hatch**[1261] was born in Hartland 16 June 1813.
1132	iv.	Zerviah **Hatch**[1262] was born 20 September 1815.

839. Brewster[8] Hill (Ralph[7], Mary[6] **Lane**, Job[5], Susanna[4] **Whipple**, Capt. John[3], Elder John[2], Matthew[1])[1263] was born 16 September 1784 and died 14 May 1879 at 94 years of age. He married **Celinda Carpenter** in Billerica, Mass. 6 October 1816.

Brewster **Hill** and Celinda **Carpenter** had the following children born in Billerica:

+ 1133	i.	Laura Williams[9] **Hill** was born 1 February 1819.
1134	ii.	Susan Blanchard **Hill**[1264] was born 12 March 1821 and married Jerome **Bock**. Jerome was from Brighton, Mass. The family was living in Burlington, Iowa in 1883.
1135	iii.	John Brewster **Hill**[1265] was born 29 October 1822 and married Mary I. **Dutton**. Mary was from Bedford, Mass. The family was living in South Boston in 1883.
+ 1136	iv.	Charles Henry **Hill** was born 20 September 1824.

852. Jonathan[8] Hill (Job[7], Mary[6] **Lane**, Job[5], Susanna[4] **Whipple**, Capt. John[3], Elder John[2], Matthew[1])[1266] was born in Billerica, Mass. 24 November 1804 and died there 17 May 1870 at 65 years of age. He married **Laura Williams Hill** in Billerica in April 1839. Laura,[1267] daughter of Brewster **Hill** and Celinda **Carpenter**, was born in Billerica 1 February 1819. Jonathan and Laura are first cousins once removed. (See. No. 1133.)

Jonathan **Hill** and Laura Williams **Hill** had the following children:

1137	i.	James Williams[9] **Hill**[1268] was born in Billerica, Mass. 20 December 1841.
1138	ii.	Laura **Hill**[1269] was born in Billerica, Mass. 26 September 1843.

863. Martha[8] Lane (Gershom Flagg[7], John[6], John[5], Susanna[4] **Whipple**, Capt. John[3], Elder John[2], Matthew[1])[1270] was born in 1788 and died in 1862 at 74 years of age. She married **Benjamin** Worcester who was born in 1783 and died in 1849 at 66 years of age.[1271]

Martha **Lane** and Benjamin **Worcester** had the following child:

+ 1139	i.	Diantha[9] **Worcester** was born in 1811.

864. Rev. John[8] Parkhurst (Betsey[7] **Hutchinson**, Rebecca[6] **Lane**, James[5], Susanna[4] **Whipple**, Capt. John[3], Elder John[2], Matthew[1])[1272] was born in Chelmsford, Mass. 17 January 1789 and died 17 February 1875 at 86 years of age. He married **Celia Burrows** in New Ipswich, N. H. 27 November 1815. Celia was born in New

Ipswich 20 May 1796 and died 29 July 1872 in Chelmsford at 76 years of age.[1273] .

Rev. John **Parkhurst** and Celia **Burrows** had the following child:
+ 1140   i. Elisabeth Ann[9] **Parkhurst** was born 11 June 1823.

865. Washington Jefferson Poor[8] **Lane** (Ebenezer[77], Samuel[6], James[5], Susanna[4] **Whipple**, Capt. John[3], Elder John[2], Matthew[1])[1274] was born in Cambridge, Mass. 16 February 1807 and died 5 August 1864 at 57 years of age. He married **Cynthia Clark** in Boston, Mass. 30 September 1830. Cynthia,[1275] daughter of Elijah **Clark** and Cynthia **Smith**, was born in Boston 1 September 1810 and died 20 July 1864 at 53 years of age.

Washington Jefferson Poor **Lane** and Cynthia **Clark** had the following child:
+ 1141   i. Mary Wellington[9] **Lane** was born 19 December 1839.

867. Charlotte Woods[8] **Stone** (Simon[7], Micah[6], Simon[5], Deacon Simon[4], Mary[3] **Whipple**, Elder John[2], Matthew[11])[1276] was born in West Boylston, Worcester Co., Mass. 20 August 1809 and married **John Whipple**. The intent to marry was published in Lancaster, Worcester Co., Mass. 16 April 1834.[1277] John,[1278] son of John **Whipple** and Eunice **Holbrook**, was born in Boylston 26 August 1811 and died 6 June 1885 in Hamilton, Mass. at 73 years of age. John and Charlotte were fifth cousins once removed. Elder John and Susanna Whipple were their common ancestors. (See No. 1104.)

John **Whipple** and Charlotte Woods **Stone** had the following children:
+ 1142   i. Alonzo Lyman[9] **Whipple** was born 18 September 1836.
   1143   ii. Lorenzo **Whipple**[1279] was born in Princeton, Worcester Co., Mass. 18 September 1836 and died the day of birth.
   1144   iii. Samuel Austin Fay **Whipple**[1280] was born in Cambridge, Mass. 9 August 1838 and died there.
   1145   iv. Adeline Louise **Whipple**[1281] was born in Cambridge, Mass. 30 May 1847 and died there 18 July 1849 at 2 years of age.

880. Lavinia[9] **Stone** (Capt. Amos[7], Amos[6], Simon[5], Deacon Simon[4], Mary[3] **Whipple**, Elder John[2], Matthew[1])[1282] was born in Steuben Co., N.Y. 6 November 1794 and died there 9 October 1871 at 77 years of age. She married **John Powers** in Bath, Steuben Co., N.Y. 3 June 1810. John's Will was proved 26 Feb. 1863 in Steuben Co.

Lavinia **Stone** and John **Powers** had the following children:
+ 1146   i. Cyrus Hale Stone[9] **Powers** was born 25 September 1815.
   1147   ii. Julia **Powers**[1283] was born abt 1820.
   1148   iii. John **Powers**[1284] was born abt 1823 and died 26 September 1881 in Jasper Co., Iowa at 58 years of age. He married Laura A. **Baldwin** in Hammondsport, N.Y. 16 January 1850.
   1149   iv. Dr. William B. **Powers**[1285] was born in New York State in 1831 and married Lovina A. **Barrett** in Hammondsport 2 October 1856. William was acting assistant surgeon for the 157th New York Inf., Co. I in the Civil War. He was drafted 15 July 1863 for a three year period and discharged for disability.
+ 1150   v. Eliza B. **Powers** was born in 1833.
   1151   vi. Ambrose **Powers**[1286] was born abt 1836. He married Caroline L. (__).

+ 1152   vii. Myron **Powers** was born abt 1837.

884. Alma Ellery[8] **Holden** (Phineas[7], Capt. Asa[6], Abigail[5] **Stone**, Deacon Simon[4], Mary[3] **Whipple**, Elder John[2], Matthew[1])[1287] was born in Shirley, Mass. 26 January 1792 and died 15 August 1879 in Harvard, Middlesex Co., Mass. at 87 years of age. She married twice. (1) **Capt. Edward Tyler** in Shirley 2 March 1814. Edward was born in Boston 10 November 1776 and died 26 December 1823 in Harvard at 47 years of age. (2) **Samuel Bacon** in Massachusetts 2 May 1826. Samuel,[1288] son of Jeremiah **Bacon**, was born in Washington, Sullivan Co., N.H. 25 April 1793 and died 23 April 1868 in Harvard at 74 years of age. He married (2) **Nancy Fairbank** in Harvard 3 June 1818. Edward married (2) **Mary Thomas** in Massachusetts in 1799. Two children were born to this union [1289] He married (3) **Susanna Thomas** in Massachusetts in 1808.

Alma Ellery **Holden** and Capt. Edward **Tyler** had the following children:

    1153   i. John Flavel[9] **Tyler**[1290].
    1154   ii. Susan **Tyler**[1291] married Luke **Pollard**. He married (2) Elizabeth Tyler, Susan's sister, after Susan died.
+ 1155   iii. Elizabeth **Tyler**.
    1156   iv. James Richard **Tyler**[1292] was born in Harvard, Mass. and died there 4 April 1905.
+ 1157   v. Harriett Newell **Tyler**.
+ 1158   vi. Alma Ellery **Tyler** was born in 1815.

Alma Ellery **Holden** and Samuel **Bacon** had the following children born in Harvard:

    1159   vii. Lucia Harlow **Bacon**[1293] was born 31 January 1827 and died 26 December 1850 in Harvard at 23 years of age.
+ 1160   viii. Samuel Newton **Bacon** was born 25 January 1829.
+ 1161   ix. Joseph Austin **Bacon** was born 4 November 1835.

885. Susanna[8] **Dunton** (Mary[7] **Jewell**, Mary[6] **Whitney**, Mary[5] **Stone**, Deacon Simon[4], Mary[3] **Whipple**, Elder John[2], Matthew[1])[1294] was born in Marlborough, Middlesex Co., Mass. 6 March 1777 and died 30 September 1861 in Stowe, Mass. at 84 years of age. She married **Ephraim Carr**. Ephraim was born in August 1775 and died 30 January 1871 at 95 years of age.[1295]

Susanna **Dunton** and Ephraim **Carr** had the following child:
+ 1162   i. Lyman[9] **Carr** was born 8 June 1798.

886. Reedsburg[8] **Stone** (David[7], Lt. James[6], James[5], John[4], Mary[3] **Whipple**, Elder John[2], Matthew[1])[1296] birth date unknown, married **Sarah Perley Treadwell**.

Reedsburg **Stone** and Sarah Perley **Treadwell** had the following child:
+ 1163   i. John Putnam[9] **Stone** was born 5 February 1847.

888. Betsey[8] **Ward** (Hannah[7] **Goddard**, Robert[6], Edward[5], Susanna[4] **Stone**, Mary[3] **Whipple**, Elder John[2], Matthew[1])[1297] was born 26 June 1778 and married **Marshall Baker**. Marshall,[1298] son of Sherebiah **Baker** and Clotilda **Daniels**, was born abt 1769 and died, either in Orange, Mass. or Plainfield, N.Y. aft 1 January 1827 at approximately 57 years of age.

Betsey **Ward** and Marshall **Baker** had the following child:

+ 1164   i. Sylvanus Ward[9] **Baker** was born 18 October 1805.

889. David[8] **Goddard** (Asa[7], Nathan[6], Edward[5], Susanna[a44] **Stone**, Mary[3] **Whipple**, Elder John[2], Matthew[1])[1299] was born in 1786 and married **Czarina White**. Czarina was born in 1790.[1300]

David **Goddard** and Czarina **White** had the following child:

+ 1165   i. Alvira C.[9] **Goddard** was born in 1807.

890. Lois[8] **Jackson** (Lois[7] **Woodward**,, Mary[6] **Stone**, Samuel[5], Ebenezer[4], Mary[3] **Whipple**, Elder John[2], Matthew[1])[1301] was born in Newton, Middlesex Co., Mass. 17 August 1765 and married **John King Jr.** 21 March 1784. John was born in Newton 8 April 1762 and died there 17 August 1824 at 62 years of age.[1302]

Lois **Jackson** and John **King, Jr.** had the following child:

+ 1166   i. John[9] **King** was born 12 December 1794.

891. Lucy[8] **Read** (Susanna [7] **Richardson**, Mary[6] **Woodward**, Mindwell[5] **Stone**, Ebenezer[4], Mary[3] **Whipple**, Elder John[2], Matthew[1])[1303] was born 2 December 1793 and married **Daniel Anthony**.

Lucy **Read** and Daniel **Anthony** had the following children:

1167   i. Hannah[9] **Anthony**[1304].

1168   ii. Jacob Merrit **Anthony**[1305].

1169   iii. Guelma Penn **Anthony**[1306] was born 1 July 1818.

1170   iv. Susan Browning **Anthony**[1307] was born in Adams, Berkshire Co., Mass. 15 February 1820 and died 13 March 1906 at 86 years of age. Susan, (5) great granddaughter of John and Susanna Whipple, may have had two more siblings than are shown. Her father, a Quaker abolitionist and a cotton manufacturer, was a stern man who believed in guiding his children. They were not allowed the normal amusements of toys, games, and music which he saw as distractions from the "inner light." He enforced self-discipline, principled convictions, and a belief in one's self-worth.

A precocious child, Susan learned to read and write at age three. The family moved to Battensville, N.Y. when she was six and when a teacher at the school refused to teach her long division, she was taken out of school and taught in a home school set up by her father. Mary Perkins, who ran the school, presented a new image of womanhood to Susan and her sisters. She later attended a boarding school near Philadelphia and then taught at a female Quaker boarding school in upstate New York.

At the first session of the 66th Congress in 1919, House Joint Resolution 1 proposed an amendment to the Constitution extending the right of suffrage to women. It was ratified 18 August 1920. That amendment guaranteed all American women the right to vote and followed a lengthy and difficult struggle that took decades of agitation and protest. Several generations of American suffrage supporters lectured, wrote, marched, lobbied, and practiced civil disobedience to achieve what many Americans considered a radical change to the Constitution.

Susan B. Anthony was one of the foremost leaders of the struggle. By the time she reached womanhood she had learned there was no such thing as women's rights. She was ruled by a government in which she had no voice and if she felt herself wronged in any way there was no provision for her to make the fact known or to suggest a remedy. She was barred from nearly all profitable jobs and paid one fourth of a man's wage in those available to her. She could not become a doctor , lawyer, or — except within the Society of Friends — a minister. If she was married, wages she earned were not hers but were given by her employer to her husband, who in every way was her master. Women were raised to lead dependent subservient lives.

She began her public crusade on behalf of temperance after moving to Rochester, N. Y. where she gave her first public speech for the Daughters of Temperance in 1849 and then helped found the Woman's State Temperance Society of New York, one of the first organizations of its kind. She met Elizabeth Cady Stanton in 1851 at a series of anti-slavery meetings in Syracuse and joined Stanton and Amelia Bloomer in campaigns for women's rights. She joined the anti slavery movement in 1854 and from 1856 to the outbreak of the Civil War was an agent for the American Anti-slavery Society. She and Stanton published the New York liberal weekly, *The Revolution* (1868-1870) which advocated equal pay for women.

Susan issued a national demand in 1872 that women be given the same civil and political rights given to black males under the 14th and 15th amendments to the constitution and led a group of women to the polls in Rochester to test their right to vote. This led to her arrest and while awaiting trial she embarked on a highly publicized lecture tour. In March 1873 she again tried to vote in city elections and was tried and convicted of violating election laws. She was successful in refusing to pay the fine assessed. From then on she campaigned throughout the country for a woman suffrage amendment through the National Woman Suffrage Association (1890-1906) and the National American Woman Suffrage Association (1890-1906).

Along with Stanton and Matilda Joslyn Gage, she published the four volume *History of Woman Suffrage* (1881-1902). She organized the International Council of Women in 1888 and the International Woman Suffrage Alliance in 1904. She did not live to see the passage of the 19th amendment but its passage was helped by her pioneering efforts.

The Susan B. Anthony House at 17 Madison St., Rochester, N. Y. 14608 is a museum with National Historical Landmark status. Readers wanting more information can call (585) 235-6124 and/or visit http://www.susanbanthonyhouse.org.

The following poem, found in Rare Books at the U. of Rochester library, was written about her:

SUSAN B. ANTHONY

No ministering angel she,
to bind up wounds
or cool the fevered brow
with soft hand of pity.

She was of sterner stuff
whereof God makes his heroes.
Stalwart, stark, yet pitiful withal
with tearless tenderness that found
    expression
in deeds of battle for the cause of right.

Hers was the warrior soul
locked in a woman's heart,
predestined to do battle.

Nobly she strove, yet sacrifices no whit
of that true womanhood
which was her high ideal.

A lady valiant she,
Semiramis of suffrage who enlarged
the boundaries that spaciously enclose
her sex's empire.

Great were her labors, great her victories,
as liberty attests. The pay be hers.

Yet this her greatest glory
that though opposing and opposed thereby
to stale conventions by the world esteemed,
she overthrew them; yet at last still held
the love of women and respect of men.

1171   v. Daniel Read **Anthony**[1308] was born 22 August 1824.

1172   vi. Mary Stafford **Anthony**[1309] was born 2 April 1829.

892. Lydia[8] **Johnson** (Abner[7], Hannah[6] **Eaton**, Lydia Abiah[5] **Starr**, Mary[4] **Stone**, Mary[3] **Whipple**, Elder John[2], Matthew[1])[1310] was born in Stafford, Conn. 27 December 1780 and died 14 January 1874 in Preble, N.Y. at 93 years of age. She married **Dr. Jabez Baldwin Phelps** in Cazenovia, N.Y. 15 January 1801. Jabez was born in Lebanon, Conn. 4 January 1777 and died 20 December 1851 in Preble at 74 years of age.[1311] He lived in Hebron, Conn. and Vernon, N.Y. before beginning a medical practice at Preble. He was Preble's first postmaster serving for five years, was assistant judge of the county court for several years, and served in the state legislature in 1841.

Lydia **Johnson** and Dr. Jabez Baldwin **Phelps** had the following children born in Preble:

1173   i. Sophia[9] **Phelps**[1312] was born 18 December 1802 and married Charles **Clark**.

1174   ii. Martin Joseph **Phelps**[1313] was born 19 November 1806 and married Emily Almira **Carey**.

1175   iii. Laura Johnson **Phelps**[1314] was born 28 March 1809 and married Dr. Phineas H. **Burdick**.

1176   iv. Cordelia Augusta **Phelps**[1315] was born 9 April 1811 and married Henry **Hobart**.

1177   v. Amanda Melvina **Phelps**[1316] was born 10 February 1815 and married Ezekiel **Chew**.

1178   vi. Abner Johnson **Phelps**[1317] was born 4 February 1817 and married Anna Minerva **Hooker**.

1179   vii. Lydia Lovina **Phelps**[1318] was born 11 May 1820 and married Dr. Alfred **Hall**.

1180   viii. Calvin Brown **Phelps**[1319] was born 23 June 1822 and married Caroline Amelia **Hooke**.

893. John[8] **Johnson** (Abner[7], Hannah[6] **Eaton**, Lydia Abiah[5] **Starr**, Mary[4] **Stone**, Mary[3] **Whipple**, Elder John[2], Matthew[1])[1320] was born in Stafford, Conn. 24 April 1783 and died 6 February 1850 in Fullerville, N.Y. at 66 years of age. He married **Zeruah Bly** in Paris, N.Y. Zeruah,[1321] daughter of Epaphroditus **Bligh** and Sarah (_), was born in Litchfield Co., Conn. abt 1790 and died 2 March 1872 in Fullerville at 81 years of age. Apparently her surname was sometimes spelled Bligh.

John **Johnson** and Zeruah **Bly** had the following children:

1181   i. Julia A.[9] **Johnson**[1322] married James **Hodgkins**.

1182   ii. John B. **Johnson**[1323] was born 24 July 1812 and died 6 August 1891 in Fowler, N.Y. at 79 years of age and married Malvina **Myers** in Rossie, N.Y. 19 January 1885.[1324]

1183   iii. Epaphroditus **Johnson**[1325] was born 3 April 1814 and married twice. (1) Martha L. **Gates** in 1838 who died in 1839.[1326] (2) Cornelia **DeWolf** after 1839 [1327]

+ 1184   iv. Sarah Jane **Johnson** was born 18 August 1818.

+ 1185   v. Grove G. **Johnson** was born 27 October 1827.

1186   vi. Abner Henry **Johnson**[1328] was born in Wilna, N.Y. 3 February 1831 and died 16 November 1906 at 75 years of age. He married twice. (1) Lydia

Glazier 29 May 1853.[1329] (2) (__) **Collins** 1870.
+ 1187   vii. Lucy Fuller **Johnson** was born 1 May 1835.

894. Laura⁸ Johnson (Abner⁷, Hannah⁶ **Eaton**, Lydia Abiah⁵ **Starr**, Mary⁴ **Stone**, Mary³ **Whipple**, Elder John², Matthew¹))[1330] was born in Stafford, Conn. 23 February 1785 and died 20 March 1856 in Preble, N.Y at 71 years of age. She married **Martin Phelps** in Preble. Martin was born in Lebanon, Conn. 5 April 1786 and died 4 December 1867 in Preble at 81 years of age.[1331] A blacksmith by trade, he settled in Preble in 1810. He was a captain of the state militia in the War of 1812 and after the war advanced through the grades achieving the rank of major general. He was a member of the Presbyterian church and taught and lead the choir for several years.

Laura **Johnson** and Martin **Phelps** had the following children born in Preble:
1188   i. Mary Ann⁹ **Phelps**[1332] was born in 1817 and died unmarried 16 December 1867 at 50 years of age.
1189   ii. Eleanor **Phelps**[1333] was born in 1819 and died unmarried 19 March 1861 at 41 years of age.
1190   iii. Avery Martin **Phelps**[1334] was born 19 May 1821 and married twice. No spouse information provided.

899. Arrunah⁸ Eaton (John⁷, John⁶, Lydia Abiah⁵ **Starr**, Mary⁴ **Stone**, Mary³ **Whipple**, Elder John², Matthew¹)[1335] was born in Cheshire, Berkshire Co., Mass. 4 February 1784 and died 7 November 1868 in Norwalk, Huron Co., Ohio at 84 years of age. He married **Candace Raymond** in Fairfield Herkimer Co., N.Y. 31 December 1807. Candace was the daughter of Lemuel **Raymond** and Hannah **Underwood**.

Arrunah **Eaton** and Candace **Raymond** had the following child:
+ 1191   i. Esther Adeline⁹ **Eaton** was born 13 December 1810.

900. Samuel Porter⁸ Grow (Joseph⁷, Abigail⁶ **Dana**, Susanna⁵ **Starr**, Mary⁴ **Stone**, Mary³ **Whipple**, Elder John², Matthew¹)[1336] was born in FitzWilliam, N.H. 23 March 1773 and died 5 March 1850 in Hartland, Vt. at 76 years of age. He married **Jerusha Stowell** 4 March 1799. Jerusha was born in Pomfret, Conn. 28 November 1778 and died in Holland, Vt.[1337] .

Samuel Porter **Grow** and Jerusha **Stowell** had the following child:
+ 1192   i. Lorenzo⁹ **Grow** was born 11 March 1806.

901. Luther⁸ Patch (Thomas⁷, Penelope⁶ **Dana**, Susanna⁵ **Starr**, Mary⁴ **Stone**, Mary33 **Whipple**, Elder John², Matthew¹)[1338] was born in Chesterfield, Mass. in 1798 and married **Elizabeth Hatter**. Elizabeth was born 1798.[1339]

Luther **Patch** and Elizabeth **Hatter** had the following child:
+ 1193   i. Edward⁹ **Patch** was born in 1823.

902. Luther⁸ Franklin (Sarah⁷ **Starr**, Capt. Comfort⁶, Comfort⁵, Mary⁴ **Stone**, Mary³ **Whipple**, Elder John², Matthew¹)[1340] birth date unknown, married **Priscilla Pinney**.

Luther **Franklin** and Priscilla **Pinney** had the following child:
+ 1194   i. Abigail⁹ **Franklin**.

903. James Bradley⁸ Ball (Abigail⁷ **Starr**, Capt. Comfort⁶, Comfort⁵, Mary⁴ **Stone**, Mary³ **Whipple**, Elder John², Matthew¹)[1341] was born in Guilford, Vt. 28 July 1781 and died 6 December 1863 in Newark, Vt. at 82 years of age. He was buried in the Packer Mountain Cemetery, Newark and his grave is plainly marked. He married **Rhoda Palmer** 15 September 1808.

James Bradley **Ball** and Rhoda **Palmer** had the following children:
- 1195   i.   James Bradley⁹ **Ball** Jr.[1342] was born in Vermont 3 October 1810.
- + 1196   ii.   Wilbur Fiske **Ball** was born 30 June 1822.
- 1197   iii.   Rhoda **Ball**[1343] was born in Vermont and married Madison **Doyle**.

910. Lucius⁸ Ball (Abigail⁷ **Starr**, Capt. Comfort⁶, Comfort⁵, Mary⁴ **Stone**, Mary³ **Whipple**, Elder John², Matthew¹)[1344] was born in Newark, Vt. 14 May 1803 and died there 26 September 1865 at 62 years of age. He was buried at the Packer Mountain Cemetery and his grave is plainly marked. He married **Harriet Humphrey** in Newark. Lucius and Harriet had seven children. Only information for James was provided.

Lucius **Ball** and Harriet **Humphrey** had the following child:
- 1198   i.   James Bradley⁹ **Ball**[1345] was born in Newark in 1836 and died 6 December 1886 at 50 years of age.

917. Lovel⁸ Starr (Comfort⁷, Capt. Comfort⁶, Comfort⁵, Mary⁴ **Stone**, Mary³ **Whipple**, Elder John², Matthew¹)[1346] was born in Colchester, Vt. 26 April 1797 and died 26 July 1858 in Summit, Marion Co., Iowa at 61 years of age. He married twice. (1) **Betsey Coon** in Vermont 25 December 1835. Betsey,[1347] daughter of Joseph **Coon** and Betsey (__), was born in 1801 and died 19 November 1841 in Russell, St. Lawrence Co., N.Y. at 40 years of age. (2) **Sarah Ann Crandall** in St. Lawrence Co., N.Y. 20 February 1844.

Lovel **Starr** and Betsey **Coon** had the following children born in Colchester:
- 1199   i.   Jane Emily⁹ **Starr**[1348] was born 16 December 1836 and died 7 June 1899 in Octavia, Butler Co., Nebr. at 62 years of age. She married William **Butler** in Russell 20 May 1854.
- 1200   ii.   Van Ness **Starr**[1349] was born 10 December 1838 and died 12 December 1861 in Sedalia, Mo. at 23 years of age of lung fever. He enlisted in Co. E., 8th Regt., Iowa Volunteers in August 1861 with the rank of sergeant.
- + 1201   iii.   Mary **Starr** was born 18 August 1841.

919. Elsie Elizabeth⁸ Starr (Ebenezer⁷, Ebenezer⁶, Comfort⁵, Mary⁴ **Stone**, Mary³ **Whipple**, Elder John², Matthew¹)[1350] was born 26 March 1807 and married twice. (1) **John West Pape** 14 September 1825.[1351] (2) **Jonas Ward** in Ashburnham, Mass. 2 November 1834. Jonas was born 15 February 1789 and died 28 April 1842 at 53 years of age.[1352]

Elsie Elizabeth **Starr** and Jonas **Ward** had the following child:
- + 1202   i.   Angeline⁹ **Ward** was born 26 February 1840.

920. John Dean⁸ Estey Jr. (John Dean⁷, Solomon⁶, Elizabeth Mary⁵ **Stearns**, Elizabeth⁴ **Stone**, Mary³ **Whipple**, Elder John², Matthew¹)[1353] was born in Kingston, Addison Co., Vt. 11 June 1800 and died 21 September 1872 in Delmar, Clinton

Co., Iowa at 72 years of age. He married twice. (1) **Charlotte Lawrence**. (2) **Charlotte Lovelace** in Clinton Co., N.Y. about 1835. Charlotte was born about 1802 and died 7 June 1864 in Maquoketa, Iowa at 61 years of age.[1354]

John Dean **Estey** Jr. and Charlotte **Lovelace** had the following children born in Clinton Co., N.Y.:

1203	i.	Charlotte[9] **Estey**[1355] was born about 1836 and died about 1858 in Maquoketa.
1204	ii.	Sarah **Estey**[1356] was born about 1839 and died about 1859 in Maquoketa.
1205	iii.	John Washington **Estey**[1357] was born 25 November 1842 and died 21 January 1915 in Missouri at 72 years of age.
+ 1206	iv.	Caroline M. **Estey** was born about 1846.

923. Harrison[8] Stearns (Phineas[7], Eliphet[6], Rev. Ebenezer[5], Elizabeth[4] **Stone**, Mary[3] **Whipple**, Elder John[2], Matthew[1])[1358] birth date unknown, married **Amanda Russell**.

Harrison **Stearns** and Amanda **Russell** had the following child:

+ 1207	i.	Abdellah M.[9] **Stearns**.

924. George[8] Smith (Hannah[7] **Wilbor**, Mary[6] **Stearns**, Jonathan[5], Elizabeth[4] **Stone**, Mary[3] **Whipple**, Elder John[2], Matthew[1])[1359] was born 2 October 1778 and died 21 August 1851 in Taunton, Mass. at 72 years of age. He married **Pamela Field** in Raynham, Mass. 4 May 1800. Pamela,[1360] daughter of James **Field** and Mary **Drew**, was born in Easton, Mass. 16 October 1783 and died 23 February 1875 in Raynham at 91 years of age.

George **Smith** and Pamela **Field** had the following child:

+ 1208	i.	James[9] **Smith** was born 1 June 1814.

925. Lucinda Chipman[8] Upham (Joseph Pierce[7], Asa[6], Hannah[5] **Stearns**, Elizabeth[4] **Stone**, Mary[3] **Whipple**, Elder John[2], Matthew[1])[1361] was born in Pawlet, Vt. 3 March 1792 and died 17 April 1867 in New York, N.Y. at 75 years of age. She was buried in Troy, N.Y. She married **Elihu Orvis** in Pawlet 4 February 1813. Elihu,[1362] son of Waitstill **Orvis** and Elizabeth **Church**, was born in Hinsdale, Vt. 25 October 1788 and died 18 May 1845 in Troy at 56 years of age. They lived in Granville, N.Y. in 1820 and in Troy in 1840.

Lucinda Chipman **Upham** and Elihu **Orvis** had the following child:

+ 1209	i.	Catherine Lorette[9] **Orvis** was born 23 February 1826.

928. Enoch Elbert[8] Goddard (Ebenezer[7], Nathan[6], Edward[5], Susanna[4] **Stone**, Mary[3] **Whipple**, Elder John[2], Matthew[1])[1363] was born 26 March 1783 and died (probably in Windam or S. Londonderry, Vt.) 3 January 1867 at 83 years of age. He married **Esther Bliss** in 1803. Esther,[1364] daughter of Timothy **Bliss** Jr. and Tamerzin **Wait**, was born in Royalston, Mass. 13 May 1771 and died (probably in Windam or S. Londonderry, Vt.) 27 December 1863 at 92 years of age.

Enoch Elbert **Goddard** and Esther **Bliss** had the following children:

1210	i.	John[9] **Goddard**[1365] died in infancy.
1211	ii.	Timothy Baxter **Goddard**[1366] married twice. (1) Fanny Jane **Abbott**. (2) Betsey **Robinson**.

1212	iii.	Bliss **Goddard**[1367] was born in Windham 10 September 1806 and died 2 August 1888 in Mazomanie, Wisc. at 81 years of age. He married Eliza **Stearns**.
1213	iv.	Lamira **Goddard**[1368] was born in Vermont 7 November 1808 and died there 19 February 1889 at 80 years of age. She married George W. **Dutton** in Vermont.
1214	v.	Emery **Goddard**[1369] was born in Vermont 11 February 1811 and died there 2 October 1819 at 8 years of age.
1215	vi.	Daniel **Goddard**[1370] was born in Windham 19 February 1812 and died there 8 February 1894 at 81 years of age. He married Delia **Waters**. He served with the Vermont Volunteers during the Civil War.
1216	vii.	Esther **Goddard**[1371] was born in Windham 21 February 1814 and died there 31 August 1900 at 86 years of age. She married Lucius **Abbott**.
+ 1217	viii.	Susan **Goddard** was born 6 April 1816.
1218	ix.	Nelson **Goddard**[1372] was born in Windham 17 December 1817 and died 23 January 1906 in Brattleboro, Vt. at 88 years of age. He married Sarah Delia **Gibson** in Gratton, Vt. 6 August 1846.
1219	x.	John William **Goddard**[1373] was born in Windham 20 July 1819 and drowned 4 July 1838 at 18 years of age.
1220	xi.	Josiah **Goddard**[1374] was born in Windham 5 May 1821 and died 18 May 1893 in S. Londonderry, Vt. at 72 years of age. He married Mary Jane **Farnum** 12 April 1843.

929. Robert[8] **Goddard** (Nahum[7], Robert[6], Edward[5], Susanna[4] **Stone**, Mary[3] **Whipple**, Elder John[2], Matthew[1])[1375] was born in Reading, Vt. 3 June 1803 and died 3 April 1865 in Monona, Iowa at 61 years of age. He married **Mary Maria Bailey** in Rutland, Vt. bef 1829. She was born in New York State in March 1811 and died 15 August 1868 in Monona at 57 years of age.

Robert **Goddard** and Mary Maria **Bailey** had the following children:

1221	i.	James Osmer[9] **Goddard**[1376] was born in Rutland, Vt. in 1829.
+ 1222	ii.	John Bailey **Goddard** was born 16 October 1830.
+ 1223	iii.	Charles Walker **Goddard** was born 8 April 1833.
+ 1224	iv.	Clark Nahum **Goddard** was born 3 May 1835.
1225	v.	Caroline E. **Goddard**[1377] was born in Rutland in 1837 and married Edwin B. **Hutchinson** in Monona 19 April 1856.[1378]

936. George[8] **Goddard** (Capt. Nathan[7], Nathan[6], Benjamin[5], Susanna[4] **Stone**, Mary[3] **Whipple**, Elder John[2], Matthew[1])[1379] was born in Framingham, Mass. 31 August 1808 and died 5 November 1877 in Upton Mass. at 69 years of age. He married **Hannah Johnson** in Upton 24 April 1833. Hannah,[1380] daughter of Rufus **Johnson** and Hannah **Newton**, was born in Upton 6 February 1812.

George **Goddard** and Hannah **Johnson** had the following children born in Upton:

1226	i.	Edwin Nathan[9] **Goddard**[1381] was born 3 February 1835 and died 14 September 1839 in Upton at 4 years of age.
+ 1227	ii.	Edwin Nathan **Goddard** was born 13 April 1842.

951. Joseph[8] **Young** (Abigail (Nabby)[7] **Howe**, Susanna[6] **Goddard**, Ebenezer[5], Susanna[4] **Stone**, Mary[3] **Whipple**, Elder John[2], Matthew[1])[1382] was born in Hopkinton, Mass. 7 April 1797 and died 16 July 1881 in Salt Lake City, Utah at 84 years of age. He had several wives including: **Jane Adeline Bicknell** who he married in Genesco., Livingston Co., N.Y. 18 February 1834. Jane,[1383] daughter of Calvin **Bicknell** and Chloe **Seymour**, was born in Utica, Oneida Co., N.Y. 14 August 1814 and died abt 1913 in Salt Lake City. Jane and Joseph moved to Kirtland, Ohio in 1834 and while he was away on a Mormon Mission, she took in washing to help feed the family. They left for Far West, Caldwell Co., Mo. in June 1838 where they survived the 30 October Mormon massacre at Haun's Mill. They stayed with family and friends in various Missouri locations until moving to Nauvoo, Hancock Co., Ill. in 1840. They left Nauvoo for Winter Quarters, Nebr. in 1849 and in the summer of 1850 left for the Salt Lake Valley.

He married **Mary Ann Huntley** in Nauvoo 6 February 1846. Mary Ann,[1384] daughter of Allen **Huntley** and Sally **Hitchcock**, was born 14 March 1816 in Waitsfield, Vt. and died 10 November 1903 in Salt Lake City at 87 years of age. Mary Ann was two when her mother died and she was raised by her **Huntley** grandparents. She later taught school to help the family financially. After she married (1) James Lewis **Burnham** 1 Dec. 1834, they moved to Illinois where they were baptized as members of the Church of Jesus Christ of Latter Day Saints (LDS) on 6 May 1843. They had five children: Luther Clinton, born 28 November 1835; Wallace Kindall, 24 January 1838; George Franklin, 26 October 1839; Marie Antoinette, 7 August 1843; Mary Ann; 12 October. 1845. After marrying Joseph Young in 1846 she remained in Nauvoo until the exodus to the Salt Lake Valley began. Her first stop was Winter Quarters where they lived in a dugout, almost starving. She sent two of her sons on to Salt Lake and followed with the rest of the family in 1852. She settled in Bountiful where she lived for nine years before moving to Richmond, Utah.[1385]

He married **Sarah Jane Snow** in Salt Lake City 6 April 1867. Sarah,[1386] daughter of James C. **Snow** and Eliza Ann **Carter**, was born in Far West 30 October 1838 and died 11 November 1910 in Provo, Utah Co., Utah at 72 years of age. Sara Jane was an infant when the family was driven from Far West to the Morley Settlement in Hancock Co., Ill where her father James and grandfather Gardner Snow ran a cooper shop. In 1844 mobs drove the Saints from Morley to Nauvoo and eventually to Winter Quarters where they lived on the plains for six years before making the trip to Utah arriving in Salt Lake 9 Ocober. 1852. Her father was in charge of the wagon train. They settled in Provo.

Sara Jane married at age 15 (1) Marshall Corrido Kinsman 5 December 1853 in Provo. They had three children born there: George Chauncy, 30 April 1855, died in 1857; Sara Ellen, 19 May 1857, married a Mr. Milner; and Emily Wheelock, 13 May 1862, married a Mr. Duggins. Marshall died 3 Feb. 1863 in Provo following a logging accident. She married Joseph Young four years later.[1387] No information provided on other wives.

Joseph **Young** and Jane Adeline **Bicknell** had the following children:

1228	i.	Jane Adeline⁹ **Young**[1388] was born in Kirtland 17 December 1834.
1229	ii.	Joseph Bicknell **Young**[1389] was born 5 February 1836.
1230	iii.	Seymour Bicknell **Young**[1390] was born 3 October 1837.
1231	iv.	Marcus LeGrande **Young**[1391] was born in Nauvoo 27 December 1840.
1232	v.	John Calvin **Young**[1392] was born 23 November 1842.
1233	vi.	Mary Lucretia **Young**[1393] was born 2 October 1844.
1234	vii.	Julia Ann Vilate **Young**[1394] was born 22 October 1845.

1235	viii.	Chloe Eliza Young[1395] was born in Winter Quarters 1 September 1848.
1236	ix.	Rhoda Young[1396] was born in Salt Lake City 19 June 1851.
1237	x.	Henrietta Young[1397] was born in Salt Lake City 5 December 1853.
1238	xi.	Brigham Bicknell Young[1398] was born in Salt Lake City 23 April 1856.

Joseph Young and Mary Ann Huntley had the following children:

| 1239 | xii. | Almira Young[1399] was born in Winter Quarters 15 February 1848 and married (_) Russell. |
| 1240 | xiii. | Clarentine Young[1400] was born in Winter Quarters 31 July 1850 and married (_) Conrad. |

Joseph Young and Sarah Jane Snow had the following children:

| 1241 | xiv. | Charles Edward Young[1401] was born in Salt Lake City 30 May 1871. |
| 1242 | xv. | Harriet May Young[1402] was born in Salt Lake City 27 April 1876 and died there in 1880 at 4 years of age. |

952. **Phineas Howe[8] Young** (Abigail (Nabby)[7] **Howe**, Susanna[6] **Goddard**, Ebenezer[5], Susanna[4] **Stone**, Mary[3] **Whipple**, Elder John[2], Matthew[1])[1403] was born in Hopkinton, Mass. 16 February 1799 and died 10 October 1879 at 80 years of age. Among his wives were: **Clarissa Hamilton** and **Phebe Groombridge Clark**. He married Phebe in Salt Lake City in November 1853. Phebe,[1404] daughter of William **Clark** and Rebecca **Groombridge**, was born in Hardway, Gosport, England 15 September 1830 and died 20 December 1901 in Salt Lake City at 71 years of age.

Phebe's parents died before she was 18 and she lived with an older sister. At 22 she attended a Mormon meeting near home and shortly thereafter was baptized in the church. She and a girl friend, despite family opposition, sailed from Liverpool for the U.S. on the *Ellen Maria* on 17 January 1853 and arrived in New Orleans 47 days later. Her friend died en-route. She joined the ninth wagon train, Elder Keddington's group, at Keokuk, Iowa and arrived in Salt Lake City 10 October 1853. Soon after her arrival she and Phineas were married in the President's Office. A widow the last 21 year of life, she was president of the Second Ward Primary, a member of the Utah Women's Press Club, Program committee of the Reapers Club, and secretary-treasurer of the Ward Relief Society. She wrote poetry, published an article on Armenia, and assisted in the development of Liberty Park.[1405]

Phineas Howe **Young** and Phebe Groombridge **Clark** had the following children born in Salt Lake City:

1243	i.	Sedenia[9] Young[1406] was born 17 October 1854 and died as a child.
1244	ii.	Phebe Celestia Young[1407] was born 5 December 1856 and married (_) Pack.
1245	iii.	Virginia Parnell Young[1408] was born 26 October 1858 and married (_) Carigan.
1246	iv.	Phineas Henry Young[1409] was born 10 September 1860.
1247	v.	Seraph Young[1410] was born 10 June 1863.
1248	vi.	Julia Dean Young[1411] was born 19 March 1866 and married Palmer Chandler.
1249	vii.	John Willard Young[1412] was born 2 April 1868 and died as a child.
1250	viii.	Joseph Seymour Young[1413] was born 4 April 1870.
1251	ix.	William Clark Young[1414] was born 25 April 1873.

953. **Brigham[8] Young** (Abigail (Nabby)[7] **Howe**, Susanna[6] **Goddard**, Ebenezer[5],

Susanna[4] **Stone**, Mary[3] **Whipple**, Elder John[2], Matthew[1]) was born in Whitingham, Windham, Co., Vt. 1 June 1801 and died 29 August 1877 in Salt Lake City at 76 years of age.[1415] He married 37 times (maybe 38) and had 56 children with 16 of the wives. The others were cared for in a temporal way. He provided them a home, listed them in his Will, and provided for their children by earlier marriages. Whether any of these were connubial marriages is not known. In addition, some 30 women were sealed to Brigham "for eternity only" with no intention that he would share earthly life with them or their children.[1416] He married:

(1) **Miriam Angeline Works** in Cayuga Co., N.Y. 8 October 1824. Miriam,[1417] daughter of Asa **Works** and Abigail **Marks**, was born in Aurelius, Cayuga Co. N.Y. 7 June 1806 and died 8 September 1832 in Mendon, Monroe Co., N.Y. at 26 years of age. She is buried at Tomlinson's Corner, Monroe Co., N.Y.

(2) **Mary Ann Angell** in Kirtland, Lake Co., Ohio, 18 February 1834. Mary,[1418] daughter of James William **Angell** and Phebe Ann **Morton**, was born in Seneca, Ontario Co., N.Y. 8 June 1803 and died 27 June 1882 in Salt Lake City at 79 years of age. She learned the art of using herbs for healing from her mother and became skilled in their use as medicine. She joined the Free Will Baptist church and taught Sunday school as a young lady. After reading the Book of Mormon in 1830 she and other members of the family joined the LDS Church. She met Brigham in Kirtland, Ohio at age 25 and they were married a year later. Brigham's first wife had died two years earlier and Mary Ann became an instant mother to his two daughters. Brigham and Mary Ann had three children together. Four days after the birth of their twins in 1836, Brigham had to flee Kirtland to escape from anti-Mormon mobs and Mary Ann had to provide for herself and the five children. Their home was ransacked and the children terrorized which caused such stress that her emotional and physical strength were affected. "It was the severest trial of my life," she said. She arrived in the Salt Lake Valley with Brigham in 1848 where she initially lived in huts and other dwellings. Brigham eventually built her a home known as the "White House." She was gifted and intelligent but did not care for her social position and chose not to take an active role as the "first lady of the Territory." The other wives called her "Mother Young" and many immigrant girls lived with her in the White House where they were trained in the art of housekeeping and caring for the sick.

(3) **Lucy Ann Decker**, Brigham's first plural wife, in Nauvoo 15 June 1842. Lucy,[1419] daughter of Isaac Perry **Decker** and Harriet Page **Wheeler**, was born in Phelps, Ontario Co., N.Y. 17 May 1822 and died 24 January 1890 in Salt Lake City at 67 years of age. Lucy's father was born in Holland and her mother in England. She was introduced to the world of work early in life. Morning household duties were completed by 8 with most of the balance of the day spent in a rigid routine of spinning, weaving, making clothes, candles, soap, and carpets. She married (1) **William Seely** when she was 15 and had three children with him: Isaac Joseph, born 25 August 1837, Harriet, born 5 Oct. 1838, and William, born abt. 1841 and died in infancy. She was widowed at 20. The Seely and Decker families moved to Portage, Ohio in 1838 were they joined the LDS Church, moved to Kirtland the next year, and thereafter followed the westward movement of the church until they reached the Salt Lake Valley. She was ill when the first pioneer company went to Utah and arrived there in September 1848. It is said her health caused her to remain in bed in the wagon from Winter Quarters to the Salt Lake Valley. The

wagon was her first Utah home and later the wagon box was made into two tables. She lived in the Lion house when it was finished in 1856 and also in the White house for a period. Brigham eventually deeded the Beehive house to her. Her daughter Clarissa Young described her as being of medium height with lovely brown eyes and hair and a dimple in each cheek. She usually had two or more immigrant girls in the home teaching them English and household routines. She took no part in public affairs but regularly attended church. She was a lover of books and devoted her spare moments to reading.[1420]

(4) **Harriett Elizabeth Cook** in Nauvoo 2 November 1843. Harriett,[1421] daughter of Archibald **Cook** and Elizabeth (Betsy) **Mosher**, was born in either Whitesborough, Oneida Co., N.Y. or Utica, N.Y. 7 November 1824 and died 5 November 1898 in Salt Lake City at 73 years of age.[1422]

(5) **Augusta Adams** in Nauvoo 2 November 1843. Augusta,[1423] daughter of John **Adams** and Mary **Ives**, was born in Lynn, Essex Co., Mass. 7 December 1802 and died 3 February 1866 in Salt Lake City at 63 years of age.

(6) **Clarissa Clara Decker** in Nauvoo 8 May 1844. Clarissa,[1424] daughter of Isaac Perry **Decker** and Harriet Page **Wheeler**, was born in either Freedom, Cattaragus Co., N.Y. or Phelps, Ontario Co., N.Y. 22 July 1828. She died 5 January 1889 in Salt Lake City at 60 years of age. The Decker family moved to Ohio in 1833, joined the Mormon church in 1834, and moved to Kirtland. Clara accompanied Joseph Smith and his family to Missouri in 1838 and was among those who were driven out by anti-Mormon mobs. She was 15 when she married Brigham Young and was among the exiles who left Nauvoo for Winter Quarters on the Missouri River in Nebraska. When Brigham led the Pioneer Company to Utah in 1847, he asked Clara to accompany them. At 19 she was the youngest of the three women on the trek. Her first home in Utah was built in the old fort and was covered with willows and dirt. She lived in the Lion House for most of her married life.[1425]

(7) **Emily Dow Partridge** in Nauvoo in September 1844. Emily,[1426] daughter of Edward **Partridge** and Lydia **Clisbee**, was born in Painesville, Geauga (now Lake) Co., Ohio 28 February 1824 and died 9 December 1899 in Salt Lake City at 75 years of age. Emily was six when her family embraced Mormonisn in 1830. The family was driven from their homes by mobs three different times and eventually arrived in Nauvoo where Emily and her sister Eliza lived with the Joseph Smith family. When plural marriage was introduced, Smith married both. After Smith's martyrdom in 1844, Emily married Brigham. She was 20, bore him seven children, and lived a widow for 22 years. She moved to Salt Lake City in 1848 and became a part of the Relief Society and did much Temple work.[1427]

(8) **Clarissa Ross** in Nauvoo 10 September 1844. Clarissa,[1428] daughter of William **Ross** and Phoebe **Ogden**, was born in Northville, Cayuga Co., N.Y. 16 June 1814 and died 17 October 1858 in Salt Lake City at 44 years of age.

(9) **Louisa Beeman or Beaman** in Nauvoo 19 September 1844. Louisa,[1429] daughter of Alva H. **Beeman** (maybe **Beaman**) and Sally **Burtts**, was born in Livonia, Livingston Co., N.Y. 7 February 1815 and died 15 May 1850 in Salt Lake City at 35 years of age.

(10) **Susannah Snively** in Nauvoo 2 November 1844. Susannah,[1430] daughter of Henry **Snively** and Mary **Heavenor**, was born in Woodstock, Shenandoah Co., Va. 30 October 1815 and died 20 November 1892 in Salt Lake City at 77 years of

age. Soon after her birth, the last of 10 children, the family moved to a farm near Clearville, Bedford Co., Penn. and it was there the family was converted to the LDS religion by Elder Erastus Snow. Suzanna and her sister Hannahette moved to Springfield, Ill. and eventually to Nauvoo where they were married in a double ceremony in the Temple before the roof had been placed. Suzanna married Brigham and Hannahette married Parley P. Pratt. After being driven from Nauvoo in 1846 they settled in Winter Quarters, Nebr and Suzanna crossed the plains to the Salt Lake Valley in 1848 in the Brigham Young wagon train, arriving 21 September. She had no children and lived in the Forest Farm House where she gave special attention to the dairy where the cheese and butter for the Young family was made. She is buried in the Brigham Young Cemetery.[1431]

(11) **Mary Harvey Pierce** in Nauvoo 16 January 1845. Mary,[1432] daughter of Robert **Pierce** and Hannah **Harvey**, was born in Willistown, Chester Co., Penn. 29 November 1821and died 16 March 1847 in Winter Quarters, Nebr. at 25 years of age.

(12) **Margaret Pierce** in Nauvoo 16 January 1845. Margaret,[1433] daughter of Robert **Pierce** and Hannah **Harvey**, was born in Ashton, Delware Co., Penn. 19 April 1823 and died 16 January 1907 in Salt Lake City at 83 years of age. Margaret was baptized a member of the LDS church 5 April 1840 and emigrated with her family to Nauvoo the next year. She married (1) **Morris Whitesides** there on 23 July 1841. He died seven months later. She traveled to the Salt Lake Valley with the Willard Snow Wagon train in the fall of 1847 where she was involved in Temple work and genealogical research. She was a member of the Genealogical Society, The Silk Association, the Deseret Hospital, the Kindergarten Association, and the Relief Society.[1434]

(13) **Sophronhia Gray Frost** in Nauvoo February 1845. Sophronhia,[1435] daughter of Aaron **Frost** and Susannah (Susan) **Gray**, was born in Bethel, Oxford Co., Maine 24 July 1816. Genealogists Gates and Sanborn give her name as Olive Grey Frost and report her death as 6 October 1845.

(14) **Ellen Rockwood** in Nauvoo in January 1846. Ellen,[1436] daughter of Albert Perry **Rockwood** and Nancy **Haven**, was born in Holliston, Middlesex Co., Mass. 23 March 1829 and died 6 January 1866 in Salt Lake City at 36 years of age.

(15) **Maria Lawrence** in Nauvoo in January 1846. Maria,[1437] daughter of Edward **Lawrence** and Margaret (__), was born in Canada abt 1805 and died in Nauvoo in 1847 at 42 years of age.

(16) **Emeline Free** in Nauvoo 14 January 1846. Emeline,[1438] daughter of Absalom Pennington **Free** and Elizabeth (Betsy) **Strait**. was born in Belleville, St. Clair Co., Ill. 28 April 1826 and died 17 July 1875 in Salt Lake City at 49 years of age. Emeline's family joined the church in 1835 and moved to Missouri the next year and then to St. Clair County, Ill. in 1840. Four years later they were living in Nauvoo and it was there at age 19 she married the 44-year-old Brigham. Emeline accompanied him on his second trip to the Salt Lake Valley in 1848. She bore 10 children, the largest of Brigham's families. She was an invalid for the last years of her life.[1439]

(17) **Margaret Maria Alley** in Nauvoo 14 January 1846. Margaret,[1440] daughter of George **Alley** and Mary **Symonds**, was born in Lynn, Essex Co., Mass. 19 December 1825 and died 5 November 1852 in Salt Lake City at 26 years of age. Margaret's family was converted to the LDS religion in 1841. She was the oldest of seven children and traveled with the family to Nauvoo where they arrived in

January 1843. The children were baptized in the Mississippi river that summer. She married Brigham when she was 21. Two years later she made the trek to the Salt Lake Valley by horse team and wagon. She died four days after the death of her son Mahonri.

(18) **Martha Bowker** in Nauvoo 21 January 1846. Martha,[1441] daughter of Samuel **Bowker** and Hannah **Atkins**, was born in Mt. Holley, Burlington Co., N.J. 24 January 1822 and died 26 September 1890 in Salt Lake City at 68 years of age.

(19) **Rebecca Greenleaf Holman** in Nauvoo 26 January 1846. Rebecca[1442] daughter of Joshua Sawyer **Holman** and Rebecca Whitcomb **Greenleaf**, was born in Stafford, Genessee, Co., N.Y. 20 February 1824 and died 11 July 1849 in Kanesville (now Council Bluffs), Potawattamie Co., Iowa at 25 years of age.

(20) **Naamah Kendall Jenkins Carter** in Nauvoo 26 January 1846. Naamah,[1443] daughter of Billings **Carter** and Betsy **Law**, was born in Wilmington, Middlesex Co., Mass. 20 March 1821. She married (1) **John Saunders Twiss.**

(21) **Mrs. Jemima (Angell) (Young) Stringham** in Nauvoo 28 January 1846. Jemima,[1444] daughter of James William **Angell** and Phebe Ann **Morton**, was born in Camden, Oneida Co., N.Y. 4 October 1804 and died 13 July 1869 in Wanship, Utah at 64 years of age. She married (1) **Valentine Young** in N. Providence, R.I. 21 March 1824. She married (2) **William Stringham** in Nauvoo 17 July 1844.

Jemima moved with her parents as a child to North Providence, R.I. where she married Valentine W. Young (no known relationship to Brigham Young). In July of 1832 her father brought two Mormon missionaries to their home, hoping that Jemima and Valentine could give them a place to stay. They couldn't because they had sold their bed and bedding in preparation to move to western New York State where they joined the Mormon church. They eventually moved to Kirtland, Ohio. When most of the Saints left Kirtland in 1838 Valentine and Jemima moved to Hanover, Licking Co., Ohio where Valentine died about 1843, leaving her with three children [one family report states they had six children; if true three died young]. Jemima and Valentine's son Nathan, 18, was a Mormon volunteer who served in the U.S. army during the War with Mexico. He had been a member of the Nauvoo Legion, a military unit. Jemima never saw her son again.

Accompanied by her two other children, she moved to Utah in 1848 and initially lived with her sister Mary Ann before getting a place of her own by 1850. Authors Mrs. Waite and Mrs. Ware in their *Biographical Sketches of Brigham Young and His Twenty-nine Wives*, published in Philadelphia in 1873 identified Jemima as wife No. 12 and wrote she was "a hearty, motherly looking woman . . . with dark hair, gray eyes, and solemn-looking but not un-pleasant face." They said her husband Stringham died out of the church and Brigham sealed her to himself to give her an exaltation "in the next world. She lives in a house by herself and Brigham seldom visits her." By 1860 she was living with her son James and family in Provo and after her health declined she moved to the mountain valley town of Wanship, 40 miles east of St. Lake City, to be near her daughter Rachel.

(22) **Elizabeth (Betsy) Fairchild** in Nauvoo 30 January 1846. Elizabeth,[1445] daughter of Joshua Junior **Fairchild** and Prudence **Fenner**, was born in Marion Co., Ohio 28 March 1828 and died 10 June 1910 in Grantsville, Tooele Co., Utah at 82 years of age.

(23) **Rhoda Richards** in Nauvoo 31 January 1846. (See No. 652.) Rhoda,[1446] daughter of Joseph **Richards** and Rhoda **Howe**, was born in Framingham,

Middlesex Co., Mass. 8 August 1784 and died 17 January 1879 in Salt Lake City at 94 years of age.

(24) **Zina Diantha Huntington** in Nauvoo 2 February 1846. Zina,[1447] daughter of William **Huntington** and Zina **Baker**, was born in Watertown, Jefferson Co., N.Y. 31 January 1821 and died 27 August 1901 in Salt Lake City at 80 years of age. She married (1) (__) **Jacobs** and they had sons Shariton and Zebulon who were reared as members of the Brigham Young family.

(25) **Mary Ann Turley** 3 February 1846. Mary,[1448] daughter of Theodore **Turley** and Frances Amelia **Kimberley**, was born in Toronto, York, Ontario, Canada 13 July 1827 and died 24 December 1904 in Utah at 77 years of age.

(26) **Nancy Crissie** (maybe **Cressy**) in Nauvoo 6 February 1846. Nancy,[1449] daughter of William **Crissie** and Hannah **Townsen**, was born in New Brunswick, Middlesex Co., N.J. 20 January 1780 and died 17 December 1871 in Minersville, Beaver Co., Utah at 91 years of age. She married (1) **Oliver Walker** 8 February 1803. He was from New York state and their first seven children (John R., Hannah, William C., Mary Ann, Alfred, Sarah, Julian) were born in New York. Diontha and Nancy R. were born in Dayton, Manchester Co., Ohio and Eveline in Winchester, Randloph Co., Ind. Oliver died in Nauvoo 13 April 1843 and Nancy and Brigham were married three years later and moved to Utah in 1848. They had no children.[1450]

(27) **Diana (Diora) Severance Chase** in Nauvoo 7 February 1846. Diana,[1451] daughter of Ezra **Chase** and Tizah **Wells**, was born in Bristol, Addison Co., Vt. 25 July 1827 and died 6 September 1886 in Ogden, Weber Co., Utah at 59 years of age.

(28) **Lucy Bigelow** in Winter Quarters Nebr. 20 March 1847. Lucy,[1452] daughter of Nahum **Bigelow** and Mary **Gibbs**, was born in Charleston, Coles Co., Ill. 3 October 1830 and died 3 February 1905 in Salt Lake City at 74 years of age. She was baptized into the LDS church at age 8 and lived through the early trying years when Mormons were outcasts every where they settled. They were living in Nauvoo when its Temple was dedicated and were settled at Winter Quarters in 1846. Her marriage to Brigham was sealed in the Endownment House in 1848 after they arrived in the Salt Lake Valley. In November 1870 she and Brigham sought the warmer climate of St. George, Utah where they built a winter home. She lived there for 21 years, presiding over the sisters in the ordinance work in the St. George Temple. She fulfilled a mission to the Sandwich Island in 1887 and traveled to the eastern states in 1888 compiling genealogical records of her family. She moved to Salt Lake City in 1891 and attended the International Council of Women Convention in February 1899. She also attended the International Congress that year and was present at the dedications of the St. George, Manati, and Salt Lake Temples.[1453]

(29) **Mary Jane Bigelow** in Winter Quarters 20 March 1847. Mary,[1454] daughter of Nahum **Bigelow** and Mary **Gibbs**, was born in Lawrenceville, Lawrence Co., Ill. 15 October 1827 and died 26 September 1868 in Salt Lake City at 40 years of age. She was the older sister of Lucy **Bigelow**, Brigham's 28th wife. Mary Jane and Brigham were divorced in Salt Lake City in 1851.[1455]

(30) **Eliza Roxey Snow** 29 June 1849. Eliza,[1456] daughter of Oliver **Snow** and Rosetta Lenora **Pettibone**, was born in Becket, Berkshire Co., Mass. 21 January 1804 and died 5 December 1887 in Salt Lake City at 83 years of age. She married (1) **Joseph Smith** in Nauvoo 29 June 1842. Eliza was a poet, teacher, organizer,

writer, and speaker and became a leader among women in advancing the cause of Mormonism after she was baptized in 1825. She left her family in 1837 to join church members in Kirtland, then on to Missouri and Nauvoo. She met Joseph Smith in Kirtland and was a governess in his home both there and in Nauvoo. When the Relief Society was organized in Nauvoo 17 March 1842, she was elected its secretary and carried its records across the plains in a wagon train to the Salt Lake Valley. She wrote some 500 poems, 22 of which are set to music and published in the LDS Hymnal. Her "O My Father" is considered to be the greatest of all LDS hymns. She lived in the Lion House in Salt Lake until her death. In 1866 Brigham asked her to assist the bishops in organizing the Relief Society in every ward and branch of the church and she served as general president of the Society from 1866-87.[1457]

(31) **Eliza Burgess** in Salt Lake City 3 October 1850. Eliza was born in Stockport, Cheshire Co., England 8 December 1827[1458] and died in August 1915 in Salt Lake City at 87 years of age.[1459] Some sources give her birth date as "about 1805."

(32) **Eliza Babcock** bef 1853. Eliza,[1460] daughter of Adolphus **Babcock** and Jerusha Jane **Rowley**, was born in Mina, N.Y. 8 October 1828 and died in 1874 at 45 years of age.

(33) **Harriet Emeline Barney** in Salt Lake City 14 March 1856. Harriet,[1461] daughter of Royal **Barney** and Sarah **Eastebrook**, was born in Amherst, Loraine Co., Ohio 13 October 1830 and died 14 February 1911 in Salt Lake City at 80 years of age. Harriet married (1) Mr. **Sagers** and had three children with him. Brigham adopted and reared them as members of his family. They were Mary, born 24 December 1847 in St. Louis, Mo., died 27 June 1849, Salt Lake City; Royal Barney, born 8 November 1851 in Tooele, Utah died 6 October 1929, Salt Lake City; and Joseph Ormal, born 15 December 1853 in Tooele, died 1 Aug. 1917 Salt Lake City.

(34) **Harriet Amelia Folsom** in Salt Lake City 24 January 1863. Harriet,[1462] daughter of William Harrison **Folsom** and Zerviah Eliza **Clark**, was born 23 August 1838 and died 11 December 1910 in Salt Lake City at 72 years of age. Harriet's family was driven from Nauvoo, losing all their property and provisions. They resettled in Council Bluffs, Iowa where they acquired a grand piano which they took across the Plains to Salt Lake in 1860. Harriet became an accomplished pianist and taught piano to some of Brigham's children. She was 25 when she married Brigham and while she had no children of her own, she was a second mother to many of his children. She assisted him in his official capacities as leader of the church and as Territorial Governor, often accompanying him on his travels throughout the territory and lived with him in St. George.[1463]

(35) **Mary Van Cott** in Salt Lake City 8 January 1868. Mary,[1464] daughter of John **Van Cott** and Lucy Lavina **Sackett**, was born in Elmira, N.Y. (maybe Canaan, Columbia, Co., N.Y.) 2 February 1844. She died either 5 or 15 January 1884 in Salt Lake City at 39 years of age. She married (1) **James Cobb**.

(36) **Ann Eliza Webb** in Salt Lake City 7 April 1868. Ann,[1465] daughter of Chauncey Griswold **Webb** and Eliza Jane **Churchill**, was born 13 September 1844. She married (1) **James L. Dee in** 1863 They had two children. Ann and Brigham were divorced in Salt Lake City in 1876.[1466]

(37) **Lydia Farnsworth** 8 May 1870. Lydia,[1467] daughter of Reuben **Farnsworth** and Lucinda **Kent**, was born in Dorset, Bennington Co., Vt. 5 February 1808 and

died 5 February 1896 in Pleasant Grove, Utah Co., Utah at 88 years of age.

He may have married **Hepzibah Richards**, younger sister of wife No. 23. Hepzibah was born in Hopkinton, Middlesex Co., Mass. 28 July 1795 and died 30 September 1838 in Far West, Mo., at 43 years of age. (See No. 652.)

Brigham is a great (5) grandson of John and Susannah Whipple. He was baptized and confirmed a member of the Church of Latter Day Saints 14 April 1832 and soon became one of the Church's earnest workers and leaders. As president of the Quorum of the Twelve Apostles he became the nominal president of the Church immediately after the martyrdom of the Prophet Joseph Smith and Joseph's brother Hyrum. He was governor of the provisional state of Deseret and of the Territory of Utah. Nearly 300 towns and settlements were founded during the 30 years between his arrival and death.

As a young man he learned the trades of carpentry, painting, and glazing. Early in his life, his parents moved from Vermont to New York where he lived in Chenango County until his first marriage when he moved to Cayuga County. Early in 1829 he moved to Mendon, Monroe County, where, in the spring of 1830, he saw his first copy of the Book of Mormon. He eventually became convinced of its divine origin and after being baptized and ordained an Elder he immediately became active in the ministry, preaching, baptizing, and organizing branches of the church. His parents and other family members also joined.

Brigham met Joseph Smith the Prophet for the first time in 1832 on a visit to Kirtland, Ohio and moved there in in the fall of 1833. He followed Joseph Smith to Far West, Mo. where he lived from 1838 until he led the Mormons (Joseph Smith and many of the other leaders were in prison at the time) to Nauvoo, Ill after anti-Mormon mobs drove them from the community. His mission to England (1839-1841) gained many converts among the urban working class. By 1841 he had so impressed Joseph Smith that he was made President of the Quorum of Twelve Apostles, the governing body of the church. This made him second in authority to Smith. He was on a mission in the eastern U.S. when Smith and his brother Hyram were murdered by an anti-Mormon mob 27 June 1844 in Carthage, Ill. On his return he played a critical role in keeping the church together by organizing an exodus that took the Mormons westward, first to Winter Quarters, Nebr. in 1846 and finally to Utah's Salt Lake Valley where he arrived with an advance party of 147 on 24 July 1847. He returned to Winter Quarters where on 27 December he was elected church president by a vote of its members in conference.

He was back in the Salt Lake Valley by September 1848 and from then on his activities were devoted to growing the church and developing the western country. He traveled extensively among the new settlements and urged the construction of temples. Four were erected in Utah: Salt Lake, St. George, Manti, and Logan. He lived to dedicate the one at St. George. Through the church he directed political decision-making, economic development, cultural affairs, law enforcement, and education. He also sought to broaden the church by establishing colonies throughout Utah Arizona, Nevada, and Idaho territories. He wanted the Mormons to be self-sufficient and encouraged the local manufacture of goods and discouraged enterprises that might require or invite outside investors.

When Utah was organized as a Territory in 1851, Young was named governor and superintendent of Indian Affairs. The 1852 announcement that plural marriage (polygamy) was a basic tenet of the church caused a public outcry throughout the nation. In 1857 president James Buchanan sent troops to Utah but by 1858 Young reached an accommodation with the federal government which allowed the Mormons to practice their religion and build their community without interference. After Young's death in 1877, the federal government renewed its attack on polygamy and the church eventually outlawed its practice.[1468]

Brigham's Will was read 3 September 1877 in the presence of 17 wives, 16 sons, 28 daughters, and a few friends. It was filed for probate on 4 September in the Salt Lake Court. Named as executors were George Q. Cannon, Brigham Young, Jr., and Albert Carrington, members of the Council of Twelve Apostles. The popular belief of the value of the estate was excessively high. It was rumored to be between $2 and $2.5 million. The attorneys who represented Ann Eliza (wife No. 36) in her divorce proceedings of 1876 estimated it a $8 million. It turned out to be $1,626,000. Deducting debts and church properties held in trust reduced it to $361,170 and after settlement including executor's fees and other deductions, the amount available to heirs was $224,242. The sum was so much less than the heirs had expected that the trustee-in-trust and the executors were forced into court to defend their settlements. A full account of the settlement is in Appendix D (pages 423-30) of *Brigham Young American Moses* by Leonard J. Arrington. For the reader who wants to know more about the life and times of Brigham Young, the libraries are full of books and articles covering all aspects of his life.

Brigham's 56 children — 32 daughters, 23 sons, and one infant who died the day of birth, sex unknown — were born over a span of 45 years. He was 24 when the first child was born and 69 when the last was born. Both were daughters with the first one age 45 when her yougest sibling was born. He fathered three sets of twins. Seven sons and three daughters did not live to become adults.

With his heavy work and travel schedule and the children living in different homes with their mothers, it must have been next to impossible for Brigham to have bonded with many other than those born to his first two wives whom he lived with in monogamous marriages.

Brigham **Young** and Miriam Angeline **Works** had the following children:

+ 1252   i. Elizabeth[9] **Young** was born 26 September 1825.
+ 1253   ii. Vilate **Young** was born 1 June 1830.

Brigham **Young** and Mary Ann **Angell** had the following children:

1254   iii. Joseph Angell **Young**[1469] was born in Kirtland, Lake Co., Ohio 13 October 1834 and died 5 August 1875 in Manti, Sampete Co., Utah at 40 years of age.

+ 1255   iv. Brigham Heber **Young** Jr. was born 18 December 1836.

1256   v. Mary Ann **Young**[1470] was born in Kirtland 18 December 1836 and died August 1843 at 6 years of age.

+ 1257   vi. Alice **Young** was born 4 September 1839.

+ 1258   vii. Eunice Caroline **Young** was born 20 August 1842.

1259   viii. John Willard **Young**[1471] was born in Nauvoo, Ill. 1 October 1844 and died 11 February 1924 in Logan, Cache Co., Utah at 79 years of age. He married Luella **Cobb**,[1472] daughter of James **Cobb** and Mary **Van Cott** and is buried in Salt Lake City

Brigham **Young** and Lucy Ann **Decker** had the following children:

1260   ix. Brigham Heber **Young**[1473] was born in Nauvoo 19 June 1845 and died

3 June 1928 at 82 years of age.

+ 1261   x.   Fanny Decker **Young** was born 25 January 1849.

  1262   xi.   Ernest Irving **Young**[1474] was born in Salt Lake City 30 April 1851 and died there 8 October 1879 at 28 years of age.

+ 1263   xii.   Shamira **Young** was born 21 January 1853.

  1264   xiii.   Arta D. Crista **Young**[1475] was born in Salt Lake City 16 April 1855 and died 7 April 1916 in Ogden, Weber Co., Utah at 60 years of age.[1476]

  1265   xiv.   Feramorz Little **Young**[1477] was born in Salt Lake City 16 September 1858 and died on a ship in the Atlantic Ocean 27 September 1881 at 23 years of age. He was buried at sea.

+ 1266   xv.   Clarissa Hamilton **Young** was born 23 July 1860.

Brigham **Young** and Emily Dow **Partridge** had the following children:

  1267   xvi.   Edward Partridge **Young**[1478] was born in Nauvoo 30 October 1845 and died 26 November 1852 in Salt Lake City at 7 years of age.

+ 1268   xvii.   Emily Augusta **Young** was born 1 March 1849.

+ 1269   xviii.   Caroline Partridge **Young** was born 1 February 1851.

  1270   xix.   Joseph Don Carlos **Young**[1479] was born in Salt Lake City 6 May 1855 and died there 19 October 1938 at 83 years of age.

+ 1271   xx.   Miriam **Young** was born 13 October 1857.

+ 1272   xxi.   Josephine **Young** was born 21 February 1860.

  1273   xxii.   Lura **Young**[1480] was born in Salt Lake City 2 April 1862 and died there 4 November 1862 at less than one year of age.[1481]

Brigham **Young** and Harriett Elizabeth **Cook** had the following child:

  1274   xxiii.   Oscar Brigham **Young** was born in Nauvoo 10 February 1846 and died 4 August 1910 in Provo at 64 years of age.

Brigham **Young** and Clarissa **Ross** had the following children:

+ 1275   xxiv.   Mary Eliza **Young** was born 8 June 1847.

+ 1276   xxv.   Clarissa Maria **Young** was born 10 December 1849.

  1277   xxvi.   Willard **Young**[1482] was born in Salt Lake City 30 April 1852 and died 30 November 1939 at 87 years of age.[1483]

+ 1278   xxvii.   Phebe Louisa **Young** was born 1 August 1854.

Brigham **Young** and Emeline **Free** had the following children:

  1279   xxviii.   Ella Elizabeth **Young**[1484] was born in Winter Quarters, Nebr. 31 August 1847 and died 7 August 1890 at 42 years of age. She married Nelson **Empey**. No children born to this union.

+ 1280   xxix.   Marinda Hyde **Young** was born 30 July 1849.

  1281   xxx.   Hyrum Smith **Young**[1485] was born in Salt Lake City 2 January 1851 and died there 28 February 1925 at 74 years of age.[1486]

  1282   xxxi.   Emeline Amanda **Young**[1487] was born in Salt Lake City 11 February 1853 and died 16 July 1895 at 42 years of age.[1488] She married William **Crosby**. No issue born to this union.

+ 1283   xxxii.   Louisa Nelle **Young** was born 30 October 1855.

  1284   xxxiii.   Lorenzo Dow **Young**[1489] was born in Salt Lake City 22 September 1856 and died 18 May 1905 at 48 years of age.[1490]

  1285   xxxiv.   Alonzo **Young**[1491] was born in Salt Lake City 20 December 1858 and died there 31 March 1918 at 59 years of age.[1492]

+ 1286   xxxv.   Ruth **Young** was born 4 March 1861.

  1287   xxxvi.   Daniel Wells **Young**[1493] was born in Salt Lake 9 February 1863 and died the day of birth.

  1288   xxxvii.   Ardelle **Young**[1494] was born in Salt Lake City 26 October 1864 and died

2 September 1900 at 35 years of age. She married Frank **Harrison**.

Brigham **Young** and Louisa Beeman or **Beaman** had the following children:

1289xxxviii. Joseph **Young**[1495] was born about 1848 and died in infancy.

1290 xxxix. Hyrum **Young**[1496] was born abt 1848 and died in infancy.

1291 xxxx. Alva **Young**[1497] was born abt 1850. and died in infancy.

1292 xli. Alma **Young**[1498] was born abt 1850 and died in infancy.

Brigham **Young** and Clarissa Clara **Decker** had the following children:

1293 xlii. Jeannette Richards **Young**[1499] was born in Salt Lake City 14 December 1849 and died 8 March 1930 at 80 years of age. She married Robert C. **Easton**. Robert was born in Scotland 22 February 1852 and died 21 June 1917 at 65 years of age.[1500] No issue born to this union.

+ 1294 xliii. Nabbie Howe **Young** was born 22 March 1852.

1295 xliv. Jedediah Grant **Young**[1501] was born in Salt Lake City either January 1854 or 21 January 1855. He died 11 January 1856.

1296 xlv. Albert Jeddie **Young** was born in Salt Lake City either 4 or 21 January 1858.[1502] He died 16 December 1864 at 6 years of age.[1503] Young family genealogists Gates and Sanborn give his death year as 1858.

1297 xlvi. Charlotte Talula **Young**[1504] was born in Salt Lake City 4 March 1861 and died 20 January 1892 at 30 years of age.[1505] She married Augustus **Woods**. No issue born to this union.

Brigham **Young** and Zina Diantha **Huntington** had the following child:

+ 1298 xlvii. Zina **Young** was born 3 April 1850.

Brigham **Young** and Margaret Maria **Alley** had the following children:

+ 1299 xlvii. Evelyn Louise **Young** was born 30 July 1850.

+ 1300 xlviii. Mahonri Moriancumber **Young** was born 1 November 1852.

Brigham **Young** and Lucy **Bigelow** had the following children:

+ 1301 xlix. Eudora Lovina **Young** was born 12 May 1852.

+ 1302 l. Susan (Susa) Amelia **Young** was born 18 March 1856.

+ 1303 li. Rhoda Mabel **Young** was born 22 February 1863.

Brigham **Young** and Eliza **Burgess** had the following child:

1304 lii. Alffales **Young**[1506] was born in Salt Lake City 3 October 1853 and died 30 March 1920 at 66 years of age.

Brigham **Young** and Margaret **Pierce** had the following child:

1305 liii. Brigham Morris **Young**[1507] was born in Salt Lake City 18 January 1854.

Brigham **Young** and Harriet Emeline **Barney** had the following children:

1306 liv. Phineas Howe **Young**[1508] was born in Salt Lake City 15 February 1863.

1307 lv. Infant **Young**[1509] was born in Salt Lake City abt 1865.

Brigham **Young** and Mary **Van Cott** had the following child:

+ 1308 lvi. Fannie Van Cott **Young** was born in 1870.

---

955. **Lorenzo Dow**[8] **Young** (Abigail (Nabby)[7] **Howe**, Susanna[6] **Goddard**, Ebenezer[5], Susanna[4] **Stone**, Mary[3] **Whipple**, Elder John[2], Matthew[1])[1510] was born in Smyrna, N.Y 19 October 1807 and died 21 November 1895 in Salt Lake City at 88 years of age. He married five times. (1) **Persis Goodall** in New York State, 6 June 1826. Persis,[1511] daughter of Joel **Goodall** and Mary (or Molly) **Swain**, was born in Watertown, Jefferson Co., N.Y. 15 March 1806 and died 16 December 1894 in Salt Lake City at 88 years of age. (2) **Harriet Page Wheeler** in Nauvoo, Ill. 9 March

1843. Harriet,[1512] daughter of Oliver **Wheeler** and Hannah **Ashby**, was born in Hillsborough, Hillsborough Co., N. H. 7 September 1803 and died 23 December 1871 in Salt Lake City at 68 years of age. She married (1) **Isaac Perry Decker** in Phelps, Ontario Co., N.Y. in 1821. They had six children: Lucy Ann, 17 May 1822; Charles Franklin, 21 June 1824; Harriet Amelia, 13 March 1826; Clarissa, 22 July 1828; Fannie Marie, 24 April 1830; and Isaac Perry, 7 August 1840. Harriet was one of the three women who went to Utah with the first Pioneer Company and was seven months pregnant when they arrived in the Salt Lake Valley. She was not impressed with what she saw and remarked that she "would rather go another 1,000 miles than stay in this barren place."[1513] (3) **Hannah Ida Hewitt** in Salt Lake City 29 April 1856. Hannah,[1514] daughter of Philip **Hewitt** and Mary Ann **Reynolds**, was born in Windham, Norfolk Co., England 11 June 1839 and died 20 September 1888 at 49 years of age. (4) **Eleanor Jones** in Salt Lake City 25 November 1856. Eleanor,[1515] daughter of Thomas **Jones** and Ruth **James**, was born in Wales, Great Britain 16 November 1830. (5) **Joanna (Anna) Larsen** in Salt Lake City 18 April 1863. Joanna,[1516] daughter of Augustus **Larsen** and Christina (_), was born in Sweden, Maine 24 August 1843.

The youngest son of John and Nabby Young, Lorenzo was baptized into the LDS Church by elder John P. Greene and soon became an energetic member of the faith. He moved to Kirtland, Ohio in the spring of 1834 where he worked in the Temple. He moved to Caldwell County, Mo. in the summer of 1837, leaving all his property there that fall because of threatening mobs and settled in Scott County, Ill. He joined the Mormon group in Nauvoo in 1841 and was a member of the advance party (known as the Pioneers) to arrive in Salt Lake Valley in 1847.[1517]

Lorenzo Dow **Young** and Persis **Goodall** had the following children:

1309	i.	William Goodall[9] **Young**[1518] was born in New York State 21 February 1827.
1310	ii.	Joseph Watson **Young**[1519] was born in New York State 12 January 1829.
1311	iii.	Lucy Ann **Young**[1520] was born in Pittsburgh, Penn. 27 November 1832 and died in August 1836 at 3 years of age.
+ 1312	iv.	Harriet Maria **Young** was born 21 July 1834.
1313	v.	John Ray **Young**[1521] was born in Kirtland, Ohio 30 April 1837.
1314	vi.	Franklin Wheeler **Young**[1522] was born in Scott Co., Ill. 17 February 1839.
1315	vii.	Lorenzo Sobiskie **Young**[1523] was born in Winchester, Scott Co., Ill. 9 March 1841.
1316	viii.	Lucius James **Young**[1524] was born 12 July 1843 and died 9 August 1844 at one year of age.
1317	ix.	Lucia Jane **Young**[1525] was born 12 July 1843.
1318	x.	Frances Elizabeth **Young**[1526] was born 27 June 1845 and died 15 July 1845 at less than one year of age.

Lorenzo Dow **Young** and Harriet Page **Wheeler** had the following children:

1319	xi.	John Brigham **Young**[1527] was born in Waynesville, Warren Co., Ohio 5 September 1844 and died the day of birth.
1320	xii.	Lorenzo Dow **Young** Jr.[1528] was born in Salt Lake City 20 September 1847 and died there 22 March 1848 at less than one year of age. Lorenzo is believed to be the first white male child born in the Salt Lake Valley and was one of the first persons to be buried in the Salt Lake Cemetery.[1529]

Lorenzo Dow **Young** and Eleanor **Jones** had the following children:

    1321   xiii. Harriet Page **Young**[1530] was born 10 April 1858 and died 4 May 1865 at 7 years of age.

    1322   xiv. Edward Jones **Young**[1531] was born 2 October 1860.

    1323   xv. George Edwin **Young**[1532] was born 12 August 1862.

    1324   xvi. James **Young**[1533] was born 12 June 1867 and died 26 June 1868 at one year of age.

Lorenzo Dow **Young** and Hannah Ida **Hewitt** had the following children:

    1325   xvii. Perry Legrand **Young**[1534] was born in Salt Lake City 1 November 1858.

    1326   xviii. Brigham Willard **Young**[1535] was born in Salt Lake City 7 February 1860 and died 20 July 1887 in Nuhak, New Zealand at 27 years of age.

 + 1327   xix. Harriet Josephine **Young** was born 24 February 1863.

    1328   xx. Ferramorz **Young**[1536] was born in Tooele Co., Utah 8 November 1867.

    1329   xxi. Clara May **Young**[1537] was born in April 1870 and married (__) **Spiers**.

Lorenzo Dow **Young** and Joanna (Anna) **Larsen** had the following children:

    1330   xxii. Harry Augustus **Young**[1538] was born in Salt Lake City 25 February 1865 and died there 6 February 1899 at 33 years of age.

    1331   xxiii. Francis Marion **Young**[1539] was born 8 April 1870.

    1332   xxiv. Albert Francis **Young**[1540] was born 15 December 1875.

959. Col. Jonathan[8] **Stone** (Lt. Jonathan[7], Jonathan[6], Jonathan[5], Jonathan[4], Mary[3] **Whipple**, Elder John[2], Matthew[1])[1541] was born in Auburn, Mass. 4 April 1793 and died in April 1845 at 52 years of age. He was lost at sea. He married **Abigail Knowlton** (see No. 1043) in Auburn, 24 May 1814. They were fifth cousins; Jonathan descending from Elder John Whipple through his daughter Mary; Abigail descending through his daughter Sarah. Abigail,[1542] daughter of Nathan **Knowlton** and Abigail **Maynard**, was born 13 March 1790 and died 15 December 1874 in Auburn at 84 years of age.

Col. Jonathan **Stone** and Abigail **Knowlton** had the following children:

    1333   i. Oliver[9] **Stone**[1543] was born in Auburn, 22 August 1815 and died 4 February 1863 in Worcester, Mass. at 47 years of age. He married twice. (1) Mary **Cudworth** 13 April 1842. (2) Melinda C. **Hook** 22 April 1856.

    1334   ii. Joseph Jackson **Stone**[1544] was born 26 December 1816 and died 2 October 1833 at 16 years of age.

    1335   iii. Prescott Brainbridge **Stone**[1545] was born 13 July 1819 and died 21 May 1886 at 66 years of age. He married Susan Platts **Crandall** 27 July 1850.

    1336   iv. Sarah Lucinda **Stone**[1546] was born 1 February 1822 and died 4 August 1885 at 63 years of age. She married George W. **Barnard**.

    1337   v. Lewis Cutting **Stone**[1547] was born 22 April 1823 and died 6 September 1900 at 77 years of age. He married Abbie Almira (Divoll) **Stockwell**.

    1338   vi. Emory **Stone**[1548] was born 9 March 1827 and died 5 March 1918 at 90 years of age. He married Catherine **Shurtleff** 5 September 1847.

 + 1339   vii. Marshall Maynard **Stone** was born 19 April 1828.

1001. Charles Hobart[8] **Stone** (Charles[7], Jonathan[6], Moses[5], Jonathan[4], Mary[3] **Whipple**, Elder John[2], Matthew[1])[1549] was born in Belmont, Mass. 25 May 1827 and died 12 June 1899 in Newton, Mass. at 72 years of age. He was a market gardener and member of the firm of Isaac Stickney & Company, produce merchants. He married **Mary Augusta Green** in Townsend, Mass. 22 November 1855. Mary,[1550] daughter of George **Green** and Polly **Baldwin**, was born in Pepperell, Mass. 8 February 1825 and died 26 December 1908 in Newton at 83 years of age.

Charles Hobart **Stone** and Mary Augusta **Green** had the following child:

+ 1340   i. Charles Augustus[9] **Stone** was born 16 January 1867.

1002. Joel[8] **Billings** (John[7], Joanna[6] **Norton**, John[5], Mary[4] **Goodhue**, Sarah[3] **Whipple**, Elder John[2], Matthew[1])[1551] was born in Berwick, York, Co., Maine 21 December 1770 and died there 13 July 1842 at 71 years of age. He married **Lydia Hussey** in Berwick 15 February 1795. Lydia,[1552] daughter of Stephen **Hussey** and Priscilla **Hanson**, was born 30 December 1775 and died 10 June 1865 in North Berwick at 89 years of age.

Joel **Billings** and Lydia **Hussey** had the following children born in North Berwick

1341   i. John H.[9] **Billings**[1553] was born 11 December 1795 and died 24 November 1859 in Scarboro, Cumberland Co., Maine at 63 years of age. He married Sophia **Fogg** in Scarboro in January 1817.

1342   ii. Susan **Billings**[1554] was born 30 August 1797.

1343   iii. Olive **Billings**[1555] was born 27 November 1798 and married Robert **Abbott** 13 August 1818.

1344   iv. Stephen **Billings**[1556] was born 24 May 1800.

1345   v. Rhoda **Billings**[1557] was born 3 April 1802.

1346   vi. Ezra **Billings**[1558] was born 8 May 1803 and was buried 13 June 1877 in North Berwick. He married Hannah **Ford** in North Berwick.

+ 1347   vii. Hiram **Billings** was born 17 May 1805.

1348   viii. Ivory **Billings**[1559] was born 9 March 1807 and was buried 4 July 1869 in North Berwick.

1003. Benjamin[8] **Swett** (Daniel[7], Moses[6], Elizabeth[5] **Norton**, Mary[4] **Goodhue**, Sarah[3] **Whipple**, Elder John[2], Matthew[1])[1560] was born in Perry, Maine 5 December 1805 and died 27 May 1895 in Stoddard, N.H. at 89 years of age. He married **Elsie Jane Shannon** who was born in 1808 and died in 1874 at 66 years of age.[1561]

Benjamin **Swett** and Elsie Jane **Shannon** had the following child:

+ 1349   i. Benjamin Frank[9] **Swett** was born 3 August 1853.

1006. Sarah (Sally)[8] **Stone** (Sarah[7] **Treadwell**, Joseph[6], Sarah[5] **Goodhue**, William[4], Sarah[3] **Whipple**, Elder John[2], Matthew[1])[1562] was born in Oxford, Worcester Co., Mass. 13 November 1783. She married **Capt. Steven Barton** there 22 April 1804. Steven,[1563] son of Dr. Stephen **Barton** and Mrs. Dorothy **Moore**, was born 18 August 1774.

Capt. Barton served as a non commissioned officer under gen. Wayne (Mad Anthony) in the French and Indian Wars on the western frontiers. In Oxford he was a farmer, horse breeder, owned the only sawmill in their section of town, and was a respected member of the community. He owned two large farms with three great barns and 25 milch cows on the home place. He was one of the first farmers in the Oxford area to introduce blooded stock — Highlanders, Virginians, and Morgans pranced the fields — and he raised his own colts.

According to his youngest child Clara, strangers and newcomers to the area naturally gravitated to their home. They were lecturers, clergymen on circuit, and anyone with a new idea to expound. She said her father's active and liberal mind inclined him to examination and toleration and his cordial hospitality was seconded by her mother's welcome to any one who could bring new thought or culture to herself or her family. Clara remembers listening "breathlessly" to her father's war stories. She said the two of them made battles and fought them. Every shade of military etiquette was regarded. Generals, colonels, captains, and sergeants were given their proper place and rank. The same with the political world: the president, cabinet, and leading officers of the government were learned by heart. She said nothing "gratified the keen humor" of her father "more than the parrot-like" way she "lisped these often difficult names and the accuracy with which I repeated them upon request." When the country was thrust into the Civil War and she had to take her part in it, she said she found herself "far less stranger to the conditions that most women, or even ordinary men" encountered.

    Sarah (Sally) **Stone** and Capt. Steven **Barton** had the following children born in Oxford:

       1350   i.   Dorothea[9] **Barton**[1564] was born 2 October 1804 and died 19 April 1846 in Oxford at 41 years of age.

  + 1351   ii. Stephen **Barton** was born 29 March 1806.

       1352   iii. David **Barton**[1565] was born 15 August 1808 and married Julia A.M. **Porter** in Oxford. The date of intent to marry was 16 August 1839. David, with access to his father's horses, was known as the Buffalo Bill of the surrounding country. Beginning when she was five, he would take Clara, his youngest sister, on "merry rides on an unsaddled colt over the fields." Clara said that during the Civil War when "she found herself on a strange horse in a trooper's saddle, flying for life or liberty in front of pursuit, I blessed the baby lessons of the wild gallops among the beautiful colts.

      When Clara was in her early teens, David, who was helping in a July barn raising, fell from the rafters into the cellar landing on his feet. He seemed none the worse for the fall but in a few days began to get severe headaches and eventually "settled fever." The treatment was to draw blood. It was then Clara had her first experience working with the ill. From the first days and nights of David's illness, she administered all his medicines including the "loathsome, crawling leeches" that sucked his blood and dressing the blisters caused by them. She was the accepted and acknowledged nurse of a man almost too ill to recover. His illness continued for two years before Dr. Asa McCullum, a "steam doctor," treated him with a vapor bath which opened the pores. The treatment worked and he was back to work in three weeks.

       1353   iv. Sally **Barton**[1566] was born 20 March 1811.

       1354   v. Clarissa Harlowe **Barton**[1567] was born 25 December 1821 and died 12 April 1912 in Glen Echo, Md. at 90 years of age. She was buried in North Oxford.

    Clara Barton, great (5) grand daughter of John and Susanna Whipple, was an American humanitarian who organized the American Red Cross. She was successively a school teacher, clerk, battlefield heroine, lecturer, organizer, and author. She attended rural schools but was chiefly educated at home by two older brothers and two sisters. Dorothy taught her spelling, Sally geography, Stephen arithmetic, and David coached her in athletics. She was such an apt pupil she started school at age 4 and could already spell three-syllable words. Formal school was so easy she was soon studying subjects such as philosophy, chemistry, and Latin. Her main problem was extreme shyness.

      Clara was born on Christmas Day in a rather newly built country house, the youngest in a family of two brothers and two sisters. The next youngest was 10 years her senior while the oldest was 17 years older. She attended two terms at school, and learned geography from *Mensuer's Geography* which included an atlas suitable for young children. "I became so interested in the maps I would wake my sisters in the cold winter morning to sit in bed and by the light of a tallow candle they would help me find mountains, rivers, counties, oceans, lakes, isthmuses, islands, channels, cities, towns, and capitals.

She later enrolled in a school taught by Lucian Burleigh where she was introduced to elementary astronomy, ancient history, and the "Science of Language." They read Milton's *Paradise Lost* and

Clara Barton, *founder of the Red Cross*

Robert Pollock's *Course of Time*.[1568] One winter she was in a school taught by Jonathan Dana, one of Oxford's most scholarly men and a teacher of note. She said "no words could describe the value of his instruction or the pains he took with his eager pupil." He had 60 students of all ages but Clara was too advanced for the customary classes so he introduced her to philosophy, chemistry, and elementary Latin — all taught outside school hours.

Clara described herself in her early years as "diffident, timid, noncommital, afraid of trouble, and difficult to understand because she wouldn't open up to people." She began teaching school at age 18 and taught in Massachusetts for 11 years (1839-50) including at a school she founded in North Oxford. She left Massachusetts to attend the Liberal Institute at Clinton, N.Y. after which she taught at Hightstown and Bordentown, N.J. She opened a free school in Bordentown and its attendance grew to more than 600. She left after the school board passed her over for a man to head the school. After the first of a series of nervous collapses, her voice failed, causing her to resign from teaching in 1854.

She moved to Washington, D.C. and worked intermittently for the U.S. Patent Office as a copyist (1854-61). Distressed at the lack of supplies and "comforts" for wounded Civil War soldiers, she resigned in 1861 and began, without official organization or affiliation, to minister to casualties on battle sites in Virginia where she soon became known as the "Angel of the Battlefield." She divided her time between caring for the wounded and feeding battle field soldiers. She rented a warehouse to hold the "comforts" she solicited from friends in New England and New Jersey.

While she gave aid to army surgeons, bandaged the wounded, and fed and nursed dying men, she viewed herself more as a provider than a nurse. It was her hot gruel and mush, sense of humor, and practical methods that endeared her to the battlefield soldiers. She was appointed superintendent of the department of nurses for the Army of the James in 1864 and nearly lost her life in the battles of Fredericksburg and Antietam when fragments of shell ripped through her clothing.

She began a missing soldier's operation after a prisoner of war brought her a list of dead from the legendary Andersonville Confederate prison camp in Georgia. Nearly 13,000 of 45,000 confined Union soldiers died from disease, filth, starvation, and exposure there. As a result of her work, Barton was able to mark the graves of thousands of dead at Andersonville. She later published a list of their names. Once people realized she had found dead soldiers, she received thousands of letters from mothers and wives seeking lost sons and husbands. Occasionally she found people who didn't want to be found. Andersonville Prison later became a National Cemetery.

In 1865 she convinced President Abraham Lincoln to commission her to compile records of missing Union soldiers becoming the first woman to run a government bureau, receiving $15,000 in congressional appropriations. Working with her own staff, she compiled lists and sent them to post offices across the country and was able to identify 22,000 soldiers between 1865-68. She combined this work with lecturing across the country and became nationally famous. While lecturing in Portland, Maine in in 1869 her voice failed again and she went to Europe to recuperate.

While in Geneva visiting a Swiss soldier she had nursed on the battlefield, officials of the International Red Cross (founded by J. Henri Dunant in 1864) called to solicit her aid in introducing the movement to the U.S. Twenty-two nations were then enrolled under the Treaty of Geneva, but the U.S., because of the Monroe Doctrine, chose not to join. She volunteered with the Red Cross to help civilian victims of the Franco-Prussian War and was honored with the Iron Cross of Germany.

She returned to Washington in 1873 and began a long struggle to bring the Red Cross movement to the U.S. She called on politicians, diplomats, generals, professors, and editors, appealed to three presidents for support, distributed brochures and pamplets at every opportunity, and little by little overcame much antagonism to her Red Cross and relief work. She stayed in close contact with the parent organization in Geneva and was invited by them in 1877 to work for affiliation of an American Society which she incorporated as the American Association of the Red Cross in 1881 in Dansville, N.Y. The U.S. Senate ratified the Geneva Treaty in 1882 and she became the first president of the American Red Cross.

As founder and leading spirit of the American Red Cross she became internationally famous. She attended international conferences, was honored at European courts, received medals from foreign governments, and wrote and lectured on such a large scale she gradually became one of the world's best known women.

Aided by a few devoted assistants but with no formal organization, she broadened the organization's scope with relief programs for victims of major disasters, issued appeals for help, and personally led many relief expeditions into devastated areas.

Her disaster operations included the Michigan forest fire (1881), the Mississippi and Ohio River floods (1884), the tornado at Mount Vernon, Ill. and the yellow fever epidemic in Florida (1888), the Johnstown, Penn. floods (1889), the Sea Islands hurricane in Georgia and South Carolina (1893), and the Galveston tidal wave (1900). During this time she also directed relief operations for the Russian (1891) and Armenian (1896) famine sufferers, and brought the Red Cross into army operations during the Spanish-American War.

Her personal leadership came under attack in 1900 and the organization was reincorporated as the American Red Cross by Congress. She remained as president until 1904 when she resigned and the society was reorganized. She had outlived the era when one pioneer could manage a growing entity but her name rests securely among the great and imaginative pioneers in philanthropic accomplishments.

Her books: *The Red Cross: A History of This Remarkable International Movement in the Interest of Humanity* (1898); *The Red Cross in Peace and War* (1899); *A Story of the Red Cross: Glimpses of Field Work* (1904); *The Story of My Childhood* (1907).

She died from complications of a cold. Her mission is life was summed up in her own words: " . . . never . . . think whether you like it or not, whether it is bearable or not; never think of anything except the need, and how to meet it." She was buried in the family plot at North Oxford, Mass.

In the fall of 1997, Gary Scott, National Park Service regional historian, found records of her work in the attic of a government building that housed her Missing Persons Office. The documents included a list with hundreds of names of missing soldiers, government records, Civil War newspapers, leftover wallpaper remnants and 19th-century clothes from embroidered slippers to a frock coat which looked like something President Lincoln would have worn. The materials were stored for a short time at Ford's theatre but since Clara is not identified with Fords they have been removed and sealed pending treatment and determination of their ownership. The General Services Administration plans to open an exhibit in the building where the items were found.

1009. **Joseph**[8] **Treadwell** (Joseph[7], Joseph[6], Sarah[5] **Goodhue**, William[4], Sarah[3] **Whipple**, Elder John[2], Matthew[1])[1569] was born in Newburyport, Mass. 12 August 1771 and died 8 June 1842 in Bangor, Maine at 70 years of age. He was a trader and builder and served as the first town clerk of Garland, Maine. At various times he lived at New Gloucester, Lewiston, Garland, and Bangor, Maine. He married **Mary Tyler** in New Gloucester, Maine 18 December 1792. Mary,[1570] daughter of John **Tyler** and Ruth **Herrick**, was born 22 February 1766 and died 3 February 1854 in Exeter, Maine at 87 years of age.

Joseph **Treadwell** and Mary **Tyler** had the following children, all born in Maine:

1355	i.	Susanna[9] **Treadwell**.[1571]
1356	ii.	Ruth **Treadwell**.[1572]
1357	iii.	Mary **Treadwell**.[1573]
1358	iv.	John **Treadwell**.[1574]
1359	v.	Joseph Tyler **Treadwell**.[1575]
1360	vi.	Sally **Treadwell**.[1576]
1361	vii.	Anna **Treadwell**.[1577]
1362	viii.	Benjamin **Treadwell**.[1578]
1363	ix.	Thomas Herrick **Treadwell**.[1579]
1364	x.	Simeon **Treadwell**.[1580]

1011. **Nathaniel**[8] **Treadwell** (Nathaniel[7], Thomas[6], Sarah[5] **Goodhue**, William[4], Sarah[3] **Whipple**, Elder John[2], Matthew[1])[1581] was born in Ipswich, Mass. 13 May 1776 and died 14 November 1808 in the West Indies, at 32 years of age. He married **Mary Pearson** in Ipswich 4 May 1800. Mary,[1582] daughter of Lieut. Enoch **Pearson** and Eunice **Marshall**, was born in Ipswich in 1784 and died there 9 June 1860 at 75 years of age.

Nathaniel **Treadwell** and Mary **Pearson** had the following children:

1365	i.	Mary[9] **Treadwell**.[1583]
1366	ii.	Sarah **Treadwell**.[1584]
1367	iii.	Thomas Warren **Treadwell**.[1585]

1012. **Thomas**[8] **Treadwell** (Nathaniel[7], Thomas[6], Sarah[5] **Goodhue**, William[4], Sarah[3] **Whipple**, Elder John[2], Matthew[1])[1586] was born in Ipswich, Mass. 1 October 1779 and died 30 March 1860 in Portsmouth, N.H. at 80 years of age. He was a hatter and felt-maker and married **Anna Passmore** in Portsmouth. 13 November 1800. Anna,[1587] daughter of Thomas **Passmore** and Mary **Whittemore**, was born in Portsmouth 28 February 1779 and died there 3 November 1855 at 76 years of age.

Thomas **Treadwell** and Anna **Passmore** had the following children:

1368	i.	Thomas Passmore[9] **Treadwell**.[1588] Died young.
1369	ii.	Elizabeth **Treadwell**.[1589]
1370	iii.	Thomas Passmore **Treadwell**.[1590]
1371	iv.	Mary Ann **Treadwell**.[1591]
1372	v.	Olive **Treadwell**.[1592]
1373	vi.	William Pepperrell **Treadwell**.[1593]
1374	vii.	Samuel Passmore **Treadwell**.[1594]
1375	viii.	Catherine Simpson **Treadwell**.[1595]
1376	ix.	Frances Dearborn **Treadwell**.[1596]

1013. **Samuel**[8] **Treadwell** (Nathaniel[7], Thomas[6], Sarah[5] **Goodhue**, William[4], Sarah[3] **Whipple**, Elder John[2], Matthew[1])[1597] was born in Ipswich, Mass. in 1781 and died in 1817 in Portsmouth, N.H. at 36 years of age. He married **Abigail Petergro** in Portsmouth 9 January 1809. Abigail died after January 1817.[1598]

Samuel **Treadwell** and Abigail **Petergro** had the following children:
1377	i.	Lucy Ann[9] **Treadwell**.[1599]
1378	ii.	Susan **Treadwell**.[1600]
1379	iii.	Elizabeth **Treadwell**.[1601]

1014. **Elizabeth**[8] **Treadwell** (Nathaniel[7], Thomas[6], Sarah[5] **Goodhue**, William[4], Sarah[3] **Whipple**, Elder John[2], Matthew[1])[1602] was born in Ipswich, Mass. 18 November 1783 and died either 29 March or 28 April 1853 at 69 years of age. She married **John Chapman Jr.** in Ipswich 30 September 1804. John,[1603] son of John **Chapman** and Mary **Woodbury**, was born in Ipswich 15 January 1781 and died there 9 April 1857 at 76 years of age.

Elizabeth **Treadwell** and John **Chapman Jr.** had the following children born in Ipswich:
1380	i.	Sally Treadwell[9] **Chapman**[1604] was born 13 June 1805.
1381	ii.	Elizabeth **Chapman**[1605] was born 1 February 1807.
1382	iii.	Hannah **Chapman**[1606] was born 30 November 1808.
1383	iv.	Mary Ann **Chapman**[1607] was born 1 October 1810.
1384	v.	Susan **Chapman**[1608] was born 15 April 1813.
1385	vi.	John **Chapman**[1609] was born 1 March 1815.
1386	vii.	Mehitable **Chapman**[1610] was born 4 July 1817.
1387	viii.	Lucy **Chapman**[1611] was born 24 February 1819.
1388	ix.	William **Chapman**[1612] was born 12 October 1821.
1389	x.	Warren **Chapman**[1613] was born 8 January 1824.
1390	xi.	Thomas Treadwell **Chapman**[1614] was born 24 June 1832.

1015. **John**[8] **Treadwell** (Nathaniel[7], Thomas[6], Sarah[5] **Goodhue**, William[4], Sarah[3] **Whipple**, Elder John[2], Matthew[1])[1615] was born in Ipswich, Mass. 27 February 1786 and died 19 December 1853 in Boston, Mass. at 67 years of age. He was a hatter and married **Hannah Jenkins** in Portsmouth, N.H. 28 June 1805. Hannah was born in Kittery, Maine 24 April 1785 and died 24 April 1864 in San Francisco, Calif. at 79 years of age.[1616]

John **Treadwell** and Hannah **Jenkins** had the following children:
1391	i.	Joseph Jenkins[9] **Treadwell**[1617].
1392	ii.	Sarah Elizabeth **Treadwell**[1618].
1393	iii.	Charles Thomas **Treadwell**[1619].

1017. **William**[8] **Treadwell** (Nathaniel[7], Thomas[6], Sarah[5] **Goodhue**, William[4], Sarah[3] **Whipple**, Elder John[2], Matthew[1])[1620] was born in Ipswich, Mass. 10 March 1791 and died there 30 September 1870 at 79 years of age. William was a mariner and married **Welcome Seward** in Ipswich 23 August 1814. Welcome,[1621] daughter of John **Seward** and Rebecca **Swett**, was born in Ipswich 10 December 1792 and died there 2 June 1883 at 90 years of age.

William **Treadwell** and Welcome **Seward** had the following children:
1394	i.	William Francis[9] **Treadwell**[1622].

1395	ii.	Abigail **Treadwell**[1623] was born 7 August 1817.
1396	iii.	John Seward **Treadwell**[1624] was born 14 September 1819
1397	iv.	Elizabeth Stone **Treadwell**[1625] was born 14 March 1822.
1398	v.	Rebecca H. **Treadwell**[1626] was born 9 April 1824.
1399	vi.	Lucy Jane **Treadwell**[1627] was born 8 November 1825.
1400	vii.	Isaac Cushing **Treadwell**[1628].
1401	viii.	Francis S. **Treadwell**[1629] was born 24 June 1831.
1402	ix.	Charles Thomas **Treadwell**[1630] was born 30 June 1833..

1018. Hannah[8] **Treadwell** (Nathaniel[7], Thomas[6], Sarah[5] **Goodhue**, William[4], Sarah[3] **Whipple**, Elder John[2], Matthew[1])[1631] was born in Ipswich, Mass. 1 September 1793 and died 18 September 1888 in Newton Highlands, Mass. at 95 years of age. She married twice. (1) **Joshua Burnham** in Ipswich 12 November 1812. He died in 1851, probably in California, at 61 years of age.[1632] (2) **Samuel Albert Lake**.

Hannah **Treadwell** and Joshua **Burnham** had the following children:
1403	i.	Elizabeth[9] **Burnham**[1633].
1404	ii.	Mary Elizabeth **Burnham**[1634].
1405	iii.	George William **Burnham**[1635].
1406	iv.	Sarah **Burnham**[1636].
1407	v.	John **Burnham**[1637].

1020. Sarah[8] **Basford** (Jonathan[7], Elizabeth[6] **Goodhue**, Jonathan[5], William[4], Sarah[3] **Whipple**, Elder John[2], Matthew[1])[1638] was born 6 April 1772 and died before 1838 in Greensville, Mercer Co., Penn. She married **Joseph Mecham** in Canaan, N.H. 6 September 1801. Joseph,[1639] son of Samuel **Mecham** and Phebe **Main**, was born in Canaan 15 June 1780 and died in 1845 in Nauvoo, Ill. at 65 years of age.

Sarah **Basford** and Joseph **Mecham** had the following children:
1408	i.	Phebe[9] **Mecham**[1640] was born in Trenton, N.H. about 1802 and died in 1852 at 50 years of age. She married Jeremiah **Mecham**. Phebe and Jeremiah were cousins.
1409	ii.	Miriam **Mecham**[1641] was born in Thornton, N.H. about 1804 and died in Cincinnati, Ohio. She married Arza **Taylor**.
+ 1410	iii.	Joseph L. **Mecham** was born 1 February 1806.
1411	iv.	Samuel **Mecham**[1642] was born in Thornton 14 November 1807 and died 18 November 1883 at 76 years of age. He married Mehitable **Knapp**.
1412	v.	Jonathan **Mecham**[1643] was born in Thornton 16 February 1810 and died in 1878 at 68 years of age. He married Eleanor **Lavery**.
1413	vi.	Susan **Mecham**[1644] was born in Thornton about 1812.

1021. Jesse W.[8] **Kimball** (Isaac[7], John[6], Isaac[5], Sarah[4] **Goodhue**, Sarah[3] **Whipple**, Elder John[2], Matthew[1])[1645] birth date unknown, died in 1817. He married **Sarah Kimball**,[1646] daughter of Jesse **Kimball** and Elizabeth **Roelofson**. She was born in 1796. Jesse and Sarah were cousins. (See 1023)

Jesse W. **Kimball** and Sarah **Kimball** had the following children:
| 1414 | i. | John[9] **Kimball**[1647] was born in 1813. |
| 1415 | ii. | Charles Jackson **Kimball**[1648] was born in 1815 and married an unnamed person. |

1022. Mary⁸ Kimball (Jesse⁷, John⁶, Isaac⁵, Sarah⁴ **Goodhue**, Sarah³ **Whipple**, Elder John², Matthew¹)[1649] was born in 1794 and married **James Gadis**.

Mary **Kimball** and James **Gadis** had the following children:
1416   i.   William⁹ **Gadis**[1650] was born in 1825.
1417   ii. Elizabeth **Gadis**[1651] was born in 1827.

1023. Sarah⁸ Kimball (Jesse⁷, John⁶, Isaac⁵, Sarah⁴ **Goodhue**, Sarah³ **Whipple**, Elder John², Matthew¹)[1652] was born in 1796 and married twice. (1) **Jesse W. Kimball**.[1653] (See No. 1021.) (2) **Hellum Jones** who died in 1897.[1654]

Jesse W. **Kimball** and Sarah **Kimball** had the following children:
1414   i.   John⁹ **Kimball**[1655] was born in 1813.
1415   ii. Charles Jackson **Kimball**[1656] was born in 1815. He married an unnamed person.

Sarah **Kimball** and Hellum **Jones** had the following children:
1418   iii. Alfred **Jones**[1657] was born in 1832.
1419   iv. Enoch **Jones**[1658] was born in 1835.
1420   v.   Smith **Jones**[1659] was born in 1838.

1024. Elisha⁸ Kimball (Jesse⁷, John⁶, Isaac⁵, Sarah⁴ **Goodhue**, Sarah³ **Whipple**, Elder John², Matthew¹)[1660] was born in 1798 and married **Mary Boyle**.

Elisha **Kimball** and Mary **Boyle** had the following children:
1421   i.   William B.⁹ **Kimball**[1661].
+ 1422   ii. Jesse C. **Kimball** was born in 1831.

1027. Easter⁸ Kimball (Jesse⁷, John⁶, Isaac⁵, Sarah⁴ **Goodhue**, Sarah³ **Whipple**, Elder John², Matthew¹)[1662] was born 15 October 1802 and died 17 October 1871 in Greenwood Co., Kans. at 69 years of age. She married **Samuel Miller** in Princeton, Gibson Co., Ind. 18 March 1819. Samuel was born in Lincoln Co., N.C. 20 February 1799 and died 27 October 1871 in Greenwood Co. at 72 years of age.[1663]

Easter **Kimball** and Samuel **Miller** had the following children:
1423   i.   William Hiram⁹ **Miller**[1664] was born in 1820 and died aft 1868 at 48 years of age. He married Lucinda **Frankes**.
1424   ii.   Isaac **Miller**[1665] was born in 1822 and died in 1859 at 37 years of age.
+ 1425   iii. Eli **Miller** was born in 1823.
1426   iv.   Mary **Miller**[1666] was born in 1826 and died in 1845 at 19 years of age.
1427   v.   Sarah **Miller**[1667] was born in 1828 and died in 1829 at one year of age.
1428   vi.   John **Miller**[1668] was born in 1830 and died in 1845 at 15 years of age.
1429   vii. Martha Jane **Miller**[1669] was born in 1833 and died in 1857 at 24 years of age. She married (_) **Chandler**.
1430   viii. Elizabeth **Miller**[1670] was born in 1835 and died in 1853 at 18 years of age. She married William M. **Glenn**.
1431   ix.   Paulina **Miller**[1671] was born in 1838.
+ 1432   x.   Elisha D. **Miller** was born 23 November 1841.
1433   xi.   Levi W. **Miller**[1672] was born in 1844 and married Rachel Ann **Dillon**.

1028. Isaac⁸ Kimball (Jesse⁷, John⁶, Isaac⁵, Sarah⁴ **Goodhue**, Sarah³ **Whipple**, Elder John², Matthew¹)[1673] was born in 1804 and married **Phyllis Low** who was born in 1796.[1674]

Isaac **Kimball** and Phyllis **Low** had the following children:

    1434   i.   Jesse[9] **Kimball**[1675] was born in 1829.
    1435   ii. William **Kimball**[1676] was born in 1831.
    1436   iii. Cynthia **Kimball**[1677] was born in 1832.
    1437   iv. Sarah Elizabeth **Kimball**[1678] was born in 1838.

1030. Cynthia[8] **Kimball** (Jesse[7], John[6], Isaac[5], Sarah[4] **Goodhue**, Sarah[3] **Whipple**, Elder John[2], Matthew[1])[1679] was born in 1809 and married **Ephraim Knowles** who was born in 1797.[1680]

Cynthia **Kimball** and Ephraim **Knowles** had the following children:

    1438   i.   Enos[9] **Knowles**[1681] was born in 1825.
    1439   ii. John W. **Knowles**[1682] was born in 1827.
    1440   iii. Francis J. **Knowles**[1683] was born in 1829.
    1441   iv. Louisa **Knowles**[1684] was born in 1831.
    1442   v.   Martha **Knowles**[1685] was born in 1833.
    1443   vi. Melissa **Knowles**[1686] was born in 1835.

1032. Walter[8] **Kimble** (Jacob[7] **Kimball**, Jacob[6], Jacob[5], Sarah[4] **Goodhue**, Sarah[3] **Whipple**, Elder John[2], Matthew[1])[1687] was born in Paupack, Pike Co., Penn. 9 June 1808 and died 3 February 1883 in Collins, N.Y. at 74 years of age. He married **Phebe Southwick** 10 October 1832. Phebe,[1688] daughter of Job **Southwick** and Sophia **Smith**, was born 23 February 1817 and died 26 April 1883 at 66 years of age.

Walter **Kimble** and Phebe **Southwick** had the following child:

 + 1444   i.   Mary Elizabeth[9] **Kimble** was born 5 April 1845.

1034. Julia Ann[8] **Stevens** (Roswell[7], Hepsibah[6] **Kilham**, Abigail[5] **Kimball**, Sarah[4] **Goodhue**, Sarah[3] **Whipple**, Elder John[2], Matthew[1])[1689] was born in Mt. Pleasant, Great Upper Canada 17 February 1830 and died 3 March 1907 in Lewisville, Jefferson Co., Idaho at 77 years of age. She married **William Alexander Fausett** 15 April 1846. William,[1690] son of John McKee **Fausett** and Margaret **Smith**, was born in Montgomery Co., Ill. 11 April 1830 and died in February 1898 in Wellington, Carbon Co., Utah at 67 years of age.

Julia Ann **Stevens** and William Alexander **Fausett** had the following child:

 + 1445   i.   Affalona Galia[9] **Fausett** was born 13 November 1853.

1035. William[8] **Stevens** (Roswell[7], Hepsibah[6] **Kilham**, Abigail[5] **Kimball**, Sarah[4] **Goodhue**, Sarah[3] **Whipple**, Elder John[2], Matthew[1])[1691] was born 14 February 1832 and died 22 May 1923 in Holden, Utah at 91 years of age. He married **Elizabeth Seeley** in Pleasant Grove, Utah Co., Utah 12 October 1854. Elizabeth was born in Canada 24 August 1837 and. died 21 March 1916 in Holden at 78 years of age.[1692]

William **Stevens** and Elizabeth **Seeley** had the following child:

 + 1446   i.   Marinda Alice[9] **Stevens** was born 31 August 1868.

1036. Samuel[8] **Goodhue** (Samuel[7], Samuel[6], George[5], Joseph[4], Sarah[3] **Whipple**, Elder John[2], Matthew[1])[1693] was born in Newburyport, Mass. in 1805 and died in 1866 at 61 years of age. He married **Mary Columbia Williams**.

Samuel **Goodhue** and Mary Columbia **Williams** had the following child:

 + 1447   i.   Francis Abbot[9] **Goodhue** was born in 1850.

1037. **Elizabeth**[8] **Upham** (Eleanor[7] **Knowlton**, Daniel[6], Robert[5], Marjory (Margery)[4] **Goodhue**, Sarah[3] **Whipple**, Elder John[2], Matthew[1])[1694] was born 8 March 1786 and married **Thomas Baird Dickson** 25 February 1820. Thomas was born in Colchester Co., N.S. 16 March 1792 and died there 7 May 1872 at 80 years of age.[1695]

Elizabeth **Upham** and Thomas Baird **Dickson** had the following children:

+ 1448   i.   Mary[9] **Dickson** was born abt 1820.
   1449   ii. Nathan Knowlton **Dickson**[1696] was born abt 1823 and died 23 August 1900 at 77 years of age. He married Elizabeth **Stiles**.

1038. **Polly**[8] **Rand** (Solomon[7], Deborah[6] **Dodge**, Margery[5] **Knowlton**, Marjory (Margery)[4] **Goodhue**, Sarah[3] **Whipple**, Elder John[2], Matthew[1])[1697] was born in Rindge, N.H. 14 March 1790 and died after 1823 in Jaffrey, N.H. She married **James Bowers** 4 January 1814. James was born in Rindge 19 March 1781 and died there abt. 1835.[1698]

Polly **Rand** and James **Bowers** had the following child:

+ 1450   i.   Nancy Mathilda[9] **Bowers** was born 29 November 1823.

1043. **Abigail**[8] **Knowlton** (Nathan[7], Joseph[6], Joseph[5], Marjory (Margery)[4] **Goodhue**, Sarah[3] **Whipple**, Elder John[2], Matthew[1])[1699] was born 13 March 1790 and died 15 December 1874 in Auburn, Mass. at 84 years of age. She married **Col. Jonathan Stone** (see No. 959) in Auburn 24 May 1814. Jonathan,[1700] son of Lt. Jonathan **Stone** and Sarah (Sally) **Hall**, was born in Auburn, Mass. 4 April 1793 and died in April 1845 at 52 years of age. He was lost at sea. Jonathan and Abigail were fifth cousins. Jonathan descended from Elder John Whipple through his daughter Mary; Abigail through his daughter Sarah.

Col. Jonathan **Stone** and Abigail **Knowlton** had the following children:

   1333   i.   Oliver[9] **Stone**[1701] was born in Auburn 22 August 1815 and died 4 February 1863 in Worcester, Mass. at 47 years of age. He married twice. (1) Mary **Cudworth** 13 April 1842. (2) Melinda C. **Hook** 22 April 1856.
   1334   ii.   Joseph Jackson **Stone**[1702] was born 26 December 1816 and died 2 October 1833 at 16 years of age.
   1335   iii. Prescott Brainbridge **Stone**[1703] was born 13 July 1819 and died 21 May 1886 at 66 years of age. He married Susan Platts **Crandall** 27 July 1850.
   1336   iv. Sarah Lucinda **Stone**[1704] was born 1 February 1822 and died 4 August 1885 at 63 years of age. She married George W. **Barnard**.
   1337   v.   Lewis Cutting **Stone**[1705] was born 22 April 1823 and died 6 September 1900 at 77 years of age. He married Abbie Almira (Divoll) **Stockwell**.
   1338   vi. Emory **Stone**[1706] was born 9 March 1827 and died 5 March 1918 at 90 years of age. He married Catherine **Shurtleff** 5 September 1847.
+ 1339 vii. Marshall Maynard **Stone** was born 19 April 1828.

1053. **Benjamin**[8] **Goodhue** (Ebenezer[7], Ebenezer[6], John[5], John[4], Sarah[3] **Whipple**, Elder John[2], Matthew[1])[1707] was born 17 July 1818 and died 24 October 1889 at 71 years of age. He married **Caroline B. Andrews** 23 November 1841.

Benjamin **Goodhue** and Caroline B. **Andrews** had the following child:

+ 1451   i.   Andrew Issachar[9] **Goodhue** was born 19 January 1848.

NINTH GENERATION

1059. Jacob⁹ Pillsbury (John Hale⁸, Rev. Edmund⁷, Moses⁶, Moses⁵, Susanna⁴ **Worth**, Susannah³ **Whipple**, Elder John², Matthew¹)[1708] was born in S. Hampton, Rockingham Co., N.H. 25 September 1791 and died 9 August 1850 in Palmyra, Somerset Co., Maine at 58 years of age. He married **Betsy Currier** in 1815 and represented Wolfboro in the New Hampshire legislature.

Jacob **Pillsbury** and Betsy **Currier** had the following children:

1452	i.	Louisa¹⁰ Pillsbury[1709] was born in 1816 and died in 1819 at 3 years of age.
1453	ii.	Jacob **Pillsbury**[1710] was born in 1819 and died that year.
1454	iii.	Louisa **Pillsbury**[1711] was born in 1821 and married John **Davis**. She died in 1849.
1455	iv.	Sarah **Pillsbury**[1712] was born in 1822 and married William **Leavitt**.
1456	v.	Lydia **Pillsbury**[1713] was born in 1825 and died in 1852 at 27 years of age. She married William **French** in 1847.
+ 1457	vi.	James **Pillsbury** was born 21 December 1826.
1458	vii.	Elvira **Pillsbury** was born in 1828 and married George **Stinson** 26 July 1848.
1459	viii.	John C. **Pillsbury**[1714] was born in 1832 and married Lizzie **Wedgwood**.
1460	ix.	Lois **Pillsbury**[1715] was born in 1834 and married Daniel **Tripp**. She died in 1852.
1461	x.	George **Pillsbury**[1716] was born in 1837 and married twice. (1) Ellen **Adams**. (2) Clara **Rackliffe**.

1060. Edmund⁹ Pillsbury (John Hale⁸, Rev. Edmund⁷, Moses⁶, Moses⁵, Susanna⁴ **Worth**, Susannah³ **Whipple**, Elder John², Matthew¹)[1717] was born in 1793 and died in 1853 in S. Hampton, N.H. at 60 years of age. He married **Eliza D. Barnard** 1 December 1819.

Edmund **Pillsbury** and Eliza D. **Barnard** had the following children:

1462	i.	Eliza¹⁰ Pillsbury[1718] was born in 1821 and died in 1891 at 70 years of age. She married Andrew **Fitts**.
1463	ii.	Oliver Perry **Pillsbury**[1719] was born in Newport, Penobscot Co., Maine 2 February 1826 and died 24 September 1890 in Milwaukee, Wisc. at 64 years of age. He married twice. (1) Catherine Stanwood **Benjamin**. (2) Vesta Ellen **Cutter**. He was a railway contractor in Ohio and Kentucky, mayor of Muskegon, Ohio in 1876, moved to Milwaukie in 1882 where he was president of the Land Log & Lumber Co. His obituary appears in the *Milwaukie Sentinel* of 25 Sept. 1890.
1464	iii.	Louisa **Pillsbury**[1720] was born in 1828 and died in 1849 at 21 years of age.
1465	iv.	John J. **Pillsbury**[1721] was born in 1828 and died in 1889 at 61 years of age. He married twice. (1) Nancy **Whitney**. (2) Rose **Whitney**.

1066. Josiah Webster⁹ Pillsbury (Oliver⁸, Parker⁷, Moses⁶, Moses⁵, Susanna⁴ **Worth**, Susannah³ **Whipple**, Elder John², Matthew¹) was born 20 March 1811 and married **Elizabeth Dinsmoor** 1 June 1841. Elizabeth, daughter of William **Dinsmoor** and Elizabeth **Barnet**, was born in Windham, N.H. 15 November 1813 and died 26 October 1894 at 80 years of age. He was graduated from Dartmouth in 1840, was a teacher and farmer, and ardent abolitionist.

Josiah Webster **Pillsbury** and Elizabeth **Dinsmoor** had the following child:
+ 1466   i. Albert Enoch[10] **Pillsbury** was born 19 August 1849.

1068. **Zacheus**[9] Hale (Zacheus[8], Joseph[7], Abigail W.[6] **Pillsbury**, Moses[5], Susanna[4] **Worth**, Susannah[3] **Whipple**, Elder John[2], Matthew[1])[1722] was born in Hudson (incorporated as Nottingham West in 1746), N.H. 27 March 1802 and died 2 August 1869 at 67 years of age. He married **Clarissa Harden**. Clarissa,[1723] daughter of John **Harden** and Jenny **Stetson**, was born in E. Bridgewater, Mass. 1 January 1804 and died there 16 September at 59 years of age. Both Zacheus and Clarissa were buried at Whitman, Mass.

Zacheus **Hale** and Clarissa **Harden** had the following children:
1467   i. Zacheus[10] **Hale**[1724] was born 13 July 1827 and buried in E. Bridgewater 10 October 1838.
1468   ii. Clarissa **Hale**[1725] was born in Riley, Oxford Co., Maine 11 November 1828 and died in 1905 at 76 years of age. She was buried in Whitman's Colebrook Cemetery. She married George **Luzarder** in E. Bridgewater 26 December 1848.
1469   iii. Nahun C. **Hale**[1726] was born in Newbry, Oxford Co., Maine 31 March 1830.
+ 1470   iv. Jane Stetson **Hale** was born 23 December 1831.
+ 1471   v. Snome Elizabeth **Hale** was born 10 September 1836.
1472   vi. Marcus Morton **Hale**[1727] was born 6 July 1839 and lived at the Old Soldiers' Home in Chelsea, Mass. in his later years.
1473   vii. Henry Z. **Hale**[1728] was born 22 July 1841.

1073. **Deborah Towne**[9] Brickett (Bernard[8], Bernard[7], Susanna[6] **Pillsbury**, Moses[5], Susanna[4] **Worth**, Susannah[3] **Whipple**, Elder John[2], Matthew[1]) was born in Haverhill, Mass. 14 July 1807 and died there 21 August 1843 at 36 years of age. She married **Thomas Dodge** in Haverhill 2 September 1830. Thomas, son of Thomas **Dodge** and Elizabeth **Manning**, was born in Ipswich, Mass. 28 January 1803 and died 29 May 1875 in Haverhill at 72 years of age.

Deborah Towne **Brickett** and Thomas **Dodge** had the following child:
+ 1474   i. Frank Brickett[10] **Dodge** was born 4 February 1835.

1076. **Dr. Hiram Pillsbury**[9] Hoyt (Judith[8] **Pillsbury**, Caleb[7], Caleb[6], Caleb[5], Susanna[4] **Worth**, Susannah[3] **Whipple**, Elder John[2], Matthew[1])[1729] was born in Danville, Caledonia Co., Vt. abt 1806 and died 15 December 1880 at 74 years of age. He married twice. (1) **Irene Sayles Randall** in Lyndon, Caldeonia Co., Vt. 11 April 1839. Irene,[1730] daughter of Job **Randall** and Irene **Sayles**, was born in Smithfield, R.I. 27 February 1803 and died 1 October 1844 at 41 years of age. (2) **Jemima M. Chesley** in Sutton, Vt. 4 October 1846. Jemima,[1731] daughter of Joel **Chesley** and Betsy **Jenness**, was born 16 October 1826 and died 10 December 1896 in Burlington, Chittenden Co., Vt. at 70 years of age. Hiram, Irene, and Jemima are buried at Lyndon Center, Vt. Jemima's mother's maiden name may have been Jenners.

Dr. Hiram Pillsbury **Hoyt** and Jemima M. **Chesley** had the following children:
1475   i. Sarah Randall[10] **Hoyt**[1732] married Austin **Bean**.
+ 1476   ii. Viola Irene **Hoyt** was born 5 December 1849.

1082. **Thomas**^9 **Blanchard Jr.** (Lois^8 **Burt**, Abiah^7 **Mooar**, Abiah^6 **Hill**, Judith^5 **Bucknam**, Judith (Jude)^4 **Worth**, Susannah^3 **Whipple**, Elder John^2, Matthew^1)[1733] was born in Andover, Mass. 1 October 1786 and married **Rebecca Gardner** 8 December 1808.

Thomas **Blanchard** Jr. and Rebecca **Gardner** had the following children:

1477	i.	Jasper P.^10 **Blanchard**[1734] was born in 1809.
1478	ii.	Allen G. **Blanchard** was born 12 August 1811.[1735]
1479	iii.	Emily M. **Blanchard**[1736] was born in 1814.
1480	iv.	Louisa M. **Blanchard**[1737] was born in 1816.

1086. **John Burt**^9 **Blanchard** (Lois^8 **Burt**, Abiah^7 **Mooar**, Abiah^6 **Hill**, Judith^5 **Bucknam**, Judith (Jude)^4 **Worth**, Susannah^3 **Whipple**, Elder John^2, Matthew^1)[1738] was born in Danville, Vt. in 1792 and died 20 December 1872 in St. Charles, Kane Co., Ill. at 80 years of age. He married **Lucy A. Thurber** in New York State in 1819. Lucy was born in 1794 and died in 1858 at 64 years of age.

John Burt **Blanchard** and Lucy A. **Thurber** had the following children:

1481	i.	Ursula^10 **Blanchard**.[1739]
1482	ii.	Fidelia **Blanchard**[1740].
1483	iii.	Louise **Blanchard**[1741] was born in 1823.
1484	iv.	Alex **Blanchard**[1742] was born in 1825.
1485	v.	Horatio **Blanchard**[1743] was born in 1826.
1486	vi.	Edward S. **Blanchard**[1744] was born in 1827.
1487	vii.	Elizabeth **Blanchard**[1745] was born in 1830.

1088. **Salma**^9 **Blanchard** (Lois^8 **Burt**, Abiah^7 **Mooar**, Abiah^6 **Hill**, Judith^5 **Bucknam**, Judith (Jude)^4 **Worth**, Susannah^3 **Whipple**, Elder John^2, Matthew^1)[1746] was born 24 September 1798 and died in 1857 in Wisconsin at 58 years of age. He married **Belinda (__)** before 1830.

Salma **Blanchard** and Belinda (__) had the following children:

1488	i.	Rodolphus^10 **Blanchard**[1747] was born in 1830.
1489	ii.	Jasper **Blanchard**[1748] was born in 1834.
1490	iii.	Thomas **Blanchard**[1749] was born in 1838.
1491	iv.	Rothland **Blanchard**[1750] was born in 1840.
1492	v.	Aaron **Blanchard**[1751] was born in 1842.

1089. **Lucy**^9 **Blanchard** (Lois^8 **Burt**, Abiah^7 **Mooar**, Abiah^6 **Hill**, Judith^5 **Bucknam**, Judith (Jude)^4 **Worth**, Susannah^3 **Whipple**, Elder John^2, Matthew^1)[1752] was born in Danville, Vt. 13 May 1801 and died 18 January 1878 in Lowell, Cherokee Co., Kans. at 76 years of age. She married **Dr. James Safford Hibbard** in June 1820. James,[1753] son of Ithamer **Hibbard** and Hannah **Wood**, was born in Fairhaven, Rutland Co., Vt. in August 1794 and died 12 September 1863 in Amesville, Athens Co., Ohio at 69 years of age. He was buried at Amesville. He practiced medicine for many years in Meigs and Athens County, Ohio and was declared insane on 8 June 1863. His son Ithamar was made his guardian. After his death, his family moved to Kansas.

Lucy **Blanchard** and Dr. James Safford **Hibbard** had the following children:

1493	i.	Thomas Birt^10 **Hibbard**[1754] was born in Sackets Harbor, Jefferson Co., N.Y. 1 December 1821 and died 26 April 1902 at 80 years of age. He married Sarah Mariah Goss **Porter** 13 August 1848.

1494	ii.	Olivia Sophia A. **Hibbard**[1755] was born in Athens, Ohio 16 September 1824 and died 29 July 1902 at 77 years of age. She married Henry **Myers** 12 April 1862.
1495	iii.	Ithamar Clark **Hibbard**[1756] was born in Ohio 11 May 1827 and married Celena L. (__).
1496	iv.	Henry **Hibbard**[1757] was born in Ohio 30 September 1829 and died 24 February 1907 at 77 years of age. He married Eliza S. (__).
1497	v.	Lucy H. **Hibbard**[1758] was born in Ohio in 1832.
1498	vi.	Juliette **Hibbard**[1759] was born in Ohio in 1834 and married Lorence **Lyons** 13 October 1859.
1499	vii.	Louisa **Hibbard**[1760] was born in Ohio in 1836.
1500	viii.	James Safford **Hibbard** Jr.[1761] was born in Ohio 8 October 1838 and died 31 July 1844 at 5 years of age.
1501	ix.	Mary A. **Hibbard**[1762] was born in Ohio in 1840 and married Jonathan A. **Gibbons** 6 September 1862.
1502	x.	Rudolph Adolph **Hibbard**[1763] was born in Ohio 6 July 1845 and died 15 October 1917 at 72 years of age. He married Margaret M. (__).

1090. Aaron[9] **Blanchard** (Lois[8] **Burt**, Abiah[7] **Mooar**, Abiah[6] **Hill**, Judith[5] **Bucknam**, Judith (Jude)[4] **Worth**, Susannah[3] **Whipple**, Elder John[2], Matthew[1])[1764] was born in Danville, Vt. 5 March 1804 and died 2 August 1886 in St. Charles, Kane Co., Ill. at 82 years of age and was buried in St. Charles' North Cemetery. He married **Annie Stonnor** 22 May 1828. Annie,[1765] daughter of J. **Stonnor**, was born in Madison Co., N.Y. 20 July 1809 and died 28 March 1891 in St. Charles at 81 years of age. She is buried in Section M., Aisle 10, Lot 46, Grave 8 of the North Cemetery.

Aaron **Blanchard** and Annie **Stonnor** had the following children:

+ 1503	i.	Zara[10] **Blanchard** was born 20 September 1829.
1504	ii.	Gustavus P. **Blanchard**[1766] was born in Cayuga Co., N.Y. 10 August 1831 and died 15 February 1900 in St. Charles at 68 years of age. He married Lucy A. **Sunderland** in St. Charles 12 October 1891. Lucy was born in 1839 and died in 1919 at 80 years of age.[1767] He was a carpenter and well driller and they had no children.
+ 1505	iii.	George Adelbert **Blanchard** was born 14 May 1834.
1506	iv.	Nelson L. **Blanchard**[1768] was born in Cleveland, Ohio 24 December 1837 and died 18 February 1862 in Alexandria, Va. at 24 years of age, apparently from service during the Civil War. He married Susan **Whipple** in Kane Co., Ill. 12 October 1861. She married (2) George L. **Renwick** 14 September 1863.[1769]

1091. Sophia[9] **Blanchard** (Lois[8] **Burt**, Abiah[7] **Mooar**, Abiah[6] **Hill**, Judith[5] **Bucknam**, Judith (Jude)[4] **Worth**, Susannah[3] **Whipple**, Elder John[2], Matthew[1])[1770] was born in Vermont 24 April 1809 and died 8 May 1899 at 90 years of age. She married **David Maynard Hagedon** in Henderson, Jefferson Co., N.Y. 1 February 1825. David was born in New York State in 1804 and died 24 December 1871 at 67 years of age.[1771] Sophia and David supposedly had 11 children; seven are listed here.

Sophia **Blanchard** and David Maynard **Hagedon** had the following children:

1507	i.	Jane L.[10] **Hagedon**[1772] was born in New York State 28 December 1830 and died 14 August 1853 at 22 years of age.
1508	ii.	Lucy **Hagedon**[1773] was born in Ohio abt. 1832 and married John

Holland 1 July 1854.

+ 1509   iii. Datus W. **Hagedon** was born abt 1834.

1510   iv. David Maynard **Hagedon** Jr.[1774] was born in Ohio abt 1837 and married Juliette **Dale** 4 April 1863.

1511   v. Louisa **Hagedon**[1775] was born in Michigan abt 1841 and married Henry F. **Fenton** 4 April 1866.

1512   vi. George S. **Hagedon**[1776] was born in Michigan in February 1848 and died 10 December 1871 at 23 years of age.

1513   vii. Clara **Hagedon**[1777] was born in Michigan abt 1850.

1092. **William Brown**[9] **Williams** (Hannah Stone[8] **Brown**, Samuel[7], William[6], Martha[5] **Whipple**, Maj. John[4], Capt. John[3], Elder John[2], Matthew[1])[1778] was born in Boston, Mass. 10 November 1835 and died 4 July 1906 in Dorchester, Mass. at 70 years of age. He married **Margaret Forrester Boak** 10 October 1871. Margaret,[1779] daughter of Sir Robert James **Boak** and Matilda Sophia **Anderson**, was born in Halifax, N.S. Canada 9 September 1848 and died 13 October 1893 in Gloucester, Mass. at 45 years of age.

William Brown **Williams** and Margaret Forrester **Boak** had the following child:

+ 1514   i. Elsie Boak[10] **Williams** was born 5 January 1882.

1099. **Susan Poor**[9] **Pearson** (Nathaniel[8], Sarah[7] **Gerrish**, Katherine[6] **Brown**, Martha[5] **Whipple**, Maj. John[4], Capt. John[3], Elder John[2], Matthew[1])[1780] was born in Newbury, Mass. 15 July 1824 and died there 10 November 1906 at 82 years of age. She married **Lorenzo Dow Stevens** in Newbury 1 May 1845. Lorenzo,[1781] son of Wiliam **Stevens** and Harriet **Nichols**, was born in West Newbury 2 September 1821 and died there 20 February 1911 at 89 years of age. There is a conflict with Lorenzo's birth. His marriage licence states he was 22 on 1 May 1845 suggesting a birth year of 1823. His obituary states he was 89 years, 5 months, 18 days old when he died 20 Feb. 1911. This indicates a birth year of 1821. Both are buried in West Newbury's Bridge Street Cemetery.

Susan Poor **Pearson** and Lorenzo Dow **Stevens** had the following children born in West Newbury:

+ 1515   i. George Nichols[10] **Stevens** was born 5 December 1845.

1516   ii. Hannah Elizabeth **Stevens**[1782] was born 1 September 1847 and married Thomas **Knight**.

1517   iii. Laura **Stevens**[1783] was born 4 April 1849 and married John A. **Bradley**.

1518   iv. Westley True **Stevens**[1784] was born 25 September 1851 and married Lizzie **Danforsth**.

1519   v. Emeline S. **Stevens**[1785] was born 25 October 1853 and married Lewis **Knight**.

1520   vi. Cora Etta **Stevens**[1786] was born 28 May 1861 and married John H. **Currier**.

1521   vii. Florence Augustus **Stevens**[1787] was born 18 June 1863 and married George **Emery**.

1522   viii. Susan Carrie **Stevens**[1788] was born 19 July 1866 and died 1 October 1887 at 21 years of age.

1100. **Grace Adams**[9] **Rogers** (George[8], John[7], Rev. John[6], Susanna[5] **Whipple**,

Maj. John[4], Capt. John[3], Elder John[2], Matthew[1])[1789] was born in Boston, Mass. 22 February 1856 and died there 22 September 1936 at 80 years of age. She married **Joseph Daniels Leland** in Boston 5 November 1879. Joseph,[1790] son of Joseph Daniels **Leland** and Mary Plimpton **Adams**, was born in Boston 9 July 1854 and died 17 January 1887 in Brookline, Norfolk Co., Mass. at 32 years of age. Grace traced her line back to rev. John and Elizabeth (Gould) Rogers of Dedham, Essex Co., England. She was schooled by private tutors at Miss Willbasby's School and in schools in Europe where she lived for several years. Owing to ill health she was unable to enjoy many activities outside her home life. She gave her time and money to the Family Welfare Society, the Salvation Army, and the Red Cross. She probably didn't know it but she and Clara Barton, founder of the American Red Cross, were sixth cousins; Elder John and Susanna Whipple being their common ancestors. She volunteered with organizations working for the blind and other charities. She was elected an annual member of the New England Historic Genealogical Society 24 June 1930. Joseph was a member of the firm of Leland, Rice, & Company, wholesale clothiers.

Grace Adams **Rogers** and Joseph Daniels **Leland** had the following children:

1523	i.	Amory[10] **Leland**.[1791] He earned an A.B. degree from Harvard in 1906 and was living in Franklin, Mass. at the time of his mother's death in 1936.
1524	ii.	Elizabeth Carter **Leland**.[1792] Elizabeth was unmarried and living in Milton, Mass. at the time of her mother's death.
1525	iii.	Joseph Daniels **Leland**.[1793] He was living in Milton at the time of his mother's death.

1103. William Ward[9] Whipple (John[8], John[7], Capt. John[6], Capt. John[5], Maj. Matthew[4], Capt. John[3], Elder John[2], Matthew[1])[1794] was born in Boylston, Worcester Co., Mass. 25 August 1811 and died 26 September 1890 in Yonkers, N.Y. at 79 years of age. He married twice. (1) **Emeline Godfrey** in October 1845. Emeline,[1795] daughter of John **Godfrey** and Sophia **Dutton**, was born in Bangor, Maine 11 November 1814 and died 22 January 1884 in Camp Point, Ill. at 69 years of age. (2) **Mary (Spofford) Wiltsie** of Yonkers, N.Y. in May 1887.

After William was graduated from Bangor, Maine Theological Seminary in 1845, he and Emeline moved from Worcester, Mass. to Qunicy, Ill., then to La Gange, Mo. where he started the Presbyterian church. His abolitionist views were unacceptable so after the start of the Civil War, he moved his family to Griggsville, Ill. They later lived in Janesville, Iowa, and Camp Point, Ill. After Emeline's death, he married Mary Wiltsie

William Ward **Whipple** and Emeline **Godfrey** had the following children:

+ 1526	i.	William Orland[10] **Whipple** was born 21 October 1846.
1527	ii.	Marie Louise **Whipple**[1796] was born in LaGrange 24 January 1850 and died 25 June 1885 at 35 years of age.
1528	iii.	John Godfrey **Whipple**[1797] was born in LaGrange 30 September 1853. and died 15 October 1865 in Griggsville at 12 years of age.

1104. John[9] Whipple (John[8], John[7], Capt. John[6], Capt. John[5], Maj. Matthew[4], Capt. John[3], Elder John[2], Matthew[1])[1798] was born in Boylston, Mass. 26 August 1811 and died 6 June 1885 in Hamilton, Mass. at 73 years of age. He married **Charlotte Woods Stone**. The intent to marry was published in Lancaster, Worcester Co.,

Mass. 16 April 1834.[1799] Charlotte,[1800] daughter of Simon **Stone** and Lydia **Rice**, was born in West Boylston 20 August 1809. John and Charlotte were fifth cousins once removed. Elder John and Susanna Whipple were their common ancestors. (See No. 867.)

John **Whipple** and Charlotte Woods **Stone** had the following children:

+ 1142   i. Alonzo Lyman[9] **Whipple** was born 18 September 1836.
   1143   ii. Lorenzo **Whipple**[1801] was born in Princeton, Worcester Co., Mass. 18 September 1836 and died the day of birth.
   1144   iii. Samuel Austin Fay **Whipple**[1802] was born in Cambridge, Mass. 9 August 1838 and died in Cambridge, Mass.
   1145   iv. Adeline Louise **Whipple**[1803] was born in Cambridge 30 May 1847 and died there 18 July 1849 at 2 years of age.

1111. **Phebe Smith**[9] **Whipple** (Stephen[8], Martha[7], Dea. Nathaniel[6], Capt. John[5], Maj. Matthew[4], Capt. John[3], Elder John[2], Matthew[1])[1804] was born in Danvers, Mass. 31 August 1818 and married twice. (1) **Thomas Wood** in Cleveland, Ohio 2 June 1838. (2) **Ovando Patterson** before 1863. Ovando was born in New York State in 1813 and married (1) **Eleanor Akin** in Trumbull Co., Ohio, 6 November 1837.[1805]

Phebe Smith **Whipple** and Thomas **Wood** had the following child:

+ 1529   i. Eunice Porter[10] **Wood** was born 1 December 1848.

Phebe Smith **Whipple** and Ovando **Patterson** had the following child:

+ 1530   ii. Proctor **Patterson** was born 5 August 1863.

1115. **James Russell**[9] **Lowell** (Harriett[8] **Spence**, Mary[7] **Traill**, Mary[6] **Whipple**, Capt. William[5], Maj. Matthew[4], Capt. John[3], Elder John[2], Matthew[1])[1806] was born in Cambridge, Mass. 22 February 1819 and died 12 August 1891 at 72 years of age. He married twice. (1) **Maria White** in December 1844. Maria, daughter of Ahijah **White**, was born 8 July 1821 and died 27 October 1853 at 31 years of age.[1807] (2) **Frances H. Dunlap** of Portland, Maine 6 September 1857. Frances,[1808] daughter of John **Dunlap** Jr. and Mrs. Lois (Cushing) **Porter**, died 19 February 1885 in London, England. Frances was his daughter's governess. No children were born to this union.

James, great (5) grandson of Elder John Whipple, was a noted American poet, critic, editor, and minister to Spain (1877-80) and England (1880-85). His collected works fill 12 volumes. He studied law at Harvard College (was graduated in 1838) but abandoned law for a career of letters. His first wife, Maria White, was a poetess.

In his early years he contributed verses and sketches to magazines, edited a few issues of the unsuccessful literary journal, *The Pioneer*, published his first volume of poems, *A Year's Life* in 1841, a second volume in 1843, and a collection of essays, *Conversations on Some of the Old Poets*, in 1844. During the nine years of his marriage to Maria, they both contributed both prose and verse to various journals, at first mostly those publishing anti-slavery propaganda. He wrote *The Biglow Papers on the Mexican War*, the first of which was published 17 June 1846 by *The Boston Courier*. A second collection of poems, the completed *Biglow Papers, and The Fable for Critics*, were published in 1848. By then he had attained both popular and critical acclaim and had won an assured place in national literature. The wit and humor in *The Biglow Papers* with their racy Yankee dialect and burning zeal against the slave-holding South assured his popularity in the North. No poems have ever more distinctly revealed the New England temper

He delivered a course of 12 lectures (unpublished) on English poetry in Boston in 1855 which resulted in his appointment to succeed Longfellow as Smith Professor of the French and Spanish Languages and Literatures and Professor of Belles Lettres at Harvard in the fall of 1856. This led to a 20-year career in teaching.

He spent two years as editor of the *Atlantic Monthly*, founded in 1857, and was a regular contributor of reviews and articles until 1863 when he joined with Charles Eliot Norton in editing *The North American Review*. For the next dozen years his essays, both political and literary, appeared mainly in this *Review*.

His chief contribution during the Civil War were the new series of *Biglow Papers* published in the *Atlantic* beginning in 1861. After the war, miscellaneous verse of the preceding 20 years was published as *Under the Willows* (1868) and odes and longer poems as *The Cathedral* (1870) and Agassiz (1874).

He began a long succession of essays of criticism of literature which are published in *Among My Books* (1870), *My Study Windows* (1871), and *Among My Books, Second Series* (1876). He addressed both literary and political themes in *Democracy and Other Addresses* (1886) and a final volume of poetry, *Heartsease and Rue* (1880).

He was a presidential elector in 1877 and was appointed by president Rutherford B. Hayes as United States Minister to Spain. This was the beginning of his diplomatic career. After three years in Spain he was transferred to the Court of St. James where his social accomplishments made him exceedingly popular in London. He was awarded honorary degrees by Harvard, Cambridge, Oxford, St. Andrew, Edinburgh, and Bologna.

His health began to fail after his return to the U.S. in 1885. He was beset with gout, sciatica, hemorrhages, and a severe type of liver disease. He was buried at Mt. Auburn in Cambridge near the graves of generations of Lowells. Henry Wadsworth Longfellow's grave is nearby. About 15 carriages were in the procession to Mt. Auburn as church bells throughout the city tolled and flags flew at half mast. A memorial service was also held at Westminster Abbey in London. In his oration, Canon Farrar said: "It is only fitting that we should gather to pay a tribute of respect and gratitude to the great and famous poet who has been called to his rest. Mr. Lowell was one of the greatest of American poets of this generation. But he was more than a poet. He had many claims on the memory of Americans and Englishmen. He was a scholar and a student of the first rank. He was also a critic, but his satire was akin to charity. Though his shafts struck home, they were never poisoned. He was a finished orator. His rich eloquence was unsurpassed in either country. He had made his second home in England, where, as well as in America, he was truly loved. He was one of the sacred unions that bound England to America more closely. The same blood ran in each of our veins; both spoke the tongue of Shakespeare, and both held faith in the morals of Milton. Mr. Lowell was one of those true Americans to whom the slaves owned their freedom, and 20,000,000 of his fellow-citizens their awakened consciousness. English universities bestowed upon him their proudest honors. He passed away loved and revered by the two mightiest nations of the world."[1809]

Joseph Foster wrote two articles on Lowell's Spence, Traill, Whipple, and Cutt ancestors which appeared in the *Portsmouth Journal* 5 Sept. 1891 and the *Critic*, published in New York 10 Oct. 1891. Professor C.E. Norton, Lowell's literary executor, characterized the articles as "a useful contribution to the history of the Lowell family" and said "many of the most striking traits of his character and genius came from his mother's (Whipple) side."

Readers interested in Lowell's relationship to a variety of well-known individuals are referred to Gary Boyd Roberts' "Notable Kin Column," *The Flowering of New England, Part Two: The Poets Bryant, Holmes, Longfellow, J.R. Lowell, and Whittier* in the New England Historical Genealogical Society *Nexus*, Vol. 6, No. 6 (December 1989), 202-06.

James Russell **Lowell** and Maria **White** had the following children:

1531 i. Mabel[10] **Lowell**[1810] was born in Cambridge 9 September 1847 and married Edward **Burnett**. He was graduated from Harvard College, class of 1871, and represented Massachusetts in the U.S. House of Representatives 1886-8.

1532 ii. Walter **Lowell**[1811] was born in Boston 22 December 1850 and died in 1853 in Rome, Italy at 2 years of age.

1118. Reuben[9] French (Reuben[8], Hannah[7] **Page**, Nathaniel[6], Susannah[5] **Lane**, Susanna[4] **Whipple**, Capt. John[3], Elder John[2], Matthew[1])[1812] was born in Billerica, Mass. 26 February 1792 and married **Abigail Holden** there 7 February 1819. Abigail,[1813] daughter of Thomas **Holden** and Mary **Munroe**, was born in Billerica 11 September 1795.

Reuben **French** and Abigail **Holden** had the following children born in Billerica:

1533 i. Henry Page[10] **French**[1814] was born 23 May 1824 and died 22 August 1824 in Billerica at less than one year of age.

1534 ii. George Page **French**[1815] was born 15 September 1829.

1126. Charles O.[9] Whitmore (William Dickman[8], John[7], Francis[6], Mary[5] **Lane**, Susanna[4] **Whipple**, Capt. John[3], Elder John[2], Matthew[1])[1816] was born 2 November 1807 and married twice. (1) **Lovice Ayres** 22 December 1830.[1817] She died 27 September 1849. (2) **Mrs. Mary (Tarbell) Blake** 30 October 1851. She was the widow of George Blake.

Charles O. **Whitmore** and Lovice **Ayres** had the following children:

1535 i. Charles J.[10] **Whitmore**[1818].
1536 ii. William H. **Whitmore**[1819].
1537 iii. Martha H. **Whitmore**[1820].
1538 iv. Anna L. **Whitmore**[1821].
1539 v. Charlotte R. **Whitmore**[1822].
1540 vi. Creighton **Whitmore**[1823] was born 16 December 1845 and died 25 April 1848 at 2 years of age.

1128. Jonathan Abbot[9] Lane (Jonathan[8], Jonathan[7], John[6], Job[5], Susanna[4] **Whipple**, Capt. John[3], Elder John[2], Matthew[1])[1824] was born in 1822 and died in 1898 at 76 years of age. He married **Sara Delia Clarke**.

Jonathan Abbot **Lane** and Sara Delia **Clarke** had the following child:

+ 1541 i. Alfred Church[10] **Lane** was born abt 1863.

1129. Paschal[9] **Hatch** (Anna[8] **Gould**, Anna[7] **Lane**, Timothy[6], Job[5], Susanna[4] **Whipple**, Capt. John[3], Elder John[2], Matthew[1])[1825] was born in Hartland, Vt. 17 October 1807 and died 22 September 1864 in Fort Pickens, Fla. at 56 years of age. He married **Roxana Cady** in Northfield, Vt. 10 May 1835. Roxana was born in Hancock, Vt. 17 January 1810 and died 22 April 1884 in Windsor, Ill. at 74 years of age.[1826]

Paschal **Hatch** and Roxana **Cady** had the following children born in Roxbury, Vt.:

1542	i.	Ellen[10] **Hatch**[1827] was born 20 April 1841.
1543	ii.	Stillman Allen **Hatch**[1828] was born 11 July 1843.
+ 1544	iii.	Alonzo Herbert **Hatch** was born 12 April 1852.

1133. Laura Williams[9] **Hill** (Brewster[8], Ralph[7], Mary[6] **Lane**, Job[5], Susanna[4] **Whipple**, Capt. John[3], Elder John[2], Matthew[1])[1829] was born in Billerica, Mass. 1 February 1819 and married **Jonathan Hill** there in April 1839. Jonathan,[1830] son of Job **Hill** and Susanna **Blanchard**, was born in Billerica 24 November 1804 and died there 17 May 1870 at 65 years of age. Jonathan and Laura are first cousins once removed, Mary Lane and Jonathan Hill being their common ancestors. (See No. 852.)

Jonathan **Hill** and Laura Williams **Hill** had the following children born in Billerica:

1137	i.	James Williams[9] **Hill**[1831] was born 20 December 1841.
1138	ii.	Laura **Hill**[1832] was born 26 September 1843.

1136. Charles Henry[9] **Hill** (Brewster[8], Ralph[7], Mary[6] **Lane**, Job[5], Susanna[4] **Whipple**, Capt. John[3], Elder John[2], Matthew[1])[1833] was born in Billerica, Mass. 20 September 1824 and married twice. (1) **Martha Whitford** in Billerica 16 December 1849. (2) **Apphia Cordelia Foster** 26 October 1861. Apphia was born in Ludlow, Vt.[1834] Charles was the proprietor of the leather-splitting machine shop in the south part of Billerica in 1883.

Charles Henry **Hill** and Martha **Whitford** had the following child:

1545	i.	Martha[10] **Hill**[1835] was born in Billerica 19 November 1851.

Charles Henry **Hill** and Apphia Cordelia **Foster** had the following children born in Billerica:

1546	ii.	Nathaniel **Hill**[1836] was born 8 August 1862 and died 18 August 1865 in Billerica at 3 years of age.
1547	iii.	Margaret Elizabeth **Hill**[1837] was born 8 February 1867.
1548	iv.	Foster Byam **Hill**[1838] was born 7 August 1869.

1139. Diantha[9] **Worcester** (Martha[8] **Lane**, Gershom Flagg[7], John[6], John[5], Susanna[4] **Whipple**, Capt. John[3], Elder John[2], Matthew[1])[1839] was born in 1811 and died in 1900 at 89 years of age. She married **Levi Pangborn** who was born in 1807 and died in 1884 at 77 years of age.[1840]

Diantha **Worcester** and Levi **Pangborn** had the following child:

+ 1549	i.	Dan Bonney[10] **Pangborn** was born in 1850.

1140. Elisabeth Ann[9] **Parkhurst** (Rev. John[8], Betsey[7] **Hutchinson**, Rebecca[6] **Lane**, James[5], Susanna[4] **Whipple**, Capt. John[3], Elder John[2], Matthew[1])[1841] was born in Chelmsford, Mass. 11 June 1823 and died 16 November 1917 at 94 years of age.

She married **Benjamin Minot Fiske** in Chelmsford 1 February 1851. Benjamin was born in Charlestown, Mass. 29 January 1826 and died 9 May 1901 at 75 years of age.[1842]

Elisabeth Ann **Parkhurst** and Benjamin Minot **Fiske** had the following child:
+ 1550   i. Frederick Augustus Parker[10] **Fiske** was born 4 October 1859.

1141. **Mary Wellington**[9] **Lane** (Washington Jefferson Poor[8], Ebenezer[7], Samuel[6], James[5], Susanna[4] **Whipple**, Capt. John[3], Elder John[2], Matthew[1])[1843] was born in West Cambridge, Mass. 19 December 1839 and married **Edward Eri Poor** 17 January 1860. Edward was the son of Benjamin **Poor** and Caroline Emily **Peabody**.[1844]

Mary Wellington **Lane** and Edward Eri **Poor** had the following child:
+ 1551   i. Edward E.[10] **Poor** was born 2 December 1868.

1142. **Alonzo Lyman**[9] **Whipple** (John[9], John[8], John[7], Capt. John[6], Capt. John[5], Maj. Matthew[4], Capt. John[3], Elder John[2], Matthew[1])[1845] was born in Princeton, Mass. 18 September 1836 and died 21 February 1911 in Foxboro, Mass. at 74 years of age. He served in the Civil War as a private from 4 Dec. 1863 to 18 Sept. 1865. He lived in Hamilton, Mass. at the time of enlistment and was a member of Co. "A" of the Massachusetts Volunteers 44th Regiment Heavy Artillery for nine months before being transferred to Co. "H" of the 3rd Mass. Heavy Artillery. He is buried in Beverly, Mass. He married **Abbie N. Kenney** in Wenham, Mass. 1 January 1860. Abbie,[1846] daughter of John **Kenney** and Martha **Nutting**, was born in Salem, Mass. 29 January 1840 and died 5 August 1888 in Hamilton at 48 years of age.

Alonzo Lyman **Whipple** and Abbie N. **Kenney** had the following children born in Hamilton:
1552   i. Lottie Woods[10] **Whipple**[1847] was born 30 August 1860 and married Lewis **Norton** in Essex, Mass. 25 January 1883.
1553   ii. Annie Louise **Whipple**[1848] was born 3 February 1863 and married George **Gibney** in Hamilton in 1887.
1554   iii. Bertha Marshall **Whipple**[1849] was born 5 June 1870 and died 9 July 1925 in Medford, Mass. at 55 years of age. She married John **Smith**.
+ 1555   iv. Cora Adalaide **Whipple** was born 13 January 1875.

1146. **Cyrus Hale Stone**[9] **Powers** (Lavinia[8] **Stone**, Capt. Amos[7], Amos[6], Simon[5], Deacon Simon[4], Mary[3] **Whipple**, Elder John[2], Matthew[1])[1850] was born in Steuben Co., N.Y. 25 September 1815 and died 6 November 1898 at 83 years of age. He married **Nancy Richmond** in Wayne, Steuben Co., N.Y. 4 July 1838. Nancy,[1851] daughter of James **Richmond** and Sarah **Cartwright**, died in September 1889 in Bureau Co., Ill. Cyrus and Nancy are buried in Section 4, Lot 11 of Bureau county's Mount Bloom Cemetery.[1852]

Cyrus Hale Stone **Powers** and Nancy **Richmond** had the following children born in Steuben Co.:
1556   i. Julia[10] **Powers**[1853] was born abt 1840 and married (__) **Young**.
+ 1557   ii. John **Powers** was born 1 November 1841.
1558   iii. Sarah **Powers**[1854] was born abt 1843 and married (__) **Carpenter**.
1559   iv. Philena **Powers**[1855] was born abt 1845 and married B. C. **Buswell**.

1560	v.	James R. **Powers**[1856] was born in 1847.
1561	vi.	Mary E. **Powers**[1857] was born in 1850 and married (__) **Hagan**.
+ 1562	vii.	Cyrus Cameron **Powers** was born 7 April 1854.
+ 1563	viii.	William B. **Powers** was born 11 April 1858.

1150. Eliza B.[9] **Powers** (Lavinia[8] **Stone**, Capt. Amos[7], Amos[6], Simon[5], Deacon Simon[4], Mary[3] **Whipple**, Elder John[2], Matthew[1])[1858] was born in New York State in 1833 and died 31 May 1891 at 57 years of age. She married **Samuel D. Davis**. Samuel,[1859] son of John **Davis** and (__) **Vanderveer**, was born in New York State and died in September 1895 in Bureau Co., Ill. Eliza and Samuel are buried in Mount Bloom Cemetery in Bureau Co.

Eliza B. **Powers** and Samuel D. **Davis** had the following children:

1564	i.	George N.[10] **Davis**[1860].
1565	ii.	Fannie H. **Davis**[1861] married (__) **Newcomb**.
+ 1566	iii.	Vanderveer **Davis** was born 18 March 1852.
1567	iv.	John J. **Davis**[1862] was born in New York State in 1856.
1568	v.	Samuel **Davis**[1863] was born in New York State in 1857.
1569	vi.	Marsell **Davis**[1864] was born in Steuben Co., N.Y. 20 September 1858 and married Honnie G. **Smith** in Deaborn Co., Ind. 23 December 1880.

1152. Myron[9] **Powers** (Lavinia[8] **Stone**, Capt. Amos[7], Amos[6], Simon[5], Deacon Simon[4], Mary[3] **Whipple**, Elder John[2], Matthew[1])[1865] was born in New York State abt 1837 and married **Ann E.** (__). Myron was mustered into service at Elmira, N.Y. in 1862 for service in the Civil War as a 1st Lieutenant in Co. I, 161st regt., New York. He was living in Jasper Co., Iowa in 1870.

Myron **Powers** and Ann E. (__) had the following child:

1570	i.	F. M.[10] **Powers**[1866] was born in New York State abt 1862.

1155. Elizabeth[9] **Tyler** (Alma Ellery[8] **Holden**, Phineas[7], Capt. Asa[6], Abigail[5] **Stone**, Deacon Simon[4], Mary[3] **Whipple**, Elder John[2], Matthew[1])[1867] birth date unknown, married **Luke Pollard** as his second wife after his first wife, Elizabeth's sister Susan, died.

Elizabeth **Tyler** and Luke **Pollard** had the following children born in Massachusetts:

1571	i.	Susan Estelle[10] **Pollard**.[1868]
1572	ii.	Molly (or Mary) Caroline **Pollard**.[1869]
1573	iii.	Sarah Elizabeth **Pollard**.[1870]
+ 1574	iv.	George Fisher **Pollard**.
1575	v.	Frederick Ellery **Pollard**.[1871]
1576	vi.	Charles Baldwin **Pollard**.[1872]
1577	vii.	Frank **Pollard**.[1873]

1157. Harriett Newell[9] **Tyler** (Alma Ellery[8] **Holden**, Phineas[7], Capt. Asa[6], Abigail[5] **Stone**, Deacon Simon[4], Mary[3] **Whipple**, Elder John[2], Matthew[1])[1874] was born in Harvard, Middlesex Co., Mass. and married **Dr. Samuel B. Kelley**.

Harriett Newell **Tyler** and Dr. Samuel B. **Kelley** had the following children:

+ 1578	i.	Edward[10] **Kelley**.
1579	ii.	Beth **Kelley**[1875].

1158. **Alma Ellery**[9] **Tyler** (Alma Ellery[8] **Holden**, Phineas[7], Capt. Asa[6], Abigail[5] **Stone**, Deacon Simon[4], Mary[3] **Whipple**, Elder John[2], Matthew[1])[1876] was born in Massachusetts in 1815 and died 21 November 1899 in Harvard, Middlesex Co., Mass. at 84 years of age. She married as his second wife **Dr. Jacob S. Eaton** in Massachusetts abt 1849. Jacob was born in Massachusetts in 1805 and died in 1888 in Massachusetts at 83 years of age.[1877]

Alma Ellery **Tyler** and Dr. Jacob S. **Eaton**, had the following children born in Massachusetts:

1580	i.	Lucien[10] **Eaton**,[1878] was born in 1850 and married Mary **Titus**.
1581	ii.	Francis **Eaton**[1879] was born in 1853 and died abt 1864.
+ 1582	iii.	James Ellery **Eaton**, was born in 1855.
+ 1583	iv.	Alma Ellery **Eaton**, was born in 1858.

1160. **Samuel Newton**[9] **Bacon** (Alma Ellery[8] **Holden**, Phineas[7], Capt. Asa[6], Abigail[5] **Stone**, Deacon Simon[4], Mary[3] **Whipple**, Elder John[2], Matthew[1])[1880] was born in Harvard, Middlesex Co., Mass. 25 January 1829 and died 11 September 1899 in Loudonville, N.Y. at 70 years of age. He married **Sarah Elizabeth Harlow** 13 February 1855. Sarah,[1881] daughter of George **Harlow** and Elizabeth Hungerford **Farrar**, was born in Westford, Mass. 12 April 1830 and died 4 June 1910 in Loudonville 80 years of age.

Samuel Newton **Bacon** and Sarah Elizabeth **Harlow** had the following children:

1584	i.	Luther Austin[10] **Bacon**[1882] was born 9 April 1857 and died 31 May 1857 at less than one year of age. He was buried in Harvard.
1585	ii.	Emma Maria **Bacon**[1883] was born in Albany, N.Y. 6 September 1858 and died 12 May 1892 in Loudonville at 33 years of age.
1586	iii.	George Newton **Bacon**[1884] was born in Albany 24 May 1860 and died 2 April 1919 in Loudonville at 58 years of age. He married twice. (1) Sarah M. **Monson** 6 January 1892. Sarah was born in 1862 and died in 1912 in Poughkeepsie, N.Y. at 50 years of age.[1885] (2) Malvina **Rorrback** in 1914. Malvina was born in 1863.[1886]
+ 1587	iv.	Allen Harlow **Bacon** was born 13 February 1864.

1161. **Joseph Austin**[9] **Bacon** (Alma Ellery[8] **Holden**, Phineas[7], Capt. Asa[6], Abigail[5] **Stone**, Deacon Simon[4], Mary[3] **Whipple**, Elder John[2], Matthew[1])[1887] was born in Harvard, Middlesex Co., Mass. 4 November 1835 and died 20 February 1875 in Loudonville, N.Y. at 39 years of age. He married **Cornelia Baldwin Chase** 25 January 1870. Cornelia,[1888] daughter of Luther A. **Chase** and Priscilla **Baldwin**, was born 14 July 1845.

Joseph Austin Bacon and Cornelia Baldwin Chase had the following children:

1588	i.	Josephine A.[10] **Bacon**[1889] was born 6 December 1871 and died in 1958 in Albany, N.Y. at 86 years of age. She married Harry T. **Crissey** in 1901. Harry was born in 1874 and died in 1960 in Albany at 86 years of age.[1890]
+ 1589	ii.	Sarah Cornelia **Bacon** was born 3 September 1873.
1590	iii.	Mary Emma **Bacon** was born April 10, 1875 and died in 1911 in Albany at 36 years of age.[1891]

1162. **Lyman**[9] **Carr** (Susanna[8] **Dunton**, Mary[7] **Jewell**, Mary[6] **Whitney**, Mary[5]

Stone, Deacon Simon^4, Mary^3 **Whipple**, Elder John^2, Matthew^1)[1892] was born in Stowe, Mass. 8 June 1798 and died 7 October 1880 in Lancaster, Worcester Co., Mass. at 82 years of age. He married **Lucy Brown** who was born 15 February 1797 and died 15 September 1844 at 47 years of age.[1893]

Lyman **Carr** and Lucy **Brown** had the following child:
+ 1591   i.   William Dustin^{10} **Carr** was born 10 October 1823.

1163. John Putnam^9 Stone (Reedsburg^8, David^7, Lt. James^6, James^5, John^4, Mary^3 **Whipple**, Elder John^2, Matthew^1)[1894] was born in Sweden, Maine 5 February 1847 and died 19 July 1925 in Reedsburg, Wisc. at 78 years of age. He was a farmer and president of the State Bank of Reedsburg for 27 years and married **Amy Angeline Phillips** in Line Ridge, Wisc. 22 April 1874. Amy,[1895] daughter of Otis **Phillips** and Janet **Whitcomb**, was born in Stanford, Vt. 5 August 1851 and died 31 May 1938 in Reedsburg at 86 years of age.

John Putnam **Stone** and Amy Angeline **Phillips** had the following child:
+ 1592   i.   Winnifred Phyllis^{10} **Stone** was born 21 July 1878.

1164. Sylvanus Ward^9 Baker (Betsey^8 **Ward**, Hannah^7 **Goddard**, Robert^6, Edward^5, Susanna^4 **Stone**, Mary^3 **Whipple**, Elder John^2, Matthew^1)[1896] was born 18 October 1805 and died 13 January 1877 in Council Bluffs, Iowa at 71 years of age. He married **Permelia Louisa Jones** 12 April 1832 who died in 1859 in Huron Co., Ohio.[1897]

Sylvanus Ward **Baker** and Permelia Louisa **Jones** had the following child:

1165. Alvira C.^{9} Goddard (David^8, Asa^7, Nathan^6, Edward^5, Susanna^4 **Stone**, Mary^3 **Whipple**, Elder John^2, Matthew^1)[1898] was born in 1807 and married **Danford Goddard** who was born in 1804.[1899]

Alvira C. **Goddard** and Danford **Goddard** had the following child:
+ 1594   i.   Nahum Parks^{10} **Goddard** was born in 1829.

1166. John^9 King (Lois^8 **Jackson**, Lois^7 **Woodward**, Mary^6 **Stone**, Samuel^5, Ebenezer^4, Mary^3 **Whipple**, Elder John^2, Matthew^1)[1900] was born in Newton, Mass. 12 December 1794 and died 12 February 1882 in Franklin, Mass. at 87 years of age. He married **Surrepta Claflin** 28 March 1820. Surrepta was born 25 September 1802.

John **King** and Surrepta **Claflin** had the following child:
+ 1595   i.   Edwin Henry^{10} **King** was born 24 November 1832.

1184. Sarah Jane^9 Johnson (John^8, Abner^7, Hannah^6 **Eaton**, Lydia Abiah^5 **Starr**, Mary^4 **Stone**, Mary^3 **Whipple**, Elder John^2, Matthew^1)[1901] was born in Paris, N.Y. 18 August 1818 and died 10 February 1899 in Gouverneur, N.Y. at 80 years of age. She married twice. (1) **Joseph Chester Jenne** in Fullerville, N.Y 4 May 1837. Joseph,[1902] son of Prince **Jenne** and Olive **Lincoln**, was born in Hadley, N.Y. 29 April 1812 and died 14 May 1853 in Fullerville at 41 years of age. He was a lumber dealer. (2) **Prince Jenne** abt 1865. He was the father of her first husband.[1903]

Sarah Jane **Johnson** and Joseph Chester **Jenne** had the following children:

    1596   i.   Julia A.^{10} **Jenne**[1904] was born in Fowler, N.Y. 20 June 1838 and died 13 March 1857 at 18 years of age. She married Calvin **Cutler**.

+ 1597   ii.   Ezra Almon **Jenne** was born 22 August 1840.

+ 1598   iii.   Jerome Adelbert **Jenne** was born 13 December 1843.

1185. Grove G.^{9} **Johnson** (John^{8}, Abner^{7}, Hannah^{6} **Eaton**, Lydia Abiah^{5} **Starr**, Mary^{4} **Stone**, Mary^{3} **Whipple**, Elder John^{2}, Matthew^{1})[1905] was born in Wilna, Jefferson Co., N.Y. 27 October 1827 and died 14 May 1866 in Fowler, N.Y. at 38 years of age. He went insane and committed suicide. He married **Amanda Malvina Wight** 23 October 1854.[1906]

Grove G. **Johnson** and Amanda Malvina **Wight** had the following children born in Fowler:

    1599   i.   Zeruah J.^{10} **Johnson**[1907] was born 26 February 1856.

    1600   ii.   Cora E. **Johnson**[1908] was born 9 September 1859.

    1601   iii.   Anna Laua **Johnson**[1909] was born 18 October 1861.

    1602   iv.   Nettie D. **Johnson**[1910] was born 5 January 1865.

    1603   v.   Myrtle M. **Johnson**[1911] was born 31 October 1871.

1187. Lucy Fuller^{9} **Johnson** (John^{8}, Abner^{7}, Hannah^{6} **Eaton**, Lydia Abiah^{5} **Starr**, Mary^{4} **Stone**, Mary^{3} **Whipple**, Elder John^{2}, Matthew^{1})[1912] was born in Fowler, N.Y. 1 May 1835 and married twice. (1) **Sylvester Wight** 4 July 1854. Sylvester,[1913] son of Jason **Wight**, was born 24 April 1833 and died 11 July 1858 in Fowler at 25 years of age. (2) **Allen Wight** in Fowler 21 September 1859. Allen,[1914] son of John **Wight**, was born 14 November 1824. He married (1) **Lucy Geer** 25 December 1853.

Lucy Fuller **Johnson** and Sylvester **Wight** had the following children born in Fowler:

    1604   i.   Corlin^{10} **Wight**[1915] was born 14 May 1855.

    1605   ii.   Isadora **Wight**[1916] was born 23 December 1857 and died 22 March 1858 in Fowler at less than one year of age.

Lucy Fuller **Johnson** and Allen **Wight** had the following children born in Fowler:

    1606   iii.   Nora Jane **Wight**[1917] was born 12 February 1861.

    1607   iv.   Julia Ann **Wight**[1918] was born 25 July 1862.

    1608   v.   John Grant **Wight**[1919] was born 15 March 1864.

    1609   vi.   Blanche **Wight**[1920] was born 8 March 1878.

1191. Esther Adeline^{9} **Eaton** (Arrunah^{8}, John^{7}, John^{6}, Lydia Abiah^{5} **Starr**, Mary^{4} **Stone**, Mary^{3} **Whipple**, Elder John^{2}, Matthew^{1})[1921] was born in Cincinnatus, Cortland Co., N.Y. 13 December 1810 and died in October 1896 in Oskaloosa, Jefferson Co., Kans. at 85 years of age. She married **John A. Patterson** in Huron Co., Ohio abt 1830. John was the son of Oliver **Patterson** and Anna **Newell**.

Esther Adeline **Eaton** and John A. **Patterson** had the following child:

+ 1610   i.   Austin Eaton^{10} **Patterson** was born 29 July 1832.

1192. Lorenzo^{9} **Grow** (Samuel Porter^{8}, Joseph^{7}, Abigail^{6} **Dana**, Susanna^{5} **Starr**, Mary^{4} **Stone**, Mary^{3} **Whipple**, Elder John^{2}, Matthew^{1})[1922] was born in Hartland, Vt. 11 March 1806 and died 10 July 1890 in Highland, Calif. at 84 years of age. He married **Harriet Felker Currier** in Old Town, Maine 5 December 1838. Harriet was born in Vasselboro, Maine in 1819 and died 22 December 1910 in Fullerton, Orange Co., Calif. at 91 years of age.[1923]

Lorenzo **Grow** and Harriet Felker **Currier** had the following child:
+ 1611   i. Mary Frances[10] **Grow** was born 23 October 1846.

1193. Edward[9] **Patch** (Luther[8], Thomas[7], Penelope[6] **Dana**, Susanna[5] **Starr**, Mary[4] **Stone**, Mary[3] **Whipple**, Elder John[2], Matthew[1])[1924] was born in Seneca Falls, N.Y. in 1823 and died in Patch Grove, Wisc. He married **Harriet Patch**. Harriet,[1925] daughter of Henry **Patch** was born in Danbury, Conn. in 1826 and died in Patch Grove.

Edward **Patch** and Harriet **Patch** had the following child:
+ 1612   i. Ralph Ernest[10] Patch was born 10 October 1869.

1194. Abigail[9] **Franklin** (Luther[8], Sarah[7] **Starr**, Capt. Comfort[6], Comfort[5], Mary[4] **Stone**, Mary[3] **Whipple**, Elder John[2], Matthew[1])[1926] birth date unknown, married **Hiram Dunlot Moor**. Hiram was the son of John **Moor** and Mary **Davis**.

Abigail **Franklin** and Hiram Dunlot **Moor** had the following child:
+ 1613   i. Victoria Josephine[10] **Moor** was born 14 March 1846.

1196. Wilbur Fiske[9] **Ball** (James Bradley[8], Abigail[7] **Starr**, Capt. Comfort[6], Comfort[5], Mary[4] **Stone**, Mary[3] **Whipple**, Elder John[2], Matthew[1])[1927] was born in Newark, Vt. 30 June 1822 and died 17 November 1893 in Newton, Rockingham Co., N.H. at 71 years of age. He married **Hannah Bean** in Vermont 19 February 1843. Hannah was the daughter of Andrew **Bean** and Hannah **Briar**.[1928]

Wilbur Fiske **Ball** and Hannah **Bean** had the following children:
1614   i. Harriet Jane[10] **Ball**[1929] was born in Vermont 23 December 1843.
+ 1615   ii. Emery Marncy DeLafayette **Ball** was born 9 May 1845.
+ 1616   iii. Hannah Iola **Ball** was born 22 March 1847.
+ 1617   iv. Wilbur Fiske **Ball** Jr. was born 23 December 1851.
+ 1618   v. Lydia Thurlow **Ball** was born 18 July 1853.
+ 1619   vi. Nellie Randilla **Ball** was born 8 January 1856.
1620   vii. Lucius Wesley **Ball**[1930] was born in Lancaster, N.H. 30 May 1858 and died 22 September 1863 at 5 years of age.
1621   viii. Rhoda Arvilla **Ball**[1931] was born in Guildhall, Vt. 22 December 1861 and died 14 September 1863 at one year of age.
+ 1622   ix. Francis Herbert **Ball** was born 20 January 1866.
1623   x. Winifred Gertrude **Ball**[1932] was born in Maidstone, Vt. 20 January 1868 and died 29 May 1931 at 63 years of age. She married Delbert E. **Allen** 19 October 1891.

1201. Mary[9] **Starr** (Lovel[8], Comfort[7], Capt. Comfort[6], Comfort[5], Mary[4] **Stone**, Mary[3] **Whipple**, Elder John[2], Matthew[1])[1933] was born in Colchester, Chittenden Co., Vt. 18 August 1841 and died in October 1928 in Pilger, Stanton Co., Nebr. at 87 years of age. She married **Oeble Pieters Viersen** in Pella, Marion Co., Iowa 18 October 1859. Oeble,[1934] son of Pieter Oebeles **Viersen** and Tjietske Jans **Wouda**, was born in Sijbrandahaus, Friesland, Holland 6 March 1839 and died 5 January 1929 in Pilger at 89 years of age.

Mary **Starr** and Oeble Pieters **Viersen** had the following children born in

Lewis, Cass Co., Iowa:

1624   i. George[10] Viersen[1935] was born 17 July 1860 and died 21 September 1861 in Lewis at one year of age.

+ 1625   ii. Mary Arvilla Viersen was born 25 February 1862.

1626   iii. Lovel Starr Viersen[1936] was born 12 June 1863 and died in May 1928 in McCook, Red Willow Co., Nebr. at 64 years of age. He married Estella Roland in Stanton, Stanton Co., Nebr. 8 October 1884.

1627   iv. Minnie Viersen[1937] was born 1 February 1868 and died 29 February 1868 in Lewis at less than one year of age.

1628   v. Milton Ernest Viersen[1938] was born 31 January 1869 and died abt 1942. He married Lucretia Hull in 1891.

1629   vi. Edgar Beecher Viersen[1939] was born 2 August 1871 and died after 1929. He married Mattie (__) in 1892.

1630   vii. Anna Estella Viersen[1940] was born 11 April 1874 and died after 1929. She married Thomas Wells in February 1898.

1631   viii. Jennie Grace Viersen[1941] was born in 1877 and died after 1929. She married Walter Seidel.

1632   ix. Lillian A. Viersen[1942] was born in 1880 and died after 1929 in Bracksburg, Nebr. She married Ira Baker.[1943]

1633   x. Ada Jane Viersen[1944] was born in 1884 and died after 1929. She married Howard Smith.

1202. Angeline[9] Ward (Elsie Elizabeth[8] Starr, Ebenezer[7], Ebenezer[6], Comfort[5], Mary[4] Stone, Mary[3] Whipple, Elder John[2], Matthew[1])[1945] was born in Oxford, Worcester Co., Mass. 26 February 1840 and married Ira David Cram in Johnston, R.I. 4 February 1855. Ira,[1946] son of Abner Cram and Nancy Jones, was born 28 April 1827 and died 7 July 1888 in Pawtucket, R.I. at 61 years of age.

Angeline Ward and Ira David Cram had the following child:

+ 1634   i. Minnie Elnora[10] Cram was born 12 February 1870.

1206. Caroline M.[9] Estey (John Dean[8], John Dean[7], Solomon[6], Elizabeth Mary[5] Stearns, Elizabeth[4] Stone, Mary[3] Whipple, Elder John[2], Matthew[1])[1947] was born in Clinton Co., N.Y. about 1846 and died 20 November 1883 in Jackson Co., Iowa at 37 years of age. She married James Ulysses Watrous in Maquoketa, Iowa 16 November 1862. James,[1948] son of Walter James Watrous and Eunice Mott, was born in Ashtabula Co., Ohio 5 November 1836 and died 9 April 1914 in Davenport, Iowa at 77 years of age.

Caroline M. Estey and James Ulysses Watrous had the following children:

+ 1635   i. Harriet Elizabeth[10] Watrous was born 1 November 1865.

1636   ii. William Watrous[1949] was born in Jackson Co., Iowa about 1869 and died 14 October 1948 in Ruthven, Palo Alto Co., Iowa at 79 years of age.

1637   iii. Walter W. Watrous[1950] was born in Jackson Co., Iowa about 1875 and married Angeline Edwards.

1207. Abdellah M.[9] Stearns (Harrison[8], Phineas[7], Eliphet[6], Rev. Ebenezer[5], Elizabeth[4] Stone, Mary[3] Whipple, Elder John[2], Matthew[1]) birth date unknown, married Abigail Dorrance.

Abdellah M. Stearns and Abigail Dorrance had the following child:

+ 1638   i. Daisie[10] Stearns.

1208. James[9] Smith (George[8], Hannah[7] **Wilbor**, Mary[6] **Stearns**, Jonathan[5], Elizabeth[4] **Stone**, Mary[3] **Whipple**, Elder John[2], Matthew[1])[1951] was born in Taunton, Mass. 1 June 1814 and died 24 June 1881 at 67 years of age. He married **Mary Bryant** in Taunton 20 October 1833. Mary,[1952] daughter of Samuel **Bryant** and Sally **Downing**, was born in Bridgewater, Mass. 28 May 1808 and died 28 June 1881 in Taunton at 73 years of age.

James **Smith** and Mary **Bryant** had the following child:
+ 1639   i. Almira D.[10] **Smith** was born 15 January 1842.

1209. Catherine Lorette[9] Orvis (Lucinda Chipman[8] **Upham**, Joseph Pierce[7], Asa[6], Hannah[5] **Stearns**, Elizabeth[4] **Stone**, Mary[3] **Whipple**, Elder John[2], Matthew[1])[1953] was born in Granville, N.Y. 23 February 1826 and died 18 June 1859 in Utica, Ind. at 33 years of age. She married **Dr. Thomas Clifford Mercer** in Woodville, Miss. 24 December 1845. Thomas,[1954] son of Carver **Mercer** and Winifred Neville **Oldham**, was born in Louisville, Ky. 16 October 1820 and died 27 February 1884 in Utica, Ind. at 63 years of age.

Catherine Lorette **Orvis** and Dr. Thomas Clifford **Mercer** had the following child:
+ 1640   i. Elizabeth Tracy[10] **Mercer** was born 22 June 1848.

1217. Susan[9] Goddard (Enoch Elbert[8], Ebenezer[7], Nathan[6], Edward[5], Susanna[4] **Stone**, Mary[3] **Whipple**, Elder John[2], Matthew[1])[1955] was born in Windham, Vt. 6 April 1816 and died 6 May 1900 in Jamaica, Vt. at 84 years of age. She married **William Hastings** 6 December 1836. William,[1956] son of Nathan **Hastings** Jr. and Esther **Woodward**, was born in Windham 4 March 1813 and died 21 February 1896 in Jamaica at 82 years of age.

Susan **Goddard** and William **Hastings** had the following children born in Jamaica:
1641   i. Lydia Ann[10] **Hastings**[1957] was born 21 July 1837 and died 1 April 1838 in Jamaica at less than one year of age.
+ 1642   ii. Almon Woodward **Hastings** was born 22 January 1839.
1643   iii. Frances Anna **Hastings**[1958] was born 29 November 1842 and died 24 February 1919 in Jamaica at 76 years of age. She married Charles P. **Stickney** in Jamaica 14 January 1869.
1644   iv. Marion E. **Hastings**[1959] was born 26 December 1847 and died 7 May 1851 in Jamaica at 3 years of age.
1645   v. William H. **Hastings**[1960] was born 15 November 1852.

1222. John Bailey[9] Goddard (Robert[8], Nahum[7], Robert[6], Edward[5], Susanna[4] **Stone**, Mary[3] **Whipple**, Elder John[2], Matthew[1])[1961] was born in Rutland, Vt. 16 October 1830 and died 13 June 1909 in Colton, S. Dak. at 78 years of age. He married twice. (1) **Caroline E. Morrill** in Danville Vt. 10 August 1852. Caroline was born in Vermont 16 March 1829 and died 21 November 1895 in South Dakota at 66 years of age. (2) **Mary E. (_)** in Colton abt 1896. She was born in Canada abt 1848.

John's obituary appeared in the Sioux Falls, S. Dak. *Argus Leader* 14 June 1909. It referred to him as a pioneer resident of the county and noted he died at the family residence at Colton after a sickness of several months. He moved from

Vermont early in life and after a dozen years in Iowa he lived in Minnesota before filling a preemption claim in Tapoi township, Minnehaha Co., S. Dak. in 1878 where he lived the last 31 years of his life. A post office called Taopi was established on his farm in December 1878 and he served as postmaster until the office was moved to Colton. In addition to farming, he operated Goddard's Store, and served as town clerk for 10 years. He was in poor health during the his final years of retirement.

John Bailey **Goddard** and Caroline E. **Morrill** had the following children:

1646	i. Addie[10] **Goddard**[1962].
+ 1647	ii. George Osmer **Goddard** was born 6 March 1856.
1648	iii. Mary Maria **Goddard**[1963] was born in Iowa in 1866.
1649	iv. Jennie V. **Goddard**[1964] was born in Iowa in 1869.

1223. Charles Walker[9] Goddard (Robert[8], Nahum[7], Robert[6], Edward[5], Susanna[4] **Stone**, Mary[3] **Whipple**, Elder John[2], Matthew[1])[1965] was born in Rochester, Windsor Co., Vt. 8 April 1833 and died 4 April 1917 in Des Moines, Iowa at 83 years of age. He married **Mary Elizabeth Bent** in Mt. Holly, Vt. 4 July 1855. Mary[1966] was the daughter of Earl **Bent** and Lephe **Clark**. Charles moved the family to Stryker, Ohio about 1860 and to Bancroft, Iowa about 1883. After the children were raised, they moved to Des Moines, Iowa around 1903.

Charles Walker **Goddard** and Mary Elizabeth **Bent** had the following children:

1650	i. Robert Earle[10] **Goddard**[1967].
1651	ii. Della M. **Goddard**[1968].
+ 1652	iii. Lora E. **Goddard** was born 24 May 1866.

1224. Clark Nahum[9] Goddard (Robert[8], Nahum[7], Robert[6], Edward[5], Susanna[4] **Stone**, Mary[3] **Whipple**, Elder John[2], Matthew[1])[1969] was born in Rutland, Vt. 3 May 1835 and died aft 1909 in Decorah, Iowa. He married **Jennie Richardson** in Iowa in 1861. He arrived in Clayton Co., Iowa in 1854 from Rutland and moved to Decorah two years later. He opened the Pioneer Store in 1860 and grew it into one of the leading dry goods store in the city. He joined with Charles Henry and Dr. E.B. Hutchinson to establish the firm of Goddard, Henry, and Hutchinson in 1862 and became the sole owner in 1874. An undated copy of his obituary in the *Decorah Republican* reported he served as postmaster and mayor of the town. He was identified as a pioneer merchant and resident since 1856. He died after an illness of 10 weeks which began with a carbuncle on one of his knees and terminated with an acute attack of Bright's disease. He was survived by his wife and children: Harry G. of Minneapolis, Mrs. Clara G. Willet of Decorah, Herbert of Abilene, Texas, and Fred R. of Nekoosa, Wisc., and a brother Charles of Des Moines, Iowa.

Clark Nahum **Goddard** and Jennie **Richardson** had the following children born in Decorah:

1653	i. Harry G.[10] **Goddard**[1970].
1654	ii. Fred R. **Goddard**[1971].
1655	iii. Clara G. **Goddard**[1972] married (__) **Willet** in Decorah.
+ 1656	iv. Herbert **Goddard** was born 22 August 1877.

1227. **Edwin Nathan**[9] **Goddard** (George[8], Capt. Nathan[7], Nathan[6], Benjamin[5], Susanna[4] **Stone**, Mary[3] **Whipple**, Elder John[2], Matthew[1])[1973] was born in Upton, Worcester Co., Mass. 13 April 1842 and died 24 July 1903 in Worcester, Mass. at 61 years of age. He married **Fannie J. Ryan** in West Boylston, Worcester Co., Mass. 2 June 1866. Fannie was born in New Ipswich, N.H. 15 March 1840 and died 30 October 1905 in Worcester at 65 years of age.[1974]

Edwin Nathan **Goddard** and Fannie J. **Ryan** had the following child:

+ 1657   i.   Clarence Ryan[10] Goddard was born 21 February 1873.

1252. **Elizabeth**[9] **Young** (Brigham[8], Abigail (Nabby)[7] **Howe**, Susanna[6] **Goddard**, Ebenezer[5], Susanna[4] **Stone**, Mary[3] **Whipple**, Elder John[2], Matthew[1])[1975] was born in either Aurelius or Port Byron, Cayuga Co., N.Y. 26 September 1825 and died 2 February 1903 in Lewisville, Jefferson Co., Idaho at 77 years of age. She married **Edmund Ellsworth** who was born in Paris, Oneida Co., N.Y. 10 July 1819.[1976]

Elizabeth **Young** and Edmund **Ellsworth** had the following children:

1658	i.	Charlotte[10] Ellsworth[1977] was born in Nauvoo, Ill. 1 July 1843 and died 24 December 1853 at 10 years of age.
+ 1659	ii.	Edmund **Ellsworth** Jr. was born 7 October 1845.
+ 1660	iii.	Rowennah W. **Ellsworth** was born 1 May 1848.
+ 1661	iv.	Brigham Henry **Ellsworth** was born 23 November 1850.
+ 1662	v.	Alice Vilate **Ellsworth** was born 22 November 1852.
+ 1663	vi.	Luna Caroline **Ellsworth** was born 17 November 1854.
1664	vii.	John W. **Ellsworth**[1978] was born 15 June 1858.
1665	viii.	Minnie **Ellsworth**[1979] was born 1 March 1861 and married Emmett **Mousley**.

1253. **Vilate**[9] **Young** (Brigham[8], Abigail (Nabby)[7] **Howe**, Susanna[6] **Goddard**, Ebenezer[5], Susanna[4] **Stone**, Mary[3] **Whipple**, Elder John[2], Matthew[1])[1980] was born in Mendon, Monroe Co., N.Y. 1 June 1830 and died either 18 or 19 November 1902 in Lewisville, Jefferson Co. Idaho at 72 years of age. She married **Charles Franklin Decker** 4 February 1847.

Vilate **Young** and Charles Franklin **Decker** had the following children:

+ 1666	i.	Miriam Vilate[10] **Decker** was born 15 January 1848.
+ 1667	ii.	Alice Luella **Decker** was born 23 July 1851.
1668	iii.	Charles Franklin **Decker**[1981] was born 24 May 1854 and married Annie **Thomas**. No issue born to this union.
1669	iv.	Louie Issac **Decker**[1982] was born 4 June 1857 and died in January 1864 at 6 years of age.
+ 1670	v.	Brigham Le Ray **Decker** was born 14 January 1859.
+ 1671	vi.	Loretta Elmina **Decker** was born 24 December 1861.
1672	vii.	Lois Elizabeth **Decker**[1983] was born 22 June 1865 and died 27 September 1867 at 2 years of age.
+ 1673	viii.	Ferra Wallace **Decker** was born 26 January 1872.

1255. **Brigham Heber**[9] **Young Jr.** (Brigham[8], Abigail (Nabby)[7] **Howe**, Susanna[6] **Goddard**, Ebenezer[5], Susanna[4] **Stone**, Mary[3] **Whipple**, Elder John[2], Matthew[1])[1984] was born in Kirtland, Ohio 18 December 1836 and died 11 April 1903 in Salt Lake City at 66 years of age.

Brigham Heber **Young** Jr. had the following child:

+ 1674   i. Albert C.[10] **Young**.

1257. Alice[9] **Young** (Brigham[8], Abigail (Nabby)[7] **Howe**, Susanna[6] **Goddard**, Ebenezer[5], Susanna[4] **Stone**, Mary[3] **Whipple**, Elder John[2], Matthew[1])[1985] was born in Montrose, Lee Co., Iowa 4 September 1839 and died 2 November 1875 in St. George, Wahn Co., Utah at 36 years of age. She married **Hiram Bradley Clawson** 26 October 1856.

Alice **Young** and Hiram Bradley **Clawson** had the following children:

+ 1675   i. John Willard[10] **Clawson** was born 18 January 1858.
+ 1676   ii. Leo Herbert **Clawson** was born 22 October 1859.
+ 1677   iii. Walter Scott **Clawson** was born 1 December 1861.
+ 1678   iv. Selden Irwin **Clawson** was born 20 March 1864.

1258. Eunice Caroline[9] **Young** (Brigham[8], Abigail (Nabby)[7] **Howe**, Susanna[6] **Goddard**, Ebenezer[5], Susanna[4] **Stone**, Mary[3] **Whipple**, Elder John[2], Matthew[1])[1986] was born in Nauvoo, Ill. 20 August 1842 and died 17 November 1922 in Logan, Cache Co., Utah at 80 years of age. She married **George Washington Thatcher** 4 April 1861. George was born in Springfield, Ill. 1 February 1840 and died 23 December 1902 at 62 years of age. He married (2) **Fanny Decker Young** in 1866.[1987]

Eunice Caroline **Young** and George Washington **Thatcher** had the following children:

+ 1679   i. Virginia Mary[10] **Thatcher** was born 15 January 1862.
  1680   ii. Alice Young **Thatcher**[1988] was born 18 July 1863 and died 13 March 1864 at less than one year of age.
+ 1681   iii. Nellie May **Thatcher** was born 12 October 1864.
  1682   iv. George Washington **Thatcher** II[1989] was born 9 August 1866 and married Emily Jane **Crismon**.
+ 1683   v. Nettie Young **Thatcher** was born 13 September 1868.
+ 1684   vi. Brigham Guy **Thatcher** was born 10 September 1870.
+ 1685   vii. Kathrine **Thatcher** was born 20 September 1873.
+ 1686   viii. Luna Angell **Thatcher** was born 17 December 1875.
+ 1687   ix. Constance **Thatcher** was born 25 November 1880.
+ 1688   x. Phylis **Thatcher** was born 16 January 1883.

1261. Fanny Decker[9] **Young** (Brigham[8], Abigail (Nabby)[7] **Howe**, Susanna[6] **Goddard**, Ebenezer[5], Susanna[4] **Stone**, Mary[3] **Whipple**, Elder John[2], Matthew[1])[1990] was born in Salt Lake City 25 January 1849 and died there 20 January 1892 at 42 years of age. She married **George Washington Thatcher** in 1866. George was born in Springfield, Ill. 1 February 1840 and died 23 December 1902 at 62 years of age. He married (2) **Eunice Caroline Young** 4 April 1861.[1991]

Fanny Decker **Young** and George Washington **Thatcher** had the following children:

+ 1689   i. Lutie[10] **Thatcher** was born 21 October 1868.
  1690   ii. Armand **Thatcher**[1992] was born 28 November 1870 and died 29 September 1871 at less than one year of age.
  1691   iii. Mary **Thatcher**[1993] was born 23 December 1873 and died 3 December 1876 at 2 years of age.
+ 1692   iv. Frank W. **Thatcher** was born 3 April 1878.

| 1693 | v. | Fera Young **Thatcher**[1994] was born 9 August 1882 and died 12 August 1882 at less than one year of age. |
| 1694 | vi. | Laurence Y. **Thatcher**[1995] was born 6 June 1885. |

1263. Shamira[9] **Young** (Brigham[8], Abigail (Nabby)[7] **Howe**, Susanna[6] **Goddard**, Ebenezer[5], Susanna[4] **Stone**, Mary[3] **Whipple**, Elder John[2], Matthew[1])[1996] was born in Salt Lake City 21 January 1853 and died 24 August 1915 at 62 years of age. She married **William A. Rossiter**.

Shamira **Young** and William A. **Rossiter** had the following children:

1695	i.	Clifford Young[10] **Rossiter**[1997] was born 21 December 1878 and died 10 May 1879 at less than one year of age.
1696	ii.	Russell Young **Rossiter**[1998] was born 29 August 1881 and died 4 September 1919 at 38 years of age. He married Clara **Junker**. No children were born to this union.
1697	iii.	Lillian **Rossiter**[1999] died in infancy.

1266. Clarissa Hamilton[9] **Young** (Brigham[8], Abigail (Nabby)[7] **Howe**, Susanna[6] **Goddard**, Ebenezer[5], Susanna[4] **Stone**, Mary[3] **Whipple**, Elder John[2], Matthew[1])[2000] was born in Salt Lake City 23 July 1860 and died there 21 August 1939 at 79 years of age.[2001] She married **John Daniel Spencer** 19 January 1882.

Clarissa Hamilton **Young** and John Daniel **Spencer** had the following children:

+ 1698	i.	John Allan[10] **Spencer** was born 9 July 1885.
+ 1699	ii.	Jean **Spencer** was born 16 June 1888.
+ 1700	iii.	Rehan **Spencer** was born 15 April 1890.
1701	iv.	Daniel Young **Spencer**[2002] was born 11 December 1893 and married Marie **Hodson**.
1702	v.	Helen Young **Spencer**[2003] was born 29 November 1896 and married Rex **Williams**.

1268. Emily Augusta[9] **Young** (Brigham[8], Abigail (Nabby)[7] **Howe**, Susanna[6] **Goddard**, Ebenezer[5], Susanna[4] **Stone**, Mary[3] **Whipple**, Elder John[2], Matthew[1])[2004] was born in Salt Lake City 1 March 1849 and died there 19 March 1926 at 77 years of age. She married **Hiram Bradley Clawson** 4 January 1868. Hiram was born 7 November 1826.

Emily Augusta **Young** and Hiram Bradley **Clawson** had the following children:

1703	i.	Victor[10] **Clawson**.
+ 1704	ii.	Carlie Louine **Clawson** was born 28 July 1869.
+ 1705	iii.	Nell Young **Clawson** was born 10 May 1872.
+ 1706	iv.	Kate Young **Clawson** was born 19 May 1874.
+ 1707	v.	Alice Young **Clawson** was born 22 January 1876.
+ 1708	vi.	Bessie Young **Clawson** was born 19 December 1878.
+ 1709	vii.	Shirley Young **Clawson** was born 15 November 1881.
+ 1710	viii.	Chester Young **Clawson** was born 5 December 1883.
+ 1711	ix.	Josephine Young **Clawson** was born 11 February 1886.
1712	x.	Scott Richmond Young **Clawson**[2005] was born in San Francisco Co., Calif. 26 December 1888 and died 5 April 1906 at 17 years of age.

1269. Caroline Partridge[9] **Young** (Brigham[8], Abigail (Nabby)[7] **Howe**,

Susanna[6] **Goddard**, Ebenezer[5], Susanna[4] **Stone**, Mary[3] **Whipple**, Elder John[2], Matthew[1])[2006] was born in Salt Lake City 1 February 1851 and died there 2 July 1903 at 52 years of age.[2007] She married twice. (1) **Mark Croxall** 7 October 1868. (2) **George Q. Cannon** in 1884. Mark married (2) **Mary Eliza Young** in Utah 4 June 1865. (See No. 1275.)

Caroline Partridge **Young** and Mark **Croxall** had the following children:
+ 1713   i.   Emily Ada Young[10] **Croxall** was born 13 August 1870.
   1714   ii. Charles Y. **Croxall**[2008] was born 17 May 1872. Died young.
   1715   iii. Maude Y. **Croxall**[2009] was born 22 October 1873.
+ 1716   iv. Caroline Y. **Croxall** was born 2 July 1875.
+ 1717   v. Mark Y. **Croxall** was born 4 August 1877.
+ 1718   vi. Tracy Y. **Croxall** was born 23 July 1879.
   1719   vii. Verna **Croxall**[2010] was born 13 October 1881 and died in infancy.
+ 1720   viii. Vera **Croxall** was born 13 October 1881.

Caroline Partridge **Young** and George Q. **Cannon** had the following children:
+ 1721   ix. Clawson Y. **Cannon** was born 27 October 1885.
+ 1722   x. Wilford Y. **Cannon** was born 4 July 1888.
+ 1723   xi. Anne Y. **Cannon** was born 13 June 1890.
   1724   xii. Georgius Y. **Cannon**[2011] was born 6 May 1892. He was an army lieutenant in WWI.

1271. Miriam[9] **Young** (Brigham[8], Abigail (Nabby)[7] **Howe**, Susanna[6] **Goddard**, Ebenezer[5], Susanna[4] **Stone**, Mary[3] **Whipple**, Elder John[2], Matthew[1])[2012] was born in Salt Lake City 13 October 1857 and died 16 October 1919 in Granite, Salt Lake Co., Utah at 62 years of age. She married **Leonard G. Hardy** in Salt Lake City 28 August 1878.

Miriam **Young** and Leonard G. **Hardy** had the following children:
+ 1725   i. Miriam Y.[10] **Hardy** was born 7 August 1879.
+ 1726   ii. Eugenia Young **Hardy** was born 30 September 1881.
+ 1727   iii. Emily Partridge **Hardy** was born 1 February 1884.
+ 1728   iv. Leonard Goodridge **Hardy** was born 25 February 1886.
   1729   v. Alice **Hardy**[2013] was born in Salt Lake City 8 December 1887 and died there 9 November 1909 at 21 years of age.
   1730   vi. Aaron Parker **Hardy**[2014] was born in Salt Lake City 14 May 1890 and married Erma Gertrude **Nichols**. Aaron served in WWI.
   1731   vii. Georgie Y. **Hardy**[2015] was born in Salt Lake City 1 January 1893.
   1732   viii. Lucile **Hardy**[2016] was born in Salt Lake City 23 April 1895 and died there 11 August 1896 at one year of age.
   1733   ix. Brigham Young **Hardy**[2017] was born in Salt Lake City 9 June 1897.
   1734   x. Edward Vernon **Hardy**[2018] was born in Sterling Alberta, Canada 7 January 1900.
   1735   xi. Dorothy Y. **Hardy**[2019] was born in Salt Lake City 23 September 1902.

1272. Josephine[9] **Young** (Brigham[8], Abigail (Nabby)[7] **Howe**, Susanna[6] **Goddard**, Ebenezer[5], Susanna[4] **Stone**, Mary[3] **Whipple**, Elder John[2], Matthew[1]) was born in Salt Lake City 21 February 1860 and married **Albert C. Young**. Albert [2020] was the son of Brigham Heber **Young** Jr. He married (2) **Mary Eliza Young Croxall**. Josephine is a half-aunt of Albert.

Albert C. **Young** and Josephine **Young** had the following children:

1736	i.	Ethel[10] Young[2021] was born in Salt Lake City 11 April 1879 and died there in December 1882 at 3 years of age.
1737	ii.	Geneva Young[2022] was born in Salt Lake City 18 March 1884.
+ 1738	iii.	Clisbee Young was born 21 March 1887.
1739	iv.	Gilbert Young[2023] was born in Salt Lake City 16 October 1891 and died there 3 May 1893 at one year of age.
1740	v.	Josephine Young[2024] was born in Salt Lake City 30 September 1896 and married George F. Harker.
1741	vi.	Virginia Young[2025] was born in Salt Lake City 15 March 1898 and married Joseph N. LaRocca.

1275. Mary Eliza[9] Young (Brigham[8], Abigail (Nabby)[7] **Howe**, Susanna[6] **Goddard**, Ebenezer[5], Susanna[4] **Stone**, Mary[3] **Whipple**, Elder John[2], Matthew[1])[2026] was born in Winter Quarters (now Florence), Nebr. 8 June 1847 and died 6 September 1871 in Salt Lake City at 24 years of age. She married **Mark Croxall** in Utah 4 June 1865. (See No. 1269). He married (1) **Caroline Partridge Young** 7 October 1868.

Mary Eliza **Young** and Mark **Croxall** had the following children:

+ 1742	i.	Mary Eliza Young[10] Croxall was born 3 March 1866.
1743	ii.	Mark Croxall Jr.[2027] was born 12 September 1867 and died 14 October 1868 at one year of age.
+ 1744	iii.	Dr. Willard Croxall was born 25 July 1869.
1745	iv.	Walter Y. Croxall[2028] was born 5 September 1871

1276. Clarissa Maria[9] Young (Brigham[8], Abigail (Nabby)[7] **Howe**, Susanna[6] **Goddard**, Ebenezer[5], Susanna[4] **Stone**, Mary[3] **Whipple**, Elder John[2], Matthew[1])[2029] was born in Salt Lake City 10 December 1849 and died 30 April 1935 at 85 years of age.[2030] She married **William Bernard Dougall** 1 June 1868. William was born in Liverpool, England in 1842 and died in April 1909 at 66 years of age.[2031]

Clarissa Maria **Young** and William Bernard **Dougall** had the following children:

+ 1746	i.	William Bernard[10] Dougall Jr. was born 7 May 1869.
+ 1747	ii.	Hugh Willard Dougall was born 6 March 1872.
+ 1748	iii.	Catherine McSweine Dougall was born 11 August 1878.
+ 1749	iv.	Clarissa Dougall was born 23 July 1884.

1278. Phebe Louisa[9] Young (Brigham[8], Abigail (Nabby)[7] **Howe**, Susanna[6] **Goddard**, Ebenezer[5], Susanna[4] **Stone**, Mary[3] **Whipple**, Elder John[2], Matthew[1])[2032] was born in Salt Lake City 1 August 1854 and died there 22 August 1931 at 77 years of age.[2033] Her name may have been spelled Phoebe. She married **Walter Josiah Beatie** 7 January 1872. He was born 31 December 1849.[2034]

Phebe Louisa **Young** and Walter Josiah **Beatie** had the following children:

1750	i.	Clarissa Marion[10] Beatie[2035] was born 21 October 1872 and died 23 November 1878 at 6 years of age.
+ 1751	ii.	Josephine Young Beatie was born 2 September 1874.
1752	iii.	Walter Josiah Beatie Jr.[2036] was born 23 October 1876 and died the day of birth.
1753	iv.	Mary Young Beatie[2037] was born 23 September 1880 and died 25 April 1887 at 6 years of age.

+ 1754   v. Hazel Young **Beatie** was born 27 November 1882.

1755   vi. Nelson Ross **Beatie**[2038] was born 26 October 1886 and served with Co. A, 16th battery, 4th division during WWI.

+ 1756   vii. Walter Sidney **Beatie** was born 12 June 1889.

1280. Marinda Hyde[9] **Young** (Brigham[8], Abigail (Nabby)[7] **Howe**, Susanna[6] **Goddard**, Ebenezer[5], Susanna[4] **Stone**, Mary[3] **Whipple**, Elder John[2], Matthew[1])[2039] was born in Salt Lake City 30 July 1849 and died there 17 August 1883 at 34 years of age. She married **Walter Karr Conrad** in Salt Lake City.

Marinda Hyde **Young** and Walter Karr **Conrad** had the following children:

1757   i. Walter K.[10] **Conrad**[2040] was born in Salt Lake City 6 September 1867 and married Winifred **Lynn**. No issue born to this union.

1758   ii. Ellie F. **Conrad**[2041] was born in Salt Lake City 25 December 1869 and died there 26 September 1873 at 3 years of age.

1759   iii. Raymond G. **Conrad**[2042] was born in Salt Lake City 29 May 1872 and died there 21 August 1872 at less than one year of age.

1760   iv. Goldie E. **Conrad**[2043] was born in Salt Lake City 30 July 1873 and died there 27 January 1874 at less than one year of age.

1761   v. Vernie Vaughn **Conrad**[2044] was born in Salt Lake City 5 May 1875 and died there 12 August 1875 at less than one year of age.

+ 1762   vi. Winifred B . **Conrad** was born 13 January 1877.

1283. Louisa Nelle[9] **Young** (Brigham[8], Abigail (Nabby)[7] **Howe**, Susanna[6] **Goddard**, Ebenezer[5], Susanna[4] **Stone**, Mary[3] **Whipple**, Elder John[2], Matthew[1])[2045] was born in Salt Lake City 30 October 1855 and died 29 August 1908 at 52 years of age. She married **James Ferguson**.

Louisa Nelle **Young** and James **Ferguson** had the following children:

1763   i. James[10] **Ferguson**[2046] was born in Salt Lake City and died young.

1764   ii. Dale **Ferguson**[2047] was born in Salt Lake City and died unmarried in New York State.

+ 1765   iii. Gladys **Ferguson**.

1766   iv. Allen **Ferguson**[2048] was born in New York State.

1286. Ruth[9] **Young** (Brigham[8], Abigail (Nabby)[7] **Howe**, Susanna[6] **Goddard**, Ebenezer[5], Susanna[4] **Stone**, Mary[3] **Whipple**, Elder John[2], Matthew[1])[2049] was born in Salt Lake City 4 March 1861 and died 8 November 1944 at 83 years of age. She married twice. (1) **Charles Johnson**. (2) **John Hopkins Healey**. Ruth and John H. Healey had no issue.

Ruth **Young** and Charles **Johnson** had the following children:

1767   i. Adella[10] **Johnson**[2050] was born 21 February 1879.

+ 1768   ii. Ellis **Johnson** was born 2 October 1880.

+ 1769   iii. Jay Elliot **Johnson** was born 16 March 1883.

1294. Nabbie Howe[9] **Young** (Brigham[8], Abigail (Nabby)[7] **Howe**, Susanna[6] **Goddard**, Ebenezer[5], Susanna[4] **Stone**, Mary[3] **Whipple**, Elder John[2], Matthew[1])[2051] was born in Salt Lake City 22 March 1852 and died there 15 March 1894 at 41 years of age. She married **Orson Spencer Clawson**.

Nabbie Howe **Young** and Orson Spencer **Clawson** had the following children:

+ 1770   i. Clara[10] **Clawson** was born 26 February 1877.

1771	ii.	Orson Spencer **Clawson** Jr.[2052] was born 29 March 1879 and died 6 May 1917 at 38 years of age.
+ 1772	iii.	Curtis Young **Clawson** was born 27 July 1884.
+ 1773	iv.	Grace **Clawson** was born 28 January 1886.
+ 1774	v.	John Neels **Clawson** was born 12 February 1888.
+ 1775	vi.	Nabbie Young **Clawson** was born 24 May 1891.

1298. Zina[9] **Young** (Brigham[8], Abigail (Nabby)[7] **Howe**, Susanna[6] **Goddard**, Ebenezer[5], Susanna[4] **Stone**, Mary[3] **Whipple**, Elder John[2], Matthew[1])[2053] was born in Salt Lake City 3 April 1850 and married twice. (1) **Thomas Williams**. Thomas was born in Wales, Great Britian 5 August 1828 and died abt 1875.[2054] (2) **Charles Ora Card**. Charles was born 5 November 1839 and died 9 September 1906 at 66 years of age.[2055]

Zina **Young** and Thomas **Williams** had the following children:

| + 1776 | i. | Sterling[10] **Williams** was born 21 September 1870. |
| 1777 | ii. | Thomas Edgar **Williams**[2056] was born 21 July 1873 and died 20 April 1882 at 8 years of age. |

Zina **Young** and Charles Ora **Card** had the following children:

+ 1778	iii.	Joseph Young **Card** was born 28 June 1885.
+ 1779	iv.	Zina Young **Card** was born 12 June 1888.
+ 1780	v.	Orson Rego **Card** was born 9 June 1891.

1299. Evelyn Louise[9] **Young** (Brigham[8], Abigail (Nabby)[7] **Howe**, Susanna[6] **Goddard**, Ebenezer[5], Susanna[4] **Stone**, Mary[3] **Whipple**, Elder John[2], Matthew[1])[2057] was born in Salt Lake City 30 July 1850 and died 30 January 1917 at 66 years of age. She married **Milton Herbert Davis**.

Evelyn Louise **Young** and Milton Herbert **Davis** had the following children:

| 1781 | i. | Milton Herbert[10] **Davis** Jr.[2058] was born 22 March 1872 and died 5 November 1872 at less than one year of age. |
| + 1782 | ii. | Margaret Alley **Davis** was born 26 January 1874. |

1300. Mahonri Moriancumber[9] **Young** (Brigham[8], Abigail (Nabby)[7] **Howe**, Susanna[6] **Goddard**, Ebenezer[5], Susanna[4] **Stone**, Mary[3] **Whipple**, Elder John[2], Matthew[1])[2059] was born in Salt Lake City 1 November 1852 and died 20 April 1884 at 31 years of age.

Mahonri Moriancumber **Young** had the following child:

| 1783 | i. | Mahonri Moriancumber[10] **Young**. He became a well-known sculptor. Among his works are the statues of Joseph and Hyrum Smith which stand in Temple Square in Salt Lake City.[2060] |

1301. Eudora Lovina[9] **Young** (Brigham[8], Abigail (Nabby)[7] **Howe**, Susanna[6] **Goddard**, Ebenezer[5], Susanna[4] **Stone**, Mary[3] **Whipple**, Elder John[2], Matthew[1])[2061] was born in Salt Lake City 12 May 1852 and died 12 November 1922 at 70 years of age. She married twice. (1) **Moreland Dunford**. (2) **Albert Hagan**.

Eudora Lovina **Young** and Moreland **Dunford** had the following children:

| + 1784 | i. | Frank Moreland[10] **Dunford** was born 2 June 1873. |
| + 1785 | ii. | George Albert **Dunford** was born 29 August 1875. |

Eudora Lovina **Young** and Albert **Hagan** had the following children:

1786	iii.	Albert **Hagan** Jr.[2062] was born in Chicago, Ill. 13 August 1882 and died 3 December 1883 at one year of age.
+ 1787	iv.	Harold Raymond **Hagan** was born 20 May 1886.
+ 1788	v.	Mabel Clara **Hagan** was born 15 May 1889.
1789	vi.	Lucy Mary **Hagan**[2063] was born 13 June 1891 and died in September 1891 at less than one year of age.

1302. Susan (Susa) Amelia[9] **Young** (Brigham[8], Abigail (Nabby)[7] **Howe**, Susanna[6] **Goddard**, Ebenezer[5], Susanna[4] **Stone**, Mary[3] **Whipple**, Elder John[2], Matthew[1])[2064] was born in Salt Lake City 18 March 1856 and died there 27 May 1933 at 77 years of age.[2065] She married twice. (1) **A. B. Dunford.** (2) **Jacob Fosberry Gates** 5 January 1880. Jacob was born 30 July 1850.[2066]

Susan (Susa) Amelia **Young** and A. B. **Dunford** had the following children:

| + 1790 | i. | Leah Eudora[10] **Dunford** was born 24 February 1874. |
| 1791 | ii. | Bailey **Dunford**[2067] was born 13 August 1875 and died abt 1895. |

Susan (Susa) Amelia **Young** and Jacob Fosberry **Gates** had the following children:

1792	iii.	Emma Lucy **Gates**[2068] was born in St. George, Wahn Co., Utah 5 November 1880 and married Albert E. **Bowen** 30 June 1916.
1793	iv.	Jacob Young **Gates**[2069] was born 11 May 1882 and died 23 February 1887 at 4 years of age.
1794	v.	Karl Nahum **Gates**[2070] was born 22 July 1883 and died 2 March 1887 at 3 years of age.
1795	vi.	Simpson Mark **Gates**[2071] was born 20 January 1885 and died 21 April 1885 at less than one year of age.
1796	vii.	Joseph Sterling **Gates**[2072] was born in Laie, Oahu, Hawaii 28 February 1886 and died there 16 June 1891 at 5 years of age.
+ 1797	viii.	Brigham Cecil **Gates** was born 17 August 1887.
+ 1798	ix.	Harvey Harris **Gates** was born 19 January 1889.
1799	x.	Sarah Beulah **Gates**[2073] was born in Provo, Utah 21 June 1891 and died 23 July 1898 at 7 years of age.
+ 1800	xi.	Franklin Young **Gates** was born 17 May 1893.
1801	xii.	Heber **Gates**[2074] was born 22 November 1894 and died the day of birth.
1802	xiii.	Brigham Young **Gates**[2075] was born 19 April 1896 and died 27 February 1900 at 3 years of age.

1303. Rhoda Mabel[9] **Young** (Brigham[8], Abigail (Nabby)[7] **Howe**, Susanna[6] **Goddard**, Ebenezer[5], Susanna[4] **Stone**, Mary[3] **Whipple**, Elder John[2], Matthew[1])[2076] was born in Salt Lake City 22 February 1863 and died 20 September 1950 at 87 years of age. She married three times. (1) **Daniel H. McAllister.** (2) **D. B. Witt.** (3) **Joseph Abbott Sanborn** 2 August 1897.

Rhoda Mabel **Young** and Daniel H. **McAllister** had the following child:

| + 1803 | i. | Daniel Handley[10] **McAllister** was born 2 August 1880. |

Rhoda Mabel **Young** and D. B. **Witt** had the following child:

| + 1804 | ii. | Brigham Winfred **Witt** was born 9 October 1889. |

Rhoda Mabel **Young** and Joseph Abbott **Sanborn** had the following children:

| 1805 | iii. | Abbott Young **Sanborn**[2077] was born 6 May 1898 and died 10 April 1901 at 2 years of age. |
| 1806 | iv. | Lucy Young **Sanborn**[2078] was born 28 May 1904. |

1807   v. Joseph Gilpen **Sanborn**[2079] was born 22 December 1908.

1308. Fannie Van Cott[9] **Young** (Brigham[8], Abigail (Nabby)[7] **Howe**, Susanna[6] **Goddard**, Ebenezer[5], Susanna[4] **Stone**, Mary[3] **Whipple**, Elder John[2], Matthew[1])[2080] was born in Salt Lake City in 1870 and died there 31 January 1950 at 79 years of age. She married **Isaac Ambrose Clayton** in Salt Lake City 22 January 1890.

Fannie Van Cott **Young** and Isaac Ambrose **Clayton** had the following children:

+ 1808   i. Isaac Ambrose[10] **Clayton** Jr. was born 17 May 1892.
   1809   ii. Frances Luella **Clayton**[2081] was born 15 December 1893 and married Richard W. **Burton**. Frances and Richard were third cousins.
   1810   iii. Vernon Van Cott **Clayton**[2082] was born 14 August 1895 and died 6 June 1896 at less than one year of age.
   1811   iv. Mary Van Cott **Clayton**[2083] was born 24 May 1897.
   1812   v. Lyndon Whitney **Clayton**[2084] was born 18 December 1898 and served with the 145th artillery in WWI.
   1813   vi. Waldemar Young **Clayton**[2085] was born 3 March 1902.
   1814   vii. Grace Young **Clayton**[2086] was born 27 August 1905.
   1815   viii. Richard Young **Clayton**[2087] was born 6 December 1910.

1312. Harriet Maria[9] **Young** (Lorenzo Dow[8], Abigail (Nabby)[7] **Howe**, Susanna[6] **Goddard**, Ebenezer[5], Susanna[4] **Stone**, Mary[3] **Whipple**, Elder John[2], Matthew[1])[2088] was born in Kirtland, Ohio 21 July 1834 and married **Joseph Guernsey Brown** 31 December 1852. Joseph was born in Tompkins Co., N.Y. 8 November 1824.[2089]

Harriet Maria **Young** and Joseph Guernsey **Brown** had the following children:

   1816   i. Homer Achilles[10] **Brown**[2090] was born in Salt Lake City 25 October 1853 and died 31 March 1886 at 32 years of age.
+ 1817   ii. Persis Ann **Brown** was born 23 December 1855.
+ 1818   iii. Joseph Guernsey **Brown** Jr. was born 17 April 1857.
+ 1819   iv. Lucy Elizabeth **Brown** was born 12 April 1859.
+ 1820   v. Angeline **Brown** was born 6 January 1861.
+ 1821   vi. Lorenzo Y. **Brown** was born 19 September 1862.
+ 1822   vii. Ebenezer **Brown** was born 10 October 1864.
   1823   viii. Juliette Little **Brown**[2091] was born in Draper, Utah 13 February 1869 and died 30 May 1870 at one year of age.
   1824   ix. Feramorz **Brown**[2092] was born 25 February 1872 and died 3 March 1893 at 21 years of age.
   1825   x. Jennie **Brown**[2093] was born in Kanab, Kane Co., Utah 9 June 1875.
   1826   xi. Willmia **Brown**[2094] was born in Kanab 15 December 1877.

1327. Harriet Josephine[9] **Young** (Lorenzo Dow[8], Abigail (Nabby)[7] **Howe**, Susanna[6] **Goddard**, Ebenezer[5], Susanna[4] **Stone**, Mary[3] **Whipple**, Elder John[2], Matthew[1])[2095] was born in Richville, Tooele Co., Utah 24 February 1863 and married **Charles S. Carter**.

Harriet Josephine **Young** and Charles S. **Carter** had the following children:

   1827   i. Charles S.[10] **Carter** Jr.[2096]
   1828   ii. Brigham W. **Carter**[2097]
   1829   iii. Fera **Carter**[2098]
   1830   iv. Clydie **Carter**[2099]
   1831   v. Gladys **Carter**[2100]

1339. **Marshall Maynard**[9] **Stone** (Col. Jonathan[8], Lt. Jonathan[7], Jonathan[6], Jonathan[5], Jonathan[4], Mary[3] **Whipple**, Elder John[2], Matthew[1])[2101] was born in Auburn, Mass. 19 April 1828 and died 16 September 1906 at 78 years of age. He married **Elsie Eldridge** in Willamantic, Conn. in July 1849. Elsie,[2102] daughter of Samuel **Eldridge** and Mary or Martha (Patty) **Welch**, was born in Brome, Quebec, Canada 11 July 1828 and died 18 October 1897 at 69 years of age.

Marshall Maynard **Stone** and Elsie **Eldridge** had the following children born in Auburn:

+ 1832   i.   Milon Gardner[10] **Stone** was born 2 June 1850.

   1833   ii. Mary Abigail **Stone**[2103] was born 30 January 1852 and died 27 March 1928 in Worcester, Mass. at 76 years of age. She is buried in the Hope Cemetery. She married John McFarlane **McCallum** in Harvard, Middlesex Co., Mass. 5 September 1871. Mary and John had five children: Lewis, Janet, Bertha, John, and Elsie.

   1834   iii. Sarah Lorinda **Stone**[2104] was born 25 November 1854 and married Ezra **Bixby** in Auburn 13 April 1872. Sarah and Ezra had two children: Ezra Marshall and Edith Gertrude.

+ 1835   iv. Arthur Davis **Stone** was born 6 March 1867.

1340. **Charles Augustus**[9] **Stone** (Charles Hobart[8], Charles[7], Jonathan[6], Moses[5], Jonathan[4], Mary[3] **Whipple**, Elder John[2], Matthew[1])[2105] was born in Newton, Middlesex Co., Mass. 16 January 1867 and died 25 February 1941 in New York, N.Y. at 74 years of age. He married **Mary Adams Leonard** in Boston, Mass. 3 June 1902. Mary,[2106] daughter of William **Leonard** and Margaret Elizabeth **Keith**, was born in Hingham, Mass. 18 August 1873 and died 6 October 1940 in Locust Valley, Long Island, N. Y. at 67 years of age.

Charles was graduated from the Massachusetts Institute of Technology with a bachelor of science degree in electrical engineering in 1888. He and Edwin S. Webster formed the firm of Stone and Webster, electrical engineers in 1889. In addition to doing consulting work for the General Electric Co., they constructed street railways, electric light and power plants, hydroelectric plants, and gas and industrial properties. They branched into finance and in 1927 purchased the investment business of Blodgett & Company which became Stone & Webster & Blodgettt, Inc.

When the U.S. entered WWI, the company constructed the cantonment at San Antonio, Texas, enlarged the U.S. arsenal at Rock River, Ill., built an ordinance base for the American Expeditionary Force in France, etc. After the war they built buildings for the Massachusetts Institute of Technology, the Ford Motor Co., Lever Bros., the Westinghouse Electric Corp., the General Electric Co., and the Johns-Manville Corp.

In addition to serving on the boards of the many firms they controlled, Charles served on the board of the Union Pacific Railroad Co., the International Acceptance Bank, Inc., and scores of other utility and industrial companies. He was director of the Federal Reserve Bank of New York, a life member of the Corporation of the Massachusetts Institute of Technology, and of the American Society of Mechanical Engineers.

He owned farms in Massachusetts, New Hampshire, and Virginia and devoted much time to improving breeds of horses and cattle. Among his many clubs were the Union of Boston, and the following in New York City: Recess, the

Technology, the University, the Bankers, The Creek, the India House, the Knickerbocker, the Piping Rock, and the New York Yacht club. He was elected a resident member 7 May 1913 and made a life member 25 Nov. 1924 of the New England Historic Genealogical Society.

Charles Augustus **Stone** and Mary Adams **Leonard** had the following children:

1836	i.	Charles Augustus[10] **Stone**[2107].
1837	ii.	Margaret **Stone**[2108] married Robert Colgate Vernon **Mann** and was living in Locus Valley, Long Island, N.Y. at the time of her father's death.
1838	iii.	Whitney **Stone**[2109] was a Harvard graduate in 1930 and was living in New York City when her father died.
1839	iv.	Janet Elizabeth **Stone**[2110] married Edward Cox **Brewster**. The Brewsters were living in New York City at the time of Charles' death.

1347. Hiram[9] **Billings** (Joel[8], John[7], Joanna[6] **Norton**, John[5], Mary[4] **Goodhue**, Sarah[3] **Whipple**, Elder John[2], Matthew[1])[2111] was born in North Berwick, Maine 17 May 1805 and died 24 October 1836 in Saco., York Co., Maine at 31 years of age. He married **Mary Fogg** in Scarboro, Cumberland Co., Maine 12 July 1827. Mary,[2112] daughter of Reuben **Fogg** and Rhoda **Moody**, was born in Scarboro 12 September 1792 and died there aft 1836. She married (1) **Ebenezer Andrews** in Scarboro 15 December 1815. They were divorced in York Co., Maine in April 1826.

Hiram **Billings** and Mary **Fogg** had the following children:

+ 1840	i.	Mary Jane[10] **Billings** was born abt 1828.
1841	ii.	Cordelia A. **Billings**[2113] was born in Scarboro abt 1833 and died 21 August 1907 in LaPorte City, Black Hawk Co., Iowa at 74 years of age. She married Thomas L. **Reed** in Woburn, Mass. 10 December 1869.

1349. Benjamin Frank[9] **Swett** (Benjamin[8], Daniel[7], Moses[6], Elizabeth[5] **Norton**, Mary[4] **Goodhue**, Sarah[3] **Whipple**, Elder John[2], Matthew[1])[2114] was born in New Hampshire 3 August 1853 and died in 1932 in Brooklyn, N.Y. at 78 years of age. He married **Eliz Earley**. Eliz was born in 1858 and died in 1940 in Brooklyn, N.Y at 82 years of age.[2115]

Benjamin Frank **Swett** and Eliz **Earley** had the following child:

+ 1842	i.	Bessie[10] **Swett** was born 11 October 1879.

1351. Stephen[9] **Barton** (Sarah (Sally)[8] **Stone**, Sarah[7] **Treadwell**, Joseph[6], Sarah[5] **Goodhue**, William[4], Sarah[3] **Whipple**, Elder John[2], Matthew[1])[2116] was born in Oxford, Worcester Co., Mass. 29 March 1806 and married **Betsey Rich** there. The intent to marry date was 3 November 1833. Betsey,[2117] daughter of Davi **Rich** and Polly (__), was born in Oxford 9 February 1818. Stephen was a noted mathematician.

Stephen **Barton** and Betsey **Rich** had the following children born in Oxford:

1843	i.	Infant[10] **Barton**[2118] was born abt March 1837 and died 1 December 1837 in Oxford at less than one year of age. The vital records indicate the baby was 10 months old at death.
1844	ii.	Samuel Rich **Barton**[2119] was born 31 May 1839.
1845	iii.	David **Barton**[2120] was born in October 1845 and died 11 November 1847 in Oxford at 2 years of age.

1410. **Joseph L.**[9] **Mecham** (Sarah[8] **Basford**, Jonathan[7], Elizabeth[6] **Goodhue**, Jonathan[5], William[4], Sarah[3] **Whipple**, Elder John[2], Matthew[1])[2121] was born in Thornton, N.H. 1 February 1806 and died 6 March 1894 in St. George, Wahn Co., Utah at 88 years of age. He married four times. (1) **Hannah Ladd Tyler** 10 February 1827. She was born in Lawrence, N.Y. 10 February 1808. (2) **Ann Elizabeth Bovee** in Nauvoo, Ill. 9 January 1845. Ann,[2122] daughter of Matthias **Bovee** and Waitstill **Hill**, was born in Hanover, N.Y. 18 April 1829 and died 17 October 1869 in Milton, Morgan Co., Utah at 40 years of age. (3) **Sarah Maria Tuttle** in Salt Lake City 4 January 1853. Sarah,[2123] daughter of Edward **Tuttle** and Sarah Mariah **Clinton**, was born in North Haven, Conn. 25 January 1825 and died 26 February 1880 in Milton at 55 years of age. (4) **Mary Katherine Green** in Salt Lake City 19 August 1885. Mary [2124] was the daughter of Charles **Green** and Mary **Ellis** and died 15 March 1912 in Moore, Idaho.

Joseph L. **Mecham** and Hannah Ladd **Tyler** had the following children:

+ 1846   i.   Ellen[10] **Mecham** was born 4 July 1836.

   1847   ii.   Loretta Sylvia **Mecham**[2125] was born 4 January 1838 and died 2 July 1914 in Bountiful, Utah at 76 years of age. She married Joseph Bates **Noble** in Salt Lake City 18 January 1857.

Joseph L. **Mecham** and Ann Elizabeth **Bovee** had the following children:

   1848   iii.   Josephine **Mecham**[2126] was born in Council Bluffs, Iowa in 1847 and died in 1849.

   1849   iv.   Ariamiah **Mecham**[2127] was born in Harris Grove, Iowa 18 April 1849 and died 23 March 1897 at 47 years of age. She married Adam **Sanberg** 14 September 1867.

   1850   v.   Joseph **Mecham**[2128] was born in Woodbine, Harrison Co., Iowa 16 February 1851 and died in 1933 in Salt Lake City at 82 years of age. He was buried in Oakley, Twin Falls Co., Idaho. He married Matilda Ann **Tuttle** in Salt Lake City 17 June 1872.

   1851   vi.   Ammon **Mecham**[2129] was born in Salt Lake City in 1853.

   1852   vii.   Ammaron **Mecham**[2130] was born in Tooele Co., Utah 6 December 1855 and died March 1867 at 11 years of age.

   1853   viii.   Emma Waitstill **Mecham**[2131] was born in Tooele Co., Utah 18 October 1858 and died 15 January 1920 in Mesa, Mariposa Co., Ariz. at 61 years of age. She married Frihoff Godfrey **Nielson** in Peterson, Morgan Co., Utah 20 October 1877.

   1854   ix.   Brigham Bovee **Mecham**[2132] was born in Etee City, Tooele Co., Utah 18 February 1860 and died 4 July 1919 in Roosevelt, Duchesne Co. Utah at 59 years of age. He married Lydia Saphronia **Lange** in St. George, Wahn Co., Utah 30 April 1885.

   1855   x.   Lucian Mormon **Mecham**[2133] was born in Milton, Utah 16 February 1862 and died 29 March 1922 in Colonia Juarez, Chihuahua, Mexico at 60 years of age. He married twice. (1) Laura Ann **Hardy** in St. George 30 May 1889. (2) (__) **Hardy** in Colonia Juarez in 1899.

   1856   xi.   Seymour B. **Mecham**[2134] was born in Milton 14 December 1864 and married Susanna **Talbot** in Salt Lake City 23 March 1882.

   1857   xii.   Desert **Mecham**[2135] was born in Milton 5 November 1865 and died 1 December 1866 at one year of age.

   1858   xiii.   Elizabeth Vilate **Mecham**[2136] was born in Milton 7 November 1867 and died 29 July 1941 in Pine Valley, Washington Co., Utah at 73 years of age. She was buried in St. George. She married Edward John Baptist

Christian in St. George 21 December 1892.

Joseph L. **Mecham** and Sarah Maria **Tuttle** had the following children:

1859   xiv. Leander **Mecham**[2137] was born in Pine Canyon , Tooele Co., Utah 18 December 1854 and died September 1855 at less than one year of age.

1860   xv. Joseph Lyman **Mecham**[2138] was born in Etee City, Utah 26 September 1856 and died 26 February 1934 in Milton at 77 years of age. He married Anna Maria **Giles** in Salt Lake City 16 February 1882.

1861   xvi. Ann Eliza **Mecham**[2139] was born in Etee City 29 November 1858 and died 2 September 1934 at 75 years of age. She married Peter **Parkinson** in Morgan 4 January 1877.

1862   xvii. Daniel Lester **Mecham**[2140] was born in Etee City Utah 7 January 1861 and died 25 November 1954 in Littleton, Morgan Co., Utah at 93 years of age. He married Martha Penelope **Richards** in Morgan 29 October 1885.

+ 1863   xviii. Luman Lehi **Mecham** was born 14 July 1863.

1864   xix. Mary Emmerett **Mecham**[2141] was born in Milton 24 April 1865 and died 15 March 1932 in Ogden, Utah at 66 years of age. She married Alexander Eddie **Sim** in Logan, Utah 30 September 1885.

1865   xx. Sarah Emily **Mecham**[2142] was born in Milton 26 February 1868 and died there September 1869 at one year of age.

Joseph L. **Mecham** and Mary Katherine **Green** had the following child:

1866   xxi. Joseph Preston **Mecham**[2143] was born in Lake Point, Utah 25 April 1857 and died 22 May 1937 in Hinckley, Utah at 80 years of age.

1422. Jesse C.[9] **Kimball** (Elisha[8], Jesse[7], John[6], Isaac[5], Sarah[4] **Goodhue**, Sarah[3] **Whipple**, Elder John[2], Matthew[1])[2144] was born in 1831 and married **Amanda E. Johnson**.

Jesse C. **Kimball** and Amanda E. **Johnson** had the following children:

1867   i. Newton[10] **Kimball**[2145].

1868   ii. Ella G. **Kimball**[2146] who died in 1914.

1425. Eli[9] **Miller** (Easter[8] **Kimball**, Jesse[7], John[6], Isaac[5], Sarah[4] **Goodhue**, Sarah[3] **Whipple**, Elder John[2], Matthew[1])[2147] was born in 1823 and died in 1874 at 51 years of age. He married twice. (1) **Lucy E. Glenn**. (2) **Mary Melissa Grey**. Mary was born in 1845 and died in 1933 at 88 years of age.[2148]

Eli **Miller** and Lucy E. **Glenn** had the following children:

1869   i. Samuel[10] **Miller**[2149] was born in 1852 and died in 1853 at one year of age.

1870   ii. John P. **Miller**[2150] was born in 1854.

1871   iii. Elisha **Miller**[2151] was born in 1857.

1872   iv. Esther A. **Miller**[2152] was born in 1860 and died in infancy.

1873   v. Levi **Miller**[2153] was born in 1861 and died in infancy.

Eli **Miller** and Mary Melissa **Grey** had the following children:

1874   vi. Martha Jane **Miller**[2154] was born in 1862 and married Frank **Wilcox**.

1875   vii. Pauline Eleanor **Miller**[2155] was born in 1864 and died in 1883 at 19 years of age.

1876   viii. Harriet Angeline **Miller**[2156] was born in 1866 and married James A. **Hutchinson**.

1877	ix.	Charles Henry **Miller**[2157] was born in 1869 and married Mary Delphine **Deniston**.
1878	x.	William Hiram **Miller**[2158] was born in 1871 and died in 1956 at 85 years of age. He married Wilma Clara **Wilcox** who was born in 1879 and died in 1958 at 79 years of age.[2159]
+ 1879	xi.	Mary Melissa **Miller** was born in 1873.

1432. Elisha D.[9] **Miller** (Easter[8] **Kimball**, Jesse[7], John[6], Isaac[5], Sarah[4] **Goodhue**, Sarah[3] **Whipple**, Elder John[2], Matthew[1])[2160] was born in Cynthiana, Posey Co., Ind. 23 November 1841 and died 17 April 1924 in Newkirk, Kay Co., Okla. at 82 years of age. He married twice. (1) **Judith Scruggs** 23 November 1859. Judith was born in Richland Township, Miami Co., Ind. 3 July 1842 and died 10 October 1907 in Cowley Co., Kans. at 65 years of age.[2161] (2) **Juliann Wilcox** in Lawton, Comanche Co., Okla. 23 November 1908. She died 30 July 1915.[2162]

Elisha D. **Miller** and Judith **Scruggs** had the following children:

1880	i.	Eliza Jane[10] **Miller**[2163] was born in 1860 and died in 1862 at two years of age.
1881	ii.	Thomas Hiram **Miller**[2164] was born in 1862 and died in 1899 at 37 years of age. He married Tabitha **Sartin**[2165] who was born in 1860 and died in 1901 at 41 years of age
+ 1882	iii.	Alexander **Miller** was born in 1864.
1883	iv.	Estella Edna **Miller**[2166] was born in 1865 and died in 1866 at one year of age.
+ 1884	v.	Samuel Martin **Miller** was born in 1868.
1885	vi.	Lillie B. **Miller**[2167] was born in 1870 and died in 1952 at 82 years of age. She married Oscar Gant who was born in 1865.[2168]
+ 1886	vii.	Benjamin Franklin **Miller** was born 9 May 1872.
1887	viii.	Rosa May **Miller**[2169] was born in 1875 and married Bert **Waller** in 1895.
1888	ix.	Mary **Miller**[2170] was born in 1880 and died in infancy.

1444. Mary Elizabeth[9] **Kimble** (Walter[8], Jacob[7] **Kimball**, Jacob[6], Jacob[5], Sarah[4] **Goodhue**, Sarah[3] **Whipple**, Elder John[2], Matthew[1])[2171] was born 5 April 1845 and died 11 April 1925 in Brant, N.Y. at 80 years of age. She married **Ulric Huch Baker** in Shirley, N.Y. 5 April 1868. Ulric,[2172] son of Sylvanus Ward **Baker** and Permelia Louisa **Jones**, was born 24 August 1844. (See No. 1593)

Ulric Huch **Baker** and Mary Elizabeth **Kimble** had the following child:

+ 1889	i.	Mary Elizabeth[10] **Baker** was born 30 November 1880.

1445. Affalona Galia[9] **Fausett** (Julia Ann[8] **Stevens**, Roswell[7], Hepsibah[6] **Kilham**, Abigail[5] **Kimball**, Sarah[4] **Goodhue**, Sarah[3] **Whipple**, Elder John[2], Matthew[1])[2173] was born in Alpine, Utah Co., Utah 13 November 1853 and died 17 March 1901 in Green River, Emery Co., Utah at 47 years of age. She married **Richmond Beeman Thompson** in Utah 30 November 1872. Richmond was born in North Carolina 14 April 1843 and died 4 June 1922 in Antelope, Duchense Co., Utah at 79 years of age.[2174]

Affalona Galia **Fausett** and Richmond Beeman **Thompson** had the following child:

+ 1890	i.	Viola Maud[10] **Thompson** was born 7 June 1884.

1446. **Marinda Alice**[9] **Stevens** (William[8], Roswell[7], Hepsibah[6] **Kilham**, Abigail[5] **Kimball**, Sarah[4] **Goodhue**, Sarah[3] **Whipple**, Elder John[2], Matthew[1])[2175] was born in Holden, Utah 31 August 1868 and died there 8 August 1904 at 35 years of age. She married **David Jones** 17 March 1891. David was born in Wisconsin 26 December 1863 and died 7 November 1927 in Bone, Idaho at 63 years of age.[2176]

Marinda Alice **Stevens** and David **Jones** had the following child:
+ 1891   i.   Maiben Stevens[10] **Jones** was born 11 March 1904.

1447. **Francis Abbot**[9] **Goodhue** (Samuel[8], Samuel[7], Samuel[6], George[5], Joseph[4], Sarah[3] **Whipple**, Elder John[2], Matthew[1])[2177] was born in 1850 and died in 1905 at 55 years of age. He married **Elizabeth Johnson Cushing**.

Francis Abbot **Goodhue** and Elizabeth Johnson **Cushing** had the following child:
+ 1892   i.   Elizabeth[10] **Goodhue** was born 11 February 1878.

1448. **Mary**[9] **Dickson** (Elizabeth[8] **Upham**, Eleanor[7] **Knowlton**, Daniel[6], Robert[5], Marjory (Margery)[4] **Goodhue**, Sarah[3] **Whipple**, Elder John[2], Matthew[1])[2178] was born in Colchester Co., N.S., Canada abt 1820 and died 6 September 1894 in Baddeck, Victoria Co. N.S. at 74 years of age. She married **Thomas McCabe** 11 June 1847. Thomas was born in West River, Pictou Co.. N.S. and died after 1848.[2179]

Mary **Dickson** and Thomas **McCabe** had the following child:
+ 1893   i.   John James[10] **McCabe** was born in 1848.

1450. **Nancy Mathilda**[9] **Bowers** (Polly[8] **Rand**, Solomon[7], Deborah[6] **Dodge**, Margery[5] **Knowlton**, Marjory (Margery)[4] **Goodhue**, Sarah[3] **Whipple**, Elder John[2], Matthew[1])[2180] was born in Rindge, N.H. 29 November 1823 and died 10 January 1908 in West Medford, Mass. at 84 years of age. She married **Charles Chandler Stevens** 30 November 1848. Charles was born in Warwick, Mass. 10 May 1820 and died 23 February 1900 in West Medford at 79 years of age.[2181]

Nancy Mathilda **Bowers** and Charles Chandler **Stevens** had the following child:
+ 1894   i.   George Gove[10] **Stevens** was born 7 December 1853.

1451. **Andrew Issachar**[9] **Goodhue** (Benjamin[8], Ebenezer[7], Ebenezer[6], John[5], John[4], Sarah[3] **Whipple**, Elder John[2], Matthew[1])[2182] was born in Hancock, N.H. 19 January 1848 and died 25 April 1923 in Burlington, Chittenden Co., Vt. at 75 years of age. He married **Lemira Barrett**. Lemira,[2183] daughter of Thomas **Barrett** and Elvira **Fretts**, was born in Nashua, N.H. 26 April 1849 and died 23 October 1929 in Northampton, Mass. at 80 years of age.

Andrew Issachar **Goodhue** and Lemira **Barrett** had the following child:
+ 1895   i.   Grace Anna[10] **Goodhue** was born 3 January 1879.

TENTH GENERATION

1457. **James**[10] **Pillsbury** (Jacob[9], John Hale[8], Rev. Edmund[7], Moses[6], Moses[5], Susanna[4] **Worth**, Susannah[3] **Whipple**, Elder John[2], Matthew[1])[2184] was born in Middleton, Strafford Co., N.H. 21 December 1826 and died 7 June 1915 in

Pasadena, Calif. at 88 years of age. He married twice. (1) **Catherine G. Wedgwood** in Lowell, Mass. 28 December 1851. (2) **Lydia Davis** in Boston, Mass. 30 September 1874. James **Pillsbury** and Catherine G. **Wedgwood** had the following children:

+ 1896   i. Harry M.[11] **Pillsbury** was born 13 November 1852.
   1897   ii. Kittie **Pillsbury** was born in 1860 and died unmarried in 1898 at 38 years of age.

James **Pillsbury** and Linda **Davis** had the following child:
   1898   iii. Oliver P. **Pillsbury** was born abt 1875 and died in 1876 at one year of age.

1466. **Albert Enoch**[10] **Pillsbury** (Josiah Webster[9], Oliver[8], Parker[7], Moses[6], Moses[5], Susanna[4] **Worth**, Susannah[3] **Whipple**, Elder John[2], Matthew[1]) was born 19 August 1849 and died 23 December 1930 in Newton, Middlesex, Co., Mass. at 81 years of age. He married twice. (1) **Louisa Fuller (Johnson) Wheeler** 9 July 1889. (2) **Elizabeth Mooney** in Edinburgh, Scotland, 1 July 1905. Elizabeth, daughter of Henry Clay **Mooney** and Lucy G. **Holbrook**, was born in North Hero, Vt. Albert attended Lawrence Academy, Groton, Mass.; two years at Harvard College; taught school in Sterling, Ill. for one year; read law in the office of Hon. James Dinsmoor (his uncle); admitted to the Illinois and Massachusetts bar; opened a law office in Boston in 1871 where he practiced until his death. Elected as a Republican to the Massachusetts house of representatives in 1876, '77, '78; state senator 1884, '85, '86, senate president his last two terms; Massachusetts attorney general 1891-93. He was a professor of constitutional law at Boston University law school 1896-1906; vice chairman of the board of directors of the United States Trust Co., vice president and trustee of the Franklin Savings Bank, and president of the corporation and a trustee of Lawrence Academy. He was vice president and director of the Massachusetts Society for the Prevention of Cruelty to Animals and held the same offices in the American Humane Education Association. Beginning in 1888, he served for several years as president of the National Association of the Pillsbury Family.

Albert Enoch **Pillsbury** and Elizabeth **Mooney** had the following children:
   1899   i. Elizabeth Dinsmoor[11] Pillsbury married Ellsworth W. **Poole**.
   1900   ii. Parker Webster **Pillsbury**.

1470. **Jane Stetson**[10] **Hale** (Zacheus[9], Zacheus[8], Joseph[7], Abigail W.[6] **Pillsbury**, Moses[5], Susanna[4] **Worth**, Susannah[3] **Whipple**, Elder John[2], Matthew[1])[2185] was born in E. Bridgewater, Mass. 23 December 1831 and died 8 September 1904 in Whitman, Mass. at 72 years of age. She married **Thomas Blackmer Sherman** 24 June 1852. Thomas,[2186] son of Kelley **Sherman** and Sally S. **Blackmer**, was born in Fairhaven, Mass. died 9 March 1832 at the Old Soldiers' Home in Togus, Maine, and was buried in Whitman 15 Jan. 1921. He was a Civil War veteran who served in the 7th, 37th, and 20th regiment of the Massachusetts volunteer infantry and was wounded in the Battle of the Wilderness. Following the war he was a member of the Grand Army of the Republic (GAR) in Whitman.

Jane Stetson **Hale** and Thomas Blackmer **Sherman** had the following children:
   1901   i. Edgar Hale[11] **Sherman** married Hattie **Pratt** and was buried 5 June 1939.

1902   ii. William Thomas **Sherman** was born 15 September 1852, died 7 August 1876 in Whitman at 23 years of age, and was buried in Colebrook Cemetery.

1903   iii. Lucy Jane **Sherman** was born 22 October 1855, died 24 January 1866 in Whitman at 10 years of age, and was buried in Colebrook Cemetery.

+ 1904   iv. Charles Herbert **Sherman** was born 14 January 1858.

1905   v. James Henry **Sherman** was born 6 June 1860.

1906   vi. Ella Mariah **Sherman** was born 13 September 1870, died 14 October 1937 at 67 years of age, and was buried in Colebrook Cemetery. She married Everett **Fullerton**.

1471. Snome Elizabeth[10] Hale (Zacheus[9], Zacheus[8], Joseph[7], Abigail W.[6] **Pillsbury**, Moses[5], Susanna[4] **Worth**, Susannah[3] **Whipple**, Elder John[2], Matthew[1])[2187] was born 10 September 1836 and married (__) **Blanchard** before 1857. She died before 1865.

Snome Elizabeth **Hale** and (__) **Blanchard** had the following children:

1907   i. Elizabeth[11] **Hale** was born in 1857.

1908   ii. Irving **Blanchard** was born in 1859.

1474. Frank Brickett[10] Dodge (Deborah Towne[9] **Brickett**, Bernard[8], Bernard[7], Susanna[6] **Pillsbury**, Moses[5], Susanna[4] **Worth**, Susannah[3] **Whipple**, Elder John[2], Matthew[1]) was born in Haverhill, Mass. 4 February 1835 and died 29 December 1891 in Woburn, Mass. at 56 years of age. He married **Harriet E. Faden** in Boston, Mass. 13 October 1858. She was born in Woburn 12 October 1837 and died in 1903 in Jamaica Plain, Suffolk Co., Mass. at 65 years of age

Frank Brickett **Dodge** and Harriet E. **Faden** had the following child:

+ 1909   i Lizzie Batchelder[11] **Dodge** was born 7 December 1865.

1476. Viola Irene[10] Hoyt (Dr. Hiram Pillsbury[9], Judith[8] **Pillsbury**, Caleb[7], Caleb[6], Caleb[5], Susanna[4] **Worth**, Susannah[3] **Whipple**, Elder John[2], Matthew[1])[2188] was born in Hardwick, Vt. 5 December 1849, died 5 April 1942 in Baltimore, Md. at 92 years of age, and is buried at Lakeview Cemetery in Burlington, Chittenden Co., Vt. She married **George Hollis Smalley** in Lyndonville, Vt. 6 April 1875. George,[2189] son of Elic **Smalley** and Joanna **Stiles**, was born in Albany, Vt. 16 June 1851 and died 24 February 1896 in Burlington at 44 years of age.

Viola Irene **Hoyt** and George Hollis **Smalley** had the following children:

1910   i. Fred Howard[11] **Smalley**[2190] was born in Lyndonville 17 June 1876 and died there 25 August 1876 at less than one year of age.

+ 1911   ii. Col. Howard Russell **Smalley** was born 21 August 1877.

1503. Zara[10] Blanchard (Aaron[9], Lois[8] **Burt**, Abiah[7] **Mooar**, Abiah[6] **Hill**, Judith[5] **Bucknam**, Judith (Jude)[4] **Worth**, Susannah[3] **Whipple**, Elder John[2], Matthew[1])[2191] was born in Jefferson Co., N.Y. 20 September 1829 and died 14 February 1897 in St. Charles, Kane Co., Ill. at 67 years of age. He married twice. (1) **Elizabeth Jordon** 3 November 1851. Elizabeth was born in 1828 and died in 1882 at 54 years of age. (2) **Sarah E. Johnson** 23 June 1875.

Zara **Blanchard** and Elizabeth **Jordon** had the following children:

1912   i. Charles L.[11] **Blanchard** was born in 1852.

1913   ii. Minnie **Blanchard** was born 14 October 1861.

1505. George Adelbert[10] Blanchard (Aaron[9], Lois[8] **Burt**, Abiah[7] **Mooar**, Abiah[6] **Hill**, Judith[5] **Bucknam**, Judith (Jude)[4] **Worth**, Susannah[3] **Whipple**, Elder John[2], Matthew[1])[2192] was born in Jefferson Co., N.Y. 14 May 1834, died 4 May 1875 in Havana, Ill. at 40 years of age, and was buried in Laurel Hill Cemetery, Block 4, Lot 2. He married **Amanda Walker** in Chicago, Ill. 17 March 1857. Amanda,[2193] daughter of James **Walker** and Elizabeth **Nichols**, was born 13 April 1835, died 18 October 1924 in Havana at 89 years of age, and was buried in Laurel Hill Cemetery. She married (2) **George W. Langford** 22 June 1878. George was decorated while serving as a captain in Co. C, 85th Ill. Vol. (Inf). during the Civil War and was a prisoner of war at the infamous Confederate prison in Andersonville, Ga. His family did not recognize him when he returned home. After the war his occupation was merchant and county clerk.

George Adelbert **Blanchard** and Amanda **Walker** had the following children:

> 1914   i.   Frank[11] **Blanchard**[2194] was born in Mason Co., Ill. 8 April 1858, died 17 April 1921 at 63 years of age, and is buried in Havana's Laurel Hill Cemetery.
>
> 1915   ii.   Harry Delbert **Blanchard**[2195] was born in Havana 17 May 1862 and died 26 June 1933 in Omaha, Nebr. at 71 years of age. He married Emma **Frances** before 1890. She was born in 1864 and died in 1925 at 61 years of age.[2196]
>
> + 1916   iii.   Nellie May **Blanchard** was born 22 February 1866.

1509. Datus W.[10] Hagedon (Sophia[9] **Blanchard**, Lois[8] **Burt**, Abiah[7] **Mooar**, Abiah[6] **Hill**, Judith[5] **Bucknam**, Judith (Jude)[4] **Worth**, Susannah[3] **Whipple**, Elder John[2], Matthew[1])[2197] was born in Ohio abt 1834 and died 20 December 1871 at 37 years of age. He married **Margaret Davidson** 3 July 1857.

Datus W. **Hagedon** and Margaret **Davidson** had the following child:

> 1917   i.   Clyde T.[11] **Hagedon**[2198].

1514. Elsie Boak[10] Williams (William Brown[9], Hannah Stone[8] **Brown**, Samuel[7], William[6], Martha[5] **Whipple**, Maj. John[4], Capt. John[3], Elder John[2], Matthew[1])[2199] was born in Boston, Mass. 5 January 1882 and died 13 August 1982 in Miami, Dade Co., Fla. at 100 years of age. She married **James Edgar Esson** in Dorchester, Mass. 16 June 1908. James,[2200] son of Charles **Esson** and Agnes **Rish**, was born in Glasgow, Scotland 24 July 1879 and died 31 August 1973 in Miami at 94 years of age.

Elsie Boak **Williams** and James Edgar **Esson** had the following children born in Chicago:

> 1918   i.   James Edgar[11] **Esson** Jr.[2201] was born 5 April 1909.
>
> 1919   ii.   Robert Boak **Esson**[2202] was born 18 October 1910 and died 27 November 1911 in Chicago at one year of age.
>
> + 1920   iii.   William Risk **Esson** was born 9 December 1912.
>
> 1921   iv.   Margaret Boak **Esson**[2203] was born 17 April 1916

1515. George Nichols[10] Stevens (Susan Poor[9] **Pearson**, Nathaniel[8], Sarah[7] **Gerrish**, Katherine[6] **Brown**, Martha[5] **Whipple**, Maj. John[4], Capt. John[3], Elder John[2], Matthew[1])[2204] was born in West Newbury, Mass. 5 December 1845 and died 30 January 1926 in Newburyport at 80 years. He married **Elizabeth Knight** in Georgetown, Mass. 29 March 1870. Elizabeth,[2205] daughter of John **Knight** and

Mary **Bryant**, was born in Abers Yehen Tienethin, Wales 3 September 1850 and died 22 June 1920 in Newburyport at 69 years of age. George and Elizabeth are buried in Belleville Cemetery.

George Nichols **Stevens** and Elizabeth **Knight** had the following children:

1922   i.   Bertha Viola[11] **Stevens**[2206] was born in West Newbury, Mass. 6 September 1870 and died in 1909 in Newburyport at 38 years of age. She married Calvin **Poore** who was born in 1866 and died in 1926 in Newburyport at 60 years of age. Bertha and Calvin are buried in Belleville Cemetery. Calvin married (2) Harriet W. **McKay**.[2207]

+ 1923   ii.   Orrin Belmont **Stevens** was born 29 December 1873.

+ 1924   iii.   Lottie Nichols **Stevens** was born 5 November 1880.

1526. William Orland[10] **Whipple** (William Ward[9], John[8], John[7], Capt. John[6], Capt. John[5], Maj. Matthew[4], Capt. John[3], Elder John[2], Matthew[1])[2208] was born in LaGrange, Mo. 21 October 1846 and died 17 March 1923 in Norton, Kans. at 76 years of age. He married **Martha Belle Coughenour** 17 August 1869. Martha,[2209] daughter of Henry **Caughenour** and Agnes **Likely**, was born in Brown Co., Ill. 26 June 1850 and died 18 May 1919 in Norton at 68 years of age. The family moved to Kansas from Mound City, Ill. in 1885. William was a farmer and their first Kansas home was a School Claim farm with sod house near New Almelo, Decatur Co. In April 1896 they began farming three miles south of Norton. After two years they moved to Lenora where William owned and operated a general store for two years. Later, they homesteaded near Aurora, five miles south of Dellvale. As an adjunct to his farming operation, William bought wild horses shipped in from the West which were broken to farm work by his sons and sold.

William Orland **Whipple** and Martha Belle **Coughenour** had the following children:

1925   i.   Mary Louise[11] **Whipple**[2210] was born in Clayton, Ill. 8 August 1870 and died 4 December 1957 in Norton at 86 years of age. She married A. A. **Bower** 23 January 1912.

+ 1926   ii.   Agnes Coughenour **Whipple** was born 14 December 1871.

+ 1927   iii.   William Henry **Whipple** was born 8 September 1874.

+ 1928   iv.   John Godfrey **Whipple** was born 5 March 1882.

+ 1929   v.   Clyde Ward **Whipple** was born 4 February 1886.

+ 1930   vi.   Carl Black **Whipple** was born 4 February 1886.

1529. Eunice Porter[10] **Wood** (Phebe Smith[9] **Whipple**, Stephen[8], Martha[7], Dea. Nathaniel[6], Capt. John[5], Maj. Matthew[4], Capt. John[3], Elder John[2], Matthew[1])[2211] was born in Cleveland, Ohio 1 December 1848 and died 12 July 1943 in Short Hills, N.H. at 94 years of age. She married **Theodore Charles Schenck** in Cleveland, Ohio. Theodore was born in Easton, Penn. 10 December 1831 and died 24 September 1888 in Canton, Ohio at 56 years of age. He was the son of Charles Morgan **Schenck** and Clarissa Antoinette **Smith**.[2212]

Eunice Porter **Wood** and Theodore Charles **Schenck** had the following child:

+ 1931   i.   Eunice[11] **Schenck** was born 22 February 1879.

1530. Proctor[10] **Patterson** (Phebe Smith[9] **Whipple**, Stephen[8], Martha[7], Dea. Nathaniel[6], Capt. John[5], Maj. Matthew[4], Capt. John[3], Elder John[2], Matthew[1])[2213] was born in Cleveland, Ohio 5 August 1863 and married **Greta Adele (Ada) Downer** in Saginaw, Mich. before 1888. Greta was born in Bay City, Bay Co., Mich. 27 March 1873.[2214]

Proctor **Patterson** and Greta Adele (Ada) **Downer** had the following child:
+ 1932   i. Ferne Catherine[11] **Patterson** was born 22 September 1889.

1541. **Alfred Church**[10] **Lane** (Jonathan Abbot[9], Jonathan[8], Jonathan[7], John[6], Job[5], Susanna[4] **Whipple**, Capt. John[3], Elder John[2], Matthew[1])[2215] was born abt 1863 and died 15 April 1948 in New York, N.Y. at 84 years of age. He married **Susanne Foster Lauriat** in Boston, Mass. 15 April 1896. Alfred attended the Boston Latin School and distinguished himself early by winning the Franklin medal. He was graduated from Harvard magna cum laude with an AB in mathematics in 1883. He instructed mathematics there until 1885. He studied for three semesters in Heidelberg, Germany and received his A.M. and Ph.D degrees from Harvard in 1887-1889. Tuffs gave him an honorary Sc.D in 1913. He taught and worked in geology at Michigan College of Mines beginning in 1889 and later served as state geologist until 1909 when he left to join the Tufts College faculty until his resignation in 1936. He was a pioneer in atomic research and credited with being the first to foresee the vast power possibilities in the destruction of atoms. In 1926 he inaugurated an international plan for the exchange of scientific information on smashing the atom. This led to a relationship with Otto Hahn, German A-bomb pioneer, and when Hahn succeeded in splitting the uranium atom in 1938, Dr. Lane was the first American to receive a complete report of the process which secret he immediately forwarded to Washington, D.C. Along with Sir James Chadwick and others, Dr. Lane was the first to make a study of neutrons, the particles which appear in the composition of the atom. This led to his appointment as head of the National Research Council's committee on the measurement of geologic time by atomic disintegration. He attracted much attention in 1936 when he resigned as Pearson Professor of Geology and Mineralogy at Tufts rather than submit to the teachers' oath law which he had opposed in legislative hearings. The college immediately elected him professor emeritus. He became an annual member of the New England Historic Genealogical Society 4 March 1924 and a corresponding member 3 Nov. 1936. He was the first appointed consultant in science in the Library of Congress, served as president of the Geological Society of America, and as an officer of the American Academy of Arts and Sciences.

Alfred Church **Lane** and Susane Foster **Lauriat** had the following children:
1933   i. Lauriat[11] **Lane**[2216] was living in Cambridge, Mass. in 1948.
1934   ii. Prof. Frederick Chapin **Lane**[2217] was teaching at John Hopkins University in 1948.
1935   iii. Harriet Page **Lane**[2218] married Clarence Dana **Rouillard**. They were living in Toronto, Canada in 1948.

1544. **Alonzo Herbert**[10] **Hatch** (Paschal[9], Anna[8] **Gould**, Anna[7] **Lane**, Timothy[6], Job[5], Susanna[4] **Whipple**, Capt. John[3], Elder John[2], Matthew[1])[2219] was born in Northfield, Vt. 12 April 1852 and died 8 December 1926 in Jefferson City, Mo. at 74 years of age. He married **Julia Ann Carney** in Gibson City, Ill. 1 March 1876. Julia was born in Winchester, Ky. 27 April 1858 and died 24 November 1938 in

Jefferson City, Mo. at 80 years of age.[2220]

Alonzo Herbert **Hatch** and Julia Ann **Carney** had the following children:

    1936   i.   Emma Alice[11] **Hatch**[2221] was born in Windsor, Ill. 20 November 1876.

+ 1937   ii. Jessamine Gertrude **Hatch** was born 2 November 1879.

1549. Dan Bonney[10] **Pangborn** (Diantha[9] **Worcester**, Martha[8] **Lane**, Gershom Flagg[7], John[6], John[5], Susanna[4] **Whipple**, Capt. John[3], Elder John[2], Matthew[1])[2222] was born in 1850 and died in 1943 at 93 years of age. He married **Sarah Adel Bowe** who was born in 1863 and died in 1934 at 71 years of age.[2223]

Dan Bonney **Pangborn** and Sarah Adel **Bowe** had the following child:

    1938   i.   Alta Ione[11] **Pangborn**[2224] was born on a farm near Shellsburg, Benton Co., Iowa 18 January 1889 and died in 1931 at 42 years of age. In addition to Elder John Whipple of Ipswich, she descends on her mother's line from two lines of Capt. John Whipple of Providence, R.I.: John Whipple Jr. and Rebecca Browne Scott and Col. Joseph Whipple and Alice Smith.

1550. Frederick Augustus Parker[10] **Fiske** (Elisabeth Ann[9] **Parkhurst**, Rev. John[8], Betsey[7] **Hutchinson**, Rebecca[6] **Lane**, James[5], Susanna[4] **Whipple**, Capt. John[3], Elder John[2], Matthew[1])[2225] was born in Chelmsford, Mass. 4 October 1859 and died there 13 January 1939 at 79 years of age. He married **Harriet Lydia Locke** in Winchester, Mass. 2 July 1890. Harriet was born in Burlington, Mass. 25 March 1862 and died 16 September 1903 in Somerville, Mass. at 41 years of age.[2226]

Frederick Augustus Parker **Fiske** and Harriet Lydia **Locke** had the following child:

+ 1939   i.   Wyman Parkhurst[11] **Fiske** was born 11 January 1900.

1551. Edward E.[10] **Poor** (Mary Wellington[9] **Lane**, Washington Jefferson Poor[8], Ebenezer[7], Samuel[6], James[5], Susanna[4] **Whipple**, Capt. John[3], Elder John[2], Matthew[1])[2227] was born in Arlington, Middlesex Co., Mass. 2 December 1868 and died 5 October 1951 in Passaic, N. J. at 82 years of age. He married twice. (1) **Susie Grimes** 18 January 1888. Susie was from North Adams, Mass. and died in 1912.[2228] (2) **Edith Adams** in 1913. Edward worked with the Denny, Poor, & Company, agents for the Passaic Print Works until 1900 when he organized the firm of Edward E. Poor & Company. The company was dissolved in 1914 and he became president and owner of a controlling interest in the Print Works. It was the first firm in the cotton industry to maintain a testing and experimental laboratory. The firm was dissolved in 1936 and Edward retired from active business. He was a member of the New England Society of New York, of the Union League of New York, a member of the New York Athletic Club, of the Balmoral Golf Club, the Merchants Club, and the Sons of the Revolution. He traces his Poor descent from John Poor of Rowley, Mass. who died about November 1684. He was elected a resident (annual) member of the New England Historic Genealogical Society 4 April 1917.

Edward E. **Poor** and Susie **Grimes** had the following children:

    1940   i.   Marion[11] **Poor**[2229]. She married (__) **Brown**.

    1941   ii. Arthur G. **Poor**[2230].

    1942   iii. Edward Eri **Poor** Jr. was born 7 November 1889.

1555. Cora Adalaide[10] **Whipple** (Alonzo Lyman[9], John[9], John[8], John[7], Capt. John[6], Capt. John[5], Maj. Matthew[4], Capt. John[3], Elder John[2], Matthew[1])[2231] was born in Hamilton, Essex Co., Mass. 13 January 1875 and died 6 July 1956 in Beverly, Essex Co., Mass. at 81 years of age. She married **William Perley Hanners** in Wenham, Essex Co., Mass. 30 June 1897. William,[2232] son of John **Hanners** and Louisa Loring **Eldredge**, was born in Beverly 21 December 1867 and died there 29 June 1944 at 76 years of age.

Cora Adalaide **Whipple** and William Perley **Hanners** had the following children:

+ 1943	i.	Roger Whipple[11] **Hanners** was born 17 July 1899.
+ 1944	ii.	Ralph Loring **Hanners** was born 9 March 1901.
+ 1945	iii.	Dwight Eldridge **Hanners** was born 24 October 1905.

1557. John[10] **Powers** (Cyrus Hale Stone[9], Lavinia[8] **Stone**, Capt. Amos[7], Amos[6], Simon[5], Deacon Simon[4], Mary[3] **Whipple**, Elder John[2], Matthew[1])[2233] was born in Steuben Co., N.Y. 1 November 1841 and died 12 April 1919 in Des Moines, Iowa of a diabetic coma at 77 years of age. He married **Eliza Augusta Partridge** in Macon, Bureau Co., Ill. 1 January 1868. Eliza,[2234] daughter of Lyman **Partridge** and Ellen **Miner**, was born in either Peacham or Montpelier, Vt. 11 April 1848 and died in June 1911 in Bureau Co. Ill. of heart disease at 63 years of age. She was educated at Peacham Academy in Vermont and Princeton Academy in Bureau Co. They are buried in adjacent graves at Mount Bloom Cemetery in Bureau Co. He was a farmer and a Mason.

John **Powers** and Eliza Augusta **Partridge** had the following children born in Bureau Co., Ill:

1946	i.	Florence Victorine[11] **Powers**[2235] was born in 1871 and married Lyman B. **Kirkpatrick**.
+ 1947	ii.	Cyrus Hale Stone **Powers** was born 5 March 1872.
1948	iii.	Nancy **Powers**[2236] was born in Tiskilwa, Bureau Co. 5 March 1872.
+ 1949	iv.	John Ellsworth **Powers** was born 19 November 1873.
1950	v.	Jerome Augustus **Powers**[2237] was born 8 July 1875 and was living in Washington State in 1908.
1951	vi.	Burton Roscoe **Powers**[2238] was born 12 December 1876 and was living in Cuba in 1908.
1952	vii.	Alice Josephine **Powers**[2239] was born 11 January 1879 and died 28 August 1929 in New Mexico at 50 years of age. She was a school teacher and is buried in Section 4, Lot 11 of Mount Bloom Cemetery, Bureau Co. (See *Lot Book* page 120).
+ 1953	viii.	Olive Evalena **Powers** was born 19 August 1880.
1954	ix.	Lawrence Clement **Powers**[2240] was born 18 August 1885 and was educated at Oberlin College.
+ 1955	x.	Dr. Wilbur Louis **Powers** was born 5 March 1887.
1956	xi.	Fred Richmond **Powers**[2241] was born 5 March 1891 and married Carrie May **Pervier** in Sheffield, Bureau Co. 14 September 1915.

1562. Cyrus Cameron[10] **Powers** (Cyrus Hale Stone[9], Lavinia[8] **Stone**, Capt. Amos[7], Amos[6], Simon[5], Deacon Simon[4], Mary[3] **Whipple**, Elder John[2], Matthew[1])[2242] was born in Steuben Co., N.Y. 7 April 1854 and died 19 January 1916 in Creston, Union Co., Iowa at 61 years of age. He married twice. (1) **Emma Brown**. (2) **Jennie**

Lind **Shepard** in Steuben Co. 3 April 1882. Jennie[2243] was the daughter of Otis **Shepard** and Lydia **Aulls**.

Cyrus Cameron **Powers** and Emma **Brown** had the following child:

    1957   i.   Claud C.[11] **Powers**[2244].

Cyrus Cameron **Powers** and Jennie Lind **Shepard** had the following children:

    1958   ii.   Katherine Myrtle **Powers**[2245] was born 6 November 1883 and married Roy **Jenks**.

    1959   iii.   Errol Jennie **Powers**[2246] was born in Union Co., Iowa 5 September 1885 and married Edward **Wilcox**.

    1960   iv.   Ermon Cameron **Powers**[2247] was born in Union Co. 5 September 1885 and died abt 1960 in San Diego, Calif..

+ 1961   v.   Leroy Cyrus **Powers** was born 1 April 1887.

    1962   vi.   Frances **Powers**[2248] was born in Union Co. 26 January 1890 and died in Creston.

+1963   vii.   Clara **Powers** was born 13 November 1894.

1563. William B.[10] **Powers** (Cyrus Hale Stone[9], Lavinia[8] **Stone**, Capt. Amos[7], Amos[6], Simon[5], Deacon Simon[4], Mary[3] **Whipple**, Elder John[2], Matthew[1])[2249] was born in Indiantown Township, Bureau Co. Ill. 11 April 1858 and married **Helen Frances Partridge** in Buda, Bureau Co., Ill. 9 November 1880. Helen was the daughter of Lyman **Partridge** and Ellen **Miner**.[2250]

William B. **Powers** and Helen Frances **Partridge** had the following children

    1964   i.   Clarence William[11] **Powers**[2251] was born 19 April 1886 and died 29 April 1886 at less than one year of age.

    1965   ii.   Howard Cameron **Powers**[2252] was born 24 October 1887.

    1966   iii.   Myrtle N. **Powers**[2253] was born 3 September 1889 and died 6 June 1890 at less than one year of age.

    1967   iv.   Hazel **Powers**[2254] was born 27 June 1891 and died 29 June 1891 at less than one year of age.

    1968   v.   Clyde **Powers**[2255] was born 2 January 1896 and died 31 December 1897 at one year of age.

    1969   vi.   Floyd Hale **Powers**[2256] was born in Kewanee, Henry Co., Ill. 12 March 1899.

1566. Vanderveer[10] **Davis** (Eliza B.[9] **Powers**, Lavinia[8] **Stone**, Capt. Amos[7], Amos[6], Simon[5], Deacon Simon[4], Mary[3] **Whipple**, Elder John[2], Matthew[1])[2257] was born 18 March 1852 and died 7 November 1890 in Waco., Nebr. at 38 years of age. He married **Alice L. Partridge** in Buda, Bureau Co., Ill., 20 January 1875. Alice[2258] was the daughter of Lyman **Partridge** and Ellen **Miner**.

Vanderveer **Davis** and Alice L. **Partridge** had the following children:

    1970   i.   Clinton DeWitt[11] **Davis**[2259].

    1971   ii.   Fannie E. **Davis**[2260] was born in Waco., Nebr. 1 October 1883.

1574. George Fisher[10] **Pollard** (Elizabeth[9] **Tyler**, Alma Ellery[8] **Holden**, Phineas[7], Capt. Asa[6], Abigail[5] **Stone**, Deacon Simon[4], Mary[3] **Whipple**, Elder John[2], Matthew[1])[2261] was born in Massachusetts.

George Fisher **Pollard** had the following children:

    1972   i.   Bessie[11] **Pollard**[2262].

    1973   ii.   Harry **Pollard** was born in 1878 and died in 1953 at 75 years of age.

1578. **Edward**[10] **Kelley** (Harriett Newell[9] **Tyler**, Alma Ellery[8] **Holden**, Phineas[7], Capt. Asa[6], Abigail[5] **Stone**, Deacon Simon[4], Mary[3] **Whipple**, Elder John[2], Matthew[1])[2263] birth date unknown.

Edward **Kelley** had the following child:
    1974   i. Dr. John S.[11] **Kelley**,[2264].

1582. **James Ellery**[10] **Eaton**, (Alma Ellery[9] **Tyler**, Alma Ellery[8] **Holden**, Phineas[7], Capt. Asa[6], Abigail[5] **Stone**, Deacon Simon[4], Mary[3] **Whipple**, Elder John[2], Matthew[1])[2265] was born in Massachusetts in 1855 and married **Flora Timpany**.

James Ellery **Eaton**, and Flora **Timpany** had the following children:
+ 1975   i. Tyler[11] **Eaton**,.
  1976   ii. Ellery T. **Eaton**,[2266].

1583. **Alma Ellery**[10] **Eaton**, (Alma Ellery[9] **Tyler**, Alma Ellery[8] **Holden**, Phineas[7], Capt. Asa[6], Abigail[5] **Stone**, Deacon Simon[4], Mary[3] **Whipple**, Elder John[2], Matthew[1])[2267] was born in S. Deerfield, Mass. in 1858 and died in 1949 at 91 years of age. She married **Dr. Herbert B. Royal** in Harvard, Middlesex Co., Mass. 19 June 1888. Herbert was born in 1863 and died in 1949 at 86 years of age.[2268]

Alma Ellery **Eaton**, and Dr. Herbert B. **Royal** had the following children:
+ 1977   i. Kent Tyler[11] **Royal**, was born 25 October 1891.
+ 1978   ii. Ellery Eaton **Royal** was born 14 July 1894.
  1979   iii. Austin Garland **Royal**, was born in Harvard 5 October 1895[2269] and died there of pneumonia 24 February 1896 at less than one year of age.[2270]

1587. **Allen Harlow**[10] **Bacon** (Samuel Newton[9], Alma Ellery[8] **Holden**, Phineas[7], Capt. Asa[6], Abigail[5] **Stone**, Deacon Simon[4], Mary[3] **Whipple**, Elder John[2], Matthew[1])[2271] was born in Albany, N.Y. 13 February 1864 and died there 18 June 1929 at 65 years of age. He married **Jennie Adelaide Mather** in Loudonville, N.Y. 17 May 1894. Jennie,[2272] daughter of Andrew Adrian **Mather** and Adelaide Julia **Birdsail**, was born in Burlington, N.Y. 2 August 1865 and died 29 January 1956 in Albany at 90 years of age.

Allen Harlow **Bacon** and Jennie Adelaide **Mather** had the following children:
+ 1980   i. Samuel Newton[11] **Bacon** was born 18 February 1895.
  1981   ii. Catharine Mather **Bacon**[2273] was born in Loudonville 2 July 1896.
+ 1982   iii. Elizabeth Harlow **Bacon** was born 2 April 1898.
  1983   iv. (Boy) **Bacon**[2274] was born in Loudonville 19 November 1899 and died the day of birth.
  1984   v. Marion **Bacon**[2275] was born in Loudonville 20 January 1901 and died 23 June 1975 in Sharon, Conn. at 74 years of age.
+ 1985   vi. Allen Harlow **Bacon**, Jr. was born 8 November 1902.

1589. **Sarah Cornelia**[10] **Bacon** (Joseph Austin[9], Alma Ellery[8] **Holden**, Phineas[7], Capt. Asa[6], Abigail[5] **Stone**, Deacon Simon[4], Mary[3] **Whipple**, Elder John[2], Matthew[1])[2276] was born 3 September 1873 and died in 1958 in Mechanicville, N.Y at 84 years of age. She married **Dr. G. Worden Crissey** in 1904. He was born in 1876 and died in 1970 in Mechanicville at 94 years of age.[2277]

Sarah Cornelia **Bacon** and Dr. G. Worden **Crissey** had the following child:

1986   i. Cornelia[11] **Crissey**,[2278] was born in 1910.

1591. William Dustin[10] **Carr** (Lyman[9], Susanna[8] **Dunton**, Mary[7] **Jewell**, Mary[6] **Whitney**, Mary[5] **Stone**, Deacon Simon[4], Mary[3] **Whipple**, Elder John[2], Matthew[1])[2279] was born in Stowe, Mass. 10 October 1823 and died 20 June 1864 in Point Lookout, Md. at 40 years of age. He married **Ellen Walsh**. Ellen was born in County Cork, Ireland 1 October 1830 and died 21 January 1903 in Lancaster, Worcester Co. Mass. at 72 years of age.[2280]

William Dustin **Carr** and Ellen **Walsh** had the following child:
+ 1987   i. Mary Olive[11] **Carr** was born 15 December 1854.

1592. Winnifred Phyllis[10] **Stone** (John Putnam[9], Reedsburg[8], David[7], Lt. James[6], James[5], John[4], Mary[3] **Whipple**, Elder John[2], Matthew[1])[2281] was born in Reedsburg, Wisc. 21 July 1878 and died 7 April 1941 in Madison, Wisc. at 62 years of age. She married **Norman Thomas Gill** 11 December 1901. Norman,[2282] son of Thomas **Gill** and Susan Hariet **Freeman**, was born in Lima, Wisc. 22 October 1876.

Following graduation from Reedsburg high school in 1896, Winnifred was graduated from the Whitewater State Teachers College in 1899. She taught school for two years following graduation. She joined the Daughters of the American Revolution in 1905 and served 13 years as regent of the Fay Robinson Chapter at Reedsburg. The family moved to Madison in 1928 where she served as treasurer, vice regent, regent, and honorary regent of the John Bell Chapter. She was also treasurer of the State Society for three years and state chair of the committee on conservation and the committee for marking historic spots. She was a founder and first president of the Wisconsin Genealogical Society organized in September 1939; associate editor of the *Wisconsin Families Magazine*, a member of the Roger Williams and the Edmond Rice Family Associations, the Founders of Hartford, the Magna Charta Dames, and the Madison branch of the National League of American Pen Women. She was also a professional genealogist of high rank and conducted a genealogical column of questions and answers in the Sunday edition of the *Wisconsin State Journal*. She was elected an annual member of the New England Historic Genealogical Society 6 Oct. 1936 and was survived by her husband and two sons.

Winnifred Phyllis **Stone** and Norman Thomas **Gill** had the following children:
1988   i. John Kenneth[11] **Gill**[2283] earned a Ph.B degree from Carrol College in 1926 and was a banker in Middleton, Wisc. at the time of his mother's death.
1989   ii. Charles H. Stone **Gill**[2284] earned a Ph.B degree at the U. of Wisconsin in 1935 and was living in Madison, Wisc. at the time of his mother's death.

1594. Nahum Parks[10] **Goddard** (Alvira C.[9], David[8], Asa[7], Nathan[6], Edward[5], Susanna[4] **Stone**, Mary[3] **Whipple**, Elder John[2], Matthew[1])[2287] was born in 1829 and married **Mary Pease Upham**.

Nahum Parks **Goddard** and Mary Pease **Upham** had the following child:
+ 1990   i.   Nahum Danforth[11] **Goddard** was born in 1859.

1595. Edwin Henry[10] **King** (John[9], Lois[8] **Jackson**, Lois[7] **Woodward**,, Mary[6] **Stone**, Samuel[5], Ebenezer[4], Mary[3] **Whipple**, Elder John[2], Matthew[1])[2288] was born in Franklin, Mass. 24 November 1832, died 2 May 1915 in Jersey City, N.J. at 82 years of age, and was buried in the Albany, N.Y. Rural Cemetery. He married **Martha Elizabeth Daniels** in Franklin, Mass. 22 October 1857. Martha,[2289] daughter of Albert Early **Daniels** and Olive Gilmore **Hills**, was born in Franklin 6 April 1836 and died 12 March 1875 in Albany at 38 years of age.

Edwin Henry **King** and Martha Elizabeth **Daniels** had the following children:
+ 1991   i.   Nellie Frances[11] **King** was born 29 May 1859.
   1992   ii.   Mary Ada **King**[2290] was born in Albany, N.Y. 27 May 1862 and died 20 August 1941 in Jersey City at 79 years of age. She married Wolf Stephen Adrian **von Borcke** 29 September 1878.

1597. Ezra Almon[10] **Jenne** (Sarah Jane[9] **Johnson**, John[8], Abner[7], Hannah[6] **Eaton**, Lydia Abiah[5] **Starr**, Mary[4] **Stone**, Mary[3] **Whipple**, Elder John[2], Matthew[1])[2291] was born in Fowler, N.Y. 22 August 1840 and died 9 April 1911 in Gouverneur, N.Y. at 70 years of age. He married **Lavilla Elva Moody** in Brooklyn, N.Y. 22 October 1874. Lavilla,[2292] daughter of Dexter **Moody** and Delia **Reed**, was born 29 December 1850. Ezra was the proprietor of a lumber yard.

Ezra Almon **Jenne** and Lavilla Elva **Moody** had the following children:
   1993   i.   Mabelle Rita[11] **Jenne**[2293] was born in Brooklyn, N.Y. 26 March 1876 and died 19 February 1904 at 27 years of age.
   1994   ii.   Hazel Preston **Jenne**[2294] was born in Gouverneur 20 July 1886.

1598. Jerome Adelbert[10] **Jenne** (Sarah Jane[9] **Johnson**, John[8], Abner[7], Hannah[6] **Eaton**, Lydia Abiah[5] **Starr**, Mary[4] **Stone**, Mary[3] **Whipple**, Elder John[2], Matthew[1])[2295] was born in Fowler, N.Y. 13 December 1843 and died 3 September 1890 in Russell, St. Lawrence Co., N.Y. at 46 years of age. He married **Anna Sarah Hazelton** in Fullerville, N.Y. 17 December 1867. Anna,[2296] daughter of Galusha **Hazelton** and Harriet **Kelley**, was born in Fowler 24 May 1846 and died 13 December 1927 in Russell at 81 years of age. Jerome, a Civil War veteran (enlisted at 17), operated a general store in Russell, N.Y.

Jerome Adelbert **Jenne** and Anna Sarah **Hazelton** had the following children:
   1995   i.   Anna Belle[11] **Jenne**[2297] was born in Fowler, 13 July 1868 and died 18 December 1930 in Russell at 62 years of age. She married Joseph **Clark** in 1883.
   1996   ii.   Frances May **Jenne**[2298] was born in Fowler 15 May 1870 and died 15 March 1962 in Massena, St. Lawrence Co., N.Y. at 91 years of age. She

married Eben **Briggs** 1 July 1888. Eben[2299] was the son of Rev. E. **Briggs**.

+ 1997   iii.   Myrtle **Jenne** was born 29 March 1872.

1998   iv.   Jerome E. **Jenne**[2300] was born in Russell 2 February 1874 and died in Yakima, Wash. He married Gertrude **Knox** in 1902. Gertrude[2301] was the daughter of William **Knox** and Martha M. **Kittie**.

1999   v.   Kittie **Jenne**[2302] was born in Russell 21 April 1876 and died there in May 1879 at 3 years of age.

+ 2000   vi.   Frank **Jenne** was born 6 April 1878.

2001   vii.   Evelyn **Jenne**[2303] was born in Russell 8 April 1882 and died there in January 1898 at 15 years of age.

2002   viii.   Bessie **Jenne**[2304] was born in Russell 18 August 1884 and died 18 February 1978 in Canton, N.Y. at 93 years of age. She married twice. (1) Knox **Smith** 3 December 1902. (2) Earle **Whitmarsh** in Carthage, N.Y. 29 May 1930.

2003   ix.   Hazelton **Jenne**[2305] was born in Russell 31 May 1886 and died in 1953 in Los Angeles, Calif. at 67 years of age.

1610. Austin Eaton[10] **Patterson** (Esther Adeline[9] **Eaton**, Arrunah[8], John[7], John[6], Lydia Abiah[5] **Starr**, Mary[4] **Stone**, Mary[3] **Whipple**, Elder John[2], Matthew[1])[2306] was born in Huron Co., Ohio 29 July 1832 and died 4 November 1896 in Oskaloosa, Jefferson Co., Kans. at 64 years of age. He married **Lydia Jane Barker** in Peru, Huron Co., Ohio 5 January 1859. Lydia was the daughter of Robert D. **Barker** and Lucy **Standish**.

Austin Eaton **Patterson** and Lydia Jane **Barker** had the following child:

+ 2004   i.   Louisa Malvina[11] **Patterson** was born 27 November 1869.

1611. Mary Frances[10] **Grow** (Lorenzo[9], Samuel Porter[8], Joseph[7], Abigail[6] **Dana**, Susanna[5] **Starr**, Mary[4] **Stone**, Mary[3] **Whipple**, Elder John[2], Matthew[1])[2307] was born in Vasselboro, Maine 23 October 1846 and married **Arthur William Newell** in Lincoln, Iowa 24 May 1868. Arthur was born in China, Maine 17 December 1844 and died 7 February 1888 in LaGrange, Cook Co., Ill. at 43 years of age.[2308]

Mary Frances **Grow** and Arthur William **Newell** had the following child:

+ 2005   i.   Nellie Eliza[11] **Newell** was born 25 March 1869.

1612. Ralph Ernest[10] **Patch** (Edward[9], Luther[8], Thomas[7], Penelope[6] **Dana**, Susanna[5] **Starr**, Mary[4] **Stone**, Mary[3] **Whipple**, Elder John[2], Matthew[1])[2309] was born 10 October 1869 and died 12 July 1956 in Patch Grove, Wisc. at 86 years of age. He married **Edna Hicklin** 2 January 1884. She died 20 April 1949 in Patch Grove at 80 years of age.[2310]

Ralph Ernest **Patch** and Edna **Hicklin** had the following children:

+ 2006   i.   James Edward[11] **Patch** was born 27 December 1901.

2007   ii.   Edna Marion **Patch**[2311] was born 6 August 1906 and died 22 June 1996 at 89 years of age.

1613. Victoria Josephine[10] **Moor** (Abigail[9] **Franklin**, Luther[8], Sarah[7] **Starr**, Capt. Comfort[6], Comfort[5], Mary[4] **Stone**, Mary[3] **Whipple**, Elder John[2], Matthew[1])[2312] was born in Ponney Hollow, Vt. 14 March 1846 and died 14 March 1885 in Plymouth, Vt. at 39 years of age. She married **Col. John Calvin Coolidge** 6 May 1868. He was born in Plymouth 31 March 1845 and died there 18 March 1926 at

80 years of age.[2313] He married (2) **Caroline Brown** 9 September 1891.

Victoria Josephine **Moor** and Col. John Calvin **Coolidge** had the following children:

+ 2008   i. Pres. John Calvin[11] **Coolidge** was born 4 July 1872.

2009   ii. Abigail Gratia **Coolidge**[2314] was born in Plymouth, Vt. 1875 and died in 1890 at 15 years of age.

1615. Emery Marncy DeLafayette[10] Ball (Wilbur Fiske[9], James Bradley[8], Abigail[7] **Starr**, Capt. Comfort[6], Comfort[5], Mary[4] **Stone**, Mary[3] **Whipple**, Elder John[2], Matthew[1])[2315] was born in Newark, Vt. 9 May 1845 and married **Sarah L. Peck** in September 1875.

Emery Marncy DeLafayette **Ball** and Sarah L. **Peck** had the following children:

2010   i. Elizabeth A.[11] **Ball**[2316] was born 17 September 1876.

2011   ii. Willard **Ball**[2317] was born 4 January 1878.

2012   iii. Frank **Ball**[2318] was born in 1880.

1616. Hannah Iola[10] Ball (Wilbur Fiske[9], James Bradley[8], Abigail[7] **Starr**, Capt. Comfort[6], Comfort[5], Mary[4] **Stone**, Mary[3] **Whipple**, Elder John[2], Matthew[1])[2319] was born in Concord, Vt. 22 March 1847 and married **Francis Pearly Johnson** 4 December 1867.

Hannah Iola **Ball** and Francis Pearly **Johnson** had the following children:

2013   i. Martha Jane[11] **Johnson**[2320] was born 6 January 1872.

2014   ii. Mabel Frances **Johnson**[2321] was born 11 March 1873.

2015   iii. Francis Perley **Johnson** Jr.[2322] was born 20 December 1882.

1617. Wilbur Fiske[10] Ball Jr. (Wilbur Fiske[9], James Bradley[8], Abigail[7] **Starr**, Capt. Comfort[6], Comfort[5], Mary[4] **Stone**, Mary[3] **Whipple**, Elder John[2], Matthew[1])[2323] was born in Littleton, Grafton Co., N.H. 23 December 1851 and died 15 June 1893 at 41 years of age. He married **Ida E. Green** 6 September 1873.

Wilbur Fiske **Ball** Jr. and Ida E. **Green** had the following children:

2016   i. Lucius W.[11] **Ball**[2324] was born 25 February 1874.

2017   ii. Walter L. **Ball**[2325] was born 2 August 1876.

2018   iii. Pearl A. **Ball**[2326] was born 22 June 1878.

2019   iv. Edwin G. **Ball**[2327] was born 9 September 1880.

2020   v. Harry W. **Ball**[2328] was born 11 April 1889.

2021   vi. Celia A. **Ball**[2329] was born 5 April 1891.

1618. Lydia Thurlow[10] Ball (Wilbur Fiske[9], James Bradley[8], Abigail[7] **Starr**, Capt. Comfort[6], Comfort[5], Mary[4] **Stone**, Mary[3] **Whipple**, Elder John[2], Mattthew[1])[2330] was born in Littleton, Grafton Co., N.H. 18 July 1853 and married **Milo A. Elliott** 2 July 1871.

Lydia Thurlow **Ball** and Milo A. **Elliott** had the following children:

2022   i. Alfred M.[11] **Elliott**[2331] was born 4 March 1872.

2023   ii. Nellie Hannah **Elliott**[2332] was born 29 May 1873.

2024   iii. Bertha May **Elliott**[2333] was born 6 October 1875.

2025   iv. Herbert Myron John **Elliott**[2334] was born 5 July 1879.

2026   v. Winifred Grace **Elliott**[2335] was born 14 April 1881.

1619. Nellie Randilla[10] Ball (Wilbur Fiske[9], James Bradley[8], Abigail[7] **Starr**,

Capt. Comfort[6], Comfort[5], Mary[4] **Stone**, Mary[3] **Whipple**, Elder John[2], Matthew[1])[2336] was born in Groveton, N.H. 8 January 1856 and died 5 December 1906 at 50 years of age. She married **A. Parker Woodman Jr.** 23 January 1877.

Nellie Randilla **Ball** and A. Parker **Woodman** Jr. had the following children:

2027	i.	Emma Judith[11] **Woodman**[2337] was born 9 February 1878.
2028	ii.	Nellie Ethelyn **Woodman**[2338] was born 30 May 1891.

1622. Francis Herbert[10] Ball (Wilbur Fiske[9], James Bradley[8], Abigail[7] **Starr**, Capt. Comfort[6], Comfort[5], Mary[4] **Stone**, Mary[3] **Whipple**, Elder John[2], Matthew[1])[2339] was born in Lancaster, N.H. 20 January 1866 and died 29 May 1931 at 65 years of age. He married **Annie W. Munsey** 24 May 1890.

Francis Herbert **Ball** and Annie W. **Munsey** had the following children:

2029	i.	Lydia Hannah[11] **Ball**[2340] was born 21 July 1891.
+ 2030	ii.	Wilbur Fiske **Ball** was born 29 August 1894
2031	iii.	Herbert Francis **Ball**[2341] was born 27 August 1900.

1625. Mary Arvilla[10] Viersen (Mary[9] **Starr**, Lovel[8], Comfort[7], Capt. Comfort[6], Comfort[5], Mary[4] **Stone**, Mary[3] **Whipple**, Elder John[2], Matthew[1])[2342] was born in Cass Co., Iowa 25 February 1862 and died 2 May 1952 in Stanton, Stanton Co., Nebr. at 90 years of age. She married **William Peter Wilson** in Atlantic, Cass Co., Iowa 27 January 1881. William,[2343] son of John P. **Wilson** and Mary Ann **Moore**, was born in Jones Co., Iowa 26 May 1856 and died 17 February 1926 in Stanton at 69 years of age. He was buried in Pilger, Stanton Co. Nebr.

Mary Arvilla **Viersen** and William Peter **Wilson** had the following children:

2032	i.	Clara Arvilla[11] **Wilson**[2344] was born in Cass Co. 9 October 1881 and died there 12 October 1882 at one year of age.
2033	ii.	Lafayette Carrol **Wilson**[2345] was born in Cass Co. 2 October 1883 and died 12 May 1968 in Stanton at 84 years of age. He married Dora **Frank** 28 March 1903.[2346]
+ 2034	iii.	Estella Grace **Wilson** was born 9 February 1886.
2035	iv.	William Peter **Wilson** Jr.[2347] was born in Nebraska 18 August 1888 and married Mary **Scherer** 16 June 1909. [2348]
2036	v.	Mattie Ethel **Wilson**[2349] was born in Nebraska in February 1891 and died 22 May 1978 at 87 years of age. She married Grant **Denny** 20 April 1910.[2350]
2037	vi.	Myrle Audrey **Wilson**[2351] was born in Pilger in July 1899 and died 2 October 1993 in Pender, Thurston Co., Nebr. at 94 years of age. She married Jesse **Lorensen** 30 June 1920.[2352]
2038	vii.	Harold Evered **Wilson**[2353] was born in Pilger 2 May 1901 and died after 1995. He married Leone **Matthes** 13 April 1922.[2354] Harold and Leone moved to Silverton, Oreg. in 1948.
2039	viii.	Howard Lovel Starr **Wilson**[2355] was born in Pilger 21 May 1903 and died 8 May 1965 in Washington State at 61 years of age. He married Lorene (__) 6 March 1929.

1634. Minnie Elnora[10] Cram (Angeline[9] **Ward**, Elsie Elizabeth[8] **Starr**, Ebenezer[7], Ebenezer[6], Comfort[5], Mary[4] **Stone**, Mary[3] **Whipple**, Elder John[2], Matthew[1])[2356] was born in Pawtucket, R.I. 12 February 1870 and died there 30 March 1959 at 89 years of age. She married **Charles Alden Spooner** in Pawtucket

6 June 1888. Charles,[2357] son of Charles Martin **Spooner** and Anna Elizabeth **Campbell**, was born in Penob Co., Maine 6 June 1867 and died 26 December 1935 in Hebronville, Mass. at 68 years of age.

Minnie Elnora **Cram** and Charles Alden **Spooner** had the following child:
+ 2040   i. Ruth Elizabeth[11] **Spooner** was born 8 July 1898.

1635. Harriet Elizabeth[10] Watrous (Caroline M.[9] **Estey**, John Dean[8], John Dean[7], Solomon[6], Elizabeth Mary[5] **Stearns**, Elizabeth[4] **Stone**, Mary[3] **Whipple**, Elder John[2], Matthew[1])[2358] was born in Jackson Co., Iowa 1 November 1865 and died 27 March 1935 in Maquoketa, Iowa at 69 years of age. She married **Joseph Thomas Wallace Brush** in Maquoketa 2 November 1881. Joseph,[2359] son of Daniel H. **Brush** and Almyra **Blackburn**, was born in Maquoketa 4 January 1855 and died 30 May 1904 at 49 years of age.

Harriet Elizabeth **Watrous** and Joseph Thomas Wallace **Brush** had the following children born in Maquoketa:
2041   i. Archie James[11] **Brush**[2360] was born 28 October 1883.
2042   ii. Myrtle Ida **Brush** was born 17 October 1886.[2361]
2043   iii. J. Earl **Brush**[2362] was born 5 May 1889 and died 20 December 1979 in Phoenix, Ariz. at 90 years of age. He married Linne **Morehead**.
2044   iv. Lula Caroline **Brush**[2363] was born 30 May 1891 and married Boulucas **Nelson**.
+ 2045   v. Norah Leona **Brush** was born 11 August 1893.

1638. Daisie[10] Stearns (Abdellah M.[9], Harrison[8], Phineas[7], Eliphet[6], Rev. Ebenezer[5], Elizabeth[4] **Stone**, Mary[3] **Whipple**, Elder John[2], Matthew[1])[2364] birth date unknown married **Frank A. Pettit Sr.**

Daisie **Stearns** and Frank A. **Pettit** Sr. had the following child:
+ 2046   i. Frank Allan[11] **Pettit**.

1639. Almira D.[10] Smith (James[9], George[8], Hannah[7] **Wilbor**, Mary[6] **Stearns**, Jonathan[5], Elizabeth[4] **Stone**, Mary[3] **Whipple**, Elder John[2], Matthew[1])[2365] was born in Taunton, Mass. 15 January 1842 and died 27 November 1914 in Brockton, Plymouth Co., Mass. at 72 years of age. She married **Norman G. Makepeace** in Raynham, Mass. 5 January 1859. Norman was born 13 June 1838 and died 15 July 1905 at 67 years of age.[2366]

Almira D. **Smith** and Norman G. **Makepeace** had the following child:
+ 2047   i. Etta Rosella[11] **Makepeace** was born 24 October 1873.

1640. Elizabeth Tracy[10] Mercer (Catherine Lorette[9] **Orvis**, Lucinda Chipman[8] **Upham**, Joseph Pierce[7], Asa[6], Hannah[5] **Stearns**, Elizabeth[4] **Stone**, Mary[3] **Whipple**, Elder John[2], Matthew[1])[2367] was born in Utica, Ind. 22 June 1848 and died 14 March 1904 in Jeffersonville, Ind. at 55 years of age. She married **Lewis Girdler** 21 December 1871. Lewis,[2368] son of John **Girdler** and Sarah Jane **Gardner**, was born in Marblehead, Essex Co., Mass. 9 May 1849 and died 7 May 1928 in Jeffersonville, Ind. at 78 years of age.

Elizabeth Tracy **Mercer** and Lewis **Girdler** had the following child:
+ 2048   i. Kate Orvis[11] **Girdler** was born 14 March 1875.

1642. Almon Woodward[10] Hastings (Susan[9] **Goddard**, Enoch

Elbert[8], Ebenezer[7], Nathan[6], Edward[5], Susanna[4] **Stone**, Mary[3] **Whipple**, Elder John[2], Matthew[1])[2369] was born in Jamaica, Vt. 22 January 1839 and died 15 July 1922 in Jefferson, Greene Co., Iowa at 83 years of age. He married **Mayette Eliz Person** in Townshend, Vt, 1 January 1862. Mayette was born in Windham, Vt. 27 October 1842 and died 15 July 1922 in Jefferson at 79 years of age.[2370]

Almon Woodward **Hastings** and Mayette Eliz **Person** had the following children:

2049   i. Nellie Marion[11] **Hastings**[2371] was born in S. Londonderry, Vt. 25 September 1862 and died 29 September 1928 in Jefferson, Iowa at 66 years of age. She married George E. **Smith** in 1883.

2050   ii. Charles Frederick **Hastings**[2372] was born in Jamaica, Vt. in 1864 and died 23 March 1942 in Syracuse, Kans. at 77 years of age.

2051   iii. Henry Arthur **Hastings**[2373] was born abt 1866 and married Ella F. **Ehrhardt**.

+ 2052   iv. Elmer William **Hastings** was born 17 June 1877.

1647. George Osmer[10] **Goddard** (John Bailey[9], Robert[8], Nahum[7], Robert[6], Edward[5], Susanna[4] **Stone**, Mary[3] **Whipple**, Elder John[2], Matthew[1])[2374] was born in Monona, Iowa 6 March 1856 and died 13 January 1907 in Colton, S. Dak. at 50 years of age. He married **Harriet Ann Kilmer** in Taopi, S. Dak. in 1878. Harriet,[2375] daughter of George Dennis **Kilmer** and Ellen **Westover**, was born in Wisconsin 3 May 1855 and died 30 October 1924 in Wessington Springs, S. Dak. at 69 years of age. According to *The History of Minnehaha County, South Dakota*, George homesteaded the northwest quarter of Section 29 in May 1878. In addition to farming, he engaged in the mercantile business with his father. He was on the town board for years, serving as chairman most of the time. He benefitted from the Timber Culture Act of 1878 when he filed application No. 3985 for a section of prairie land devoid of timber. He agreed to use the land to grow timber and stated he made the application in good faith, "and not for the purpose of speculation" or for the use and benefit of any other person. The application was dated 29 Oct. 1879 at the Land Office at Sioux Falls, Dakota Territory. His obituary in the Sioux Falls *Argus Leader* of 15 January 1907 listed the cause of death as abscess of the brain caused by tuberculosis. He was ill for two weeks before his death.

George Osmer **Goddard** and Harriet Ann **Kilmer** had the following children:

+ 2053   i. Charles Edmund[11] **Goddard** was born 28 October 1879.

+ 2054   ii. John Osmer **Goddard** was born 28 August 1884.

+ 2055   iii. Clara May **Goddard** was born 7 August 1889.

+ 2056   iv. George Francis **Goddard** was born 11 January 1895.

1652. Lora E.[10] **Goddard** (Charles Walker[9], Robert[8], Nahum[7], Robert[6], Edward[5], Susanna[4] **Stone**, Mary[3] **Whipple**, Elder John[2], Matthew[1])[2376] was born in Stryker, Ohio 24 May 1866 and died 28 November 1936 in Seattle, Wash. at 70 years of age. She married **Charles Richmond Morehouse** in Bancroft, Iowa 4 May 1885. Charles was the son of Andrew **Morehouse** and Vesta **Richmond**.[2377]

Lora E. **Goddard** and Charles Richmond **Morehouse** had the following children:

2057   i. Lila[11] **Morehouse** was born 13 May 1886.

+ 2058   ii. Cecil Goddard **Morehouse** was born 1 July 1888.

+ 2059   iii. Dorothy **Morehouse** was born 5 September 1895.

   2060   iv. Charles Wilmont **Morehouse**[2378] was born in Bancroft, Iowa 18 March 1898 and died 13 February 1919 in Italy at 20 years of age. He was a casualty of World War I.

   2061   v. David Hugh **Morehouse**[2379] was born in Bancroft 4 May 1903 and died there 28 September 1907 at 4 years of age.

1656. Herbert[10] **Goddard** (Clark Nahum[9], Robert[8], Nahum[7], Robert[6], Edward[5], Susanna[4] **Stone**, Mary[3] **Whipple**, Elder John[2], Matthew[1])[2380] was born in Decorah, Iowa 22 August 1877 and died 31 May 1946 in Des Moines, Iowa at 68 years of age. He married **Mary Ayres** in Iowa 18 June 1907.

Herbert **Goddard** and Mary **Ayres** had the following child:

   2062   i. Philip Ayres[11] **Goddard**[2381].

1657. Clarence Ryan[10] **Goddard** (Edwin Nathan[9], George[8], Capt. Nathan[7], Nathan[6], Benjamin[5], Susanna[4] **Stone**, Mary[3] **Whipple**, Elder John[2], Matthew[1])[2382] was born in Worcester, Worcester Co., Mass. 21 February 1873 and died there 18 February 1929 at 55 years of age. He married, as her second husband, **Annie Blanche Allen** in Worcester 14 October 1910. Annie was born in Brookfield, Worcester Co., Mass. 24 January 1874 and died 24 August 1961 in Vero Beach, Indian River Co., Fla. at 87 years of age.[2383] She married (1) **Harry W. Boardman** before 1910.

Clarence Ryan **Goddard** and Annie Blanche **Allen** had the following children:

+ 2063   i. Mary Virginia[11] **Goddard** was born 24 June 1912

   2064   ii. Edwin N. **Goddard**[2384] was born in Worcester 4 July 1915 and died there in 1916 at less than one year of age.

1659. Edmund[10] **Ellsworth Jr.** (Elizabeth[9] **Young**, Brigham[8], Abigail (Nabby)[7] **Howe**, Susanna[6] **Goddard**, Ebenezer[5], Susanna[4] **Stone**, Mary[3] **Whipple**, Elder John[2], Matthew[1])[2385] was born in Nauvoo, Hancock Co., Ill. 7 October 1845 and married **Ellen C. Blair**.

Edmund **Ellsworth** Jr. and Ellen C. **Blair** had the following children:

   2065   i. Edmund[11] **Ellsworth**[2386] was born 7 August 1868.

   2066   ii. Seth Millington **Ellsworth**[2387] was born 30 August 1870.

   2067   iii. Frank Blair **Ellsworth**[2388] was born 28 August 1872.

   2068   iv. Clara Cornelia **Ellsworth**[2389] was born 31 October 1874.

   2069   v. John Willard **Ellsworth**[2390] was born 31 October 1878.

   2070   vi. Elizabeth Young **Ellsworth**[2391] was born 6 July 1880.

   2071   vii. Alonzo Sheridan **Ellsworth**[2392] was born 16 September 1883.

   2072   viii. Preston B. **Ellsworth**[2393] was born 6 May 1887.

1660. Rowennah W.[10] **Ellsworth** (Elizabeth[9] **Young**, Brigham[8], Abigail (Nabby)[7] **Howe**, Susanna[6] **Goddard**, Ebenezer[5], Susanna[4] **Stone**, Mary[3] **Whipple**, Elder John[2], Matthew[1])[2394] was born 1 May 1848 and died 10 April 1880 at 31 years of age. She married **John Howard**.

Rowennah W. **Ellsworth** and John **Howard** had the following child:

   2073   i. John Henry[11] **Howard**[2395] was born 21 November 1870.

1661. **Brigham Henry**[10] **Ellsworth** (Elizabeth[9] **Young**, Brigham[8], Abigail (Nabby)[7] **Howe**, Susanna[6] **Goddard**, Ebenezer[5], Susanna[4] **Stone**, Mary[3] **Whipple**, Elder John[2], Matthew[1])[2396] was born 23 November 1850 and married **Helen Adelia Gibson**.

Brigham Henry **Ellsworth** and Helen Adelia **Gibson** had the following children:

2074	i.	John Willard[11] **Ellsworth**.
2075	ii.	Alice Elizabeth **Ellsworth**[2397] was born 25 September 1870.
2076	iii.	Brigham **Ellsworth**[2398] was born 11 August 1872.
2077	iv.	Charles Eliot **Ellsworth**[2399] was born 10 August 1874.
2078	v.	John Willard **Ellsworth**[2400] was born 28 December 1876.
2079	vi.	Joseph **Ellsworth**[2401] was born 24 April 1877.
2080	vii.	Marian Vilate **Ellsworth**[2402] was born 27 October 1879.
2081	viii.	Claude William **Ellsworth**[2403] was born 27 February 1881.
2082	ix.	Lovill Edgar **Ellsworth**[2404] was born 21 May 1883.
2083	x.	Curtis K. **Ellsworth**[2405] was born 11 September 1885.
2084	xi.	Crystal Vere **Ellsworth**[2406] was born 11 December 1888.
2085	xii.	Sara Eliza **Ellsworth**[2407] was born 23 June 1890.

1662. **Alice Vilate**[10] **Ellsworth** (Elizabeth[9] **Young**, Brigham[8], Abigail (Nabby)[7] **Howe**, Susanna[6] **Goddard**, Ebenezer[5], Susanna[4] **Stone**, Mary[3] **Whipple**, Elder John[2], Matthew[1])[2408] was born 22 November 1852 and married **James O. Swift**.

Alice Vilate **Ellsworth** and James O. **Swift** had the following children:

2086	i.	Alice[11] **Swift**[2409] was born 25 September 1873.
2087	ii.	James **Swift**.[2410]
2088	iii.	Luna **Swift**.[2411]
2089	iv.	William **Swift**[2412] was born 16 May 1876.
2090	v.	Owen **Swift**.[2413]
2091	vi.	Joseph **Swift**.[2414]
2092	vii.	Lewis **Swift**.[2415]
2093	viii.	Lorenzo **Swift**.[2416]

1663. **Luna Caroline**[10] **Ellsworth** (Elizabeth[9] **Young**, Brigham[8], Abigail (Nabby)[7] **Howe**, Susanna[6] **Goddard**, Ebenezer[5], Susanna[4] **Stone**, Mary[3] **Whipple**, Elder John[2], Matthew[1])[2417] was born 17 November 1854 and married **Richard Franklin Jardine**.

Luna Caroline **Ellsworth** and Richard Franklin **Jardine** had the following children:

2094	i.	Luna[11] **Jardine**[2418] was born 13 January 1871.
2095	ii.	Richard Franklin **Jardine**[2419] was born 3 November 1872.
2096	iii.	James Leo **Jardine**[2420] was born 17 July 1875.
2097	iv.	Rowennah Wilmont **Jardine**[2421] was born 10 July 1877.
2098	v.	Edmund Laroy **Jardine**[2422] was born 16 October 1879.
2099	vi.	Elizabeth Young **Jardine**[2423] was born 19 January 1882.
2100	vii.	John William **Jardine**[2424] was born 8 March 1884.
2101	viii.	Minnie Bell **Jardine**[2425] was born 21 April 1886.
2102	ix.	Joseph Arthur **Jardine**[2426] was born 21 May 1888.
2103	x.	Ellen **Jardine**[2427] was born 7 January 1891.
2104	xi.	Hamilton Lester **Jardine**[2428] was born 15 September 1892.
2105	xii.	Mary Mildred **Jardine**[2429] was born 22 March 1897.

2106   xiii.   Ruth **Jardine**[2430] was born 21 January 1900.

1666. Miriam Vilate[10] **Decker** (Vilate[9] **Young**, Brigham[8], Abigail (Nabby)[7] **Howe**, Susanna[6] **Goddard**, Ebenezer[5], Susanna[4] **Stone**, Mary[3] **Whipple**, Elder John[2], Matthew[1])[2431] was born 15 January 1848 and died 12 January 1888 at 39 years of age. She married twice. (1) **Louie Granger**. (2) **George Benton Davis**.

Miriam Vilate **Decker** and Louie **Granger** had the following children:
2107   i.   Louie Edwin[11] **Granger**[2432] was born in March 1873.
2108   ii.   Henry Corydon **Granger**[2433].

Miriam Vilate **Decker** and George Benton **Davis** had the following children:
2109   iii.   Ray **Davis**[2434] was born 5 May 1881.
2110   iv.   Charlie Decker **Davis**[2435] was born 4 May 1883.
2111   v.   George Benton **Davis** Jr.[2436] was born 1 December 1885.

1667. Alice Luella[10] **Decker** (Vilate[9] **Young**, Brigham[8], Abigail (Nabby)[7] **Howe**, Susanna[6] **Goddard**, Ebenezer[5], Susanna[4] **Stone**, Mary[3] **Whipple**, Elder John[2], Matthew[1])[2437] was born 23 July 1851 and married three times. (1) **John A. Raine**. (2) **Charles Scott Cunningham**. (3) **Joseph Pitt**.

Alice Luella **Decker** and John A. **Raine** had the following child:
2112   i.   Genevieve[11] **Raine**[2438] was born 28 April 1879.

Alice Luella **Decker** and Charles Scott **Cunningham** had the following children:
2113   ii.   Charles Scott **Cunningham** II[2439] was born 19 April 1882.
2114   iii.   Katie Vilate **Cunningham**[2440] was born 31 August 1884.

1670. Brigham LeRay[10] **Decker** (Vilate[9] **Young**, Brigham[8], Abigail (Nabby)[7] **Howe**, Susanna[6] **Goddard**, Ebenezer[5], Susanna[4] **Stone**, Mary[3] **Whipple**, Elder John[2], Matthew[1])[2441] was born 14 January 1859 and died in November 1910 at 51 years of age. He married twice. (1) **Fannie Caroline Taylor**. (2) **Emma Kammerman**.

Brigham LeRay **Decker** and Fannie Caroline **Taylor** had the following child:
2115   I.   Bessie[11] **Decker**[2442] was born in April 1885.

Brigham Le Ray **Decker** and Emma **Kammerman** had the following children:
2116   ii.   Rawlins K. **Decker**[2443] was born 15 November 1894.
2117   iii.   Eric K. **Decker**[2444] was born 19 February 1898.
2118   iv.   Louie K. **Decker**[2445] was born 8 January 1902.
2119   v.   Harold K. **Decker**[2446] was born 30 July 1904.

1671. Loretta Elmina[10] **Decker** (Vilate[9] **Young**, Brigham[8], Abigail (Nabby)[7] **Howe**, Susanna[6] **Goddard**, Ebenezer[5], Susanna[4] **Stone**, Mary[3] **Whipple**, Elder John[2], Matthew[1])[2447] was born 24 December 1861 and died 4 June 1897 at 35 years of age. She married **Heber Charles Sorenson**.

Loretta Elmina **Decker** and Heber Charles **Sorenson** had the following children:
2120   i.   Frank[11] **Sorenson**[2448] was born in November 1880.
2121   ii.   Fred Dale **Sorenson**[2449] was born 7 January 1882.
2122   iii.   Guy Erwin **Sorenson**[2450] was born in October 1883.
2123   iv.   Wilamina Christina **Sorenson**[2451] was born in March 1889.

2124   v. Heber Custer **Sorenson**[2452] was born in December 1890.

2125   vi. Bryan Bland **Sorenson**[2453] was born 23 February 1897.

1673. Ferra Wallace[10] **Decker** (Vilate[9] **Young**, Brigham[8], Abigail (Nabby)[7] **Howe**, Susanna[6] **Goddard**, Ebenezer[5], Susanna[4] **Stone**, Mary[3] **Whipple**, Elder John[2], Matthew[1])[2454] was born 26 January 1872 and married **Leila Rogers.**

Ferra Wallace **Decker** and Leila **Rogers** had the following child:

2126   i. Loretta[11] **Decker**[2455] was born in October 1897.

1674. Albert C.[10] **Young** (Brigham Heber[9], Brigham[8], Abigail (Nabby)[7] **Howe**, Susanna[6] **Goddard**, Ebenezer[5], Susanna[4] **Stone**, Mary[3] **Whipple**, Elder John[2], Matthew[1])[2456] birth date unknown married twice. (1) **Josephine Young**, his half-aunt. She was the daughter of Brigham **Young** and Emily Dow **Partridge** and was born in Salt Lake City, Utah 21 February 1860. (2) **Mary Eliza Young Croxall**, his half first cousin (see No. 1742). Mary,[2457] daughter of Mark **Croxall** and Mary Eliza **Young**, was born 3 March 1866. She also married **Abram H. Cannon.** (See. No. 1272.)

Albert C. **Young** and Josephine **Young** had the following children born in Salt Lake City:

1736   i. Ethel[10] **Young**[2458] was born 11 April 1879 and died in Salt Lake City in December 1882 at 3 years of age.

1737   ii. Geneva **Young**[2459] was born 18 March 1884.

+ 1738   iii. Clisbee **Young** was born 21 March 1887.

1739   iv. Gilbert **Young**[2460] was born 16 October 1891 and died 3 May 1893 in Salt Lake City at one year of age.

1740   v. Josephine **Young**[2461] was born 30 September 1896 and married George F. **Harker.**

1741   vi. Virginia **Young**[2462] was born 15 March 1898 and married Joseph N. **LaRocca.**

1675. John Willard[10] **Clawson** (Alice[9] **Young**, Brigham[8], Abigail (Nabby)[7] **Howe**, Susanna[6] **Goddard**, Ebenezer[5], Susanna[4] **Stone**, Mary[3] **Whipple**, Elder John[2], Matthew[1])[2463] was born 18 January 1858 and married **Mary Alice Clark.** Mary was born 18 August 1863.[2464] John became an eminent portrait painter and was well-known throughout the country.

John Willard **Clawson** and Mary Alice **Clark** had the following children:

2127   i. Willard Wesley[11] **Clawson**[2465] was born 28 November 1882.

2128   ii. Louise Davenport **Clawson**[2466] was born 31 May 1886.

2129   iii. Consuella **Clawson**[2467] was born 16 December 1909.

1676. Leo Herbert[10] **Clawson** (Alice[9] **Young**, Brigham[8], Abigail (Nabby)[7] **Howe**, Susanna[6] **Goddard**, Ebenezer[5], Susanna[4] **Stone**, Mary[3] **Whipple**, Elder John[2], Matthew[1])[2468] was born 22 October 1859 and married **Lizzie S. Watson** 15 October 1885. Lizzie was born 21 June 1863.[2469]

Leo Herbert **Clawson** and Lizzie S. **Watson** had the following children:

2130   i. Marion Sutherland[11] **Clawson**[2470] was born 8 September 1886.

2131   ii. Alice Young **Clawson**[2471] was born 21 August 1888.

2132   iii. Leone **Clawson**[2472] was born 15 January 1890.

2133   iv. Roburta **Clawson**[2473] was born 12 January 1893.

2134   v. Watson Monroe **Clawson**[2474] was born 21 March 1896.

2135   vi.   Elizabeth **Clawson**[2475] was born 4 June 1898.
2136   vii. Leo Herbert **Clawson**[2476] was born 23 July 1900.

1677. Walter Scott[10] **Clawson** (Alice[9] **Young**, Brigham[8], Abigail (Nabby)[7] **Howe**, Susanna[6] **Goddard**, Ebenezer[5], Susanna[4] **Stone**, Mary[3] **Whipple**, Elder John[2], Matthew[1])[2477] was born 1 December 1861 and married **May Allen**. May was born 4 September 1868.[2478]

Walter Scott **Clawson** and May **Allen** had the following child:
2137   i.   Walter Allen[11] **Clawson**[2479] was born 30 October 1887.

1678. Selden Irwin[10] **Clawson** (Alice[9] **Young**, Brigham[8], Abigail (Nabby)[7] **Howe**, Susanna[6] **Goddard**, Ebenezer[5], Susanna[4] **Stone**, Mary[3] **Whipple**, Elder John[2], Matthew[1])[2480] was born 20 March 1864 and married **Clara Morris** 19 November 1885. Clara was born 9 March 1869.[2481]

Selden Irwin **Clawson** and Clara **Morris** had the following children:
2138   i.   Cora[11] **Clawson**[2482] was born 6 October 1888.
2139   ii.   Helen **Clawson**[2483] was born 27 December 1890.
2140   iii. Irwin **Clawson**[2484] was born 13 January 1892.
2141   iv.   Julion **Clawson**[2485] was born 21 October 1898.

1679. Virginia Mary[10] **Thatcher** (Eunice Caroline[9] **Young**, Brigham[8], Abigail (Nabby)[7] **Howe**, Susanna[6] **Goddard**, Ebenezer[5], Susanna[4] **Stone**, Mary[3] **Whipple**, Elder John[2], Matthew[1])[2486] was born 15 January 1862 and died 5 December 1886 at 24 years of age. She married **Edmund Burke Spencer**.

Virginia Mary **Thatcher** and Edmund Burke **Spencer** had the following children:
2142   i.   Gladys[11] **Spencer**[2487] was born 7 May 1882.
2143   ii. Edmund B. **Spencer**[2488] was born 2 November 1884.

1681. Nellie May[10] **Thatcher** (Eunice Caroline[9] **Young**, Brigham[8], Abigail (Nabby)[7] **Howe**, Susanna[6] **Goddard**, Ebenezer[5], Susanna[4] **Stone**, Mary[3] **Whipple**, Elder John[2], Matthew[1])[2489] was born 12 October 1864 and married **George Elias Blair**

Nellie May **Thatcher** and George Elias **Blair** had the following children:
2144   i.   Virginia[11] **Blair**[2490] was born 29 April 1890.
2145   ii. Millington **Blair**[2491] was born 4 February 1894.
2146   iii. Phillip T. **Blair**[2492] was born 24 April 1896.
2147   iv. Kathryn **Blair**[2493] was born 28 July 1899.
2148   v.   George W.T. **Blair**[2494] was born 21 August 1903.

1683. Nettie Young[10] **Thatcher** (Eunice Caroline[9] **Young**, Brigham[8], Abigail (Nabby)[7] **Howe**, Susanna[6] **Goddard**, Ebenezer[5], Susanna[4] **Stone**, Mary[3] **Whipple**, Elder John[2], Matthew[1])[2495] was born 13 September 1868 and married **Robert Wallace Sloan**.

Nettie Young **Thatcher** and Robert Wallace **Sloan** had the following children:
2149   i.   George E.[11] **Sloan**[2496] was born 2 November 1892.
2150   ii. Robert Wallace **Sloan** II[2497] was born 5 May 1899.
2151   iii. Richard T. **Sloan**[2498] was born 5 July 1900.

1684. **Brigham Guy**[10] **Thatcher** (Eunice Caroline[9] **Young**, Brigham[8], Abigail (Nabby)[7] **Howe**, Susanna[6] **Goddard**, Ebenezer[5], Susanna[4] **Stone**, Mary[3] **Whipple**, Elder John[2], Matthew[1])[2499] was born 10 September 1870 and married **Florence Bell Beatie**.

Brigham Guy **Thatcher** and Florence Bell **Beatie** had the following child:
2152   i.   Guy[11] **Thatcher**[2500] was born 8 March 1896.

1685. **Kathrine**[10] **Thatcher** (Eunice Caroline[9] **Young**, Brigham[8], Abigail (Nabby)[7] **Howe**, Susanna[6] **Goddard**, Ebenezer[5], Susanna[4] **Stone**, Mary[3] **Whipple**, Elder John[2], Matthew[1])[2501] was born 20 September 1873 and married **David H.L. Thomas**.

Kathrine **Thatcher** and David H.L. **Thomas** had the following children:
2153   i.   Lallis Young[11] **Thomas**[2502] was born 5 April 1894.
2154   ii.   Winifred W. **Thomas**[2503] was born 24 February 1896.
2155   iii.   Luna Jocelyn **Thomas**[2504] was born 26 April 1902.
2156   iv.   David T. **Thomas**[2505] was born 21 February 1908.

1686. **Luna Angell**[10] **Thatcher** (Eunice Caroline[9] **Young**, Brigham[8], Abigail (Nabby)[7] **Howe**, Susanna[6] **Goddard**, Ebenezer[5], Susanna[4] **Stone**, Mary[3] **Whipple**, Elder John[2], Matthew[1])[2506] was born 17 December 1875 and married **Alfred L. Farrell**.

Luna Angell **Thatcher** and Alfred L. **Farrell** had the following children:
2157   i.   Luna C.[11] **Farrell**[2507] was born 17 July 1898.
2158   ii.   Alfred T. **Farrell**[2508] was born in March 1900.
2159   iii.   Maxwell T. **Farrell**[2509] was born in October 1902.
2160   iv.   Janet E. **Farrell**[2510] was born 28 July 1905.
2161   v.   William S. **Farrell**[2511] was born in April 1908.

1687. **Constance**[10] **Thatcher** (Eunice Caroline[9] **Young**, Brigham[8], Abigail (Nabby)[7] **Howe**, Susanna[6] **Goddard**, Ebenezer[5], Susanna[4] **Stone**, Mary[3] **Whipple**, Elder John[2], Matthew[1])[2512] was born 25 November 1880 and died 3 May 1905 at 24 years of age. She married **Alexander Nibley**.

Constance **Thatcher** and Alexander **Nibley** had the following child:
2162   i.   Constance T.[11] **Nibley**[2513] was born 23 May 1904.

1688. **Phylis**[10] **Thatcher** (Eunice Caroline[9] **Young**, Brigham[8], Abigail (Nabby)[7] **Howe**, Susanna[6] **Goddard**, Ebenezer[5], Susanna[4] **Stone**, Mary[3] **Whipple**, Elder John[2], Matthew[1])[2514] was born 16 January 1883 and married **William Spicker**.

Phylis **Thatcher** and William **Spicker** had the following children:
2163   i.   William G.[11] **Spicker**[2515] was born 1 March 1910.
2164   ii.   Mary Angell **Spicker**[2516] was born 31 August 1914.
2165   iii.   Mark Guy **Spicker**[2517] was born 14 August 1916.
2166   iv.   Fred Elmer **Spicker**[2518] was born 14 November 1918.

1742. **Mary Eliza Young**[10] **Croxall** (Mary Eliza[9] **Young**, Brigham[8], Abigail (Nabby)[7] **Howe**, Susanna[6] **Goddard**, Ebenezer[5], Susanna[4] **Stone**, Mary[3] **Whipple**, Elder John[2], Matthew[1])[2519] was born 3 March 1866 and married twice. (1) **Abram**

H. **Cannon.** (2) **Albert C. Young** (see No. 1674). Albert [2520] was the son of Brigham Heber **Young** Jr. Mary Eliza and Albert are half first cousins.

Mary Eliza Young **Croxall** and Abram H. **Cannon** had the following children:

2167	i.	Mary C.[11] **Cannon**[2521] was born 11 November 1887.
2168	ii.	Lillian C. **Cannon**[2522] was born 9 December 1888.
2169	iii.	Williard L. **Cannon**[2523] was born 8 April 1890.
2170	iv.	Gene C. **Cannon**[2524] was born 14 September 1891.
2171	v.	Claire C. **Cannon**[2525] was born 20 November 1892.
2172	vi.	Spencer C. **Cannon**[2526] was born 16 December 1894.

1744. Dr. Willard[10] **Croxall** (Mary Eliza[9] **Young**, Brigham[8], Abigail (Nabby)[7] Howe, Susanna[6] **Goddard**, Ebenezer[5], Susanna[4] **Stone**, Mary[3] **Whipple**, Elder John[2], Matthew[1])[2527] was born 25 July 1869 and married **Gertrude M. Pierce.**

Dr. Willard **Croxall** and Gertrude M. **Pierce** had the following child:

2173	i.	Willard Rufus[11] **Croxall**[2528] was born 11 November 1910.

1689. Lutie[10] **Thatcher** (Fanny Decker[9] **Young**, Brigham[8], Abigail (Nabby)[7] Howe, Susanna[6] **Goddard**, Ebenezer[5], Susanna[4] **Stone**, Mary[3] **Whipple**, Elder John[2], Matthew[1])[2529] was born 21 October 1868 and married **Stephen H. Lynch.**

Lutie **Thatcher** and Stephen H. **Lynch** had the following children:

2174	i.	Stephen Herbert[11] **Lynch**[2530] was born 7 January 1891.
2175	ii.	Brent Thatcher **Lynch**[2531] was born 11 May 1892.
2176	iii.	Moses Thatcher **Lynch**[2532] was born 26 July 1894.
2177	iv.	Phyllis **Lynch**[2533] was born 30 September 1896.
2178	v.	Fanny Thatcher **Lynch**[2534] was born 26 November 1898.
2179	vi.	Evelyn **Lynch**[2535] was born 5 September 1901.
2180	vii.	George Thatcher **Lynch**[2536] was born 6 March 1905.

1692. Frank W.[10] **Thatcher** (Fanny Decker[9] **Young**, Brigham[8], Abigail (Nabby)[7] Howe, Susanna[6] **Goddard**, Ebenezer[5], Susanna[4] **Stone**, Mary[3] **Whipple**, Elder John[2], Matthew[1])[2537] was born 3 April 1878 and married twice. (1) **Mary Jean McAlister.** (2) **Velva Snyder.**

Frank W. **Thatcher** and Mary Jean **McAlister** had the following children:

2181	i.	Frank W.[11] **Thatcher** II[2538] was born in 1904.
2182	ii.	Mary Jean **Thatcher**[2539] was born in 1906.

1704. Carlie Louine[10] **Clawson** (Emily Augusta[9] **Young**, Brigham[8], Abigail (Nabby)[7] **Howe**, Susanna[6] **Goddard**, Ebenezer[5], Susanna[4] **Stone**, Mary[3] **Whipple**, Elder John[2], Matthew[1])[2540] was born in Salt Lake City, Utah 28 July 1869 and married **Seymour B. Young** who was born there 11 January 1868.[2541]

Carlie Louine **Clawson** and Seymour B. **Young** had the following child:

+ 2183	i.	Scott Richmond[11] **Young.**

1705. Nell Young[10] **Clawson** (Emily Augusta[9] **Young**, Brigham[8], Abigail (Nabby)[7] **Howe**, Susanna[6] **Goddard**, Ebenezer[5], Susanna[4] **Stone**, Mary[3] **Whipple**, Elder John[2], Matthew[1])[2542] was born 10 May 1872 and married three times. (1) **Leigh Richmond Brown** 9 March 1892. He died 5 December 1899 in Salt Lake City.[2543] (2) **John Silver.** (3) **Morris Rosenbaum.**

Nell Young **Clawson** and Leigh Richmond **Brown** had the following children:

2184 i. Leigh Richmond[11] **Brown Jr.**[2544] was born 4 December 1892.

2185 ii. Nellie Louine **Brown**[2545] was born 4 December 1892.

2186 iii. Thedora Beatie **Brown**[2546] was born 10 January 1895 and married Byron **McKay** 4 May 1912.

Nell Young **Clawson** and John **Silver** had the following children:

2187 iv. William C. **Silver**[2547] was born in Raymond, Canada 1 April 1905.

2188 v. Mary Askie **Silver**[2548] was born 20 January 1907.

2189 vi. Hiram C. **Silver**[2549] was born in Lethbridge, Canada 2 July 1908.

2190 vii. John C. **Silver**[2550] was born 23 February 1910.

1706. Kate Young[10] **Clawson** (Emily Augusta[9] **Young**, Brigham[8], Abigail (Nabby)[7] **Howe**, Susanna[6] **Goddard**, Ebenezer[5], Susanna[4] **Stone**, Mary[3] **Whipple**, Elder John[2], Matthew[1])[2551] was born in Salt Lake City, Utah 19 May 1874 and died 14 March 1914 at 39 years of age. She married **George C. Lambert** Jr. 23 June 1898.

Kate Young **Clawson** and George C. **Lambert** Jr. had the following children:

2191 i. Katherine[11] **Lambert**[2552] was born 9 October 1901.

2192 ii. William Needham **Lambert**[2553] was born 1 October 1904.

2193 iii. Scott Richmond **Lambert**[2554] was born 15 November 1910.

2194 iv. Martin Clawson **Lambert**[2555] was born 11 December 1912.

1707. Alice Young[10] **Clawson** (Emily Augusta[9] **Young**, Brigham[8], Abigail (Nabby)[7] **Howe**, Susanna[6] **Goddard**, Ebenezer[5], Susanna[4] **Stone**, Mary[3] **Whipple**, Elder John[2], Matthew[1])[2556] was born 22 January 1876 and married **Alexander S. Campbell**.

Alice Young **Clawson** and Alexander S. **Campbell** had the following children:

2195 i. Virginia[11] **Campbell**[2557] was born 27 March 1902.

2196 ii. Alexander Stewart **Campbell**[2558] was born 18 August 1903.

2197 iii. Alice C. **Campbell**[2559] was born 29 May 1905.

2198 iv. Mary C. **Campbell**[2560] was born 16 November 1907.

2199 v. John C. **Campbell**[2561] was born 25 January 1910.

2200 vi. Kate C. **Campbell**[2562] was born in Idaho Falls, Idaho 23 November 1914.

1708. Bessie Young[10] **Clawson** (Emily Augusta[9] **Young**, Brigham[8], Abigail (Nabby)[7] **Howe**, Susanna[6] **Goddard**, Ebenezer[5], Susanna[4] **Stone**, Mary[3] **Whipple**, Elder John[2], Matthew[1])[2563] was born in Salt Lake City, Utah 19 December 1878 and married **LeRoy Bland Hughes**.

Bessie Young **Clawson** and LeRoy Bland **Hughes** had the following children:

2201 i. Miriam[11] **Hughes**[2564] was born 30 July 1904.

2202 ii. Edward Bland **Hughes**[2565] was born 6 June 1906.

2203 iii. Margaret C. **Hughes**[2566] was born 29 March 1909.

2204 iv. Elizabeth **Hughes**[2567] was born 28 December 1911.

2205 v. Eyleen **Hughes**[2568] was born 21 October 1913.

2206 vi. Robert Bland **Hughes**[2569] was born 6 November 1914.

1709. Shirley Young[10] **Clawson** (Emily Augusta[9] **Young**, Brigham[8], Abigail (Nabby)[7] **Howe**, Susanna[6] **Goddard**, Ebenezer[5], Susanna[4] **Stone**, Mary[3] **Whipple**, Elder John[2], Matthew[1])[2570] was born 15 November 1881 and married **Gertrude May Romney**.

Shirley Young **Clawson** and Gertrude May **Romney** had the following children:

2207   i.   Frances Romney[11] **Clawson**[2571] was born 19 December 1911.

2208   ii. Orson Douglas **Clawson**[2572] was born 21 July 1913.

2209   iii. Scott Romney **Clawson**[2573] was born 6 April 1917.

1710. Chester Young[10] **Clawson** (Emily Augusta[9] **Young**, Brigham[8], Abigail (Nabby)[7] **Howe**, Susanna[6] **Goddard**, Ebenezer[5], Susanna[4] **Stone**, Mary[3] **Whipple**, Elder John[2], Matthew[1])[2574] was born 5 December 1883 and married **Esther Vida Fox**.

Chester Young **Clawson** and Esther Vida **Fox** had the following children:

2210   i.   Emily Fox[11] **Clawson**[2575] was born 25 March 1911.

2211   ii. Ruth Fox **Clawson**[2576] was born 12 February 1914.

2212   iii. Vida Elizabeth **Clawson**[2577] was born 31 December 1916.

1711. Josephine Young[10] **Clawson** (Emily Augusta[9] **Young**, Brigham[8], Abigail (Nabby)[7] **Howe**, Susanna[6] **Goddard**, Ebenezer[5], Susanna[4] **Stone**, Mary[3] **Whipple**, Elder John[2], Matthew[1])[2578] was born 11 February 1886 and married **Alvin Paul Thompson**.

Josephine Young **Clawson** and Alvin Paul **Thompson** had the following children:

2213   i.   Ruth[11] **Thompson**[2579] was born 30 August 1911.

2214   ii. Josephine Martha **Thompson**[2580] was born 22 January 1917.

1762. Winifred B.[10] **Conrad** (Marinda Hyde[9] **Young**, Brigham[8], Abigail (Nabby)[7] **Howe**, Susanna[6] **Goddard**, Ebenezer[5], Susanna[4] **Stone**, Mary[3] **Whipple**, Elder John[2], Matthew[1])[2581] was born in Salt Lake City, Utah 13 January 1877 and died 21 December 1918 at 41 years of age. She married **Amasa Lyman Haymond II**.

Winifred B . **Conrad** and Amasa Lyman **Haymond** II had the following children:

2215   i.   Ella LaVaun[11] **Haymond**[2582] was born in Salt Lake City 6 March 1897.

2216   ii. Walter Conrad **Haymond**[2583] was born 23 October 1898.

2217   iii. Allen Dilworth **Haymond**[2584] was born 9 June 1900.

2218   iv. Ferdinand Fabian **Haymond**[2585] was born 30 May 1902.

2219   v. Harold Edgar **Haymond**[2586] was born 8 July 1905.

2220   vi. Winifred **Haymond**[2587] was born 6 January 1907.

2221   vii. Edward Lyman **Haymond**[2588] was born 1 June 1911.

2222   viii. Marian **Haymond**[2589] was born 16 September 1913.

1746. William Bernard[10] **Dougall Jr.** (Clarissa Maria[9] **Young**, Brigham[8], Abigail (Nabby)[7] **Howe**, Susanna[6] **Goddard**, Ebenezer[5], Susanna[4] **Stone**, Mary[3] **Whipple**, Elder John[2], Matthew[1])[2590] was born 7 May 1869 and died 10 April 1906 at 36 years of age. He married **Hattie Richards**.

William Bernard **Dougall** Jr. and Hattie **Richards** had the following children:

2223   i.   Marie[11] **Dougall**[2591] was born 12 September 1897.

2224   ii. D. Grant **Dougall**[2592] was born 11 September 1901.

2225   iii. Bernard Richards **Dougall**[2593] was born in October 1903.

2226   iv. Alice **Dougall**[2594] was born 26 August 1905.

1747. Hugh Willard[10] **Dougall** (Clarissa Maria[9] **Young**, Brigham[8], Abigail

(Nabby)[7] **Howe**, Susanna[6] **Goddard**, Ebenezer[5], Susanna[4] **Stone**, Mary[3] **Whipple**, Elder John[2], Matthew[1])[2595] was born 6 March 1872 and married **Ella Smith**.

Hugh Willard **Dougall** and Ella **Smith** had the following children:
    2227   i.   William Bernard[11] **Dougall**[2596] was born 6 April 1908.
    2228   ii.   Virginia **Dougall**[2597] was born 3 March 1912.

1748. Catherine McSweine[10] **Dougall** (Clarissa Maria[9] **Young**, Brigham[8], Abigail (Nabby)[7] **Howe**, Susanna[6] **Goddard**, Ebenezer[5], Susanna[4] **Stone**, Mary[3] **Whipple**, Elder John[2], Matthew[1])[2598] was born 11 August 1878 and married **Frankin B. Platt.**

Catherine McSweine **Dougall** and Franklin B. **Platt** had the following children:
    2229   i.   Catherine Virginia[11] **Platt**[2599] was born 5 November 1910.
    2230   ii.   Frances Elizabeth **Platt**[2600] was born 14 February 1913.
    2231   iii.   Lawrence Harmon **Platt**[2601] was born 30 October 1915.

1749. Clarissa[10] **Dougall** (Clarissa Maria[9] **Young**, Brigham[8], Abigail (Nabby)[7] **Howe**, Susanna[6] **Goddard**, Ebenezer[5], Susanna[4] **Stone**, Mary[3] **Whipple**, Elder John[2], Matthew[1])[2602] was born 23 July 1884 and married **Hyrum Bergtrom.**

Clarissa **Dougall** and Hyrum **Bergstrom** had the following children:
    2232   i.   Justin D.[11] **Bergstrom**[2603] was born 10 August 1906.
    2233   ii   Julian **Bergstrom**[2604] was born 28 January 1912.
    2234   iii.   Mary Elizabeth **Bergstrom**[2605] was born 22 November 1914.

1776. Sterling[10] **Williams** (Zina[9] **Young**, Brigham[8], Abigail (Nabby)[7] **Howe**, Susanna[6] **Goddard**, Ebenezer[5], Susanna[4] **Stone**, Mary[3] **Whipple**, Elder John[2], Matthew[1])[2606] was born 21 September 1870 and married **Attena Bates.**

Sterling **Williams** and Attena **Bates** had the following children:
    2235   i.   Thomas[11] **Williams**.[2607]
    2236   ii.   Edgar **Williams**.[2608]
    2237   iii.   Sterling **Williams**.[2609]
    2238   iv.   Ora **Williams**.[2610]
    2239   v.   Karl Morgan **Williams**.[2611]
    2240   vi.   Loila **Williams**.[2612]
    2241   vii.   Brigham Young **Williams**.[2613].
    2242   viii.   Seymour **Williams**.[2614]

1778. Joseph Young[10] **Card** (Zina[9] **Young**, Brigham[8], Abigail (Nabby)[7] **Howe**, Susanna[6] **Goddard**, Ebenezer[5], Susanna[4] **Stone**, Mary[3] **Whipple**, Elder John[2], Matthew[1])[2615] was born in Logan, Cache Co., Utah 28 June 1885 and married twice. (1) **Leona Ballantyne**. (2) **Pearl Christensen**.

Joseph Young **Card** and Leona **Ballantyne** had the following child:
    2243   i.   Joseph **Ballantyne**[11] was born in Cardston, Alberta, Canada 14 May 1906.[2616]

Joseph Young **Card** and Pearl **Christensen** had the following children born in Cardson:
    2244   ii.   Brigham Young **Card** was born 11 March 1914.[2617]
    2245   iii.   Eldon Joseph **Card** was born 23 October 1915.[2618]

2246   iv. Ruth **Card** was born 27 June 1917.[2619]

1779. Zina Young[10]**Card** (Zina[9] Young, Brigham[8], Abigail (Nabby)[7] Howe, Susanna[6] Goddard, Ebenezer[5] Susanna[4] Stone, Mary[3] Whipple, Elder John[2], Matthew[1])[2620] was born in Cardston, Alberta, Canada 12 June 1888 and married **Maj. Hugh H. Brown**. Hugh was born in Salt Lake City 24 October 1883 and commanded a squadron of Canadian Mounted Infantry in Europe during WWI.[2621]

Zina Young **Card** and Maj. Hugh H. **Brown** had the following children;
2247   i. Zina Lydia[11]**Brown** was born in July 1909.[2622]
2248   ii. Zola Grace **Brown**.[2623]
2249   iii. LaJune **Brown**.[2624]
2250   iv. Mary **Brown**.[2625]
2251   v. Hugh Card **Brown** was born 20 October 1919.[2626]

1780. Orson Rego[10]**Card** (Zina[9] Young, Brigham[8], Abigail (Nabby)[7] Howe, Susanna[6] Goddard, Ebenezer[5] Susanna[4] Stone, Mary[3] Whipple, Elder John[2], Matthew[1])[2627] was born in Cardston, Alberta, Canada 9 June 1891 and married **Lucena Richards** who was born 9 August 1893.[2628]

Orson Rego **Card** and Lucena **Richards** had the following children:
2252   i. Richard Young **Card**[11] was born 24 September 1915.[2629]
2253   ii. Delpha **Card** was born in Salt Lake City 8 November 1918.[2630]

1782. Margaret Alley[10] **Davis** (Evelyn Louise[9] Young, Brigham[8], Abigail (Nabby)[7] Howe, Susanna[6] Goddard, Ebenezer[5] Susanna[4] Stone, Mary[3] Whipple, Elder John[2], Matthew[1])[2631] was born 26 January 1874 and married **George M. Marshall**.

Margaret Alley **Davis** and George M. **Marshall** had the following children:
2254   i. Margaret **Marshall**[11] was born 16 March 1897.
2555   ii. Katherine **Marshall** was born 12 December 1898 and married Dwight Lewis **Sawyer** 3 January 1920.
2256   iii. Clara Clawson **Marshall** was born 8 November 1902.

1713. Emily Ada Young[10] **Croxall** (Caroline Partridge[9] **Young**, Brigham[8], Abigail (Nabby)[7] **Howe**, Susanna[6] **Goddard**, Ebenezer[5], Susanna[4] **Stone**, Mary[3] **Whipple**, Elder John[2], Matthew[1])[2632] was born 13 August 1870 and married **William Tenny Cannon** 27 April 1892.

Emily Ada Young **Croxall** and William Tenny **Cannon** had the following children:
+ 2257   i. Helen Mae[11] **Cannon** was born 14 May 1894.
+ 2258   ii. Alma Eliza **Cannon** was born 29 May 1896.
2259   iii. William Tenny **Cannon** Jr.[2633] was born 21 July 1898 and married Geneve **Anderson** in April 1919.
2260   iv. Richard Callister **Cannon**[2634] was born 15 November 1902.
2261   v. Emily Ada **Cannon**[2635] was born 9 August 1904.
2262   vi. George Quail **Cannon**[2636] was born 28 May 1908.
2263   vii. Warren Croxal **Cannon**[2637] was born 9 March 1911.

1716. Caroline Y.[10] **Croxall** (Caroline Partridge[9] Young, Brigham[8], Abigail (Nabby)[7] **Howe**, Susanna[6] **Goddard**, Ebenezer[5], Susanna[4] **Stone**, Mary[3] **Whipple**,

Elder John[2], Matthew[1])[2638] was born 2 July 1875 and married **Willare Telle Cannon** 4 April 1900.

> Caroline Y. **Croxall** and Willare Telle **Cannon** had the following children:
>
> 2264   i. Roger Willard[11] **Cannon**[2639] was born 12 March 1901.
> 2265   ii. Caroline **Cannon**[2640] was born 14 May 1902.
> 2666   iii. Phyllis **Cannon**[2641] was born 21 April 1905.
> 2267   iv. Gerald Quintin **Cannon**[2642] was born 4 October 1906.
> 2268   v. Ethelyn **Cannon**[2643] was born 12 December 1907.
> 2269   vi. Arthur Quayle **Cannon**[2644] was born 29 January 1910.
> 2270   vii. Barbara **Cannon**[2645] was born 30 May 1912 and died 5 April 1913 at less than one year of age.

1717. **Mark Y.**[10] **Croxall** (Caroline Partridge[9] **Young**, Brigham[8], Abigail (Nabby)[7] **Howe**, Susanna[6] **Goddard**, Ebenezer[5], Susanna[4] **Stone**, Mary[3] **Whipple**, Elder John[2], Matthew[1])[2646] was born 4 August 1877 and married **Gertrude Winder** 27 November 1900.

> Mark Y. **Croxall** and Gertrude **Winder** had the following children:
>
> 2271   i. Lucile[11] **Croxall**[2647] was born in September 1901.
> 2272   ii. Hayden **Croxall**[2648] was born in 1903 and died 24 March 1920 at 16 years of age.
> 2273   iii. Elizabeth **Croxall**[2649] was born in 1905.
> 2274   iv. Virginia **Croxall**[2650] was born in 1906.
> 2275   v. Eloise **Croxall**[2651] was born 11 December 1907.
> 2276   vi. Helen **Croxall**[2652] was born in 1909.
> 2277   vii Robert Ward **Croxall**[2653] was born in 1911.
> 2278   viii. Caroline **Croxall**[2654] was born in 1913.
> 2279   ix. John Winder **Croxall**[2655] was born in August 1917.

1718. **Tracy Y.**[10] **Croxall** (Caroline Partridge[9] **Young**, Brigham[8], Abigail (Nabby)[7] **Howe**, Susanna[6] **Goddard**, Ebenezer[5], Susanna[4] **Stone**, Mary[3] **Whipple**, Elder John[2], Matthew[1])[2656] was born 23 July 1879 and married twice. (1) **Elsie Riter** 12 September 1905. She died 27 May 1908. [2657] (2) **Lettie Taylor**.[2658]

> Tracy Y. **Croxall** and Lettie **Taylor** had the following children:
>
> 2280   i. Trace Taylor[11] **Croxall**[2659] was born 10 February 1912.
> 2281   ii. Melvin **Croxall**[2660] was born 25 July 1913.
> 2282   iii. Ralph Taylor **Croxall**[2661] was born 22 April 1915.
> 2283   iv. Judith **Croxall**[2662] was born 19 September 1916.
> 2284   v. Frances **Croxall**[2663] was born 18 May 1919.

1720. **Vera**[10] **Croxall** (Caroline Partridge[9] **Young**, Brigham[8], Abigail (Nabby)[7] **Howe**, Susanna[6] **Goddard**, Ebenezer[5], Susanna[4] **Stone**, Mary[3] **Whipple**, Elder John[2], Matthew[1])[2664] was born 13 October 1881 and married **Heber C. Sharp** 16 September 1902.

> Vera **Croxall** and Heber C. **Sharp** had the following children:
>
> 2285   i. James Cannon[11] **Sharp**[2665] was born 4 September 1903.
> 2286   ii. Heber Cannon **Sharp**[2666] was born 24 November 1904.
> 2287   iii. Anthony Cannon **Sharp**[2667] was born 18 April 1908.
> 2288   iv. Florence Cannon **Sharp**[2668] was born 2 May 1911.
> 2289   v. George Cannon **Sharp**[2669] was born 20 February 1915.

1721. Clawson Y.[10] **Cannon** (Caroline Partridge[9] **Young**, Brigham[8], Abigail (Nabby)[7] **Howe**, Susanna[6] **Goddard**, Ebenezer[5], Susanna[4] **Stone**, Mary[3] **Whipple**, Elder John[2], Matthew[1])[2670] was born 27 October 1885 and married **Winifred Morrell.**

Winifred **Morrell** had the following children:

2290   i.   Rowland Morrell[11] **Cannon**[2671] was born 2 June 1914.

2291   ii.   Robert Young **Cannon**[2672] was born 11 September 1917.

2292   iii.   Winifred **Cannon**[2673] was born 14 November 1919.

1722. Wilford Y.[10] **Cannon** (Caroline Partridge[9] **Young**, Brigham[8], Abigail (Nabby)[7] **Howe**, Susanna[6] **Goddard**, Ebenezer[5], Susanna[4] **Stone**, Mary[3] **Whipple**, Elder John[2], Matthew[1])[2674] was born 4 July 1888 and married **Delores Stohl.**

Wilford Y. **Cannon** and Delores **Stohl** had the following child:

2293   i.   Wilfred Stohl[11] **Cannon**[2675] was born 19 April 1919.

1723. Anne Y.[10] **Cannon** (Caroline Partridge[9] **Young**, Brigham[8], Abigail (Nabby)[7] **Howe**, Susanna[6] **Goddard**, Ebenezer[5], Susanna[4] **Stone**, Mary[3] **Whipple**, Elder John[2], Matthew[1])[2676] was born 13 June 1890 and married **John Rex Winder** 20 October 1914.

Anne Y. **Cannon** and John Rex **Winder** had the following children:

2294   i.   Anne[11] **Winder**[2677] was born 30 August 1915.

2295   ii.   John Rex **Winder** Jr.[2678] was born 18 November 1918 and died 12 February 1920 at one year of age.

1770. Clara[10] **Clawson** (Nabbie Howe[9] **Young**, Brigham[8], Abigail (Nabby)[7] **Howe**, Susanna[6] **Goddard**, Ebenezer[5], Susanna[4] **Stone**, Mary[3] **Whipple**, Elder John[2], Matthew[1])[2679] was born 26 February 1877 and died 28 February 1903 at 26 years of age. She married **Chauncey Benedict.**

Clara **Clawson** and Chauncey **Benedict** had the following child:

2296   i.   Joseph Clawson[11] **Benedict**[2680] was born 8 February 1903.

1772. Curtis Young[10] **Clawson** (Nabbie Howe[9] **Young**, Brigham[8], Abigail (Nabby)[7] **Howe**, Susanna[6] **Goddard**, Ebenezer[5], Susanna[4] **Stone**, Mary[3] **Whipple**, Elder John[2], Matthew[1])[2681] was born 27 July 1884 and married **Louise Parkinson.** He served with the 145th artillery as a major in WWI.

Curtis Young **Clawson** and Louise **Parkinson** had the following children:

2297   i.   Nabbie Louise[11] **Clawson**[2682] was born 5 April 1912.

2298   ii.   Jeannette **Clawson**[2683] was born 16 April 1914.

2299   iii.   William Curtis **Clawson**[2684] was born 12 December 1919.

1773. Grace[10] **Clawson** (Nabbie Howe[9] **Young**, Brigham[8], Abigail (Nabby)[7] **Howe**, Susanna[6] **Goddard**, Ebenezer[5], Susanna[4] **Stone**, Mary[3] **Whipple**, Elder John[2], Matthew[1])[2685] was born 28 January 1886 and married **Ralph Woolley.**

Grace **Clawson** and Ralph **Woolley** had the following children:

2300   i.   Easton Clawson[11] **Woolley**[2686] was born 8 January 1904.

2301   ii.   Peter Brenton **Woolley**[2687] was born 17 March 1915.

1774. John Neels[10] **Clawson** (Nabbie Howe[9] **Young**, Brigham[8], Abigail

(Nabby)[7] **Howe**, Susanna[6] **Goddard**, Ebenezer[5], Susanna[4] **Stone**, Mary[3] **Whipple**, Elder John[2], Matthew[1])[2688] was born 12 February 1888 and married **Nora Wiscomb**.

> John Neels **Clawson** and Nora **Wiscomb** had the following children:
> 2302   i.   Spencer Wiscomb[11] **Clawson**[2689] was born 7 November 1915.
> 2303   ii.   Robert Wiscomb **Clawson**[2690] was born 21 March 1919.

1775. Nabbie Young[10] Clawson (Nabbie Howe[9] **Young**, Brigham[8], Abigail (Nabby)[7] **Howe**, Susanna[6] **Goddard**, Ebenezer[5], Susanna[4] **Stone**, Mary[3] **Whipple**, Elder John[2], Matthew[1])[2691] was born 24 May 1891 and married **Frank McMaster**.

> Nabbie Young **Clawson** and Frank **McMaster** had the following child:
> 2304   i.   Alexander Spencer[11] **McMaster**[2692] was born 27 December 1916.

1784. Frank Moreland[10] Dunford (Eudora Lovina[9] **Young**, Brigham[8], Abigail (Nabby)[7] **Howe**, Susanna[6] **Goddard**, Ebenezer[5], Susanna[4] **Stone**, Mary[3] **Whipple**, Elder John[2], Matthew[1])[2693] was born 2 June 1873 and married **Irene Bellew**.

> Frank Moreland **Dunford** and Irene **Bellew** had the following children:
> 2305   i.   Francis Bellew[11] **Dunford**[2694] was born 24 August 1899.
> 2306   ii.   John Moreland **Dunford**[2695] was born 10 December 1906.

1785. George Albert[10] Dunford (Eudora Lovina[9] **Young**, Brigham[8], Abigail (Nabby)[7] **Howe**, Susanna[6] **Goddard**, Ebenezer[5], Susanna[4] **Stone**, Mary[3] **Whipple**, Elder John[2], Matthew[1])[2696] was born 29 August 1875 and died 20 December 1901 at 26 years of age. He married **Mary Ann Phillips**.

> George Albert **Dunford** and Mary Ann **Phillips** had the following children:
> 2307   i.   Marie Lucile[11] **Dunford**[2697] was born 19 November 1896.
> 2308   ii.   Albert Phillips **Dunford**[2698] was born 24 February 1898 and served in the U.S. Navy during WWI and was invalided home at the close of the hostilities.
> 2309   iii.   Dorothy Emmeline **Dunford**[2699] was born 2 February 1901.

1787. Harold Raymond[10] Hagan (Eudora Lovina[9] **Young**, Brigham[8], Abigail (Nabby)[7] **Howe**, Susanna[6] **Goddard**, Ebenezer[5], Susanna[4] **Stone**, Mary[3] **Whipple**, Elder John[2], Matthew[1])[2700] was born in Coeur 'd Alene, Idaho 20 May 1886 and married **Blanche Young**, his third cousin. Blanche was the daughter of Isaac **Young**.

> Harold Raymond **Hagan** and Blanche **Young** had the following children:
> 2310   i.   Frances Marie[11] **Hagan**[2701] was born 1 August 1910 and died in July 1911 at less than one year of age.
> 2311   ii.   Harold Raymond **Hagan** Jr.[2702] was born 1 November 1915.

1788. Mabel Clara[10] Hagan (Eudora Lovina[9] **Young**, Brigham[8], Abigail (Nabby)[7] **Howe**, Susanna[6] **Goddard**, Ebenezer[5], Susanna[4] **Stone**, Mary[3] **Whipple**, Elder John[2], Matthew[1])[2703] was born in Coeur 'd Alene, Idaho 15 May 1889 and married **Roy Farnes**. Roy was born 21 August 1886.[2704]

> Mabel Clara **Hagan** and Roy **Farnes** had the following children:
> 2312   i.   Albert Hagen[11] **Farnes**[2705] was born 14 April 1907.
> 2313   ii.   Harold Raymond **Farnes**[2706] was born 1 June 1908.

2314   iii. Dora Mary **Farnes**[2707] was born 25 December 1911.

1751. Josephine Young[10] **Beatie** (Phebe Louisa[9] **Young**, Brigham[8], Abigail (Nabby)[7] **Howe**, Susanna[6] **Goddard**, Ebenezer[5], Susanna[4] **Stone**, Mary[3] **Whipple**, Elder John[2], Matthew[1])[2708] was born 2 September 1874 and married **Charles S. Burton**. Charles was born 18 May 1855.[2709]

Josephine Young **Beatie** and Charles S. **Burton** had the following children:

2315   i. Richard Wells[11] **Burton**[2710] was born 17 March 1894.
2316   ii. Julian Young **Burton**[2711] was born 11 February 1896.
2317   iii. Josephine Lou **Burton**[2712] was born 1 December 1906.

1754. Hazel Young[10] **Beatie** (Phebe Louisa[9] **Young**, Brigham[8], Abigail (Nabby)[7] **Howe**, Susanna[6] **Goddard**, Ebenezer[5], Susanna[4] **Stone**, Mary[3] **Whipple**, Elder John[2], Matthew[1])[2713] was born 27 November 1882 and married **Edward Partridge Kimball**. Edward was born 12 June 1882.[2714]

Hazel Young **Beatie** and Edward Partridge **Kimball** had the following children:

2318   i. Marion Young[11] **Kimball**[2715] was born 6 May 1906.
2319   ii. Edward Beatie **Kimball**[2716] was born 17 February 1910.
2320   iii. Willard Young **Kimball**[2717] was born 16 February 1917.

1756. Walter Sidney[10] **Beatie** (Phebe Louisa[9] **Young**, Brigham[8], Abigail (Nabby)[7] **Howe**, Susanna[6] **Goddard**, Ebenezer[5], Susanna[4] **Stone**, Mary[3] **Whipple**, Elder John[2], Matthew[1])[2718] was born 12 June 1889 and married **Margaret Gay Taylor**. Margaret was born 19 November 1892.[2719]

Walter Sidney **Beatie** and Margaret Gay **Taylor** had the following children:

2321   i. Virginia[11] **Beatie**[2720] was born 7 January 1912.
2322   ii. Richard Sidney **Beatie**[2721] was born 8 October 1913.

1765. Gladys[10] **Ferguson** (Louisa Nelle[9] **Young**, Brigham[8], Abigail (Nabby)[7] **Howe**, Susanna[6] **Goddard**, Ebenezer[5], Susanna[4] **Stone**, Mary[3] **Whipple**, Elder John[2], Matthew[1])[2722] was born in New York State and married **Benjamin Edwards**.

Gladys **Ferguson** and Benjamin **Edwards** had the following children:

2323   i. Mildred[11] **Edwards**[2723].
2324   ii. Audrey **Edwards**[2724].

1790. Leah Eudora[10] **Dunford** (Susan (Susa) Amelia[9] **Young**, Brigham[8], Abigail (Nabby)[7] **Howe**, Susanna[6] **Goddard**, Ebenezer[5], Susanna[4] **Stone**, Mary[3] **Whipple**, Elder John[2], Matthew[1])[2725] was born 24 February 1874 and married **Dr. J. A. Widtoe**. He was born 31 January 1872 in Froien, Norway which is off the north coast of Norway. [2726]

Leah Eudora **Dunford** and Dr. J. A. **Widtoe** had the following children:

2325   i. Anna Gaarden[11] **Widtoe**[2727] was born in Gottingen, Germany 23 April 1899.
2326   ii. John Andreas **Widtoe** Jr.[2728] was born in Logan, Cache Co., Utah 8 April 1901 and died there 10 February 1902 at less than one year of age.
2327   iii. Karl Marselius **Widtoe**[2729] was born in Logan 27 November 1902.
2328   iv. Mark Adriel **Widtoe**[2730] was born 18 May 1904 and died 27 August

1906 at 2 years of age.

2329   v.   Helen **Widtoe**[2731] was born 22 August 1907 and died the day after birth.

2330   vi.   Mary **Widtoe**[2732] was born 15 November 1909 and died the day of birth.

2331   vii.   Leah Eudora **Widtoe**[2733] was born 4 July 1912.

1797. Brigham Cecil[10] **Gates** (Susan (Susa) Amelia[9] **Young**, Brigham[8], Abigail (Nabby)[7] **Howe**, Susanna[6] **Goddard**, Ebenezer[5], Susanna[4] **Stone**, Mary[3] **Whipple**, Elder John[2], Matthew[1])[2734] was born in Laie, Oahu, Hawaii 17 August 1887 and married **Gweneth Gibbs** 30 June 1917.

Brigham Cecil **Gates** and Gweneth **Gibbs** had the following children:

2332   i.   Gweneth[11] **Gates**[2735] was born 23 April 1918.

2333   ii.   Emma Lucy **Gates**[2736] was born 8 September 1919.

1798. Harvey Harris[10] **Gates** (Susan (Susa) Amelia[9] **Young**, Brigham[8], Abigail (Nabby)[7] **Howe**, Susanna[6] **Goddard**, Ebenezer[5], Susanna[4] **Stone**, Mary[3] **Whipple**, Elder John[2], Matthew[1])[2737] was born in Laie, Oahu, Hawaii 19 January 1889 and marrried **Lucie Jenne Genez** 21 December 1912.

Harvey Harris **Gates** and Lucie Jenne **Genez** had the following children:

2334   i.   Victor Cecil[11] **Gates**[2738] was born in New York State 28 November 1913.

2335   ii.   Beulah Suzanne **Gates**[2739] was born in Hollywood, Calif. 23 June 1915.

2336   iii.   Jacob Harvey **Gates**[2740] was born in Hollywood 31 December 1916.

1800. Franklin Young[10] **Gates** (Susan (Susa) Amelia[9] **Young**, Brigham[8], Abigail (Nabby)[7] **Howe**, Susanna[6] **Goddard**, Ebenezer[5], Susanna[4] **Stone**, Mary[3] **Whipple**, Elder John[2], Matthew[1])[2741] was born 17 May 1893 and married **Florence Keate**.

Franklin Young **Gates** and Florence **Keate** had the following children:

2337   i.   Lurene Keliilalanikulani[11] **Gates**[2742] was born in Hilo, Hawaii 25 September 1914.

2338   ii.   Franklin Young **Gates** Jr.[2743] was born in Logan, Cache Co., Utah 21 June 1916.

2339   iii.   James Keate **Gates**[2744] was born in August 1919 and died 18 June 1920 at less than one year of age.

1725. Miriam Y.[10] **Hardy** (Miriam[9] **Young**, Brigham[8], Abigail (Nabby)[7] **Howe**, Susanna[6] **Goddard**, Ebenezer[5], Susanna[4] **Stone**, Mary[3] **Whipple**, Elder John[2], Matthew[1])[2745] was born in Salt Lake City, Utah 7 August 1879 and married **Riego Stay Hawkins** there.

Miriam Y. **Hardy** and Riego Stay **Hawkins** had the following children born in Salt Lake City, Utah:

2340   I.   Miriam Charlotte[11] **Hawkins**[2746] was born 30 August 1906.

2341   ii.   Lillian **Hawkins**[2747] was born 24 March 1908 and died 6 November 1908 in Salt Lake City at less than one year of age.

2342   iii.   Riego Curtis **Hawkins**[2748] was born 20 December 1909.

2343   iv.   Eugene **Hawkins**.[2749]

2344   v.   Lucile **Hawkins**.[2750]

1726. Eugenia Young[10] **Hardy** (Miriam[9] **Young**, Brigham[8], Abigail (Nabby)[7] **Howe**, Susanna[6] **Goddard**, Ebenezer[5], Susanna[4] **Stone**, Mary[3] **Whipple**, Elder John[2], Matthew[1])[2751] was born 30 September 1881 and married **James Henry Rampton.**

Eugenia Young **Hardy** and James Henry **Rampton** had the following children:

2345   i.   Henry Hardy[11] **Rampton**[2752] was born in Sterling Alberta, Canada 19 December 1904.

2346   ii.   Leonard Hardy **Rampton**[2753] was born in Taylorville, Canada 26 December 1906.

2347   iii.   James Paul **Rampton**[2754] was born in Centerville, Utah 11 November 1909.

2348   iv.   Richard Hardy **Rampton**[2755] was born in Bountiful, Utah 13 May 1911.

2349   v.   Edward **Rampton**[2756].

1727. Emily Partridge[10] **Hardy** (Miriam[9] **Young**, Brigham[8], Abigail (Nabby)[7] **Howe**, Susanna[6] **Goddard**, Ebenezer[5], Susanna[4] **Stone**, Mary[3] **Whipple**, Elder John[2], Matthew[1])[2757] was born in Salt Lake City, Utah 1 February 1884 and married **Thomas Blair.**

Emily Partridge **Hardy** and Thomas **Blair** had the following children born in Salt Lake City, Utah:

2350   i.   Thomas[11] **Blair Jr.**[2758]

2351   ii.   Alice Hardy **Blair.**[2759]

2352   iii.   Mary Elizabeth **Blair.**[2760]

2353   iv.   Blanche Florence **Blair.**[2761].

1728. Leonard Goodridge[10] **Hardy** (Miriam[9] **Young**, Brigham[8], Abigail (Nabby)[7] **Howe**, Susanna[6] **Goddard**, Ebenezer[5], Susanna[4] **Stone**, Mary[3] **Whipple**, Elder John[2], Matthew[1])[2762] was born in Salt Lake City, Utah 25 February 1886 and married **Lucetta Morton Bromley.**

Leonard Goodridge **Hardy** and Lucetta Morton **Bromley** had the following children born in Salt Lake City:

2354   i.   Elizabeth (Betty)[11] **Hardy**[2763] was born 2 February 1915.

2355   ii.   Barbara Jean **Hardy**[2764] was born 12 February 1917.

2356   iii.   Leonard Goodridge **Hardy** III[2765] was born 30 December 1918.

1738. Clisbee[10] **Young** (Josephine[9], Brigham[8], Abigail (Nabby)[7] **Howe**, Susanna[6] **Goddard**, Ebenezer[5], Susanna[4] **Stone**, Mary[3] **Whipple**, Elder John[2], Matthew[1])[2766] was born in Salt Lake City, Utah 21 March 1887 and married **Artemacy Mariger.**

Clisbee **Young** and Artemacy **Mariger** had the following child:

2357   i.   Audrey[11] **Mariger**[2767] was born in Salt Lake City, Utah 25 July 1910.

1698. John Allan[10] **Spencer** (Clarissa Hamilton[9] **Young**, Brigham[8], Abigail (Nabby)[7] **Howe**, Susanna[6] **Goddard**, Ebenezer[5], Susanna[4] **Stone**, Mary[3] **Whipple**, Elder John[2], Matthew[1])[2768] was born 9 July 1885 and married **Alice Young.**

John Allan **Spencer** and Alice **Young** had the following children:

2358   i.   John Allan[11] **Spencer Jr.**[2769] was born 10 December 1912.

2359   ii.   Claire **Spencer**[2770] was born 24 May 1916.

1699. **Jean**[10] **Spencer** (Clarissa Hamilton[9] **Young**, Brigham[8], Abigail (Nabby)[7] **Howe**, Susanna[6] **Goddard**, Ebenezer[5], Susanna[4] **Stone**, Mary[3] **Whipple**, Elder John[2], Matthew[1])[2771] was born 16 June 1888 and married **Morrill Newton Farr**.

Jean **Spencer** and Morrill Newton **Farr** had the following children:
    2360   i. Morrill Spencer[11] **Farr**[2772] was born 13 March 1910.
    2361   ii. Frances Jean **Farr**[2773] was born 14 June 1913.
    2362   iii. Richard Spencer **Farr**[2774] was born 21 May 1915.

1700. **Rehan**[10] **Spencer** (Clarissa Hamilton[9] **Young**, Brigham[8], Abigail (Nabby)[7] **Howe**, Susanna[6] **Goddard**, Ebenezer[5], Susanna[4] **Stone**, Mary[3] **Whipple**, Elder John[2], Matthew[1])[2775] was born 15 April 1890 and married Archie **West**.

Rehan **Spencer** and Archie **West** had the following child:
    2363   i. James Spencer[11] **West**[2776] was born 1 October 1915.

1768. **Ellis**[10] **Johnson** (Ruth[9] **Young**, Brigham[8], Abigail (Nabby)[7] **Howe**, Susanna[6] **Goddard**, Ebenezer[5], Susanna[4] **Stone**, Mary[3] **Whipple**, Elder John[2], Matthew[1])[2777] was born 2 October 1880 and married **Bessie Pinkerton**.

Ellis **Johnson** and Bessie **Pinkerton** had the following children:
    2364   i. Harry Ellis[11] **Johnson**[2778] was born 2 July 1908.
    2365   ii. Dovey Marian **Johnson**[2779] was born 16 April 1914.
    2366   iii. Lee Scott **Johnson**[2780] was born 20 November 1919.

1769. **Jay Elliot**[10] **Johnson** (Ruth[9] **Young**, Brigham[8], Abigail (Nabby)[7] **Howe**, Susanna[6] **Goddard**, Ebenezer[5], Susanna[4] **Stone**, Mary[3] **Whipple**, Elder John[2], Matthew[1])[2781] was born 16 March 1883 and married **Elizabeth May Snyder**.

Jay Elliot **Johnson** and Elizabeth May **Snyder** had the following children:
    2367   i. Ruth Elizabeth[11] **Johnson**[2782] was born 23 August 1913.
    2368   ii. Ella May **Johnson**[2783] was born 16 September 1916.

1803. **Daniel Handley**[10] **McAllister** (Rhoda Mabel[9] **Young**, Brigham[8], Abigail (Nabby)[7] **Howe**, Susanna[6] **Goddard**, Ebenezer[5], Susanna[4] **Stone**, Mary[3] **Whipple**, Elder John[2], Matthew[1])[2784] was born 2 August 1880 and married **Beulah Keeler**.

Danniel Handley **McAllister** and Beulah **Keeler** had the following children:
    2369   i. Joseph Daniel[11] **McAllister**[2785] was born 23 July 1909.
    2370   ii. Helen **McAllister**[2786] was born 27 April 1912.
    2371   iii. Martha **McAllister**[2787] was born 9 December 1914.

1804. **Brigham Winfred**[10] **Witt** (Rhoda Mabel[9] **Young**, Brigham[8], Abigail (Nabby)[7] **Howe**, Susanna[6] **Goddard**, Ebenezer[5], Susanna[4] **Stone**, Mary[3] **Whipple**, Elder John[2], Matthew[1])[2788] was born 9 October 1889 and married **Anna Lundsted**. He was with the 1st Division for 22 months in England during WWI.

Brigham Winfred **Witt** and Anna **Lundsted** had the following child:
    2372   i. Winifred Utahna[11] **Witt**[2789] was born 28 January 1912.

1808. **Isaac Ambrose**[10] **Clayton Jr.** (Fannie Van Cott[9] **Young**, Brigham[8], Abigail (Nabby)[7] **Howe**, Susanna[6] **Goddard**, Ebenezer[5], Susanna[4] **Stone**, Mary[3] **Whipple**, Elder John[2], Matthew[1])[2790] was born 17 May 1892 and married **Marguerite Bassett**.

Isaac Ambrose **Clayton** Jr. and Marguerite **Bassett** had the following child:

2373   i.   Norman^{11} **Clayton**[2791] was born 3 November 1917.

1817. Persis Ann^{10} Brown (Harriet Maria^{9} **Young**, Lorenzo Dow^{8}, Abigail (Nabby)^{7} **Howe**, Susanna^{6} **Goddard**, Ebenezer^{5}, Susanna^{4} **Stone**, Mary^{3} **Whipple**, Elder John^{2}, Matthew^{1})[2792] was born in Draper, Utah 23 December 1855 and married **Howard Orson Spencer**. Howard was born in Middlefield, Hampshire Co., Mass. 16 June 1838.[2793]

Persis Ann **Brown** and Howard Orson **Spencer** had the following children born in Orderville, Kane Co., Utah:

2374   i.   Harriet^{11} **Spencer**[2794] was born 4 March 1877.
2375   ii.   Joseph Guernsey **Spencer**[2795] was born 29 June 1881.
2376   iii.   Nabby **Spencer**[2796] was born 1 March 1883.
2377   iv.   Bessie **Spencer**[2797] was born 6 April 1886.
2378   v.   Homer B. **Spencer**[2798] was born 13 June 1888.

1818. Joseph Guernsey^{10} Brown Jr. (Harriet Maria^{9} **Young**, Lorenzo Dow^{8}, Abigail (Nabby)^{7} **Howe**, Susanna^{6} **Goddard**, Ebenezer^{5}, Susanna^{4} **Stone**, Mary^{3} **Whipple**, Elder John^{2}, Matthew^{1})[2799] was born in Draper, Utah 17 April 1857 and died 23 July 1887 at 30 years of age. He married **Clara Ann Little** 10 January 1884. She married (2) **Ebenezer Brown**.

Joseph Guernsey **Brown** Jr. and Clara Ann **Little** had the following children:

2379   i.   Clara Curtis^{11} **Brown**[2800] was born in Tooele Co., Utah 3 December 1884 and died 30 September 1889 at 4 years of age.
2380   ii.   Joseph Guernsey **Brown** III[2801] was born in Kanab, Kane Co., Utah 14 May 1886.

1819. Lucy Elizabeth^{10} Brown (Harriet Maria^{9} **Young**, Lorenzo Dow^{8}, Abigail (Nabby)^{7} **Howe**, Susanna^{6} **Goddard**, Ebenezer^{5}, Susanna^{4} **Stone**, Mary^{3} **Whipple**, Elder John^{2}, Matthew^{1})[2802] was born in Draper, Utah 12 April 1859 and married **William Derby Johnson II**. William was born in Kanesville, Potawattamie Co., Iowa 2 May 1850.[2803]

Lucy Elizabeth **Brown** and William Derby **Johnson** II had the following children:

2381   i.   Zeno Martel^{11} **Johnson**[2804] was born in Kanab, Kane Co., Utah 16 April 1878.
2382   ii.   Annie **Johnson**[2805] was born in Kanab 23 November 1880 and died the day of birth.
2383   iii.   Ruby **Johnson**[2806] was born in Kanab 16 December 1882 and died there 17 July 1883 at less than one year of age.
2384   iv.   Rupert Fay **Johnson**[2807] was born in Kanab 2 February 1885 and died 30 January 1886 at less than one year of age.
2385   v.   Jane Cadwalader **Johnson**[2808] was born in LaSension, Chihuahua, Mexico 22 June 1886.
2386   vi.   Kathe **Johnson**[2809] was born in Diaz Bravos, Mexico 15 August 1888 and died there 2 June 1891 at 2 years of age.
2387   vii.   Viva **Johnson**[2810] was born in Diaz Bravos 15 October 1890.
2388   viii.   Ivy **Johnson**[2811] was born in Diaz Bravos 16 May 1892.
2389   ix.   Karl Maeser **Johnson**[2812] was born in Diaz Bravos 22 May 1895 and

died 19 August 1897 at 2 years of age.

2390   x. Harriet Persis **Johnson**[2813] was born 21 November 1898.

1820. Angeline[10] **Brown** (Harriet Maria[9] **Young**, Lorenzo Dow[8], Abigail (Nabby)[7] **Howe**, Susanna[6] **Goddard**, Ebenezer[5], Susanna[4] **Stone**, Mary[3] **Whipple**, Elder John[2], Matthew[1])[2814] was born in Draper, Utah 6 January 1861 and married **William J.F. Macalister**. William was born 4 August 1845.[2815]

Angeline **Brown** and William J.F. **Macalister** had the following children:

2391   i. Graham B.[11] **Macalister**[2816] was born in Kanab, Kane Co., Utah 4 March 1880.

2392   ii. Nellie **Macalister**[2817] was born in Kanab 13 December 1881.

2393   iii. Clara **Macalister**[2818] was born in 5 April 1884.

2394   iv. Seymour Y. **Macalister**[2819] was born in Kanab 17 May 1888.

2395   v. Persis **Macalister**[2820] was born in Fredonia, Ariz. 17 September 1894.

1821. Lorenzo Y.[10] **Brown** (Harriet Maria[9] **Young**, Lorenzo Dow[8], Abigail (Nabby)[7] **Howe**, Susanna[6] **Goddard**, Ebenezer[5], Susanna[4] **Stone**, Mary[3] **Whipple**, Elder John[2], Matthew[1])[2821] was born in Draper, Utah 19 September 1862 and died 13 December 1893 at 31 years of age. He married **Mary Elizabeth Haycock** 27 January 1885.

Lorenzo Y. **Brown** and Mary Elizabeth **Haycock** had the following children:

2396   i. Homer[11] **Brown**[2822] was born 22 March 1887 and died the day of birth.

2397   ii. Afton **Brown**[2823] was born 19 May 1889.

2398   iii. Lorenzo D. **Brown**[2824] was born 28 April 1891.

2399   iv. Feramorz Y. **Brown**[2825] was born 28 April 1891.

2400   v. Kenneth **Brown**[2826] was born 4 September 1892.

1822. Ebenezer[10] **Brown** (Harriet Maria[9] **Young**, Lorenzo Dow[8], Abigail (Nabby)[7] **Howe**, Susanna[6] **Goddard**, Ebenezer[5], Susanna[4] **Stone**, Mary[3] **Whipple**, Elder John[2], Matthew[1])[2827] was born in Draper, Utah 10 October 1864 and married as her second husband **Clara Ann Little**. She married (1) **Joseph Guernsey Brown Jr.** 10 January 1884.

Ebenezer **Brown** and Clara Ann **Little** had the following children:

2401   i. Eben Ray[11] **Brown**[2828] was born 11 August 1889.

2402   ii. Chill **Brown**[2829] was born in Kanab, Kane Co., Utah 31 August 1891.

2403   iii. George Little **Brown**[2830] was born in Kanab 14 July 1893.

2404   iv. Basil **Brown**[2831] was born in Kanab 26 November 1895 and died 26 February 1899 at 3 years of age.

2405   v. Ruel Elgin **Brown**[2832] was born in Kanab 9 May 1897.

2406   vi. Feramorz Little **Brown**[2833] was born in Kanab 24 March 1899.

1832. Milon Gardner[10] **Stone** (Marshall Maynard[9], Col. Jonathan[8], Lt. Jonathan[7], Jonathan[6], Jonathan[5], Jonathan[4], Mary[3] **Whipple**, Elder John[2], Matthew[1])[2834] was born in Auburn, Mass. 2 June 1850 and died 1 May 1940 in Spartanburg, S.C. at 89 years of age. He married twice. (1) **Mary Ann Evans** in Providence, R.I. 17 June 1871. Mary, daughter of Smith **Evans** and Sarah **Simmons**, was born in Smithfield, R.I. 5 February 1851 and died 19 July 1892 in Spartanburg at 41 years of age.[2835] (2) **Mrs. Eliza (Christman) Esty** in Spartanburg 5 December 1893. Eliza,[2836] daughter of Johann Ferdinand **Christman** and Maria

Elizabeth **Pricken**, was born in New York, N.Y. 30 July 1858 and died 1 December 1938 in Spartanburg at 80 years of age. She married (1) **Newell F. Esty** before 1893.

Milon Gardner **Stone** and Mary Ann **Evans** had the following children:

2407   i.   Elsie Maria[11] **Stone**[2837] was born in Putnam, Conn. 25 June 1872 and died in 1949 in Spartanburg, S.C. at 77 years of age. She married Matthew **Pettigrew** in Spartanburg.

2408   ii.   Ida Estella **Stone**[2838] was born in Putnam 22 October 1874 and died there 24 February 1875 at less than one year of age.

+ 2409   iii.   Sarah Mary (Mai) **Stone** was born 12 March 1876.

Milon Gardner **Stone** and Mrs. Eliza (Christman) **Esty** had the following children born in Spartanburg, S.C.:

2410   iv.   Maud Elizabeth **Stone**[2839] was born 5 October 1894 and died in Spartanburg 16 February 1979 at 84 years of age. She married Reuben Walker **Porter** in Spartanburg 23 December 1924. No children born to this union.

2411   v.   Milon Gardner **Stone**[2840] was born 30 December 1895 and died 12 May 1896 in Spartanburg at less than one year of age.

+ 2412   vi.   Marshall Christman **Stone** was born 4 December 1897.

1835. Arthur Davis[10] **Stone** (Marshall Maynard[9], Col. Jonathan[8], Lt. Jonathan[7], Jonathan[6], Jonathan[5], Jonathan[4], Mary[3] **Whipple**, Elder John[2], Matthew[1])[2841] was born in Auburn, Mass. 6 March 1867 and married **Lily Etta Collier** in Worcester, Worcester Co., Mass. 15 June 1887.

Arthur Davis **Stone** and Lily Etta **Collier** had the following children:

2413   i.   William Arthur[11] **Stone**[2842] was born 21 July 1888.

2414   ii.   Milon Marshall **Stone**[2843] was born 25 June 1889.

2415   iii.   Lilly Thelma **Stone**[2844] was born 23 September 1905.

1840. Mary Jane[10] **Billings** (Hiram[9], Joel[8], John[7], Joanna[6] **Norton**, John[5], Mary[4] **Goodhue**, Sarah[3] **Whipple**, Elder John[2], Matthew[1])[2845] was born in Scarboro, Cumberland Co., Maine abt 1828 and died 18 May 1864 in Bath, Sagadahoc Co., Maine at 35 years of age. She married **Oliver Hazard Perry** in Portland, Maine 15 October 1849. Oliver was born in New Hampshire abt 1821.[2846] He married (2) **Elizabeth Felker** in Bath 4 November 1865. Oliver died aft 1870.

Mary Jane **Billings** and Oliver Hazard **Perry** had the following child:

+ 2416   i.   Mary Alice[11] **Perry** was born 25 October 1852.

1842. Bessie[10] **Swett** (Benjamin Frank[9], Benjamin[8], Daniel[7], Moses[6], Elizabeth[5] **Norton**, Mary[4] **Goodhue**, Sarah[3] **Whipple**, Elder John[2], Matthew[1])[2847] was born in Auburn, Maine 11 October 1879 and died 4 June 1931 in East Rockaway, N.Y. at 51 years of age. She married **George M. Wilde**. George was born in New York State in 1881 and died in 1942 in The Bronx, N.Y. at 61 years of age.[2848]

Bessie **Swett** and George M. **Wilde** had the following child:

+ 2417   i.   George H.[11] **Wilde** was born 11 September 1904.

1846. Ellen[10] **Mecham** (Joseph L.[9], Sarah[8] **Basford**, Jonathan[7], Elizabeth[6] **Goodhue**, Jonathan[5], William[4], Sarah[3] **Whipple**, Elder John[2], Matthew[1])[2849] was born 4 July 1836 and died 1 August 1872 in Woods Cross, Davis Co., Utah at 36 years of age. She married **Ormus Ephraim Bates** in Salt Lake City, Utah 5 January 1853. Ormus,[2850] son of Cyrus **Bates** and Lydia **Harrington**, was born 25 March 1815 and died 4 August 1873 in Tooele Co., Utah at 58 years of age.

Ellen **Mecham** and Ormus Ephraim **Bates** had the following children born in Tooele Co., Utah:

2418	i.	Armintha[11] **Bates**[2851] was born in 1855 and married twice. (1) . W. Pettit. (2) Henry **Shields**.
2419	ii.	Oliver **Bates**[2852] was born in1856 and married Lu Juana **Kelley**.
2420	iii.	Albert **Bates**[2853] was born in 1860 and married Irene **Day**.
2421	iv.	Lillian May **Bates**[2854] was born 9 May 1868 and died 24 May 1940 in Kailspell, Mont. at 72 years of age. She married Dr. Henry Wylie **Brant**.

1863. Luman Lehi[10] **Mecham** (Joseph L.[9], Sarah[8] **Basford**, Jonathan[7], Elizabeth[6] **Goodhue**, Jonathan[5], William[4], Sarah[3] **Whipple**, Elder John[2], Matthew[1])[2855] was born in Milton, Morgan Co., Utah 14 July 1863 and died 14 April 1939 in Logan, Cache Co., Utah at 75 years of age. He was buried in Paris, Bear Lake Co., Idaho. He married **Mary Ann Hess** in Logan 16 November 1892. Mary,[2856] daughter of Jacob **Hess** and Hannah **Thornock**, was born in Bloomington, Oneida Co., Idaho 28 February 1872 and died 29 January 1935 in Paris at 62 years of age.

Luman Lehi **Mecham** and Mary Ann **Hess** had the following children:

+ 2422	i.	Ella Lovenia[11] **Mecham** was born 23 November 1893.
+ 2423	ii.	Everett Hess **Mecham** was born 15 June 1895.
+ 2424	iii.	Mary Eurilla **Mecham** was born 10 August 1898.
+ 2425	iv.	Dora Artenchia **Mecham** was born 1 August 1901.
2426	v.	(__) **Mecham**[2857] was born in Fairview, Wyo. 26 January 1903 and died the day of birth.
+ 2427	vi.	Lester Eugene **Mecham** was born 20 October 1905.

1879. Mary Melissa[10] **Miller** (Eli[9], Easter[8] **Kimball**, Jesse[7], John[6], Isaac[5], Sarah[4] **Goodhue**, Sarah[3] **Whipple**, Elder John[2], Matthew[1])[2858] was born in 1873 and died in 1950 at 77 years of age. She married **William Becker**. William was born in 1855 and died in 1925 at 70 years of age.[2859]

Mary Melissa **Miller** and William **Becker** had the following child:

+ 2428	i.	Vivian[11] **Becker** was born in 1892.

1882. Alexander[10] **(Tink) Miller** (Elisha D.[9], Easter[8] **Kimball**, Jesse[7], John[6], Isaac[5], Sarah[4] **Goodhue**, Sarah[3] **Whipple**, Elder John[2], Matthew[1])[2860] was born in 1864 and died in 1952 at 88 years of age. He married twice. (1) **Mary Ellen Hooser**. Mary was born in 1866 and died in 1921 at 55 years of age.[2861] (2) **Rebecca Leeann Auttereson** who died in 1945.[2862]

Alexander **Miller** and Mary Ellen **Hooser** had the following children:

+ 2429	i.	Glenn Dora[11] **Miller** was born in 1886.
+ 2430	ii	Lillie Maude **Miller** was born in 1888.
+ 2431	iii.	Mary Frances **Miller** was born in 1890.
2432	iv.	Bessie Blanche **Miller**[2863] was born in 1892 and died in 1893 at one year of age.
+ 2433	v.	James Alexander **Miller** was born in 1893.

+ 2434   vi.   Frederick Dean **Miller** was born in 1896.

2435   vii.   George Elisha **Miller**[2864] was born in 1898 and died in 1985 at 87 years of age.

2436   viii.   Earl Charles **Miller**[2865] was born in 1899 and married Mae **Keathley**. Mae was born in 1921.[2866]

+ 2437   ix.   Martha Judith **Miller** was born in 1902.

2438   x.   Earnest **Miller**[2867] was born in 1904 and died in infancy.

+ 2439   xi.   Elmer Cecil **Miller** was born in 1905 .

+ 2440   xii.   Roy Elvin **Miller** was born in 1907.

2441   xiii.   Verna Lucille **Miller**[2868] was born in 1908 and married Elmer Virgil **Jestes**. Elmer was born in 1900 and died in 1966 at 66 years of age [2869]

+ 2442   xiv.   Edwin Lee **Miller** was born in 1910.

1884. Samuel Martin[10] **Miller** (Elisha D.[9], Easter[8] **Kimball**, Jesse[7], John[6], Isaac[5], Sarah[4] **Goodhue**, Sarah[3] **Whipple**, Elder John[2], Matthew[1])[2870] was born in 1868 and died in 1941 at 73 years of age. He married **Emma Malinda Craig**. Emma was born in 1871 and died in 1952 at 81 years of age.[2871]

Samuel Martin **Miller** and Emma Malinda **Craig** had the following children:

2443   i.   Gladys[11] **Miller**[2872].

2444   ii.   Vera **Miller**[2873].

+ 2445   iii.   Carl Otis **Miller** was born in 1893.

1886. Benjamin Franklin[10] **Miller** (Elisha D.[9], Easter[8] **Kimball**, Jesse[7], John[6], Isaac[5], Sarah[4] **Goodhue**, Sarah[3] **Whipple**, Elder John[2], Matthew[1])[2874] was born in Otter Township, Cowley Co., Kans. 9 May 1872 and died 10 February 1951 in Pawnee, Okla. at 78 years of age. He married twice. (1) **Mary B. Richards** in Sedan, Chautauqua Co., Kans. 1 December 1897. Mary was born in Kansas 12 July 1874 and died 17 April 1905 in Cedar Vale, Chautauqua Co., Kans. at 30 years of age.[2875] (2) **Cora Gillespie** in Chatuauqua Co., Kans. 16 August 1906. Cora was born in Guthrie, Tenn. 4 July 1885 and died 14 November 1971 in Pawnee, Okla. at 86 years of age.[2876]

Benjamin Franklin **Miller** and Mary B. **Richards** had the following children:

2446   i.   Edna K.[11] **Miller**[2877] was born in Chautauqua, Co. in October 1898 and married (__) **Whorton**.

2447   ii.   Clarence E. **Miller**[2878] was born in Cedar Vale 23 May 1900 and died 2 May 1955 at 54 years of age. He married Marie LaFloss **Hibbs** 16 August 1918. Marie was born in Davis Co., Mo. 16 September 1893 and died 8 May 1980 in Lees Summit, Mo. at 86 years of age.[2879]

+ 2448   iii.   Madison Theodore **Miller** was born 29 September 1902.

+ 2449   iv.   Orville Cecil Miller **Mansfield** was born 5 April 1905.

Benjamin Franklin **Miller** and Cora **Gillespie** had the following children:

2450   v.   Otis Leroy **Miller**[2880] was born in 1912.

2451   vi.   Stella M. **Miller**[2881] was born in 1915 and married (__) **Royster**.

1889. Mary Elizabeth[9] **Baker** (Walter[8], Jacob[7], **Kimball**, Jacob[6], Jacob[5], Sarah[4] **Goodhue**, Sarah[3] **Whipple**, Elder John[2], Matthew[1])[2882] was born in North Collins, N.Y. 30 November 1880 and died 25 August 1952 in Lawtons, N.Y. at 71 years of age. She married **Wilbor Alonzo Tanner** 1 January 1900. Wilbor,[2883] son of Edgar Peabody **Tanner** and Betsy

Corinna **Camp**, was born in Evans, N.Y. 20 September 1875 and died 15 January 1938 in North Collins at 62 years of age.

Mary Elizabeth **Baker** and Wilbor Alonzo **Tanner** had the following children:
+ 2452   i. Blanche May[11] **Tanner** was born 16 May 1901.
+2453   ii. Bernice Louise **Tanner** was born 2 December 1902.

1890. Viola Maud[10] **Thompson** (Affalona Galia[9] **Fausett**, Julia Ann[8] **Stevens**, Roswell[7], Hepsibah[6] **Kilham**, Abigail[5] **Kimball**, Sarah[4] **Goodhue**, Sarah[3] **Whipple**, Elder John[2], Matthew[1])[2884] was born in Wellington, Carbon Co., Utah 7 June 1884 and died 13 April 1941 in Alturas, Modoc Co., Calif. at 56 years of age. She married **William Smith** in Vernal, Utah Co., Utah 7 February 1906. William,[2885] son of Abraham Owen **Smith** Sr. and Malong **Draper**, was born in Maroni, Sanpeta Co., Utah 23 October 1879 and died 16 May 1957 in Cedarville, Modoc Co., Calif. at 77 years of age.

Viola Maud **Thompson** and William **Smith** had the following child:
+ 2454   i. Viola Beal[11] **Smith** was born 23 December 1906.

1891. Maiben Stevens[10] **Jones** (Marinda Alice[9] **Stevens**, William[8], Roswell[7], Hepsibah[6] **Kilham**, Abigail[5] **Kimball**, Sarah[4] **Goodhue**, Sarah[3] **Whipple**, Elder John[2], Matthew[1])[2886] was born in Holden, Utah 11 March 1904 and married **Ethel Leda Sayer** 28 February 1925. Ethel was born in Rigby, Idaho 20 November 1904.[2887]

Maiben Stevens **Jones** and Ethel Leda **Sayer** had the following child:
+ 2455   i. Alice LuZella[11] **Jones** was born 3 August 1925.

1892. Elizabeth[10] **Goodhue** (Francis Abbot[9], Samuel[8], Samuel[7], Samuel[6], George[5], Joseph[4], Sarah[3] **Whipple**, Elder John[2], Matthew[1])[2888] was born in Malden, Middlesex Co., Mass. 11 February 1878 and died 26 July 1943 in Boston, Mass. at 65 years of age. She was educated in Brookline public schools and at Abbot Academy. She married **Claude Moore Fuess** 27 June 1911. He was headmaster of Phillips Academy at Andover, Mass. at the time of his wife's death.[2889]

Elizabeth **Goodhue** and Claude Moore **Fuess** had the following child:
2456   i. John Cushing[11] **Fuess**.[2890] John was United States vice consul in Belfast at the time of his mother's death.

1893. John James[10] **McCabe** (Mary[9] **Dickson**, Elizabeth[8] **Upham**, Eleanor[7] **Knowlton**, Daniel[6], Robert[5], Marjory (Margery)[4] **Goodhue**, Sarah[3] **Whipple**, Elder John[2], Matthew[1])[2891] was born in Onslow, N.S. Canada in 1848 and died 26 April 1913 in St. John's Newfoundland at 64 years of age. He married **Matilda Harold** in Glace Bay, N.S. 19 July 1878. Matilda was born in Sydney, N.S. Canada in June 1850 and died 2 January 1942 in Alabama at 91 years of age.[2892]

John James **McCabe** and Matilda **Harold** had the following child:
+ 2457   i. Charlotte Georgina[11] **McCabe** was born 15 June 1881.

1894. George Gove[10] **Stevens** (Nancy Mathilda[9] **Bowers**, Polly[8] **Rand**, Solomon[7], Deborah[6] **Dodge**, Margery[5] **Knowlton**, Marjory (Margery)[4] **Goodhue**, Sarah[3] **Whipple**, Elder John[2], Matthew[1])[2893] was born in Warwick, Mass. 7

December 1853 and died 20 January 1894 in Indianapolis, Ind. at 40 years of age. He married **Julia Maria Stanclift** 17 October 1881. Julia was born in Allegan Co., Mich. 31 December 1849.[2894]

George Gove **Stevens** and Julia Maria **Stanclift** had the following child:
+ 2458   i. Samuel Stanclift[11] **Stevens** was born 17 February 1889.

1895. **Grace Anna**[10] **Goodhue** (Andrew Issachar[9], Benjamin[8], Ebenezer[7], Ebenezer[6], John[5], John[4], Sarah[3] **Whipple**, Elder John[2], Matthew[1])[2895] was born in Burlington, Chittenden Co., Vt. 3 January 1879 and died 8 July 1957 in Northampton, Mass. at 78 years of age. She was buried in Plymouth, Vt. She married **Pres. John Calvin Coolidge** 4 October 1905. Calvin,[2896] son of Col. John Calvin **Coolidge** and Victoria Josephine **Moor**, was born in Plymouth, Vt. 4 July 1872 and died 5 January 1933 in Northampton, Mass. at 60 years of age.

Grace was graduated from the U. of Vermont with a Ph.D in 1902 and was awarded an honorary LL.D. by the University in 1929. Honorary LL.Ds were also given her by Boston University in 1924, Smith College in 1929, and George Washington University in 1939. She taught in the Clark School for the Deaf in Northampton from 1902-15.[2897] Later she was a trustee of the school as well as a trustee of Mercersburg Academy. Her husband, who was noted for his economy of speaking, paid her a tribute when he said that "having taught the deaf to hear, Miss Goodhue might perhaps cause the mute to speak." (See No. 2008)

Pres. John Calvin **Coolidge** and Grace Anna **Goodhue** had the following children:
+ 2459   i. John[11] **Coolidge** was born 7 September 1906.
  2460   ii. Calvin **Coolidge**[2898] was born in Northampton, Mass. 13 April 1908 and died 7 July 1924 in Washington, D.C. at 16 years of age.

ELEVENTH GENERATION

1896. **Harry M.**[11] **Pillsbury** (James[10], Jacob[9], John Hale[8], Rev. Edmund[7], Moses[6], Moses[5], Susanna[4] **Worth**, Susannah[3] **Whipple**, Elder John[2], Matthew[1]) was born in Lowell, Mass. 13 November 1852 and died 9 January 1903 in Milwaukie, Wisc. at 50 years of age. He was sec.-treas. of the Land Log & Lumber Co. and died of Bright's (kidney) disease. Immediate cause of death was cerebral apoplexy. His obituary appears in the *Milwaukie Sentinel* of 10 January 1903. He was buried at the Forest Home Cemetery. He married **Kate Cutter** in Brewer, Penobscot Co., Maine 31 May 1881.

Harry M. **Pillsbury** and Kate **Cutter** had the following children:
  2461   i. Eleanor Benjamin[12] **Pillsbury** was born in Milwaukie, Wisc. and died 19 January 1919. She married Henry Beaumont **Pennell** Jr. They had a daughter and son. Mother and son died two days before her 2-year-old daughter in the 1919 influenza epidemic.
+ 2462   ii. Helen Cutter **Pillsbury** was born 17 September 1883.
+ 2463   iii. Alice Wedgwood **Pillsbury** was born 17 October 1886.
  2464   iv. James Marcellus **Pillsbury** was born 2 December 1887 and died 19 March 1888 at less than one year of age.

1904. **Charles Herbert**[11] **Sherman** (Jane Stetson[10] **Hale**, Zacheus[9], Zacheus[8],

Joseph[7], Abigail W.[6] **Pillsbury**, Moses[5], Susanna[4] **Worth**, Susannah[3] **Whipple**, Elder John[2], Matthew[1])[2899] was born in Whitman, Mass. 14 January 1858 and died 8 March 1933 in Whitman at 75 years of age. He married **Deborah Mande Nicoll** in Whitman 31 May 1885. Deborah was born in Gaburus, Sidney, Cape Breton, Nova Scotia 31 July 1862 and died 28 June 1940 in Whitman at 77 years of age. Charles and Deborah were buried at Colebrook Cemetery.

Charles Herbert **Sherman** and Deborah Mande **Nicoll** had the following children:

2465   i.   Carrie M.[12] **Sherman**[2900] was born 10 March 1886 and died 13 July 1929 in N. Troy, N.Y. at 43 years of age. She was buried at Colebrook Cemetery. She married twice. (1) Harry **Phillips** 27 October 1906. (2) Charles **Whitman** 25 June 1927.

+2466   ii.   Herbert Blackmer **Sherman** was born 10 September 1889.

1909. **Lizzie Batchelder**[11] **Dodge** (Frank Brickett[10], Deborah Towne[9] **Brickett**, Bernard[8], Bernard[7], Susanna[6] **Pillsbury**, Moses[5], Susanna[4] **Worth**, Susannah[3] **Whipple**, Elder John[2], Matthew[1]) was born in Woburn, Mass. 7 December 1865 and died there 22 July 1916 at 50 years of age. She married **Harrison Gray Blake** in Woburn 19 February 1890. Harrison, son of Ebenezer Norton **Blake** and Harriet **Cummings**, was born in Woburn 26 January 1864 and died there 26 January 1922 at 58 years of age.

Lizzie Batchelder **Dodge** and Harrison Gray **Blake** had the following child:

+ 2467   i.   Clarence Dodge[12] **Blake** was born 17 January 1904.

1911. **Col. Howard Russell**[11] **Smalley** (Viola Irene[10] **Hoyt**, Dr. Hiram Pillsbury[9], Judith[8] **Pillsbury**, Caleb[7], Caleb[6], Caleb[5], Susanna[4] **Worth**, Susannah[3] **Whipple**, Elder John[2], Matthew[1])[2901] was born in Lyndonville, Vt. 21 August 1877 and died 2 January 1967 in San Francisco, Calif. at 89 years of age. He married **Frances Elizabeth Norrington** in Bay City, Bay Co., Mich. 20 November 1909. Frances,[2902] daughter of Henry Huddie **Norrington** and Frances Elizabeth **White**, was born in Bay City 25 February 1882 and died 3 December 1961 in Portsmouth, Va. at 79 years of age. Howard, who served in the cavalry, retired from the army as a colonel.

Col. Howard Russell **Smalley** and Frances Elizabeth **Norrington** had the following child:

+ 2468   i.   Col. Howard Norrington[12] **Smalley** was born 18 September 1912.

1916. **Nellie May**[11] **Blanchard** (George Adelbert[10], Aaron[9], Lois[8] **Burt**, Abiah[7] **Mooar**, Abiah[6] **Hill**, Judith[5] **Bucknam**, Judith (Jude)[4] **Worth**, Susannah[3] **Whipple**, Elder John[2], Matthew[1])[2903] was born in Havana, Ill. 22 February 1866 and died 24 February 1943 in Havana at 77 years of age. She married **Dr. Lawford Gard Pullen** in Havana 21 December 1893. Lawford,[2904] son of John Tyson **Pullen** and Mary Druce **Gard**, was born in Stony Creek, Ontario, Canada 27 November 1861 died 21 November 1944 in Havana at 82 years of age. Nellie and Lawford were buried in Havana's Laurel Hill Mausoleum. He was a dentist.

Nellie May **Blanchard** and Dr. Lawford Gard **Pullen** had the following children:

+ 2469   i.   Helena[12] **Pullen** was born 19 May 1895.

2470   ii.   Deb Adelbert Pullen[2905] was born in Havana 31 March 1903 and died

8 August 1962 in Dwight, Ill. at 59 years of age. He died in a Veterans Hospital and was buried in the Laurel Hill Mausoleum. He married Edythe **Stevenson** in Ohio 6 January 1945. They were divorced after 1946. No children were born to this union.[2906]

1920. **William Risk**[11] **Esson** (Elsie Boak[10] **Williams**, William Brown[9], Hannah Stone[8] **Brown**, Samuel[7], William[6], Martha[5] **Whipple**, Maj. John[4], Capt. John[3], Elder John[2], Matthew[1])[2907] was born in Chicago, Ill. 9 December 1912 and died 3 October 1982 in Portland, Maine at 69 years of age. He married **Zelda Norine McIntyre** in West Newton, Mass. 11 April 1942. Zelda,[2908] daughter of Frederick **McIntyre** and Frances **Booth**, was born in Chicago, Ill. 1 May 1912 and died 15 July 1994 in Wolfeboro, N.H. at 82 years of age.

William Risk **Esson** and Zelda Norine **McIntyre** had the following children born in Newton, Mass:

    2471   i.   Barbara Ann[12] **Esson**[2909] was born 20 March 1943.
\+ 2472   ii. Donald Boak **Esson** was born 2 July 1946.
    2473   iii. Richard **Esson**[2910] was born 2 July 1947.

1923. **Orrin Belmont**[11] **Stevens** (George Nichols[10], Susan Poor[9] **Pearson**, Nathaniel[8], Sarah[7] **Gerrish**, Katherine[6] **Brown**, Martha[5] **Whipple**, Maj. John[4], Capt. John[3], Elder John[2], Matthew[1])[2911] was born in West Newbury, Mass. 29 December 1873 and died 20 September 1927 in Newburyport, Essex Co., Mass. at 53 years of age. He married **Ella Florence Bent** in Boston, Mass. 3 October 1907. Ella,[2912] daughter of Joel Woodbury **Bent** and Elizabeth **Huston**, was born in Brighton, Mass. 13 February 1879 and died 30 March 1965 in Salisbury, Essex Co., Mass. at 86 years of age. Orrin and Ella are buried at Brighton's Evergreen Cemetery.

Orrin Belmont **Stevens** and Ella Florence **Bent** had the following child:

\+ 2474   i.   Donald Belmont[12] **Stevens** was born 4 November 1911.

1924. **Lottie Nichols**[11] **Stevens** (George Nichols[10], Susan Poor[9] **Pearson**, Nathaniel[8], Sarah[7] **Gerrish**, Katherine[6] **Brown**, Martha[5] **Whipple**, Maj. John[4], Capt. John[3], Elder John[2], Matthew[1])[2913] was born in West Newbury, Mass. 5 November 1880. She married twice. (1) **Arthur Tibbetts**. (2) **Walter Brown**.

Lottie Nichols **Stevens** and Walter **Brown** had the following child:

\+ 2475   i.   Earle Bryant[12] **Brown**.

1926. **Agnes Coughenour**[11] **Whipple** (William Orland[10], William Ward[9], John[8], John[7], Capt. John[6], Capt. John[5], Maj. Matthew[4], Capt. John[3], Elder John[2], Matthew[1])[2914] was born in Clayton, Ill. 14 December 1871 and died 10 November 1948 at 76 years of age. She married **Emery D. Moody** in 1903. Emery was born 9 April 1871 and died in June 1959 at 88 years of age.[2915]

Agnes Coughenour **Whipple** and Emery D. **Moody** had the following children:

    2476   i.   Zelma Lucile[12] **Moody**[2916] was born 24 April 1904 and died after 1980 in Amity, Mo. She married Carl **Lawson** in Fairbury, Nebr. 31 August 1935.
\+ 2477   ii. Mildred Irene **Moody** was born 7 February 1906.

1927. William Henry[11] Whipple (William Orland[10], William Ward[9], John[8], John[7], Capt. John[6], Capt. John[5], Maj. Matthew[4], Capt. John[3], Elder John[2], Matthew[1])[2917] was born in Mound Station, Ill. 8 September 1874 and died 16 May 1938 in Lebanon, Mo. at 63 years of age. He married **Rosetta Moye** in Lenora, Kans. 28 January 1903. She died there 14 February 1975. [2918]

William Henry **Whipple** and Rosetta **Moye** had the following children:

+ 2478   i.   Esther Louise[12] **Whipple** was born 17 August 1904.
    2479   ii.   Eunice Marie **Whipple**[2919] was born in Lenora 6 July 1906 and died 20 May 1979 at 72 years of age. She married Thomas **Summers** in Albuquerque, N. Mex. in August 1938. Thomas was born in 1906 and and died in1980 at 74 years of age..[2920]
+ 2480   iii.   Ruth Isabel **Whipple** was born 6 May 1908.
    2481   iv.   Walter William **Whipple**[2921] was born in Lenora 2 December 1909 and died in 1985 at 75 years of age. He married twice. (1) Roxie (__) in Lenora . (2) Lillian (__).
+ 2482   v.   Frances Irene **Whipple** was born 1 March 1911.
+ 2483   vi.   Marjorie Eula **Whipple** was born 29 July 1912.
+ 2484   vii.   Harold Paul **Whipple** was born 24 December 1914.
+ 2485   viii.   Melvin Eugene **Whipple** was born 9 January 1917.
+ 2486   ix.   Earl Lawrence **Whipple** was born 22 January 1919.
+ 2487   x.   Evelyn Eugenia **Whipple** was born 3 October 1920.
+ 2488   xi.   Carl Henry **Whipple** was born 3 May 1922.
+ 2489   xii.   Rosetta **Whipple** was born 11 June 1925.
+ 2490   xiii.   Grace Katherine **Whipple** was born 5 July 1927.
    2491   xiv.   Betty Jean **Whipple**[2922] was born in Lebanon, Mo. in June 1931 and died the month of birth.

1928. John Godfrey[11] Whipple (William Orland[10], William Ward[9], John[8], John[7], Capt. John[6], Capt. John[5], Maj. Matthew[4], Capt. John[3], Elder John[2], Matthew[1])[2923] was born in Mound Station, Ill. 5 March 1882 and died 2 August 1948 in Greeley, Colo. at 66 years of age. He married **Ola Bull** in Norton, Kans. 29 May 1906. Ola was born in Lenora, Kans. 26 May 1886 and died 19 November 1974 in Hemet, Calif. at 88 years of age.[2924]

John Godfrey **Whipple** and Ola **Bull** had the following children:

+ 2492   i.   Jerald Howard[12] **Whipple** was born 12 March 1909.
+ 2493   ii.   Paul Warren **Whipple** was born 21 January 1915.
    2494   iii.   Dorothy Lois **Whipple**[2925] was born in Greeley, Colo. 25 December 1924 and was living there in 1997.
+ 2495   iv.   Martha Belle **Whipple** was born 1 May 1928.

1929. Clyde Ward[11] Whipple (William Orland[10], William Ward[9], John[8], John[7], Capt. John[6], Capt. John[5], Maj. Matthew[4], Capt. John[3], Elder John[2], Matthew[1])[2926] was born in Decatur Co., Kans. 4 February 1886 and died 17 November 1949 in Parkville, Mo. at 63 years of age. He married **Myrtle Launa Smith** in Enterprise, Kans. 24 June 1914. Myrtle,[2927] daughter of Henry **Smith** and Clara Eliza **Hofmeister**, was born in Hoisington, Kans. 1 February 1887 and died 14 April 1984 in Parkville at 97 years of age.

Clyde was born in a sod house near New Almelo and during his formative years he, his twin brother Carl, and older brother Will, did farm work for their father. Clyde worked on the family farm for the first 20 years of his life and among his jobs was breaking wild horses which his father sold to the army. He attended school in Kansas, graduating from the eighth grade at Aurora District #96, from Norton high school in 1909, and attended Kansas State Agricultural College. He taught school for one year at School District #30 in Norton County before attending Kansas Commercial College in Kansas City, Kans. He was an accountant at the C.B. Hoffman Milling Co. in Enterprise, Kans. in 1911 where he met and married Martha.

Clyde Ward **Whipple** and Myrtle Launa **Smith** had the following children:
+ 2496   i. Ward Deal[12] **Whipple** was born 10 May 1915.
+ 2497   ii. Claribel **Whipple** was born 19 November 1916.
+ 2498   iii. Grant Dodge **Whipple** was born 24 January 1919.
+ 2499   iv. Launa May **Whipple** was born 23 May 1921.
+ 2500   v. Lyle Marion **Whipple** was born 23 May 1921.
+ 2501   vi. Clyde David **Whipple** was born 3 October 1927.

1930. **Carl Black[11] Whipple** (William Orland[10], William Ward[9], John[8], John[7], Capt. John[6], Capt. John[5], Maj. Matthew[4], Capt. John[3], Elder John[2], Matthew[1])[2928] was born in Decatur Co., Kans. 4 February 1886 and died 30 April 1922 in Stratton, Nebr. at 36 years of age. He married **Eva Knapp** in Loveland, Colo. 21 March 1910.

Carl Black **Whipple** and Eva **Knapp** had the following child:
2502   i. Mildred Denise[12] **Whipple**[2929].

1931. **Eunice[11] Schenck** (Eunice Porter[10] **Wood**, Phebe Smith[9] **Whipple**, Stephen[8], Martha[7], Dea. Nathaniel[6], Capt. John[5], Maj. Matthew[4], Capt. John[3], Elder John[2], Matthew[1])[2930] was born in Cleveland, Ohio 22 February 1879 and died 15 August 1972 in Ft. Lauderdale, Fla. at 93 years of age. She married **Henry Richard Ahrens**. Henry,[2931] son of Richard William **Ahrens** and Emma **Wetzel**, was born in Cleveland, Ohio 14 December 1879 and died 3 March 1963 in Ft. Lauderdale at 83 years of age.

Eunice **Schenck** and Henry Richard **Ahrens** had the following child:
+ 2503   i. Henry Richard[12] **Ahrens** Jr. was born 11 June 1907.

1932. **Ferne Catherine[11] Patterson** (Proctor[10], Phebe Smith[9] **Whipple**, Stephen[8], Martha[7], Dea. Nathaniel[6], Capt. John[5], Maj. Matthew[4], Capt. John[3], Elder John[2], Matthew[1])[2932] was born in Chicago, Ill. 22 September 1889 and died 20 June 1968 in Cleveland, Ohio at 78 years of age. She married **John Beverly Jones** in Cleveland 30 September 1913. John was born in Montreal, Canada 5 January 1880 and and died 6 October 1955 in Cleveland at 75 years of age.[2933]

Ferne Catherine **Patterson** and John Beverly **Jones** had the following children:
+ 2504   i. Proctor Patterson[12] **Jones** was born 25 May 1916.
2505   ii. Ferne Beverly **Jones**[2934] was born in Lakewood, Ohio 19 June 1917.

1937. **Jessamine Gertrude[11] Hatch** (Alonzo Herbert[10], Paschal[9], Anna[8] **Gould**, Anna[7] **Lane**, Timothy[6], Job[5], Susanna[4] **Whipple**, Capt. John[3], Elder John[2], Matthew[1])[2935] was born in Windsor, Ill. 2 November 1879 and died 4 January 1972 in Helena, Mont. at 92 years of age. She married **Harry Arthur Nelson** in Jefferson City, Mo. 24 May 1901. Harry was born in Monmouth, Ill. 15 December 1875 and

and died 6 August 1909 in Denver, Colo. at 33 years of age.[2936]

Jessamine Gertrude **Hatch** and Harry Arthur **Nelson** had the following child:
+ 2506   i.   Robert Hatch[12] **Nelson** was born 20 November 1902.

1939. Wyman Parkhurst[11] **Fiske** (Frederick Augustus Parker[10], Elisabeth Ann[9] **Parkhurst**, Rev. John[8], Betsey[7] **Hutchinson**, Rebecca[6] **Lane**, James[5], Susanna[4] **Whipple**, Capt. John[3], Elder John[2], Matthew[1])[2937] was born in Somerville, Mass. 11 January 1900 and died 13 July 1972 in New York, N.Y. at 72 years of age. He married **Ruth Nichols** in Dorchester, Mass. 16 July 1927. Ruth was born in Portland, Maine 15 July 1900.[2938]

Wyman Parkhurst **Fiske** and Ruth **Nichols** had the following child:
+ 2507   i.   John Wyman[12] **Fiske** was born 3 July 1928.

1943. Roger Whipple[11] **Hanners** (Cora Adalaide[10] **Whipple**, Alonzo Lyman[9], John[9], John[8], John[7], Capt. John[6], Capt. John[5], Maj. Matthew[4], Capt. John[3], Elder John[2], Matthew[1])[2939] was born in Beverly, Essex Co., Mass. 17 July 1899 and died there 5 April 1984 at 84 years of age. He married twice. (1) **Gladys Wilson Frost** in Marblehead, Essex Co., Mass. 6 September 1926. Gladys,[2940] daughter of James P. **Frost** and Edith A.C. **Waring**, was born in Marblehead 6 September 1896 and died there 17 October 1939 at 43 years of age.[2941] (2) **Florence E. Smith** 6 September 1941. Florence was born in Lynn, Essex Co., Mass. 15 January 1906.[2942]

Roger Whipple **Hanners** and Gladys Wilson **Frost** had the following child:
+ 2508   i.   Asenath Waring[12] **Hanners** was born 13 October 1939.

1944. Ralph Loring[11] **Hanners** (Cora Adalaide[10] **Whipple**, Alonzo Lyman[9], John[9], John[8], John[7], Capt. John[6], Capt. John[5], Maj. Matthew[4], Capt. John[3], Elder John[2], Matthew[1])[2943] was born in Beverly, Essex Co., Mass. 9 March 1901 and died 12 November 1980 in St. Petersburg, Fla. at 79 years of age. He married **Dorothy May Howard** in Beverly 24 September 1927. Dorothy,[2944] daughter of John **Howard** and Margaret **Bushey**, was born in Beverly 11 August 1904 and died 2 October 1999 in Lakewood, Colo. at 95 years of age. She is buried in Beverly.

Ralph Loring **Hanners** and Dorothy May **Howard** had the following children:
+ 2509   i.   Priscilla Ann[12] **Hanners** was born 22 October 1929.
+ 2510   ii. Howard Whipple **Hanners** was born 8 June 1931.

1945. Dwight Eldridge[11] **Hanners** (Cora Adalaide[10] **Whipple**, Alonzo Lyman[9], John[9], John[8], John[7], Capt. John[6], Capt. John[5], Maj. Matthew[4], Capt. John[3], Elder John[2], Matthew[1])[2945] was born in Beverly, Essex Co., Mass. 24 October 1905 and died 11 January 1976 in Santa Fe, N. Mex. at 70 years of age. He married **Eleanor Johannes** in New York, N.Y. 14 July 1937. Eleanor was born in Baltimore, Md. 7 October 1910 and died 25 May 1996 in Austin, Texas at 85 years of age.[2946]

Dwight Eldridge **Hanners** and Eleanor **Johannes** had the following children:
+ 2511   i.   William Eldredge[12] **Hanners** was born 20 August 1940.
  2512   ii.   Sally Mitchell **Hanners**[2947] was born in Colon, Panama 28 March 1943 and married James Leon **Phillips** in Plainville, Texas 16 June 1962. James was born in Shamrock, Texas 17 November 1945.[2948]
+ 2513   iii. Douglas Guy **Hanners** was born 17 November 1945.

1947. Cyrus Hale Stone[11] Powers (John[10], Cyrus Hale Stone[9], Lavinia[8] **Stone**, Capt. Amos[7], Amos[6], Simon[5], Deacon Simon[4], Mary[3] **Whipple**, Elder John[2], Matthew[1])[2949] was born in Tiskilwa, Bureau Co., Ill. 5 March 1872 and died 18 August 1950 in Creston, Union Co., Iowa at 78 years of age. He married **Evva Julio Saylor** in Creston 27 December 1899. Evva,[2950] daughter of Benjamin **Saylor** and Clarissa **Hollock**, was born in Creston 22 March 1876 and died there. Cyrus moved to Creston in 1892 and became a successful farmer and stockman. He and Evva are buried side-by-side at Creston's Prairie Lawn Cemetery.

Cyrus Hale Stone **Powers** and Evva Julio **Saylor** had the following children:

- \+ 2514 i. Edwin Cyrus[12] **Powers** was born 16 October 1900.
- \+ 2515 ii. Bert E. **Powers** was born 26 July 1902.
- \+ 2516 iii. Aretta Viola **Powers** was born 17 April 1904.
- \+ 2517 iv. Mabel S. **Powers** was born 2 July 1906.
- \+ 2518 v. Wesley Raymond **Powers** was born 28 April 1908.

1949. John Ellsworth[11] Powers (John[10], Cyrus Hale Stone[9], Lavinia[8] **Stone**, Capt. Amos[7], Amos[6], Simon[5], Deacon Simon[4], Mary[3] **Whipple**, Elder John[2], Matthew[1])[2951] was born in Bureau Co., Ill. 19 November 1873 and died 23 January 1944 at 70 years of age. He married **Edith H. Fisher** in Bureau Co. 24 February 1898. She was born in Buda, Bureau Co., Ill.[2952] John is buried in Section 6, Lot N 1/2 of 26 in Mount Bloom Cemetery, Bureau Co.

John Ellsworth **Powers** and Edith H. **Fisher** had the following child:

- 2519 i. Hazel B.[12] **Powers**[2953] was born in Illinois in January 1899.

1953. Olive Evalena[11] Powers (John[10], Cyrus Hale Stone[9], Lavinia[8] **Stone**, Capt. Amos[7], Amos[6], Simon[5], Deacon Simon[4], Mary[3] **Whipple**, Elder John[2], Matthew[1])[2954] was born in Tiskilwa, Bureau Co., Ill. 19 August 1880 and died 9 July 1971 in Afton, Union Co., Iowa at 90 years of age. She married **Nelson P. Pratt** in Tiskilwa 26 December 1900. Nelson,[2955] son of William **Pratt** and Rosalia **Goodale**, was born in Bradford, Ill. 30 January 1874 and died 8 February 1956 in Cromwell, Iowa at 82 years of age. He was a farmer and worked as a liaison between the the U.S. Post Office and the Chicago, Burlington, and Quincy Railroad. Both Olive and Nelson are buried in Cromwell's Maple Hill Cemetery.

Olive Evalena **Powers** and Nelson P. **Pratt** had the following children:

- \+ 2520 i. Orville Powers[12] **Pratt** was born 5 June 1905.
- 2521 ii. Ethel Maxine **Pratt**[2956] was born in Bureau Co., Ill. 21 September 1908 and died 15 March 1969 in Union Co., Iowa at 60 years of age. She married Alexander **Craig** abt 1929. They were divorced in Union Co. 27 January 1931. She is buried in Maple Hill Cemetery, Cromwell, Iowa.
- 2522 iii. Jerome Clarence **Pratt**[2957] was born in Spaulding, Iowa 1 July 1911 and died 31 December 1977 in Omaha, Nebr. at 66 years of age. He married twice. (1) Aurella **Lawn**. (2) Wanda **Moore-Morr** in Newton, Jasper Co., Iowa 2 November 1968. He was buried in Maple Hill Cemetery, Cromwell, Iowa.

1955. Dr. Wilbur Louis[11] Powers (John[10], Cyrus Hale Stone[9], Lavinia[8] **Stone**, Capt. Amos[7], Amos[6], Simon[5], Deacon Simon[4], Mary[3] **Whipple**, Elder John[2], Matthew[1])[2958] was born in Bureau Co., Ill. 5 March 1887 and married **Mabel**

Hayes,[2959] daughter of James **Hayes** and Mary **Blessing**. Wilbur was a professor of agriculture at both Washington State University (Pullman, Wash.) and Oregon State University (Corvallis, Oreg.).

Dr. Wilbur Louis **Powers** and Mabel **Hayes** had the following child:

+ 2523   i.   Dr. Myron J.[12] **Powers** was born 29 April 1911.

1961. Leroy Cyrus[11] **Powers** (Cyrus Cameron[10], Cyrus Hale Stone[9], Lavinia[8] **Stone**, Capt. Amos[7], Amos[6], Simon[5], Deacon Simon[4], Mary[3] **Whipple**, Elder John[2], Matthew[1])[2960] was born in Union Co., Iowa 1 April 1887 and died in 1940 in Creston, Union Co., Iowa at 53 years of age. He married **Gladys Anna Coakley** in Creston 5 June 1916.

Leroy Cyrus **Powers** and Gladys Anna **Coakley** had the following children:

+ 2524   i.   William Cameron[12] **Powers** was born in 1919.
+ 2525   ii. Catherine Ann **Powers** was born in 1926.

1963. Clara[11] **Powers** (Cyrus Cameron[10], Cyrus Hale Stone[9], Lavinia[8] **Stone**, Capt. Amos[7], Amos[6], Simon[5], Deacon Simon[4], Mary[3] **Whipple**, Elder John[2], Matthew[1])[2961] was born in Union Co., Iowa 13 November 1894 and died abt 1944 in Des Moines, Iowa. She married **Zee Munson**.

Clara **Powers** and Zee **Munson** had the following children born in Creston, Union Co., Iowa:

2526   i.   Robert Powers[12] **Munson**[2962] died in California.
2527   ii. John Cameron **Munson**[2963] died in California.
2528   iii. Janet **Munson**[2964] died in California.

1975. Tyler[11] **Eaton**, (James Ellery[10], Alma Ellery[9] **Tyler**, Alma Ellery[8] **Holden**, Phineas[7], Capt. Asa[6], Abigail[5] **Stone**, Deacon Simon[4], Mary[3] **Whipple**, Elder John[2], Matthew[1])[2965] birth date unknown, married **Harriet (__)**.

Tyler **Eaton**, and Harriet (__) had the following child:

2529   i.   James Ellery[12] **Eaton**,[2966].

1977. Kent Tyler[11] **Royal**, (Alma Ellery[10] **Eaton**,, Alma Ellery[9] **Tyler**, Alma Ellery[8] **Holden**, Phineas[7], Capt. Asa[6], Abigail[5] **Stone**, Deacon Simon[4], Mary[3] **Whipple**, Elder John[2], Matthew[1])[2967] was born in Harvard, Middlesex Co., Mass. 25 October 1891 and married **Dr. Lila Jane Benjamin** in 1920.

Kent Tyler **Royal**, and Dr. Lila Jane **Benjamin**, had the following children:

2530   i.   Betty Ann[12] **Royal**[2968] was born in 1921.
2531   ii. Janet **Royal**[2969] was born in 1928.

1978. Ellery Eaton[11] **Royal** (Alma Ellery[10] **Eaton**,, Alma Ellery[9] **Tyler**, Alma Ellery[8] **Holden**, Phineas[7], Capt. Asa[6], Abigail[5] **Stone**, Deacon Simon[4], Mary[3] **Whipple**, Elder John[2], Matthew[1])[2970] was born in Harvard, Middlesex Co., Mass. 14 July 1894 and married twice. (1) **Harriett Burdett Thayer** 1 June 1918. Harriett was born in 1894 and died in 1951 at 57 years of age.[2971] (2) **Aini Marie Hendricks** after 1934. Aini was born in 1908.[2972]

Ellery Eaton **Royal** and Harriett Burdett **Thayer** had the following children:

+ 2532   i.   Nancy Tyler[12] **Royal** was born 8 August 1921.

+ 2533   ii. Virginia **Royal** was born 18 May 1923.

+ 2534   iii. Ellery Thayer **Royal** was born 20 November 1934.

1980. Samuel Newton[11] **Bacon** (Allen Harlow[10], Samuel Newton[9], Alma Ellery[8] **Holden**, Phineas[7], Capt. Asa[6], Abigail[5] **Stone**, Deacon Simon[4], Mary[3] **Whipple**, Elder John[2], Matthew[1])[2973] was born in Loudonville, N.Y. 18 February 1895 and married twice. (1) **Caroline Fitch Lansing** in Albany, N.Y. 9 October 1920. Caroline,[2974] daughter of Charles Edgar **Lansing** and Harriette Emeline **Fitch**, was born in Albany 24 March 1895 and died 14 April 1965 in San Francisco., Calif. at 70 years of age. (2) **Mrs. Georgie (Howell) Mang** in Albany 30 October 1965. Georgie was born 11 December 1897 and died 6 November 1982 in Albany at 84 years of age. She married (1) **Harry Mang** before 1965 and is buried with him.[2975]

Samuel Newton **Bacon** and Caroline Fitch **Lansing** had the following children:

+ 2535   i. Samuel Newton[12] **Bacon, Jr.** was born 5 June 1922.

+ 2536   ii. Charles Lansing **Bacon** was born 22 August 1923.

+ 2537   iii. Richard Mather **Bacon** was born 14 January 1928.

1982. Elizabeth Harlow[11] **Bacon** (Allen Harlow[10], Samuel Newton[9], Alma Ellery[8] **Holden**, Phineas[7], Capt. Asa[6], Abigail[5] **Stone**, Deacon Simon[4], Mary[3] **Whipple**, Elder John[2], Matthew[1])[2976] was born in Loudonville, N.Y. 2 April 1898 and died 24 September 1986 in Santa Cruz, Santa Cruz Co., Calif. at 88 years of age. She married **Donald Newman Swain** in Loudonville 23 August 1924. Donald,[2977] son of Charles Elwood **Swain** and Fannie Maria **Stone**, was born in Roxbury, Mass. 18 May 1894 and died 26 July 1962 at 68 years of age.

Elizabeth Harlow **Bacon** and Donald Newman **Swain** had the following children:

2538   i. Harlow Newman[12] **Swain**[2978] was born 23 August 1926.

+ 2539   ii. Lorna Mather **Swain** was born 17 December 1927.

+ 2540   iii. Robert David **Swain** was born 8 October 1931.

1985. Allen Harlow[11] **Bacon, Jr.** (Allen Harlow[10] **Bacon**, Samuel Newton[9], Alma Ellery[8] **Holden**, Phineas[7], Capt. Asa[6], Abigail[5] **Stone**, Deacon Simon[4], Mary[3] **Whipple**, Elder John[2], Matthew[1])[2979] was born in Loudonville, N.Y. 8 November 1902. He married **Dorothy Gross Jagel** in Albany, N.Y. 6 April 1929. Dorothy,[2980] daughter of Arthur Garfield **Jagel** and Elsie **Gross**, was born in Waterbury, Conn. 4 May 1904.

Allen Harlow **Bacon**, Jr. and Dorothy Gross **Jagel** had the following children:

+ 2541   i. Catharine Mather[12] **Bacon**, was born 18 January 1930.

+ 2542   ii. Marian Jagel **Bacon**, was born 20 August 1937.

1987. Mary Olive[11] **Carr** (William Dustin[10], Lyman[9], Susanna[8] **Dunton**, Mary[7] **Jewell**, Mary[6] **Whitney**, Mary[5] **Stone**, Deacon Simon[4], Mary[3] **Whipple**, Elder John[2], Matthew[1])[2981] was born in Lancaster, Worcester Co., Mass. 15 December 1854 and died there 19 January 1915 at 60 years of age. She married **James Edward Wise**. James was born in Lancaster 10 April 1854 and died there 20 January 1909 at 54 years of age.[2982]

Mary Olive **Carr** and James Edward **Wise** had the following child:

+ 2543   i. William Oliver[12] **Wise** was born 22 March 1884.

1990. Nahum Danforth[11] **Goddard** (Nahum Parks[10], Alvira C.[9], David[8], Asa[7], Nathan[6], Edward[5], Susanna[4] **Stone**, Mary[3] **Whipple**, Elder John[2], Matthew[1])[2983] was born in 1859 and married **Fannie Louise Hoyt**.

Nahum Danforth **Goddard** and Fannie Louise **Hoyt** had the following children:

2544   i. Robert Hutchings[12] **Goddard**[2984] was born in Maple Hill, Worcester Co., Mass. 5 October 1882 and died 14 August 1945 of cancer in Baltimore, Md. at 62 years of age. He is buried in Hope Cemetery, Worcester, Mass. He married Esther **Kisk** in June 1924.

During his 63 years of life, Robert, great (8) grandson of Elder John and Susannah Whipple and a pioneer in rocket research, was inspired by Sir Isaac Newton's Third Law which states that "for every action there is always an equal and opposite reaction." He believed that this law operated universally, whether in or out of a vacuum or atmospheric space. This belief led him to achieve a number of firsts in his chosen field of rocketry. He was first:

1. To prove that a rocket needs no air to push against and will work in a vacuum.
2. To include a barometer and camera in a rocket flight.
3. To use vanes in the rocket motor blast for guidance.
4. To develop gyro control apparatus for rocket flight.
5. To receive a U.S. patent with an idea for a multi-stage rocket and to conceive the multi-stage rocket.
6. To successfully launch a rocket with a motor pivoted on gimbals under the influence of a gyro mechanism.
7. To invent the prototype of the Bazooka.
8. To fire a liquid fuel rocket that traveled faster than the speed of sound.
9. To develop the turbo-pumps for a liquid propellant rocket.

This talented and extremely private man's research efforts included work on solar energy, vacuum tubes, railroad transportation, and radio tube oscillators. A liquid fuel rocket constructed on the principles developed by Goddard helped man land on the moon in 1969. He was director of research of the Bureau of Aeronautics for the U.S. navy during World War II and for the last two years of his life was a consultant engineer for the Curtiss-Wright corporation. He was also responsible for the procurement, development, and verification and testing of the geostationary operational environmental satellite.

By age 5, Robert, the only surviving child of his parents – his younger brother Richard was born and died in 1894 – was reading books and magazines on science. He became enamored by the lives of scientists and their discoveries and inventions and was motivated to study physics in later life. He was graduated from South high school at Worcester, Mass. in 1904 and from Worcester's Polytechnic Institute in 1908 where his scientific and investigative mind began to analyze the possibilities of rocket flight. He was noticed when he fired a powder rocket in the basement of the Institute and was encouraged by school officials to do further experiments and analysis of rockets.

He began graduate studies at Worcester's Clark University in the fall of 1908 where his major was physics and his minor mathematics while also conducting static tests with small solid fuel rockets. The title of his master's thesis was "Theory of Diffraction" and he was awarded his degree in June 1910. He earned his doctorate in 1911 after completing a thesis on "Current Rectification at Contacts of Dissimilar Solids." He taught at Princeton in 1912 and began serious work on rocket development by exploring mathematically the practicability of using rocket escape velocity for space flight. He developed the detailed mathematical theory of rocket propulsion in 1912 and was granted the first of 214 rocket patents in 1914.

He then set out to prove experimentally that a rocket could operate in space by building a large closed loop evacuated test chamber and fired more than 50 small rockets in it. The rockets readily lifted themselves in this vacuum proving his theories. In 1916 the Smithsonian Institution gave him a grant for continued work on solid propellant rockets and to begin the development of liquid propellants. He developed and demonstrated the basic idea of a Bazooka-type weapon to the U.S. army during WW I.

He joined the faculty at Clark University in 1914 as an instructor in physics and eventually became head of the department and director of its physical laboratories. By 1925 he had successfully fired a rocket motor which lifted itself in its test frame. He launched the world's first liquid-fueled rocket in Auburn, Mass. 16 March 1926 and on 17 July 1929 he launched a liquid-filled rocket with a payload. He took a leave of absence from Clark in 1929 and moved to Roswell, N. M. where, with a $100,000 grant from financier Harry Guggenheim, he established a rocket lab and for the next 12 years constructed and flight tested many rockets and solved many complicated technical problems. His work for the U.S. navy during WW II was researching rocket motors for jet assisted take off for aircraft.

His talent in creative sciences and practical engineering brought him wide acclaim and many awards and honors:

1.   The 80th congress authorized a gold medal in his honor on 16 Sept. 1959.
2.   The Langley Medal in 1960 and the Daniel Guggenheim Medal in 1964.
3   The National Space Hall of Fame and the Aviation Hall of Fame Awards in 1966.
4.   A major space science laboratory, NASA's Goddard space flight center in Greenbelt, Md. was established in his honor 1 May 1959.

Quotations attributed to Goddard include:

"It is difficult to say what is impossible, for the dream of yesterday is the hope of today and the reality of tomorrow." June 1904 at his high school reunion. "The years forever fashion new dreams when old ones go. God pity a one-dream man." "How many more years I shall be able to work on the problem I do not know; I hope as long as I live. There can be no thoughts of finishing for 'aiming at the stars' both literally and figuratively is a problem to occupy generations, so that no matter how much progress one makes, there is always the thrill of just beginning." In a 1932 letter to H. G. Wells. "I feel we are going to enter a new era, it is just a matter of imagination how far we can go with rockets. I think it is fair to say 'you haven't seen anything yet.'" On his last day of life: "Every vision is a joke until the first man accomplished it."

A recluse, Goddard was unwilling to share his work with other pioneers and worked in isolation without the engineering resources of a major institution. When he finished each new round of research he'd file it under a deliberately misleading title — "Formulae for Silvering Mirrors," for example — lest it fall into the wrong hands. The realization of his dream fell to others with military and other national support and though he did not live to see the age of space flight, he was the one to take the first steps to make space travel possible.

His wife Esther was his photographer, lab assistant, secretary, and confidante. Readers interested in further information on Robert Goddard should check the Web site at http://www.nasm.edu/galleries/gal100/goddard.htm for descriptions of exhibits of Goddard's rockets at the National Air and Space Museum (part of the Smithsonian Institution) in Washington, D. C.

   2545   ii. Richard **Goddard** was born and died in Maple Hill, Worcester Co., Mass. in 1884 at less than one year of age.

1991. Nellie Frances[11] **King** (Edwin Henry[10], John[9], Lois[8] **Jackson**, Lois[7]

Woodward,, Mary[6] **Stone**, Samuel[5], Ebenezer[4], Mary[3] **Whipple**, Elder John[2], Matthew[1])[2985] was born in Albany, N.Y. 29 May 1859 and died there 9 July 1950 at 91 years of age. She married **Charles Augustus Croissant** in Albany 13 June 1882. Charles,[2986] son of Johann Martin **Croissant** III and Anna Phillippina **Gunther**, was born in Albany 12 January 1859 and died there 19 March 1950 at 91 years of age.

Nellie Frances **King** and Charles Augustus **Croissant** had the following children born in Albany:

2546	i.	Dr. Charles Augustus[12] **Croissant**[2987] was born 8 April 1883 and died 20 February 1967 in Worcester, Worcester Co., Mass. at 83 years of age. He married Carrie Louise **Bender** in Yonkers, N.Y. 18 July 1908.
2547	ii.	Martha Elizabeth **Croissant**[2988] was born 22 October 1885 and died 5 March 1974 in Port Charlotte, Fla. at 88 years of age. She married George Conrad **Hammer** in Albany 24 December 1912.
+ 2548	iii.	Martin **Croissant** was born 16 November 1887.
2549	iv.	Mary Ada **Croissant**[2989] was born 13 September 1889 and died 28 June 1930 in Jersey City, N.J. at 40 years of age.

1997. Myrtle[11] **Jenne** (Jerome Adelbert[10], Sarah Jane[9] **Johnson**, John[8], Abner[7], Hannah[6] **Eaton**, Lydia Abiah[5] **Starr**, Mary[4] **Stone**, Mary[3] **Whipple**, Elder John[2], Matthew[1])[2990] was born in Russell, St. Lawrence Co., N.Y. 29 March 1872 and died 24 May 1940 in Edwards, N.Y. at 68 years of age. She married **Daniel MacPhearson Barraford** in Canton, N.Y. 30 December 1891. Daniel was born in Edwards 4 August 1867 and died 14 May 1953 in Bedminister, N.J. at 85 years of age. He was buried in Edwards. [2991]

Myrtle **Jenne** and Daniel MacPhearson **Barraford** had the following children:

2550	i.	Daniel Everett[12] **Barraford**[2992] was born and died in 1891 at less than one year of age.
+ 2551	ii.	Ruth **Barraford** was born in 1892.
+ 2552	iii.	Jennie **Barraford** was born in 1898.
2553	iv.	Everett Daniel **Barraford**[2993] was born in 1898 and died in August 1979 at 81 years of age. He married Ruth **Giffin** in 1944.
+ 2554	v.	Evelyn Rebecca **Barraford** was born in 1902.
2555	vi.	Jerome **Barraford**[2994] was born in 1907 and married Josephine **Fedorowicz** in 1937.
+ 2556	vii.	William **Barraford** was born in 1909.
+ 2557	viii.	Daniel MacPherson **Barraford** Jr. was born in 1914.
+ 2558	ix.	Myrtle Annabelle **Barraford** was born in 1920.

2000. Frank[11] **Jenne** (Jerome Adelbert[10], Sarah Jane[9] **Johnson**, John[8], Abner[7], Hannah[6] **Eaton**, Lydia Abiah[5] **Starr**, Mary[4] **Stone**, Mary[3] **Whipple**, Elder John[2], Matthew[1])[2995] was born in Russell, St. Lawrence Co., N.Y. 6 April 1878 and died in December 1959 in Canton, N.Y. at 81 years of age. He married twice. (1) **Charlotte Williams** in Bucks Bridge, N.Y. 24 March 1906. Charlotte,[2996] daughter of Richard **Williams** and Ellen **Shaw**, was born in Bucks Bridge 7 February 1884 and died 2 April 1916 in Clare, N.Y. at 32 years of age and was buried in Russell. (2) **Leta Brown** in Russell 22 February 1921. Leta,[2997] daughter of Albert E. **Brown** and Linda M. **Curtis**, died 13 May 1949 at 49 years of age. He operated a boarding house for lumber workers from 1907-20 after which he was a barber in Russell.

Frank **Jenne** and Charlotte **Williams** had the following children:

2559   i.   Anna S.[12] **Jenne**[2998] was born in Bucks Bridge 7 November 1907 and died 30 November 1990 at 83 years of age. She married twice. (1) James **Diez** in Texas 31 August 1941. (2) Perry **Medford** in Big Lake, Texas 19 December 1951.

+ 2560   ii.   Francis Richard **Jenne** was born 1 January 1910.

2561   iii.   Charlotte **Jenne**[2999] was born in Clare. 29 October 1911 and died there 27 August 1919 at 7 years of age.

2562   iv.   Jerome Hazelton **Jenne**[3000] was born in Clare 2 May 1914 and died 31 July 1996 at 82 years of age. He married Irene **Burnham** in Canton 3 December 1941.

Frank **Jenne** and Leta **Brown** had the following children:

2563   v.   Roy **Jenne**[3001] was born in Russell 27 November 1921 and married twice. (1) Harrriet **Johnson** 10 November 1946. (2) June **Loope**.

2564   vi.   Leo **Jenne**[3002] was born 22 May 1928 and married Isabel **Cole** in 1947.

2565   vii.   Bernard **Jenne**[3003] was born 26 October 1932 and married Phyllis **Chase** in Russell 21 July 1957.

2004. Louisa Malvina[11] **Patterson** (Austin Eaton[10], Esther Adeline[9] **Eaton**, Arrunah[8], John[7], John[6], Lydia Abiah[5] **Starr**, Mary[4] **Stone**, Mary[3] **Whipple**, Elder John[2], Matthew[1])[3004] was born in Oskaloosa, Jefferson Co., Kans. 27 November 1869 and died in 1932 in Topeka, Shawnee Co., Kans. at 62 years of age. She married **William Sherman Wills** in Jefferson Co. 28 November 1888. He was the son of Louis T. **Wills** and Nancy **Kendall**.

Louisa Malvina **Patterson** and William Sherman **Wills** had the following child:

+ 2566   i.   Lydia Irene[12] **Wills** was born 4 August 1897.

2005. Nellie Eliza[11] **Newell** (Mary Frances[10] **Grow**, Lorenzo[9], Samuel Porter[8], Joseph[7], Abigail[6] **Dana**, Susanna[5] **Starr**, Mary[4] **Stone**, Mary[3] **Whipple**, Elder John[2], Matthew[1])[3005] was born in Omaha, Nebr. 25 March 1869 and married **Frederick Myron Baldwin** in LaGrange, Cook Co., Ill. 1 November 1888. Frederick,[3006] son of Myron Tuttle **Baldwin** and Mary Cornelia **Harvey**, was born in Utica, Oneida Co., N.Y. 13 October 1867 and died 17 January 1942 in Alhambra, Calif. at 74 years of age.

Nellie Eliza **Newell** and Frederick Myron **Baldwin** had the following child:

+ 2567   i.   Eunice Mae[12] **Baldwin** was born 25 May 1891.

2006. James Edward[11] **Patch** (Ralph Ernest[10], Edward[9], Luther[8], Thomas[7], Penelope[6] **Dana**, Susanna[5] **Starr**, Mary[4] **Stone**, Mary[3] **Whipple**, Elder John[2], Matthew[1])[3007] was born 27 December 1901 and died 10 February 1965 at 63 years of age. He married **Ethel McFatridge** in 1932. Ethel was born 13 February 1903 and died 1 May 1990 at 87 years of age.[3008]

James Edward **Patch** and Ethel **McFatridge** had the following children:

+ 2568   i.   Emily Carol[12] **Patch** was born 16 December 1939.

+ 2569   ii.   Jimmie, Ralph James **Patch** was born 2 June 1941.

2008. Pres. John Calvin[11] **Coolidge** (Victoria Josephine[10] **Moor**, Abigail[9] **Franklin**, Luther[8], Sarah[7] **Starr**, Capt. Comfort[6], Comfort[5], Mary[4] **Stone**, Mary[3] **Whipple**, Elder John[2], Matthew[1])[3009] was born in Plymouth, Vt. 4 July 1872 and died 5 January 1933 in Northampton, Mass. at 60 years of age. He married **Grace Anna Goodhue** 4 October 1905. (See No. 1895.) Calvin was the 30th president of the United States, succeeding to the office 2 August 1923 upon the death of President Warren G. Harding. The oath of office was administered by his father, a justice of the peace, at the paternal home in Plymouth in the early morning of Friday, 3 August. Calvin and Grace were distant cousins, their common ancestor being Matthew Whipple, Clothier, of Bocking, England. Calvin descends from both of Matthew's sons, Matthew, Jr. and Elder John. Grace descends from Elder John. The brothers settled in Ipswich, Mass.

Pres. John Calvin **Coolidge** and Grace Anna **Goodhue** had the following children:

 + 2459 i. John[11] **Coolidge** was born 7 September 1906.
   2460 ii. Calvin **Coolidge**[3010] was born in Northampton, Mass. 13 April 1908 and died 7 July 1924 in Washington, D.C. at 16 years of age.

2030. Wilbur Fiske[11] **Ball** (Francis Herbert[10], Wilbur Fiske[9], James Bradley[8], Abigail[7] **Starr**, Capt. Comfort[6], Comfort[5], Mary[4] **Stone**, Mary[3] **Whipple**, Elder John[2], Matthew[1])[3011] was born in Haverhill, Mass. 29 August 1894 and died there in 1958 at 63 years of age. He married twice. (1) **Philantha Whipple Torey** in 1914. (2) **Beatrice Emma George** in Newton, Rockingham Co., N.H. 23 July 1924. Beatrice was the daughter of Elmer **George** and Mary **Grace**.[3012]

Wilbur Fiske **Ball** and Philantha Whipple **Torey** had the following children:
   2570 i. Russell[12] **Ball**[3013].
   2571 ii. Winifred **Ball**[3014] was born in Haverhill, Mass.

Wilbur Fiske **Ball** and Beatrice Emma **George** had the following children:
 + 2572 iii. Raymond Ellsworth **Ball** was born 7 January 1926.
 + 2573 iv. Phyllis **Ball** was born in 1930.
 + 2574 v. Wilbur Fiske **Ball** Jr. was born 26 May 1934.

2034. Estella Grace[11] **Wilson** (Mary Arvilla[10] **Viersen**, Mary[9] **Starr**, Lovel[8], Comfort[7], Capt. Comfort[6], Comfort[5], Mary[4] **Stone**, Mary[3] **Whipple**, Elder John[2], Matthew[1])[3015] was born in Omaha, Nebr. 9 February 1886 and died 8 December 1972 in Stanton, Stanton Co., Nebr. at 86 years of age. She married **John Cox Carson** in Pilger, Stanton Co., 16 September 1903. John,[3016] son of Edwin **Carson** and Sena **Edwards**, was born in St. Clair, Va. 15 March 1882 and died 1 August 1951 in Norfolk, Madison Co., Nebr. at 69 years of age. He was a farmer, rural mail carrier, and operated an oil station in Pilger. Estella and John were members of the Baptist church and were buried at Pilger.

Estella Grace **Wilson** and John Cox **Carson** had the following children:
   2575 i. Wilma May[12] **Carson**[3017] was born in Stanton 1 November 1904 and died 7 October 1968 of a blood clot in Norfolk at 63 years of age. She was buried in Wisner, Cuming Co., Nebr. She married Ross **Faubel** in West Point, Cuming Co., Nebr. 29 May 1928. [3018]
   2576 ii. Wayne William **Carson**[3019] was born in Stanton 9 September 1906 and died 17 July 1989 of lung cancer in Cherokee, Iowa at 82 years of age.

He married Esther **Schneider** in Council Bluffs, Iowa 29 June 1927.[3020] A Methodist, he was a grocery supervisor.

2577   iii.   Leland Stanford **Carson**[3021] was born in Stanton 19 January 1909 and died 2 May 1978 of a cerebral hemorrhage in Omaha at 69 years of age. He was buried in Norfolk He married Norine **Mitchel** 4 November 1933.[3022] He was manager of the Wheeler Lumber & Bridge Co.

+ 2578   iv.   Helen Beatrice **Carson** was born 9 February 1911.

2579   v.   Irma Mildred **Carson**[3023] was born in Stanton 30 May 1914 and died 8 July 1984 in Palm Desert, Calif. at 70 years of age. She was buried in Pilger. She married Ralph **Butterfield** in Los Angeles, Calif. 9 June 1937.[3024]

2580   vi.   Eldon John **Carson**[3025] was born in Stanton 22 January 1917 and died 4 March 1987 of a brain tumor in Newport News, Va. at 70 years of age. He married Dorothy **Cain** in Vicksburg, Miss. 30 November 1944.[3026] He was a career army officer and a member of the Baptist church.

2581   vii.   Joyce Evon **Carson**[3027] was born in Pilger 15 October 1927 and died 24 November 1955 of myasthemia gravis. in Sioux City, Woodbury Co., Iowa at 28 years of age. She was buried in New Castle, Dixon Co., Nebr. She married Edward F. **Livingston** in Hartington, Cedar Co., Nebr. 23 May 1946.[3028] She was a school teacher and a member of the Catholic church.

2040. **Ruth Elizabeth**[11] **Spooner** (Minnie Elnora[10] **Cram**, Angeline[9] **Ward**, Elsie Elizabeth[8] **Starr**, Ebenezer[7], Ebenezer[6], Comfort[5], Mary[4] **Stone**, Mary[3] **Whipple**, Elder John[2], Matthew[1])[3029] was born in Pawtucket, R.I. 8 July 1898 and died there 19 May 1981 at 82 years of age. She was buried as Ruth E. Fairweather. She married twice. (1) **Frederick Raymond Fairweather** in Pawtucket 22 December 1918. Frederick,[3030] son of James Robertson **Fairweather** and Lydia Ann **Beachen**, was born in Pawtucket 16 January 1891 and died 28 April 1975 in Cumberland, R.I. at 84 years of age. (2) **John Beech** in Pawtucket after 1975.[3031]

Ruth Elizabeth **Spooner** and Frederick Raymond **Fairweather** had the following child:

+ 2582   i.   Carol Lydia[12] **Fairweather** was born 12 November 1933.

2045. **Norah Leona**[11] **Brush** (Harriet Elizabeth[10] **Watrous**, Caroline M.[9] **Estey**, John Dean[8], John Dean[7], Solomon[6], Elizabeth Mary[5] **Stearns**, Elizabeth[4] **Stone**, Mary[3] **Whipple**, Elder John[2], Matthew[1])[3032] was born in Maquoketa, Iowa 11 August 1893 and died 30 November 1978 in Bellevue, Jackson Co., Iowa at 85 years of age. She married **Emil Frederick Westensee** in Davenport, Iowa before 1915. He married (1) and divorced Cora Engel. Emil,[3033] son of Johann Heinrich **Westensee** and Auguste Christina Frederica **Ahrens**, was born in Davenport 8 January 1894 and died 30 November 1978 in Bellevue at 84 years of age. He was buried in Rock Island, Ill.

Norah Leona **Brush** and Emil Frederick **Westensee** had the following children:

+ 2583   i.   Emil John[12] **Westensee** was born 29 April 1915.

2584   ii.   Phyllis Hope **Westensee**[3034] was born in Davenport 4 February 1917 and married Clifford K. **Sleeper** in Jackson Co., Iowa 17 November 1934.

2046. **Frank Allan**[11] **Pettit** (Daisie[10] **Stearns**, Abdellah M.[9], Harrison[8], Phineas[7], Eliphet[6], Rev. Ebenezer[5], Elizabeth[4] **Stone**, Mary[3] **Whipple**, Elder John[2], Matthew[1])[3035] birth date unknown, married **E. Mary Franzen**.

Frank Allan **Pettit** and E. Mary **Franzen** had the following child:
    2585   i. Alana[12] **Pettit**[3036].

2047. **Etta Rosella**[11] **Makepeace** (Almira D.[10] **Smith**, James[9], George[8], Hannah[7] **Wilbor**, Mary[6] **Stearns**, Jonathan[5], Elizabeth[4] **Stone**, Mary[3] **Whipple**, Elder John[2], Matthew[1])[3037] was born in N. Bridgewater, Mass. 24 October 1873 and died 5 August 1941 in Brockton, Plymouth Co., Mass. at 67 years of age. She married **Horace Sherman Packard** 15 December 1888. Horace,[3038] son of Ebenezer James **Packard** and Rosanda Jane **Ayers**, was born in Hobrook, Mass. 1 February 1870 and died 20 August 1953 in Brockton at 83 years of age.

Etta Rosella **Makepeace** and Horace Sherman **Packard** had the following child:
  + 2586   i. Merle Everett[12] **Packard** was born 19 July 1895.

2048. **Kate Orvis**[11] **Girdler** (Elizabeth Tracy[10] **Mercer**, Catherine Lorette[9] **Orvis**, Lucinda Chipman[8] **Upham**, Joseph Pierce[7], Asa[6], Hannah[5] **Stearns**, Elizabeth[4] **Stone**, Mary[3] **Whipple**, Elder John[2], Matthew[1])[3039] was born in Clark Co., Ind. 14 March 1875 and died 11 April 1966 in Versailles, Ky. at 91 years of age. She married **Jefferson Howard Fitch** in Jeffersonville, Ind. 7 September 1898. Jefferson was born in Jeffersonville 18 November 1867 and died 26 March 1936 in Lexington, Ky. at 68 years of age.[3040]

Kate Orvis **Girdler** and Jefferson Howard **Fitch** had the following child:
  + 2587   i. Girdler Brent[12] **Fitch** was born 30 October 1899.

2052. **Elmer William**[11] **Hastings** (Almon Woodward[10], Susan[9] **Goddard**, Enoch Elbert[8], Ebenezer[7], Nathan[6], Edward[5], Susanna[4] **Stone**, Mary[3] **Whipple**, Elder John[2], Matthew[1])[3041] was born in Jefferson, Greene Co., Iowa 17 June 1877 and died there 17 November 1949 at 72 years of age. He married twice. (1) **Dell Kelley** in Jefferson. (2) **Mary E. Hall** in Jefferson 15 March 1911. Mary,[3042] daughter of Alexander **Hall** and Nancy **Fox**, **Kelley**, was born in Kendrick Township, Iowa 19 November 1879 and died 12 April 1960 in Jefferson at 80 years of age.

Elmer William **Hastings** and Dell **Kelley** had the following child:
    2588   i. Charles Almon[12] **Hastings**[3043] was born in Greene Co., Iowa 3 September 1902 and died in 1949 in Jefferson at 46 years of age. He married twice. (1) Isa Helen **Davis** in Greene Co. (2) an unnamed person in Greene Co. 11 March 1936.

Elmer William **Hastings** and Mary E. **Hall** had the following children born in Greene Co., Iowa:
    2589   ii. Elmer Dean **Hastings**[3044] was born 19 August 1912 and died in 1975 in Chicago, Ill. at 62 years of age. He married Gwendolyn **Townsley** in Chicago 28 February 1942. He earned a Bachelor of Science degree from the U. of Iowa.
    2590 iii. Maryetta Ruth **Hastings**[3045] was born 4 May 1915 and married Judge William **Hanson** in Jefferson 18 September 1935. She is a Phi Betta Kappa graduate of the U. of Iowa. Her husband is a federal judge.

2591   iv.   Corinne Marion **Hastings**[3046] was born 18 October 1917 and married Frank **Griffey** in Iowa City, Iowa 4 May 1940.

+ 2592   v.   Beatrice Nancy **Hastings** was born 21 January 1920.

2053. Charles Edmund[11] **Goddard** (George Osmer[10], John Bailey[9], Robert[8], Nahum[7], Robert[6], Edward[5], Susanna[4] **Stone**, Mary[3] **Whipple**, Elder John[2], Matthew[1])[3047] was born in Taopi (now Colton), S. Dak. 28 October 1879 and died 24 July 1951 of asthmatic heart failure in Sioux Falls, S. Dak. at 71 years of age. He married **Carrie Elizabeth Aldrich** in South Dakota abt 1896. He was a mail carrier and died at Lees Nursing Home, 1019 Grange, Sioux Falls.

Charles Edmund **Goddard** and Carrie Elizabeth **Aldrich** had the following children born in Colton:

2593   i.   Eunice Harriett[12] **Goddard**[3048] was born in May 1897.

2594   ii. George Alvin **Goddard**[3049] was born abt 1902.

2054. John Osmer[11] **Goddard** (George Osmer[10], John Bailey[9], Robert[8], Nahum[7], Robert[6], Edward[5], Susanna[4] **Stone**, Mary[3] **Whipple**, Elder John[2], Matthew[1])[3050] was born in Taopi (now Colton), S. Dak. 28 August 1884 and died in 1953 in South Dakota at 68 years of age. He married **Ida D. Aldrich** 11 November 1903.

John Osmer **Goddard** and Ida D. **Aldrich** had the following children:

2595   i.   George Aldrich[12] **Goddard**[3051].

2596   ii. Hazel May **Goddard**[3052] was born in Colton, S. Dak. in 1904.

2597   iii. Clarence Osmer **Goddard**[3053] was born abt 1906 and died 5 April 1923 at 16 years of age.

2055. Clara May[11] **Goddard** (George Osmer[10], John Bailey[9], Robert[8], Nahum[7], Robert[6], Edward[5], Susanna[4] **Stone**, Mary[3] **Whipple**, Elder John[2], Matthew[1])[3054] was born in Taopi (now Colton), S. Dak. 7 August 1889 and died 3 December 1932 at 43 years of age. She married **Benjamin H. Jennings** 23 September 1908.

Clara May **Goddard** and Benjamin H. **Jennings** had the following child:

2598   i.   Verda Blanch[12] **Jennings**. She was adopted and died in February 1937 at 2 years of age.

2056. George Francis[11] **Goddard** (George Osmer[10], John Bailey[9], Robert[8], Nahum[7], Robert[6], Edward[5], Susanna[4] **Stone**, Mary[3] **Whipple**, Elder John[2], Matthew[1])[3055] was born in Taopi (now Colton), S. Dak. 11 January 1895 and died 14 June 1948 of acute coronary occlusion in Rhinelander, Wisc. at 53 years of age. He married **Minnie Ophelia Helgerson** in Sioux Falls, S. Dak. 3 November 1915. Minnie,[3056] daughter of Per Helgesen **Muruaasen** and Iverdina Amundsdatter **Instenas**, was born in Sioux Falls 14 August 1896 and died 4 April 1993 in Rhinelander at 96 years of age. George farmed and operated a hardware store and lumber yard in South Dakota for many years before moving to Esmond, S. Dak. in 1925. The family moved to Pierson, Iowa in 1931 where he was manager of the Joyce Lumber Co. He was treasurer to the WPA when it was formed in 1934, was president of the Community Club, and president of the school board. In the latter position, he was instrumental in introducing shorthand, typing, and bookkeeping to the high school. The family moved to Three Lakes, Wisc. in 1942 where he managed a lumber yard. Their final move was to Rhinelander, Wisc. where he was again employed at a lumber yard.

George Francis **Goddard** and Minnie Ophelia **Helgerson** had the following children:

+ 2599	i.	Frances Harriet[12] **Goddard** was born 17 December 1917.
+ 2600	ii.	Jean Doris **Goddard** was born 10 March 1920.
+ 2601	iii.	Helen Maurine **Goddard** was born 22 February 1921.
+ 2602	iv.	Donald Wray **Goddard** was born 8 April 1925.
+ 2603	v.	Marjorie Arlene **Goddard** was born 25 January 1927.
+ 2604	vi.	Dean Alan **Goddard** was born 18 March 1928.
+ 2605	vii.	Kenneth Charles **Goddard** was born 19 October 1929.
+ 2606	viii.	Verda Joann **Goddard** was born 18 December 1930.
+ 2607	ix.	Bethel Beryl **Goddard** was born 5 May 1932.
+ 2608	x.	Beverly Joy **Goddard** was born 28 October 1933.

2057. Lila[11] **Morehouse** (Lora E.[10] **Goddard**, Charles Walker[9], Robert[8], Nahum[7], Robert[6], Edward[5], Susanna[4] **Stone**, Mary[3] **Whipple**, Elder John[2], Matthew[1])[3057] was born in Bancroft, Iowa 13 May 1886 and died 14 August 1943 in Eugene, Lane Co., Oreg. at 57 years of age. She married **Robert C. Hall** in Bancroft 17 August 1911. Robert was the son of Alfonso **Hall** and Louisa **Carr**.[3058]

Lila **Morehouse** and Robert C. **Hall** had the following children:

2609	i.	Ruth[12] **Hall**[3059].
2610	ii.	Robert Morehouse **Hall**[3060] was born in Del Norte, Colo. 7 May 1912 and married twice. (1) Betty **Schaaf**. (2) Marion **Chapman** in Eugene, Oreg. 12 October 1933.

2058. Cecil Goddard[11] **Morehouse** (Lora E.[10] **Goddard**, Charles Walker[9], Robert[8], Nahum[7], Robert[6], Edward[5], Susanna[4] **Stone**, Mary[3] **Whipple**, Elder John[2], Matthew[1])[3061] was born in Bancroft, Iowa 1 July 1888 and died 11 March 1924 in Everett, Wash. at 35 years of age. He married **Edith Glick** in Seattle, Wash. 11 March 1919.

Cecil Goddard **Morehouse** and Edith **Glick** had the following children:

2611	i.	Charles Richmond[12] **Morehouse** II[3062] who married Emma Lou **Feckley**.
2612	ii.	Dorothy Lucille **Morehouse**[3063] who married twice. (1) Vernon Lewis **Abrahamson**. (2) Lyle **Grieb**.
2613	iii.	Laura Glick **Morehouse**[3064] who married Norman **Tupper**.

2059. Dorothy[11] **Morehouse** (Lora E.[10] **Goddard**, Charles Walker[9], Robert[8], Nahum[7], Robert[6], Edward[5], Susanna[4] **Stone**, Mary[3] **Whipple**, Elder John[2], Matthew[1])[3065] was born in Bancroft, Iowa 5 September 1895 and died 18 January 1985 in Seattle, Wash. at 89 years of age. She married **Frederick Vincent Lockman** in Seattle 21 August 1921. Frederick was the son of George **Lockman** and Genevieve **Keeny**.[3066]

Dorothy **Morehouse** and Frederick Vincent **Lockman** had the following children:

2614	i.	Richard Morehouse[12] **Lockman** married twice. (1) Bonnie Lavisa **Dalton**. (2) Carline **Lechner**.

2615   ii. Marshall Frederick **Lockman**[3067]. married twice. (1) Peggy Ruth **Dudek**. (2) Edith Kading **Ermatinger**.

2616   iii. George Roland **Lockman**[3068] married Camilla Ann **Amsbaugh**.

2617   iv. Genevieve **Lockman**[3069] married George Benjamin **Pitteklau**.

2063. Mary Virginia[11] **Goddard** (Clarence Ryan[10], Edwin Nathan[9], George[8], Capt. Nathan[7], Nathan[6], Benjamin[5], Susanna[4] **Stone**, Mary[3] **Whipple**, Elder John[2], Matthew[1])[3070] was born in Worcester, Worcester Co., Mass. 24 June 1912 and married **Alfred A. Scott** in Ft. Lauderdale, Fla. 18 September 1942. Alfred,[3071] son of William David **Moffatt** and Edith A. **Tallman**, was born in Lexington, Mich. 5 June 1906 and died 19 September 1978 in Franklin, N.C. at 72 years of age. His birth name was William David Tallman and he was placed in an orphanage in Coldwater, Mich. as an infant. He was given the Scott name by a foster family.

Mary Virginia **Goddard** and Alfred A. **Scott** had the following children:

+ 2618   i. Patricia Ann[12] **Scott** was born 30 August 1942.
+ 2619   ii. Cricket Annie Rae **Scott** was born 12 November 1943.
+ 2620   iii. June Darleen **Scott** was born 14 May 1947.
  2621   iv. Mary Virginia **Scott**[3072] was born in Vero Beach, Indian River Co., Fla. 25 March 1951 and died 21 February 1973 in Marion, Mitchell Co., N.C. at 21 years of age. She was buried in Atlanta, Ga.
+ 2622   v. Edwin Goddard **Scott** was born 15 January 1954.

2183. Scott Richmond[11] **Young** (Carlie Louine[10] **Clawson**, Emily Augusta[9] **Young**, Brigham[8], Abigail (Nabby)[7] **Howe**, Susanna[6] **Goddard**, Ebenezer[5], Susanna[4] **Stone**, Mary[3] **Whipple**, Elder John[2], Matthew[1])[3073] birth date unknown married **Louise Leonard**.

Scott Richmond **Young** and Louise **Leonard** had the following child:

+ 2623   i. LeGrande[12] **Young**.

2257. Helen Mae[11] **Cannon** (Emily Ada Young[10] **Croxall**, Caroline Partridge[9] **Young**, Brigham[8], Abigail (Nabby)[7] **Howe**, Susanna[6] **Goddard**, Ebenezer[5], Susanna[4] **Stone**, Mary[3] **Whipple**, Elder John[2], Matthew[1])[3074] was born 14 May 1894 and married **Lynne Phillips Walker** 3 April 1919.

Helen Mae **Cannon** and Lynne Phillips **Walker** had the following child:

  2624   i. Lynne[12] **Walker Jr.**[3075] was born 5 May 1920.

2258. Alma Eliza[11] **Cannon** (Emily Ada Young[10] **Croxall**, Caroline Partridge[9] **Young**, Brigham[8], Abigail (Nabby)[7] **Howe**, Susanna[6] **Goddard**, Ebenezer[5], Susanna[4] **Stone**, Mary[3] **Whipple**, Elder John[2], Matthew[1])[3076] was born 29 May 1896 and married **Edwin Kent** 24 June 1919.

Alma Eliza **Cannon** and Edwin **Kent** had the following child:

  2625   i. Barbara[12] **Kent**[3077] was born 19 May 1920.

2409. Sarah Mary (Mai)[11] **Stone** (Milon Gardner[10], Marshall Maynard[9], Col. Jonathan[8], Lt. Jonathan[7], Jonathan[6], Jonathan[5], Jonathan[4], Mary[3] **Whipple**, Elder John[2], Matthew[1])[3078] was born in Putnam, Conn. 12 March 1876 and died 16 November 1896 in Spartanburg, S.C. at 20 years of age. She married **Frederick Christman** in Spartanburg 12 March 1894. Frederick,[3079] son of Johann Ferdinand

Christman and Maria Elizabeth **Pricken**, was born in Charleston, S.C. 1 January 1866 and died 4 March 1898 in Spartanburg at 32 years of age.

Sarah Mary (Mai) **Stone** and Frederick **Christman** had the following child:
+ 2626   i.   Milon Stone[12] **Christman** was born 30 August 1895.

2412. Marshall Christman[11] **Stone** (Milon Gardner[10], Marshall Maynard[9], Col. Jonathan[8], Lt. Jonathan[7], Jonathan[6], Jonathan[5], Jonathan[4], Mary[3] **Whipple**, Elder John[2], Matthew[1])[3080] was born in Spartanburg, S.C. 4 December 1897 and died 11 September 1966 in Palo Alto, Santa Clara Co., Calif. at 68 years of age. He married twice. (1) **Bennie Maxwell Brown** in Spartanburg 10 November 1921. Bennie,[3081] daughter of James Fleming **Brown** and Bennie Moore **Scurry**, was born in Spartanburg 16 September 1897 and died 18 June 1985 in Spartanburg at 87 years of age. They were divorced in Spartanburg before 1963. She was known as Maxie. (2) **Lolita (__) McDonald** in Nevada in 1963. He was a textile executive.

Marshall Christman **Stone** and Bennie Maxwell **Brown** had the following children:
+ 2627   i.   Bennie Scurry[12] **Stone** was born 27 April 1923.
+ 2628   ii.   Marshall Christman **Stone** Jr. was born 25 April 1927.

2416. Mary Alice[11] **Perry** (Mary Jane[10] **Billings**, Hiram[9], Joel[8], John[7], Joanna[6] **Norton**, John[5], Mary[4] **Goodhue**, Sarah[3] **Whipple**, Elder John[2], Matthew[1])[3082] was born in Portland, Maine 25 October 1852 and died 3 August 1924 in Woodend, Estevan, Saskatchewan, Canada at 71 years of age. She married **William Henry Makee** in LaPorte City, Black Hawk Co., Iowa 4 October 1869. William,[3083] son of William **Makee** and Tryphena (__), was born in Rochester, Monroe Co., N.Y. 16 August 1840 and died 3 April 1920 in San Diego, Calif. at 79 years of age. They were buried in Kenmare, Ward Co., N. Dak. Lakeview Cemetery. A Civil War veteran, he later owned and operated a drug store and lived in New York, Wisconsin, Iowa, and North Dakota.

Mary Alice **Perry** and William Henry **Makee** had the following children:
2629   i.   Galen Perry[12] **Makee**[3084] was born in LaPorte City, Black Hawk Co., Iowa 2 August 1870 and died 3 April 1935 in San Gabriel, Orange Co., Calif. at 64 years of age. He married Phebe Mae Ann **Davidson** in Assinoibia Territory, Saskatchewan, Canada 19 May 1901.
2630   ii.   William Francis Luther **Makee** was born in LaPorte City 2 February 1872 and died 14 February 1926 in Kenmare at 54 years of age. He married Lillie Augusta **Crum**.
+ 2631   iii.   Albert Henry **Makee** was born 11 October 1873.
2632   iv.   Lendel Reed **Makee**[3085] was born in LaPorte City 18 September 1875 and died 22 December 1902 in Portal, Burke Co., N. Dak. at 27 years of age. He is buried in Kenmare. He married Annie **Kotschevar** in Dunseith, Rollette Co., N. Dak. 27 June 1901.

2417. George H.[11] **Wilde** (Bessie[10] **Swett**, Benjamin Frank[9], Benjamin[8], Daniel[7], Moses[6], Elizabeth[5] **Norton**, Mary[4] **Goodhue**, Sarah[3] **Whipple**, Elder John[2], Matthew[1])[3086] was born in Richmond Hill, N.Y. 11 September 1904 and died 14 January 1995 in Hollywood, Fla. at 90 years of age. He married **Irma Baumann** who was born in New York State in 1904 and died there in 1991 at 87 years of age.[3087]

George H. **Wilde** and Irma **Baumann** had the following child:

    2633   i.   Roy H.[12] **Wilde**[3088] was born in Uniondale, N.Y. 17 September 1927 and married an unnamed person in 1954. They were divorced in 1980.

2422. Ella Lovenia[11] **Mecham** (Luman Lehi[10], Joseph L.[9], Sarah[8] **Basford**, Jonathan[7], Elizabeth[6] **Goodhue**, Jonathan[5], William[4], Sarah[3] **Whipple**, Elder John[2], Matthew[1])[3089] was born in Bloomington, Bear Lake Co., Idaho 23 November 1893 and died 26 February 1982 in St. George, Wahn Co., Utah at 88 years of age. She was buried 1 March 1982 in Ogden, Weber Co., Utah Aultorest Memorial Park. She married **Henry Fuchs** 11 June 1919. Henry,[3090] son of John Michael **Fuchs** and Christiana **Lugensland**, was born in Paris, Bear Lake Co., Idaho 28 February 1884 and died 7 November 1968 in Ogden, Weber Co., Utah at 84 years of age.

Ella Lovenia **Mecham** and Henry **Fuchs** had the following children born in Paris, Bear Lake Co., Idaho:

    2634   i.   Cleo Lothaire[12] **Fuchs**[3091] was born 21 March 1920 and died 30 January 1951 in California at 30 years of age. She was buried in Ogden.

+ 2635   ii. Delone **Fuchs** was born 2 April 1922.

+ 2636   iii. Ruth Mae **Fuchs** was born 3 September 1924.

+ 2637   iv. Arda **Fuchs** was born 5 May 1927.

    2638   v.   Henry Everett **Fuchs**[3092] was born 10 January 1929 and died in Paris.

    2639   vi. June Norma **Fuchs**[3093] was born 4 June 1934 and died in Paris.

2423. Everett Hess[11] **Mecham** (Luman Lehi[10], Joseph L.[9], Sarah[8] **Basford**, Jonathan[7], Elizabeth[6] **Goodhue**, Jonathan[5], William[4], Sarah[3] **Whipple**, Elder John[2], Matthew[1])[3094] was born in Paris, Bear Lake Co., Idaho 15 June 1895 and died 25 September 1970 in Logan, Cache Co., Utah at 75 years of age. He married **Lillie Elizabeth Dunford** in Salt Lake City, Utah 1 September 1921. Lillie,[3095] daughter of Moroni **Dunford** and Sarah **Bridwell**, was born in Bloomington, Bear Lake Co., Idaho 14 January 1902 and died 11 November 1971 in Logan at 69 years of age.

Everett Hess **Mecham** and Lillie Elizabeth **Dunford** had the following children:

    2640   i.   Sarah Merle[12] **Mecham**[3096] was born in Bloomington 16 May 1924 and married Le Roy I. **Jorgenson** 14 June 1946.

    2641   ii. Melvin Everett **Mecham**[3097] was born in Salt Lake City 23 July 1928 and married Janet **Pond** 12 June 1952.

    2642   iii. Norman Dunford **Mecham**[3098] was born in Logan 9 August 1932 and married Karmon Rae **Rex** 7 June 1956.

    2643   iv. Glenn Jefferson **Mecham**[3099] was born in Logan 11 December 1935 and married Anna Mae **Parson** 5 June 1957.

    2644   v.   Edward Moroni **Mecham**[3100] was born in Logan 28 December 1941 and married Vicci **Hullinger** 17 December 1964.

    2645   vi. Kenneth Luman **Mecham**[3101] was born in Logan 18 September 1943.

2424. Mary Eurilla[11] **Mecham** (Luman Lehi[10], Joseph L.[9], Sarah[8] **Basford**, Jonathan[7], Elizabeth[6] **Goodhue**, Jonathan[5], William[4], Sarah[3] **Whipple**, Elder John[2], Matthew[1])[3102] was born in Garden City, Utah 10 August 1898 and died 3 July 1989 in Boise, Idaho at 90 years of age. She married twice. (1) **Lavell Hyrum Rich** in Salt Lake City, Utah 8 October 1919. Lavell,[3103] son of Hyrum Smith **Rich** and Amanda Angelia **Allred**, was born in Afton, Wyo. 25 July 1896 and died 14 September 1925 in Afton at 29 years of age. (2) **Joy Sylvester Wilson** in Logan, Cache Co., Utah 4 December 1929. Joy,[3104] son of Ervin **Wilson** and Mary Jane **Davis**, was born in Jackson, Wyo. 14 September 1894 and died 21 April 1972 in Boise Idaho at 77 years of age. Mary and Joy were buried in Meridan, Ada Co., Idaho.

Mary Eurilla **Mecham** and Lavell Hyrum **Rich** had the following children:
+ 2646   i. Verla Eurilla[12] **Rich** was born 22 May 1920.
+ 2647   ii. Doyle Hyrum **Rich** was born 25 March 1923.
+ 2648   iii. Lavell Mecham **Rich** was born 6 October 1925.

Mary Eurilla **Mecham** and Joy Sylvester **Wilson** had the following children:
+ 2649   iv. Byron Joy **Wilson** was born 2 February 1931.
+ 2650   v. Dean Ervin **Wilson** was born 9 November 1932.

2425. **Dora Artenchia**[11] **Mecham** (Luman Lehi[10], Joseph L.[9], Sarah[8] **Basford**, Jonathan[7], Elizabeth[6] **Goodhue**, Jonathan[5], William[4], Sarah[3] **Whipple**, Elder John[2], Matthew[1])[3105] was born in Fairview, Wyo. 1 August 1901 and died 8 April 1985 in Clearfield, Utah at 83 years of age. She married **Guy Boyce** in Lovell, Wyo. 31 December 1924. Guy was born 28 March 1896 and died 7 September 1984 in Kaysville, Weber Co., Utah at 88 years of age.[3106] They were buried in Kaysville's City Cemetery.

Dora Artenchia **Mecham** and Guy **Boyce** had the following children:
+ 2651   i. Derald Mecham[12] **Boyce** was born 30 June 1925.
+ 2652   ii. Grant Mecham **Boyce** was born 21 March 1928.
  2653   iii. Vernon Milford **Boyce**[3107] was born in Shelley, Bingham Co., Idaho 2 November 1933 and married Carol **Holmes** in Salt Lake City, Utah 6 September 1963.
+ 2654   iv. Shirley Doris **Boyce** was born 3 February 1945.

2427. **Lester Eugene**[11] **Mecham** (Luman Lehi[10], Joseph L.[9], Sarah[8] **Basford**, Jonathan[7], Elizabeth[6] **Goodhue**, Jonathan[5], William[4], Sarah[3] **Whipple**, Elder John[2], Matthew[1])[3108] was born in Paris, Bear Lake Co., Idaho 20 October 1905 and died 1 August 1949 in San Francisco., Calif. at 43 years of age. He was buried in San Francisco's Colma Cemetery. He married **Ann Marie Leeming** in Deer Lodge, Mont. 4 March 1930. Ann, daughter of John **Leeming**, was born in Butte, Mont. 23 September 1907 and died 3 March 1985 in Montana at 77 years of age.

Lester Eugene **Mecham** and Ann Marie **Leeming** had the following child:
+ 2655   i. Leora Ann[12] **Mecham** was born 12 March 1932.

2428. **Vivian**[11] **Becker** (Mary Melissa[10] **Miller**, Eli[9], Easter[8] **Kimball**, Jesse[7], John[6], Isaac[5], Sarah[4] **Goodhue**, Sarah[3] **Whipple**, Elder John[2], Matthew[1])[3109] was born in 1892 and died in 1963 at 71 years of age. She married **George Leonard**.

Vivian **Becker** and George **Leonard** had the following child:
+ 2656   i. Melvin Addison[12] **Leonard** was born in 1920.

2429. **Glenn Dora**[11] **Miller** (Alexander[10], Elisha D.[9], Easter[8] **Kimball**, Jesse[7], John[6], Isaac[5], Sarah[4] **Goodhue**, Sarah[3] **Whipple**, Elder John[2], Matthew[1])[3110] was born in 1886 and died in 1977 at 91 years of age. She married **George Lebeous Custer**. He was born in 1883 and died in 1964 at 81 years of age.[3111]

Glenn Dora **Miller** and George Lebeous **Custer** had the following children:

2657   i. Laura Luella[12] **Custer**[3112] was born in 1906 and married Hiram Leroy **Harris** who was born in 1905.[3113]

2658   ii. Orval Earl **Custer**[3114] was born in 1908 and died in 1910 at 2 years of age.

2659   iii. George Harley **Custer**[3115] was born in 1910 and married Margaret Sue **Cooley**. Margaret was born in 1915 and died in 1978 at 63 years of age.[3116]

2660   iv. Orval Merle **Custer**[3117] was born in 1911 and died in 1980 at 69 years of age. He married Denzyle Anna **Carter**. She was born in 1913.[3118]

2661   v. Ruby Ellen **Custer**[3119] was born in 1914 and married Morgan L. **Williams**. He was born in 1912.[3120]

2662   vi. Naomi Lucille **Custer**[3121] was born in 1916 and married Vern Everett **Maze**. He was born in 1911 and died in 1975 at 64 years of age.[3122]

2663   vii. Glen Levi **Custer**[3123] was born in 1920 and married Betty Jean **Wheeler**. She was born in 1922.[3124]

2664   viii. Morris Dewayne **Custer**[3125] was born in 1925 and married Ceil **Kelly**. She was born in 1931.[3126]

2665   ix. David Warren **Custer**[3127] was born in 1928 and married Marilyn Jane **Taylor**. She was born in 1933.[3128]

2666   x. Jack **Custer**[3129] was born in 1932 and died in infancy.

2430. Lillie Maude[11] **Miller** (Alexander[10], Elisha D.[9], Easter[8] **Kimball**, Jesse[7], John[6], Isaac[5], Sarah[4] **Goodhue**, Sarah[3] **Whipple**, Elder John[2], Matthew[1])[3130] was born in 1888 and died in 1963 at 75 years of age. She married **Henry White**. He was born in 1884 and died in 1962 at 78 years of age.[3131]

Lillie Maude **Miller** and Henry **White** had the following children:

2667   i. Leland A.[12] **White**[3132] was born in 1906 and married Bessie M. **Calvin**. She was born in 1904.[3133]

2668   ii. Elvin Ford **White**[3134] was born in 1912 and married Lola Lee **Coomer**. She was born in 1913.[3135]

2669   iii. Everett Leslie **White**[3136] was born in 1917 and died in 1988 at 71 years of age. He married Lillian **Strunk**.

2670   iv. Donald Henry **White**[3137] was born in 1926 and died in 1928 at 2 years of age.

2431. Mary Frances[11] **Miller** (Alexander[10], Elisha D.[9], Easter[8] **Kimball**, Jesse[7], John[6], Isaac[5], Sarah[4] **Goodhue**, Sarah[3] **Whipple**, Elder John[2], Matthew[1])[3138] was born in 1890 and died in 1952 at 62 years of age. She married **Hugh Allison Long**. He was born in 1885.[3139]

Mary Frances **Miller** and Hugh Allison **Long** had the following children:

2671   i. Millard Lee[12] **Long**[3140] was born in 1915 and married Mary Maurine **Smith**. She was born in 1914.[3141]

2672   ii. Vera Mae **Long**[3142] was born in 1917 and died in 1961 at 44 years of age. She married Fwoege **Vaeth**.

2673   iii. Winfred Allison **Long**[3143] was born in 1919 and married Ruby Goldie **Raley**.

2433. James Alexander[11] **Miller** (Alexander[10], Elisha D.[9], Easter[8] **Kimball**, Jesse[7], John[6], Isaac[5], Sarah[4] **Goodhue**, Sarah[3] **Whipple**, Elder John[2], Matthew[1])[3144] was born in 1893 and died in 1976 at 83 years of age. He married twice. (1) **Laura Mae Ferguson**. She was born in 1896.[3145] (2) **Blanche Meurice Stoneberger**. She was born in 1896 and died in 1987 at 91 years of age.[3146]

James Alexander **Miller** and Laura Mae **Ferguson** had the following children:

2674   i.   James Alexander[12] **Miller** Jr.[3147] was born in 1916 and died in infancy.

2675   ii.   Laura Marie **Miller**[3148] was born in 1918 and married Melvin Clyde **Syfert**. He was born in 1910.[3149]

2676   iii.   Harold Wray **Miller**[3150] born in 1920 and married Zora Irene **McNeese**.

2677   iv.   Elizabeth Marilla **Miller**[3151] was born in 1921 and married David Laurance **Davidson**. He was born in 1922.[3152]

James Alexander **Miller** and Blanche Meurice **Stoneberger** had the following child:

2678   v.   Howard Lee **Miller**[3153] was born in 1931 and married Marianne **Kolshorn**.

2434. **Frederick Dean**[11] **Miller** (Alexander[10], Elisha D.[9], Easter[8] **Kimball**, Jesse[7], John[6], Isaac[5], Sarah[4] **Goodhue**, Sarah[3] **Whipple**, Elder John[2], Matthew[1])[3154] was born in 1896 and died in 1976 at 80 years of age. He married **Mabel Clara Anderson**. She was born in 1898 and died in 1968 at 70 years of age.[3155]

Frederick Dean **Miller** and Mabel Clara **Anderson** had the following children:

2679   i.   Maedean Ivanette[12] **Miller**[3156] was born in 1918 and died in 1971 at 53 years of age. She married Charles Lawrence **Roberts** Sr.

2680   ii.   Kenneth Maynard **Miller**[3157] was born in 1919 and married Helen Louise **Hawkins**. She was born in 1921.[3158]

2681   iii.   Henry Alexander **Miller**[3159] was born in 1923 and married Claire LaVaun **Towers**. She was born in 1922.[3160]

2682   iv.   Frederick Dean **Miller** Jr.[3161] was born in 1923 and died in infancy.

2437. **Martha Judith**[11] **Miller** (Alexander[10], Elisha D.[9], Easter[8] **Kimball**, Jesse[7], John[6], Isaac[5], Sarah[4] **Goodhue**, Sarah[3] **Whipple**, Elder John[2], Matthew[1])[3162] was born in 1902 and died in 1982 at 80 years of age. She married **Ray Elmer Foster**. He was born in 1897 and died in 1979 at 82 years of age.[3163]

Martha Judith **Miller** and Ray Elmer **Foster** had the following children:

2683   i.   Raymond Keith[12] **Foster**[3164] was born in 1922 and married Edna Inabelle **Gilly**. She was born in 1922.[3165]

2684   ii.   Lorene Odessa **Foster**[3166] was born in 1924 and married Norman **Yordi**. He was born in 1916.[3167]

2685   iii.   Orval Jack **Foster**[3168] was born in 1927 and married Beverly (__).

2686   iv.   Helen Golda **Foster**[3169] was born in 1932 and married Thomas Leroy **Perryman**. He was born in 1930.

2687   v.   Loyd Dean **Foster**[3170] was born in 1934. and married Alfred Luther **Rainey**. He was born in 1906 and died in 1972 at 66 years of age.[3171]

2439. **Elmer Cecil**[11] **Miller** (Alexander[10], Elisha D.[9], Easter[8] **Kimball**, Jesse[7], John[6], Isaac[5], Sarah[4] **Goodhue**, Sarah[3] **Whipple**, Elder John[2], Matthew[1])[3172] was born in 1905 and died in 1985 at 80 years of age. He married **Priscilla L. Waller**. She was born in 1908.[3173]

Elmer Cecil **Miller** and Priscilla L. **Waller** had the following child:

2688   i. Patsy Ruth[12] **Miller**[3174] was born in 1928 and married Harold Wallace **McGee.**

2440. **Roy Elvin**[11] **Miller** (Alexander[10], Elisha D.[9], Easter[8] **Kimball**, Jesse[7], John[6], Isaac[5], Sarah[4] **Goodhue**, Sarah[3] **Whipple**, Elder John[2], Matthew[1])[3175] was born in 1907 and married twice. (1) **Marguerite Adams.** (2) **Evelyn Eileen Milsom.** Evelyn was born in 1914.[3176]

Roy Elvin **Miller** and Marguerite **Adams** had the following child:

2689   i. Jack[12] **Miller**[3177] was born in 1934.

Roy Elvin **Miller** and Evelyn Eileen **Milsom** had the following children:
2690   ii. Roileen Jeanette **Miller**[3178] was born in 1940 and married Vernon T. **Baumgardner.** He was born in 1944.[3179]
2691   iii. David John **Miller**[3180] was born in 1942 and married Paula **Monte.**
2692   iv. Shirley Darlene **Miller**[3181] was born in 1957 and married Thomas **Pfrimmer.** He was born in 1941.

2442. **Edwin Lee**[11] **Miller** (Alexander[10], Elisha D.[9], Easter[8] **Kimball**, Jesse[7], John[6], Isaac[5], Sarah[4] **Goodhue**, Sarah[3] **Whipple**, Elder John[2], Matthew[1])[3182] was born in 1910 and died in 1991 at 81 years of age. He married **Eva Lorraine Jamison.** She was born in 1909 and died in 1993 at 84 years of age.[3183]

Edwin Lee **Miller** and Eva Lorraine **Jamison** had the following children:
2693   i. Carolyn Pauline[12] **Miller**[3184] was born in 1937 and married John Merton **Goode.** He was born in 1936.[3185]
2694   ii. Kenneth Edwin **Miller**[3186] was born 1940. and died in 1975 at 35 years of age.

2445. **Carl Otis**[11] **Miller** (Samuel Martin[10], Elisha D.[9], Easter[8] **Kimball**, Jesse[7], John[6], Isaac[5], Sarah[4] **Goodhue**, Sarah[3] **Whipple**, Elder John[2], Matthew[1])[3187] was born in 1893 and died in 1971 at 78 years of age. He married **Rosetta Johanna Balsters.** She was born in 1892 and died in 1980 at 88 years of age.[3188]

Carl Otis **Miller** and Rosetta Johanna **Balsters** had the following child:

+ 2695   i. Clark Henry[12] **Miller** was born in 1914.

2448. **Madison Theodore**[11] **Miller** (Benjamin Franklin[10], Elisha D.[9], Easter[8] **Kimball**, Jesse[7], John[6], Isaac[5], Sarah[4] **Goodhue**, Sarah[3] **Whipple**, Elder John[2], Matthew[1])[3189] was born in Cedar Vale, Chautauqua Co., Kans. 29 September 1902 and died 10 January 1987 in Harrisonville, Cass Co., Mo. at 84 years of age. He married **Edna L. Arney** 16 June 1927. She was born in Madras, Jefferson Co., Oreg. 21 February 1907 and died 26 February 1981 at 74 years of age.[3190]

Madison Theodore **Miller** and Edna L. **Arney** had the following child:
+ 2696   i. Marilyn Kay[12] **Miller** was born in 1935.

2449. **Orville Cecil Miller**[11] **Mansfield** (Benjamin Franklin[10] **Miller**, Elisha D.[9], Easter[8] **Kimball**, Jesse[7], John[6], Isaac[5], Sarah[4] **Goodhue**, Sarah[3] **Whipple**, Elder John[2], Matthew[1])[3191] was born in Cedar Vale, Co., Kans. 5 April 1905 and was adopted by Frank Emerson Mansfield and Della Hanby Mansfield on 5 Nov. 1905 in Chautauqua Co., Kans. The adoption papers are on file in Sedan, Chautauqua Co., Kans. He died 14 February 1934 in Independence, Mo. at 28 years of age. He married **Musa Marie Porter** in Independence, Montgomery Co., Kans. 7 November 1925. She was born in Aberdeen, S. Dak. 26 December 1904 and died 21 May 1990 in La Jolla, Calif. at 85 years of age.[3192]

Orville Cecil Miller **Mansfield** and Musa Marie **Porter** had the following children:

+ 2697   i.   Marilyn Ann[12] **Mansfield** was born 19 November 1926.
+ 2698   ii.   William Duane **Mansfield** was born 17 July 1931.

2452. Blanche May[11] **Tanner** (Mary Elizabeth[10] **Baker**, Ulric Huch[10], Sylvanus Ward[9], Betsey[8] **Ward**, Hannah[7] **Goddard**, Robert[6], Edward[5], Susanna[4] **Stone**, Mary[3] **Whipple**, Elder John[2], Matthew[1])[3193] was born in Brant, N.Y. 16 May 1901 and died 8 July 1937 at 36 years of age. She married **Wilson Americk Grennell** in Evans, N.Y. 1 June 1926. Wilson,[3194] son of Chapman H. **Grennell** and Rachel Amsdell **Mills**, was born in Brant 12 August 1873 and died 21 April 1959 in Silver Creek, N.Y. at 85 years of age.

Blanche May **Tanner** and Wilson Americk **Grennell** had the following children:

2699   i.   Mable[12] **Grennell**[3195] was born in Gowanda, N.Y. 24 April 1934 and married Donald Howland **McMahon** in Derby, N.Y. 11 September 1954. Donald,[3196] son of Arthur P. **McMahon** and Elnora **Langley**, was born 18 April 1934.
+ 2700   ii.   Richard Henry **Grennell** was born 25 January 1936.

2453. Bernice Louise[11] **Tanner** (Mary Elizabeth[10] **Baker**, Ulric Huch[10], Sylvanus Ward[9], Betsey[8] **Ward**, Hannah[7] **Goddard**, Robert[6], Edward[5], Susanna[4] **Stone**, Mary[3] **Whipple**, Elder John[2], Matthew[1])[3197] was born 2 December 1902 and married **John Morris Horton** 11 October 1926.

Bernice Louise **Tanner** and John Morris **Horton** had the following children:

+ 2701   i.   Ruth May[12] **Horton** was born 4 August 1927.
+ 2702   ii.   Dorothy Marietta **Horton** was born 20 March 1930.
+ 2703   iii.   Marvin Morris **Horton** was born 11 August 1940.

2454. Viola Beal[11] **Smith** (Viola Maud[10] **Thompson**, Affalona Galia[9] **Fausett**, Julia Ann[8] **Stevens**, Roswell[7], Hepsibah[6] **Kilham**, Abigail[5] **Kimball**, Sarah[4] **Goodhue**, Sarah[3] **Whipple**, Elder John[2], Matthew[1])[3198] was born in Myton, Duchesne Co., Utah 23 December 1906 and died 12 May 1982 in Lakeview, Lake Co., Oreg. at 75 years of age. She married **Clifford Robert Thayer** in Eureka, Humboldt Co., Calif. 11 January 1941 Clifford,[3199] son of Joseph Frank **Thayer** and Hallie May **Linton**, was born in Adin, Modoc Co., Calif. 11 October 1918.

Viola Beal **Smith** and Clifford Robert **Thayer** had the following child:

+ 2704   i.   Patricia Andrea[12] **Thayer** was born 11 July 1946.

2455. Alice LuZella[11] **Jones** (Maiben Stevens[10], Marinda Alice[9] **Stevens**, William[8], Roswell[7], Hepsibah[6] **Kilham**, Abigail[5] **Kimball**, Sarah[4] **Goodhue**, Sarah[3] **Whipple**, Elder John[2], Matthew[1])[3200] was born in Ucon, Idaho 3 August 1925 and married **Harry Sidney Day** in Salt Lake City, Utah 2 February 1946. Harry,[3201] son of Abraham John **Day** and Lucy May **Bloxham**, was born in Idaho Falls, Idaho 28 February 1926 and died 16 December 1981 in Stevensville, Mont. at 55 years of age. He was buried in Victor, Ravali Co., Montana.

Alice LuZella **Jones** and Harry Sidney **Day** had the following children:

+ 2705   i. Dennis[12] **Day** was born 1 September 1946.
  2706   ii. Dallas J **Day**[3202] was born in Idaho Falls 20 October 1947 and died 4 March 1971 in Salt Lake City at 23 years of age. He was buried in Victor, Montana.
+ 2707   iii. Steven R. **Day** was born 24 January 1951.
+ 2708   iv. Cody Delene **Day** was born 1 September 1953.
+ 2709   v. Kelly Jean **Day** was born 26 November 1958.

2457. **Charlotte Georgina**[11] **McCabe** (John James[10], Mary[9] **Dickson**, Elizabeth[8] **Upham**, Eleanor[7] **Knowlton**, Daniel[6], Robert[5], Marjory (Margery)[4] **Goodhue**, Sarah[3] **Whipple**, Elder John[2], Matthew[1])[3203] was born 15 June 1881 and died 25 January 1958 in Ocala, Fla. at 76 years of age. She married **Oscar Ray Hunter** in Cristobal, Canal Zone, Panama 2 April 1921. Oscar was born in Woodstock, Cherokee Co., Ga. 2 August 1884 and died 18 August 1963 in St. Petersburg, Fla. at 79 years of age.[3204]

Charlotte Georgina **McCabe** and Oscar Ray **Hunter** had the following child:

+ 2710   i. William Ray[12] **Hunter** was born 24 October 1924.

2458. **Samuel Stanclift**[11] **Stevens** (George Gove[10], Nancy Mathilda[9] **Bowers**, Polly[8] **Rand**, Solomon[7], Deborah[6] **Dodge**, Margery[5] **Knowlton**, Marjory (Margery)[4] **Goodhue**, Sarah[3] **Whipple**, Elder John[2], Matthew[1])[3205] was born in Indianapolis, Ind. 17 February 1889 and died 16 October 1970 in Oakland, Calif. at 81 years of age. He married **Lois Voswinkel** in New York, N.Y. 30 January 1917. Lois was born in Council Bluffs, Iowa 17 April 1892 and died 25 April 1970 in Piedmont, Calif. at 78 years of age.[3206]

Samuel Stanclift **Stevens** and Lois **Voswinkel** had the following child:

+ 2711   i. Samuel Phillips[12] **Stevens** was born 3 May 1918.

2459. **John**[11] **Coolidge** (Pres. John Calvin[11], Victoria Josephine[10] **Moor**, Abigail[9] **Franklin**, Luther[8], Sarah[7] **Starr**, Capt. Comfort[6], Comfort[5], Mary[4] **Stone**, Mary[3] **Whipple**, Elder John[2], Matthew[1])[3207] was born in Northampton, Mass. 7 September 1906 and married **Florence Trumbull** 23 September 1929. Florence,[3208] daughter of Gov. John H. **Trumbull** and Maude **Usher**, was born 30 November 1904. John received a Bachelor of Arts degree from Amherst and was a corporation executive and a director and trustee of various corporations. He was retired in 1975 and living in Farmington, Conn.

John **Coolidge** and Florence **Trumbull** had the following children:

+ 2712   i. Cynthia[12] **Coolidge** was born 28 October 1933.
+ 2713   ii. Lydia **Coolidge** was born 14 August 1939.

TWELFTH GENERATION

2462. Helen Cutter[12] Pillsbury (Harry M.[11], James[10], Jacob[9], John Hale[8], Rev. Edmund[7], Moses[6], Moses[5], Susanna[4] **Worth**, Susannah[3] **Whipple**, Elder John[2], Matthew[1]) was born in Muskegon, Muskegon Co., Mich. 17 September 1883 and died 16 October 1948 at 65 years of age. She married **Pearson Wells**. Pearson was born 2 August 1883 and died 1 November 1963 at 80 years of age. Helen and Pearson were divorced in 1935. He married (2) **Lucy Skelton White** after 1948.

Helen Cutter **Pillsbury** and Pearson **Wells** had the following children:

+ 2714   i. Catherine[13] **Wells** was born in 1907.
  2715   ii. Louise **Wells** was born in 1908 and died in 1979 at 71 years of age. She married George C. **Chandler** Jr.
+ 2716   iii. Clark Thompson **Wells** was born in 1910.
+ 2717   iv. Cyrus Curtis **Wells** was born in 1914.

2463. Alice Wedgwood[12] Pillsbury (Harry M.[11], James[10], Jacob[9], John Hale[8], Rev. Edmund[7], Moses[6], Moses[5], Susanna[4] **Worth**, Susannah[3] **Whipple**, Elder John[2], Matthew[1]) was born in Milwaukee, Wisc. 17 October 1886 and died 21 April 1965 in LaJolla, Calif. at 78 years of age. She married **John C. Martin** in Milwaukee 12 April 1909. Alice was a member of the Acorn Club of Philadelphia, the National Society of Colonial Dames, and the National Society of Magna Carta Dames. She was active in charitable work with the Salvation Army, responsible for the restoration of the "Powell House" in Philadelphia, and she and her husband gave a room from "Sutton Scarsdale" England to the Philadelphia Museum of Art.

Alice Wedgwood **Pillsbury** and John C. **Martin** had the following children:

  2718   i. Isabel Wedgwood[13] **Martin** was born in Milwaukee 23 January 1910 and married twice. (1) W. Porter **Ogelsby** in 1930. They were divorced in 1949. (2) Whitson M. **Jones** in 1954.
+ 2719   ii. Harrison Pillsbury **Martin** was born in 1911.
  2720   iii. Edith C. **Martin** was born in Wyncote, Penn. in 1914 and married Gerard H. **Cox** II.
+ 2721   iv. John Stanwood **Martin** was born 18 December 1915.
+ 2722   v. David Cutter **Martin** was born 18 January 1919.

2466. Herbert Blackmer[12] Sherman (Charles Herbert[11], Jane Stetson[10] **Hale**, Zacheus[9], Zacheus[8], Joseph[7], Abigail W.[6] **Pillsbury**, Moses[5], Susanna[4] **Worth**, Susannah[3] **Whipple**, Elder John[2], Matthew[1])[3209] was born in Whitman, Mass. 10 September 1889 and died 7 September 1982 in Brockton, Plymouth Co., Mass. at 92 years of age. He was buried in Whitman's. Colebrook Cemetery. He married **Lerola Ailene Spring** in Omaha, Nebr. 18 February 1918. Lerola, daughter of James Walter **Spring** and Eva Olive **Scholey**, was born in Clarinda, Iowa 1 December 1896. Herbert was an accountant and musician.

Herbert Blackmer **Sherman** and Lerola Ailene **Spring** had the following children:

  2723   i. Charles James[13] **Sherman**[3210] was born in Norfolk, Madison Co., Nebr. 15 April 1923 and married Edna Arlean **Cochran** in Las Vegas, Clark Co., Nev. 5 June 1978. Edna,[3211] daughter of Dewey **Cochran** and Maudie **Mears**, was born in Time, Texas 23 November 1923. She married (2) Walter A. Tranah. Charles fought in France and Germany during WWII (1943-47) and was with the first units of Paton's Third Army to cross the Rhine River. He was awarded three campaign ribbons and three battle stars. He attended Boston University and California State College in Northridge, and retired from the Los Angeles County, Calif. Probation Department. He is a member of the Sons of the American Revolution and the Mayflower Society.

2724 ii. Ailene Ruth **Sherman**[3212] was born 14 October 1926 and married twice. (1) Kenneth **Orcutt** 11 September 1946. (2) Richard **Marshall** 12 October 1964.

2725 iii. Herbert Thomas **Sherman**[3213] was born 4 April 1928 and married Louise **Sinclair** 3 January 1988.

2726 iv. Helen May **Sherman**[3214] was born in Elkhorn, Wisc. 4 January 1929 and married Peter **Brigida** in Whitman, Mass. 9 December 1949.

2467. Clarence Dodge[12] **Blake** (Lizzie Batchelder[11] **Dodge**, Frank Brickett[10], Deborah Towne[9] **Brickett**, Bernard[8], Bernard[7], Susanna[6] **Pillsbury**, Moses[5], Susanna[4] **Worth**, Susannah[3] **Whipple**, Elder John[2], Matthew[1]) was born in Woburn, Mass. 17 January 1904 and died there 7 November 1977 at 73 years of age. He married **Lauretta Dolliver** 17 June 1928. Lauretta, daughter of Currie Duncan **Dolliver** and Katherine **Deasy**, was born in Boston, Mass. 24 November 1903 and died 21 February 1975 in Waltham, Middlesex Co., Mass. at 71 years of age.

Clarence Dodge **Blake** and Lauretta **Dolliver** had the following child:
+ 2727 i. Priscilla June[13] **Blake** was born 2 April 1929.

2468. Col. Howard Norrington[12] **Smalley** (Col. Howard Russell[11], Viola Irene[10] Hoyt, Dr. Hiram Pillsbury[9], Judith[8] **Pillsbury**, Caleb[7], Caleb[6], Caleb[5], Susanna[4] **Worth**, Susannah[3] **Whipple**, Elder John[2], Matthew[1])[3215] was born in Detroit, Mich. 18 September 1912 and married **Gladys Alice McCoskrie** at Schofield Barracks, Oahu, Hawaii 30 April 1938. Peggy,[3216] daughter of Frank Unsworth **McCoskrie** and Gladys Jessie **Jordan**, was born in Spokane, Wash. 1 January 1915 and died 27 July 1995 in Marin, Calif. at 80 years of age. She is buried at the Golden Gate National Cemetery, San Bruno, Calif. Howard attended the U. of Rochester and Bradens West Point Preparatory School and was graduated from the U.S. Military Academy at West Point in June 1937. He attended West Point through appointment by President Herbert Hoover. He retired from the U.S. army in 1967 with the rank of colonel and was living in Greenbrae, California in 1999.

Col. Howard Norrington **Smalley** and Gladys Alice **McCoskrie** had the following children:
+ 2728 i. Barbara[13] **Smalley** was born 2 May 1939.
2729 ii. Richard Norrington Smalley[3217] was born in Augusta, Ga. 15 May 1942 and married Avril Glynes **Davey** in Harrogate, England 3 February 1968.

2469. Helena[12] **Pullen** (Nellie May[11] **Blanchard**, George Adelbert[10], Aaron[9], Lois[8] **Burt**, Abiah[7] **Mooar**, Abiah[6] **Hill**, Judith[5] **Bucknam**, Judith (Jude)[4] **Worth**, Susannah[3] **Whipple**, Elder John[2], Matthew[1])[3218] was born in Havana, Ill. 19 May 1895 and died 23 October 1972 in Pekin, Ill. at 77 years of age. She was a school teacher and homemaker and is buried in Laurel Hill Mausoleum, Havana. She married three times. (1) **Maurice Pote Horstman** in Chicago, Ill. 1 January 1920.

Maurice was born in New Harmony, Ind. 2 October 1895 and died 4 February 1969 in Los Angeles, Calif. at 73 years of age. (2) **Eric Kirby** in 1927. (3) **H. H. Worner** in Pekin, Ill. in 1945. Maurice married (2) **Zella Gray**.

Helena **Pullen** and Maurice Pote **Horstman** had the following child:
+ 2730   i.   Janet[13] **Horstman** was born 6 September 1920.

2472. Donald Boak[12] **Esson** (William Risk[11], Elsie Boak[10] **Williams**, William Brown[9], Hannah Stone[8] **Brown**, Samuel[7], William[6], Martha[5] **Whipple**, Maj. John[4], Capt. John[3], Elder John[2], Matthew[1])[3219] was born in Newton, Middlesex Co., Mass. 2 July 1946 and married **Beverly Jean Nash** in Lancaster, N.H. 15 October 1977. Beverly,[3220] daughter of Victor **Nash** and Doris **Martin**, was born 6 June 1951.

Donald Boak **Esson** and Beverly Jean **Nash** had the following children:
2731   i.   James William[13] **Esson** was born in Hartford, Conn. 2 June 1983.[3221]
2732   ii.   Thomas Boak **Esson** was born 10 November 1988.[3222]

2474. Donald Belmont[12] **Stevens** (Orrin Belmont[11], George Nichols[10], Susan Poor[9] **Pearson**, Nathaniel[8], Sarah[7] **Gerrish**, Katherine[6] **Brown**, Martha[5] **Whipple**, Maj. John[4], Capt. John[3], Elder John[2], Matthew[1])[3223] was born in Newburyport, Essex Co., Mass. 4 November 1911 and married **Priscilla Bartlett Safford** there 3 September 1938. Priscilla,[3224] daughter of John **Safford** and Martha **Rowe**, was born in Newburyport 26 May 1911.

Donald Belmont **Stevens** and Priscilla Bartlett **Safford** had the following children:
+ 2733   i.   John Belmont[13] **Stevens Jr.** was born 15 July 1942.
+ 2734   ii.   Peter Bartlett **Stevens** was born 6 January 1946.

2475. Earle Bryant[12] **Brown** (Lottie Nichols[11] **Stevens**, George Nichols[10], Susan Poor[9] **Pearson**, Nathaniel[8], Sarah[7] **Gerrish**, Katherine[6] **Brown**, Martha[5] **Whipple**, Maj. John[4], Capt. John[3], Elder John[2], Matthew[1]) birth date unknown.

Earle Bryant **Brown** had the following child:
2735   i.   Lawrence[13] **Brown**.

2477. Mildred Irene[12] **Moody** (Agnes Coughenour[11] **Whipple**, William Orland[10], William Ward[9], John[8], John[7], Capt. John[6], Capt. John[5], Maj. Matthew[4], Capt. John[3], Elder John[2], Matthew[1])[3225] was born 7 February 1906 and died after 1970 in Glendale, Ariz. She married twice. (1) **LeRoy Whitaker** in 1935. They were divorced before 1958. (2) **Gordon Towne** 1 November 1958.

Mildred Irene **Moody** and LeRoy **Whitaker** had the following children:
2736   i.   Jon Michael[13] **Whitaker**.
2737   ii.   Lucile Ann **Whitaker**.

2478. Esther Louise[12] **Whipple** (William Henry[11], William Orland[10], William Ward[9], John[8], John[7], Capt. John[6], Capt. John[5], Maj. Matthew[4], Capt. John[3], Elder John[2], Matthew[1])[3226] was born in Lenora, Kans. 17 August 1904 and died after 1980. She married **John Franklin Zumwalt** 24 June 1927. John was born 20 June 1888 and died 31 December 1935 at 47 years of age.[3227]

Esther Louise **Whipple** and John Franklin **Zumwalt** had the following child:

+ 2738   i. Orlow R.[13] **Zumwalt** was born 1 June 1928.

2480. **Ruth Isabell**[12] **Whipple** (William Henry[11], William Orland[10], William Ward[9], John[8], John[7], Capt. John[6], Capt. John[5], Maj. Matthew[4], Capt. John[3], Elder John[2], Matthew[1])[3228] was born in Lenora, Kans. 6 May 1908 and died in 1989 at 81 years of age. She married **Carl F. Johnson** 19 April 1932. He died 12 January 1960.[3229]

Ruth Isabell **Whipple** and Carl F. **Johnson** had the following children:

+ 2739   i. Karl Fredrick[13] **Johnson** was born 19 February 1938.
+ 2740   ii. Martha Ann **Johnson** was born 21 August 1939.
  2741   iii. William Don **Johnson** was born 11 January 1948.

2482. **Frances Irene**[12] **Whipple** (William Henry[11], William Orland[10], William Ward[9], John[8], John[7], Capt. John[6], Capt. John[5], Maj. Matthew[4], Capt. John[3], Elder John[2], Matthew[1])[3230] was born in Lenora, Kans. 1 March 1911 and died in 1994 in Lebanon, Mo. at 83 years of age. She married **George Ellis Wedge** in Lebanon 31 May 1930. George was born in Lenora 1 March 1911.[3231]

Frances Irene **Whipple** and George Ellis **Wedge** had the following children:

+ 2742   i. LeRoy Ellis[13] **Wedge** was born 9 July 1934.
+ 2743   ii. Helen Louise **Wedge** was born 20 January 1944.
  2744   iii. Leslie Lynn **Wedge**[3232] was born in Lebanon, Mo. 10 February 1952 and died in Diamond Point, N.Y. She married Marshall **Green** 25 June 1977. He was born in New York, N.Y. 10 May 1935 and died in Diamond Point.[3233]

2483. **Marjorie Eula**[12] **Whipple** (William Henry[11], William Orland[10], William Ward[9], John[8], John[7], Capt. John[6], Capt. John[5], Maj. Matthew[4], Capt. John[3], Elder John[2], Matthew[1])[3234] was born 29 July 1912 and married **Fay (Otto) Hopkins** in Marshfield, Mo., 11 July 1931. Fay was born in Philipsburg, Mo. 29 January 1908 and died in 1990 in Lebanon, Mo. at 82 years of age.[3235]

Marjorie Eula **Whipple** and Fay (Otto) **Hopkins** had the following children

+ 2745   i. Doris Jean[13] **Hopkins** was born 9 March 1932.
+ 2746   ii. Dora Dean **Hopkins** was born 13 July 1933.
+ 2747   iii. Melba Paulene **Hopkins** was born 25 November 1934.
+ 2748   iv. Eula Faye **Hopkins** was born 17 April 1938.
+ 2749   v. Mirian Frances **Hopkins** was born 16 November 1939.
+ 2750   vi. William Otto **Hopkins** was born 1 December 1941.
+ 2751   vii. Elizabeth Irene **Hopkins** was born 26 June 1945.

2484. **Harold Paul**[12] **Whipple** (William Henry[11], William Orland[10], William Ward[9], John[8], John[7], Capt. John[6], Capt. John[5], Maj. Matthew[4], Capt. John[3], Elder John[2], Matthew[1])[3236] was born 24 December 1914 and died in 1992 in Lebanon, Mo. at 77 years of age. He married **Dena Vay Pline** 23 June 1934. She was born 27 September 1907.[3237]

Harold Paul **Whipple** and Dena Vay **Pline** had the following children:

+ 2752   i. Carol Dena[13] **Whipple** was born 11 April 1937 .
  2753   ii. Harold Dean **Whipple**[3238] was born in Lebanon, Mo. 3 April 1938 and married Jeannette Elaine **Millers** 25 August 1962. They were divorced and he remarried in 1993. Jeannette was born 26 January 1941.[3239]

2485. **Melvin Eugene**[12] **Whipple** (William Henry[11], William Orland[10], William Ward[9], John[8], John[7], Capt. John[6], Capt. John[5], Maj. Matthew[4], Capt. John[3], Elder John[2], Matthew[1])[3240] was born in Wamego, Kans. 9 January 1917 and married **LaVeta Hart** 15 February 1943. LaVeta was born 12 December 1919.[3241]

Melvin Eugene **Whipple** and LaVeta **Hart** had the following children:
+ 2754   i.   Thomas William[13] **Whipple** was born 10 September 1945.
+ 2755   ii. Linda Marie **Whipple** was born 1 July 1948.

2486. **Earl Lawrence**[12] **Whipple** (William Henry[11], William Orland[10], William Ward[9], John[8], John[7], Capt. John[6], Capt. John[5], Maj. Matthew[4], Capt. John[3], Elder John[2], Matthew[1])[3242] was born in Lebanon, Mo. 22 January 1919 and married twice. (1) **Ruth Long** 15 May 1942. She was born 12 May 1921.[3243] They were divorced after 1950. (2) **Beverly (__)** after 1951.

Earl Lawrence **Whipple** and Ruth **Long** had the following children:
+ 2756   i.   Marjorie Diane[13] **Whipple** was born 19 September 1943.
+ 2757   ii. Patricia Ann **Whipple** was born 10 January 1945.
  2758   iii. Richard Earl **Whipple**[3244] was born in 1950 and married twice. (1) Laura (__). They were divorced before 1978. (2) Mrs. Beverly (__) **Purcell in** 1978. Beverly was divorced from her first husband, Thomas Purcell.

2487. **Evelyn Eugenia**[12] **Whipple** (William Henry[11], William Orland[10], William Ward[9], John[8], John[7], Capt. John[6], Capt. John[5], Maj. Matthew[4], Capt. John[3], Elder John[2], Matthew[1])[3245] was born in Lebanon, Mo. 3 October 1920 and died there in 1992 at 71 years of age. She married **William Herbert West** 7 June 1941. He was born 5 January 1915 and died 12 March 1978 at 63 years of age.[3246]

Evelyn Eugenia **Whipple** and William Herbert **West** had the following child:
+ 2759   i.   Lawrence Willliam[13] **West** was born 14 August 1943.

2488. **Carl Henry**[12] **Whipple** (William Henry[11], William Orland[10], William Ward[9], John[8], John[7], Capt. John[6], Capt. John[5], Maj. Matthew[4], Capt. John[3], Elder John[2], Matthew[1])[3247] was born in Lebanon, Mo. 3 May 1922 and died in 1984 at 62 years of age. He married **JoAnn Rae Schermerhorn** 11 February 1942. She was born 29 May 1922.[3248]

Carl Henry **Whipple** and JoAnn Rae **Schermerhorn** had the following children:
+ 2760   i.   Stephen Allen[13] **Whipple** was born 23 October 1944.
+ 2761   ii. Michael William **Whipple** was born 24 January 1947.

2489. **Rosetta**[12] **Whipple** (William Henry[11], William Orland[10], William Ward[9], John[8], John[7], Capt. John[6], Capt. John[5], Maj. Matthew[4], Capt. John[3], Elder John[2], Matthew[1])[3249] was born in Lebanon, Mo. 11 June 1925 and died in 1982 at 57 years of age. She married **Alger Kuchin** abt 1948. He was born 23 November 1915.[3250]

Rosetta **Whipple** and Alger **Kuchin** had the following children:
+ 2762   i.   Joseph Terrance[13] **Kuchin** was born 8 September 1949.
  2763   ii. Jonathan Peter **Kuchin**[3251] was born 3 July 1951.

2490. **Grace Katherine**[12] **Whipple** (William Henry[11], William Orland[10], William Ward[9], John[8], John[7], Capt. John[6], Capt. John[5], Maj. Matthew[4], Capt. John[3], Elder John[2], Matthew[1])[3252] was born in Lebanon, Mo. 5 July 1927 and married twice. (1) **Keith Donigan** 1 November 1946. They were divorced before 1978. (2) **Eugene Stefan Valian** 27 May 1978.

Grace Katherine **Whipple** and Keith **Donigan** had the following children:

2764   i.   Ronald Ray[13] **Donigan**[3253] was born 10 November 1947. He married Donna **Wall** in 1991.
2765   ii.   Joseph Dwain **Donigan**[3254] was born 10 June 1949.
+ 2766   iii. Pamela Kay **Donigan** was born 3 February 1951.

2492. **Jerald Howard**[12] **Whipple** (John Godfrey[11], William Orland[10], William Ward[9], John[8], John[7], Capt. John[6], Capt. John[5], Maj. Matthew[4], Capt. John[3], Elder John[2], Matthew[1])[3255] was born in Topeka, Shawnee Co., Kans. 12 March 1909 and died 19 September 1993 in Lewiston, Idaho at 84 years of age. He married **Elma Florence Duncan** in Portland, Multnomah Co., Oreg. 29 December 1937. Elma was born in Red Deer, Alberta, Canada 15 May 1914.[3256]

Jerald Howard **Whipple** and Elma Florence **Duncan** had the following children:

+ 2767   i.   Barbara Kay[13] **Whipple** was born 19 December 1939.
2768   ii.   Howard Duncan **Whipple**[3257] was born 4 July 1944 and married Tomika **Ikuma** 26 March 1976. She was born 14 May 1941 [3258]

2493. **Paul Warren**[12] **Whipple** (John Godfrey[11], William Orland[10], William Ward[9], John[8], John[7], Capt. John[6], Capt. John[5], Maj. Matthew[4], Capt. John[3], Elder John[2], Matthew[1])[3259] was born in Tonganoxie, Kans. 21 January 1915 and married **Irma Stark** in Washington, D.C. 20 November 1948. Irma was born 18 May 1914 and died in Washington, D.C.[3260]

Paul Warren **Whipple** and Irma **Stark** had the following children:

2769   i.   Sarah Elizabeth[13] **Whipple**[3261] was born in Washington, D.C. 13 August 1952.
2770   ii.   Laura Melanie **Whipple**[3262] was born in Washington, D.C. 15 May 1955.

2495. **Martha Belle**[12] **Whipple** (John Godfrey[11], William Orland[10], William Ward[9], John[8], John[7], Capt. John[6], Capt. John[5], Maj. Matthew[4], Capt. John[3], Elder John[2], Matthew[1])[3263] was born in Weldona, Colo. 1 May 1928 and married **Cyril Clement Munsch** in Denver, Colo. 15 November 1947. She was born in Schoenchen, Kans. 31 August 1922.[3264]

Martha Belle **Whipple** and Cyril Clement **Munsch** had the following children:

+ 2771   i.   Margaret Leah[13] **Munsch** was born 8 August 1948.
2772   ii.   Michael Douglas **Munsch**[3265] was born in Greeley, Colo. 27 November 1949 and married Pamela Rae **Palin** in Richland, Wash. 28 August 1992. She was born in Hamilton, Mont. 12 March 1950 and was previously married; no details provided.[3266]
2773   iii. Patrick Cyril **Munsch**[3267] was born in Denver, Colo. 23 April 1951.
+ 2774   iv.   Timothy John **Munsch** was born 6 April 1955.
+ 2775   v.   Melody Ann **Munsch** was born 29 August 1956.

2496. **Ward Deal**[12] **Whipple** (Clyde Ward[11], William Orland[10], William Ward[9], John[8], John[7], Capt. John[6], Capt. John[5], Maj. Matthew[4], Capt. John[3], Elder John[2], Matthew[1])[3268] was born 10 May 1915 and married **Letty Elizabeth Wagner** in Huntington, W. Va, 2 July 1955. She was born in Pike Co., Ky. 10 December 1918.[3269] Ward earned a A.B. degree at Park College, Parkville, Mo. and a master's degree in 1940 from Northwestern University in Chicago. He did additional graduate work at Columbia College in New York City. At various times he worked as a teacher, editor, and sales representative.

Ward Deal **Whipple** and Letty Elizabeth **Wagner** had the following children:

    2776   i.   William Ward[13] **Whipple**[3270] was born in Washington, D.C. 6 October 1956 and married Merri Grace **McLeroy** in Atlanta, Ga. 31 May 1986. They were divorced after 1987.

+ 2777   ii.   Margaret Beth **Whipple** was born 4 September 1958.

2497. **Claribel**[12] **Whipple** (Clyde Ward[11], William Orland[10], William Ward[9], John[8], John[7], Capt. John[6], Capt. John[5], Maj. Matthew[4], Capt. John[3], Elder John[2], Matthew[1])[3271] was born 19 November 1916 and married **Leonard L. Carpenter** 10 April 1942. Leonard,[3272] son of Lawrence L. **Carpenter** and Alice **Tilsley**, was born in Amoret, Mo. 7 December 1917.

Claribel **Whipple** and Leonard L. **Carpenter** had the following children:

+ 2778   i.   Lendell LeRoy[13] **Carrpenter** was born 22 April 1945.
+ 2779   ii.   Craig Ward **Carpenter** was born 19 March 1947.
+ 2780   iii.   Rev. Keith Whipple **Carpenter** was born 21 May 1952.
+ 2781   iv.   Scott Lawrence **Carpenter** was born 24 August 1954.

2498. **Grant Dodge**[12] **Whipple** (Clyde Ward[11], William Orland[10], William Ward[9], John[8], John[7], Capt. John[6], Capt. John[5], Maj. Matthew[4], Capt. John[3], Elder John[2], Matthew[1])[3273] was born 24 January 1919 and married twice. (1) **Patricia Baldwin** in East Orange, Essex Co., N.J. 23 February 1946. Patricia,[3274] daughter of Donald **Baldwin** and Winfred **Barrett**, was born in Orange 13 July 1924 and died 2 December 1982 in Cape Neddick, Maine at 58 years of age. (2) **Emily (Whaley) Balentine** in Charleston, S.C. 21 March 1987. Emily,[3275] daughter of Ben Scott **Whaley** and Emily Sinkle **Fishburne**, was born in Charleston 14 July 1939. She married (1) **Douglas Balentine** before 1987.

Grant was graduated from Parkville (Mo.) high school in 1937, attended Park College at Parkville for two years, and was graduated from the U. of Michigan (Ann Arbor) in 1942 where he earned a Bachelor of Science degree in electrical engineering. He was hired by the Sperry Gyroscope Co. as a civilian technician and assigned to work with the U.S. navy in the South Pacific. After their 1945 marriage, Grant and Patricia lived Little Neck, N.Y., Rocky River, Ohio, Locust Valley, N.Y. and Cape Neddick, Maine. They owned and operated the York Harbor Marine Service in Cape Neddick from 1967 through 1975. Grant purchased a cottage at Yeamans Hall Club in Charleston, S.C. in 1983 and he and Emily winter there and summer in Maine.

Grant's interest in his family genealogy motivated him to communicate with various family members and over the past 30 years, he has compiled group sheets for each family. He has copies of the Darling Paper Collection a genealogy of the early Whipple generations housed in the Ipswich, Mass. public library. Another of his sources on earlier generations is a "Whipple Genealogy," written by George

Albert Whipple in the 1920s. Grant has an original copy of this genealogy and has personally checked Whipple records in Massachusetts, Maine Illinois, Missouri, and Kansas.

Grant Dodge **Whipple** and Patricia **Baldwin** had the following child:
+ 2782   i.   Joan Morgan[13] **Whipple** was born 12 September 1946.

2499. **Launa May**[12] **Whipple** (Clyde Ward[11], William Orland[10], William Ward[9], John[8], John[7], Capt. John[6], Capt. John[5], Maj. Matthew[4], Capt. John[3], Elder John[2], Matthew[1])[3276] was born 23 May 1921 and married **Lawrence Delbert Weeks** in Parkville, Mo. 28 December 1948. Lawrence,[3277] son of William Joseph **Weeks** and Lucy Mae **Wright**, was born in Kankakee, Ill. 7 December 1918.

Launa May **Whipple** and Lawrence Delbert **Weeks** had the following children:
+ 2783   i.   Susan Launa[13] **Weeks** was born 2 May 1953.
+ 2784   ii. Jane Lucy **Weeks** was born 25 November 1954.

2500. **Lyle Marion**[12] **Whipple** (Clyde Ward[11], William Orland[10], William Ward[9], John[8], John[7], Capt. John[6], Capt. John[5], Maj. Matthew[4], Capt. John[3], Elder John[2], Matthew[1])[3278] was born 23 May 1921 and married **Victoria Verne Petschulat Shely** in Plymouth, Mich. 28 June 1957. She was the widow of Robert Delbert Shely. Victoria was born in Grand Rapids, Mich. 7 July 1930.[3279]

Lyle Marion **Whipple** and Victoria Verne Petschulat **Shely** had the following children:
2785   i.   Ellen Elizabeth[13] **Whipple** was born in Detroit, Mich. 18 September 1959 and married Steven Ernst **Nickoloff** in Plymouth, Mich. 20 August 1983. He was born in Detroit 7 October 1958.[3280] They divorced before 1996..[3281]
+ 2786   ii. Victor Ward **Whipple** was born 9 July 1962.

2501. **Clyde David**[12] **Whipple** (Clyde Ward[11], William Orland[10], William Ward[9], John[8], John[7], Capt. John[6], Capt. John[5], Maj. Matthew[4], Capt. John[3], Elder John[2], Matthew[1])[3282] was born 3 October 1927 and married **Isabel Anne Wellington** in Chatham, N.J. 26 December 1953. Isabel,[3283] daughter of Alex Robertson Wellington and Mary Ellen **Kindegan**, was born in East Orange, Essex Co., N.J. 29 December 1931. He was graduated from Parkville, Mo. high school in 1945, earned a BA degree from Baker University, Baldwin City, Kans. in 1950, and was awarded a law degree by the U. of Missouri, Kansas City in 1952. He served with the US Army in Korea, was mayor of Parkville, Mo. 1952-58, and practiced law in Kansas City, Mo. from 1952 to the present.

Clyde David **Whipple** and Isabel Anne **Wellington** had the following children
+ 2787   i.   David Wellington[13] **Whipple** was born 29 March 1955
+ 2788   ii.   Anne Margaret **Whipple** was born 20 April 1956.
2789   iii. Mary Lynn **Whipple**[3284] was born 21 September 1959.

2503. **Henry Richard**[12] **Ahrens Jr.** (Eunice[11] **Schenck**, Eunice Porter[10] **Wood**, Phebe Smith[9] **Whipple**, Stephen[8], Martha[7], Dea. Nathaniel[6], Capt. John[5], Maj. Matthew[4], Capt. John[3], Elder John[2], Matthew[1])[3285] was born in New York, N.Y. 11 June 1907 and died 18 June 1967 in Appleton, Wisc. at 60 years of age. He married **Virginia Payne**.

Henry Richard **Ahrens** Jr. and Virginia **Payne** had the following child:

2790   i.   Richard William[13] **Ahrens**[3286] was born in New York, N.Y. 7 April 1932 and is the ninth great grandson of both Elder John Whipple and his older brother Matthew Whipple of Ipswich.

2504. Proctor Patterson[12] **Jones** (Ferne Catherine[11] **Patterson**, Proctor[10], Phebe Smith[9] **Whipple**, Stephen[8], Martha[7], Dea. Nathaniel[6], Capt. John[5], Maj. Matthew[4], Capt. John[3], Elder John[2], Matthew[1])[3287] was born in Lakewood, Ohio 25 May 1916 and died 2 April 1999 in San Francisco., Calif. at 82 years of age. He married three times. (1) **Betty Weber** in Lakeland, Fla. 15 August 1942. Betty was born in Cleveland, Ohio in 1915.[3288] They were divorced before November 1947. (2) **Martha Eloise Martin** in Zanesville, Ohio 29 November 1947. Martha was born in Zanesville, Ohio 6 July 1921.[3289] They were divorced after November 1947. (3) **Marion** (__) after November 1947, probably in San Francisco. He moved to northern California after law school and was secretary to Otto Preminger who was an attorney before entering the film industry. He served in the U.S. Army during WWII in the European and Mediterranean theatres as a special services officer with the rank of captain. He learned to speak French in Algeria while serving with Air Force Intelligence which led to his eventual appointment as honorary counsul general of Tunisia. After the war he became active with the Young Republicans and unsuccessfully ran for sheriff of San Mateo County. He began his professional career writing legal texts for publisher Bancroft Whitney and subsequently worked as a professional photographer, film maker, and author. He founded Proctor Jones Publishing Company of San Francisco., publisher of fine art books and mystery novels. He wrote and published *Idylls of France*, a book about the French countryside; *Classic Russian Idylls*, a book about the scenery of Russia; *At the Dawn of Glasnot: Soviet Portraits*, with an introduction by Armand Hammer. President Richard Nixon presented pres. Gorbaschev of the USSR a copy on his first visit to the U.S. He also wrote and published *Ransom of the Golden Bridge*, and *Napoleon: An Intimate Account of the Years of Supremacy 1800-1814* with an introduction by Jean Tulard of Paris (1992). This book won the 1992 Literary Award of the Napoleonic Society. He was an active member of the Bohemian Club, the Union Club, the San Francisco Rotary, the San Francisco Yacht Club, and the National Society of the Sons of the American Revolution. He was survived by his wife Marion, daughters Melinda of Greensboro, N.C., Greta of Raleigh, N.C., Jessica of San Francisco and Martha (Jones) Griffinger of Piedmont, Calif; sons John of Los Angeles and Proctor, Jr. of San Francisco.

Proctor Patterson **Jones** and Betty **Weber** had the following children:

+ 2791   i.   Melinda[13] **Jones** was born 25 May 1943.
+ 2792   ii.   Greta Patterson **Jones** was born 27 January 1946.

Proctor Patterson **Jones** and Martha Eloise **Martin** had the following children:

+ 2793   iii.   John Beverly **Jones** was born 29 January 1949.
   2794   iv.   Martha **Jones** was born 6 July 1950.
   2795   v.   Proctor Patterson **Jones** Jr.[3290] was born in Palo Alto, Santa Clara Co., Calif. 17 July 1952.
   2796   vi.   Jessica Haig **Jones**[3291] was born in Palo Alto 11 September 1955.

2506. **Robert Hatch**[12] **Nelson** (Jessamine Gertrude[11] **Hatch**, Alonzo Herbert[10], Paschal[9], Anna[8] **Gould**, Anna[7] **Lane**, Timothy[6], Job[5], Susanna[4] **Whipple**, Capt. John[3], Elder John[2], Matthew[1])[3292] was born in Minneapolis, Minn. 20 November 1902 and died 9 September 1984 in Helena, Mont. at 81 years of age. He married twice. (1) **Catherine Jane Babcock** in Glenwood Springs, Colo. 6 March 1926. Catherine was born in Chadron, Nebr. 2 January 1901 and died 15 June 1952 in San Diego, Calif. at 51 years of age. She was buried in Chadron.[3293] They were divorced in Butte, Mont. in 1936. (2) **Margaret Kennedy Lemmon** in Anaconda, Mont. 6 April 1937. She married (1). Bernie Sevener. Margaret was born in Anaconda 20 March 1910 and died in September 1992 in Missoula, Mont. at 82 years of age

Robert Hatch **Nelson** had the following children:
+ 2797   i.   Barbara Jane[13] **Nelson** was born 7 December 1926.
  2798   ii.   Robert Babcock **Nelson**[3294] was born in Aspen, Colo. 7 December 1926 and died 22 March 1996 in Fayetteville, N.C. at 69 years of age.

Robert Hatch **Nelson** and Margaret Kennedy **Lemmon** had the following child:
+ 2799   iii.   Eric Hatch **Nelson** was born 27 May 1942.

2507. **John Wyman**[12] **Fiske** (Wyman Parkhurst[11], Frederick Augustus Parker[10], Elisabeth nn[9] **Parkhurst**, Rev. John[8], Betsey[7] **Hutchinson**, Rebecca[6] **Lane**, James[5], Susanna[4] **Whipple**, Capt. John[3], Elder John[2], Matthew[1])[3295] was born in Boston, Mass. 3 July 1928 and married **Jane Scoop Fletcher**. She was born 26 December 1930.[3296]

John Wyman **Fiske** and Jane Scoop **Fletcher** had the following child:
  2800   i.   William Wyman[13] **Fiske**[3297] was born 2 March 1956.

2508. **Asenath Waring**[12] **Hanners** (Roger Whipple[11], Cora Adalaide[10] **Whipple**, Alonzo Lyman[9], John[9], John[8], John[7], Capt. John[6], Capt. John[5], Maj. Matthew[4], Capt. John[3], Elder John[2], Matthew[1])[3298] was born in Marblehead, Essex Co., Mass. 13 October 1939 and married **Allen G. Torsey** in Ipswich, Essex Co., Mass. 19 August 1961. Allen,[3299] son of Leon **Torsey** and Dorothy D. **Dearborn**, was born in Plymouth, N.H. 25 July 1936.

Asenath Waring **Hanners** and Allen G. **Torsey** had the following children:
+ 2801   i.   David Allen[13] **Torsey** was born 8 January 1966.
  2802   ii.   Mark Steven **Torsey**[3300] was born 22 May 1969.

2509. **Priscilla Ann**[12] **Hanners** (Ralph Loring[11], Cora Adalaide[10] **Whipple**, Alonzo Lyman[9], John[9], John[8], John[7], Capt. John[6], Capt. John[5], Maj. Matthew[4], Capt. John[3], Elder John[2], Matthew[1])[3301] was born in Beverly, Essex Co., Mass. 22 October 1929 and married twice. (1) **Vernon LeRoy Nelms** in Balboa, Canal Zone, Panama 19 June 1948. Vernon, son of Jacob **Foos** and Amelia **Loos**, was born in Ft. Morgan, Colo. 7 September 1927. They were divorced in Golden, Colo. in April 1971.[3302] (2) **Richard Leroy Johnson** in Lakewood, Colo. 27 October 1972. He was born in Leonardville, Kans. 10 March 1924.[3303]

Priscilla Ann **Hanners** and Vernon Leroy **Nelms** had the following children:
+ 2803   i.   Susan Priscilla[13] **Nelms** was born 28 May 1949.[3304]

2804   ii, Douglas Vernon **Nelms** was born in Ancon, Canal Zone, Panama 8 October 1951 and married Sylvia **Perez** in Commerce City, Colo. 24 December 1984.[3305]

+ 2805   iii. Debra Louise **Nelms** was born 20 June 1954.[3306]

+ 2806   iv. Judith Ann **Nelms** was born 16 January 1957.[3307]

+ 2807   v. Mark Ralph **Nelms** was born 28 April 1960.[3308]

2510. Howard Whipple[12] Hanners (Ralph Loring[11], Cora Adalaide[10] **Whipple**, Alonzo Lyman[9], John[9], John[8], John[7], Capt. John[6], Capt. John[5], Maj. Matthew[4], Capt. John[3], Elder John[2], Matthew[1])[3309] was born in Beverly, Essex Co., Mass. 8 June 1931 and married **Jean Brown** in Midland, Mich. 13 August 1956. Jean was born in Midland.

Howard Whipple **Hanners** and Jean **Brown** had the following children:
+ 2808   i. Stephen[13] **Hanners** was born 22 July 1957.
+ 2809   ii. John David **Hanners** was born 22 September 1959.

2511. William Eldredge[12] Hanners (Dwight Eldridge[11], Cora Adalaide[10] **Whipple**, Alonzo Lyman[9], John[9], John[8], John[7], Capt. John[6], Capt. John[5], Maj. Matthew[4], Capt. John[3], Elder John[2], Matthew[1])[3310] was born in Boston, Mass. 20 August 1940 and married **Oda Lee Lowery** in Niagra Falls, N.Y. 12 February 1961. Oda[3311] is the daughter of Charles W. **Lowery** and Dorothy Arlene **Nelms**.

William Eldredge **Hanners** and Oda Lee **Lowery** had the following children:
2810   i; William[13] **Hanners**[3312] was born 7 June 1969.
2811   ii. Elizabeth **Hanners**[3313] was born 7 April 1971.

2513. Douglas Guy[12] Hanners (Dwight Eldridge[11], Cora Adalaide[10] **Whipple**, Alonzo Lyman[9], John[9], John[8], John[7], Capt. John[6], Capt. John[5], Maj. Matthew[4], Capt. John[3], Elder John[2], Matthew[1])[3314] was born in Salem, Mass. 17 November 1945 and married **Mary Janice Keys** in Austin, Texas 20 August 1973. Mary,[3315] daughter of Arch **Keys** and Mary **Moore**, was born in Lubbock, Texas 24 November 1947.

Douglas Guy **Hanners** and Mary Janice **Keys** had the following child:
2812   i. Nathaniel Keys[13] **Hanners**[3316] was born in Austin, Texas 10 June 1975.

2514. Edwin Cyrus[12] Powers (Cyrus Hale Stone[11], John[10], Cyrus Hale Stone[9], Lavinia[8] **Stone**, Capt. Amos[7], Amos[6], Simon[5], Deacon Simon[4], Mary[3] **Whipple**, Elder John[2], Matthew[1])[3317] was born in Creston, Union Co., Iowa 16 October 1900 and died there 31 October 1997 at 97 years of age. He married **Areta Ethel Bender**.

Edwin Cyrus **Powers** and Areta Ethel **Bender** had the following children:
+ 2813   i. Areta Mae[13] **Powers**.
+ 2814   ii. Clarissa Louise **Powers** was born abt 1935.

2515. Bert E.[12] Powers (Cyrus Hale Stone[11], John[10], Cyrus Hale Stone[9], Lavinia[8] **Stone**, Capt. Amos[7], Amos[6], Simon[5], Deacon Simon[4], Mary[3] **Whipple**, Elder John[2], Matthew[1])[3318] was born in Spaulding Township, Union Co., Iowa 26 July 1902 and died there 30 March 1983 at 80 years of age. He married **Gladys Holt**,[3319] daughter of John **Holt** and Carrie (__).

Bert E. **Powers** and Gladys **Holt** had the following children:
2815   i. Duane J.[13] **Powers**[3320] was born 28 April 1933.

2816   ii. Dean E. **Powers**[3321] was born 23 August 1935.

+ 2817   iii. Leo John **Powers** was born 28 April 1938,

2818   iv. Calen B. **Powers**[3322] was born 31 July 1941.

2516. Aretta Viola[12] **Powers** (Cyrus Hale Stone[11], John[10], Cyrus Hale Stone[9], Lavinia[8] **Stone**, Capt. Amos[7], Amos[6], Simon[5], Deacon Simon[4], Mary[3] **Whipple**, Elder John[2], Matthew[1])[3323] was born in Creston, Union Co., Iowa 17 April 1904 and died there 28 January 1994 at 89 years of age. She married **Irvin Hiatt Hazen** in Creston 15 February 1931.

Aretta Viola **Powers** and Irvin Hiatt **Hazen** had the following children:

+ 2819   i. Ralph Irvin[13] **Hazen**.

+ 2820   ii. Mary Evva **Hazen**.

+ 2821   iii. Martha Ola **Hazen**.

+ 2822   iv. Ruth Ruby **Hazen**.

2823   v. Hugh **Hazen**[3324].

2517. Mabel S.[12] **Powers** (Cyrus Hale Stone[11], John[10], Cyrus Hale Stone[9], Lavinia[8] **Stone**, Capt. Amos[7], Amos[6], Simon[5], Deacon Simon[4], Mary[3] **Whipple**, Elder John[2], Matthew[1])[3325] was born in Spaulding Township, Union Co., Iowa 2 July 1906 and died in June 1986 in Minnesota at 79 years of age. She married twice. (1) **Philip Bender**. (2) **Charles Fackas**.

Mabel S. **Powers** and Philip **Bender** had the following children:

+ 2824   i. Vaneta Lorraine[13] **Bender**.

2825   ii. Dixie **Bender**[3326]

2518. Wesley Raymond[12] **Powers** (Cyrus Hale Stone[11], John[10], Cyrus Hale Stone[9], Lavinia[8] **Stone**, Capt. Amos[7], Amos[6], Simon[5], Deacon Simon[4], Mary[3] **Whipple**, Elder John[2], Matthew[1])[3327] was born in Spaulding Township, Union Co., Iowa 28 April 1908 and died 27 August 1987 in Greenfield, Adair Co., Iowa at 79 years of age. He married twice. (1) **Viola Cleone White**. (2) **Florence Irene White**.

Wesley Raymond **Powers** and Viola Cleone **White** had the following children:

+ 2826   i. Harold Cyrus[13] **Powers**.

+ 2827   ii. Marilyn Lou **Powers**.

2828   iii. Helen Joan **Powers**[3328] was born in 1932 and died in 1935 at 3 years of age.

2520. Orville Powers[12] **Pratt** (Olive Evalena[11] **Powers**, John[10], Cyrus Hale Stone[9], Lavinia[8] **Stone**, Capt. Amos[7], Amos[6], Simon[5], Deacon Simon[4], Mary[3] **Whipple**, Elder John[2], Matthew[1])[3329] was born in Tiskilwa, Arispie Township, Bureau Co., Ill. 5 June 1905 and died 12 August 1979 in Springville, Henry Co., Tenn. at 74 years of age. He died of cancer of the colon that metastasized to the liver on his 50th wedding anniversary and is buried at Mount Emblem Cemetery, Elmhurst, Ill. He married **Ellen Elizabeth Watson** in Des Moines, Iowa 12 August 1929. Ellen,[3330] daughter of James **Watson** II and Margaret **Ritchie**, was born in Bluff Creek Township, Monroe Co., Iowa 21 October 1903. Orville earned a BA from Simpson College and did graduate work at the U. of Iowa and taught school until June of 1936 when he became a railway postal clerk retiring 32 years later as assistant district superintendent in Chicago. They lived on Whipple street in

Chicago when he worked at Midway Airport. He was a 50-year member of Cornerstone Masonic Lodge (twice past master), member of the Faith United Methodist Church, member of the Chicago Federation of Musicians Local 10-208 (Life Member), and member of the National Assn. of Postal Supervisors, Chicago Branch 14.

Orville Powers **Pratt** and Ellen Elizabeth **Watson** had the following child:
+ 2829   i.   Thomas Nelson[13] **Pratt** was born 10 August 1937.

2523. **Dr. Myron J.**[12] **Powers** (Dr. Wilbur Louis[11], John[10], Cyrus Hale Stone[9], Lavinia[8] **Stone**, Capt. Amos[7], Amos[6], Simon[5], Deacon Simon[4], Mary[3] **Whipple**, Elder John[2], Matthew[1])[3331] was born 29 April 1911 and married **Margaret Teissen**.

Dr. Myron J. **Powers** and Margaret **Teissen** had the following child:
2830   i.   Karen[13] **Powers**.[3332]

2524. **William Cameron**[12] **Powers** (Leroy Cyrus[11], Cyrus Cameron[10], Cyrus Hale Stone[9], Lavinia[8] **Stone**, Capt. Amos[7], Amos[6], Simon[5], Deacon Simon[4], Mary[3] **Whipple**, Elder John[2], Matthew[1])[3333] was born in 1919 and married twice. (1) **Florence Colleen McCoy.** (2) **Linda Rutlege Ultang.**

William Cameron **Powers** and Florence Colleen **McCoy** had the following children:
+ 2831   i.   Errol Kathleen[13] **Powers** was born in 1949.
+ 2832   ii.   Kathryn Lee **Powers** was born in 1951.

William Cameron **Powers** and Linda Rutlege **Ultang** had the following children:
2833   iii.   Josua Cameron **Powers**[3334] was born in 1971.
2834   iv.   Seth Baird **Powers**[3335] was born in 1975.
2835   v.   Jedd Rutlege Davis **Powers**[3336] was born in 1979.
+ 2836   vi.   Sarah Hale **Powers** was born in 1981.

2525. **Catherine Ann**[12] **Powers** (Leroy Cyrus[11], Cyrus Cameron[10], Cyrus Hale Stone[9], Lavinia[8] **Stone**, Capt. Amos[7], Amos[6], Simon[5], Deacon Simon[4], Mary[3] **Whipple**, Elder John[2], Matthew[1])[3337] was born in 1926 and died in 1991 at 65 years of age. She married **Paul O. Grodt**.

Catherine Ann **Powers** and Paul O. **Grodt** had the following children:
+ 2837   i.   Douglas[13] **Grodt** was born in 1951.
+ 2838   i.   Mary **Grodt** was born in 1952.

2532. **Nancy Tyler**[12] **Royal** (Ellery Eaton[11], Alma Ellery[10] **Eaton,**, Alma Ellery[9] Tyler, Alma Ellery[8] **Holden**, Phineas[7], Capt. Asa[6], Abigail[5] **Stone**, Deacon Simon[4], Mary[3] **Whipple**, Elder John[2], Matthew[1])[3338] was born 8 August 1921 and married **John Donaldson**. He was born in 1922.[3339]

Nancy Tyler **Royal** and John **Donaldson** had the following children:
2839   i.   Susan[13] **Donaldson**[3340] was born in 1950.
2840   ii.   Deborah **Donaldson**[3341] was born in 1951.
2841   iii.   James **Donaldson**[3342] was born in 1954.
2842   iv.   John **Donaldson**[3343] was born in 1958.

2533. **Virginia**[12] **Royal** (Ellery Eaton[11], Alma Ellery[10] **Eaton,**, Alma Ellery[9] **Tyler**,

Alma Ellery[8] **Holden**, Phineas[7], Capt. Asa[6], Abigail[5] **Stone**, Deacon Simon[4], Mary[3] **Whipple**, Elder John[2], Matthew[1])[3344] was born 18 May 1923 and married **William E. Pierce**. He was born in 1920.[3345]

Virginia **Royal** and William E. **Pierce** had the following children:
2843   i. Nancy Lee[13] **Pierce**[3346] was born in 1951.
2844   ii. Jeannie **Pierce**[3347] was born in 1955.

2534. Ellery Thayer[12] Royal (Ellery Eaton[11], Alma Ellery[10] **Eaton**,, Alma Ellery[9] **Tyler**, Alma Ellery[8] **Holden**, Phineas[7], Capt. Asa[6], Abigail[5] **Stone**, Deacon Simon[4], Mary[3] **Whipple**, Elder John[2], Matthew[1])[3348] was born 20 November 1934 and married **Sandra Bartlett**. She was born in 1938.[3349]

Ellery Thayer **Royal** and Sandra **Bartlett** had the following children:
2845   i. Pamela[13] **Royal**[3350] was born in 1958.
2846   ii. Jennifer **Royal**[3351] was born in 1964.

2535. Samuel Newton[12] Bacon, Jr. (Samuel Newton[11] **Bacon**, Allen Harlow[10], Samuel Newton[9], Alma Ellery[8] **Holden**, Phineas[7], Capt. Asa[6], Abigail[5] **Stone**, Deacon Simon[4], Mary[3] **Whipple**, Elder John[2], Matthew[1])[3352] was born in Albany, N.Y. 5 June 1922 and died 31 October 1983 in San Francisco., Calif. at 61 years of age. He married **Carol Hazeltine** in New London, Conn. 30 May 1953. Carol,[3353] daughter of Frank Albert **Hazeltine** and Fanny **Brown**, was born in New London 21 September 1928. They were divorced in 1965.

Samuel Newton **Bacon**, Jr. and Carol **Hazeltine** had the following children:
2847   i. Samuel Newton[13] **Bacon**[3354] was born in New York, N.Y. 10 May 1954.
+ 2848   ii. Joni Lansing **Bacon** was born 26 July 1955.
2849   iii. Alexandra Hazeltine **Bacon**[3355] was born in Pittsfield, Berkshire Co., Mass. in April 1959 and died there in June (maybe July) 1959 at less than one year of age. She is buried in Williamstown, Mass.
+ 2850   iv. Peter Hazeltine **Bacon** was born 7 December 1960.

2536. Charles Lansing[12] Bacon (Samuel Newton[11], Allen Harlow[10], Samuel Newton[9], Alma Ellery[8] **Holden**, Phineas[7], Capt. Asa[6], Abigail[5] **Stone**, Deacon Simon[4], Mary[3] **Whipple**, Elder John[2], Matthew[1])[3356] was born in Albany, N.Y. 22 August 1922 and married **Eleanor Bringhurst Tinsley** in Durham, Strafford Co., N.H. 8 September 1951. Eleanor,[3357] daughter of Vernon French **Tinsely** and Marjorie **Blish**, was born in Des Moines, Iowa 22 February 1924.

Charles Lansing **Bacon** and Eleanor Bringhurst **Tinsley** had the following children born in Amesbury, Mass. :
2851   i. Elizabeth Allen[13] **Bacon**[3358] was born 3 April 1953.
2852   ii Karen Tinsley **Bacon**[3359] was born 20 February 1955 and married twice. (1) Robert Edward **Weeks** in Bangor, Maine 1 March 1976. Robert,[3360] son of Eugene **Weeks** and Ruth **Butterfield**, was born in Bangor 4 October 1951. They were divorced in 1980. (2) Thomas Reginald **Mitchell** in Amherst, N.H. 20 September 1986. Thomas,[3361] son of Perry Nelson **Mitchell** and Sophia **Poplaski**, was born in Dover, N.J. 2 January 1948. He married (1) Alice **Moore** 23 August 1969. They were divorced in 1985.
+ 2853   iii. Deborah Lansing **Bacon** was born 14 June 1957.

2537. **Richard Mather**[12] **Bacon** (Samuel Newton[11], Allen Harlow[10], Samuel Newton[9], Alma Ellery[8] **Holden**, Phineas[7], Capt. Asa[6], Abigail[5] **Stone**, Deacon Simon[4], Mary[3] **Whipple**, Elder John[2], Matthew[1])[3362] was born in Albany, N.Y. 14 January 1928 and married twice. (1) **Rosa Lynn Law** in Maryville, Tenn. 8 August 1953. Rosa[3363] is the daughter of Enoch Waters **Law**. They were divorced before 1960. (2) **Mary Neale Joyce** in Norfolk, Va. 27 August 1960. Mary,[3364] daughter of James Justin **Joyce** and Eugenia **Portlock**, was born in Norfolk 16 August 1933. They were divorced in 1981

Richard Mather **Bacon** and Mary Neale **Joyce** had the following children:
+ 2854   i.   Timothy Mather[13] **Bacon** was born 13 September 1962.
   2855   ii.   James Justin **Bacon**[3365] was born in Fitchburg, Worcerster Co., Mass. 26 January 1964.
   2856   iii.   Caroline Lansing **Bacon**[3366] was born in Philadelphia, Penn. 18 January 1967.

2539. **Lorna Mather**[12] **Swain** (Elizabeth Harlow[11] **Bacon**, Allen Harlow[10], Samuel Newton[9], Alma Ellery[8] **Holden**, Phineas[7], Capt. Asa[6], Abigail[5] **Stone**, Deacon Simon[4], Mary[3] **Whipple**, Elder John[2], Matthew[1])[3367] was born 17 December 1927 and married **Gene Edson Washburn** in Montgomery, Mass. 30 January 1960. Gene,[3368] son of Levi Edwin **Washburn** and Lena Louise **Pueschel**, was born in Westfield, Mass. 15 April 1932.

Lorna Mather **Swain** and Gene Edson **Washburn** had the following children:
+ 2857   i.   Linda Jean[13] **Washburn** was born 2 February 1961.
   2858   ii.   Donald Edson **Washburn**[3369] was born in Westfield, Mass. 10 November 1962.

2540. **Robert David**[12] **Swain** (Elizabeth Harlow[11] **Bacon**, Allen Harlow[10], Samuel Newton[9], Alma Ellery[8] **Holden**, Phineas[7], Capt. Asa[6], Abigail[5] **Stone**, Deacon Simon[4], Mary[3] **Whipple**, Elder John[2], Matthew[1])[3370] was born 8 October 1931 and married **Linn Davis** in Cleveland, Ohio 24 November 1956. Linn,[3371] daughter of James Cox **Davis** and Elizabeth Stevens **Linn**, was born in Des Moines, Iowa 15 April 1933.

Robert David **Swain** and Linn **Davis** had the following children:
+ 2859   i.   David Newman[13] **Swain** was born 12 June 1958.
   2860   ii.   Nancy Linn **Swain**[3372] was born in Evanston, Ill. 17 May 1960.
   2861   iii.   Scott Davis **Swain**[3373] was born in White Plains, N.Y. 30 December 1962 and married Tamara Lynn **Hendrickson** in Tacoma, Pierce Co., Wash. 28 May 1988. Tamara,[3374] daughter of Dr. Leonard Andrew **Hendrickson** and Serena Ellen **Lawson**, was born in Seattle, Wash. 20 August 1964
   2862   iv.   Clark Davis **Swain**[3375] was born in White Plains, N.Y. 30 December 1962 .

2541. **Catharine Mather**[12] **Bacon**, (Allen Harlow[11], Allen Harlow[10] **Bacon**, Samuel Newton[9], Alma Ellery[8] **Holden**, Phineas[7], Capt. Asa[6], Abigail[5] **Stone**, Deacon Simon[4], Mary[3] **Whipple**, Elder John[2], Matthew[1])[3376] was born in Albany, N.Y. 18 January 1930 and married **Thomas Richards Foster** in Greenwich, N.Y. 21 July 1951. Thomas,[3377] son of Myron McAuley **Foster** and Alice Catherine **Richards**, was born 29 April 1929.

Catharine Mather **Bacon**, and Thomas Richards **Foster** had the following children:

+ 2863   i.   Susan Elizabeth[13] **Foster** was born 16 March 1953.

    2864   ii.   Nancy Allen **Foster**[3378] was born in Glens Falls, N.Y. 4 November 1954 and died there 12 August 1986 at 31 years of age. She is buried in Greenwich, N.Y.

+ 2865   iii.   Catharine Mather **Foster** was born 17 April 1957.

2542. Marian Jagel[12] **Bacon**, (Allen Harlow[11], Allen Harlow[10] **Bacon**, Samuel Newton[9], Alma Ellery[8] **Holden**, Phineas[7], Capt. Asa[6], Abigail[5] **Stone**, Deacon Simon[4], Mary[3] **Whipple**, Elder John[2], Matthew[1])[3379] was born in Albany, N.Y. 20 August 1937 and married **John Samuel Gillis** in Greenwich, N.Y. 23 August 1958. John,[3380] son of Joseph A. **Gillis** and Alice **Mosher**, was born 14 April 1936.

Marian Jagel **Bacon**, and John Samuel **Gillis** had the following children:

+ 2866   i.   John Peter[13] **Gillis** was born 11 October 1961.

    2867   ii.   Matthew Bacon **Gillis**[3381] was born in Saratoga Springs, N.Y. 23 November 1964 and married Jennifer Estelle **Reycroft** 20 August 1988. Jennifer,[3382] daughter of Louis Manning **Reycroft**, Jr. and Gloria Florence **Johnson**, was born in Framingham, Middlesex Co., Mass. 28 November 1964.

2543. William Oliver[12] **Wise** (Mary Olive[11] **Carr**, William Dustin[10], Lyman[9], Susanna[8] **Dunton**, Mary[7] **Jewell**, Mary[6] **Whitney**, Mary[5] **Stone**, Deacon Simon[4], Mary[3] **Whipple**, Elder John[2], Matthew[1])[3383] was born in Lancaster, Worcester Co., Mass. 22 March 1884 and died 8 September 1971 in Ithaca, N.Y. at 87 years of age. He married **Anna Hale Ellis** in Braintree, Norfolk Co., Mass. 10 September 1912. Anna was born in Braintree 3 June 1883 and died 30 December 1963 in Winter Park, Fla. at 80 years of age. [3384]

William Oliver **Wise** and Anna Hale **Ellis** had the following children:

+ 2868   i.   Robert E.[13] **Wise** was born 26 December 1913.

+ 2869   ii.   Miriam **Wise** was born 17 November 1916.

+ 2870   iii.   William Oliver **Wise** Jr. was born 24 July 1919.

2548. Martin[12] **Croissant** (Nellie Frances[11] **King**, Edwin Henry[10], John[9], Lois[8] **Jackson**, Lois[7] **Woodward**,, Mary[6] **Stone**, Samuel[5], Ebenezer[4], Mary[3] **Whipple**, Elder John[2], Matthew[1])[3385] was born in Albany, N.Y. 16 November 1887 and died 2 October 1976 in Pittsburgh, Penn. at 88 years of age. He married **Virginia Smith Carson** 2 June 1919. Virginia,[3386] daughter of Edward Geary **Carson** and Anna Mary **Lang**, was born in Chartiers, Penn. 7 September 1898 and died 23 February 1979 in Albany, N.Y. at 80 years of age

Martin **Croissant** and Virginia Smith **Carson** had the following child:

+ 2871   i.   Virginia Anne[13] **Croissant** was born 30 March 1920.

2551. Ruth[12] **Barraford** (Myrtle[11] **Jenne**, Jerome Adelbert[10], Sarah Jane[9] **Johnson**, John[8], Abner[7], Hannah[6] **Eaton**, Lydia Abiah[5] **Starr**, Mary[4] **Stone**, Mary[3] **Whipple**, Elder John[2], Matthew[1])[3387] was born in 1892 and died 14 December 1948 in Florida, at 56 years of age. She married **George Javall** abt 1911. They were divorced in 1936.

Ruth **Barraford** and George **Javall** had the following children:

    2872   i. Lester[13] **Javall**.[3388]

    2873   ii. Hester **Javall**.[3389]

    2874   iii. Vaneshia **Javall**.[3390]

2552. Jennie[12] **Barraford** (Myrtle[11] **Jenne**, Jerome Adelbert[10], Sarah Jane[9] **Johnson**, John[8], Abner[7], Hannah[6] **Eaton**, Lydia Abiah[5] **Starr**, Mary[4] **Stone**, Mary[3] **Whipple**, Elder John[2], Matthew[1])[3391] was born in 1898 and died in 1958 at 60 years of age. She married **Glen Hance** in 1913 .

Jennie **Barraford** and Glen **Hance** had the following children:

    2875   i. Geraldine[13] **Hance**.[3392]

    2876   ii. Gwendolyn **Hance**.[3393]

    2877   iii. Glenn **Hance**.[3394]

    2878   iv. Jenne **Hance**.[3395]

    2879   v. Gloria **Hance**.[3396]

    2880   vi. Everett **Hance**[3397] died in February 1984 at 4 years of age.

2554. Evelyn Rebecca[12] **Barraford** (Myrtle[11] **Jenne**, Jerome Adelbert[10], Sarah Jane[9] **Johnson**, John[8], Abner[7], Hannah[6] **Eaton**, Lydia Abiah[5] **Starr**, Mary[4] **Stone**, Mary[3] **Whipple**, Elder John[2], Matthew[1])[3398] was born in 1902 and married **Leone Watson** in 1920.

Evelyn Rebecca **Barraford** and Leone **Watson** had the following children:

    2881   i. Robert[13] **Watson**.[3399]

    2882   ii. Joanne **Watson**.[3400]

    2883   iii. Marlene **Watson**[3401]

    2884   iv. Roderick **Watson**.[3402]

2556. William[12] **Barraford** (Myrtle[11] **Jenne**, Jerome Adelbert[10], Sarah Jane[9] **Johnson**, John[8], Abner[7], Hannah[6] **Eaton**, Lydia Abiah[5] **Starr**, Mary[4] **Stone**, Mary[3] **Whipple**, Elder John[2], Matthew[1])[3403] was born in 1909 and married **Jessie Strait** in 1937.

William **Barraford** and Jessie **Strait** had the following children:

    2885   i. William[13] **Barraford**.[3404]

    2886   ii. Sherrill **Barraford**.[3405]

    2887   iii. Maureen **Barraford**.[3406]

    2888   iv. Margery **Barraford**.[3407]

2557. Daniel MacPherson[12] **Barraford Jr.** (Myrtle[11] **Jenne**, Jerome Adelbert[10], Sarah Jane[9] **Johnson**, John[8], Abner[7], Hannah[6] **Eaton**, Lydia Abiah[5] **Starr**, Mary[4] **Stone**, Mary[3] **Whipple**, Elder John[2], Matthew[1])[3408] was born in 1914 and married **Nora M. McDonnell** in Larne, Northern Ireland in 1942.

Daniel MacPherson **Barraford** Jr. and Nora M. **McDonnell** had the following children:

    2889   i. Daniel[13] **Barraford**.[3409]

    2890   ii. Andrew **Barraford**.[3410]

    2891   iii. Thomas **Barraford**.[3411]

    2892   iv. Eulalie **Barraford**[3412] was born in 1945 and died in 1971 at 26 years of age.

    2893   v. Theodore **Barraford**[3413] was born in 1954 and died in 1979 at 25 years of age.

2558. Myrtle Annabelle[12] Barraford (Myrtle[11] **Jenne**, Jerome Adelbert[10], Sarah Jane[9] **Johnson**, John[8], Abner[7], Hannah[6] **Eaton**, Lydia Abiah[5] **Starr**, Mary[4] **Stone**, Mary[3] **Whipple**, Elder John[2], Matthew[1])[3414] was born in 1920 and married **Wayne Patterson** in 1939.

Myrtle Annabelle **Barraford** and Wayne **Patterson** had the following children:

2894	i.	Ronald[13] **Patterson**.[3415]
2895	ii.	Darla **Patterson**.[3416]
2896	iii.	Gayle Marie **Patterson**.[3417]
2897	iv.	Trudi Lynn **Patterson**.[3418]
2898	v.	Winford **Patterson**[3419] was born in 1939 and died in August 1979 at 40 years of age.

2560. Francis Richard[12] Jenne (Frank[11], Jerome Adelbert[10], Sarah Jane[9] **Johnson**, John[8], Abner[7], Hannah[6] **Eaton**, Lydia Abiah[5] **Starr**, Mary[4] **Stone**, Mary[3] **Whipple**, Elder John[2], Matthew[1])[3420] was born in Clare, N.Y. 1 January 1910 and died 24 March 1992 at 82 years of age. He was a barber and married twice. (1) **Juanita Maxine Flanders** in Hannawa Falls, N.Y. 24 December 1935. Juanita,[3421] daughter of Erwin Webster **Flanders** and Alta Sophia **Whitford**, was born in Potsdam, N.Y. 12 August 1915 and died 9 November 1967 in Cornwall, Ontario, Canada at 52 years of age. She was buried in Hannawa Falls. She was a school teacher. (2) **Ruth (Hatch) Brothers** in Brasher Falls, N.Y. 20 June 1970. Ruth[3422] is the daughter of Roy C. **Hatch** and Mae **Burcurne**.

Francis Richard **Jenne** and Juanita Maxine **Flanders** had the following children born in Potsdam, N.Y.:

+ 2899	i.	Francis Richard[13] **Jenne** was born 22 November 1936.
2900	ii.	Duane Erwin **Jenne**[3423] was born 2 March 1939 and was married three times; no information on wives provided.
2901	iii.	Nancy Eleanor **Jenne**[3424] was born 30 January 1941 and married Richard **Demo** 22 October 1966.
2902	iv.	Karen Lee **Jenne**[3425] was born in November 1942 and died the day of birth.
2903	v.	Sharon Ann **Jenne**[3426] was born 9 November 1944 and married Thomas **Tyo** in 1969.

2566. Lydia Irene[12] Wills (Louisa Malvina[11] **Patterson**, Austin Eaton[10], Esther Adeline[9] **Eaton**, Arrunah[8], John[7], John[6], Lydia Abiah[5] **Starr**, Mary[4] **Stone**, Mary[3] **Whipple**, Elder John[2], Matthew[1])[3427] was born in Leavenworth, Leavenworth Co., Kans. 4 August 1897 and died 1 November 1976 in Lombard, DuPage Co., Ill. at 79 years of age. She married **Donald Connet Stubbs** in Ackerland, Lawrence Co., Kans. 5 March 1915. Donald was the son of George Walter **Stubbs** and Winifred Adams **Connet**.

Lydia Irene **Wills** and Donald Connet **Stubbs** had the following child:

+ 2904	i.	Jessie Arline[13] **Stubbs**.

2567. Eunice Mae[12] Baldwin (Nellie Eliza[11] **Newell**, Mary Frances[10] **Grow**, Lorenzo[9], Samuel Porter[8], Joseph[7], Abigail[6] **Dana**, Susanna[5] **Starr**, Mary[4] **Stone**, Mary[3] **Whipple**, Elder John[2], Matthew[1])[3428] was born 25 May 1891 and died 9 February 1980 in Porterville, Calif. at 88 years of age. She married **John William McIntosh** in California in September 1912. John,[3429] son of Charles Cummin

Mackintosh and Sarah Ann **Bell**, was born in Prince Edward Island, Canada 17 September 1880 and died 4 January 1977 in Porterville at 96 years of age.

Eunice Mae **Baldwin** and John William **McIntosh** had the following child:
+ 2905   i. Victoria Anne[13] **McIntosh** was born 19 May 1919.

2568. Emily Carol[12] **Patch** (James Edward[11], Ralph Ernest[10], Edward[9], Luther[8], Thomas[7], Penelope[6] **Dana**, Susanna[5] **Starr**, Mary[4] **Stone**, Mary[3] **Whipple**, Elder John[2], Matthew[1])[3430] was born 16 December 1939 and married **Thomas Baker** in 1973.

Emily Carol **Patch** and Thomas **Baker** had the following child:
2906   i. Cassandra Marion[13] **Baker**[3431] was born 31 August 1977. Adopted.

2569. Jimmie, Ralph James[12] **Patch** (James Edward[11], Ralph Ernest[10], Edward[9], Luther[8], Thomas[7], Penelope[6] **Dana**, Susanna[5] **Starr**, Mary[4] **Stone**, Mary[3] **Whipple**, Elder John[2], Matthew[1])[3432] was born 2 June 1941 and married **Susan Winters** 12 July 1973.

Jimmie, Ralph James **Patch** and Susan **Winters** had the following children:
2907   i. Susan Ai Nan Marion[13] **Patch**[3433] was born 24 August 1976. Adopted.
2908   ii. Michelle Elizabeth Bo Yung Kak **Patch**[3434] was born 12 December 1981. Adopted.

2572. Raymond Ellsworth[12] **Ball** (Wilbur Fiske[11], Francis Herbert[10], Wilbur Fiske[9], James Bradley[8], Abigail[7] **Starr**, Capt. Comfort[6], Comfort[5], Mary[4] **Stone**, Mary[3] **Whipple**, Elder John[2], Matthew[1])[3435] was born in Haverhill, Mass. 7 January 1926 and died in December 1993 in Claremont, Calif. at 67 years of age.

Raymond Ellsworth **Ball** had the following children:
2909   i. Jeffery[13] **Ball**[3436] was born in 1953.
2910   ii. Jennifer **Ball**[3437] was born in 1957.

2573. Phyllis[12] **Ball** (Wilbur Fiske[11], Francis Herbert[10], Wilbur Fiske[9], James Bradley[8], Abigail[7] **Starr**, Capt. Comfort[6], Comfort[5], Mary[4] **Stone**, Mary[3] **Whipple**, Elder John[2], Matthew[1])[3438] was born in Haverhill, Mass. in 1930 and married **John Williams** there.

Phyllis **Ball** and John **Williams** had the following children:
2911   i. Linda[13] **Williams**.[3439]
2912   ii. Diane **Williams**.[3440]
2913   iii. Stephen **Williams**.[3441]
2914   iv. John **Williams** Jr.[3442]

2574. Wilbur Fiske[12] **Ball Jr.** (Wilbur Fiske[11], Francis Herbert[10], Wilbur Fiske[9], James Bradley[8], Abigail[7] **Starr**, Capt. Comfort[6], Comfort[5], Mary[4] **Stone**, Mary[3] **Whipple**, Elder John[2], Matthew[1])[3443] was born in Haverhill, Mass. 26 May 1934 and married **Dorothy Jane Graham** in Portland, Maine 13 November 1953. Dorothy[3444] is the daughter of Thomas **Graham** and Gladys **Massie**.

Wilbur Fiske **Ball** Jr. and Dorothy Jane **Graham** had the following children:
+ 2915   i. Thomas William[13] **Ball** was born 28 February 1954.
+ 2916   ii. Susan Lynne **Ball** was born 16 May 1955.
+ 2917   iii. Cherryl Ann **Ball** was born 9 October 1956.

2918   iv. David Michael **Ball**[3445] was born in Haverhill, Mass. 28 December 1957.

2578. Helen Beatrice[12] **Carson** (Estella Grace[11] **Wilson**, Mary Arvilla[10] **Viersen**, Mary[9] **Starr**, Lovel[8], Comfort[7], Capt. Comfort[6], Comfort[5], Mary[4] **Stone**, Mary[3] **Whipple**, Elder John[2], Matthew[1])[3446] was born in Stanton Co., Nebr. 9 February 1911 and married **Boyd Dee Jones** in Glidden, Carroll Co., Iowa 30 May 1931. Boyd,[3447] son of Emory Lee **Jones** and Margaret **Rennick**, was born in Pilger, Stanton Co., Nebr. 9 January 1913.

Helen Beatrice **Carson** and Boyd Dee **Jones** had the following children:
+ 2919   i. Donald Dee[13] **Jones** was born 27 November 1932.
  2920   ii. Leland Boyd **Jones**[3448] was born in Pilger 21 November 1935 and married Valerie **Soule** in Athens, Ga. 23 July 1960.
  2921   iii. Larry Dean **Jones**[3449] was born in Pilger 19 March 1938 and married Beverly Rae **Meyer** in Grand Island, Nebr. 25 August 1957.[3450]

2582. Carol Lydia[12] **Fairweather** (Ruth Elizabeth[11] **Spooner**, Minnie Elnora[10] **Cram**, Angeline[9] **Ward**, Elsie Elizabeth[8] **Starr**, Ebenezer[7], Ebenezer[6], Comfort[5], Mary[4] **Stone**, Mary[3] **Whipple**, Elder John[2], Matthew[1])[3451] was born in Pawtucket, R.I. 12 November 1933 married **Rev. Robert Emerson Andrews** there 7 June 1953. Robert,[3452] son of George Robert **Andrews** and Laura Violet **Byron**, was born in Providence, R.I. 20 July 1933.

Carol Lydia **Fairweather** and Rev. Robert Emerson **Andrews** had the following children:
+ 2922   i. George Robert[13] **Andrews** was born 22 April 1954.
+ 2923   ii. Sharon Leslie **Andrews** was born 10 June 1955.

2583. Emil John[12] **Westensee** (Norah Leona[11] **Brush**, Harriet Elizabeth[10] **Watrous**, Caroline M.[9] **Estey**, John Dean[8], John Dean[7], Solomon[6], Elizabeth Mary[5] **Stearns**, Elizabeth[4] **Stone**, Mary[3] **Whipple**, Elder John[2], Matthew[1])[3453] was born in Davenport, Iowa 29 April 1915 and married **Betty Ruth Ferong** there 8 April 1939. Betty,[3454] daughter of Henry Luther **Ferong** and Anna Wilhemina **Johnson**, was born in Swedona, Mercer Co., Ill. 12 March 1921.

Emil John **Westensee** and Betty Ruth **Ferong** had the following children:
  2924   i. Anna Christine[13] **Westensee**[3455] was born in Moline, Ill. 7 November 1942.
  2925   ii. Carol Noreen **Westensee**[3456] was born in Moline, Ill. 21 December 1944.
+ 2926   iii. John Henry **Westensee** was born 22 July 1947.

2586. Merle Everett[12] **Packard** (Etta Rosella[11] **Makepeace**, Almira D.[10] **Smith**, James[9], George[8], Hannah[7] **Wilbor**, Mary[6] **Stearns**, Jonathan[5], Elizabeth[4] **Stone**, Mary[3] **Whipple**, Elder John[2], Matthew[1])[3457] was born in Holbrook, Mass. 19 July 1895 and died 10 September 1972 at 77 years of age. He married **Amelia Julia Rose Preskins** in Salem Depot, N.H. 28 April 1923. Amelia,[3458] daughter of William **Preskins** and Louise M. **Kulesus**, was born in Bossier City, La. 20 September 1903.

Merle Everett **Packard** and Amelia Julia Rose **Preskins** had the following children:

+ 2927   i. Lila Lee[13] **Packard** was born 30 September 1924.

2928   ii. Kathleen Lorraine **Packard**[3459] was born in Haverhill, Mass. 22 October 1925 and died 23 June 1989 in West Palm Beach, Fla. at 63 years of age. She married Anthony T. **Guliano** in Barrington, R.I.

2587. Girdler Brent[12] **Fitch** (Kate Orvis[11] **Girdler**, Elizabeth Tracy[10] **Mercer**, Catherine Lorette[9] **Orvis**, Lucinda Chipman[8] **Upham**, Joseph Pierce[7], Asa[6], Hannah[5] **Stearns**, Elizabeth[4] **Stone**, Mary[3] **Whipple**, Elder John[2], Matthew[1])[3460] was born in Jeffersonville, Ind. 30 October 1899 and died 11 March 1969 in Charleston, S.C. at 69 years of age. He married **Alice Estella Habden** in Lexington, Ky. 2 September 1927. Alice,[3461] daughter of John Fogg **Habden** and Jean **Slater**, was born in Louisville, Ky. 28 January 1903 and died 5 November 1995 in Spartanburg, S.C. at 92 years of age. Alice earned an A.B. degree from the U. of Kentucky in 1924. Her public service included Chair of the Charleston County Library Board, and Boards of the Charleston County and the South Carolina League of Women Voters. She is Registered as a Democrat.[3462] Girdler received the A.B. degree in 1921 from Translvania College, Lexington, Ky., a M.A. in 1923 from the U. of Chicago, a Ph.D in 1937 from Ohio State, and attended Yale Drama School 1928/29. He taught foreign languages and literature at Transylvania 1923/30, taught at Ohio State 1930/39 and joined the faculty at The Citadel, Charleston, S.C. in 1939 where he became a full professor. He was honorary consul for Uruguay in Charleston 1942/56 and served in the student army training corps during WWI. He was a member of the Episcopal Church.

Girdler Brent **Fitch** and Alice Estella **Habden** had the following children:

2929   i. Lewis Thomas[13] **Fitch**.

+ 2930   ii. Nancy Marian **Fitch** was born 28 June 1936.

2592. Beatrice Nancy[12] **Hastings** (Elmer William[11], Almon Woodward[10], Susan[9] **Goddard**, Enoch Elbert[8], Ebenezer[7], Nathan[6], Edward[5], Susanna[4] **Stone**, Mary[3] **Whipple**, Elder John[2], Matthew[1])[3463] was born in Jefferson, Greene Co., Iowa 21 January 1920 and married **Dean Alan Billigmeier** in San Francisco., Calif. 18 July 1959. Dean,[3464] son of Henry **Billigmeier** and Meta **Masuger**, was born in McClusky, N. Dak. 10 October 1920. He married (2) **Susan (__)**.

Beatrice Nancy **Hastings** and Dean Alan **Billigmeier** had the following child:

2931   i. Scott Dean[13] **Billigmeier** was born in San Rafael, Marin Co., Calif. 9 September 1961 and married Jessica Marion **Bradley**, daughter of Samuel Arthur **Bradley** and Ivy Mabel **Allen**. She was was born in Gorefield, Cambs, England 11 April 1957.[3465]

2599. Frances Harriet[12] **Goddard** (George Francis[11], George Osmer[10], John Bailey[9], Robert[8], Nahum[7], Robert[6], Edward[5], Susanna[4] **Stone**, Mary[3] **Whipple**, Elder John[2], Matthew[1])[3466] was born in Hartford, S. Dak. 17 December 1917 and married **Bryce Jay Stevens** in Hollywood, Calif. in 1941 After graduation from the Pierson, Iowa high school in 1936, Frances became a bookkeeper at Farmers Savings Bank in Pierson until 1940 when she joined Woodbury County Savings Bank at Sioux City, Iowa. After her marriage, she was employed by the Security Bank and Surety Savings and Loan in Burbank, Calif. She later became a vice president, managing the loan processing department, of the Valley Federal

Savings and Loan in Van Nuys, Calif.

Frances Harriet **Goddard** and Bryce Jay **Stevens** had the following children:

+ 2932   i.   Cheryl Maureen[13] **Stevens** was born 4 March 1945.
+ 2933   ii.   Diane Eileen **Stevens** was born 25 April 1948.
   2934   iii.   Jeffrey Jay **Stevens**[3467] was born in California 29 August 1953 and died 15 November 1978 at 25 years of age.

2600. Jean Doris[12] Goddard (George Francis[11], George Osmer[10], John Bailey[9], Robert[8], Nahum[7], Robert[6], Edward[5], Susanna[4] **Stone**, Mary[3] **Whipple**, Elder John[2], Matthew[1])[3468] was born in Sioux Falls, S. Dak. 10 March 1920 and married three times. (1) **Bill Hardie**. (2) **Harold Reinking** in 1938. (3) **Walter Ploen** in 1970.

Jean Doris **Goddard** and Harold **Reinking** had the following children:

+ 2935   i.   Judith Ann[13] **Reinking** was born 18 June 1939.
+ 2936   ii.   Karen Jean **Reinking** was born 7 May 1942.

2601. Helen Maurine[12] Goddard (George Francis[11], George Osmer[10], John Bailey[9], Robert[8], Nahum[7], Robert[6], Edward[5], Susanna[4] **Stone**, Mary[3] **Whipple**, Elder John[2], Matthew[1])[3469] was born in Colton, S. Dak. 22 February 1921 and married **Russel John Sobieski** 2 March 1940.

Helen Maurine **Goddard** and Russel John **Sobieski** had the following children:

+ 2937   i.   Russel Allen[13] **Sobieski** was born 29 December 1940.
+ 2938   ii.   Gary Lee **Sobieski** was born 13 May 1942.
+ 2939   iii.   Linda Maurine **Sobieski** was born 21 February 1954.

2602. Donald Wray[12] Goddard (George Francis[11], George Osmer[10], John Bailey[9], Robert[8], Nahum[7], Robert[6], Edward[5], Susanna[4] **Stone**, Mary[3] **Whipple**, Elder John[2], Matthew[1])[3470] was born in Madison, S. Dak. 8 April 1925 and married twice. (1) **Joyce (__)**. (2) **Luette Baugous**.

Donald Wray **Goddard** and Luette **Baugous** had the following children:

+ 2940   i.   Dennis Wray[13] **Goddard** was born 12 July 1949.
   2941   ii.   Roger Lynn **Goddard**[3471] was born 23 June 1953.
   2942   iii.   Michael Lee **Goddard** was born 11 March 1956.

2603. Marjorie Arlene[12] Goddard (George Francis[11], George Osmer[10], John Bailey[9], Robert[8], Nahum[7], Robert[6], Edward[5], Susanna[4] **Stone**, Mary[3] **Whipple**, Elder John[2], Matthew[1])[3472] was born in Esmond, Kingsbury Co., S. Dak. 25 January 1927 and married **David Olander**.

Marjorie Arlene **Goddard** and David **Olander** had the following children:

+ 2943   i.   Sandra Jean[13] **Olander** was born 28 December 1946.
+ 2944   ii.   Bethel **Olander** was born 10 November 1948.
+ 2945   iii.   David John **Olander** was born 6 June 1951.
+ 2946   iv.   Paul Carney **Olander** was born 12 April 1953.

2604. Dean Alan[12] Goddard (George Francis[11], George Osmer[10], John Bailey[9], Robert[8], Nahum[7], Robert[6], Edward[5], Susanna[4] **Stone**, Mary[3] **Whipple**, Elder John[2], Matthew[1])[3473] was born in Esmond, Kingsbury Co., S. Dak. 18 March 1928 and died 10 April 1991 at 63 years of age. He married **Carlyn Clark**.

Dean Alan **Goddard** and Carlyn **Clark** had the following children:

+ 2947   i.   Dawn Maurine[13] **Goddard** was born 2 December 1950.
+ 2948   ii.   Alan Clark **Goddard** was born 7 February 1953.
   2949   iii.   Kerry Lynne **Goddard**[3474] was born 8 November 1957 and married (_) **Coverly**.
+ 2950   iv.   Robert Wray **Goddard** was born 16 March 1960.

2605. Kenneth Charles[12] **Goddard** (George Francis[11], George Osmer[10], John Bailey[9], Robert[8], Nahum[7], Robert[6], Edward[5], Susanna[4] **Stone**, Mary[3] **Whipple**, Elder John[2], Matthew[1])[3475] was born in Esmond, Kingsbury Co., S. Dak. 19 October 1929 and married **Leona Anderson**.

Kenneth Charles **Goddard** and Leona **Anderson** had the following children:

   2951   i.   Cynthia Lee[13] **Goddard**[3476] was born 16 March 1954 and died 26 March 1954 at 10 days of age.
   2952   ii.   Scot Alan **Goddard**[3477] was born 26 August 1957.
   2953   iii.   Lori Kay **Goddard**[3478] was born 8 March 1959 and died 18 December 1966 at 7 years of age.
   2954   iv.   Gene Francis **Goddard**[3479] was born 29 September 1959.

2606. Verda Joann[12] **Goddard** (George Francis[11], George Osmer[10], John Bailey[9], Robert[8], Nahum[7], Robert[6], Edward[5], Susanna[4] **Stone**, Mary[3] **Whipple**, Elder John[2], Matthew[1])[3480] was born in Esmond, Kingsbury Co., S. Dak. 18 December 1930 and married **Donald Heise**.

Verda Joann **Goddard** and Donald **Heise** had the following children:

+ 2955   i.   Linda Jean[13] **Heise** was born 4 December 1949.
+ 2956   ii.   Keryl Anne **Heise** was born 13 May 1952.
+ 2957   iii.   Donna Jo **Heise** was born 27 February 1954.
+ 2958   iv.   Kathryn Marie **Heise** was born 30 August 1955.
+ 2959   v.   Douglas Dean **Heise** was born 12 March 1957.
+ 2960   vi.   Mary Ann **Heise** was born 27 October 1958.
+ 2961   vii.   Stephen Kent **Heise** was born 7 October 1960.
+ 2962   viii.   Robert John **Heise** was born 5 December 1961.
+ 2963   ix.   Nancy Jean **Heise** was born 19 June 1963.
+ 2964   x.   Karen Maureen **Heise** was born 26 August 1964.
+ 2965   xi.   Philip Ray **Heise** was born 10 April 1966.
+ 2966   xii.   Timothy Paul **Heise** was born 22 December 1967.

2607. Bethel Beryl[12] **Goddard** (George Francis[11], George Osmer[10], John Bailey[9], Robert[8], Nahum[7], Robert[6], Edward[5], Susanna[4] **Stone**, Mary[3] **Whipple**, Elder John[2], Matthew[1])[3481] was born in Pierson, Iowa 5 May 1932 and married **Harold Nystrom**.

Bethel Beryl **Goddard** and Harold **Nystrom** had the following children:

   2967   i.   Debra Kay[13] **Nystrom**[3482] was born 4 September 1952 and died the day after birth.
+ 2968   ii.   Harold Kenneth **Nystrom** Jr. was born 6 October 1953.
+ 2969   iii.   Pamela Beth **Nystrom** was born 9 November 1955.
+ 2970   iv.   Theresa Jean **Nystrom** was born 26 October 1956.
+ 2971   v.   Peggy Sue **Nystrom** was born 25 January 1958.
+ 2972   vi.   Toni Corrine **Nystrom** was born 27 March 1961.

2608. **Beverly Joy**[12] **Goddard** (George Francis[11], George Osmer[10], John Bailey[9], Robert[8], Nahum[7], Robert[6], Edward[5], Susanna[4] **Stone**, Mary[3] **Whipple**, Elder John[2], Matthew[1])[3483] was born in Pierson, Iowa 28 October 1933 and married **Richard Edward Gaber** in Rhinelander, Wisc. 30 June 1951. Richard,[3484] son of Frank Edward **Gaber** and Clara Sadie **Villiesse**, was born in Rhinelander 26 January 1930. He was a Wisconsin State patrol officer, chief of police at Washburn, Wisc., owned a video store, and a real estate firm. Beverly had a varied career. She worked as a secretary , paralegal, real estate sales agent, owned a knit shop, and was clerk of courts in Bayfield Co., Wisc.

Beverly Joy **Goddard** and Richard Edward **Gaber** had the following children:

+ 2973   i.   Richard Francis[13] **Gaber** was born 5 February 1952.
+ 2974   ii.   Denise Eileen **Gaber** was born 28 February 1953.
+ 2975   iii.   Brian Keith **Gaber** was born 30 January 1955.
   2976   iv.   Donald Howand **Gaber**[3485] was born in Wausau, Wisc. 25 August 1959 and married Laurie **Zehe**.
+ 2977   v.   Thomas Stanley **Gaber** was born 27 March 1962.
+ 2978   vi.   Kurt Erwin **Gaber** was born 16 March 1965.

2618. **Patricia Ann**[12] **Scott** (Mary Virginia[11] **Goddard**, Clarence Ryan[10], Edwin Nathan[9], George[8], Capt. Nathan[7], Nathan[6], Benjamin[5], Susanna[4] **Stone**, Mary[3] **Whipple**, Elder John[2], Matthew[1])[3486] was born in Deland, Valusia Co., Fla. 30 August 1942 and married **William Frederick Long** in Beaufort, S.C. 9 April 1964.

Patricia Ann **Scott** and William Frederick **Long** had the following children:

   2979   i.   Gregory Scott[13] **Long**[3487]
   2980   ii.   Bambi Denise **Long**[3488] died young.
   2981   iii.   Patrice Danielle **Long**[3489].

2619. **Cricket Annie Rae**[12] **Scott** (Mary Virginia[11] **Goddard**, Clarence Ryan[10], Edwin Nathan[9], George[8], Capt. Nathan[7], Nathan[6], Benjamin[5], Susanna[4] **Stone**, Mary[3] **Whipple**, Elder John[2], Matthew[1])[3490] was born in Miami, Dade Co., Fla. 12 November 1943 and married **Phillip Clinton Platt** in December 1961.

Cricket Annie Rae **Scott** and Phillip Clinton **Platt** had the following child:

   2982   i.   Parrish Christopher[13] **Platt**[3491].

2620. **June Darleen**[12] **Scott** (Mary Virginia[11] **Goddard**, Clarence Ryan[10], Edwin Nathan[9], George[8], Capt. Nathan[7], Nathan[6], Benjamin[5], Susanna[4] **Stone**, Mary[3] **Whipple**, Elder John[2], Matthew[1])[3492] was born in Vero Beach, Indian River Co., Fla. 14 May 1947 and married twice. (1) **William Brian Tegreeny** 4 December 1965. They were divorced in 1970. (2) **Ronald Chris Brown** in Kingsport, Sullivan Co., Tenn. 12 June 1976. Ronald,[3493] son of John Harding **Brown** and Lillian Loraine **Lingenfelter**, was born in Knoxville, Tenn. 17 December 1949.

June Darleen **Scott** and William Brian **Tegreeny** had the following child:

   2983   i.   Wendy Caprice[13] **Tegreeny**[3494] was born in Cocoa Beach, Fla. 2 April 1967 and married Craig Stephen **Quinn** in Ft. Lauderdale, Fla. 25 November 1989.

June Darleen **Scott** and Ronald Chris **Brown** had the following child:

   2984   ii.   Kathleen Alicia **Brown**[3495] was born 29 July 1987.

2622. **Edwin Goddard**[12] **Scott** (Mary Virginia[11] **Goddard**, Clarence Ryan[10], Edwin Nathan[9], George[8], Capt. Nathan[7], Nathan[6], Benjamin[5], Susanna[4] **Stone**, Mary[3] **Whipple**, Elder John[2], Matthew[1])[3496] was born in Vero Beach, Indian River Co., Fla. 15 January 1954 and married **Tracey Webster** in Jupiter, Fla. 7 March 1987.

Edwin Goddard **Scott** and Tracey **Webster** had the following child:
    2985   i.   Trevor Goddard[13] **Scott**[3497].

2623. **LeGrande**[12] **Young** (Scott Richmond[11], Carlie Louine[10] **Clawson**, Emily Augusta[9] **Young**, Brigham[8], Abigail (Nabby)[7] **Howe**, Susanna[6] **Goddard**, Ebenezer[5], Susanna[4] **Stone**, Mary[3] **Whipple**, Elder John[2], Matthew[1])[3498] birth date unknown, married **Sherry Steed**.

LeGrande **Young** and Sherry **Steed** had the following children:
    2986   i.   Michael[13] **Young**[3499].
    2987   ii.   Thomas **Young**[3500].
    2988   iii.   Melissa **Young**[3501].
    2989   iv.   James **Young**[3502].
    2990   v.   Jon Steven (Steve) **Young**[3503] was born in Salt Lake City, Utah 11 October 1961. He was the award-winning quarterback of the San Francisco '49er professional football team.

2626. **Milon Stone**[12] **Christman** (Sarah Mary (Mai)[11] **Stone**, Milon Gardner[10], Marshall Maynard[9], Col. Jonathan[8], Lt. Jonathan[7], Jonathan[6], Jonathan[5], Jonathan[4], Mary[3] **Whipple**, Elder John[2], Matthew[1])[3504] was born in Spartanburg, S.C. 30 August 1895 and died there 28 August 1966 at 70 years of age. He married **Virginia Pickney Jennings** in Spartanburg 21 July 1917. Virginia,[3505] daughter of Henry Burritt **Jennings** and Martha Glen **Reeves**, was born in Charleston, S.C. 19 October 1895 and died 1 April 1981 in Spartanburg at 85 years of age.

Milon Stone **Christman** and Virginia Pickney **Jennings** had the following children:
  + 2991   i.   Virginia Jennings[13] **Christman** was born 21 April 1919.
  + 2992   ii.   Milon Stone **Christman** Jr. was born 29 August 1920.

2627. **Bennie Scurry**[12] **Stone** (Marshall Christman[11], Milon Gardner[10], Marshall Maynard[9], Col. Jonathan[8], Lt. Jonathan[7], Jonathan[6], Jonathan[5], Jonathan[4], Mary[3] **Whipple**, Elder John[2], Matthew[1])[3506] was born in Gainesville, Ga. 27 April 1923 and married twice. (1) **Marion Littleton Meeks** in Gainesville, Ga. 24 May 1944. Marion,[3507] son of Jesse Littleton **Meeks** and Ione **Tumlin**, was born in Gainesville 1 October 1923. They were divorced in Cambridge, Mass. in June 1970. (2) **Vladimir Larj** in Waltham, Middlesex Co., Mass. 25 June 1971. Vladimir was born in Uzhorod, Czechoslavakia and died 7 August 1985 in Waltham, Middlesex Co., Mass.[3508] They were divorced in Cambridge in June 1980

Bennie Scurry **Stone** and Marion Littleton **Meeks** had the following children:
  + 2993   i.   Marshall Stone[13] **Meeks** was born 27 December 1947.
  + 2994   ii.   Fleming Littleton **Meeks** was born 15 June 1951.
  + 2995   iii.   Marion Littleton **Meeks** Jr. was born 5 May 1955.

2628. **Marshall Christman**[12] **Stone Jr.** (Marshall Christman[11], Milon

Gardner[10], Marshall Maynard[9], Col. Jonathan[8], Lt. Jonathan[7], Jonathan[6], Jonathan[5], Jonathan[4], Mary[3] **Whipple**, Elder John[2], Matthew[1])[3509] was born in Spartanburg, S.C. 25 April 1927 and married twice. (1) **Edith Elizabeth Hemeter** in Hattiesburg, Miss. 24 May 1952. Betty was born in Hattiesburg 2 June 1926 and and died 2 March 1989 at 62 years of age.[3510] They were divorced before 1984. (2) **Amanda Marie (Hayes) Lanford** in Spartanburg in 1984.[3511]

Marshall Christman **Stone** Jr. and Edith Elizabeth **Hemeter** had the following children:

+ 2996   i.   Elizabeth Leighton[13] **Stone** was born 10 April 1953.
2997   ii.   Marshall Christman **Stone** III[3512] was born in Spartanburg 6 February 1955 and married Krista **Sifter** in Atlanta, Ga. 16 October 1993. Krista, daughter of George David **Sifter** and Gay Ann **Nissen**, was born in Philadelphia, Penn. 24 October 1968.[3513]
2998   iii.   Ben Maxwell **Stone**[3514] was born in Spartanburg 17 August 1958.

2631. Albert Henry[12] **Makee** (Mary Alice[11] **Perry**, Mary Jane[10] **Billings**, Hiram[9], Joel[8], John[7], Joanna[6] **Norton**, John[5], Mary[4] **Goodhue**, Sarah[3] **Whipple**, Elder John[2], Matthew[1])[3515] was born in LaPorte City, Black Hawk Co., Iowa 11 October 1873 and died 2 October 1951 in Noonan, Divide Co., N. Dak. at 77 years of age. He married **Ida Caroline Carlson** in Oxbow, Assinoibia Territory, Saskatchewan, Canada 2 May 1898. She was born in Winnipeg, Canada 5 May 1880 and died 12 April 1939 in Noonan at 58 years of age. Her parentage is unknown. She was adopted by the Carlson family.[3516] Albert and Ida were buried in Lakeview Cemetery in Kenmare, Ward Co., N. Dak.

Albert Henry **Makee** and Ida Caroline **Carlson** had the following children:

2999   i.   William Perry[13] **Makee**[3517] was born in Portal, Burke Co., N. Dak. 8 May 1898 and died 27 September 1918 in Varennes, France at 20 years of age during WWI. He was buried in Lakeview Cemetery in Kenmare.
3000   ii.   Lendall Billlings **Makee**[3518] was born in LaPorte City, Iowa 29 November 1900 and died died 22 April 1968 in Umatilla, Umatilla Co., Oreg. at 67 years of age. He married twice. (1) Evaline **Giles** in North Dakota abt 1920. (2) Hettie (__).
3001   iii.   Albert Fayette **Makee**[3519] was born in Portal 19 October 1902 and died 15 December 1963 in Estevan, Saskatchewan, Canada at 61 years of age. He was buried in the Zion Luthern Cemetery in Noonan. He married twice. (1) Cora **Heitman**. (2) Florence **Melby** 4 August 1934. She was buried in Zion Luthern Cemetery. [3520]
+ 3002   iv.   Mary Esther **Makee** was born 13 July 1904.

2635. Delone[12] **Fuchs** (Ella Lovenia[11] **Mecham**, Luman Lehi[10], Joseph L.[9], Sarah[8] **Basford**, Jonathan[7], Elizabeth[6] **Goodhue**, Jonathan[5], William[4], Sarah[3] **Whipple**, Elder John[2], Matthew[1])[3521] was born in Paris, Bear Lake Co., Idaho 2 April 1922 and married twice. (1) **Albert Frederick Mohr** in Salt Lake City, Utah 28 July 1944. (2) **Lorin Tueller Schoss** 31 May 1968. Lorin,[3522] son of Fred William **Schoss** and Viola **Tueller**, was born in Geneva, Bear Lake Co., Idaho 10 March 1919.

Delone **Fuchs** and Albert Frederick **Mohr** had the following children:

3003   i.   Albert Jerald[13] **Mohr**[3523] was born in Brigham, Utah 3 January 1946 and married Sandra **Johnson** in Salt Lake City 30 March 1973.
3004   ii.   Janice Carol **Mohr**[3524] was born in Chicago, Ill. 25 December 1946 and

married Gary Leon **High** in Ogden, Weber Co., Utah 3 January 1969. Gary,[3525] son of Leon Jesse **High** and Mildred **Brown**, was born in Yreka, Calif. 31 July 1947.

3005   iii.   Keith Russell **Mohr**[3526] was born in Ogden 10 August 1953.

2636. Ruth Mae[12] **Fuchs** (Ella Lovenia[11] **Mecham**, Luman Lehi[10], Joseph L.[9], Sarah[8] **Basford**, Jonathan[7], Elizabeth[6] **Goodhue**, Jonathan[5], William[4], Sarah[3] **Whipple**, Elder John[2], Matthew[1])[3527] was born in Paris, Bear Lake Co., Idaho 3 September 1924 and married twice. (1) **Eldon Leon Eliason** in Paris 23 November 1942. Eldon,[3528] son of Frederick L. **Eliason**, was born in Ogden, Utah 23 July 1914 (2) **James Lavere Hill** in Salt Lake City, Utah 22 October 1949.[3529]

Ruth Mae **Fuchs** and Eldon Leon **Eliason** had the following child:
+ 3006   i.   Ronald Brent[13] **Eliason** was born 2 February 1944.

Ruth Mae **Fuchs** and James Lavere **Hill** had the following children:
+ 3007   ii.   Paul James **Hill** was born 13 July 1950.
3008   iii.   Glenn Brian **Hill**[3530] was born in Murray, Utah 7 July 1955.
3009   iv.   Shana Diane **Hill**[3531] was born in Utah 17 October 1960.

2637. Arda[12] **Fuchs** (Ella Lovenia[11] **Mecham**, Luman Lehi[10], Joseph L.[9], Sarah[8] **Basford**, Jonathan[7], Elizabeth[6] **Goodhue**, Jonathan[5], William[4], Sarah[3] **Whipple**, Elder John[2], Matthew[1])[3532] was born in Paris, Bear Lake Co., Idaho 5 May 1927 and married **Woodruff Ballard Pollock** in Las Vegas, Clark Co., Nev. 4 June 1945. Woodruff,[3533] son of Loran **Pollock** and Maggie **Johnson**, was born in Tropic, Garfield Co., Utah 3 April 1922.

Arda **Fuchs** and Woodruff Ballard **Pollock** had the following children:
3010   i.   Dale Bruce[13] **Pollock**[3534] was born in Ogden, Weber Co., Utah 18 May 1948 and married Shauna Mai **Gibson** in St George, Wahn Co., Utah 5 December 1970.
3011   ii.   Sharon Lorraine **Pollock**[3535] was born in Las Vegas, 11 February 1951 and married Robert Milton **Thomas** 20 November 1971.
3012   iii.   Lynn Ray **Pollock**[3536] was born in Las Vegas 14 March 1953.

2646. Verla Eurilla[12] **Rich** (Mary Eurilla[11] **Mecham**, Luman Lehi[10], Joseph L.[9], Sarah[8] **Basford**, Jonathan[7], Elizabeth[6] **Goodhue**, Jonathan[5], William[4], Sarah[3] **Whipple**, Elder John[2], Matthew[1])[3537] was born in Afton, Wyo. 22 May 1920 and married **Thomas Franklin Murphy** in Logan, Cache Co., Utah 7 May 1940. Thomas was born in Grovont, Teton Co., Wyo. 22 October 1913[3538]

Verla Eurilla **Rich** and Thomas Franklin **Murphy** had the following children:
+ 3013   i.   Rich Eugene[13] **Murphy** was born 4 June 1942.
+ 3014   ii.   Cheryl Kay **Murphy** was born 22 April 1944.
+ 3015   iii.   Marva Dene **Murphy** was born 29 May 1948.

2647. Doyle Hyrum[12] **Rich** (Mary Eurilla[11] **Mecham**, Luman Lehi[10], Joseph L.[9], Sarah[8] **Basford**, Jonathan[7], Elizabeth[6] **Goodhue**, Jonathan[5], William[4], Sarah[3] **Whipple**, Elder John[2], Matthew[1])[3539] was born in Afton, Wyo. 25 March 1923 and married twice. (1) **Norma Jean Packard** in Logan, Cache Co., Utah 22 September 1942. Norma was born in Kuna, Ada Co., Idaho 19 May 1925.[3540] (2) **Lillian Loveland** in Idaho Falls, Idaho, 27 February 1947. Lillian was born in Chesterfield,

Caribou Co., Idaho 29 May 1921.[3541]

Doyle Hyrum **Rich** and Norma Jean **Packard** had the following child:

+ 3016   i.   Sharon LaRay[13] **Rich** was born 5 September 1943.

Doyle Hyrum **Rich** and Lillian **Loveland** had the following children:

+ 3017   ii.   Rhonda Lee **Rich** was born 11 February 1949.
+ 3018   iii. JoAnn **Rich** was born 9 May 1952.
+ 3019   iv. Marsha Lynn **Rich** was born 14 July 1953.
+ 3020   v.   Mark Hyrum **Rich** was born 11 October 1956.

2648. **Lavell Mecham**[12] **Rich** (Mary Eurilla[11] **Mecham**, Luman Lehi[10], Joseph L.[9], Sarah[8] **Basford**, Jonathan[7], Elizabeth[6] **Goodhue**, Jonathan[5], William[4], Sarah[3] **Whipple**, Elder John[2], Matthew[1])[3542] was born in Afton, Wyo. 6 October 1925 and married **Imogene Lindsay** in Logan, Cache Co., Utah 21 September 1950. Imogene,[3543] daughter of Hyrum Lester **Lindsay** and Vara **Mouritsen**, was born in Bennington, Bear Lake Co., Idaho 21 September 1925.

Lavell Mecham **Rich** and Imogene **Lindsay** had the following children:

+ 3021   i.   Lester Lavell[13] **Rich** was born 1 July 1951.
+ 3022   ii.   Ardeana Jean **Rich** was born 4 April 1953.
+ 3023   iii. Robert Wayne **Rich** was born 9 March 1955.
+ 3024   iv. Boyd Lindsay **Rich** was born 28 July 1956.

2649. **Byron Joy**[12] **Wilson** (Mary Eurilla[11] **Mecham**, Luman Lehi[10], Joseph L.[9], Sarah[8] **Basford**, Jonathan[7], Elizabeth[6] **Goodhue**, Jonathan[5], William[4], Sarah[3] **Whipple**, Elder John[2], Matthew[1])[3544] was born in Jackson, Wyo. 2 February 1931 and married **Elizabeth Jane Rauback** in West Frankfort, Franklin Co., Ill. 12 June 1958. Elizabeth was born in West Frankfort 1 August 1936.[3545]

Byron Joy **Wilson** and Elizabeth Jane **Rauback** had the following children:

3025   i.   Lee David[13] **Wilson**[3546] was born in Seattle, Wash. 2 December 1960.
3026   ii.   Bruce Eric **Wilson**[3547] was born in Nashville, Tenn. 22 March 1962.
+ 3027   iii. Ross Evan **Wilson** was born 7 August 1963.
+ 3028   iv. Kathleen **Wilson** was born 5 June 1965.
3029   v.   Kevin Wade **Wilson**[3548] was born in Provo, Utah Co., Utah 14 December 1968 and married Audrey **Davis** in Salt Lake City, Utah 19 July 1991. Audrey was born 9 July 1971.[3549]
3030   vi. Reed Owen **Wilson**[3550] was born in Provo 28 May 1971 and married Geneal **Woods** there 7 June 1996. Geneal was born in Provo 10 July 1976. [3551]
3031   vii. Jennifer **Wilson**[3552] was born in Provo 5 May 1975.

2650. **Dean Ervin**[12] **Wilson** (Mary Eurilla[11] **Mecham**, Luman Lehi[10], Joseph L.[9], Sarah[8] **Basford**, Jonathan[7], Elizabeth[6] **Goodhue**, Jonathan[5], William[4], Sarah[3] **Whipple**, Elder John[2], Matthew[1])[3553] was born in Jackson, Wyo. 9 November 1932 and married **Karen Marie Gundestrup** in Los Angeles, Calif. 30 December 1961. Karen,[3554] daughter of Frank William **Gundestrup** and Elaine **Hiatt**, was born in Vacaville, Calif. 4 July 1941

Dean Ervin **Wilson** and Karen Marie **Gundestrup** had the following children:

+ 3032   i.   Brent Ervin[13] **Wilson** was born 23 April 1963.
3033   ii.   Frank Edward **Wilson**[3555] was born in Nampa, Canyon Co., Idaho 28 May 1964.

+ 3034   iii. Christina Marie **Wilson** was born 2 December 1966.

   3035   iv. Todd Evan **Wilson**[3556] was born in Portland, Multnomah Co., Oreg. 2 March 1970.

2651. Derald Mecham[12] **Boyce** (Dora Artenchia[11] **Mecham**, Luman Lehi[10], Joseph L.[9], Sarah[8] **Basford**, Jonathan[7], Elizabeth[6] **Goodhue**, Jonathan[5], William[4], Sarah[3] **Whipple**, Elder John[2], Matthew[1])[3557] was born in Lovell, Wyo. 30 June 1925 and married twice. (1) **Arlene Shultz**.[3558] (2) **Bertie Ellen Holmes** in Salt Lake City, Utah. Bertie,[3559] daughter of Frank L. **Holmes** and Norma Maria **Philips**, was born 19 October 1926.

    Derald Mecham **Boyce** and Bertie Ellen **Holmes** had the following children:

+ 3036   i. Patricia Lynne[13] **Boyce** was born 22 September 1950.
   3037   ii. David Derald **Boyce**[3560] was born in Provo, Utah Co., Utah 9 July 1952 and married Shauna Lee **Pebley**. Shauna[3561] is the daughter of Victor E. **Pebley**.
   3038   iii. Craig Allen **Boyce**[3562] was born in Inglewood, Calif. 18 December 1954 and married Jan **Clark** in Oakland, Calif, 21 August 1976. Jan is the daughter of Jack W. **Clark**.[3563]
   3039   iv. Kevin **Boyce**[3564] was born in Torrance, Calif. 27 February 1958 and married Julia **Clark** in Oakland, Calif. 14 June 1980.

2652. Grant Mecham[12] **Boyce** (Dora Artenchia[11] **Mecham**, Luman Lehi[10], Joseph L.[9], Sarah[8] **Basford**, Jonathan[7], Elizabeth[6] **Goodhue**, Jonathan[5], William[4], Sarah[3] **Whipple**, Elder John[2], Matthew[1])[3565] was born in Lovell, Wyo. 21 March 1928 and married **Lola Dean Larsen** in Monroe, Utah in 1951. Lola,[3566] daughter of Hans Peter **Larsen** and Ida **Peterson**, was born in Glenwood, Utah 7 October 1929.

    Grant Mecham **Boyce** and Lola Dean **Larsen** had the following children:

   3040   i. Terri Lynne[13] **Boyce**[3567] was born in Salt Lake City, Utah 5 January 1954 and married David L. **Kurill** in Sunset, Weber Co., Utah 17 May 1975. David,[3568] son of Joseph L. **Kurill**, was born in Utah.
+ 3041   ii. Merdene **Boyce** was born 6 April 1957.

2654. Shirley Doris[12] **Boyce** (Dora Artenchia[11] **Mecham**, Luman Lehi[10], Joseph L.[9], Sarah[8] **Basford**, Jonathan[7], Elizabeth[6] **Goodhue**, Jonathan[5], William[4], Sarah[3] **Whipple**, Elder John[2], Matthew[1])[3569] was born in Filer, Jerome Co., Idaho 3 February 1945 and married **Gaylyn W. Bergstrom** in Salt Lake City, Utah 6 January 1966. Gaylyn,[3570] son of Walter Bergstrom and Mary Juanita **Nielson**, was born in Salt Lake City 6 December 1941.

    Shirley Doris **Boyce** and Gaylyn W. **Bergstrom** had the following children:

   3042   i. Destry Leon[13] **Bergstrom**[3571] was born in Denver, Colo. 18 June 1968.
   3043   ii. Katie Sarika **Bergstrom**[3572] was born in India 12 September 1982.

2655. Leora Ann[12] **Mecham** (Lester Eugene[11], Luman Lehi[10], Joseph L.[9], Sarah[8] **Basford**, Jonathan[7], Elizabeth[6] **Goodhue**, Jonathan[5], William[4], Sarah[3] **Whipple**, Elder John[2], Matthew[1])[3573] was born in Butte, Mont. 12 March 1932 and married **Peter Charles Brinig** there 9 July 1950. Peter,[3574] son of Peter **Brinig** and Ann Catharine **Weis**, was born in Butte 23 June 1926 and died there 13 July 1986 at 60 years of age.

Leora Ann **Mecham** and Peter Charles **Brinig** had the following children:

+ 3044   i.   David[13] **Brinig** was born 12 March 1952

  3045   ii.   Paul Thomas **Brinig**[3575] was born in Butte 17 August 1955 and married Denise **Hull** in Billings, Mont. 28 January 1984. Denise,[3576] daughter of William **Hull**, was born in Cody Park, Wyo..

  3046   ii.   Andrew Nathan **Brinig**[3577] was born in Butte, Mont. 28 May 1963.

2656. Melvin Addison[12] **Leonard** (Vivian[11] **Becker**, Mary Melissa[10] **Miller**, Eli[9], Easter[8] **Kimball**, Jesse[7], John[6], Isaac[5], Sarah[4] **Goodhue**, Sarah[3] **Whipple**, Elder John[2], Matthew[1])[3578] was born in 1920 and married **Edna Biggs**. She was born in 1928.[3579]

Melvin Addison **Leonard** and Edna **Biggs** had the following children:

  3047   i.   LaWayne[13] **Leonard**[3580] married Anita **Baca**

  3048   ii.   Stacey **Leonard**[3581] married Michael **Peaters**.

2695. Clark Henry[12] **Miller** (Carl Otis[11], Samuel Martin[10], Elisha D.[9], Easter[8] **Kimball**, Jesse[7], John[6], Isaac[5], Sarah[4] **Goodhue**, Sarah[3] **Whipple**, Elder John[2], Matthew[1])[3582] was born in 1914 and married **Bernice Pauline Wallace**. She was born in 1919.[3583]

Clark Henry **Miller** and Bernice Pauline **Wallace** had the following child:

  3049   i.   Dorothy June[13] **Miller**[3584] was born in 1940 and married Jerald Lee **Hurst**. He was born in 1934.[3585]

2696. Marilyn Kay[12] **Miller** (Madison Theodore[11], Benjamin Franklin[10], Elisha D.[9], Easter[8] **Kimball**, Jesse[7], John[6], Isaac[5], Sarah[4] **Goodhue**, Sarah[3] **Whipple**, Elder John[2], Matthew[1])[3586] was born in 1935 and died in 1987 at 52 years of age. She married (_) **Johnson**.

Marilyn Kay **Miller** and (_) **Johnson** had the following child:

  3050   i.   David[13] **Johnson**[3587].

2697. Marilyn Ann[12] **Mansfield** (Orville Cecil Miller[11], Benjamin Franklin[10] **Miller**, Elisha D.[9], Easter[8] **Kimball**, Jesse[7], John[6], Isaac[5], Sarah[4] **Goodhue**, Sarah[3] **Whipple**, Elder John[2], Matthew[1])[3588] was born in Longton, Elk Co., Kans. 19 November 1926 and married **Leroy Riggs** 1 September 1946. Leroy,[3589] son of William **Riggs** and Berta Josephine **Forester**, was born 25 February 1927.

Marilyn Ann **Mansfield** and Leroy **Riggs** had the following children:

+ 3051   i.   Frances Louise[13] **Riggs** was born 27 June 1947.

+ 3052   ii.   Cynthia Ann **Riggs** was born 16 October 1949.

2698. William Duane[12] **Mansfield** (Orville Cecil Miller[11], Benjamin Franklin[10] **Miller**, Elisha D.[9], Easter[8] **Kimball**, Jesse[7], John[6], Isaac[5], Sarah[4] **Goodhue**, Sarah[3] **Whipple**, Elder John[2], Matthew[1])[3590] was born in Independence, Montgomery Co., Kans. 17 July 1931 and died 14 September 1990 in San Vicente, Baja California, Mexico at 59 years of age. He married **Ramona Contreras** Taylor in Las Vegas, Clark Co., Nev. 1 March 1956. Ramona was born in Sultana, Tulare Co., Calif. 31 August 1930.[3591]

William Duane **Mansfield** and Ramona Contreras **Taylor** had the following children:

+ 3053   i. Karen Lynn[13] **Mansfield** was born 16 July 1957.

3054   ii. Lesly Alana **Mansfield**[3592] was born in Orange, Orange Co., Calif. 11 July 1959 and married Christopher Patrick **Gunz** in Corona Del Mar, Colo. 3 November 1990. Christopher was born in Seattle, Wash. 2 July 1957.[3593]

3055   iii. Jan Marie **Mansfield**[3594] was born in Anaheim, Calif. 30 September 1961 and married Bradley Roland **Garrett** in Las Vegas, Clark Co., Nev. 29 February 1984 (leap year). Bradley was born in Glendale, Calif. 14 September 1960.[3595]

2700. Richard Henry[12] **Grennell** (Blanche May[11] **Tanner**, Mary Elizabeth[10] **Baker**, Ulric Huch[10], Sylvanus Ward[9], Betsey[8] **Ward**, Hannah[7] **Goddard**, Robert[6], Edward[5], Susanna[4] **Stone**, Mary[3] **Whipple**, Elder John[2], Matthew[1])[3596] was born in Gowanda, N.Y. 25 January 1936 and died 4 May 1973 in Ithaca, N.Y. at 37 years of age. He died as a consequence of an auto accident and is buried at Brookdale, N.Y. He married **Helen Jones** in Norwalk, Conn. 10 February 1961. Helen,[3597] daughter of Archie **Jones** and Edna **Fish**, was born 8 February 1940. She married (2) **Edward Shackett** in 1976. They were divorced in 1985.

Richard Henry **Grennell** and Helen **Jones** had the following children:

3056   i. Esther Helen[13] **Grennell**[3598] was born in Nashville, Tenn. 25 January 1962 and married William Edward **Cochell** in Salt Lake City, Utah 29 September 1985

3057   ii. Stephen Wilson **Grennell**[3599] was born in Ithaca, N.Y. 15 July 1963 and married Browyn Marie **Cassidy** in Connecticut 25 June 1988. They were divorced in October 1990.

3058   iii. David Paul **Grennell**[3600] was born in Suffolk, Va. 2 June 1966.

2701. Ruth May[12] **Horton** (Bernice Louise[11] **Tanner**, Mary Elizabeth[10] **Baker**, Ulric Huch[10], Sylvanus Ward[9], Betsey[8] **Ward**, Hannah[7] **Goddard**, Robert[6], Edward[5], Susanna[4] **Stone**, Mary[3] **Whipple**, Elder John[2], Matthew[1])[3601] was born 4 August 1927 and married **Henry G. Metzler** in Eden, Erie Co., N.Y. 4 September 1948. Henry,[3602] son of Charles D. **Metzler** and Ottillia **Kieffer**, was born in Lackawanna, Erie Co., N.Y. 14 May 1927.

Ruth May **Horton** and Henry G. **Metzler** had the following children:

3059   i. Kathleen Ruth[13] **Metzler**[3603] was born in Peoria, Ill. 18 June 1949 and married Ross James **Bower** in Canberra, Australia 12 December 1968.

3060   ii. Ronald Charles **Metzler**[3604] was born in Peoria 6 December 1951 and married L Linda **Godfrey** in Rochester, Monroe Co., N.Y. 25 September 1976.

3061   iii. Janice Anne **Metzler**[3605] was born in Wilmington, Clinton Co., Ohio 19 February 1953 and married Neil W. **Comstra** in Rochester 19 July 1975.

3062   iv. Margaret Lynn **Metzler**[3606] was born in Wilmington 7 April 1955 and married Donald G. **Mauer** in Rochester 11 September 1982.

2702. Dorothy Marietta[12] **Horton** (Bernice Louise[11] **Tanner**, Mary Elizabeth[10] **Baker**, Ulric Huch[10], Sylvanus Ward[9], Betsey[8] **Ward**, Hannah[7] **Goddard**, Robert[6], Edward[5], Susanna[4] **Stone**, Mary[3] **Whipple**, Elder John[2], Matthew[1])[3607] was born in Eden, Erie Co., N.Y. 20 March 1930 and married **Maynard Lester Clapp** there 27 June 1951. Maynard,[3608] son of Lester Lincoln **Clapp** and Margaret Pearl **Valentine**, was born 19 December 1927.

Dorothy Marietta **Horton** and Maynard Lester **Clapp** had the following children:

> 3063   i.   Daniel Wayne[13] **Clapp**[3609] was born in San Benito, Texas 22 November 1952 and married Susan **Kaemer** 15 October 1971.
>
> 3064   ii.   Kenneth James **Clapp**[3610] was born 12 June 1954 and married Kathy Ford **Thompson** in Texas 28 August 1987.
>
> 3065   iii   Thomas George **Clapp**[3611] was born 2 January 1958 and married Patricia **Rollison** in Houston, Texas 23 July 1977.

2703. **Marvin Morris**[12] **Horton** (Bernice Louise[11] **Tanner**, Mary Elizabeth[10] **Baker**, Ulric Huch[10], Sylvanus Ward[9], Betsey[8] **Ward**, Hannah[7] **Goddard**, Robert[6], Edward[5], Susanna[4] **Stone**, Mary[3] **Whipple**, Elder John[2], Matthew[1])[3612] was born in Angola, Erie Co., N.Y. 11 August 1940 and married **Patricia Lee** in Seoul, Korea 3 December 1965. Patricia was born in Mak Po, Korea 22 January 1941.[3613]

Marvin Morris **Horton** and Patricia **Lee** had the following children:

> 3066   i.   Sharon Lee[13] **Horton**[3614] was born 30 December 1968.
>
> 3067   ii.   Lisa Lynn **Horton**[3615] was born 12 January 1972.

2704. **Patricia Andrea**[12] **Thayer** (Viola Beal[11] **Smith**, Viola Maud[10] **Thompson**, Affalona Galia[9] **Fausett**, Julia Ann[8] **Stevens**, Roswell[7], Hepsibah[6] **Kilham**, Abigail[5] **Kimball**, Sarah[4] **Goodhue**, Sarah[3] **Whipple**, Elder John[2], Matthew[1])[3616] was born in Alturas, Modoc Co., Calif. 11 July 1946 and married **Donald Philip Munro** in Lakeview, Lake Co., Oreg. 26 August 1967. Donald,[3617] son of Dorth Paulum **Muno** and Vera Marie **Blackiston**, was born in Oregon City, Clackamas Co., Oreg. 9 October 1944.

Patricia Andrea **Thayer** and Donald Philip **Munro** had the following children:

> 3068   i.   Brent Paul[13] **Munro**[3618] was born in Seaside, Clatsop Co., Oreg. 26 August 1970.
>
> 3069   ii.   Bethany Nanette **Munro**[3619] was born in Oregon City 7 October 1973.
>
> 3070   iii.   Nathan Reed **Munro**[3620] was born in Oregon City 4 July 1976.
>
> 3071   iv.   Todd Clifford **Munro**[3621] was born in Klamath Falls, Klamath Co., Oreg. 10 July 1979.

2705. **Dennis**[12] **Day** (Alice LuZella[11] **Jones**, Maiben Stevens[10], Marinda Alice[9] **Stevens**, William[8], Roswell[7], Hepsibah[6] **Kilham**, Abigail[5] **Kimball**, Sarah[4] **Goodhue**, Sarah[3] **Whipple**, Elder John[2], Matthew[1])[3622] was born in Idaho Falls, Idaho 1 September 1946 and married twice. (1) **Judith Ann McAlpine** in Stevensville, Mont. 18 June 1968.[3623] They were divorced 19 September 1976. (2) **Joy Elaine Novick** in Twin Bridges, Mont. 14 March 1981.

Dennis **Day** and Judith Ann **McAlpine** had the following children:

> + 3072   i.   Nicole Marie[13] **Day** was born 23 December 1968.
>
> + 3073   ii.   Cory Morgan **Day** was born 16 March 1970.

2707. **Steven R.**[12] **Day** (Alice LuZella[11] **Jones**, Maiben Stevens[10], Marinda Alice[9] **Stevens**, William[8], Roswell[7], Hepsibah[6] **Kilham**, Abigail[5] **Kimball**, Sarah[4] **Goodhue**, Sarah[3] **Whipple**, Elder John[2], Matthew[1])[3624] was born in Idaho Falls, Idaho 24 January 1951 and died 7 April 1983 in Stevensville, Mont. at 32 years of age. He was buried in Victor, Ravali Co., Mont. He married **Elizabeth Skarecki** in Victor 16 June 1979.

Steven R. **Day** and Elizabeth **Skarecki** had the following children:

3074   i.   Sarah Elizabeth[13] **Day**[3625] was born in Missoula, Mont. 6 November 1978.

3075   ii. Evan Steven **Day**[3626] was born in Missoula 7 April 1982.

2708. Cody Delene[12] **Day** (Alice LuZella[11] **Jones**, Maiben Stevens[10], Marinda Alice[9] **Stevens**, William[8], Roswell[7], Hepsibah[6] **Kilham**, Abigail[5] **Kimball**, Sarah[4] **Goodhue**, Sarah[3] **Whipple**, Elder John[2], Matthew[1])[3627] was born in Hamilton, Mont. 1 September 1953 and married **Stuart Raymond Foster** in Salt Lake City, Utah 28 May 1974.

Cody Delene **Day** and Stuart Raymond **Foster** had the following children born in Coeur d'Alene, Idaho:

3076   i.   Monica Ray[13] **Foster**[3628] was born 18 May 1976.

3077   ii. Travis Grant **Foster**[3629] was born 18 October 1978.

3078   iii. Melissa Kay **Foster**[3630] was born 2 November 1984.

2709. Kelly Jean[12] **Day** (Alice LuZella[11] **Jones**, Maiben Stevens[10], Marinda Alice[9] **Stevens**, William[8], Roswell[7], Hepsibah[6] **Kilham**, Abigail[5] **Kimball**, Sarah[4] **Goodhue**, Sarah[3] **Whipple**, Elder John[2], Matthew[1])[3631] was born 26 November 1958 and married twice. (1) **Shane R. Flinders** 17 December 1980. They were divorced in 1981.[3632] (2) **Gordon Roy Levandoske** in Stevensville, Mont. 23 December 1982.

Kelly Jean **Day** and Shane R. **Flinders** had the following child:

3079   i.   Cassandra Rae[13] **Flinders** was born in Hamilton, Mont. 11 November 1981.[3633]

2710. William Ray[12] **Hunter** (Charlotte Georgina[11] **McCabe**, John James[10], Mary[9] **Dickson**, Elizabeth[8] **Upham**, Eleanor[7] **Knowlton**, Daniel[6], Robert[5], Marjory (Margery)[4] **Goodhue**, Sarah[3] **Whipple**, Elder John[2], Matthew[1])[3634] was born in Cristobal, Canal Zone, Panama 24 October 1924 and married **Dorothy G. Edmondson** in Ocala, Fla. 27 July 1949. Dorothy was born in Memphis, Tenn. 26 November 1928.[3635]

William Ray **Hunter** and Dorothy G. **Edmondson** had the following children:

3080   i.   William Robert[13] **Hunter**[3636] was born 16 February 1951 .

3081   ii. Charlotte Elizabeth **Hunter**[3637] was born 4 December 1954.

3082   iii. Edward Allen **Hunter**[3638] was born 13 February 1960.

3083   iv. Laurence McCabe **Hunter**[3639] was born 16 September 1965.

2711. Samuel Phillips[12] **Stevens** (Samuel Stanclift[11], George Gove[10], Nancy Mathilda[9] **Bowers**, Polly[8] **Rand**, Solomon[7], Deborah[6] **Dodge**, Margery[5] **Knowlton**, Marjory (Margery)[4] **Goodhue**, Sarah[3] **Whipple**, Elder John[2], Matthew[1])[3640] was born in Oakland, Calif. 3 May 1918 and married **Mary Elizabeth Allen** in Piedmont, Calif. 19 March 1941. Mary was born in Oakland, Calif. 18 November 1918.[3641]

Samuel Phillips **Stevens** and Mary Elizabeth **Allen** had the following children:

3084   i.   Elizabeth Sharon[13] **Stevens**[3642] was born in Oakland, Calif. 14

February 1942.

+ 3085   ii.   Samuel Stanclift **Stevens** II was born 11 May 1945.

+ 3086   iii.   Martha Stuart **Stevens** was born 2 December 1947.

     3087   iv.   Anne Phillips **Stevens**[3643] was born in Oakland 5 February 1955.

2712. Cynthia[12] **Coolidge** (John[11], Pres. John Calvin[11], Victoria Josephine[10] **Moor**, Abigail[9] **Franklin**, Luther[8], Sarah[7] **Starr**, Capt. Comfort[6], Comfort[5], Mary[4] **Stone**, Mary[3] **Whipple**, Elder John[2], Matthew[1])[3644] was born in New Haven, Conn. 28 October 1933 and married **S. Edward Jeter** in Farmington, Conn. 26 September 1964. The son of Sherwood F. **Jeter**, Jr. and Edwina **Pabst**, Edward was born in Hartford, Conn. 1 September 1937.[3645]

Cynthia **Coolidge** and S. Edward **Jeter** had the following child:

     3088   i.   Christopher Coolidge[13] **Jeter**[3646] was born in Hartford, Conn. 3 January 1967.

2713. Lydia[12] **Coolidge** (John[11], Pres. John Calvin[11], Victoria Josephine[10] **Moor**, Abigail[9] **Franklin**, Luther[8], Sarah[7] **Starr**, Capt. Comfort[6], Comfort[5], Mary[4] **Stone**, Mary[3] **Whipple**, Elder John[2], Matthew[1])[3647] was born in New Haven, Conn. 14 August 1939 and married **Jeremy Whitman Sayles** in Farmington, Conn. 17 June 1966. Jeremy,[3648] son of Phil Whitman **Sayles** and Mildred **Jones**, was born in Schenectady, N.Y. 9 June 1937.

Lydia **Coolidge** and Jeremy Whitman **Sayles** had the following child:

     3089   i.   Jennifer Coolidge[13] **Sayles**[3649] was born in Boston, Mass. 27 July 1970.

THIRTEENTH GENERATION

2714. Catherine[13] **Wells** (Helen Cutter[12] **Pillsbury**, Harry M.[11], James[10], Jacob[9], John Hale[8], Rev. Edmund[7], Moses[6], Moses[5], Susanna[4] **Worth**, Susannah[3] **Whipple**, Elder John[2], Matthew[1]) was born in 1907 and died in 1963 at 56 years of age. She married **Joseph Lawrence Buell** II who died in 1981.

Catherine **Wells** and Joseph Lawrence **Buell** II had the following children:

+ 3090   i.   Eleanor[14] **Buell** was born 8 January 1928.

+ 3091   ii.   Joseph Lawrence **Buell** III was born in 1934.

+ 3092   iii.   Elizabeth **Buell** was born 25 August 1936.

2716. Clark Thompson[13] **Wells** (Helen Cutter[12] **Pillsbury**, Harry M.[11], James[10], Jacob[9], John Hale[8], Rev. Edmund[7], Moses[6], Moses[5], Susanna[4] **Worth**, Susannah[3] **Whipple**, Elder John[2], Matthew[1]) was born in 1910 and died in 1994 at 84 years of age. He married **Elizabeth Leone Cavanaugh** in 1935.

Clark Thompson **Wells** and Elizabeth Leone **Cavanaugh** had the following children:

     3093   i.   Anne[14] **Wells** was born in 1938 and married twice. (1) Jack **Rosch**. (2) Dr. John **Roberts**.

     3094   ii.   Clark Thompson **Wells** Jr. was born in 1940. He married Janet **Knost**.

     3095   iii.   David C. **Wells** was born in 1947. He married twice. (1) Mary Elizabeth **Thurber**. (2) Pamela **Loomis**.

+ 3096   iv.   Mary **Wells** was born 1 November 1947.

2717. Cyrus Curtis[13] Wells (Helen Cutter[12] **Pillsbury**, Harry M.[11], James[10], Jacob[9], John Hale[8], Rev. Edmund[7], Moses[6], Moses[5], Susanna[4] **Worth**, Susannah[3] **Whipple**, Elder John[2], Matthew[1]) was born in 1914 and died in 1991 at 77 years of age. He married **Barbara Holt** in 1936.

Cyrus Curtis **Wells** and Barbara **Holt** had the following children:

+ 3097   i. Peter C.[14] **Wells** was born 2 November 1940.
+ 3098   ii. Wendy **Wells** was born 13 November 1942.
+ 3099   iii. Christopher B. **Wells** was born 26 November 1948.

2719. Harrison Pillsbury[13] Martin (Alice Wedgwood[12] **Pillsbury**, Harry M.[11], James[10], Jacob[9], John Hale[8], Rev. Edmund[7], Moses[6], Moses[5], Susanna[4] **Worth**, Susannah[3] **Whipple**, Elder John[2], Matthew[1]) was born in Milwaukee, Wisc. in 1911 and died in 1964 at 53 years of age. He married **Joyce E. Newbill** in Milwaukee. Joyce was born in Portland, Multnomah Co., Oreg. in 1910 and died in 1996 at 86 years of age.

Harrison Pillsbury **Martin** and Joyce E. **Newbill** had the following child:

3100   i. Thomas Wedgwood[14] **Martin** was born in 1937 and married Karen V. **Crownover** in 1982.

2721. John Stanwood[13] Martin (Alice Wedgwood[12] **Pillsbury**, Harry M.[11], James[10], Jacob[9], John Hale[8], Rev. Edmund[7], Moses[6], Moses[5], Susanna[4] **Worth**, Susannah[3] **Whipple**, Elder John[2], Matthew[1]) was born in Wyncote, Penn. 18 December 1915 and married **Mary Elizabeth Newkirk** before 1951. Mary was born in Philadelphia, Penn. 7 February 1928.

John Stanwood **Martin** and Mary Elizabeth **Newkirk** had the following children:

3101   i. Eliz Pillsbury[14] **Martin** was born in Philadelphia, Penn. in 1951 and married John S. **Barber** in 1977.
+ 3102   ii. Harris Warthman **Martin** was born 7 November 1954.
3103   iii. John Charles **Martin** II was born in Wayne, Penn. in 1956.
3104   iv. Theodore Taft **Martin** was born in Wayne, Penn. in 1958.

2722. David Cutter[13] Martin (Alice Wedgwood[12] **Pillsbury**, Harry M.[11], James[10], Jacob[9], John Hale[8], Rev. Edmund[7], Moses[6], Moses[5], Susanna[4] **Worth**, Susannah[3] **Whipple**, Elder John[2], Matthew[1]) was born in Wyncote, Penn. 18 January 1919 and died 16 December 1987 in Haverford, Penn. at 68 years of age. He married **Helen L. Wright**. She was born in State College, Penn. 24 December 1922.

David Cutter **Martin** and Helen L. **Wright** had the following child:

+ 3105   i. Brandon Cutter[14] **Martin** was born 10 September 1947.

2727. Priscilla June[13] Blake (Clarence Dodge[12], Lizzie Batchelder[11] **Dodge**, Frank Brickett[10], Deborah Towne[9] **Brickett**, Bernard[8], Bernard[7], Susanna[6] **Pillsbury**, Moses[5], Susanna[4] **Worth**, Susannah[3] **Whipple**, Elder John[2], Matthew[1]) was born in Boston, Mass. 2 April 1929 and married **Lawrence Archibald Haines** in Winchester, Mass. 3 June 1950. Lawrence, son of William Laurence **Haines** and Doris Alma **Snyder**, was born in Boston 4 May 1928.

Priscilla June **Blake** and Lawrence Archibald **Haines** had the following children:

+ 3106	i.	William Blake[14] **Haines** was born 26 December 1950.
3107	ii.	Robert Lawrence **Haines** was born in Boston 8 March 1953 and married four times. (1) Terry Lynn **Sunquist**. They were divorced before 1985. (2) Mary **Hoyle** in Las Vegas, Clark Co., Nev. in June 1974. They were divorced after 1974. (3) Mary Jane **Knittle** after 1975. (4) Linda Susan **Wren** 31 May 1985.
+ 3108	iii.	Susan June **Haines** was born 30 May 1955.
+ 3109	iv.	Sandra Dale **Haines** was born 2 January 1958.
+ 3110	v.	Linda Ann **Haines** was born 2 January 1958.
+ 3111	vi.	Bradford Blake **Haines** was born 21 January 1962.
3112	vii.	Brent Blake **Haines** was born in Provo, Utah Co., Utah 17 March 1967 and married Julia Ann **Tanner** in Mapleton, Utah 4 February 1989. Julia, daughter of Dale Louis **Tanner** and Wilma Nettie **Roberts**, was born in Terre Haute, Vigo Co., Ind. 29 September 1967.
3113	viii.	Christopher Blake **Haines** was born in Provo 9 October 1970.
3114	ix.	Darelyn Ruth **Haines** was born in Provo 23 May 1972 and married William **Guinn** in Mapleton, Utah 17 November 1990.

2728. **Barbara**[13] **Smalley** (Col. Howard Norrington[12], Col. Howard Russell[11], Viola Irene[10] **Hoyt**, Dr. Hiram Pillsbury[9], Judith[8] **Pillsbury**, Caleb[7], Caleb[6], Caleb[5], Susanna[4] **Worth**, Susannah[3] **Whipple**, Elder John[2], Matthew[1])[3650] was born at Schofield Barracks, Oahu, Hawaii 2 May 1939 and married **Robert Ernst Seyfarth** in San Francisco., Calif. 17 June 1961. Robert,[3651] son of Ernst Oskar Emil Karl **Seyfarth** and Gertrude Sarah **Freeman**, was born in Cambridge, Mass. 25 July 1939. He was graduated from the U.S. Naval Academy with a bachelor of science degree in June 1961, earned a master of business administration degree from Golden Gate University in May 1973, and a doctor of education degree from the U. of Nevada at Reno in August 1980. He retired from the U.S. Navy in June 1981 with the rank of Lt. Commander and became a professor of computer science/management science and accounting.

Barbara **Smalley** and Robert Ernst **Seyfarth** had the following children:

3115	i.	Karin Marie[14] **Seyfarth**[3652] was born in Portsmouth, Va. 12 October 1962 and married Adam Grant **Kremers** in Carson City, Nev. 17 June 1990.
3116	ii.	Suzanne **Seyfarth**[3653] was born in San Francisco, Calif. 15 January 1966 and married Walter Jay **Leshinskie** in Shamokin, Northumberland Co., Pa. 19 October 1991.

2730. **Janet**[13] **Horstman** (Helena[12] **Pullen**, Nellie May[11] **Blanchard**, George Adelbert[10], Aaron[9], Lois[8] **Burt**, Abiah[7] **Mooar**, Abiah[6] **Hill**, Judith[5] **Bucknam**, Judith (Jude)[4] **Worth**, Susannah[3] **Whipple**, Elder John[2], Matthew[1])[3654] was born in Chicago, Ill. 6 September 1920 and was baptized in an Episcopalian church in New Harmony, Ind. in 1921. She married **James Allen Anderson Jr.** in Havana, Ill. 18 June 1941. James,[3655] son of James Allen **Anderson** Sr. and Norma **Caillordt**, was born in Opelousas, St. Landry Parish, La. 9 October 1919. He earned a bachelor of science degree before 1941 from the U. of Illinois and later a master of arts from Penn State. He worked as a chemical engineer. Janet earned a bachelor of science degree with an education major from the U. of Illinois in 1941.

Janet **Horstman** and James Allen **Anderson** Jr. had the following children:

+ 3117	i.	Merilee Joan[14] **Anderson** was born 31 August 1942.
+ 3118	ii.	Carole Helena **Anderson** was born 13 October 1944.
+ 3119	iii.	James Lawford **Anderson** was born 2 December 1947.

2733. **John Belmont**[13] **Stevens** Jr. (Donald Belmont[12], Orrin Belmont[11], George Nichols[10], Susan Poor[9] **Pearson**, Nathaniel[8], Sarah[7] **Gerrish**, Katherine[6] **Brown**, Martha[5] **Whipple**, Maj. John[4], Capt. John[3], Elder John[2], Matthew[1])[3656] was born in Newburyport, Essex Co., Mass. 15 July 1942 and married twice. (1) **Carolyn Griffin** in Buckhannon, W. Va. 21 September 1968. Carolyn,[3657] daughter of Ambrose **Griffin** and Elaine **Avington**, was born in Buckhannon 4 May 1946. (2) **Kristina Lynn Bailey** in Purcellville, Va. 27 May 1995. Kristina,[3658] daughter of Ronald T. **Bailey** and Carol **Vollmer**, was born in Syracuse, N.Y. 29 January 1969.

John Belmont **Stevens** Jr. and Carolyn **Griffin** had the following children:

3120	i.	John Belmont[14] **Stevens** Jr.[3659] was born in Buckhannon 19 June 1970.
3121	ii.	Philip Ambrose **Stevens**[3660] was born in Austin, Texas 6 November 1973.
3122	iii.	Katherine Elizabeth **Stevens**[3661] was born in Houston, Texas 8 June 1977.
3123	iv.	Paul Safford **Stevens**[3662] was born in Northfield, Vt. 21 May 1980.

John Belmont **Stevens** Jr. and Kristina Lynn **Bailey** had the following child:

| 3124 | v. | Jennifer Mary Ann **Stevens**[3663] was born in Sterling, Va. 13 September 1996. |

2734. **Peter Bartlett**[13] **Stevens** (Donald Belmont[12], Orrin Belmont[11], George Nichols[10], Susan Poor[9] **Pearson**, Nathaniel[8], Sarah[7] **Gerrish**, Katherine[6] **Brown**, Martha[5] **Whipple**, Maj. John[4], Capt. John[3], Elder John[2], Matthew[1])[3664] was born in Newburyport, Essex Co., Mass. 6 January 1946 and married twice. (1) **Carol Ann Delaney** 1 February 1975. Carol,[3665] daughter of John W. **Delaney** and Lillian **Cushing**, was born 24 June 1948. They were divorced 11 February 1986. (2) **Vittoria Bruni** 9 December 1989. Vittoria,[3666] daughter of Antonio **Bruni** and Lillian **McDonald**, was born in Portland, Maine 21 April 1960.

Peter Bartlett **Stevens** and Carol Ann **Delaney** had the following children:

3125	i.	Matthew Bartlett[14] **Stevens**[3667] was born in Wilton, Maine 4 July 1978.
3126	ii.	Ethan Allen Delaney **Stevens**[3668] was born in Wilton 24 March 1980.
3127	iii.	Krystal Ann **Stevens**[3669] was born in No. Tonawanda, N.Y. 12 June 1982.

Peter Bartlett **Stevens** and Vittoria **Bruni** had the following child:

| 3128 | iv. | Scarlett **Stevens**[3670] was born in Bradford, Maine 1 July 1992. |

2738. **Orlow R.**[13] **Zumwalt** (Esther Louise[12] **Whipple**, William Henry[11], William Orland[10], William Ward[9], John[8], John[7], Capt. John[6], Capt. John[5], Maj. Matthew[4], Capt. John[3], Elder John[2], Matthew[1])[3671] was born 1 June 1928 and married **Jeri N. West** after 1940. She died in 1991 in Baltimore, Md. [3672]

Orlow R. **Zumwalt** and Jeri N. **West** had the following children:

+ 3129	i.	Eric[14] **Zumwalt** was born 20 July 1951.
3130	ii.	Marta Jo **Zumwalt**[3673] was born 3 January 1954.
3131	iii.	Janeen Lea **Zumwalt**[3674] was born 29 May 1955.
3132	iv.	Kurt Detric **Zumwalt**[3675] was born 8 May 1958.
3133	v.	Elise Lyn **Zumwalt**[3676] was born 24 September 1961.

2739. **Karl Fredrick**[13] **Johnson** (Ruth Isabell[12] **Whipple**, William Henry[11], William Orland[10], William Ward[9], John[8], John[7], Capt. John[6], Capt. John[5], Maj. Matthew[4], Capt. John[3], Elder John[2], Matthew[1])[3677] was born 19 February 1938 and married **Helen Spalding** 28 November in1980. Helen was born 19 February 1938.[3678]

Karl Fredrick **Johnson** and Helen **Spalding** had the following child:
    3134   i. Kjerstin[14] **Johnson-Spalding**[3679] was born 13 January 1986.

2740. **Martha Ann**[13] **Johnson** (Ruth Isabell[12] **Whipple**, William Henry[11], William Orland[10], William Ward[9], John[8], John[7], Capt. John[6], Capt. John[5], Maj. Matthew[4], Capt. John[3], Elder John[2], Matthew[1])[3680] was born 21 August 1939 and married twice. (1) **Rinaldo John Redstrom** 30 December 1958. Rinaldo was born in Baraboo, Wisc. 3 March 1936 and died 9 April 1980 at 44 years of age.[3681] (2) **Peter Plourd** 1 January 1983. Peter was born in Upper Frenchville, Maine 24 May 1938.[3682]

Martha Ann **Johnson** and Rinaldo John **Redstrom** had the following children:
    3135   i. Rinaldo John William[14] **Redstrom Jr.**[3683] was born in Farmington, Mo. 20 February 1963 and married, as her second husband, Rebecca Sue **Walker** 2 April 1990. Rebecca was born in Charlotte, N.C. 5 January 1967.[3684]
    3136   ii. Venita Marinal **Redstrom**[3685] was born in Farmington, Mo. 15 August 1964.[3686] She married Matthew **Mitchell** 31 August 1991.

2741. **William Don**[13] **Johnson** (Ruth Isabell[12] **Whipple**, William Henry[11], William Orland[10], William Ward[9], John[8], John[7], Capt. John[6], Capt. John[5], Maj. Matthew[4], Capt. John[3], Elder John[2], Matthew[1])[3687] was born in Independence, Mo. 11 January 1948 and married **Mary Calder** in November 1977. Mary was born 10 October 1949.[3688]

William Don **Johnson** and Mary **Calder** had the following child:
    3137   i. Zachary Calder[14] **Johnson**[3689] was born 4 April 1980.

2742. **LeRoy Ellis**[13] **Wedge** (Frances Irene[12] **Whipple**, William Henry[11], William Orland[10], William Ward[9], John[8], John[7], Capt. John[6], Capt. John[5], Maj. Matthew[4], Capt. John[3], Elder John[2], Matthew[1])[3690] was born in Oakland, Mo. 9 July 1934 and married **Martha Joyce Simmons** 30 June 1957. Martha was born 3 July 1935.[3691] They were divorced after 1966.

LeRoy Ellis **Wedge** and Martha Joyce **Simmons** had the following children:
  + 3138   i. Deborah Michele Simmons[14] **Wedge** was born 8 September 1963.
    3139   ii. Edith **Wedge**[3692] was born in Owensboro, Ky. 3 October 1966 and married John **Collins** in August 1994.

2743. **Helen Louise**[13] **Wedge** (Frances Irene[12] **Whipple**, William Henry[11], William Orland[10], William Ward[9], John[8], John[7], Capt. John[6], Capt. John[5], Maj. Matthew[4], Capt. John[3], Elder John[2], Matthew[1])[3693] was born in Lebanon, Mo. 20 January 1944 and married **Gary Frenchie Fisher** in Brandsville, Mo. 8 June 1963. Gary was born 20 January 1944.[3694]

Helen Louise **Wedge** and Gary Frenchie **Fisher** had the following children:
    3140   i. John Gary[14] **Fisher**[3695] was born in Independence, Mo. 20 April 1967

and married Kerry Ann **Imsland** in June 1994.

3141   ii.   James Ellis **Fisher**[3696] was born in Columbia, Mo. 8 October 1971.

3142   iii.   Thomas Jason **Fisher**[3697] was born in Columbia 21 October 1973.

2745. Doris Jean[13] Hopkins (Marjorie Eula[12] **Whipple**, William Henry[11], William Orland[10], William Ward[9], John[8], John[7], Capt. John[6], Capt. John[5], Maj. Matthew[4], Capt. John[3], Elder John[2], Matthew[1])[3698] was born 9 March 1932 and married **Dennis Michael** 27 February 1952. Dennis was born 6 January 1935.[3699]

Doris Jean **Hopkins** and Dennis **Michael** had the following children:

+ 3143   i.   Richard Lee[14] **Michael** was born 5 April 1955.

    3144   ii.   Ronald Eugene **Michael**[3700] was born 13 April 1956.

2746. Dora Dean[13] Hopkins (Marjorie Eula[12] **Whipple**, William Henry[11], William Orland[10], William Ward[9], John[8], John[7], Capt. John[6], Capt. John[5], Maj. Matthew[4], Capt. John[3], Elder John[2], Matthew[1])[3701] was born in Lebanon, Mo. 13 July 1933 and married **Russel Weatherly** 3 July 1951. Russel was born 8 March 1928 and died in 1993 at 65 years of age. [3702]

Dora Dean **Hopkins** and Russel **Weatherly** had the following children:

+ 3145   i.   Russel[14] **Weatherly** Jr. was born 16 June 1952.

+ 3146   ii.   James Fay **Weatherly** was born 6 January 1954.

+ 3147   iii.   Marjorie Diana **Weatherly** was born 20 June 1956.

+ 3148   iv.   Pamela Sue **Weatherly** was born 29 September 1960.

2747. Melba Paulene[13] Hopkins (Marjorie Eula[12] **Whipple**, William Henry[11], William Orland[10], William Ward[9], John[8], John[7], Capt. John[6], Capt. John[5], Maj. Matthew[4], Capt. John[3], Elder John[2], Matthew[1])[3703] was born in Lebanon, Mo. 25 November 1934 and married twice. (1) **Lavelle Jones** in Lebanon 25 March 1952. He died there 25 March 1956.[3704] (2) **Mitchell Chaffin** 3 September 1960.[3705] They were divorced after 1972.

Melba Paulene **Hopkins** and Lavelle **Jones** had the following children:

+ 3149   i.   Paul Eugene[14] **Jones** was born 17 March 1953.

    3150   ii.   Eddie Lee **Jones**[3706] was born in Lebanon, Mo. 2 June 1954 and died in a traffic accident near Kansas City, Mo. 26 August 1989 at 35 years of age.

+ 3151   iii.   Charles Steven **Jones** was born 9 October 1955.

Melba Paulene **Hopkins** and Mitchell **Chaffin** had the following children:

+ 3152   iv.   JoAnne **Chaffin** was born 7 January 1959.

+ 3153   v.   Larry Dale **Chaffin** was born 17 April 1961.

+ 3154   vi.   Mary Chrystine **Chaffin** was born 25 December 1962.

+ 3155   vii.   William Fay **Chaffin** was born 22 March 1964.

    3156   viii.   Joyce Elaine **Chaffin**[3707] was born 13 October 1972.

2748. Eula Faye[13] Hopkins (Marjorie Eula[12] **Whipple**, William Henry[11], William Orland[10], William Ward[9], John[8], John[7], Capt. John[6], Capt. John[5], Maj. Matthew[4], Capt. John[3], Elder John[2], Matthew[1])[3708] was born in Lebanon, Mo. 17 April 1938 and married **Harold Lee Beal** 3 September 1957. Harold was born 22 June 1934.[3709]

Eula Faye **Hopkins** and Harold Lee **Beal** had the following children:

+ 3157   i. Bruce Lee[14] **Beal** was born 7 November 1960.
+ 3158   ii. Bryan **Beal** was born 15 February 1962.

2749. Mirian Frances[13] Hopkins (Marjorie Eula[12] **Whipple**, William Henry[11], William Orland[10], William Ward[9], John[8], John[7], Capt. John[6], Capt. John[5], Maj. Matthew[4], Capt. John[3], Elder John[2], Matthew[1])[3710] was born in Lebanon, Mo. 16 November 1939 and married **Glen Williams** 25 September 1960. Glen was born in April 1936.[3711]

Mirian Frances **Hopkins** and Glen **Williams** had the following children:
+ 3159   i. Kimberly Sue[14] **Williams** was born 17 November 1959.
+ 3160   ii. Dareatha Denise **Williams** was born 19 February 1961.
   3161   iii. Nicholas Glen **Williams**[3712] was born in Germany 15 September 1962 and married Laurie **Williams**.

2750. William Otto[13] Hopkins (Marjorie Eula[12] **Whipple**, William Henry[11], William Orland[10], William Ward[9], John[8], John[7], Capt. John[6], Capt. John[5], Maj. Matthew[4], Capt. John[3], Elder John[2], Matthew[1])[3713] was born in Lebanon, Mo. 1 December 1941 and married **Charlene Davis** 29 January 1965. Charlene was born 19 February 1928.[3714]

William Otto **Hopkins** and Charlene **Davis** had the following child:
+ 3162   i. Melissa[14] **Hopkins** was born 20 September 1965.

2751. Elizabeth Irene[13] Hopkins (Marjorie Eula[12] **Whipple**, William Henry[11], William Orland[10], William Ward[9], John[8], John[7], Capt. John[6], Capt. John[5], Maj. Matthew[4], Capt. John[3], Elder John[2], Matthew[1])[3715] was born in Lebanon, Mo. 26 June 1945 and married **James Carl Grimes** there 9 August 1962. They were divorced after 1963.

Elizabeth Irene **Hopkins** and James Carl **Grimes** had the following children:
   3163   i. Jacque[14] **Grimes**[3716].
+ 3164   ii. Jacque **Grimes** was born 15 December 1962.
+ 3165   iii. James Carl **Grimes** was born 22 June 1963.

2752. Carol Dena[13] Whipple (Harold Paul[12], William Henry[11], William Orland[10], William Ward[9], John[8], John[7], Capt. John[6], Capt. John[5], Maj. Matthew[4], Capt. John[3], Elder John[2], Matthew[1])[3717] was born in Lebanon, Mo. 11 April 1937 and married **Melvin Norton** there 2 July 1961. Melvin was born 5 December 1933.[3718]

Carol Dena **Whipple** and Melvin **Norton** had the following children:
   3166   i. Cynthia Marie[14] **Norton**[3719] was born 24 December 1964.
   3167   ii. Stephanie Lea **Norton**[3720] was born 3 April 1970.

2754. Thomas William[13] Whipple (Melvin Eugene[12], William Henry[11], William Orland[10], William Ward[9], John[8], John[7], Capt. John[6], Capt. John[5], Maj. Matthew[4], Capt. John[3], Elder John[2], Matthew[1])[3721] was born in Durham, N.C. 10 September 1945 and married **Jane Bittner** in Athens, Ohio before 1970. She was born in Freeport, Ill. 19 May 1945.[3722]

Thomas William **Whipple** and Jane **Bittner** had the following child:
   3168   i. Timothy Scott[14] **Whipple**[3723] was born 2 July 1970.

2755. **Linda Marie**[13] **Whipple** (Melvin Eugene[12], William Henry[11], William Orland[10], William Ward[9], John[8], John[7], Capt. John[6], Capt. John[5], Maj. Matthew[4], Capt. Jon[3], Elder John[2], Matthew[1])[3724] was born in Chicago, Ill. 1 July 1948 and married twice. (1) **Floyd Washborn** 3 March 1966. They were divorced before 1984. (2) **Randall Grogan** in 1984.

Linda Marie **Whipple** and Floyd **Washborn** had the following children:

    3169   i.   Laura Denice[14] **Washborn**[3725] was born 13 September 1966.
    3170   ii. Melisua Valerie **Washborn** was born in Oklahoma City, Okla. 31 August 1971.

2756. **Marjorie Diane**[13] **Whipple** (Earl Lawrence[12], William Henry[11], William Orland[10], William Ward[9], John[8], John[7], Capt. John[6], Capt. John[5], Maj. Matthew[4], Capt. John[3], Elder John[2], Matthew[1])[3726] was born 19 September 1943 and married twice. (1) **Kenneth Ray Whitmire** 8 April 1962. They were divorced after 1966. (2) (_) **Johnston** after 1967. They were divorced after 1967.

Marjorie Diane **Whipple** and Kenneth Ray **Whitmire** had the following children:

    3171   i.   Stephen Ray[14] **Whitmire**[3727] was born 7 May 1965 and married Colleen (_) 9 February 1991. They were divorced
    3172   ii. Deborah Diane **Whitmire**[3728] was born 13 October 1966.

2757. **Patricia Ann**[13] **Whipple** (Earl Lawrence[12], William Henry[11], William Orland[10], William Ward[9], John[8], John[7], Capt. John[6], Capt. John[5], Maj. Matthew[4], Capt. John[3], Elder John[2], Matthew[1])[3729] was born 10 January 1945 and married **Vaughan Visser** 4 October 1964. Vaughan was born 14 June 1944.[3730]

Patricia Ann **Whipple** and Vaughan **Visser** had the following children:

  + 3173   i.   Del Reese[14] **Visser** was born 3 September 1966.
    3174   ii. Cameron Kip **Visser**[3731] was born 11 May 1969.

2759. **Lawrence Willliam**[13] **West** (Evelyn Eugenia[12] **Whipple**, William Henry[11], William Orland[10], William Ward[9], John[8], John[7], Capt. John[6], Capt. John[5], Maj. Matthew[4], Capt. John[3], Elder John[2], Matthew[1])[3732] was born 14 August 1943 and married **Janie Kay Miller** 26 June 1964. Janie was born 15 August 1946.[3733]

Lawrence Willliam **West** and Janie Kay **Miller** had the following child:

    3175   i.   Julie Kay[14] **West**[3734] was born 7 April 1965 and married Robert **Edwards** 16 April 1994.

2760. **Stephen Allen**[13] **Whipple** (Carl Henry[12], William Henry[11], William Orland[10], William Ward[9], John[8], John[7], Capt. John[6], Capt. John[5], Maj. Matthew[4], Capt. John[3], Elder John[2], Matthew[1])[3735] was born 23 October 1944 and married twice. (1) **Ruby** (_) in 1965. They were divorced in 1988. (2) **Chirre** (_) in 1990.

Stephen Allen **Whipple** and Ruby (_) had the following children:

    3176   i.   Edgar Carl[14] **Whipple**[3736] was born 5 August 1966.
    3177   ii. Grant Michael **Whipple**[3737] was born 3 February 1971.

2761. **Michael William**[13] **Whipple** (Carl Henry[12], William Henry[11], William Orland[10], William Ward[9], John[8], John[7], Capt. John[6], Capt. John[5], Maj. Matthew[4], Capt. John[3], Elder John[2], Matthew[1])[3738] was born 24 January 1947 and married

Diane (__) abt 1975.

Michael William **Whipple** and Diane (__) had the following child:
3178   i.   Michelle Diane[14] **Whipple**[3739] was born 11 August 1975.

2762. **Joseph Terrance**[13] **Kuchin** (Rosetta[12] **Whipple**, William Henry[11], William Orland[10], William Ward[9], John[8], John[7], Capt. John[6], Capt. John[5], Maj. Matthew[4], Capt. John[3], Elder John[2], Matthew[1])[3740] was born 8 September 1949 and married **Stacy (__)** abt 1984.

Joseph Terrance **Kuchin** and Stacy (__) had the following children:
3179   i.   Christopher[14] **Kuchin**[3741] was born in 1985.
3180   ii.   Adam **Kuchin**[3742] was born in 1988.
3181   iii. Heidi **Kuchin**[3743] was born in 1990.
3182   iv.   Gretchin **Kuchin**[3744] was born in 1994.

2766. **Pamela Kay**[13] **Donigan** (Grace Katherine[12] **Whipple**, William Henry[11], William Orland[10], William Ward[9], John[8], John[7], Capt. John[6], Capt. John[5], Maj. Matthew[4], Capt. John[3], Elder John[2], Matthew[1])[3745] was born 3 February 1951 and married **Walter Lyles** in 1983.

Pamela Kay **Donigan** and Walter **Lyles** had the following child:
3183   i.   Wyatt P.[14] **Lyles**[3746] was born in 1990.

2767. **Barbara Kay**[13] **Whipple** (Jerald Howard[12], John Godfrey[11], William Orland[10], William Ward[9], John[8], John[7], Capt. John[6], Capt. John[5], Maj. Matthew[4], Capt. John[3], Elder John[2], Matthew[1])[3747] was born in Pendleton, Oreg. 19 December 1939 and married twice. (1) (__) **Buchan** before 1963. They were divorced after 1965. (2) **Bill Biddle** 23 May 1994.

Barbara Kay **Whipple** and **Buchan** had the following children:
+ 3184   i.   Elizabeth Diane[14] **Buchan** was born 29 January 1963.
  3185   ii.   Robin **Buchan**[3748] was born 2 February 1964.

2771. **Margaret Leah**[13] **Munsch** (Martha Belle[12] **Whipple**, John Godfrey[11], William Orland[10], William Ward[9], John[8], John[7], Capt. John[6], Capt. John[5], Maj. Matthew[4], Capt. John[3], Elder John[2], Matthew[1])[3749] was born in Greeley, Colo. 8 August 1948 and married **Norman Andrew Dahl** in Tukwila, Wash. 21 June 1969. Norman was born in Seattle, Wash. 16 February 1948.[3750]

Margaret Leah **Munsch** and Norman Andrew **Dahl** had the following child:
3186   i.   Louise Marie[14] **Dahl**[3751] was born in Olympia, Wash. 26 July 1984.

2774. **Timothy John**[13] **Munsch** (Martha Belle[12] **Whipple**, John Godfrey[11], William Orland[10], William Ward[9], John[8], John[7], Capt. John[6], Capt. John[5], Maj. Matthew[4], Capt. John[3], Elder John[2], Matthew[1])[3752] was born in Renton, Wash. 6 April 1955 and married, as her second husband, **Stephanie Ann Waugh** in Anderson Island, Wash. 29 February 1984. She was born 31 August 1956.[3753]

Timothy John **Munsch** and Stephanie Ann **Waugh** had the following children:
3187   i.   Morgen Lynn[14] **Munsch**[3754] was born in Olympia, Wash. 25 September 1984.

3188   ii. Timothy John **Munsch**[3755] was born in Olympia 7 October 1985.

3189   iii. Jeffrey James **Munsch**[3756] was born in Federal Way, Wash. 26 December 1987.

2775. Melody Ann[13] **Munsch** (Martha Belle[12] **Whipple**, John Godfrey[11], William Orland[10], William Ward[9], John[8], John[7], Capt. John[6], Capt. John[5], Maj. Matthew[4], Capt. John[3], Elder John[2], Matthew[1])[3757] was born in Renton, Wash. 29 August 1956 and married **David Edmund Butzner** in Steilacoom, Wash. 20 August 1977. He was born in Baltimore, Md. 2 February 1955.[3758]

Melody Ann **Munsch** and David Edmund **Butzner** had the following child:

3190   i. Alexis Marie[14] **Butzner**[3759] was born in Olympia, Wash. 18 January 1984.

2777. Margaret Beth[13] **Whipple** (Ward Deal[12], Clyde Ward[11], William Orland[10], William Ward[9], John[8], John[7], Capt. John[6], Capt. John[5], Maj. Matthew[4], Capt. John[3], Elder John[2], Matthew[1])[3760] was born in Washington, D.C. 4 September 1958 and married **David Michael Equi** in Richmond, Va. 20 October 1984. David,[3761] son of William Daniel **Equi III** and Frances Jean **Dowdy**, was born in Roanoke, Va. 2 October 1953.

Margaret Beth **Whipple** and David Michael **Equi** had the following children:

3191   i. Brian[14] **Equi**[3762] was born in Richmond, Va. 12 June 1987.

3192   ii. Courtney Elizabeth **Equi**[3763] was born in Richmond, Va. 26 July 1989.

2778. Lendell LeRoy[13] **Carpenter** (Claribel[12] **Whipple**, Clyde Ward[11], William Orland[10], William Ward[9], John[8], John[7], Capt. John[6], Capt. John[5], Maj. Matthew[4], Capt. John[3], Elder John[2], Matthew[1])[3764] was born in Lincoln, Nebr. 22 April 1945 and married three times. (1) **Joy Diane Watson** in Portland, Multnomah Co., Oreg. 25 June 1966. Joy,[3765] daughter of Clarence **Watson** and Hazel (__), was born in Portland 8 August 1946. They were divorced in Portland, after 1972. (2) **Deborah Ann Bronkey** in Portland 12 July 1975. Deborah,[3766] daughter of Vern **Bronkey** and Marjorie (__), was born in The Dalles, Wasco Co., Oreg. 6 April 1953. They were divorced in Portland after 1978. (3) **Christy Larson** in Portland 18 June 1992. Christy was born 17 June 1945 and was married and divorced before marrying Lendell.[3767]

Lendell LeRoy **Carpenter** and Joy Diane **Watson** had the following children:

+ 3193   i. Bradley Lendell[14] **Carpenter** was born 17 June 1969.

3194   ii. Todd **Carpenter**[3768] was born in Portland 13 March 1972.

Lendell LeRoy **Carpenter** and Deborah Ann **Bronkey** had the following child:

3195   iii. Ariane **Carpenter**[3769] was born in Portland 11 May 1978.

2779. Craig Ward[13] **Carpenter** (Claribel[12] **Whipple**, Clyde Ward[11], William Orland[10], William Ward[9], John[8], John[7], Capt. John[6], Capt. John[5], Maj. Matthew[4], Capt. John[3], Elder John[2], Matthew[1])[3770] was born in Des Moines, Iowa 19 March 1947 and married **Marilyn Lee Mitchell** in Portland, Multnomah Co., Oreg. 29 June 1968. Marilyn,[3771] daughter of Vern **Mitchell** and Evelyn (__), was born in Portland, 30 January 1947.

Craig Ward **Carpenter** and Marilyn Lee **Mitchell** had the following children:

3196   i. Troy[14] **Carpenter**[3772] was born in Portland 17 May 1971 and married

Deborah **Wolfe** in Eaton, Colo. 18 September 1993.

3197   ii. Matthew Branden **Carpenter**[3773] was born in Eugene, Lane Co., Oreg. 10 September 1974.

3198   iii. Casey Mitchell **Carpenter**[3774] was born in Phoenix, Ariz. 26 September 1978.

3199   iv. Sean **Carpenter**[3775] was born in Phoenix 8 March 1980.

2780. **Rev. Keith Whipple**[13] **Carpenter** (Claribel[12] **Whipple**, Clyde Ward[11], William Orland[10], William Ward[9], John[8], John[7], Capt. John[6], Capt. John[5], Maj. Matthew[4], Capt. John[3], Elder John[2], Matthew[1])[3776] was born in Portland, Multnomah Co., Oreg. 21 May 1952 and married **Michelle Baugh** in Spokane, Wash. 5 March 1983. Michelle,[3777] daughter of Odin **Baugh** and Dedee **Marcus**, was born in Spokane 22 August 1951.

Rev. Keith Whipple **Carpenter** and Michelle **Baugh** had the following children:

3200   i. Kirk[14] **Carpenter**[3778] was born 19 October 1985.

3201   ii. Jeffrey Marcus **Carpenter**[3779] was born in Renton, Wash. 29 April 1988.

3202   iii. Marisa Michelle **Carpenter**[3780] was born in Renton after 1989.

2781. **Scott Lawrence**[13] **Carpenter** (Claribel[12] **Whipple**, Clyde Ward[11], William Orland[10], William Ward[9], John[8], John[7], Capt. John[6], Capt. John[5], Maj. Matthew[4], Capt. John[3], Elder John[2], Matthew[1])[3781] was born in Portland, Multnomah Co., Oreg. 24 August 1954 and married **Jane Lemieux** in Portland 16 August 1975. Jane,[3782] daughter of Gerald **Lemieux** and Margaret (__), was born in Minneapolis, Minn. 11 March 1954.

Scott Lawrence **Carpenter** and Jane **Lemieux** had the following children born in Portland:

3203   i. Ryan[14] **Carpenter**[3783] was born 21 April 1982.

3204   ii. Claire **Carpenter**[3784] was born 10 October 1985.

3205   iii. Emily Jane **Carpenter**[3785] was born 21 October 1988.

2782. **Joan Morgan**[13] **Whipple** (Grant Dodge[12], Clyde Ward[11], William Orland[10], William Ward[9], John[8], John[7], Capt. John[6], Capt. John[5], Maj. Matthew[4], Capt. John[3], Elder John[2], Matthew[1])[3786] was born in Mineola, Long Island, N.Y. 12 September 1946 and married four times. (1) **Peter Pierce Rice** in Locus Valley, N.Y. in September 1966. They were divorced before 1968. (2) **Samuel Walter Gregg III** in New Hampshire 1 February 1968. Samuel had been married and divorced prior to marrying Joan. He was born 25 April 1942.[3787] (3) **Richard Gerrity** 1 September 1988. Richard was married and divorced prior to his marriage to Joan.[3788] Joan and Richard were divorced after 1989. (4) **Henry W. Trimble III** in Cape Neddick, Maine 10 June 1990. Henry was married and divorced prior to his marriage to Joan.

Joan Morgan **Whipple** and Peter Pierce **Rice** had the following child:

+ 3206   i. Christina Baldwin[14] **Rice** was born 21 November 1966.

Joan Morgan **Whipple** and Samuel Walter **Gregg** III had the following children:

3207   ii. Patricia Barrett **Gregg**[3789] was born in Norristown, Pa. 28 April 1969 and married Stewart Andrew **Young** in Cape Neddick 8 August 1992. Stewart was born in Enfield, England 14 March 1963.[3790]

3208   iii.   Brian Whipple **Gregg**[3791] was born in Portsmouth, Rockingham Co., N.H. 30 March 1972.

Joan Morgan **Whipple** and Richard **Gerrity** had the following child:
3209   iv.   Thomas Barrett **Gerrity**[3792] was born in Portland, Maine 17 September 1989 and died 18 September 1989 at less than one year of age.

Joan Morgan **Whipple** and Henry W. **Trimble** III had the following child:
3210   v.   Laura Tucker Barrett **Trimble**[3793] was born 4 January 1993.

2783. **Susan Launa**[13] **Weeks** (Launa May[12] **Whipple**, Clyde Ward[11], William Orland[10], William Ward[9], John[8], John[7], Capt. John[6], Capt. John[5], Maj. Matthew[4], Capt. John[3], Elder John[2], Matthew[1])[3794] was born in Kankakee, Ill. 2 May 1953 and married twice. (1) **Gary Schnell** in Kankakee 24 May 1975. The were divorced before 1984. (2) **William Scott Roleson** in San Diego, Calif. 21 November 1984. He was born 17 January 1949.

Susan Launa **Weeks** and William Scott **Roleson** had the following child:
3211   i.   Ryan Scott[14] **Roleson**[3795] was born in Poway, Calif. 27 September 1986.

2784. **Jane Lucy**[13] **Weeks** (Launa May[12] **Whipple**, Clyde Ward[11], William Orland[10], William Ward[9], John[8], John[7], Capt. John[6], Capt. John[5], Maj. Matthew[4], Capt. John[3], Elder John[2], Matthew[1])[3796] was born in Kankakee, Ill. 25 November 1954 and married **John Francis Randazzo** in New York, N.Y. 10 April 1980. John,[3797] son of Ted Francis **Randazzo** and Barbara Ann **Zahn**, was born in Brooklyn, N.Y. 7 July 1954.

Jane Lucy **Weeks** and John Francis **Randazzo** had the following children:
3212   i.   Kelly Frances[14] **Randazzo**[3798] was born in New York, N.Y. 4 March 1981.
3213   ii.   Alexis Catherine **Randazzo**[3799] was born in Hartford, Conn. 25 June 1986.
3214   iii.   Ted Lawrence **Randazzo**[3800] was born in Santa Monica, Calif. 23 January 1990.
3215   iv.   Jack Thomas **Randazzo**[3801] was born in Santa Monica 3 December 1991.

2786. **Victor Ward**[13] **Whipple** (Lyle Marion[12], Clyde Ward[11], William Orland[10], William Ward[9], John[8], John[7], Capt. John[6], Capt. John[5], Maj. Matthew[4], Capt. John[3], Elder John[2], Matthew[1])[3802] was born in Detroit, Mich. 9 July 1962 and married **Julie Ann Stevens** in Plymouth, Mich. 24 March 1984. Julie,[3803] daughter of Lawrence Dennis **Stevens** and Lorna May **McCabe**, was born 30 August 1962.

Victor Ward **Whipple** and Julie Ann **Stevens** had the following children:
3216   i.   Jared David[14] **Whipple**[3804] was born in Dearborn, Mich. 11 April 1990.
3217   ii.   Tyler Jordon **Whipple**[3805] was born in Dearborn 13 September 1995.

2787. **David Wellington**[13] **Whipple** (Clyde David[12], Clyde Ward[11], William Orland[10], William Ward[9], John[8], John[7], Capt. John[6], Capt. John[5], Maj. Matthew[4], Capt. John[3], Elder John[2], Matthew[1])[3806] was born 29 March 1955 and married **Bonnie Jill Allen** in Ogden, Weber Co., Utah 10 August 1978. Bonnie,[3807] daughter of Khalil Leon **Allen** and Ivaloo **Downs**, was born in Ogden 5 November 1955. David is an associate with his father's law firm, Whipple Law Firm, P.C., in Kansas

City, Missouri .

David Wellington **Whipple** and Bonnie Jill **Allen** had the following children:
3218	i.	Kristan Jill[14] **Whipple**[3808] was born 30 May 1979.
3219	ii.	Amie Leigh **Whipple**[3809] was born 11 July 1982.
3220	iii.	Daniel Wellington **Whipple**[3810] was born 21 June 1984.
3221	iv.	Timothy David **Whipple**[3811] was born 18 April 1986.
3222	v.	Jonathan Matthew **Whipple**[3812] was born 29 December 1988.

2788. **Anne Margaret**[13] **Whipple** (Clyde David[12], Clyde Ward[11], William Orland[10], William Ward[9], John[8], John[7], Capt. John[6], Capt. John[5], Maj. Matthew[4], Capt. John[3], Elder John[2], Matthew[1])[3813] was born 20 April 1956 and married **Richard John LaMar** in Parkville, Mo. 20 May 1989. Richard,[3814] son of Frank William **LaMar** and Marjorie (__), was born 10 November 1955.

Anne Margaret **Whipple** and Richard John **LaMar** had the following children:
3223	i.	Ashlee Anne[14] **LaMar**[3815] was born 19 May 1990.
3224	ii.	Brandon William **LaMar**[3816] was born 31 July 1992.

2791. **Melinda**[13] **Jones** (Proctor Patterson[12], Ferne Catherine[11] **Patterson**, Proctor[10], Phebe Smith[9] **Whipple**, Stephen[8], Martha[7], Dea. Nathaniel[6], Capt. John[5], Maj. Matthew[4], Capt. John[3], Elder John[2], Matthew[1])[3817] was born in Cleveland, Ohio 25 May 1943 and married **David Windisch**.

Melinda **Jones** and David **Windisch** had the following children:
+ 3225	i.	Katherine Patterson[14] **Windisch** was born 10 January 1963.
3226	ii.	David Anthony **Windisch** II[3818] was born in Miami, Dade Co., Fla. 31 May 1970.
3227	iii.	Matthew Anthony **Windisch**[3819] was born in Miami 1 August 1971.

2792. **Greta Patterson**[13] **Jones** (Proctor Patterson[12], Ferne Catherine[11] **Patterson**, Proctor[10], Phebe Smith[9] **Whipple**, Stephen[8], Martha[7], Dea. Nathaniel[6], Capt. John[5], Maj. Matthew[4], Capt. John[3], Elder John[2], Matthew[1])[3820] was born in Cleveland, Ohio 27 January 1946 and married **Michael Jones** in Winston-Salem, N.C. 2 June 1968.

Greta Patterson **Jones** and Michael **Jones** had the following child:
3228	i.	Andrew Petree[14] **Jones**[3821] was born in Wilson 18 February 1976.

2793. **John Beverly**[13] **Jones** (Proctor Patterson[12], Ferne Catherine[11] **Patterson**, Proctor[10], Phebe Smith[9] **Whipple**, Stephen[8], Martha[7], Dea. Nathaniel[6], Capt. John[5], Maj. Matthew[4], Capt. John[3], Elder John[2], Matthew[1])[3822] was born in Palo Alto, Santa Clara Co., Calif. 29 January 1949 and married **Roslyn Lewis** in Los Angeles, Calif. 4 March 1984. She was born 24 April 1953.[3823]

John Beverly **Jones** and Roslyn **Lewis** had the following children:
3229	i.	Austin Patterson[14] **Jones**[3824] was born in Santa Monica, Calif. 28 August 1984.
3230	ii.	Sydney Mara **Jones**[3825] was born in Santa Monica 16 April 1987.

2794. **Martha**[13] **Jones** (Proctor Patterson[12], Ferne Catherine[11] **Patterson**, Proctor[10], Phebe Smith[9] **Whipple**, Stephen[8], Martha[7], Dea. Nathaniel[6], Capt. John[5], Maj. Matthew[4], Capt. John[3], Elder John[2], Matthew[1])[3826] was born in Palo Alto, Santa

Clara Co., Calif. 6 July 1950 and married **Theodore A. Griffinger** Jr. in San Francisco., Calif. 3 July 1973.

Martha **Jones** and Theodore A. **Griffinger** Jr. had the following children:

3231   i.   Whitney Armstrong[14] **Griffinger**[3827] was born in San Francisco 27 October 1977.

3232   ii.   Elisabeth Patterson **Griffinger**[3828] was born in Berkeley, Calif. 3 September 1979.

2797. **Barbara Jane**[13] **Nelson** (Robert Hatch[12], Jessamine Gertrude[11] **Hatch**, Alonzo Herbert[10], Paschal[9], Anna[8] **Gould**, Anna[7] **Lane**, Timothy[6], Job[5], Susanna[4] **Whipple**, Capt. John[3], Elder John[2], Matthew[1])[3829] was born in Aspen, Colo. 7 December 1926 and married twice. (1) **Theodore G. Wege** in Bangor, Wisc. 8 June 1948. He was born in Barre Mills, Wisc. 8 June 1919.[3830] They were divorced in Cavalier, Pembina Co., N. Dak. 28 December 1976. (2) **Henry E. Grieser** in Minneapolis, Minn. 14 October 1977. Henry was born in Duluth, Minn. 12 January 1927.[3831]

Barbara Jane **Nelson** and Theodore G. **Wege** had the following children:

3233   i.   Linda Marie[14] **Wege**[3832] was born in Salt Lake City, Utah 11 January 1950 and married Alfred **Fisher** in Boston, Mass. 8 October 1982. Alfred was born in New York, N.Y. 1 March 1933.[3833]

3234   ii.   Anne Elizabeth **Wege**[3834] was born in Salt Lake City 30 April 1951.

+ 3235   iii.   Deborah Louise **Wege** was born 24 September 1952.

2799. **Eric Hatch**[13] **Nelson** (Robert Hatch[12], Jessamine Gertrude[11] **Hatch**, Alonzo Herbert[10], Paschal[9], Anna[8] **Gould**, Anna[7] **Lane**, Timothy[6], Job[5], Susanna[4] **Whipple**, Capt. John[3], Elder John[2], Matthew[1])[3835] was born in Washington, D.C. 27 May 1942 and married **Roberta Cauthron** in Miles City, Mont. 17 October 1964. They were divorced in Missoula, Mont. 25 October 1982.

Eric Hatch **Nelson** and Roberta **Cauthron** had the following children born in Missoula, Mont:

3236   i.   Misty Daniele[14] **Nelson**[3836] was born 24 June 1976.

3237   ii.   Morgan Eric **Nelson**[3837] was born 3 January 1978.

2801. **David Allen**[13] **Torsey** (Asenath Waring[12] **Hanners**, Roger Whipple[11], Cora Adalaide[10] **Whipple**, Alonzo Lyman[9], John[9], John[8], John[7], Capt. John[6], Capt. John[5], Maj. Matthew[4], Capt. John[3], Elder John[2], Matthew[1])[3838] was born 8 January 1966. and married **Heather Struss** in Salem, Mass. 9 August 1997. Heather was born in Beverly, Essex Co., Mass. 9 October 1972.[3839]

David Allen **Torsey** and Heather **Struss** had the following child:

3238   i.   Brendon[14] **Torsey**[3840] was born in Beverly in November 1999.

2803. **Susan Priscilla**[13] **Nelms** (Priscilla Ann[12] **Hanners**, Ralph Loring[11], Cora Adalaide[10] **Whipple**, Alonzo Lyman[9], John[9], John[8], John[7], Capt. John[6], Capt. John[5], Maj. Matthew[4], Capt. John[3], Elder John[2], Matthew[1])[3841] was born in Ancon, Canal Zone, Panama 28 May 1949 and married twice. (1) **Jay Gillette** in Marin Co., Calif. in November 1971. Jay,[3842] son of Charles **Gillette** and Penny (__), was born 1 May 1949. (2) **Richard Murphy** in Golden, Colo. 28 April 1989. Richard was born in Nyack, N.Y. 15 August 1940.[3843]

Susan Priscilla **Nelms** and Jay **Gillette** had the following children:
    3239   i.   Jared Douglas[14] **Gillette**[3844] was born in Walnut Creek, Contra Costa Co., Calif. 12 February 1978.
    3240   ii.   Katie Katherine **Gillette**[3845] was born in Denver, Colo. 13 December 1979.
    3241   iii.   Jesse Leann **Gillette**[3846] was born in Denver 30 June 1982.

2805. Debra Louise[13] **Nelms** (Priscilla Ann[12] **Hanners**, Ralph Loring[11], Cora Adalaide[10] **Whipple**, Alonzo Lyman[9], John[9], John[8], John[7], Capt. John[6], Capt. John[5], Maj. Matthew[4], Capt. John[3], Elder John[2], Matthew[1])[3847] was born in Denver, Colo. 20 June 1954 and married twice. (1) **Ricky Eugene Hubler** in Denver, Colo, 24 May 1975. Ricky was born in Newton, Jasper Co., Iowa 17 October 1952.[3848] (2) **David Emerson Kaylor**. He was born in New Philadelphia, Ohio.[3849]

Debra Louise **Nelms** and Ricky Eugene **Hubler** had the following child:
    3242   i.   Kara Michelle[14] **Hubler**[3850] was born in Denver, Colo. 6 August 1979 and married Steven Josiah **Dolos** in Las Vegas, Clark Co., Nev. 1 November 1997. They were divorced in Golden, Colo. in August 1999.

2806. Judith Ann[13] **Nelms** (Priscilla Ann[12] **Hanners**, Ralph Loring[11], Cora Adalaide[10] **Whipple**, Alonzo Lyman[9], John[9], John[8], John[7], Capt. John[6], Capt. John[5], Maj. Matthew[4], Capt. John[3], Elder John[2], Matthew[1])[3851] was born in Denver, Colo. 16 January 1957 and married twice. (1) **Wayne Gomez** in Denver 13 December 1975. Wayne,[3852] son of Samuel **Gomez** and Della (__), was born in Denver 7 February 1956. (2) **Clay Sharp** in Lakewood, Colo. 21 November 1992. He was born in Wyoming 16 March 1961.[3853]

Judith Ann **Nelms** and Wayne **Gomez** had the following child:
    3243   i.   Joslyn Nicole[14] **Gomez**[3854] was born in Denver, Colo. 16 August 1981.

2807. Mark Ralph[13] **Nelms** (Priscilla Ann[12] **Hanners**, Ralph Loring[11], Cora Adalaide[10] **Whipple**, Alonzo Lyman[9], John[9], John[8], John[7], Capt. John[6], Capt. John[5], Maj. Matthew[4], Capt. John[3], Elder John[2], Matthew[1])[3855] was born in Denver, Colo. 28 April 1960 and married **Deborha Dawn Peterson** in Arvada, Colo. 29 June 1984. Deborha is the daughter of Peter **Peterson** and Sharon (__). [3856] Mark and Deborah were divorced in February 1992

Mark Ralph **Nelms** and Deborha Dawn **Peterson** had the following children:
    3244   i.   Tyler Justin[14] **Nelms**[3857] was born in Wheatridge, Colo. 18 June 1986.
    3245   ii.   Jaime Lynn **Nelms**[3858] was born in Wheatridge 16 May 1989.

2808. Stephen[13] **Hanners** (Howard Whipple[12], Ralph Loring[11], Cora Adalaide[10] **Whipple**, Alonzo Lyman[9], John[9], John[8], John[7], Capt. John[6], Capt. John[5], Maj. Matthew[4], Capt. John[3], Elder John[2], Matthew[1])[3859] was born in Midland, Mich. 22 July 1957 and married **Nancy Merrill** in Bainbridge Island, Wash. 9 July 1989.

Stephen **Hanners** and Nancy **Merrill** had the following children:
    3246   i.   Angla Loring[14] **Hanners**[3860] was born in Bremerton, Wash. 27 April 1992.
    3247   ii.   Crystal Ann **Hanners**[3861] was born in Bremerton 19 September 1994.

2809. John David[13] **Hanners** (Howard Whipple[12], Ralph Loring[11], Cora

Adalaide[10] **Whipple**, Alonzo Lyman[9], John[9], John[8], John[7], Capt. John[6], Capt. John[5], Maj. Matthew[4], Capt. John[3], Elder John[2], Matthew[1])[3862] was born in Midland, Mich. 22 September 1959 and married **Julie Schilter** in Seattle, Wash. 27 July 1996.

John David **Hanners** and Julie **Schilter** had the following children:
- 3248   i. John David[14] **Hanners** Jr.[3863] was born in Seattle, Wash. 10 August 1997.
- 3249   ii. Jessica **Hanners**[3864] was born in Snoqualmie, Wash. 16 January 2000.

2813. Areta Mae[13] **Powers** (Edwin Cyrus[12], Cyrus Hale Stone[11], John[10], Cyrus Hale Stone[9], Lavinia[8] **Stone**, Capt. Amos[7], Amos[6], Simon[5], Deacon Simon[4], Mary[3] **Whipple**, Elder John[2], Matthew[1])[3865] birth date unknown, married (__) **Baker**.

Areta Mae **Powers** and (__) **Baker** had the following child:
- 3250   i. Margaret[14] **Baker**[3866] married (__) **Christmas**.

2814. Clarissa Louise[13] **Powers** (Edwin Cyrus[12], Cyrus Hale Stone[11], John[10], Cyrus Hale Stone[9], Lavinia[8] **Stone**, Capt. Amos[7], Amos[6], Simon[5], Deacon Simon[4], Mary[3] **Whipple**, Elder John[2], Matthew[1])[3867] was born abt 1935 and married twice. (1) **Frederick Charles Green**. (2) **Robert Eugene Sexton**.

Clarissa Louise **Powers** and Frederick Charles **Green** had the following child:
- + 3251   i. Frederick Lee[14] **Green**.

Clarissa Louise **Powers** and Robert Eugene **Sexton** had the following children:
- + 3252   ii. Lonni Rae **Sexton**.
- + 3253   iii. Karen Jill **Sexton**.
- + 3254   iv. Patty Jo **Sexton**.

2817. Leo John[13] **Powers** (Bert E.[12], Cyrus Hale Stone[11], John[10], Cyrus Hale Stone[9], Lavinia[8] **Stone**, Capt. Amos[7], Amos[6], Simon[5], Deacon Simon[4], Mary[3] **Whipple**, Elder John[2], Matthew[1])[3868] was born 28 April 1938 and died 8 March 1985 at 46 years of age. He married **Patricia Brown** 27 July 1958.

Leo John **Powers** and Patricia **Brown** had the following children:
- 3255   i. Sherri[14] **Powers**.[3869]
- 3256   ii. Kendall **Powers**.[3870]
- 3257   iii. Dana **Powers**.[3871]

2819. Ralph Irvin[13] **Hazen** (Aretta Viola[12] **Powers**, Cyrus Hale Stone[11], John[10], Cyrus Hale Stone[9], Lavinia[8] **Stone**, Capt. Amos[7], Amos[6], Simon[5], Deacon Simon[4], Mary[3] **Whipple**, Elder John[2], Matthew[1])[3872] birth date unknown, married **Alice Reece**.

Ralph Irvin **Hazen** and Alice **Reece** had the following children:
- 3258   i. Jeni Kay[14] **Hazen**[3873] married twice. (1) (__) **Huddleston**. (2) Wayne **Shymanski**.
- 3259   ii. James Reece **Hazen**.[3874]

2820. Mary Evva[13] **Hazen** (Aretta Viola[12] **Powers**, Cyrus Hale Stone[11], John[10], Cyrus Hale Stone[9], Lavinia[8] **Stone**, Capt. Amos[7], Amos[6], Simon[5], Deacon Simon[4], Mary[3] **Whipple**, Elder John[2], Matthew[1])[3875] birth date unknown, married **Lloyd LeRoy Jones**.

Mary Evva **Hazen** and Lloyd LeRoy **Jones** had the following children:

    3260   i.   Diane Louise[14] **Jones**[3876] married Lonny Dean **Riley**.

    3261   ii. Linda Kay **Jones**[3877] married Arlan Wayne **Preston**.

    3262   iii. Donna Marie **Jones**[3878] married Skyler Dean **Criss**.

2821. Martha Ola[13] **Hazen** (Aretta Viola[12] **Powers**, Cyrus Hale Stone[11], John[10], Cyrus Hale Stone[9], Lavinia[8] **Stone**, Capt. Amos[7], Amos[6], Simon[5], Deacon Simon[4], Mary[3] **Whipple**, Elder John[2], Matthew[1])[3879] birth date unknown, married **John Albert Musmaker**.

Martha Ola **Hazen** and John Albert **Musmaker** had the following children:

    3263   i.   Bruce Allan[14] **Musmaker**[3880] married Chrystal Ann **Christenson**.

    3264   ii. Brian Earl **Musmaker**[3881].

2822. Ruth Ruby[13] **Hazen** (Aretta Viola[12] **Powers**, Cyrus Hale Stone[11], John[10], Cyrus Hale Stone[9], Lavinia[8] **Stone**, Capt. Amos[7], Amos[6], Simon[5], Deacon Simon[4], Mary[3] **Whipple**, Elder John[2], Matthew[1])[3882] birth date unknown, married **Robert Arthur Long**.

Ruth Ruby **Hazen** and Robert Arthur **Long** had the following children:

    3265   i.   Raymond Andrew[14] **Long**.[3883]

    3266   ii. Ryan Arthur **Long**.[3884]

    3267   iii. Randall Abraham **Long**.[3885]

2824. Vaneta Lorraine[13] **Bender** (Mabel S.[12] **Powers**, Cyrus Hale Stone[11], John[10], Cyrus Hale Stone[9], Lavinia[8] **Stone**, Capt. Amos[7], Amos[6], Simon[5], Deacon Simon[4], Mary[3] **Whipple**, Elder John[2], Matthew[1])[3886] birth date unknown, married **Carl LeRoy Perkins**.

Vaneta Lorraine **Bender** and Carl LeRoy **Perkins** had the following children:

    3268   i.   Carl Richard[14] **Perkins**[3887]. married Mary Margaret **Quinn**.

    3269   ii. Robert Dennis **Perkins**[3888] married Ceryl Ann **Duckworth**.

2826. Harold Cyrus[13] **Powers** (Wesley Raymond[12], Cyrus Hale Stone[11], John[10], Cyrus Hale Stone[9], Lavinia[8] **Stone**, Capt. Amos[7], Amos[6], Simon[5], Deacon Simon[4], Mary[3] **Whipple**, Elder John[2], Matthew[1])[3889] birth date unknown, married **Patricia Darlene Shawgo**.

Harold Cyrus **Powers** and Patricia Darlene **Shawgo** had the following children:

    3270   i.   Michael Harold[14] **Powers**[3890] married Peggy J. **Payne**.

 + 3271   ii. Lisa Carol **Powers**.

 + 3272   iii. Jill Kay **Powers**.

    3273   iv. Beth Ann **Powers**.[3891]

2827. Marilyn Lou[13] **Powers** (Wesley Raymond[12], Cyrus Hale Stone[11], John[10], Cyrus Hale Stone[9], Lavinia[8] **Stone**, Capt. Amos[7], Amos[6], Simon[5], Deacon Simon[4], Mary[3] **Whipple**, Elder John[2], Matthew[1])[3892] birth date unknown, married **Robert D. Hulbert**.

Marilyn Lou **Powers** and Robert D. **Hulbert** had the following children:

    3274   i.   Terry[14] **Hulbert**.[3893]

3275   ii. Mark **Hulbert**.[3894]
3276   iii. Sheila **Hulbert**.[3895]

2829. Thomas Nelson[13] **Pratt** (Orville Powers[12], Olive Evalena[11] **Powers**, John[10], Cyrus Hale Stone[9], Lavinia[8] **Stone**, Capt. Amos[7], Amos[6], Simon[5], Deacon Simon[4], Mary[3] **Whipple**, Elder John[2], Matthew[1])[3896] was born in Oak Park Cook Co., Ill. 10 August 1937 and married **Marilyn Jeanne Sorensen** there 28 November 1959. Marilyn,[3897] daughter of Sidney **Sorensen** and Oline **Kvanvic**, was christened in Oak Park 14 May 1939. Thomas earned a Bachelor of Mechanical Engineering degree from the General Motors Institute, a Master of Science in Mechanical Engineering from Purdue University, and a management degree from Illinois Benedictine College. An engineer, he was a supervisor and manager for the electro-motive division of General Motors Corp. until his retirement in September 1991. His avocation is genealogy.

Thomas Nelson **Pratt** and Marilyn Jeanne **Sorensen** had the following children:

+ 3277   i. Thomas Jeffrey[14] **Pratt** was born 24 November 1962.
+ 3278   ii. Karen Ellen **Pratt** was born 8 July 1965.

2831. Errol Kathleen[13] **Powers** (William Cameron[12], Leroy Cyrus[11], Cyrus Cameron[10], Cyrus Hale Stone[9], Lavinia[8] **Stone**, Capt. Amos[7], Amos[6], Simon[5], Deacon Simon[4], Mary[3] **Whipple**, Elder John[2], Matthew[1])[3898] was born in 1949 and married **Jeff Buis**.

Errol Kathleen **Powers** and Jeff **Buis** had the following children:

3279   i. Daniel[14] **Buis**[3899] was born in 1983.
3280   ii. Collin **Buis**[3900] was born in 1986.

2832. Kathryn Lee[13] **Powers** (William Cameron[12], Leroy Cyrus[11], Cyrus Cameron[10], Cyrus Hale Stone[9], Lavinia[8] **Stone**, Capt. Amos[7], Amos[6], Simon[5], Deacon Simon[4], Mary[3] **Whipple**, Elder John[2], Matthew[1])[3901] was born in 1951 and married **Scott Vroom**.

Kathryn Lee **Powers** and Scott **Vroom** had the following children:

3281   i. Katie[14] **Vroom**[3902] was born in 1984.
3282   ii. Corey **Vroom**[3903] was born in 1988.

2836. Sarah Hale[13] **Powers** (William Cameron[12], Leroy Cyrus[11], Cyrus Cameron[10], Cyrus Hale Stone[9], Lavinia[8] **Stone**, Capt. Amos[7], Amos[6], Simon[5], Deacon Simon[4], Mary[3] **Whipple**, Elder John[2], Matthew[1])[3904] was born in 1981.

Sarah Hale **Powers** had the following child:

3283   i. Cameron Alexander[14] **Powers**[3905] was born in Des Moines, Iowa 23 June 1998.

2837. Douglas[13] **Grodt** (Catherine Ann[12] **Powers**, Leroy Cyrus[11], Cyrus Cameron[10], Cyrus Hale Stone[9], Lavinia[8] **Stone**, Capt. Amos[7], Amos[6], Simon[5], Deacon Simon[4], Mary[3] **Whipple**, Elder John[2], Matthew[1])[3906] was born in 1951 and married **Tina Jesperson**.

Douglas **Grodt** and Tina **Jesperson** had the following children:

3284   i. Caroline[14] **Grodt**[3907] was born in 1980.

3285 ii. Paul **Grodt**[3908] was born in 1982.

2838. Mary[13] **Grodt** (Catherine Ann[12] **Powers**, Leroy Cyrus[11], Cyrus Cameron[10], Cyrus Hale Stone[9], Lavinia[8] **Stone**, Capt. Amos[7], Amos[6], Simon[5], Deacon Simon[4], Mary[3] **Whipple**, Elder John[2], Matthew[1])[3909] was born in 1952 and married **Radia Suku**.

Mary **Grodt** and Radia **Suku** had the following children:
3286 i. Ryan Charles[14] **Suku**[3910] was born in 1986.
3287 ii. Renee Catherine **Suku**[3911] was born in 1988.
3288 iii. Matalie Paige **Suku**[3912] was born in 1992.

2848. Joni Lansing[13] **Bacon** (Samuel Newton[12] **Bacon,**, Samuel Newton[11] **Bacon**, Allen Harlow[10], Samuel Newton[9], Alma Ellery[8] **Holden**, Phineas[7], Capt. Asa[6], Abigail[5] **Stone**, Deacon Simon[4], Mary[3] **Whipple**, Elder John[2], Matthew[1])[3913] was born in Pittsfield, Berkshire Co., Mass. 26 July 1955 and married **Robert Joseph Lawless** in Washington, D.C. 25 August 1979. Robert,[3914] son of Joseph Francis **Lawless** and Ethel **Sliney**, was born in Lynn, Essex Co., Mass. 27 December 1946.

Joni Lansing **Bacon** and Robert Joseph **Lawless** had the following child:
3289 i. Alessandra Christinia[14] **Lawless**[3915] was born in Atlanta, Ga. 10 April 1983.

2850. Peter Hazeltine[13] **Bacon** (Samuel Newton[12] **Bacon,**, Samuel Newton[11] **Bacon**, Allen Harlow[10], Samuel Newton[9], Alma Ellery[8] **Holden**, Phineas[7], Capt. Asa[6], Abigail[5] **Stone**, Deacon Simon[4], Mary[3] **Whipple**, Elder John[2], Matthew[1])[3916] was born in North Adams, Mass. 7 December 1960 and married **Diana Lyn Caton** in South Lake Tahoe, Calif. 9 March 1988. Diana,[3917] daughter of Albert William **Caton** and Evelyn Royal **Smith**, was born 12 May 1953.

Peter Hazeltine **Bacon** and Diana Lyn **Caton** had the following child:
3290 i. Peter Jonathan[14] **Bacon**[3918] was born 20 August 1988.

2853. Deborah Lansing[13] **Bacon** (Charles Lansing[12], Samuel Newton[11], Allen Harlow[10], Samuel Newton[9], Alma Ellery[8] **Holden**, Phineas[7], Capt. Asa[6], Abigail[5] **Stone**, Deacon Simon[4], Mary[3] **Whipple**, Elder John[2], Matthew[1])[3919] was born in Amesbury, Essex Co., Mass. 14 June 1957 and married **Francis Joseph Mohr, Jr.** in Amherst, Mass. 24 April 1976. Francis,[3920] son of Francis Joseph **Mohr** and Elizabeth **O'Hara**, was born in Queens, Long Island, N.Y. 23 July 1947.

Deborah Lansing **Bacon** and Francis Joseph **Mohr, Jr.** had the following children:
3291 i. Daniel Francis[14] **Mohr**,[3921] was born in Brattleboro, Vt. 25 September 1978.
3292 ii. Jeffrey Samuel **Mohr**,[3922] was born in Brattleboro 11 September 1981.

2854. Timothy Mather[13] **Bacon** (Richard Mather[12], Samuel Newton[11], Allen Harlow[10], Samuel Newton[9], Alma Ellery[8] **Holden**, Phineas[7], Capt. Asa[6], Abigail[5] **Stone**, Deacon Simon[4], Mary[3] **Whipple**, Elder John[2], Matthew[1])[3923] was born in Concord, Rockingham Co., N.H. 13 September 1962 and married **Kaylynn Fellows** 9 June 1988. Kaylynn,[3924] daughter of Joseph **Fellows** and Saralee **Wood**, was born in Concord 21 June 1964.

Timothy Mather **Bacon** and Kaylynn **Fellows** had the following child:
 3293 i. Katrina Lynn[14] **Bacon**[3925] was born in Concord 28 January 1990.

2857. Linda Jean[13] **Washburn** (Lorna Mather[12] **Swain**, Elizabeth Harlow[11] **Bacon**, Allen Harlow[10], Samuel Newton[9], Alma Ellery[8] **Holden**, Phineas[7], Capt. Asa[6], Abigail[5] **Stone**, Deacon Simon[4], Mary[3] **Whipple**, Elder John[2], Matthew[1])[3926] was born in Westfield, Mass. 2 February 1961 and married **Matthew Putnam Stone** in Paxton, Mass. 14 May 1988. Matthew,[3927] son of James Russell **Stone** Jr. and Carolyn Ann **Everleth**, was born in Worcester, Worcester Co., Mass. 12 March 1958.

Linda Jean **Washburn** and Matthew Putnam **Stone** had the following child:
 3294 i. Russell Putnam[14] **Stone**[3928] was born in Worcester 11 November 1991.

2859. David Newman[13] **Swain** (Robert David[12], Elizabeth Harlow[11] **Bacon**, Allen Harlow[10], Samuel Newton[9], Alma Ellery[8] **Holden**, Phineas[7], Capt. Asa[6], Abigail[5] **Stone**, Deacon Simon[4], Mary[3] **Whipple**, Elder John[2], Matthew[1])[3929] was born in Evanston, Ill. 12 June 1958 and married **Dorothy Ann Richter** in Harvard, Middlesex Co., Mass. 2 May 1987. Dorothy,[3930] daughter of Edwin William **Richter** and Margaret Carrick **Wright**, was born in Concord, Mass. 20 January 1960.

David Newman **Swain** and Dorothy Ann **Richter** had the following child:
 3295 i. Carrie Elizabeth[14] **Swain**[3931] was born in Concord 13 August 1989.

2863. Susan Elizabeth[13] **Foster** (Catharine Mather[12] **Bacon**,, Allen Harlow[11], Allen Harlow[10] **Bacon**, Samuel Newton[9], Alma Ellery[8] **Holden**, Phineas[7], Capt. Asa[6], Abigail[5] **Stone**, Deacon Simon[4], Mary[3] **Whipple**, Elder John[2], Matthew[1])[3932] was born in Glens Falls, N.Y. 16 March 1953 and married **Curtis Lee Forsyth** in South Glens Falls, N.Y. 24 May 1975. Curtis,[3933] son of George Lewis **Forsyth** and Joanne **Chamberlin**, was born in Lowville, N.Y. 8 July 1953.

Susan Elizabeth **Foster** and Curtis Lee **Forsyth** had the following child:
 3296 i. Thomas Richards[14] **Forsyth**[3934] was born in Syracuse, N.Y. 7 October 1982. Adopted.

2865. Catharine Mather[13] **Foster** (Catharine Mather[12] **Bacon**,, Allen Harlow[11], Allen Harlow[10] **Bacon**, Samuel Newton[9], Alma Ellery[8] **Holden**, Phineas[7], Capt. Asa[6], Abigail[5] **Stone**, Deacon Simon[4], Mary[3] **Whipple**, Elder John[2], Matthew[1])[3935] was born in Rutland, Rutland Co., Vt. 17 April 1957 and married **Bradford Lee Parker** in Greenwich, N.Y. 7 August 1982. Bradford,[3936] son of Bruce L. **Parker** and Judythe Ann **Daggett**, was born at Camp LeJeune, N.C. 23 March 1956.

Catharine Mather **Foster** and Bradford Lee **Parker** had the following child:
 3297 i. Joshua Lee[14] **Parker**[3937] was born in Burlington, Chittenden Co., Vt. 19 July 1990.

2866. John Peter[13] **Gillis** (Marian Jagel[12] **Bacon**,, Allen Harlow[11], Allen Harlow[10] **Bacon**, Samuel Newton[9], Alma Ellery[8] **Holden**, Phineas[7], Capt. Asa[6], Abigail[5] **Stone**, Deacon Simon[4], Mary[3] **Whipple**, Elder John[2], Matthew[1])[3938] was born in Albany, N.Y. 11 October 1961 and married **Deborah Anne Flanagan** 29 August

1987. Deborah,[3939] daughter of James William **Flanagan** and Margaret Mary **Flynn**, was born in Kittery, Maine 14 June 1962.

John Peter **Gillis** and Deborah Anne **Flanagan** had the following children:

3298   i.   Connor Flanagan[14] **Gillis**[3940] was born in Worcester, Worcester Co., Mass. 9 December 1989.

3299   ii.   Macaulay Flanagan **Gillis**[3941] was born in Worcester 26 January 1991.

2868. **Robert E.**[13] **Wise** (William Oliver[12], Mary Olive[11] **Carr**, William Dustin[10], Lyman[9], Susanna[8] **Dunton**, Mary[7] **Jewell**, Mary[6] **Whitney**, Mary[5] **Stone**, Deacon Simon[4], Mary[3] **Whipple**, Elder John[2], Matthew[1])[3942] was born in St. Albans, Vt. 26 December 1913 and married **Charlotte Cutts**. Charlotte was born in New York, N.Y. 26 December 1912.[3943] Robert descends from both John and Matthew Whipple of Ipswich. His descent from John is through his daughter Mary who married Deacon Simon Stone. He descends from two of Matthew's children: John and his his third wife Mary Stevens and Elizabeth and her husband Jacob Perkins.

Robert E. **Wise** and Charlotte **Cutts** had the following children:

+ 3300   i.   Eugenia[14] **Wise** was born 14 January 1942.

+ 3301   ii.   Barbara **Wise** was born 2 March 1944.

+ 3302   iii.   John O. **Wise** was born 17 November 1953.

2869. **Miriam**[13] **Wise** (William Oliver[12], Mary Olive[11] **Carr**, William Dustin[10], Lyman[9], Susanna[8] **Dunton**, Mary[7] **Jewell**, Mary[6] **Whitney**, Mary[5] **Stone**, Deacon Simon[4], Mary[3] **Whipple**, Elder John[2], Matthew[1])[3944] was born 17 November 1916 and married **Byron W. Saunders**. He was born in June 1914 and died 4 January 1987 at 72 years of age.[3945]

Miriam **Wise** and Byron W. **Saunders** had the following children:

+ 3303   i.   William C.[14] **Saunders** was born 18 March 1945.

+ 3304   ii.   Martha **Saunders** was born 10 May 1947.

+ 3305   iii.   Carolyn **Saunders** was born 5 June 1951.

2870. **William Oliver**[13] **Wise Jr.** (William Oliver[12], Mary Olive[11] **Carr**, William Dustin[10], Lyman[9], Susanna[8] **Dunton**, Mary[7] **Jewell**, Mary[6] **Whitney**, Mary[5] **Stone**, Deacon Simon[4], Mary[3] **Whipple**, Elder John[2], Matthew[1])[3946] was born 24 July 1919 and married **Ruby Kent**. Ruby was born 11 March 1923.[3947]

William Oliver **Wise** Jr. and Ruby **Kent** had the following children:

+ 3306   i.   William Oliver[14] **Wise III** was born in 1954.

3307   ii.   Cynthia Anne **Wise**[3948] was born in 1955.

2871. **Virginia Anne**[13] **Croissant** (Martin[12], Nellie Frances[11] **King**, Edwin Henry[10], John[9], Lois[8] **Jackson**, Lois[7] **Woodward**,, Mary[6] **Stone**, Samuel[5], Ebenezer[4], Mary[3] **Whipple**, Elder John[2], Matthew[1])[3949] was born in Albany, N.Y. 30 March 1920 and married **Charles Henry Wolfe** in Pittsfield, Berkshire Co., Mass. 29 May 1941. Charles,[3950] son of Charles Lesley **Wolfe** and Edna Hannah **Sibley**, was born in Little Falls, Herkimer Co., N.Y. 14 November 1918 and died 14 November 1990 in Malone, Franklin Co., N.Y. at 72 years of age.

Virginia Anne **Croissant** and Charles Henry **Wolfe** had the following children:

+ 3308   i.   Leslie Anne[14] **Wolfe** was born 7 January 1947.

3309   ii. Charles Henry **Wolfe** II[3951] was born in Malone 29 January 1954 and married Joyce **Guthrie**.

2899. Francis Richard[13] **Jenne** (Francis Richard[12], Frank[11], Jerome Adelbert[10], Sarah Jane[9] **Johnson**, John[8], Abner[7], Hannah[6] **Eaton**, Lydia Abiah[5] **Starr**, Mary[4] **Stone**, Mary[3] **Whipple**, Elder John[2], Matthew[1])[3952] was born in Potsdam, N.Y. 22 November 1936 and married twice. (1) **Geraldine Davies** in Canton, N.Y. 27 July 1963. Geraldine,[3953] daughter of Earl **Davies** and Marion **Bamberger**, was born in Utica, Oneida Co., N.Y. 28 November 1941. Geraldine also married **Charles Baker**. (2) **Patricia (LaClair) Marsjanik** in 1977. Francis, a Korean War veteran, was a public accountant in Potsdam, N.Y. in 1997.

Francis Richard **Jenne** and Geraldine **Davies** had the following children:
    3310   i. Beth-Anne[14] **Jenne**[3954] was born 25 July 1964.
    3311   ii. Jodie-Lyn **Jenne**[3955] was born 11 August 1967.

2904. Jessie Arline[13] **Stubbs** (Lydia Irene[12] **Wills**, Louisa Malvina[11] **Patterson**, Austin Eaton[10], Esther Adeline[9] **Eaton**, Arrunah[8], John[7], John[6], Lydia Abiah[5] **Starr**, Mary[4] **Stone**, Mary[3] **Whipple**, Elder John[2], Matthew[1])[3956] was born in Kansas City, Jackson Co., Mo. and married **Richard Holt Rolls** there 24 November 1937. Richard is the son of Hurbert Reason **Rolls** and Alma Gertrude **Holt**.

Jessie Arline **Stubbs** and Richard Holt **Rolls** had the following child:
    3312   i. Sally Arline[14] **Rolls**[3957] was born in Kansas City and married Jerry William **Pavia** in Whittier, Los Angeles Co., Calif. 21 June 1957. Jerry is the son of Vincent James **Pavia** and Lucille C. **Lawler**.

2905. Victoria Anne[13] **McIntosh** (Eunice Mae[12] **Baldwin**, Nellie Eliza[11] **Newell**, Mary Frances[10] **Grow**, Lorenzo[9], Samuel Porter[8], Joseph[7], Abigail[6] **Dana**, Susanna[5] **Starr**, Mary[4] **Stone**, Mary[3] **Whipple**, Elder John[2], Matthew[1])[3958] was born in Bishop, Calif. 19 May 1919 and married **James Rife Hayden** 25 September 1940. James,[3959] son of Dory **Hayden** and Gertrude Alma **Rife**, was born in Monessan, Pa. 1 March 1916.

Victoria Anne **McIntosh** and James Rife **Hayden** had the following child:
  + 3313   i. Ruth Anne[14] **Hayden** was born 12 January 1946.

2915. Thomas William[13] **Ball** (Wilbur Fiske[12], Wilbur Fiske[11], Francis Herbert[10], Wilbur Fiske[9], James Bradley[8], Abigail[7] **Starr**, Capt. Comfort[6], Comfort[5], Mary[4] **Stone**, Mary[3] **Whipple**, Elder John[2], Matthew[1])[3960] was born in Haverhill, Mass. 28 February 1954 and married **Joy Lynn Combs** in Finneytown, Ohio in 1983.

Thomas William **Ball** and Joy Lynn **Combs** had the following children:
    3314   i. Lisa Marie[14] **Ball**[3961] was born 17 August 1985.
    3315   ii. Rachel Lee Ann **Ball**[3962] was born 27 September 1988.

2916. Susan Lynne[13] **Ball** (Wilbur Fiske[12], Wilbur Fiske[11], Francis Herbert[10], Wilbur Fiske[9], James Bradley[8], Abigail[7] **Starr**, Capt. Comfort[6], Comfort[5], Mary[4] **Stone**, Mary[3] **Whipple**, Elder John[2], Matthew[1])[3963] was born in Haverhill, Mass. 16 May 1955 and married **Thomas Lucas** in Smyrna, Ga. 4 July 1987.

Susan Lynne **Ball** and Thomas **Lucas** had the following child:

3316   i. Joshua David[14] **Lucas**[3964] was born in New Orleans, La. 27 November 1983.

2917. Cherryl Ann[13] **Ball** (Wilbur Fiske[12], Wilbur Fiske[11], Francis Herbert[10], Wilbur Fiske[9], James Bradley[8], Abigail[7] **Starr**, Capt. Comfort[6], Comfort[5], Mary[4] **Stone**, Mary[3] **Whipple**, Elder John[2], Matthew[1])[3965] was born in Haverhill, Mass. 9 October 1956 and married **Kirk Robert Wallbillich** in Belle Chasse, Plaquimine Parish, La. 18 June 1994. Kirk is the son of Robert **Wallbillich** and Joanna **Grior**.

Cherryl Ann **Ball** and Kirk Robert **Wallbillich** had the following children:

3317   i. Graham[14] **Ball**[3966] was born in New Orleans, La. 13 February 1981.
3318   ii. Elizabeth **Wallbillich**[3967] was born in Dallas, Texas 22 November 1994.

2919. Donald Dee[13] **Jones** (Helen Beatrice[12] **Carson**, Estella Grace[11] **Wilson**, Mary Arvilla[10] **Viersen**, Mary[9] **Starr**, Lovel[8], Comfort[7], Capt. Comfort[6], Comfort[5], Mary[4] **Stone**, Mary[3] **Whipple**, Elder John[2], Matthew[1])[3968] was born in Pilger, Stanton Co., Nebr. 27 November 1932 and married **Joan Carolyn Reifschneider** in Omaha, Nebr. 22 August 1953. Joan,[3969] daughter of M. S. **Reifschneider** and Ivy **Nelson**, was born in Omaha 5 May 1933. She is a graduate of the U. of Nebraska where she was a member of Phi Upsilon Omicron and is a retired pharmacy bookkeeper. Donald earned a B.S. from the U. of Nebraska where he was a member of Rho Chi and Sigma Xi. He is a U.S. Army veteran and a pharmacist at Carroll Clinic Pharmacy, Carroll, Iowa .

Donald Dee **Jones** and Joan Carolyn **Reifschneider** had the following children:

+ 3319   i. Carolyn Christine[14] **Jones** was born 12 June 1955.
+ 3320   ii. Laurie Grace **Jones** was born 21 January 1957.
+ 3321   iii. Susan Marie **Jones** was born 7 May 1958.
+ 3322   iv. Philip Lee **Jones** was born 7 May 1960.
  3323   v. Elizabeth Ann **Jones**[3970] was born in Carroll, Carroll Co., Iowa 8 August 1961 and married Joseph Patrick **Eaker** in Omaha 4 April 1992. Joseph,[3971] son of Edward E. **Eaker** and Margarita **Corn**, was born in Ft. Oglethorpe, Catoosa Co., Ga. 25 March 1963. He earned a B.S. from the U. of Tennessee and a M.S. from Case Western Reserve and is a hydro-geologist for the state of N.J. Elizabeth earned a B.A. at Iowa State University, a M.A. from Case Western Reserve, and is working for a Ph.D in anthropology at Rutgers University graduate school.

2922. George Robert[13] **Andrews** (Carol Lydia[12] **Fairweather**, Ruth Elizabeth[11] **Spooner**, Minnie Elnora[10] **Cram**, Angeline[9] **Ward**, Elsie Elizabeth[8] **Starr**, Ebenezer[7], Ebenezer[6], Comfort[5], Mary[4] **Stone**, Mary[3] **Whipple**, Elder John[2], Matthew[1])[3972] was born in Pawtucket, R.I. 22 April 1954. and married twice. (1) **Karen Seals** in Bolivar, Mo. 8 February 1975. Karen was born 28 October 1953.[3973] They were divorced in Miami, Okla. in 1980. (2) **Tena Faye Bivens** 24 August 1981. Tena,[3974] daughter of Tony Arthur **Bivens** and Jacquelle **Maye**, was born in Pamps, Texas 5 March 1958

George Robert **Andrews** and Tena Faye **Bivens** had the following children:

3324   i. Robert Arthur[14] **Andrews**[3975] was born 5 November 1985.
3325   ii. Nicole Marie **Andrews**[3976] was born in Raleigh, N.C. 25 May 1988.

2923. **Sharon Leslie**[13] **Andrews** (Carol Lydia[12] **Fairweather**, Ruth Elizabeth[11] **Spooner**, Minnie Elnora[10] **Cram**, Angeline[9] **Ward**, Elsie Elizabeth[8] **Starr**, Ebenezer[7], Ebenezer[6], Comfort[5], Mary[4] **Stone**, Mary[3] **Whipple**, Elder John[2], Matthew[1])[3977] was born in Pawtucket, R.I. 10 June 1955 and married **Joseph Donald Riesenberg** in Cincinnati, Ohio 17 April 1977. Joseph was born in Cincinnati 26 February 1951.[3978]

Sharon Leslie **Andrews** and Joseph Donald **Riesenberg** had the following children born in Cincinnati, Ohio:

3326   i. Amy Nicole[14] **Riesenberg**[3979] was born 9 April 1978.
3327   ii. Justin Craig **Riesenberg**[3980] was born 13 April 1981.
3328   iii. Allison Maria **Riesenberg**[3981] was born 11 April 1986.
3329   iv. Ashley Laura **Riesenberg**[3982] was born 29 March 1988.

2926. **John Henry**[13] **Westensee** (Emil John[12], Norah Leona[11] **Brush**, Harriet Elizabeth[10] **Watrous**, Caroline M.[9] **Estey**, John Dean[8], John Dean[7], Solomon[6], Elizabeth Mary[5] **Stearns**, Elizabeth[4] **Stone**, Mary[3] **Whipple**, Elder John[2], Matthew[1])[3983] was born in Moline, Ill. 22 July 1947 and married **Colette Ann Yogele** there 21 August 1976. Colette was born in Moline 25 October 1952.[3984]

John Henry **Westensee** and Colette Ann **Yogele** had the following children born in Rock Island, Ill.:

3330   i. Jay Andrew[14] **Westensee**[3985] was born 9 May 1981.
3331   ii. Erin Kathleen **Westensee**[3986] was born 26 February 1983.
3332   iii. Laura Ann **Westensee**[3987] was born 19 March 1986.

2927. **Lila Lee**[13] **Packard** (Merle Everett[12], Etta Rosella[11] **Makepeace**, Almira D.[10] **Smith**, James[9], George[8], Hannah[7] **Wilbor**, Mary[6] **Stearns**, Jonathan[5], Elizabeth[4] **Stone**, Mary[3] **Whipple**, Elder John[2], Matthew[1])[3988] was born in Boston, Mass. 30 September 1924 and married twice. (1) **Harry George Woodworth Jr.** in Brown Co., Texas 10 April 1943. Harry,[3989] son of Harry George **Woodworth** and Agnes Frances **Samuelson**, was born 1 June 1924 and died 25 December 1944 in Europe at 20 years of age. He was killed in the Battle of the Bulge during WWII. (2) **Tony Raymond Papara** in Brockton, Plymouth Co., Mass. 26 June 1965. Tony was born in Brockton 20 March 1921[3990]

Lila Lee **Packard** and Harry George **Woodworth** Jr. had the following child:

3333   i. Harry George Joseph[14] **Woodworth**[3991] was born in Brockton 13 December 1943. He also descends from Matthew Whipple of Ipswich through his great grandfather Horace Sherman Packard, husband of Etta Rosella Makepeace.

2930. **Nancy Marian**[13] **Fitch** (Girdler Brent[12], Kate Orvis[11] **Girdler**, Elizabeth Tracy[10] **Mercer**, Catherine Lorette[9] **Orvis**, Lucinda Chipman[8] **Upham**, Joseph Pierce[7], Asa[6], Hannah[5] **Stearns**, Elizabeth[4] **Stone**, Mary[3] **Whipple**, Elder John[2], Matthew[1])[3992] was born in Columbus, Ohio 28 June 1936 and died 10 July 1993 in Spartanburg, S.C. at 57 years of age. She married **James Geraty Harrison Jr.** 11 August 1961. James,[3993] son of James Geraty **Harrison** and Evelyn **Eichhorn**, was born in Charleston, S.C. 30 September 1936.

Nancy Marian **Fitch** and James Geraty **Harrison** Jr. had the following children born in Durham, N.C.:

3334   i. Rachel Hebden[14] **Harrison**[3994] was born 7 June 1966 and married John Joseph **DiLutis** Jr. in Spartanburg 2 June 1990. He died 29 March 1993 in San Francisco., Calif.[3995] Rachel is a graduate of the Eastman School of Music in Rochester, N.Y. and earned a Master's Degree from Juilliard in New York, N.Y.

3335   ii. Robert Girdler **Harrison**[3996] was born 29 January 1970 and married Thomasine Richards **Hahn** in Aiken, S.C. 24 March 1994.[3997] He was awarded a B.A. by Davidson (N.C.) College in 1992 with a major in French.

2932. Cheryl Maureen[13] **Stevens** (Frances Harriet[12] **Goddard**, George Francis[11], George Osmer[10], John Bailey[9], Robert[8], Nahum[7], Robert[6], Edward[5], Susanna[4] **Stone**, Mary[3] **Whipple**, Elder John[2], Matthew[1])[3998] was born in California 4 March 1945 and married (__) **Augustine**.

Cheryl Maureen **Stevens** and (__) **Augustine** had the following children:

+ 3336   i. David Edward[14] **Augustine** was born 2 April 1961.
3337   ii. Todd Henry Lee **Augustine**[3999] was born 28 June 1964.
3338   iii. Ryan Bryce **Augustine**[4000] was born 10 January 1968.

2933. Diane Eileen[13] **Stevens** (Frances Harriet[12] **Goddard**, George Francis[11], George Osmer[10], John Bailey[9], Robert[8], Nahum[7], Robert[6], Edward[5], Susanna[4] **Stone**, Mary[3] **Whipple**, Elder John[2], Matthew[1])[4001] was born in California 25 April 1948 and married twice. (1) (__) **Glupker**. (2) (__) **Parker**.

Diane Eileen **Stevens** and (__) **Glupker** had the following children:

3339   i. Christopher[14] **Glupker**[4002] was born 7 May 1968.
3340   ii. Kimberly Joy **Glupker**[4003] was born 23 October 1971.

2935. Judith Ann[13] **Reinking** (Jean Doris[12] **Goddard**, George Francis[11], George Osmer[10], John Bailey[9], Robert[8], Nahum[7], Robert[6], Edward[5], Susanna[4] **Stone**, Mary[3] **Whipple**, Elder John[2], Matthew[1])[4004] was born in Pierson, Iowa 18 June 1939 and married **Jim Darby**.

Judith Ann **Reinking** and Jim **Darby** had the following children:

3341   i. Mark Lee[14] **Darby**[4005] was born 19 November 1958 and died the day after birth.
+ 3342   ii. Julie Kay **Darby** was born 17 November 1959.
+ 3343   iii. Joni Sue **Darby** was born 22 May 1961.
+ 3344   iv. Jill Anette **Darby** was born 21 February 1963.

2936. Karen Jean[13] **Reinking** (Jean Doris[12] **Goddard**, George Francis[11], George Osmer[10], John Bailey[9], Robert[8], Nahum[7], Robert[6], Edward[5], Susanna[4] **Stone**, Mary[3] **Whipple**, Elder John[2], Matthew[1])[4006] was born in Pierson, Iowa 7 May 1942 and married (__) **Wilson**.

Karen Jean **Reinking** and (__) **Wilson** had the following children:

+ 3345   i. William Ray[14] **Wilson** was born 23 June 1961.
+ 3346   ii. Kathryn Ann **Wilson** was born 22 February 1963.
+ 3347   iii. Linda Marie **Wilson** was born 13 March 1966.
+ 3348   iv. Jodel Christine **Wilson** was born 9 January 1969.
+ 3349   v. Kenneth Ray **Wilson** was born 14 June 1971.

2937. Russel Allen[13] **Sobieski** (Helen Maurine[12] **Goddard**, George Francis[11], George Osmer[10], John Bailey[9], Robert[8], Nahum[7], Robert[6], Edward[5], Susanna[4] **Stone**, Mary[3] **Whipple**, Elder John[2], Matthew[1])[4007] was born 29 December 1940 and married **Carol Marie Heath** 21 November 1965.

Russel Allen **Sobieski** and Carol Marie **Heath** had the following children:

    3350   i.   Michael Allen[14] **Sobieski**[4008] was born 18 January 1970.
+ 3351   ii. Monica Marie **Sobieski** was born 1 September 1972.

2938. Gary Lee[13] **Sobieski** (Helen Maurine[12] **Goddard**, George Francis[11], George Osmer[10], John Bailey[9], Robert[8], Nahum[7], Robert[6], Edward[5], Susanna[4] **Stone**, Mary[3] **Whipple**, Elder John[2], Matthew[1])[4009] was born 13 May 1942 and married **Alice Mae Gothier** 9 February 1963.

Gary Lee **Sobieski** and Alice Mae **Gothier** had the following children:

    3352   i.   Tamara Lynn[14] **Sobieski**[4010] was born 27 June 1963.
+ 3353   ii. Thomas Lee **Sobieski** was born 16 July 1964.
    3354   iii. Everett Allen **Sobieski**[4011] was born 25 April 1969.

2939. Linda Maurine[13] **Sobieski** (Helen Maurine[12] **Goddard**, George Francis[11], George Osmer[10], John Bailey[9], Robert[8], Nahum[7], Robert[6], Edward[5], Susanna[4] **Stone**, Mary[3] **Whipple**, Elder John[2], Matthew[1])[4012] was born 21 February 1954 and married **Mark Alan Chmelar** 18 June 1977.

Linda Maurine **Sobieski** and Mark Alan **Chmelar** had the following children:

    3355   i.   Jessica Ann[14] **Chmelar**[4013] was born 11 April 1980.
    3356   ii. Nathan Alan **Chmelar**[4014] was born 27 March 1982.
    3357   iii. Brian Lee **Chmelar**[4015] was born 5 July 1984.
    3358   iv. Daniel Joseph **Chmelar**[4016] was born 24 July 1987.

2940. Dennis Wray[13] **Goddard** (Donald Wray[12], George Francis[11], George Osmer[10], John Bailey[9], Robert[8], Nahum[7], Robert[6], Edward[5], Susanna[4] **Stone**, Mary[3] **Whipple**, Elder John[2], Matthew[1])[4017] was born 12 July 1949 and died 7 December 1992 at 43 years of age.

Dennis Wray **Goddard** had the following child:

    3359   i.   Dane Michael[14] **Goddard**[4018] was born 5 June 1979.

2942. Michael Lee[13] **Goddard** (Donald Wray[12], George Francis[11], George Osmer[10], John Bailey[9], Robert[8], Nahum[7], Robert[6], Edward[5], Susanna[4] **Stone**, Mary[3] **Whipple**, Elder John[2], Matthew[1])[4019] was born 11 March 1956.

Michael Lee **Goddard** had the following children:

    3360   i.   Jason Lee[14] **Goddard**[4020] was born 3 June 1982.
    3361   ii. Robert Wayne **Goddard**[4021] was born 18 September 1983.
    3362   iii. David Michael **Goddard**[4022] was born 25 May 1988.

2943. Sandra Jean[13] **Olander** (Marjorie Arlene[12] **Goddard**, George Francis[11], George Osmer[10], John Bailey[9], Robert[8], Nahum[7], Robert[6], Edward[5], Susanna[4] **Stone**, Mary[3] **Whipple**, Elder John[2], Matthew[1])[4023] was born 28 December 1946 and married **Kurt Ebert**.

Sandra Jean **Olander** and Kurt **Ebert** had the following children:

    3363   i.   Dawn Marie[14] **Ebert**[4024] was born 16 May 1980. Adopted.

3364   ii. Mark Curtis **Ebert**[4025] was born 12 March 1982.

2944. Bethel[13] **Olander** (Marjorie Arlene[12] **Goddard**, George Francis[11], George Osmer[10], John Bailey[9], Robert[8], Nahum[7], Robert[6], Edward[5], Susanna[4] **Stone**, Mary[3] **Whipple**, Elder John[2], Matthew[1])[4026] was born 10 November 1948 and married (__) **Fredrickson**.

Bethel **Olander** and (__) **Fredrickson** had the following children:
3365   i.   Stephanie Lynn[14] **Fredrickson**[4027] was born 11 November 1972.
3366   ii. Kerri Ann **Fredrickson**[4028] was born 24 July 1977.
3367   iii. James Thomas **Fredrickson**[4029] was born 3 November 1978 and died 28 May 1993 at 14 years of age.

2945. David John[13] **Olander** (Marjorie Arlene[12] **Goddard**, George Francis[11], George Osmer[10], John Bailey[9], Robert[8], Nahum[7], Robert[6], Edward[5], Susanna[4] **Stone**, Mary[3] **Whipple**, Elder John[2], Matthew[1])[4030] was born 6 June 1951.

David John **Olander** had the following children:
3368   i.   David Sean[14] **Olander**[4031] was born 14 July 1974.
3369   ii. Erin Daniele **Olander**[4032] was born 28 October 1976.

2946. Paul Carney[13] **Olander** (Marjorie Arlene[12] **Goddard**, George Francis[11], George Osmer[10], John Bailey[9], Robert[8], Nahum[7], Robert[6], Edward[5], Susanna[4] **Stone**, Mary[3] **Whipple**, Elder John[2], Matthew[1])[4033] was born 12 April 1953.

Paul Carney **Olander** had the following children:
3370   i.   Katie Lynn[14] **Olander**[4034] was born 27 April 1981.
3371   ii. Andrew John **Olander**[4035] was born 9 June 1983.

2947. Dawn Maurine[13] **Goddard** (Dean Alan[12], George Francis[11], George Osmer[10], John Bailey[9], Robert[8], Nahum[7], Robert[6], Edward[5], Susanna[4] **Stone**, Mary[3] **Whipple**, Elder John[2], Matthew[1])[4036] was born 2 December 1950 and married (__) **Morgan**.

Dawn Maurine **Goddard** and (__) **Morgan** had the following children:
+ 3372   i.   Richard Dean Godard[14] **Morgan** was born 5 December 1970.
3373   ii. Todd Justin **Morgan**[4037] was born 31 January 1982.
3374   iii. Kymberly Dawn **Morgan**[4038] was born 21 April 1984.

2948. Alan Clark[13] **Goddard** (Dean Alan[12], George Francis[11], George Osmer[10], John Bailey[9], Robert[8], Nahum[7], Robert[6], Edward[5], Susanna[4] **Stone**, Mary[3] **Whipple**, Elder John[2], Matthew[1])[4039] was born 7 February 1953.

Alan Clark **Goddard** had the following children:
3375   i.   Amber Lynn[14] **Goddard**[4040] was born 27 August 1981.
3376   ii. Jeffry Alan **Goddard**[4041] was born 5 May 1987.

2950. Robert Wray[13] **Goddard** (Dean Alan[12], George Francis[11], George Osmer[10], John Bailey[9], Robert[8], Nahum[7], Robert[6], Edward[5], Susanna[4] **Stone**, Mary[3] **Whipple**, Elder John[2], Matthew[1])[4042] was born 16 March 1960.

Robert Wray **Goddard** had the following child:
3377   i.   Brianna Marie[14] **Goddard**[4043] was born 21 February 1983.

2955. **Linda Jean**[13] **Heise** (Verda Joann[12] **Goddard**, George Francis[11], George Osmer[10], John Bailey[9], Robert[8], Nahum[7], Robert[6], Edward[5], Susanna[4] **Stone**, Mary[3] **Whipple**, Elder John[2], Matthew[1])[4044] was born 4 December 1949 and married (__) **Michaels**.

Linda Jean **Heise** and (__) **Michaels** had the following children:
- 3378   i. Kelly Lynn[14] **Michaels**[4045] was born 10 March 1984.
- 3379   ii. Melissa Ann **Michaels**[4046] was born 22 December 1985.
- 3380   iii. Nicole Marie **Michaels**[4047] was born 4 October 1988.

2956. **Keryl Anne**[13] **Heise** (Verda Joann[12] **Goddard**, George Francis[11], George Osmer[10], John Bailey[9], Robert[8], Nahum[7], Robert[6], Edward[5], Susanna[4] **Stone**, Mary[3] **Whipple**, Elder John[2], Matthew[1])[4048] was born 13 May 1952 and married (__) **Ketter**.

Keryl Anne **Heise** and (__) **Ketter** had the following children:
- 3381   i. Andrew Dylan[14] **Ketter**[4049] was born 7 August 1974.
- 3382   ii. Eric Jon **Ketter**[4050] was born 2 December 1976.
- 3383   iii. Donald Joseph **Ketter**[4051] was born 8 November 1978.
- 3384   iv. Sarah Cathryn **Ketter**[4052] was born 14 August 1982.
- 3385   v. Bethany Ann **Ketter**[4053] was born 24 October 1990.

2957. **Donna Jo**[13] **Heise** (Verda Joann[12] **Goddard**, George Francis[11], George Osmer[10], John Bailey[9], Robert[8], Nahum[7], Robert[6], Edward[5], Susanna[4] **Stone**, Mary[3] **Whipple**, Elder John[2], Matthew[1])[4054] was born 27 February 1954 and married twice. (1) (__) **McDonald**. (2) (__) **King**.

Donna Jo **Heise** and (__) **McDonald** had the following children:
- 3386   i. Ryan James[14] **McDonald**[4055] was born 5 March 1978.
- 3387   ii. Kristin Marie **McDonald**[4056] was born 15 October 1981.

2958. **Kathryn Marie**[13] **Heise** (Verda Joann[12] **Goddard**, George Francis[11], George Osmer[10], John Bailey[9], Robert[8], Nahum[7], Robert[6], Edward[5], Susanna[4] **Stone**, Mary[3] **Whipple**, Elder John[2], Matthew[1])[4057] was born 30 August 1955 and married (__) **Glover**.

Kathryn Marie **Heise** and (__) **Glover** had the following child:
- 3388   i. Jenna Marie[14] **Glover**[4058] was born 28 April 1985.

2959. **Douglas Dean**[13] **Heise** (Verda Joann[12] **Goddard**, George Francis[11], George Osmer[10], John Bailey[9], Robert[8], Nahum[7], Robert[6], Edward[5], Susanna[4] **Stone**, Mary[3] **Whipple**, Elder John[2], Matthew[1])[4059] was born 12 March 1957.

Douglas Dean **Heise** had the following child:
- 3389   i. Christopher James[14] **Heise**[4060] was born 9 October 1984.

2960. **Mary Ann**[13] **Heise** (Verda Joann[12] **Goddard**, George Francis[11], George Osmer[10], John Bailey[9], Robert[8], Nahum[7], Robert[6], Edward[5], Susanna[4] **Stone**, Mary[3] **Whipple**, Elder John[2], Matthew[1])[4061] was born 27 October 1958 and married (__) **Bennett**.

Mary Ann **Heise** and (__) **Bennett** had the following child:
- 3390   i. Patricia Gail[14] **Bennett**[4062] was born 16 June 1985.

2961. **Stephen Kent**[13] **Heise** (Verda Joann[12] **Goddard**, George Francis[11], George Osmer[10], John Bailey[9], Robert[8], Nahum[7], Robert[6], Edward[5], Susanna[4] **Stone**, Mary[3] **Whipple**, Elder John[2], Matthew[1])[4063] was born 7 October 1960.

Stephen Kent **Heise** had the following children:
3391   i.   Jessica Ann[14] **Heise**[4064] was born 11 September 1990.
3392   ii. Alyson Marie **Heise**[4065] was born 23 September 1993.

2962. **Robert John**[13] **Heise** (Verda Joann[12] **Goddard**, George Francis[11], George Osmer[10], John Bailey[9], Robert[8], Nahum[7], Robert[6], Edward[5], Susanna[4] **Stone**, Mary[3] **Whipple**, Elder John[2], Matthew[1])[4066] was born 5 December 1961.

Robert John **Heise** had the following children:
3393   i.   Erin Elizabeth[14] **Heise**[4067] was born 31 January 1993.
3394   ii. Amy Linn **Heise**[4068] was born 7 November 1995.

2963. **Nancy Jean**[13] **Heise** (Verda Joann[12] **Goddard**, George Francis[11], George Osmer[10], John Bailey[9], Robert[8], Nahum[7], Robert[6], Edward[5], Susanna[4] **Stone**, Mary[3] **Whipple**, Elder John[2], Matthew[1])[4069] was born 19 June 1963 and married (__) **Grys**.

Nancy Jean **Heise** and (__) **Grys** had the following children:
3395   i.   Cassandra Jean[14] **Grys**[4070] was born 1 March 1990.
3396   ii. Samantha Joann **Grys**[4071] was born 13 September 1991.

2964. **Karen Maureen**[13] **Heise** (Verda Joann[12] **Goddard**, George Francis[11], George Osmer[10], John Bailey[9], Robert[8], Nahum[7], Robert[6], Edward[5], Susanna[4] **Stone**, Mary[3] **Whipple**, Elder John[2], Matthew[1])[4072] was born 26 August 1964 and married (__) **Young**.

Karen Maureen **Heise** and (__) **Young** had the following children:
3397   i.   Joshua David[14] **Young**[4073] was born 5 June 1990.
3398   ii. Benjamin Donald **Young**[4074] was born 12 March 1993.

2965. **Philip Ray**[13] **Heise** (Verda Joann[12] **Goddard**, George Francis[11], George Osmer[10], John Bailey[9], Robert[8], Nahum[7], Robert[6], Edward[5], Susanna[4] **Stone**, Mary[3] **Whipple**, Elder John[2], Matthew[1])[4075] was born 10 April 1966.

Philip Ray **Heise** had the following children:
3399   i.   Justin Wrae[14] **Heise**[4076] was born 17 September 1989.
3400   ii. Kyle Andrew **Heise**[4077] was born 23 October 1991.

2966. **Timothy Paul**[13] **Heise** (Verda Joann[12] **Goddard**, George Francis[11], George Osmer[10], John Bailey[9], Robert[8], Nahum[7], Robert[6], Edward[5], Susanna[4] **Stone**, Mary[3] **Whipple**, Elder John[2], Matthew[1])[4078] was born 22 December 1967.

Timothy Paul **Heise** had the following children:
3401   i.   Timothy Paul[14] **Heise Jr.**[4079] was born 19 October 1988.
3402   ii. Kevin Matthew **Heise**[4080] was born 30 March 1991.
3403   iii. Heather Ann **Heise**[4081] was born 22 July 1994.

2968. **Harold Kenneth**[13] **Nystrom Jr.** (Bethel Beryl[12] **Goddard**, George Francis[11], George Osmer[10], John Bailey[9], Robert[8], Nahum[7], Robert[6], Edward[5], Susanna[4] **Stone**, Mary[3] **Whipple**, Elder John[2], Matthew[1])[4082] was born 6 October 1953.

Harold Kenneth **Nystrom** Jr. had the following children:

3404　i.　Angela Beth[14] **Nystrom**[4083] was born 10 October 1973.
3405　ii.　Daniel Lewis **Nystrom**[4084] was born 10 November 1976.
3406　iii.　Asa Eric **Nystrom**[4085] was born 8 July 1981 and died 6 August 1981 at less than one month of age.
3407　iv.　Amanda Joy **Nystrom**[4086] was born in January 1983.
3408　v.　Harold Kenneth **Nystrom**[4087] was born 30 July 1985.
3409　vi.　Emilee Ruth **Nystrom**[4088] was born 12 November 1990.
3410　vii.　Erin Michelle **Nystrom**[4089] was born 8 February 1993.
3411　viii.　Deborah Kay **Nystrom**[4090] was born 17 April 1996.

2969. Pamela Beth[13] **Nystrom** (Bethel Beryl[12] **Goddard**, George Francis[11], George Osmer[10], John Bailey[9], Robert[8], Nahum[7], Robert[6], Edward[5], Susanna[4] **Stone**, Mary[3] **Whipple**, Elder John[2], Matthew[1])[4091] was born 9 November 1955 and died 11 September 1991 at 35 years of age. She married (__) **Stagg**.

Pamela Beth **Nystrom** and (__) **Stagg** had the following children:

3412　i.　Jesse Rebecca[14] **Stagg**[4092] was born 10 January 1981.
3413　ii.　Carmen Paige **Stagg**[4093] was born 3 June 1982.
3414　iii.　Margaret Stacey **Stagg**[4094] was born 14 January 1984.

2970. Theresa Jean[13] **Nystrom** (Bethel Beryl[12] **Goddard**, George Francis[11], George Osmer[10], John Bailey[9], Robert[8], Nahum[7], Robert[6], Edward[5], Susanna[4] **Stone**, Mary[3] **Whipple**, Elder John[2], Matthew[1])[4095] was born 26 October 1956 and married (__) **Harman**.

Theresa Jean **Nystrom** and (__) **Harman** had the following children:

3415　i.　Thomas Jonathan[14] **Harman**[4096] was born 12 February 1982.
3416　ii.　Christopher Todd **Harman**[4097] was born 2 November 1985.

2971. Peggy Sue[13] **Nystrom** (Bethel Beryl[12] **Goddard**, George Francis[11], George Osmer[10], John Bailey[9], Robert[8], Nahum[7], Robert[6], Edward[5], Susanna[4] **Stone**, Mary[3] **Whipple**, Elder John[2], Matthew[1])[4098] was born 25 January 1958 and married **Andrew Donald Benyo Jr.**.

Peggy Sue **Nystrom** and Andrew Donald **Benyo** Jr. had the following children:

3417　i.　Katelyn Beryl[14] **Benyo**[4099] was born 29 June 1988.
3418　ii.　Andrew Donald **Benyo** III[4100] was born 9 December 1991.

2972. Toni Corrine[13] **Nystrom** (Bethel Beryl[12] **Goddard**, George Francis[11], George Osmer[10], John Bailey[9], Robert[8], Nahum[7], Robert[6], Edward[5], Susanna[4] **Stone**, Mary[3] **Whipple**, Elder John[2], Matthew[1])[4101] was born 27 March 1961 and married (__) **Diaz**.

Toni Corrine **Nystrom** and (__) **Diaz** had the following child:

3419　i.　Marabella Inez[14] **Diaz**[4102] was born 13 November 1982 and died in April 1983 at less than one year of age.

2973. Richard Francis[13] **Gaber** (Beverly Joy[12] **Goddard**, George Francis[11], George Osmer[10], John Bailey[9], Robert[8], Nahum[7], Robert[6], Edward[5], Susanna[4] **Stone**, Mary[3] **Whipple**, Elder John[2], Matthew[1])[4103] was born in Baraboo, Wisc. 5 February 1952 and married **Patricia Voltz**. Patricia is the daughter of Roger **Voltz** and

Madge (__). Richard earned a bachelor's degree from the U. of Wisconsin and a Ph.D. from the Massachusetts Institute of Technology. He was an associate professor of Microbiology at Northwestern University in 1998.

Richard Francis **Gaber** and Patricia **Voltz** had the following children:
- 3420   i.   Rikky Shannon[14] **Gaber**[4104] was born 20 August 1989.
- 3421   ii.   Charles Earl **Gaber**[4105] was born 11 April 1991.

2974. Denise Eileen[13] **Gaber** (Beverly Joy[12] **Goddard**, George Francis[11], George Osmer[10], John Bailey[9], Robert[8], Nahum[7], Robert[6], Edward[5], Susanna[4] **Stone**, Mary[3] **Whipple**, Elder John[2], Matthew[1])[4106] was born in Baraboo, Wisc. 28 February 1953 and married **Richard Allen Beebe** in Washburn, Bayfield Co., Wisc. 3 July 1971.

Denise Eileen **Gaber** and Richard Allen **Beebe** had the following children:
- 3422   i.   Jessie Lyn[14] **Beebe**[4107] was born 11 November 1974.
- 3423   ii.   Jaimie Lea **Beebe**[4108] was born 11 April 1977.
- 3424   iii.   Jorran Lee **Beebe**[4109] was born 14 December 1982.

2975. Brian Keith[13] **Gaber** (Beverly Joy[12] **Goddard**, George Francis[11], George Osmer[10], John Bailey[9], Robert[8], Nahum[7], Robert[6], Edward[5], Susanna[4] **Stone**, Mary[3] **Whipple**, Elder John[2], Matthew[1])[4110] was born in Rhinelander, Wisc. 30 January 1955 and married **Petra Deckert** in Schoeningen, Germany 7 August 1976. Petra,[4111] daughter of Gerhard **Deckert** and Ingebog **Heinrich**, was born in Helmstedt, Landkreis Helmstedt, Germany 11 August 1957

Brian Keith **Gaber** and Petra **Deckert** had the following children born in Helmstedt, Germanu:
- 3425   i.   Sandy Denise[14] **Gaber**[4112] was born 27 September 1980.
- 3426   ii.   Rebekka **Gaber**[4113] was born 6 October 1981.

2977. Thomas Stanley[13] **Gaber** (Beverly Joy[12] **Goddard**, George Francis[11], George Osmer[10], John Bailey[9], Robert[8], Nahum[7], Robert[6], Edward[5], Susanna[4] **Stone**, Mary[3] **Whipple**, Elder John[2], Matthew[1])[4114] was born in Wausau, Wisc. 27 March 1962 and married **Christine Korseuburg** in Washburn, Bayfield Co., Wisc.

Thomas Stanley **Gaber** and Christine **Korseuburg** had the following children:
- 3427   i.   Scott Thomas[14] **Gaber**[4115] was born 17 May 1987.
- 3428   ii.   Malorie Christine **Gaber**[4116] was born 29 December 1991.
- 3429   iii.   Lisa Joy **Gaber**[4117] was born 23 October 1993.

2978. Kurt Erwin[13] **Gaber** (Beverly Joy[12] **Goddard**, George Francis[11], George Osmer[10], John Bailey[9], Robert[8], Nahum[7], Robert[6], Edward[5], Susanna[4] **Stone**, Mary[3] **Whipple**, Elder John[2], Matthew[1])[4118] was born in Washburn, Bayfield Co., Wisc. 16 March 1965. He married **Natalie Andrews** in Washburn Wisc.

Kurt Erwin **Gaber** and Natalie **Andrews** had the following children:
- 3430   i.   Lindsay Marie[14] **Gaber**[4119] was born 17 October 1990.
- 3431   ii.   Hunter Reed **Gaber**[4120] was born 30 April 1995.

2991. Virginia Jennings[13] **Christman** (Milon Stone[12], Sarah Mary (Mai)[11] **Stone**, Milon Gardner[10], Marshall Maynard[9], Col. Jonathan[8], Lt. Jonathan[7], Jonathan[6], Jonathan[5], Jonathan[4], Mary[3] **Whipple**, Elder John[2], Matthew[1])[4121] was born in Spartanburg, S.C. 21 April 1919 and married twice. (1) **John Davis Smith**

in Spartanburg 1 July 1939. John,[4122] son of Dwight Arthur **Smith** and Myra **Crocker**, was born in Greenville, S.C. 27 February 1916 and died 16 August 1979 in Wilmington, N.C. at 63 years of age. (2) **W. Pickney Irwin Jr.** in Spartanburg 12 July 1986. He was born in Spartanburg 10 September 1917 and is the son of W. Pickney **Irwin** and Ann **Page**.[4123]

Virginia Jennings **Christman** and John Davis **Smith** had the following children:

+ 3432   i.   Reeves[14] **Smith** was born 15 December 1941.
   3433   ii.   John Davis **Smith**[4124] was born in Spartanburg 2 September 1945.
+ 3434   iii.   Milon Christman **Smith** was born 15 August 1950.

2992. Milon Stone[13] **Christman Jr.** (Milon Stone[12], Sarah Mary (Mai)[11] **Stone**, Milon Gardner[10], Marshall Maynard[9], Col. Jonathan[8], Lt. Jonathan[7], Jonathan[6], Jonathan[5], Jonathan[4], Mary[3] **Whipple**, Elder John[2], Matthew[1])[4125] was born in Spartanburg, S.C. 29 August 1920 and married **Betty Jean Adams** in Meridian, Miss. 7 June 1947. Betty,[4126] daughter of Forrest Baughman **Adams** and Dorothy Vernon **Rush**, was born in Meridian 15 March 1925.

Milon Stone **Christman** Jr. and Betty Jean **Adams** had the following children:

   3435   i.   Dorothy Adams[14] **Christman**[4127] was born in Meridian 11 June 1948.
+ 3436   ii.   Virginia Jennings **Christman** was born 14 October 1949.
+ 3437   iii.   Milon Stone **Christman** III was born 23 March 1954.

2993. Marshall Stone[13] **Meeks** (Bennie Scurry[12] **Stone**, Marshall Christman[11], Milon Gardner[10], Marshall Maynard[9], Col. Jonathan[8], Lt. Jonathan[7], Jonathan[6], Jonathan[5], Jonathan[4], Mary[3] **Whipple**, Elder John[2], Matthew[1])[4128] was born in Spartanburg, S.C. 27 December 1947 and married **Catherine Dorothy Fitzgerald** in Lincoln, Mass. 27 October 1979. Catherine,[4129] daughter of Frederick Priestly **Fitzgerald** and Elizabeth **Croy**, was born 20 December 1949.

Marshall Stone **Meeks** and Catherine Dorothy **Fitzgerald** had the following children born in Spartanburg, S.C.:

   3438   i.   Jesse Fitzgerald[14] **Meeks**[4130] was born 11 July 1981.
   3439   ii.   Sarah Elizabeth **Meeks**[4131] was born 10 August 1984.

2994. Fleming Littleton[13] **Meeks** (Bennie Scurry[12] **Stone**, Marshall Christman[11], Milon Gardner[10], Marshall Maynard[9], Col. Jonathan[8], Lt. Jonathan[7], Jonathan[6], Jonathan[5], Jonathan[4], Mary[3] **Whipple**, Elder John[2], Matthew[1])[4132] was born in Spartanburg, S.C. 15 June 1951 and married twice. (1) **Martha Wescott Driver** in Waterloo Village, N.J. 12 June 1982. No children born to this marriage.[4133] They were divorced in New York, N.Y. about 1992. (2) **Elinor Freda Schull** in New York, N.Y. 30 January 1994. Elinor,[4134] is the daughter of Eugene Arnold **Schull** and Rebecca Anna **Wattenberg**, was born in Ocean Side, N.Y. 24 May 1956.

Fleming Littleton **Meeks** and Elinor Freda **Schull** had the following child:

   3440   i.   Henry Isaac[14] **Meeks**[4135] was born in New York, N.Y. 26 July 1995.

2995. Marion Littleton[13] **Meeks Jr.** (Bennie Scurry[12] **Stone**, Marshall Christman[11], Milon Gardner[10], Marshall Maynard[9], Col. Jonathan[8], Lt. Jonathan[7], Jonathan[6], Jonathan[5], Jonathan[4], Mary[3] **Whipple**, Elder John[2], Matthew[1])[4136] was born in Atlanta, Ga. 5 May 1955 and married **Helen Moore Laughinghouse** in Gainesville, Ga, 14 November 1981. Helen,[4137] daughter of Hayward Dail **Laughinghouse**, Jr. and Minnie Mae **Moore**, was born in Greenville N.C. 4 March 1955.

Marion Littleton **Meeks** Jr. and Helen Moore **Laughinghouse** had the following child:

    3441   i.   Jennifer Dail[14] **Meeks**[4138] was born in Gainesville 24 January 1985.

2996. Elizabeth Leighton[13] **Stone** (Marshall Christman[12], Marshall Christman[11], Milon Gardner[10], Marshall Maynard[9], Col. Jonathan[8], Lt. Jonathan[7], Jonathan[6], Jonathan[5], Jonathan[4], Mary[3] **Whipple**, Elder John[2], Matthew[1])[4139] was born in Spartanburg, S.C. 10 April 1953 and married **Robert Payne Richardson** V there 4 February 1978. Robert, [4140] son of Robert Payne **Richardson** IV and Elizabeth **McGee** was born in Spartanburg 9 November 1953.

Elizabeth Leighton **Stone** and Robert Payne **Richardson** V had the following children born in Spartanburg:

    3442   i.   Robert Payne[14] **Richardson** VI[4141] was born 8 April 1981.
    3443   ii.   Caroline Christman **Richardson**[4142] was born 11 August 1984.

3002. Mary Esther[13] **Makee** (Albert Henry[12], Mary Alice[11] **Perry**, Mary Jane[10] **Billings**, Hiram[9], Joel[8], John[7], Joanna[6] **Norton**, John[5], Mary[4] **Goodhue**, Sarah[3] **Whipple**, Elder John[2], Matthew[1])[4143] was born in Portal, Burke Co., N. Dak. 13 July 1904 and died 4 June 1993 in Portland, Multnomah Co., Oreg. at 88 years of age. She married **Arthur Oliver Bakke** in Noonan, Divide Co., N. Dak. 30 June 1926. Arthur,[4144] son of Hans Jenson **Bakke** and Arnikke Lovise Christensdatter **Lone**, was born in Maddock, Benson Co., N. Dak. 24 January 1900 and died 25 April 1984 in Portland at 84 years of age.

Mary Esther **Makee** and Arthur Oliver **Bakke** had the following children.:

    3444   i.   Arthur Oliver[14] **Bakke**[4145] was born in Minneapolis, Minn. 25 March 1927 and married Shirley **Kanzler** in Portland 27 January 1951.
+ 3445   ii.   Jerry Duane **Bakke** was born 6 June 1931.
    3446   iii.   Karen Dorothy **Bakke**[4146] was born in Portland 26 February 1946 and married twice. (1) William **Englestadter** in Yakima, Wash., 5 November 1966. They were divorced about 1989. (2) Clayton **Harris** in Reno, Nev. 14 February 1997.

3006. Ronald Brent[13] **Eliason** (Ruth Mae[12] **Fuchs**, Ella Lovenia[11] **Mecham**, Luman Lehi[10], Joseph L.[9], Sarah[8] **Basford**, Jonathan[7], Elizabeth[6] **Goodhue**, Jonathan[5], William[4], Sarah[3] **Whipple**, Elder John[2], Matthew[1])[4147] was born in Ogden, Weber Co. Utah 2 February 1944 and married **Kathy Lou Imlay**. Kathy,[4148] daughter of Thomas Fredrick **Imlay** and Maced Doris **Peterson**, was born in Taylorville, Utah 18 July 1945.

Ronald Brent **Eliason** and Kathy Lou **Imlay** had the following children:

    3447   i.   Clinton Brent[14] **Eliason**[4149] was born in Salt Lake City, Utah 13 October 1968.
    3448   ii.   Shane Glen **Eliason**[4150] was born 17 March 1972.

3007. Paul James[13] **Hill** (Ruth Mae[12] **Fuchs**, Ella Lovenia[11] **Mecham**, Luman

Lehi[10], Joseph L.[9], Sarah[8] **Basford**, Jonathan[7], Elizabeth[6] **Goodhue**, Jonathan[5], William[4], Sarah[3] **Whipple**, Elder John[2], Matthew[1])[4151] was born in Salt Lake City, Utah 13 July 1950 and married **Sue Shirley Swartz**.

Paul James **Hill** and Sue Shirley **Swartz** had the following child:
3449   i. Brandon James[14] Hill[4152] was born 20 May 1972.

3013. Rich Eugene[13] Murphy (Verla Eurilla[12] **Rich**, Mary Eurilla[11] **Mecham**, Luman Lehi[10], Joseph L.[9], Sarah[8] **Basford**, Jonathan[7], Elizabeth[6] **Goodhue**, Jonathan[5], William[4], Sarah[3] **Whipple**, Elder John[2], Matthew[1])[4153] was born in Nampa, Canyon Co. Idaho 4 June 1942 and married **Wilda Dee Bledsoe** in Mesa, Mariposa Co. Ariz. 25 January 1966. Wilda was born in Nampa 13 January 1946.[4154]

Rich Eugene **Murphy** and Wilda Dee **Bledsoe** had the following children:
3450   i. Penny Dee[14] Murphy[4155] was born in Lincoln, Nebr. 21 August 1967 and married Daniel Ray **Hall** in West Jordan, Utah 2 May 1997. Daniel is the son of Wayne **Hall** and Lorraine (__).[4156]
3451   ii. Shane Rich Murphy[4157] was born in Henrietta, Okla. 19 February 1970.
3452   iii. Kiska Rae Murphy[4158] was born in Caldwell, Idaho 28 February 1972.
3453   iv. B. Jay Murphy[4159] was born 12 March 1972.

3014. Cheryl Kay[13] Murphy (Verla Eurilla[12] **Rich**, Mary Eurilla[11] **Mecham**, Luman Lehi[10], Joseph L.[9], Sarah[8] **Basford**, Jonathan[7], Elizabeth[6] **Goodhue**, Jonathan[5], William[4], Sarah[3] **Whipple**, Elder John[2], Matthew[1])[4160] was born in Nampa, Canyon Co., Idaho 22 April 1944 and married **Mark Linden Billings** in Mesa, Mariposa Co., Ariz. 6 June 1970. Mark was born in Salt Lake City, Utah 8 November 1946.[4161]

Cheryl Kay **Murphy** and Mark Linden **Billings** had the following children:
3454   i. Rebecca[14] Billings[4162] was born in Logan, Cache Co., Utah 2 May 1972.
3455   ii. Rex Linden Billings[4163] was born at Fort Hood, Texas 12 July 1974.
3456   iii. David Murphy Billings[4164] was born in Bountiful, Utah 20 June 1977.
3457   iv. Craig Nicholas Billings[4165] was born in Renton, Wash. 11 June 1980 and died 20 June 1980 in Seattle, Wash. at less than one month of age.

3015. Marva Dene[13] Murphy (Verla Eurilla[12] **Rich**, Mary Eurilla[11] **Mecham**, Luman Lehi[10], Joseph L.[9], Sarah[8] **Basford**, Jonathan[7], Elizabeth[6] **Goodhue**, Jonathan[5], William[4], Sarah[3] **Whipple**, Elder John[2], Matthew[1])[4166] was born in Nampa, Canyon Co., Idaho 29 May 1948 and married **Steven Ray Bard** in Los Angeles, Calif. 1 June 1974. Steven was born 20 July 1952.[4167]

Marva Dene **Murphy** and Steven Ray **Bard** had the following children:
3458   i. Paul Lynn[14] Bard[4168] was born in Mesa, Mariposa Co., Ariz. 24 July 1975.
3459   ii. Lesa Dawn Bard[4169] was born in Longview, Wash. 11 1977.

3016. Sharon LaRay[13] Rich (Doyle Hyrum[12], Mary Eurilla[11] **Mecham**, Luman Lehi[10], Joseph L.[9], Sarah[8] **Basford**, Jonathan[7], Elizabeth[6] **Goodhue**, Jonathan[5], William[4], Sarah[3] **Whipple**, Elder John[2], Matthew[1])[4170] was born in Nampa, Canyon Co., Idaho 5 September 1943 and married **Bruce Frank Holley** in Salt Lake City,

Utah 5 November 1964. Bruce,[4171] son of Earl Henry **Holley** and Lilyan Lorraine **Dorr.**, was born in Los Angeles, Calif. 13 September 1942.

Sharon LaRay **Rich** and Bruce Frank **Holley** had the following children:

+ 3460   i.   Nicole LaRai[14] **Holley** was born in 1969.
   3461   ii.   Wendi Jene **Holley**[4172] was born at Cherry Pt. USMCA, Havelock Co., N.C. 11 December 1969 and married Steven Scott **Tye** in American Fork, Utah 10 January 1997. Steven was born in Salt Lake City 6 December 1971.[4173]
   3462   iii.   Cari Carlene **Holley**[4174] was born in Provo, Utah Co., Utah 20 December 1970.
+ 3463   iv.   Erik David **Holley** was born 14 January 1973.
   3464   v.   Kristina Marie **Holley**[4175] was born in Provo 4 September 1975.
   3465   vi.   Katrina Leigh **Holley**[4176] was born in Provo 31 July 1978.
   3466   vii.   Michael Wayne **Holley**[4177] was born in Provo 12 November 1980.
   3467   viii.   Daniel James **Holley**[4178] was born in Provo 18 August 1982.

3017. Rhonda Lee[13] **Rich** (Doyle Hyrum[12], Mary Eurilla[11] **Mecham**, Luman Lehi[10], Joseph L.[9], Sarah[8] **Basford**, Jonathan[7], Elizabeth[6] **Goodhue**, Jonathan[5], William[4], Sarah[3] **Whipple**, Elder John[2], Matthew[1])[4179] was born in Nampa, Canyon Co., Idaho 11 February 1949 and married **Merle Delwin Rust** in Seattle, Wash. 27 February 1982. Merle was born in 1939.[4180]

Rhonda Lee **Rich** and Merle Delwin **Rust** had the following children:

   3468   i.   Cindy Marie[14] **Rust**[4181] was born in Junction City, Lane Co., Oreg. 7 February 1965.
   3469   ii.   Tina Marie **Rust**[4182] was born 1 May 1973.
   3470   iii.   Abby Katolina **Rust**[4183] was born 21 April 1978.
   3471   iv.   Jeri Ann **Rust**[4184] was born in Eugene, Lane Co., Oreg. 5 April 1983.
   3472   v.   Josi Rae **Rust**[4185] was born in Eugene 2 August 1986.
   3473   vi.   Joni Lynn **Rust**[4186] was born in Eugene 30 January 1991.

3018. JoAnn[13] **Rich** (Doyle Hyrum[12], Mary Eurilla[11] **Mecham**, Luman Lehi[10], Joseph L.[9], Sarah[8] **Basford**, Jonathan[7], Elizabeth[6] **Goodhue**, Jonathan[5], William[4], Sarah[3] **Whipple**, Elder John[2], Matthew[1])[4187] was born in Roseburg, Douglas Co., Oreg. 9 May 1952 and married **Ken Michael Christopherson** in Idaho Falls, Idaho 27 July 1972. Ken was born in Cody Park, Wyo. 7 September 1950.

JoAnn **Rich** and Ken Michael **Christopherson** had the following children:

+ 3474   i.   Dustin Michael[14] **Christopherson** was born 11 June 1973.
   3475   ii.   Raundi Pearl **Christopherson**[4188] was born at Ellsworth AFB, Meade, S. Dak. 17 December 1974.
   3476   iii.   Cory Rich **Christopherson**[4189] was born in Boise, Idaho 21 August 1978.
   3477   iv.   Aaron Grant **Christopherson**[4190] was born in Boise 30 March 1981.
   3478   v.   Carol Ann **Christopherson**[4191] was born in Boise 14 March 1983.

3019. Marsha Lynn[13] **Rich** (Doyle Hyrum[12], Mary Eurilla[11] **Mecham**, Luman Lehi[10], Joseph L.[9], Sarah[8] **Basford**, Jonathan[7], Elizabeth[6] **Goodhue**, Jonathan[5], William[4], Sarah[3] **Whipple**, Elder John[2], Matthew[1])[4192] was born in Roseburg, Douglas Co., Oreg. 14 July 1953 and married **Duane Oler** in Cardston, Alberta, Canada 24 February 1973.

Marsha Lynn **Rich** and Duane **Oler** had the following children:

3479   i.   Julie Anne[14] **Oler**[4193] was born 19 November 1973 and married Tyler **Snow** in Cardston 6 May 1995. Tyler was born 1 October 1973. [4194]

3480   ii.   Daniel Thomas **Oler**[4195] was born 20 September 1976.

3481   iii.   Neil Christopher **Oler**[4196] was born 26 October 1979.

3482   iv.   Andrew Joseph **Oler**[4197] was born 30 May 1981.

3483   v.   Caroline **Oler**[4198] was born 18 March 1984.

3020. Mark Hyrum[13] **Rich** (Doyle Hyrum[12], Mary Eurilla[11] **Mecham**, Luman Lehi[10], Joseph L.[9], Sarah[8] **Basford**, Jonathan[7], Elizabeth[6] **Goodhue**, Jonathan[5], William[4], Sarah[3] **Whipple**, Elder John[2], Matthew[1])[4199] was born in Roseburg, Douglas Co., Oreg. 11 October 1956 and married **Cynthia Greenland** in Salt Lake City, Utah 22 December 1984. She was born 3 May 1957.[4200]

Mark Hyrum **Rich** and Cynthia **Greenland** had the following children:

3484   i.   Mindi Lee[14] **Rich**[4201] was born in Provo, Utah Co., Utah 21 October 1985.

3485   ii.   Spencer Hyrum **Rich**[4202] was born 5 December 1987.

3486   iii.   Jennifer **Rich**[4203] was born 17 March 1990.

3487   iv.   Stephanie **Rich**[4204] was born in Orem, Utah 6 March 1992.

3021. Lester Lavell[13] **Rich** (Lavell Mecham[12], Mary Eurilla[11] **Mecham**, Luman Lehi[10], Joseph L.[9], Sarah[8] **Basford**, Jonathan[7], Elizabeth[6] **Goodhue**, Jonathan[5], William[4], Sarah[3] **Whipple**, Elder John[2], Matthew[1])[4205] was born in Nampa, Canyon Co., Idaho 1 July 1951 and married **LaRae Roberts** in Provo, Utah Co., Utah 16 March 1974. LaRae was born in Boise, Idaho 27 February 1952.[4206]

Lester Lavell **Rich** and LaRae **Roberts** had the following children:

3488   i.   Kimberly Ann[14] **Rich**[4207] was born in Boise, Idaho 9 September 1975.

3489   ii.   Ryan Charles **Rich**[4208] was born in Boise 11 April 1977.

3490   iii.   Darin Lavell **Rich**[4209] was born 9 January 1979.

3491   iv.   Karynn **Rich**[4210] was born 1 April 1981.

3022. Ardeana Jean[13] **Rich** (Lavell Mecham[12], Mary Eurilla[11] **Mecham**, Luman Lehi[10], Joseph L.[9], Sarah[8] **Basford**, Jonathan[7], Elizabeth[6] **Goodhue**, Jonathan[5], William[4], Sarah[3] **Whipple**, Elder John[2], Matthew[1])[4211] was born in Nampa, Canyon Co., Idaho 4 April 1953 and married **Brian Sterling Hansen** in Logan, Cache Co., Utah 7 June 1974. Brian,[4212] son of Ephriam Albert **Hansen** and Kathern **Peterson**, was born in Boise, Idaho 20 October 1952.

Ardeana Jean **Rich** and Brian Sterling **Hansen** had the following children:

3492   i.   Jacob Rich[14] **Hansen**[4213] was born in Rupert, Idaho 23 February 1977.

3493   ii.   Nolan Jay **Hansen**[4214] was born in Rupert 2 January 1978.

3494   iii.   Benjamin Tyrel **Hansen**[4215] was born in Boise 8 June 1980.

3495   iv.   Christopher James **Hansen**[4216] was born in Boise 28 December 1982.

3496   v.   Steven Wade **Hansen**[4217] was born in Rupert 29 August 1984.

3497   vi.   Joseph Wayne **Hansen** was born in Twin Falls, Idaho 21 July 1986.

3498   vii.   Jennifer **Hansen**[4218] was born in Twin Falls 9 September 1988.

3023. Robert Wayne[13] **Rich** (Lavell Mecham[12], Mary Eurilla[11] **Mecham**, Luman Lehi[10], Joseph L.[9], Sarah[8] **Basford**, Jonathan[7], Elizabeth[6] **Goodhue**, Jonathan[5], William[4], Sarah[3] **Whipple**, Elder John[2], Matthew[1])[4219] was born in Nampa, Canyon

Co., Idaho 9 March 1955 and died 24 September 1993 in Draper, Utah at 38 years of age. He was buried in Orem, Utah. He married **Marguerite Cora Howard** in Logan, Utah 28 July 1979. Marguerite,[4220] daughter of William Bailey **Howard** and Ella Marie **Christensen**, was born in Missoula, Mont. 8 October 1956.

Robert Wayne **Rich** and Marguerite Cora **Howard** had the following children:
- 3499   i.   Brandon Wayne[14] **Rich**[4221] was born in Provo, Utah Co., Utah 10 November 1980.
- 3500   ii.   Brady Michael **Rich**[4222] was born in Orem, Utah 17 September 1982.
- 3501   iii.   Kyle Lavell **Rich**[4223] was born in Heber, Utah 1 September 1984.
- 3502   iv.   Cory Allan **Rich**[4224] was born 27 October 1986.
- 3503   v.   Devin Bailey **Rich**[4225] was born in Provo 22 January 1990.

3024. Boyd Lindsay[13] **Rich** (Lavell Mecham[12], Mary Eurilla[11] **Mecham**, Luman Lehi[10], Joseph L.[9], Sarah[8] **Basford**, Jonathan[7], Elizabeth[6] **Goodhue**, Jonathan[5], William[4], Sarah[3] **Whipple**, Elder John[2], Matthew[1])[4226] was born in Nampa, Canyon Co., Idaho 28 July 1956 and married three times. (1) **Mary Elizabeth Young** in Boise, Idaho 12 March 1980. (2) **Joleen Mae Carlson** in Boise 24 October 1980. Joleen was born in Seattle, Wash. 27 April 1958.[4227] (3) **Beverly June McMillin** in Meridan, Ada Co., Idaho 4 January 1997. Beverly was born in Nampa 24 December 1954.[4228]

Boyd Lindsay **Rich** and Joleen Mae **Carlson** had the following children:
- 3504   i.   Nicholas Paul[14] **Rich**[4229] was born in Layton, Utah 1 October 1981.
- 3505   ii.   Lindsey Marie **Rich**[4230] was born in Boise 19 April 1982.

3027. Ross Evan[13] **Wilson** (Byron Joy[12], Mary Eurilla[11] **Mecham**, Luman Lehi[10], Joseph L.[9], Sarah[8] **Basford**, Jonathan[7], Elizabeth[6] **Goodhue**, Jonathan[5], William[4], Sarah[3] **Whipple**, Elder John[2], Matthew[1])[4231] was born in Nashville, Tenn. 7 August 1963 and married **Lynnanne Janette Taylor** in Salt Lake City, Utah 8 August 1986. Lynnanne was born in Salt Lake City 1 July 1964.[4232]

Ross Evan **Wilson** and Lynnanne Janette **Taylor** had the following children:
- 3506   i.   Taylor Clark[14] **Wilson**[4233] was born in Provo, Utah Co., Utah 1 March 1988.
- 3507   ii.   Brooke Janette **Wilson**[4234] was born in Portland, Multnomah Co., Oreg. 19 December 1989.
- 3508   iii.   Covey Stephen **Wilson**[4235] was born in Portland 31 January 1992.
- 3509   iv.   John Ross **Wilson**[4236] was born in Beaverton, Washington Co., Oreg. 24 May 1994.

3028. Kathleen[13] **Wilson** (Byron Joy[12], Mary Eurilla[11] **Mecham**, Luman Lehi[10], Joseph L.[9], Sarah[8] **Basford**, Jonathan[7], Elizabeth[6] **Goodhue**, Jonathan[5], William[4], Sarah[3] **Whipple**, Elder John[2], Matthew[1])[4237] was born in Nashville, Tenn. 5 June 1965 and married **Jose Avila** in Provo, Utah Co., Utah 4 May 1991. Jose,[4238] son of Francisco J. **Avila**, was born 28 January 1964.

Kathleen **Wilson** and Jose **Avila** had the following children born in Provo, Utah:
- 3510   i.   Susanna[14] **Avila**[4239] was born 1 February 1992.
- 3511   ii.   Sara **Avila**[4240] was born 24 January 1993.
- 3512   iii.   Noah Benjamin **Avila**[4241] was born 8 December 1995.

3032. **Brent Ervin**[13] **Wilson** (Dean Ervin[12], Mary Eurilla[11] **Mecham**, Luman Lehi[10], Joseph L.[9], Sarah[8] **Basford**, Jonathan[7], Elizabeth[6] **Goodhue**, Jonathan[5], William[4], Sarah[3] **Whipple**, Elder John[2], Matthew[1])[4242] was born in Nampa, Canyon Co., Idaho 23 April 1963 and married **Kelli Sue Bleichner** in Seattle, Wash. 6 July 1990. Kelli,[4243] daughter of James Richard **Bleichner** and Judith Ann **McIntyre**, was born in Kennewick, Wash. 29 August 1969.

Brent Ervin **Wilson** and Kelli Sue **Bleichner** had the following children:

    3513   i.   Jena Lynn[14] **Wilson**[4244] was born in Bremerton, Wash. 12 February 1993.

    3514   ii. Benjamin Dean **Wilson**[4245] was born in Naples, Italy 24 October 1996.

3034. **Christina Marie**[13] **Wilson** (Dean Ervin[12], Mary Eurilla[11] **Mecham**, Luman Lehi[10], Joseph L.[9], Sarah[8] **Basford**, Jonathan[7], Elizabeth[6] **Goodhue**, Jonathan[5], William[4], Sarah[3] **Whipple**, Elder John[2], Matthew[1])[4246] was born in Portland, Multnomah Co., Oreg. 2 December 1966 and married **Robert Foster Zoller** in Mesa, Mariposa Co., Ariz, 6 July 1989. Robert,[4247] son of Sanford Foster **Zoller** and Ann Marie **Herschede**, was born 12 December 1964.

Christina Marie **Wilson** and Robert Foster **Zoller** had the following child:

    3515   i.   Jason Robert[14] **Zoller**[4248] was born in Phoenix, Ariz. 8 November 1995.

3036. **Patricia Lynne**[13] **Boyce** (Derald Mecham[12], Dora Artenchia[11] **Mecham**, Luman Lehi[10], Joseph L.[9], Sarah[8] **Basford**, Jonathan[7], Elizabeth[6] **Goodhue**, Jonathan[5], William[4], Sarah[3] **Whipple**, Elder John[2], Matthew[1])[4249] was born in Provo, Utah Co., Utah 22 September 1950 and married **Robyn Lyman** in Reno, Nev. 1 March 1969. Robyn was born in Monticello, San Juan Co., Utah 10 January 1948.[4250]

Patricia Lynne **Boyce** and Robyn **Lyman** had the following children:

    3516   i.   Ellen Marie[14] **Lyman**[4251] was born in California 21 October 1969.

    3517   ii. Tricin Lynne **Lyman**[4252] was born in Salt Lake City, Utah 29 November 1971.

    3518   iii. Christopher Robyn **Lyman**[4253] was born in Salt Lake City 10 December 1973.

3041. **Merdene**[13] **Boyce** (Grant Mecham[12], Dora Artenchia[11] **Mecham**, Luman Lehi[10], Joseph L.[9], Sarah[8] **Basford**, Jonathan[7], Elizabeth[6] **Goodhue**, Jonathan[5], William[4], Sarah[3] **Whipple**, Elder John[2], Matthew[1])[4254] was born in Fort Worth, Texas 6 April 1957 and married **Dennis Perkins** in Ray, Davis Co., Utah 8 June 1974. Dennis is the son of Ray B. **Perkins**.

Merdene **Boyce** and Dennis **Perkins** had the following child:

    3519   i.   Robert Grant[14] **Perkins**[4255] was born in Ogden, Weber Co., Utah 21 December 1974.

3044. **David**[13] **Brinig** (Leora Ann[12] **Mecham**, Lester Eugene[11], Luman Lehi[10], Joseph L.[9], Sarah[8] **Basford**, Jonathan[7], Elizabeth[6] **Goodhue**, Jonathan[5], William[4], Sarah[3] **Whipple**, Elder John[2], Matthew[1])[4256] was born in Butte, Mont. 12 March 1952 and married **Karrell Irish** in Virginia City, Mont. 22 June 1973. Karrell, born in Livingston, Mont. 1 July 1956, is the daughter of Gordon **Irish**. [4257]

David **Brinig** and Karrell **Irish** had the following child:

    3520   i.   Sarah Elizabeth[14] **Brinig**[4258] was born in Livingston, Mont. 25 September 1978.

3051. **Frances Louise**[13] **Riggs** (Marilyn Ann[12] **Mansfield**, Orville Cecil Miller[11], Benjamin Franklin[10] **Miller**, Elisha D.[9], Easter[8] **Kimball**, Jesse[7], John[6], Isaac[5], Sarah[4] **Goodhue**, Sarah[3] **Whipple**, Elder John[2], Matthew[1])[4259] was born in El Paso, Texas 27 June 1947. and married **William Howard Fenical** 17 December 1967. William,[4260] son of Maruice Sylvester **Fenical** and Gertrude Agnes **Adams**, was born in Chicago, Ill. 24 June 1941.

Frances Louise **Riggs** and William Howard **Fenical** had the following child:
>   3521   i.   Scott William[14] **Fenical**[4261] was born in Fontana, Calif. 30 May 1971.

3052. **Cynthia Ann**[13] **Riggs** (Marilyn Ann[12] **Mansfield**, Orville Cecil Miller[11], Benjamin Franklin[10] **Miller**, Elisha D.[9], Easter[8] **Kimball**, Jesse[7], John[6], Isaac[5], Sarah[4] **Goodhue**, Sarah[3] **Whipple**, Elder John[2], Matthew[1])[4262] was born 16 October 1949 and married twice. (1) **Ronald Coleman Young** in Seal Beach, Calif. 5 August 1972. Ronald,[4263] son of James Kent **Young** and Leota Marie **Maddox**, was born in 1942. They were divorced in 1991. (2) **Richard Allen Craig** in Jamestown, Tuolumne Co., Calif. 20 June 1986. Richard was born in 1942.[4264]

Cynthia Ann **Riggs** and Ronald Coleman **Young** had the following children:
>   3522   i.   Rebekah Elisabeth[14] **Young**[4265] was born in Fountain Valley, Calif. 11 April 1976 and married James Arthur **Keighley** in Clovis, Fresno Co., Calif. 2 December 1995. Jay was born in Fresno, Calif. 18 June 1975.[4266] They were divorced in 1997.
>   3523   ii.   Rachel Christine **Young**[4267] was born in Fountain Valley, Calif. 3 April 1978.
>   3524   iii. Christopher David **Young**[4268] was born in Fresno 14 January 1980.

3053. **Karen Lynn**[13] **Mansfield** (William Duane[12], Orville Cecil Miller[11], Benjamin Franklin[10] **Miller**, Elisha D.[9], Easter[8] **Kimball**, Jesse[7], John[6], Isaac[5], Sarah[4] **Goodhue**, Sarah[3] **Whipple**, Elder John[2], Matthew[1])[4269] was born in Berkeley, Calif. 16 July 1957 and married **Randall Keith Dowis** in Laguna Beach, Calif. 7 August 1982. Randall was born in Phoenix, Ariz. 13 May 1950.[4270]

Karen Lynn **Mansfield** and Randall Keith **Dowis** had the following children:
>   3525   i.   Blair Marie[14] **Dowis**[4271] was born in Orange, Orange Co., Calif. 15 August 1988.
>   3526   ii.   Carly Jane **Dowis**[4272] was born in Newport Beach, Calif. 15 January 1990.
>   3527   iii. Dru Helena **Dowis**[4273] was born in Newport Beach 8 March 1993.

3072. **Nicole Marie**[13] **Day** (Dennis[12], Alice LuZella[11] **Jones**, Maiben Stevens[10], Marinda Alice[9] **Stevens**, William[8], Roswell[7], Hepsibah[6] **Kilham**, Abigail[5] **Kimball**, Sarah[4] **Goodhue**, Sarah[3] **Whipple**, Elder John[2], Matthew[1])[4274] was born in Dillon Beaverhead Co., Mont. 23 December 1968 and married **Marcus Stauduhar**.

Nicole Marie **Day** had the following child:
>   3528   i.   Colton Jacob[14] **Day**[4275] was born in St Louis, St. Clair Co., Ill. 16 August 1993.

3073. **Cory Morgan**[13] **Day** (Dennis[12], Alice LuZella[11] **Jones**, Maiben Stevens[10], Marinda Alice[9] **Stevens**, William[8], Roswell[7], Hepsibah[6] **Kilham**, Abigail[5] **Kimball**, Sarah[4] **Goodhue**, Sarah[3] **Whipple**, Elder John[2], Matthew[1])[4276] was born in Havre,

Blaine Co., Mont. 16 March 1970.

Cory Morgan **Day** had the following child:

3529   i.   Alexa Lee Ann[14] **Day**[4277] was born in Portland, Multnomah Co., Oreg. 21 April 1992.

3085. Samuel Stanclift[13] **Stevens** II (Samuel Phillips[12], Samuel Stanclift[11], George Gove[10], Nancy Mathilda[9] **Bowers**, Polly[8] **Rand**, Solomon[7], Deborah[6] **Dodge**, Margery[5] **Knowlton**, Marjory (Margery)[4] **Goodhue**, Sarah[3] **Whipple**, Elder John[2], Matthew[1])[4278] was born in Oakland, Calif. 11 May 1945 and married **Jane McCarthy** in Piedmont, Calif. Jane was born 12 January 1945.[4279]

Samuel Stanclift **Stevens** II and Jane **McCarthy** had the following children born in Santa Cruze, Santa Cruz, Co., Calif.:

3530   i.   Charles Luke[14] **Stevens**[4280] was born 24 March 1971.
3531   ii.   William McCarthy **Stevens**[4281] was born 13 April 1973.
3532   iii.   Jessica Clara **Stevens**[4282] was born 27 September 1976.

3086. Martha Stuart[13] **Stevens** (Samuel Phillips[12], Samuel Stanclift[11], George Gove[10], Nancy Mathilda[9] **Bowers**, Polly[8] **Rand**, Solomon[7], Deborah[6] **Dodge**, Margery[5] **Knowlton**, Marjory (Margery)[4] **Goodhue**, Sarah[3] **Whipple**, Elder John[2], Matthew[1])[4283] was born in Oakland, Calif. 2 December 1947 and married **Lawrence Crager Bennett**.

Martha Stuart **Stevens** and Lawrence Crager **Bennett** had the following children:

3533   i.   Samuel Crager[14] **Bennett**[4284] was born in Berkeley, Calif. 4 July 1983.
3534   ii.   James Allen **Bennett**[4285] was born in Berkeley 2 March 1986.

FOURTEENTH GENERATION

3090. Eleanor[14] **Buell** (Catherine[13] **Wells**, Helen Cutter[12] **Pillsbury**, Harry M.[11], James[10], Jacob[9], John Hale[8], Rev. Edmund[7], Moses[6], Moses[5], Susanna[4] **Worth**, Susannah[3] **Whipple**, Elder John[2], Matthew[1]) was born 8 January 1928 and married **John H. Stephenson Jr.** before 1953. John was born 7 December 1921.

Eleanor **Buell** and John H. **Stephenson** Jr. had the following children:

3535   i.   Catherine Wells[15] **Stephenson** was born 8 January 1953.
+ 3536   ii.   Janet L. **Stephenson** was born 15 February 1956.

3091. Joseph Lawrence[14] **Buell** III (Catherine[13] **Wells**, Helen Cutter[12] **Pillsbury**, Harry M.[11], James[10], Jacob[9], John Hale[8], Rev. Edmund[7], Moses[6], Moses[5], Susanna[4] **Worth**, Susannah[3] **Whipple**, Elder John[2], Matthew[1]) was born in 1934 and died in 1989 at 55 years of age. He married **Sandra Smith** 27 December 1957.

Joseph Lawrence **Buell** III and Sandra **Smith** had the following children:

3537   i.   Joseph Lawrence[15] **Buell** IV was born 31 May 1959.
3538   ii.   Pearson W. **Buell** was born 2 September 1960 and married Lisa Michelle **Leak** 29 September 1985.
3539   iii.   Herbert Burling **Buell** was born 29 May 1963.

3092. Elizabeth[14] **Buell** (Catherine[13] **Wells**, Helen Cutter[12] **Pillsbury**, Harry

M.[11], James[10], Jacob[9], John Hale[8], Rev. Edmund[7], Moses[6], Moses[5], Susanna[4] **Worth**, Susannah[3] **Whipple**, Elder John[2], Matthew[1]) was born 25 August 1936 and married **Dr. Harold Drinkhaus** 5 October 1962. Harold was born 13 March 1936.

Elizabeth **Buell** and Dr. Harold **Drinkhaus** had the following children:

3540   i. Dr. Philip Harold[15] **Drinkhaus** was born 11 August 1964.
3541   ii. Lawrie W. **Drinkhaus** was born 3 October 1968.

3096. **Mary**[14] **Wells** (Clark Thompson[13], Helen Cutter[12] **Pillsbury**, Harry M.[11], James[10], Jacob[9], John Hale[8], Rev. Edmund[7], Moses[6], Moses[5], Susanna[4] **Worth**, Susannah[3] **Whipple**, Elder John[2], Matthew[1]) was born 1 November 1947 and married **James Vournakis**. They were divorced 1 November 1947.

Mary **Wells** and James **Vournakis** had the following child:

3542   i. Nicholas[15] **Vournakis** was born 5 September 1973.

3097. **Peter C.**[14] **Wells** (Cyrus Curtis[13], Helen Cutter[12] **Pillsbury**, Harry M.[11], James[10], Jacob[9], John Hale[8], Rev. Edmund[7], Moses[6], Moses[5], Susanna[4] **Worth**, Susannah[3] **Whipple**, Elder John[2], Matthew[1]) was born 2 November 1940.

Peter C. **Wells** had the following children:

3543   i. Jonathon[15] **Wells** was born 22 November 1970.
3544   ii. Deborah D. **Wells** was born 24 March 1972.

3098. **Wendy**[14] **Wells** (Cyrus Curtis[13], Helen Cutter[12] **Pillsbury**, Harry M.[11], James[10], Jacob[9], John Hale[8], Rev. Edmund[7], Moses[6], Moses[5], Susanna[4] **Worth**, Susannah[3] **Whipple**, Elder John[2], Matthew[1]) was born 13 November 1942 and married (__) **Oakes**.

Wendy **Wells** and (__) **Oakes** had the following children:

3545   i. Timothy Wade[15] **Oakes** was born 28 November 1967.
3546   ii. Anthony Dean **Oakes** was born 19 September 1969.

3099. **Christopher B.**[14] **Wells** (Cyrus Curtis[13], Helen Cutter[12] **Pillsbury**, Harry M.[11], James[10], Jacob[9], John Hale[8], Rev. Edmund[7], Moses[6], Moses[5], Susanna[4] **Worth**, Susannah[3] **Whipple**, Elder John[2], Matthew[1]) was born 26 November 1948 and died abt 1988.

Christopher B. **Wells** had the following children:

3547   i. Tina Nicole[15] **Wells** was born 30 January 1970.
3548   ii. Julie Joan **Wells** was born 22 July 1972.

3102. **Harris Warthman**[14] **Martin** (John Stanwood[13], Alice Wedgwood[12] **Pillsbury**, Harry M.[11], James[10], Jacob[9], John Hale[8], Rev. Edmund[7], Moses[6], Moses[5], Susanna[4] **Worth**, Susannah[3] **Whipple**, Elder John[2], Matthew[1]) was born in Wayne, Penn. 7 November 1954 and married **Ruth (Davis) Meurer** as her second husband 27 June 1981. Ruth was born in Portsmouth, Va. 1 March 1951. She married (1) **Jack R. Meurer** in 1970. Ruth was a widow when she married Harris. They were divorced after 1985 and Ruth married (3) Gary Neal and following his death (4) Robert Davenport.

Harris Warthman **Martin** and Ruth **Davis** had the following children:

3549   i. Rachel Elizabeth[15] **Martin** was born in Newark, Del. 27 February 1982.

3550   ii.   Stanwood Warthman Davis **Martin** was born in Gainesville, Fla. 13 April 1984.

3105. Brandon Cutter[14] **Martin** (David Cutter[13], Alice Wedgwood[12] **Pillsbury**, Harry M.[11], James[10], Jacob[9], John Hale[8], Rev. Edmund[7], Moses[6], Moses[5], Susanna[4] **Worth**, Susannah[3] **Whipple**, Elder John[2], Matthew[1]) was born in Philadelphia, Penn. 10 September 1947 and married **Alice T. Squires** 21 April 1973. Alice was born 3 March 1949.

Brandon Cutter **Martin** and Alice T. **Squires** had the following children:

3551   i.   John Charles[15] **Martin** III was born in Petersburg, Va. 24 November 1978.
3552   ii.   Emily Tappey **Martin** was born in Petersburg 5 June 1988.

3106. William Blake[14] **Haines** (Priscilla June[13] **Blake**, Clarence Dodge[12], Lizzie Batchelder[11] **Dodge**, Frank Brickett[10], Deborah Towne[9] **Brickett**, Bernard[8], Bernard[7], Susanna[6] **Pillsbury**, Moses[5], Susanna[4] **Worth**, Susannah[3] **Whipple**, Elder John[2], Matthew[1]) was born in Boston, Mass. 26 December 1950 and married **Nancy Elaine Ferris** in Springville, Utah 18 September 1970. Nancy, daughter of Edmund La Var **Ferris** and Elaine Ila **Ewell**, was born in Provo, Utah Co., Utah 4 February 1952.

William Blake **Haines** and Nancy Elaine **Ferris** had the following children:

+ 3553   i.   Madelline Grace[15] **Haines** was born 2 August 1971.
3554   ii.   Tonia Elaine **Haines** was born in Provo 5 November 1973.
3555   iii.   Lori Ruth **Haines** was born in Provo 25 August 1980.
3556   iv.   Blake Lawrence **Haines** was born 19 January 1983.
3557   v.   Amber Rae **Haines** was born in San Bernardino, Calif. 19 May 1986.
3558   vi.   Thomas William **Haines** was born in Provo 8 April 1991.

3108. Susan June[14] **Haines** (Priscilla June[13] **Blake**, Clarence Dodge[12], Lizzie Batchelder[11] **Dodge**, Frank Brickett[10], Deborah Towne[9] **Brickett**, Bernard[8], Bernard[7], Susanna[6] **Pillsbury**, Moses[5], Susanna[4] **Worth**, Susannah[3] **Whipple**, Elder John[2], Matthew[1]) was born in Weymouth, Norfolk Co., Mass. 30 May 1955 and married **Randy Dean Gordon** in Mapleton, Utah 5 April 1974. Randy was previously married and divorced. Randy was born in Provo, Utah Co., Utah 21 November 1953.

Susan June **Haines** and Randy Dean **Gordon** had the following children:

3559   i.   Nathaniel Lawrence[15] **Gordon** was born 5 November 1974.
3560   ii.   Corry **Gordon** was born in Provo 31 July 1978.
3561   iii.   Joshua **Gordon** was born in Orem, Utah 13 June 1981.
3562   iv.   Joel **Gordon** was born in Orem 3 June 1984.

3109. Sandra Dale[14] **Haines** (Priscilla June[13] **Blake**, Clarence Dodge[12], Lizzie Batchelder[11] **Dodge**, Frank Brickett[10], Deborah Towne[9] **Brickett**, Bernard[8], Bernard[7], Susanna[6] **Pillsbury**, Moses[5], Susanna[4] **Worth**, Susannah[3] **Whipple**, Elder John[2], Matthew[1]) was born in Brockton, Plymouth Co., Mass. 2 January 1958 and married **Kendall C. Taylor** 9 April 1977. Kendall was born in Provo, Utah Co., Utah 9 May 1955.

Sandra Dale **Haines** and Kendall C. **Taylor** had the following children:

3563	i.	Casey Lawrence[15] **Taylor** was born in Provo 15 February 1978.
3564	ii.	Kimberly Ann **Taylor** was born Provo 18 May 1979.
3565	iii.	Kendra Lee **Taylor** was born in Provo 9 September 1980.
3566	iv.	Justin William **Taylor** was born in Provo 29 June 1983.
3567	v.	Matthew Charles **Taylor** was born in Provo 13 November 1986.
3568	vi.	Kelli Leann **Taylor** was born in Mt. Vernon, Wash. 14 May 1990.

3110. Linda Ann[14] **Haines** (Priscilla June[13] **Blake**, Clarence Dodge[12], Lizzie Batchelder[11] **Dodge**, Frank Brickett[10], Deborah Towne[9] **Brickett**, Bernard[8], Bernard[7], Susanna[6] **Pillsbury**, Moses[5], Susanna[4] **Worth**, Susannah[3] **Whipple**, Elder John[2], Matthew[1]) was born in Brockton, Plymouth Co., Mass. 2 January 1958 and married **Steven Spencer** 29 April 1977. Steven, son of Norman Darwin **Spencer** and Colleen **Nielsen**, was born in Provo, Utah Co., Utah 21 May 1955.

Linda Ann **Haines** and Steven **Spencer** had the following children:
3569	i.	Kristie Ann[15] **Spencer** was born in Provo 19 December 1978.
3570	ii.	Kirk Allen **Spencer** was born in Provo 22 April 1980.
3571	iii.	Katie Mae **Spencer** was born in San Angelo, Texas 23 January 1982.
3572	iv.	Kathy Marie **Spencer** was born in San Angelo 12 April 1986.
3573	v.	Lisa Kay **Spencer** was born in Redding, Calif. 27 August 1989.

3111. Bradford Blake[14] **Haines** (Priscilla June[13] **Blake**, Clarence Dodge[12], Lizzie Batchelder[11] **Dodge**, Frank Brickett[10], Deborah Towne[9] **Brickett**, Bernard[8], Bernard[7], Susanna[6] **Pillsbury**, Moses[5], Susanna[4] **Worth**, Susannah[3] **Whipple**, Elder John[2], Matthew[1]) was born in Weymouth, Norfolk Co., Mass. 21 January 1962 and married **Kelly Verdeana Kinyon** in Mapleton, Utah 3 June 1982.

Bradford Blake **Haines** adopted the following child in 1984:
| 3574 | i. | Jaycellyn[15] **Haines** was born in Payson, Utah 2 September 1981. |

Bradford Blake **Haines** and Kelly Verdeana **Kinyon** had the following children:
| 3575 | ii | Aaron Bradford **Haines** was born in Payson 3 April 1984. |
| 3576 | iii. | Delicia Ann **Haines** was born in Payson 1 October 1986. |

3117. Merilee Joan[14] **Anderson** (Janet[13] **Horstman**, Helena[12] **Pullen**, Nellie May[11] **Blanchard**, George Adelbert[10], Aaron[9], Lois[8] **Burt**, Abiah[7] **Mooar**, Abiah[6] Hill, Judith[5] **Bucknam**, Judith (Jude)[4] **Worth**, Susannah[3] **Whipple**, Elder John[2], Matthew[1])[4286] was born in Goose Creek, Harris Co., Texas 31 August 1942 and married **David F. Thorman** in Baytown, Harris Co., Texas 16 April 1966. David,[4287] son of Otto Henry **Thorman** and Adelia **Field**, was born in El Paso, Texas 17 July 1938. Merilee received a degree from the U. of Texas in Austin in 1965 and has been a teacher, artist, and decorator.

Merilee Joan **Anderson** and David F. **Thorman** had the following children:
| 3577 | i. | Caillouet F.[15] **Thorman**[4288] was born in Baltimore, Md. 25 October 1969 and married Gokhan **Ozaqacli** 29 December 1993. She went to Turkey on a Watson Fellowship and while there met her future husband, an archeologist. She received a degree in 1999. |
| 3578 | ii. | Kendall Field **Thorman**[4289] was born 12 March 1973. |

3118. Carole Helena[14] **Anderson** (Janet[13] **Horstman**, Helena[12] **Pullen**, Nellie May[11] **Blanchard**, George Adelbert[10], Aaron[9], Lois[8] **Burt**, Abiah[7] **Mooar**, Abiah[6]

Hill, Judith[5] **Bucknam**, Judith (Jude)[4] **Worth**, Susannah[3] **Whipple**, Elder John[2], Matthew[1])[4290] was born in Goose Creek, Harris Co., Texas 13 October 1944 and married **Jonathan Lowry Gilbreath** in Baytown, Harris Co., Texas 24 August 1968. Jonathan, son of Lowry E. **Gilbreath** and Doris **Sand**, was born in Seattle, Wash. 21 September 1945. Carole received a degree in U. of Colorado in 1967.

Carole Helena **Anderson** and Jonathan Lowry **Gilbreath** had the following children:

> 3579   i. Janet Elaine[15] **Gilbreath**[4291] was born in 1969, is a graduate of the U. of Virginia (1992), and was awarded a Masters' of Business Administration by Harvard College in June 1996.
>
> 3580   ii. Wendy Helena **Gilbreath**[4292] was born in Summit, N.J. 25 May 1972 and married Robert **Wilson** 25 May 1996.[4293] She received a degree at Southern Methodist University in 1994.

3119. James Lawford[14] **Anderson** (Janet[13] **Horstman**, Helena[12] **Pullen**, Nellie May[11] **Blanchard**, George Adelbert[10], Aaron[9], Lois[8] **Burt**, Abiah[7] **Mooar**, Abiah[6] Hill, Judith[5] **Bucknam**, Judith (Jude)[4] **Worth**, Susannah[3] **Whipple**, Elder John[2], Matthew[1])[4294] was born in Goose Creek, Harris Co., Texas 2 December 1947 and married twice. (1) **Cynthia Louise Pullen** in San Antonio, Texas, 23 May 1970. Cynthia, daughter of Judson Lee **Pullen** and Martha Jean **Allen**, was born in Columbus, Ohio 29 January 1947 and was graduated from Trinity University. They were divorced in Los Angeles, Calif. in August 1991. (2) **Jean Morrison** in Pasadena, Calif. 6 June 1992. Jean, daughter of Milner Bowden **Morrison** and Etta Marie **Hayball**, was born in Pauling, N.Y. 19 May 1957. James is a graduate of both Trinity University, San Antonio, Texas (1970) and the University of Wisconsin at Madison (1975) and is a professor of geology at the University of Southern California. Jean is also a professor of geology at the U. of Southern California

James Lawford **Anderson** and Cynthia Louise **Pullen** had the following children:

> 3581   i. Tyson James[15] **Anderson**[4295] was born in Madison, Wisc. 23 April 1974.
> 3582   ii. Christopher Michael **Anderson**[4296] was born in Los Angeles, Calif. 3 March 1976.
> 3583   iii. Jonathan Lee **Anderson**[4297] was born in Los Angeles 20 August 1979.

James Lawford **Anderson** and Jean **Morrison** had the following child:

> 3584   iv. Sarah Marie **Anderson**[4298] was born in Pasadena, Calif. 13 June 1995.

3129. Eric[14] **Zumwalt** (Orlow R.[13], Esther Louise[12] **Whipple**, William Henry[11], William Orland[10], William Ward[9], John[8], John[7], Capt. John[6], Capt. John[5], Maj. Matthew[4], Capt. John[3], Elder John[2], Matthew[1])[4299] was born 20 July 1951 and married **Susan (__)** 1 August 1975. They were divorced after 1976.

Eric **Zumwalt** and Susan (__) had the following children:

> 3585   i. Jenny[15] **Zumwalt**[4300].
> 3586   ii. Jill **Zumwalt**[4301] was born 1 December 1977.

3138. Deborah Michele Simmons[14] **Wedge** (LeRoy Ellis[13], Frances Irene[12] **Whipple**, William Henry[11], William Orland[10], William Ward[9], John[8], John[7], Capt. John[6], Capt. John[5], Maj. Matthew[4], Capt. John[3], Elder John[2], Matthew[1])[4302] was born in Owensboro, Ky. 8 September 1963 and married **Patrick O'shaughnessey** in

Rolla, Mo. in January 1992.

Deborah Michele Simmons **Wedge** and Patrick **O'shaughnessey** had the following children born in Rolla:

    3587   i.   Megan Marie[15] **O'shaughnessey**[4303] was born 28 July 1992.

    3588   ii.   Olivia Joye **O'shaughnessey**[4304] was born 28 July 1992.

3143. Richard Lee[14] Michael (Doris Jean[13] Hopkins, Marjorie Eula[12] **Whipple**, William Henry[11], William Orland[10], William Ward[9], John[8], John[7], Capt. John[6], Capt. John[5], Maj. Matthew[4], Capt. John[3], Elder John[2], Matthew[1])[4305] was born 5 April 1955 and married **Valorie Lynn Hedrick** 27 February 1980.

Richard Lee **Michael** and Valorie Lynn **Hedrick** had the following children:

    3589   i.   Ryan Christopher[15] **Michael**[4306] was born 14 February 1988.

    3590   ii.   Cady Lynn **Michael**[4307] was born 30 May 1993.

3145. Russel[14] Weatherly Jr. (Dora Dean[13] Hopkins, Marjorie Eula[12] **Whipple**, William Henry[11], William Orland[10], William Ward[9], John[8], John[7], Capt. John[6], Capt. John[5], Maj. Matthew[4], Capt. John[3], Elder John[2], Matthew[1])[4308] was born in Lebanon, Mo. 16 June 1952 and married **Deborah Story** in Lebanon, Mo. 21 August 1971. Deborah was born 1 March 1954.[4309]

Russel **Weatherly** Jr. and Deborah **Story** had the following children:

    3591   i.   Monoca Dawn[15] **Weatherly**[4310] was born in Texas in August 1972.

    3592   ii.   Monoca **Weatherly**[4311] was born in Texas in August 1972.

    3593   iii.   Russel Andrew **Weatherly**[4312] was born in San Angelo, Texas 28 April 1974.

3146. James Fay[14] Weatherly (Dora Dean[13] Hopkins, Marjorie Eula[12] **Whipple**, William Henry[11], William Orland[10], William Ward[9], John[8], John[7], Capt. John[6], Capt. John[5], Maj. Matthew[4], Capt. John[3], Elder John[2], Matthew[1])[4313] was born at Ft. Riley, Kans. 6 January 1954 and married twice. (1) **Ladonna Sumner** 20 June 1972. They were divorced after 1974. (2) **Mary Ellen Wills** after 1975.

James Fay **Weatherly** and Ladonna **Sumner** had the following child:

    3594   i.   Timothy James[15] **Weatherly**[4314] was born 17 February 1974.

3147. Marjorie Diana[14] Weatherly (Dora Dean[13] Hopkins, Marjorie Eula[12] **Whipple**, William Henry[11], William Orland[10], William Ward[9], John[8], John[7], Capt. John[6], Capt. John[5], Maj. Matthew[4], Capt. John[3], Elder John[2], Matthew[1])[4315] was born 20 June 1956 and married **Lawrence Karl Patz**.

Marjorie Diana **Weatherly** and Lawrence Karl **Patz** had the following children:

    3595   i.   Jessica Marie[15] **Patz**[4316] was born 17 September 1981.

    3596   ii.   Karl Allen **Patz**[4317] was born 18 August 1983.

    3597   iii.   Richard Andrew **Patz**[4318] was born 15 August 1985.

3148. Pamela Sue[14] Weatherly (Dora Dean[13] Hopkins, Marjorie Eula[12] **Whipple**, William Henry[11], William Orland[10], William Ward[9], John[8], John[7], Capt. John[6], Capt. John[5], Maj. Matthew[4], Capt. John[3], Elder John[2], Matthew[1])[4319] was born 29 September 1960 and married **Richard Odom Jr.** before 1980. They were divorced after 1981.

Pamela Sue **Weatherly** and Richard **Odom** Jr. had the following child:

    3598   i. Diane Michele[15] **Odom**[4320] was born 19 June 1980.

3149. Paul Eugene[14] **Jones** (Melba Paulene[13] **Hopkins**, Marjorie Eula[12] **Whipple**, William Henry[11], William Orland[10], William Ward[9], John[8], John[7], Capt. John[6], Capt. John[5], Maj. Matthew[4], Capt. John[3], Elder John[2], Matthew[1])[4321] was born in Lebanon, Mo. 17 March 1953 and married **Shirley Miller** there 18 January 1974. Shirley was born 18 November 1956.[4322]

Paul Eugene **Jones** and Shirley **Miller** had the following children:

    3599   i. Jeffery Paul[15] **Jones**[4323] was born in Lebanon, 2 April 1977.
    3600   ii. Bethany Ann **Jones**[4324] was born in Jefferson City, Mo. 18 March 1981.
    3601   iii. Travis Lavelle **Jones**[4325] was born in Jefferson City 23 May 1989.

3151. Charles Steven[14] **Jones** (Melba Paulene[13] **Hopkins**, Marjorie Eula[12] **Whipple**, William Henry[11], William Orland[10], William Ward[9], John[8], John[7], Capt. John[6], Capt. John[5], Maj. Matthew[4], Capt. John[3], Elder John[2], Matthew[1])[4326] was born 9 October 1955 and married **Bonita Hendrix** in October 1973. Bonita was born 22 May 1956.[4327]

Charles Steven **Jones** and Bonita **Hendrix** had the following children:

    3602   i. Amy Leigh[15] **Jones**[4328] was born 17 May 1974 and married Chuck **Bryant**.
    3603   ii. Lori Brooke **Jones**[4329] was born 10 June 1982.

3152. JoAnne[14] **Chaffin** (Melba Paulene[13] **Hopkins**, Marjorie Eula[12] **Whipple**, William Henry[11], William Orland[10], William Ward[9], John[8], John[7], Capt. John[6], Capt. John[5], Maj. Matthew[4], Capt. John[3], Elder John[2], Matthew[1])[4330] was born 7 January 1959 and married **William Glen Gillis** before 1979. They were divorced after 1992.

JoAnne **Chaffin** and William Glen **Gillis** had the following child:

    3604   i. Paula Michaelle[15] **Gillis**[4331] was born 20 April 1979.

JoAnne **Chaffin** had the following child:

    3605   ii. Jessica Michale **Chaffin**[4332] was born 20 October 1992.

3153. Larry Dale[14] **Chaffin** (Melba Paulene[13] **Hopkins**, Marjorie Eula[12] **Whipple**, William Henry[11], William Orland[10], William Ward[9], John[8], John[7], Capt. John[6], Capt. John[5], Maj. Matthew[4], Capt. John[3], Elder John[2], Matthew[1])[4333] was born 17 April 1961 and married **Carla O'Neal** 9 October 1982. Larry is a member of the U.S. army.

Larry Dale **Chaffin** and Carla **O'Neal** had the following children:

    3606   i. Larry Dale[15] **Chaffin** Jr.[4334] was born 4 November 1983.
    3607   ii. Jonathan Michael **Chaffin**[4335] was born 8 September 1985.
    3608   iii. Gregory William **Chaffin**[4336] was born 28 January 1989.
    3609   iv. Carrie Jodee **Chaffin**[4337] was born 2 March 1990.

3154. Mary Chrystine[14] **Chaffin** (Melba Paulene[13] **Hopkins**, Marjorie Eula[12] **Whipple**, William Henry[11], William Orland[10], William Ward[9], John[8], John[7], Capt. John[6], Capt. John[5], Maj. Matthew[4], Capt. John[3], Elder John[2], Matthew[1])[4338] was born 25 December 1962 and married **Thomas Allen McClanahan**.

Mary Chrystine **Chaffin** and Thomas Allen **McClanahan** had the following children:

  3610 i. Bridget Dawn[15] **McClanahan**[4339] was born 10 November 1982.
  3611 ii. Chad Allen **McClanahan**[4340] was born 7 February 1986.

3155. William Fay[14] **Chaffin** (Melba Paulene[13] **Hopkins**, Marjorie Eula[12] **Whipple**, William Henry[11], William Orland[10], William Ward[9], John[8], John[7], Capt. John[6], Capt. John[5], Maj. Matthew[4], Capt. John[3], Elder John[2], Matthew[1])[4341] was born 22 March 1964 and married **Karen Florenski** 2 May 1986.

William Fay **Chaffin** and Karen **Florenski** had the following children:

  3612 i. Brock Edward[15] **Chaffin**[4342] was born 18 December 1989.
  3613 ii. Breet Dean **Chaffin**[4343] was born 14 April 1992.

3157. Bruce Lee[14] **Beal** (Eula Faye[13] **Hopkins**, Marjorie Eula[12] **Whipple**, William Henry[11], William Orland[10], William Ward[9], John[8], John[7], Capt. John[6], Capt. John[5], Maj. Matthew[4], Capt. John[3], Elder John[2], Matthew[1])[4344] was born in Spain 7 November 1960 and married **Robin Tyndal**.

Bruce Lee **Beal** and Robin **Tyndal** had the following child:

  3614 i. Brittany Elizabeth[15] **Beal**[4345] was born 26 December 1989.

3158. Bryan[14] **Beal** (Eula Faye[13] **Hopkins**, Marjorie Eula[12] **Whipple**, William Henry[11], William Orland[10], William Ward[9], John[8], John[7], Capt. John[6], Capt. John[5], Maj. Matthew[4], Capt. John[3], Elder John[2], Matthew[1])[4346] was born in Spain 15 February 1962 and married **Christina Ojhi**.

Bryan **Beal** and Christina **Ojhi** had the following children:

  3615 i. Sarah Ashley[15] **Beal**[4347] was born 13 April 1988.
  3616 ii. Chelsea **Beal**[4348] was born 27 May 1991.

3159. Kimberly Sue[14] **Williams** (Mirian Frances[13] **Hopkins**, Marjorie Eula[12] **Whipple**, William Henry[11], William Orland[10], William Ward[9], John[8], John[7], Capt. John[6], Capt. John[5], Maj. Matthew[4], Capt. John[3], Elder John[2], Matthew[1])[4349] was born in Peoria, Ill. 17 November 1959 and married twice. (1) **Hilton Thomas Wells** before 1982. They were divorced after 1983. (2) **Chris Bowling** after 1984.

Kimberly Sue **Williams** and Hilton Thomas **Wells** had the following child:

  3617 i. April Denise[15] **Wells**[4350] was born 9 April 1982.

3160. Dareatha Denise[14] **Williams** (Mirian Frances[13] **Hopkins**, Marjorie Eula[12] **Whipple**, William Henry[11], William Orland[10], William Ward[9], John[8], John[7], Capt. John[6], Capt. John[5], Maj. Matthew[4], Capt. John[3], Elder John[2], Matthew[1])[4351] was born in Germany 19 February 1961 and married twice. (1) **Gary Runge** abt 1987. They were divorced after 1987. (2) **Gerald Gann** after 1988.

Dareatha Denise **Williams** and Gary **Runge** had the following child:

  3618 i. Nicholas Cole[15] **Runge**[4352] was born in Lebanon, Mo. 2 August 1987. Adopted by Gerald Gann.

3162. Melissa[14] **Hopkins** (William Otto[13], Marjorie Eula[12] **Whipple**, William Henry[11], William Orland[10], William Ward[9], John[8], John[7], Capt. John[6], Capt. John[5], Maj. Matthew[4], Capt. John[3], Elder John[2], Matthew[1])[4353] was born 20 September

1965 and married **Wendell D. Perryman** 14 December 1984.

> Melissa **Hopkins** and Wendell D. **Perryman** had the following children:
>
> 3619   i. Wesley Dwayne[15] **Perryman**[4354] was born 3 December 1987.
> 3620   ii. Tyler William **Perryman**[4355] was born 29 January 1992.
> 3621   iii. Eryn Michele **Perryman**[4356] was born 8 January 1994.

3164. Jacque[14] **Grimes** (Elizabeth Irene[13] **Hopkins**, Marjorie Eula[12] **Whipple**, William Henry[11], William Orland[10], William Ward[9], John[8], John[7], Capt. John[6], Capt. John[5], Maj. Matthew[4], Capt. John[3], Elder John[2], Matthew[1])[4357] was born 15 December 1962 and married **Robert Berthurem**. They were divorced.

> Jacque **Grimes** had the following child:
>
> 3622   i. Jaclyn[15] **Grimes**[4358] was born in Lebanon, Mo. 20 January 1993.

3165. James Carl[14] **Grimes** (Elizabeth Irene[13] **Hopkins**, Marjorie Eula[12] **Whipple**, William Henry[11], William Orland[10], William Ward[9], John[8], John[7], Capt. John[6], Capt. John[5], Maj. Matthew[4], Capt. John[3], Elder John[2], Matthew[1])[4359] was born 22 June 1963 and married **Tammy Tabors**.

> James Carl **Grimes** and Tammy **Tabors** had the following children born in Lebanon, Mo.:
>
> 3623   i. Elizabeth Joann[15] **Grimes**[4360] was born 21 October 1983.
> 3624   ii. Jayson Everett **Grimes**[4361] was born 14 August 1985.

3173. Del Reese[14] **Visser** (Patricia Ann[13] **Whipple**, Earl Lawrence[12], William Henry[11], William Orland[10], William Ward[9], John[8], John[7], Capt. John[6], Capt. John[5], Maj. Matthew[4], Capt. John[3], Elder John[2], Matthew[1])[4362] was born 3 September 1966 and married **Dena (__)** abt 1987.

> Del Reese **Visser** and Dena (__) had the following children:
>
> 3625   i. Brookie Ashly[15] **Visser**[4363] was born in 1988.
> 3626   ii. Skyler **Visser**[4364] was born in 1994.

3184. Elizabeth Diane[14] **Buchan** (Barbara Kay[13] **Whipple**, Jerald Howard[12], John Godfrey[11], William Orland[10], William Ward[9], John[8], John[7], Capt. John[6], Capt. John[5], Maj. Matthew[4], Capt. John[3], Elder John[2], Matthew[1])[4365] was born in Middlesex Co., England 29 January 1963 and married **Victor Garcia** in Orcas Island, Wash. in December 1992.

> Elizabeth Diane **Buchan** and Victor **Garcia** had the following child:
>
> 3627   i. Kestrel[15] **Garcia**[4366] was born in Nashville, Tenn. 15 August 1992.

3193. Bradley Lendell[14] **Carpenter** (Lendell LeRoy[13], Claribel[12] **Whipple**, Clyde Ward[11], William Orland[10], William Ward[9], John[8], John[7], Capt. John[6], Capt. John[5], Maj. Matthew[4], Capt. John[3], Elder John[2], Matthew[1])[4367] was born in Portland, Multnomah Co., Oreg. 17 June 1969 and married **Annette Marie Johnson** in Kent, Wash. 2 January 1993.[4368]

> Bradley Lendell **Carpenter** and Annette Marie **Johnson** had the following child:
>
> 3628   i. Madeline Faith[15] **Carpenter**[4369] was born in Forest Grove, Washington Co., Oreg. 24 February 1994.

3206. **Christina Baldwin**[14] **Rice** (Joan Morgan[13] **Whipple**, Grant Dodge[12], Clyde Ward[11], William Orland[10], William Ward[9], John[8], John[7], Capt. John[6], Capt. John[5], Maj. Matthew[4], Capt. John[3], Elder John[2], Matthew[1])[4370] was born 21 November 1966.

Christina Baldwin **Rice** had the following child:
    3629   i. Hannah Elizabeth Barrett[15] **Rice**[4371] was born 29 June 1994.

3225. **Katherine Patterson**[14] **Windisch** (Melinda[13] **Jones**, Proctor Patterson[12], Ferne Catherine[11] **Patterson**, Proctor[10], Phebe Smith[9] **Whipple**, Stephen[8], Martha[7], Dea. Nathaniel[6], Capt. John[5], Maj. Matthew[4], Capt. John[3], Elder John[2], Matthew[1])[4372] was born 10 January 1963 and married **Rayburn Ingle**.[4373]

Katherine Patterson **Windisch** and Rayburn Ingle had the following child:
    3630   i. Cara Dawn[15] **Ingle**[4374] was born 20 October 1982.

3235. **Deborah Louise**[14] **Wege** (Barbara Jane[13] **Nelson**, Robert Hatch[12], Jessamine Gertrude[11] **Hatch**, Alonzo Herbert[10], Paschal[9], Anna[8] **Gould**, Anna[7] **Lane**, Timothy[6], Job[5], Susanna[4] **Whipple**, Capt. John[3], Elder John[2], Matthew[1])[4375] was born in Salt Lake City, Utah 24 September 1952 and married **Stephan Alfred Tribull** in Chicago, Ill. 22 November 1980. Stephan was born in Wuppertal, West Germany 18 July 1946.[4376]

Deborah Louise **Wege** and Stephan Alfred **Tribull** had the following children:
    3631   i. Sean Andreas[15] **Tribull** was born in Frankfurt/Hochst, West Germany 13 January 1988.
    3632   ii. Sven Alexander **Tribull**[4377] was born in Frankfurt/Hochst 5 January 1990.

3251. **Frederick Lee**[14] **Green** (Clarissa Louise[13] **Powers**, Edwin Cyrus[12], Cyrus Hale Stone[11], John[10], Cyrus Hale Stone[9], Lavinia[8] **Stone**, Capt. Amos[7], Amos[6], Simon[5], Deacon Simon[4], Mary[3] **Whipple**, Elder John[2], Matthew[1])[4378] birth date unknown married **Karen Ann Castor**.

Frederick Lee **Green** and Karen Ann **Castor** had the following children:
    3633   i. Ranae Lynn[15] **Green**[4379].
    3634   ii. Beau Michael **Green**[4380].

3252. **Lonni Rae**[14] **Sexton** (Clarissa Louise[13] **Powers**, Edwin Cyrus[12], Cyrus Hale Stone[11], John[10], Cyrus Hale Stone[9], Lavinia[8] **Stone**, Capt. Amos[7], Amos[6], Simon[5], Deacon Simon[4], Mary[3] **Whipple**, Elder John[2], Matthew[1])[4381] birth date unknown married **Tod Lenz Balkovich**.

Lonni Rae **Sexton** and Tod Lenz **Balkovich** had the following children:
    3635   i. Robert Michael[15] **Balkovich**[4382].
    3636   ii. Halley Rose **Balkovich**[4383].

3253. **Karen Jill**[14] **Sexton** (Clarissa Louise[13] **Powers**, Edwin Cyrus[12], Cyrus Hale Stone[11], John[10], Cyrus Hale Stone[9], Lavinia[8] **Stone**, Capt. Amos[7], Amos[6], Simon[5], Deacon Simon[4], Mary[3] **Whipple**, Elder John[2], Matthew[1])[4384] birth date unknown married **Patrick Lee Holihan**.

Karen Jill **Sexton** and Patrick Lee **Holihan** had the following children:

3637   i.   Jamie Kay[15] **Holihan**[4385].
3638   ii.   Natalie **Holihan**[4386].
3639   iii.   Joseph Patrick **Holihan**[4387].

3254. Patty Jo[14] **Sexton** (Clarissa Louise[13] **Powers**, Edwin Cyrus[12], Cyrus Hale Stone[11], John[10], Cyrus Hale Stone[9], Lavinia[8] **Stone**, Capt. Amos[7], Amos[6], Simon[5], Deacon Simon[4], Mary[3] **Whipple**, Elder John[2], Matthew[1])[4388] birth date unknown married twice. (1) **Kenneth Arthur Wells.** (2) **Ronald Allen McFarlane.**

Patty Jo **Sexton** and Kenneth Arthur **Wells** had the following children:
3640   i.   Kristarae Mackenzi[15] **Wells**[4389].
3641   ii.   Kaylee Marie **Wells**[4390].

3271. Lisa Carol[14] **Powers** (Harold Cyrus[13], Wesley Raymond[12], Cyrus Hale Stone[11], John[10], Cyrus Hale Stone[9], Lavinia[8] **Stone**, Capt. Amos[7], Amos[6], Simon[5], Deacon Simon[4], Mary[3] **Whipple**, Elder John[2], Matthew[1])[4391] birth date unknown married twice. (1) **James A. Gottschalk.** (2) James **Dallmeyer.**

Lisa Carol **Powers** and James A. **Gottschalk** had the following child:
3642   i.   Jonathan[15] **Gottschalk**[4392] was born 1 January 1991.

3272. Jill Kay[14] **Powers** (Harold Cyrus[13], Wesley Raymond[12], Cyrus Hale Stone[11], John[10], Cyrus Hale Stone[9], Lavinia[8] **Stone**, Capt. Amos[7], Amos[6], Simon[5], Deacon Simon[4], Mary[3] **Whipple**, Elder John[2], Matthew[1])[4393] birth date unknown married **Robert Powell.**

Jill Kay **Powers** and Robert **Powell** had the following child:
3643   i.   John Robert[15] **Powell**[4394] was born in Lake Forest, Ill. 25 February 1998.

3277. Thomas Jeffrey[14] **Pratt** (Thomas Nelson[13], Orville Powers[12], Olive Evalena[11] **Powers**, John[10], Cyrus Hale Stone[9], Lavinia[8] **Stone**, Capt. Amos[7], Amos[6], Simon[5], Deacon Simon[4], Mary[3] **Whipple**, Elder John[2], Matthew[1])[4395] was born in LaGrange, Cook Co., Ill. 24 November 1962 and married **Jennifer Susan Le Sueur** in River Forest, Ill. 4 June 1988. Jennifer,[4396] daughter of Robert Le **Sueur** and Betty **Moore**, was born in Chicago, Ill. Thomas is a graduate of Purdue University.

Thomas Jeffrey **Pratt** and Jennifer Susan Le **Sueur** had the following children:
3644   i.   Taylor Thomas[15] **Pratt**[4397] was born in Oak Park, Cook Co., Ill. 25 October 1991.
3645   ii.   Alexa Lyndsey **Pratt**[4398] was born 1 May 1995.

3278. Karen Ellen[14] **Pratt** (Thomas Nelson[13], Orville Powers[12], Olive Evalena[11] **Powers**, John[10], Cyrus Hale Stone[9], Lavinia[8] **Stone**, Capt. Amos[7], Amos[6], Simon[5], Deacon Simon[4], Mary[3] **Whipple**, Elder John[2], Matthew[1])[4399] was born in LaGrange, Cook Co., Ill. 8 July 1965 and married **Scott Merlin Allen** in Oak Park, Cook Co., Ill. 13 June 1992. Scott,[4400] son of Frederick **Allen** and Barbara **Dangel**, was born in Chicago, Ill. He was adopted by Frederick and Barbara Allen in 1962. He is a commodity trader and salesman. Karen is a graduate of Eastern Illinois University and works in pre-school education.

Karen Ellen **Pratt** and Scott Merlin **Allen** had the following children born in Oak Park, Cook Co., Ill:

3646   i.   John Frederick^{15} **Allen**[4401] was born 25 August 1997.

3647   ii.   Thomas Scott **Allen**[4402] was born 21 March 2001.

3300. Eugenia^{14} **Wise** (Robert E.^{13}, William Oliver^{12}, Mary Olive^{11} **Carr**, William Dustin^{10}, Lyman^9, Susanna^8 **Dunton**, Mary^7 **Jewell**, Mary^6 **Whitney**, Mary^5 **Stone**, Deacon Simon^4, Mary^3 **Whipple**, Elder John^2, Matthew^1)[4403] was born 14 January 1942 and married **Orson S. Hathaway.**

Eugenia **Wise** and Orson S. **Hathaway** had the following children:

3648   i.   Danforth O.^{15} **Hathaway**[4404] was born 23 December 1964.

3649   ii.   Paul D. **Hathaway**[4405] was born 25 March 1970.

3301. Barbara^{14} **Wise** (Robert E.^{13}, William Oliver^{12}, Mary Olive^{11} **Carr**, William Dustin^{10}, Lyman^9, Susanna^8 **Dunton**, Mary^7 **Jewell**, Mary^6 **Whitney**, Mary^5 **Stone**, Deacon Simon^4, Mary^3 **Whipple**, Elder John^2, Matthew^1)[4406] was born 2 March 1944 and married **John M. Lynch III.** John was born 16 January 1945.[4407]

Barbara **Wise** and John M. **Lynch** III had the following children:

3650   i.   Christina^{15} **Lynch**[4408] was born 29 April 1972.

3651   ii.   Michael F. **Lynch**[4409] was born 5 December 1974.

3652   iii.   Matthew P. **Lynch**[4410] was born 8 March 1982.

3302. John O.^{14} **Wise** (Robert E.^{13}, William Oliver^{12}, Mary Olive^{11} **Carr**, William Dustin^{10}, Lyman^9, Susanna^8 **Dunton**, Mary^7 **Jewell**, Mary^6 **Whitney**, Mary^5 **Stone**, Deacon Simon^4, Mary^3 **Whipple**, Elder John^2, Matthew^1)[4411] was born 17 November 1953 and married **Lisa Marson.** Lisa was born 28 June 1957.[4412]

John O. **Wise** and Lisa **Marson** had the following children:

3653   i.   Julia A.^{15} **Wise**[4413] was born 3 November 1987.

3654   ii.   Rachel G. **Wise**[4414] was born 29 November 1989.

3303. William C.^{14} **Saunders** (Miriam^{13} **Wise**, William Oliver^{12}, Mary Olive^{11} **Carr**, William Dustin^{10}, Lyman^9, Susanna^8 **Dunton**, Mary^7 **Jewell**, Mary^6 **Whitney**, Mary^5 **Stone**, Deacon Simon^4, Mary^3 **Whipple**, Elder John^2, Matthew^1)[4415] was born 18 March 1945 and married **Susan Thrasher.**

William C. **Saunders** and Susan **Thrasher** had the following children:

3655   i.   Peter^{15} **Saunders**[4416] was born 15 October 1977.

3656   ii.   Brynn **Saunders**[4417] was born 26 September 1982.

3304. Martha^{14} **Saunders** (Miriam^{13} **Wise**, William Oliver^{12}, Mary Olive^{11} **Carr**, William Dustin^{10}, Lyman^9, Susanna^8 **Dunton**, Mary^7 **Jewell**, Mary^6 **Whitney**, Mary^5 **Stone**, Deacon Simon^4, Mary^3 **Whipple**, Elder John^2, Matthew^1)[4418] was born 10 May 1947 and married **Bahram Nabatian.**

Martha **Saunders** and Bahram **Nabatian** had the following children:

3657   i.   Kaveh^{15} **Nabatian**[4419] was born 16 June 1976.

3658   ii.   Sohrob **Nabatian**[4420] was born 10 July 1980.

3659   iii.   Shireen **Nabatian**[4421] was born 22 November 1982.

3305. Carolyn^{14} **Saunders** (Miriam^{13} **Wise**, William Oliver^{12}, Mary Olive^{11} **Carr**, William Dustin^{10}, Lyman^9, Susanna^8 **Dunton**, Mary^7 **Jewell**, Mary^6 **Whitney**, Mary^5 **Stone**, Deacon Simon^4, Mary^3 **Whipple**, Elder John^2, Matthew^1)[4422] was born 5 June

1951 and married **Robert Munger.**

Carolyn **Saunders** and Robert **Munger** had the following child:
3660   i.   Loren[15] **Munger**[4423] was born 11 November 1988.

3306. **William Oliver**[14] **Wise III** (William Oliver[13], William Oliver[12], Mary Olive[11] **Carr**, William Dustin[10], Lyman[9], Susanna[8] **Dunton**, Mary[7] **Jewell**, Mary[6] **Whitney**, Mary[5] **Stone**, Deacon Simon[4], Mary[3] **Whipple**, Elder John[2], Matthew[1])[4424] was born in March 1954 and married **Janis Miller.**

William Oliver **Wise** III and Janis **Miller** had the following children:
3661   i.   Robert[15] **Wise**[4425].
3662   ii.   Kent **Wise**[4426].
3663   iii.   Sean **Wise**[4427].

3308. **Leslie Anne**[14] **Wolfe** (Virginia Anne[13] **Croissant**, Martin[12], Nellie Frances[11] **King**, Edwin Henry[10], John[9], Lois[8] **Jackson**, Lois[7] **Woodward,**, Mary[6] **Stone**, Samuel[5], Ebenezer[4], Mary[3] **Whipple**, Elder John[2], Matthew[1])[4428] was born in Malone, Franklin Co. N.Y. 7 January 1947 and married **Albert Leonard Pfeifer** in McLean, Va. 12 June 1984.

Leslie Anne **Wolfe** and Albert Leonard **Pfeifer** had the following children:
3664   i.   Christopher Alexander[15] **Pfeifer**[4429] was born in Brasilia, Brazil 29 January 1986.
3665   ii.   Amanda Marie **Pfeifer**[4430] was born 22 October 1987.

3313. **Ruth Anne**[14] **Hayden** (Victoria Anne[13] **McIntosh**, Eunice Mae[12] **Baldwin**, Nellie Eliza[11] **Newell**, Mary Frances[10] **Grow**, Lorenzo[9], Samuel Porter[8], Joseph[7], Abigail[6] **Dana**, Susanna[5] **Starr**, Mary[4] **Stone**, Mary[3] **Whipple**, Elder John[2], Matthew[1])[4431] was born in Alhambra, Calif. 12 January 1946 and married **Ronald Norman Hancock** in Garden Grove, Orange Co., Calif. 30 July 1966. Ronald,[4432] son of Harold Russell **Hancock** and Kathrine **Rehner**, was born in Detroit, Mich. 21 September 1942. Ronald was in the U.S. Navy 1962-66 and now is a fire captain. Ruth is a Registered nurse.

Ruth Anne **Hayden** and Ronald Norman **Hancock** had the following children:
3666   i.   Kenneth Martin[15] **Hancock**[4433] was born 21 August 1967 and is a mortgage broker in Seattle, Wash.
3667   ii.   Dean Russell **Hancock**[4434] was born 13 January 1970. He was in the book publishing business before becoming a computer network manager in Seattle, Wash.
3668   iii.   Gregory Scott **Hancock**[4435] was born in Coupeville Island, Wash. 2 September 1971 and is an inventor, free lance writer, and artist.

3319. **Carolyn Christine**[14] **Jones** (Donald Dee[13], Helen Beatrice[12] **Carson**, Estella Grace[11] **Wilson**, Mary Arvilla[10] **Viersen**, Mary[9] **Starr**, Lovel[8], Comfort[7], Capt. Comfort[6], Comfort[5], Mary[4] **Stone**, Mary[3] **Whipple**, Elder John[2], Mattthew[1])[4436] was born in Lincoln, Nebr. 12 June 1955 and married **Gary William Koch** in Carroll, Carroll Co., Iowa 22 May 1976. Gary,[4437] son of Edward **Kich** and Bonnie **Menafe**, was born in Hampton, Franklin Co., Iowa 9 October 1954. They were divorced after 1982. Gary was graduated with a B.A. and a law degree at the U. of Iowa where he was a member of Phi Beta Kappa and practiced law in New Ulm, Minn. Carolyn was Governor of Iowa Girls State in 1972 and earned a B.A. at the U. of Iowa where she was Phi Beta Kappa, student senate president, and member of the Mortar Board and Order of Coif. She earned a JD degree from the University in 1982 and later a ULM degree from Yale. She was a law professor at St. Louis University beginning in 1982, a visiting professor at the U. of Iowa in 1986, a law professor at St. Louis University in 1987 and joined the law faculty at the U. of Connecticut in 1989.

Carolyn Christine **Jones** and Gary William **Koch** had the following child:

> 3669   i. Allison Elizabeth[15] **Koch**[4438] was born in New Haven, Conn. 24 November 1981.

3320. Laurie Grace[14] **Jones** (Donald Dee[13], Helen Beatrice[12] **Carson**, Estella Grace[11] **Wilson**, Mary Arvilla[10] **Viersen**, Mary[9] **Starr**, Lovel[8], Comfort[7], Capt. Comfort[6], Comfort[5], Mary[4] **Stone**, Mary[3] **Whipple**, Elder John[2], Matthew[1])[4439] was born in Omaha, Nebr. 21 January 1957 and married **Elias Inez Vasquez** in Phoenix, Ariz. 13 March 1982. Elias,[4440] son of Elias Vasquez, was born in El Paso, Texas 17 August 1955. They were divorced in Phoenix, Ariz. after 1983. He earned an undergraduate degree at Northern Arizona University and a M.S. and Ph.D. at the U. of Arizona and became a professor of nursing at the U. of Texas. Laurie is a graduate of the U. of Iowa where she was a member of Sigma Theta Tau. She is the head neo-natal nurse at Phoenix's Children's Hospital.

Laurie Grace **Jones** and Elias Inez **Vasquez** had the following child:

> 3670   i. Nicole Rene[15] **Vasquez**[4441] was born in Phoenix, Ariz. 9 September 1987.

3321. Susan Marie[14] **Jones** (Donald Dee[13], Helen Beatrice[12] **Carson**, Estella Grace[11] **Wilson**, Mary Arvilla[10] **Viersen**, Mary[9] **Starr**, Lovel[8], Comfort[7], Capt. Comfort[6], Comfort[5], Mary[4] **Stone**, Mary[3] **Whipple**, Elder John[2], Matthew[1])[4442] was born in Carroll, Carroll Co., Iowa 7 May 1958 and married **Todd Paul Semla** there 23 August 1980. Todd,[4443] son of Donald **Semla** and Faith **Metzler**, was born in Newark, Licking Co., Ohio 20 November 1958. He is a graduate of the U. of Iowa with both a Bachelor and Master of Science degrees and is a professor of pharmacy at the U. of Ill. Chicago. Susan earned both a BS and Ph.D. degree from the U. of Iowa and is a research pharmacist for Abbott Labs where is is a senior project manager.

Susan Marie **Jones** and Todd Paul **Semla** had the following children born in Evanston, Ill:

> 3671   i. Marie Christine[15] **Semla**[4444] was born. 4 October 1988.
> 3672   ii. Colleen Jennifer **Semla**[4445] was born 5 March 1993.
> 3673   iii. Peter Donald **Semla**[4446] was born 25 October 1995.

3322. Philip Lee[14] **Jones** (Donald Dee[13], Helen Beatrice[12] **Carson**, Estella Grace[11] **Wilson**, Mary Arvilla[10] **Viersen**, Mary[9] **Starr**, Lovel[8], Comfort[7], Capt. Comfort[6], Comfort[5], Mary[4] **Stone**, Mary[3] **Whipple**, Elder John[2], Matthew[1])[4447] was born in Carroll, Carroll Co., Iowa 7 May 1960 and married **Patricia Wightman** in Sioux City, Woodbury Co., Iowa 4 June 1985. Patricia,[4448] daughter of Richard **Wightman** and Virginia **Egger**, was born in Sioux City, 12 January 1962. She is a graduate of Iowa State University and the University of Minnesota and is a certified public accountant in Eagan, Minn. Philip attended Iowa State University and earned a bachelor of science degree from the U. of Iowa in engineering. He is a computer engineer at Terradyne Corporation.

Philip Lee **Jones** and Patricia **Wightman** had the following children born in Burnsville, Dakota Co., Minn:

3674	i.	Samuel Philip[15] **Jones**[4449] was born 1 August 1989.
3675	ii.	Hannah Grace **Jones**[4450] was born 14 February 1992.
3676	iii.	Olivia Christine **Jones**[4451] was born 19 September 1996.
3677	iv.	Benjamin Lee **Jones**[4452] was born 19 September 1996.

3336. David Edward[14] **Augustine** (Cheryl Maureen[13] **Stevens**, Frances Harriet[12] **Goddard**, George Francis[11], George Osmer[10], John Bailey[9], Robert[8], Nahum[7], Robert[6], Edward[5], Susanna[4] **Stone**, Mary[3] **Whipple**, Elder John[2], Matthew[1])[4453] was born 2 April 1961.

David Edward **Augustine** had the following child:

3678	i.	David Jeffrey[15] **Augustine**[4454].

3342. Julie Kay[14] **Darby** (Judith Ann[13] **Reinking**, Jean Doris[12] **Goddard**, George Francis[11], George Osmer[10], John Bailey[9], Robert[8], Nahum[7], Robert[6], Edward[5], Susanna[4] **Stone**, Mary[3] **Whipple**, Elder John[2], Matthew[1])[4455] was born 17 November 1959 and married **Tom Foss**.

Julie Kay **Darby** and Tom **Foss** had the following children:

3679	i.	Jessie Johanna[15] **Foss**[4456].
3680	ii.	Katie Jo **Foss**[4457].
3681	iii.	Ben Thomas **Foss**[4458].

3343. Joni Sue[14] **Darby** (Judith Ann[13] **Reinking**, Jean Doris[12] **Goddard**, George Francis[11], George Osmer[10], John Bailey[9], Robert[8], Nahum[7], Robert[6], Edward[5], Susanna[4] **Stone**, Mary[3] **Whipple**, Elder John[2], Matthew[1])[4459] was born 22 May 1961 and married twice. (1) (_) **Woodruff**. (2) (_) **Haynes**.

Joni Sue **Darby** and (_) **Woodruff** had the following children:

3682	i.	Travis James[15] **Woodruff**[4460].
3683	ii.	Jenna Kristine **Woodruff**[4461].

3344. Jill Anette[14] **Darby** (Judith Ann[13] **Reinking**, Jean Doris[12] **Goddard**, George Francis[11], George Osmer[10], John Bailey[9], Robert[8], Nahum[7], Robert[6], Edward[5], Susanna[4] **Stone**, Mary[3] **Whipple**, Elder John[2], Matthew[1])[4462] was born 21 February 1963 and married **Robert Andrea**.

Jill Anette **Darby** and Robert **Andrea** had the following child:

3684	i.	Jared Blaine[15] **Andrea**[4463].

3345. William Ray[14] **Wilson** (Karen Jean[13] **Reinking**, Jean Doris[12] **Goddard**, George Francis[11], George Osmer[10], John Bailey[9], Robert[8], Nahum[7], Robert[6], Edward[5], Susanna[4] **Stone**, Mary[3] **Whipple**, Elder John[2], Matthew[1])[4464] was born 23 June 1961.

William Ray **Wilson** had the following children:

3685	i.	Brandie Michelle[15] **Wilson**[4465] was born 3 March 1984.

3686   ii. Tyrel David **Wilson**[4466] was born 30 November 1986. Adopted.

3687   iii. Lee Mark **Wilson**[4467] was born 13 February 1988. Adopted.

3688   iv. Steven Scott **Wilson**[4468] was born 18 September 1989. Adopted.

3689   v. Sarah Jean Marie **Wilson**[4469] was born 31 July 1993. Adopted.

3346. Kathryn Ann[14] **Wilson** (Karen Jean[13] **Reinking**, Jean Doris[12] **Goddard**, George Francis[11], George Osmer[10], John Bailey[9], Robert[8], Nahum[7], Robert[6], Edward[5], Susanna[4] **Stone**, Mary[3] **Whipple**, Elder John[2], Matthew[1])[4470] was born 22 February 1963 and married (__) **Peer**.

Kathryn Ann **Wilson** and (__) **Peer** had the following children:

3690   i. Zecheriah Scott[15] **Peer**[4471] was born 18 July 1983.

3691   ii. Lacey Ann **Peer**[4472] was born 19 September 1984.

3692   iii. Megan Christine **Peer**[4473] was born 20 March 1987.

3693   iv. Ashley Elizabeth **Peer**[4474] was born 8 August 1989.

3347. Linda Marie[14] **Wilson** (Karen Jean[13] **Reinking**, Jean Doris[12] **Goddard**, George Francis[11], George Osmer[10], John Bailey[9], Robert[8], Nahum[7], Robert[6], Edward[5], Susanna[4] **Stone**, Mary[3] **Whipple**, Elder John[2], Matthew[1])[4475] was born 13 March 1966 and married (__) **Corrigan**.

Linda Marie **Wilson** and (__) **Corrigan** had the following children:

3694   i. Michael Allen[15] **Corrigan**[4476] was born 18 June 1990.

3695   ii. Carisse Marie **Corrigan**[4477] was born 30 April 1993.

3348. Jodel Christine[14] **Wilson** (Karen Jean[13] **Reinking**, Jean Doris[12] **Goddard**, George Francis[11], George Osmer[10], John Bailey[9], Robert[8], Nahum[7], Robert[6], Edward[5], Susanna[4] **Stone**, Mary[3] **Whipple**, Elder John[2], Matthew[1])[4478] was born 9 January 1969 and married (__) **Thatcher**.

Jodel Christine **Wilson** and (__) **Thatcher** had the following children:

3696   i. Kenneth Ray[15] **Thatcher**[4479].

3697   ii. Kristine Nicole **Thatcher**[4480] was born 3 September 1989.

3698   iii. Jessica Dawn **Thatcher**[4481] was born 10 May 1991.

3699   iv. Brianna Rae **Thatcher**[4482] was born 12 November 1994.

3700   v. Maddison Renee **Thatcher**[4483] was born 24 December 1996.

3349. Kenneth Ray[14] **Wilson** (Karen Jean[13] **Reinking**, Jean Doris[12] **Goddard**, George Francis[11], George Osmer[10], John Bailey[9], Robert[8], Nahum[7], Robert[6], Edward[5], Susanna[4] **Stone**, Mary[3] **Whipple**, Elder John[2], Matthew[1])[4484] was born 14 June 1971.

Kenneth Ray **Wilson** had the following child:

3701   i. Taya Marie[15] **Wilson**[4485] was born 17 February 1997.

3351. Monica Marie[14] **Sobieski** (Russel Allen[13], Helen Maurine[12] **Goddard**, George Francis[11], George Osmer[10], John Bailey[9], Robert[8], Nahum[7], Robert[6], Edward[5], Susanna[4] **Stone**, Mary[3] **Whipple**, Elder John[2], Matthew[1])[4486] was born 1 September 1972 and married (__) **Miller**.

Monica Marie **Sobieski** and (__) **Miller** had the following children:

3702   i. Kelli Jo[15] **Miller**[4487] was born 6 August 1991.

3703   ii. Amanda **Miller**[4488] was born 19 October 1992.

3704   iii. Abbie Marie **Miller**[4489] was born 27 April 1996.

3353. Thomas Lee[14] **Sobieski** (Gary Lee[13], Helen Maurine[12] **Goddard**, George Francis[11], George Osmer[10], John Bailey[9], Robert[8], Nahum[7], Robert[6], Edward[5], Susanna[4] **Stone**, Mary[3] **Whipple**, Elder John[2], Matthew[1])[4490] was born 16 July 1964.

Thomas Lee **Sobieski** had the following child:
3705   i. Brittany Leigh[15] **Sobieski**[4491] was born 4 December 1990.

3372. Richard Dean Godard[14] **Morgan** (Dawn Maurine[13] **Goddard**, Dean Alan[12], George Francis[11], George Osmer[10], John Bailey[9], Robert[8], Nahum[7], Robert[6], Edward[5], Susanna[4] **Stone**, Mary[3] **Whipple**, Elder John[2], Matthew[1])[4492] was born 5 December 1970.

Richard Dean Godard **Morgan** had the following child:
3706   i. Megan Leeann[15] **Morgan**[4493] was born 7 December 1993.

3432. Reeves[14] **Smith** (Virginia Jennings[13] **Christman**, Milon Stone[12], Sarah Mary (Mai)[11] **Stone**, Milon Gardner[10], Marshall Maynard[9], Col. Jonathan[8], Lt. Jonathan[7], Jonathan[6], Jonathan[5], Jonathan[4], Mary[3] **Whipple**, Elder John[2], Matthew[1])[4494] was born in Spartanburg, S.C. 15 December 1941 and married twice. (1) **James Renwick Wilkes III** in Spartanburg 8 August 1964. James,[4495] son of James Renwick **Wilkes**, Jr. and Elizabeth **Triplett**, was born in Charlotte, N.C. 5 February 1939 and died 1 October 1982 in Spartanburg at 43 years of age. (2) **Jerry Ray Blackburn** in Spartanburg 9 June 1984. Jerry,[4496] son of Eli Grant **Blackburn** and Lucille **Garres**, was born in Elkin, N.C. 19 December 1942.

Reeves **Smith** and James Renwick **Wilkes** III had the following children:
3707   i. Virginia Reeves[15] **Wilkes**[4497] was born in Atlanta, Ga. 14 November 1968.
3708   ii. James Renwick **Wilkes** IV[4498] was born in Spartanburg 23 January 1971

3434. Milon Christman[14] **Smith** (Virginia Jennings[13] **Christman**, Milon Stone[12], Sarah Mary (Mai)[11] **Stone**, Milon Gardner[10], Marshall Maynard[9], Col. Jonathan[8], Lt. Jonathan[7], Jonathan[6], Jonathan[5], Jonathan[4], Mary[3] **Whipple**, Elder John[2], Matthew[1])[4499] was born in Spartanburg, S.C. 15 August 1950 and married **Mary Lou Hodges** there 14 April 1974. Mary,[4500] daughter of Robert Fike **Hodges** and Elna **Leonard**, was born in Spartanburg 23 June 1950.

Milon Christman **Smith** and Mary Lou **Hodges** had the following children:
3709   i. David Fiske[15] **Smith**[4501] was born in Columbia, S.C. 30 June 1978.
3710   ii. Creighton Reeves **Smith**[4502] was born in Charleston, S.C. 9 July 1981.

3436. Virginia Jennings[14] **Christman** (Milon Stone[13], Milon Stone[12], Sarah Mary (Mai)[11] **Stone**, Milon Gardner[10], Marshall Maynard[9], Col. Jonathan[8], Lt. Jonathan[7], Jonathan[6], Jonathan[5], Jonathan[4], Mary[3] **Whipple**, Elder John[2], Matthew[1])[4503] was born in Meridian, Miss. 14 October 1949 and married three times. (1) **Steven Wayne Seaman** in Atlanta, Ga. 9 October 1971. They were divorced before 1984. (2) **Robert Mitchell Fowler** in Atlanta 10 March 1984. They were divorced before 1989. (3) **David Mark Schreiber** in Atlanta 16 September 1989.

Virginia Jennings **Christman** and Steven Wayne **Seaman** had the following child:

    3711   i.   Bennett Adams[15] **Seaman**[4504] was born in Atlanta 6 April 1980.

3437. Milon Stone[14] **Christman III** (Milon Stone[13], Milon Stone[12], Sarah Mary (Mai)[11] **Stone**, Milon Gardner[10], Marshall Maynard[9], Col. Jonathan[8], Lt. Jonathan[7], Jonathan[6], Jonathan[5], Jonathan[4], Mary[3] **Whipple**, Elder John[2], Matthew[1])[4505] was born in Gainesville, Ga. 23 March 1954 and married **Catherine Elaine Kicidis** in Union, S.C. 3 November 1979. They were divorced after 1984.

Milon Stone **Christman** III and Catherine Elaine **Kicidis** had the following child:

    3712   i.   Nicholas Kicidis[15] **Christman**[4506] was born in Myrtle Beach, S.C. 6 August 1984.

3445. Jerry Duane[14] **Bakke** (Mary Esther[13] **Makee**, Albert Henry[12], Mary Alice[11] **Perry**, Mary Jane[10] **Billings**, Hiram[9], Joel[8], John[7], Joanna[6] **Norton**, John[5], Mary[4] **Goodhue**, Sarah[3] **Whipple**, Elder John[2], Matthew[1])[4507] was born in Minneapolis, Minn. 6 June 1931 and married twice. (1) **Karen Soderberg** in Portland, Multnomah Co. Oreg. 17 December 1960. Karen was born in Portland 7 June 1935.[4508] They were divorced in Portland in 1971. (2) **Sharon L. Diffendaffer Essex** in Portland 13 June 1972. Sharon, daughter of James M. **Diffendaffer** and Marguerite Louise **Moore**, was born in Boise, Idaho 10 March 1942.

Jerry Duane **Bakke** and Karen **Soderberg** had the following children born in Portland, Oreg.:

    3713   i.   Dana[15] **Bakke**[4509] was born 13 July 1961 and married Michael **Boswell** in Portland 5 August 1985.

    3714   ii.   Kyle Duane **Bakke**[4510] was born 13 July 1961.

  + 3715   iii. Melissa Elaine **Bakke** was born 5 April 1963.

3460. Nicole LaRai[14] **Holley** (Sharon LaRay[13] **Rich**, Doyle Hyrum[12], Mary Eurilla[11] **Mecham**, Luman Lehi[10], Joseph L.[9], Sarah[8] **Basford**, Jonathan[7], Elizabeth[6] **Goodhue**, Jonathan[5], William[4], Sarah[3] **Whipple**, Elder John[2], Matthew[1])[4511] was born in 1969 and married **Stephen Martel Bay** in Salt Lake City, Utah 10 October 1991. Stephen, son of Elvon Leone **Bay** and Janel **Anderson**, was born in Chula Vista, San Diego Co., Calif. 19 September 1967.

Nicole LaRai **Holley** and Stephen Martel **Bay** had the following children:

    3716   i.   Benjamin Elvon[15] **Bay**[4512] was born in Provo, Utah 2 September 1992.

    3717   ii.   Miriam LaRae **Bay**[4513] was born in Provo 13 January 1994.

    3718   iii. Asher Anderson **Bay**[4514] was born in Salt Lake City in 1997.

3463. Erik David[14] **Holley** (Sharon LaRay[13] **Rich**, Doyle Hyrum[12], Mary Eurilla[11] **Mecham**, Luman Lehi[10], Joseph L.[9], Sarah[8] **Basford**, Jonathan[7], Elizabeth[6] **Goodhue**, Jonathan[5], William[4], Sarah[3] **Whipple**, Elder John[2], Matthew[1])[4515] was born in Provo, Utah Co., Utah 14 January 1973 and married **Susan Baumann** 23 November 1994. Susan,[4516] daughter of Richard William **Baumann** and Myrna Rae **Morrill**, was born in Fairfax, Va. 6 September 1974.

Erik David **Holley** and Susan **Baumann** had the following children born in Provo, Utah:

3719   i.   Rachel Anne[15] **Holley**[4517] was born 14 October 1995.

3720   ii. Sarah Michelle **Holley**[4518] was born 18 December 1996.

3474. Dustin Michael[14] **Christopherson** (JoAnn[13] **Rich**, Doyle Hyrum[12], Mary Eurilla[11] **Mecham**, Luman Lehi[10], Joseph L.[9], Sarah[8] **Basford**, Jonathan[7], Elizabeth[6] **Goodhue**, Jonathan[5], William[4], Sarah[3] **Whipple**, Elder John[2], Matthew[1])[4519] was born in Wichita Falls, Texas 11 June 1973 and married **Heather Kingdon** in Boise, Idaho 14 January 1994. Heather was born in South Haven, Mich. 14 January 1974.

Dustin Michael **Christopherson** and Heather **Kingdon** had the following child:

3721   i.   Robert Michael[15] **Christopherson**[4520] was born in Boise, Idaho 3 December 1995.

Fifteenth Generation

3536. Janet L.[15] **Stephenson** (Eleanor[14] **Buell**, Catherine[13] **Wells**, Helen Cutter[12] **Pillsbury**, Harry M.[11], James[10], Jacob[9], John Hale[8], Rev. Edmund[7], Moses[6], Moses[5], Susanna[4] **Worth**, Susannah[3] **Whipple**, Elder John[2], Matthew[1]) was born 15 February 1956 and married **John Carlock**.

Janet L. **Stephenson** and John **Carlock** had the following children:

3722   i.   Sydney Wells[16] **Carlock** was born 1 October 1983.

3723   ii. Madelline McCartel **Carlock** was born 9 January 1986.

3553. Madelline Grace[15] **Haines** (William Blake[14], Priscilla June[13] **Blake**, Clarence Dodge[12], Lizzie Batchelder[11] **Dodge**, Frank Brickett[10], Deborah Towne[9] **Brickett**, Bernard[8], Bernard[7], Susanna[6] **Pillsbury**, Moses[5], Susanna[4]**Worth**, Susannah[3] **Whipple**, Elder John[2], Matthew[1]) was born in Provo, Utah Co., Utah 2 August 1971 and married **Allen Victor Searl** 21 March 1990.

Madelline Grace **Haines** and Allen Victor **Searl** had the following child:

3724   i.   Chelsey Rae[16] **Searl** was born in Provo 15 June 1991.

3715. Melissa Elaine[15] **Bakke** (Jerry Duane[14], Mary Esther[13] **Makee**, Albert Henry[12], Mary Alice[11] **Perry**, Mary Jane[10] **Billings**, Hiram[9], Joel[8], John[7], Joanna[6] **Norton**, John[5], Mary[4] **Goodhue**, Sarah[3] **Whipple**, Elder John[2], Matthew[1])[4521] was born in Portland, Multnomah Co., Oreg. 5 April 1963 and married **Brian G. Moran** in Portland, Multnomah Co., Oreg, 14 September 1991.

Melissa Elaine **Bakke** and Brian G. **Moran** had the following children born in Portland:

3725   i.   Margaret Mary[16] **Moran**[4522] was born 19 June 1993.

3726   ii. McKenzie Irene **Moran**[4523] was born 7 October 1995.

ENDNOTES

1. *Parish Registers, Bocking, St. Mary's Church* (Salt Lake City, UT: Family History Library. Film #1471886, Item 12 (1588-1639): baptisms (1561- 1605), burials (1558- 1628), marriages (1593-1639). Original records at the Essex Record Office, Chelmsford, England. A second Register with baptisms from 1606-1654 is missing. A third Register, Item 13 on the film, includes baptisms from 1655-68 and marriages and burials 1655- 70.). [Hereafter cited as *Parish Records*, Bocking.]).

2. Anne (Anna) 1583-1646; Margaret 1585-1608; Johane 1587-?; Jane (Jana) 1587-?; Matthew abt. 1590-1647; Elizabeth 1594-?; Mary abt. 1599-abt. 1663; Amy abt. 1604-?.

3. *Parish Records*, Bocking, Matthew Whipple's will dated 19 June 1616, proved in the Superior Probate Court, the Prerogative Court of Canterbury in 1619; Mary Lovering Holman and George R. Marvin, editors, *Abstracts of English Records Gathered Principally in Devonshire and Essex in a Search for the Ancestry of Roger Dearing c 1624-1676 and Matthew Whipple c. 1560-1618*, Boston, 1929; *Boyd's Marriage Index*; Henry Burdett Whipple, *A Partial List of the Descendants of Matthew Whipple, the Elder, of Bocking Essex Co., England*, 2 volumes, High Point, NC: 1965 and 1969; professional research by Debrett Ancestry Research Limited of Winchester, England. (Hereafter cited as Matthew Whipple, Clothier, *Various sources*).

4. Joseph B. Felt, *History of Ipswich, Essex, and Hamilton, Massachusetts*, Ipswich: The Clamshell Press, 1966, 159. First published in Cambridge, MA in 1834. (Hereafter cited as Felt, *History of Ipswich & Hamilton.*)

5. Henry Burdett Whipple, *A Partial List of the Descendants of Matthew Whipple, the Elder, of Bocking Essex Co., England*, 2 volumes, High Point, NC: 1965 and 1969; 1:8 [hereafter Henry Whipple]; *Parish Records*, Bocking, and Essex Co., MA, *Vital Records*, Salem, births, 414.

6. *Parish Records*, Bocking; New England Historic Genealogical Society *Register* (New England Historical Genealogical Society, Boston), 8:69-70; 10:229-30; 11:238; 23:61; 73:xlv; 86:140-41; 109;140-41, 307; 148:31. [Hereafter cited as *Register*); Essex Co., MA, *Vital Records*, Salem births, 424; J. Gardner Bartlett, comp., *Simon Stone Genealolgy - Ancestry and Descendants of Simon Stone of Watertown, Massachusetts* (Boston: Stone Family Association, 1926), 65. [Hereafter cited as J.G. Bartlett]; and Mellinde Lutz Sanborn, transcriber from the original by W.P. Upham, *Essex County, Massachusetts Probate Index 1638-1840*, Vol. II. Probate file 2259. [Hereafter cited as *Probate Index*, Essex Co., MA)].

7. *Parish Records*, Bocking.

8. *Parish Records*, Bocking, and Essex Co., MA, *Vital Records*, Salem births, 424.

9. Henry Whipple, 1:8.

10. *Parish Records*, Bocking; and Essex Co., MA, *Vital Records*, Salem births, 424.

11. Henry Whipple, 1:8.

12. Parish *Records*, Bocking and Essex Co., MA *Vital Records*,, Newbury deaths, 756.

13. Essex Co. Probate Files, Document at 30,700. A copy of the estate inventory is in Ipswich Quarterly Court Record 5:52. Susannah is listed in the Estate of Robert Coker of Newbury as having meadow at Plumb Island at the Sandy beach., *Ipswich Deeds*, 4:390.

14. Henry Whipple, II:2. He cites Mary Lovering Holman, *The Pillsbury Ancestry* (1938) as his source.

15. *Ibid*, II:2; Newbury births, 56, Salisbury marriages, 520.

16. *Ibid.*, II:2; Newbury marriages, 256.

17. Henry Whipple, 1:8-50; *Parish Registers*, Bocking; Records compiled by E. E. Fewkes, known as the *Darling Collection*, in the Ipswich, MA public library; Amos Everett Jewett and Emily Mabel Adams Jewett, comp., *Rowley, Massachusetts Mr. Ezechi Rogers' Plantation 1639-1850*, Salem, MA: The Jewett Family of America, Newcomb & Gauss Co. Printer, 1946; and George Brainard Blodgett, comp., and Amos Everett Jewett, ed., *Early Settlers of Rowley, Massachusetts,* Rowley: the editor, 1933, 321.

18. Abraham Hammatt, *The Hammatt Papers Early Inhabitants of Ipswich, Massachusetts 1633-1700*, Baltimore, MD: Genealogical Publishing Co., Inc., 1980. (Reprint from the original published in seven parts at Ipswich, MA, 1880-89 with an added index), 276. Clarence Almon Torrey, comp., *New England Marriages Prior to 1700*, Genealogical Publishing Co., Inc, 1985, 803; *Vital Early Records of the Commonwealth of Massachusetts to the Year 1850*, Ipswich deaths, 709; *Register*, 156:316.

19. . *Early Vital Records of the Commonwealth of Massachusetts to the Year 1850*, Ipswich marriages, 325.

20. Henry Whipple, 1:9; *Early Vital Records of the Commonwealth of Massachusetts to the Year 1850*, Ipswich deaths, 709.

21 *Register*, 53:345-50. David H. Brown, A.B. of West Medford, MA was the author of the article in Vol. 53. His sources included: Bond's *History of Watertown; The Early Records of Watertown;* Savage's *Genealogical Dictionary*, Vol iv; Massachusetts Archives at the State House; Probate Offices and Registry of Deeds Offices at East Cambridge, Boston, Salem, and Worcester; *Quinquennial Catalogue of Harvard University;* Bodge's *Soldiers in the King Phillip's War;* Butler's *History of Groton, MA;* Green's *Early Records of Groton, MA;* Paige's *History of Cambridge, MA;* Jackson's *Newton, MA;* Barry's *Framingham, MA;* Temple's *Framingham, MA;* Hudson's *Sudbury, MA;* Marvin's *Lancaster, MA;* the printed *Records of Lancaster;* Freeman's *Cape Cod;* Deyo's *History of Barnstable County;* and Rev. Nathan Stone's (1707-8-1781) *Almanac.* Vol. 10, 229-30; J.G. Bartlett; *Parish Records, Bocking, Essex Co., England;* and Essex Co., MA, *Vital Records*, Salem births, 424.

22. J.G. Bartlett; and *Register*, 10:299-30; 53:345-50.

23. J.G. Bartlett; and *Register*, 53:345-50.

24. J.G. Bartlett, Includes birth and death information.

25. William R. Hunter-Dorothy Edmondson family group sheet, supplied 29 Jan. and 17 April 1992 by Dorothy (Edmondson) Hunter, 6705 Caneel Court, Springfield, VA 22152. This sheet cites documentation as follows: " Whipple Ancestry Chart" by J. Gardner Bartlett; *Matthew Whipple of Bocking, England* by Henry B. Whipple; *Goodhue and Allied Families* by Elizabeth Goodhue Fuess; *History and Genealogy of the Goodhue Family* by Rev. Jonathan Goodhue; *Vital Records of Ipswich, MA; History and Genealogy of the Knowltons of England and America* by Rev. Charles H.W. Stocking; *Knowlton Ancestry* by Rona Duncan Creelman; *International Genealogical Index*; *Vital Records of Ashford, CT; Descendants of John Upham of Massachusetts* by F.K. Upham; *Historical and Genealogical Record of the First Settlers of Colchester County Nova Scotia, Canada* by Thomas Miller; *James McCabe Genealogy* by Allan E. Marble; birth and death certificates; and marriage licenses. (Hereafter cited as Wm. R. Hunter, *Family Group Sheet*).

26. *Ibid.*; Essex Co., MA, *Vital Records*, Ipswich marriages, 188; and *Register*, 10:229- 30.

27. Felt, 171.

28. Marilyn Riggs to Blaine Whipple. Letter dated 22 July 1998 at 3952 Santa Nella Place, San Digeo, CA 92130-2288. In possession of Whipple (2003). Included family group sheets and descendancy chart. Documentation includes Ipswich, MA *Vital Records*, Clarence Torrey's *New England Marriages*, and a genealogy on *Kimballs in America.*). (Hereafter cited as Riggs to Whipple, *Letter 22 July 1998*).

29. Dean E. Wilson to Blaine Whipple. Letters dated 11 June 1996 and 18 June & 2 July 1997 at 3303 SE 66th, Portland, OR 97206. In possession of Whipple at 236 NW Sundown Way, Portland, OR 97229 (2003). Wilson's sources: Leonidas Devon Mechan, comp., *Family Book of Remembrances & Genealogy with Allied Lines*, 2nd edition, (1967); Mary Eurilla (Mecham) Wilson, *Family Book of Remembrances & Family Record*; Thomas Franklin Waters, *Ipswich in the Massachusetts Bay Colony*, Ipswich, (1905); S. Noyes, C. Libby, & W. Davis, *Genealogical Dictionary of Maine & New Hampshire*, Baltimore, (1991); Abraham Hammatt, *The Hammatt Papers, Early Inhabitants of Ipswich, Massachusetts 1633-1700*, Baltimore, (1980); Clarence A. Torrey, *New England Marriages Prior to 1700*, Baltimore, (1992); William Goodhue, comp., *Goodhue Family Biography of the First Settlement of the Family of the Name of Goodhue, at Ipswich, Mass. in 1636 with Genealogy to 1833*; Frank R. Holmes, comp., *Directoy of the Ancestral Heads of New England Families*, Baltimore; James Savage, *A Genealogical Dictionary of the First Settlers of New England*, Vol. IV, Baltimore; Frederick Adams Virkus, *Immigrant Ancestors*, Baltimore (1986); George Madison Bodge, *Soldiers in King Philip's War*; Charles Henry Pope, *The Pioneers of Massachusetts*, Baltimore; "FGRC LDS Archives," Salt Lake City; and Family Group Sheets submitted to Dean Wilson in 1995 & 1996.). (Hereafter cited as Wilson to Whipple, *Letters, June 1996 & 1967*); and Riggs to Whipple, *Letter 22 July 1998*.

30. Henry Whipple, , II:2. He cites Mary Lovering Holman, *The Pillsbury Ancestry* (1938) as his source.

31. (1) Janet H. Anderson, Certified Genealogist (C.G.), (2) J. Stanwood Martin, (3) Priscilla Blake Haines, (4) Charles J. Sherman to Blaine Whipple. Letters dated Jan. 1993 and Aug. 1996 from Anderson; Jan. 1992 and Aug. 1996 from Martin; Jan. 1993 from Haines; and Dec. 1991 from Sherman at the following addresses: Anderson at 3155 Las Palmas, Houston, Tex. 77027; Martin at 308 Devon Lane, West Chester, Pa. 19830; Haines at 1000 South 1000 East, Mapleton,

Utah 84665; and Sherman at 147 N. Murray, Porterville, Calif. 93257-4066. In possession of Whipple at 236 N.W. Sundown Way, Portland, Oreg. 97229-6575 (2003). Sources cited for the Pillsbury, Blake, Haines, and Martin familes as they descend from Susannah Whipple and Lionel Worth were: Haverhill and Newbury, Mass. *Vital Records*; James Savage, *Genealogical Dictionary of New England*, Baltimore: Genealogical Publishing Co., reprint, 1986; Clarence Almon Torrey, *New England Marriages Prior to 1700*, Genealogical Publishing, 1985; Henry B. Whipple, *Matthew Whipple of Bocking, England & Descendants*, High Point, N.C.: 1969; Burton W. Spear, *Search for the Passengers of the 'Mary and John*, Toledo, Ohio, 1987; Ezra S. Stearns, *Genealogical and Family History of the State of New Hampshire*, Whitcher & Parker, 1908; David W. Hoyt, *The Old Families of Salisbury and Amesbury, Somerworth*: New England History Press, 1981; Mary Lovering Holman, *Ancestry of Charles Stinson Pillsbury and John Sargent Pillsbury*, Concord, N.H.: Concord Press, 2 vols, 1938; David Pillsbury and Emily Gelchel, *Pillsbury Family*, 1898; Robert S. Hale, *Thomas Hale the Glover of Newbury, Mass.*; Robert S. Hale, *Descendants of Thomas Hale of Walton, England and of Newbury, Mass*; Ezra S. Stearns, *Thirty Dunstable Families*, "*Deaths and Marriages in Dunstable, N.H.* Each of the four contributors also provided family group sheets and pedigree charts. Anderson states Lionel Worth was born in Devonshire, England and is the source for the daughter, Hannah. Martin believes Lionel was born in Yoevil, Somerset, England and that the couple had twins born and died in 1659. Martin apparently has more specific dates and places in his files. He wrote in his letter of 27 Aug. 1996 that he had "been inconsistent in adding the month and day to dates [as] I don't believe it worth the time and disk space to include them."). (Hereafter cited as Letters from, four individuals).

32.   Robert Ernst Seyfarth-Barbara Smalley Family Group Sheet, supplied July 1991 by Barbara (Smalley) Seyfarth, 2 Crestview Dr., Lock Haven, PA 17745. Pedigree sheets also provided; no documentation included. (Hereafter cited as Smalley - Seyfarth, Family Group Sheet).

33.   through 37. *Ibid.*

38.   Janet (Horstman) (Mrs. James A.) Anderson to Blaine Whipple. letters dated 3 Feb. 1993, 20 Aug. 1996, and 2 Sept. 1996 at 3155 Las Palmas, Houston, Tex. 77027. in possession of Whipple at 236 NW Sundown Way, Portland, Oreg. 97229 (2003). (Hereafter cited as Anderson to Whipple, *Letter, 02-3-1993*); and Henry Whipple, *Whipple Descendents*, II:2.

39.   through 44. *Ibid.*

45.   Charles H. Preston, "Genealogy of the Whipples of Ipswich for Five Generations," *Putnam's Monthly Historical Magazine Devoted To Genealogy, History and Archaeology* II (Sept. 1893 - Aug. 1894): 5-14; 62-66 (Hereafter cited as *Putnam's Monthly*,); *Vital Records of Ipswich, Massachusetts to the end of the Year 1849.*, (Salem, MA: The Essex Institute, 1910) births, 391; marriages, 454; deaths, 710 (Hereafter cited as Ipswich Births, *Vital Records*); and Arthur Warren Johnson and Ralph Elbridge Ladd, Jr. comp., *Memento Mori Part The First being An Accurate Transcription of the Tomb-Stones, Monuments, Foot- Stones, and other Memorials in the Ancient Old North Burial Yard in the Town of Ipswich, County of Essex, Massachusetts, From its Beginnings in the Year Anno. Domi. 1634 to the Present Day, With a Chart of the Location of the Same that any Grave Therein May be Located with Ease and Accuracy, Together with a History and Description of this Ancient Burial Yard* (Decorah, IA: The Anundsen Publishing Co., 1988 Reprint. Originally published by the Ipswich Historical Society in 1935), 247 (Hereafter cited as Johnson & Ladd, *Ipswich Burials*).

46.   *Putnam's Monthly*,; *Vital Records of Ipswich, Massachusetts to the end of the year 1840. Vol III, Deaths*, (Salem, MA: The Essex Institute, 1910), 710. (Hereafter cited as Ipswich Deaths, *Vital Records*); Johnson & Ladd, *Ipswich Burials*, 247; and Essex Antiquarian (The), *Monthly Magazine*, 7:45.

47.   *Putnam's Monthly*,.

48.   Henry Whipple, 1;10; *Putnam's Monthly*,; and Johnson & Ladd, *Ipswich Burials*, 247.

49.   Henry Whipple, 1:10; and Johnson & Ladd, *Ipswich Burials*, 247.

50.   Henry Whipple, 1:10; and *Putnam's Monthly*,.

51.   Henry Whipple, 1:10.

52.   *Putnam's Monthly*,, 2:14.

53.   Rev. Henry A. Hazen, comp., *A History of Billerica, Massachuetts, With A Genealogical Register* (Boston: A. Williams and Co., 1883), 89 (Hereafter cited as Billerica, MA, *History*); *Vital Records of Ipswich, Massachusetts to the end of the Year 1849. Vol. II, Marriages*, (Salem, MA: The Essex Institute, 1910), 453. and *Vital Records, deaths*, 710 (Hereafter cited as Ipswich Marriages, *Vital Records*); *Register*, 11:234; Felt., *History of Ipswich, & Hamilton*, 176-77); and Melinde Lutz Sanborn, comp., *Essex County, Massachusetts Probate Index 1638-1840* (Original by W.P. Upham: Salem, MA 1920), No. 29516 (Hereafter cited as Sanborn, *Probate, Essex Co., MA*).

54. *Register*, 10:234, 357; and Billerica, MA, *History*, 89.

55. Henry Whipple, 1:12; *Essex Antiquarian (The), Monthly Magazine*, Vol. IV, No. 1, January 1900, 1-2.; and Genealogical research project completed by James W. Petty, Certified American Lineage Specialist and Accredited Genealogist, at PO Box 893, Salt Lake City, UT 84110, telephone 801-572-4049 dated 20 April 1989 for Proctor P. Jones, 3401 Sacramento St., San Francisco., CA 94118-1999 . (Hereafter cited as Petty to Jones, *Research Project*).

56. Henry Whipple, I:12.

57. *Putnam's Monthly*, and Felt, *History of Ipswich & Hamilton*, 176-77.

58. *Putnam's Monthly*, Henry Whipple, I:12 ; and Essex Co., MA, *Vital Records*, Ipswich deaths, 710.

59. *Putnam's Monthly* and Essex Co., MA, *Vital Records*, Ipswich marriages, 454.

60. Henry Whipple, 1:12; and Ipswich Deaths, *Vital Records*, 710.

61. Ipswich Births, *Vital Records*.

62. Warren Brown, comp., *History of the Town of Hampton Falls, New Hampshire From the Time of the First Settlement Within Its Borders 1640 Until 1900* (Manchester, NH: John B. Clarke Company, 1900), See also Vol. 1, *Hampton Falls, NH*); Joseph Crook Anderson II and Lois Ware Thurston, C.G. editors., *Vital Records of Kittery, Maine to the Year 1892* (Camden, ME: Maine Genealogical Society, Special Publication No. 8, Picton Press, 1991), 61 (Hereafter cited as Kittery, ME, *Vital Records*); Brown, Vol. 1, *Hampton Falls, NH*, 31-33, 40; Warren Brown, comp., *History of Hampton Falls, N.H. Containing the Church History and Many Other Things Not Previously Recorded* (Concord, NH: The Rumford Press, 1918), 19-25 (Hereafter cited as Brown, Vol. 2, *Hampton Falls, NH*); and Ruth L. Nichipor, comp, *Vital Statistics from the Town Records of Hampton Falls, N. H. Through 1899*, (Hampton Falls Free Library), (Hereafter cited as Vital Statistics, *Hampton Falls, NH*).

63. Brown, Vol. 2, *Hampton Falls, NH*, 24; and Essex Co., MA, *Vital Records*, Newbury marriages, 508.

64. L. H. Butterfield, ed., *The Earliest Diary of John Adams*, Cambridge, Mass: The Belknap Press of Harvard University Press, 1961, 49-51.

65. Ipswich, *Vital Records*, births, 392; deaths, 710.

66. *Putnam's Monthly*; and Henry Whipple, 1:12.

67. Family group sheet, supplied 27 November 1991 by Barbara J. (Nelson) Grieser, 2318 N. Elm St, Greensboro, NC 27408. This sheet cites the following documentation: *Register*, vol 10; *Compendium of American Genealogy*, vol 3; James Hill Fitts, *Lane Genealogies*, vol. 3 (1902); Frances Cowles, *The Family of Ruggles* (1912); Franklin L. Bailey, *The Genealogy of Thomas Ruggles of Roxbury, 1637*; Horace Davis, *Dolor Davis, a Sketch of His Life* (1881); Charles H.S. Davis, *Davis Family Records* (1867); Benjamin A. Gould, *Family of Zaccheus Gould of Topsfield* (1895); Massachusetts and Vermont *Vital Records*, Daughters of the American Republic (DAR) *Patriot Index* and application for membership in DAR of Gertrude Hatch Nelson, Roxbury, VT cemetery records, and various documents at the New England Historic Genealogical Society, Boston, MA (Hereafter cited as Whipple-Lane, *Family Group Sheet*); and Billerica, MA, *History*, 89.

68. *Register*, 10:357; 11:235-6; 17:331-3; Billerica, MA, *History*, 88-89; and Whipple-Lane, *Family Group Sheet*.

69. *Register*, 10:356 gives the date as 17 Jan. 1714-15 and as 7 Jan. 1715 on p. 357.

70. *Register*, 10:357.

71. Ibid., 10:357; Billerica, MA, *History*, 89; and Henry Whipple, 2:7.

72. Billerica, MA, *History, Genealogical Register*, 88.

73. *Register*, 10:257; and Henry Whipple, 2:7.

74. *Putnam's Monthly* and Ipswich Marriages, *Vital Records*.

75. *Putnam's Monthly*.

76. *Register*, 1:9; and Essex Co., MA, *Vital Records*, Ipswich deaths, 701.

77. *Putnam's Monthly*, Essex Co., MA, *Vital Records*, Ipswich births, 378; Ipswich marriages, 453; Ipswich deaths, 701; and Thomas Franklin Waters, *Ipswich in the Massachusetts Bay Colony 1700-1917*, 2 vols. (Salem, Mass.: The Ipswich Historical Society, Newcomb & Gauss, Printers, 1917), Vol. 2 (Hereafter cited as Waters, *Ipswich in MA Bay*).

78. Felt, 173.

79. and 80. *Putnam's Monthly*.

81. Essex Co., MA, *Vital Records*, Ipswich births, 378.

82. *Putnam's Monthly* and Essex Co., MA, *Vital Records*, Ipswich births, 378; Ipswich marriages, 440.

83. Essex Co., MA, *Vital Records*, Ipswich births, 378; Ipswich deaths, 701.

84. *Putnam's Monthly* and Essex Co., MA, *Vital Records*, Ipswich deaths, 701.

85. Essex Co., MA, *Vital Records*, Ipswich births, 378.

86. J.G. Bartlett, *Register*, 10:229-30; 53:346-50; and Cotton Mather, *Magnalia Christi Americana or the Ecclesiastical History of New England in Seven Books* (London: 1702), II:606 (Hereafter cited as Mather, *Magnalia*).

87. *Register*, 53:347.

88. *Register*, 10:229.

89. through 93. *Register* 53:345-60.

94. *J.G. Bartlett*; and *Register*, 53:345-50.

95. and 96. *Register*, 53:345-50.

97. *J.G. Bartlett*; and *Register*, 53:345-50.

98. *Register*, 53:347.

99. Ibid., 53:345-50.

100. *J.G. Bartlett*; and *Register*, 10:229-30 and 53:345-50.

101. *Register*, 53:345-50.

102. *Register*, 53:347-48.

103. through 105. *Register*, 53:345-50.

106. *J.G. Bartlett*; and Register, 10:229-30 and 53:348.

107. through 120. *Register*, 53:345-50.

121. Joan (Mrs. Donald) Jones to Blaine Whipple. letters dated Dec. 1991, 9 April 1993, and 12 May and 26 June 1997 at 1601 Pike Ave., Carroll, IA 51401. In possession of Whipple at 236 NW Sundown Way, Portland, OR 97229 (1997). Her sources include: Hosea Starr Ballou, *Early Starrs in Kent & New England*, Concord, NH: The Rumford Press, 1944; Burgis Pratt Starr, *History of the Starr Family of New England*, (1879); M.V.B. Perley, *History and Genealogy of the Perley Family*, (1906); J. Gardner Bartlett, *Simon Stone Genealogy. Ancestry and Descendants of Deacon Simon Stone of Watertown, Massachusetts, 1320-1926*, (1926); *Official History of Guilford, Vermont 1678-1961*, Brattleboro, VT, 1961; Kathleen Kamm Jones and Donale E. Jones, *Some Ancestors of Pearl Griggs Kamm, Part 1-Colonial New England Lineages*, Limited Run Publishing Solutions, (1993); Henry B. Whipple, *A Partial List of the Descendants of Matthew Whipple, The Elder, of Bocking, Essex County, England*, Vol I, (1965); *History of Cass County (Iowa) 1884*; U.S. Census (1880) Cass County, Iowa, 729-730; U.S. Census (1900) Stanton County, NE; obituaries in the Pilger (Nebraska) *Herald*; marriage and death records, family Bibles, and professional research in The Netherlands.). (Hereafter cited as J. Jones to Wh, *Letters 1991, 1993 & 1997*); and Burgess Pratt Starr, comp., *Starr Genealogy* (Hereafter cited as Starr, *Starr Genealogy*). *Register*, Vol. 64, 73-4.

122. through 131. J. Jones to Wh, *Letters 1991, 1993 & 1997*.

132. *J.G. Bartlett*; and *Register*, 10:229-30 and 53:345-50.

133. and 134. *Register*, 53:345-50.

135. Ibid., 10:229-30.

136. and 137. *Register*, 53:345-50.

138. *Register*, 53:345-50; 10:229-30.

139. through 141. *Register*, 53:350.

142. through 145. *Register*, 53:345-50; 10:229-30.

146. Ibid., 53:345-50; and James G. Harrison, Jr. to Blaine Whipple. letter dated 5 Dec. 1991 & 14 Jan. 1997 at 828 Rutledge Ave., Spartanburg, SC 29302 in possession of Whipple at 236 NW Sundown Way, Portland, OR 97229. His sources include the 1926 Simon Stone Genealogy by J. Gardner Bartlett; the 1901 *Genealogy and Memoirs of Isaac Stearns and his Descendants* by Avis Stearns Van Wagenen; the 1892 *Upham Genealogy* by F.K. Upham; the 1976 *Pawlet, Vermont for One Hundred Years* by Hiel Hollister; the 1922 *A History of the Orvis Family in America* by Francis Wayland Orvis; and the *Abridged Compendium of American Genealogy* by Virkus for the ancestry of Jefferson Howard Fitch (p 190) (1997). (Hereafter cited as Harrison to Whipple, *Letter, 12-5-1991 & 01-14-1997*).

147. Alana (Lani) Pettit to Blaine Whipple. Letter dated 7 January 1990 at 3412 Old Lakeport Rd.,

Sioux City, IA 51106. In possession of Whipple at 236 NW Sundown Way, Portland, OR 97229-6575 (1998). (Hereafter cited as Pettit, *Letter 7 Jan. 1990*); and Harrison to Whipple, *Letter, 12-5-1991 & 01-14-1997*.

148. J.G. Bartlett; and *Register*, 10:229-30 and 53:345-50.

149. Scott D. Billigmeier to Blaine Whipple. letters dated 29 April and 3 July 1992 at 3744 Bonny Bridge Pl., Endicott City, MD 21043. in possession of Whipple at 236 NW Sundown Way, Portland, OR 97229. (1997). His sources included the Stone and Goddard genealogies, Bond's 1855 *Watertown, MA Genealogies*, and *The Hastings Memorial* published in 1866). (Hereafter cited as Billigmeier to Whipple, *2 Letters 1992*); and *Register*, 10:229-30.

150. June D. Brown to Blaine Whipple. letter dated 1 Jan. 1992 at 1008 Bjork Dr., New Lenox, IL 60451. In possession of Whipple at 236 NW Sundown Way, Portland, OR 97229 (1997). (Hereafter cited as Brown to Whipple, *1 Jan. 1992*); and Susa Young Gates and Mabel Young Sanborn, daughters of Brigham Young, "Brigham Young Genealogy"., *The Utah Genealogical and Historical Magazine: Vol. XI* (Salt Lake City, UT: Genealogical Society of Utah published quarterly, *The Deseret News Press*, 1920), April 1930:58-64 (Hereafter cited as *Utah Magazine*, "Brigham Young").

151. Brown to Whipple, *1 Jan. 1992*; and *Utah Magazine*, "Brigham Young," April 1930:58-64.

152. *Register*, 53:345-50 and *Utah Magazine*, "Brigham Young," April 1930:58-64.

153. *Register*, 53:345-50.

154. Brown to Whipple, *1 Jan. 1992* and *Utah Magazine*, "Brigham Young," April 1930:58-64.

155. through 157. *Utah Magazine*, "Brigham Young," April 1930:58-64.

158. *Register*, 10:229-30; 53:345-50; 95:179-80.

159. and 160. *Register*, 53:345-50.

161. Ibid., 53:345-50; 77:275-76.

162. through 164. *Register*, 53:345-50.

165. J.G. Bartlett and *Register*, 10:229-30 and 53:345-50.

166. *Register*, 53:345-50.

167. Ibid., 53:345-50; and *Utah Magazine*, "Brigham Young," April 1930:58-64.

168. and 169. *Register*, 53:345-50.

170. Roy Wilde to Blaine Whipple. letters dated 10 and 22 April 1997 at 3-11th Ave. N., Jensen Beach, FL 34957 in possession of Whipple at 236 NW Sundown Way, Portland, OR 97229 (1997). (Hereafter cited as Wilde to Whipple, *Letters 04/ 10 & 22/ 1997*); and Wilson to Whipple, *Letters, June 1996 & 1967*.

171. *Essex Probate Records,* iii:168; *Essex Deeds,* xxi:137.

172. *Register*, 13:225-30.

173. *Register*, 27:60.

174. *Essex Probate Records*, x:271; *Register*, 9:113; 43:366.

175. *Register*, 13:229.

176. Jerry D. Bakke-Karen Soderberg Family Group Sheet, supplied 13 June 1995 and 9 Dec. 1997 by Mrs. Sharon l. Bakke, 8102 Skeena Way, Blaine, WA 98230-9558. Sources include: Savage's *General Dictionary of First Settlers of New England*, Vol. 4; Bank's *Topographical Dictionary of 2885 Emigrants to New England, 1620-1650*; Pope's *Pioneers of Massachusetts*; *Register*, 3:187, 242, 13:225-30; *Vital Records of Ipswich, MA*; "Marriages & Deaths — Ipswich, MA" (1910); *Probate Records of the Province of NH*; Libby, Noyes, & Davis, *General Dictionary of Maine and New Hampshire*; Stackpole's *Old Kittery and Her Families*; Lebanon, Maine Vital Records; York Co., *ME Genealogical Society Journal*, July 1987, 43; Phillis O. Whitten, *Samuel Fogg 1628- 1672*; *York Co. Probate & Orphan Court Records*; *Maine Historical & Genealogical Record*; Scarborough, ME Town Records; Cumberland Co., ME Marriages; various church records, wills, obituaries, deeds, death certificates, journals, and other family records; census records: Berwick, York Co., ME, 1790, 1840, 1850, 1860; Portland, Cumberland Co., ME, 1850; Sagadahoe Co. ME, 1860; Blackhawk Co., ME, 1870; WS Territorial Census, Jefferson Co., 1846; Jefferson Co., WS, 1850; Manitowoc Co., WS, 1860'; Blackhawk Co., IA, 1870; Cass Co., ND, 1880; Rollette Co., ND Territorial Census, 1885; Ward Co., ND, 1910; Blackhawk Co., IA Marriage Records; Civil War Pension Records; Masonic Lodge Records; (Hereafter cited as Bakke - Whipple, *Family Group Sheet*).

177. *Register*, 13:229.

178. Bakke - Whipple, *Family Group Sheet.*

179. and 180. *Register,* 13:229.

181. Wilson to Whipple, *Letters, June 1996 & 1967*; and Johnson & Ladd, *Ipswich Burials,* 94.

182. through 191. Wilson to Whipple, *Letters, June 1996 & 1967.*

192. Harry S. Day-Alice L. Jones family group sheet, supplied 20 May 1989, 19 July 1994, and 4 Oct. 1996 by Alice J. Day, 146 Auto Bahn Dr., Stevensville, MT 59870. This sheet does not verify the information with documentation (Hereafter cited as Alice J. Day, *Family Group Sheet*); and Wilson to Whipple, *Letters, June 1996 & 1967.*

193. Mabel M. McMahon to Blaine Whipple. Letters dated 25 April and 8 May 1989 and 12 April 1993 at 1 Lafond, Gansevoort, NY 12831. In possession of Whipple at 236 NW Sundown Way, Portland, OR 97229-6575 (1999). Extensive pedigree and family group sheets provided, however, no documentation was included. Mrs. McMahon said most of her research was done at the New England Historic Genealogical Library in Boston when she lived in Carlisle, MA.). (Hereafter cited as McMahon to Whipple, *3 Letters*); and Alice J. Day, *Family Group Sheet.*

194. through 196. Riggs to Whipple, *Letter 22 July 1998.*

197. *Register,* 97:389.

198. Wm. R. Hunter, *Family Group Sheet*; and Stevens to Whipple, *3 Letters, 1992 & 1996.*

199. Wm. R. Hunter, *Family Group Sheet*; and Bennie S. Larj to Blaine Whipple. letters dated 25 Aug., 15 Sept., 6 Oct. 1991 & 25 Jan. 1997 at 785 Plume St., Spartanburg, SC 29302-1451 Her letters cite the following sources: *The Simon Stone Genealogy* by J.G. Bartlett (Boston, 1926); *The History and Genealogy of the Goodhue Family* by Rev. Jonathan E. Goodhue (Rochester, NY, 18910); *The History and Genealogy of the Knowltons of England and America* by Rev. Charles Henry Wright Stocking (New York, 1897); *Errata and Addenda* by George Henry Knowlton (Boston, 1903); *The Livermore Family of America* by Walter Eliot Thwing; various vital records; and personal knowledge. in possession of Blaine Whipple at 236 NW Sundown Way, Portland, OR 97229 (1997). (Hereafter cited as Larj to Whipple, *3 letters in 1991, 1 in 1997*).

200 *Register,* 112:143.

201. through 204. Riggs to Whipple, *Letter 22 July 1998.*

205. Wilson to Whipple, *Letters, June 1996 & 1967*; Riggs to Whipple, *Letter 22 July 1998*; and Jonathan E. Goodhue., *History and Genealogy of the Goodhue Family in England and America to the year 1890* (Rochester, NY, 1891), (Hereafter cited as Goodhue Family, *Genealogy*).

206. Riggs to Whipple, *Letter 22 July 1998.*

207. Ibid.; and Essex Co., MA, *Vital Records,* Ipswich marriages, 253.

208. Riggs to Whipple, *Letter 22 July 1998*; and Essex Co., MA, *Vital Records,* Ipswich deaths, 602.

209. Riggs to Whipple, *Letter 22 July 1998*; and Essex Co., MA, *Vital Records,* Ipswich marriages, 256.

210. Riggs to Whipple, *Letter 22 July 1998*; and Essex Co., MA, *Vital Records,* Ipswich deaths, 603.

211. Riggs to Whipple, *Letter 22 July 1998.*

212. Essex Co., MA, *Vital Records,* Ipswich, 2:255.

213. through 215. Riggs to Whipple, *Letter 22 July 1998.*

216. through 230. Smalley - Seyfarth, *Family Group Sheet.*

231. through 245. Anderson to Whipple, *Letter, 02-3-1993.*

246. *Putnam's Monthly*; Ipswich Births, *Vital Records,* 392; and Ipswich Marriages, *Vital Records,* 454.

247. Donald B. Stevens to Blaine Whipple. Letters dated 16 and 31 Oct. 1991 at 25 Gardner Ter., Delmar, NY 12054-1027. In possession of Whipple at 236 NW Sundown Way, Portland, OR 97229-6575 (1999). His sources: Georgetown, Haverhill, Ipswich, Newbury, W. Newbury, Reading, & Sudbury MA Vital Records; Coffin, *Sketch of the History of Newbury, Newburyport, & W. Newbury*; C. Smith, *Report to the Brown Assn. of USA*; *Genealogy & History of the Brown/Browne Family of Granville, NY and Granville, WI*; *Essex Antiquarian,* 8:105, 9:160, 13: No. 4; J.B. Felt, *History of Ipswich, Essex, and Hamilton*; A.S. Hudson, *History of Sudbury, MA*; O.M. Whipple, *Brief Genealogy of the Whipple Family*; G.T. Little, *Descendants of George Little*; Blodgette & Jenett, *Early Settlers of Rowley, MA*; *Hammatt Papers*; various wills; gravestone inscriptions.). (Hereafter cited as Stevens to Whipple, *2 Letters*); and Beverly Esson to Blaine Whipple, letters dated 2 and 15 Jan. 1992 and 21 Nov. 1996 at 31 Tote Rd., Wells, ME 04090. In possession of Whipple at 236 NW Sundown Way, Portland, OR 97229 (1997). Her main source of information is vital records.). (Hereafter cited as Esson to Whipple, *Letters, Jan. 1992 & Nov. 1996*).

248. *Putnam's Monthly*; Stevens to Whipple, *2 Letters*; *Vital Records of Ipswich, Massachusetts to the End of 1849. Vol. II, Marriages* (Salem, MA: The Essex Institute, 1910), Ipswich marriages,475; Newbury births, 70; Hamilton deaths, 109 (Hereafter cited as Ipswich Vital Records, *Marriages, Vol. II*); and *Essex Antiquarian (The), Monthly Magazine*, 13:170.

249. *Putnam's Monthly* and Stevens to Whipple, *2 Letters*.

250. *Putnam's Monthly*.

251. through 253. Stevens to Whipple, *2 Letters*.

254. Essex Co., MA, *Vital Records*, Ipswich marriages, 454; Ipswich deaths, 533; and Johnson & Ladd, *Ipswich Burials*, 53.

255. Henry Whipple, 1:11 and Johnson & Ladd, *Ipswich Burials*, 57.

256. *Register*, 6:71.

257. Waters, Vol. II.

258. Henry Whipple, 1:11.

259. Ibid., 1:10; Essex Co., MA, *Vital Records*, Ipswich births, 393; and *Register*, 5:320.

260. Essex Co., MA, *Vital Records*, Ipswich births, 661; and *Register*, 5:320.

261. J.L.M. Ellis, comp., *Old Elliott, Book One 1897-1899* (Somersworth, New England History Press, 1985. This is a reprinting in three books of the 60 historical and genealogical magazines published in Eliot, Maine between 1879 and 1909.), 163 (Hereafter cited as Willis, *Old Elliot, ME*); *Register*, 5:327; and Essex Co., MA, *Vital Records*, Gloucester marriages, 466; Gloucester deaths, 265.

262. *Register*, 5:327 and Essex Co., MA, *Vital Records*, Gloucester deaths, 264.

263. Essex Co., MA, *Vital Records*, Gloucester marriages, 466.

264. through 269. Willis, *Old Elliot, ME*, 163; and *Register*, 5:327.

270. Ipswich Births, *Vital Records*, births; marriages, 453; death, 710; and Sanborn, *Probate, Essex Co., MA*, No. 29,497; 11:983.

271. Henry Whipple, 1:12; and Essex Co., MA, *Vital Records*, Ipswich births, 391; Ipswich deaths, 709.

272. *Putnam's Monthly* and Essex Co., MA, *Vital Records*, Ipswich births, 394; deaths, 710.

273. Ipswich Births, *Vital Records*, 393; Kittery, ME, *Vital Records*, 52; *Maine Wills 1640-1760* (Portland, ME: Brown Thurston & Company, 1887), 656-58 (Hereafter cited as *Maine Wills, 1640-1760*); and *Register*, 4:37.

274. *Register*, 4:37.

275. Kittery, ME, *Vital Records*, Marriages, 151.

276. J. Farmer and J.B. Moore, *Collections, Historical and Miscellaneous*, II.Concord, 1823, 20-21.

277. *New Hampshire Gazette*, 15 Feb. 1771, 214-15. Isaac W. Hammond, Editor, *New Hampshire Provincial and State Papers*, Vol. XII. Parsons B. Cogswell, State Printer. Concord, 1884, 23. Clifton K. Shipton, Sibley's *Harvard Graduates. Biographical Sketches of Those Who Attended Harvard College in the Classes of 1751-1755 With Bibliographical and Other Notes*. Vol. XIII. Massachusetts Historical Society. Boston, 1942, 197-201.

278. Ibid., 87 and Register, 4:37.

279. Kittery, ME, *Vital Records*, 87.

280. *Register*, 93:158; Kittery, ME, *Vital Records*, 226; and Suffolk Deeds, 177:262.

281. Chester B. Jordan, "Col. Joseph B. Whipple," *Proceedings of the NewHampshire Historical Society*, II:293-314.

282. Rev. B. G. Wiley, *Sketches of the White Mountains,* 1885, 20-30.

283. Richard M. Candee, "An Old Town by the Sea," *Urban Landscapes and Vernacular Building in Portsmouth, N.H. 1660 - 1990* ; Portsmouth, 1992: 26-8.

284. Elizabeth was the daughter of John Langdon, a prominent leader in revolutionary New Hampshire, a delegate to the constitutional convention, and the state's first U.S. senator. He was elected the president of the first session of the senate and counted the votes of the electoral college, informed Washington of his election, and administered the oath of office to him 30 April 1789. He also served six terms as the state's governor.

285. "A Quiet Abiding Place," a manuscript by Paul Hughes. Available at the Weeks Public Library, 36 Post Road, Greenland, NH 03840; (603) 436-8548;

http://weekslibrary.org/ona_maria_judge.htm.

286. *Putnam's Monthly*, Derick S. Hartshorn, III., *The Hartshorn Families in America* (Baltimore, MD: Gateway Press, Inc.), 33,57 (Hereafter cited as Hartshorn Families, *Genealogy*); and *Early Vital Records of Massachusetts to about 1850*, (Wheat Ridge CO: Search Research Publishing Corp., CD ROM, 1998), Concord marriages, 148 (Hereafter cited as Massachusetts, *Vital Records*).

287. Hartshorn Families, *Genealogy*, 33,57; and Essex Co., MA, *Vital Records*, Concord births, 148.

288. Hartshorn Families, *Genealogy*, 57; and Massachusetts, *Vital Records*, Concord births, 148.

289. Hartshorn Families, *Genealogy*, 57; and Massachusetts, *Vital Records*, Concord births, 148; Deaths, 332.

290. Hartshorn Families, *Genealogy*, 57.

291. Massachusetts, *Vital Records*, Concord: 151.

292. Hartshorn Families, *Genealogy*, 57; and Massachusetts, *Vital Records*, Concord births, 163; Marriages, 232.

293. through 300. Billerica, MA, *History*, Genealogical Register, 52, 89, 102-03.

301. Register, 10:357; and Billerica, MA, *History*, Genealogical Register, 89.

302. through 307. *Register*, 10:356.

308. Whipple-Lane, *Family Group Sheet*; Billerica, MA, *History*, Genealogical Register, 89; and *Register*, 102:162.

309. Whipple-Lane, *Family Group Sheet*.

310. Billerica, MA, *History*, Genealogical *Register*, 89; and Whipple-Lane, *Family Group Sheet*.

311. through 313. Whipple-Lane, *Family Group Sheet*.

314. Billerica, MA, *History*, Genealogical Register, 89.

315. Ibid. and Whipple-Lane, *Family Group Sheet*.

316. Whipple-Lane, *Family Group Sheet*.

317. Ibid.

318. *Register*, 10:357; Billerica, MA, *History*, 89; and Henry Whipple, 2:7.

319. through 327. Billerica, MA, *History*, Genealogical Register, 89, 157.

328. *Register*, 10;357; 106:224-25; and Henry Whipple, 2:7.

329. Billerica, MA, *History*, Genealogical Register, 89; and *Register*, 106:225.

330. through 336. Billerica, MA, *History*, Genealogical Register, 89.

337. *Putnam's Monthly* and Ipswich Marriages, *Vital Records*, 453.

338. The *Register* 23:271 lists them in "A Record of Births, Marriages, and Deaths in Portsmouth, N. H. from 1706 to 1742."

339. *Putnam's Monthly*.

340. Ibid.

341. *Register*, 53:345-50; and Thomas N. Pratt to Blaine Whipple. Letter dated 5 Feb. 1999 at 427 N. Taylor Ave., Oak Park, IL 60302-2419. In possession of Whipple at 236 NW Sundown Way, Portland, OR 97229-6575 (1999). His sources: J. Gardner Bartlett, *Simon Stone Genealogy - Ancestry and Descendants of Simon Stone of Watertown, MA*, Boston: Stone Family Assn., 1926; *Early Settlers of New York State*, Vol. II, July 1938; *A History of Steuben County, New York, and Its People*, Irvin W. Near, vol. I, Chicago, The Lewis Publishing Co., 1911; *History of the Settlement of Steuben County, NY*, Guy H. McMaster, Geneva, NY, Steuben Co. Historical Society, W.F. Humphrey Press, Inc., 1975; *Part First, Historical Gazetteer, Steuben County, New York*, Millard F. Roberts, Syracuse, NY, 1891; *Abstracts of Graves of Revolutionary Patriots*, vol. 4; *New York Pensioners of 1835, Records 5041-5050*; *Tree Talks* vol. 23, No. 4, 1893 Central New York Genealogical Society, Syracuse, NY; *Revolutionary War Soldiers Buried in Steuben County, New York*, vol. xi, *Gemini-Twin Tiers* Genealogical Society, Elmira, NY, No. 2, June 1982; *Thomas Hale, 1637 Emigrant*, Louise G. Walker, Chicago, 1978; *Genealogy of Descendants of Thomas Hale of Watton, England, and of Newbury*, Mass. Robert Safford Hale, Albany, NY, Weed, Parsons and Company, Printers, 1889; *Tombstone Inscriptions, Gulf Stream Cemetery, Jefferson Co., NY*, Broderbund Software, Banner Blue Division, CD #183; Mrs. Edna Stone Parker, DAR ID #57117; DAR Lineage Books, National No. 320369, 2; Will of Amos Stone; Yvonne E. Martin, *Marriages and Deaths from Steuben Co., NY Newspapers 1797-1868*, Heritage Books, Inc., 8 & 102; Gary Boyd Roberts, *Ancestors of American Presidents*, Santa Clarita, CA: *Register*, 1995, 292; *Prairie Lawn Cemetery Tombstones*; *Genealogy of the Descendants of John White of Wenham and Lancaster, Massachusetts 1638-1900*, 2 volumes, by Almira Larkin White, Haverhill, Chase Brothers, Printers, 1900; *Voters and Tax-Payers of Bureau County*,

Illinois, Chicago, H.F. Kett and Co., 1877; *The Richmond Family 1594-1896* and *Pre-American Ancestors 1040-1594*, by Joshua Bailey Richmond, Boston, 1897; *10,000 Vital Records of Western New York 1809-1850*, Fred Q. Bowman, Baltimore, Genealogical Publishing Co., Inc., 1986; various birth, marriage, and death records; internment records; and newspaper obituaries.). (Hereafter cited as Pratt to Whipple, *Letter, 5 Feb. 1999*).

342. through 346. Pratt to Whipple, *Letter, 5 Feb. 1999.*

347. *Register*, 53:345-50; and Pratt to Whipple, *Letter, 5 Feb. 1999.*

348. *Register*, 53:345-50; and Charles L. Bacon to Blaine Whipple. letter dated 4 Dec. 1991 at Peabody Mill, 66 Brook Rd., Amherest, NH 03031. in possession of Whipple at 236 NW Sundown Way, Portland, OR 97229 (1997.) Letter included family groups and cited the following sources: Mary Lovering Holman, *The Pillsbury Ancestry* (1938); David H. Brown, *Simon and Joan (Clarke) Stone of Watertown, Mass. and Three Generations of Their Descendants*, (Reprint from *Register*, July, 1899); Eben Putnam, *The Holden Genealogy*, (Murray Printing, Boston, 1923); Thomas W. Baldwin, *Michael Bacon of Dedham, 1640, and His Descendants*, (Murray & Emery Co., Cambridge, MA, 1915). [This shows the line of descent from Michael Bacon through Allen Harlow Bacon. Baldwin's claim of an 1844 marriage of Nancy Maria Bacon to Volney Green does not agree with either family records or the vital records of Harvard, MA, which do not show such a marriage or even mention a Volney Green. They do, however, show the 1848 marriage of Nancy Maria Bacon to Luther A. Chase]. *Holy Bible Record* for Samuel N. and Sarah E. Bacon, (Lippincott, Grambo & Co., Philadelphia, 1842); cemetery inscriptions from Rural Cemetery, Albany, NY, Harvard, MA, and Hancock and Washington, NH; Town Histories from Harvard, MA and Hancock, Hillsboro, & Washington, NH; probate records from Hillsborough Co., NH; Vital Records from the various towns). (Hereafter cited as Bacon to Whipple, *Letter 12-04-1991*).

349. Bacon to Whipple, *Letter 12-04-1991.*

350. *Register*, 53:345-50; and Robert E. Wise to Blaine Whipple. Letters dated 20 Dec. 1991; 1 Jan. 1992; 2 April 1993 at 54 Ellis Farm Lane, Melrose, MA 02176. In possession of Whipple at 236 NW Sundown Way, Portland, OR 97229- 6575 (1999.) Sources included *Ipswich Vital Records*; *Candlewood* by Franklin Waters; Bow, NH Town Records; Essex Co., MA Registry of Deeds; various gravestone in Brewer, ME, Stow, MA, and Marlborough, MA; *Some of the Descendants of John and Elinor Whitney* by William L. Whitney; *Jewell Register* by Thomas Jewell; family *Bible* and various other family records.). (Hereafter cited as Wise to Whipple, *3 Letters*).

351. Wise to Whipple, *3 Letters.*

352. *Register*, 53:345-50; and *J.G. Bartlett*, 61.

353. *J.G. Bartlett*, 61.

354. through 360. *Register*, 53:345-50.

361. Ibid., 53:345-50; McMahon to Whipple, *3 Letters*; and *J.G. Bartlett*, 84-5.

362. McMahon to Whipple, *3 Letters*; and *J.G. Bartlett*, 84-5.

363. *Register*, 53:345-50; and Virginia Anne (Croissant) Wolfe to Blaine Whipple. letters dated 7 Feb. and 24 March 1994 at PO Box 6, Malone, NY 12953-0006. in possession of Whipple at 236 NW Sundown Way, Portland, OR 97229 (1997). (Hereafter cited as Wolfe to Whipple, *Letters, 2-7 & 3-24-1994*).

364. Wolfe to Whipple, *Letters, 2-7 & 3-24-1994.*

365. *Register*, 53:345-50.

366. Jonathan Richardson-Mary Woodward Family Pedigree sheet, supplied 15 May 1998 by Michael Dobson to Weldon Whipple, web master www.whipple.org, E-mail dobfam4@juno.com. The source for this pedigree was the *International Genealogical Index* and J. Gardner Bartlett, *Simon Stone Genealogy*, Boston, 1926, 66 (Hereafter cited as Richardson - Woodward, *Pedigree Sheet*).

367. Ibid.

368. *Register*, 53:348.

369. Richardson - Woodward, *Pedigree Sheet.*

370. through 380. Francis R. Jenne, CPA, to Blaine Whipple. Letters dated 5 Sept. 1992 and 22 & 24 July 1997 at One Chestnut St., Potsdam, NY 13676. In possession of Whipple at 236 NW Sundown Way, Portland, OR 97229 (1997). His sources included *Barraford-Jenne, A Multilineal Genealogy*, Vol. I, comp. & edited by Nora M. Barraford, Ph.D., Francis R. Jenne, CPA, Jessie Barraford, 1986; *John Jenney of Plymouth, and his Descendants*, edited by Judith Jenney Gurney, Gateway Press, Baltimore; *The Wights,"* by *William Ward Wight*, Swain & Tate Printers, Milwaukie,

1890). (Hereafter cited as Jenne to Whipple, *Letters, 5 Sept. 1992 and 22 & 24 July 1997*).

381. J. Jones to Wh, *Letters 1991, 1993 & 1997*; and Ruth (Hayden) Hancock to Blaine Whipple. letter dated 28 October 1993 & 7 Feb. 1997 at 1710 S.E. Pioneer Way, Oak Harbor, WA 98277. in possession of Whipple at 236 NW Sundown Way, Portland, OR 97229 (1997) (Hereafter cited as Hancock to Whipple, *Letters, 10-28-1993 & 02-07- 1997*).

382. Hancock to Whipple, *Letters, 10-28-1993 & 02-07-1997*.

383. J. Jones to Wh, *Letters 1991, 1993 & 1997*.

384. Starr, *Starr Genealogy*.

385. through 390. J. Jones to Wh, *Letters 1991, 1993 & 1997*.

391. *Register*, 53:349; 53:345-50.

392. and 393. *Register.*, 10:229-30.

394. and 395. *Register*, 53:349-50; 10:229-30.

396. and 397. *Register* , 10:229-30.

398. through 406. Betty (Mrs. Emil J.) Westensee to Blaine Whipple. Letters dated 28 Dec. 1991 & 26 Jan. 1992 at 2330 - 24 1/2 St., Rock Island, IL 61201. In possession of Whipple at 236 NW Sundown Way, Portland, OR 97229 (1997). (Hereafter cited as Westensee to Whipple, *Letters 1991 & 1992*).

407. Pettit, *Letter 7 Jan. 1990*.

408. Harry G. Woodworth to Blaine Whipple. Letters dated 11 and 22 Dec. 1991 and 14 April 1993 at 60 Bell St., Orange, NJ 07050. In possession of Whipple at 236 NW Sundown Way, Portland, OR 97229-6575 (1999.) Extensive pedigree charts included. Sources included *The Darling Papers; The Paine Genealogy; Register; Ipswich Vital Records*; Hammatt's *History of Ipswich; Bassett Genealogy*; Bocking parish records.). (Hereafter cited as Woodworth to Whipple, *3 Letters*).

409. Ibid.

410. Harrison to Whipple, *Letter, 12-5-1991 & 01-14-1997*.

411. Ibid.

412. Billigmeier to Whipple, *2 Letters 1992*; *Utah Magazine*, "Brigham Young", April 1930:58-64; and *Early Vital Records of Worcester Co., Mass. to About 1850*, (Wheat Ridge, Colo.: Search & Research Publishing Corporation, (1999), Shrewsbury deaths, 252 (Hereafter cited as Vital Records, *Worcester Co., MA*).

413. through 415. Billigmeier to Whipple, *2 Letters 1992*; and *Vital Records, Worcester Co., MA*, Shrewsbury births, 39, 40; marriages, 155; deaths, 252.

416. through 420. *Vital Records, Worcester Co., MA*, Shrewsbury births, 29, 39, 40, 41; deaths, 252, 253.

421. Brown to Whipple, *1 Jan. 1992*; and *Utah Magazine*, "Brigham Young", April 1930:58-64.

422. through 430. Brown to Whipple, *1 Jan. 1992*.

431. Ibid.; and *Utah Magazine*, "Brigham Young", April 1930:58-64.

432. *Utah Magazine*, "Brigham Young," Oct. 1920:186-7.

433. through 444. *Utah Magazine*. "Brigham Young,", April 1930:58-64.

445. through 447. *J.G.* Bartlett; and *Register*, 53:345-50.

448. through 450. Bakke - Whipple, *Family Group Sheet*.

451. *Register*, 13:229; Bakke - Whipple, *Family Group Sheet*; and Wilde to Whipple, *Letters 04/ 10 & 22/ 1997*.

452. Wilde to Whipple, *Letters 04/ 10 & 22/ 1997*.

453. *Register*, 13:229; 43:366-7.

454. through 462. *Register.*, 43:366-7.

463. through 466. *Register.*, 60:52.

467. through 469. Wilson to Whipple, *Letters, June 1996 & 1967*.

470. through 482. Riggs to Whipple, *Letter 22 July 1998*.

483. and 484. McMahon to Whipple, *3 Letters*.

485. Alice J. Day, *Family Group Sheet*.

486. Donald Philip Muno-Patricia Andrea Thayer Family Group Sheet, supplied 8 Dec. 1990 by Patricia (Thayer) Muno, 6885 SW 161 Ave., Beaverton, OR 97007. Pedigree sheets back to Matthew Whipple of Bocking, England also provided. No documentation included. (Hereafter

cited as Muno - Thayer, *Family Group Sheet*); and Alice J. Day, *Family Group Sheet*.

487. *Register*, 97:389.

488. and 489. Wm. R. Hunter, *Family Group Sheet*.

490. Stevens to Whipple, *3 Letters, 1992 & 1996*.

491. Thomas Knowlton-Margery Goodhue Family group sheet, supplied 15 Jan. 1992 by Samuel P. Stevens, 312 Sheridan Ave., Piedmont, CA 94611. This sheet does not cite evidence or document the information in any way. (Hereafter cited as Stevens, *Family Group Sheet*).

492. and 493. Larj to Whipple, *3 letters in 1991, 1 in 1997*.

494. *Register*, 112:143.

495. Riggs to Whipple, *Letter 22 July 1998*; and *Ipswich Vital Records*, Marriages, 252.

496. through 499. Riggs to Whipple, *Letter 22 July 1998*.

500. Ibid.; and Essex Co., MA, *Vital Records*, Ipswich marriages, 256.

501. through 504. Riggs to Whipple, *Letter 22 July 1998*.

505. Anderson to Whipple, *Letter, 02-3-1993*.

506. through 515. Smalley - Seyfarth, *Family Group Sheet*.

516. Anderson to Whipple, *Letter, 02-3-1993*.

517. through 521. Ibid., Sources include the Andover, Mass *Vital Records* and the *Mooar Genealogy*, by Charles H. Pope, Boston, 1901, 19-22.

522. and 523. Esson to Whipple, *Letters, Jan. 1992 & Nov. 1996*.

524. through 531. Stevens to Whipple, *2 Letters*.

532. Ipswich Births, *Vital Records*, Ipswich marriages, 104; Ipswich deaths, 533; Essex Co., MA, *Vital Records*, Ipswich marriages, 117; and Johnson & Ladd, *Ipswich Burials*, 58.

533. Henry Whipple, 1:10; and Essex Co., MA, *Vital Records*, Ipswich deaths, 533.

534. Essex Co., MA, *Vital Records*, Ipswich deaths, 533; and Johnson & Ladd, *Ipswich Burials*, 57.

535. Essex Co., MA, *Vital Records*, Ipswich births, 104; marriages, 117; deaths, 483.

536. Ibid., Ipswich deaths, 483.

537. Ipswich Births, *Vital Records*, Ipswich births, 104.

538. Essex Co., MA, *Vital Records*, Ipswich births, 104; and Henry Whipple, 2:9.

539. Essex Co., MA, *Vital Records*, Ipswich births, 105.

540. Ipswich Births, *Vital Records*, Ipswich births, 104.

541. Essex Co., MA, *Vital Records*, Ipswich births, 104.

542. Ibid., Ipswich births, 104.

543. Ibid., Ipswich births, 104; and Johnson & Ladd, *Ipswich Burials*, 57.

544. *Putnam's Monthly*; Register, 5:327; and Essex Co., MA, *Vital Records*, Gloucester marriages, 465, Gloucester deaths, 264.

545. Essex Co., MA, *Vital Records*, Gloucester marriages, 465; Gloucester deaths, 265.

546. Ibid., Gloucester marriages, 465; Gloucester deaths, 264.

547. Ibid., Gloucester marriages, 465; Gloucester deaths, 263.

548. Ibid., Gloucester deaths, 265.

549. Willis, *Old Elliot, ME*; *Register*, 5:327; and Essex Co., MA, *Vital Records*, Gloucester marriages, 464; Gloucester deaths, 263.

550. *Register*, 5:327; and Essex Co., MA, *Vital Records*, Gloucester marriages, 464; Gloucester deaths, 264.

551. Essex Co., MA, *Vital Records*, Gloucester marriages, 464; Gloucester deaths, 265.

552. Ibid., Gloucester births, 599.

553. Ibid., Gloucester births, 598.

554. Ibid., Gloucester births, 597.

555. Ibid., Gloucester births, 597; Gloucester deaths, 263.

556. Ibid., Gloucester births, 597; Gloucester deaths, 265.

557. Ibid., Gloucester births, 600.

558. Ibid., Gloucester births, 599; Gloucester deaths, 264.

559. Ibid., Gloucester births, 598.

560. Ibid., Gloucester births, 600.

561. Ibid., Gloucester births, 597.

562. Ibid., Gloucester births, 600.

563. Ibid., Gloucester births, 599.

564. through 566. Ibid., Gloucester births, 600.

567. Ibid., Gloucester births, 598; Gloucester deaths, 264.

568. and 569. Ibid., Gloucester births, 599.

570. Ibid., Gloucester births, 598.

571. *Putnam's Monthly* and Essex Co., MA, *Vital Records*, Ipswich births, 392; marriages, 453.

572. Family group sheet, supplied 3 May 1993 and 30 Oct. 1996 by Grant Dodge Whipple, winter address, PO Box 9455, Charleston, SC 29410; summer address R.F.D. 1, Box 96, Shore Rd., Cape Nededick ME 03902. Sources include the *Darling Papers* at the Ipswich, MA public library and various Massachusetts vital records (Hereafter cited as Grant Dodge Whipple, *Family Group Sheet*); and Ipswich Deaths, *Vital Records*.

573. Essex Co., MA, *Vital Records*, Ipswich births, 391.

574. Ipswich *Vital Records*, Marriages, Vol. 2, page 453.

575. *Ipswich Vital Records*, Births, 393; Marriages, 454; and Petty to Jones, *Research Project*.

576. *Ipswich, Essex County, Massachusetts War Records*, Salt Lake City: LDS Church, film #878659.

577. Henry Whipple, 1:12; and *Register*, 115:80.

578. *Putnam's Monthly*.

579. Ipswich Births, *Vital Records*, 392; and Petty to Jones, *Research Project*.

580. *Ipswich Vital Records*, births, 391; and Petty to Jones, *Research Project*.

581. Petty to Jones, *Research Project*; and Ipswich Marriages, *Vital Records*.

582. Henry Whipple, 1:13; and Ipswich Marriages, *Vital Records*.

583. Petty to Jones, *Research Project*; and Ipswich Marriages, *Vital Records*.

584. Ipswich Deaths, *Vital Records*.

585. Kittery, ME, *Vital Records*, Births, 87; Marriages, 120; and Willis, *Old Elliot, ME*, 186.

586. *Laws of New Hampshire*, 4:177-80.

587. Kittery, ME, *Vital Records*, 87; and *Register*, 151:234. *The Parish Records of the First Church and Society of Kittery, Maine* 1714 to 1791. William Whipple was baptized 14 Feb. 1730/31.

588. Billerica, MA, *History*, Genealogical Register, 102-3.

589. and 590. Ibid., Genealogical Register, 103.

591. and 592. *Register*, 10:356.

593. Whipple-Lane, *Family Group Sheet*; and Billerica, MA, *History*, 89.

594. through 603. Whipple-Lane, *Family Group Sheet*.

604. Billerica, MA, *History*, Genealogical Register, 70, 89; and Whipple-Lane, *Family Group Sheet*.

605. through 614. Billerica, MA, *History*, 70, 72.

615. Ibid., Genealogical Register, 89; and Janet Martin to Blaine Whipple. E-mail dated 16 May 1999 at janmartin@austin.rr.com. In possession of Whipple at 236 N.W. Sundown Way, Portland, Oreg. 97229-6575 (2002). (Hereafter cited as Martin to Whipple, *E-mail 16 May 1999*).

616. Billerica, MA, *History*, Genealogical Register, 89; and William W. Fiske to Blaine Whipple. E-mail dated 30 Jan. 1999 at 56 Rendevous Ln, Barnstable, Mass. 02630; E- mail wfiske@capecod.net. In possession of Whipple at 236 NW Sundown Way, Portland, Oreg. 97229-6576 (2002). (Hereafter cited as Fiske to Whipple, *E-mail 30 Jan. 1999*).

617. Fiske to Whipple, *E-mail 30 Jan. 1999*.

618. Billerica, MA, *History*, Genealogical Register, 89.

619. *Register*, 106:225.

620. *J.G. Bartlett*, 203.

621. through 630. Pratt to Whipple, *Letter, 5 Feb. 1999*.

631. and 632. Bacon to Whipple, *Letter 12-04-1991*.

633. and 634. Wise to Whipple, *3 Letters*.

635. through 638. J.G. Bartlett, 61.

639. *1850 U.S.Census, Population Schedule, Eugene Township, Vermillion Co., Ind.*, 95:347, (Hereafter cited as 1850, *U.S. Census*).

640. *Register*, 53:345-50.

641. Ibid., 53:345-50.

642. Brian Gaber to Blaine Whipple by letters dated 3, 13, 18, and 19 Jan. 1998 at Uber dem Thie 2, 38388 Twieflingen, Germany. In possession of Whipple at 236 NW Sundown Way, Portland, OR 97229-6575 (1998). His sources include vital records beginning with Robert Goddard (1803) and John W. Harms and Pearl Goddard Harms, *The Goddard Book*, Vol 1, 1984, Vol. 2, 1990. Baltimore, MD: Gateway Press, Vermont vital records, various U.S. Census records, Goddard *Bible*, Wisconsin, Iowa, and South Dakota vital records, various obituaries in his possession.). (Hereafter cited as Gaber to Whipple, *Letters, Jan. 1998*); and McMahon to Whipple, *3 Letters*.

643. Gaber to Whipple, *Letters, Jan. 1998*; and Billigmeier to Whipple, *2 Letters 1992*.

644. *Worcester Co. Vital Records* under Shrewsbury Births (p. 41) state he was born on this date in Shrewsbury.

645. Gaber to Whipple, *Letters, Jan. 1998*.

646. J.G. Bartlett, 84-5.

647. Ibid., 84-5; and *Vital Records, Worcester Co., MA*, Shrewsbury births, 39.

648. through 653. J.G. Bartlett, 654. Wolfe to Whipple, *Letters, 2-7 & 3-24-1994*.

654. and 655. Ibid.

656. through 666. Richardson - Woodward, *Pedigree Sheet*.

667. through 675. Jenne to Whipple, *Letters, 5 Sept. 1992 and 22 & 24 July 1997*.

676. Ibid.; and Sally Pavia to Blaine Whipple. E-mail dated 14 June 1999 at pavia@futureone.com. In possession of Blaine Whipple at 236 N.W. Sundown Way, Portland, Oreg. 97229-6575 (2002). (Hereafter cited as Pavia to Whipple, *E-mail 14 June 1999*).

677. and 678. Hancock to Whipple, *Letters, 10-28-1993 & 02-07-1997*.

679. and 680. Emily Patch to Blaine Whipple. E-mail letters dated 22, 24, 29 November 1998 at E5path@teleport.com, mailing address 5815 SW Logan Ct., Portland, OR 97219. In possession of Whipple at 236 NW Sundown Way, Portland, OR 97229-6575 (1999). Her sources included *The Dana Family in America* by Elizabeth Ellery Dana, Wright & Potter Printing Co., 32 Deme St., Boston, 1940.). (Hereafter cited as Patch to Whipple, *3 Letters*).

681. through 690. J. Jones to Wh, *Letters 1991, 1993 & 1997*.

691. Starr, *Starr Genealogy*.

692. through 694. *Register*, 53:345-50.

695. Ibid., 53:345-50; 10:230.

696. through 698. Westensee to Whipple, *Letters 1991 & 1992*.

699. Pettit, *Letter 7 Jan. 1990*.

700. and 701. Woodworth to Whipple, *3 Letters*.

702. and 703. Harrison to Whipple, *Letter, 12-5-1991 & 01-14-1997*.

704. Billigmeier to Whipple, *2 Letters 1992*; and *Vital Records, Worcester Co., MA*, Shrewsbury births, 40.

705. through 708. Billigmeier to Whipple, *2 Letters 1992*.

709. Gaber to Whipple, *Letters, Jan. 1998*; and Billigmeier to Whipple, *2 Letters 1992*.

710. *Worcester Co. Vital Records*, Shrewsbury Births (p. 41) state he was born on this date in Shrewsbury

711. Gaber to Whipple, *Letters, Jan. 1998*; and McMahon to Whipple, *3 Letters*.

712. through 724. Gaber to Whipple, *Letters, Jan. 1998*.

725. J.G. Bartlett, 84-5; and *Vital Records*, Worcester Co., MA, Shrewsbury births, 39.

726. through 732. J.G. Bartlett, 84-5.

733. *Vital Records, Worcester Co., MA*, Shrewsbury births, 39; Shrewsbury marriages, 155; Grafton marriages, 211; Shrewsbury deaths, 252.

734. Ibid., Shrewsbury deaths, 253.

735. Ibid., Shrewsbury births, 40; deaths, 253.

736. Ibid., Shrewsbury births, 39; deaths, 252.

737. Ibid., Shrewsbury births, 40.
738. Ibid., Shrewsbirths, 40; deaths, 252.
739. Ibid., Shrewsbury births, 39.
740. Ibid., Shrewsbury births, 40; deaths, 253.
741. Ibid., Shrewsbury births, 39; marriages, 155; deaths, 252.
742. Ibid., Shrewsbury deaths, 253.
743. Ibid., Shrewsbury births, 41.
744. Ibid., Shrewsbury births, 40.
745. Ibid., Shrewsbury births, 41; deaths, 253.
746. and 747. Brown to Whipple, *1 Jan. 1992*.
748. and 749. *Utah Magazine*, "Brigham Young," Oct. 1920: 180-7.
750. through 758. *Utah Magazine*, "Brigham Young,," July 1929: 97-114.
759. J.G. Bartlett.
760. Larj to Whipple, *3 letters in 1991, 1 in 1997*; and J.G. Bartlett.
761. through 766. J.G. Bartlett.
767. and 768. Ibid., 99, 169-70.
769. through 778. J. G. Bartlett, 171-72.
779. *Register*, 95:179-80.
780. through 788. Bakke - Whipple, *Family Group Sheet*.
789. Wilde to Whipple, *Letters 04/ 10 & 22/ 1997*.
790. Ibid.
791. *Register*, 60:52, 192.
792. through 794. *Register*, 60:192.
795. through 804. *Register*., 60:52.
805. through 808. *Register*, 60:192.
809. through 816. Wilson to Whipple, *Letters, June 1996 & 1967*.
817. through 822. Riggs to Whipple, *Letter 22 July 1998*.
823. McMahon to Whipple, *3 Letters*.
824. Alice J. Day, *Family Group Sheet*.
825. Muno - Thayer, *Family Group Sheet*.
826. *Register*, 97:389.
827. and 828. Wm. R. Hunter, *Family Group Sheet*.
829. and 830. Stevens to Whipple, *3 Letters, 1992 & 1996*.
831. and 832. Larj to Whipple, *3 letters in 1991, 1 in 1997*.
833. *Register*, 112:143.
834. through 849. Smalley - Seyfarth, *Family Group Sheet*.
850. through 868. Anderson to Whipple, *Letter, 02-3-1993*.
869. and 870. Esson to Whipple, *Letters, Jan. 1992 & Nov. 1996*.
871. through 874. Stevens to Whipple, *2 Letters*.
875. Essex Co., MA, *Vital Records*, Ipswich births, 105; marriages, 117; and Henry Whipple, 2:9.
876. and 877. Henry Whipple, 2:9.
878. Essex Co., MA, *Vital Records*, Ipswich births, 104; and Henry Whipple, 2:9.
879. and 880. Henry Whipple, 2:9.
881. Essex Co., MA, *Vital Records*, Ipswich births, 104; marriages, 222; deaths, 586.
882. Ibid., Ipswich deaths, 695.
883. Ibid., Ipswich deaths, 586.
884. Ibid., Ipswich births, 370.
885. Ibid., Ipswich births, 369; deaths, 696.
886. and 887. Ibid., Ipswich births, 369.
888. and 889. Ibid., Ipswich births, 368.

890.   *Register*, 92:184-85.

891.   through 895. Grant Dodge Whipple, *Family Group Sheet*.

896.   Petty to Jones, *Research Project*; and Ipswich Marriages, *Vital Records*.

897.   Sanborn, *Probate, Essex Co., MA*; *Ipswich, Essex, Mass. War Records 1776-1777*; Family History Library (Church of Jesus Christ of Latter-Day Saints, Salt Lake City, UT), (Hereafter cited as Ipswich, MA, *War Records 1776-1777*); Archives, Commonwealth of Massachusetts., *Massachusetts Soldiers and Sailors of the Revolutionary War* (Secretary of the Commonwealth; Wright & Potter Printing Co., State Printers; (Boston, 1908)), (Hereafter cited as Massachusetts, *Rev. War Veterans*); and Petty to Jones, *Research Project*.

898.   Ipswich Births, *Vital Records*.

899.   Ibid. and Petty to Jones, *Research Project*.

900.   Ipswich Births, *Vital Records*; and Petty to Jones, *Research Project*.

901.   and 902. Petty to Jones, *Research Project*.

903.   Ipswich Births, *Vital Records*; and Petty to Jones, *Research Project*.

904.   and 905. Petty to Jones, *Research Project*.

906.   Willis, *Old Elliot, ME*, 187.

907.   through 914. Billerica, MA, *History*, Genealogical Register, 58, 96, 103.

915.   *Register*, 10:356 .

916.   Ibid., 162.

917.   through 923. Whipple-Lane, *Family Group Sheet*.

924.   through 933. Billerica, MA, *History*, Genealogical Register, 70.

934.   Ibid., Genealogical Register, 12, 89.

935.   through 940. Ibid., Genealogical Record, 71.

941.   Ibid., Genealogical Register, 71, 142.

942.   Ibid., Genealogical Register, 142.

943.   Ibid., Genealogical Register, 70.

944.   through 948. Ibid., Genealogical Register, 71.

949.   Ibid., Genealogical Register, 70, 135.

950.   through 954. Ibid., Genealogical Register, 135.

955.   Ibid., Genealogical Register, 70, 143.

956.   and 957. Ibid., Genealogical Register, 143.

958.   Martin to Whipple, *E-mail 16 May 1999*.

959.   and 960. Fiske to Whipple, *E-mail 30 Jan. 1999*.

961.   *Register*, 106:224-25.

962.   and 963. Ibid., 106:225.

964.   J.G. Bartlett, 203.

965.   *Vital Records, Worcester Co., MA*, Boylston births, 55.

966.   Ibid., Boylston births, 55.

967.   Ibid., Boylton births, 55; deaths, 149.

968.   Ibid., Boylton births, 54.

969.   Ibid., West Boylston Births: 55; Deaths: 149.

970.   and 971. Ibid., Boylton births, 55.

972.   and 973. Pratt to Whipple, *Letter, 5 Feb. 1999*.

974.   through 983. J. G. Bartlett, Pension Application S11489, Va. Records, NARA, Group 15, Roll 2301; *Massachusetts Soldiers and Sailors of the Revolutionary War*, 15:84; US Pension Records, Treasury Dept., Accounting Office, Records Group 217, NARA, Washington, D.C.; *Census of United States Pensioners in 1840*, 98; New York Council of Appointment, 1:708.

984.   and 985. Bacon to Whipple, *Letter 12-04-1991*.

986.   Wise to Whipple, *3 Letters*.

987.   and 988. *Register*, 95:347.

989.   and 990. Ibid., 53:345-50.

991.   Gaber to Whipple, *Letters, Jan. 1998*; and McMahon to Whipple, *3 Letters*.

992.   McMahon to Whipple, *3 Letters*.

993.   J.G. Bartlett, 85.

994.   Billigmeier to Whipple, *2 Letters 1992*.

995.   and 996. Wolfe to Whipple, *Letters, 2-7 & 3-24-1994*.

997.   Richardson - Woodward, *Pedigree Sheet*.

998.   through 1003. Jenne to Whipple, *Letters, 5 Sept. 1992 and 22 & 24 July 1997*.

1004. Pavia to Whipple, *E-mail 14 June 1999*.

1005. and 1006. Hancock to Whipple, *Letters, 10-28-1993 & 02-07-1997*.

1007. and 1008. Patch to Whipple, *3 Letters*.

1009. J. Jones to Wh, *Letters 1991, 1993 & 1997*.

1010. through 1018. Cherryl Ball to Blaine Whipple. Letters dated 2 and 11 Feb. 1999 at 8517 Moraine Dr., Frisco., TX 75034-5847. In possession of Whipple at 236 NW Sundown Way, Portland, OR 97229-6575 (1999.) Sources cited: *History of Watertown, Mass;* Hosea Starr Gallou, *Early Starrs in Kent & New England* Concord, NH: The Romford Press, 1944; *History of Vermont* by Hemenway, vol. 1, 356-7; *History of Caldonia County, Vermont,* by Child, 261). (Hereafter cited as Ball to Whipple, *Letters, 2 & 11 Feb. 1999*).

1019. through 1027. J. Jones to Wh, *Letters 1991, 1993 & 1997*.

1028. Carol L. (Fairweather) Andrews to Blaine Whipple. letters dated 12 Jan. 1992 and 12 May 1997 at 788 Glebe Rd., Westmoreland, NH 03467. In possession of Whipple at 236 NW Sundown Way, Portland, OR 97229 (1997). (Hereafter cited as Andrews to Whipple, *Letters 1992 & 1997*).

1029. Starr, *Starr Genealogy*.

1030. through 1032. Westensee to Whipple, *Letters 1991 & 1992*.

1033. Pettit, *Letter 7 Jan. 1990*.

1034. and 1035. Woodworth to Whipple, *3 Letters*.

1036. and 1037. Harrison to Whipple, *Letter, 12-5-1991 & 01-14-1997*.

1038. through 1042. Billigmeier to Whipple, *2 Letters 1992*.

1043. J.G. Bartlett, 85.

1044. and 1045. Gaber to Whipple, *Letters, Jan. 1998*.

1046. *Vital Records, Worcester Co., MA*, Shrewsbury births, 39; marriages, 155.

1047. through 1049. Ibid., Shrewsbury births, 40.

1050. through 1059. Brown to Whipple, *1 Jan. 1992*.

1060. *Utah Magazine*, "Brigham Young", July 1929:97-114.

1061. Brigham Young-various wives Family Group Record, various dates Family Search, a genealogy web site owned and operated by the Church of Jesus Christ of Latter-Day Saints. This information found in *Ancestral File* 4:19 on 29 Jan. 2000, Salt Lake City, UT. (Hereafter cited as Brigham Young, *Family Group Record*).

1062. *Utah Magazine*, "Brigham Young", April 1920:52.

1063. Ibid., Oct. 1920:180-3.

1064. *Deseret News*, vol. 3. Salt Lake City, Utah 1852.

1065. See Gene A. Sessions, "John Young: Soldier of the Revolution," in *Latter Day Patriots: Nine Mormon Families and Their Revolutionary War Heritage*. Salt Lake City: 1975, 20-41; also John Young Revolutionary War Pension File, No. W,11908 BLWT 101. 305-160-55, National Archives, Washington, D. C.

1066. through 1073. *Utah Magazine*, "Brigham Young", July 1929;97-114.

1074. through 1088. J.G. Bartlett.

1089. through 1102, J.G. Bartlett. 170.

1103. through 1125. J. B. Bartlett., 171.

1126. Ibid., 171; John A. Garraty and Mark C. Carnes, eds., *American National Biography*, 24 vols. (New York: Oxford University Press, 1999), 17:809 (Hereafter cited as AmNatBi, *Garraty & Carnes*); and Obituary of Charles Pratt, *New York Times*, New York City, N.Y. (5 May 1891), Page 1, col. 7 (Hereafter cited as Charles Pratt obit, *New York Times*).

1127. and 1128. AmNatBi, *Garraty & Carnes*, 17:809.

1129. *Encyclopedia of Biography of New York*, vol. 1, 145-46. (1916.)

1130. Charles Pratt obit, *New York Times*, Page 1, col. 7.

1131. through 1133. J.G. Bartlett, 172.

1134. *Register*, 95:179-80.

1135. Bakke - Whipple, *Family Group Sheet*.

1136. and 1137. Wilde to Whipple, *Letters 04/ 10 & 22/ 1997*.

1138. *Register*, 60:192.

1139. Ibid., 60:192; and *Vital Records, Worcester Co., MA*, Oxford marriages, 131; Oxford deaths, 309.

1140. *Register*, 60:192; and *Vital Records, Worcester Co., MA*, Oxford births, 108; marriages, 241; deaths, 309.

1141. *Register*, 60:192; and *Vital Records, Worcester Co., MA*, Oxford births, 108; marriages, 242.

1142. *Register*, and *Vital Records, Worcester Co., MA*, Oxford births, 108; marriages, 141.

1143. *Register*, 60:192; and *Vital Records, Worcester Co., MA*, Oxford births, 108; marriages, 242.

1144. and 1145. *Register*, 60:297.

1146. through 1149. Ibid., 60:298.

1150. and 1151. Wilson to Whipple, *Letters, June 1996 & 1967*.

1152. through 1156. Riggs to Whipple, *Letter 22 July 1998*.

1157. and 1158. McMahon to Whipple, *3 Letters*.

1159. and 1160. Alice J. Day, *Family Group Sheet*; and Muno - Thayer, *Family Group Sheet*.

1161. and 1162. Muno - Thayer, *Family Group Sheet*.

1163. *Register*, 97:389.

1164. and 1165. Wm. R. Hunter, *Family Group Sheet*.

1166. and 1167. Stevens to Whipple, *3 Letters, 1992 & 1996*.

1168. through 1185. Larj to Whipple, *3 letters in 1991, 1 in 1997*.

1186. *Register*, 112:143.

1187. through 1196. Anderson to Whipple, *Letter, 02-3-1993*.

1197. Sources for information on the Zacheus Hale family include: *U.S. New Hampshire census for 1800, 1810, and 1820*; the N.H. Bureau of Vital Records; *Dunstable, N.H. Births, Deaths, and Marriages*; *Seven Generations of the Descendants of Agvila and Thomas Chase*, by Joan Carroll Chase and G.W. Chamberlain; and *Agvila Chase and His Descendants*, by John C. Chase and G. W. Chamberlain.

1198. through 1204. Smalley - Seyfarth, *Family Group Sheet*.

1205. through 107. Anderson to Whipple, *Letter, 02-3-1993*.

1208. through 1215. Ibid., The following are cited as sources: *Andover, Mass. Vital Records*; *Danville, Vt. Vital Records*; U.S. Vermont Census for 1800 and 1810; U.S. N.Y. Census for Jefferson Co., for 1820, 1830, 1840, and *1850*; *U.S. Illinois Census for Kane Co. for 1850, 1860, 1870, and 1880*; *Past and Present Kane County, Illinois*, by H. B. Peirce (1878); and the St. Charles, Ill. *Chronicle*.

1216. and 1217. Esson to Whipple, *Letters, Jan. 1992 & Nov. 1996*.

1218. through 1227. Stevens to Whipple, *2 Letters*.

1228. and 1229. *Register*, 92;184-85.

1230. through 1234. Grant Dodge Whipple, *Family Group Sheet*.

1235. Ibid.; and Dwane W. Norris, comp., *The Whipple Family Tree Through Matthew Whipple of Bocking, England Family. Captain John Whipple of England Family and Other Whipple Families* (Jackson, Mich.: Dwane V. Norris, 4540 Hendee Rd., 1993), (Hereafter cited as D.W. Norris, *Whipple Family Tree*).

1236. Petty to Jones, *Research Project*; and Ipswich Births, *Vital Records*.

1237. Petty to Jones, *Research Project*.

1238. through 1241. *Vital Records of Danvers Massachusetts to the end of the year 1849*. (The Essex Institute, Salem, MA, 1909), (Hereafter cited as Danvers, MA, *Vital Records*).

1242. *Register*, 53:376; 91:341.

1243. Harold Blodgett, "Robert Traill Spence Lowell," *The New England Quarterly* 16 (December 1943): 578-91 (Hereafter cited as Robt. T.S. Lowell, Harold Blodgett).

1244. through 1252. Billerica, MA, *History*, Genealogical Register, 58-9.

1253. through 1256. *Register*, 10:356.

1257. Ibid., 102:162.

1258. through 1262.Whipple-Lane, *Family Group Sheet.*

1263. through 1269. Billerica, MA, *History*, Genealogical Register, 70, 71, 72.

1270. and 1271. Martin to Whipple, *E-mail 16 May 1999.*

1272. and 1273. Fiske to Whipple, *E-mail 30 Jan. 1999.*

1274. *Register*, 106:224-5.

1275. Ibid., 106:225.

1276. J.G. Bartlett, 203; *Vital Records, Worcester Co., MA*, Boylston births, 54; and Ibid., Northborough marriages, 119.

1277. Lancaster, Mass. *Vital Record*, 2 31.

1278. Grant Dodge Whipple, *Family Group Sheet*; and Priscilla Ann Hanners-Vernon LeRoy Nelms Family Group Sheet, supplied 1 May 2000 by Priscilla Ann (Hanners- Nelms) Johnson, 1160 S. Eaton Ct., Denver, CO 80232. (Hereafter cited as Hanners- Nelms, *Family Group Sheet*).

1279. through 1281. Alonzo Lyman Whipple-Abbie N. Kenney Family Group Sheet, supplied 1 May 2000 by Asenath Hanners Torsey, 14 Lincoln St., Beverly, Mass 01915-1126. This sheet lists generic references to vital records, marriage and death certificates, Civil War Pension affidavits, and family letters. (Hereafter cited as Kenney - Whipple, *Family Group Sheet*).

1282. through 1286. Pratt to Whipple, *Letter, 5 Feb. 1999.*

1287. through 1293. Bacon to Whipple, *Letter 12-04-1991.*

1294. and 1295. Wise to Whipple, *3 Letters.*

1296. *Register*, 95:347.

1297. McMahon to Whipple, *3 Letters.*

1298. Ibid.

1299. and 1300. David Goddard-Czarina White Pedigree Sheet, supplied 15 May 1998 to Weldon Whipple, web master, www.whipple.org by Michael Dobson, E-mail: dobfam4@juno.com;. The pedigree is from the *International Genealogical Index* and cites no documentation (Hereafter cited as White- Goddard, *Pedigree Sheet*).

1301. and 1302. Wolfe to Whipple, *Letters, 2-7 & 3-24-1994.*

1303. through 1309. Richardson - Woodward, *Pedigree Sheet.*

1310 through 1334.Jenne to Whipple, *Letters, 5 Sept. 1992 and 22 & 24 July 1997.*

1335. Pavia to Whipple, *E-mail 14 June 1999.*

1336. and 1337. Hancock to Whipple, *Letters, 10-28-1993 & 02-07-1997.*

1338. and 1339. Patch to Whipple, *3 Letters.*

1340. Pratt to Whipple, *Letter, 5 Feb. 1999.*

1341. through 1345. Ball to Whipple, *Letters, 2 & 11 Feb. 1999.*

1346. through 1349. J. Jones to Wh, *Letters 1991, 1993 & 1997.*

1350. through 1352. Starr, *Starr Genealogy.*

1353. through 1357. Westensee to Whipple, *Letters 1991 & 1992.*

1358. Pettit, *Letter 7 Jan. 1990.*

1359. and 1360. Woodworth to Whipple, *3 Letters.*

1361. and 1362. Harrison to Whipple, *Letter, 12-5-1991 & 01-14-1997.*

1363. through 1374. Billigmeier to Whipple, *2 Letters 1992.*

1375. through 1378. Gaber to Whipple, *Letters, Jan. 1998.*

1379. through 1381. Brown to Whipple, *1 Jan. 1992.*

1382. *Utah Magazine*, "Brigham Young," July 1929:97-114.

1383. International Society Daughters of Utah Pioneers., *Pioneer Women of Faith and Fortitude, S to Z* (Salt Lake City, Utah: Publishers Press, 1998), 4:3506 (Hereafter cited as Pioneer Women, *of Utah*).

1384. Ibid., 4:3514-15.

1385. *Pioneer Women of Utah* 3414-15.

1386. and 1387. Ibid., 4:3519-29.

1388. through 1398. *Pioneer Women of Utah*, 4:3506.

1399. and 1400. Ibid., 4:3514.

1401. and 1402. Ibid., 4:3519.
1403. Utah Magazine, *Brigham Young*, July 1929:97-114.
1404. and 1405. *Pioneer Women, of* Utah 4:3517-18.
1406. through 1414. Ibid., 4:3517.
1415. *Utah Magazine* "Brigham Young," April 1920:52.
1416. Leonard J. Arrington, *Brigham Young: American Moses.* Urbana and Chicago: U. of Illinois Press, 1986, 421.
1417. *Utah Magazine* "Brigham Young," April 1920: 49-50.
1418. Ibid., April 1920:52; Brigham Young, *Family Group Record*; Register, 587:211- 233; and *Pioneer Women of Utah* 4:3513.
1419. *Utah Magazine*, "Brigham Young," April 1920:53.
1420. *Pioneer Women of Utah* 3507-8.
1421. Ibid., April 1920:54.
1422. through 1424. Brigham Young, *Family Group Record.*
1425. *Pioneer Women of Utah* 3498.
1426. Brigham Young, *Family Group Record.*
1427. *Pioneer Women of Utah* 3503.
1428. Ibid.; and *Utah Magazine* "Brigham Young," April 1920:54.
1429. Ibid.
1430. *Utah Magazine* "Brigham Young," July 1920:130; and Brigham Young, *Family Group Record.*
1431. *Pioneer Women of Utah* 3520-21.
1432. Brigham Young, *Family Group Record.*
1433. *Utah Magazine* "Brigham Young," July 1920:130-1.
1434. *Pioneer Women of Utah* 3512.
1435. Brigham Young, *Family Group Record.*
1436. *Utah Magazine* "Brigham Young," July 1920:131; and Brigham Young, *Family Group Record.*
1437. *Utah Magazine* "Brigham Young," July 1920:131.
1438. Brigham Young, *Family Group Record.*
1439. *Pioneer Women of Utah* 3502.
1440. *Utah Magazine* "Brigham Young," July 1920:130.
1441. Ibid., July 1920:131.
1442. Brigham Young, *Family Group Record.*
1443. *Utah Magazine* "Brigham Young," July 1920:132.
1444. *Register*, 587:217-18, 221-23.
1445. and 1446. Brigham Young, *Family Group Record.*
1447. *Utah Magazine* "Brigham Young," July 1920:131.
1448. and 1449. Brigham Young, *Family Group Record.*
1450. and 1451. *Pioneer Women of Utah* 3516-17.
1452. *Utah Magazine* "Brigham Young," July 1920:132.
1453. *Pioneer Women of Utah* 3508-9.
1454. Ibid., July 1920:132.
1455 Arrington, 421.
1456. *Utah Magazine* "Brigham Young," July 1920:133.
1457. *Pioneer Women of Utah* 3499-3500.
1458. Ibid., July 1920:133.
1459. and 1460. Brigham Young, *Family Group Record.*
1461. *Utah Magazine* "Brigham Young," July 1920:133.
1462. Ibid., July 1920:133; and Brigham Young, *Family Group Record.*
1463. *Pioneer Women of Utah* 3503-4.
1464. *Utah Magazine* "Brigham Young," July 1920:133.

1465. Ibid., July 1920:134.

1466. Arrington, 421.

1467. Brigham Young, *Family Group Record*.

1468. Susa Young Gates and Mabel Young Sanborn, "Brigham Young Genealogy," *The Utah Genealogical and Historical Magazine*, vol. XI, April 1920, 49-50. [Hereafter *Utah Genealogical Magazine*].

1469. *Utah Magazine* "Brigham Young," April 1920:52.

1470. Ibid., April 1920:52; and Brigham Young, *Family Group Record*.

1471. *Utah Magazine* "Brigham Young," April 1920:53; and Brigham Young, *Family Group Record*.

1472. *Utah Magazine* "Brigham Young," July 1920:133-4.

1473. Ibid., April 1920:53; and Brigham Young, *Family Group Record*.

1474. and 1475. Utah Magazine, *Brigham Young*, April 1920:53.

1476. Brigham Young, *Family Group Record*.

1477. *Utah Magazine* "Brigham Young," April 1920:53.

1478. Ibid., July 1920:127; and Brigham Young, *Family Group Record*.

1479. Brigham Young, *Family Group Record*.

1480. *Utah Magazine* "Brigham Young," July 1920:129.

1481. Brigham Young, *Family Group Record*.

1482. *Utah Magazine* "Brigham Young," April 1920:55.

1483. Brigham Young, *Family Group Record*.

1484. and 1485. *Utah Magazine* "Brigham Young," July 1920:129.

1486. Brigham Young, *Family Group Record*.

1487. *Utah Magazine* "Brigham Young," July 1920:130.

1488. Brigham Young, *Family Group Record*.

1489. *Utah Magazine* "Brigham Young," July 1920:130.

1490. Brigham Young, *Family Group Record*.

1491. *Utah Magazine* "Brigham Young," July 1920:130.

1492. Brigham Young, *Family Group Record*.

1493. and 1494. *Utah Magazine* "Brigham Young," July 1920:130.

1495. through 1498. Ibid., April 1920:54-5.

1499. Ibid., April 1920:54; and Brigham Young, *Family Group Record*.

1500. Brigham Young, *Family Group Record*.

1501. and 1502. *Utah Magazine* "Brigham Young," April 1920:54.

1503. Brigham Young, *Family Group Record*.

1504. *Utah Magazine* "Brigham Young," April 1920:54.

1505. Brigham Young, *Family Group Record*.

1506. *Utah Magazine* "Brigham Young," July 1920:133.

1507. Ibid., July 1920:130-1.

1508. Ibid., July 1920:133.

1509. Brown to Whipple, *1 Jan. 1992*.

1510. *Utah Magazine* "Brigham Young," October 1920:177-80.

1511. Ibid., October 1920:178.

1512. Brigham Young, *Family Group Record*.

1513. *Pioneer Women of Utah* 3505.

1514. through 1516. *Utah Magazine* "Brigham Young," October 1920:179.

1517. For a biography of Lorenzo See James A. Little, "Biography of Lorenzo Dow Young," *Utah Historical Quarterly*, 14, 1946.

1518. through 1528. *Utah Magazine* "Brigham Young," October 1920:178-79.

1529. *Pioneer Women of Utah* 3505.

1530. through 1540. *Utah Magazine*, "Brigham Young," October 1920:179-80.

1541. through 1548. J.G. Bartlett.

1549. and 1550. *Register*, 95:179-80.

1551. through 1559. Bakke - Whipple, *Family Group Sheet*.

1560. and 1561. Wilde to Whipple, *Letters 04/ 10 & 22/ 1997*.

1562. *Register*, 60:192; and *Vital Records, Worcester Co., MA*, Oxford births, 109; Oxford marriages, 131.

1563. Clara Barton, *The Story of My Childhood* (New York: The Baker & Taylor Co., 1907. Reprint by Arno Press, A New York Times Company. New York, 1980), 17-22, 57-64, 92, 109-10 (Hereafter cited as Clara Barton, *My Childhood*); and *Vital Records, Worcester Co., MA*, Oxford births, 16.

1564. *Vital Records, Worcester Co., MA*, Oxford births, 15; deaths, 269.

1565. Clara Barton, *My Childhood*, 17-20, 79-87. Dr. Samuel Thompson was the first American doctor to advance the theory that fever was not the foe, but the friend of the patient. He reasoned that drawing blood would not purify the remaining blood and that creating blisters — which was supposed to soothe a nervous patient to sleep or reduce pain — caused greater pain. He created "Thompson's Steam Box" and soon generated a following of young doctors. Most older doctors opposed Thompson's cure. Clara said it was fortunate David and her father were willing to try the treatment.; and *Vital Records, Worcester Co., MA*, Oxford births, 15; Marriages, 131.

1566. *Vital Records, Worcester Co., MA*, Oxford births, 16.

1567. Clara Barton, *My Childhood*, 12, 23, 27-8, 96-99, 112; and *Vital Records, Worcester Co., MA*, Oxford births, 15.

1568. A poem in 10 books first published in Edinburgh, Scotland in 1827 with 24 or more editions published by 1863. It can be purchased today for approximately ƒ150.

1569. through 1603. *Register*, 60:297-98.

1604. Ibid., 60:298 and *Essex Co., Mass. Vital Records*, Ipswich births, 84.

1605. Ibid., 60:298 and Ipswich births, 82.

1606. Ibid., 60:298 and Ipswich births, 83.

1607. Ibid., 60:298 and Ipswich births, 84.

1608. Ibid., 60:298 and Ipswich births, 85.

1609. Ibid., 60:298 and Ipswich births, 83.

1610. and 1611. Ibid., 60:298 and Ipswich births, 84.

1612. through 1614. Ibid., 60:298 and Ipswich births, 85.

1615. through 1622. *Register.*, 60:298.

1623. Ibid., 60:298 and *Essex Co., Mass. Vital Records*, Ipswich births 368..

1624. Ibid., 60:298 and Ipswich births, 369.

1625. Ibid., 60:298 and Ipswich births, 368.

1626. Ibid., 60:298 and Ipswich births, 370.

1627. Ibid., 60:298 and Ipswich births, 369.

1628. Ibid., 60:298.

1629. and 1630. Ibid., 60:298 and Ipswich births, 368.

1631. through 1637. *Register*, 60:298.

1638. through 1644. Wilson to Whipple, *Letters, June 1996 & 1967*.

1645. through 1686. Riggs to Whipple, *Letter 22 July 1998*.

1687. and 1688. McMahon to Whipple, *3 Letters*.

1689. and 1690. Muno - Thayer, *Family Group Sheet*.

1691. and 1692. Alice J. Day, *Family Group Sheet*.

1693. *Register*, 97:389.

1694. through 1696. Wm. R. Hunter, *Family Group Sheet*.

1697. and 1698. Stevens to Whipple, *3 Letters, 1992 & 1996*.

1699. through 1706. J.G. Bartlett.

1707. *Register*, 112:143.

1708. through 1721. Anderson to Whipple, *Letter, 02-3-1993*.

1722. through 1728. Charles J. Sherman to Blaine Whipple. (2000). Sources: *New Hampshire Vital Records: Dunstable Births, Deaths, and Marriages; Town Records of E. Bridgewater, Mass; History of Early Settlement of Bridgewater in Plymouth County*, by Nahum Mitchell; *Descendants of Cornet Robert*

Stetson; 1830 U.S. Census for Riley, Oxford, Co., Maine; and 1855 and 1865 Massachusetts State Census.). (Hereafter cited as Sherman to Whipple, *Letter*).

1729. through 1732. Smalley - Seyfarth, *Family Group Sheet.*

1733. through 1777. Anderson to Whipple, letter, 02-03-1993. Sources: *Washington Co., Ohio Marriage Records,* 2:279; *Genealogy of the Hibbard Family,* by Augusting Hibbard; *History of Marietta and Washington County, Ohio and Representative Citizens,* by M. Andrews; *Athens County, Ohio Land and Property Index 1790-1866; Athens County, Ohio Probate Court Journal 1858-1870; Athens County, Ohio Marriage Records 1822-1866; History of Athens County, Ohio* by C. M. Walker (1869); *1860 and 1870 U.S. Census of Belpre, Washington Co., Ohio; 1860 U.S. Census of Ames, Athens Co., Ohio; 1880 U.S. Census of Cherokee Co., Kansas; Past and Present Kane County, Illinois,* by H. B. Peirce (1878); petition for probate of Aaron Blanchard; obituary for A. Blanchard; death certificate for Aaron Blanchard; death certificate for Charles L. Blanchard; "Proof of Heirship" of the estate of Gustavus B. Blanchard; "Biography of David M. Hagedon" in *History of St. Clair County, Michigan,* A.T. Andreas & Co., Chicago 1883, 306; obituary of David M. Hagedon and Datus Hagedon, *Times Herald,* Port Huron, Mich., 28 Dec. 1871; obituary of Sophia Hagedon, *Ibid,* 8 May 1899; *Michigan Pioneer and Historical Collection,* 2:114; *St. Clair County, Michigan Death Records,* 1:65-6, 2:264, and 3:194; *Lakeside Cemetery Records,* comp. by the St. Clair County Family History Group; *St Clair County Marriage Records,* 1:442, 629, 2:313, and 3:25; *1830 U.S. Census for Penfield, Monroe Co., N.Y.; 1840 U.S. Census for Port Huron, St. Clair Co., Mich.,* 240 and 1850, 190R.

1778. and 1779. Esson to Whipple, *Letters, Jan. 1992 & Nov. 1996.*

1779. Ibid.

1780. through 1788. Stevens to Whipple, *2 Letters.*

1789. through 1793. *Register,* 92:184-86.

1794. through 1797. Grant Dodge Whipple, *Family Group Sheet.*

1798. Ibid.; and Hanners-Nelms, *Family Group Sheet.*

1799. Lancaster, Mass *Vital Records,* 231.

1800. J.G. Bartlett, 203; *Vital Records, Worcester Co., MA,* Boylston births, 54; and *Vital Records, Worcester Co., MA,* Northborough marriages, 119.

1801. through 1803. Kenney - Whipple, *Family Group Sheet.*

1804. Danvers, MA, *Vital Records;* Petty to Jones, *Research Project;* and Proctor Patterson Jones to Blaine Whipple. letter dated 21 May 1991 & 16 Feb. 1997 at 3625 Sacramento St., San Francisco, CA 94118-1914. in possession of Whipple at 236 NW Sundown Way, Portland, OR 97229 (2000). (Hereafter cited as Jones to Whipple, *Letter 05/21/1991 & 01/16/1997*).

1805. Jones to Whipple, *Letter 05/21/1991 & 01/16/1997;* and Petty to Jones, *Research Project.*

1806. *Register,* 46:92; and *Cambridge History of American Literature,* (New York: the Macmillian Company, 1918), 2:245-57 (Hereafter cited as History, *American Literature*).

1807. *Register,* 93:253.

1808. Ibid., 74:103.

1809, *The Critic,* vol. 19, July-Dec. 1891. No. 399, 22 August, 92-99; No. 403, 19 September, 144-45; No. 400, 10 October, 189-90.

1810. Ibid., 93:255.

1811. Ibid., 93:257.

1812. through 1815. Billerica, MA, *History,* Genealogical Register, 59-73.

1816. through 1823. *Register,* 10:356.

1824. Ibid., 102:162.

1825. through 1828. Whipple-Lane, *Family Group Sheet.*

1829. through 1838. Billerica, MA, *History,* Genealogical Register, 71-72.

1839. and 1840. Martin to Whipple, *E-mail 16 May 1999.*

1841. and 1842. Fiske to Whipple, *E-mail 30 Jan. 1999.*

1843. and 1844. Register, 106:225.

1845. through 1849. Kenney - Whipple, *Family Group Sheet.*

1850. and 1851. Pratt to Whipple, *Letter, 5 Feb. 1999.*

1852. through 1866. Bureau Co., Ill. Cemetery Records, 119-120.

1867. through 1891. Bacon to Whipple, *Letter 12-04-1991.*

1892. and 1893. Wise to Whipple, *3 Letters.*

1894. and 1895. *Register*, 95:347.

1896. and 1897. McMahon to Whipple, *3 Letters.*

1898. and 1899. White - Goddard, *Pedigree Sheet.*

1900. Wolfe to Whipple, *Letters, 2-7 & 3-24-1994.*

1901. through 1920. Jenne to Whipple, *Letters, 5 Sept. 1992 and 22 & 24 July 1997.*

1921. Pavia to Whipple, *E-mail 14 June 1999.*

1922. and 1923. Hancock to Whipple, *Letters, 10-28-1993 & 02-07-1997.*

1924. and 1925. Patch to Whipple, *3 Letters.*

1926. Pratt to Whipple, *Letter, 5 Feb. 1999*; and Ibid.

1927. through 1932. Ball to Whipple, *Letters, 2 & 11 Feb. 1999.*

1933. through 1944. J. Jones to Wh, *Letters 1991, 1993 & 1997.*

1945. and 1946. Starr, *Starr Genealogy.*

1947. and 1948. Westensee to Whipple, *Letters 1991 & 1992.*

1949. 1850, *U.S. Census.*

1950. Westensee to Whipple, *Letters 1991 & 1992.*

1951. and 1952. Woodworth to Whipple, *3 Letters.*

1953. and 1954. Harrison to Whipple, *Letter, 12-5-1991 & 01-14-1997.*

1955. through 1960. Billigmeier to Whipple, *2 Letters 1992.*

1961. through 1972. Gaber to Whipple, *Letters, Jan. 1998.*

1973. and 1974. Brown to Whipple, *1 Jan. 1992.*

1975. *Utah Magazine,* "Brigham Young," April 11920:51; and Brigham Young, *Family Group Record.*

1976. through 1985. *Utah Magazine,* "Brigham Young," April 1920:51.

1986. Ibid., April 1920:52; and Brigham Young, *Family Group Record.*

1987. through 1989. *Utah Magazine,* "Brigham Young," April 1920:52.

1990. Ibid., April 1920:53; and Brigham Young, *Family Group Record.*

1991. through 2000. *Utah Magazine,* "Brigham Young, "April 1920:52-53.

2001. Brigham Young, *Family Group Record.*

2002. and 2003. *Utah Magazine,* "Brigham Young,", April 1920:53.

2004. Ibid., July 1920:127; and Brigham Young, *Family Group Record.*

2005. *Utah Magazine,* "Brigham Young,", July 1920:127-8.

2006. Ibid., July 1920:128.

2007. Brigham Young, *Family Group Record.*

2008. through 2011. *Utah Magazine,* "Brigham Young," July 1920:128.

2012. Ibid., July 1920:128-9; and Brigham Young, *Family Group Record.*

2013. through 2019 *Utah Magazine,* "Brigham Young," July 1920:129.

2020. Ibid., April 1920:55.

2021. through 2025. Ibid., July 1920:129.

2026. through 2029. Ibid., April 1920:55.

2030. Brigham Young, *Family Group Record.*

2031. and 2032. *Utah Magazine,* "Brigham Young,", April 1920:55.

2033. Brigham Young, *Family Group Record.*

2034. through 2038. *Utah Magazine,* "Brigham Young," April 1920:55.

2039. through 2044. Ibid., July 1920:129.

2045. through 2050. Ibid., July 1920:130.

2051. and 2052. Ibid., April 1920:54.

2053. through 2056. Ibid., July 1920:131.

2057. and 2058. Ibid., July 1920:130.

2059. Ibid., July 1920:130; and *Pioneer Women of Utah.*

2060. *Pioneer Women of Utah* 3511-12.

2061. *Utah Magazine,* "Brigham Young," July 1920:132; and Brigham Young, *Family Group Record.*

2062. through 2064. Ibid, July 1920:54

2065. Brigham Young, *Family Group Record.*

2066. through 2075. *Utah Magazine,* "Brigham Young," July 1920:132-33.

2076. Ibid., July 1920:133; and Brigham Young, *Family Group Record.*

2077. through 2079. *Utah Magazine,* "Brigham Young," July 1920:133.

2080. Ibid., July 1920:133-4; and Brown to Whipple, *1 Jan. 1992.*

2081. through 2087. *Utah Magazine,* "Brigham Young," July 1920:133-4.

2088. through 2100. Ibid., October 1920:178-79.

2101. and 2102. J.G. Bartlett.

2103. Larj to Whipple, *3 letters in 1991, 1 in 1997.*

2104. J.G. Bartlett.

2105. through 2110. *Register,* 95:179-80.

2111. through 2113. Bakke - Whipple, *Family Group Sheet.*

2114. and 2115. Wilde to Whipple, *Letters 04/ 10 & 22/ 1997.*

2116. *Vital Records, Worcester Co., MA,* Oxford births, 16; marriages, 225.

2117. Ibid., Oxford births, 96.

2118. Ibid., Oxford Deaths: 269.

2119. Ibid., Oxford births, 16.

2120. Ibid., Oxford births, 15; deaths, 269.

2121. through 2143. Wilson to Whipple, *Letters, June 1996 & 1967.*

2144. through 2170. Riggs to Whipple, *Letter 22 July 1998.*

2171. and 2172. McMahon to Whipple, *3 Letters.*

2173. and 2174, Muno - Thayer, *Family Group Sheet.*

2175. and 2176. Alice J. Day, *Family Group Sheet.*

2177. *Register,* 97:389.

2178. and 2179. Wm. R. Hunter, *Family Group Sheet.*

2180. Stevens to Whipple, *3 Letters, 1992 & 1996.*

2181. Stevens, *Family Group Sheet.*

2182. and 2183. *Register,* 112:143.

2184. Anderson to Whipple, *Letter, 02-3-1993.*

2185. through 2187. Sherman to Whipple, *Letter.*

2188. through 2190. Smalley - Seyfarth, *Family Group Sheet.*

2191. Anderson to Whipple, *Letter, 02-3-1993.*

2192. through 2198. Ibid., Sources: Blanchard family *Bible*; 1850, 1870, and *1880 U.S. Illinois Census*; Blanchard pension record; administration of Geo. A. Blanchard estate; cemetery records; *Past and Present Kane County, Illinois,* by H.B. Peirce (1878)..

2199. through 2203. Esson to Whipple, *Letters, Jan. 1992 & Nov. 1996.*

2204. through 2207. Stevens to Whipple, *2 Letters.*

2208. through 2210. Grant Dodge Whipple, *Family Group Sheet.*

2211. and 2112. Richard W. Ahrens to Blaine Whipple. Letter dated 25 May 1990 at 4235 Norton Ave., Oakland, CA 94602. In possession of Whipple at 236 NW Sundown Way, Portland, OR 97229-6575 (1998). (Hereafter cited as Ahrens to Whipple, *Letter, 25 May 1990*).

2213. and 2114. Jones to Whipple, *Letter 05/21/1991 & 01/16/1997.*

2215. through 2218. *Register,* 102:161-162.

2219. through 2221. Whipple-Lane, *Family Group Sheet.*

2222. through 2224. Martin to Whipple, *E-mail 16 May 1999.*

2225. and 2226. Fiske to Whipple, *E-mail 30 Jan. 1999.*

2227. through 2230. *Register,* 106:224-25.

2231. Kenney - Whipple, *Family Group Sheet*; and Hanners-Nelms, *Family Group Sheet.*

2232. Kenney - Whipple, *Family Group Sheet.*

2233. through 2260. Pratt to Whipple, *Letter, 5 Feb. 1999.*

2261. through 2278. Bacon to Whipple, *Letter 12-04-1991.*

2279. and 2280. Wise to Whipple, *3 Letters.*

2281. through 2284. *Register,* 95:347-48.

2285. and 2286. McMahon to Whipple, *3 Letters.*

2287. White - Goddard, *Pedigree Sheet.*

2288. through 2290. Wolfe to Whipple, *Letters, 2-7 & 3-24-1994.*

2291. through 2305. Jenne to Whipple, *Letters, 5 Sept. 1992 and 22 & 24 July 1997.*

2306. Pavia to Whipple, *E-mail 14 June 1999.*

2307. and 2308. Hancock to Whipple, *Letters, 10-28-1993 & 02-07-1997.*

2309. through 2311. Patch to Whipple, *3 Letters.*

2312. through 2314. *Burke's Presidential Families of the United States of America* (London: Burke's Peerage Limited, First Edition, 1975) (Hereafter cited as Burke's, *Presidential Families*), 472-73

2315. through 2341. Ball to Whipple, *Letters, 2 & 11 Feb. 1999.*

2342. through 2355. J. Jones to Wh, *Letters 1991, 1993 & 1997.*

2356. and 2357, Andrews to Whipple, *Letters 1992 & 1997.*

2358. through 2363. Westensee to Whipple, *Letters 1991 & 1992.*

2364. Pettit, *Letter 7 Jan. 1990.*

2365. and 2366. Woodworth to Whipple, *3 Letters.*

2367. and 2368. Harrison to Whipple, *Letter, 12-5-1991 & 01-14-1997.*

2369. through 2373. Billigmeier to Whipple, *2 Letters 1992.*

2374. through 2381. Gaber to Whipple, *Letters, Jan. 1998.*

2382. through 2384. Brown to Whipple, *1 Jan. 1992.*

2385. through 2415. *Utah Magazine,* "Brigham Young," April 1920:51.

2416. Ibid., May 1920:51.

2417. through 2457. Ibid., April 1920:51-55.

2458. through 2462. Ibid., July 1920:129.

2463. through 2539. Ibid., April 1920:52-55..

2540. Ibid., July 1920:127.

2541. Dick Harmon, *Steve Young: Staying in the Pocket* (Salt Lake City: Black Moon Publishing, 1995), 13 (Hereafter cited as Harmon, *Steve Young*).

2542. through 2589. *Utah Magazine,* "Brigham Young," July 1920:127.

2590. through 2605. Ibid., April 1920:55.

2606. through 2630. Ibid., July 1920:131.

2631. through 2678. Ibid., July 1920:128.

2679. through 2692. Ibid., April 1920:54.

2693. through 2707. Ibid., July 1920:132.

2708. through 2721. Ibid., April 1920:55.

2722. through 2724. Ibid., July 1920:130.

2725. through 2744. Ibid., July 1920:132.

2745. through 2767. Ibid., July 1920: 129.

2768. through 2776. Ibid., April 1920:53.

2777. through 2783. Ibid., July 1920:130.

2784. through 2791. Ibid., July 1920:133.

2792. through 2833. Ibid., October 1920:178.

2834. Larj to Whipple, *3 letters in 1991, 1 in 1997.*

2835. J.G. Bartlett.

2836. Larj to Whipple, *3 letters in 1991, 1 in 1997.*

2837. Ibid.

2838. J.G. Bartlett.

2839. Larj to Whipple, *3 letters in 1991, 1 in 1997.*

2840. through 2844. J.G. Bartlett.

2845. Bakke - Whipple, *Family Group Sheet.*

2846. Ibid.

2847. Wilde to Whipple, *Letters 04/ 10 & 22/ 1997.*

2848. Ibid.

2849. through 2857. Wilson to Whipple, *Letters, June 1996 & 1967.*

2858. through 2881. Riggs to Whipple, *Letter 22 July 1998.*

2882. and 2883. McMahon to Whipple, *3 Letters.*

2884. and 2885. Muno - Thayer, *Family Group Sheet.*

2886. and 2887. Alice J. Day, *Family Group Sheet.*

2888. through 2890. *Register*, 97:389.

2891. and 2892. Wm. R. Hunter, *Family Group Sheet.*

2893. and 2894. Stevens to Whipple, *3 Letters, 1992 & 1996.*

2895. *Register*, 112:143.

2896. Ibid., 77:270-304; 112:143.

2897. *Register*, 112:143.

2898. Burke's, *Presidential Families*, 473.

2899. and 2900. Sherman to Whipple, *Letter*, Sources: Certificate of marriage and Charles Herbert Sherman's Will probated in Plymouth Co., Mass. in 1933.

2901. and 2902. Smalley - Seyfarth, *Family Group Sheet.*

2903. Anderson to Whipple, *Letter, 02-3-1993.*

2904. and 2905. Ibid., Sources: Family *Bible*, L.G. Pullen obituary, divorce decree, and death certificates.

2906. Anderson to Whipple Letter, 02-3-1993.

2907. through 2910. Esson to Whipple, *Letters, Jan. 1992 & Nov. 1996.*

2911. through 2913. Stevens to Whipple, *2 Letters.*

2914. through 2929. Grant Dodge Whipple, *Family Group Sheet.*

2930. and 2931. Ahrens to Whipple, *Letter, 25 May 1990.*

2932. through 1934. Jones to Whipple, *Letter 05/21/1991 & 01/16/1997.*

2935. and 2936. Whipple-Lane, *Family Group Sheet.*

2937. and 2938. Fiske to Whipple, *E-mail 30 Jan. 1999.*

2939. and 2940. Kenney - Whipple, *Family Group Sheet.*

2941. and 2942. Kenney - Whipple, *Family Group Sheet.* and Hanners-Nelms, *Family Group Sheet.*

2943. Kenney - Whipple, *Family Group Sheet.*

2944. Ibid.; and Hanners-Nelms, *Family Group Sheet.*

2945. Kenney - Whipple, *Family Group Sheet.*

2946. Ibid.; and Hanners-Nelms, *Family Group Sheet.*

2947. and 2948. Kenney - Whipple, *Family Group Sheet.*

2949. through 2964. Pratt to Whipple, *Letter, 5 Feb. 1999.*

2965. through 2980. Bacon to Whipple, *Letter 12-04-1991.*

2981. and 2982. Wise to Whipple, *3 Letters.*

2983. White - Goddard, *Pedigree Sheet.*

2984. "Robert Goddard," http://www.top-biography.com/9 131- Robert%20Goddard/life.htm and "Rocket Scientist Robert Goddard. He launched the space age with a 10-ft. rocket in a New England cabbage field." http://www.time.com/time/time1 00/scientist/profile/goddard.html

2985. through 2989. Wolfe to Whipple, *Letters, 2-7 & 3-24-1994.*

2990. through 3003. Jenne to Whipple, *Letters, 5 Sept. 1992 and 22 & 24 July 1997.*

3004. Pavia to Whipple, *E-mail 14 June 1999.*

3005. Hannah Hart entry, 1860 U.S. census, Population Schedule (county-level copy), Walworth County, Wisconsin, Village of Elkhorn, dwelling 46, family 60, (National Archives, Laguna

Niguel, Calif. (Hereafter cited as Hannah Chamberlain, *1860 US Census*).

3006. Hancock to Whipple, *Letters, 10-28-1993 & 02-07-1997*.

3007. and 3008. Patch to Whipple, *3 Letters*.

3009. *Register*, 77:270-304; 112:143.

3010. Burke's, *Presidential Families*, 473.

3011. through 3014. Ball to Whipple, *Letters, 2 & 11 Feb. 1999*.

3015. through 3028. J. Jones to Wh, *Letters 1991, 1993 & 1997*.

3029. through 3031. Andrews to Whipple, *Letters 1992 & 1997*.

3032. through 3034. Westensee to Whipple, *Letters 1991 & 1992*.

3035. and 3036. Pettit, *Letter 7 Jan. 1990*.

3037. and 3038. Woodworth to Whipple, *3 Letters*.

3039. and 3040. Harrison to Whipple, *Letter, 12-5-1991 & 01-14-1997*.

3041. through 3046. Billigmeier to Whipple, *2 Letters 1992*.

3047. through 3069. Gaber to Whipple, *Letters, Jan. 1998*.

3070. through 3072. Brown to Whipple, *1 Jan. 1992*.

3073. Harmon, *Steve Young*, 13.

3074. through 3077. *Utah Magazine*, "Brigham Young," July 1920:128.

3078. and 3079. J.G. Bartlett.

3080. and 3081. Larj to Whipple, *3 letters in 1991, 1 in 1997*.

3082. through 3085. Bakke - Whipple, *Family Group Sheet*.

3086. through 3088. Wilde to Whipple, *Letters 04/ 10 & 22/ 1997*.

3089. through 3108. Wilson to Whipple, *Letters, June 1996 & 1967*.

3109. through 3165. Riggs to Whipple, *Letter 22 July 1998*.

3166. Andrew H. Ward, comp., *The Rice Family* (1858), (Hereafter cited as Rice Family, *Genealogy*).

3167. through 3192. Riggs to Whipple, *Letter 22 July 1998*.

3193. through 3197. McMahon to Whipple, *3 Letters*.

3198. and 3199. Muno - Thayer, *Family Group Sheet*.

3200. through 3202. Alice J. Day, *Family Group Sheet*.

3203. and 3204. Wm. R. Hunter, *Family Group Sheet*.

3205. and 3206. Stevens, *Family Group Sheet*.

3207. and 3208. Burke's, *Presidential Families*, 473.

3209. through 3214. Sherman to Whipple, *Letter*.

3215. through 3217. Smalley - Seyfarth, *Family Group Sheet*.

3218. Anderson to Whipple, *Letter, 02-3-1993*, Sources: *The History of Horstman Family*, by Kay Lawler, divorce papers, and a death certificate..

3219. and 3220. Esson to Whipple, *Letters, Jan. 1992 & Nov. 1996*.

3221. and 3222. Donald Boak Esson-Beverly Jean Nash family group sheet, supplied 15 January 1992 by Beverly (Nash) Esson, RR1, Box 580, Wells, ME 04090. This sheet does not cite documentation for the information furnished (Hereafter cited as Esson-Nash, *Family Group Sheet*).

3223. and 3224. Stevens to Whipple, *2 Letters*.

3225. through 3267. Grant Dodge Whipple, *Family Group Sheet*.

3268. and 3269. Family group sheet, supplied 28 July 1993 by Ward Deal Whipple, 1135 Lake Dr., Roswell, GA 30075.This sheet does not cite documentation (Hereafter cited as Ward D. Whipple, *Family Group Sheet*).

3270. through 3280. Grant Dodge Whipple, *Family Group Sheet*.

3281. Lyle M. Whipple to Blaine Whipple. letter dated 6 Feb. 1997 at 51291 Murray Hill Dr., Canton, MI 48187-1026. in possession of B. Whipple at 236 NW Sundown Way, Portland, OR 97229 (1997). (Hereafter cited as L.M. Whipple to B. Whipple, *Letter, 02- 06-1997*).

3282. Grant Dodge Whipple, *Family Group Sheet*; and C. David Whipple to Blaine Whipple. Letter dated 10 Feb. 1997 at 400 Scarritt Bldg., 818 Gand Ave., Kansas City, MO 64106. In possession of Whipple at 236 NW Sundown Way, Portland, OR 97229 (1997). (Hereafter cited as C.D.

Whipple to Whipple, *Letter, 02/10/1997*).

3283. and 3284. Grant Dodge Whipple, *Family Group Sheet.*

3285. and 3286. Ahrens to Whipple, *Letter, 25 May 1990.*

3287. Jones to Whipple, *Letter 05/21/1991 & 01/16/1997*; and Obituary of Proctor Patterson Jones, *The Chronicle*, San FrancisCo., Calif. (8 April 1999), (Hereafter cited as Proctor Jones Obit, *San Francisco Chronicle*).

3288. through 3291. Jones to Whipple, *Letter 05/21/1991 & 01/16/1997.*

3292. through 3294. Whipple-Lane, *Family Group Sheet.*

3295. through 3297. Fiske to Whipple, *E-mail 30 Jan. 1999.*

3298. Kenney - Whipple, *Family Group Sheet.*

3299. Ibid.; and Hanners-Nelms, *Family Group Sheet.*

3300. Kenney - Whipple, *Family Group Sheet.*

3301. through 3308. Ibid.; and Hanners-Nelms, *Family Group Sheet.*

3309. and 3310. Kenney - Whipple, *Family Group Sheet.*

3311. Hanners-Nelms, *Family Group Sheet.*

3312. through 3314. Kenney - Whipple, *Family Group Sheet.*

3315. Ibid.; and Hanners-Nelms, *Family Group Sheet.*

3316. Kenney - Whipple, *Family Group Sheet*; and Hanners-Nelms, *Family Group Sheet.*

3317. through 3337. Pratt to Whipple, *Letter, 5 Feb. 1999.*

3338. through 3382. Bacon to Whipple, *Letter 12-04-1991.*

3383. and 3384. Wise to Whipple, *3 Letters.*

3385. and 3386. Wolfe to Whipple, *Letters, 2-7 & 3-24-1994.*

3387. through 3426. Jenne to Whipple, *Letters, 5 Sept. 1992 and 22 & 24 July 1997.*

3427. Pavia to Whipple, *E-mail 14 June 1999.*

3428. and 3429. Hancock to Whipple, *Letters, 10-28-1993 & 02-07-1997.*

3430. through 3434. Patch to Whipple, *3 Letters.*

3435. through 3445. Ball to Whipple, *Letters, 2 & 11 Feb. 1999.*

3446. through 3450. J. Jones to Wh, *Letters 1991, 1993 & 1997.*

3451. and 3452. Andrews to Whipple, *Letters 1992 & 1997.*

3453. through 3456. Westensee to Whipple, *Letters 1991 & 1992.*

3457. through 3459. Woodworth to Whipple, *3 Letters.*

3460. and 3461. Harrison to Whipple, *Letter, 12-5-1991 & 01-14-1997.*

3462. Louise Jones Dubose, ed., *South Carolina Lives*, Historical Record Assn. Hopkinsville, Ky. 1963, 191.

3463. through 3465. Billigmeier to Whipple, *2 Letters 1992.*

3466. through 3485. Gaber to Whipple, *Letters, Jan. 1998.*

3486. through 3497. Brown to Whipple, *1 Jan. 1992.*

3498. Harmon, *Steve Young*, 13.

3499. through 3503. Laurey Livsey, *The Steve Young Story* (Rocklin, CA: Prima Publishing, 1996), 7 (Hereafter cited as Livsey, *Steve Young*).

3504. through 3514. Larj to Whipple, *3 letters in 1991, 1 in 1997.*

3515. through 3520. Bakke - Whipple, *Family Group Sheet.*

3521. through 3577. Wilson to Whipple, *Letters, June 1996 & 1967.*

3578. through 3595. Riggs to Whipple, *Letter 22 July 1998.*

3596. through 3615. McMahon to Whipple, *3 Letters.*

3616. through 3621. Muno - Thayer, *Family Group Sheet.*

3622. through 3633. Alice J. Day, *Family Group Sheet.*

3634. through 3639. Wm. R. Hunter, *Family Group Sheet.*

3640. Stevens to Whipple, *3 Letters, 1992 & 1996.*

3641. Stevens, *Family Group Sheet.*

3642. and 3643. Stevens to Whipple, *3 Letters, 1992 & 1996.*

3644. through 3649. Burke's, *Presidential Families*, 473.

3650. through 3653. Smalley - Seyfarth, *Family Group Sheet*.

3654. and 3655. Anderson to Whipple, *Letter, 02-3-1993*.

3656. through 3670. Stevens to Whipple, *2 Letters*.

3671. through 3759. Grant Dodge Whipple, *Family Group Sheet*.

3760. Ibid.; and Ward D. Whipple, *Family Group Sheet*.

3761. through 3805. Grant Dodge Whipple, *Family Group Sheet*.

3806. Ibid.; and C.D. Whipple to Whipple, *Letter, 02/10/1997*.

3807. through 3816. Grant Dodge Whipple, *Family Group Sheet*.

3817. through 3828. Jones to Whipple, *Letter 05/21/1991 & 01/16/1997*.

3829. through 3837. Whipple-Lane, *Family Group Sheet*.

3838. Kenney - Whipple, *Family Group Sheet*; and Hanners-Nelms, *Family Group Sheet*.

3839. and 3840. Hanners-Nelms, *Family Group Sheet*.

3841. and 3842. Kenney - Whipple, *Family Group Sheet*; and Hanners-Nelms, *Family Group Sheet*.

3843. Kenney - Whipple, *Family Group Sheet*.

3844. Ibid.; and Hanners-Nelms, *Family Group Sheet*.

3845. through 3847. Kenney - Whipple, *Family Group Sheet*; and Hanners-Nelms, *Family Group Sheet*.

3848. through 3850. Kenney - Whipple, *Family Group Sheet*.

3851. Ibid.; and Hanners-Nelms, *Family Group Sheet*.

3852. Kenney - Whipple, *Family Group Sheet*; and Hanners-Nelms, *Family Group Sheet*.

3853. Hanners-Nelms, *Family Group Sheet*.

3854. Kenney - Whipple, *Family Group Sheet*.

3855. Ibid.; and Hanners-Nelms, *Family Group Sheet*.

3856. Hanners-Nelms, *Family Group Sheet*.

3857. through 2859. Kenney - Whipple, *Family Group Sheet*.

3860. Ibid.; and Hanners-Nelms, *Family Group Sheet*.

3861. Kenney - Whipple, *Family Group Sheet*; and Hanners-Nelms, *Family Group Sheet*.

3862. and 3863. Kenney - Whipple, *Family Group Sheet*.

3864. Hanners-Nelms, *Family Group Sheet*.

3865. through 3912. Pratt to Whipple, *Letter, 5 Feb. 1999*.

3913. through 3941. Bacon to Whipple, *Letter 12-04-1991*.

3942. through 3948. Wise to Whipple, *3 Letters*.

3949. through 3951. Wolfe to Whipple, *Letters, 2-7 & 3-24-1994*.

3952. through 3955. Jenne to Whipple, *Letters, 5 Sept. 1992 and 22 & 24 July 1997*.

3956. and 3957, Pavia to Whipple, *E-mail 14 June 1999*.

3958. and 3959. Hancock to Whipple, *Letters, 10-28-1993 & 02-07-1997*.

3960. through 2967. Ball to Whipple, *Letters, 2 & 11 Feb. 1999*.

3968. through 3971. J. Jones to Wh, *Letters 1991, 1993 & 1997*.

3972. through 3982. Andrews to Whipple, *Letters 1992 & 1997*.

3983. through 3987. Westensee to Whipple, *Letters 1991 & 1992*.

3988. through 3991. Woodworth to Whipple, *3 Letters*.

3992. through 3997. Harrison to Whipple, *Letter, 12-5-1991 & 01-14-1997*.

3998. through 4120. Gaber to Whipple, *Letters, Jan. 1998*.

4121. through 4142. Larj to Whipple, *3 letters in 1991, 1 in 1997*.

4143. through 4146. Bakke - Whipple, *Family Group Sheet*.

4147. through 4258. Wilson to Whipple, *Letters, June 1996 & 1967*.

4259. through 4273. Riggs to Whipple, *Letter 22 July 1998*.

4274. through 4277. Alice J. Day, *Family Group Sheet*.

4278. Stevens to Whipple, *3 Letters, 1992 & 1996*.

4279. and 4280. Stevens, *Family Group Sheet*.

4281. through 4285. Stevens to Whipple, *3 Letters, 1992 & 1996*.

4286. through 4298. Anderson to Whipple, *Letter, 02-3-1993*.

4299. through 4371. Grant Dodge Whipple, *Family Group Sheet*.

4372. through 4374. Jones to Whipple, *Letter 05/21/1991 & 01/16/1997*.

4375. through 4377. Whipple-Lane, *Family Group Sheet*.

4378. through 4401. Pratt to Whipple, *Letter, 5 Feb. 1999*.

4402. Thomas Nelson Pratt to Blaine Whipple. e-mail dated 8 April 2001 at tnpratt@mediaone.net (mailing address: 427 N. Taylor Ave., Oak Park, Ill 60302-2419). in possession of Whipple at 236 NW Sundown Way, Portland, OR 97229-6575 (2001). (Hereafter cited as Pratt to Whipple, *e-mail 8 April 2001*).

4403. through 4427. Wise to Whipple, *3 Letters*.

4428. through 4430. Wolfe to Whipple, *Letters, 2-7 & 3-24-1994*.

4431. through 4435. Hancock to Whipple, *Letters, 10-28-1993 & 02-07-1997*.

4436. through 4452. J. Jones to Wh, *Letters 1991, 1993 & 1997*.

4453. through 4493. Gaber to Whipple, *Letters, Jan. 1998*.

4494. through 4506. Larj to Whipple, *3 letters in 1991, 1 in 1997*.

4507. through 4510. Bakke - Whipple, *Family Group Sheet*.

4511. through 4520. Wilson to Whipple, *Letters, June 1996 & 1967*.

4521. through 4523. Bakke - Whipple, *Family Group Sheet*.

INDEX TO HISTORY

D

E

N

O

P

T

V

W

Y

INDEX TO GENEALOGY

Figures enclosed in square brackets are assigned genealogical numbers, superscript numbers indicate generation, and page numbers in bold indicate significant biographical treatment of the subject.

Anderson, Jean (Morrison), G306
Anderson, Jonathan Lee[15] [3583], G306
Anderson, Leona. *See* Goddard, Leona (Anderson)
Anderson, Mabel Clara. *See* Miller, Mabel Clara (Anderson)
Anderson, Merilee Joan[14]. *See* Thorman, Merilee Joan (Anderson)[14] [3117]
Anderson, Norma (Caillordt), G265
Anderson, Sarah Marie[15] [3584], G306
Anderson, Tyson James[15] [3581], G306
Andrea, Jared Blaine[15] [3684], G316
Andrea, Jill Anette (Darby)[14] [3344], G287, G316
Andrea, Robert, G316
Andrews, Carol Lydia (Fairweather)[12] [2582], G217, G249
Andrews, Caroline B. *See* Goodhue, Caroline B. (Andrews)
Andrews, Ebenezer, G158
Andrews, George Robert, G249
Andrews, George Robert[13] [2922], G249, G286
Andrews, Karen (Seals), G285
Andrews, Laura Violet (Byron), G249
Andrews, Mary (Fogg). *See* Billings, Mary (Fogg)
Andrews, Natalie. *See* Gaber, Natalie (Andrews)
Andrews, Nicole Marie[14] [3325], G285
Andrews, Robert Arthur[14] [3324], G285
Andrews, [Rev.] Robert Emerson, G249
Andrews, Sharon Leslie[13]. *See* Riesenberg, Sharon Leslie (Andrews)[13] [2923]
Andrews, Tena Faye (Bivens), G285
Angell, James William, G107, G110
Angell, Jemima. *See* Young, Jemima (Angell)
Angell, Mary Ann. *See* Young, Mary Ann (Angell)
Angell, Phebe Ann (Morton), G107, G110
Ansley, Anna. *See* Kimball, Anna (Ansley)
Ansley, Eunice (———), G87
Ansley, John, G87
Anthony, Daniel, G98
Anthony, Daniel Read[9] [1171], G100
Anthony, Guelma Penn[9] [1169], G98
Anthony, Hannah[9] [1167], G98
Anthony, Jacob Merrit[9] [1168], G98
Anthony, Lucy (Read)[8] [891], G75, G98
Anthony, Mary Stafford[9] [1172], G100
Anthony, Susan Browning[9] [1170], **G98–99**

Appleton, Johanna. *See* Whipple, Johanna (Appleton)
Appleton, John, G9
Appleton, Mary. *See* Whipple, Mary (Appleton)
Appleton, Mary (Oliver), G9
Appleton, Mehitable (Crocker)[7], G47
Appleton, [Lt.] Oliver, G49
Appleton, Samuel, G9
Appleton, Sarah (Perkins), G49
Appleton, Thomas, G47
Arney, Edna L. *See* Miller, Edna L.
Augustine, ——— [married Cheryl Maureen[13] Stevens], G287
Augustine, Cheryl Maureen (Stevens)[13] [2932], G251, G287
Augustine, David Edward[14] [3336], G287, G316
Augustine, David Jeffrey[15] [3678], G316
Augustine, Ryan Bryce[14] [3338], G287
Augustine, Todd Henry Lee[14] [3337], G287
Austin, Henry, G77
Austin, Mary (Starr)[8] [916], G77
Auttereson, Rebecca Leeann. *See* Miller, Rebecca Leeann (Auttereson)
Avery, John, G75
Avery, Lydia. *See* Johnson, Lydia (Avery)
Avery, Mehitable (Buell), G75
Avila, Francisco J., G299
Avila, Jose, G299
Avila, Kathleen (Wilson)[13] [3028], G257, G299
Avila, Noah Benjamin[14] [3512], G299
Avila, Sara[14] [3511], G299
Avila, Susanna[14] [3510], G299
Ayres, Lovice. *See* Whitmore, Lovice (Ayres)

B

Babcock, Adolphus, G112
Babcock, Catherine Jane. *See* Nelson, Catherine Jane (Babcock)
Babcock, Eliza. *See* Young, Eliza (Babcock)
Babcock, Jerusha Jane (Rowley), G112
Baca, Anita. *See* Leonard, Anita (Baca)
Bacon, ——— [11] [1983], G171
Bacon, Alexandra Hazeltine[13] [2849], G243
Bacon, Allen Harlow[10] [1587], G141, G171
Bacon, Allen Harlow[11] Jr. [1985], G171, G211
Bacon, Alma Ellery (Holden)[8] [884], G74, G97
Bacon, Carol (Hazeltine), G243

Ball, Winifred Gertrude[10]. *See* Allen, Winifred Gertrude (Ball)[10] [1623]

Ball, Winifred[12] [2571], G216

Ballantyne, Joseph[11] [2243], G188

Ballantyne, Leona. *See* Card, Leona (Ballantyne)

Ballou, Asahel, G77

Ballou, Hosea[8] [918], G77

Ballou, Martha (Starr)[7] [613], G56, G77

Balsters, Rosetta Johanna. *See* Miller, Rosetta Johanna (Balsters)

Bangs, David, G19

Bangs, Eunice (Stone)[5] [141], G19

Bangs, Seth, G19

Bangs, Thankful (Stone), G19

Barber, Eliz Pillsbury (Martin)[14] [3101], G264

Barber, John S., G264

Barber, Peter, G14

Bard, Lesa Dawn[14] [3459], G296

Bard, Marva Dene (Murphy)[13] [3015], G256, G296

Bard, Paul Lynn[14] [3458], G296

Bard, Steven Ray, G296

Barker, Lucy (Standish), G174

Barker, Lydia Jane. *See* Patterson, Lydia Jane (Barker)

Barker, Robert D., G174

Barnard, Eliza D. *See* Pillsbury, Eliza D. (Barnard)

Barnard, George W., G118, G128

Barnard, Hannah. *See* Stone, Hannah (Barnard)

Barnard, Hannah (Stowell), G61

Barnard, Jonathan, G61

Barnard, Sarah Lucinda (Stone)[9] [1336], G118, G128

Barnard, [Rev.] Thomas, G11

Barney, Harriet Emeline. *See* Young, Harriet Emeline (Barney)

Barney, Royal, G112

Barney, Sarah (Eastebrook), G112

Barraford, Andrew[13] [2890], G246

Barraford, Daniel Everett[12] [2550], G214

Barraford, Daniel MacPhearson, G214

Barraford, Daniel MacPherson[12] Jr. [2557], G214, G246

Barraford, Daniel[13] [2889], G246

Barraford, Eulalie[13] [2892], G246

Barraford, Evelyn Rebecca[12]. *See* Watson, Evelyn Rebecca (Barraford)[12] [2554]

Barraford, Everett Daniel[12] [2553], G214

Barraford, Jennie[12]. *See* Hance, Jennie (Barraford)[12] [2552]

Barraford, Jerome[12] [2555], G214

Barraford, Jessie (Strait), G246

Barraford, Josephine (Fedorowicz), G214

Barraford, Margery[13] [2888], G246

Barraford, Maureen[13] [2887], G246

Barraford, Myrtle Annabelle[12]. *See* Patterson, Myrtle Annabelle (Barraford)[12] [2558]

Barraford, Myrtle (Jenne)[11] [1997], G174, G214

Barraford, Nora M. (McDonnell), G246

Barraford, Ruth (Giffin), G214

Barraford, Ruth[12]. *See* Javall, Ruth (Barraford)[12] [2551]

Barraford, Sherrill[13] [2886], G246

Barraford, Theordore[13] [2893], G246

Barraford, Thomas[13] [2891], G246

Barraford, William[12] [2556], G214, G246

Barraford, William[13] [2885], G246

Barrett, Elvira (Fretts), G162

Barrett, Lemira. *See* Goodhue, Lemira (Barrett)

Barrett, Lovina A. *See* Powers, Lovina A. (Barrrett)

Barrett, Thomas, G162

Barrows, Huldah (Whitmore)[9] [1124], G94

Barrows, William G., G94

Bartlett, Sandra. *See* Royal, Sandra (Bartlett)

Barton, Betsey (Rich), G158

Barton, Clarissa [Clara] Harlowe[9] [1354], G119, **G120–122**

Barton, David[9] [1352], **G120**

Barton, David[10] [1845], G158

Barton, Dorothea[9] [1350], G120

Barton, Dorothy Moore, G119

Barton, [infant][10] [1843], G158

Barton, Julia A. M. (Porter), G120

Barton, Sally[9] [1353], G120

Barton, Samuel Rich[10] [1844], G158

Barton, Sarah [Sally] (Stone)[8] [1006], G85, G119

Barton, [Dr.] Stephen, G119

Barton, Stephen[9] [1351], G120, G158

Barton, [Capt.] Steven, **G119–120**

Basford, Aaron[7] [715], G63

Basford, Benjamin[7] [712], G63

Basford, Elizabeth (Goodhue)[6] [427], G42, G63

Basford, Elizabeth[7] [713], G63

Brown, William[6] [246], G26, G46

Brown, William, G70

Brown, Willmia[10] [1826], G156

Brown, Zina Lydia[11] [2247], G189

Brown, Zina Young (Card)[10] [1779], G154, G189

Brown, Zola Grace[11] [2248], G189

Bruni, Antonio, G266

Bruni, Lillian (McDonald), G266

Bruni, Vittoria. See Stevens, Vittoria (Bruni)

Brush, Almyra (Blackburn), G177

Brush, Archie James[11] [2041], G177

Brush, Daniel H., G177

Brush, Harriet Elizabeth (Watrous)[10] [1635], G145, G177

Brush, J. Earl[11] [2043], G177

Brush, Linne (Morehead), G177

Brush, Lula Caroline[11]. See Nelson, Lula Caroline (Brush)[11] [2044]

Brush, Myrtle Ida[11] [2042], G177

Brush, Norah Leona[11]. See Westensee, Norah Leona (Brush)[11] [2045]

Brush, Thomas Wallace, G177

Bryant, Hannah. See Brickett, Hannah (Bryant)

Bryant, Mary. See Smith, Mary (Bryant)

Bryant, Sally (Downing), G146

Bryant, Samuel, G146

Buchan, ––– [married Barbara Kay[13] Whipple], G271

Buchan, Barbara Kay (Whipple)[13] [2767], G235, G271

Buchan, Elizabeth Diane[14]. See Garcia, Elizabeth Diane (Buchan)[14] [3184]

Buchan, Robin[14] [3185], G271

Bucklin, Jerusha (Eaton)[6] [342], G37

Bucklin, John, G37

Bucknam, [Lt.] Samuel[5] [54], G8, G25

Bucknam, Abigail[6] [232], G25

Bucknam, Benjamin[6] [238], G25

Bucknam, Deborah (Millen), G25

Bucknam, Debra[6] [239], G25

Bucknam, Edward[5] [58], G8

Bucknam, John[6] [236], G25

Bucknam, Judith [Jude] (Worth)[4] [16], G5, G8

Bucknam, Judith[5]. See Blanchard, Judith (Bucknam)[5] [55]

Bucknam, Lydia[5] [59], G8

Bucknam, Lydia[6] [233], G25

Bucknam, Mehitable[6] [234], G25

Bucknam, Phebe[6] [231], G25

Bucknam, Samuel[6] [240], G25

Bucknam, Sarah (Wilkinson), G8

Bucknam, Susanna[5] [56], G8

Bucknam, William[5] [57], G8

Bucknam, William, G8

Bucknam, William[6] [235], 25, G25

Bucknam, William[6] [237], G25

Buell, Catherine (Wells)[13] [2714], G230, G263

Buell, Eleanor[14]. See Stephenson, Eleanor (Buell)[14] [3090]

Buell, Elizabeth[14]. See Drinkhaus, Elizabeth (Buell)[14] [3092]

Buell, Herbert Burling[15] [3539], G302

Buell, Joseph Lawrence II, G263

Buell, Joseph Lawrence[14] III [3091], G263, G302

Buell, Joseph Lawrence[15] IV [3537], G302

Buell, Lisa Michelle (Leak), G302

Buell, Pearson W.[15] [3538], G302

Buell, Sandra (Smith), G302

Buis, Collin[14] [3280], G280

Buis, Daniel[14] [3279], G280

Buis, Errol Kathleen (Powers)[13] [2831], G242, G280

Buis, Jeff, G280

Bull, Ola. See Whipple, Ola (Bull)

Burdick, Laura Johnson (Phelps)[9] [1175], G100

Burdick, [Dr.] Phineas H., G100

Burgess, Eliza. See Young, Eliza (Burgess)

Burley, Mehitable. See Crocker, Mehitable (Burley)

Burnett, Edward, G137

Burnett, Mabel (Lowell)[10] [1531], G137

Burnham, Elizabeth[9] [1403], G125

Burnham, George William[9] [1405], G125

Burnham, Hannah (Treadwell)[8] [1018], G86, G125

Burnham, Irene. See Jenne, Irene (Burnham)

Burnham, James Lewis, G105

Burnham, John[9] [1407], G125

Burnham, Joshua, G125

Burnham, Mary Ann (Huntley). See Young, Mary Ann (Huntley)

Burnham, Mary Elizabeth[9] [1404], G125

Burnham, Sarah[9] [1406], G125

Burrows, Celia. See Parkhurst, Celia (Burrows)

Burt, Abiah (Mooar)[7] [468], G46, G67

Burt, Abiah[8]. See Dane, Abiah (Burt)[8] [767]

Cannon, Wilfred Stohl[11] [2293], G191
Cannon, Wilfred Y.[10] [1722], G151, G191
Cannon, Willare Telle, G190
Cannon, William Tenny, G189
Cannon, William Tenny[11] Jr. [2259], G189
Cannon, Williard L.[11] [2169], G185
Cannon, Winifred (Morrell), G191
Cannon, Winifred[11] [2292], G191
Card, Brigham Young[11] [2244], G188
Card, Charles Ora, G154
Card, Delpha[11] [2253], G189
Card, Eldon Joseph[11] [2245], G188
Card, Joseph Young[10] [1778], G154, G188
Card, Leona (Ballantyne), G188
Card, Lucena (Richards), G189
Card, Orson Rego[10] [1780], G154, G189
Card, Pearl (Christensen), G188
Card, Richard Young[11] [2252], G189
Card, Ruth[11] [2246], G189
Card, Zina (Young)[9] [1298], G154, GG116
Card, Zina Young[10]. See Brown, Zina Young
   (Card)[10] [1779]
Carey, Emily Almira. See Phelps, Emily
   Almira (Carey)
Carigan, ——— [married Virginia Parnell[9]
   Young], G106
Carigan, Virginia Parnell (Young)[9] [1245],
   G106
Carlock, Janet L. (Stephenson)[15] [3536],
   G302, G320
Carlock, John, G320
Carlock, Madelline McCartel[16] [3723], G320
Carlock, Sydney Wells[16] [3722], G320
Carlson, Ida Caroline. See Makee, Ida
   Caroline (Carlson)
Carlson, Joleen Mae. See Rich, Joleen Mae
   (Carlson)
Carlton, Mary. See Burt, Mary (Carlton)
Carney, Julia Ann. See Hatch, Julia Ann
   (Carney)
Carpenter, ——— [married Sarah[10] Powers],
   G139
Carpenter, Alice (Tilsley), G236
Carpenter, Annette Marie (Johnson), G310
Carpenter, Ariane[14] [3195], G272
Carpenter, Bradley Lendell[14] [3193], G272,
   G310
Carpenter, Casey Mitchell[14] [3198], G273
Carpenter, Celinda. See Hill, Celinda
   (Carpenter)
Carpenter, Christy (Larson), G272
Carpenter, Claire[14] [2304], G273

Carpenter, Claribel (Whipple)[12] [2497],
   G207, G236
Carpenter, Craig Ward[13] [2779], G236,
   G272
Carpenter, Deborah Ann (Bronkey), G272
Carpenter, Deborah (Wolfe), G273
Carpenter, Emily Jane[14] [2305], G273
Carpenter, Jane (Lemieux), G273
Carpenter, Jeffrey Marcus[14] [3201], G273
Carpenter, Joy Diane (Watson), G272
Carpenter, [Rev.] Keith Whipple[13] [2780],
   G236, G273
Carpenter, Kirk[14] [3200], G273
Carpenter, Lawrence L., G236
Carpenter, Lendell LeRoy[13] [2778], G236,
   G272
Carpenter, Leonard L., G236
Carpenter, Madeline Faith[15] [3628], G310
Carpenter, Marilyn Lee (Mitchell), G272
Carpenter, Marisa Michelle[14] [3202], G273
Carpenter, Matthew Branden[14] [3197],
   G273
Carpenter, Michelle (Baugh), G273
Carpenter, Ryan[14] [2303], G273
Carpenter, Sarah (Powers)[10] [1558], G139
Carpenter, Scott Lawrence[13] [2781], G236,
   G273
Carpenter, Sean[14] [3199], G273
Carpenter, Todd[14] [3194], G272
Carpenter, Troy[14] [3196], G272
Carr, Ellen (Walsh), G172
Carr, Ephraim, G97
Carr, Fanny (Young)[8]. See Murray, Fanny
   (Young)[8] [946]
Carr, Lucy (Brown), G142
Carr, Lyman[8] [1162], G97, G141-142
Carr, Mary Olive[11]. See Wise, Mary Olive
   (Carr)[11] [1987]
Carr, Robert, G80
Carr, Susanna (Dunton)[8] [885], G74, G97
Carr, William Dustin[10] [1591], G142, G172
Carrington, Albert, G114
Carson, Anna Mary (Lang), G245
Carson, Dorothy (Cain), G217
Carson, Edward Geary, G245
Carson, Edwin, G216
Carson, Eldon John[12] [2580], G217
Carson, Estella Grace (Wilson)[11] [2034],
   G176, G216
Carson, Esther (Schneider), G217
Carson, Helen Beatrice[12]. See Jones, Helen
   Beatrice (Carson)[12] [2578]

Chapman, William⁹ [1388], G124
Chase, Anna K. *See* Starr, Anna (Chase)
Chase, Cornelia Baldwin. *See* Bacon, Cornelia Baldwin (Chase)
Chase, Diana [Diora] Severance. *See* Young, Diana [Diora] Severance (Chase)
Chase, Emery, G46
Chase, Ezra, G111
Chase, Joshua, G89
Chase, Luther A., G141
Chase, Mary (Hadley), G89
Chase, Mary [Polly]. *See* Hale, Mary [Polly] (Chase)
Chase, Mehitable (Mooar)⁷. *See* Blanchard, Mehitable (Mooar)⁷ [472]
Chase, Phyllis. *See* Jenne, Phyllis (Chase)
Chase, Priscilla (Baldwin), G141
Chase, Tizah (Wells), G111
Chesley, Betsey (Jenness), G130
Chesley, Jemima M. *See* Hoyt, Jemima M. (Chesley)
Chesley, Joel, G130
Chew, Amanda Melvina (Phelps)⁹ [1177], G100
Chew, Ezekiel, G100
Chmelar, Brian Lee¹⁴ [3357], G288
Chmelar, Daniel Joseph¹⁴ [3358], G288
Chmelar, Jessica Ann¹⁴ [3355], G288
Chmelar, Linda Maurine (Sobieski)¹³ [2939], G251, G288
Chmelar, Mark Alan, G288
Chmelar, Nathan Alan¹⁴ [3356], G288
Christensen, Pearl. *See* Card, Pearl (Christensen)
Christenson, Chrystal Ann. *See* Musmaker, Chrystal Ann (Christenson)
Christian, Edward John Baptist, G159-160
Christian, Elizabeth Vilate (Mecham)¹⁰ [1858], G159
Christman, Betty Jean (Adams), G294
Christman, Catherine Elaine (Kicidis), G319
Christman, Dorothy Adams¹⁴ [3435], G294
Christman, Eliza. *See* Stone, Eliza (Christman)
Christman, Frederick, G221-222
Christman, Johann Ferdinand, G198, G221-222
Christman, Maria Elizabeth (Pricken), G198-199, G222
Christman, Milon Stone¹² [2626], G222, G254

Christman, Milon Stone¹³ Jr. [2992], G254, G294
Christman, Milon Stone¹⁴ III [3437], G294, G319
Christman, Nicholas Kicidis¹⁵ [3712], G319
Christman, Sarah Mary [Mai] (Stone)¹¹ [2409], G199, G221
Christman, Virginia Jennings¹³. *See* Smith, Virginia Jennings (Christman)¹³ [2991]
Christman, Virginia Jennings¹⁴. *See* Seaman, Virginia Jennings (Christman)¹⁴ [3436]
Christman, Virginia Pickney (Jennings), G254
Christopherson, Aaron Grant¹⁴ [3477], G297
Christopherson, Carol Ann¹⁴ [3478], G297
Christopherson, Cory Rich¹⁴ [3476], G297
Christopherson, Dustin Michael¹⁴ [3474], G297, G320
Christopherson, Heather (Kingdon), G320
Christopherson, JoAnn (Rich)¹³ [3018], G257, G297
Christopherson, Ken Michael, G297
Christopherson, Raundi Pearl¹⁴ [3475], G297
Christopherson, Robert Michael¹⁵ [3721], G320
Claflin, Surrepta. *See* King, Surrepta (Claflin)
Clapp, Daniel Wayne¹³ [3063], G261
Clapp, Dorothy Marietta (Horton)¹² [2702], G228, G260-261
Clapp, Kathy Ford (Thompson), G261
Clapp, Kenneth James¹³ [3064], G261
Clapp, Lester Lincoln, G260
Clapp, Margaret Pearl (Valentine), G260
Clapp, Maynard Lester, G260-261
Clapp, Patricia (Rollison), G261
Clapp, Susan (Kaemer), G261
Clapp, Thankful. *See* Stearns, Thankful (Clapp)
Clapp, Thomas George¹³ [3065], G261
Clark, Anna Belle (Jenne)¹¹ [1995], G173
Clark, Carlyn. *See* Goddard, Carlyn (Clark)
Clark, Charles, G100
Clark [Clerke], Susanna. *See* Whipple, Susanna [wife of John² Whipple]
Clark, Cynthia. *See* Lane, Cynthia (Clark)
Clark, Cynthia (Smith), G96
Clark, Elijah, G96

D

G235, G271

Dahl, Norman Andrew, G271

Dale, Juliette. *See* Hagedon, Juliette (Dale)

Dallmeyer, James, G312

Dallmeyer, Lisa Carol (Powers)[14]. *See* Gottschalk, Lisa Carol (Powers)[14] [3271]

Dalton, Bonnie Lavisa. *See* Morehouse, Bonnie Lavisa (Dalton)

Dana, Abigail[6]. *See* Grow, Abigail (Dana)[6] [349]

Dana, Jonathan, G121

Dana, Penelope[6]. *See* Patch, Penelope (Dana)[6] [350]

Dana, Samuel, G37

Dana, Susanna (Starr)[5] [126], G18, G37

Dane, Abiah (Burt)[8] [767], G67

Dane, Francis, G67

Dane, Lucy (Burt)[8] [776], G67

Dane, Mary Baldwin[9] [1079], G90

Dane, Peter Osgood, G67

Dane, Susanna (Burt)[8] [766], G67, G90

Dane, William Jr., G90

Danforsth, Lizze. *See* Stevens, Lizze (Danforsth)

Daniels, Albert Early, G173

Daniels, Martha Elizabeth. *See* King, Martha Elizabeth (Daniels)

Daniels, Olive Gilmore (Hills), G173

Darby, Jill Anette[14]. *See* Andrea, Jill Anette (Darby)[14] [3344]

Darby, Jim, G287

Darby, Joni Sue[14]. *See* Woodruff, Joni Sue (Darby)[14] [3343]

Darby, Judith Ann (Reinking)[13] [2935], G251

Darby, Julie Kay[14]. *See* Foss, Julie Kay (Darby)[14] [3342]

Darby, Mark Lee[14] [3341], G287

Davenport, Robert, G303

Davenport, Ruth (Davis). *See* Martin, Ruth (Davis)

Davey, Avril Glynes. *See* Smalley, Avril Glynes

Davidson, David Laurance, G226

Davidson, Elizabeth Marilla (Miller)[12] [2677], G226

Davidson, Margaret. *See* Hagedon, Margaret (Davidson)

Davidson, Phebe Mae Ann. *See* Makee, Phebe Mae Ann (Davidson)

Davies, Earl, G284

Davies, Geraldine. *See* Jenne, Geraldine (Davies)

Davies, Honnie G. (Smith), G140

Davies, Marion (Bamberger), G284

Davis, ——— (Vanderveer), G140

Davis, Alice L. Partridge, G170

Davis, Audrey. *See* Wilson, Audrey (Davis)

Davis, Charlene. *See* Hopkins, Charlene (Davis)

Davis, Charlie Decker[11] [2110], G181

Davis, Clinton DeWitt[11] [1970], G170

Davis, Eliza B. (Powers)[9] [1150], G96, G140

Davis, Elizabeth (Brown), G52

Davis, Elizabeth (Hammond). *See* Treadwell, Elizabeth (Hammond)

Davis, Elizabeth Stevens (Linn), G244

Davis, Evelyn Louise (Young)[9] [1299], G116, G154

Davis, Fannie E.[11] [1971], G170

Davis, Fannie H.[10]. *See* Newcomb, Fannie H. (Davis)[10] [1565]

Davis, George Benton[11] Jr. [2111], G181

Davis, George N.[10] [1564], G140

Davis, Isa Helen. *See* Hastings, Isa Helen (Davis)

Davis, James Cox, G244

Davis, John, G129, G140

Davis, John J.[10] [1567], G140

Davis, Linn. *See* Swain, Linn (Davis)

Davis, Louisa (Pillsbury)[10] [1454], G129

Davis, Lydia. *See* Lane, Lydia (Davis)

Davis, Marsell[10] [1569], G140

Davis, Milton Herbert, G154

Davis, Milton Herbert[10] Jr. [1781], G154

Davis, Miriam Vilate (Decker)[10] [1666], G148, G181

Davis, Ray[11] [2109], G181

Davis, Ruth. *See* Lane, Ruth (Davis); Martin, Ruth (Davis)

Davis, Samuel D., G140

Davis, Samuel[10] [1568], G140

Davis, Stephen, G52

Davis, Vanderveer[10] [1566], G140, G170

Davis, Walter, G62

Day, Abraham John, G229

Day, Alexa Lee Ann[14] [3529], G302

Day, Alice LuZella (Jones)[11] [2455], G202, G228-229

Day, Cody Delene[12]. *See* Foster, Cody Delene (Day)[12] [2708]

Day, Colton Jacob[14] [3528], G301

Day, Cory Morgan[13] [3073], G261, G301-302

Day, Dallas J.[12] [2706], G229
Day, Dennis[12] [2705], G229, G261
Day, Elizabeth (Skarecki), G262
Day, Evan Steven[13] [3075], G262
Day, Harry Sidney, G229
Day, Irene. *See* Bates, Irene (Day)
Day, Joy Elaine (Novick), G261
Day, Judith Ann (McAlpine), G261
Day, Kelly Jean[12]. *See* Flinders, Kelly Jean
    (Day)[12] [2709]
Day, Lucy May (Bloxham), G229
Day, Nicole Marie[13] [3072], G261, G301
Day, Sarah Elizabeth[13] [3074], G262
Day, Steven R.[12] [2707], G229, G261–262
Dean, Joanna (Whitcomb), G57
Dean, Phebe. *See* Estey, Phebe (Dean)
Dean, Silas, G57
Death, Anna. *See* Goddard, Anna (Death)
Death, Hannah. *See* Goddard, Hannah
    (Death)
Decker, Alice Luella[10]. *See* Cunningham,
    Alice Luella (Decker)[10] [1667]
Decker, Annie (Thomas), G148
Decker, Bessie[11] [2115], G181
Decker, Brigham Le Ray[10] [1670], G148,
    G181
Decker, Charles Franklin, G117, G148
Decker, Charles Franklin[10] [1668], G148
Decker, Clarissa, G117
Decker, Clarissa Clara. *See* Young,
    Clarissa Clara (Decker)
Decker, Emma (Kammerman), G181
Decker, Eric K.[11] [2117], G181
Decker, Fannie Caroline (Taylor), G181
Decker, Fannie Marie, G117
Decker, Ferra Wallace[10] [1673], G148, G182
Decker, George Davis, G181
Decker, Harold K.[11] [2119], G181
Decker, Harriet Amelia, G117
Decker, Harriet Page (Wheeler), G107, G108
Decker, Isaac Perry, G107, G108, G117
Decker, Leila (Rogers), G182
Decker, Lois Elizabeth[10] [1672], G148
Decker, Loretta Elmina[10]. *See* Sorensen,
    Loretta Elmina (Decker)[10] [1671]
Decker, Loretta[11] [2126], G182
Decker, Louie Isaac[10] [1669], G148
Decker, Louie K.[11] [2118], G181
Decker, Lucy Ann [daughter of Lorenzo
    Dow Young], G117
Decker, Lucy Ann [wife of Brigham
    Young]. *See* Young, Lucy Ann (Decker)

Decker, Miriam Vilate[10]. *See* Davis,
    Miriam Vilate (Decker)[10] [1666]
Decker, Rawlins K.[11] [2116], G181
Decker, Vilate (Young)[9] [1253], G114, G148
Deckert, Gerhard, G293
Deckert, Ingebog (Heinrich), G293
Deckert, Petra. *See* Gaber, Petra (Deckert)
Dee, Ann Eliza (Webb). *See* Young, Ann
    Eliza (Webb)
Dee, James L., G112
Delaney, John W., G266
Delaney, Lillian (Cushing), G266
Delany, Carol Ann. *See* Stevens, Carol Ann
    (Delany)
Demo, Nancy Eleanor (Jenne)[13] [2901],
    G247
Demo, Richard, G247
Denison, Daniel, G9
Denison, John, G9
Denison, Martha. *See* Whipple, Martha
    (Denison)
Denison, Martha (Symonds), G9
Deniston, Mary Delphine. *See* Miller,
    Mary Delphine (Deniston)
Dennis, Hannah. *See* Young, Hannah
    (Dennis)
Denny, Grant, G176
Denny, Mattie Ethel (Wilson)[11] [2036],
    G176
DeWolf, Cornelia. *See* Johnson, Cornelia
    (DeWolf)
Diaz, ——— [married Toni Corrine[13]
    Nystrom], G292
Diaz, Marabella Inez[14] [3419], G292
Diaz, Toni Corrine (Nystrom)[13] [2972],
    G252, G292
Dickinson, Jennet (Brook) [wife of John[2]
    Whipple], G4
Dickinson, Sarah. *See* Pillsbury, Sarah
    (Dickinson)
Dickinson, Thomas, G4
Dickson, Elizabeth (Stiles), G128
Dickson, Elizabeth (Upham)[8] [1037], G87,
    G128
Dickson, Mary[9]. *See* McCabe, Mary
    (Dickson)[9] [1448]
Dickson, Nathan Knowlton[9] [1449], G128
Dickson, Thomas Baird, G128
Diez, Anna S. (Jenne)[12]. *See* Medford,
    Anna S. (Jenne)[12] [2559]
Diez, James, G215
Diffendaffer, James M., G319

Diffendaffer, Marguerite Louise (Moore), G319

Diffendaffer, Sharon L. *See* Bakke, Sharon L. (Diffendaffer)

DiLutis, Joseph Jr., G287

DiLutis, Rachel Hebden (Harrison)[14] [3334], G287

Dinsmoor, Elizabeth. *See* Pillsbury, Elizabeth (Dinsmoor)

Dinsmoor, Elizabeth (Barnet), G129

Dinsmoor, James, G163

Dinsmoor, William, G129

Divoll, Abbie Almira. *See* Stone, Abbie Almira (Divoll)

Doane, Sarah Caroline (Hovey). *See* Rogers, Sarah Caroline (Hovey)

Dodge, Deborah Towne (Brickett)[9] [1073], G90, G130

Dodge, Deborah[6]. *See* Rand, Deborah (Dodge)[6]

Dodge, Elizabeth (Manning), G130

Dodge, Frank Brickett[10] [1474], G130, G164

Dodge, Hannah (Whipple)[8] [813], G70

Dodge, Harriet E. (Faden), G164

Dodge, Isaac, G70

Dodge, Jabez, G43

Dodge, Levi W., G30

Dodge, Lizzie Batchelder[11]. *See* Blake, Lizzie Batchelder (Dodge)[11] [1909]

Dodge, Margery (Knowlton)[5] [197], G23, G43

Dodge, Thomas [Jr.], G130

Dodge, Thomas [Sr.], G130

Dolliver, Currie Duncan, G231

Dolliver, Katherine (Deasy), G231

Dolliver, Lauretta. *See* Blake, Lauretta (Dolliver)

Dolos, Kara Michelle (Hubler)[14] [3242], G277

Dolos, Steven Josiah, G277

Donaldson, Deborah[13] [2840], G242

Donaldson, James[13] [2841], G242

Donaldson, John, G242

Donaldson, John[13] [2842], G242

Donaldson, Nancy Tyler (Royal)[12] [2532], G210, G242

Donaldson, Susan[13] [2839], G242

Donigan, Donna (Wall), G235

Donigan, Grace Katherine (Whipple)[12] [2490], G206, G235

Donigan, Keith, G235

Donigan, oseph Dwain[13] [2765], G235

Donigan, Pamela Kay[13]. *See* Lyles, Pamela Kay (Donigan)[13] [2766]

Donigan, Ronald Ray[13] [2764], G235

Dorrance, Abigail. *See* Stearns, Abigail (Dorrance)

Dougall, Alice[11] [2226], G187

Dougall, Bernard Richards[11] [2225], G187

Dougall, Catherine McSweine[10]. *See* Platt, Catherine McSweine (Dougall)[10] [1748]

Dougall, Clarissa Maria (Young)[9] [1276], G115, G152

Dougall, Clarissa[10]. *See* Bergstrom, Clarissa (Dougall)[10] [1749]

Dougall, D. Grant[11] [2224], G187

Dougall, Hattie (Richards), G187

Dougall, Hugh Willard[10] [1747], G152, G187–188

Dougall, Marie[11] [2223], G187

Dougall, Virginia[11] [2228], G188

Dougall, William Bernard, G152

Dougall, William Bernard[10] Jr. [1746], G152, G187

Dougall, William Bernard[11] [2227], G188

Dow, Betsey Fitts. *See* Pillsbury, Betsey Fitts (Dow)

Dowis, Blair Marie[14] [3525], G301

Dowis, Carly Jane[14] [3526], G301

Dowis, Dru Helena[14] [3527], G301

Dowis, Karen Lynn (Mansfield)[13] [3053], G260, G301

Dowis, Randall Keith, G301

Downing, Emanuel, G22

Downing, Lucy (Winthrop), G22

Doyle, John, G87

Doyle, Madison, G102

Doyle, Mariah. *See* Stevens, Mariah (Doyle)

Doyle, Polly (———), G87

Doyle, Rhoda (Ball)[9] [1197], G102

Drinkhaus, Elizabeth (Buell)[14] [3092], G263, G302–303

Drinkhaus, [Dr.] Harold, G303

Drinkhaus, Lawrie W.[15] [3541], G303

Drinkhaus, [Dr.] Philip Harold[15] [3540], G303

Driver, Martha Wescott. *See* Meeks, Martha Wescott (Driver)

Drurg, Grace (Goddard)[7] [650], G60

Duane, Judge, G93

Duane, Mary Ann. *See* Lowell, Mary Ann (Duane)

Duckworth, Ceryl Ann. *See* Perkins, Ceryl Ann (Duckworth)

Dudek, Peggy Ruth. *See* Lockman, Peggy Ruth (Dudek)

Duggins, Emily Wheelock (Duggins), G105

Dummer, Shubel, G14

Duncan, Elma Florence. *See* Whipple, Elma Florence (Duncan)

Dunford, A. B., G155

Dunford, Albert Phillips[11] [2308], G192

Dunford, Bailey[10] [1791], G155

Dunford, Dorothy Emmeline[11] [2309], G192

Dunford, Eudora Lovina (Young)[9]. *See* Hagan, Eudora Lovina (Young)[9] [1301]

Dunford, Francis Bellew[11] [2305], G192

Dunford, Frank Moreland[10] [1784], G154, G192

Dunford, George Albert[10] [1785], G154, G192

Dunford, Irene (Bellew), G192

Dunford, John Moreland[11] [2306], G192

Dunford, Leah Eudora[10]. *See* Widtoe, Leah Eudora (Dunford)[10] [1790]

Dunford, Lillie Elizabeth. *See* Mecham, Lillie Elizabeth (Dunford)

Dunford, Marie Lucile[11] [2307], G192

Dunford, Mary Ann (Phillips), G192

Dunford, Moreland, G154

Dunford, Moroni, G223

Dunford, Sarah (Bridwell), G223

Dunford, Susan [Susa] Amelia (Young)[9]. *See* Gates, Susan [Susa] Amelia (Young)[9] [1302]

Dunlap, Frances H. *See* Lowell, Frances H. (Dunlap)

Dunlap, John Jr., G135

Dunlap, Lois (Cushing) Porter, G135

Dunton, Abner, G74

Dunton, Jewell, Mary[7]. *See* Dunton, Mary (Jewell)[7] [570]

Dunton, Mary (Jewell)[7] [570], G53, G74

Dunton, Susanna[8]. *See* Carr, Susanna (Dunton)[8] [885]

Dutton, George W., G104

Dutton, Lamira (Goddard)[9] [1213], G104

Dutton, Mary I. *See* Hill, Mary I. (Dutton)

Dyke, Priscilla. *See* Stone, Priscilla (Dyke)

E

Eaker, Edward E., G285

Eaker, Elizabeth Ann (Jones)[14] [3323], **G285**

Eaker, Joseph Patrick, **G285**

Eaker, Margarita (Corn), G285

Eames, Ruthy. *See* Howe, Ruthy (Eames)

Earley, Eliz. *See* Swett, Eliz Earley

Easton, Jeannette Richards (Young)[9] [1293], G116

Easton, Robert C., G116

Eaton, Alice (———), G36

Eaton, Alice[6]. *See* Leavens, Alice (Eaton)[6] [340]

Eaton, Alma Ellery (Tyler)[9] [1158], G97, G141

Eaton, Alma Ellery[10]. *See* Royal, Alma Ellery (Eaton)[10] [1583]

Eaton, Arrunah[8] [899], G76, G101

Eaton, Candace (Raymond), G101

Eaton, Comfort[6] [347], G37

Eaton, Deliverance (Cleveland), G37

Eaton, Elizabeth (Lyon), G37

Eaton, Ellery T.[11] [1976], G171

Eaton, Esther Adeline[9]. *See* Patterson, Esther Adeline (Eaton)[9] [1191]

Eaton, Flora (Timpany), G171

Eaton, Francis[10] [1581], G141

Eaton, Hannah[6]. *See* Johnson, Hannah (Eaton)[6] [343]

Eaton, Harriet (———), G210

Eaton, [Dr.] Jacob S., G141

Eaton, James Ellery[10] [1582], G141, G171

Eaton, James Ellery[12] [2529], G210

Eaton, Jerusha[6]. *See* Bucklin, Jerusha (Eaton)[6] [342]

Eaton, John, G36

Eaton, John[6] [345], G37, G55

Eaton, John[7] [603], G55, G76

Eaton, Jonathan, G36

Eaton, Jonathan[6] [344], G37

Eaton, Keziah[6] [339], G37

Eaton, Lucien[10] [1580], G141

Eaton, Lydia Abiah (Starr)[5] [122], G18, G36

Eaton, Lydia[6]. *See* Goodale, Lydia (Eaton)[6] [338]

Eaton, Marston[6] [348], G37

Eaton, Mary (Starr)[5] [121], G18

Eaton, Mehitable (Richardson), G76

Eaton, Mehitable (Whitmore), G37

Eaton, Penelope[6] [346], G37

Eaton, Rufus[7] [602], G55

Eaton, Sarah (Johnson), G37, G55

Eaton, Susanna[6]. *See* Grou, Susanna (Eaton)[6] [341]

Eaton, Tyler[11] [1975], G171, G210

Eaton, William, G18

Ebert, Dawn Marie[14] [3363], G288
Ebert, Kurt, G288
Ebert, Mark Curtis[14] [3364], G289
Ebert, Sandra Jean (Olander)[13] [2943], G251, G288
Eddy Amos, G85
Eddy, Anna (Stone)[8] [1007], G85
Eddy, Ruth. *See* Stone, Ruth (Eddy)
Eddy, Samuel, G20
Eddy, Sarah (Mead), G20
Edmondson, Dorothy G. *See* Hunter, Dorothy G. (Edmondson)
Edson, Mary. *See* Johnson, Mary (Edson)
Edwards, Angeline. *See* Watrous, Angeline (Edwards)
Edwards, Audrey[11] [2324], G193
Edwards, Benjamin, G193
Edwards, Gladys (Ferguson)[10] [1766], G153, G193
Edwards, Joseph, G7
Edwards, Julie Kay (West)[14] [3175], G270
Edwards, Mildred[11] [2323], G193
Edwards, Robert, G270
Eggleston, (———). *See* Starr, (———) Eggleston
Ehrhardt, Ella F. *See* Hastings, Ella F. (Ehrhardt)
Eldridge, Elsie. *See* Maynard, Elsie (Eldridge)
Eldridge, Mary [Martha?] [Patty] (Welch), G157
Eldridge, Samuel, G157
Eliason, Clinton Brent[14] [3447], G295
Eliason, Eldon Leon, G256
Eliason, Frederick L., G256
Eliason, Kathy Lou (Imlay), G295
Eliason, Ronald Brent[13] [3006], G256, G295
Eliason, Ruth Mae (Fuchs)[12]. *See* Hill, Ruth Mae (Fuchs)[12] [2636]
Eliason, Shane Glen[14] [3448], G295
Elkins, Rachel. *See* Towle, Rachel (Elkins)
Ellery, Mary. *See* Roger, Mary (Ellery)
Ellery, Rachel. *See* Rogers, Rachel Ellery
Elliott, Alfred M.[11] [2022], G175
Elliott, Bertha May[11] [2024], G175
Elliott, Herbert Myron John[11] [2025], G175
Elliott, Lydia Thurlow (Ball)[10] [1618], G144, G175
Elliott, Milo A., G175
Elliott, Nellie Hannah[11] [2023], G175
Elliott, Winifred Grace[11] [2026], G175
Ellis, Anna Hale. *See* Wise, Anna Hale (Ellis)

Ellsworth, Alice Elizabeth[11] [2075], G180
Ellsworth, Alice Vilate[10]. *See* Swift, Alice Vilate (Ellsworth)[10] [1662]
Ellsworth, Alonzo Sheridan[11] [2071], G179
Ellsworth, Brigham Henry[10] [1661], G148, G180
Ellsworth, Brigham[11] [2076], G180
Ellsworth, Charles Eliot[11] [2077], G180
Ellsworth, Charlotte[10] [1658], G148
Ellsworth, Clara Cornelia[11] [2068], G179
Ellsworth, Claude William[11] [2081], G180
Ellsworth, Crystal Vere[11] [2084], G180
Ellsworth, Curtis K.[11] [2083], G180
Ellsworth, Edmund, G148
Ellsworth, Edmund[10] Jr. [1659], G148, G179
Ellsworth, Edmund[11] [2065], G179
Ellsworth, Elizabeth (Young)[9] [1252], G114, G148
Ellsworth, Elizabeth Young[11] [2070], G179
Ellsworth, Ellen C. (Blair), G179
Ellsworth, Frank Blair[11] [2067], G179
Ellsworth, Helen Adelia (Gibson), G180
Ellsworth, John Willard[11] [2069], G179
Ellsworth, John Willard[11] [2074], G180
Ellsworth, John Willard[11] [2078], G180
Ellsworth, John W.[10] [1664], G148
Ellsworth, Joseph[11] [2079], G180
Ellsworth, Lovill Edgar[11] [2082], G180
Ellsworth, Luna Caroline[10]. *See* Jardine, Luna Caroline (Ellsworth)[10] [1663]
Ellsworth, Marian Vilate[11] [2080], G180
Ellsworth, Minnie[10]. *See* Mousley, Minnie (Ellsworth)[10] [1665]
Ellsworth, Preston B.[11] [2072], G179
Ellsworth, Rowennah W.[10]. *See* Howard, Rowennah W. (Ellsworth)[10] [1660]
Ellsworth, Sara Eliza[11] [2085], G180
Ellsworth, Seth Millington[11] [2066], G179
Emery, David, G24
Emery, Florence Augustus (Stevens)[10] [1518], G133
Emery, George, G133
Emery, Mary (Pillsbury)[6] [219], G24
Empey, Ella Elizabeth (Young)[9] [1279], G115
Empey, Nelson, G115
Englestadter, Karen Dorothy (Bakke)[14]. *See* Harris, Karen Dorothy (Bakke)[14] [3446]
Englestadter, William, G295
Epes, [Maj.] Symonds, G34
Epes, Elizabeth[6] [315], G34
Epes, Mary (Whipple)[5]. *See* Holyoke,

F

Farnsworth, Matthew, G15
Farnsworth, Matthias Jr., G16
Farnsworth, Reuben, G112
Farnsworth, Sarah. See Stone, Sarah (Farnsworth)
Farnsworth, Sarah (Nutting). See Stone, Sarah (Nutting) Farnsworth
Farnum, Mary Jane. See Goddard, Mary Jane (Farnum)
Farr, Frances Jean[11] [2361], G196
Farr, Jemima[6] [316], G34
Farr, Joseph[6] [317], G34
Farr, Mary (Taylor), G34
Farr, Morrill Newton, G196
Farr, Morrill Spencer[11] [2360], G196
Farr, Richard Spencer[11] [2362], G196
Farr, Sarah (Stone)[5] [93], G16, G34
Farr, Sarah[6] [319], G35
Farr, Stephen, G34
Farr, Stephen [Sr.], G34
Farr, Susanna[6] [318], G34
Farrell, Alfred L., G184
Farrell, Alfred T.[11] [2158], G184
Farrell, Janet E.[11] [2160], G184
Farrell, Luna Angell (Thatcher)[10] [1686], G149, G184
Farrell, Luna C.[11] [2157], G184
Farrell, Maxwell T.[11] [2159], G184
Farrell, William S.[11] [2161], G184
Farwell, Elizabeth. See Stone, Elizabeth Farwell
Farwell, Hannah (———), G16, G35
Farwell, Joseph, G16, G35
Farwell, Mary. See Stone, Mary (Farwell)
Fassett, Joanna (Page)[6] [279], G32
Fassett, Josiah, G32
Fassett, Josiah [Sr.], G32
Faubel, Ross, G216
Faubel, Wilma May (Carson)[12] [2575], G216
Fausett, Affalona Galia[9]. See Thompson, Affalona Galia (Fausett)[9] [1445]
Fausett, John McKee, G127
Fausett, Julia Ann (Stevens)[8] [1034], G87, G127
Fausett, Margaret (Smith), G127
Fausett, William Alexander, G127
Fay, C., G88
Fay, Olive (Knowlton)[8] [1048], G88
Feckley, Emma Lou. See Morehouse, Emma Lou (Feckley)
Fedorowicz, Josephine. See Barraford, Josephine (Fedorowicz)

Fellows, Joseph, G281
Fellows, Kaylynn. See Bacon, Kaylynn (Fellows)
Fellows, Saralee (Wood), G281
Fenical, Frances Louise (Riggs)[13] [3051], G259, G301
Fenical, Gertrude Agnes (Adams), G301
Fenical, Maurice Sylvester, G301
Fenical, Scott William[14] [3521], G301
Fenical, William Howard, G301
Fenton, Henry F., G133
Fenton, Louisa (Hagedon)[10] [1511], G133
Ferguson, Allen[10] [1766], G153
Ferguson, Dale[10] [1764], G153
Ferguson, James, G153
Ferguson, James[10] [1763], G153
Ferguson, Laura Mae. See Miller, Laura Mae (Ferguson)
Ferguson, Louisa Nelle (Young)[9] [1283], G115, G153
Fernald, Mercy. See Billings, Mercy (Fernald)
Ferong, Anna Wilhemina (Johnson), G249
Ferong, Betty Ruth. See Westensee, Betty Ruth (Ferong)
Ferong, Henry Luther, G249
Ferris, Edmund La Var, G304
Ferris, Elaine Ila (Ewell), G304
Ferris, Nancy Elaine. See Haines, Nancy Elaine (Ferris)
Field, James, G103
Field, Mary (Drew), G103
Field, Pamela. See Smith, Pamela (Field)
Fisher, Alfred, G276
Fisher, Anna Maria Bird[8] [985], G82
Fisher, Charles Lowell[8] [989], G82
Fisher, Davenport[8] [988], G82
Fisher, Edith H. See Powers, Edith H. (Fisher)
Fisher, Eveline[8] [984], G82
Fisher, Gary Frenchie, G267
Fisher, George Jabez[8] [986], G82
Fisher, Harriet Louisa[8] [982], G82
Fisher, Helen Louise (Wedge)[13] [2743], G233, G267
Fisher, Jabez, G82
Fisher, Jabez George[8] [983], G82
Fisher, Jabin, G82
Fisher, James Ellis[14] [3141], G268
Fisher, James Tucker[8] [980], G82
Fisher, John Gary[14] [3140], G267-268
Fisher, Kerry Ann (Imsland), G268

Fuller, Elizabeth (McNeal). *See* Treadwell, Elizabeth (McNeal)

Fullerton, Ella Mariah (Sherman)[11] [1906], G164

Fullerton, Everett, G164

G

Gaber, Beverly Joy (Goddard)[12] [2608], G220, G253

Gaber, Brian Keith[13] [2975], G253, G293

Gaber, Charles Earl[14] [3421], G293

Gaber, Christine (Korseuburg), G293

Gaber, Clara Sadie (Villiesse), G253

Gaber, Donald Howand[13] [2976], G253

Gaber, Frank Edward, G253

Gaber, Hunter Reed[14] [3431], G293

Gaber, Kurt Erwin[13] [2978], G253, G293

Gaber, Laurie (Zehe), G253

Gaber, Lindsay Marie[14] [3430], G293

Gaber, Lisa Joy[14] [3429], G293

Gaber, Malorie Christine[14] [3428], G293

Gaber, Natalie (Andrews), G293

Gaber, Patricia (Voltz), G292

Gaber, Petra (Deckert), G293

Gaber, Rebekka[14] [3426], G293

Gaber, Richard Edward, G253

Gaber, Richard Francis[13] [2973], G253, G292–293

Gaber, Rikky Shannon[14] [3420], G293

Gaber, Sandy Denise[14] [3425], G293

Gaber, Scott Thomas[14] [3427], G293

Gaber, Thomas Stanley[13] [2977], G253, G293

Gadis, Elizabeth[9] [1417], G126

Gadis, James, G126

Gadis, Mary (Kimball)[8] [1022], G86, G126

Gadis, William[9] [1416], G126

Gann, Dareatha Denise (Williams)[14]. *See* Runge, Dareatha Denise (Williams)[14] [3160]

Gann, Gerald, G309

Garcia, Elizabeth Diane (Buchan)[14] [3184], G271, G310

Garcia, Kestrel[15] [3627], G310

Garcia, Victor, G310

Gardiner, [Capt.] Joseph, G22

Gardner, Rebecca. *See* Blanchard, Rebecca (Gardner)

Garrett, Bradley Roland, G260

Garrett, Jan Marie (Mansfield)[13] [3055], G260

Gates, Beulah Suzanne[11] [2335], G194

Gates, Brigham Cecil[10] [1797], G155, G194

Gates, Brigham Young[10] [1802], G155

Gates, Emma Lucy[10]. *See* Bowen, Emma Lucy (Gates)[10] [1792]

Gates, Emma Lucy[11] [2333], G194

Gates, Florence (Keate), G194

Gates, Franklin Young[10] [1800], G155, G194

Gates, Franklin Young[11] Jr. [2338], G194

Gates, Gweneth (Gibbs), G194

Gates, Gweneth[11] [2332], G194

Gates, Harvey Harris[10] [1798], G155, G194

Gates, Heber[10] [1801], G155

Gates, Jacob Fosberry, G155

Gates, Jacob Harvey[11] [2336], G194

Gates, Jacob Young[10] [1793], G155

Gates, James Keate[11] [2339], G194

Gates, Joseph Sterling[10] [1796], G155

Gates, Karl Nahum[10] [1794], G155

Gates, Lucie Jenne (Genez), G194

Gates, Lurene Keliilalanikulani[11] [2337], G194

Gates, Martha L. *See* Johnson, Martha L. Gates

Gates, Mary (Clark). *See* Stone, Mary (Clark)

Gates, Sally. *See* Knowlton, Sally (Gates)

Gates, Sarah Beulah[10] [1799], G155

Gates, Simpson Mark[10] [1795], G155

Gates, Susan [Susa] Amelia (Young)[9] [1302], G116, G155

Gates, Susannah. *See* Knowlton, Susannah (Gates)

Gates, Victor Cecil[11] [2334], G194

Genez, Lucie Jenne. *See* Gates, Lucie Jenne (Genez)

George, (———) [wife of Mary[5] Stone], G17

George, Beatrice Emma. *See* Ball, Beatrice Emma (George)

George, Elmer, G216

George, Mary (Grace), G216

George, Mary Stone* [107], G17

Gerrish, Jacob[7] [479], G46

Gerrish, Jane[7] [476], G46

Gerrish, [Col.] Joseph, G46

Gerrish, Katherine (Brown)[6] [248], G26, G46

Gerrish, Katherine[7] [477], G46

Gerrish, Martha[7] [480], G46

Gerrish, Mary[7] [478], G46

Gerrish, Sarah[7]. *See* Pearson, Sarah (Gerrish)[7] [482]

Gould, Betsey[8] [836], G71
Gould, Ebenezer[8] [832], G71
Gould, John[8] [833], G71
Gould, Patty[8] [835], G71
Gould, Rachel[8] [834], G71
Graham, Dorothy Jane. *See* Ball, Dorothy Jane (Graham)
Graham, Gladys (Massie), G248
Graham, Thomas, G248
Granger, Henry Corydon[11] [2108], G181
Granger, Louie, G181
Granger, Louie Edwin[11] [2107], G181
Granger, Miriam Vilate (Decker)[10]. *See* Davis, Miriam Vilate (Decker)[10] [1666]
Grant, Lillie B. (Miller)[10] [1885], G161
Grant, Oscar, G161
Green, Adeline (Whipple)[9] [1102], G92
Green, Beau Michael[15] [3634], G311
Green, Charles, G159
Green, Clarissa Louise (Powers)[13]. *See* Sexton, Clarissa Louise (Powers)[13] [2814]
Green, Frederick Charles, G278
Green, Frederick Lee[14] [3251], G278, G311
Green, George, G119
Green, Ida E. *See* Ball, Ida E. (Green)
Green, John Portinus, G80
Green, Karen Ann (Castor), G311
Green, Leslie Lynn (Wedge)[13] [2744], G233
Green, Marshall, G233
Green, Mary Augusta. *See* Stone, Mary Augusta (Green)
Green, Mary (Ellis), G159
Green, Mary Katherine. *See* Mecham, Mary Katherine (Green)
Green, Polly (Baldwin), G119
Green, Ranae Lynn[15] [3633], G311
Green, Rhoda (Young)[8] [947], G80
Green, William, G92
Greene, John P., G117
Gregg, Brian Whipple[14] [3208], G274
Gregg, Joan Morgan (Whipple)[13]. *See* Trimble, Joan Morgan (Whipple)[13] [2782]
Gregg, Samuel Walter III, G273
Gregory, (———) [married Lucinda[8] Stone], G74
Gregory, Lucinda (Stone)[8] [877], G74
Grennell, Blanche May (Tanner)[11] [2452], G202, G228
Grennell, Browyn Marie (Cassidy), G260
Grennell, Chapman H., G228
Grennell, David Paul[13] [3058], G260
Grennell, Esther Helen[13]. *See* Cochell,

Esther Helen (Grennell)[13] [3056]
Grennell, Helen (Jones), G260
Grennell, Mable[12]. *See* McMahon, Mable (Grennell)[12] [2699]
Grennell, Rachel Amsdell (Mills), G228
Grennell, Richard Henry[12] [2700], G228, G260
Grennell, Stephen Wilson[13] [3057], G260
Grennell, Wilson Americk, G228
Grey, Mary Melissa. *See* Miller, Mary Melissa (Grey)
Grieb, Dorothy Lucille (Morehouse)[12] [2612], G220
Grieb, Lyle, G220
Grieser, Henry E., G276
Griffey, Corinne Marion (Hastings)[12] [2591], G219
Griffey, Frank, G219
Griffin, Ambrose, G265
Griffin, Carolyn. *See* Stevens, Carolyn (Griffin)
Griffin, Elaine (Avington), G265
Griffinger, Elisabeth Patterson[14] [3232], G276
Griffinger, Martha (Jones)[13] [2794], G238, G275-276
Griffinger, Theodore A. Jr., G276
Griffinger, Whitney Armstrong[14] [3231], G276
Grimes, Elizabeth Irene (Hopkins)[13] [2751], G233, G269
Grimes, Elizabeth Joann[15] [3623], G310
Grimes, Jaclyn[15] [3622], G310
Grimes, Jacque[14] [3163], G269
Grimes, Jacque[14] [3164], G269, G310
Grimes, James Carl, G269
Grimes, James Carl[14] [3165], G269, G310
Grimes, Jayson Everett[15] [3624], G310
Grimes, Mary. *See* Page, Mary (Grimes)
Grimes, Susie. *See* Poor, Susie (Grimes)
Grimes, Tammy (Tabors), G310
Grodt, Caroline[14] [3284], G280
Grodt, Catherine Ann (Powers)[12] [2525], G210, G242
Grodt, Douglas[13] [2837], G242, G280
Grodt, Mary[13]. *See* Suku, Mary (Grodt)[13] [2838]
Grodt, Paul O., G242
Grodt, Paul[14] [3285], G281
Grodt, Tina (Jesperson), G280
Grogan, Linda Marie (Whipple)[13]. *See* Washborn, Linda Marie (Whipple)[13]

Grogan, Randall, G270

Grosvenor, Hannah. *See* Goddard, Hannah (Grosvenor)

Grou, Susanna (Eaton)[6] [341], G37

Grou, Thomas, G37

Grove, Amanda Malvina (Wight), G143

Grow, Abigail (Dana)[6] [349], G37, G55

Grow, Harriet Felker (Currier), G143-144

Grow, Jerusha (Stowell), G101

Grow, Joseph, G55-56

Grow, Joseph[7] [604], G56, G76

Grow, Lorenzo[9] [1192], G101, G143-144

Grow, Mary Frances[10]. *See* Newell, Mary Frances (Grow)[10] [1611]

Grow, Rebecca (Holt), G55

Grow, Samuel Porter[8] [900], G76, G101

Grow, Thomas, G55

Grow, Tirzah (Sanger), G76

Grys, ——— [married Nancy Jean[13] Heise], G291

Grys, Cassandra Jean[14] [3395], G291

Grys, Nancy Jean (Heise)[13] [2963], G252, G291

Grys, Samantha Joann[14] [3396], G291

Guggenheim, Harry, G213

Guinn, Darelyn Ruth (Haines)[14] [3114], G265

Guinn, William, G265

Guliano, Anthony T., G250

Guliano, Kathleen Lorraine (Packard)[13] [2928], G250

Gundestrup, Elaine (Hiatt), G257

Gundestrup, Frank William, G257

Gundestrup, Karen Marie. *See* Wilson, Karen Marie (Gundestrup)

Gunnison, Joseph, G26

Gunnison, Mary (Crocker)[6] [253], G26

Gunz, Christopher Patrick, G260

Gunz, Lesly Alana (Mansfield)[13] [3054], G260

Guthrie, Joyce. *See* Wolfe, Joyce (Guthrie)

H

Habden, Alice Estella. *See* Fitch, Alice Estella (Habden)

Habden, Jean (Slater), G250

Habden, John Fogg, G250

Hagan, ——— [married Mary E.[10] Powers], G140

Hagan, Albert, G154

Hagan, Albert[10] Jr. [1786], G155

Hagan, Blanche (Young), G191

Hagan, Eudora Lovina (Young)[9] [1301], G116, G154

Hagan, Frances Marie[11] [2310], G192

Hagan, Harold Raymond[10] [1787], G155, G192

Hagan, Harold Raymond[11] Jr. [2311], G192

Hagan, Lucy Mary[10] [1789], G155

Hagan, Mabel Clara[10]. *See* Farnes, Mabel Clara (Hagan)[10] [1788]

Hagan, Mary E. (Powers)[10] [1561], G140

Hagedon, Clara[10] [1513], G133

Hagedon, Clyde T.[11] [1917], G165

Hagedon, Datus W.[10] [1509], G133, G165

Hagedon, David Maynard, G132

Hagedon, David Maynard[10] Jr. [1510], G133

Hagedon, George S.[10] [1512], G133

Hagedon, Jane L.[10] [1507], G132

Hagedon, Juliette (Dale), G133

Hagedon, Louisa[10]. *See* Fenton, Louisa (Hagedon)[10] [1511]

Hagedon, Lucy[10]. *See* Holland, Lucy (Hagedon)[10] [1508]

Hagedon, Maragaret (Davidson), G165

Hagedon, Sophia (Blanchard)[9] [1091], G91, G132

Hahn, Otto, G167

Hahn, Thomasine Richards. *See* Harrison, Thomasine Richards (Hahn)

Haines, Aaron Bradford[15] [3575], G305

Haines, Amber Rae[15] [3557], G304

Haines, Blake Lawrence[15] [3556], G304

Haines, Bradford Blake[14] [3111], G265, G305

Haines, Brent Blake[14] [3112], G265

Haines, Christopher Blake[14] [3113], G265

Haines, Darelyn Ruth[14]. *See* Guinn, Darelyn Ruth (Haines)[14] [3114]

Haines, Delicia Ann[15] [3576], G305

Haines, Doris Alma (Snyder), G264

Haines, Jaycellyn[15] [3574], G305

Haines, Julia Ann (Tanner), G265

Haines, Kelly Verdeana (Kinyon), G305

Haines, Lawrence Archibald, G264

Haines, Linda Ann[14]. *See* Spencer, Linda Ann (Haines)[14] [3110]

Haines, Linda Susan (Wren), G265

Haines, Lori Ruth[15] [3555], G304

Haines, Madelline Grace[15]. *See* Searl, Madelline Grace (Haines)[15] [3553]

Haines, Mary (Hoyle), G265

Haines, Mary Jane (Knittle), G265

Haines, Nancy Elaine (Ferris), G304

G195

Hardy, Lucile[10] [1732], G151

Hardy, Miriam (Young)[9] [1271], G115, G151

Hardy, Miriam Y.[10]. *See* Hawkins, Miriam Y. (Hardy)[10] [1725]

Harker, George F., G152, G182

Harker, Josephine (Young)[10] [1740], G152, G182

Harlow, Elizabeth Hungerford (Farrar), G141

Harlow, George, G141

Harlow, Sarah Elizabeth. *See* Bacon, Sarah Elizabeth (Harlow)

Harman, ——— [married Theresa Jean[13] Nystrom], G292

Harman, Christopher Todd[14] [3416], G292

Harman, Theresa Jean (Nystrom)[13] [2970], G252, G292

Harman, Thomas Jonathan[14] [3415], G292

Harold, Matilda. *See* McCabe, Matilda (Harold)

Harrington, Francis[8] [956], G81

Harrington, Jonathan[8] [957], G81

Harrington, Mary. *See* Stone, Mary (Harrington)

Harrington, Nathaniel, G81

Harrington, Ruth (Stone)[7] [663], G60, G81

Harrington, Sarah[8] [958], G81

Harris, Clayton, G295

Harris, Hiram Leroy, G225

Harris, Karen Dorothy (Bakke)[14] [3446], G295

Harris, Laura Luella (Custer)[12] [2657], G225

Harrison, Ardelle (Young)[9] [1288], G115–116

Harrison, Evelyn (Eichhorn), G286

Harrison, Frank, G116

Harrison, James Geraty Jr., G286

Harrison, James Geraty [Sr.], G286

Harrison, Nancy Marian (Fitch)[13] [2930], G250, G286

Harrison, Rachel Hebden[14]. *See* DiLutis, Rachel Hebden (Harrison)[14] [3334]

Harrison, Robert Girdler[14] [3335], G287

Harrison, Thomasine Richards (Hahn), G287

Hart, LeVeta. *See* Whipple, LeVeta (Hart)

Hartshorn, Ebenezer, G32

Hartshorn, Ebenezer[6] [273], G32

Hartshorn, Elizabeth[6]. *See* Remington,

Elizabeth (Hartshorn)[6] [274]

Hartshorn, Eunice (Hapgood), G32

Hartshorn, John Denison[6] [271], G32

Hartshorn, Martha (Whipple)[5] [76], G32

Hartshorn, Martha[6] [272], G32

Hartwell, Philemon, G77

Hartwell, Sally (Ball)[8] [906], G77

Harvey, Judith (Pillsbury)[6] [229], G25

Harvey, William, G25

Haskell, Dorothy. *See* Goodhue, Dorothy (Haskell)

Haskell, Joseph, G22

Haskell, Mary (Graves), G22

Hastings, Almon Woodward[10] [1642], G146, G178

Hastings, Beatrice Nancy[12]. *See* Billigmeier, Beatrice Nancy (Hastings)[12] [2592]

Hastings, Charles Almon[12] [2588], G218

Hastings, Charles Frederick[11] [2050], G178

Hastings, Corinne Marion[12]. *See* Griffey, Corinne Marion (Hastings)[12] [2591]

Hastings, Dell (Kelley), G218

Hastings, Ella F. (Ehrhardt), G178

Hastings, Elmer Dean[12] [2589], G218

Hastings, Elmer William[11] [2052], G178, G218

Hastings, Esther (Woodward), G146

Hastings, Frances Anna[10]. *See* Stickney, Frances Anna (Hastings)[10] [1642]

Hastings, Gwendolyn (Townsley), G218

Hastings, Henry Arthur[11] [2051], G178

Hastings, Isa Helen (Davis), G218

Hastings, Isaac, G54, G58

Hastings, Lydia Ann[10] [1641], G146

Hastings, Marion E.[10] [1644], G146

Hastings, Mary E. (Hall), G218

Hastings, Maryetta Ruth[12]. *See* Hanson, Maryetta Ruth (Hastings)[12] [2590]

Hastings, Mayette Eliz (Person), G178

Hastings, Nathan Jr., G146

Hastings, Nellie Marion[11]. *See* Smith, Nellie Marion (Hastings)[11] [2049]

Hastings, Sarah (Goddard)[7] [576], G54, G58

Hastings, Susan (Goddard)[9] [1217], G104, G146

Hastings, William, G146

Hastings, William H.[10] [1645], G146

Hatch, Allen[9] [1130], G95

Hatch, Alonzo Herbert[10] [1544], G138, G167–168

Hatch, Anna (Gould)[8] [831], G71, G95
Hatch, Darius, G95
Hatch, Ellen[10] [1542], G138
Hatch, Emma Alice[11] [1936], G168
Hatch, Franklin[9] [1131], G95
Hatch, Jessamine Gertrude[11]. *See* Jessamine Gertrude (Hatch)[11] [1937]
Hatch, Julia Ann (Carney), G167–168
Hatch, Mae (Burcurne), G247
Hatch, Paschal[9] [1129], G95, G138
Hatch, Roxana (Cady), G138
Hatch, Roy C., G247
Hatch, Ruth. *See* Jenne, Ruth (Hatch)
Hatch, Stillman Allen[10] [1543], G138
Hatch, Zerviah[9] [1132], G95
Hathaway, Danforth O.[15] [3648], G313
Hathaway, Eugenia (Wise)[14] [3300], G283, G313
Hathaway, Orson S., G313
Hathaway, Paul D.[15] [3649], G313
Hatter, Elizabeth. *See* Patch, Elizabeth (Hatter)
Haven, Betsey (Howe)[7], G60
Haven, John, G60
Haven, Joseph, G20
Haven, [Dr.] Samuel, G32
Haven, Susanna (Goddard)[5] [152], G20
Hawkins, Eugene[11] [2343], G194
Hawkins, Helen Louise. *See* Miller, Helen Louise (Hawkins)
Hawkins, Lillian[11] [2341], G194
Hawkins, Lucile[11] [2344], G194
Hawkins, Miriam Charlotte[11] [2340], G194
Hawkins, Miriam Y. (Hardy)[10] [1725], G151, G194
Hawkins, Riego Curtis[11] [2342], G194
Hawkins, Riego Stay, G194
Hawse, Luella. *See* Stone, Luella (Hawse)
Haycock, Mary Elizabeth. *See* Brown, Mary Elizabeth (Haycock)
Hayden, Dory, G284
Hayden, Gertrude Alma (Rife), G284
Hayden, James Rife, G284
Hayden, Victoria Anne (McIntosh)[13] [2905], G248, G284
Hayes, Amanda Marie. *See* Stone, Amanda Marie (Hayes)
Hayes, James, G210
Hayes, Mabel. *See* Powers, Mabel (Hayes)
Hayes, Mary (Blessing), G210
Haymond, Allen Dilworth[11] [2217], G187
Haymond, Amasa Lyman II, G187

Haymond, Edward Lyman[11] [2221], G187
Haymond, Ella LaVaun[11] [2215], G187
Haymond, Ferdinand Fabian[11] [2218], G187
Haymond, Harold Edgar[11] [2219], G187
Haymond, Marian[11] [2222], G187
Haymond, Walter Conrad[11] [2216], G187
Haymond, Winifred B. (Conrad)[10] [1762], G153, G187
Haymond, Winifred[11] [2220], G187
Haynes, ——— [married Joni Sue[14] Darby], G316
Haynes, Joni Sue (Darby)[14]. *See* Woodruff, Joni Sue (Darby)[14] [3343]
Hazeltine, Carol. *See* Bacon, Carol (Hazeltine)
Hazeltine, Fanny (Brown), G243
Hazeltine, Frank Albert, G243
Hazelton, Anna Sarah. *See* Jenne, Anna Sarah (Hazelton)
Hazelton, Galusha, G173
Hazelton, Harriet (Kelley), G173
Hazen, Alice (Reece), G278
Hazen, Aretta Viola (Powers)[12] [2516], G209, G241
Hazen, Hugh[13] [2823], G241
Hazen, Irvin Hiatt, G241
Hazen, James Reece[14] [3259], G278
Hazen, Jeni Kay[14]. *See* Shymanski, Jeni Kay (Hazen)[14] [3258]
Hazen, Martha Ola[13]. *See* Musmaker, Martha Ola (Hazen)[13] [2821]
Hazen, Mary Evva[13]. *See* Jones, Mary Evva (Hazen)[13] [2820]
Hazen, Ralph Irvin[13] [2819], G241, G278
Hazen, Ruth Ruby[13]. *See* Long, Ruth Ruby (Hazen)[13] [2822]
Heald, Hannah (French)[8] [826], G70
Heald, Jonathan, G70
Healey, John Hopkins, G153
Healey, Ruth (Young)[9]. *See* Johnson, Ruth (Young)[9] [1286]
Heath, Carol Marie. *See* Sobieski, Carol Marie (Heath)
Hedrick, Valorie Lynn. *See* Michael, Valorie Lynn (Hedrick)
Heise, Alyson Marie[14] [3392], G291
Heise, Amy Linn[14] [3394], G291
Heise, Christopher James[14] [3389], G290
Heise, Donald, G252
Heise, Donna Jo[13]. *See* McDonald, Donna Jo (Heise)[13] [2957]

Holden, Miriam (Longley), G74
Holden, Nathaniel, G35
Holden, Phineas[7] [569], G53, G74
Holden, Thomas, G137
Holiday, Elizabeth. *See* Stone, Elizabeth (Holiday)
Holihan, Jamie Kay[15] [3637], G312
Holihan, Joseph Patrick[15] [3639], G312
Holihan, Karen Jill (Sexton)[14] [3253], G278, G311
Holihan, Natalie[15] [3638], G312
Holihan, Patrick Lee, G311
Holland, John, G132-133
Holland, Lucy (Hagedon)[10] [1508], G132
Holley, Bruce Frank, G296-297
Holley, Cari Carlene[14] [3462], G297
Holley, Daniel James[14] [3467], G297
Holley, Earl Henry, G297
Holley, Erik David[14] [3463], G297, G319
Holley, Katrina Leigh[14] [3465], G297
Holley, Kristina Marie[14] [3464], G297
Holley, Lilyan Lorraine (Dorr), G297
Holley, Michael Wayne[14] [3466], G297
Holley, Nicole LaRai[14]. *See* Bay, Nicole LaRai (Holley)[14] [3460]
Holley, Rachel Anne[15] [3719], G320
Holley, Sarah Michelle[15] [3720], G320
Holley, Sharon LaRay (Rich)[13] [3016], G257, G296-297
Holley, Susan (Baumann), G319
Holley, Wendi Jene[14]. *See* Tye, Wendi Jene (Holley)[14] [3461]
Holman, Joshua Sawyer, G110
Holman, Rebecca Greenleaf. *See* Young, Rebecca Greenleaf (Holman)
Holman, Rebecca Whitcomb (Greenleaf), G110
Holmes, Bertie Ellen. *See* Boyce, Bertie Ellen (Holmes)
Holmes, Carol. *See* Boyce, Carol (Holmes)
Holmes, Frank L., G258
Holmes, Norma Maria (Philips), G258
Holt, Barbara. *See* Wells, Barbara (Holt)
Holt, Gladys. *See* Powers, Gladys (Holt)
Holyoke, [Rev.] Edward, G34
Holyoke, Mary (Whipple)[5] [85], G12, G34
Hook, Melinda C. *See* Stone, Melinda C. (Hook)
Hooke, Caroline Amelia. *See* Phelps, Caroline Amelia (Hooke)
Hooker, Anna Minerva. *See* Phelps, Anna Minerva (Hooker)

Hooser, Mary Ellen. *See* Miller, Mary Ellen (Hooser)
Hopkins, Charlene (Davis), G269
Hopkins, Dora Dean[13]. *See* Weatherly, Dora Dean (Hopkins)[13] [2746]
Hopkins, Doris Jean[13] [2745]. *See* Michael, Doris Jean (Hopkins)[13] [2745]
Hopkins, Elizabeth Irene[13]. *See* Grimes, Elizabeth Irene (Hopkins)[13] [2751]
Hopkins, Eula Faye[13]. *See* Beal, Eula Faye (Hopkins)[13] [2748]
Hopkins, Fay [Otto], G233
Hopkins, Marjorie Eula (Whipple)[12] [2493], G206, G233
Hopkins, Melba Paulene[13]. *See* Chaffin, Melba Paulene (Hopkins)[13] [2747]
Hopkins, Melissa[14]. *See* Perryman, Melissa (Hopkins)[14] [3162]
Hopkins, Mirian Frances[13]. *See* Williams, Mirian Frances (Hopkins)[13] [2749]
Hopkins, William Otto[13] [2750], G233, G269
Horstman, Helena (Pullen)[12] [2469], G204, G231-232
Horstman, Janet[13]. *See* Anderson, Janet (Horstman)[13] [2730]
Horstman, Maurice Pote, G231-232
Horstman, Zella (Gray), G232
Horton, Bernice Louise (Tanner)[11] [2453], G202, G228
Horton, Dorothy Marietta[12]. *See* Clapp, Dorothy Marietta (Horton)[12] [2702]
Horton, John Morris, G228
Horton, Lisa Lynn[13] [3067], G261
Horton, Marvin Morris[12] [2703], G228, G261
Horton, Patricia (Lee), G261
Horton, Ruth May[12]. *See* Metzler, Ruth May (Horton)[12] [2701]
Horton, Sharon Lee[13] [3066], G261
Hovey, Esther. *See* Treadwell, Esther (Hovey)
Hovey, Hannah (Fossee), G63
Hovey, Luke, G7
Hovey, Nathaniel, G63
Hovey, Sarah Caroline. *See* Rogers, Sarah Caroline (Hovey)
Hovey, Sarah (Johnson), G91
Hovey, Solomon, G91
Hovey, Sussannah (Pillsbury)[5] [49], G7
How, Margaret. *See* Goddard, Margaret (How)

Huntley, Allen, G105

Huntley, Mary Ann. *See* Young, Mary Ann (Huntley)

Huntley, Sally (Hitchcock), G105

Hurst, Dorothy June (Miller)[13] [3049], G259

Hurst, Jerald Lee, G259

Hussey, Lydia. *See* Billings, Lydia (Hussey)

Hussey, Priscill (Hanson), G119

Hussey, Stephen, G119

Hutchinson, Benjamin Jr., G52

Hutchinson, Betsey[7]. *See* Parkhurst, Betsey (Hutchinson)[7] [557]

Hutchinson, Caroline E. (Goddard)[9] [1225], G104

Hutchinson, [Dr.] E. B., G147

Hutchinson, Edwin B., G104

Hutchinson, Harriet Angeline (Miller)[10] [1875], G160

Hutchinson, James A., G160

Hutchinson, Rebecca[6] [307], G34, G52

Hyde, Elizabeth (Starr)[5] [131], G18

Hyde, Jonathan, G18

Hyde, Lydia, G17

I

Ikuma, Tomika. *See* Whipple, Tomika (Ikuma)

Imlay, Kathy Lou. *See* Eliason, Kathy Lou (Imlay)

Imlay, Maced Doris (Peterson), G295

Imlay, Thomas Frederick, G295

Imsland, Kerry Ann. *See* Fisher, Kerry Ann (Imsland)

Ingle, Cara Dawn[15] [3630], G311

Ingle, Katherine Patterson (Windisch)[14] [3225], G275

Ingle, Rayburn, G311

Irish, Karrell. *See* Brinig, Karrell (Irish)

Irwin, Ann (Page), G294

Irwin, Virginia Jennings (Christman)[13]. *See* Smith, Virginia Jennings (Christman)[13] [2991]

Irwin, W. Pickney, G294

Ives, (———) [wife of Amos[7] Stone]. *See* Stone, (———) (Ives)

J

Jackson, Lois (Woodward)[7] [584], G54, G75

Jackson, Lois[8]. *See* King, Lois (Jackson)[8] [890]

Jackson, Samuel, G75

Jacobs, ——— [married Zina Diantha Huntington], G111

Jacobs, Zina Diantha Huntington. *See* Young, Zina Diantha (Hungtington)

Jagel, Arthur Garfield, G211

Jagel, Dorothy Gross. *See* Bacon, Dorothy Gross (Jagel)

Jagel, Elsie (Gross), G211

Jamison, Miller, Eva Lorraine. *See* Miller, Eva Lorraine (Jamison)

Jaquith, Joseph, G70

Jaquith, Susanna (French)[8] [828], G70

Jardine, Edmund Laroy[11] [2098], G180

Jardine, Elizabeth Young[11] [2099], G180

Jardine, Ellen[11] [2103], G180

Jardine, Hamilton Lester[11] [2104], G180

Jardine, James Leo[11] [2096], G180

Jardine, John William[11] [2100], G180

Jardine, Joseph Arthur[11] [2102], G180

Jardine, Luna Caroline (Ellsworth)[10] [1663], G148, G180

Jardine, Luna[11] [2094], G180

Jardine, Mary Mildred[11] [2105], G180

Jardine, Minnie Bell[11] [2101], G180

Jardine, Richard Franklin, G180

Jardine, Richard Franklin[11] [2095], G180

Jardine, Rowennah Wilmont[11] [2097], G180

Jardine, Ruth[11] [2106], G181

Javall, George, G245–246

Javall, Hester[13] [2873], G246

Javall, Lester[13] [2872], G246

Javall, Ruth (Barraford)[12] [2551], G214, G245–246

Javall, Vaneshia[13] [2874], G246

Jenkins, Hannah. *See* Treadwell, Hannah (Jenkins)

Jenks, Katherine Myrtle (Powers)[11] [1958], G170

Jenks, Roy, G170

Jenne, Anna Belle[11]. *See* Clark, Anna Belle (Jenne)[11] [1995]

Jenne, Anna Sarah (Hazelton), G173

Jenne, Anna S.[12]. *See* Medford, Anna S. (Jenne)[12] [2559]

Jenne, Bernard[12] [2565], G215

Jenne, Bessie[11]. *See* Whitmarsh, Bessie (Jenne)[11] [2002]

Jenne, Beth-Anne[14] [3310], G284

Jenne, Charlotte (Williams), G214

Jenne, Charlotte[12] [2561], G215

Jenne, Duane Erwin[13] [2900], G247

Jenne, Evelyn[11] [2001], G174

Johnson, Elizabeth[8]. *See* Corbin, Elizabeth (Johnson)[8] [895]

Johnson, Ella May[11] [2368], G196

Johnson, Ellis[10] [1768], G153, G196

Johnson, Epaphroditus[9] [1183], G100

Johnson, Esther. *See* Towle, Esther (Johnson)

Johnson, Francis Pearly, G175

Johnson, Francis Perley[11] Jr. [2015], G175

Johnson, Grove G.[9] [1185], G100, G143

Johnson, Hannah. *See* Goddard, Hannah (Johnson)

Johnson, Hannah (Eaton)[6] [343], G37, G55

Johnson, Hannah Iola (Ball)[10] [1616], G144, G175

Johnson, Hannah (Newton), G104

Johnson, Hannah[7] [598], G55

Johnson, Harriet. *See* Jenne, Harriet (Johnson)

Johnson, Harriet Persis[11] [2390], G198

Johnson, Harry Ellis[11] [2364], G196

Johnson, Helen (Spalding), G257

Johnson, Ivy[11] [2388], G197

Johnson, Jane Cadwalader[11] [2385], G197

Johnson, Jay Elliot[10] [1769], G153, G196

Johnson, John B. [1182], G100

Johnson, John[8] [893], G76, G100

Johnson, Jonathan[7] [597], G55

Johnson, Julia A.[9]. *See* Hodgkins, Julia A. (Johnson)[9] [1181]

Johnson, Karl Fredrick[13] [2739], G233, G267

Johnson, Karl Maeser[11] [2389], G197–198

Johnson, Kathe[11] [2386], G197

Johnson, Laura[8]. *See* Phelps, Laura (Johnson)[8] [894]

Johnson, Lee Scott[11] [2366], G196

Johnson, Lucy Elizabeth (Brown)[10] [1819], G156, G197

Johnson, Lucy Fuller[9]. *See* Wight, Lucy Fuller (Johnson)[9] [1187]

Johnson, Lydia[7] [601], G55

Johnson, Lydia (Avery), G75–76

Johnson, Lydia (Glazier), G100–101

Johnson, Lydia[8]. *See* Phelps, Lydia (Johnson)[8] [892]

Johnson, Mabel[7] [599], G55

Johnson, Mabel[8] [896], G76

Johnson, Mabel Frances[11] [2014], G175

Johnson, Malvina (Myers), G100

Johnson, Marilyn Kay (Miller)[12] [2696], G227, G259

Johnson, Martha Ann[13]. *See* Redstrom, Martha Ann (Johnson)[13] [2740]

Johnson, Martha Jane[11] [2013], G175

Johnson, Martha L. Gates, G100

Johnson, Mary (Calder), G267

Johnson, Mary (Edson), G55

Johnson, Mehitable (Guile), G55

Johnson, Mehitable[7] [596], G55

Johnson, Myrtle M.[10] [1603], G143

Johnson, Nathaniel, G55

Johnson, Nettie D.[10] [1602], G143

Johnson, Priscilla Ann (Hanners)[12]. *See* Nelms, Priscilla Ann (Hanners)[12] [2509]

Johnson, Richard Leroy, G239

Johnson, Ruby[11] [2383], G197

Johnson, Rufus, G104

Johnson, Rupert Fay[11] [2384], G197

Johnson, Ruth Elizabeth[11] [2367], G196

Johnson, Ruth Isabel (Whipple)[12] [2480], G206, G233

Johnson, Ruth (Young)[9] [1286], G115, G153

Johnson, Sandra. *See* Mohr, Sandra (Johnson)

Johnson, Sarah. *See* Eaton, Sarah (Johnson)

Johnson, Sarah E. *See* Blanchard, Sarah E. (Johnson)

Johnson, Sarah Jane[9]. *See* Jenne, Sarah Jane (Johnson)[9] [1184]

Johnson, Seth, G55

Johnson, Viva[11] [2387], G197

Johnson, Welthy[8] [898], G76

Johnson, William Derby II, G197

Johnson, William Don[13] [2741], G233, G267

Johnson, Zachary Calder[14] [3137], G267

Johnson, Zeno Martel[11] [2381], G197

Johnson, Zeruah (Bly), G100

Johnson, Zeruah J.[10] [1599], G143

Johnson-Spalding, Kjerstin[14] [3134], G267

Johnston, ——— [married Marjorie Diane[13] Whipple], G270

Johnston, Marjorie Diane (Whipple)[13]. *See* Whitmire, Marjorie Diane (Whipple)[13] [2756]

Jones, Abigail. *See* Stone, Abigail (Jones)

Jones, Alice LuZella[11]. *See* Day, Alice LuZella (Jones)[11] [2455]

Jones, Amy Leigh[15] [3602], G308

Jones, Andrew Petree[14] [3228], G275

K

Kady, Delia. *See* Goddard, Delia (Kady)

Kaemer, Susan. *See* Clapp, Susan (Kaemer)

Kammerman, Emma. *See* Decker, Emma (Kammerman)

Kanzler, Shirley. *See* Bakke, Shirley (Kanzler)

Kaylor, David Emerson, G276

Keate, Florence. *See* Gates, Florence (Keate)

Keathley, Mae. *See* Miller, Mae (Keathley)

Keeler, Beulah. *See* McAllister, Beulah (Keeler)

Keene, Huldah (Stone)[7] [560], G53

Keene, Zebulon, G53

Keighley, James Arthur, G301

Keighley, Rebekah Elisabeth (Young)[14] [3522], G301

Kelley, Beth[10] [1579], G140

Kelley, Dell. *See* Hastings, Dell (Kelley)

Kelley, Edward[10] [1578], G140, G171

Kelley, Harriett Newell (Tyler) [1157], G97, G140

Kelley, [Dr.] John S.[11] [1974], G171

Kelley, Lu Juana. *See* Bates, Lu Juana (Kelley)

Kelley, [Dr.] Samuel B., G140

Kelly, Ceil. *See* Custer, Ceil (Kelly)

Kelsey, Eunice B. (Pillsbury)[8] [762], G67

Kelsey, James, G67

Kenney, Abbie N. *See* Whipple, Abbie N. (Kenney)

Kenney, John, G139

Kenney, Martha (Nutting), G139

Kent, Alma Eliza (Cannon)[11] [2258], G189, G221

Kent, Barbara[12] [2625], G221

Kent, Daniel, G80

Kent, Edwin, G221

Kent, Nancy (Young)[8] [945], G80

Kent, Ruby. *See* Wise, Ruby (Kent)

Kerby, Helena (Pullen)[12]. *See* Horstman, Helena (Pullen)[12] [2469]

Ketter, ——— [married Keryl Anne[13] Heise], G290

Ketter, Andrew Dylan[14] [3381], G290

Ketter, Bethany Ann[14] [3385], G290

Ketter, Donald Joseph[14] [3383], G290

Ketter, Eric Jon[14] [3382], G290

Ketter, Keryl Anne (Heise)[13] [2956], G252, G290

Ketter, Sarah Cathryn[14] [3384], G290

Keys, Arch, G240

Keys, Mary Janice. *See* Hanners, Mary Janice (Keys)

Keys, Mary (Moore), G240

Kicidis, Catherine Elaine. *See* Christman, Catherine Elaine (Kicidis)

Kilham, Abigail (Kimball)[5] [194], G23, G43

Kilham, Hepsibah[6]. *See* Stevens, Hepsibah (Kilham)[6] [438]

Kilham, John, G43

Kilmer, Ellen (Westover), G178

Kilmer, George Dennis, G178

Kilmer, Harriet Ann. *See* Goddard, Harriet Ann (Kilmer)

Kimbale, Walter[8] [1032], G87, G127

Kimball, Aaron[5] [205], G24, G44

Kimball, Abigail[5]. *See* Kilham, Abigail (Kimball)[5] [194]

Kimball, Alfred[9] [1418], G126

Kimball, Amanda E. (Johnson), G160

Kimball, Amy[8] [1025], G86

Kimball, Anna (Ansley), G87

Kimball, Azuba[7] [719], G63

Kimball, Bethia (Shepard), G45

Kimball, Charles Jackson[9] [1415], G125, G126

Kimball, Cynthia[8]. *See* Knowles, Cynthia (Kimball)[8] [1030]

Kimball, Cynthia[9] [1436], G127

Kimball, David[5] [190], G23, G42

Kimball, David[6] [433], G43

Kimball, Easter[8]. *See* Miller, Easter (Kimball)[8] [1027]

Kimball, Ebenezer[5] [207], G24

Kimball, Ebenezer[6] [449], G44

Kimball, Ebenezer[6] [451], G44

Kimball, Edward Beatie[11] [2319], G193

Kimball, Edward Partridge, G193

Kimball, Elisha[8] [1024], G86, G126

Kimball, Elizabeth (Roelofson), G86, G125

Kimball, Ella G.[10] [1868], G160

Kimball, Enoch[8] [1029], G86

Kimball, Enoch[9] [1419], G126

Kimball, Esther (Phillips), G64

Kimball, Eunice[6] [431], G43

Kimball, Ezekiel[5] [209], G24

Kimball, Hazel Young (Beatie)[10] [1754], G153, G193

Kimball, Isaac[5] [192], G23, G43

Kimball, Isaac[7] [716], G63, G86

Kimball, Isaac[8] [1028], G86, G126-127

Kimball, Jacob[5] [194], G23, G43

Kimball, Jacob[6] Jr. [437], G43, G64

Jennifer Susan (Le Sueur)
Le Sueur, Robert, G312
Leak, Lisa Michelle. *See* Buell, Lisa
Michelle (Leak)
Lear, Tobias, G31
Learned, Martha. *See* Treadwell, Martha
(Learned)
Leatherland, John, G24
Leatherland, Sarah (Kimball)[5] [204], G24
Leavens, Alice (Eaton)[6] [340], G37
Leavens, Joseph, G37
Leavitt, Sarah (Pillsbury)[10] [1455], G129
Leavitt, William, G129
Lechner, Carline. *See* Morehouse, Carline
(Lechner)
Lee, Hannah (Thurber). *See* Starr,
Hannah (Thurber)
Lee, Patricia. *See* Horton, Patricia (Lee)
Lee, [Rev.] Richard, G77
Leeming, Ann Marie. *See* Mecham, Ann
Marie (Leeming)
Leeming, John, G224
Leighton, Katherine (Rogers)[6] [257], G27
Leighton, Kathrin [Ketherin]. *See*
Whipple, Kathrin [Ketherin] (Layton)
Leighton, William Jr., G27
Leland, Amory[10] [1523], G134
Leland, Elizabeth Carter[10] [1524], G134
Leland, Grace Adams (Rogers) [1100], G91,
G133–134
Leland, Joseph Daniels, G134
Leland, Joseph Daniels[10] [1525], G134
Lemieux, Gerald, G273
Lemieux, Jane. *See* Carpenter, Jane
(Lemieux)
Lemieux, Margaret (———), G273
Lemmon, Margaret Kennedy. *See* Nelson,
Margaret Kennedy (Lemmon)
Leonard, Anita (Baca), G259
Leonard, Edna (Briggs), G259
Leonard, George, G224
Leonard, LaWayne[13] [3047], G259
Leonard, Louise. *See* Young, Louise
(Leonard)
Leonard, Margaret Elizabeth (Keith), G157
Leonard, Mary Adams. *See* Stone, Mary
Adams (Leonard)
Leonard, Melvin Addison[12] [2656], G224,
G259
Leonard, Vivian (Becker)[11] [2428], G200,
G224
Leonard, William, G157

Leshinskie, Suzanne (Seyfarth)[14] [3116],
G265
Leshinskie, Walter Jay, G265
Levandoske, Gordon Roy, G262
Levandoske, Kelly Jean (Day)[12]. *See*
Flinders, Kelly Jean (Day)[12] [2709]
Lewis, Ezekiel, G13
Lewis, Roslyn. *See* Jones, Roslyn (Lewis)
Lincoln, (———) Briggs, G39
Lincoln, Experience. *See* Stearns,
Experience (Lincoln)
Lincoln, Isaac, G19
Lincoln, Kezia (Stone)[5] [136], G19
Lincoln, Samuel, G39
Lindsay, Hyrum Lester, G257
Lindsay, Imogene. *See* Rich, Imogene
(Lindsay)
Lindsay, Vara (Mouritsen), G257
Little, Clara Ann. *See* Brown, Clara Ann
(Little)
Little, [Rev.] Daniel, G29
Little, James, G80
Little, Susannah (Young)[8]. *See* Stilson,
Susannah (Young)[8] [950]
Livermore, Oliver, G60
Livermore, Ruth. *See* Stone, Ruth
(Livermore)
Livermore, Ruth (———) Bowman, G60
Livermore, Sarah (Nevinson) (Stearns).
See Stone, Sarah (Nevinson) (Stearns)
Livermore
Livingston, Edward F., G217
Livingston, Joyce Evon (Carson)[12] [2581],
G217
Locke, Harriet Lydia. *See* Fiske, Harriet
Lydia (Locke)
Lockman, Camilla Ann (Amsbaugh), G221
Lockman, Dorothy (Morehouse)[11] [2059],
G179, G220
Lockman, Edith Kading (Ermatinger),
G221
Lockman, Frederick Vincent, G220
Lockman, Genevieve (Keeny), G220
Lockman, Genevieve[12]. *See* Pitteklau,
Genevieve (Lockman)[12] [2617]
Lockman, George, G220
Lockman, George Roland[12] [2616], G221
Lockman, Marshall Frederick[12] [2615],
G221
Lockman, Peggy Ruth (Dudek), G221
Lockman, Richard Morehouse[12] [2614],
G220

M

Makee, Albert Fayette[13] [3001], G255
Makee, Albert Henry[12] [2631], G222, G255
Makee, Annie (Kotschevar), G222
Makee, Cora (Heitman), G255
Makee, Evaline (Giles), G255
Makee, Florence (Melby), G255
Makee, Galen Perry[12] [2629], G222
Makee, Hettie (———), G255
Makee, Ida Caroline (Carlson), G255
Makee, Lendall Billings[13] [3000], G255
Makee, Lendel Reed[12] [2632], G222
Makee, Lillie Augusta (Crum), G222
Makee, Mary Alice (Perry)[11] [2416], G199,
    G222
Makee, Phebe Mae Ann (Davidson), G222
Makee, Tryphena (———), G222
Makee, William, G222
Makee, William Francis Luther[12] [2630],
    G222
Makee, WIlliam Henry, G222
Makee, William Perry[13] [2999], G255
Makepeace, Almira D.[10] [1639], G146, G177
Makepeace, Etta Rosella[11]. See Packard,
    Etta Rosella (Makepeace)[11] [2047]
Makepeace, Norman G., G177
Mang, Georgie (Howell). See Bacon,
    Georgie (Howell)
Mang, Harry, G211
Mann, Margaret (Stone)[10] [1837], G158
Mann, Robert Colgate Vernon, G158
Manning, Sarah. See Burt, Sarah
    (Manning)
Mansfield, Jan Marie[13]. See Garrett, Jan
    Marie (Mansfield)[13] [3055]
Mansfield, Karen Lynn[13]. See Dowis,
    Karen Lynn (Mansfield)[13] [3053]
Mansfield, Lesly Alana[13]. See Gunz, Lesly
    Alana (Mansfield)[13] [3054]
Mansfield, Marilyn Ann[12]. See Riggs,
    Marilyn Ann (Mansfield)[12] [2697]
Mansfield, Musa Marie (Porter), G228
Mansfield, Orville Cecil Miller[11] [2447],
    G201, G227-228
Mansfield, Ramona (Contreras), G259
Mansfield, William Duane[12] [2698], G228,
    G259
Marcus, Dedee. See Baugh, Dedee (Marcus)
Marden, Ruth. See Towle, Ruth (Marden)
Mariger, Artemacy, G195
Mariger, Audrey[11] [2357], G195
Mariger, Clisbee (Young)[10] [1738], G152,
    G182, G195

Marshall, Abigail (Brown), G70
Marshall, Ailene Ruth (Sherman)[13] [2724],
    G231
Marshall, Anne (Mooar)[7] [473], G46
Marshall, Clara Clawson[11] [2256], G189
Marshall, George M., G189
Marshall, Isaac, G70
Marshall, Joel, G46
Marshall, Katherine[11]. See Sawyer,
    Katherine (Marshall)[11] [2255]
Marshall, Margaret Alley (Davis)[10] [1782],
    G154, G189
Marshall, Margaret[11] [2254], G189
Marshall, Rebecca. See French, Rebecca
    (Marshall)
Marshall, Richard, G231
Marsjanik, Patricia (LaClair). See Jenne,
    Patricia (LaClair)
Marson, Lisa. See Wise, Lisa (Marson)
Martin, Alice T. (Squires), G304
Martin, Alice Wedgwood (Pillsbury)[12]
    [2463], G203, G230
Martin, Brandon Cutter[14] [3105], G264,
    G304
Martin, David Cutter[13] [2722], G230, G264
Martin, Edith C.[13]. See Cox, Edith C.
    (Martin)[13] [2720]
Martin, Eliz Pillsbury[14]. See Barber, Eliz
    Pillsbury (Martin)[14] [3101]
Martin, Emily Tappey[15] [3552], G304
Martin, Harris Warthman[14] [3102], G264,
    G303
Martin, Helen L. (Wright), G264
Martin, Isabel Wedgwood[13]. See Jones,
    Isabel Wedgwood (Martin)[13] [2718]
Martin, John C., G230
Martin, John Charles[13] II [3103], G264
Martin, John Charles[15] III [3551], G304
Martin, Joyce E. (Newbill), G264
Martin, Karen V. (Crownover), G264
Martin, Martha Eloise. See Jones, Martha
    Eloise (Martin)
Martin, Mary Elizabeth (Newkirk), G264
Martin, Rachel Elizabeth[15] [3549], G303
Martin, Ruth (Davis), G303
Martin, Stanwood Warthman Davis[15]
    [3550], G304
Martin, Theodore Taft[14] [3104], G264
Martin, Thomas Wedgwood[14] [3100], G264
Mather, Adelaide Julia (Birdsail), G171
Mather, Adrian, G171
Mather, [Rev.] Cotton, G15

Mather, Jennie Adelaide. *See* Bacon, Jennie Adelaide (Mather)

Matthes, Leone. *See* Wilson, Leone (Matthes)

Mauer, Donald G., G260

Mauer, Margaret Lynn (Metzler)[13] [3062], G260

Maxey [slave], G14

Maynard, Abigail. *See* Knowlton, Abigail (Maynard)

Maynard, Abigail (Rice), G87–88

Maynard, Benjamin, G87

Maynard, Elsie (Eldridge), G157

Maze, Naomi Lucille (Custer)[12] [2662], G225

Maze, Vern Everett, G225

McCoy, Florence Colleen. *See* Powers, Florence Colleen (McCoy)

McLeroy, Merri Grace. *See* Whipple, Merri Grace (McLeroy)

McNeal, Elizabeth. *See* Treadwell, Elizabeth (McNeal)

Mecham, ––– (Hardy) [wife of Lucian Mormon[10] Mecham], G159

Mecham, Ammaron[10] [1852], G159

Mecham, Ammon[10] [1851], G159

Mecham, Ann Elizabeth (Bovee), G159

Mecham, Ann Eliza[10]. *See* Parkinson, Ann Eliza (Mecham)[10] [1861]

Mecham, Ann Marie (Leeming), G224

Mecham, Anna Mae (Parson), G223

Mecham, Anna Maria (Giles), G160

Mecham, Ariamiah[10]. *See* Sanberg, Ariamiah (Mecham)[10] [1849]

Mecham, Bates, Ellen[10]. *See* Bates, Ellen (Mecham)[10] [1846]

Mecham, Brigham Bovee[10] [1854], G159

Mecham, Daniel Lester[10] [1862], G160

Mecham, Desert[10] [1857], G159

Mecham, Dora Artenchia. *See* Boyce, Dora Artenchia (Mecham)[11] [2425]

Mecham, Edward Moroni[12] [2644], G223

Mecham, Eleanor (Lavery), G125

Mecham, Elizabeth Vilate[10]. *See* Christian, Elizabeth Vilate (Mecham)[10] [1858]

Mecham, Ella Lovenia[11]. *See* Fuchs, Ella Lovenia (Mecham)[11] [2422]

Mecham, Emma Waitstill[10]. *See* Nielson, Emma Waitstill (Mecham)[10] [1853]

Mecham, Everett Hess[11] [2423], G200, G223

Mecham, Glenn Jefferson[12] [2643], G223

Mecham, Hanna Ladd (Tyler), G159

Mecham, Janet (Pond), G223

Mecham, Jeremiah, G125

Mecham, Jonathan[9] [1412], G125

Mecham, Joseph, G125

Mecham, Joseph Lyman[10] [1860], G160

Mecham, Joseph L.[9] [1410], G125, G159–160

Mecham, Joseph Preston[10] [1866], G160

Mecham, Josephine[10] [1848], G159

Mecham, Joseph[10] [1850], G159

Mecham, Karmon Rae (Rex), G223

Mecham, Kenneth Luman[12] [2645], G223

Mecham, Laura Ann (Hardy), G159

Mecham, Leander[10] [1859], G160

Mecham, Leora Ann[12]. *See* Brinig, Leora Ann (Mecham)[12] [2655]

Mecham, Lester Eugene[11] [2427], G200, G224

Mecham, Lillie Elizabeth (Dunford), G223

Mecham, Loretta Sylvia[10]. *See* Noble, Loretta Sylvia (Mecham)[10] [1847]

Mecham, Lucian Mormon[10] [1855], G159

Mecham, Luman Lehi[10] [1863], G160, G200

Mecham, Lydia Saphronia (Lange), G159

Mecham, Martha Penelope (Richards), G160

Mecham, Mary Ann (Hess), G200

Mecham, Mary Emmerett[10]. *See* Sim, Mary Emmerett Mecham[10] [1864]

Mecham, Mary Eurilla[11]. *See* Wilson, Mary Eurilla (Mecham)[11] [2424]

Mecham, Mary Katherine (Green), G159

Mecham, Matilda Ann (Tuttle), G159

Mecham, Mehitable (Knapp), G125

Mecham, Melvin Everett[12] [2641], G223

Mecham, Miriam[9]. *See* Taylor, Miriam (Mecham)[9] [1409]

Mecham, Norman Dunford[12] [2642], G223

Mecham, Phebe (Main), G125

Mecham, Phebe[9] (Mecham) [1408], G125

Mecham, Samuel, G125

Mecham, Samuel[9] [1411], G125

Mecham, Sarah (Basford)[8] [1020], G86, G125

Mecham, Sarah Emily[10] [1865], G160, G200

Mecham, Sarah Maria (Tuttle), G159

Mecham, Sarah Merle[12]. *See* Jorgenson, Sarah Merle (Mecham)[12] [2640]

Mecham, Seymour B.[10] [1856], G159

Mecham, Susanna (Talbot), G159

Mecham, Susan[9] [1413], G125

Mecham, Vicci (Hullinger), G223
Mecham, ———[11] [2426], G200
Medford, Anna S. (Jenne)[12] [2559], G215
Medford, Perry, G215
Meeks, Bennie Scurry (Stone)[12] [2627],
    G222, G254
Meeks, Catherine Dorothy (Fitzgerald),
    G294
Meeks, Elinor Freda (Schull), G294
Meeks, Fleming Littleton[13] [2994], G254,
    G294
Meeks, Helen Moore (Laughinghouse),
    G295
Meeks, Henry Isaac[14] [3440], G294
Meeks, Ione (Tumlin), G254
Meeks, Jennifer Dail[14] [3441], G295
Meeks, Jesse Fitzgerald[14] [3438], G294
Meeks, Jesse Littleton, G254
Meeks, Marion Littleton, G254
Meeks, Marion Littleton[13] Jr. [2994], G254,
    G294
Meeks, Marshall Stone[13] [2993], G254,
    G294
Meeks, Martha Wescott (Driver), G294
Meeks, Sarah Elizabeth[14] [3439], G294
Melby, Florence. See Makee, Florence
    (Melby)
Mercer, Carver, G146
Mercer, Catherine Lorette (Orvis)[9] [1209],
    G103, G146
Mercer, Elizabeth Tracy[10]. See Girdler,
    Elizabeth Tracy (Mercer)[10] [1640]
Mercer, [Dr.] Thomas Clifford, G146
Mercer, Winifred Neville (Oldham), G146
Merrill, Nancy. See Hanners, Nancy
    (Merrill)
Metzler, Charles D., G260
Metzler, Henry G., G260
Metzler, Janice Anne[13]. See Comstra,
    Janice Anne (Metzler)[13] [3061]
Metzler, Kathleen Ruth[13]. See Bower,
    Kathleen Ruth (Metzler)[13] [3059]
Metzler, Linda (Godfrey), G260
Metzler, Margaret Lynn[13]. See Mauer,
    Margaret Lynn (Metzler)[13] [3062]
Metzler, Ottillia (Kieffer), G260
Metzler, Ronald Charles[13] [3060], G260
Metzler, Ruth May (Horton)[12] [2701],
    G228, G260
Meurer, Jack R., G303
Meurer, Ruth (Davis). See Martin, Ruth
    (Davis)

Meyer, Beverly Rae. See Jones, Beverly Rae
    (Meyer)
Michael, Cady Lynn[15] [3590], G307
Michael, Dennis, G268
Michael, Doris Jean (Hopkins)[13] [2745],
    G233, G268
Michael, Richard Lee[14] [3143], G268, G307
Michael, Ronald Eugene[14] [3144], G268
Michael, Ryan Christopher[15] [3589], G307
Michael, Valorie Lynn (Hedrick), G307
Michaels, ——— [married Linda Jean[13]
    Heise], G290
Michaels, Kelly Lynn[14] [3378], G290
Michaels, Linda Jean (Heise)[13] [2955],
    G252, G290
Michaels, Melissa Ann[14] [3379], G290
Michaels, Micole Marie[14] [3380], G290
Millen, Deborah. See Bucknam, Deborah
    (Millen)
Miller, ——— [married Monica Marie[14]
    Sobieski], G317
Miller, Abbie Marie[15] [3704], G318
Miller, Alexander[10] [1882], G161, G200
Miller, Amanda[15] [3703], G317
Miller, Benjamin Franklin[10] [1886], G161,
    G201
Miller, Bernice Pauline (Wallace), G259
Miller, Bessie Blanche[11] [2432], G200
Miller, Blance Meurice (Stoneberger),
    G226
Miller, Carl Otis[11] [2444], G201, G227
Miller, Carolyn Pauline[12]. See Goode,
    Carolyn Pauline (Miller)[12] [2693]
Miller, Charles Henry[10] [1877], G161
Miller, Claire LaVaun (Towers), G226
Miller, Clarence E.[11] [2447], G201
Miller, Clark Henry[12] [2695], G227, G259
Miller, Cora (Gillespie), G201
Miller, David John[12] [2691], G227
Miller, Dorothy June[13]. See Hurst,
    Dorothy June (Miller)[13] [3049]
Miller, Earl Charles[11] [2436], G201
Miller, Earnest[11] [2438], G201
Miller, Easter (Kimball)[8] [1027], G86, G126
Miller, Edna K.[11]. See Whorton, Edna K.
    (Miller)[11] [2446]
Miller, Edna L., G227
Miller, Edwin Lee[11] [2442], G201, G227
Miller, Elisha D.[9] [1432], G126, G161
Miller, Elisha[10] [1871], G160
Miller, Eliza Jane[10] [1880], G161
Miller, Elizabeth Marilla[12]. See Davidson,

Moore-Morr, Wanda. *See* Pratt, Wanda (Moore-Morr)

Moors, Edmund Jr., G7

Moors, Judith (Pillsbury)[5] [50], G7

Moran, Brian G., G320

Moran, McKenzie Irene[16] [3726], G320

Moran, Margaret Mary[16] [3725], G320

Moran, Melissa Elaine (Bakke)[15] [3715], G319, G320

Morehead, Linne. *See* Brush, Linne (Morehead)

Morehouse, Andrew, G178

Morehouse, Bonnie Lavisa (Dalton), G220

Morehouse, Carline (Lechner), G220

Morehouse, Cecil Goddard[11] [2058], G179, G220

Morehouse, Charles Richmond, G178

Morehouse, Charles Richmond[12] II [2611], G220

Morehouse, Charles Wilmont[11] [2060], G179

Morehouse, David Hugh[11] [2061], G179

Morehouse, Dorothy Lucille[12]. *See* Grieb, Dorothy Lucille (Morehouse)[12] [2612]

Morehouse, Dorothy[11]. *See* Lockman, Dorothy (Morehouse)[11] [2059]

Morehouse, Edith (Glick), G220

Morehouse, Emma Lou (Feckley), G220

Morehouse, Laura Glick[12]. *See* Tupper, Laura Glick (Morehouse)[12] [2613]

Morehouse, Lora E. (Goddard)[10] [1652], G147

Morehouse, Vesta (Richmond), G178

Morgan, ――― [married Dawn Maurine[13] Goddard], G289

Morgan, Dawn Maurine (Goddard)[13] [2947], G252, G289

Morgan, Megan Leeann[15] [3706], G318

Morgrage, Rebecca (Billings)[7] [691], G62

Morgrage, Thomas, G62

Morrell, Samuel, G45

Morrell, Sarah (Pillsbury)[7] [462]. *See* Brown, Sarah (Pillsbury)[7] [462]

Morrell, Winifred. *See* Cannon, Winifred (Morrell)

Morrill, Caroline E. *See* Goddard, Caroline E.

Morrill, John, G67

Morrill, Martha (Pillsbury)[8] [761], G66–67

Morris, Clara. *See* Clawson, Clara (Morris)

Morrison, Etta Marie (Hayball), G306

Morrison, Jean. *See* Anderson, Jean

(Morrison)

Morrison, Milner Bowden, G306

Morse, Benjamin, G24

Morse, [David or Moses], G66

Morse, Elisha, G60

Morse, Elizabeth (Pillsbury)[8] [757], G66

Morse, John, G18

Morse, Judith (Starr)[5] [128], G18

Morse, Patty (Howe)[7] [655], G60

Morse, Ruth (Sawyer), G24

Morse, Samuel, G18

Morse, Sarah. *See* Pillsbury, Sarah (Morse)

Morse, Sarah (Starr)[5] [124], G18

Morton, Abner, G40

Morton, Easter (Goddard)[6] [402], G40

Morton, Samuel, G40

Morton, Sophia (Goddard)[6] [400], G40

Moulton, Dorothy. *See* Whipple, Dorothy (Moulton)

Moulton, Sarah. *See* Stone, Sarah (Moulton)

Mousley, Emmett, G148

Mousley, Minnie (Ellsworth)[10] [1665], G148

Munger, Carolyn (Saunders)[14] [3305], G283, G313–314

Munger, Loren[15] [3660], G314

Munger, Robert, G314

Munro, Bethany Nanette[13] [3069], G261

Munro, Brent Paul[13] [3068], G261

Munro, Donald Philip, G261

Munro, Dorth Paulum, G261

Munro, Nathan Reed[13] [3070], G261

Munro, Patricia Andrea (Thayer)[12] [2704], G228, G261

Munro, Todd Clifford[13] [3071], G261

Munro, Vera Marie (Blackiston), G261

Munsch, Cyril Clement, G235

Munsch, Jeffrey James[14] [3189], G272

Munsch, Margaret Leah[13]. *See* Dahl, Margaret Leah (Munsch)[13] [2771]

Munsch, Martha Belle (Whipple)[12] [2495], G206, G235

Munsch, Melody Ann[13]. *See* Butzner, Melody Ann (Munsch)[13] [2775]

Munsch, Michael Douglas[13] [2772], G235

Munsch, Morgen Lynn[14] [3187], G271

Munsch, Pamela Rae (Palin), G235

Munsch, Patrick Cyril[13] [2773], G235

Munsch, Stephanie Ann (Waugh), G271

Munsch, Timothy John[13] [2774], G235, G271

Munsch, Timothy John[14] [3188], G272

Munsey, Annie W. *See* Ball, Annie W. (Munsey)

Munson, Clara (Powers)[11] [1963], G170, G210

Munson, Jane[12] [2528], G210

Munson, John Cameron[12] [2527], G210

Munson, Robert Powers[12] [2526], G210

Munson, Zee, G210

Murphy, B. Jay[14] [3453], G296

Murphy, Cheryl Kay[13]. *See* Billings, Cheryl Kay (Murphy)[13] [3014]

Murphy, Kiska Rae[14] [3452], G296

Murphy, Marva Dene[13]. *See* Bard, Marva Dene (Murphy)[13] [3015]

Murphy, Penny Dee[14]. *See* Hall, Penny Dee (Murphy)[14] [3450]

Murphy, Rich Eugene[13] [3013], G256, G296

Murphy, Richard, G276

Murphy, Shane Rich[14] [3451], G296

Murphy, Susan Priscilla (Nelms)[13]. *See* Gillette, Susan Priscilla (Nelms)[13] [2803]

Murphy, Thomas Franklin, G256

Murphy, Verla Eurilla (Rich)[12] [2646], G224, G256

Murphy, Wilda Dee (Bledsoe), G296

Murray, Fanny (Young)[8] [946], G80

Murray, Roswell, G80

Muruaasen, Iverdina Amundsdatter (Instenas), G219

Muruaasen, Per Helgesen, G219

Musmaker, Brian Earl[14] [3264], G279

Musmaker, Bruce Allan[14] [3263], G279

Musmaker, Chrystal Ann (Christenson), G279

Musmaker, John Albert, G279

Musmaker, Martha Ola (Hazen)[13] [2821], G241, G279

Myers, Henry, G132

Myers, Malvina. *See* Johnson, Malvina (Myers)

Myers, Olivia Sophia A. (Hibbard)[10] [1494], G132

N

Nabatian, Bahram, G312

Nabatian, Kaveh[15] [3657], G313

Nabatian, Martha (Saunders)[14] [3304], G283, G313

Nabatian, Shireen[15] [3659], G313

Nabatian, Sohrob[15] [3658], G313

Nash, Beverly Jean. *See* Esson, Beverly Jean (Nash)

Nash, Doris (Martin), G232

Nash, Victor, G232

Neal, Gary, G303

Neal, Ruth (Davis). *See* Martin, Ruth (Davis)

Nelms, Deborha Dawn (Peterson), G277

Nelms, Debra Louise[13]. *See* Hubler, Debra Louise (Nelms)[13] [2805]

Nelms, Douglas Vernon[13] [2804], G240

Nelms, Jaime Lynn[14] [3245], G277

Nelms, Mark Ralph[13] [2807], G240, G277

Nelms, Priscilla Ann (Hanners)[12] [2509], G208, G239

Nelms, Susan Priscilla[13]. *See* Gillette, Susan Priscilla (Nelms)[13] [2803]

Nelms, Sylvia (Perez), G240

Nelms, Tyler Justin[14] [3244], G277

Nelms, Vernon LeRoy, G239

Nelson, Barbara Jane[13]. *See* Wege, Barbara Jane (Nelson)[13] [2797]

Nelson, Boulucas, G177

Nelson, Catherine Jane (Babcock), G239

Nelson, Eric Hatch[13] [2799], G239, G276

Nelson, Harry Arthur, G207–208

Nelson, Lula Caroline (Brush)[11] [2044], G177

Nelson, Margaret Kennedy (Lemmon), G239

Nelson, Misty Daniele[14] [3236], G276

Nelson, Morgan Eric[14] [3237], G276

Nelson, Nancy. *See* Pillsbury, Nancy (Nelson)

Nelson, Robert Babcock[13] [2798], G239

Nelson, Robert Hatch[12] [2506], G208, G239

Nelson, Roberta (Cauthron), G276

Newbill, Joyce E. *See* Martin, Joyce E. (Newbill)

Newcomb, ——— [married Fannie H.[10] Davis], G140

Newcomb, Fannie H. (Davis)[10] [1565], G140

Newell, Arthur William, G174

Newell, Mary Frances (Grow)[10] [1611], G144, G174

Newell, Nellie Eliza[11]. *See* Baldwin, Nellie Eliza (Newell)[11] [2005]

Newkirk, Mary Elizabeth. *See* Martin, Mary Elizabeth (Newkirk)

Newman, Robert, G63

Nibley, Alexander, G184

Nibley, Constance (Thatcher)[10] [1687],

O

P

Woodworth, Lila Lee (Packard)[13] [2927]
Papara, Tony Raymond, G286
Pape, Elsie Elizabeth (Starr)[8]. *See* Ward, Elsie Elizabeth (Starr)[8] [919]
Pape, John West, G102
Parke, Hannah (Witter), G43
Parke, Mary. *See* Kimball, Mary (Parke)
Parke, Prudence. *See* Kimball, Prudence (Parke)
Parke, Thomas, G43
Parker, ——— [married Diane Eileen[13] Stevens], G287
Parker, Ann (Howe)[7] [656], G60
Parker, Betsey. *See* Snow, Betsey (Parker)
Parker, Bradford Lee, G282
Parker, Bruce L., G282
Parker, Catharine Mather (Foster)[13] [2865], G245, G282
Parker, Daniel, G25
Parker, Diane Eileen (Stevens)[13]. *See* Glupker, Diane Eileen (Stevens)[13] [2933]
Parker, Emme. *See* Stone, Emme (Parker)
Parker, Esther (Pillsbury)[6] [225], G25
Parker, Jereboam, G60
Parker, John, G50
Parker, Joshua Lee[14] [3297], G282
Parker, Judythe Ann (Daggett), G282
Parker, Mary. *See* Pillsbury, Mary (Parker)
Parkhurst, Betsey (Hutchinson)[7] [557], G52, G73
Parkhurst, Celia (Burrows), G95–96
Parkhurst, Elisabeth Ann[9]. *See* Fiske, Elisabeth Ann (Parkhurst)[9] [1140]
Parkhurst, [Dr.] John[8] [864], G73, G95–96
Parkhurst, Samuel, G73
Parkinson, Ann Eliza (Mecham)[10] [1861], G160
Parkinson, Louise. *See* Clawson, Louise (Parkinson)
Parkinson, Peter, G160
Parson, Anna Mae. *See* Mecham, Anna Mae (Parson)
Partridge, Alice L. *See* Davis, Alice L. Partridge
Partridge, Edward, G108
Partridge, Eliza, G108
Partridge, Eliza Augusta. *See* Powers, Eliza Augusta (Partridge)
Partridge, Ellen (Miner), G169, G170
Partridge, Emily Dow. *See* Young, Emily Dow (Partridge)
Partridge, Helen Frances. *See* Powers,

Helen Frances (Partridge)
Partridge, Katherine. *See* Stone, Katherine (Partridge)
Partridge, Lydia (Clisbee), G108
Partridge, Lyman, G169, G170
Passmore, Anna. *See* Treadwell, Anna (Passmore)
Passmore, Mary (Whittemore), G123
Passmore, Thomas, G123
Patch, Desire (Cowing), G76
Patch, Edna (Hicklin), G174
Patch, Edna Marion[11] [2007], G174
Patch, Edward[9] [1193], G101, G144
Patch, Elizabeth (Hatter), G101
Patch, Emily Carol[12]. *See* Baker, Emily Carol (Patch)[12] [2568]
Patch, Ephraim, G56
Patch, Ethel (McFatridge), G215
Patch, Harriet (Patch), G144
Patch, Henry, G144
Patch, James Edward[11] [2006], G174, G215
Patch, Luther[8] [901], G76, G101
Patch, Michelle Elizabeth Bo Yung Kak[13] [2908], G248
Patch, Penelope (Dana)[6] [350], G37, G56
Patch, Ralph Ernest[10] [1612], G144, G174
Patch, Ralph James[12] [2569], G215, G248
Patch, Susan Ai Nan Marion[13] [2907], G248
Patch, Susan (Winters), G248
Patch, Thomas[7] [605], G56, G76
Patterson, Anna (Newell), G143
Patterson, Austin Eaton[10] [1610], G143, G174
Patterson, Darla[13] [2895], G246
Patterson, Eleanor Akin, G135
Patterson, Esther Adeline (Eaton)[9] [1191], G101, G143
Patterson, Ferne Catherine[11]. *See* Jones, Ferne Catherine (Patterson)[11] [1932]
Patterson, Gayle Marie[13] [2896], G246
Patterson, John A., G143
Patterson, Louisa Malvina[11]. *See* Wills, Louisa Malvina (Patterson)[11] [2004]
Patterson, Lydia Jane (Barker), G173
Patterson, Myrtle Annabelle (Barraford)[12] [2558], G214, G247
Patterson, Oliver, G143
Patterson, Ovando, G135
Patterson, Phebe Smith (Whipple)[9] [1111], G92, G135
Patterson, Proctor[10] [1530], G135,

G163

Pillsbury, Catherine Stanwood (Benjamin), G129

Pillsbury, Clara (Rackliffe), G129

Pillsbury, Daniel[6] [216], G24

Pillsbury, Dorothy (Crosby), G7

Pillsbury, Dorothy[5]. See Poor, Dorothy (Pillsbury)[5] [48]

Pillsbury, Edmund[6] [220], G24

Pillsbury, [Rev.] Edmund[7] [453], G45, G65

Pillsbury, Edmund[9] [1060], G89, G129

Pillsbury, Eleanor Benjamin[12]. See Pennell, Eleanor Benjamin (Pillsbury)[12] [2461]

Pillsbury, Eliz (Rowell), G89

Pillsbury, Eliza D. (Barnard), G129

Pillsbury, Eliza (Godfrey), G7

Pillsbury, Elizabeth (Dinsmoor), G129, G130

Pillsbury, Elizabeth Dinsmoor[11]. See Poole, Elizabeth Dinsmoor (Pillsbury)[11] [1899]

Pillsbury, Elizabeth (Mooney), G163

Pillsbury, Elizabeth (Sawyer), G45

Pillsbury, Elizabeth (Stuart), G7

Pillsbury, Elizabeth[7]. See Webster, Elizabeth (Pillsbury)[7] [465]

Pillsbury, Elizabeth[8]. See Morse, Elizabeth (Pillsbury)[8] [757]

Pillsbury, Eliza[10]. See Fitts, Eliza (Pillsbury)[10] [1462]

Pillsbury, Eliz[9]. See Currier, Eliz (Pillsbury)[9] [1062]

Pillsbury, Ellen (Adams), G129

Pillsbury, Ellinore[6] [227], G25

Pillsbury, Elvira[10]. See Stinson, Elvira (Pillsbury)[10] [1458]

Pillsbury, Enoch[8] [731], G65

Pillsbury, Enoch[9] [1061], G89

Pillsbury, Eunice B.[8]. See Kelsey, Eunice B. (Pillsbury)[8] [762]

Pillsbury, Ezra[6] [217], G24

Pillsbury, George Washington[9] [1065], G89

Pillsbury, George[9] [1055], G89

Pillsbury, George[10] [1461], G129

Pillsbury, Hannah[5]. See Hoit, Hannah (Pillsbury)[5] [52]

Pillsbury, Hannah[6] [226], G25

Pillsbury, Harry M.[11] [1896], G163, G203

Pillsbury, Helen Cutter[12]. See Wells, Helen Cutter (Pillsbury)[12] [2462]

Pillsbury, Hepzieth (Twombly), G65

Pillsbury, Isaac[7] [467], G46

Pillsbury, Jacob[9] [1059], G89, G129

Pillsbury, Jacob[10] [1453], G129

Pillsbury, James Marcellus[12] [2464], G203

Pillsbury, James[8] [734], G65

Pillsbury, James[9] [1054], G89

Pillsbury, James[9] [1057], G89

Pillsbury, James[10] [1457], G129, G162

Pillsbury, John[8] [729], G65

Pillsbury, John Hale[8] [730], G65, G89

Pillsbury, John[9] [1058], G89

Pillsbury, John C.[10] [1459], G129

Pillsbury, John J.[10] [1465], G129

Pillsbury, Joseph[5] [46], G7

Pillsbury, Joshua[7] [460], G45

Pillsbury, Josiah Webster[9] [1066], G89, G129

Pillsbury, Judith (Sargent), G66

Pillsbury, Judith[5]. See Moors, Judith (Pillsbury)[5] [50]

Pillsbury, Judith[6]. See Harvey, Judith (Pillsbury)[6] [229]

Pillsbury, Judith[8]. See Hoyt, Judith (Pillsbury)[8] [756]

Pillsbury, Kate (Cutter), G203

Pillsbury, Kittie M.[11] [1897], G163

Pillsbury, Lizze (Wedgwood), G129

Pillsbury, Lois[9]. See Currier, Lois (Pillsbury)[9] [1056]

Pillsbury, Lois[10]. See Tripp, Lois (Pillsbury)[10] [1460]

Pillsbury, Louisa Fuller (Johnson) Wheeler, G163

Pillsbury, Louisa[10] [1452], G129

Pillsbury, Louisa[10] [1454]. See Davis, Louisa (Pillsbury)[10] [1454]

Pillsbury, Louisa[10] [1464], G129

Pillsbury, Lydia B.[8]. See Chamberlain, Lydia B. (Pillsbury)[8] [763]

Pillsbury, Lydia[10]. See French, Lydia (Pillsbury)[10] [1456]

Pillsbury, Martha (Hale)[7] [458], G45, G65

Pillsbury, Martha[8]. See Batchelder, Martha (Pillsbury)[8]; Morrill, Martha (Pillsbury)[8] [761]

Pillsbury, Mary (Parker), G44, G65

Pillsbury, Mary (Smith), G46

Pillsbury, Mary[6]. See Emery, Mary (Pillsbury)[6] [219]

Pillsbury, Mary[8]. See Robbins, Mary (Pillsbury)[8] [758]

Pillsbury, Mehitable (Buswell), G45

Pillsbury, Mercy (Watson), G24

Pillsbury, Micajah[7] [466], G45

Pratt, George D., G83, G84
Pratt, Hannahette (Snively), G109
Pratt, Henry A. [8] [998], G84
Pratt, Herbert L., G83, G84
Pratt, Jennifer Susan (Le Sueur), G312
Pratt, Jerome Clarence[12] [2522], G209
Pratt, John T., G83, G84
Pratt, Karen Ellen[14]. *See* Allen, Karen Ellen (Pratt)[14] [3277]
Pratt, Lydia Ann (Richardson), G83
Pratt, Lydia [daughter of Charles[8] Pratt], G83
Pratt, Marilyn Jeanne (Sorensen), G280
Pratt, Mary Helen (Richardson), G83
Pratt, Nelson P., G209
Pratt, Olive Evalena (Powers)[11] [1953], G169, G209
Pratt, Orville Powers[12] [2520], G209, **G241–242**
Pratt, Parley P., G109
Pratt, Rosalia (Goodale), G209
Pratt, Sherman. *See* Sherman, Hattie (Pratt)
Pratt, Taylor Thomas[15] [3644], G312
Pratt, Thomas Jeffrey[14] [3277], G280, G312
Pratt, Thomas Nelson[13] [2829], G242, **G280**
Pratt, Wanda (Moore-Morr), G209
Pratt, William, G209
Prescott, Mary. *See* Stone, Mary (Prescott)
Preskins, Amelia Julia Rose. *See* Packard, Amelia Julia Rose (Preskins)
Preskins, Louise M. (Kulesus), G249
Preskins, William, G249
Preston, Arlan Wayne, G279
Preston, Linda Kay (Jones)[14] [3261], G279
Pride, Sarah. *See* Kimball, Sarah (Pride)
Prince, Elizabeth (Starr)[6] [355], G37
Proctor, Mary. *See* Hill, Mary (Proctor)
Puffer, James, G40
Puffer, Mary [Mercy, May]. *See* Goddard, Mary [Mercy, May] (Puffer)
Puffer, Submit (Goddard)[6] [394], G40
Pullen, Cynthia Louise. *See* Anderson, Cynthia Louise (Pullen)
Pullen, Deb Adelbert[12] [2470], G204–205
Pullen, Edythe (Stevenson), G205
Pullen, Henena[12]. *See* Horstman, Helena (Pullen)[12] [2469]
Pullen, John Tyson, G204
Pullen, Judson Lee, G306
Pullen, [Dr.] Lawford Gard, G204
Pullen, Martha Jean (Allen), G306

Pullen, Mary Druce (Gard), G204
Pullen, Nellie May (Blanchard)[11] [1916], G165, G204
Putnam, Mary Traill Spence (Lowell)[9] [1112], G92
Putnam, S. R., G92

Q

Quinn, Craig Stephen, G253
Quinn, Mary Margaret. *See* Perkins, Mary Margaret (Quinn)
Quinn, Wendy Caprice (Tegreeny)[13] [2983], G253

R

Rackliffe, Clara. *See* Pillsbury, Clara (Rackliffe)
Raine, Alice Luella (Decker)[10]. *See* Cunningham, Alice Luella (Decker)[10] [1667]
Raine, Genevieve[11] [2112], G181
Raine, John A., G181
Rainey, Alfred Luther, G226
Rainey, Loyd Dean (Foster)[12] [2687], G226
Raley, Ruby Goldie. *See* Long, Ruby Goldie (Raley)
Rampton, Edward[11] [2349], G195
Rampton, Eugenia Young (Hardy)[10] [1726], G151, GG195
Rampton, Henry Hardy[11] [2345], G195
Rampton, James Henry, G195
Rampton, James Paul[11] [2347], G195
Rampton, Leonard Hardy[11] [2346], G195
Rampton, Richard Hardy[11] [2348], G195
Rand, Deborah (Dodge)[6], G43, G64
Rand, Polly[8]. *See* Bowers, Polly (Rand)[8] [1038]
Rand, Sarah (Adams), G87
Rand, Solomon, G64
Rand, Solomon[7] [726], G64, G87
Randall, Irene Sayles. *See* Hoyt, Irene Sayles (Randall)
Randall, Irene (Sayles), G130
Randall, Job, G130
Randall, Judkins, G67
Randall, Ploomy (Pillsbury) [765], G67
Randazzo, Alexis Catherine[14] [3213], G274
Randazzo, Barbara Ann (Zahn), G274
Randazzo, Jack Thomas[14] [3215], G274
Randazzo, Jane Lucy (Weeks)[13] [2784], G237, G274
Randazzo, John Francis, G274
Randazzo, Kelly Frances[14] [3212], G274

(Ripley)

Riter, Elsie. *See* Croxall, Elsie (Riter)

Robbins, Caroline (Stone)[7] [684], G61

Robbins, George M., G61

Robbins, Isaac, G66

Robbins, Mary (Pillsbury)[8] [758], G66

Robbins, Sally. *See* Pillsbury, Sally (Robbins)

Roberts, Anne (Wells)[14] [3093], G263

Roberts, Charles Lawrence Sr., G226

Roberts, John, G14

Roberts, [Dr.] John, G263

Roberts, LaRae. *See* Rich, LaRae (Roberts)

Roberts, Maedean Ivanette (Miller)[12] [2679], G226

Robinson, Betsey. *See* Goddard, Betsey (Robinson)

Robinson, Hannah. *See* Knowlton, Hannah (Robinson)

Rockwood, David, G88

Rockwood, Ellen. *See* Young, Ellen (Rockwood)

Rockwood, Joanna (Knowlton)[8] [1045], G88

Rockwood, Nancy (Haven), G109

Rockwood, Perry, G109

Roelofson, Elizabeth. *See* Kimball, Elizabeth (Roelofson)

Roger, Mary (Ellery), G47

Rogers, Abigail (Hammond), G27

Rogers, Abigail (Woodward), G47

Rogers, Charles[7] [499], G48

Rogers, Daniel[6] [261], G27, G48

Rogers, Daniel[7] [500], G48

Rogers, Daniel[7] [505], G48

Rogers, Elizabeth (Gorham), G48

Rogers, Eliza[7] [498], G48

Rogers, Esther (———), G27

Rogers, Esther[7] [503], G48

Rogers, Eunice. *See* Swett, Eunice (Rogers)

Rogers, Fanny[7] [514], G48

Rogers, George[7] [511], G48

Rogers, George[8] [806], G69, G91

Rogers, Gideon, G91

Rogers, Grace Adams[9]. *See* Leland, Grace Adams (Rogers) [1100]

Rogers, Hannah (Flood), G91

Rogers, Henry H., G83

Rogers, John, G13, G15

Rogers, [Rev.] John, G26

Rogers, [Rev.] John [Sr.], G26

Rogers, [Rev.] John[6] [254], G26, G47–48

Rogers, John[7] [495], G48, G69

Rogers, John Gorham[7] [497], G48

Rogers, Judith[7] [512], G48

Rogers, Katherine[6], Katherine (Rogers)[6] [257], Leighton

Rogers, Leila. *See* Decker, Leila (Rogers)

Rogers, Lucy (———), G27

Rogers, Lucy[7] [496], G48

Rogers, Martha (Whittingham), G26

Rogers, Martha[6]. *See* Hill, Martha (Rogers)[6] [260]

Rogers, Mary[6]. *See* Hammond, Mary (Rogers)[6] [262]

Rogers, Mary[7] [507], G48

Rogers, Nathaniel[6] [258], G27

Rogers, Nathaniel[6] [259], G27

Rogers, [Rev.] Nathaniel, G47

Rogers, Rachel Ellery, G48

Rogers, Rachel[7] [502], G48

Rogers, Rachel[7] [513], G48

Rogers, Rebekah. *See* Pearson, Rebekah (Rogers)

Rogers, Samuel[7] [508], G48

Rogers, Sarah Caroline (Hovey), G91

Rogers, Sarah (Smith), G69

Rogers, Shubael Gorham[7] [509], G48

Rogers, Susanna (Whipple)[5] [66], G8, G26

Rogers, Susannah (Allen), G47

Rogers, Susannah[7] [494], G47–48

Rogers, Susanna[7] [504], G48

Rogers, [Capt.] Timothy[6] [255], G26

Rogers, Timothy[7] [506], G48

Rogers, William[6] [256], G27

Rogers, William[7] [510], G48

Rogers, [unamed child][7] [501], G48

Roland, Estella. *See* Viersen, Estella (Roland)

Roleson, Ryan Scott[14] [3211], G274

Roleson, Susan Launa (Weeks)[13] [2783], G237, G274

Roleson, William Scott, G274

Rolfe, Abigail. *See* Pillsbury, Abigail (Rolfe)

Rolfe, Abigail (Bond), G24

Rolfe, Ezra, G24

Rollison, Patricia. *See* Clapp, Patricia (Rollison)

Rolls, Alma Gertrude (Holt), G284

Rolls, Hurbert Reason, G284

Rolls, Jessie Arline [Stubbs][13], G247, G284

Rolls, Richard Holt, G284

Rolls, Sally Arline[14]. *See* Pavia, Sally Arline (Rolls)[14] [3312]

Romney, Gertrude May. *See* Clawson,

Gertrude May (Romney)

Rorrback, Malvina. *See* Bacon, Malvina (Rorrback)

Rosch, Anne (Wells)[14]. *See* Roberts, Anne (Wells)[14] [3093]

Rosch, Jack, G263

Rose, Anna Stevens. *See* Starr, Anna Stevens (Rose)

Rose, Asa, G78

Rosenbaum, Morris, G185

Rosenbaum, Nell Young (Clawson)[10]. *See* Silver, Nell Young (Clawson)[10] [1705]

Ross, Clarissa. *See* Young, Clarissa (Ross)

Ross, Phoebe (Ogden), G108

Ross, William, G108

Rossiter, Clara (Junker), G150

Rossiter, Clifford Young[10] [1695], G150

Rossiter, Lillian[10] [1697], G150

Rossiter, Russell Young[10] [1696], G150

Rossiter, Shamira (Young)[9] [1263], G115, G150

Rossiter, William A., G150

Rouillard, Clarence Dana, G167

Rouillard, Harriet Page (Lane)[11] [1935], G167

Rowell, Eliz. *See* Pillsbury, Eliz (Rowell)

Rowley, Jane Jewett. *See* Whipple, Jane Jewett (Rowley)

Royal, Aini Marie (Hendricks), G210

Royal, Alma Ellery (Eaton)[10] [1583], G141, G171

Royal, Austin Garland[11] [1979], G171

Royal, Betty Ann[12] [2530], G210

Royal, Ellery Eaton[11] [1978], G171, G210

Royal, Ellery Thayer[12] [2534], G211, G243

Royal, Harriett Burdett (Thayer), G210

Royal, [Dr.] Herbert B., G171

Royal, Janet[12] [2531], G210

Royal, Jennifer[13] [2846], G243

Royal, Kent Tyler[11] [1977], G171, G210

Royal, [Dr.] Lila Jane (Benjamin), G210

Royal, Pamela[13] [2845], G243

Royal, Sandra (Bartlett), G243

Royal, Virginia[12]. *See* Pierce, Virginia (Royal)[12] [2533]

Royster, ——— [married Stella M.[11] Miller], G201

Royster, Stella M. (Miller)[11] [2451], G201

Ruggles, Martha. *See* Lane, Martha (Ruggles)

Runge, Dareatha Denise (Williams)[14] [3160], G269, G309

Runge, Gary, G309

Runge, Nicholas Cole[15] [3618], G309

Russell, ——— [married Amira [9] Young], G106

Russell, Almira (Young)[9] [1239], G106

Russell, Anna. *See* Stearns, Anna (Russel)

Rust, Abby Katolina[14] [3470], G297

Rust, Cindy Marie[14] [3468], G297

Rust, Jeri Ann[14] [3471], G297

Rust, Joni Lynn[14] [3473], G297

Rust, Josi Rae[14] [3472], G297

Rust, Merle Delwin, G297

Rust, Rhonda Lee (Rich)[13] [3017], G257, G297

Rust, Tina Marie[14] [3469], G297

Ryan, Fannie J. *See* Goddard, Fannie J. (Ryan)

S

Sabin, Hannah Starr[5] [124], G18

Sabin, [Dr.] John, G18

Safford, John, G232

Safford, Martha (Rowe), G232

Safford, Priscilla Bartlett. *See* Stevens, Priscilla Bartlett (Safford)

Sagers, ——— [married Harriet Emeline Barney], G112

Sagers, Harriet Emeline (Barney). *See* Young, Harriet Emeline (Barney)

Sagers, Joseph Ormal, G112

Sagers, Mary, G112

Sagers, Royal Barney, G112

Sanberg, Adam, G159

Sanberg, Ariamiah (Mecham)[10] [1849], G159

Sanborn, Abbott Young[10] [1805], G155

Sanborn, Joseph Abbott, G155

Sanborn, Joseph Gilpen[10] [1807], G156

Sanborn, Lucy Young[10] [1806], G155

Sanborn, Rhoda Mabel (Young)[9] [1303], G116, G155

Sanders, Ruhumah. *See* Kimball, Ruhumah (Sanders)

Sanford, Joel, G81

Sanford, Louisa (Young)[8] [954], G81

Sanger, Tirzah. *See* Grow, Tirzah (Sanger)

Sarah (Treadwell)[7] [697], G62, G85

Sarah (Watson). *See* Stone, Sarah (Watson)

Sargent, Benjamin, G66

Sargent, Judith. *See* Pillsbury, Judith (Sargent)

Sargent, Ruth (Moulton), G66

Diane Eileen (Stevens)[13] [2933]

Stevens, Donald Belmont[12] [2474], G205, G232

Stevens, Dorothy. *See* Goddard, Dorothy (Stevens)

Stevens, Elizabeth (Knight), G165

Stevens, Elizabeth (Seeley), G127

Stevens, Elizabeth Sharon[13] [3084], G262

Stevens, Ella Florence (Bent), G205

Stevens, Ethan Allen Delaney[14] [3126], G266

Stevens, Florence Augustus[10]. *See* Emery, Florence Augustus (Stevens)[10] [1518]

Stevens, Frances, Harriet (Goddard)[12] [2599], G220, **G250-251**

Stevens, Francis, G60

Stevens, George Gove[10] [1894], G162, G202-203

Stevens, George Nichols[10] [1515], G133, G165-166

Stevens, Hannah Elizabeth[10]. *See* Knight, Hannah Elizabeth (Stevens)[10] [1516]

Stevens, Harriet [Nichols], G133

Stevens, Hepsibah (Kilham)[6] [438], G43, G64

Stevens, Jane (McCarthy), G302

Stevens, Jeffrey Jay[13] [2934], G251

Stevens, Jennifer Mary Ann[14] [3124], G266

Stevens, Jessica Clara[14] [3532], G302

Stevens, John Belmont[13] Jr. [1733], G232, G266

Stevens, John Belmont[14] [3120], G266

Stevens, Julia Ann[8]. *See* Fausett, Julia Ann (Stevens)[8] [1034]

Stevens, Julia Maria (Stanclift), G203

Stevens, Julie Ann. *See* Whipple, Julie Ann (Stevens)

Stevens, Katherine Elizabeth[14] [3122], G266

Stevens, Kristina Lynn (Bailey), G266

Stevens, Krystal Ann[14] [3127], G266

Stevens, Laura[10]. *See* Bradley, Laura (Stevens)[10] [1517]

Stevens, Lizze (Danforsth), G133

Stevens, Lois (Voswinkel), G229

Stevens, Lorenzo Dow, G133

Stevens, Lorna May (McCabe), G274

Stevens, Lottie Nichols[11]. *See* Brown, Lottie Nichols (Stevens)[11] [1924]

Stevens, Mariah (Doyle), G87

Stevens, Marinda Alice[9]. *See* Jones, Marinda Alice (Stevens)[9] [1446]

Stevens, Martha Stuart[13]. *See* Bennett, Martha Stuart (Stevens)[13] [3086]

Stevens, Mary. *See* Starr, Mary (Stevens)

Stevens, Mary Elizabeth (Allen), G262

Stevens, Mary (Mooar)[7] [474], G46

Stevens, Mary (Stone)[7] [669], G60

Stevens, Matthew Bartlett[14] [3125], G266

Stevens, Nancy Mathilda (Bowers)[9] [1450], G128, G162

Stevens, Nehemiah, G64

Stevens, Orrin Belmont[11] [1923], G166, G205

Stevens, Paul Safford[14] [3123], G266

Stevens, Peter Bartlett[13] [1734], G232, G266

Stevens, Philip Ambrose[14] [3121], G266

Stevens, Priscilla Bartlett (Safford), G232

Stevens, Robert, G56

Stevens, Roswell[7] [723], G64, G87

Stevens, Roswell[8] Jr. [1033], G87

Stevens, Samuel, G46

Stevens, Samuel Phillips[12] [2711], G229, G262

Stevens, Samuel Stanclift[11] [2458], G203, G229

Stevens, Samuel Stanclift[13] II [3085], G262, G302

Stevens, Sarah. *See* Hill, Sarah (Stevens)

Stevens, Scarlett[14] [3128], G266

Stevens, Susan Carrie[10] [1518], G133

Stevens, Susan Poor (Pearson)[9] [1099], G91, G133

Stevens, Sybell (Spencer), G87

Stevens, Vittoria (Bruni), G266

Stevens, Westley True[10] [1518], G133

Stevens, William[8] [1035], G87, G127

Stevens, William, G133

Stevens, William McCarthy[14] [3531], G302

Stevenson, Edythe. *See* Pullen, Edythe (Stevenson)

Stickney, Charles P., G146

Stickney, Frances Anna (Hastings)[10] [1642], G146

Stiles, Elizabeth. *See* Dickson, Elizabeth (Stiles)

Stilson, Susannah (Young)[8] [950], G80

Stilson, William, G80

Stinson, Elvira (Pillsbury)[10] [1458], G129

Stockwell, Abbie Almira (Divoll). *See* Stone, Abbie Almira (Divoll)

Stohl, Delores. *See* Cannon, Delores (Stohl)

Stone, (———) (Ives), G73

Stone, Abbie Almira (Divoll), G118, G128

Stone, Abigail (Jones), G81

Syfert, Laura Marie (Miller)[12] [2675], G226

Syfert, Melvin Clyde, G226

Symonds, Mary. *See* Whipple, Mary (Symonds)

Symonds, William, G12

Synder, Elizabeth May. *See* Johnson, Elizabeth May (Snyder)

T

Tabors, Tammy. *See* Grimes, Tammy (Tabors)

Tainter, Hannah. *See* Stone, Hannah (Tainter)

Tainter, [Capt.] John, G41

Talbot, Susanna. *See* Mecham, Susanna (Talbot)

Tallman, Edith A., G221

Tanner, Bernice Louise[11]. *See* Horton, Bernice Louise (Tanner)[11] [2453]

Tanner, Betsy Corinna (Camp), G201–202

Tanner, Blanche May[11]. *See* Grennell, Blanche May (Tanner)[11] [2452]

Tanner, Dale Louis, G265

Tanner, Edgar Peabody, G201

Tanner, Julia Ann. *See* Haines, Julia Ann (Tanner)

Tanner, Mary Elizabeth (Baker)[10] [1889], G161, G173, G201–202

Tanner, Wilbor Alonzo, G201

Tanner, Wilma Nettie (Roberts), G265

Taylor, Arza, G125

Taylor, Emma (Hill)[8] [844], G71

Taylor, Fannie Caroline. *See* Decker, Fannie Caroline (Taylor)

Taylor, Isaac, G51

Taylor, Justin William[15] [3566], G305

Taylor, Kelli Leann[15] [3568], G305

Taylor, Kendall C., G304

Taylor, Kendra Lee[15] [3565], G305

Taylor, Kimberly Ann[15] [3564], G305

Taylor, Lawrence[15] [3563], G305

Taylor, Lettie. *See* Croxall, Lettie (Taylor)

Taylor, Lucy (Hill)[7] [548], G52

Taylor, Lynnanne Janette. *See* Wilson, Lynnanne Janette (Taylor)

Taylor, Margaret Gay. *See* Beatie, Margaret Gay (Taylor)

Taylor, Marily Jane. *See* Custer, Marily Jane (Taylor)

Taylor, Mary (Goddard)[6] [399], G40

Taylor, Matthew Charles[15] [3567], G305

Taylor, Miriam (Mecham)[9] [1409], G125

Taylor, Rufus, G40

Taylor, Sandra Dale (Haines)[14] [3109], G265, G304

Taylor, Stephen, G71

Tebold, Richard, G3

Tegreeny, June Darleen (Scott)[12]. *See* Brown, June Darleen (Scott)[12] [2620]

Tegreeny, Wendy Caprice[13]. *See* Quinn, Wendy Caprice (Tegreeny)[13] [2983]

Tegreeny, William Brian, G253

Teissen, Margaret. *See* Powers, Margaret (Teissen)

Thatcher, ——— [married Jodel Christine[14] Wilson], G317

Thatcher, Alice Young[10] [1680], G149

Thatcher, Armand[10] [1690], G149

Thatcher, Brianna Rae[15] [3699], G317

Thatcher, Brigham Guy[10] [1684], G149, G184

Thatcher, Constance[10]. *See* Nibley, Constance (Thatcher)[10] [1687]

Thatcher, Eunice Caroline (Young)[9] [1258], G114, G149

Thatcher, Fanny Decker (Young)[9] [1261], G115, G149

Thatcher, Fera Young[10] [1693], G150

Thatcher, Florence Bell (Beatie), G184

Thatcher, Frank W.[10] [1692], G149, G185

Thatcher, Frank W.[11] II [2181], G185

Thatcher, George Washington, G149

Thatcher, George Washington[10] II [1680], G149

Thatcher, Guy[11] [2152], G184

Thatcher, Jessica Dawn[15] [3698], G317

Thatcher, Jodel Christine (Wilson)[14] [3348], G287, G317

Thatcher, Kathrine[10]. *See* Thomas, Kathrine (Thatcher)[10] [1685]

Thatcher, Kenneth Ray[15] [3696], G317

Thatcher, Kristine Nicole[15] [3697], G317

Thatcher, Laurence Y.[10] [1694], G150

Thatcher, Luna Angell[10]. *See* Farrell, Luna Angell (Thatcher)[10] [1686]

Thatcher, Lutie[10]. *See* Lynch, Lutie (Thatcher)[10] [1689]

Thatcher, Maddison Rennee[15] [3700], G317

Thatcher, Mary. *See* Stone, Mary (Thatcher)

Thatcher, Mary Jean[11] [2182], G185

Thatcher, Mary[10] [1691], G149

Thatcher, Nellie May[10]. *See* Blair, Nellie May (Thatcher)[10] [1681]

(Treadwell)[6] [424]

Treadwell, Sarah[7]. See Sarah (Treadwell)[7] [697]

Treadwell, Sarah[9] [1366], G123

Treadwell, Simeon[9] [1364], G123

Treadwell, Susanna (———), G85

Treadwell, Susanna[9] [1355], G123

Treadwell, Susan[9] [1378], G124

Treadwell, Thomas, G42

Treadwell, Thomas Herrick[9] [1363], G123

Treadwell, Thomas[6] [426], G42, G63

Treadwell, Thomas[8] [1012], G86, G123

Treadwell, Thomas Passmore[9] [1368], G123

Treadwell, Thomas Passmore[9] [1370], G123

Treadwell, Thomas Warren[9] [1367], G123

Treadwell, Welcome (Seward), G124

Treadwell, William[8] [800], G69

Treadwell, William[8] [1017], G86, G124

Treadwell, William Francis[9] [1394], G124

Treadwell, William Pepperrell[9] [1373], G123

Tribull, Deborah Louise (Wege)[14] [3235], G276, G311

Tribull, Sean Andreas[15] [3631], G311

Tribull, Stephan Alfred, G311

Tribull, Sven Alexander[15] [3632], G311

Trimble, Henry W. III, G273

Trimble, Joan Morgan (Whipple)[13] [2782], G237, G273–274

Trimble, Laura Tucker Barrett[14] [3210], G274

Tripp, Daniel, G129

Tripp, Lois (Pillsbury)[10] [1460], G129

Trumbull, Florence. See Coolidge, Florence (Trumbull)

Trumbull, [Gov.] John H., G229

Trumbull, Maude (Usher), G229

Tryal, George, G62

Tryal, Mary (Treadwell)[7] [696], G62

Tupper, Laura Glick (Morehouse)[12] [2613], G220

Tupper, Norman, G220

Turley, Frances Amelia (Kimberley), G111

Turley, Mary Ann. See Young, Mary Ann (Turley)

Turley, Theodore, G111

Tuttle, Edward, G159

Tuttle, Matilda Ann. See Mecham, Matilda Ann (Tuttle)

Tuttle, Sarah Maria. See Mecham, Sarah Maria (Tuttle)

Tuttle, Sarah Mariah (Clinton), G159

Twiss, John Saunders, G110

Twiss, Naamah Kendall Jenkins (Carter). See Young, Naamah Kendall Jenkins (Carter)

Twombly, Hepzieth. See Pillsbury, Hepzieth (Twombly)

Tye, Steven Scott, G297

Tye, Wendi Jene (Holley)[14] [3461], G297

Tyler, Alma Ellery (Holden)[8]. See Bacon, Alma Ellery (Holden)[8] [884]

Tyler, Alma Ellery[9]. See Eaton, Alma Ellery (Tyler)[9] [1158]

Tyler, [Capt.] Edward, G97

Tyler, Elizabeth[9]. See Pollard, Elizabeth (Tyler)[9] [1155]

Tyler, Hannah Ladd. See Mecham, Hanna Ladd (Tyler)

Tyler, Harriett Newell[9]. See Kelley, Harriett Newell (Tyler) [1157]

Tyler, James Richard[9] [1156], G97

Tyler, John, G123

Tyler, John Flavel[9] [1153], G97

Tyler, Mary. See Treadwell, Mary (Tyler)

Tyler, Mary (Thomas), G97

Tyler, Ruth (Herrick), G123

Tyler, Susanna (Thomas), G97

Tyler, Susan[9]. See Pollard, Susan (Tyler)[9] [1154]

Tyndal, Robin. See Beal, Robin (Tyndal)

Tyo, Sharon Ann (Jenne)[13] [2903], G247

Tyo, Thomas, G247

U

Ultang, Linda Rutlege. See Powers, Linda Rutlege (Ultang)

Upham, Abigail (———), G39

Upham, Asa[6] [373], G39, G57

Upham, Eleanor (Knowlton)[7] [725], G64, G87

Upham, Elizabeth[8]. See Dickson, Elizabeth (Upham)[8] [1037]

Upham, Ezekiel, G39

Upham, Hannah (Stearns)[5] [150], G19, G39

Upham, Huldah Rosabella (Smith), G78

Upham, John, G39

Upham, Joseph Pierce[7] [621], G57, G78

Upham, Lucinda Chipman[8]. See Orvis, Lucinda Chipman (Upham)[8] [925]

Upham, Lydia (Pierce), G57

Upham, Mary Pease. See Goddard, Mary Pease (Upham)

Upham, Nathan, G87

V

W

G189, G221

Walker, James, G165

Walker, John R., G111

Walker, Julian, G111

Walker, Lynne Jr.[12] [2624], G221

Walker, Lynne Phillips, G221

Walker, Mary Ann, G111

Walker, Nancy (Crissie). *See* Young, Nancy (Crissie)

Walker, Nancy R., G111

Walker, Oliver, G111

Walker, Rebecca Sue. *See* Redstrom, Rebecca Sue (Walker)

Walker, Sarah, G111

Walker, Susannah (Pillsbury)[6] [224], G25

Walker, William C., G111

Wall, Donna. *See* Donigan, Donna (Wall)

Wallace, Bernice Pauline. *See* Miller, Bernice Pauline (Wallace)

Wallbillich, Cherryl Ann (Ball)[13] [2917], G248, G285

Wallbillich, Joanna (Grior), G285

Wallbillich, Kirk Robert, G285

Wallbillich, Robert, G285

Waller, Bert, G161

Waller, Priscilla L. *See* Miller, Priscilla L. (Waller)

Waller, Rosa May (Miller)[10] [1887], G161

Wallis, Sarah. *See* Towle, Sarah (Wallis)

Walsh, Ellen. *See* Carr, Ellen (Walsh)

Ward, Angeline[9]. *See* Cram, Angeline (Ward)[9] [1202]

Ward, Anna (Goddard)[8] [926], G79

Ward, Asbel, G79

Ward, Betsey[8]. *See* Baker, Betsey (Ward)[8] [888]

Ward, Elsie Elizabeth (Starr)[8] [919], G78, G102

Ward, Ephraim, G17

Ward, Experience (Stone)[5] [120], G17

Ward, Hannah. *See* Knowlton, Hannah Ward

Ward, Hannah (Goddard)[7] [575], G54, G58, G75

Ward, Jonas, G102

Ward, Jospeh, G17

Ward, Mary (Stone)[5] [117], G17

Ward, Sylvanus, G75

Warner, Elizo. *See* Starr, Elizo (Warner)

Warner, Sarah. *See* Kimball, Sarah (Warner)

Washborn, Floyd, G270

Washborn, Laura Denice[14] [3169], G270

Washborn, Linda Marie (Whipple)[13], G234, G270

Washborn, Melisua Valerie[14] [3170], G270

Washburn, Donald Edson[13] [2858], G244

Washburn, Gene Edson, G244

Washburn, Lena Louise (Pueschel), G244

Washburn, Levi Edwin, G244

Washburn, Lorna Mather (Swain)[12] [2539], G211 G244

Washington, George, G30–32

Washington, Martha, G31

Waters, Delia. *See* Goddard, Delia (Waters)

Waters, Luther, G88

Waters, Mary (Knowlton)[8] [1050], G88

Watkins, Zerviah. *See* Knowlton, Zerviah (Watkins)

Watrous, Angeline (Edwards), G145

Watrous, Caroline (Estey)[9] [1206], G103, G145

Watrous, Eunice (Mott), G145

Watrous, Harriet Elizabeth[10]. *See* Brush, Harriet Elizabeth (Watrous)[10] [1635]

Watrous, James Ulysses, G145

Watrous, Walter James, G145

Watrous, Walter W.[10] [1637], G145

Watrous, William[10] [1636], G145

Watson, Clarence, G272

Watson, Ellen Elizabeth. *See* Pratt, Ellen Elizabeth (Watson)

Watson, Evelyn Rebecca (Barraford)[12] [2554], G214, G246

Watson, Hazel (———), G272

Watson, James II, G241

Watson, Joanne[13] [2882], G246

Watson, Joy Diane. *See* Carpenter, Joy Diane (Watson)

Watson, Leone, G246

Watson, Lizzie S. *See* Clawson, Lizzie S. (Watson)

Watson, Margaret (Ritchie), G241

Watson, Marlene[13] [2883], G246

Watson, Mercy. *See* Pillsbury, Mercy (Watson)

Watson, Robert[13] [2881], G246

Watson, Roderick[13] [2884], G246

Waugh, Stephanie Ann. *See* Munsch, Stephanie Ann (Waugh)

Weare, Elizabeth (Shaw), G10

Weare, Mechech, G10, G11

Weare, Mehitable Wainwright, G10

Weatherly, Deborah (Story), G307

Weatherly, Dora Dean (Hopkins)[13] [2746], G233, G268
Weatherly, James Fay[14] [3146], G268, G307
Weatherly, Ladonna (Summer), G307
Weatherly, Marjorie Diana[14]. *See* Patz, Marjorie Diana (Weatherly)[14] [3147]
Weatherly, Mary Ellen (Wills), G307
Weatherly, Monoca Dawn[15] [3591], G307
Weatherly, Monoca[15] [3592], G307
Weatherly, Pamela Sue[14]. *See* Odom, Pamela Sue (Weatherly)[14] [3148]
Weatherly, Russel, G268
Weatherly, Russel Andrew[15] [3593], G307
Weatherly, Russel[14] Jr. [3145], G268, G307
Weatherly, Timothy James[15] [3594], G307
Webb, Ann Eliza. *See* Young, Ann Eliza (Webb)
Webb, Chauncey Griswold, G112
Webb, Eliza Jane (Churchill), G112
Weber, Betty. *See* Jones, Betty (Weber)
Weber, Susanna. *See* Page, Susanna (Weber)
Webster, Elizabeth, G5
Webster, Elizabeth (Pillsbury)[7] [465], G45
Webster, Samuel, G45
Webster, Tracey. *See* Goddard, Tracey (Webster)
Wedge, Deborah Michele Simmons[14]. *See* O'Shaughnessey, Deborah Michele Simmons (Wedge)[14] [3138]
Wedge, Edith[14]. *See* Collins, Edith (Wedge)[14] [3139]
Wedge, Frances, Irene (Whipple)[12] [2482], G206, G233
Wedge, George Ellis, G233
Wedge, Helen Louise[13]. *See* Fisher, Helen Louise (Wedge)[13] [2743]
Wedge, LeRoy Ellis[13] [2742], G233, G267
Wedge, Leslie Lynn[13]. *See* Green, Leslie Lynn (Wedge)[13] [2744]
Wedge, Martha Joyce (Simmons), G267
Wedgwood, Catherine G. *See* Pillsbury, Catherine G. (Wedgwood)
Wedgwood, Lizze. *See* Pillsbury, Lizze (Wedgwood)
Weeks, Eugene, G243
Weeks, Jane Lucy[13]. *See* Randazzo, Jane Lucy (Weeks)[13] [2784]
Weeks, Karen Tinsley (Bacon)[13]. *See* Mitchell, Karen Tinsley (Bacon)[13] [2852]
Weeks, Launa May (Whipple)[12] [2499], G207, G237
Weeks, Lawrence Delbert, G237

Weeks, Lucy Mae (Wright), G237
Weeks, Robert Edward, G243
Weeks, Ruth (Butterfield), G243
Weeks, Susan Launa[13]. *See* Roleson, Susan Launa (Weeks)[13] [2783]
Weeks, William Joseph, G237
Wege, Anne Elizabeth[14] [3234], G276
Wege, Barbara Jane (Nelson)[13] [2797], G239, G276
Wege, Linda Marie[14]. *See* Fisher, Linda Marie (Wege)[14] [3233]
Wege, Theodore G., G276
Wellington, Alex Robertson, G237
Wellington, Charity. *See* Lane, Charity (Wellington)
Wellington, Isabel Anne. *See* Whipple, Isabel Anne (Wellington)
Wellington, Mary Ellen (Kindegan), G237
Wells, Anna Estella (Viersen)[10] [1630], G145
Wells, Anne[14]. *See* Roberts, Anne (Wells)[14] [3093]
Wells, April Denise[15] [3617], G309
Wells, Barbara (Holt), G264
Wells, Catherine[13]. *See* Buell, Catherine (Wells)[13] [2714]
Wells, Christopher B. [3099], G264, G303
Wells, Clark Thompson[13] [2716], G230, G263
Wells, Clark Thompson[14] Jr. [3094], G263
Wells, Cyrus Curtis[13] [2717], G230, G264
Wells, David C.[14] [3095], G263
Wells, Deborah D.[15] [3544], G303
Wells, Elizabeth Leone (Cavanaugh), G263
Wells, Helen Cutter (Pillsbury)[12] [2462], G203, G230
Wells, Hilton Thomas, G309
Wells, Janet (Knost), G263
Wells, Jonathon[15] [3543], G303
Wells, Julie Joan[15] [3548], G303
Wells, Kaylee Marie[15] [3641], G312
Wells, Kenneth Arthur, G312
Wells, Kimberly Sue (Williams)[14] [3159], G269, G309
Wells, Kristarae Mackenzi[15] [3640], G312
Wells, Louise[12]. *See* Chandler, Louise (Wells)[12]
Wells, Lucy Skelton (White), G230
Wells, Mary Elizabeth (Thurber), G263
Wells, Mary[14]. *See* Vournakis, Mary (Wells)[14] [3096]
Wells, Pamela (Loomis), G263
Wells, Patty Jo (Sexton)[14] [3254], G278,

Wilson, Myrle Audrey[11]. *See* Lorenson, Myrle Audrey (Wilson)[11] [2037]

Wilson, Rebecca. *See* Norton, Rebecca (Wilson)

Wilson, Reed Owen[13] [3030], G257

Wilson, Rhoda (Goddard)[7] [628], G58

Wilson, Robert, G306

Wilson, Ross Evan[13] [3027], G257, G299

Wilson, Sarah Jean Marie[15] [3689], G317

Wilson, Solomon, G58

Wilson, Steven Scott[15] [3688], G317

Wilson, Taya Marie[15] [3701], G317

Wilson, Taylor Clark[14] [3506], G299

Wilson, Todd Evan[13] [3035], G258

Wilson, Tyrel David[15] [3686], G317

Wilson, Wendy Helena (Gilbreath)[15] [3580], G306

Wilson, William Peter, G176

Wilson, William Peter[11] Jr. [2035], G176

Wiltsie, Mary (Spofford). *See* Whipple, Mary (Spofford)

Winder, Anne Y. (Cannon)[10] [1723], G151, G191

Winder, Anne[11] [2294], G191

Winder, Gertrude. *See* Croxall, Gertrude (Winder)

Winder, John Rex, G191

Winder, John Rex[11] Jr. [2295], G191

Windisch, David Anthony[14] II [3226], G275

Windisch, Katherine Patterson[14]. *See* Ingle, Katherine Patterson (Windisch)[14] [3225]

Windisch, Matthew Anthony[14] II [3227], G275

Windisch, Melinda (Jones)[13] [2791], G238, G275

Winters, Susan. *See* Patch, Susan (Winters)

Winthrop, [Gov.] John, 22

Wiscomb, Nora. *See* Clawson, Nora (Wiscomb)

Wise, Anna Hale (Ellis), G245

Wise, Barbara[14]. *See* Lynch, Barbara (Wise)[14] [3301]

Wise, Charlotte (Cutts), G283

Wise, Cynthia Anne[14] [3307], G283, G314

Wise, Eugenia[14]. *See* Hathaway, Eugenia (Wise)[14] [3300]

Wise, James Edward, G211

Wise, Janis (Miller), G314

Wise, John O.[14] [3302], G283, G313

Wise, Julia A.[15] [3653], G313

Wise, Kent[15] [3662], G314

Wise, Lisa (Marson), G313

Wise, Mary Olive (Carr)[11] [1987], G172, G211

Wise, Miriam[13]. *See* Saunders, Miriam (Wise)[13] [2869]

Wise, Rachel G.[15] [3654], G313

Wise, Robert E.[13] [2868], G245, G283

Wise, Robert[15] [3661], G314

Wise, Ruby (Kent), G283

Wise, Sean[15] [3663], G314

Wise, William Oliver[12] [2543], G212, G245

Wise, William Oliver[13] Jr. [2870], G245, G283

Wise, William Oliver[14] III [3306], G283, G314

Witt, Anna (Lundsted), G196

Witt, Brigham Winfred[10] [1804], G155, G196

Witt, D. B., G155

Witt, Rhoda Mabel (Young)[9]. *See* Sanborn, Rhoda Mabel (Young)[9] [1303]

Witt, Winifred Utahna[11] [2372], G196

Wolcott, Oliver, G31

Wolfe, Charles Henry, G283

Wolfe, Charles Henry[14] II [3309], G284

Wolfe, Charles Lesley, G283

Wolfe, Deborah. *See* Carpenter, Deborah (Wolfe)

Wolfe, Edna Hannah (Sibley), G283

Wolfe, Joyce (Guthrie), G284

Wolfe, Virginia Anne (Croissant)[13] [2871], G245, G283

Wood, Eunice Porter[10]. *See* Schenck, Eunice Porter (Wood)[10] [1529]

Wood, Phebe Smith (Whipple)[9]. *See* Patterson, Phebe Smith (Whipple)[9] [1111]

Wood, Sally. *See* Goddard, Sally (Wood)

Wood, Thomas, G135

Woodbury, Martha (Whipple)[8] [817], G70

Woodbury, Mary. *See* Whipple, Mary (Woodbury)

Woodbury, Polly. *See* Whipple, Polly (Woodbury)

Woodbury, Robert, G70

Woodman, A. Parker Jr., G176

Woodman, Emma Judith[11] [2027], G176

Woodman, Nellie Ethelyn[11] [2028], G176

Woodman, Nellie Randilla (Ball)[10] [1619], G144, G176

Woodruff, ——— [married Joni Sue[14] Darby], G316

Woodruff, Jenna Kristine[15] [3683], G316

Woodruff, Joni Sue (Darby)[14] [3343],

Y

Young, Nancy[8]. *See* Kent, Nancy (Young)[8] [945]

Young, Nathan, G110

Young, Oscar Brigham[9] [1274], G115

Young, Patricia Barrett (Rice)[14] [3207], G273, G311

Young, Perry Legrand[9] [1325], G118

Young, Persis (Goodall), G116, G117

Young, Phebe Celestia[9]. *See* Pack, Phebe Celestia (Young)[9] [1244]

Young, Phebe Groombridge (Clark), G106

Young, Phebe Louisa[9]. *See* Beatie, Phebe Louisa [9] [1278]

Young, Phineas Henry[9] [1246], G106

Young, Phineas Howe[8] [952], G81, G106

Young, Phineas Howe[9] [1306], G116

Young, Rachel Christine[14] [3523], G301

Young, Rebecca Greenleaf (Holman), G110

Young, Rebekah Elisabeth[14]. *See* Keighley, Rebekah Elisabeth (Young)[14] [3522]

Young, Rhoda Mabel[9]. *See* Sanborn, Rhoda Mabel (Young)[9] [1303]

Young, Rhoda (Richards)[8] [943], G80, G110-111

Young, Rhoda[8]. *See* Green, Rhoda (Young)[8] [947]

Young, Rhoda[9] [1236], G106

Young, Ronald Coleman, G301

Young, Ruth[9]. *See* Johnson, Ruth (Young)[9] [1286]

Young, Sarah Jane (Snow), G105

Young, Scott Richmond[11] [2183], G185, G221

Young, Sedenia[9] [1243], G106

Young, Seraph[9] [1247], G106

Young, Seymour B., G185

Young, Seymour Bicknell[9] [1230], G105

Young, Shamira[9]. *See* Rossiter, Shamira (Young)[9] [1263]

Young, Sherry (Steed), G254

Young, Sophronhia Gray (Frost), G109

Young, Stewart Andrew, G273

Young, Susan [Susa] Amelia[9]. *See* Gates, Susan [Susa] Amelia (Young)[9] [1302]

Young, Susannah (Cotton), G80

Young, Susannah (Snively), G108

Young, Susannah[8]. *See* Stilson, Susannah (Young)[8] [950]

Young, Theodocia (Kimball), G80

Young, Thomas[13] [2987], G254

Young, Valentine, G110

Young, Vilate[9]. *See* Decker, Vilate (Young)[9]

Young, Virginia Parnell[9]. *See* Carigan, Virginia Parnell (Young)[9] [1245]

Young, Virginia[10]. *See* LaRocca, Virginia (Young)[10] [1741]

Young, Willard[9] [1277], G115

Young, William, G80

Young, William Clark[9] [1250], G106, G116

Young, William Goodall[9] [1309], G117

Young, Zina Diantha (Hungtington), G111

Young, Zina[9]. *See* Card, Zina (Young)[9] [1298]

Young, [infant][9] [1307], G116

Z

Zehe, Laurie.   Gaber, Laurie (Zehe)

Zoller, Christina Marie (Wilson)[13] [3034], G258, G300

Zoller, Jason Robert[14] [3515], G300

Zumwalt, Elise Lyn[14] [3133], G266

Zumwalt, Eric[14] [3129], G266, G306

Zumwalt, Esther Louise (Whipple)[12] [2478], G206, G232

Zumwalt, Janeen Lea[14] [3131], G266

Zumwalt, Jenny[15] [3585], G306

Zumwalt, Jeri N. (West), G266

Zumwalt, Jill[15] [3586], G306

Zumwalt, John Franklin, G232

Zumwalt, Kurt Detric[14] [3132], G266

Zumwalt, Marta Jo[14] [3130], G266

Zumwalt, Orlow R.[13] [2738], G233, G266

Zumwalt, Susan (———), G306

ISBN 155395676-1

9 781553 956761